Praise for *Play Your Bes*

"The definitive book on 9 Ball and 10 B
Tom Shaw – Pool & Billiard Magazine

"I think that Phil Capelle should be in the Hall of Fame for his contributions to this wonderful game. Just when you thought he was done, here he comes with yet another gem."
Tony Robles – Pro Player/Instructor, Owner - Predator Tour and National Pool League

"Play Your Best 9&10 Ball is a must have for any aspiring player. The insightful analysis of how to play these games is a roadmap towards achieving highly advanced levels of play."
Todd Fleitman – Instructor, Consultant

Praise for *Play Your Best 9 Ball* - First Edition

"You would have to pay thousands of dollars for professional lessons to obtain the information in this book."
Mike Zuglan – Joss Northeast Nine Ball Tour

"This is the most comprehensive book on 9 ball. It is a must read for all players."
Tommy Kennedy – 1992 U.S. Open Champion

"So you want to learn how to play 9 ball? If that is your goal, reading Phil Capelle's latest book, Play Your Best Nine Ball is THE BEST way to begin."
The National Billiard News

"The book covers pretty much every facet of the game that a player, regardless of skill level, needs to know to play nine-ball to the best of their ability."
InsidePOOL

"As someone who is striving to improve my own 9 Ball game, I know I'll be keeping this book handy."
Rhonda Jackman – Chalk & Cue

"Phil Capelle's new book on nine ball is an encyclopedia of information on this fascinating game. It's huge, detailed, and clear. The book is organized in a way that will be useful to any player who wants to improve his/her nine ball skills."
On the Wire

"You will find instructions on all facets of the game that will move your game to the next level."
On the Break

"Another great book from Phil Capelle. His insights into the game of 9 Ball are unparalleled."
John Horsfall – Sands Reno Open Nine Ball Champion, 1996 and 2000

Play Your Best
9 & 10 Ball

Phil Capelle

Second Edition
Billiards Press, New York City

Play Your Best 9 & 10 Ball

Phil Capelle

Copyright © 2014

Publication Date: November, 2014

Published by: Billiards Press
　　　　　　　Park Ave. S., #94307
　　　　　　　New York, NY 10003

First Printing

All rights reserved. No part of this book may be reproduced or transmitted in any form or by any means, electronic or mechanical, including photocopying, recording or by an information and retrieval system without written permission from the author, except for the inclusion of quotations in a review.

Printed in the United States of America

10 9 8 7 6 5 4 3 2 1

Library of Congress Catalog Card Number 2014918194

ISBN 978-0989891776

Dedication

I dedicate this book to the late Jay Swanson. Watching "Swanee" play 9 Ball was one of the true joys of my pool career. He was a good friend, a genuinely nice guy, and an awesome player.

Acknowledgements

Working on this book was a true labor of love. Every day I looked forward to diagramming, writing, researching and learning something new about the great games of 9 Ball and 10 Ball. Once again I was blessed with the support of friends and associates who share my passion for the game. I was fortunate to have them work with me, for there is no way the book would have turned out nearly as well without their contributions.

Pat Fleming of Accu-Stats Video Productions and his team have toured the country for over 25 years filming the very best professionals in tournament competition. Pat has supported my efforts every step of the way and has been kind enough to allow me to make use of shots and comments that appear on Accu-Stats' extensive library of tapes.

Janet Tedesco was my assistant for this second edition. She created the new cover, drew the new diagrams, and laid out the book. I am very thankful for her tireless effort in creating the book.

Jonathan Meltzer worked long hours proofing the text and making some editorial suggestions that improved the clarity of the ideas. Thank you for your time and expertise.

Todd Fleitman, a top instructor from New Jersey, consulted on the first and second editions. Todd provided numerous ideas for improving the quality of the book, and his keen eye for detail was instrumental in ensuring the accuracy of the illustrations. John Leyman, a leading tournament director, helped to update the section on the rules.

Paul Harris worked on the first edition of the book, turning my hand drawn work into the splendid diagrams that are one of the most important features of the book. And thanks again to Shari Stauch and Tom Shaw at *Pool & Billiard Magazine* for supporting my work.

Roy Yamane, a well-known instructor on the West Coast, and I spent several afternoons testing many of the shots in the book and discussing pool theory for the first edition. Roy had the unique ability to take a good idea and expand and improve upon it. Roy sadly passed away in 2014.

Paul Gray and I conducted numerous research sessions at Danny Kuykendall's poolroom for the first edition. He provided valuable assistance in running many of the tests that ensured the accuracy of the diagrams in the book.

Longtime friends Rachel Brown, Regina Girardot, and Melinda Bailey were very helpful in providing ideas for the women's perspective on pool. Thanks also go to anyone who I may have failed to mention, and to the hundreds of pool players I've met over the last 45+ years who are a part of the pages that follow.

Introduction

History

In the movie "The Hustler", which came out in 1961, Minnesota Fats and Eddie Felson were featured in two titanic duels of Straight Pool. When the "The Color of Money" was released in 1986, the featured game had switched to 9-Ball. While Eight Ball continues to be the most widely played game, 9 Ball emerged as the game of choice for the majority of serious pool players. Then, in the new century, 10 Ball began to grow in popularity. The easiest way to describe 10 Ball is as 9 Ball – only with ten balls (naturally) – which are racked in the shape of a triangle, not a diamond. Today both 9 Ball and 10 Ball are the games played at almost every major professional tournament around the world. 9 Ball is still the most widely played of the two games at the amateur level, but the number of competitions in 10 Ball has grown rapidly over the last five to ten years.

There were many great 9 Ball players prior to 1970 who avoided the limelight of tournament play, preferring instead to play high stakes games in relative obscurity. Because these great players avoided tournaments in years past, it is difficult to rank them with a high degree of accuracy. Most observers, however, are in agreement that Luther Lassiter was the greatest 9 Ball player in the era before the game achieved the widespread popularity it enjoys today. And many still feel he was the best ever.

I believe that the best test of a player's game is their performance in tournament competition. Tournaments demand that a player bring their best game to the table against a variety of opponents. This, of course, eliminates some of the great money players who are only able to access their "A" game after several hours of uninterrupted competition against a solitary opponent.

The record book shows that from the 1970s on, the best players in tournament completion were Jim Rempe, Mike Sigel, Earl Strickland, Buddy Hall, Nick Varner, Johnny Archer, Efren Reyes, Mika Immonen, Ralf Souquet, Thorsten Hohmann, Francisco Bustamante, Darren Appleton, and Shane Van Boening (with apologies to those who I may have overlooked). Most of these great champions are still active and both games have gone global, so it is now common for winners of major events to come from all over the globe.

While it would be great for fans of the sport to see the top men pros live on TV on a regular basis, such is not the case as this is being written. Serious students and fans of the game, however, can watch these marvels in tournament competition thanks to the efforts of Pat Fleming and his team at Accu-Stats, which has filmed pro events for over a dozen years.

On the women's side, Jean Balukas was dominant in 9 Ball in the 1980's before women's pool was televised on a regular basis. From the mid-1990s on, Allison Fisher has logged more TV time than any other player while dominating the ladies tour. Other fine players who have captured world titles or are well known to fans include Loree Jon Jones, Jeanette Lee, Robin Dodson, Ewa Mataya-Laurence, Karen Corr, Kelly Fisher, Xiao Ting Pan, and Ga Young Kim.

9 Ball and 10 Ball

9 Ball and 10 Ball (which I will refer to as 9&10 Ball from now on) are fast paced games that provide a stern test of your skills. You need to shoot with great accuracy, play pinpoint position, play killer safeties and be able to kick or jump your way out of a jam. And at the higher levels of play, it helps to have a powerful and dependable break.

The object in 9 Ball is to sink the 9-ball, and in 10 Ball you win when you make the 10-ball. You can win at any time as long as you hit the lowest numbered ball first. This unique feature brings in an element of luck and a degree of excitement to both games that makes them unlike any other game of pool. (It should be noted, however, that in some competitions you must call the gamewinning shot.)

The 500 Game Study

I conducted a study of 500 pro games of 9 Ball as part of my research for this book. The study consisted largely of the exploits of the players whose names I mentioned a few moments ago. The purpose of the study was to shed some light on how the game is played at the very highest levels. My findings, several of which are sprinkled throughout the book, should be useful to players of all levels.

The 424 Game Study

I conducted research on 424 games of 10 Ball for the three chapters on 10 Ball that make up Book 2 of the second edition of this book. Although several professional events of 10 Ball have been played on a 5' x 10' table (which is very fun to watch), I confined my analysis to tournaments that were played on a 4.5' x 9' table because that size is most relevant to amateur players. The study was comprised of 312 games from the Derby City 10-Ball tournaments from 2009-2012, and 112 games from Pat Fleming's Make It Happen All-Stars event in 2014.

How to Use This Book

This book is intended to be your one stop reference guide to playing 9&10-Ball. It is for players of at all levels of skill who have a sincere desire to improve at both games. The book is also designed to complement my previous books, *Play Your Best Pool*, *A Mind For Pool*, and *Capelle's Practicing Pool*, which give you a well-rounded course in all aspects of the game.

I suggest you develop your own specific course of study based on your game and your goals by making extensive use of the detailed table of contents. Read through it and make a list of the things that you need to work on. Once you have mastered the subject matter, pick out your next course of study.

Like a doctor or lawyer, it takes a long time to earn your degree in pool, so I recommend that you take your time while incorporating the material into your game. I also suggest that you view the book as a reference source and as a refresher course.

You can play a respectable game of 9 Ball or 10 Ball by mastering 30-50% of the material in the book. But if you wish to play your very best, you will need to be able to execute everything in the book – and more, for no book can cover everything. Keep in mind, however, that you have a lifetime to enjoy the fruits of your labor.

The ABC System

Players' skills vary widely, so each level should employ strategies that correspond to their game. Average players may see the same shot in several different ways because of their knowledge about what to do in a given situation. As a rule of thumb, the better you play 9&10-Ball, the more your choices of shots will mirror other players at your level. At the pro level, there is usually one best shot in most positions, and the pros are capable of recognizing it.

Players are divided into three broad categories that are based on their level of skill. I often refer to the ratings so that you can tailor the instruction to your current level of play. Below is a guide to rating your current level of play. For a more detailed explanation of my ABC rating system, please see pages 324-325.

Player Ratings
C Player – is an average player. Your typical daily high run is 5-6 balls.
B Player – is an advanced player: You can consistently run 5-7 balls, and are capable of running the easier layouts.
A Player – is an expert player. You can run complete racks with consistency.

I mentioned that you should design your course based on your game and level of play. The suggestions below should be helpful.
C Players – Begin by brushing up on your fundamentals starting with the first 10 pages of Chapter 1. The most critical ingredient to playing these games is position play. Master the position routes labeled C in Chapter 3, then move on to the Bs. Learn the basics of safety play because this will enable you to outsmart your fellow C Players.
B Players – Start by diagnosing your game. Pick out those areas you feel need work using the expanded table of contents. Include items that could use a refresher. Design your curriculum, and begin filling in the gaps in your game.
A Players – Evaluate your game to discover what still needs work. Look throughout the complete contents and the book for the fine points that can add an extra dimension to your game. Remember, the learning never stops if you want to reach your full potential as a player.

You can raise your winning percentage in competition right away with no increase in your skills simply by taking a more strategic approach to the game. In Chapter 13, The ABCs of Strategy, you will find a game plan for competing against opponents at all three levels of play.

The Illustrations

The illustrations complement the text. They have been drawn perfectly to scale so that you can see exactly how the shots and strategies really work on the table. Over 230 of the 550 illustrations are of shots played in competition by the world's best players. They were chosen for their instructive value, but you will find the exploits of the great champions to be entertaining as well.

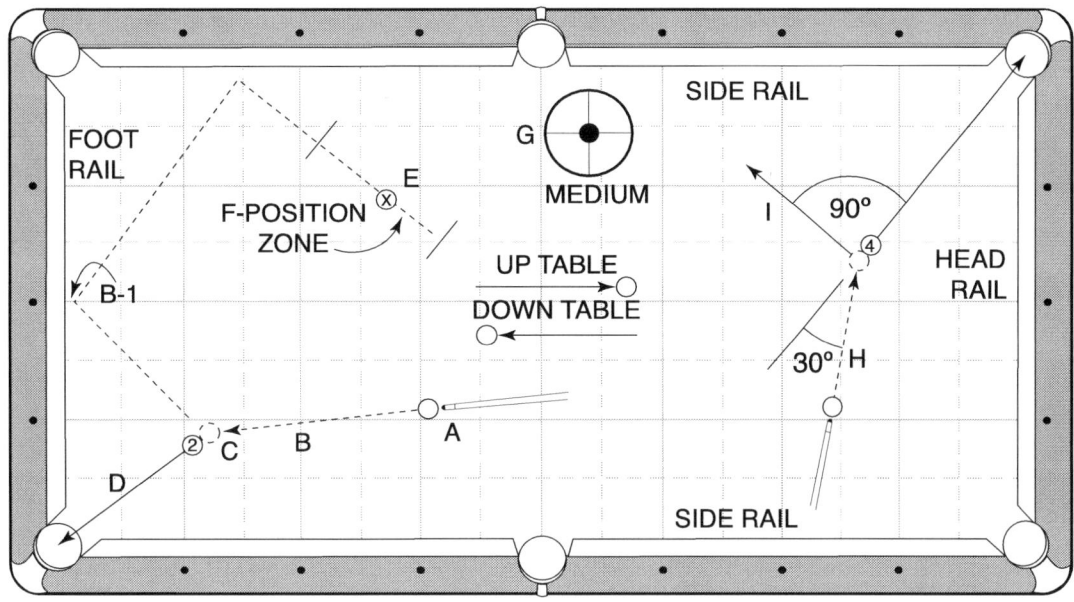

A The cue shows the direction in which the cue ball is being shot. When english is used, the cue will be positioned to the left or right of center. You can gain the shooter's perspective by turning the book so you are looking straight down the cue stick, just as if you were playing the shot.

B The dashed line shows the path of the cue ball to the object ball, as well as its path after contact.

B-1 The cue ball's path is shown by where its center is traveling. As a result, the line will never touch the rail.

C The dashed circle shows the cue ball's position at contact with the object ball.

D The solid line shows the path of the object ball. In most cases, it will be to the called pocket. On certain shots, the line into the pocket will be purposefully drawn to one side of the pocket.

E The cue ball with an X inside shows where it has come to rest. A series of cue balls with an X on one shot shows several possible stopping points. On straight in shots when the cue ball stops dead at the point of contact, the X cue ball is used to show both contact and the cue ball's ending location.

F Descriptive text appears on the diagrams where appropriate.

G Whenever the speed of stroke and cueing are particularly important to your understanding of a shot, you will find a box with a cue ball inside.

H It is important for you to understand the ideal cut angle for a wide variety of shots, so cut angles have been labeled throughout the book.

I You will find numerous references to the tangent line, which shows the cue ball's path after contact at a 90-degree angle from the object ball's line to the pocket.

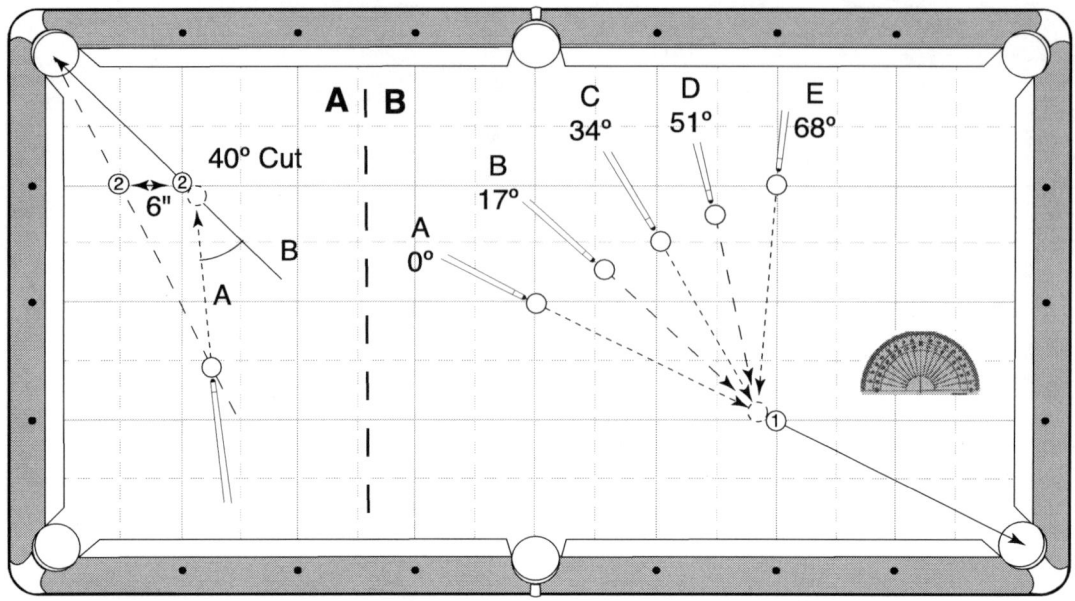

Pool Geometry Lesson 101

A working knowledge of angles is essential for position play in 9&10 Ball. You needn't carry a protractor (a device for measuring angles), but I do recommend that you be able to tell the difference in angles within at least a few (3-5) degrees of accuracy. I will refer to cut angles throughout the book, so if you are not comfortable with angles yet, please take the lesson below.

An angle measures the relationship between two straight lines. Angles are measured in degrees. In Part A, the straight in shot has no cut angle (0-degrees). If you move the 2-ball 6" to the right, the shot now has a 40-degree cut angle. This angle is computed by comparing Line A, which is the cue ball's path to the 2-ball, to Line B, which is the path of the 2-ball to the pocket.

Set up the shots in Part B so you can become acquainted with five significantly different cut angles. The 1-ball is 1 diamond off the bottom side rail and two diamonds from the end rail. Cue Ball A is in the exact middle of the table. Cue Ball E is one diamond off the top side rail and two diamonds from the end rail. Cue Balls B, C, and D are spaced three balls apart between Cue Balls A and E. You can put them in the exact positions by placing two balls between each cue ball.

- Cue Ball A shows a straight in shot on the 1-ball (0-degrees angle).
- Cue Ball B shows a shallow 17-degree cut shot.
- Cue Ball C is at 34-degrees to the 1-ball line to the pocket. A good percentage of your position play will use angles of 30-40 degrees.
- Cue Ball D shows a 51-degree cut angle. This angle is quite steep, and is one that you would almost never intentionally play for.
- Cue Ball E shows a cut shot that is at about the maximum angle that most players feel comfortable shooting.

x

The Spectrum of Speeds

The first and most important subject in the chapter on the Principles of Position Play is about speed control – your ability to send the cue ball the necessary distance for shape on the next ball. The Spectrum of Speeds for position play runs from extremely soft (a 1) to extremely hard (a 9). Most shots in 9 Ball and 10 Ball are played in the 4-7 range. Still, for a complete game, you must master all speeds. I reference the speeds on many shots.

The Spectrum of Speeds

Speed	MPH	Speed	MPH
1 Extremely Soft	1.0	**6** Medium Hard	6.0
2 Very Soft	2.0	**7** Hard	7.0
3 Soft	3.0	**8** Very Hard	8.0
4 Medium Soft	4.0	**9** Extremely Hard	9.0
5 Medium	5.0	**10** The Break	10.0

Glossary

There are many terms that are used for pool in general, and many more that are specifically used in 9&10 Ball. If you have any question on the terminology used in the book, look for the definition in the appendix.

Tips

A series of tips throughout the book are designed to provide you with a concise lesson related to the topic discussed just above it. They can also be read independently of the text.

Using the Donuts

Roy Yamane first gave me the idea for using the hole reinforcements that you use for three ring binder paper as an inexpensive but powerful training tool for pool. The "donuts", as I (and others) like to call them, enable you to quickly and accurately mark the position of the balls when practicing so you can play the same shots over and over.

Use of the Masculine Pronoun

I am 100% in favor of women playing pool. For style purposes only, however, I chose to use the masculine pronoun throughout the book because I find it awkward to be constantly alternating between he and she. To women readers I ask that you understand that he really means he or she.

A Word with Phil Capelle

Play Your Best 9 & 10 Ball is the culmination of my over 45 years of continuous involvement in pool. Along the way I learned by playing, watching players of all levels, reading books on pool, and from teaching.

I can honestly say that I looked forward to getting up every single day to work on this book, and that writing and producing it was indeed a labor of love. I hope you enjoy the book and that it helps you to play these two games better than you ever imagined possible.

Reader Comments

I would like to hear your comments and suggestions for improving future editions. You can write to me at: capellepublishing@gmail.com.

Abridged Table of Contents

BOOK 1 - Play Your Best 9 Ball

1 Shotmaking 3

2 The Break 41

3 Position Routes 59

4 Principles of Position 123

5 Pattern Play 159

6 Cluster Management 205

7 Reading the Table 213

8 Push Out Strategy 225

9 Safety Play 241

10 The Kicking Game 295

11 The ABCs of Strategy 323

12 Competitive 9 Ball....................................337

13 Practicing 9 Ball..359

BOOK 2 - Play Your Best 10 Ball

14 About 10 Ball 391

15 Derby City 10 Ball Challenge 409

16 Make It Happen All-Stars 463

Appendix..495

Complete Table of Contents

BOOK 1
Play Your Best 9 Ball

CHAPTER 1

Shotmaking 1
- Position Play or Shotmaking? 3
- The Fundamentals 4
- Stance 4
- Grip 4
- The Bridge 5
- The Stroke 7
- 12 Keys for Getting in Stroke 9
- Shot Selection 9
- Difficult Shots 10
- Extending Your Comfort Range 10
- Use Feedback from Missed Shots 12
- Missed Shot Tendencies 12
- Classifying Shots By Difficulty 13
- Shots You Must Master 14
- Maximum Practical Cut Angles 14
- Side Pocket Cut Angles 15
- Thin Cuts Rail First 15
- **Off the Rail (P)** 16
- Jacked Up Near the Rail 17
- **Basics of Banking** 18
- Short Rail Banks 18
- Try this Bank for Fun (P) 19
- Long Rail Bank Cut Angles 20
- Crossover Bank Shots 20
- Bank Combos Offer a Big Target (P) 21
- Aiming Factors 22
- Using the Aiming Factors 21
- Combining Aiming Factors 23
- **Billiards** 24
- Billiards Using the Tangent Line 24
- The Draw Back Billiard 25
- The Diversion Billiard 25
- A Long Distance Billiard (P) 26
- **Caroms** 27
- **Combinations** 28
- Difficulty of Various Combos 29
- Combo or Partially Blocked Shot? 30
- **Rail First Shots** 31
- **Curve Shots** 32
- A Masse/Curve Shot (P) 33
- **Jump Shots** 34
- The Pros' Use of the Jump Shot 34
- Jump Cues 34
- Practicing the Jump Shot 35
- Technique 35
- The Cue Ball's Flight Pattern 36
- Playing Position on Jump Shots 37
- When Not to Jump 38
- **Shooting the Gamewinner** 39
- Ideal Position on the 9-Ball 39

CHAPTER 2

The Break 41
- The Importance of the Break 42
- C Players 42
- B Players 42
- A Players 42
- The Pool & Billiard Study 43
- Your Optimum Break Speed 43
- The Strong Breaker's Advantage 42
- Goals for the Break Shot 44
- Where the Balls Go on the Break 45
- Playing Position After the Break 46
- Losing the Cue Ball on the Break 46
- Where the Pros Scratch 47
- Cue Ball Location 48
- Looking for the "Sweet Spot" 48
- Looking for the Best Speed 49
- The Control Break 49
- Setting Up for the Break Shot 50
- The Break Shot Stroke 51
- Johnny Archer's Break 52
- The Cue Balls Flight Pattern 54
- The Sardo Rack 53
- Racking is as Easy as 1-2-3 55
- Reading a Table for Tendencies 54
- Racking Technique 55
- Accept Imperfection 55
- The Racker – It Takes All Kinds 56
- When to Play Rack Inspector 57

CHAPTER 3

Position Routes 59
- The Run Out Game Plan 59
- The Sequence for Learning Position 60
- **Cueing - Learn to Become Multi Dimensional** .. 60
- English and Position Play 61
- Rules for Using English 61
- How English Affects the Cue Ball 62
- How English Affects the Rebound Angle ... 62
- The Cue Ball's Traveling Distance 63
- Mixing the Right Ingredients for Position .. 64
- The Primary Emphasis 65
- Don't Fight the Physics of Pool 66
- ABCs of Position Plays 67
- Recovery Shape 67
- **Setting Your Positional Goals** 67
- Average Players 68
- Advanced Players 68
- Expert Players 68
- Learn Both Sides of the Shot 69
- Formulas for Position Play 69
- **No Rail Position Routes** 70
- Stop Shots (C) 70
- Soft Follow Shots (C) 70
- Power Floaters (A) 71
- Follow Stun (B-A) 72
- Basic Short Range Draw Shots (C) 72

XIV

Long Draw Shots (A & B)	73
The Return Path on Draw Shots	74
Draw Floater (B)	74
Stun/Draw (B)	75
One-Rail Position Routes	**76**
Basic Follow Routes (C)	76
Balls Near a Pocket (C)	77
Pocket Speed Position and the Lag Shot (C)&(A)	78
One-Rail Follow on a 30-Degree Cut (C)	79
Inside English and the 90-Degree Reference Line	80
How the Angle Naturally Widens (B)	80
Long Distance One Rail Follow (B)	81
Targeting the Contact Point (B)	81
Long Distance Finesse Stun/Follow (A)	82
Basic Side Pocket One-Railers (C)	82
Creeper Follow (B)-(P)	83
Inside Power Follow (A)-(P)	83
One-Rail and Out (C & A)	84
Draw Across Table and Out (B)	84
Backcut Draw Across Table and Out (B)	85
Draw to the Rail and Out (B)	85
Draw Up the Side Rail (C)	86
Finesse Draw Outside English (B)	86
Draw Kill Shot (A) and (B)	87
Side Pocket to the End Rail (C)	87
The Pound Shot (A) – RR	88
Super Hard Pound & Draw (A)	88
Creating an Angle (B)	89
Two-Rail Position Routes	**90**
Two Rails with Follow (C)	90
Cueing and Speed Affects the Follow Route (B)	90
Two Rails with Inside Follow (B)	91
Shallow Angle Two-Railer (B, B, & A)	92
Small Cut Angle Two-Railer (A, A, & B)	92
Crossing the Table with English	93
Long Distance Side Rail Follow Shots - (B & A)	94
Avoiding a Common Scratch (C)	94
A Natural Centerball Two Railer (A)	95
Going Deep into the Corners – (P)	95
Reversing with Outside English (A)(P)	96
Across and Down with Inside English (A), (P)	96
Two Rails with Draw (C)	97
Stun/Draw Two Railer (B)	98
Two Rails Across with Draw Outside (B)	98
Stun Across and Down the Table (B)	99
Basic Side Pocket Two-Railer (A)	100
Side Pocket Inside English Two-Railers (B)	100
Inside Draw Two Rails (A), (P)	101
Three Rail Position Routes	**102**
Power Three-Railer (B &A)	102
Off Side Rail Three-Railer (B)	103
Three Rails Across (B &A)	103
Three Rails After a Thin Cut (A) (P)	104
Power Three Rail Position (A) (P)	104
Side Pocket Three-Railer (C)	105
Inside English Side Rail Three-Railer (A)	105
Inside English Three-Railer (B) (P)	106
Inside Draw off the Side Rail (A) (P)	106
Cross Table Twice (A) (P)	107
Massive Three Rail Draw (A) (P)	107
Four-Rail Position Routes	**108**
Draw Four-Railer (A)	108
Four Rails to the Short Side (A) (P)	108
Inside English 4 Rails to the Short Side (A) (P)	109
Four Rails with Inside Spin (2) (A)(P)	110
Long Distance Four-Railer (A) (P)	110
Follow/Pound Around the Table (A) (P)	111
Thin Cut Four Rail Route – (A) (P)	111
Position off of Bank Shots	**112**
Cross Corner Bank Routes	113
Long Rail Bank Routes	113
Crossover Side Pocket Bank	114
Intentionally Banking for Shape	114
Around the Table Bank Shape (A) (P)	115
Draw to Rail and Out off of a Cut Bank (A) (P)	115
Draw for Shape off the End Rail (A) (P)	116
Bank and Go Three Rails – (A) (P)	116
Position Play Errors	**117**
Why Errors Happen	117
The Corrective Cycle	117
Specific Error Tendencies	118
General Error Tendencies	118
Shots with High Error Potential	118
Landing Behind the Big Ball	119
Undercutting for Position	120
Overcutting for Position	120
Hitting Another Ball	120
Choosing the Wrong Route	121
Speed Control	122

CHAPTER 4
Principles of Position 123

#1 Speed Control	124
#2 The Correct Cut Angle Optimizes Position	126
#3 Know the Boundaries of a Position Zone	128
#4 Margin for Error	131
#5 When to Play Area Shape	133
#6 Survey the Table Before Shooting	134
#7 Playing for Three Balls at a Time	135
#8 Play the High Percentage Sequence	136
#9 Right Side/Wrong Side	138
#10 Play to the Long Side When Possible and Practical	140
#11 Ball in Hand Shape	143
#12 Playing Down the Line of a Position Zone	144
#13 Enter the Wide Part of a Position Zone	146
#14 Play Natural Shape as Often as Possible	148
#15 Plan Your Route and Avoid Obstructions	148
#16 Use Rail Targets	150
#17 Avoid Scratching	151
#18 Keep the Cue Ball Away from the Rails and Other Balls	154
#19 Pay Attention to Details	155
#20 Play Your Game	156
#21 Use Your Imagination	157
#22 Know the Exceptions to the First 21 Principles	158

CHAPTER 5
Pattern Play 159

The Run Out Game Plan	**159**
Pattern Recognition	**159**
The Primary Skill of Pattern Play	160
Position Routes as Tools	160

Key Principles of Position for Planning Patterns 160
A Tale of Two Players 161
Become a Skillful Navigator 161
Choosing the Optimal Route 162
Distance Affects Your Choice of Routes 162
Obstruction Creates a Gap in Position Zones 162
Connecting Naturally to the Next Ball.....................163
Using a Natural Route to Avoid a Combo (P) 164
Drawing to the Right Side (P).....................................164
Setting Up the Zorro Shot (P) 165
Setting Up a One Rail Route (P)................................165
Three Ball Patterns 166
Good Speed to Get on the Right Side 166
Setting up Two Way Position....................................166
When A Sharper Angle Works Better 167
A Multiple Option Pattern – Two Way Position.....168
End-to-End 168
4 Ball Patterns..169
Second Ball Cut Angle 169
The Second Ball's Cut Angle is Key 170
Setting Up Down-the-Line Shape 170
One Good Angle Leads to Another 171
Don't Fight the Table..172
Accept what the Table Gives You (P).......................172
Cinching Position with a Long Shot (P)...................172
Play Shape for a Combo 173
Simple is Often Best 174
Don't Needlessly Play Shape When You Have Shape..174
Keep it Simple to Avoid Trouble (P).........................174
A Sensible but Overlooked Pattern 175
The Easiest and Best Sequence (P) 176
The Right Choice is a One-Railer 176
Shoot Easy Combos to Simplify Things 177
Pocket Choice 178
Setting Up the Short Side (P)....................................192
Use All Six Pockets (P) 178
Multiple Pocket Shape (P)...179
Managing Risk and Avoiding Trouble 180
Weighing Risk and Reward.......................................180
Going Near a Pocket for Shape 181
Balls Together Away From the Rail 181
Shape Versus Scratch 182
Shape for a Safety (P) 182
Avoiding Trouble with the High % Route (P) 183
The Gap Past the Side Pocket..................................183
Precision Pattern Play 184
Precision Pattern Play (P)...184
Top Flight Planning and Execution (P) 185
Precision Short Side Shape (P) 185
Across and Out to a Small Zone (P).........................186
Setting Up a Precision Follow Shot (P) 186
Ultra Precise One-Railer (P) 187
Draw Control (P) 187
Improving the Layout by Moving a Ball 188
Optional and Mandatory Layout Improvement 188
Looking Ahead 188
Getting a Ball off the Rail (P) 189
End of Rack Pattern Play 190
End of Game Run Out %s 190
The 9-Ball Determines the Correct Route 190
When to Play for a Cut on the 9-Ball 191

End to End on the Last Three Balls (P) 192
The Last Two are on the Same Rail 192
End of Rack Pattern (P) 193
Sending the Cue Ball to Center Table (P) 194
Side Versus Corner Pocket 194
Side Versus Corner 195
Patterning Balls in the Middle................................196
Ball in the Middle (P)..196
Shaping a Ball in the Middle of the Table (P) 197
Two Consecutive Balls on the Same Rail 198
Two Consecutive Balls on the Same Side Rail (1)...198
Two Consecutive Balls on the Same Side Rail (2)...199
Either Side of the Ball Can Work 200
Either Side Works Just Fine.....................................200
One Side Is Better 200
End Rail Position..201
End Rail Position (2) 202
Setting Up for a Bank 202
Bank Shape Zones 202
Playing for a Bank (P) 203
Miss Position then Play a Bank (P) 204

CHAPTER 6

Cluster Management 205
Cluster Management 205
Reading Clusters 206
High % Breakouts 206
Low % Breakouts 206
Avoid High Risk Cluster Busting...............................207
Controlling the Path to the Cluster 208
Timing a Break Is Critical 208
The Ideal Cluster Busting Scenario.........................209
Use Ball in Hand to Break Clusters 210
Breaking a Cluster with BIH (P) 210
How to Break a Cluster (P) 211
Precision Cluster Breaking 211
Break a Cluster with a Safety (P) 212
Use a Bank to Break a Cluster 212

CHAPTER 7

Reading the Table 213
The Football Analogy 213
The Stop Light Analogy 214
A Simplified Decision Matrix...................................214
Know Your Game and Play Your Game 214
Get to Know the Table..215
Where the Balls Tend to Locate 216
Reading the Table...216
How to Read the Table...217
The Various Types of Layouts.................................217
The Roadmap (or Cosmo) (P) 218
Tough Racks that Appear Easy 218
Precision Run Out is Possible 219
A Traveling Rack 219
A Tough Position Play (P) 220
The Out Shot (P)..220
Short Rack Opportunities (P) 221
Congestion Rules from the Start 222
Congestion at the End 223
The Improbable Dream (P)..224

CHAPTER 8

Pushout Strategy 225
- **Professional's Use of the Push Out** 226
- **The Push Out is a Valuable Strategic Weapon** 226
- **Common Errors** 227
- **The 40-60 Rule of Push Outs** 227
- Push Out Decision Making Matrix 263
- **Developing a Winning Push Out Game** 228
- Basics of Cue Ball Control 229
- Shoot Don't Push 230
- Leave Two Tough Shots 230
- Bank or Cut – What's Your Preference? 231
- When to Kick at a Pocket Hanger 231
- Accept Free Shots 232
- Get It Close to the Rail 232
- Push to an Uncertain Hook 233
- Sucker Shot versus Smart Safety 233
- Combo in the Lowest Numbered Ball 234
- Make the Run Much Tougher 234
- Pocket a 9-Ball in the Jaws 235
- Tying Balls Up 235
- The Beginner's Big Mistake 236
- Pushing to a Semi-Easy Hook Opportunity (P) 236
- Be Wary of the Congestion Factor 237
- A Bluff Could Lead to a Mental Mistake 237
- Push Out to a Better Kick Shot (P) 238
- Combining Elements of a Push Out 238
- Jump or Kick? 239
- Cluster Balls Past Your Money Ball 240
- Get Your Money Ball in Front of a Pocket 240

CHAPTER 9

Safety Play 241
- **Mindset for Safety Play** 241
- Defensive Goals 242
- **Rating the Quality of Your Safeties** 242
- The Spectrum of Safeties 243
- **Skills for Excelling at Safety Play** 244
- Mastering the Basics 244
- Hitting the Object Ball the Correct Thickness 244
- Controlling the Cue Ball's Path off the Rails 245
- The Angle of Departure 246
- The Thin Hit 247
- Draw Control 248
- **Safety Skills Inventory** 249
- **Knowing When to Play Safe** 249
- Safety Over a Shot 250
- **Selecting the Best Safety** 250
- Which Safety is the Better Choice? 251
- **Basic Hook Safeties** 252
- Hitting the Hook Zone 252
- Hitting the Hook Zone (2) 253
- Eliminating Options 254
- Block the Natural Kick Route 254
- Hooking Behind the "Big Ball" 255
- Basic Hook (P) 256
- Off the Side Rail and Down Table (P) 256
- Multiple Ball Hook Safeties 257
- Risk Versus Reward 258
- Multi Rail Hook Safeties 259
- **Controlling the Right Ball is Key** 260
- Airtight Safety (P) 260
- Controlling the Cue Ball at Long Range (P) 261
- Beware of the Returning Object Ball 262
- Control Both on a Billiard (P) 262
- Don't Accidentally Make a Bank 263
- Control Both Balls (P) 264
- Thin Hit Across Table (P) 264
- An Effective Long Distance Safety (P) 265
- **Using Available Blockers** 266
- Using Available Blockers (P) 266
- Window Free (P) 266
- Banking Past a Big Ball 267
- **Soft Follow Shot Safeties** 268
- Lock'em Up Tight 268
- Super Soft Hit Safety (P) 268
- A Finesse Follow Shot Safety 269
- Inside English Kill Shot Safety 270
- **Finesse Draw Safeties** 270
- Soft Draw Hook Safety (P) 270
- Draw Spin Finesse Safety 271
- **Thin Hit Safeties** 272
- Thin Hit at Short Range 272
- Frozen Ball Safety 273
- Ball in Hand Thin Hit Safety 274
- Thin Hit Safety or Bank Shot? 274
- Perfect Speed Avoids Possible Scratch (P) 275
- **Crossover Bank Safeties** 276
- **Safes with a Carom** 278
- A Carom Safety 278
- A "Dead" Carom Bank Safety 278
- Carom Safety at Long Range (P) 279
- **Kick Safeties** 280
- Two Rail Kick Safety (P) 280
- Short Rail Kick and Stick 280
- Thin Hit Kick Shot 281
- **Missing Safe (1/2 Safe, 1/2 Shot)** 282
- Overcut to Miss Safe 282
- Miss Short Rail Banks on the Pro Side 282
- Cross Side Bank Safeties 283
- Cross Side Safety Bank 284
- Missing Long Rail Banks on the Pro Side 284
- Leave a Tough Shot after a Bank (P) 285
- **End Game** 286
- Long Distance End Game Warfare (P) 286
- Two End Game Bank Safeties 287
- **Strategic Safeties** 288
- Pass on a Shot that Leads Nowhere 288
- Pass on Shot, Hook at Long Range (P) 288
- Pass on Shot for Sure Safe (P) 289
- Simplify the Rack with Ball In Hand (P) 290
- Leave Shots Your Opponent Doesn't Like 290
- Set Up Combo on the 9-Ball (P) 291
- **Creative Safety Play** 292
- Imagination Creates a Winning Safety 292
- Grady's Near Masterpiece (P) 292
- Jump and Hook (P) 293
- Rail First Safety (P) 294
- Use a Second Ball as a Stopper 294

CHAPTER 10

The Kicking Game 295
Your Attitude Towards Kicking 296
The Possible Outcome – How You View a Kick Shot .. 296
A Game Plan for the Kicking Game 297
Basics of Kicking 298
The Importance of Speed Control 298
Adjusting for Speed of the Table 298
Combining Adjustments 299
English Pick Up 300
Testing a Table 300
The ABCs of Kicking Targets 302
Kicking to Hit 302
The Triangle Method 302
The Dominant Rail 303
Kicking Past Obstructers 304
Two or Three Rails is Often Better than One 304
Aim at the Big Ball 305
Long Distance Side Rail Kicks 305
The Side Pocket Gap 306
Corner Pocket Gaps 306
"The Shot Heard Around the Pool World" (P) 307
Kick to Separate the Balls 308
The Big Ball Ensures a Hit 308
Separate the Balls 308
Separate the Balls (P) 309
Kick to Hook 310
Kicking at Balls Near a Rail 310
Kick and Stick (P) 310
Two Rail Stick and Hook at High Speed (P) 311
A Soft Hit Kick Safety 312
Kick and Hook One-Rail (P) 312
Kick and Hook (P) 313
A Perfect Kick and Hook (P) 313
Kick to Pocket 314
Tough, But Easier than it Looks 314
Ride the 9-Ball (P) 314
Kick to Pocket off the Side Rail 315
Skill Lets You Get Lucky Sometimes (P) 315
Creative Tactics 316
Creative Use of Spin Plus Great Execution (P) 316
Draw Bender 316
Jump/Kick and Hook (P) 317
Curve Kick Shot (P) 317
Kicking Errors 318
Don't Kick Softly to an Open Area of the Table 318
Avoid Scratching 318
Using the Correct Speed (P) 319
A Common Scratch on a Kick (P) 319
Be Wary of the Point (1) 320
Be Wary of the Point (2) 320
Hitting the Wrong Side 321
A Sure Safety Beats a Sucker's Kick Shot 321
Short Distance to the First Rail 322
Trying to Hit Balls Thinly and Missing Altogether .. 322

CHAPTER 11

The ABCs of Strategy 323
Rating Your Game and Testing Your Skill 324
Measuring Your Ability By the # of Racks Run 324
How to Measure a Run 324
Your Typical Good Runs 325
Personal Bests 325
The Three Phases of a Rack 325
Phase 1: The Beginning 326
Phase 2: The Middle 326
Phase 3: The End 326
The ABCs of Strategy 326
Strategy for All Levels of Players 327
Strategies for C Players 327
C Player vs. C Player 327
C Player vs. B Player 328
C Player vs. A Player 329
Strategies for B Players 330
B Player vs. B Player 330
B Player vs. C Player 331
B Player vs. A Player 331
Strategies for A Players 332
A Player vs. A Player 332
A Player vs. B Player 333
A Player vs. C Player 334

CHAPTER 12

Competitive 9 Ball 337
Intimidation – The Mental Side of Nine-Ball 338
Qualities that Opponents Find Intimidating 338
The Battle for Intimidation 340
Levels of Intimidation – the Spectrum 340
9 Ball is a Battle of Skill Sets 341
Scouting Your Opponent 341
The Mini-Max Strategy 342
The Score – All About that Most Vital Statistic 343
Categories of Games 344
Accessing Your Top Gear and Closing a Match 345
Rolls, Mistakes and Great Shots 345
Developing the Killer Instinct 346
Men and Women in Today's World of Pool 347
Tournaments 348
Types of Tournaments 348
Manage Your Expectations 349
How to win Tournaments 392
Single Elimination 350
Double Elimination 350
Preparing for a Big Tournament 350
Money Games 352
Handicapping 352
Spotting 353
Combination Spots 353
Format 354
Money Management 354
The Rules 355
Time 355
Backers 355
Hustles and Shark Moves 355
The Collection Department 355
League Play 356
An Introduction 356
Your Team 356
Team Goals 357

Individual Goals 357
League Night 357

CHAPTER 13
Practicing 9 Ball 359
Rating Your Game in the Key Competencies 359
Champions Checklist 360
A Sample Comparison of Skills 361
Practice Environment 361
Increase Your Awareness 362
Solitary Practice 362
How to Structure Each Session 363
Practice Tips for Solitary Sessions 364
The ABCs of Practicing with a Partner 365
How to Practice with Your Partner 366
Having a Teacher, Coach or Mentor 367
Tips for Being a Great Student 367
Practicing Your Fundamentals 368
5 Donuts in a Row 368
Cue Over the Diamond Drill 369
Shotmaking Practice 370
Test Your Cut Shots 370
The Long Green Practice Drill 371
Position Practice 372
One Rail Rebound Pathways 372
Soft Follow One Rail 373
Draw Off One Rail 373
No Rail Position 374
Stop Shot 374
Follow Shots 374
Progressive Draw 375
Two Rail Position 376
Across and Down the Table 377
Hitting a Target Ball 378
Avoid Obstructers 378
Opposites Add Variety 379
Pattern Play 380
Build Your Run Out Power 380
Use Cosmos to Build Concentration 381
Practice the Key Principles 382
A Useful Run Out Drill 383
Additional Pattern Play Drills 423
Practice Drills For Safety Play 384
Controlling Sideways Drift 384
Float and Hook 385
The Cue Ball's Route After Contact (1) 386
The Cue Ball's Route After Contact (2) 386
Long Distance Hook Safeties 387
Kicking Practice 388
Break Shot Practice 388

BOOK 2
Play Your Best 10 Ball

CHAPTER 14
About 10 Ball 391
The Game 391
Who Should Play 10 Ball 392
My 424 Game Study: 9 Ball vs. 10 Ball 392

The Break in 10 Ball 394
Practicing Your Break 394
Van Boening: Pool's Most Powerful Second ... 396
Bustamante's High Powered Break Stroke ... 398
An Intro. to the Following Sections and Chapters ... 400
The Derby City and Make It Happen Tournaments .. 400
Derby City and Make It Happen Shot Titles ... 400
Capelle's Analysis 401
Features of the Presentations 402
Pool's Unique Challenge 404
Black Cue Ball Exercises 405
Ideas for Your BCB Practice Sessions 406
A Rated Black Cue Ball Exercises 407

CHAPTER 15
Derby City 10 Ball 409
#1 – Corteza (15) vs. Souquet (11) – Finals ... 410
Corteza Makes a Statement! 410
Balls in the Middle 410
Balls in the Middle 411
Shape After the Combo 412
Souquet's Combo Clinic 412
Two-Way Billiard is a Winner 413
Souquet: Phase 1 - Diag. A 414
One Pocket in 10-Ball - Diag. B 414
#2 – Reyes (15) vs. Archer (11) – Semi-Final ... 415
4 Balls at a Time! 415
The Magician Plies his Trade 416
Efren Threads the Needle 416
Precision Draw Position 417
A 4-Rail Escape 418
Like a Diamond Cutter! 418
Archer Runs to the Bank 419
#3 – Reyes (15) vs. Shuff (8) – Finals 420
Efren's Two-Rail Reverse 420
Use those Blockers 420
Side Pocket 10 Ball! – Diag. A 421
Side Pocket 10 Ball! – Diag. B 423
#4 – Van Boening (15) vs. Souquet (14) 422
Half Ball Bank Safety – Diag. A 422
Shane Opens the Window – Diag. B 423
Send in Souquet! 424
Ultra-Thin Safety! 424
Set that Angle! 425
Power Follow and Across 426
#5 – Bustamante (15) vs. Martinez (1) 426
Off to the Races! 426
Controlling a Hanger! 427
This Judge Gives it a 10!! 428
A Certified Jaw Dropper!! 428
#6 – Corteza (15) vs. Moore (8) 429
World Class Pattern Play!! 429
World Class, Part II 430
That 40 Degree Angle! 430
An Impossible Runout! – Diag. A 431
Corteza's Reward – Diag. B 432
Two Way Position off a Combo 432
#7 – Appleton (15) vs. Bustamante (13) – Semi-F. .. 433
"Banking" in a Billiard 433
Matching Wits on Defense 434

Pushing Out to a Shot – Diag. A 434
Going Airborne! – Diag. B 435
Coming with a Big Shot 436
Straight Back Power Draw!! 436
The Bustamante Show!! 437
A One Shot Lesson in Kicking 438
#8 – Morris (15) vs. Appleton (11) – Finals 438
Pattern Play Genius – Diag. A 438
Pattern Play Genius – Diag. B 439
Unusual, But Very Effective! 440
Three Rails in the Side 440
High Speed Firepower! 441
Super Spinner! 442
#9 – Bustamante (15) vs. Van Boening (9) 442
Punch and Counterpunch! 442
Squeaking in the Widow 443
Power Hop and Run! 444
Targeting the Cue Ball 444
Game Winning Billiard! 445
70-Degree Table Length Cut 446
Inside Spin Power 4-Railer! 446
Combo Simplifies the Pattern 447
#10 – Pagulayan (15) vs. Morris (9) 448
Position for a Breakout 448
Runout Over Combo 448
High Octane Recovery Route 449
The Cluster and Hook Bunt Shot! 450
Super 4 Rail Route 450
A Rail First (Kick) Billiard 451
Draw + Spin = Position 452
#11 – Moore (15) vs. Pagulayan (12) – Semi-F. 452
Precision Push Out 452
Duel "Out Shots" 453
Fan it in to Win! 454
More Gems by Moore!   Diag. A 454
Closing the Deal in Style   Diag. B 455
#12 – Bustamante (15) vs. Morra (5) – Semi-F. 456
Rail First at Long Range 456
Through Traffic to a Combo 456
Draw/Stun to a Frozen Cut 457
Identify the Big Hurdle – Diag. A 458
Identify the Big Hurdle – Diag. B 458
#13 – Bustamante (15) vs. Moore (5) – Finals 459
All Out Strategic Warfare! 459
A Big Z Safety! 460
Five Rail Position Play 460

CHAPTER 16

Make It Happen All-Stars 463
#1 – Van Boening (11) vs. Hohmann (9) 464
Super Soft Position Play 464
Shane's Draw & Jump Show! 464
Hohmann's Extravaganza! 465
4-Rail Super Bank Safety! 466
Incidence Equals Reflection! 466
A 26 Foot Journey! 467
Shane's Variety Act! (Diag. A) 468
Rail First Cheat Shot! (Diag. B) 468
#2 – Orcollo (11) vs. Hohmann (9) 469

Kick, Stick, and Hook! 469
A Pinball Safety 470
Great Opening Sequence!! 470
Middle of a Super Tough Run 471
The Hardest Shot of All!!! (Diag. A) 472
The Hardest Shot of All!!! (Diag. B) 472
Power Follow Shot 473
Bad Push to Textbook Safety 474
#3 – Orcollo (11) vs. Van Boening (7) 474
Playing Perfect Pool 474
A Great Exchange: Kick and Safety 475
Multiple Objectives! 476
Fortune Favors the Bold! 476
#4 – Appleton (11) vs. Orcollo (8) 477
Spectacular Recovery Route 477
Hook and Counter-Hook! (Diag. A) 478
Precision Long Range Draw! (Diag. B) 478
The One Inch Push Out (Diag. A) 479
Wrong Side Position Play (Diag. B) 480
Play that Combo! 480
Super Strong Opening 481
Setting a Rail Target! 482
Winning Won Games! 482
Setting Up the Key Shot! 483
#5 – Van Boening (11) vs. Appleton (5) 484
Classic Side Rail Stun Shot 484
Long Range Recovery Route 484
Accepting a Push Out 485
Big Draw Leads to a B&R 486
Power Follow Past an Obstructer 486
Super Draw/Bender Shot 487
Setting Up the Angle 488
#6 – Appleton (11) vs. Hohmann (8) 488
Pattern to a Safety 488
Going Deep into the Corner 489
Big Position Play 490
Draw Outside Special 490
An Aiming/Power-Draw Shot! 491
On the Wrong Side 492
A Strong Opening Act 493

APPENDIX

Rules 495
Glossary 498
A Pool Player's Cue Case 506
Bar Table 9 Ball 507
Ring Games 510
Player Index 511
Where to Play 9 Ball and 10 Ball 512
Accu-Stats DVDs 513
How to Order DVDs 515
How to Learn from Watching DVDs 515
Black Cue Ball Closing Run Out Patterns 516
Phil Capelle 520
Billiards Press 520

BOOK 1

Play Your Best 9 BALL

CHAPTER 1

Shotmaking

*" I remember when I was playing my best pool when
I got a simple shot I beared down on it.
And it kept me going, going."*
Bill Incardona

9 Ball is for shotmakers. Each demands that you consistently pocket tough shots. Indeed, even if you play excellent position, you will still have to play at least a couple of moderately challenging shots in all but the easiest layouts. One of your primary objectives, therefore, is to make sure that the tough shots come up because of your opponent's leaves, or due to the inherent difficulty of the layout, not because of your lack of cue ball control.

My analysis of over a thousand games by top pros shows that the best position players in the world still face an average of nearly one very difficult shot per rack. A fair percentage of runouts studied included at least two difficult shots. The typical amateur may face several challenging shots in an average rack because of errors in position, but many of these shots can be eliminated through improved position play.

Position Play or Shotmaking?

To excel at 9 Ball you've got to **be a position playing shotmaker more than a shotmaking position player**. No matter how accurate your shotmaking skills become, you cannot consistently string together runs of more than 2-4 shots without playing adequate position. Still, even if you become an expert position player, you will still need to pocket a variety of challenging shots to initiate and sustain all but the simplest of layouts – so learn to enjoy the challenge each one presents!

The Fundamentals

The upcoming sections discuss the fundamentals as they relate to 9 Ball. A complete discussion of the fundamentals is beyond the scope of this book, but can be found in *Play Your Best Pool* and *Capelle's Practicing Pool*.

Stance

While largely a matter of personal preference, **your stance should feel natural, comfortable, and stable. Your head should be in a position where you can aim accurately**. Lastly, a good stance will put your shooting arm in a position where you can swing it straight through contact and beyond.

The three basic heights for the stance are low, medium, and high. A low stance, with your chin on or just above your cue, enables you to achieve a more consistent alignment, which is crucial in aiming. A low stance, however, can restrict your arm swing, especially on power shots, which can lead to jumping up prematurely. Your chin is about 6-8" above the cue with a medium height stance. This allows for a free arm swing for ample power, and it enables you to aim with accuracy. Your chin will be over a foot above the cue with a high stance. This stance promotes a very free arm swing with which you can apply plenty of power, but it is not recommended for 9 Ball because of the precise aiming that the game requires.

Variable Stance Height

You should consider **matching the height of your stance to the requirements of each shot**. For example, when the cue ball is very close to the object ball, a high stance can improve depth perception and your aim. When you have a long shot off the rail, a low stance enables you to look back and forth between the cue ball and object ball without having to move your head up and down to any great degree.

Your height, and the height of your stance, will affect the distance of your grip hand from your bridge hand, and the position of your grip hand relative to the cue. A tall player's hands will be further apart than those of a shorter player. And those players with a low stance will have a longer distance between their two hands than those who use a more upright stance.

Grip

The grip is largely an individual matter, as can be seen by the grips of some of the world's top professionals and the many opponents you will encounter. If, however, you have neither the talent nor the time to master any of the non-textbook grips, I suggest that you stick to a grip like the one I recommend in *Play Your Best Pool*.

Your grip for 9 Ball should be loose and flexible. You need a supple wrist so you can release the cue with authority into contact with the cue ball. Tension in your grip hand will reduce the action you can impart on the cue ball, and it will lead to twisting the cue on the forward stroke. Remember, **the lighter you grip the cue, the more you will feel the weight of the cue**. A light grip creates the feeling that the cue is doing a large share of the work.

The Bridge
Bridge Length
9 Ball is a full table game in which you must regularly play long shots, often using a powerful stroke. Because of the power required, **the average professional uses an 11" bridge** according to a study conducted by *Pool & Billiard Magazine*. This is considerably longer than the 8" bridge length favored the great Straight Pool players of yesteryear. Eight Ball, which is much more closely related to Straight Pool, is also played with a shorter bridge. And those who play mostly on a bar table also tend to favor a shorter bridge because this version of 9 Ball is more about finesse than power.

Compromises Between Short and Long
In 9 Ball you must play with power and accuracy, shot characteristics which are at odds with one another! A long bridge enables you to smoothly generate plenty of power, but at the expense of accuracy. A short bridge increases your accuracy, but limits your ability to generate power with a smooth delivery. Players who use an extremely short bridge tend to muscle the ball when they need extra power.

You need to strike the ideal balance between accuracy and power. In the beginning, I suggest you use a slightly shorter bridge than the pros, say about 9-10". As your stroke develops power and accuracy, you can lengthen your bridge to the 10-11" range. Since bridge length is largely a matter of personal preference, those of you with exceptional hand/eye coordination may be able to mimic the bridges of pros who use a 12"+ long bridge.

Benefits of a Long Bridge
A long bridge enables you to accelerate smoothly without having to force the action, or to make a conscious effort to apply extra power. This can help improve your speed control across a wider range of the Spectrum of Speeds. **A long bridge can also improve your view down the cue and to the cue ball** because the closed bridge loop does not interfere nearly as much with your line of sight.

On every shot the cue ball goes airborne for a short distance after contact even though its flight cannot be seen by the human eye. A short bridge can cause a more downward hit, which causes the cue ball to fly higher. In addition, stroke errors will be magnified. A long bridge enables you to use a more level stroke, which reduces unwanted sidespin or stun caused by an error in your stroke.

On draw shots you will always be hitting slightly down on the cue ball due to the height of the rails. In addition, most players use a closed bridge on draw shots, which automatically raises the cue at their bridge to 1.5" or more above the cloth. Meanwhile, when you are using a full tip of draw, the middle of your tip is only 5/8" off the table. In other words, your cue is angled downward into the cue ball on draw shots, which naturally creates a downward hit on the cue ball.

A longer bridge enables you to decrease your cue's angle to the table, which reduces the amount that the cue ball jumps after contact. This can be especially important if you have large hands, as they create a more elevated bridge. With an 8" bridge that is elevated 1.5" from the table, the cue will be at a 6.5-degree angle when one tip of draw is used. Using the same bridge elevation, an 11" bridge and one tip of draw would create a cue angle of only 4.5-degrees!

Open Bridge

An open bridge has many advantages. **Your line of sight to the cue ball is unobstructed, which makes aiming easier.** Less friction between the cue and your bridge leads to a smoother stroke. You can bridge lower on draw shots, which decreases the cue's angle into the cue ball. On stretch shots it is easier to reach the cue ball. Finally, an open bridge helps to expose errors in your technique. For example, if you twist your arm or wrist, or if you rise up slightly, the cue will come flying off the "Vee" of your bridge hand. Even if you don't use an open bridge in competition, practicing with it will help you groove a nearly flawless stroke.

Despite the advantages of the open bridge, nearly all top players **use a closed bridge for power shots** because they like the feeling of stability and confidence that the closed bridge gives them.

Variable Bridge Length

Golfers use a narrower stance for their short irons than they do for their driver. Similarly, **you may wish to consider varying the length of your bridge** to match the shot you are playing. On a finesse follow shot you can smoothly generate the power you need with a 7" bridge and stroke. On a long draw shot, you might extend your bridge to 10-11 inches. To use the variable bridge technique, you would have to either:

- Feel comfortable using strokes of varying lengths or,
- Use a backstroke on power shots that is no longer than the longest stroke you use when using a short bridge.

Changing Your Bridge Length

After evaluating your game, you may decide that a longer or shorter bridge would be better. **You can adjust you bridge by regulating the position of your grip hand**. Both hands should move the same distance up or down the cue when you make the change. Let's say that you want to lengthen your bridge by 2". Here's how to do it:

- Take your normal shooting stance for a medium length shot.
- Take your bridge hand off your cue and grip the butt end of the cue next to your grip hand (at the side closest to the joint).
- Place a rubber band 2" towards the butt end of the cue.
- When you take your stance, your grip hand should be next to the rubber band. Your bridge hand will naturally follow your grip hand back down the shaft toward the joint!

The Stroke

The game of 9 Ball requires you to play shots at different speeds. At times you will need the touch of a surgeon while on other occasions you must power the cue ball at upwards of 10 MPH for position. Most new players like to hit the cue ball at high speeds, which seems to meet the requirements for 9 Ball. To play this game correctly, however, you need the kind of power that is generated by a fluid stroke, not from a muscular stab at the ball.

Graceful Power

A graceful swing of the arm and a release of your wrist prior to contact can produce the power that you need to play any shot in 9 Ball (with the exception of the break). And yet, all too many players try to add power to their shots by muscling the cue ball with their arm – an error that usually begins at the beginning of the transition from the backstroke to the forwardstroke. The tensing of the arm and wrist actually slows down the arm, reducing power and accuracy!

The secret to power is to stay relaxed as you swing the arm forward and let your wrist accelerate the cue just prior to the moment of contact. This timed release of the cue helps you to avoid steering the cue, and it provides extra power precisely at the moment it is needed.

Become a Pool Shooting Machine

A smooth and powerful stroke is a product of the steps in your shooting routine that have preceded it. We've already discussed the stance, grip, bridge and stroke. Another important element is your preshot routine. So, I recommend that you **begin your shooting routine by facing directly down the line of aim before assuming your stance**. Land on the table with your bridge hand the same way every time. Once you have mastered these steps, you will be well on your way to becoming a pool shooting machine. Three pros who especially embody this technique are Efren Reyes, Mika Immonen, and Cory Deuel.

Warm Up Strokes

An entire chapter could be written on the various sequences of warm up strokes. Some players use the same back and forth motion on every warm up stroke. Others mix things up with a series of short and long strokes. If you are not already comfortable with your pattern, **I recommend a full series of warm up strokes that most closely resembles your final stroke** because this acts as a rehearsal for the stroke you are going to use. Or, you can try experimenting with the various techniques of the pros until you find the pattern that works best for you.

Briefly, warm up strokes:
- Give you enough time to lock in your aim.
- Allow you to make any last second adjustments in your position.
- Give you time to develop a feel for the speed of stroke.
- Enable you to gain the feeling that your stroke is on track.
- Loosen up your arm and wrist.

The items on the list above will largely become instinctual after a while. Still, you will have to consciously focus on some of them during your shooting routine.

The Transition

The transition from the final backstroke (once the warm up strokes are over) to the final forwardstroke is the make or break point of most players' strokes. A smooth and unhurried transition helps give you a longer look at the object ball. It also insures against a muscle bound lurch into the cue ball. It is amazing how so many players with a series of silky smooth warm-up strokes will end up making a spastic stab at the cue ball on the final stroke.

The culprit is the "hit impulse", which takes over during the transition from backstroke to forwardstroke. To solve this problem, **consciously slow the transition phase of the final stroke, and then accelerate smoothly** so that you generate maximum power and speed at contact with the cue ball – not at the start of your forwardstroke.

Finding "It", Losing "It", and Finding "It" Again

Sports like pool, tennis, and golf depend on a player's ability to repeat certain movements with a very high level of consistency. **You are a human and not a machine, so you will be forever finding your stroke, having it, losing it, and finding it again**. It is a never-ending cycle. Your stroke will come and go. Hopefully, you'll spend most of the time in stroke instead of searching for the lost magic. Your efforts to maintain a consistent stroke – one that will stay with you for long periods of time, will be greatly aided if you:
- Develop a fundamentally sound stroke.
- Know your game and your negative tendencies. This allows you to quickly spot flaws and apply corrective measures before you sink into an extended period of poor play – a slump!
- Visualize and imagine the feel of your stroke so you can utilize the benefits of muscle memory.

12 Keys for Getting in Stroke

You can quickly get back in the groove if you focus your attention on a specific fundamental. Your key thought may be a technique that has worked in the past, or something new.

1. **Relax Your Grip** - Let your shooting arm hang naturally at your side. Curl your fingers at the second joint. Then lay the cue across the middle pad of your first two fingers. Your thumb acts only as a support.

2. **Set Up Correctly** - Set up precisely for each shot as this eliminates the need to shuffle around excessively in order to find your comfort zone.

3. **Cue Perfectly** - Try positioning your tip with extra care when setting up for your shots.

4. **Silky Smooth Stroke** - As you settle into your stance, think about making the smoothest stroke imaginable.

5. **Swing Only Your Arm** - Unwanted body movements can ruin your shots. To eliminate this fault, concentrate on moving only your shooting arm and wrist.

6. **Use Extra Warm-up Strokes** - If you tend to rush your shots, add a couple of extra warm-up strokes into your shooting routine.

7. **Slow the Transition** —You can eliminate the tendency to tighten up at this critical stage by beginning your final forwardstroke in the same relaxed manner that you use during your warm up strokes.

8. **Stare Intently Down the Line of Aim** — Try to stare holes through the Shot Picture, including the object ball, during your final stroke

9. **Feel The Tip At Contact** - You can learn about your stroke and cue ball action by focusing on the feel of the tip at contact. Does the tip mesh with the cue ball in a crisp, satisfying manner?

10. **Drop Your Elbow After Contact** - After contact the elbow should drop as the arm swings forward, and as it glides to a stop.

11. **Follow Through Straight** - Extend your cue directly down the line of aim. Hold your follow through as if posing for a picture and check to see if your cue is perfectly on line. This works best on shots cued on the vertical axis.

12. **Stay Down** - Try to stay down until the object ball is in the pocket. This will keep you from taking your eyes off the target prematurely.

Shot Selection

When playing 9 Ball, you must be able to gauge the difficulty of a shot so you can make correct decisions as to whether to play offense or defense. Which shot or safety gives you the best odds of winning? **You must know which shots are a go, and which are not**. Your decisions will vary depending on how you are playing, the equipment, and the pressure.

Difficult Shots

It is a common mistake for amateurs and pros to give difficult shots their worst stroke. A poor effort results from a lack of confidence in their ability to make the shot, and because they are anticipating a poor result. How many times have you seen someone jump up when playing a tough shot? Do you do it yourself? Unfortunately, **poor execution often happens when you need to perform your fundamentals at your very best level**!

You can solve this problem by understanding that **no one plays perfect pool**. Everybody misses difficult shots. So, while your goal on tough shots is to make the ball, you are still going to miss your share. Knowing that you will miss some of your tough shots reduces the pressure as you prepare to shoot them. It's ok to miss. Everybody does.

Once you believe that, you can now **focus your efforts on giving difficult shots your very best effort**. No jumping up or spasmodic arm-twisting is allowed. Aim carefully, use your very best, smoothest, and straightest stroke. And be sure to stay down as you follow through. If you do this, you will give yourself your best chance of pocketing the shot. If you are now pocketing 40 percent of your difficult shots, you could conceivably raise your average to 60 percent, or even higher.

In sum, understand that no matter how well you play, not all tough shots are destined for the pocket. So be willing to accept the results before you play the shot. Then go ahead and give it your very best stroke.

Extending Your Comfort Range

You may have read stories of leading pros who, after missing a shot in competition, will go shoot it a hundred times in a row in practice. They put themselves through such an exacting regime because: 1) they don't want to miss that shot ever again, and 2) they don't want any routine shots to eat at their confidence, which must be extremely high to compete at the pro level.

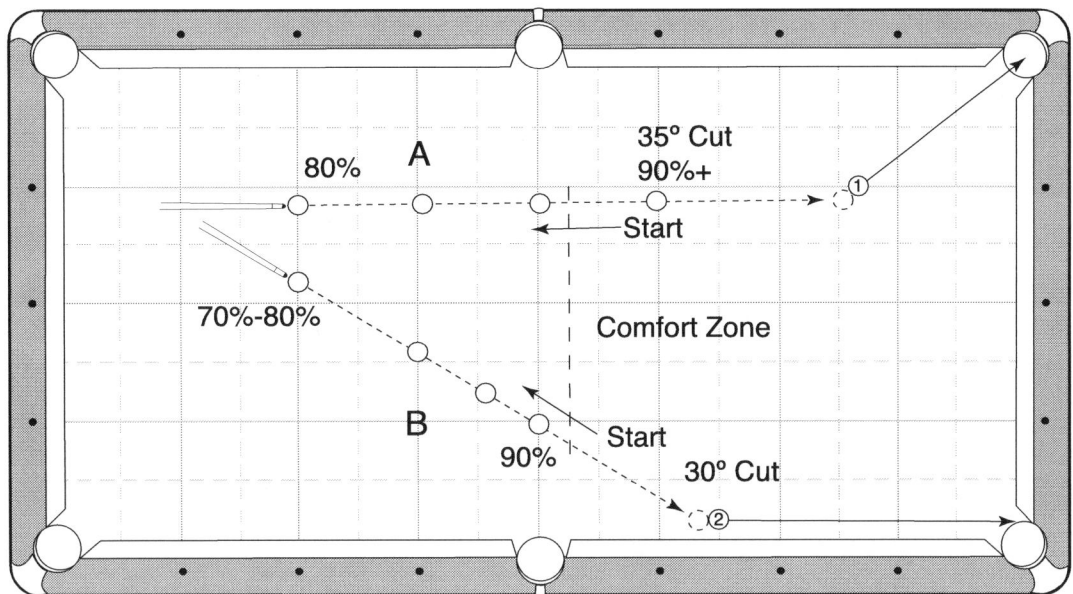

You are probably not as obsessive about your game, but you can employ a simple routine to discover where the hard shot syndrome begins to affect your shotmaking. The diagram shows two of the most commonly played shots in 9 Ball. Shot A is a follow shot while Shot B is a draw shot. You may wish to add several other shots to this exercise, especially those that give you the most trouble.

Start with the cue ball closest to the object ball. Play the shot 10 times using a medium firm stroke. How many did you make? Did you stay down and execute the shot with a smooth stroke? Did you feel any apprehension about the shot, or were you totally confident? You should make at least 9 out of 10 of each shot before moving the cue ball back for a longer version of the shot.

You are looking to discover the minimum distance at which you are no longer 90-100% certain that you will pocket the shot. This is where your comfort zone ends. Carefully assess the quality of your misses at this distance. How close are they to the pocket? If the misses are at the edge of the pocket that means your execution is still relatively good. If at some point your misses are several inches wide of the pocket, your execution is faltering because of the perceived difficulty of the shot.

After a miss, evaluate you technique. Was it up to your usual standards, which you employed at shorter distances? If not, what did you do differently? Now try the shot again, only this time give it your very best effort. Don't worry about whether it goes in or not. The objective is to **give the longer versions the same quality of execution that you used at the shorter ranges where your confidence was high**. This will enable you to extend your comfort zone, and to improve your shotmaking on more difficult shots.

Use Feedback from Missed Shots

You can improve your shotmaking and reduce your misses by discovering the reason(s) for your missed shots. This is more productive than cursing the fact that you are off your game, or that you made a stupid mistake. After a miss, evaluate the shot using the checklist below. You may discover that:

- The feel of your stroke was off.
- Your sense of aim was incorrect, or you were just guessing where to aim.
- You took your eyes off the shot.
- You felt uneasy before you pulled the trigger. Something wasn't right, perhaps with your stance or grip.
- You didn't feel comfortable over the shot, which led to a mechanical error in your stroke.
- You committed some combination of the above errors.
- You did not have a definite plan before executing the shot.

Your objective is to **become aware of what you do so that you can initiate a self-corrective process** to get your game back on track.

Missed Shot Tendencies

On a great many shots most players have a tendency to miss the shot on the same side. For example, most players overcut shots using inside english at high speeds. The list below gives you some other shots for consideration. Do you miss where most other players do? Do your misses favor either side of the pocket? Or do you go completely against the norm by missing a certain shot on the list on the opposite side of the pocket?

Shot Error Tendencies

- Shots played with inside english and a hard stroke are almost always overcut, due to deflection.
- Undercut thin cut banks.
- Overcut down the rail cut shots due to an optical illusion.
- Overcut combos.
- Hit billiards too fully.
- Jump up on cut shots down the rail and overcut the shot.
- Undercut shots when you are trying to restrict the cue ball's traveling distance.

There is a reason why error tendencies exist: prior to playing the shot, your mind's eye obviously is telling you that your aim is correct. Otherwise you would adjust your aim. Right? Well, not always, and therein lies the problem. Shots with dominant error tendencies built into them just don't look right when you are aiming correctly!

What's the solution? You need to single out the shots on the list and others that habitually give you trouble. Then you need to practice each one until you have discovered the correct line of aim. You need to convince your pool memory that the new point of aim is indeed correct so that when the shot comes up again in competition, you will not revert to your previous tendency, which is to aim incorrectly.

Classifying Shots By Difficulty

The difficulty of any non-hanger is an individual matter. A routine shot for Earl Strickland may be a challenging shot for the average player. It can help your efforts in competition if you have a good idea of where each shot rests on your degree of difficulty scale as this will enable you to make smarter decisions. You will know which shots you are justified in taking, which are on the borderline, and those where the odds favor a safety.

You must occasionally go for tough shots because there is no better choice available. However, I suggest that you consider the probability of success for the "typical" shot. When figuring your percentages you must allow for the quality of the competition that you face on a regular basis. If you play with C Players, then it is okay to go for shots in the 60-70% range and above. B Players should play mostly shots in the 75-80%+ range. A Players should attempt shots in the 85%+ range.

The rankings below offer perspectives on the difficulty of each shot.
- **Easy shot**. Always play these unless there is a better option.
- **Average difficulty**. Always play these unless there is a better option.
- **Above average in difficulty**. Play these some of the time. Your decision depends on how you are playing, the conditions, the situation, and what other options are available.
- **Very difficult shots**. Pass on these and play safe most of the time. Play these only when you have little or no choice.
- **Extremely difficult shots**. You should almost never play these as they are not a part of your game. Look for a safety no matter what the circumstances. Play only as a last resort.

Chapter 1 - Shotmaking

Shots You Must Master

Accurate shotmaking is a valuable weapon for 9 Ball, so you should strive to raise your competency in all areas of this part of the game. The more shots you master, the more opportunities you give yourself to remain at the table and to finish runouts. Your ability to consistently make a variety of shots can also help you to avoid those safety battles where the outcome is often in doubt. Below is a checklist of shots that can turn you into an offensive powerhouse.

____The long green	____Easier combos
____Thin cuts	____Rail first
____Off the rail shots	____Curve shots
____Jacked up	____Jump
____Basic short rail banks	____Power draw
____Basic long rail banks	____Power follow
____Billiards	____The break shot (see Chapter 2)
____Caroms	____Kick shots (see Chapter 10)

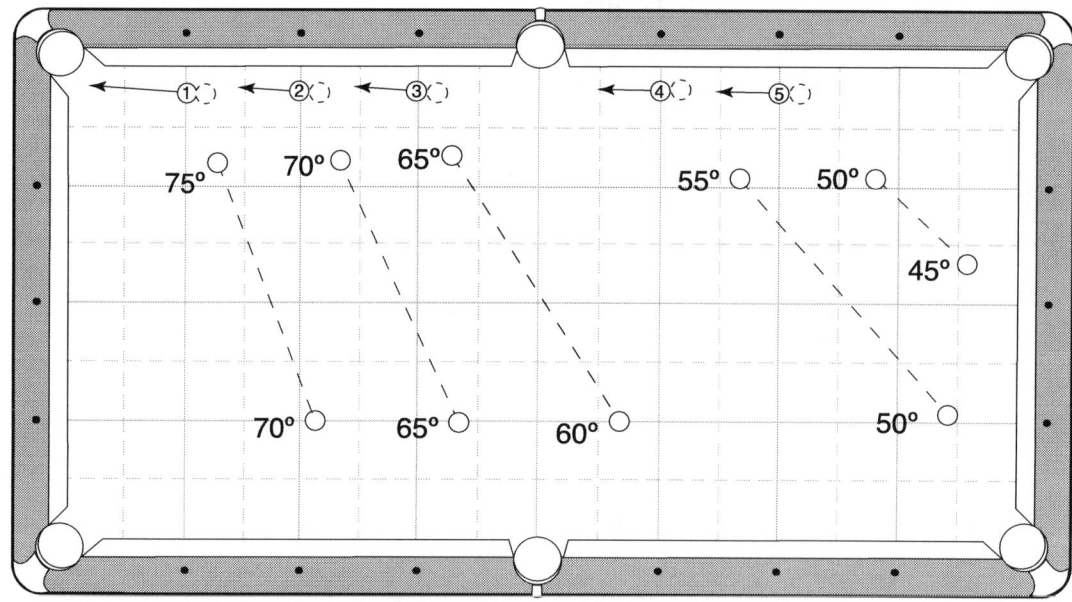

Maximum Practical Cut Angles

At some point a moderate cut angle quickly turns into a very thin cut, and the odds of making the shot drop precipitously. The distance of the object ball from the pocket and the distance of the cue ball from the object ball are big factors in determining the point at which a shot goes from very makeable to very missable. In the diagram above, the 1-ball is close to the pocket, so this shot not so difficult even though the cut angle is 70 degrees. Notice how the recommended practical cut angle decreases as the object ball rests further from the pocket. When the 5-ball is six diamonds from the pocket, the recommended maximum practical cut angle drops to about 30 degrees.

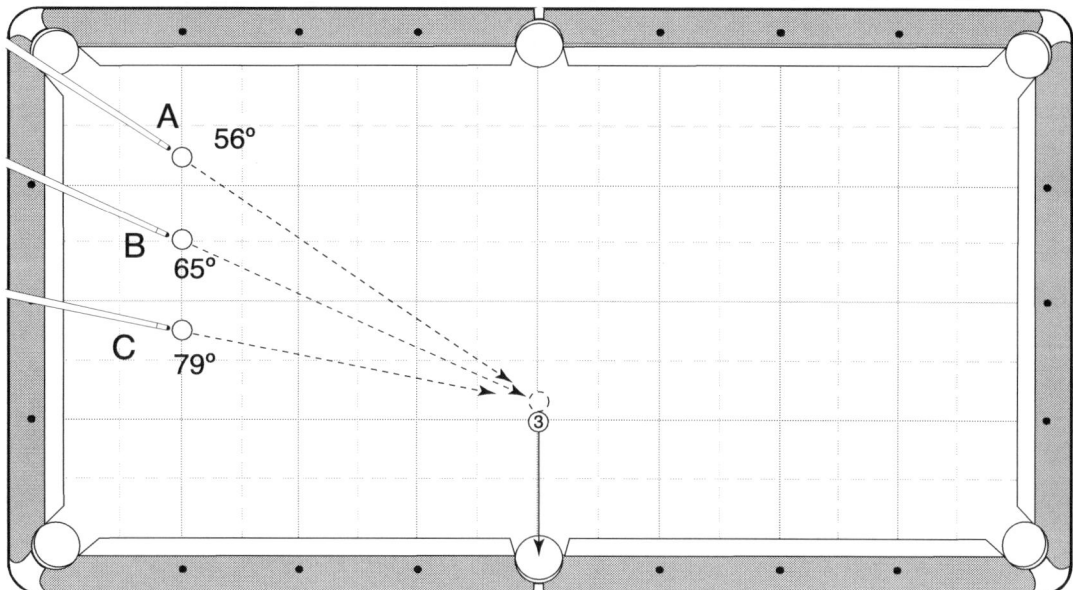

Side Pocket Cut Angles
Most thin cut shots into the side are not so difficult because of the large opening of the pocket, and because the object ball is usually close to the pocket. Check out the cut angles from the shooter's view by turning the book. The 56-degree cut is not difficult, and even the 65-degree cut is highly makeable. It is only above 70-degrees that the shot becomes a challenge.

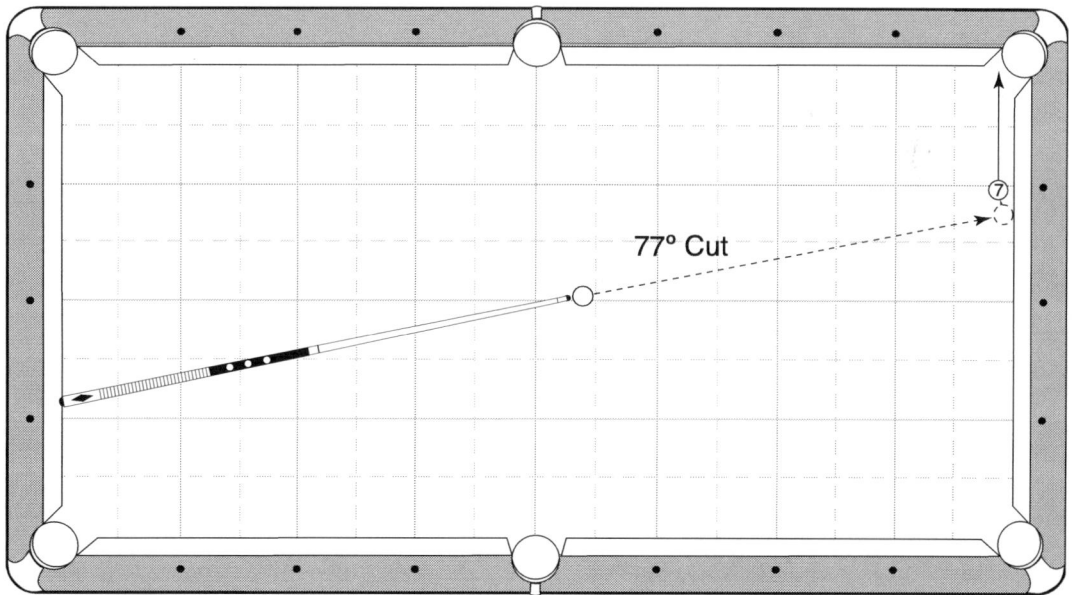

Thin Cuts Rail First
The diagram shows a 77-degree cut shot. This cut angle may be too much for most players if it is played directly into the edge of the 7-ball. An effective technique for making this shot is to aim at the rail. Use inside english (left in this example).

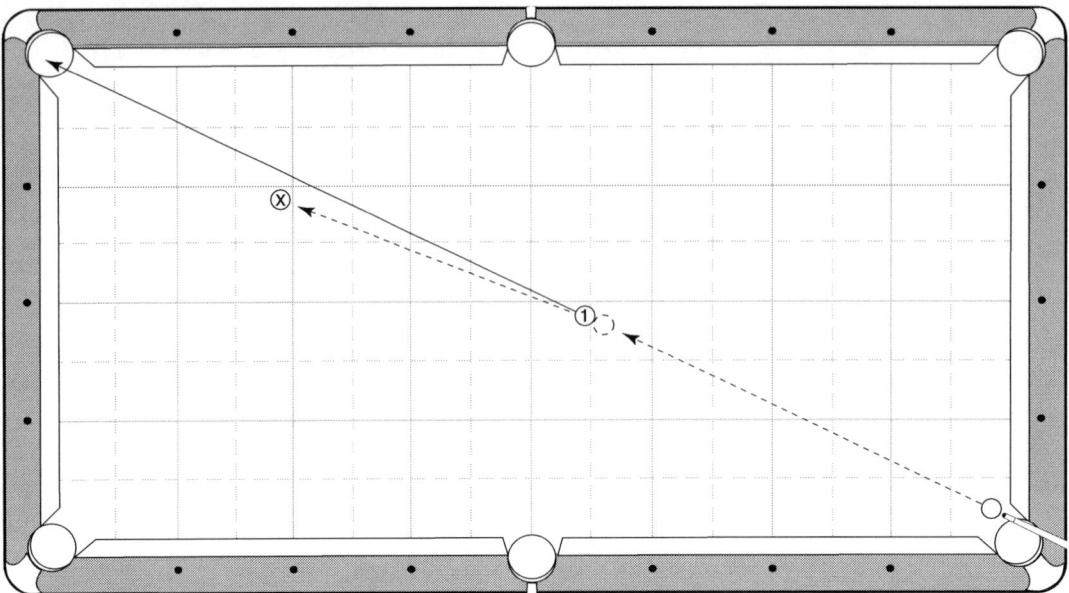

Off the Rail

You will occasionally find the cue ball on or near the rail as a result of positional error, which happens because it is difficult to control cue ball speed over long distances, as you must often do in 9 Ball. In addition, your opponent may push out to rail shots if they are good at them, or if they feel you are not. So, while I advise you try to avoid the rail shots, you will wind up shooting them quite often

When playing shots off the rail, if you can play position without elevating your cue it will improve your accuracy. Johnny Archer led Ismael Paez 7-6 in a race 11, in the 1997 U.S. Open when he was left with the table length shot shown in the diagram. Archer calmly rolled it into the pocket using a medium soft stroke. The cue ball rolled forward for excellent position, and he went on to run the rack (not shown) and to win the match. The keys to making difficult off the rail shots are to:

- Keep your cue as level as possible.
- Set up a little lower to the shot, if you normally have your head several inches above the cue.
- Use a short stroke.
- Accelerate smoothly.
- Use a medium soft to medium speed stroke. Try to avoid using higher speeds unless absolutely necessary.
- Stay down on the shot.

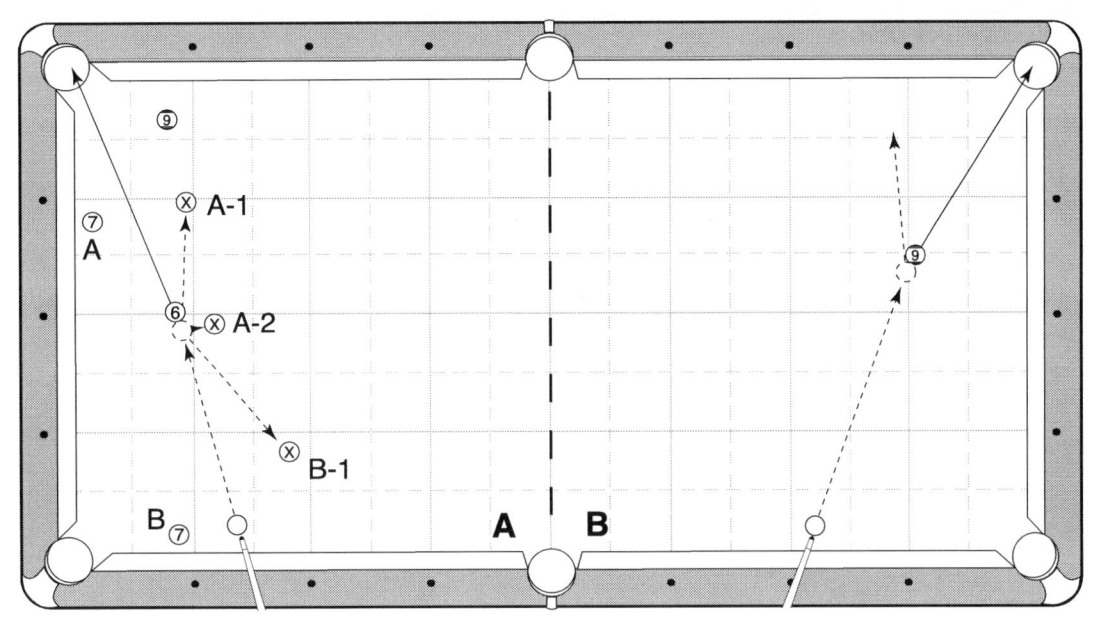

Jacked Up Near the Rail

On most shots with the cue ball near the rail, you will need to elevate your cue in order to get position on the next ball. The diagram above shows several of the most common uses of the jack up shot. In Part A, if you roll forward you will lose position on the 7-ball (A) at A-1. The solution is to jack up and play a stop shot, which will leave the cue ball at A-2. If the 7-ball was at (B), you would need to jack up and draw the cue ball back to B-1.

In Part B, the shot is on the 9-ball (in a game of 9-Ball), so you do not need to play position. The shot has a 10- degree cut angle, which eliminates the possibility of scratching with a follow shot. Even though you could roll in this shot, many players still prefer to elevate the cue slightly and to use a firm stroke. A harder stroke is better for many players under pressure, and it eliminates the chance that the shot might roll off.

When jacking up, avoid elevating the cue any more than is needed to accomplish the objective of the shot. **Excessive elevation will magnify any stroke errors**, resulting in an almost certain miss. I also advise that you to take a little extra time in setting up for the shot so you can make the adjustments necessary to obtain the correct alignment over the shot. Be sure to choke up on the cue, and use your smoothest stroke. This should keep you from jabbing at the cue ball, which is a problem for many players on jack up shots. In sum, your fundamentals must be rock solid when playing jack up shots.

Jack up shots offer players with exceptional skills a chance to gain a significant advantage over their opponents as they can execute position plays that their opponents can only dream about. If you possess such skills, you are blessed with a powerful offensive weapon. If not, it's time for some serious practice.

Basics of Banking

Skill at bank shots can enable you to run out games from positions where many of your opponents would have to play safe or run the risk selling out. The majority of banks played in 9 Ball are fairly routine compared to the kind that you must pocket regularly in Bank Pool or One-Pocket.

The bank shots you play in 9 Ball should carry a success rate of about 50-85%. If your pocketing percentage is under this range, you are playing overly difficult bank shots, or you are missing too many of the easy ones. If that is the case, the suggestions below and some time at the practice table could yield immediate and substantial results.

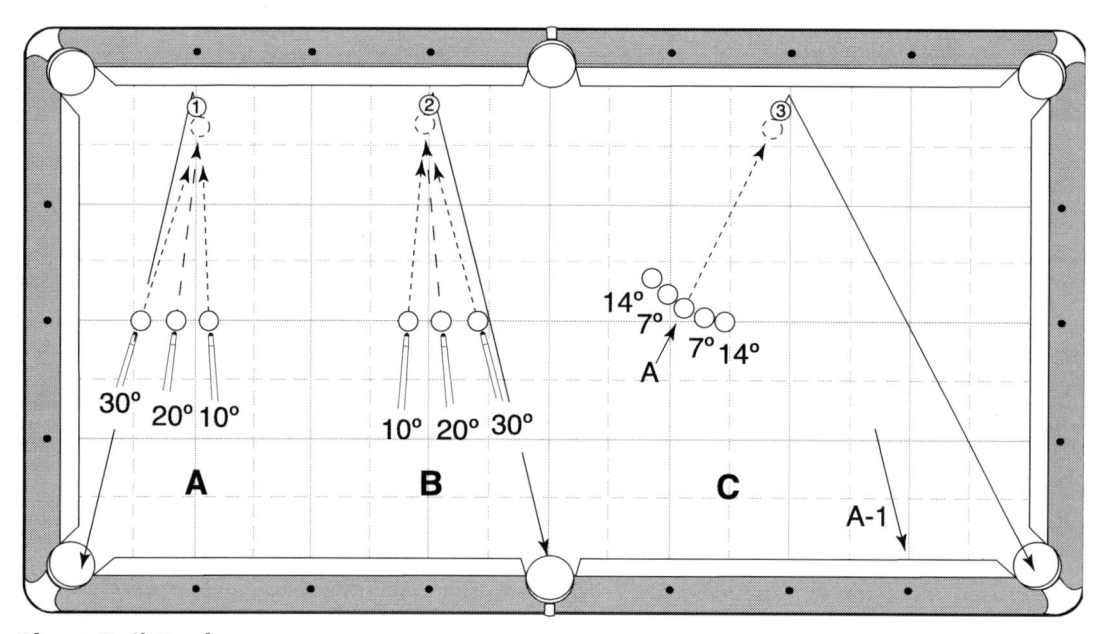

Short Rail Banks

In our discussion on cut shots we established that the difficulty factor rises quickly on cut shots over 60-70 degrees. In contrast, **on most bank shots you will be aiming to hit the object ball rather fully**. And in no instances are you required to cut the paint off the ball in order to pocket a bank.

Parts A and B in the diagram show two of the most common object ball locations for bank shots in 9 Ball. Both positions show cut angles of 10, 20, and 30 degrees. Notice the fullness of the hit on cut angles of 10 or 20 degrees. With a cut angle of 30 degrees, you are still hitting slightly more than half of the object ball (to allow for contact induced throw). You will seldom cut a bank shot more than 30-degrees in competition. Remember that **most players have a tendency to undercut bank shots with relatively thin cut angles** (25 degrees+).

Bank shot cut angles are confined to a narrow range on the object ball when you are aiming them compared to regular cut shots. **Banking is largely guesswork, albeit very educated guesswork**, so it should comfort you to know that you need only consider a small part of the object ball's equator.

Part C shows a variety of cut angles when the object ball is further up the rail. Notice that the cut angles in this position go up to around 14 degrees on either side of the ball. When the object ball is in this position, each degree your aim is off translates into an additional inch that the ball will travel off of the center of the pocket. As an example, if you hit the 3-ball fully from Cue Ball A, it would hit the opposite side rail at A-1.

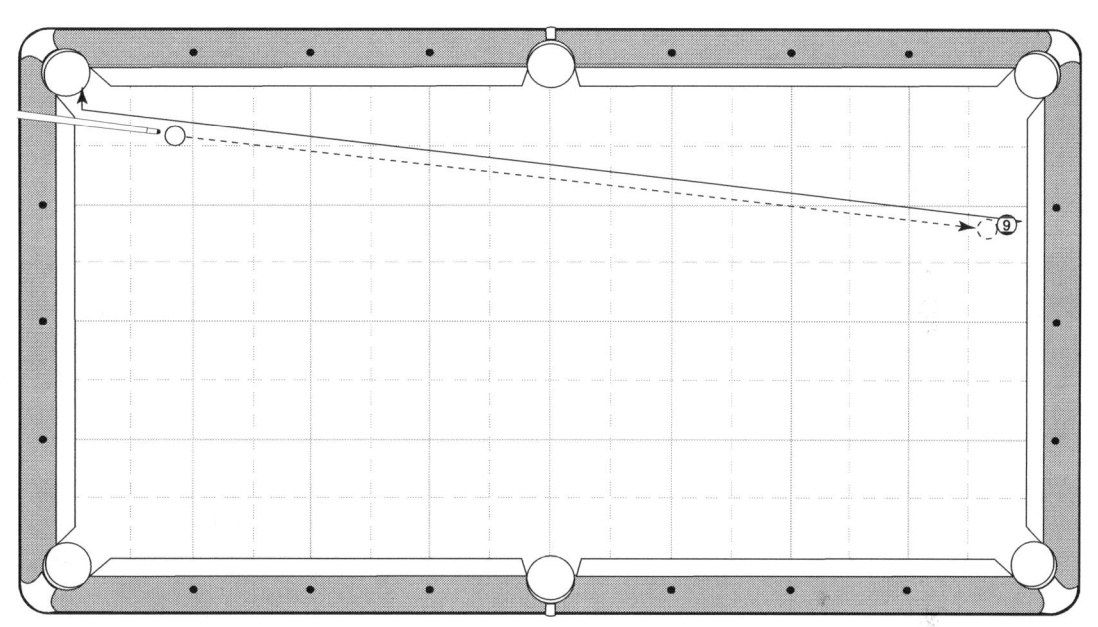

Try this Bank for Fun
Mika Immonen and Jim Rempe were tied at 10 in a race to 11 late in the 1998 U.S. Open when Immonen stepped to the table for this long rail bank on the 9-ball. He barely coaxed the shot into the far edge of the pocket as shown. This clutch shot helped him to a third place finish. Rempe finished in a tie for fifth place. I suggest you set the balls up in this position and give yourself one shot. Imagine you are shooting this on double hill against a world-class competitor. Did you make it? Congratulations! I knew you would!

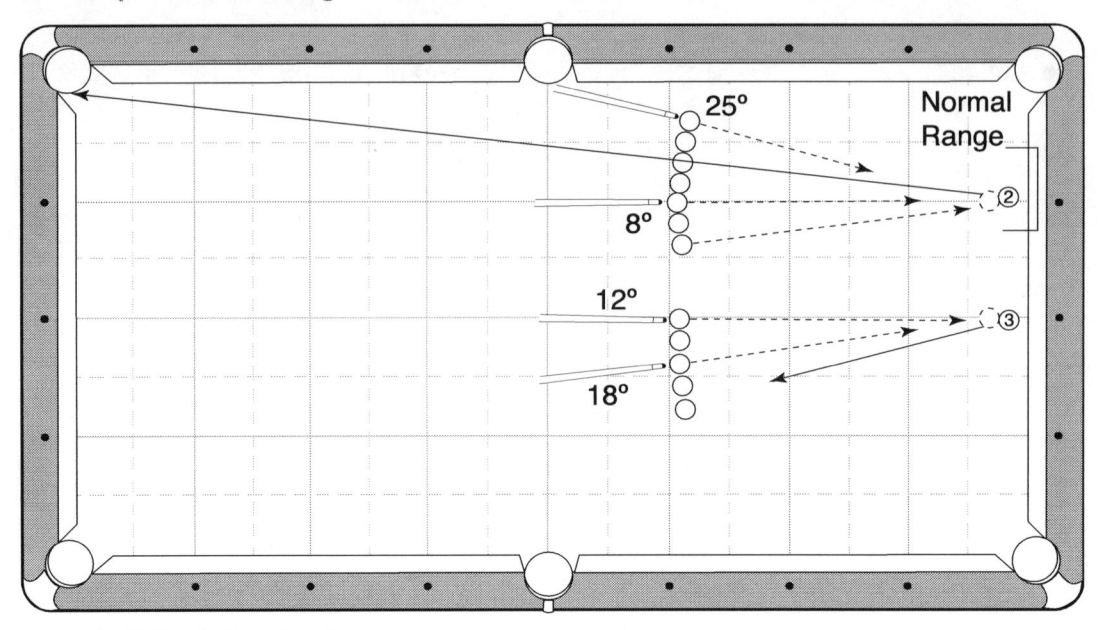

Long Rail Bank Cut Angles

Cut angles on long rail bank shots are usually less than on short rail banks as they typically range from 8-25 degrees. **On most long rail banks aim for a little less than a full ball hit on the object ball**. Just how much less than full, however, is the big challenge to making these shots. On most long rail banks the object ball is between one-half diamond and one and a quarter diamonds up the rail from the opposite corner pocket.

One of the great joys in pool is the sight of a long rail bank whizzing towards the pocket. Table length banks take a long time to unfold, which raises your level of anticipation as you wonder if your shot is about to split the pocket. When long rail banks are successful, they give you a sense of satisfaction that few other shots in the game can match.

Crossover Bank Shots

The diagram at the top of page 21 shows a two common crossover bank shots. The cue ball will be traveling across the object ball's path to the pocket after it rebounds off the cushion. On these bank shots there is no risk of the cue ball hitting the object ball. **Crossover banks must be played with a firm stroke** because you are contacting only a small portion of the object ball. The cue ball will also travel a long distance, so you need to plot your route with care.

Both of these banks are normally shot from the other side of the ball. However, because the cue ball is approaching from the opposite side of the object ball, you must allow for contact throw by aiming for a thinner hit than usual. For example, the side pocket bank must be aimed about three degrees further to the left. You can also play the shot by aiming normally and using a hard stroke.

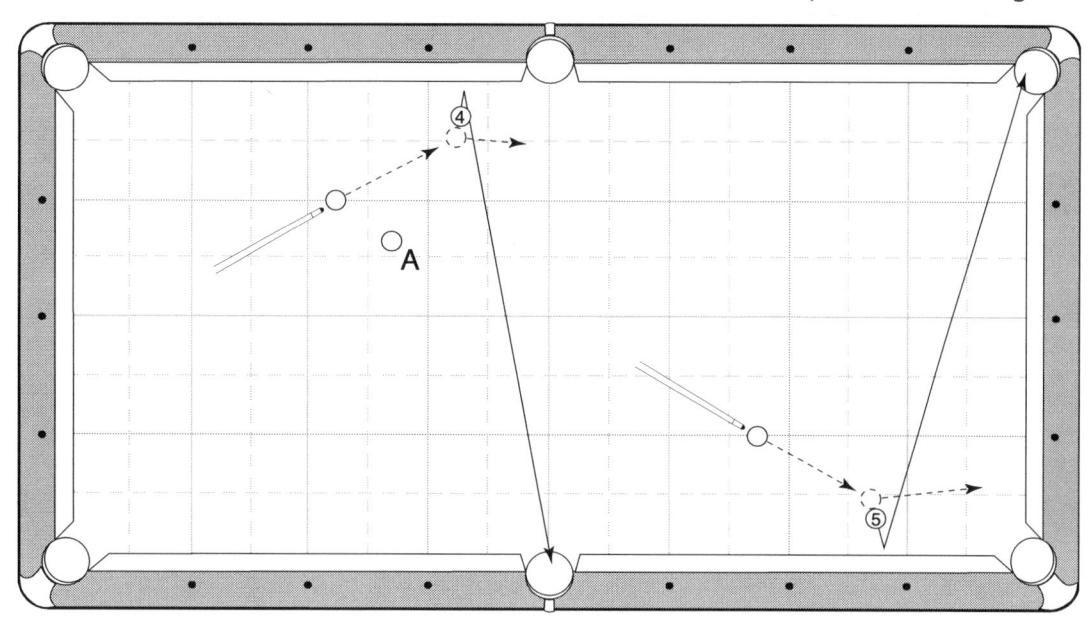

If the cue ball is in Position A for the side pocket bank, there is a chance that the cue ball would collide with the object ball after it rebounds off the rail. I suggest that you **experiment with several positions for the cue ball and object ball to determine when a crossover bank is possible**, and when a collision with the cue ball cannot be avoided. A collision generally occurs when half or more of the cue ball strikes half or more of the object ball.

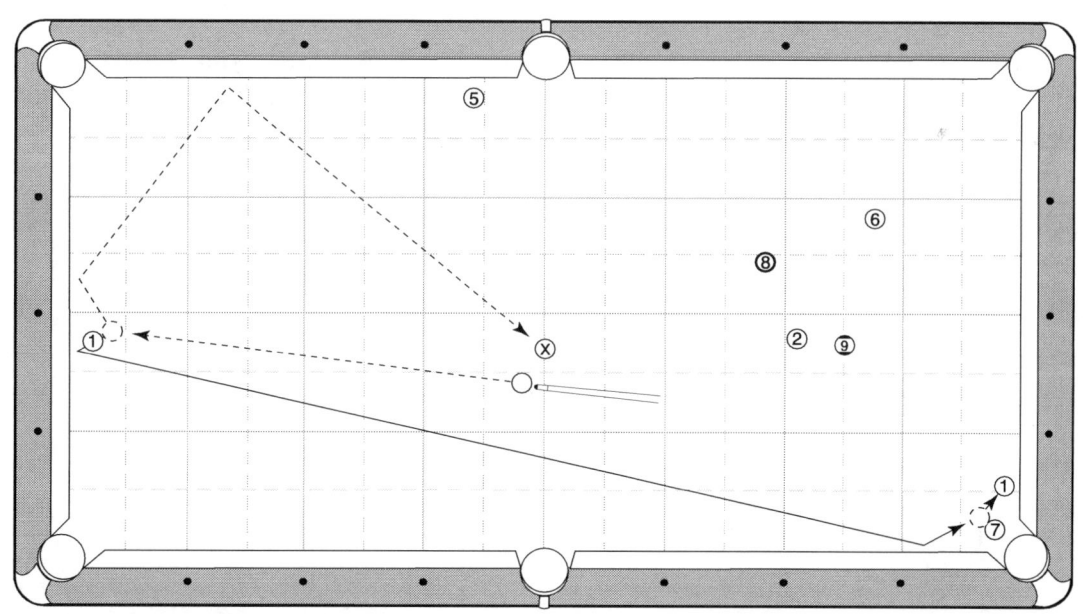

Bank Combos Offer a Big Target
When an object ball is close to the corner pocket, it becomes an inviting target for a bank combination because the margin for error is so large. Jeanette Lee played the long rail bank combo shown in the diagram below. Even though the 1-ball hit well up the cushion, she was still able to pocket the 7-ball. She ran this rack while on her way to winning the 1994 U.S. Open.

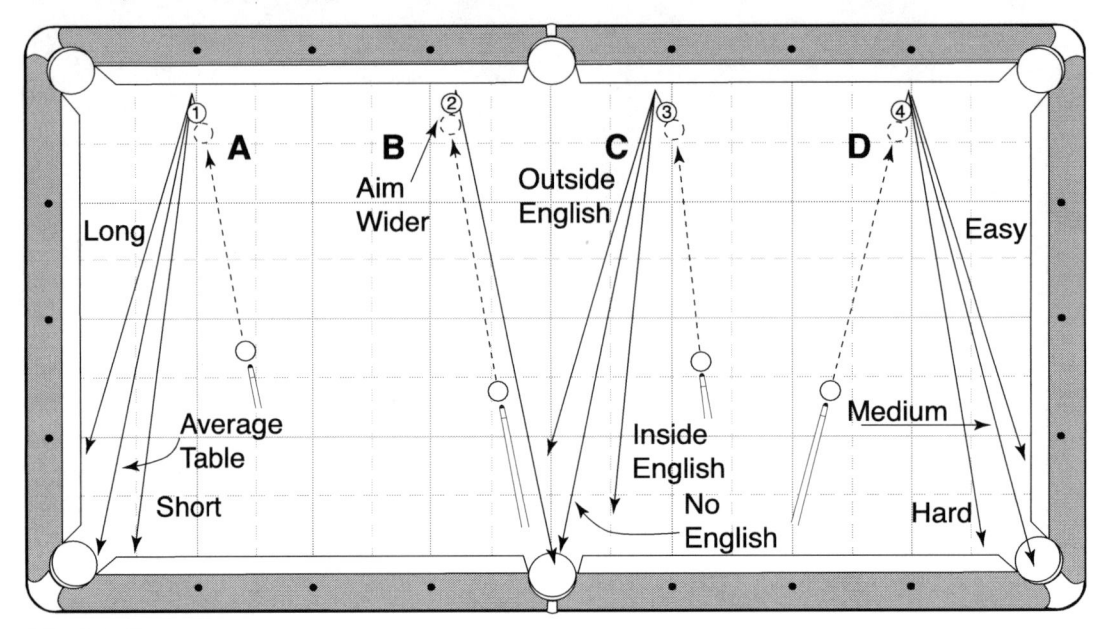

Aiming Factors
Four major factors complicate the aiming equation on bank shots, each one capable of changing your aim by a couple of degrees or more.

Factor #1 – The Table
Part A shows three results for a bank that is struck with medium speed. If the table banks like an "average" table, it will split the pocket. If it banks "short" the ball will hit the bottom side rail. In this case you must cut the shot a little to the right to allow for the table, or you can hit the shot easier. If the table banks "long," the ball will strike the end rail. You can adjust for this by aiming slightly to the left, or you can hit the shot firmer.

Factor #2 – Contact Induced Throw
Part B shows a cross-side bank with a 15-degree cut angle. The shot is played with a medium speed stroke. On banks with fairly pronounced cut angles you must factor in contact throw, which can alter the path of the object ball by about 3-6 degrees (see *Play Your Best Pool*). On this shot you must overcut the ball (aim to the left about 3 degrees more) to compensate for contact throw.

Factor #3 English
Part C shows a relatively straight bank hit, once again, with a medium speed stroke. If you apply outside english to the shot (right in this example), the bank will miss to the far side as shown. You can compensate for this by aiming for a fuller hit on the object ball and throwing it in the pocket. In fact, many excellent bankers prefer to shoot most of their banks shot with outside english. If you use inside english (left in this example), the bank will miss to the short side as shown. You can compensate for this by aiming for a slightly thinner hit on the object ball (a little more to the right in this example).

Factor #4 Speed of Stroke
The bank in Part D is lined up for a full hit on the object ball (a 0 degree cut). To pocket the shot, hit the object ball fully with a medium speed stroke. If you were to lag the ball to the pocket, it could bank long and hit the end rail. If you hit the shot with a hard stroke, it would bank short as shown. **Many top players prefer to hit banks with a hard stroke** because they feel that this improves their accuracy. A firm stroke is typically used when they are confident of making the shot, and when the shot carries little or no defensive components to it. If you use this approach, be sure aim for a slightly thinner hit on the object ball to compensate for its sharper rebound angle off the rail.

Using the Aiming Factors
You can use english and/or additional speed of stroke to reduce or eliminate the effects of contact throw. You can also use speed of stroke and/or english to create a successful shot. For example, you can hit the ball with a harder stroke to offset a table's tendency to bank long. And you could use outside english to throw a bank along a wider path if a table tends to bank short.

Combining Aiming Factors
It is possible to combine factors that cancel each other out. This could be done by using outside english and a hard stroke. You can also change the point of aim greatly by combining factors to influence a bank in the same direction. For example, to open up the rebound angle of a bank as much as possible use a soft stroke with lots of outside english. And to create the sharpest rebound angle possible, use a hard stroke with a tip of inside english.

Aiming Factors

Influence	Opens the angle	Closes the angle
Speed of stroke	Easy stroke	Hard stroke
English	Outside english	Inside english
Table	Banks long	Banks short

Combining Aiming Factors

Goal Sought	Action
Open angle greatly	Outside english/soft stroke
Close angle greatly	Inside english/hard stroke
Avoid double kiss	Inside english/hard stroke

Billiards

A billiard is a shot in which the cue ball strikes the lowest numbered ball first and glances off I into the ball you wish to pocket. There are infinite uses for billiard shots in 9 Ball, which naturally includes shots on the game ball.

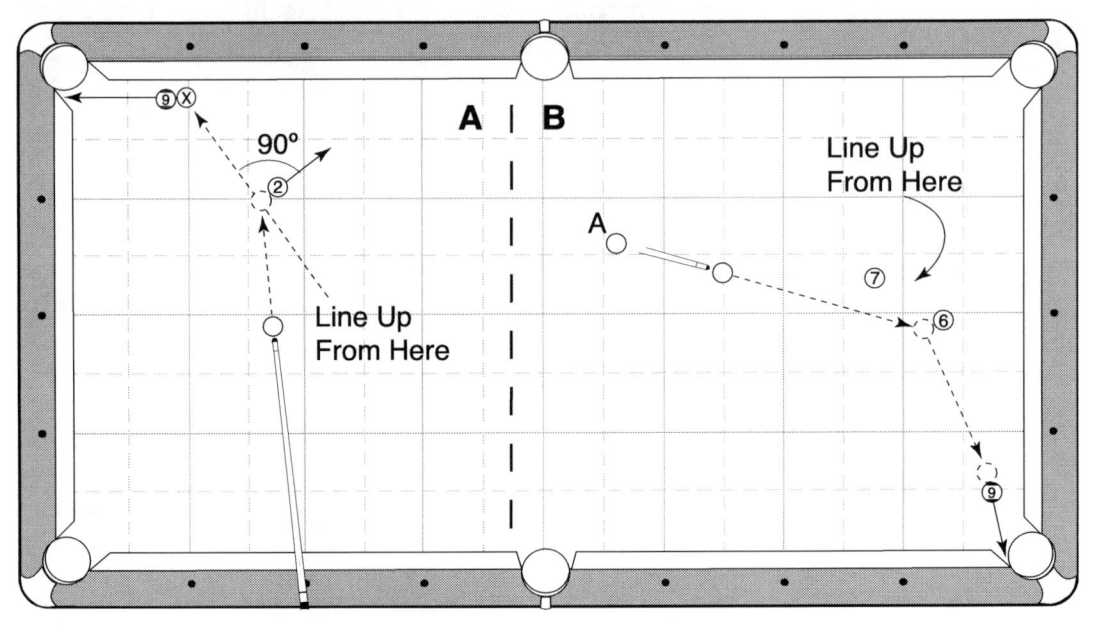

Billiards Using the Tangent Line

When the cue ball is struck firmly with centerball, after contact with the object ball it travels at a 90- degree angle compared to the direction of the object ball. You can use this bit of pocket billiard physics to create the desired path for the cue ball into a ball that you wish to pocket.

In Part A of the diagram, the 2-9 combo is way too difficult to consider playing. The billiard, however, is quite makeable. View the shot from the line that the cue ball must take after contacting the 2-ball in order to pocket the 9-ball. Your point of aim is the far left edge on the 2-ball when viewed from this position. Play the shot with centerball and a medium firm stroke.

Part B shows another billiard, only this time the 9-ball is much closer to the pocket. Walk over and view the direct line that the cue ball must take into the 9-ball. This will help you to gauge where to send the cue ball into the 6-ball so that it will shoot off to the right and into the 9-ball. Use a medium firm stroke and centerball. This example shows the maximum distance you can play a centerball billiard with an acceptable degree of accuracy. If the cue ball was further back, such as at Position A, you would need to use a very hard stroke or a little bit of draw to make the shot. In either case, the shot would become much less reliable.

The Draw Back Billiard

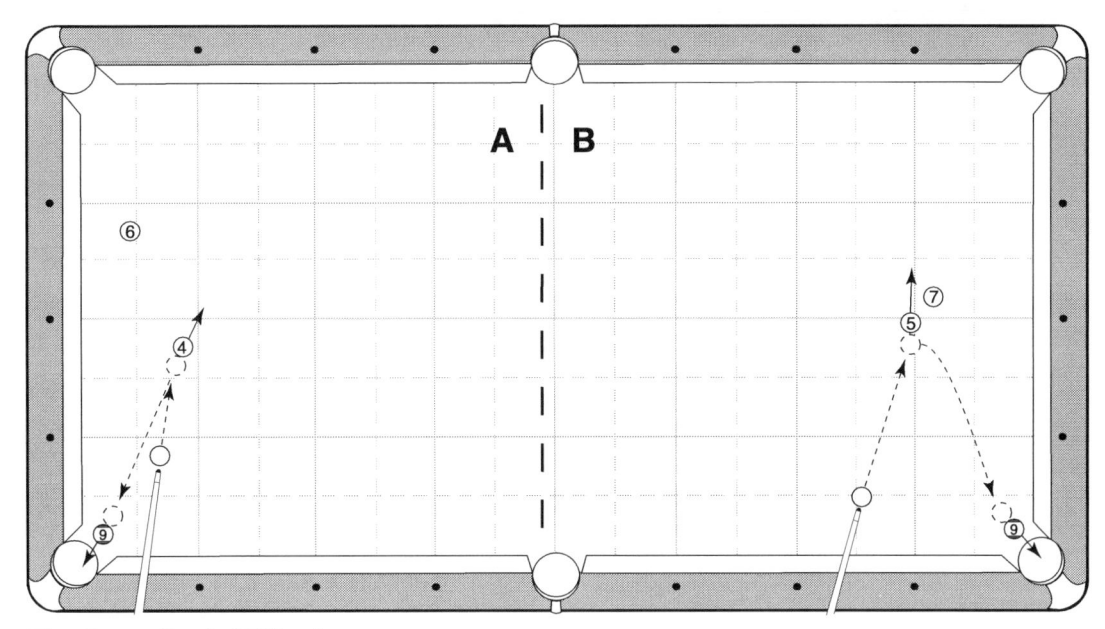

The draw back billiard is a very useful shot when you encounter the following conditions:

- The ball you wish to pocket is very close to the pocket.
- The ball you will be contacting first is within about two feet from the ball you wish to pocket.
- The cue ball is on or not far from a line that runs from the ball you will be contacting to the ball you wish to pocket.

All of these conditions have been met in Part A of the diagram. If the cue ball was on the dashed line that runs between the balls, you could simply shoot straight at the 4-ball with draw and the cue ball would pull back into the 9-ball. However, the cue ball rests just to the right of the dashed line, so you need to hit the 4-ball just slightly to the left of center. If you aim a couple of hairs too far to the left, the cue ball will travel just a fraction to the left before drawing back, causing it to strike the end rail instead of the 9-ball. So, the key to this shot is to hit the first ball just a fraction less than full.

The draw back shot in Part B is much more difficult than the one in Part A even though the 9-ball is hanging in the jaws. The problem is gauging the cue ball's path after it contacts the 5-ball. In this case, a 15-degree cut on the 5-ball will result in about a 30-degree rebound angle. On this shot most players fail to compensate for the wide return angle by hitting the 5-ball too thinly. This aiming error would cause the cue ball to hit the end rail.

26 Chapter 1 - **Shotmaking**

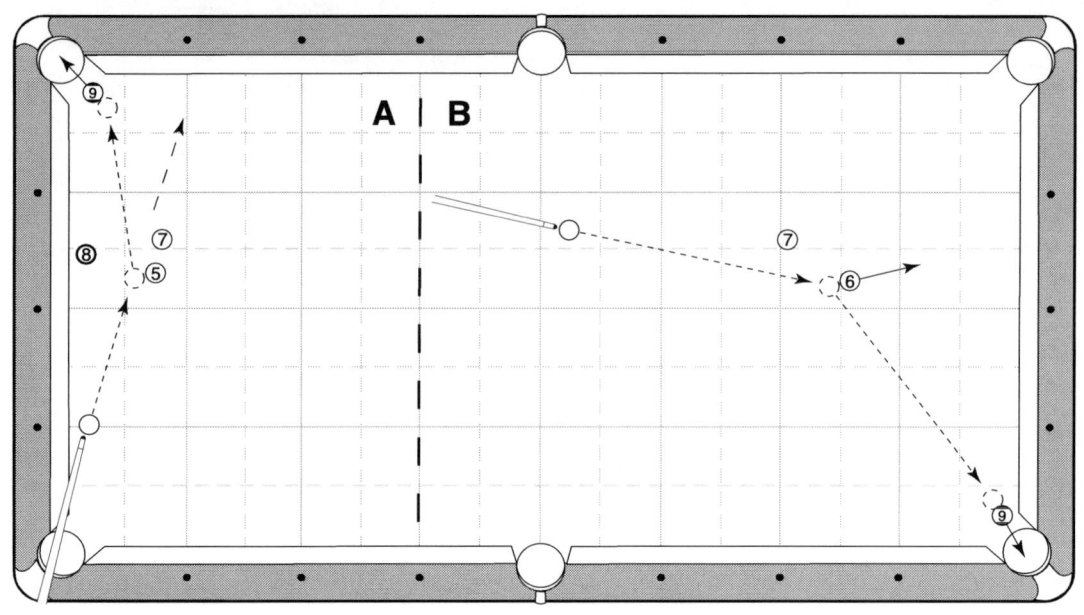

The Diversion Billiard
The diagram shows two examples of what could be called a diversion billiard. Use a soft follow stroke and roll the cue ball into contact with the lowest numbered ball. Rolling the cue ball eliminates most of the bend in the cue ball's path that occurs after contact, which simplifies the aiming process. The key in guestimating how much of the ball you need to hit to "divert" the cue ball onto a path towards the ball you wish to pocket. A thin hit on the 5-ball in Part A will divert the cue ball slightly to the left and along a path into the 9-ball. In Part B a half ball hit on the 6-ball will send the cue ball to the right and towards the 9-ball.

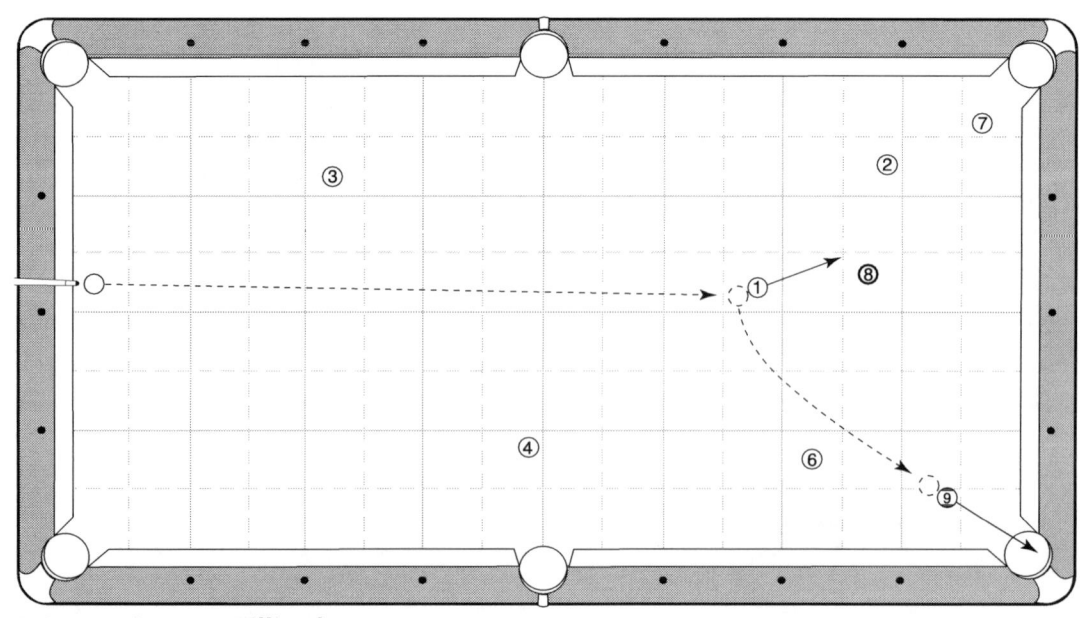

A Long Distance Billiard
Sometimes you need to play a risky shot when you are trailing in a match, you need to build some momentum, and you don't see a good safety. Perhaps that was Takeshi Okumura's reasoning when he approached the table trailing Earl Strickland in the finals

of the 2000 U.S. Open. Okumura used a hard follow stroke, aimed for about a 2/3 full hit on the 1-ball, and dazzled the crowd with the spectacular follow/curve billiard into the 9-ball on page 26.

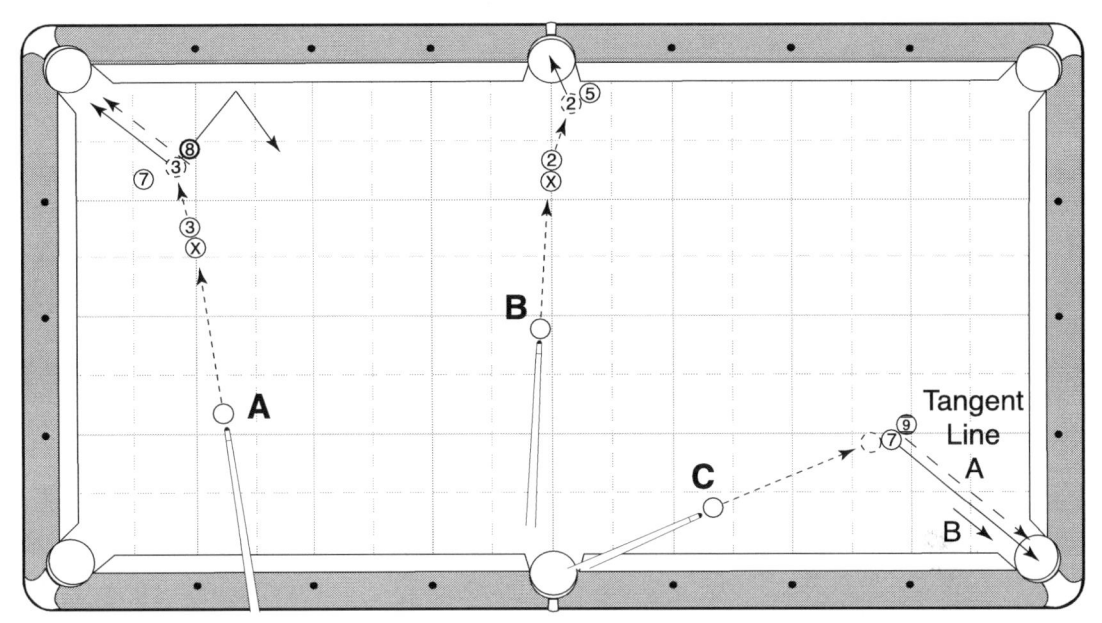

Caroms
On a carom shot the cue ball is shot into an object ball, and the object ball then glances off another ball and into the pocket. Carom shots can also be useful in playing safe. On a safety, your objective is to play the first ball into a second ball and have the first ball continue to a position where your opponent has little or nothing with which to work (for more on carom safeties see chapter 11).

Part A shows a basic carom shot. The 7-ball prevents you from cutting the 3-ball into the corner, but you can carom it off the 8-ball, which is in the ideal position for this kind of shot. A medium hard stroke will keep the 3-ball on the correct line after it contacts the 8-ball. The 8-ball should be hit on the edge of the tangent line that lines up with the outside portion of the pocket as shown by the dashed line.

You could play the 2-ball directly into the side pocket in Part B, but that would leave the 5-ball in the worst spot on the table. The smart move is to get the 5-ball off the rail by caroming the 2-ball off of it and into the pocket.

Part C shows a dead carom shot. The tangent line, Line A, runs between the 7 and 9-balls and points at the inside of the corner pocket. You can pocket the 7-ball with a soft follow stroke while hitting the left side of the 7-ball. Avoid using draw. If the tangent line was pointing down line B, you could still pocket the 7-ball. Hit the 7 about 2/3 full and use a sharp draw stroke.

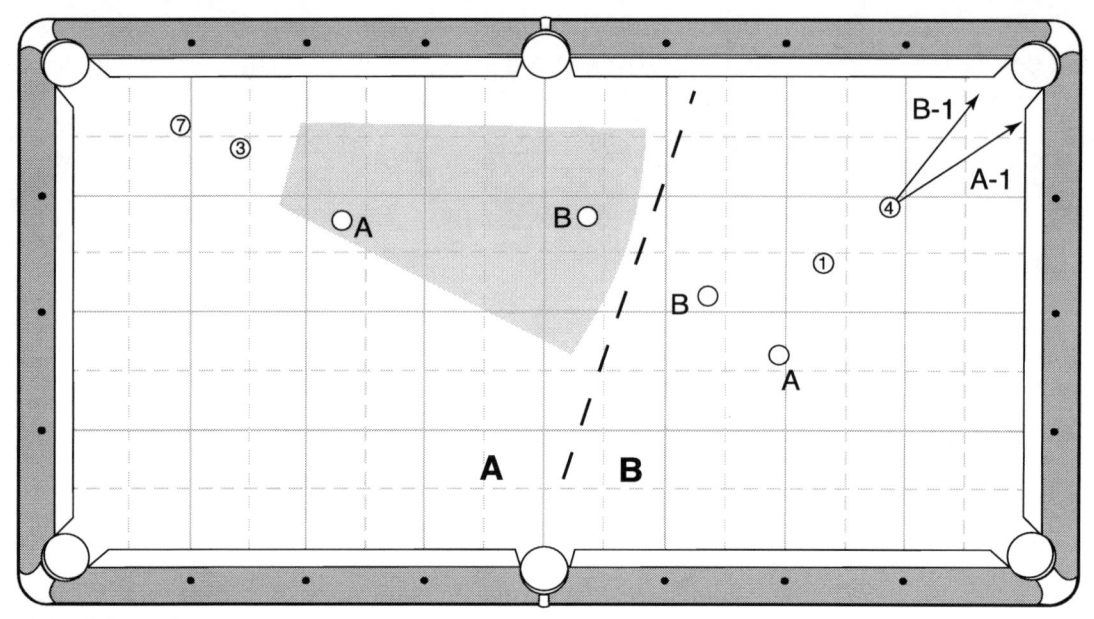

Combinations

There are fewer chances to play combos in 9 Ball than in other games because there are only 9 balls, at most, on the table after the break. In addition, the balls are spread more widely down the table. Combinations appear most often when a player possesses a weak break as this leads to congestion around the area of the rack. Those of you who play on bar tables will play more combinations for obvious reasons. Despite the shortage of combos in 9 Ball, skill at them can provide you with a means for winning short racks, and for completing your run outs.

I spent hours studying the shot selection of top pros, who are almost all quite skilled at combos. My findings indicate that even the pros routinely avoid combos. So, **you should also consider only playing combos when the percentages are substantially in your favor**. If a particular combo lies too difficult, you are usually better off playing safe or choosing another offensive option.

Part A shows a fairly easy combination. The 3-7 combination is lined up nearly straight at the pocket and the balls are only 4 inches apart. The 7-ball is a little less than a diamond from the pocket. This shot is an easy combo, but it still must still be played with great care. When the cue ball is in the position zone, the shot is not overly difficult. And yet, I would guess that the odds of the average player pocketing if are about 70 percent with the cue ball in Position A, and about 40 percent with it in Position B.

Players line up combos from all angles, including pointing their cue at the spot where they hope to hit on the first ball. But few, I would wager, have factored in contact induced throw into their calculations.

Part B on page 28 shows a difficult 1-4 combo. If you fail to allow for contact throw, the 4-ball will be missed to the right of the pocket at A-1 when the cue ball is shot from Position A. The 4 would travel down Line B-1 if the cue ball was shot from Position B and the player failed to allow for contact induced throw.

Combos exert a hypnotic lure over many players, especially when they are on the game ball. **If you find that shooting anything but the easiest combos is costing you games, then your shot selection needs an overhaul.**

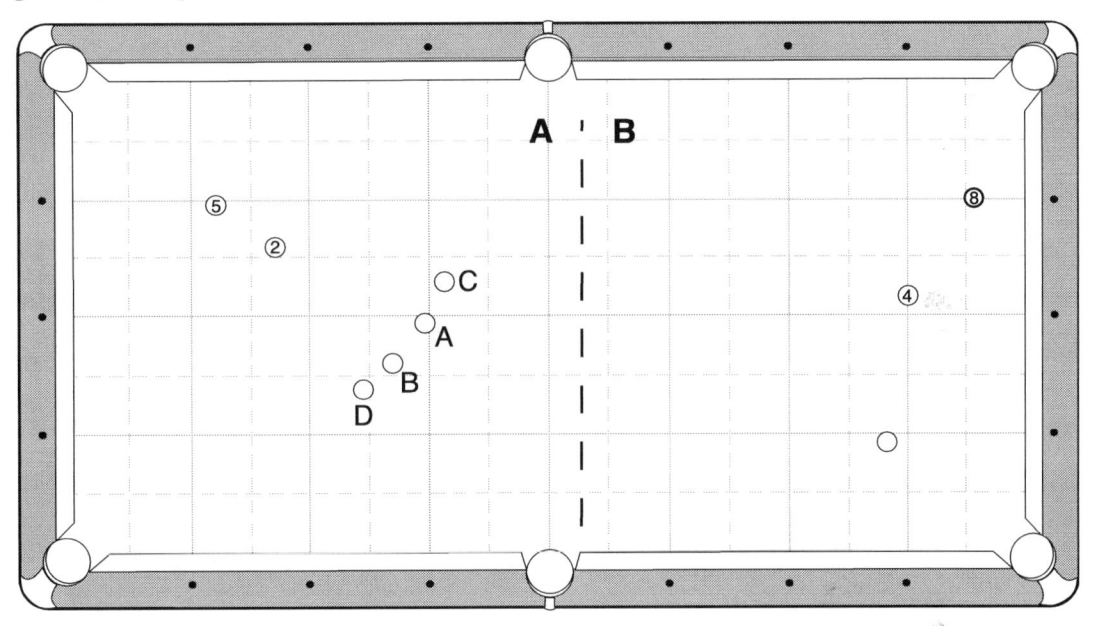

Difficulty of Various Combos

The 2 and 5 balls are 5 inches apart in Part A. The 5-ball is 18 inches from the pocket. The 2-ball is an inch to the right of lining up with the 5-ball and the pocket. Despite these minor differences, this combo lies much tougher than the ones in the previous example. With the cue ball in Position A, you can shoot directly at the 2-ball. This is the easiest angle from which to play this combo.

Position B is next in difficulty as you must cut the 2-ball slightly to the left to pocket the 5-ball. With the cue ball in Position C you are cutting the two in the direction of the 5-ball, but this is still a very missable shot. When the cue ball is in Position D you must backcut the 2-ball into the 5-ball, which is quite troublesome for most players.

The difficulty of the shots in Part A is at about the limit of those that you should attempt. The combo in Part B should carry a label "For Suckers Only." Hopefully this discussion has alerted you to the potential hazards of playing any but the easiest combos.

"You can miss a combo no matter how easy it looks." **Jim Rempe**

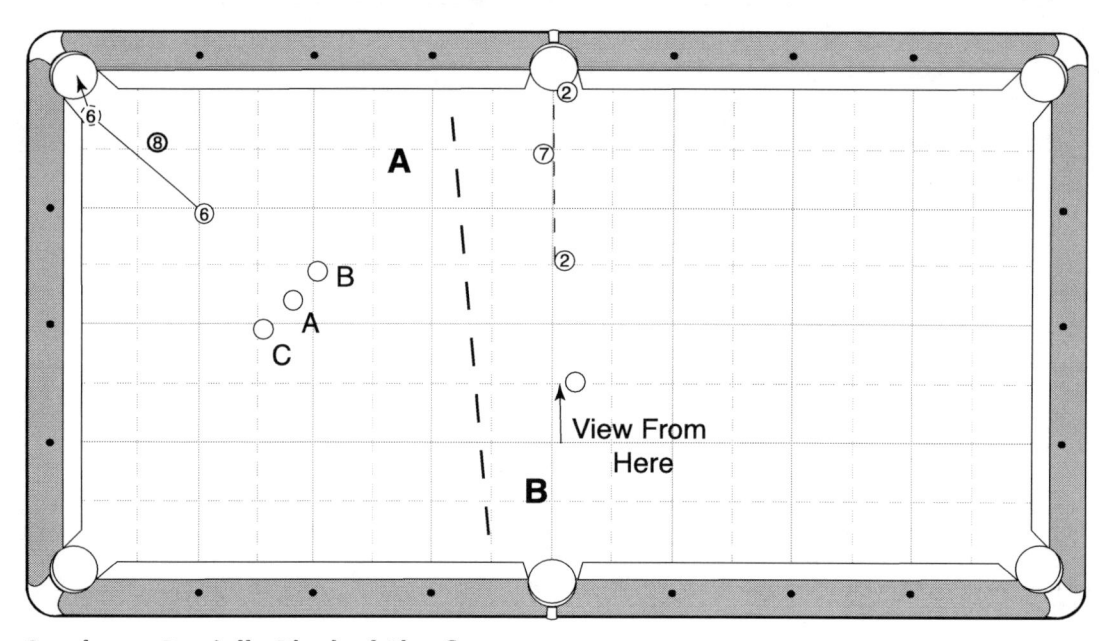

Combo or Partially Blocked Shot?

The position in Part A presents a tough decision: should you play the 6-ball directly into a partially blocked pocket or play a combo into a full pocket? When only a third of the pocket is blocked, then you are better off shooting the ball directly into the pocket. When half the pocket is blocked (assuming a corner pocket of 4.75 inches), then your margin for error is about .25 inch on either side of the ball. When playing to a half pocket, remember that the outside edge of the object ball can graze the point of the pocket and the shot will still fall.

The position of the cue ball has a big impact on your decision. When the cue ball is lined up straight with the pocket and the object ball (see cue ball A) then you should play the ball straight into the pocket. When the cue ball is at Position B, you should also play the 6-ball directly into the pocket. When the cue ball is in Position C, then the combo is the better choice.

You may fall victim to a visual distortion that can trick you into believing that a ball won't go into a partially blocked pocket when it will. In Part B, stand with your head at just above table level and imagine a line that runs from the inside of the ball you wish to pocket (in this case the 2-ball) and the outside edge of the obstructer (the 7-ball). Extend the line to the pocket opening. Is there at least enough room for the ball (2.25 inches) with a little room to spare? If so, then you can play the shot directly into the pocket.

Rail First Shots

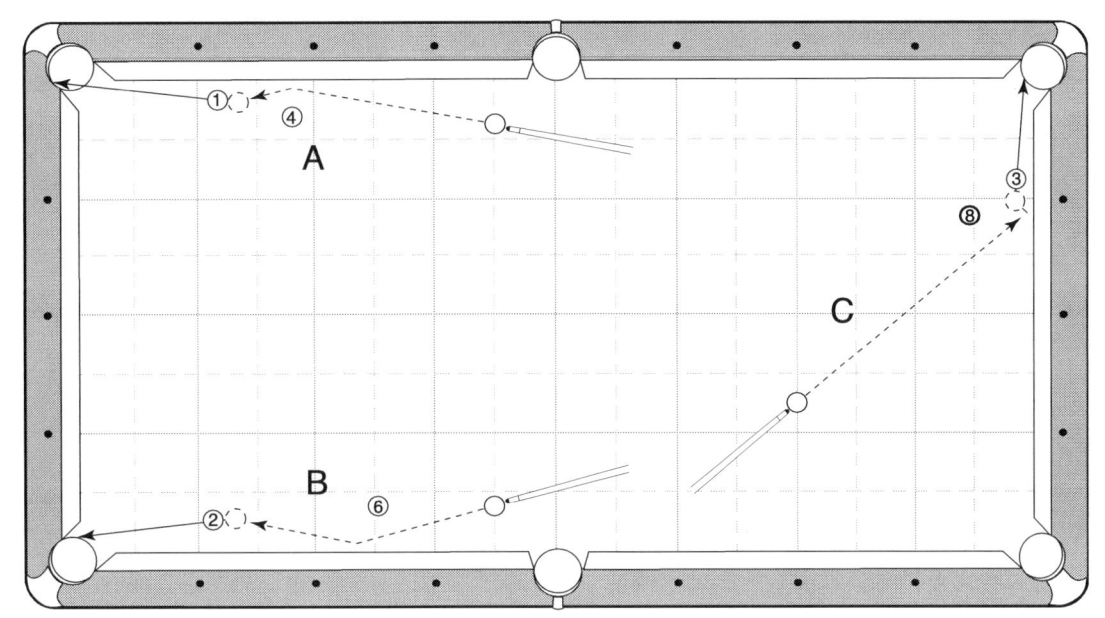

Rail first shots are used when the path to the object ball is blocked by an obstructer, the object ball is close to the rail, and the ball is within a couple of diamonds of the pocket. In Part A, the 1-ball is blocked by the 4-ball. The 1-ball is also a little less than an inch from the rail and the cue ball is close to the rail. These factors make for an easy rail first shot. Aim at the spot on the rail as indicated and avoid using english. Use a soft stroke when possible because it makes the pocket play bigger.

I advise that you avoid english, but some of you may discover that you have more success when you apply outside english. If you prefer this approach, you may need to adjust your aim to compensate for the throw that is applied to the object ball, and for the shallower rebound angle that the cue ball takes off the cushion. Keep in mind that the throw effect and the shallower angle of approach may largely offset each other.

In Part B, the 2-ball is significantly further from the rail than the 1-ball was in Part A. The cue ball is about the same distance from the rail as in Part A. Notice that you must aim much further up the rail. The 2-ball is about the maximum distance that a ball should rest from the rail for you to consider a rail first shot.

The cue ball is at a sharp angle to the rail for the shot in Part C. When you have an angle this steep, play a rail first shot only if the object ball is very close to the rail as shown by the 3-ball. When the angle of approach is very steep, the cue ball must hit the rail very close to the object ball. I suggest that you use inside english on this type of shot.

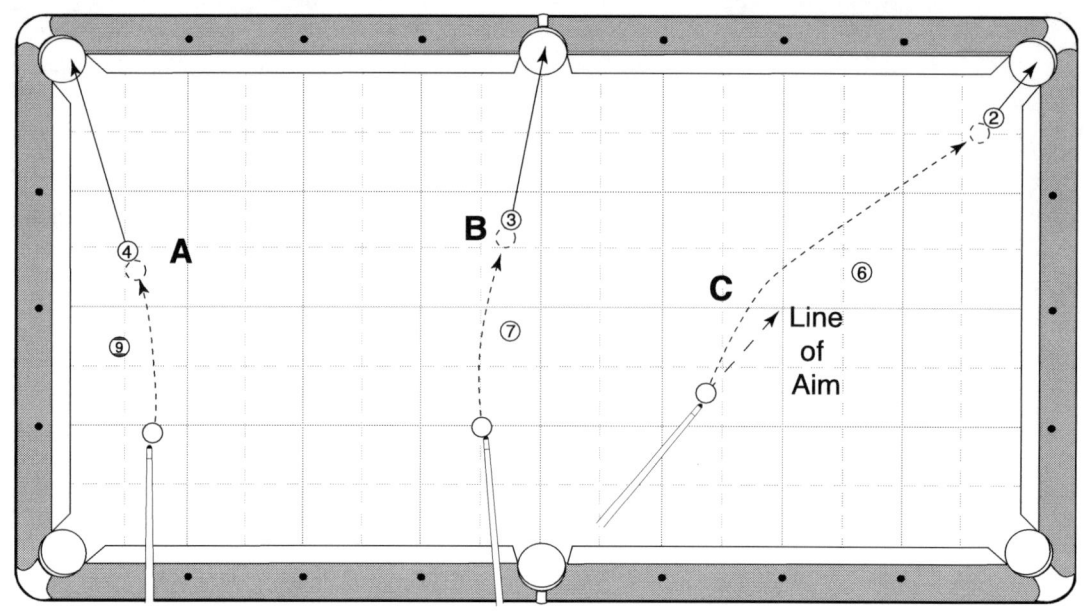

Curve Shots

When an obstructer blocks any part of the cue ball's path to the object ball, conditions may be ripe for a curve shot. **When a curve shot and a jump shot are possible, a curve shot may be the better choice** because the cue ball never leaves the table, and it usually rolls a short distance after contact, which makes it easier to play position.

Curve Shot Factors:
- The distance from the cue ball to the object ball.
- The amount of curve needed to avoid the obstructer with a little room to spare.
- The cue stick's angle of elevation.
- The force of the stroke.
- The amount of english you are applying.
- Cue ball deflection before it starts to curve back.
- The amount that the object ball will be thrown.

Wow! Now before you enlist a computer programmer to calculate the effect of these variables, understand that curve shots are not as complicated as you might imagine. Thanks to the wonders of our subconscious mind it is possible to weigh these variables and arrive at an accurate guesstimate of how to play the shot. This assumes that you have spent enough time at the practice table working on these shots.

It will improve your view of curve shots if you realize that you are going to miss some no matter what you do. But, with practice, and a working knowledge of the factors that influence these shots, you will begin to start pocketing your share.

In the shot in Part A of the diagram on page 32, you can pocket the 4-ball without using a curve shot, but you only have 1/16 inch of clearance past the 9-ball. In this position, the 9 can act like a magnet for the cue ball. The solution is to aim a half inch or so wide of the 9-ball and play a soft curve shot around it. A quarter tip of left english and a modest degree of elevation (10-degrees) should work.

The 7-ball blocks a quarter of the cue ball's path to the 3-ball in Part B. Now you must aim a ball's width to the left of the 7-ball. Elevate your cue to about 20-degrees and apply a half tip of right english. Use a medium soft stroke. The cue ball should curve around the 7-ball and into the 3-ball. At contact the 3-ball is thrown to the left (because of the english) and into the side pocket.

Part C is a long distance curve shot which requires that you bend the cue ball around the 6-ball to pocket the 2-ball. Long curve shots like this should only be played when the object ball is close to the pocket. Aim about 3.5 inches outside of the 6-ball. Elevate to 25-degrees, use a tip of low right english, and use a firm stroke. You want the cue ball to squirt to the left beyond your line of aim. and then curve back along the path shown.

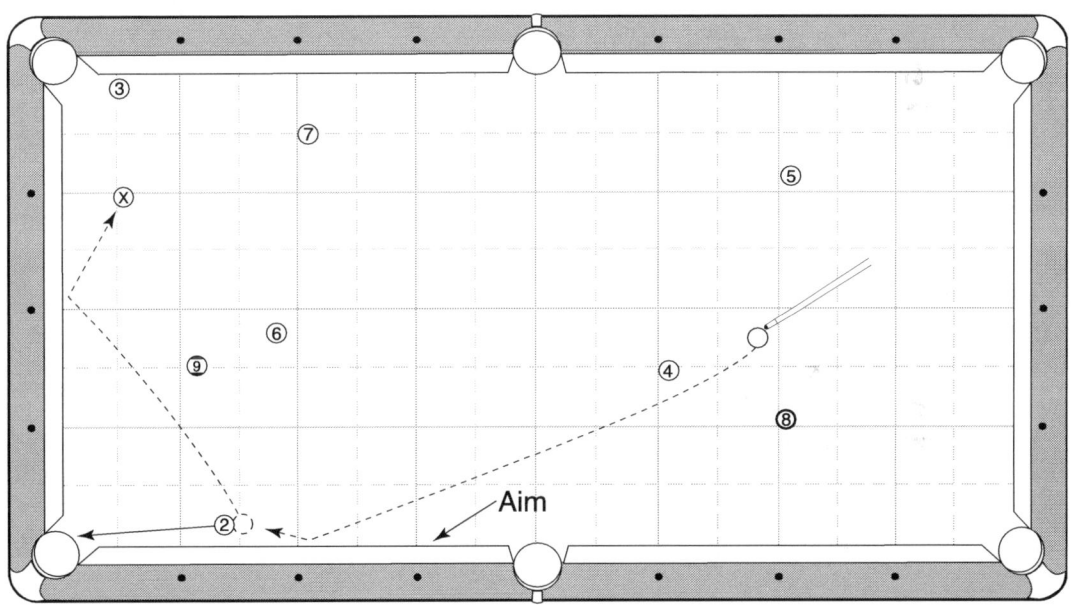

A Masse/Curve Shot

Fong-Pang Chao of Chinese Taipei was forced to go for this difficult shot on his way to defeating Corey Deuel in the 2000 World 9-Ball Championships. Chao elevated his cue to about 50-degrees and played a spectacular masse/curve shot. The cue ball twisted around the 4-ball and into a rail first shot on the 2-ball. The cue ball's path changed 12-degrees from the point of aim and its point of contact with the rail. As I said, curve shots are no sure thing, but they do give you a fighting chance to stay at the table and to continue your run.

Jump Shots

Jump shots have spiraled in popularity as serious players view them as the best way to escape from safeties and bad leaves, and as jump cues have improved in recent years. **Jump shots also give you a direct line to the object ball, eliminating the guesswork that accompanies some kick shots.** In addition, you have a much better chance of pocketing the ball with a jump shot as opposed to a kick shot. The negatives are that a jump shot may fail to reach proper elevation and crash into the blocker, or fly off the table.

Amateur players tend to play more jump shots than the pros because they: 1) lack skill at kicking; 2) face more hooks than the pros (because their games have more innings); 3) feel jumping is the thing to do; 4) have fallen in love with jump shots and play them at every opportunity despite the risks involved.

The Pros' Use of the Jump Shot

In a study I conducted of 500 pro games in 2000, the jump shot was used only 22 times in 20 of those 500 games. The jumper won only 6 of the 20 games, and five of those wins came on run outs after making a ball. This shows that the pros are hesitant to pull out the short stick and, when they do, they win only about 30% of the time. In contrast, the pros played 241 kick shots in 159 games of the 500 that I studied.

Efren Reyes, the world's best kicker, almost never plays jump shots, but why should he with his kicking skills. On the other hand, Earl Strickland and Johnny Archer are extremely proficient at jump shots, but can't match Reyes' kicking game.

Jump Cues

The evidence above suggests that you should **become proficient at kicking before jump shots** (see chapter 10). Still, jump shots come up enough in amateur competition that you should be well rewarded for your skill, providing you pick your spots wisely.

If you haven't already purchased a jump cue or are not satisfied with your current make, I suggest that you ask your friends what brands they are using and search on the forums to see what jumps well.

Practicing the Jump Shot

Before you work on perfecting your jump shot in the local poolroom, consider that these shots are probably not that popular with your poolroom owner or players on the tables nearby. After all, it doesn't take long for a series of constant explosions and flying cue balls to grate on anyone's nerves. So, in consideration of those around you and your poolroom owner's fine slate, I suggest that you practice it at home, or in off hours at the poolroom, with the manager's permission, and not on the table(s) they reserve for big games.

Technique

Jump shots are played by elevating your cue and striking down on the cue ball. Aim below the center of the cue ball, when viewed from the angle at which your cue is pointing when elevated, as shown in the illustration. **Use a light grip and a definite snap of the wrist**. While you need to use a medium to medium hard stroke, you don't need to "kill the cue ball." You can achieve sufficient elevation by elevating the cue to about 30-40 degrees. However, when you must get the ball up quickly, you may need as much as 55-60 degrees of elevation.

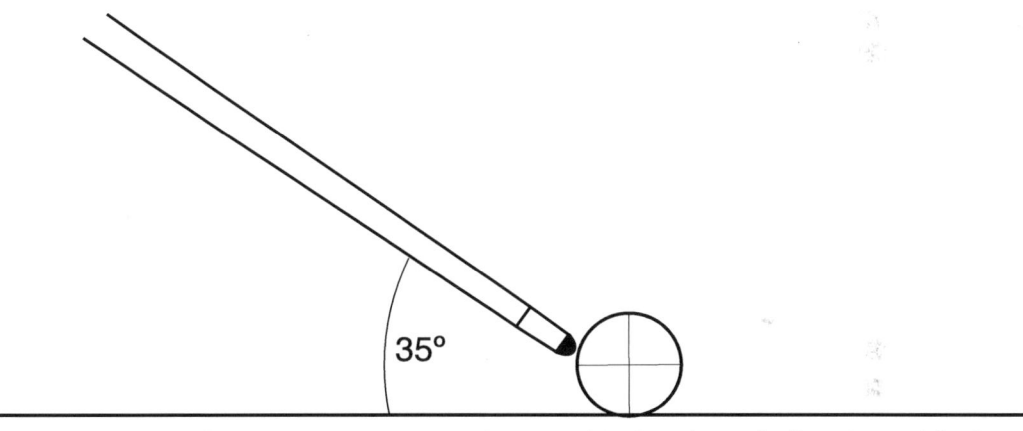

On most jump shots, your primary goals are to hit the object ball and avoid fouling, which can be accomplished with no special attention to aiming. If your goal is to pocket the ball, however, you will need to aim with even more care than you use on a regular shot. Some players find it helps to line up the shot with their cue as level as possible, and then to elevate the butt end to the desired angle.

When aiming at a straight in jump shot, you can pocket the ball whether the cue ball is on or off the table at the moment of contact. On cut shots, however, the cue ball will most likely be in the air when it makes contact. Your accuracy will be determined in part by the cue ball's distance from the cloth at the moment of contact. To compensate for this you must aim for a slightly fuller hit on the object ball. **Your aiming adjustment on jump/cut shots is a guessing game** as it is impossible to predict exactly how far off the table the cue ball will be at contact.

Chapter 1 - Shotmaking

The Cue Ball's Flight Pattern

The more you elevate your cue, the higher the cue ball will fly, causing the first bounce to be higher after the ball lands on the table. On most jump shots, the object ball is hit after the initial bounce. When the landing strip is particularly long, there is a chance that the cue ball will bounce two or three times. Each successive bounce will be lower, and the distance between each bounce will be considerable shorter. You can expect the distance between the first and second bounces to be roughly 40-50% of the distance from where the cue ball was struck to where it first landed on the table.

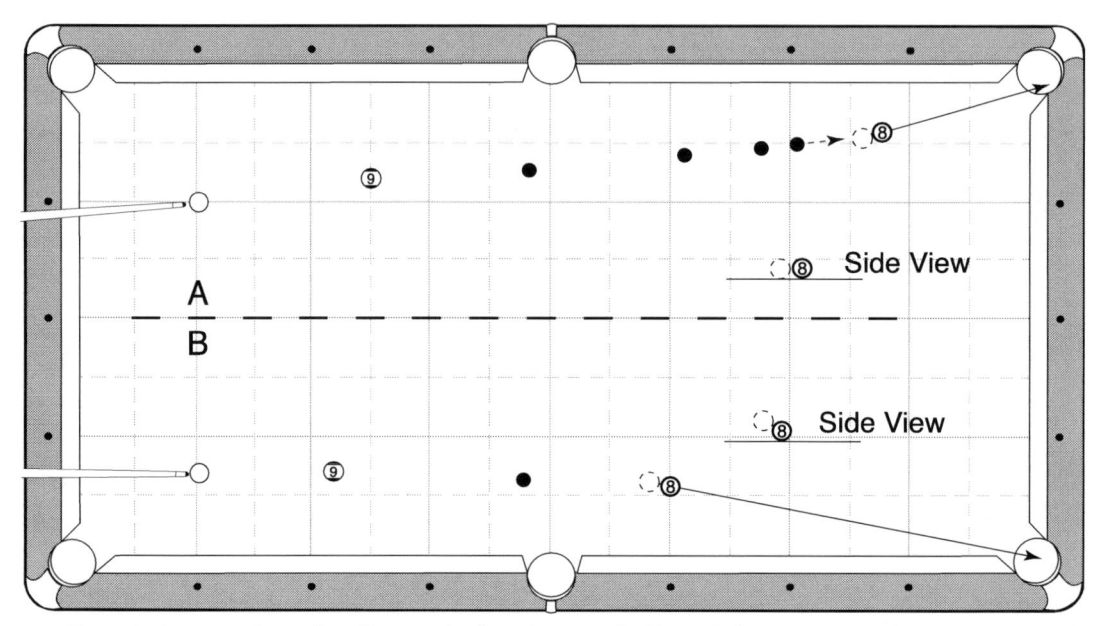

Part A shows a long landing strip for the cue ball, so it has room to bounce several times before contacting the 8-ball. This is the ideal scenario because the risk of the cue ball leaving the table is nil. In addition, **the cut angle is much more predictable when the object ball is being struck while the cue ball is at table level**. The ideal contact position is shown in the side view.

The 9-ball is closer to the cue ball in Part B, so your cue must be angled up a little more to produce more immediate elevation. The cue ball will bounce higher, which results in a downward hit on the 8-ball after the first bounce.

On short-range jump shots, the big skill is in controlling the flight of the cue ball when there is little or no room for a bounce. You want to avoid having the cue ball hit close to the object ball on its first bounce because it could easily glance off the top of the object ball and fly off the table. This is especially true on cut shots. You can avoid fouling if you can make the cue ball fly down onto the object ball before it lands on the table. This requires expert technique and detailed knowledge of the cue ball's flight pattern.

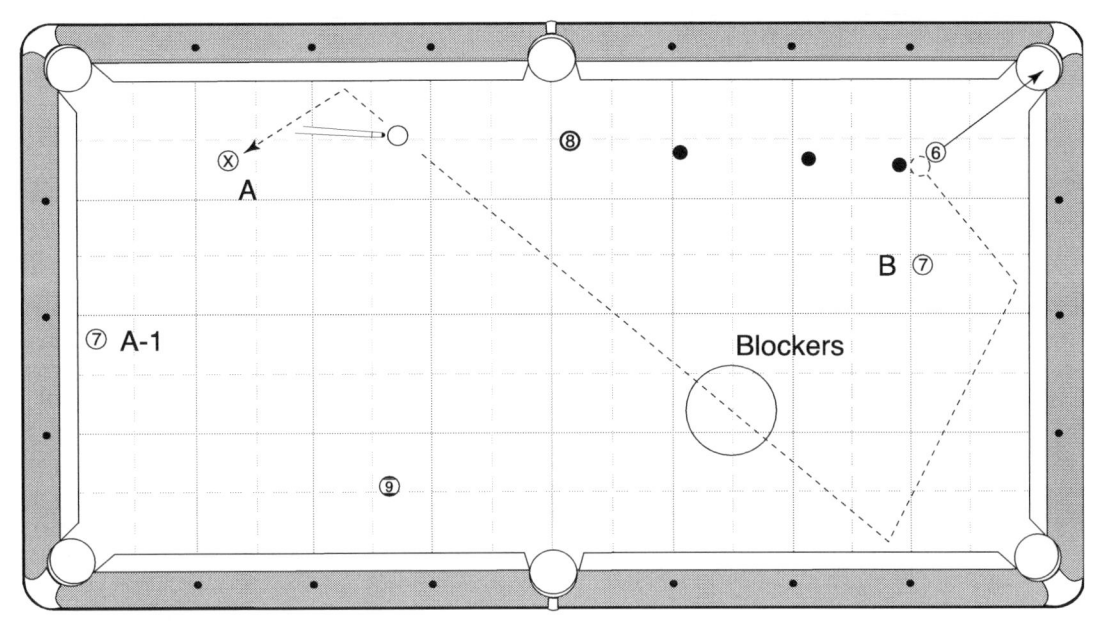

Playing Position on Jump Shots
The ultimate goals on any jump shot are to make the ball and to play position for a shot or a safety. When you are cutting the object ball, be prepared for the cue ball to travel a long distance after contact. In the illustration, the cue ball stopped at Position A for excellent shape on the 7-ball at Position A-1. If the 7-ball had been at Position B, you would have a big problem. Now let's assume the 7-ball was at Position B and there were one or more blockers around the area covered by the circle. These balls could be used to stop the cue ball for position on the 7-ball. In sum, your chances of playing position on jump shots are linked to the position of the balls.

If you are playing a straight or nearly straight in jump shot, you can bring the cue ball back as the draw spin that you applied will still be on the cue ball when it contacts the object ball. It is difficult to apply follow unless you are jumping over an obstructer at a shallow angle, which allows you to hit higher on the cue ball.

When to Jump
A realistic appraisal of your skills helps in determining when you should go skywards as opposed to playing a kicking shot. Some love jumping, others hate it, and then there are those who view jump shots as a necessary evil. In short, **what is a kick shot for some is a jump for another**. Below are the conditions when a jump shot may be your best bet:
- There is a long landing strip for the cue ball.
- The object ball that must be carried is in the ideal range (not to far or too close) from the cue ball so that there is no need for excessive elevation.
- The object ball is close to a pocket.
- You only have to clear the edge of the blocker.
- There is a good chance of making the ball and getting position on the next ball for a shot or safety.
- The cue ball will hit the object ball fully, which minimizes the risk of it flying off the table.

- The primary kicking lanes are blocked.
- A possible kick requires that you use a difficult route to the object ball.
- The table is conducive to jump shots. Thicker slate generally leads to a higher bounce.

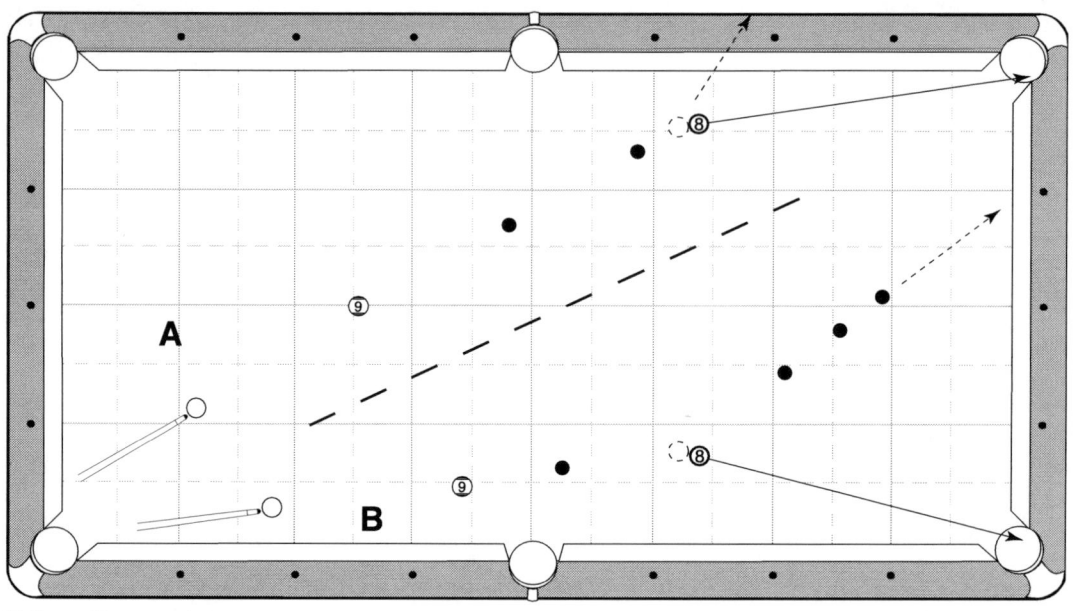

When Not to Jump

The conditions which make a jump shot a risky proposition are pretty much the opposite of those listed above. If you have a short landing strip and the cue ball is likely to hit well up on the object ball or on the upswing after a short hop, the cue ball could be headed to the poolroom floor. In addition, you must pay special attention to the object ball's location.

Part A shows a partially successful jump shot: the 8-ball was pocketed (note the fuller hit to compensate for the airborne cue ball). The cue ball flew off the table because the object ball was close to the rail and the shot was being played towards the cushion. Notice that there were only a few inches for the cue ball to land.

In Part B, the cue ball flew into the upper half of the 8-ball, but it still stayed on the table thanks to the lengthy landing strip. **Ideally you will have a long area for the cue ball to land on after it contacts the object ball**. View the landing zone, after contact with the object ball, as a secondary landing strip.

Shooting the Gamewinner

My 500 game study of top pros showed that they missed only four 9-balls in the 426 games that went the distance, or less than 1 percent! This is irrefutable evidence as to their ability to play position and to consistently pocket the gamewinner under tournament pressure. In contrast, I can't recall how many zillions of times I've heard a novice complain that they can't make the 8-ball at the finish of a game of Eight Ball.

Well, the same aversion to pocketing the gamewinner also holds true for many players who are relatively inexperienced at 9 Ball. But they are not alone, for even seasoned veterans have been known to cough up the 9-ball (or 10-ball) when on the verge of an important title. In short, **players at all levels have suffered from "moneyball-it is."**

The game ball is usually a routine shot for A Players. They do miss more than the pros when they are competing against less skilled players because lower rated players have a tendency to miss at the end of a game and to leave long, tough shots. The 9 ball can be even more of an adventure for B Players who are more prone to positional errors. And for C Players, the gamewinner is often a journey into the unknown.

I can't offer you a foolproof cure for "money-ball-it is," but I can provide you with some insights into playing the money ball that will help you cope successfully with the game's most stressful shot. These ideas should save you a game here or there. And these tips could someday spell the difference between winning and losing a double hill match for some big title!

Ideal Position on the 9 Ball

Let me first state the obvious: **acceptable or excellent position is your best insurance against missing the money ball**. Furthermore, the game ball should be the easiest ball to get shape on because:

- You don't have to worry about setting up the correct angle or playing position for another shot.
- You needn't worry about getting hooked behind any other balls when playing position.
- You can play area position.

Your position on the game ball should be to a rather sizeable zone that enables you to pocket it with little concern about the cue ball.

"I want to see the collision." **Nick Varner** on watching the 9-ball go into the pocket.

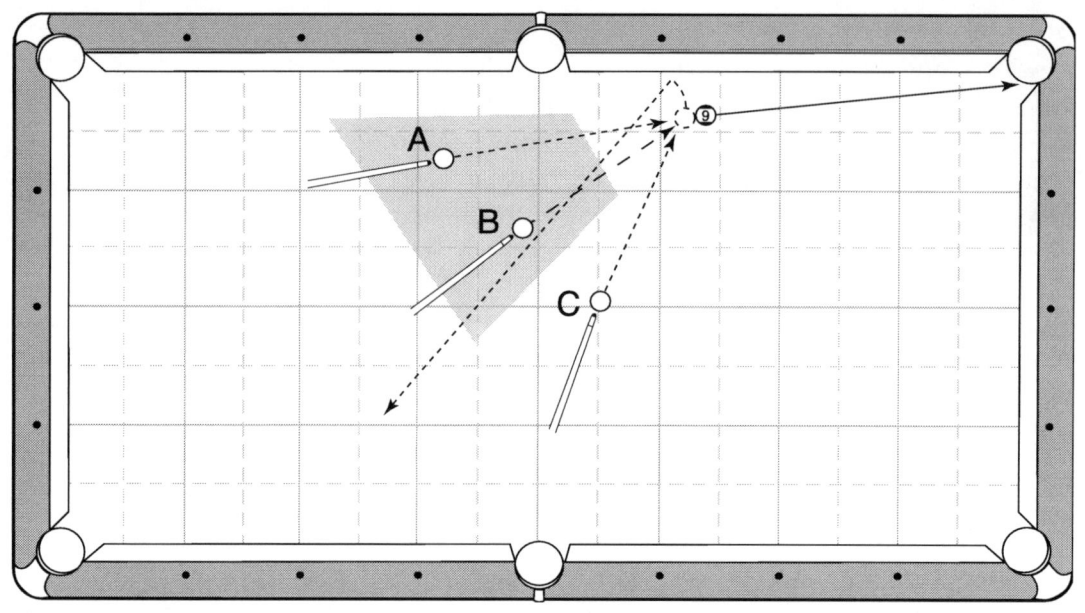

The diagram shows a typically large zone for the 9-ball. The cue ball in Position A presents you with **the ideal scenario for shooting the game ball, which is an easy shot with a small cut angle**. A shot like this enables you to concentrate your energies on making the ball since there is no chance of scratching. Play this shot with the speed of stroke that you feel gives you the best chance of making the ball. On this shot most good players will use a medium soft stroke to a medium firm stroke.

When your position is a little less than perfect, you must expend a little energy worrying about the cue ball. With the cue ball in Position B you must now control its direction to avoid scratching in the opposite side pocket. Some players like to play this shot with draw while others use follow. You don't need shape, so you should play this shot with the speed with which you are most comfortable. This also holds true for most shots on the game ball: play the shape that allows you to use the speed of stroke with which you are the most comfortable. The cue ball in Position C is well out of the ideal zone. The 60-degree cut angle makes this shot very missable. In addition, you must now apply right or left english to avoid scratching in the opposite side pocket.

When you have a difficult shot on the money ball, be sure to complete your shooting routine. Take enough time to get comfortable over the shot. Then concentrate on giving it your best effort with the understanding that this will give you your best chance of making the ball.

CHAPTER 2

The Break

*"The cardinal rule of Nine-Ball is
don't foul on the break."*
Steve Mizerak

Breaking of racks of 9 Ball is like a golfer's driving or a basketball player's jump shot: sometimes you've got it and sometimes you don't. At times you'll consistently pocket balls and separate the pack across the table while on others you can't buy a ball on the break. And sometimes the conditions are breaker friendly while at others the table is as stingy as Scrooge at Christmas.

In one pro match I saw the wing ball go straight into the corner pocket 21 straight games! Before another match, the commentators at the 1992 Bicycle Club Invitational were reciting the super-fast radar gun readings of Earl Strickland and Francisco Bustamante as proof of their breaking prowess, alerting viewers to the upcoming break and run show. So what happens? These two ball blasters failed to break and run one single rack in 23 games!

The pros work on their break as much as any other shot, and yet their results are highly inconsistent. This is due to changing conditions and minor fluctuations in their technique. In sum, you've got to perfect your break so you can wring as much from the table as possible, and so you won't be at a disadvantage when playing an opponent with a powerhouse buster.

When you possess a strong break, you always have a chance to stage a comeback providing the table is breaker friendly. A great break can also intimidate an opponent. If you break poorly, your opponent will gain confidence because they know they will have a chance at winning most games.

The Importance of the Break

C Players

According to several studies, including mine, the 9-ball goes on the break about once in every 40-50 racks. The 10-ball goes even less often. At the C Player level, a break and run rarely happens, so there are few opportunities for these players to win a game in the first inning. C Players, however, can lose games by scratching. If they foul against a fellow C Player, their opponent may line up a combo or some other shot on the money ball. And, if they are playing a B Player or better, their opponent could run out. As a result, a C Player's main objective when breaking should be to make a solid hit on the 1-ball, and to keep the cue ball on the table. This can be accomplished by employing a softer break. Ironically, many top players will go to a soft break under certain playing conditions. When a C Player is getting weight, however, they should use a power break if they are being spotted two or more extra money balls.

B Players

B players can consistently break and run the easier racks of 9-Ball, but not when playing 10-Ball. When a B Player is on their game, they are also fully capable of running tougher racks and making combos or other shots on the game ball. As a result, a B Player with an effective break can gain a significant advantage over an opponent with a comparatively poor break. A B Player who is breaking well can completely dominate a match with a C Player. Against an A Player, they will need their very best break to have any chance of winning unless, of course, they are receiving sufficient weight. The last thing a B Player wants to do is to give an A Player ball in hand after their break.

A Players

A Players are a threat to run out the majority of the time when they make a ball and have a reasonable shot at the lowest numbered ball, providing the layout has few, if any, complications. Their skill at shotmaking and position play make the break an extremely valuable weapon. **At the A level, many matches are won by the player whose break is working better** during the match. Since A Players mostly compete with other top players, fouling on the break is perhaps the biggest single mistake they can make. When their break is working an A Player will completely dominate C and B Players even when they are giving them a sizeable spot.

In sum, **the break becomes more of a factor the better you play**. If you are a C Player, your practice time is better spent on other parts of your game. B Players can significantly raise their winning percentage by improving their break. Those who aspire to the A Player level and above must plan on developing a consistent and powerful break that enables them to counter their opponent's run outs.

LAW: The greater the ability of the players, the more of a role the break plays in determining the outcome of the match, and vice versa.

The Pool & Billiard Study

Scientific evidence on break shot speed was lacking until *Pool & Billiard Magazine* conducted a break speed contest at the 1996 BCA Trade Show. Karin Kaltofen (then the editor of the magazine) and engineer Steve Kasten measured the speed of the break shots of over 300 hundred amateurs and professionals using his "Laser Speed Meter." The 23 male pros averaged 24.9 MPH while the 15 female pros averaged 19.3 MPH. Sammy Jones recorded the fastest break with a speed of 31.1 MPH while Jeanette Lee lead the ladies with a speed of 23.8 MPH.

High-speed hits with accuracy produced more balls on the break. Imagine that! The test also revealed that going all out for speed creates a big variable in your results. A controlled, yet powerful break speed gives you consistency. The table below summarizes the results of their contest/study.

Summary of the Pool & Billiard Study

MPH	%	MPH	%	MPH	%
28	1.1	22	12.4	16	3.6
27	1.1	21	11.7	15	1.8
26	2.1	20	12.1	12-14	2.1
25	5.3	19	14.2	< 12	1.1
24	5.3	18	13.5		
23	6.4	17	6.4		

All Breakers Approximate Ranges
16.0 – 25.8 MPH 90%   17.2 – 24.9 MPH 80%

Your Optimum Break Speed

Some people are born with bodies that enable them to run 100 meters in under 10 seconds, or that enable them to throw a baseball at 90+MPH. Those lacking a certain muscle structure can never hope to become a Nolan Ryan or a Michael Phelps. Similarly, you possess strength, muscle structure, and other elements of biomechanics that place natural limitations on the maximum speed that you can ever hope to obtain on the break.

Once you have come close to mastering the elements of the power break, you are probably within 1-2 MPH of your absolute top speed. From that point on, improvement will come only from focusing on a training regimen designed to enable you to reach your maximum. Since you have so many other things to master in pool, as a practical matter, your practice time is better spent elsewhere instead of trying to squeeze another mile or two per hour out of your break.

Goals for the Break Shot

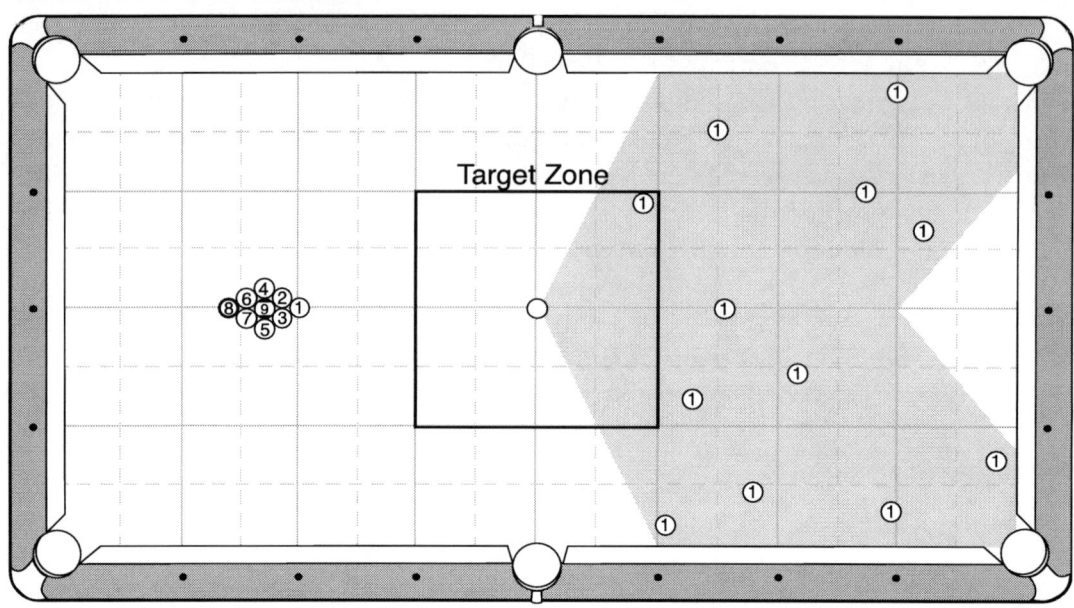

Your goals for the break shot depend on your level of skill. The primary goal of C Players, as I mentioned, is avoiding a foul. B Players and above should be looking to accomplish the following:
- Make at least one ball.
- Have the balls spread so that the rack can be run.
- Have a makeable shot on the lowest numbered ball.
- Park the cue ball in the center portion of the table.

The diagram shows the ideal zone for the cue ball after the break in both 9 and 10 ball. Let's assume that the cue ball parked in the dead center of the table. The 1-ball almost always banks off the side rail to the opposite end of the table when it does not go on the break. Notice the huge zone in which the 1-ball is a very makeable shot when the cue ball is in the Target Zone.

Where the Balls Go on the Break

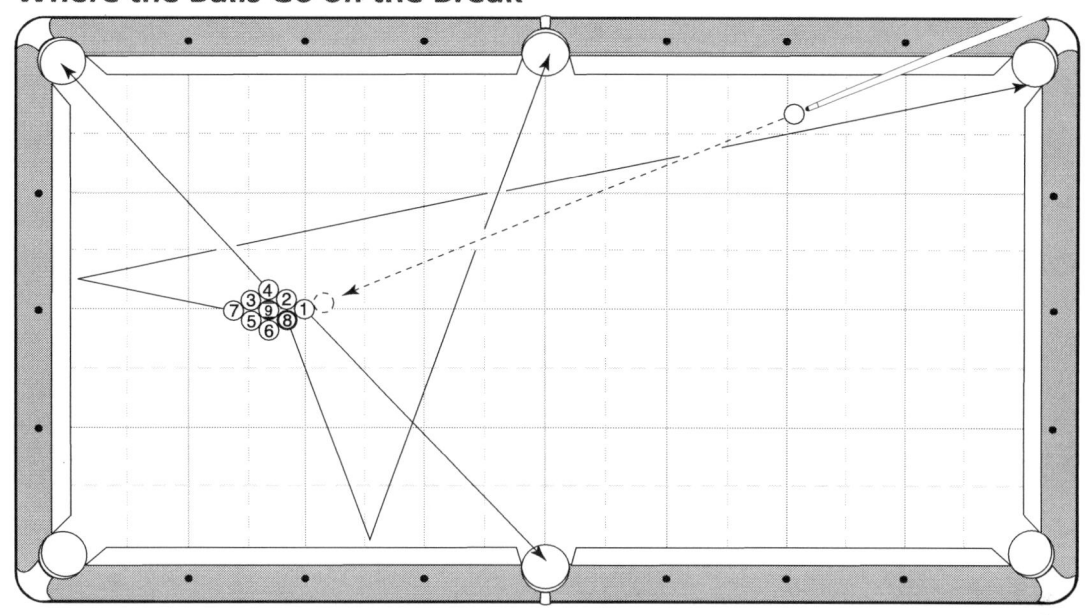

The majority of balls that fall on the break in 9-Ball go mostly into a few predictable destinations. When the rack is broken from the right side, as in the example, the wing ball or corner ball (the 4-ball) will drop into the corner pocket on the same side of the breaker much more often than any other ball.

The 1-ball goes mostly in the opposite side pocket, and it is the second most pocketed ball. The 8-ball in this rack occasionally goes cross side. If you are receiving a spot ball, you should break from the opposite side of the table. If you are giving up a spot and your opponent always breaks from the same side of the table, you should always place his money ball on the same side behind the 1-ball. The ball at the end of the rack (the 7-ball) occasionally banks into the far corner.

Playing Position After the Break

Your attempts to make a ball should be focused on the wing ball or the 1-ball. Any other balls that fall are usually a result of the unpredictable collisions. If the corner ball is going on nearly every break, you can put even more effort into controlling the cue ball. Try taking a little speed off the break. If the wing ball still goes with a softer break, you can really zero in on position for the 1-ball.

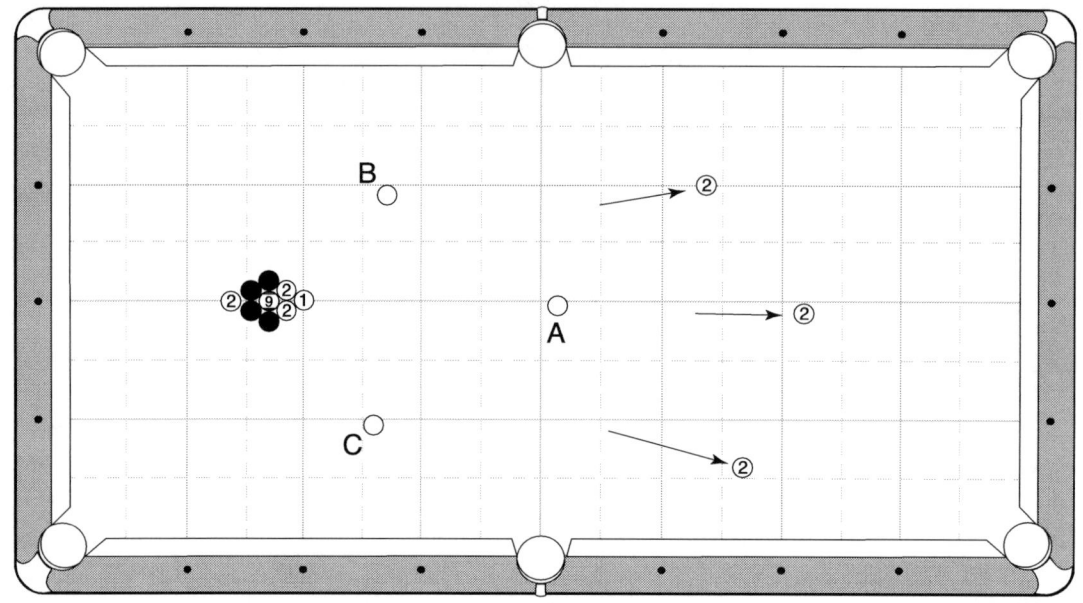

Many players prefer to go for the 1-ball in the side. If it is dropping regularly, focus on how to play shape on the 2-ball. If the 2-ball is racked right behind the 1-ball or at the bottom of the rack, as in the example above, it should join Cue Ball A at the breakers end of the table. Your opponent may attempt to neutralize your strategy by placing the 2-ball in the positions shown by the solid balls. If that is the case, you may wish to send the cue ball to Position B or C.

Losing the Cue Ball on the Break

A less than perfect hit on the cue ball and/or 1-ball can lead to a loss of control of the cue ball. The cue ball in Position A in the diagram at the top of page 45 continued forward because it was hit too high. The obvious solution is to lower your tip at address. The cue ball scratched in Position B thanks to a less than perfect hit on the 1-ball combined with follow. Adjust your aim slightly to the right and hit the cue ball a bit lower.

The cue ball disappears into the opposite side pocket (Position C) on most scratches. Hitting to the right of the ideal line of aim caused this scratch. For some reason, many players (even the pros) have a very difficult time correcting for this error. If you have this problem, try overcompensating for a while until you slowly work your way back to the proper line. Hitting the cue ball too far below center caused the corner pocket scratch in Position D. Finally, the cue ball in Position E near the end rail was also caused by hitting the cue ball too low. This is the least damaging of all the errors since the cue ball is still on the table and there is a good chance that the 1-ball could be in the same area of the table.

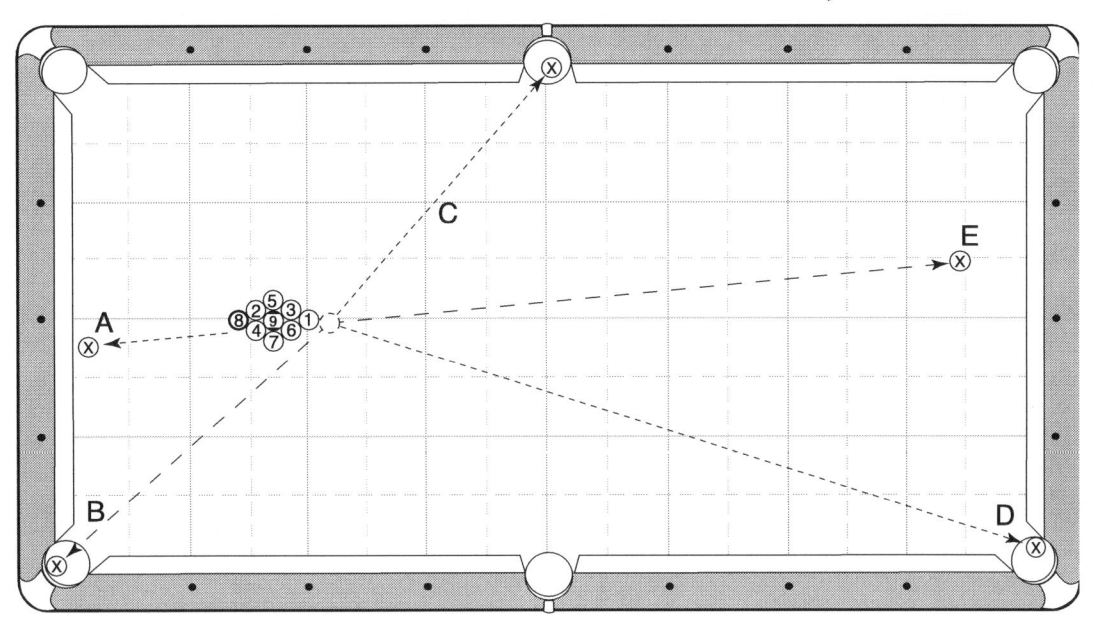

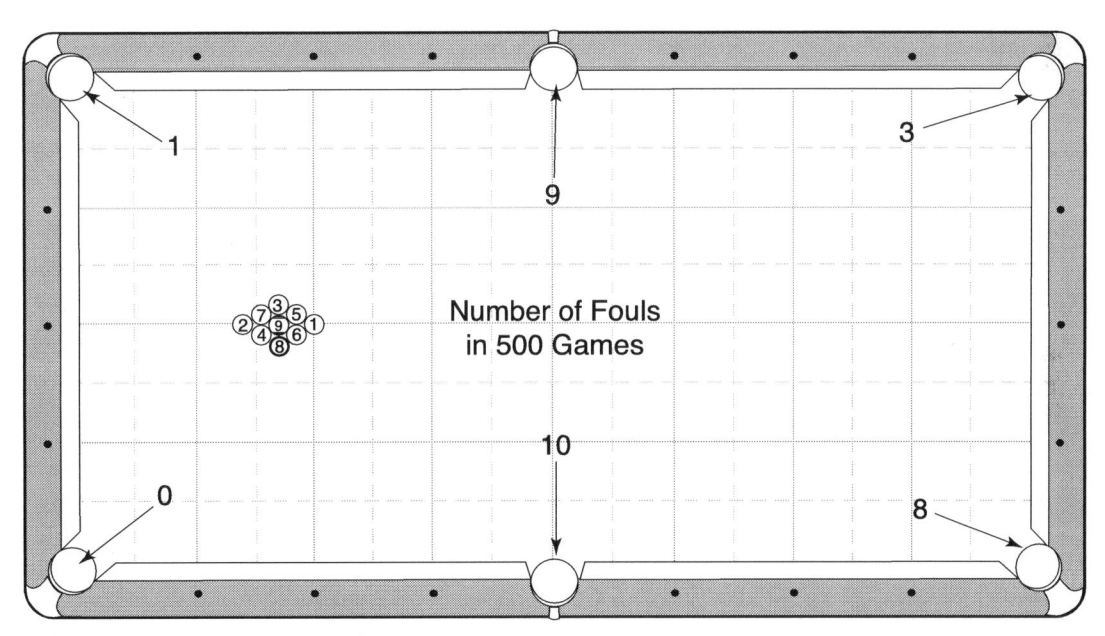

Where the Pros Scratch

In a study I conducted of 500 games, the pros fouled on only 7.6% of their breaks, or once in every 13.2 attempts. The cue ball flew off the table 7 times, or only once in every 71.4 breaks! The remaining 31 fouls were scratches into the various pockets shown above. The cue ball traveled directly into a pocket 21 times, and it was kissed in 10 times. The study shows the pros' remarkable skill at hitting the cue ball and 1-ball on target. The one scratch at the foot end reveals that **the pros almost never let the cue ball travel forward on the break**!

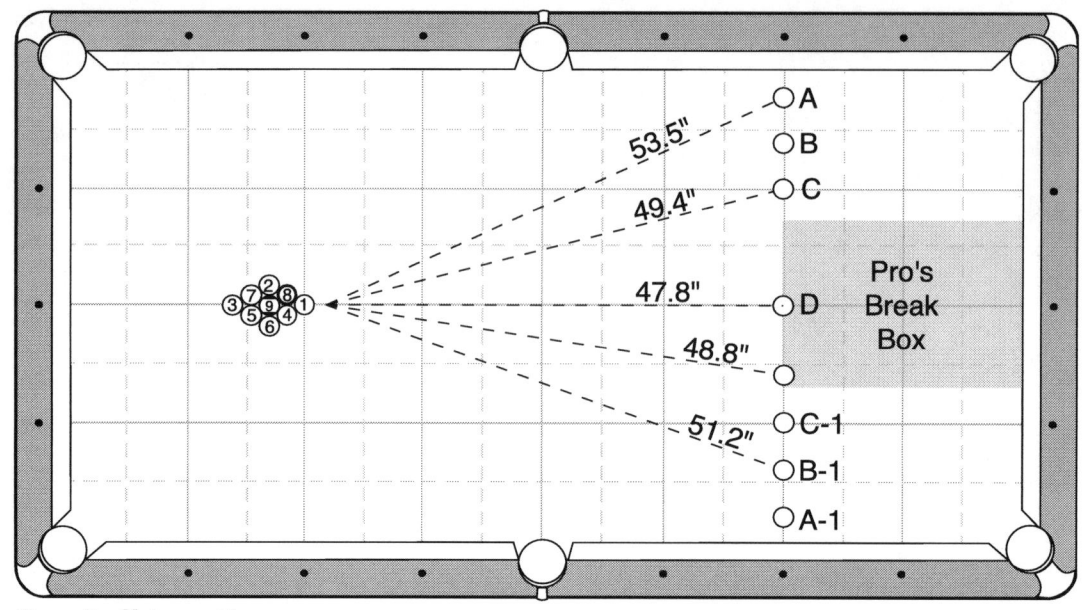

Cue Ball Location
Most players prefer one side of the table for breaking because they feel that they can line up better with the rack. Positions A, B, C and their opposites on the other side of the table are the most popular spots for the break. Position D in the center offers two big advantages: it is the shortest distance to the rack; it is easier to aim directly at the 1-ball. Even so, this position is seldom used because it yields the least number of balls on the break.

The cue balls in Positions A and A-1, next to the side rail, are furthest from the rack but are very popular locations because they raise your chances of making a wing ball. Many players also like bridging on the side rail. Positions B and B-1 are popular because they permit you to use a bridge on the bed of the table while still giving you a good chance to pocket the corner ball. Positions C and C-1 are good for control because they give you a more direct line on the 1-ball, plenty of room to use your normal bridge, and an even shorter distance to the 1-ball than the positions closer to the rail.

The rectangle shows the break box, which is used in some pro events. The purpose of the break box is to create more balance in Nine Ball by reducing the number of balls on the break, thus increasing the value of the other components of the game. According to my study, the break box has cut the balls pocketed from an average of 1.04 (in 350 games) to .75 (in 150 games)!

Looking for the "Sweet Spot"
When you are evaluating a table before a match, **look for the track lines to the 1-ball**. These lines show the spot from which other players have been breaking – and it is fair to assume that they kept breaking from this location because it was working. So, this could be a good place to begin your quest for the "sweet spot."

When balls aren't falling, your mechanics may be to blame. **Before you abandon a break spot that has worked for you in the past, evaluate your mechanics**. If you are still certain your break stroke is in fine working order, then it's time to hunt for a new location.

You should have at least two or three positions that you feel comfortable using. And be sure to **consider the position that your opponent is using if they are getting good results**. When you switch locations, monitor the hit on the 1-ball and make any adjustments, if needed. Your break stroke mechanics should not be affected by switching locations. In sum, the ability to break well from multiple locations is a skill which must be learned if you are to compete at higher levels.

A Players cannot afford to come up empty on more than a couple of breaks in succession against opponents of their caliber when their opponent's break is working. If it takes you too long to figure out the break, your opponent could have built a lead that will be hard to overcome. **You must avoid the scenario where you lose on your break as well as on theirs** because that is too much "weight" to give an excellent player.

TIP: If you are pocketing balls other than the wing ball or 1-ball, you may wish to consider switching positions before the well runs dry.

TIP: When evaluating your opponent's break, look for: 1) cue ball location; 2) contact with the 1-ball (full or partial); 3) where they are hitting the cue ball.

Looking for the Best Speed

When you have tried all of your favorite locations and the balls still aren't falling, change the speed of the break. **If your soft break isn't making balls, increase the speed. If you have been using a power break, back off on the speed**. A soft break can be especially successful in making the 1-ball in the side. If making the 1-ball is your plan for the break, you need to know where the 2-ball is going. You should also pay close attention to the speed of your opponent's break, especially if they are getting good results.

The Control Break

If you are having trouble making solid contact with the 1-ball, try reducing the speed of your break. Strive for solid contact with the 1-ball by using about 80% of your available power. You may be surprised at the power you generate. The control break can help you to loosen up and restore your timing. Once you are consistently making solid contact with the 1-ball, you can begin to apply more power if balls still aren't falling.

Setting Up for the Break Shot

If you are a C Player, work on hitting the 1-ball accurately and on developing a controlled break shot. Those of you who play at the B level or above are ready to work on the power break.

The power break shot is like no other shot in pool because you will be hitting the cue ball about twice as hard as on the most forceful of position plays. As the *Pool & Billiard Magazine* study showed, the average pro breaks at nearly 25 MPH. The hardest stroke I encountered on over 3,000 position plays was only a little over half that fast at 13 MPH.

You will obviously need to modify your shooting technique to achieve speeds of roughly double what you will use for the most powerfully struck of position plays. This begins with the set up.

The Break Stance

When your cue contacts the cue ball on the break, your head will be considerably higher than it was at address. This is especially true if you use a low stance when setting up for the break. With a low stance you must raise your head considerably as your arm begins to swing forward. I recommend that you position your head several inches higher when setting up for the break shot. A higher head position reduces the amount that you will have to raise up during the forward stroke.

Your feet should be positioned several inches closer together than in your normal stance because you will be more upright at contact than with a normal shot. A narrower stance enables you to push off your back foot, which is an additional source of power. You should feel like you are in an explosive position, much like a sprinter who is ready to explode out of the blocks. I suggest you experiment with various stance widths until you find the right distance for you.

Front Arm

Some players like to bend their front arm when taking their regular stance, but most players keep it fairly straight. Some players even prefer to lock their front arm at the elbow. When taking your break stance, however, I suggest that you bend your front arm so that your forearm is at roughly a 40-degree angle to your upper arm. Bending your front arm makes it easier for your body to move forward with the stroke. If you keep your front arm locked, you will block your body from moving into the shot, robbing your break of a big source of power.

Bridge Length

Your bridge for a break shot needs to be long enough so that you can smoothly accelerate to the moment of contact, at which point you want to experience an explosive burst of power that comes from whipping your wrist with perfect timing. The bridge length you use for position plays requiring a hard stroke should be sufficiently long. If you use an extra-long bridge for the break, what little extra power you gain could be more than offset by an unhealthy percentage of miss hits.

Grip

A major source of power on the break comes from releasing your wrist a split second prior to contact. This kind of action can only be produced with a loose grip. Francisco Bustamante's break has been clocked at upwards of 30 MPH despite his slight stature. He uses a long bridge, but his primary source of power is the supplest wrist in pool. He uses a super light grip, which enables him to blast the balls all over the table.

Most players who fail to produce the desired action tend to tighten the muscles in their arm and wrist on the forward swing. Their attempt to muscle the balls and to hit the rack with all their might accomplishes the opposite effect. Remember, **loose and relaxed muscles are fast muscles, and fast equals power**.

I trust that I've convinced you to use a loose grip, perhaps even more relaxed than the one that you use for your normal shots. **Your grip hand should be placed a couple of inches further up on the butt of your cue than on normal shots** to accommodate your more upright body position at contact. If you rise up on your forward swing (as you should) with your grip hand and it is in its normal position, it will be a few inches behind perpendicular at contact. If your grip hand is too far "behind," it will be harder, if not impossible, to achieve maximum power.

Cueing

I discussed earlier how hitting the cue ball in the wrong spot can lead to a complete loss of control. It follows that one of your primary goals is to hit the cue ball exactly where intended. You should **make a habit of observing the cue ball's path after contact** with great interest. If it is traveling forward after contact, you need to lower your bridge when setting up for the break. You will need to raise your bridge slightly if the cue ball is drawing back to the head of the table.

The cue ball will be ramming into a mass of balls, which provides much resistance. As a result, the cue ball will bounce back at least a foot when hit in the center. If you want the cue ball to return past the center of the table, strike it just a hair below center. Understand that **regulating the cue ball's exact return distance on the break is one of the hardest skills to master in pool**.

A number of top players like to set up with their tip well below center. As they swing forward, their arm drops and their cue strikes the cue ball near the center. Contacting the cue ball in the center will enable you to achieve maximum power.

The Break Shot Stroke

The break stroke is a well-timed swing that, in some ways, is more like a golf swing than a pool stroke because your entire body gets into the act. The break shot is played with a stroke that is 3-5 times as hard as the stroke used for medium speed position plays. Since you will use your break stroke on only 7-10% of your shots, you should follow the pros and **take a little more time to get set for the break shot**. I suggest that you use between 1.5 and 3 times as many warm up strokes as on a typical shot so that you will have enough time to lock in your aim on the 1-ball and to loosen up your shooting arm for the final stroke. The remaining fundamentals will be covered in my analysis of the breaking techniques of Johnny Archer and Shane Van Boening.

Johnny Archer's Break

Johnny Archer had the best power break in pool during the 1990s and 2000s. His break is still formidable and worth studying even though the experts now concede the break crown to Shane Van Boening. These photos are from the finals of the Sand Regency Open 20, December, 1994. We pick up the action after Archer has completed a lengthy series of warm up strokes.

1 Archer's head is about a foot above his cue prior to beginning the final stroke, which is much higher than it is for a normal shot. His knees are flexed and his legs are ready to drive his body forward.

2 Archer's body starts to rise up in preparation for the transition. This is a critical move, and it starts in the middle of the final backstroke.

3 As Archer nears the end of his backstroke, his lower body begins to shift forward. This sets the timing for his powerful release through the cue ball. He avoids the impulse to crush the rack in the transition – a fault that can cause a player to tighten up and to lose power.

4 Archer's cue explodes into the cue ball, sending it flying into the rack at over 25MPH. The stroke features a strong release of the wrist, which adds power. His head is higher than at address, which allows him to extend his shooting arm for power. The cue is slightly inclined, as it must be, because the rail is above his contact point on the cue ball.

5 The cue tip brushes the cloth and Archer's body is going up. The cue ball is flying down the table.

6 His back foot is off the ground, indicating how much forward momentum he puts into the break shot. His grip hand is about a foot above the table, eliminating the chance that he might ram it into the table.

7 Both of Archer's hands are now well above the table. His cue is extended to the center of the table, which is another sign of his tremendous forward momentum. The cue ball is now three quarters of the way to the rack!

8 The cue ball is smashing into the 1-ball and is about to reach an elevation of about 6 inches above the table. Archer's cue has now extended past the side pocket, and he is hovering above the table. A full follow through is a must for maximum power.

The Result: Archer watches as the balls roll around the table for 5.7 seconds. The cue ball is a few inches from dead center. Archer has an easy shot on the 1-ball, and he indeed proceeded to run out.

Chapter 2 - The Break

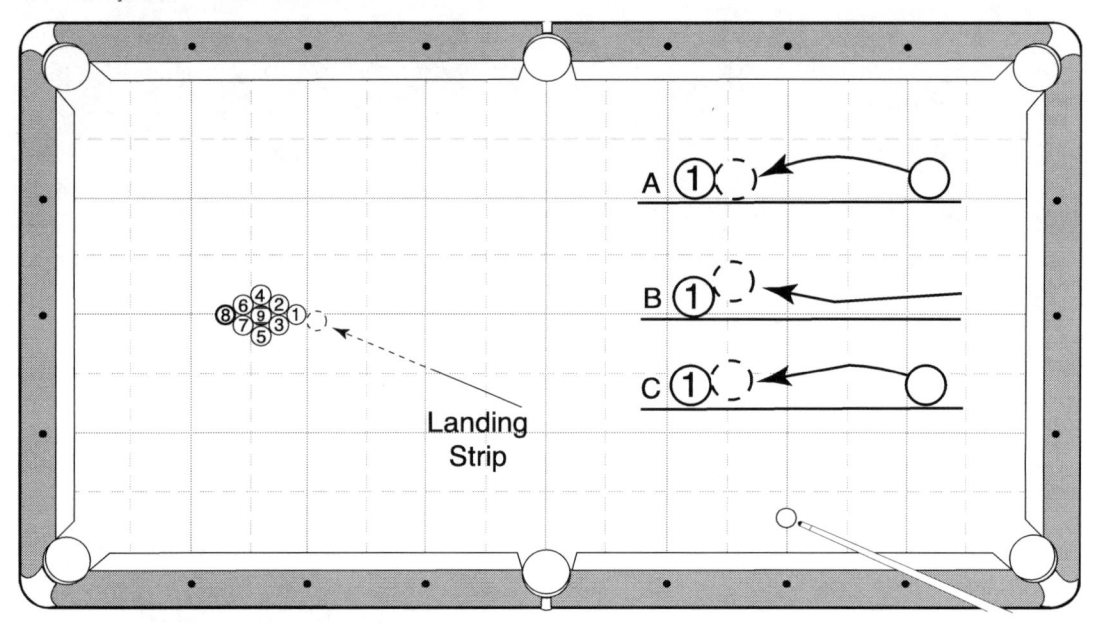

The Cue Ball's Flight Pattern

The cue ball should be struck in the dead center or just a hair below center to keep it from rolling forward after the break. The center of your tip will be about 1 1/8" above the slate at contact. The rail is higher than the center of the cue ball, so the butt will be slightly higher than the tip at contact. The cue ball is struck with a slightly descending blow, sending it flying down the table.

The flight pattern is visible on tables where the break is being played from the same spot thanks to the marks that the cue ball leaves upon landing. The diagram shows the landing strip for the cue ball when a power break is employed. After its first bounce, the cue ball will fly the rest of the way into the 1-ball or take one more bounce before making contact.

Position A shows the cue ball hitting the 1-ball and the table at the exact same moment. This allows the cue ball to impart maximum energy into the rack, and there is no risk of the cue ball leaving the table.

The cue ball in Position B has struck the 1-ball with an uppercut after bouncing in front of the rack. This type of contact minimizes the transfer of the cue ball's energy into the rack and also causes the cue ball to fly off the table when the 1-ball is hit off center. Hitting the cue ball with an excessively downward blow causes this flight pattern.

The cue ball in Position C struck the 1-ball at a downward angle after bouncing well down the table. The less than pure contact with the 1-ball will result in a loss of power, but there is little chance that the cue ball will fly off the table. Hitting the cue ball at an excessively downward angle causes this error. It is difficult to regulate the flight of the cue ball into the rack when your cue is at an overly steep angle at contact. Your best bet for solid contact is to **minimize the altitude of the cue ball's flight by hitting it with your cue as level as possible**.

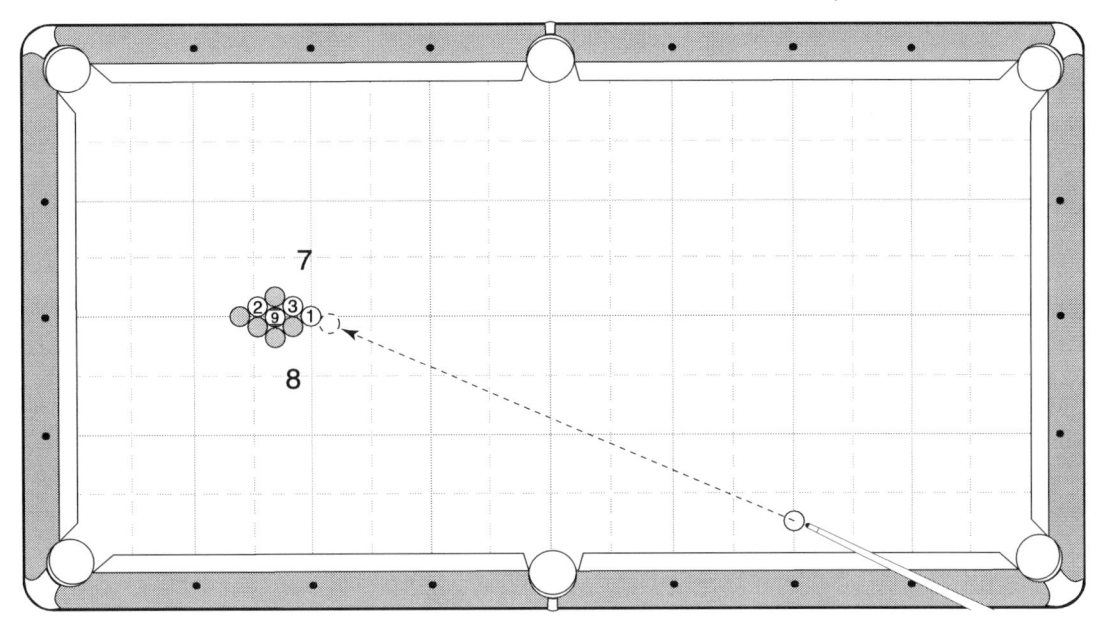

Racking is as Easy as 1-2-3
You can make life more difficult for your opponent if you place the balls in the positions in the diagram. When your opponent breaks from the left side, place the 2 and 3-balls where shown. This will often cause them to be spread across the table, forcing your opponent play long distance position through traffic on his first couple of shots. If your opponent breaks from the other side of the table, switch the 2 and 3-balls to the other side of the rack.

Reading a Table for Tendencies
The playing conditions and you and/or your opponent's breaking skill can lead to a variety of layouts, so watch how the balls are breaking on the first few games of a match. This can help you to manage your expectations and to adopt the appropriate strategy.

Wide Open Layout and Balls Are Falling
When you see this happening, you must gear up for an offensive match. Now is the time to bear down on the break, and to adopt a mindset that prepares you to run out. And don't be surprised if your opponent also plays well and runs out often under these conditions.

The Table is Stingy and the Balls Are Clustering
Perhaps your and/or your opponent's break are not working, or perhaps the playing conditions are not conducive to making balls on the break. When this happens and the balls are clustering towards the rack end of the table, be set to play more defense. Take advantage of the additional opportunities to hook your opponent. Look for combos and billiards when you get ball-in-hand, especially if there is a safety that can be built into the shot.

Racking Technique
Before pushing the rack into place, occasionally take a little time to **rub the cloth in the area of the rack to remove unwanted particles of chalk or other debris** that could keep the balls from settling into place. This procedure can also condition the cloth. The

next step is to put the balls in the proper places within the rack. Obviously the 1-ball goes up front and the 9-ball in the middle.

You should consider where you place the other balls, especially if you are playing someone who runs out regularly. **Proper ball placement makes it more difficult for your opponent to run out** should they be lucky enough to make a ball or two on your tight and honest racks! If you are getting a spot and you are racking for your opponent, be sure to place your "money balls" in the row right behind the 1-ball.

The worst offense in racking Nine-Ball happens when the 1-ball has broken loose from the rest of the rack. A gap between the 1-ball and the rest of the rack causes a marshmallow break which is accompanied by a sickening thud. You can avoid this "mistake" by following the proper racking technique. Once you have positioned the balls in the rack, put the 1-ball on the spot and let it settle into place. Slide the top edge of the rack up against the 1-ball. Then push the second row of balls and the remainder of the rack carefully into place. Keep your eyes on the 1-ball to make sure it doesn't move. If the 1-ball does move, you will have to start over. Press the rack together and observe the results. If they are satisfactory, push the rack slightly forward and lift it from the table.

Accept Imperfection

The pros play with new sets of balls that are nearly perfectly round on brand new cloth from the world's finest manufacturers. At many tournaments the balls are racked with devices and racks that lead to the tightest rack possible – and, the pros these days insist (sometimes beyond reason) that the balls be perfectly placed. In your poolroom, the balls may not be exactly the same size due to wear and tear. In addition, the cloth will be pitted in several locations because the balls are not always racked in the exact same spot. As a result, **it is often impossible to get every ball to fit perfectly together**. This means that you shouldn't expect a perfect rack, nor should your opponent expect one from you.

You and your opponent can save each other a lot of grief by agreeing where the balls should be racked, and on the acceptable standard of quality. In some events, rack your own rules eliminate the troubles that come from having your opponent rack for you when they have such an obvious conflict of interest.

The Racker – It Takes All Kinds

The wide variety of the quality of racks demonstrates differences in equipment and the spectrum of character in humans. **Your racker will range from an honest good citizen to an outright crook**. The good citizen is a true sportsman who makes a legitimate effort to give you the best rack possible. Most players probably will make a decent attempt to give you a good rack, but do not like to spend much time fiddling with the balls. And then there are the slug artists, who view their ability to slip their opponent an occasional bad rack as an integral part of their strategy.

"With some people you don't really have to worry about the slug so you can just play pool." **Bill Incardona**

"I come to a tournament to play pool, not to rack balls." **Grady Mathews**

The devilish streak in pool players comes out most often when racking the balls. Many players take a special delight in watching their opponent blast away at their carefully crafted slug racks with no favorable results. Many slug artists may even find it hard to keep from chuckling at the sound of the cue ball going splat upon contact with the 1-ball.

When to Play Rack Inspector

Less than perfect racks can be the fault of imperfect equipment and your opponent, who may be simply careless or unskilled at racking the balls. Still, **you must insist on your right to a reasonably tight rack** if winning is important to you. So, I recommend that you check the rack periodically, especially if you are breaking well but balls aren't falling.

In baseball, a brush back pitch is used to keep a skilled hitter back from the plate. The slug rack is pool's answer to the brush back pitch. Here is a set of circumstances in which you are ripe for receiving a slug rack:
- When your opponent is mad after losing a game and takes little time racking.
- When you've been breaking and running regularly.
- When you've just made the 9-Ball.

"I find it kind of insulting to have someone eyeballing every little bit of space in the balls. It is kind of degrading." **Grady Mathews**

I recommend that you **occasionally conduct rack inspections, especially if you suspect foul play**. In most cases, however, a spot inspection is all that is necessary. But I certainly don't advise you to slow down the game to a snail's pace by making your opponent rack the balls over and over again. In fact, those who inspect every rack and force their beleaguered opponent to rerack the balls constantly are probably a bigger nuisance than all but the dastardliest of slug artists.

TIP: Conduct spot inspections to keep the racker honest.

Rack Classifications

A rack's quality falls into one of four categories. You should factor in the conditions when determining the minimum quality that you will accept.

1. **Perfect** – All balls are frozen, the 1-ball is on the spot, and the rack is perfectly straight. It is not realistic to expect this kind of rack unless you are playing under perfect conditions.
2. **Near Perfect** – There is a small gap in a non-critical location, or in a place that could actually help you make a ball. A rack of this quality is the best either you or your opponent can expect under normal playing conditions.
3. **Satisfactory** – An acceptable rack under the conditions, but it could be slightly better. When your opponent is giving you less than the best rack possible, then they must be willing to accept the same quality.
4. **Unacceptable** – This is a slug or a close cousin. There are one or more gaps that will severely limit your ability to make a ball and to get a good spread.

You Come Up Empty Over and Over Again

If you are hitting the break perfectly time and again, and nothing is going, change you break spot and/or speed, as we discussed earlier. If the balls still won't go, it could be that the table is stingy. However, if your opponent is consistently making balls, and you are getting a good spread but are not making anything, your opponent could be a master of the racking arts – so you would be wise to take a closer look at their handiwork. Make sure that the 1-ball is touching the second row, and also make sure the second row is touching the 9-ball on at least one side.

The Rack Is Not Straight

A rack artist may tilt the rack slightly if you have a habit of always breaking from the same side. You can take advantage of this by changing sides – after he has racked the balls! If you discover the rack is pointing to the right (from your vantage point at the head of the table), break from the right side as this will give you a good chance to make the wing ball. You will want to break from the left side if the rack is tilted to the left.

Bad Sound on the Break

If your break lacks that explosive sound that you expect to hear when you hit the 1-ball just right, there is a good chance that one or more balls were loose.

High and Low Racks

When the balls are racked above the spot, your chances of making a corner ball are severely reduced or eliminated. However, you now have a better chance of making the 1-ball in the side pocket! Sometimes a good portion of the spot is visible after the balls have been racked, which indicates that they have been racked low. When this happens, the chances of making the wing ball go up, so you are advised to leave this "bad rack" alone. It could even be smart for you to use a medium speed for control if the corner ball is going every time

Pounding the Balls

According to the rules, you and your opponent must "refrain from tapping the object balls more than is absolutely necessary." If your opponent is pounding the balls into the slate, you are within your rights to ask them to stop.

Beware of Slow Rackers

It may be a little disconcerting to see your opponent throw together the rack while giving you no time to revel in your victory. **Fast rackers are either very good or very careless.** The quality of your break is an excellent indicator as to the quality of their work.

Do not be fooled by those who exercise the care of a diamond cutter in assembling the rack. They may be pretending to take the time necessary to give you a perfect rack when, in fact, they could be trying to arrange a slug rack that could pass your inspection. I get a kick out of the players that peer at the rack from all angles to make sure they are giving you a gap free experience. If the racker is honest, but slow, you should walk away from the table and start your break shot routine over again once they are done racking.

CHAPTER 3

Position Routes

"If you are playing with confidence you can control the cue ball within inches."
Jim Rempe

Superior shotmaking skills will only take you so far in 9 Ball. After 2-3 tough shots in succession, even the most talented ball pocketers will succumb to the pressure or the odds. In fact, all but the easiest runouts will quickly terminate due to lack of position after a few tough shots. So, while position play is important in all pool games, it is extremely critical in 9 Ball because you must play shape on a specific ball. This requires that you master a variety of routes that can send the cue ball anywhere on the table.

Since you are using only nine or ten balls and they are usually spread across the table, a typical rack is far less congested than in other pool games. As a result, you don't always have to be as precise with your position. However, you do have to fall within certain boundaries or zones on most shots if you want to keep matters simple and be able to consistently run out. And you must pay close attention to the cut angles that you leave yourself.

In this chapter we'll discuss playing position from one ball to the next. If you master the basic routes and have a working knowledge of several of the advanced routes, you will have the tools to play patterns and to consistently run out. If you then add the expert routes to your arsenal and learn to recognize a variety of patterns, you will be able to run racks that the average player only dreams about running.

The Run Out Game Plan

Position Play is how you get on the next ball. This includes the route, the target zone, and measures to reduce risk.
Patterns are recognizable sequences of shots that tend to repeat themselves.
Run Outs are the end result of stringing position plays and patterns together.

The Sequence for Learning Position

One of the great mysteries of pool to the casual observer is how easy the masters make the game appear. In truth, position play is deceptively difficult. However, an aspiring player can learn to control the cue ball with consummate skill if he follows a logical sequence and patiently learns the skills that are needed to proceed to each successive level. So, **as long as you keep learning, perfecting, and expanding your skills, you will be on the path to mastering control of the cue ball**. To play position well you must follow these steps:

- Become proficient in the fundamentals of the game.
- Learn basic stroking with fairly straight shots.
- Learn to pocket cut shots.
- Learn to hit the cue ball above and below center.
- Learn to feel comfortable using different speeds of stroke.
- Learn to recognize the various position routes. This includes the speed and cueing that each route requires.
- Learn to execute the position route.
- Learn variations of the position route.

Cueing - Learn to Become Multi-Dimensional

The cue ball's ending location results from cueing (where your tip strikes the cue ball) and the speed with which you stroke the shot. In other words, **cueing + speed of stroke = position**.

You can play adequate shape for most shots by cueing on the vertical axis and by using a few basic speeds of stroke. **Once you have mastered the basic routes, you will be prepared to extend your position play repertoire** by adding english and by using an even wider variety of speeds of stroke.

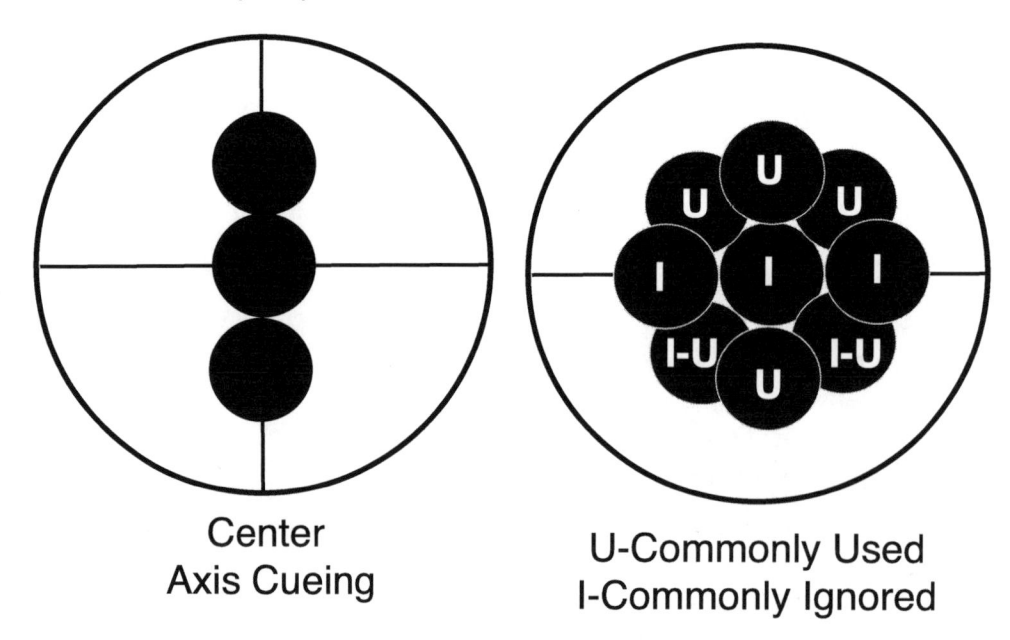

Center Axis Cueing

U-Commonly Used
I-Commonly Ignored

The cue ball on the right shows the nine points of contact. Those labeled with a U are the most commonly used locations. The areas labeled with an I are avoided by a great number of players. The tip positions labeled I-U indicate low inside english and low outside english. For example, Low right english is commonly used when it is outside english, but not when it is inside english.

Many players fall into the trap of using only a few of the cueing options. They may use draw on shots where follow is the better choice. Or, they may avoid inside english even when it is essential to the success of the shot. If you restrict your cueing to a few pet shots, you will not have routes available to you that you will need to play some layouts. To master position play you must expand your skills so that you feel confident cueing on any of the nine basic locations on the cue ball (and on variations of these locations) with a wide range of speeds of stroke.

English and Position Play

In 9 Ball, shotmaking takes priority. English increases the difficulty of pocketing balls, but it must be used regularly to play position. As a result, the big challenge is to use english effectively when shotmaking accuracy is at a premium.

Many players use english as a crutch, a bad habit that is exaggerated when they are out of stroke. Should you fall out of stroke, I advise that you play as many shots as possible on the vertical axis until your stroke returns. And don't use side spin to make up for deficiencies in your stroke. In sum, **strive for the perfect balance between shotmaking accuracy and cue ball control**. The following rules will help guide your use of english:

Rules for Using English:
- Avoid english on long shots unless it is absolutely necessary. Exceptions are long shots when the object ball is close to the pocket.
- On long shots, try to use no more than a half tip, if possible. Try experimenting with a quarter tip.
- Avoid the temptation on short shots to apply extreme english just because the shot is relatively easy.
- On short shots, use what you need, but go no further than a tip off center.
- If you tend to use a firm stroke, use less english.
- You may wish to spin balls in with english as a matter of personal preference, but don't overdo it.
- A smooth stroke enables you to hit closer to center axis and still get the required action on the cue ball.

TIP: Remember: **vertical axis and speed of stroke = shotmaking accuracy and cue ball control**, which is all that is needed on most position plays.

How English Affects the Cue Ball

English is essential to the success of many position plays, and it enables you to fine tune your position routes. English has a small effect on the cue ball's path prior to contact with the rail. The major influence of english on the cue ball's path comes after it contacts one or more cushions. After contacting the rail, english can:
- Add speed to the cue ball.
- Slow down the cue ball.
- Open up the rebound angle.
- Close the rebound angle.

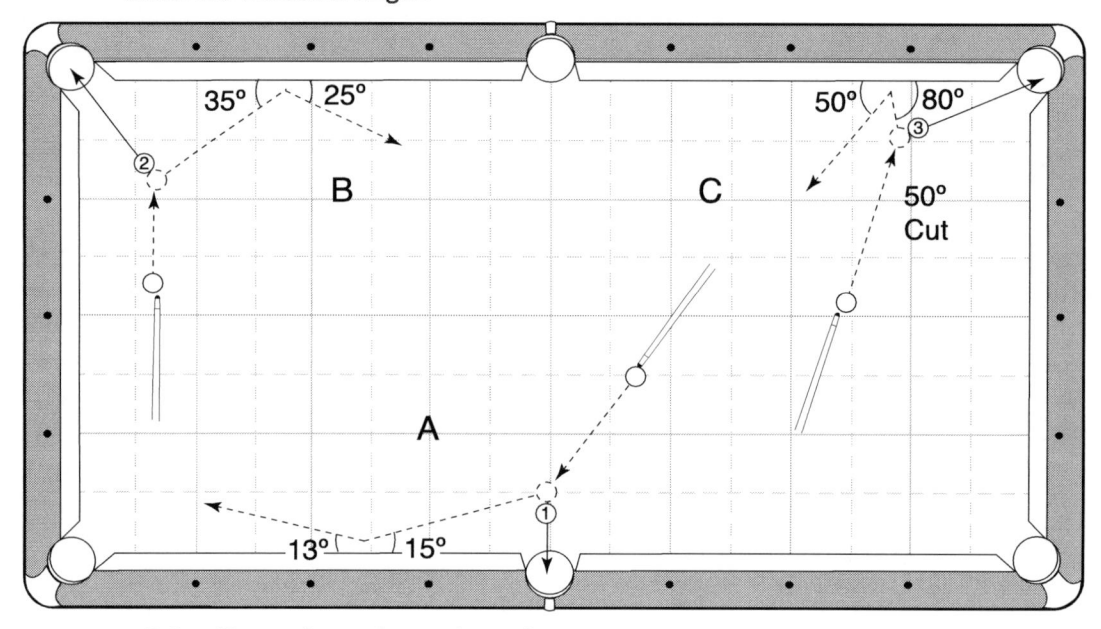

How English Affects the Rebound Angle

The diagram shows three examples of how english affects the rebound angle. When the approach angle is shallow as in Position A, then there is little impact on the rebound angle. In this case, right (outside) english is used primarily to speed up the cue ball. In Position B the cue ball entered the rail at 35-degrees and exited at only 25-degrees thanks to the outside english. Position C shows how english can radically affect the rebound angle when the cue ball enters at a steep angle. Notice that the rebound angle is a full 30-degrees shallower than the entrance angle. **It is important that you have a working knowledge of how english affects the cue ball's path after it strikes the rail.**

Entrance Angles		Impact of English
Very Shallow	1-18	Very Little
Shallow	19-36	Some change in direction
Medium	37-54	A fair amount of change in direction
Sharp	55-72	Pronounced
Very Sharp	73-90	Very Pronounced

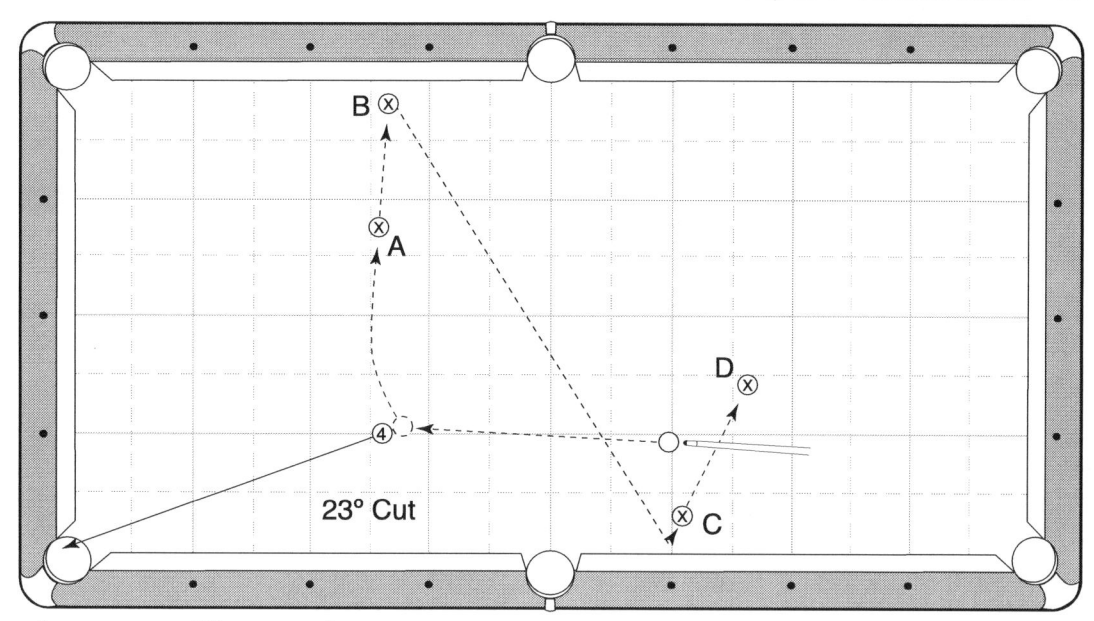

The Cue Ball's Traveling Distance

In 9 Ball, angles are used to facilitate position play. **On every position route with a cut angle you need to learn the cue ball's range of traveling distances for that shot**. The example shows a medium long 23-degree cut shot. Let's assume we're going to play the shot with draw and a half tip of right english. The cue ball in Position A shows the Minimum Traveling Distance it will go when hit with low right english along this path. This shot takes great finesse and it is not a practical shot for most players. When the cue ball is struck with the slowest speed that most players would feel comfortable using, it would stop at Position B. This is the Minimum Practical Traveling Distance.

The cue ball at Position C shows the Longest Practical Traveling Distance for this shot. While you could send the cue ball to Position D with an extremely hard stroke, this is beyond the capabilities of most players. The normal range for playing this route is the line that stretches from the cue ball at Position B to the one at Position C.

The minimum and longest practical traveling distances for any position play will be affected by the playing conditions. Lively rails or a slow table are just a couple of factors that could add or subtract from the length that the cue ball travels.

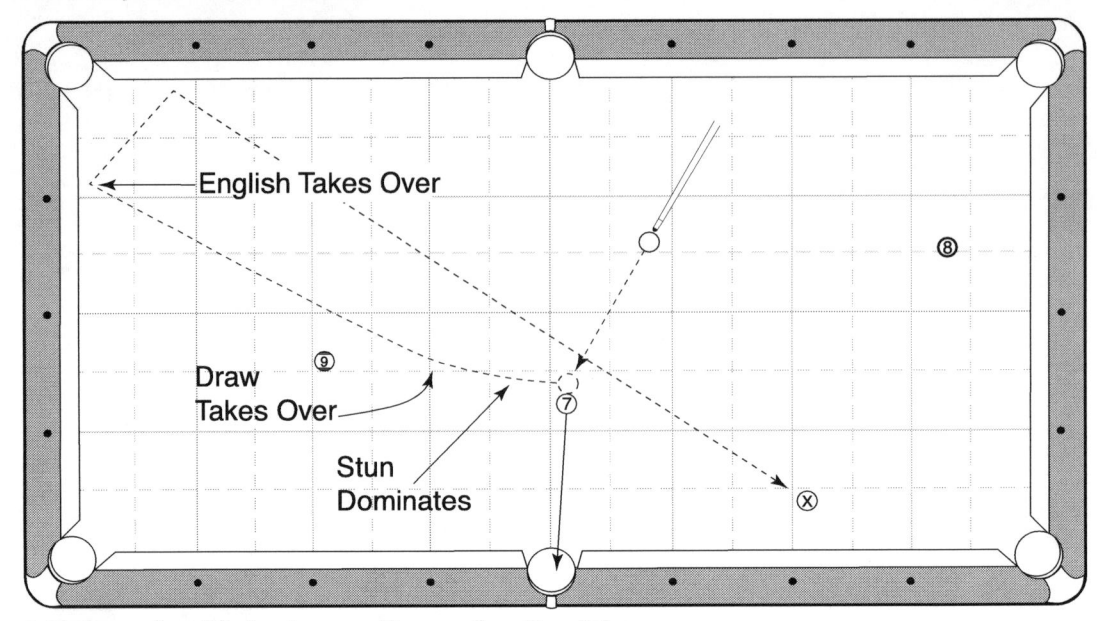

Mixing the Right Ingredients for Position

Planning a position route is like creating a perfect recipe. When the cue ball is going to contact one or more rails, you must map out its route to the first rail, and its subsequent path after it strikes the rail(s). If you fail to mix the ingredients correctly then scratches, hooks, or lack of position could take place.

The first step is to select the cue ball's destination, which is at Position X in this example. Then you must select the correct ingredients. In this case, mix a hard stroke with stun, a half tip draw, and a half tip of right english to produce the route shown. The stun created the first part of the cue ball's path to the first rail. But after it traveled a short distance, the draw spin took over, causing the cue ball to curve to the right. When the cue ball hit the rail the right english took over. Notice that three different forces (stun, draw, english) took turns dominating the action of the cue ball. **Understanding the timing and magnitude of each component force is a big key to mastering position play**.

All three components exerted a profound influence on the cue ball's journey to Position X. On other shots, one component (such as draw or english) must have a significantly large impact in order for the shot to be a success. Even so, all components are needed to make the shot work. For example, a shot might require a hard stroke, a tip of follow, but only one quarter tip of english. While the english is the smallest ingredient, it could still be vital to the success of the shot.

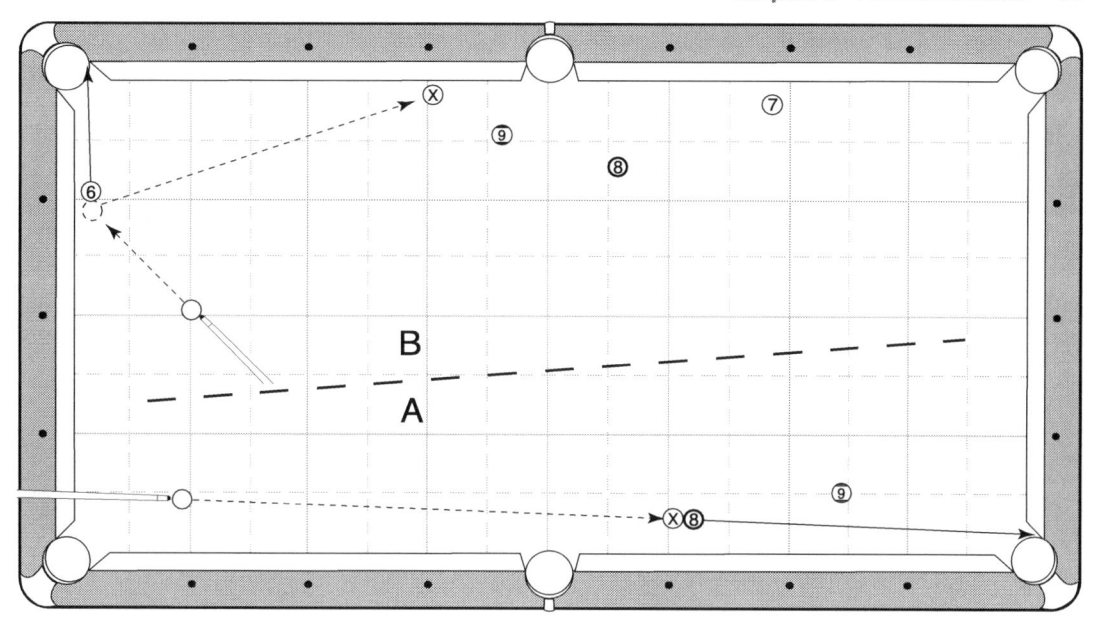

The Primary Emphasis

Successful position plays in 9 Ball are a combination of:
- Speed control.
- Directional control.
- Pocketing accuracy.

On any position play one of the three elements could be particularly crucial to the success of the shot. That element then becomes the Primary Emphasis of the shot. It is always important, of course, to pocket the ball. But when a shot is easy to pocket, the primary emphasis could be on:
- Directional control (to avoid an obstacle or a scratch).
- Speed control (to perhaps get the best angle for the next ball).
- Strategy (two way shot).

The success of the shot could rest on the precise execution of two or three challenging components. As a 9-Ball and/or 10-Ball player, you must learn which component(s) needs to be emphasized on any given shot.

The position play in Part A of the diagram is pretty straightforward: if you can make the 8-ball with a stop shot, the game is essentially over. Your emphasis should be 99% on pocketing the ball and 1% on shape.

In Part B the Primary Emphasis is split evenly between speed control and directional control because both elements are needed to avoid getting hooked behind the 9-ball. Let's say each requires 45% of your attention. The shot is a hanger, so about 10% of your attention is on making the ball. I give pocketing the shot 10% because you must always make sure to make the ball.

On the toughest shots the Primary Emphasis is split between two or more components, each of which must be executed to near perfection. An example would be a long shot using english, which must be hit three rails with perfect speed. The ability to accomplish several challenging objectives on a single position play is the stuff of champions.

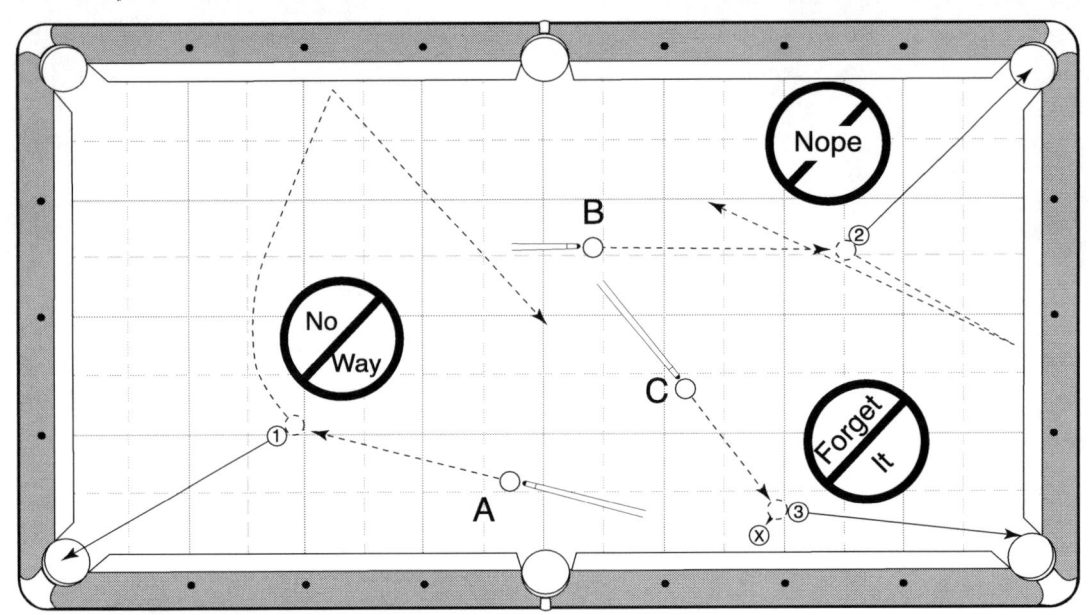

Don't Fight the Physics of Pool
Your efforts to control the cue ball will meet with failure if you insist on fighting the physics of the game. The three shots in the diagram are slightly exaggerated, but they illustrate how you can wage a losing battle with the balls. The 45-degree cut angle in Position A rules out any possibility of drawing back down the table off the side rail. Inside english can be used to work some eye popping miracles, but none like reversing the cue ball's direction off the end rail as shown in Position B. The 50-degree cut angle in Position C means that there is no chance of killing the stone at Position X.

It takes a while to distinguish between possible position routes and those that are totally unrealistic. So pay close attention to what the balls can and can't do when you are playing position. The idea is to: 1) learn what the balls can do, and what routes are natural and reliable based on the position of the balls; and 2) learn what routes (like those in the diagram) have no chance of working.

A Few Shots Where You Can't Fight the Physics of Pool
- Holding the cue ball close to the rail on thin cuts.
- Trying to play routes that aren't available when the object ball is frozen to the rail.
- Attempting to draw the cue ball 2.5 table lengths.
- Expecting the cue ball to change the rebound angle by an unreasonable amount.
- Expecting the cue ball to follow an impossible route immediately after contact.

ABCs of Position Plays

The sections in the pages ahead cover the basic position routes and advanced position plays that will enable you to send the cue ball to almost any part of the table. The learning starts with the basic routes (C Routes), which provide you with the foundation for position play. Skill at the basic routes will enable you to run the easiest racks with little difficulty.

The typical rack, however, consists of at least a couple of advanced position plays (B Routes). When you have mastered a number of Cs and Bs, you will be able to consistently run at least 5-6 balls. The toughest position plays are the A Routes. These usually appear at the start of a run, or in the middle of a run-out due to positional errors. They can also appear in a runout simply because the balls are lying tough.

A number of factors can influence the difficulty of a position route:

Degree of Difficulty Factors
The Shot
- Cut angle
- Distance
- Jacked up, on the rail

Cueing
- Draw, follow, stun
- English, inside english
- English
- Extreme english

Speed of Stroke
- A comfortable speed
- A finesse stroke
- A hard or power stroke

The Position Route
- The difficulty of the route
- Pocketing correctly
- Obstructions
- Avoiding scratches

The Conditions
- The table (cloth and rails)
- The pressure of a match

Recovery Routes

In an ideal world you would only encounter routine position routes because of your expert cue ball control. In the real world, however, you will often miss position by several inches or more. The players call this getting out of line. **You can get back in line and in sync with the layout with a Recovery Route.** These are not the position routes you would normally choose for your pattern, but they can enable you to get back in line providing you can execute a challenging shot. Recovery Routes will be labeled by a **RR** throughout the upcoming sections on position routes.

Setting Your Positional Goals

I suggest that you put aside any illusions about your ability so you can make a serious attempt to grade your current level of play. Objectively placing yourself in one of our three categories is a big step in evaluating your game, and it will enable you to select the position routes for practice that coincide with your current level of skill.

The position routes in the sections that follow have all been graded. Your success with each shot and the various categories (draw or follow, for example) will guide you towards those position plays that deserve your valuable practice time. The table below gives you some general guidelines as to the expected ratio of success.

Success Rates

Player/Route	C Route	B Route	A Route
C Player	70%	50%	10%
B Player	85%	70%	40%
A Players	98%	85%	70%

The table below will help you to create a practice regimen for your game.

Average Players
C- Players should work exclusively on the Cs
C Players should work on the Cs and easier Bs.
C+ Players should work on the Cs and easy to moderately difficult 's.

Advanced Players
B- Players should master the Cs and become very familiar with a wide variety of the Bs.
B Players should maintain their mastery of the Cs. In addition, they should become familiar with most of the Bs. They may also begin learning a few of the easier A's.
B+ Players should continue practicing the easier routes they have mastered while gaining proficiency at the tougher Bs and easier As.

Expert Players
A- Players should spend as much time as necessary maintaining their mastery of the routes they already know. They should also be perfecting the tougher Bs and adding to their list of As.
A Players should spend time perfecting the tougher routes they already know while adding additional As to their arsenal. They should also spend as much time as necessary maintaining their mastery of a wide range of routes.
A+ Players have mastered all but the very toughest position routes. Their goal is to maintain their level of skill across the board while continuing to add additional routes and fine points to their game.

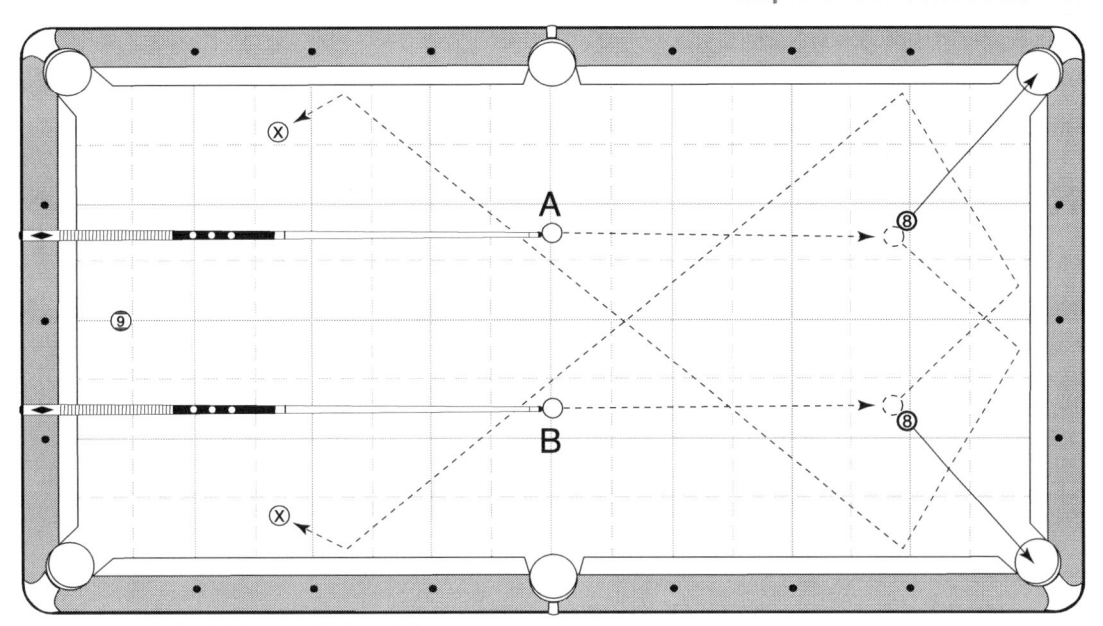

Learn Both Sides of the Shot

The position routes in the sections that follow are diagrammed with a cut to either the left or the right. However, **you should learn both sides of a shot**. For example, the illustration with the cue ball at Position A shows a cut shot to the left. The mirror image of this route is shown with the cue ball at Position B, which is obviously a cut to the right.

Many players are more comfortable using left english as opposed to right english on a particular shot. Others prefer cutting to the right versus cutting to the left. To master each route, you must know both "sides" of the shot.

Practice tips:
- Set up both versions with the donuts.
- Play each route 5 times from each side.
- Note which side is your good side, and which side of the shot gives you trouble (if any).
- Practice until you are equally skilled at both sides of a shot.

Formulas for Position Play

Before we venture into the world of position play diagrams, it may help for you to ingrain these two simple formulas for position play into your pool playing mind, for they embody the essence of cue ball control. Once you have chosen the correct route, you must simply hit the cue ball in the right location with the correct speed to send it to the intended location. Hence, formula #1:

#1) Cueing + Speed of Stroke = Position

In order for the cue ball to arrive at the desired location it must be sent along the correct path with the right speed. This gives us formula #2:

#2) Directional Control + Distance Control = Position

No-Rail Position Routes
Introduction
According to my research, 23.8% of the position plays by top pros in Nine Ball are routes in which the cue ball does not strike a cushion. (I would expect that a study of 10-Ball would yield similar results.) While no-rail routes are among the easiest position plays, there are those that require expert handling of the cue ball. These include draw shots in which good speed control is essential, and stun shots. Since the cue ball is not going to a cushion, you rarely need to use english. This should lead to accurate shotmaking.

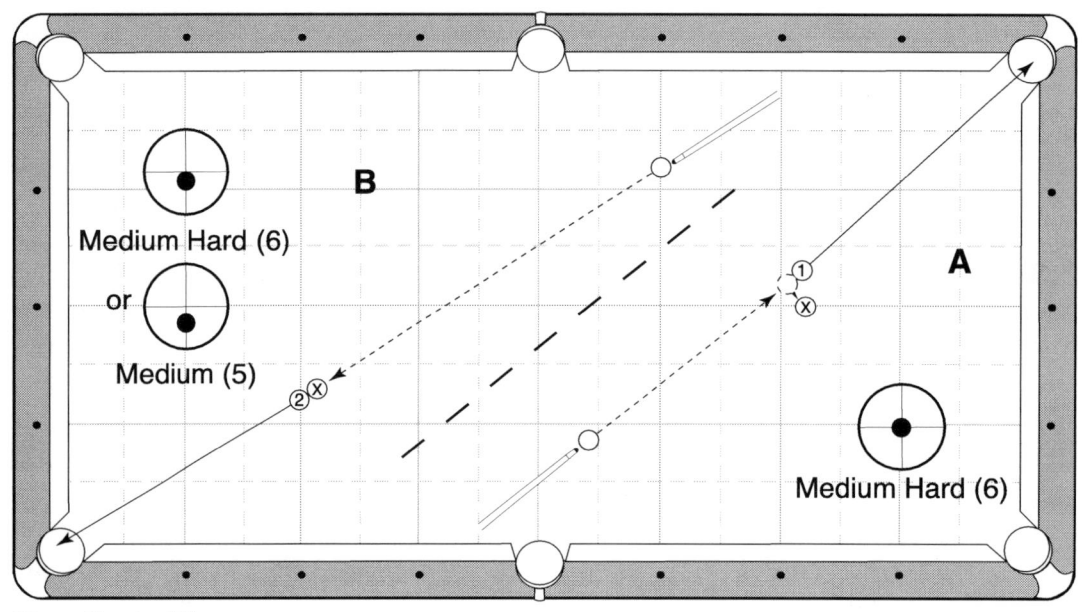

Stop Shots (C)
If you can execute a stop shot when the shot is straight in, you know exactly where the cue ball will be for the next shot. If the cue ball is within 3 feet of the object ball, you can make the cue ball stop dead in its tracks by using centerball and a medium hard stroke.

Shots with very small cut angles in which the cue ball is going to travel only a few inches sideways are also referred to as stop shots. Part A shows a "stop shot" with a 3-degree cut angle.

Part B shows a long-range stop shot. Shots like this must be played with some combination of draw and speed in order for the cue ball to stop dead. The lower you hit the cue ball, the less speed you need, and vice versa.

Soft Follow Shots (C)
The soft follow shot is one of the easiest and most valuable positional weapons. Soft follow shots enable you to control the rolling distance of the cue ball with great precision. On the follow shots shown in Parts A and B, you should be able to send the cue ball to within a few inches of the bull's eye. Play soft follow shots with a shorter stroke and accelerate smoothly. When the cue ball is on the rail, as in Part C, use a 3-4 inch backstroke and a very smooth stroke.

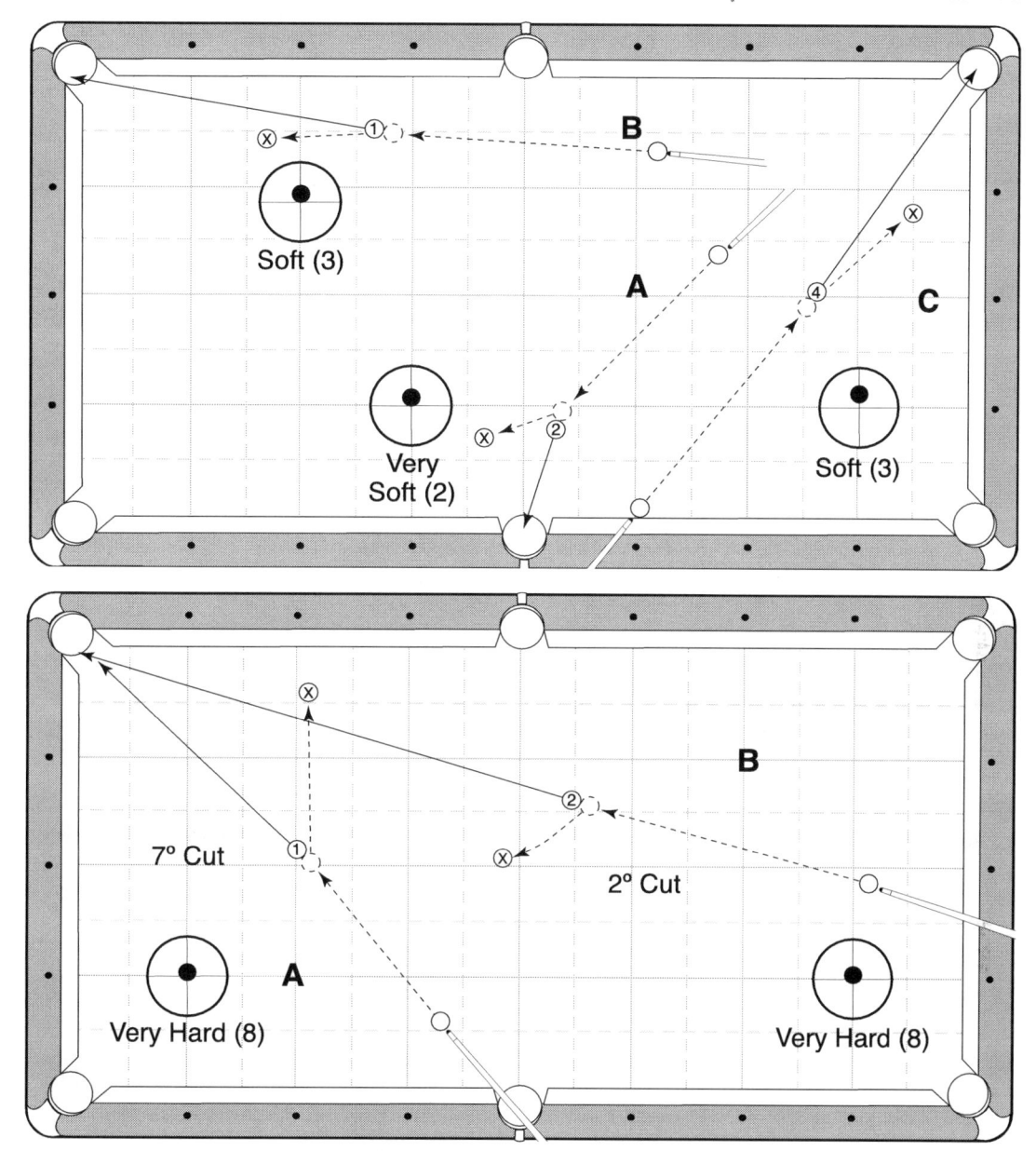

Power Floaters (A)
The power follow floater is an advanced position play that requires a very hard stroke. The idea is to squeeze the cue ball sideways after contact, and to then have it float forward on shots with very little cut angle. In essence, you are creating something out of almost nothing. The shots in Parts A and B were played with a very hard stroke. Notice how much further the cue ball slid sideways with a cut angle of 7-degrees (Part A) compared to the shot with only a 2-degree cut angle in Part B.

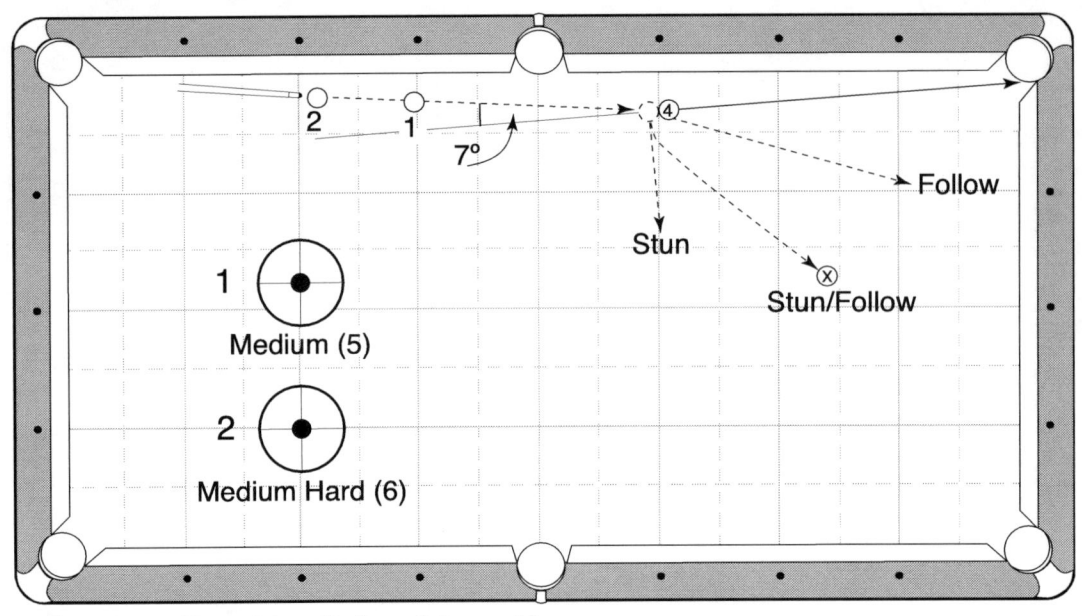

Follow Stun (Part 1 is a B, Part 2 is an A)
The follow/stun shot is one of the trickiest position plays. The goal is to send the cue ball to a location in between where it would go if the shot was played with straight follow and where it would go on a stun shot. This is a feel shot that takes much practice. With the cue ball in Position 1 (rated B), use a medium stroke with a half tip of follow. With the cue ball further back at Position 2 (rated A), use a medium hard stroke and cue an eighth of a tip above center. **While practicing the follow stun shot, take note of how small adjustments in cueing and speed of stroke affect where the cue ball comes to rest.**

Basic Short Range Draw Shots (C)
Precise short-range draw control is one of the hallmarks of a fine player. Making the shots at the top of page 73 is the easy part, but regulating your cueing and speed of stroke to get the desired return distance requires great touch.

The draw shot in Part A is played with a medium soft stroke. In Part B, a medium speed draw stroke will pull the cue ball back about a foot on this nearly straight in shot.

Part C shows a pinch shot. The goal is to minimize the cue ball's sideways movement after contact. Cue a tip or more below center and **use the softest stroke that will still keep the cue ball from rolling forward, which from this distance is a medium soft, give or take a little speed**.

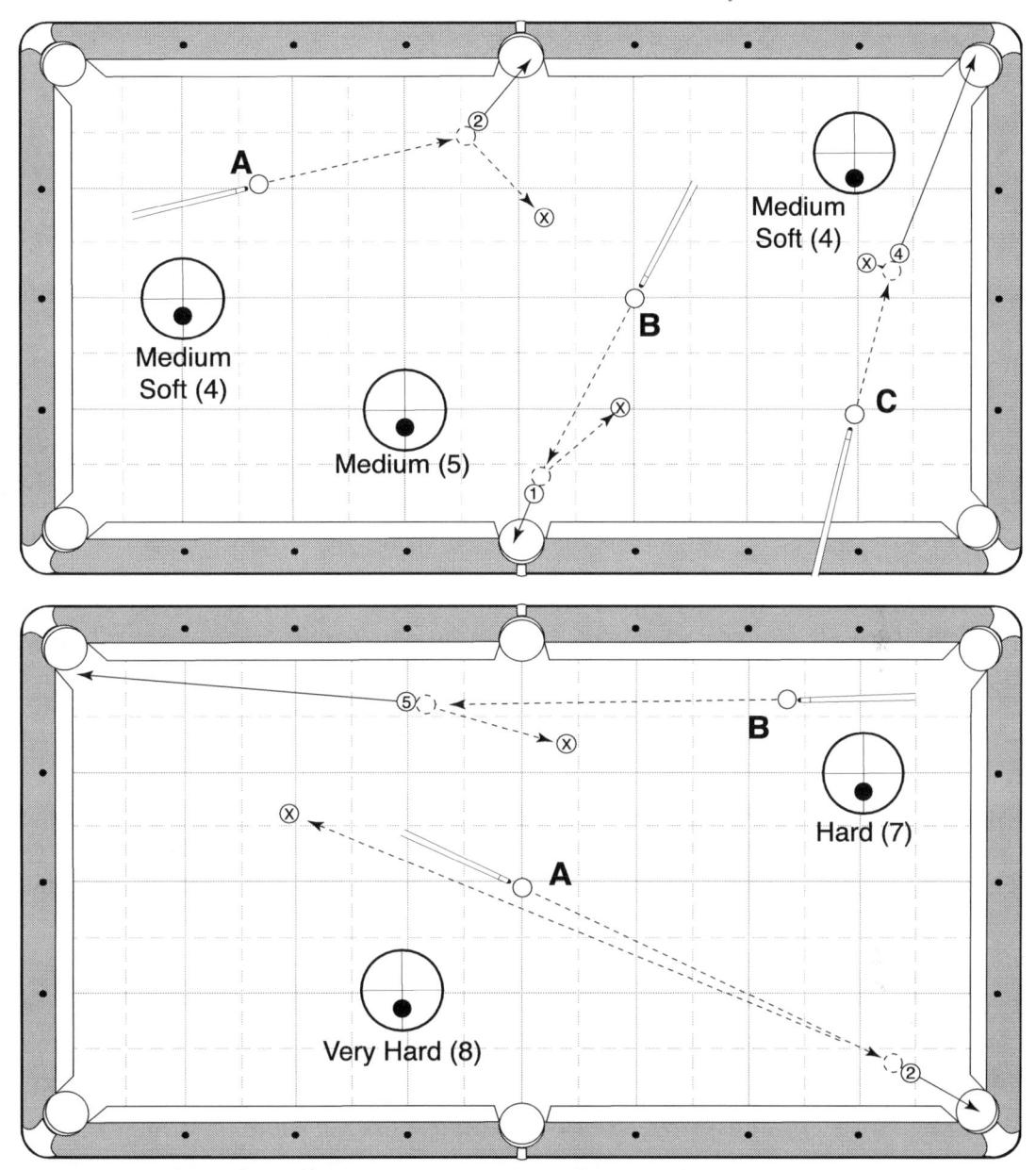

Long Draw Shots (Part A is an A, Part B is a B)

Long draw shots require great technique, and yet these challenging position plays often bring out a player's worst effort. Long draw shots should be played with a smooth and authoritative stroke for decisive draw action. Do not poke at the ball because that will likely result in the cue ball dribbling back only a few inches.

Keep your arm and wrist relaxed so that you can whip your cue smoothly and powerfully through the cue ball. Remember to stay down and follow through completely. The draw shot in Part A requires a very hard stroke to produce the backspin necessary to pull the cue ball 6' back. The long-range draw shot in Part B is played with a hard stroke.

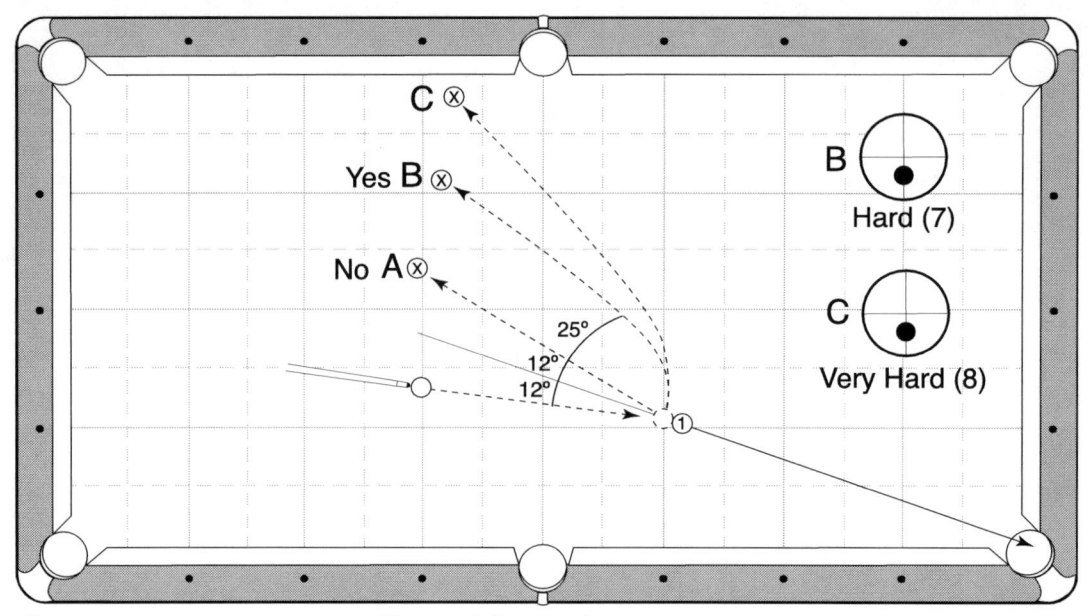

The Return Path on a Draw Shot Widens (B)
The cue ball travels at a much wider angle on its return path on draw shots with a relatively small cut angle. The example shows a 12-degree cut shot. If the cue ball's return path mirrored the cut angle, it would have come back to Position A. In fact, the cue ball will draw back on a much wider angle.

A medium hard draw stroke will send the cue ball to Position B, a path that is about 25-degrees to the other side of the line that runs straight to the pocket!

When you hit draw shots with an even harder stroke, the cue ball will travel further down the tangent line before it completes its turn and comes back toward you. This creates an even wider return angle as shown by the cue ball in Position C.

Draw Floater (B)
The illustration at the top of page 75 shows the path for three basic routes: a follow shot, a stun shot, and a draw shot. It also shows a route between the follow and stun shot that can be accessed with a draw floater shot, also known as a drag draw shot. The draw floater is an "in between" shot that many players avoid, but that can help you in executing routes your competition can't match. A medium soft stroke and a tip of draw produces a quasi-follow shot as the cue ball rolls between the paths that would be created by using either a follow shot or a stun shot.

Even though the draw floater is not that difficult, it is used mostly by advanced players. Twenty to thirty minutes of practice will get you started towards mastering this route.

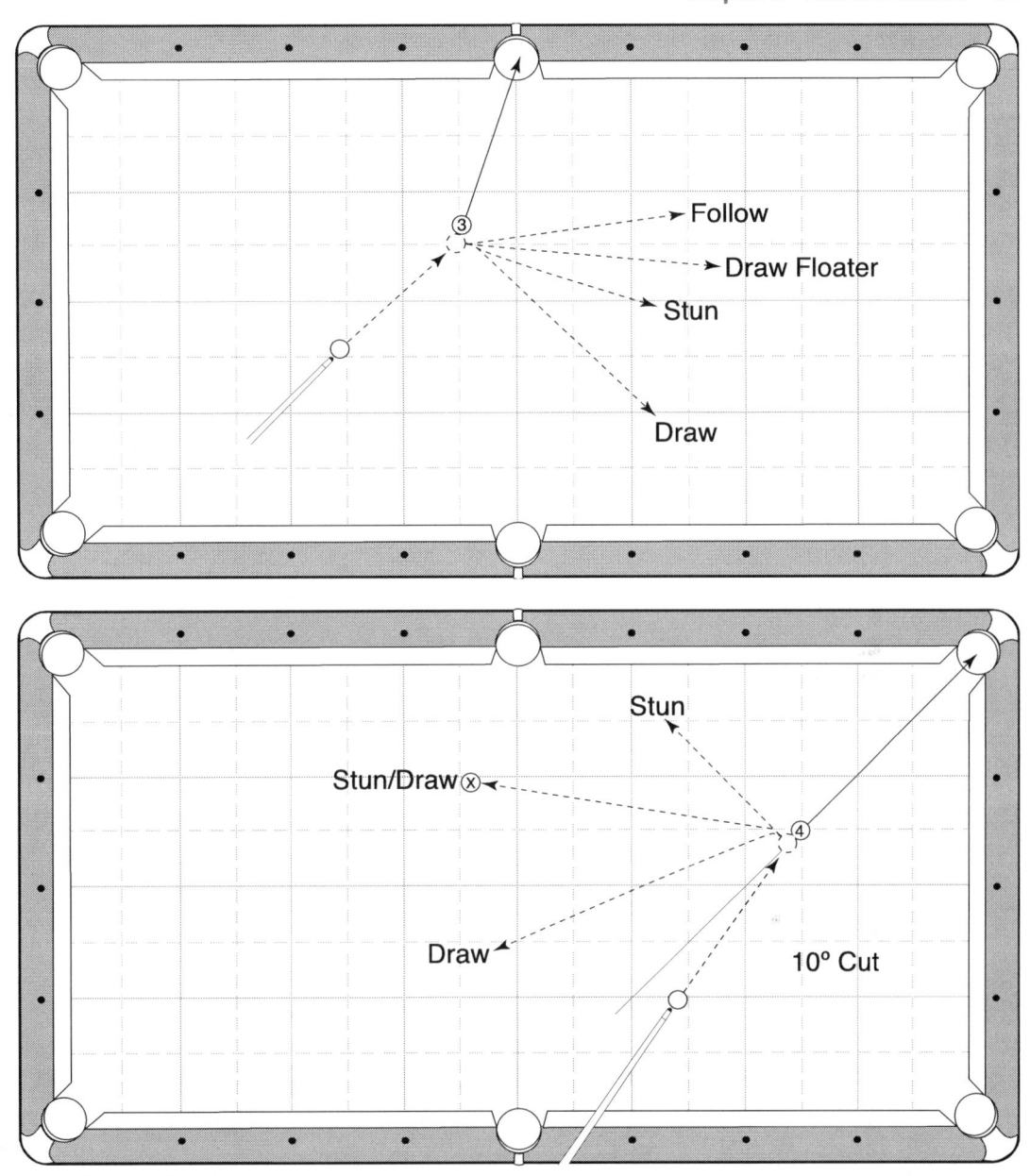

Stun/Draw (B)

The stun/draw shot is a difficult but necessary position play for top level 9 Ball. The diagram shows the two cue ball return paths for a 10-degree cut – one played with stun, and the other with straight draw. Notice that there is a large gap between the two paths. The area between these two routes can be accessed with a draw/stun shot, which is played with varying amounts of draw and speed. The correct mixture depends on where you must send the cue ball. This is a feel shot that takes much practice, so be patient while you experiment with the different variables.

Chapter 3 - Position Routes

One-Rail Position Routes

The tops pros play one-rail position on nearly half (48.5%) of their position plays in Nine Ball. These results prove that **the ability to control the cue ball off one rail is the foundation of position play in 9 Ball**. I suspect that the number would be very similar for a study of 10 Ball.

In the pages ahead you'll learn one-rail routes from the most basic to the kind of advanced position plays that can enable you to run out the more difficult racks. I advise that you master the C routes before tackling the more difficult position routes.

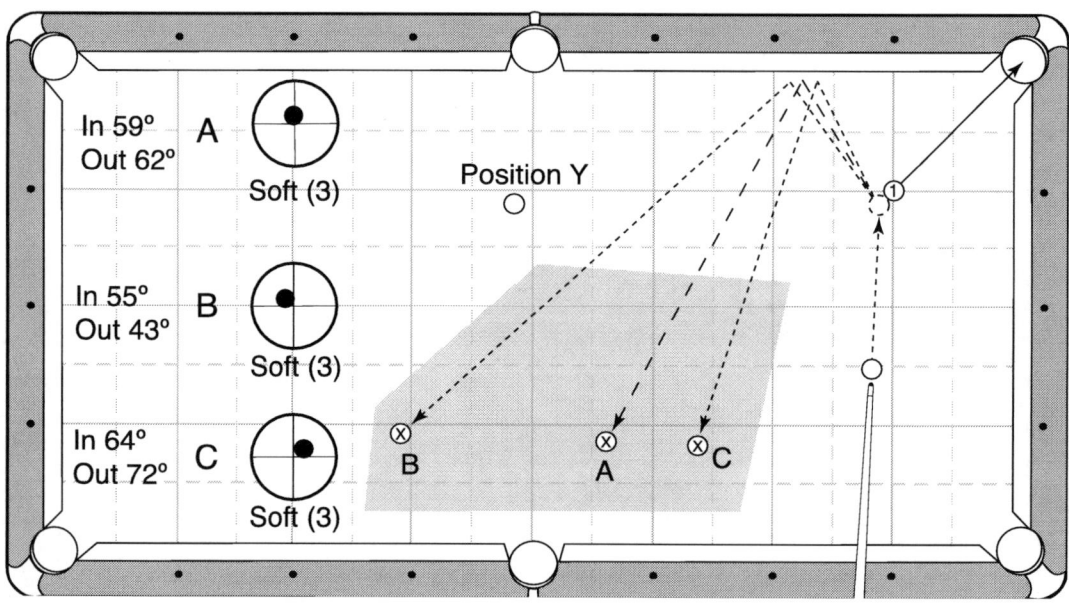

Basic Follow Routes (C)

These one-rail routes, which require a soft follow stroke, are some of the most reliable position plays. Route A shows the cue ball's path when follow is used on the vertical axis. The rebound angle is a shade wider than the angle of entry.

One of the primary reasons for using english in 9 Ball is that it enables you to adjust the cue ball's rebound angle after it contacts a rail. Outside english (left in this case) was applied to create Route B. Notice that the cue ball rebounded at a shallower angle, causing it to travel further up the table than it did in Route A. Route C shows how inside english (right in this example) creates a steeper rebound angle.

Varying amounts of english can be used to fine tune the cue ball's path off the cushion. When you combine cueing with expert speed control, you will be able to access any point within the position zone.

TIP: You can maximize the effects of english on position plays like this by cueing on the horizontal axis.

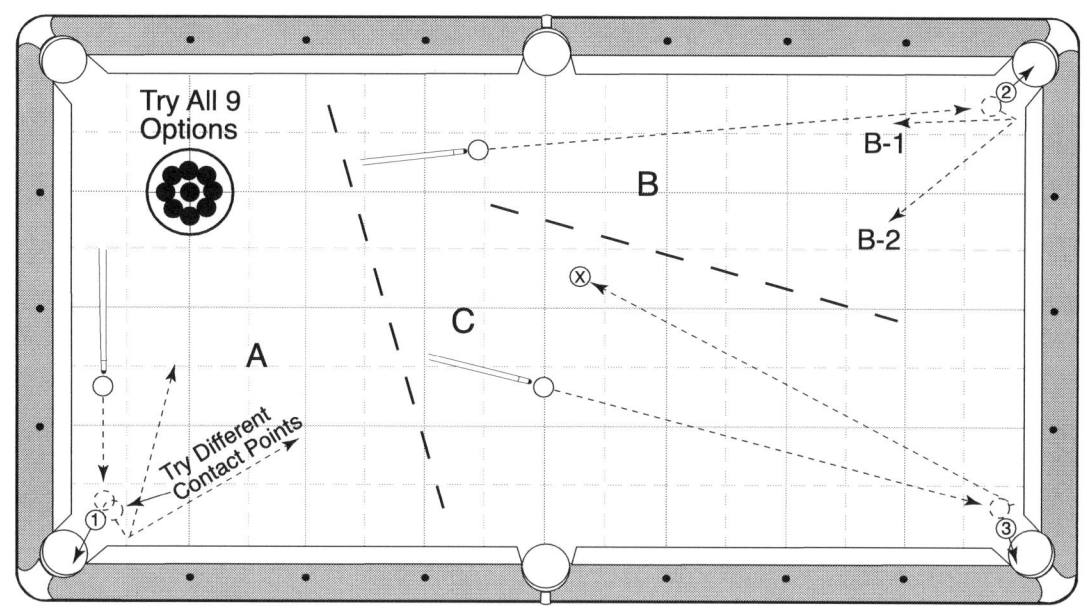

Balls Near a Pocket (C)

Experienced players execute pocket hangers with great care because they know that even though making the ball is a cinch, controlling the cue ball is not. There are countless ways to play pocket hangers because you can hit the object ball on so many places and still make the shot, and because you have so much latitude in where you strike the cue ball.

You can begin to learn to play pocket hangers by setting up the balls as shown in Position A. (Note: you can also try this exercise with the cue ball next to the side rail.)

When you combine different contact points on the object ball with a wide range of cueing options and speeds of stroke, you will discover many ways for playing position. Once you have learned the basic variations at close range, try playing them from longer distances. You should quickly discover that **distance adds a great degree of difficulty to pocket hangers – especially when you use english**.

The longer range version in Position B requires precise cueing and aim. You could send the cue ball down Route B-1 by either hitting the 2-ball very fully, or by hitting a third of the object ball with left english. Route B-2 shows the natural path on a half ball hit with no english. Position C shows the best way for creating an exact route when you must send the cue ball a long distance back down the table. Use a thin hit on the object ball with no english. Let the contact with the object ball dictate the cue ball's direction. If you use english on this shot and hit the object ball too fully, it will die well short of the position zone.

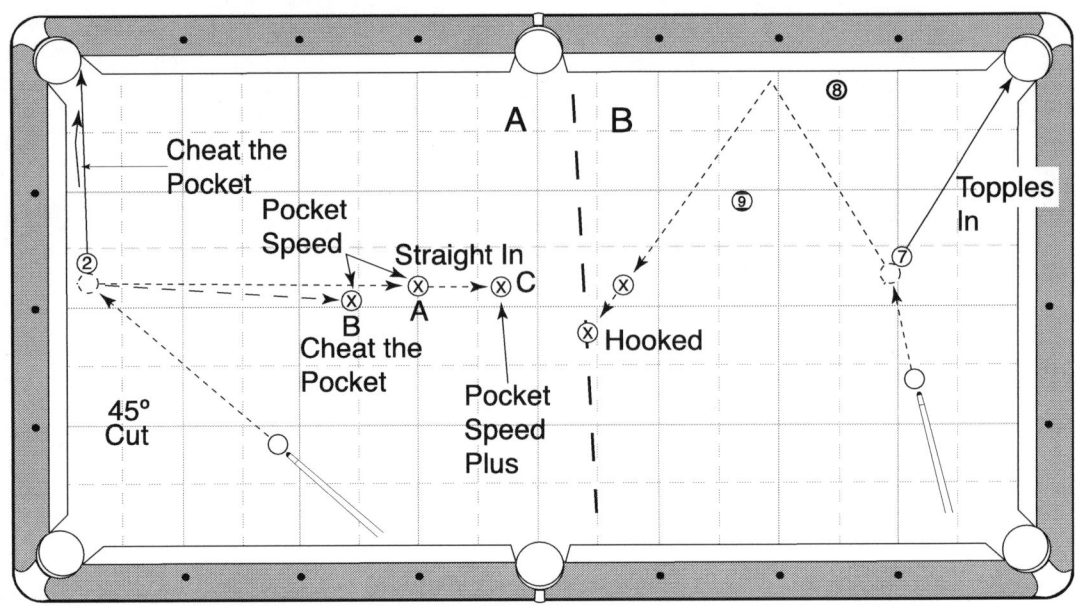

Pocket Speed Position and the Lag Shot (B, B, C, B)

Even though our two games mostly use higher speed position plays, a soft touch is needed to complete your arsenal. In Part A (B rated), the 45-degree cut was played with just enough force to send the 2-ball over the lip of the pocket. The cue ball drifted to Position A. When the object ball barely gets to the pocket, it is hit with what is called pocket speed. You can further reduce the cue ball's traveling distance by playing the shot with pocket speed and by cheating the pocket, which reduces the cut angle. The cue ball will then stop at Position B (also rated B).

It takes a very fine touch and nerves of steel to play shots at pocket speed. So, **if rolling balls in at very slow speeds is not your forte, play them at pocket speed plus.** In the example, a shot hit with pocket speed plus would send the cue ball to Position C (rated C). When using this speed, the shot is hit hard enough so that the object ball would hit the back of the pocket if the slate extended that far. Pocket speed plus helps avoid roll offs, which can be a problem when the ball nears the pocket on softly hit shots.

Part B shows a lag shot on a 40-degree cut, which is rated as a B despite its apparent simplicity. The hard part on cut shots when you are lagging the ball at pocket speed is in gauging the speed so that it topples into the pocket. If this shot had been hit even a whisker harder, the cue ball would have rolled a few inches further, resulting in a hook behind the 9-ball.

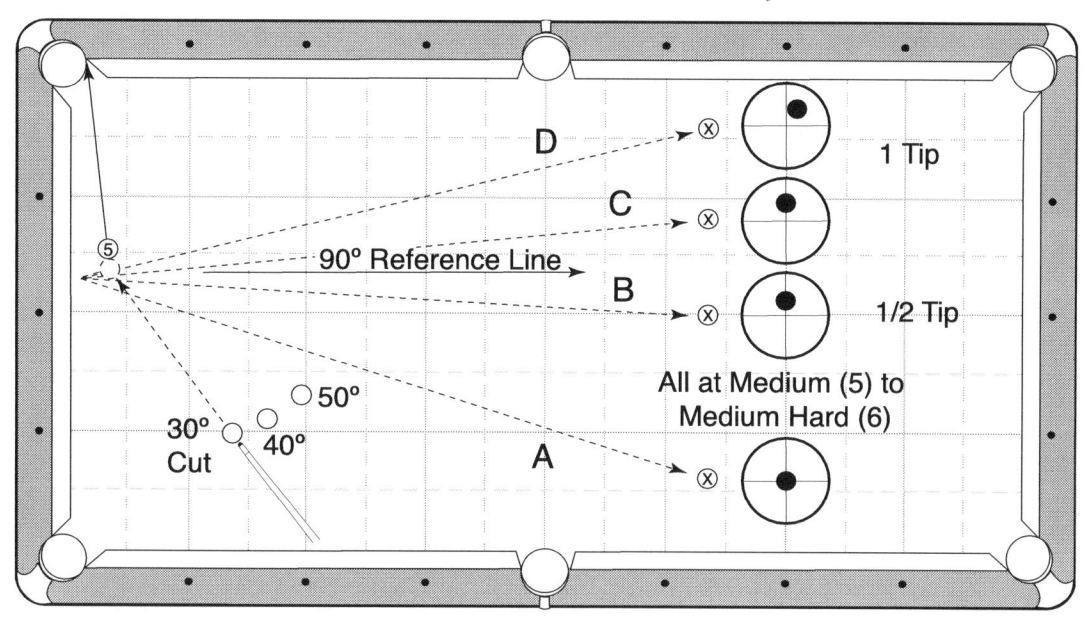

One-Rail Follow on a 30-Degree Cut (B)

The cue ball must often travel a long distance after rebounding off the end rail, such as on the position plays in the example. When the object ball is a few inches from the rail you must take active measures to control its direction off the cushion. The first step is to **construct a 90-degree reference line off the rail and then determine how far the cue ball needs to travel on either side of the line**, if at all. Next, choose the cueing and speed that will create the desired direction. A medium to medium hard stroke and centerball will send the cue ball down Route A. Route B was played with a half tip of follow. Route C resulted from using follow. Route D required the use of right english. I rate all of these routes as Bs.

The examples show a 30 degree cut. It is easier to control the cue ball's path when the cut angle is a little sharper, such as 40 or 50-degrees. Experiment with different cut angles, and with the object ball at various distances from the rail. A few practice sessions devoted to learning all of the variations of these valuable routes will pay big dividends.

Once you get proficient at these routes, add some speed. You will discover that **many two-rail and three-rail routes are merely extensions of the basic one-rail routes**. For example, if the cue ball traveling down Route A continued to the side rail and then off the end rail, you would have a three-rail route that is a natural extension of the one-rail route in the diagram.

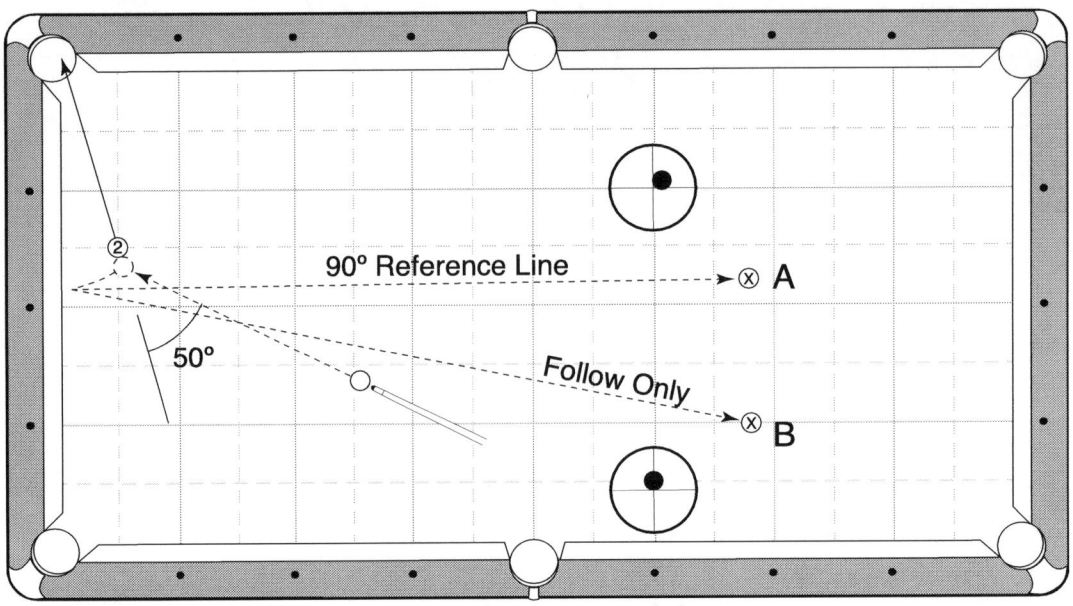

Inside English and the 90-Degree Reference Line (B)
When the object ball is several inches from the rail, inside english is needed to send it down the 90-degree reference line (see Position A). Long distance inside english one-rail follow shots with large cut angles require a fairly soft stroke. This keeps deflection to a minimum. Try aiming with no allowance for english (see Position B). Then try using a quarter tip, and then a half tip. These routes are B rated.

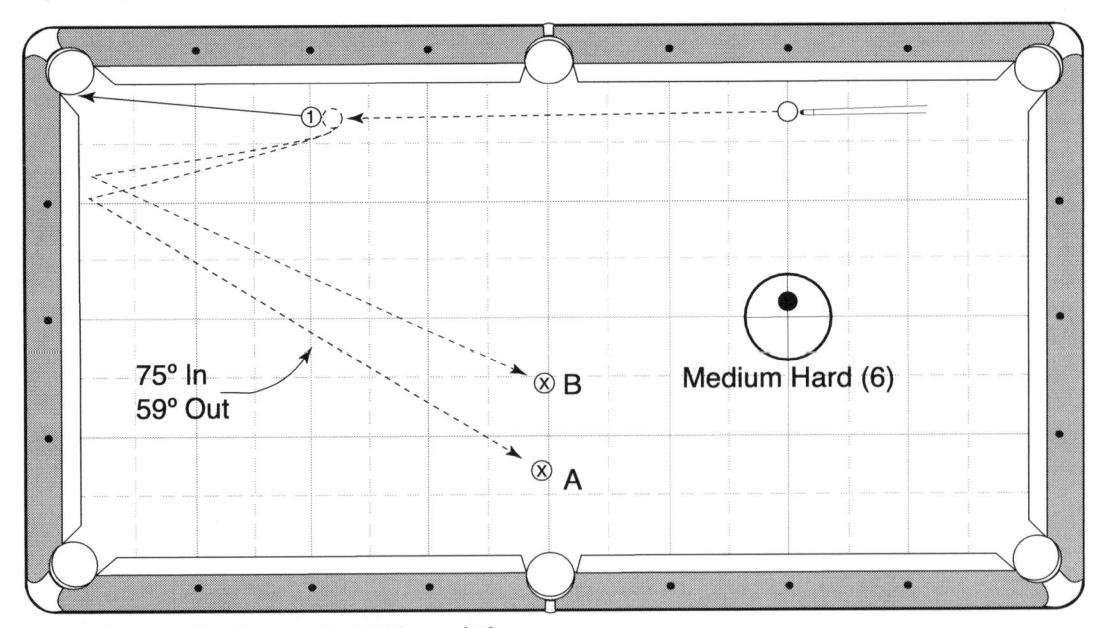

How the Angle Naturally Widens (B)
This long range B rated follow shot catches many players by surprise because they are expecting that the cue ball will rebound at a much sharper angle off the end rail. Notice that the angle opens up significantly even though no english is used. Positions A and B demonstrate the difference that pocketing makes on this shot. Position A results from cutting the shot a bit more.

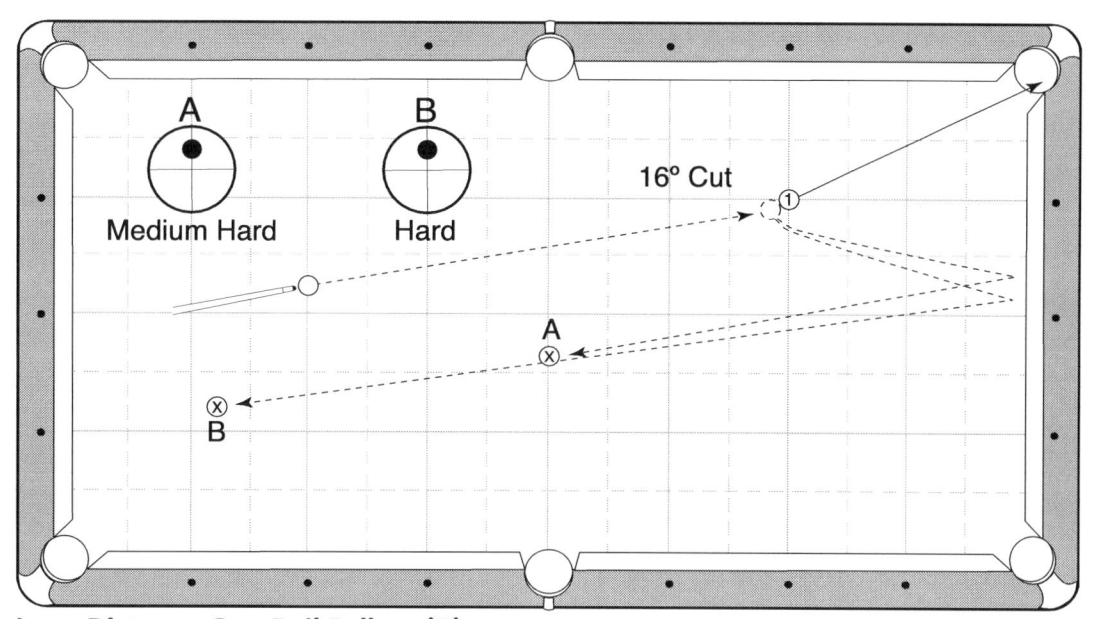

Long Distance One Rail Follow (B)
Long distance follow shots require an extra smooth stroke with a full follow through. Practice both the short range (Position A) and long-range (Position B) versions. The smooth and authoritative stroke you develop with these position plays will come in handy on other less challenging shots.

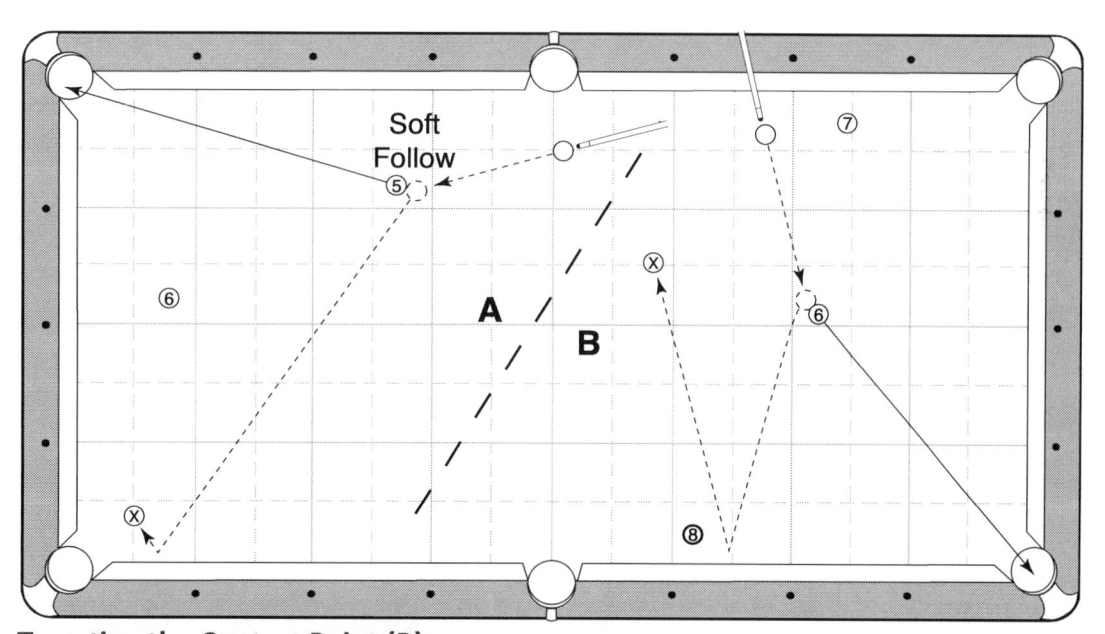

Targeting the Contact Point (B)
When the cue ball will be traveling a long distance across the table to the rail after contacting the object ball, try to gauge where it will strike the rail. Mapping out the cue ball's path to the rail can enable you to play the shot with the assurance that you won't scratch, as in Part A, or that you will avoid a potential obstacle, as shown in Part B.

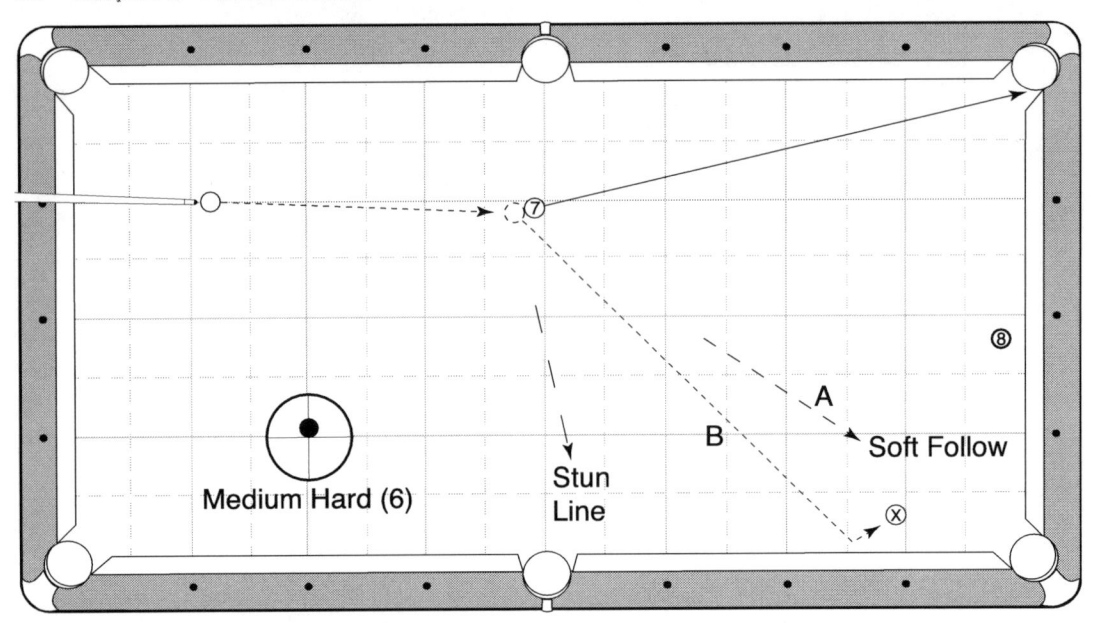

Long Distance Finesse Stun/Follow (A)

If this long range shot is played with a soft follow stroke, the cue ball would travel down Route A towards the corner pocket. You can avoid a scratch on this shot by stunning the cue ball so that it follows Route B. Set up the balls in the positions shown and play the soft follow shot. Then use a little less follow and a medium hard stroke. The cue ball should hit the side rail as shown.

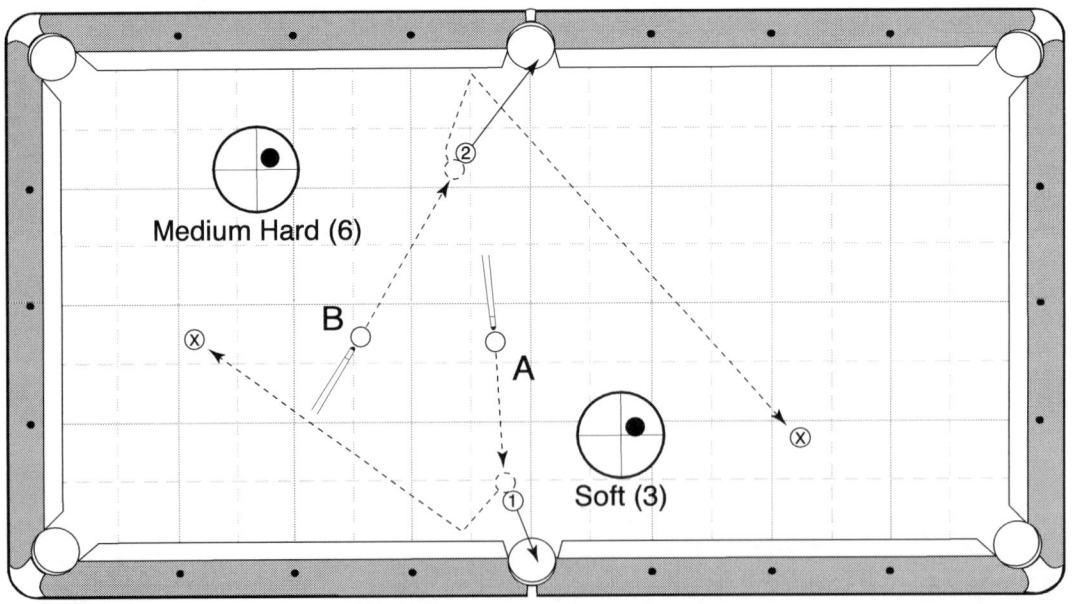

Basic Side Pocket One Railers (C)

The diagram shows two basic side pocket one-rail position plays. Route A is played with a soft stroke and outside english. Route B takes a medium hard stroke with follow and inside english. **The side pockets allow for an extremely wide range of possible routes,** especially when the object ball is straight out from the pocket.

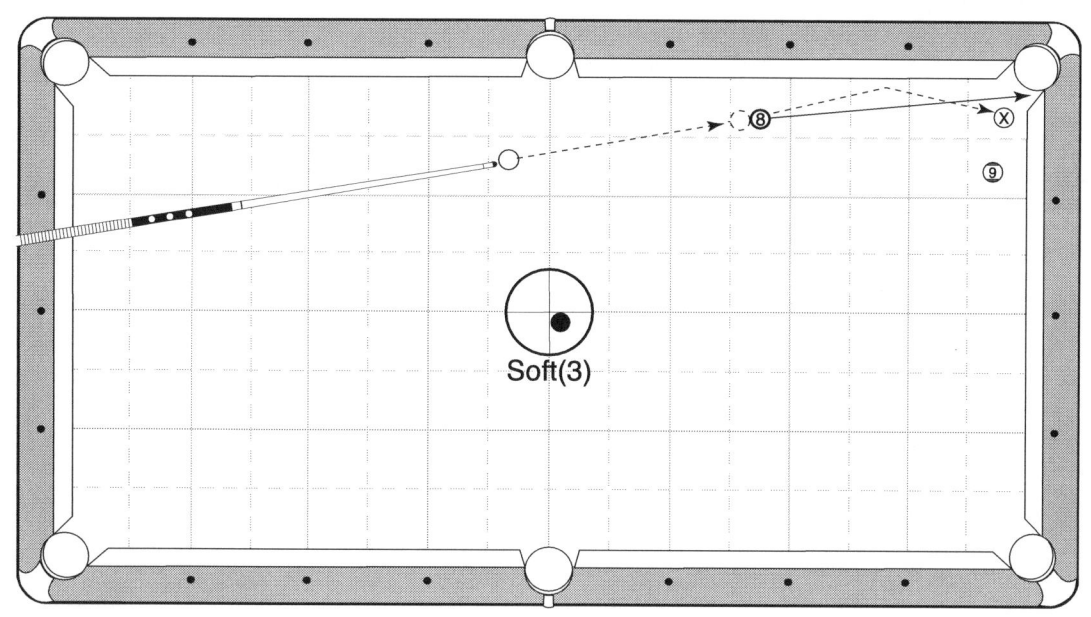

Creeper Follow (B)
Francisco Bustamante played short side shape on the 9-ball using this finesse follow shot in a match against Earl Strickland at the Bicycle Club in 1992. This shot is struck with low inside english and a very soft stroke. The draw helps to keep the cue ball close to the rail, but it obviously does not act as "normal" draw.

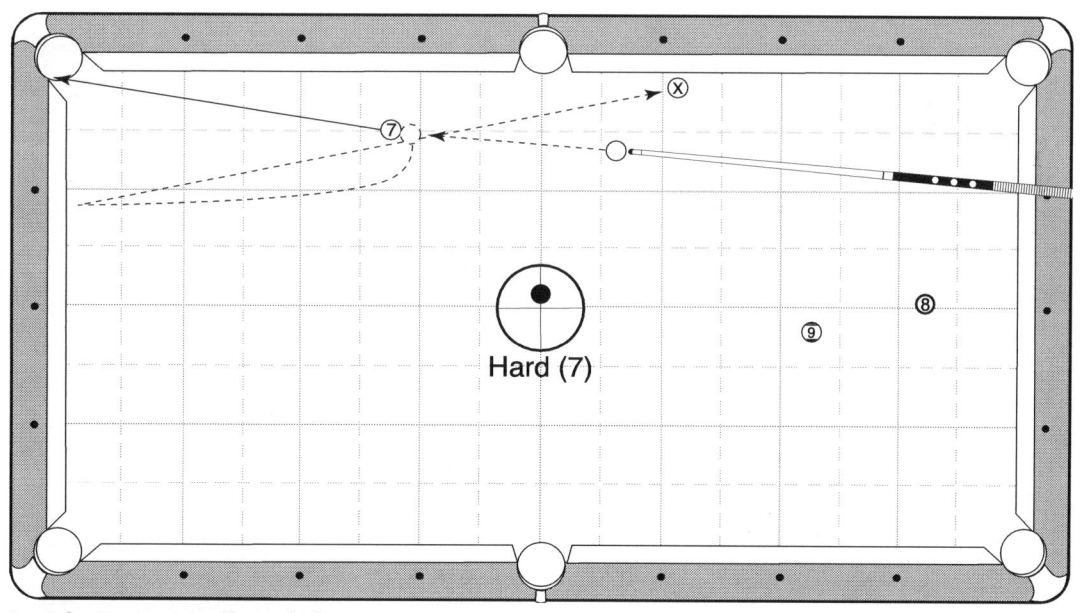

Inside Power Follow (A)
Jeremy Jones used a hard stroke with inside follow to get back down table for the 8-ball in the finals of the 1999 U.S. Open against Johnny Archer. Notice how the cue ball bent back towards the end rail and how the right english took over upon contact with the cushion. If you can consistently execute shots like this A rated position play, you surely must possess great fundamentals!

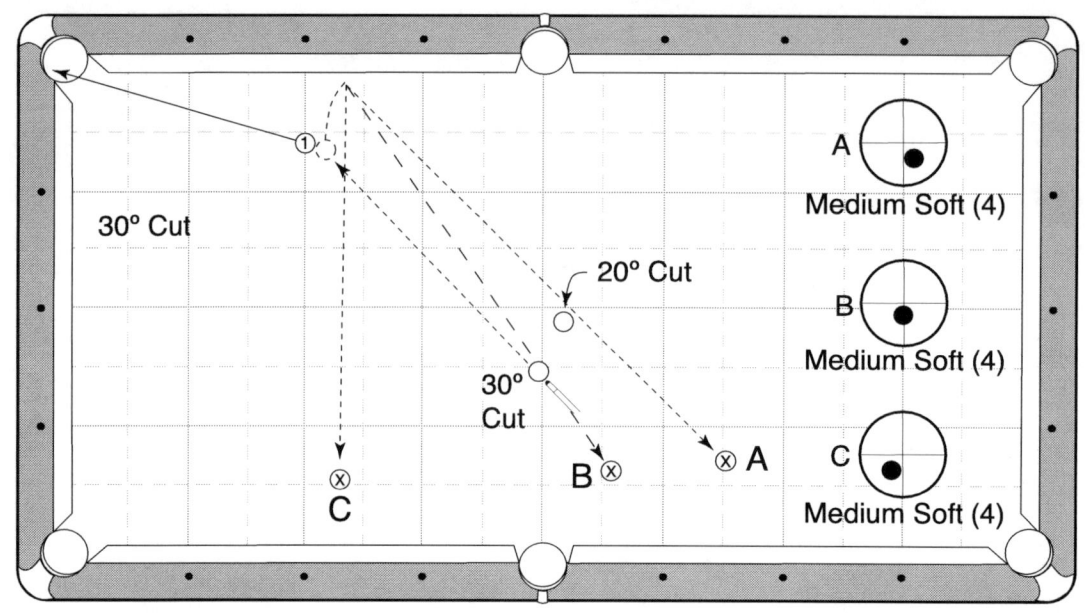

One-Rail and Out (C, C, A)

The 1-rail and out draw shot is a valuable position route. The illustration shows a 30-degree cut angle with the object ball about 7 inches off the rail. Master Routes A and B first, which are rated C. Practice the shot with cut angle of 30-degrees (as shown) and 20-degrees. When the ball is close to the rail, there is less variety in the return path.

Route C (rated A) is played with low inside english and is only for advanced players.

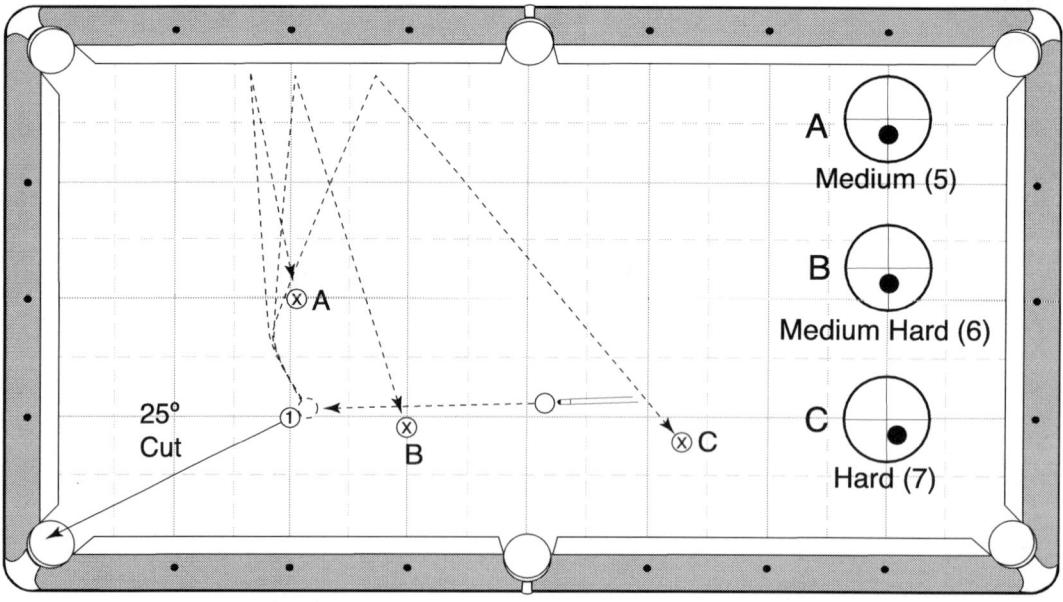

Draw Across Table and Out (B)

The cue ball will travel a long distance to the side rail after contacting the object ball, making this a challenging position play. Route A will send the cue ball straight back across the table. Route B, which requires a firm draw stroke, will bring the cue ball back up the table a little. Draw and outside english with a hard stroke produces Route C. All of these routes are B rated.

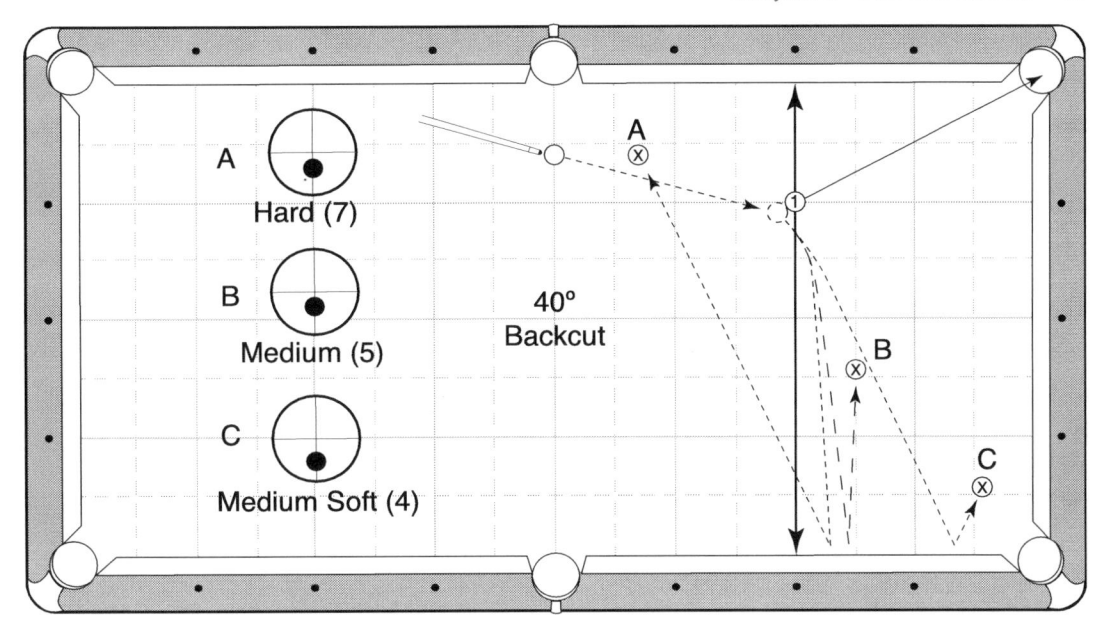

Backcut Draw Across Table and Out (B)

This shot is a variation of the previous position play, but now you face a 40-degree back cut, which limits the "comeback" distance to Position A. Observe that the cue ball is further down the table in Positions B and C, which both rest beneath the reference line that runs from side rail to side rail through the 1-ball.

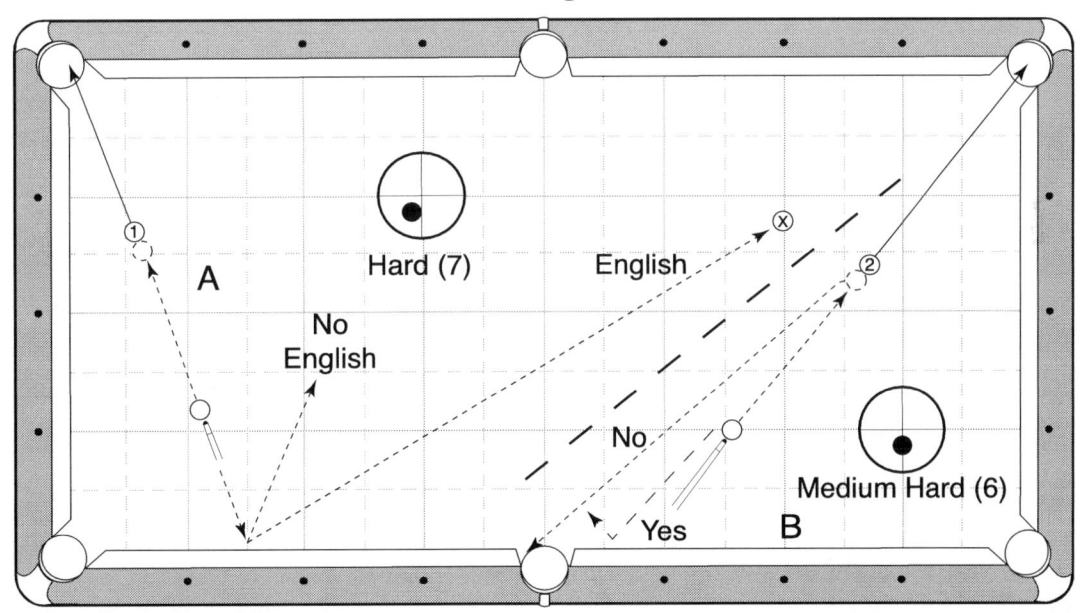

Draw to the Rail and Out (B)

Straight in position, as shown in Part A, usually results from an error. However, you can still send the cue ball far down the table by using draw and outside english. Use a very smooth stroke. The cue ball will grab the rail and shoot back down the table. Part B shows how you can make a straight in shot and scratch even though the shot was not lined up to go into the side pocket. To avoid a scratch, you must make an extra effort to hit the 2-ball squarely, and you should consider favoring the left side of the pocket.

Chapter 3 - Position Routes

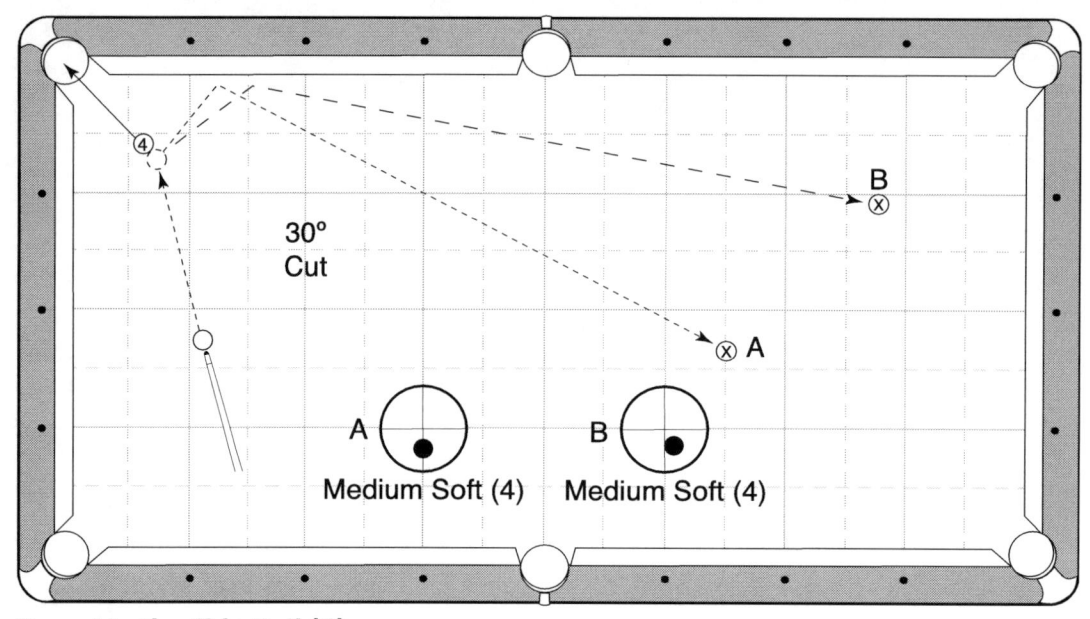

Draw Up the Side Rail (C)

Most players have a tendency to overshoot their position zone when sending the cue ball down Route A, and especially when using outside (running) english, as in Route B. When you practice these routes, mark 3-4 targets along them. Observe carefully where the cue ball stops, and make the necessary adjustments until you have dialed in your speed of stroke.

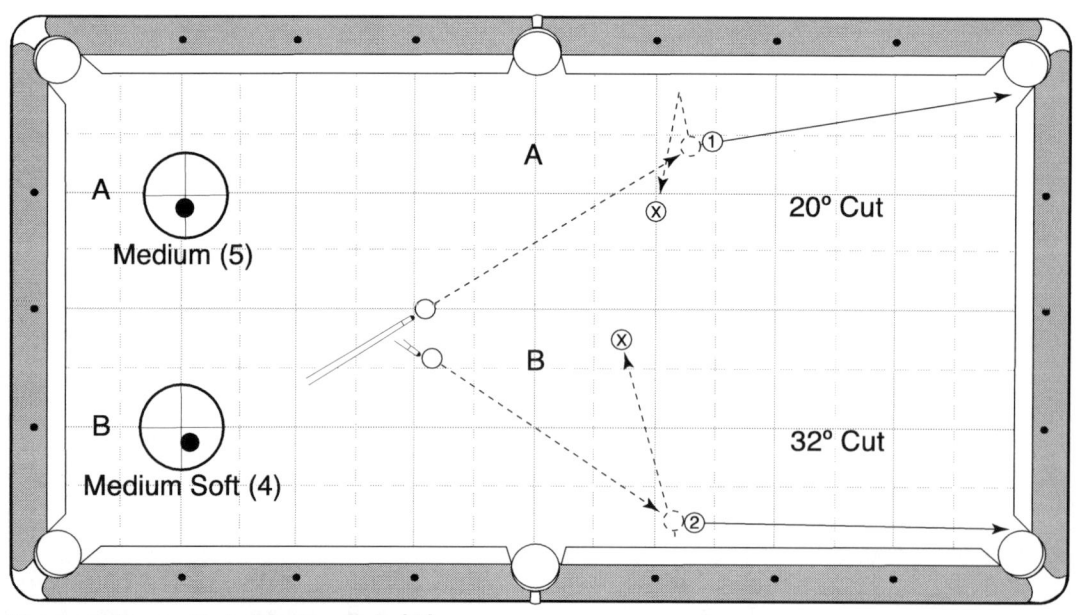

Finesse Draw Outside English (B)

Use a finesse draw stroke with outside english to float the cue ball gently off the rail and into the middle of the table. Route A is played with a medium speed and a half tip of draw. Route B requires a medium soft stroke and a half tip of low right english. In both cases, the draw enables you to shoot with greater authority, but is not used to bring the cue ball back up table.

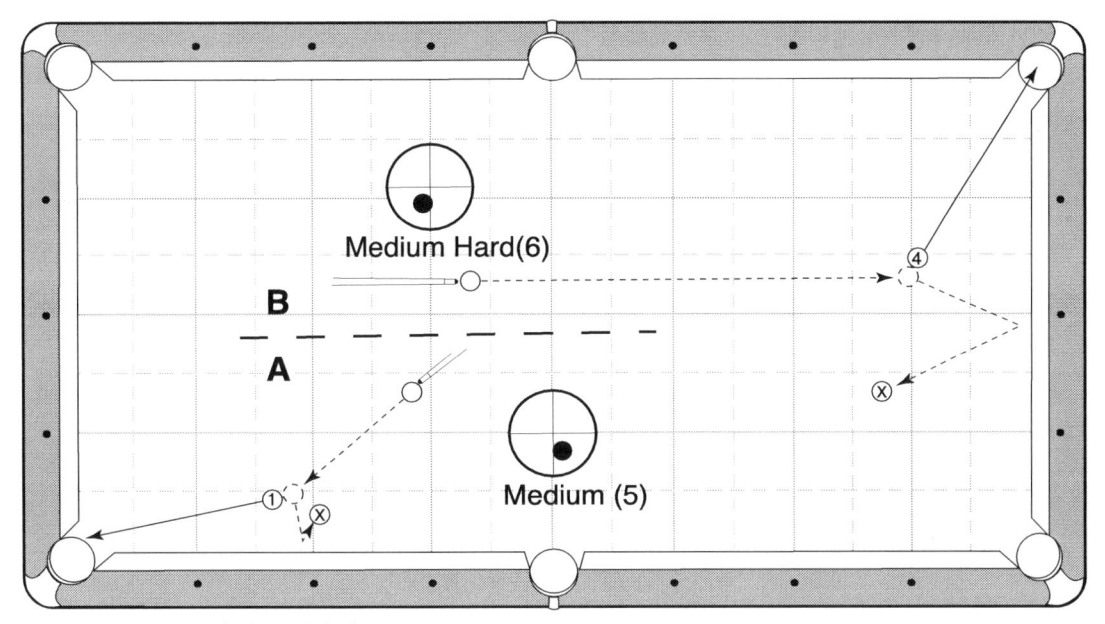

Draw Kill Shot (B) and (A)
When the draw kill shot is executed well, the cue ball will travel only a short distance after bouncing off the rail. Part A is B rated since it is played from short range. Use inside english and draw, and release your wrist for extra spin. Part B is rated A because it is difficult to aim with low inside english from this distance. Use a smooth stroke and release your wrist as your tip nears contact.

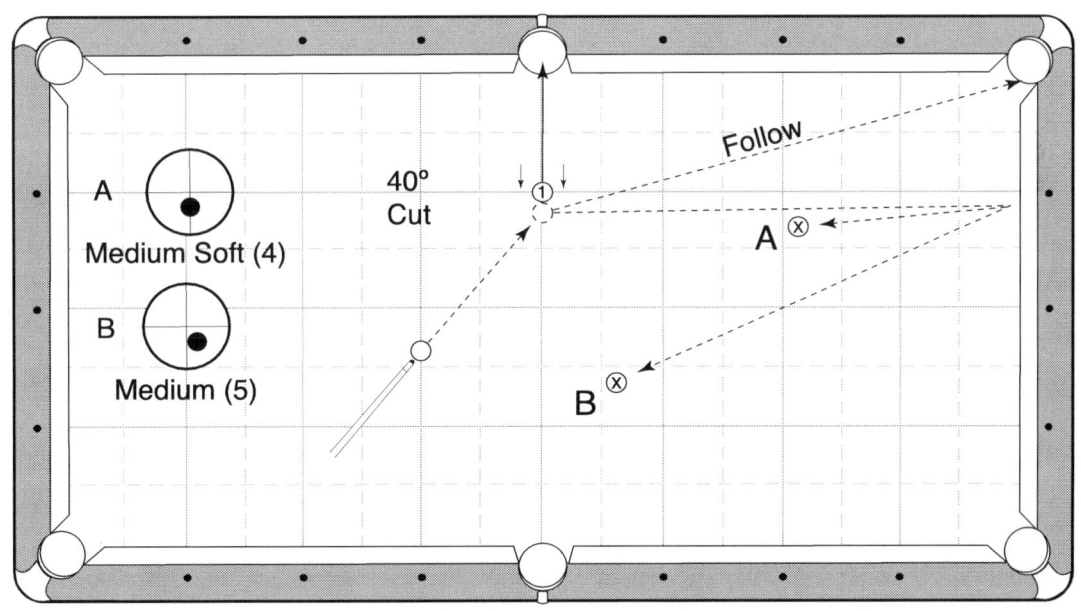

Side Pocket to the End Rail (C)
A soft follow stroke could lead to a scratch in the corner pocket. If you use the same speed of stroke with draw, the backspin will hold the cue ball on a straight line to the end rail, resulting in Position A. Draw with outside english will pull the cue ball across the table to Position B. After mastering these shots, try them with the 1-ball over a ball's width to either side of its current position as shown by the two arrows.

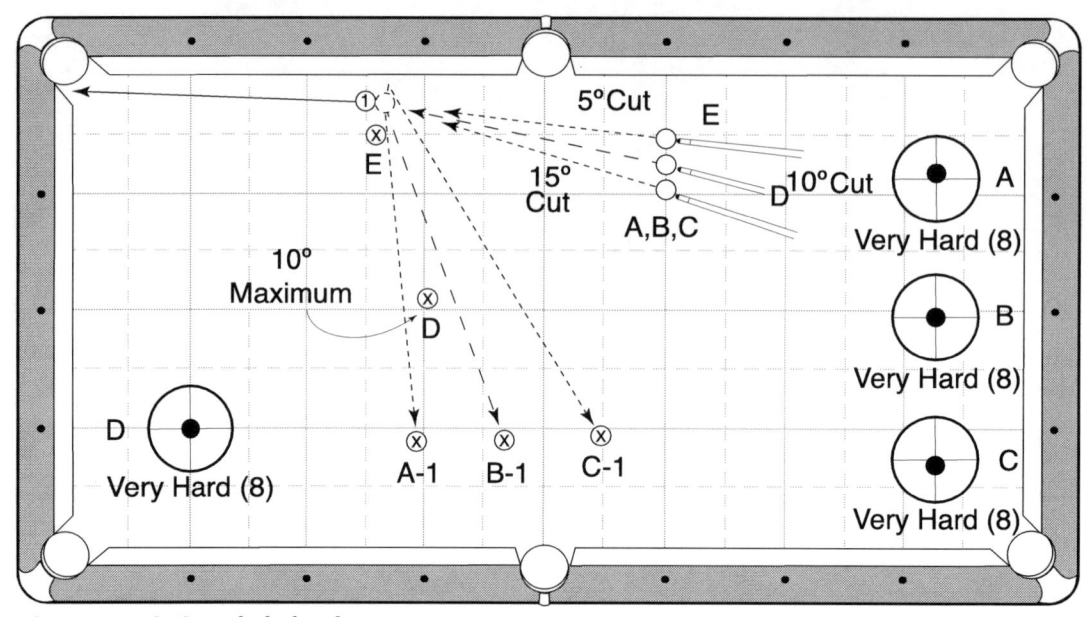

The Pound Shot (A) (RR)
A pound shot can help you to get the cue ball back in line when you have left yourself with an overly shallow cut angle. Pound shots are normally played when the object ball is close to the rail, but they can also be used when the object ball is several inches from the cushion. Pound shots are played with a very high speed of stroke. When you combine a high speed with the smaller effective pocket opening for shots down the rail, you have the ingredients for a shot that requires your very best technique.

The thinnest of the three cut shots in the diagram is only 15 degrees. A very hard stroke with a quarter tip of follow will send the cue ball to A-1. A centerball hit will result in Position B-1. A very hard stroke with a quarter tip of draw will send the cue ball to Position C-1. Begin practicing this shot using a medium hard speed until your stroke is loosened up and in the groove. Gradually add speed providing you continue to pocket the ball. Keep adding speed until the cue ball reaches the three locations.

When the cut angle is reduced to 10 degrees, the maximum distance that you can realistically expect to send the cue ball off the rail is shown by the cue ball in Position D. With a cut angle of only 5-degrees, Position E is about the best you can hope for. When the cut angle ranges from about 7-12 degrees, your results can vary significantly. What may seem like the same stroke could result in about a 6-12 inch difference in position, due in part to where the ball enters the pocket.

Super Hard Pound & Draw (A) (RR)
Part A shows a pound draw shot using an extremely hard stroke. Pocketing the 1-ball is a challenge because of the high speed of stroke.

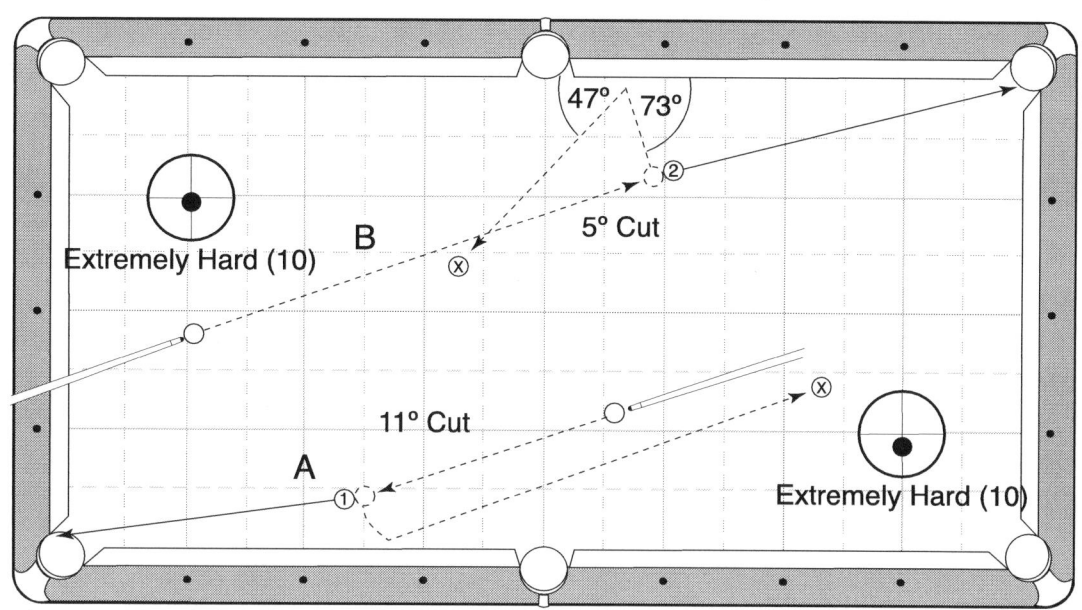

The pound and draw shot in Part B takes one of the hardest strokes that you will ever use for any shot other than a break shot. The shot is hit with a quarter tip of draw. Notice that the rebound angle is much shallower than the entrance angle. This shows how the cue ball picks up english at contact on high speed shots with a nearly full hit. This monster of a shot is rated A++.

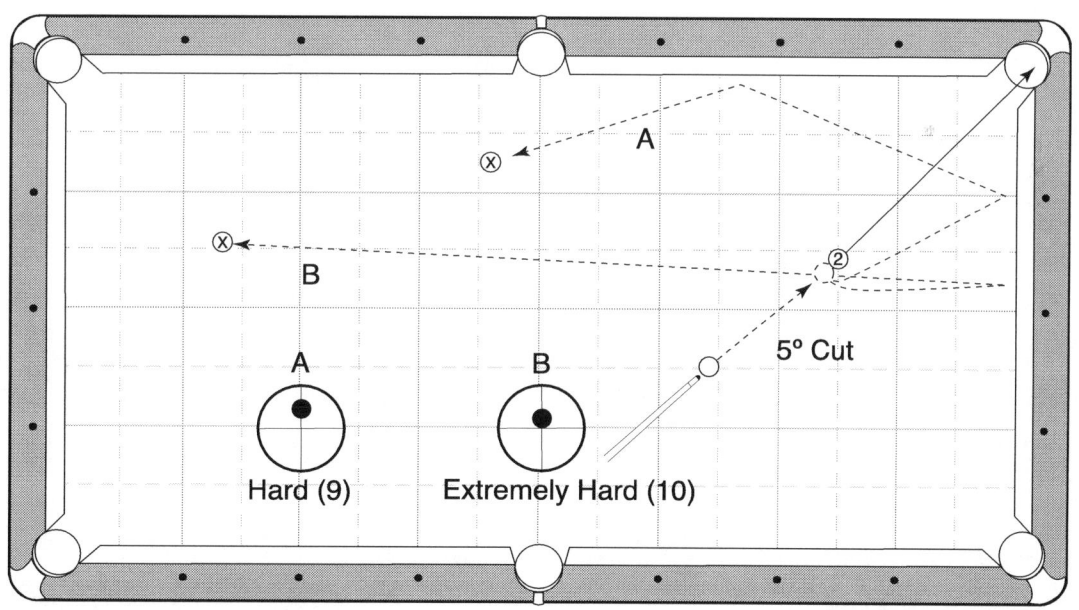

Creating an Angle (B) (RR)
The cue ball would normally follow the two-rail route to Position A when struck with a hard follow stroke. If this route is not available, you can create a new angle of departure from the rail by playing the shot with an extremely hard stroke and a half tip of follow, which will send the cue ball to Position B.

Two-Rail Position Routes

Two-rail position plays, at 22.0 percent, are the routes that are third most commonly used by the top pros when playing 9-Ball. On the majority of two-rail position plays the cue ball will hit an end rail and then a side rail before continuing out towards the center portion of the table. The ability to fine tune your two-rail routes is a huge asset to your game. In addition, **a number of two-rail routes can be easily extended to create three-rail position plays**. So, when you are learning two-rail shape you are also, in many instances, laying the groundwork for three-rail routes!

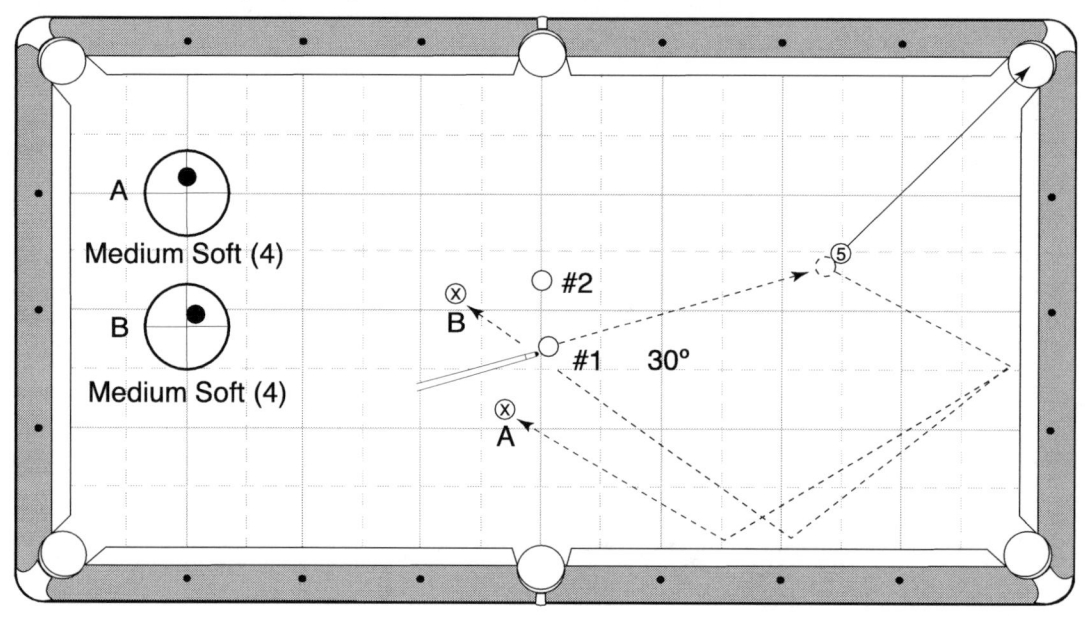

Two Rails with Follow (C)

This useful position route enables you to easily access a large portion of the center of the table. This is a natural route that, when played with follow and a medium soft stroke, will result in Position A. If you add a half tip of outside english, the cue ball will follow a shallower path off the first rail, resulting in Position B. These are 30-degree cuts, which are half ball hits before you adjust for contact induced throw, and english.

When you can consistently send the cue ball to Positions A and B, add and then subtract one foot from the targets (X) to develop a feel for other distances. After you complete these versions, repeat the same steps with the cue ball at #2, which is a 40-degree cut. This will teach you how a small difference in the position of the balls can influence a position route.

Cueing and Speed Affects the Follow Route (B)

Your choice of cueing and speed can have a significant impact on the cue ball's path as shown by the two-rail position plays at the top of page 91. All three routes were hit with a medium hard stroke. Position A resulted from using follow and a half tip of right english. A half tip of follow on the vertical axis was used to send the cue ball to Position B. A full tip of follow on the vertical axis was the ticket to Position C. The difference between Positions A and C, which is nearly a half a table width, was the result of slight modifications in cueing.

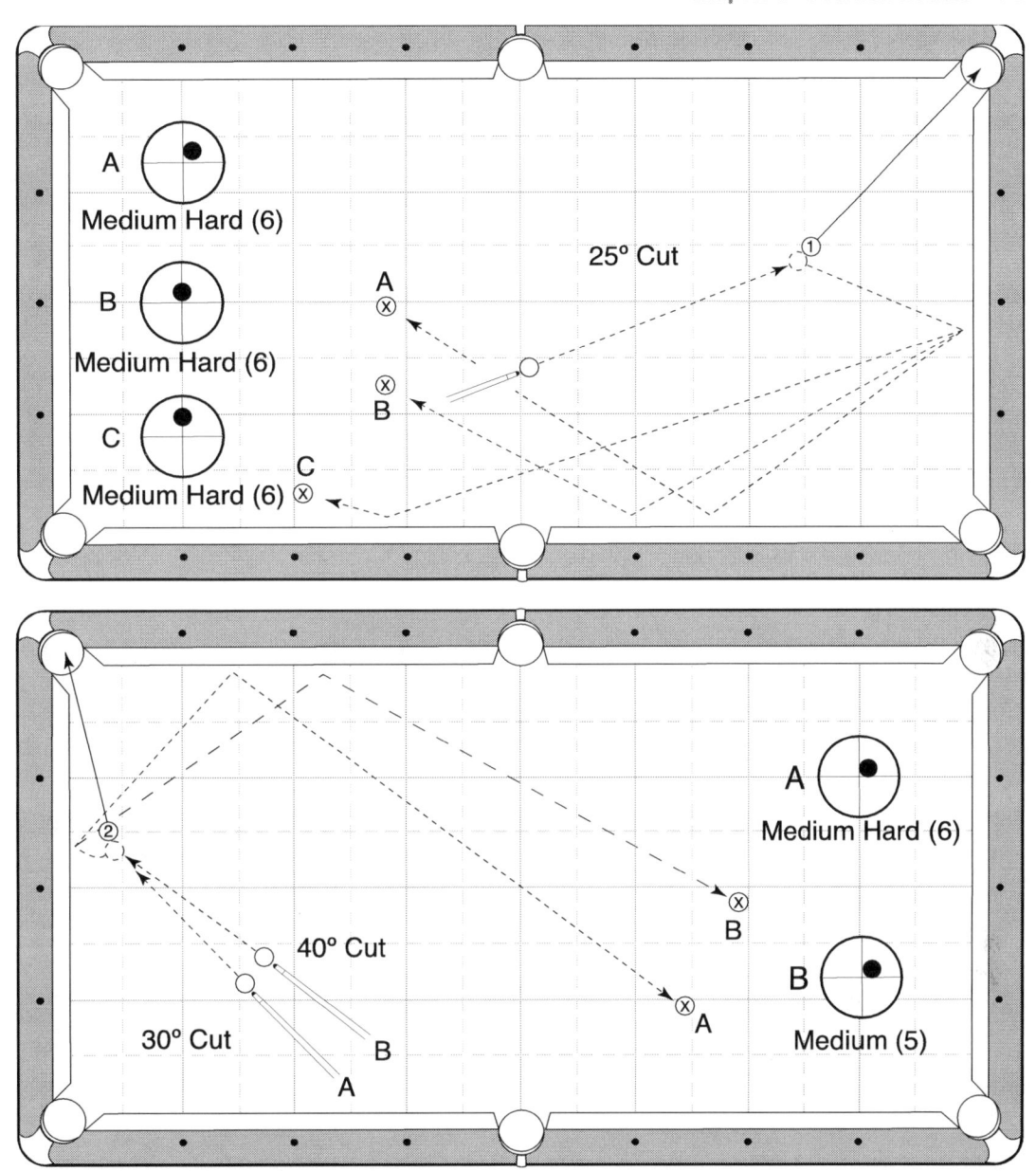

Two Rails with Inside Follow (B)

The key to these position plays is adjusting your aim for inside english. You must aim for a fuller hit on the 2-ball because deflection will cause the cue ball to squirt to the left. A smooth stroke will create sufficient inside spin with less force, and less deflection. Notice that the shot with the 30-degree cut angle in Position A required a firmer stroke than the 40-degree cut in Position B to propel the cue ball to about the same location.

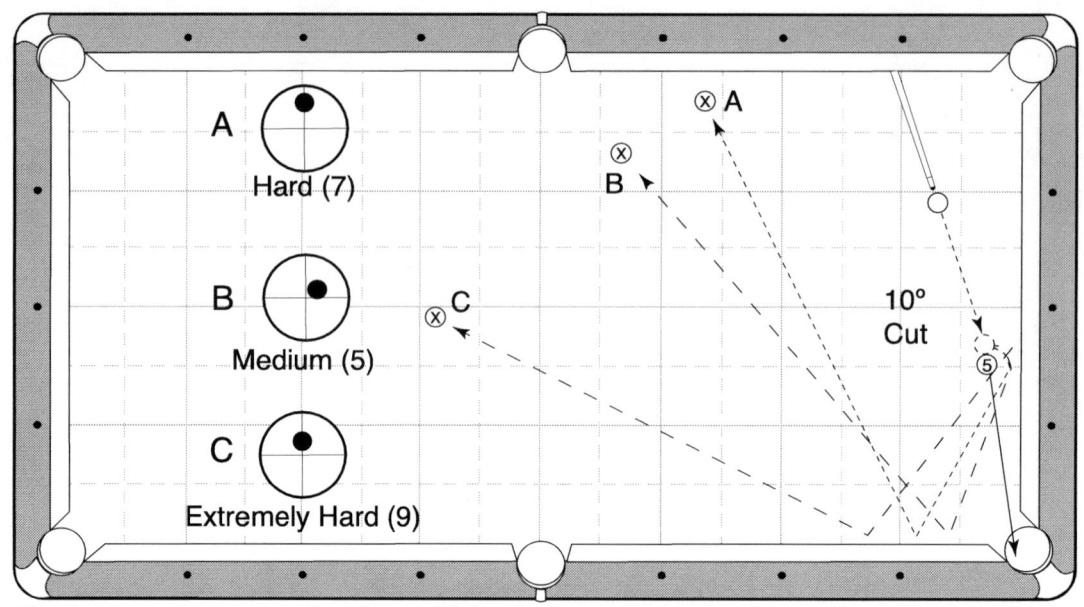

Shallow Angle Two Railer (B, B, A) (RR)

These position plays give you several ways to escape the end rail when you have left yourself an overly shallow cut angle. These recovery routes demonstrate how cueing and speed of stroke can exert a huge influence on a shot.

Use a hard stroke with one and a quarter tips of follow (A) to send the cue ball to Position A. This route requires a hard stroke to send the cue ball a relatively short distance, and you must guard against a tendency to come up short. The cue ball in Position B traveled a little further up the table. Play this route with only a medium speed. Use a half tip of inside (running) english, which adds speed to the cue ball after it strikes the cushions.

Now for the fun part, which requires that you send the cue ball all of the way to Position C! This A rated route requires a full tip of follow and an extremely hard stroke. The extra power produces a stun like effect to the first rail, at which point the follow takes over. The cue ball will strike much further up the side rail than on Routes A and B.

Small Cut Angle Two Railer (A, A, B) (RR)

You can reach a number of destinations even though the shot is relatively straight in (see the top of page 93) thanks to the magic of cueing and speed of stroke. Route A (rated A) is played with a hard follow stroke. No english is needed. **It is important to know where the cue ball will strike each cushion as this can help you to avoid obstructers.** In this case, the cue ball hits the end rail opposite the first diamond.

A very hard follow stroke with a full tip of follow will send the cue ball further up table to Position B (also rated A). This time the cue ball hit the end rail 1.25 feet from the corner pocket. This is a dangerous route because the cue ball must flirt with the side pocket. A half tip of inside english and a medium hard follow stroke combine to create a completely different path to Position C (rated B). Notice that the cue ball is almost all of the way across the table.

Chapter 3 - **Position Routes**

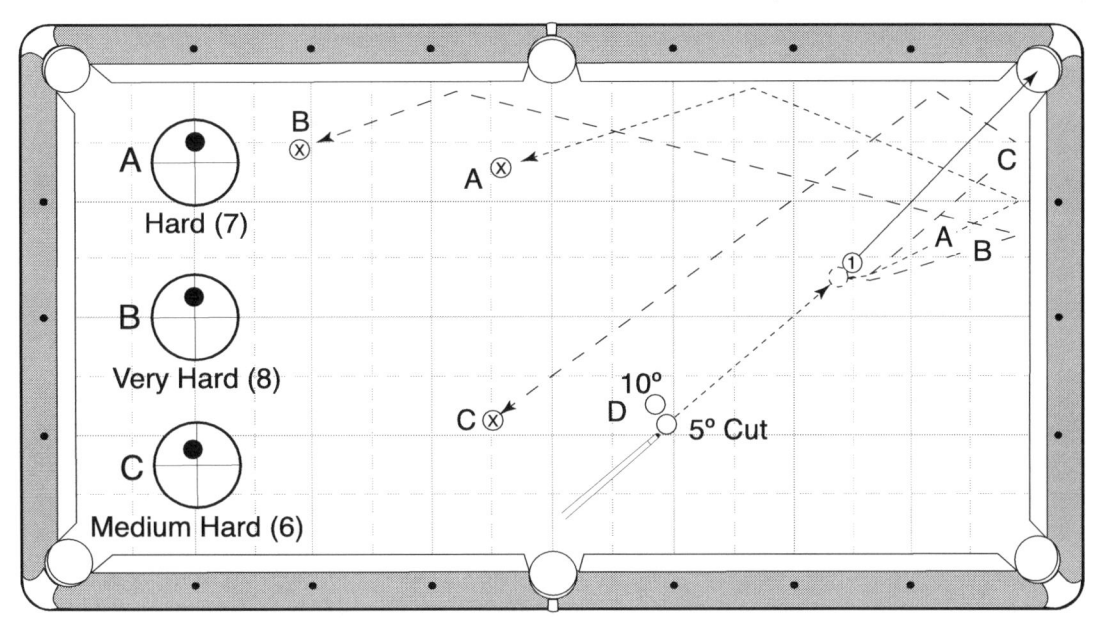

Practice these shots with the balls in the positions as shown. Use a shallow 5-degree cut angle. Then move the cue ball over a ball width to Position D, which is a 10-degree cut. The dynamics of these shots are similar to the previous shots. They begin to change radically once the cut angle exceeds 12-degrees.

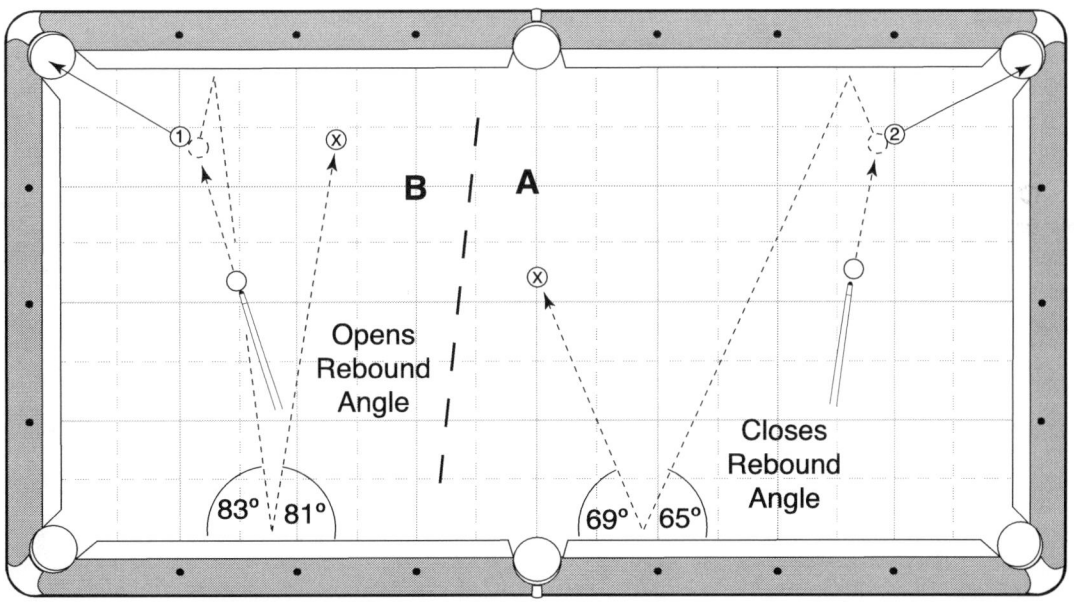

Crossing the Table with English
When you apply sufficient sidespin to the cue ball and it is traveling back and forth across the table, it will retain some of that spin from one cushion to the next. When outside english is applied, as in Part A, the rebound angle will open up off the first side rail and it will close slightly off the opposite side rail. The opposite is true in Part B where inside english was used.

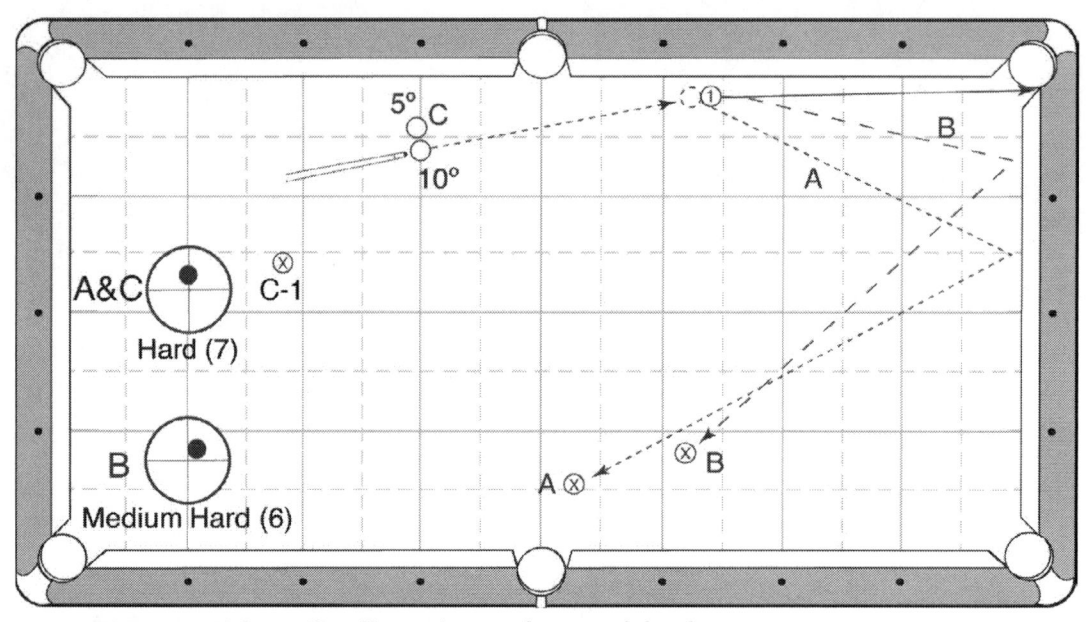

Long Distance Side Rail Follow Shots - (A, A, A) (RR)

These three recovery routes are all rated A. Route A, with a cut of 10-degrees, shows the cue ball's path when the shot is played with hard follow. Route B shows how the cue ball will swing across the table when inside english combines with a medium hard stroke. A hard follow stroke will send the cue ball to Position C-1 from Position C. This is a 5-degree cut.

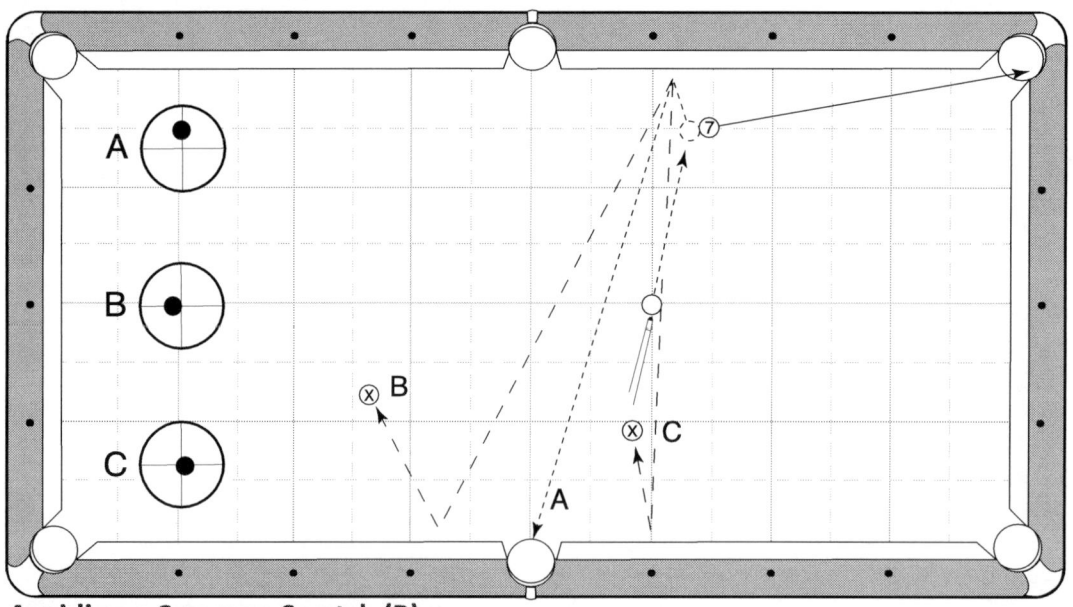

Avoiding a Common Scratch (B)

The cue ball will follow a path up the table from the point where it strikes the cushion on shots like the 7-ball (see Route A) when played with straight follow. You can avoid this common scratch with outside english, which will send the cue ball above the side pocket along Route B. You can keep the cue ball below the side pocket by using inside english, sending it down Route C.

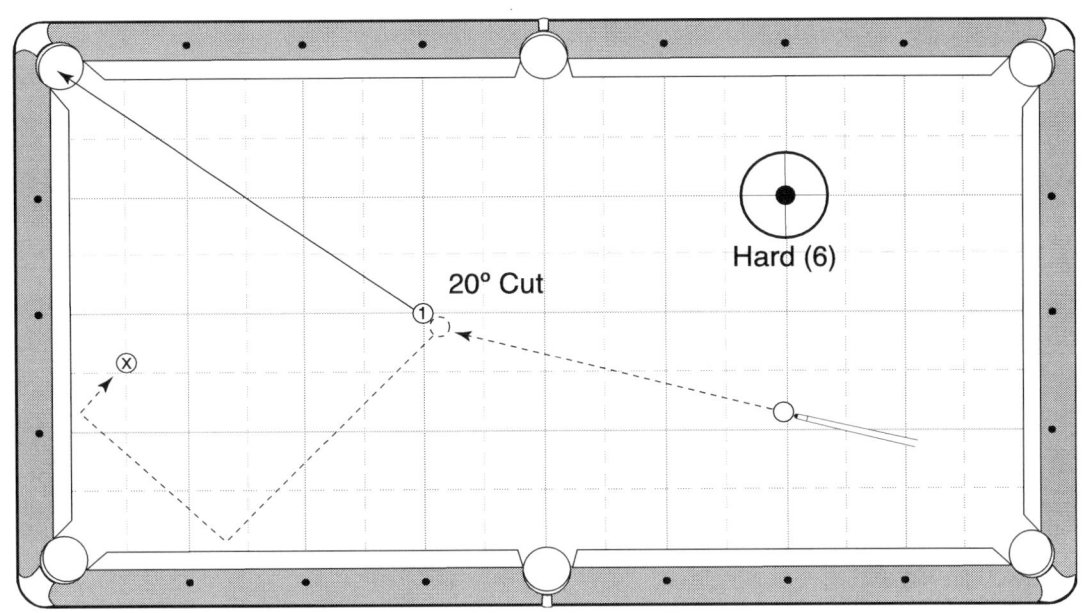

A Natural Centerball Two Railer (A)

This A rated route is played with centerball and a hard stroke. The cue ball's path looks very similar to a follow shot. The cue ball will pick up a little topspin because of the distance from the cue ball to the object ball. Distance and the use of centerball, which is foreign to many players, conspire to make this a challenging position play.

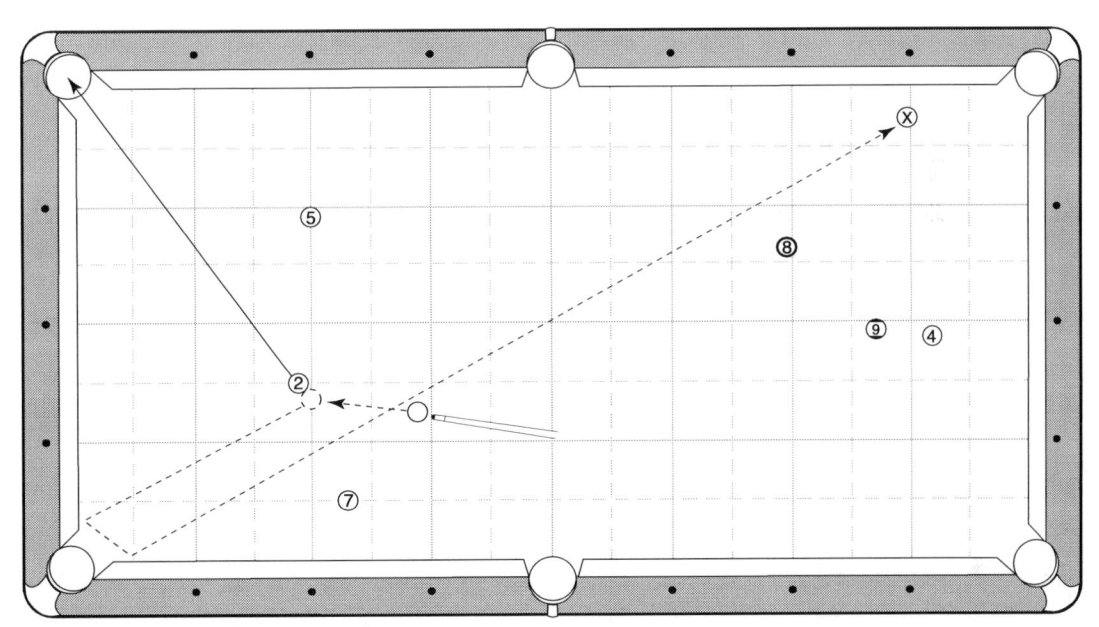

Going Deep into the Corners (A)

Nick Varner demonstrated exceptional cue ball control on this two-rail position play in a match with Mike Sigel at the 1990 U.S. Open. He had little margin for error as he barely avoided scratching. When you can purposefully play this close to a pocket without scratching, it is a strong indicator that your positional skills are approaching, or are at, a very high level.

Chapter 3 - Position Routes

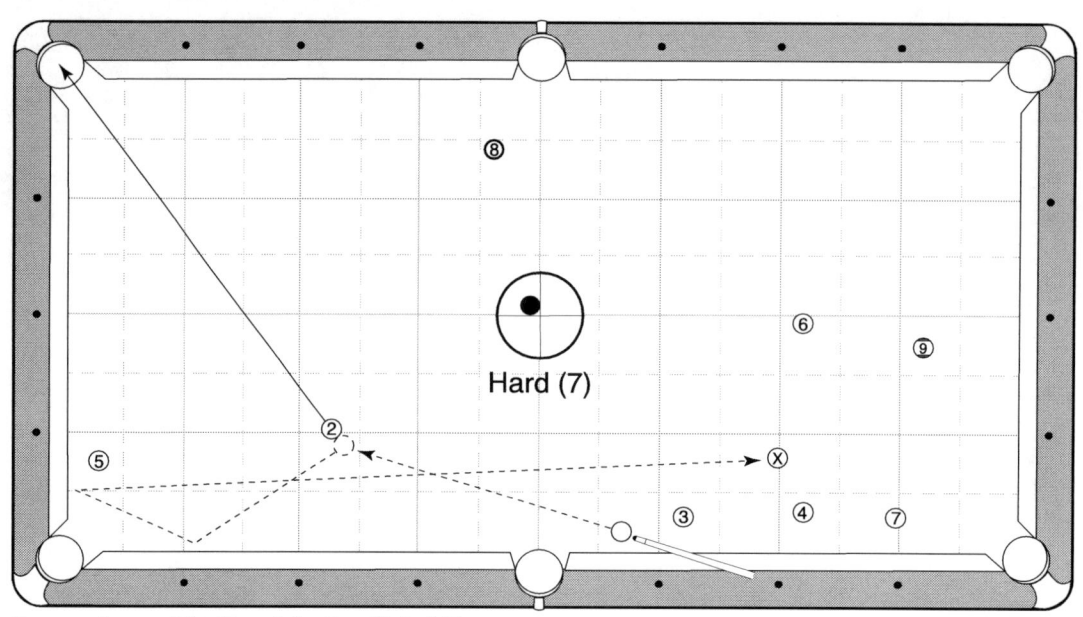

Reversing with Outside English (A)
This brilliant shot was executed by Earl Strickland against Efren Reyes in the 1997 U.S. Open. His unusual position play demonstrates the possibilities when you learn to "think out of the box." Outside (left) english was used to reverse the cue ball's path off the second rail.

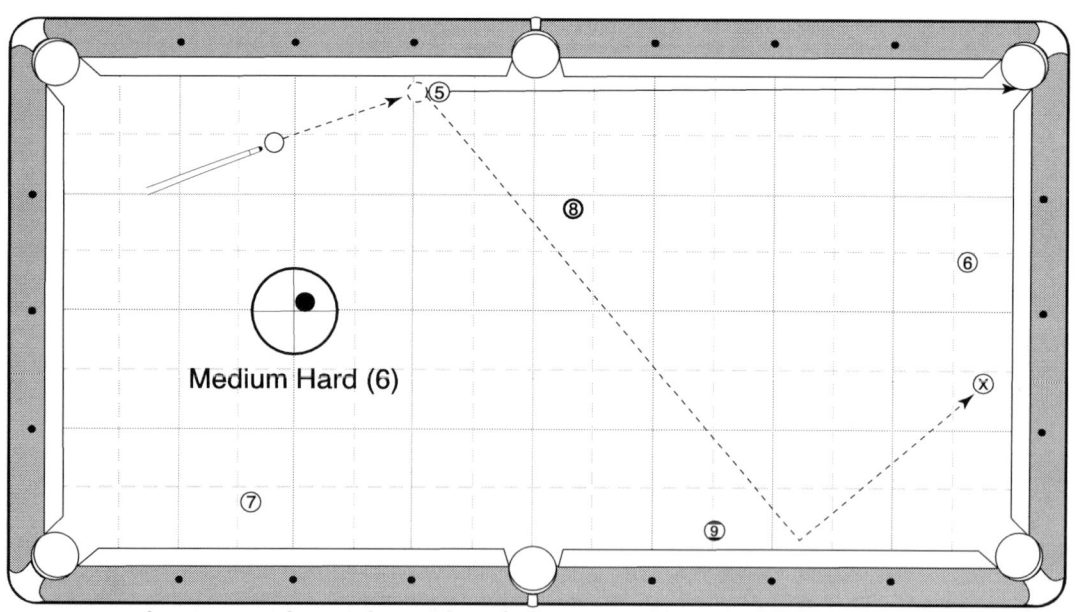

Across and Down with Inside English (A)
Here's another gem from Strickland that took place against Buddy Hall at the Sands Regency Open 12, 1990. His route enabled him to avoid both the 8 and 9-balls. Too much spin and the cue ball would have hit the 8-ball. If he had not applied enough inside english, then the cue ball could have run into the 9-ball, which could have resulted in a hook.

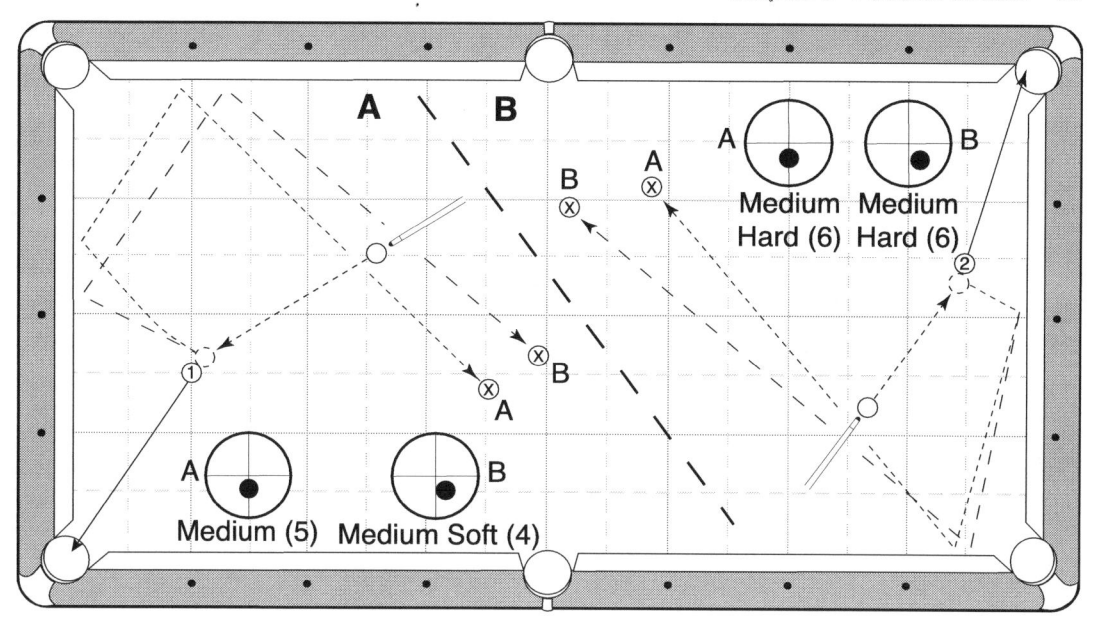

Two Rails with Draw (C & B)

Two-rail draw shots are some of the most commonly played position routes in 9 Ball, so they are a must for your arsenal. Part A shows a pair of two-rail routes on a 30-degree cut shot. Route A (rated C) is played with a medium speed draw stroke. A medium soft stroke with outside running english sent the cue ball down Route B (rated C). Notice that the cue ball ended up in almost the same place using either route, but that it's path was slightly different.

Changing your routes on two-rail position plays can enable you to avoid obstacles while sending the cue ball to essentially the same location. You can fine-tune your routes to play pinpoint position. You may also develop a preference for using only draw. Or perhaps you can achieve better speed control by using running english, which enables you to use a softer stroke.

The two-rail routes in Part A are excellent vehicles for sending the cue ball to the middle portion of the table, from which you can play balls in a wide variety of positions across the table. **Two-rail draw routes can be extended to create three rail routes** which, in turn, can enable you to play position on balls at the opposite end of the table. For example, imagine that the cue ball in either Routes A or B (in Part A) had continued to the bottom side rail and out.

Part B is a different version of the two-rail draw shot. This time the cut angle is only 20-degrees and the object ball is much closer to the rail. A firmer stroke is needed to bring the cue ball out to the center of the table. Route A (rated B) is played with draw. Route B (rated B) is played using draw and outside (right) english. Notice that their paths diverge as the cue ball exits the second rail.

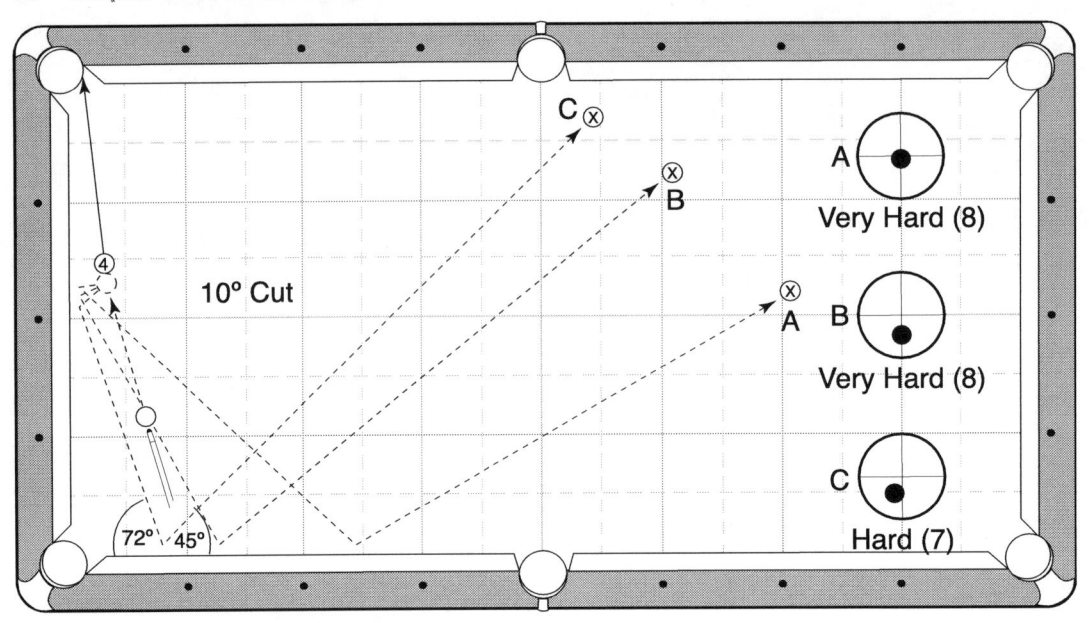

Stun/Draw Two Railer (B) (RR)

When you have a small angled cut shot on the end rail, you can employ one of the recovery routes in the diagram to propel the cue ball far up the table. Use a very hard stroke and a quarter tip of draw to send the cue ball down Route A. Notice that the cue ball hit the side rail 2.5 diamonds up from the corner pocket.

A stun/draw shot will send the cue ball to Position B. Use a very hard stroke and a full tip of draw. Notice that the cue ball struck the side rail much closer to the corner pocket compared to Route A.

A hard stun/draw stoke with a half tip of outside english should result in Position C. This shot must be aimed with extra care as it is always difficult to use english with the higher speeds of stroke. Notice that the cue ball entered the rail at a 72-degree angle and departed at 45-degrees thanks to the hard hit and the outside english.

Two Rails Across with Outside Draw (B)

Drawing the cue ball across and down the table is seldom easy, and the task is even more difficult when you must contend with the side pocket. The key is to **know when you can draw past the side, and when you must play to the near side to avoid scratching**

The object ball's distance from the rail and the cut angle determine how far you can bring the cue ball back down the table. When the object ball is close to the rail and the cut angle is sharp, this limits how far you can bring the cue ball back down the table.

The 2-ball is a half a ball's width off the rail for each of these position plays. Position A shows a 20-degree cut shot. A medium hard draw stroke with a half tip of outside english will send the cue ball four diamonds down the table, and well past the side pocket. When the cue ball is in Position B, you have a 60-degree cut, which makes it far more difficult to avoid the side pocket. This route is played with low left english and a medium speed stroke. You must really spin the cue ball to get past the side, so english (not draw) is the key to this position play. Practice this shot from all five angles in the diagram and take note of how far you can bring the cue ball down table.

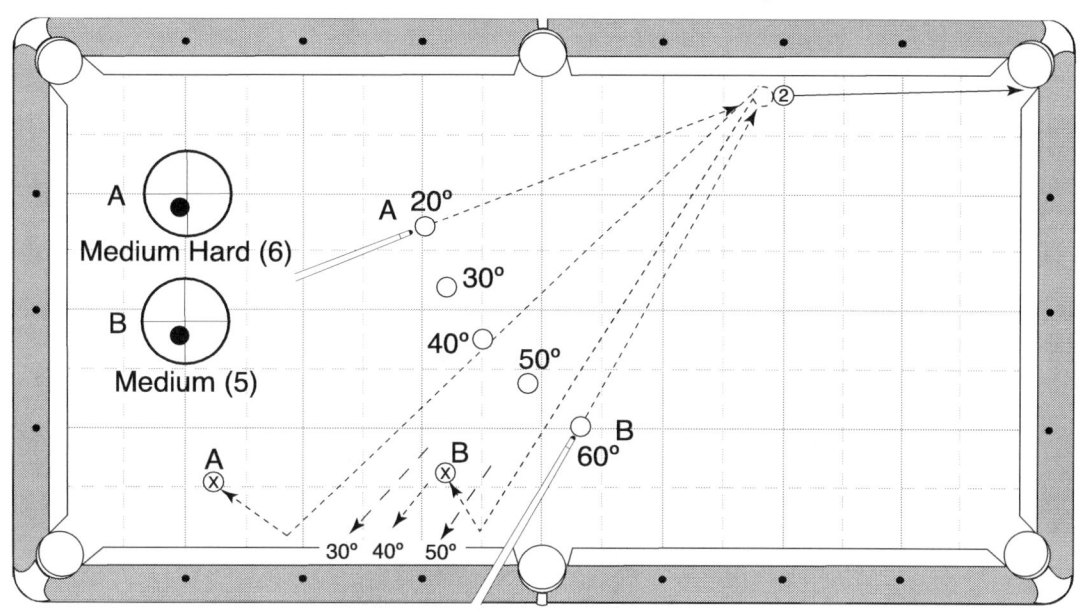

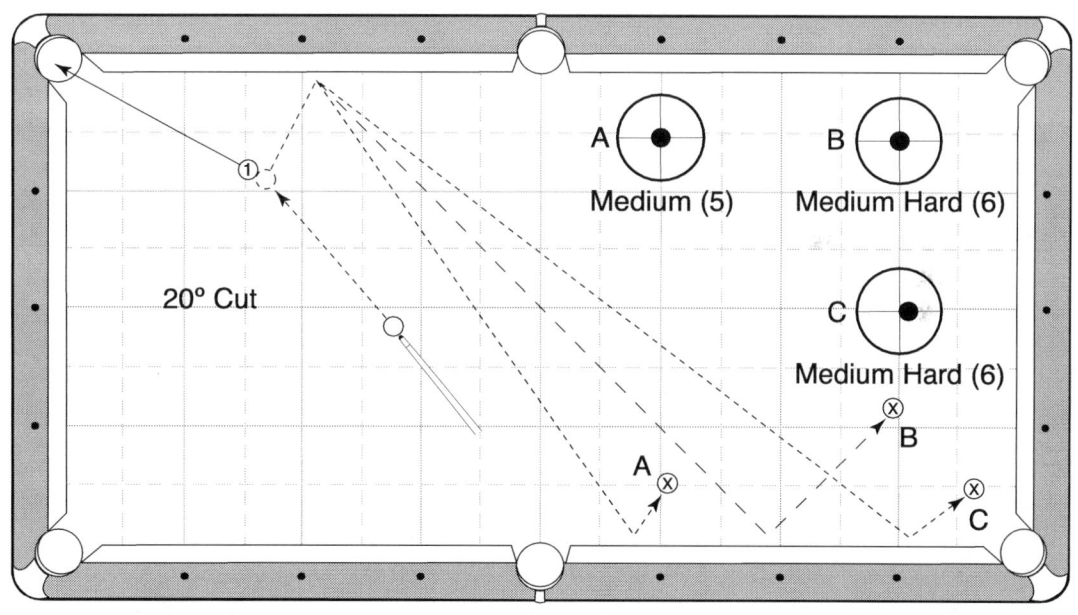

Stun Across and Down the Table (B)
These valuable position plays give you very effective methods for sending the cue ball across and down the table. The key ingredients are a firm stroke, centerball, and a relatively small cut, such as the 20-degree angle shown. Routes A and B are created by sending the cue ball down the tangent line to the rail, and by the running english that comes from contact with the object ball. Route C is created by using a half tip of outside english.

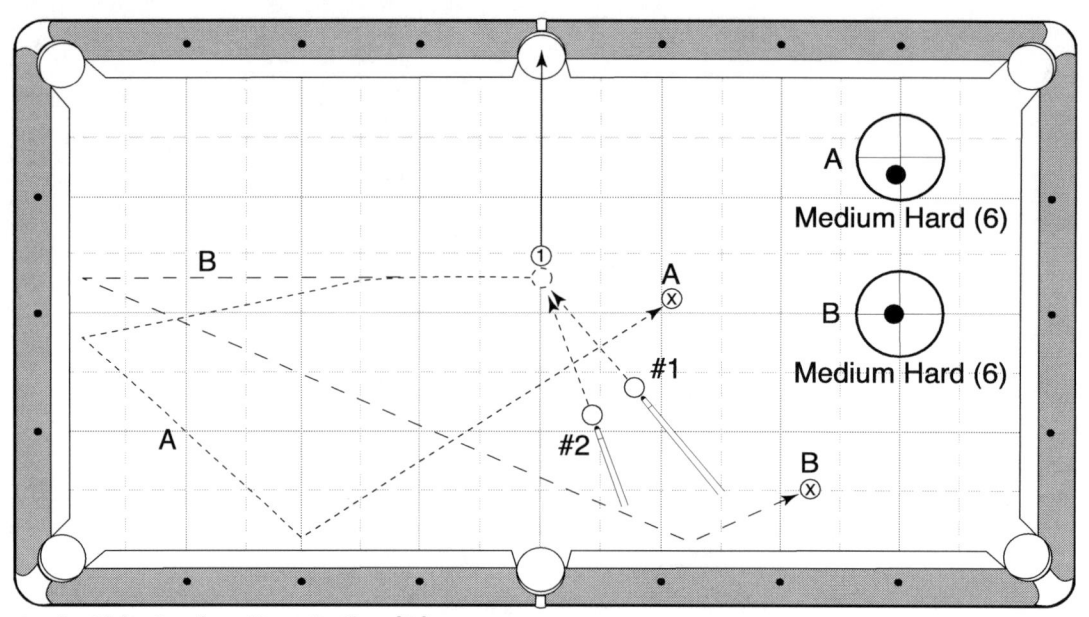

Basic Side Pocket Two Railer (B)

A big plus for these routes is that the object ball is directly opposite the side pocket, which makes pocketing the ball not too difficult. Controlling the cue ball, however, is another matter.

Route A is played with draw and outside english when the cue ball is in Position #1. This position play is not as challenging as it appears because you need not worry about scratching. In addition, the route to Position A on this 40-degree cut is fairly predictable even though the cue ball must travel four diamonds to the end rail.

The path to the end rail is very predictable in Route B since the shot is being played on the horizontal axis with outside english and a medium hard stroke. The trick in Route B is to regulate the english so that you strike the side rail safely past the side pocket.

For the next version, move the cue ball to Position #2. The cue ball's path is much less predictable on this 20 degree cut because small errors in cueing will be greatly magnified by the time the cue ball reaches the end rail. From Position #2, use a quarter tip of draw and a medium hard stroke to send the cue ball down Route A.

Side Pocket Inside English Two Railers (B)

You can achieve a variety of positional objectives on this side pocket shot by adjusting your cueing. The illustration at the top of page 101 shows two valuable but underused position plays. In Part A, a medium speed stroke with inside (right) english will send the cue ball to the end rail, then off the side rail and down table. Play the shot with enough force so that the stun does not convert into follow because this could lead to a scratch.

In Part B, use a medium speed stroke with follow and inside (right) english. The cue ball will strike the side rail first, then the end rail. The english will straighten out the cue ball's rebound angle off of the end rail.

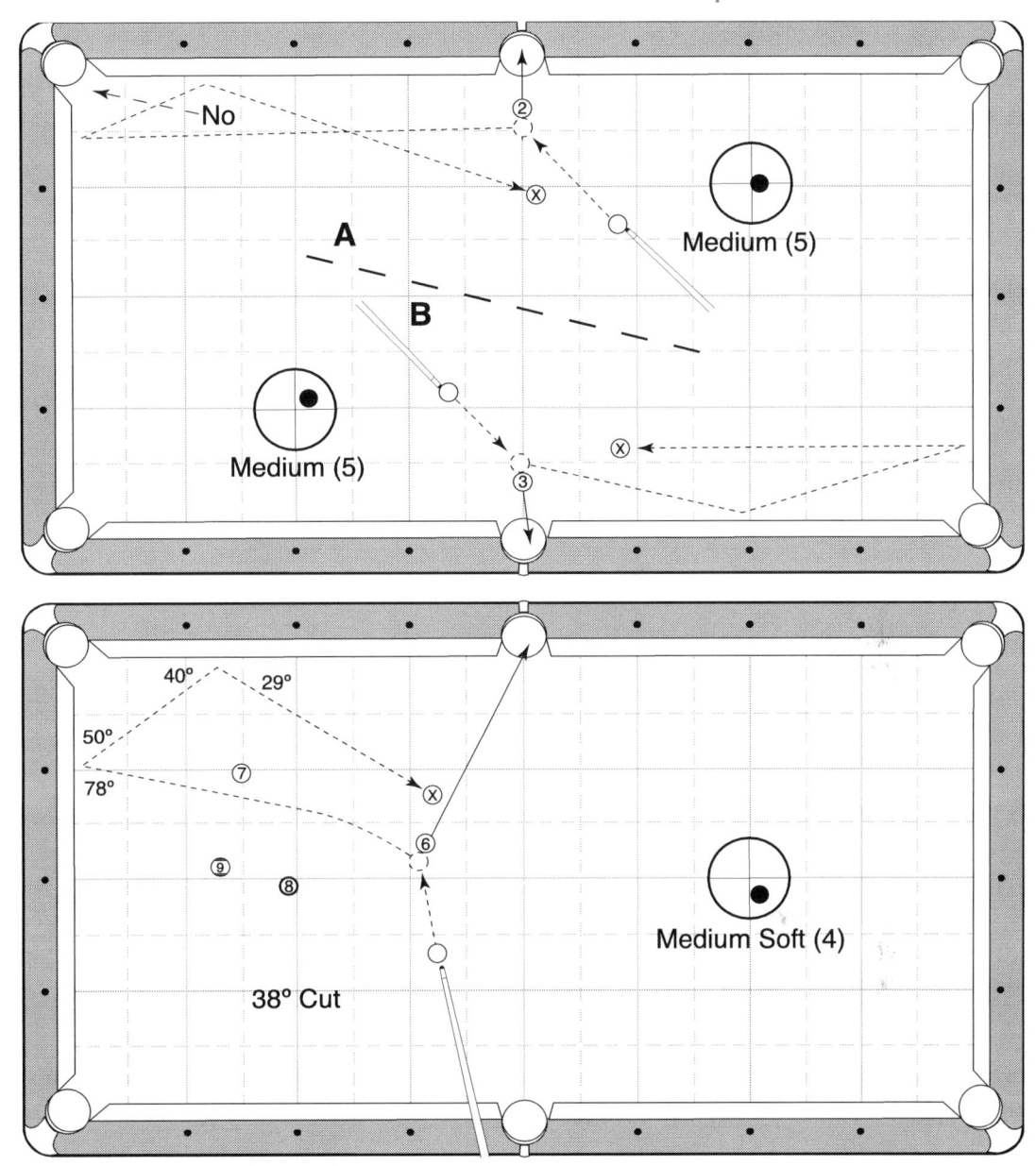

Inside Draw Two Rails (A)

Efren Reyes displayed his artistry in the finals of the 1994 U.S. Open in his match with Nick Varner. The Magician was facing an awkward situation when he concocted the route shown in the illustration. A medium soft draw stroke put enough bend on the cue ball so that it barely avoided the 7-ball. If Reyes had hit the shot a little harder, the cue ball would have crashed into the 7-ball. When the cue ball struck the end rail, the inside english widened the rebound angle by a full 28 degrees (78 in, 50 out). The english propelled the cue ball off the side rail and to the middle of the table for excellent position on the 7-ball. The lesson: **inside draw shots are valuable positional tools that can give your game an added dimension**.

Three-Rail Position Routes

The professionals use three-rail routes on 5.1 percent of their position plays, about 1 in 20. This means that, on average, you will need one in every four games. While three-rail routes are not the mainstay of a 9 Ball player's game, they come up often enough that you should still master the ones that we'll be covering in this section

Many of the three-rail routes are natural extensions of the one and two-rail routes that we've covered in previous sections. **The cue ball usually travels a long distance on three-rail routes, so use rail targets whenever possible to help plan your route.** In addition, guard against scratching, especially when the cue ball will be traveling a long distance to the second and/or third rails.

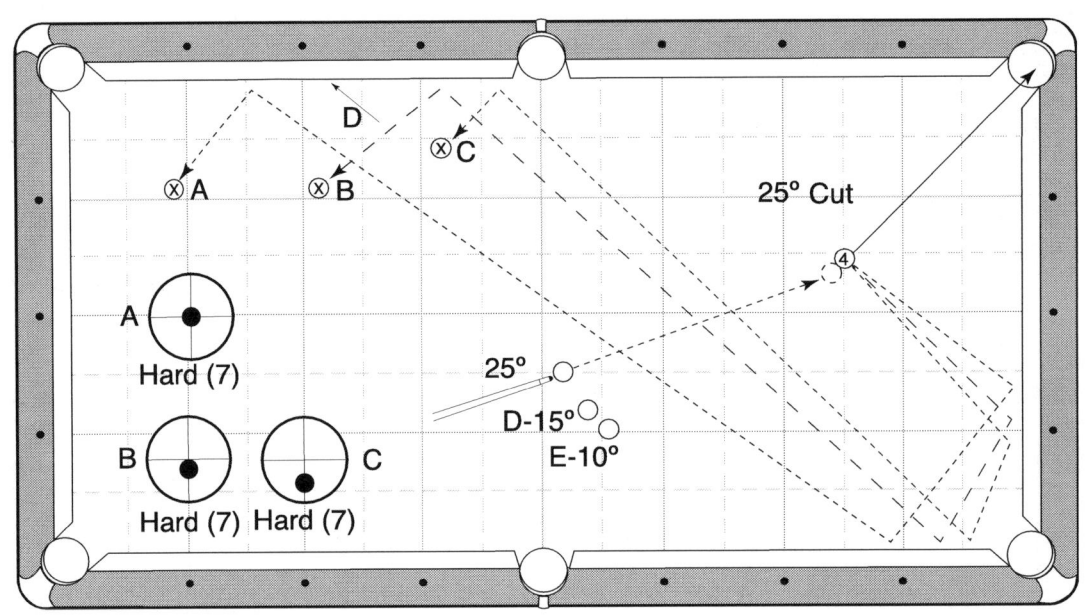

Power Three-Railer (B, A)

The first three shots feature a 25-degree cut angle. A dead centerball hit with a hard stroke will send the cue ball to Position A (rated B). Variations of this route with even larger cut angles are among the most commonly used three rail routes. You can adjust the contact point on the third rail by applying a half tip of draw. Again, use a hard stroke, which will send the cue ball to Position B (rated B). Notice that the cue ball hit much further up the side rail. Cue one full tip below center with a hard stroke to send the cue ball to Position C (rated B).

Next, place the cue ball in Position D, which is a 15-degree cut. Centerball and a very hard stroke will send the cue ball to the third rail at the second diamond, as shown by the arrow. Now try the shot with the cue ball at Position E, which is only a 10-degree cut! A centerball hit with an extremely hard stroke will send the cue ball into the third rail at about the same place as on the previous shot. The routes from Positions D and E are rated A because of the distance and because each one requires a high speed of stroke.

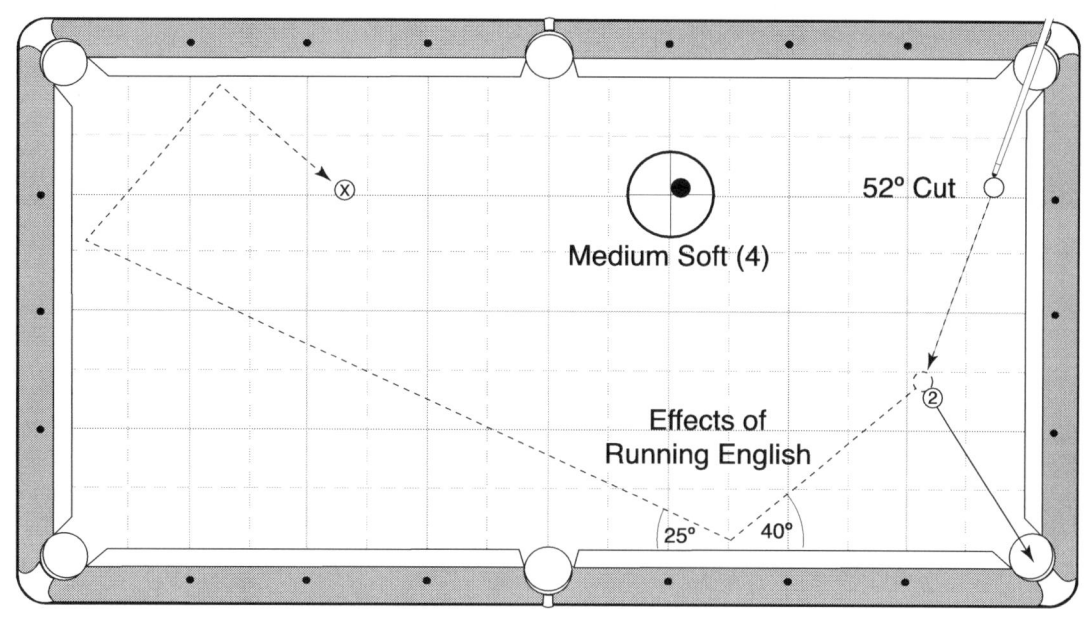

Off a Side Rail Three-Railer (B)
The cue ball is going to travel a long distance on this shot even though it requires only a medium soft stroke thanks to the 52-degree cut angle and a half tip of outside (running) english. It is not easy to play pinpoint shape on a long distance route like this, but the cue ball will slow down quickly after hitting the last rail, which is a big help.

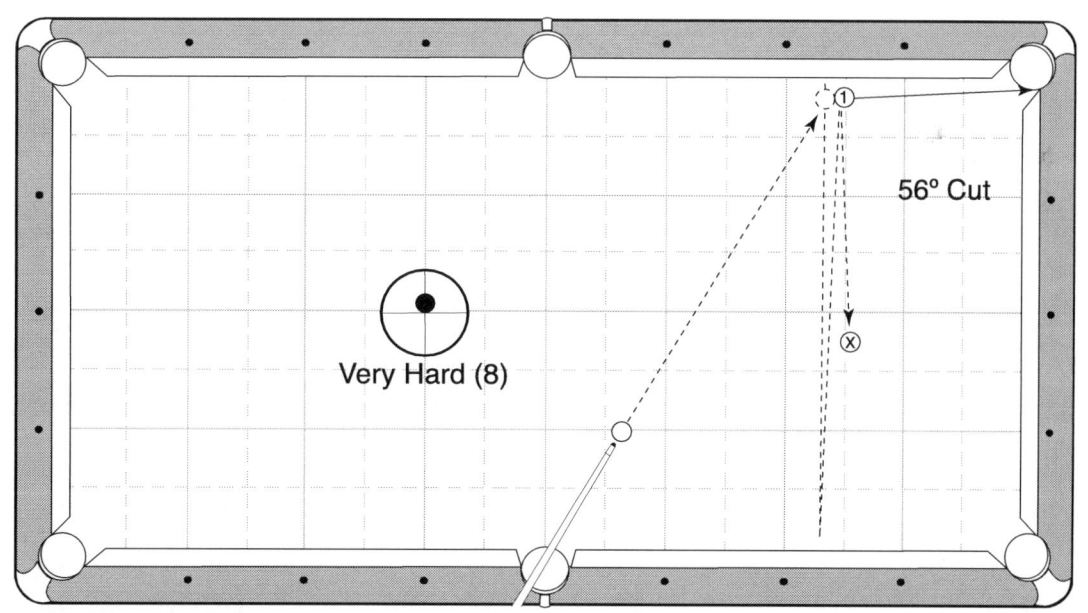

Three Rails Across (A)
Three rail routes can be used to send the cue ball across the table multiple times as shown by this demanding position play. This 56-degree cut requires a very hard stroke to ensure that the object ball reaches the pocket. But what makes shots like this so difficult is that it is hard to figure out where the cue ball will come to rest. So, when practicing shots like this, pay special attention to where the cue ball stops and the speed with which the object ball enters the pocket.

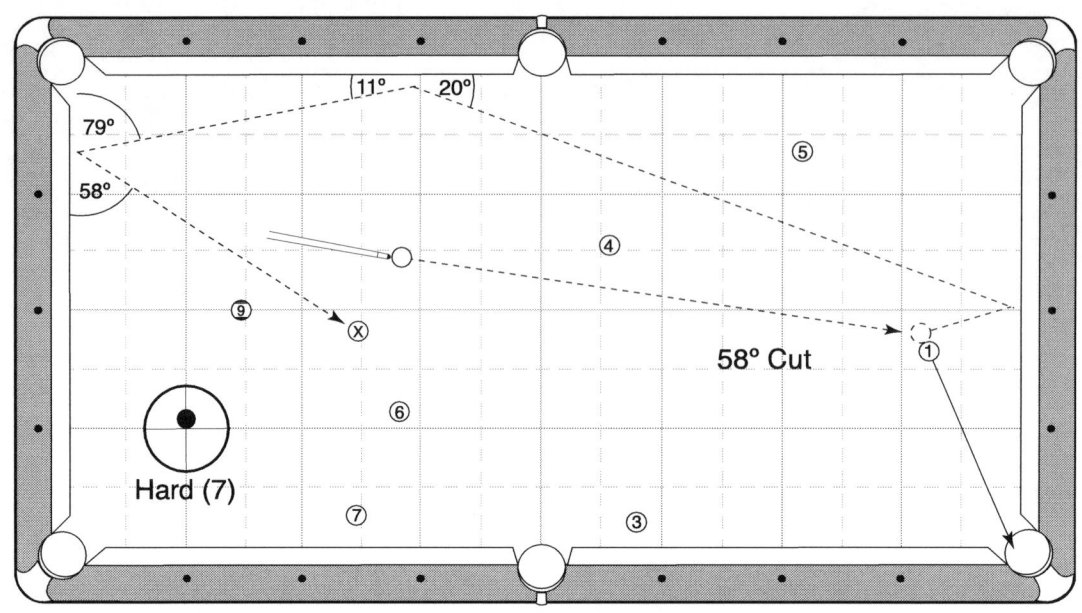

Three Rails After a Thin Cut (A)
This masterpiece by Mike Sigel came against Johnny Archer at the 1993 U.S. Open. Sigel played this 58-degree cut with straight follow and a hard stroke. No english was used, but **the cue ball was able to pick up plenty of spin after contacting the rails**, as evidenced by the opening of the rebound off the last cushion. This A+ rated route required accurate long-range shotmaking, a hard stroke, and incredibly precise routing.

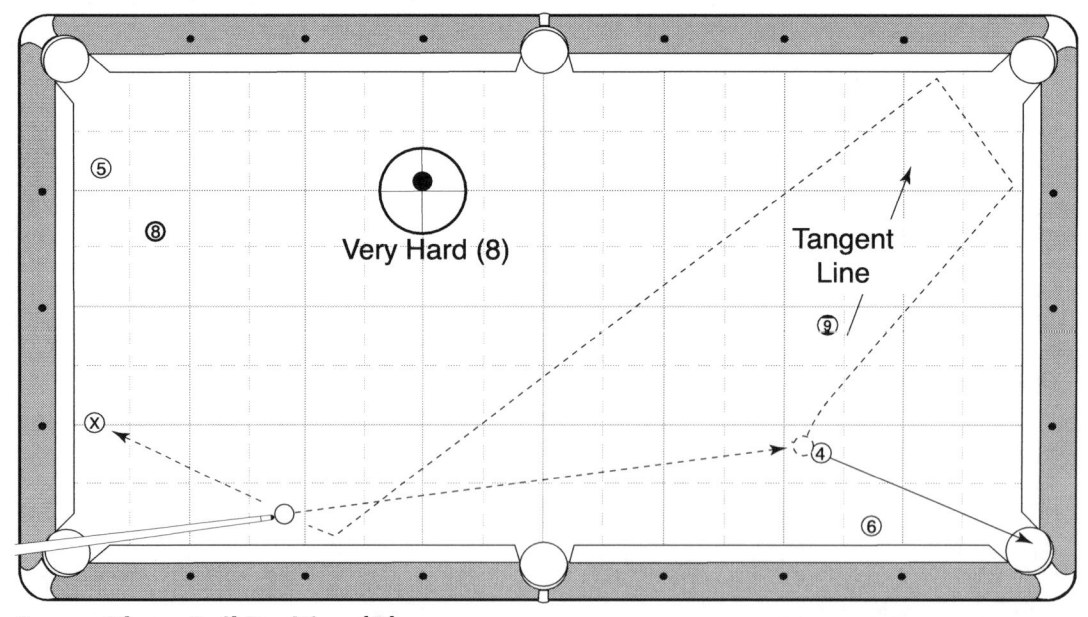

Power Three Rail Position (A)
Chuck Altomare drilled home this powerful three-railer at the 1999 U.S. Open against Kunihiko Takahashi. **When the cue ball is hit hard with follow, and it is going to travel across the table, is has plenty of time to bend forward to contact with the end rail, and avoid a scratch, as shown.**

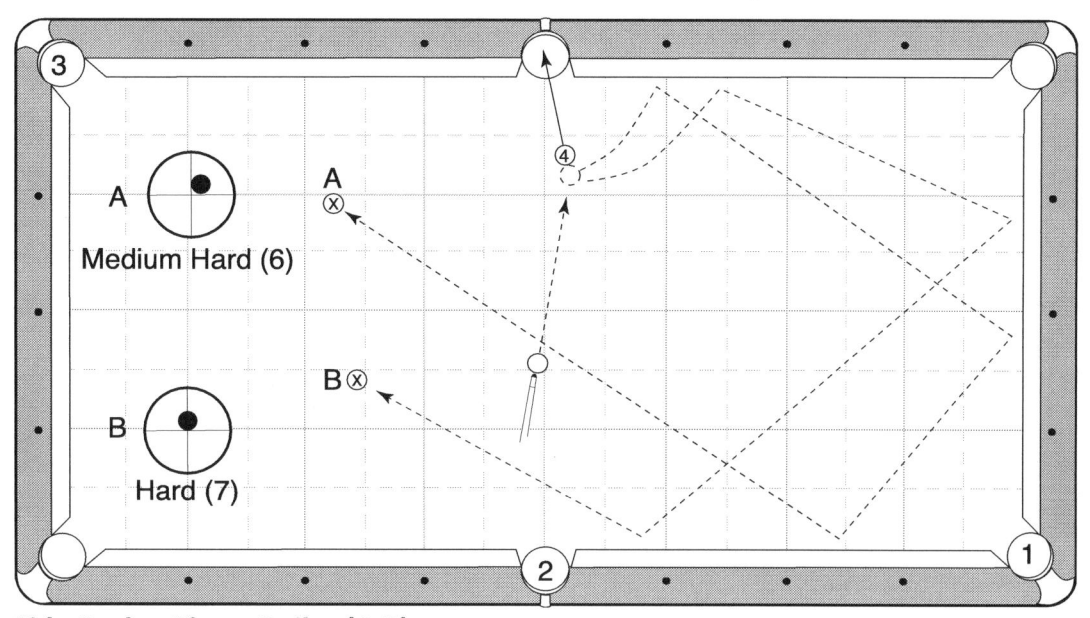

Side Pocket Three-Railer (C-B)
Three-rail side pocket position plays are often used as recovery routes when you have played position to the wrong side of the ball. The diagram shows two of these routes. The short shot to a big side pocket gives you plenty of options in planning your route. Notice the difference that cuing and speed made when playing to Positions A and B. Your main considerations are obstacles in route, and scratching in pockets #2 or #3. The chances of a scratch depend on the route you are playing, and on the position of the balls.

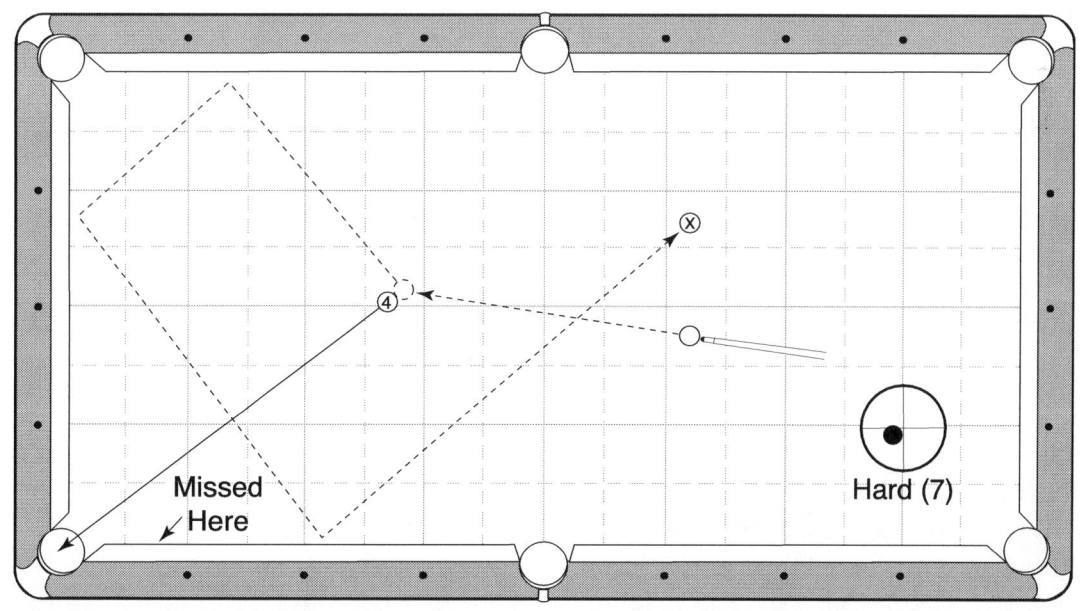

Inside English Side Rail Three-Railer (A)
This long distance position play requires a hard stroke with inside english. The tendency among 99.9 percent of all players is to overcut the shot because of a failure to compensate enough for deflection. You must force yourself to aim for a fuller hit even when it looks wrong to you. The big secret is practice.

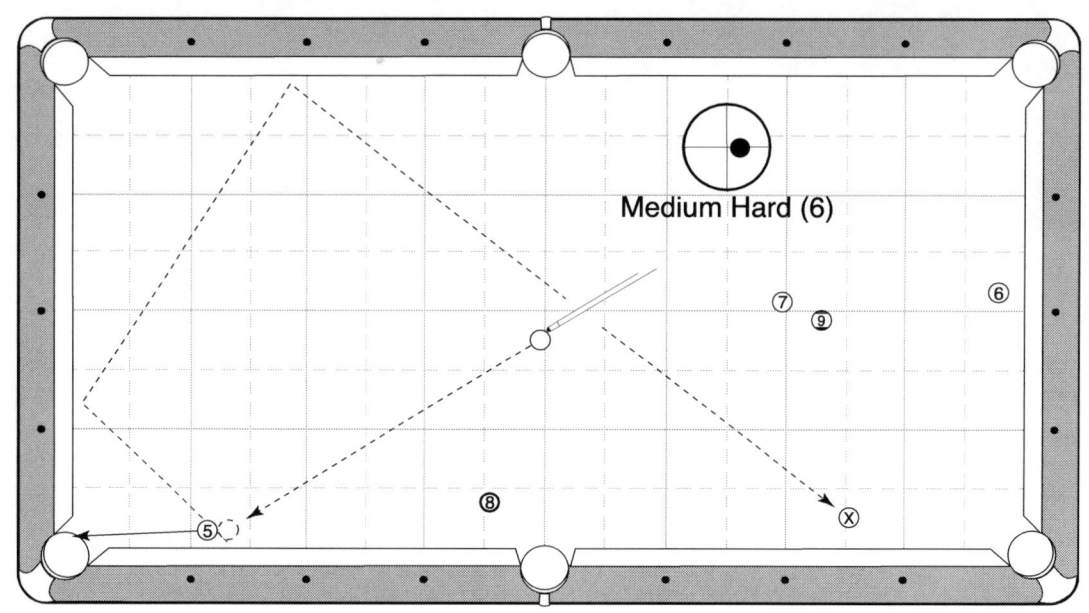

Inside English Three-Railer (B)

German wizard Ralf Souquet played this difficult three-rail position play against Efren Reyes on his way to capturing the Sands Regency Open 27 in 1998. The shot is played with a medium hard stroke on the horizontal axis with inside english. Again, you must allow sufficiently for deflection, which often causes this shot to be overcut.

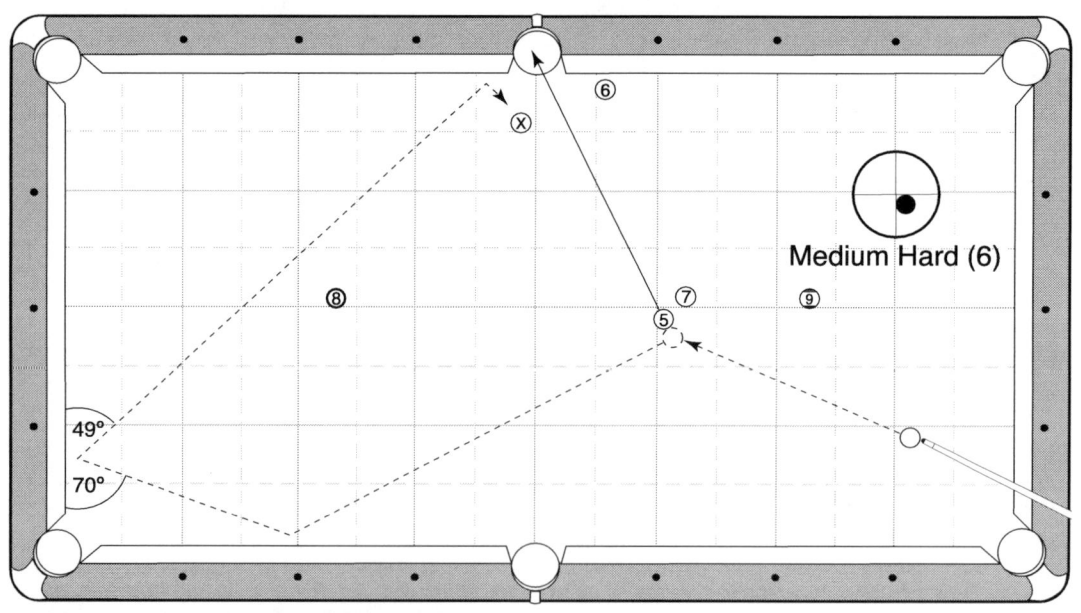

Inside Draw off the Side Rail (A)

Nick Varner uncorked this gem on Johnny Archer on his way to winning the Sands Regency Open 23, 1996. He used draw to avoid a corner pocket scratch and so that the cue ball would strike far enough up on the side rail to keep from going into the opposite side pocket. The inside english kicked in on the second rail as shown by the opening of the angle off the end rail. Varner's perfect execution led to his fine position on the 6-ball.

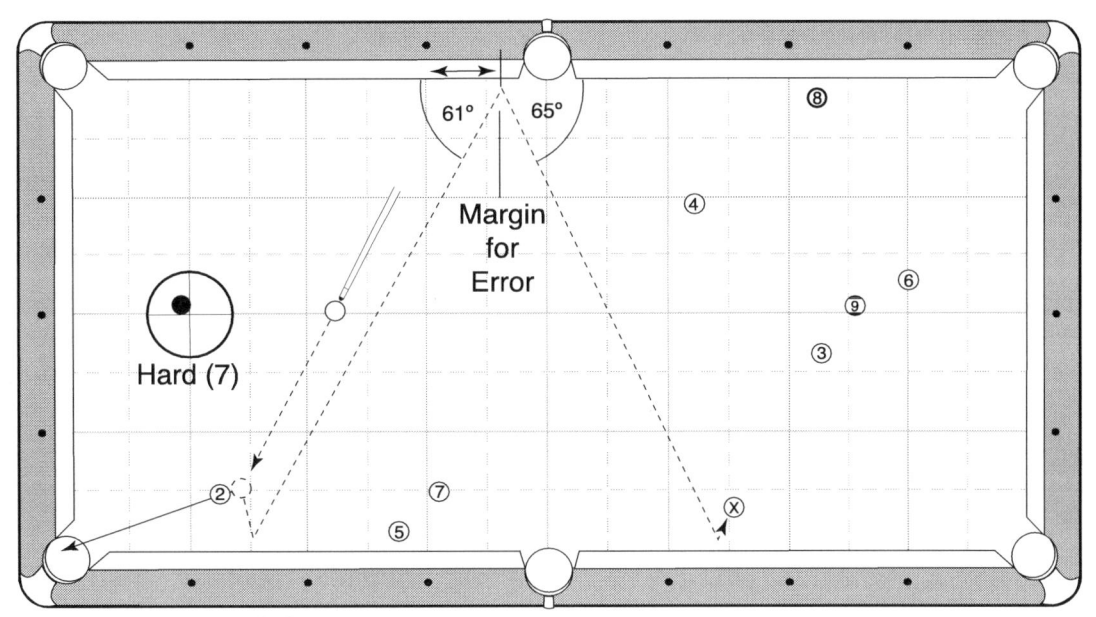

Cross Table Twice (A)

Loree Jon Jones set up a 3-9-ball combination with this twice across and out position route against Allison Fisher at the 1999 Prescott Resort Classic. Jones probably came a little closer to the side than she had planned, but a player of her caliber is able to operate with a small margin for error like this. A hard stroke with left english opened up the rebound angle off the bottom rail and it closed slightly off the second rail.

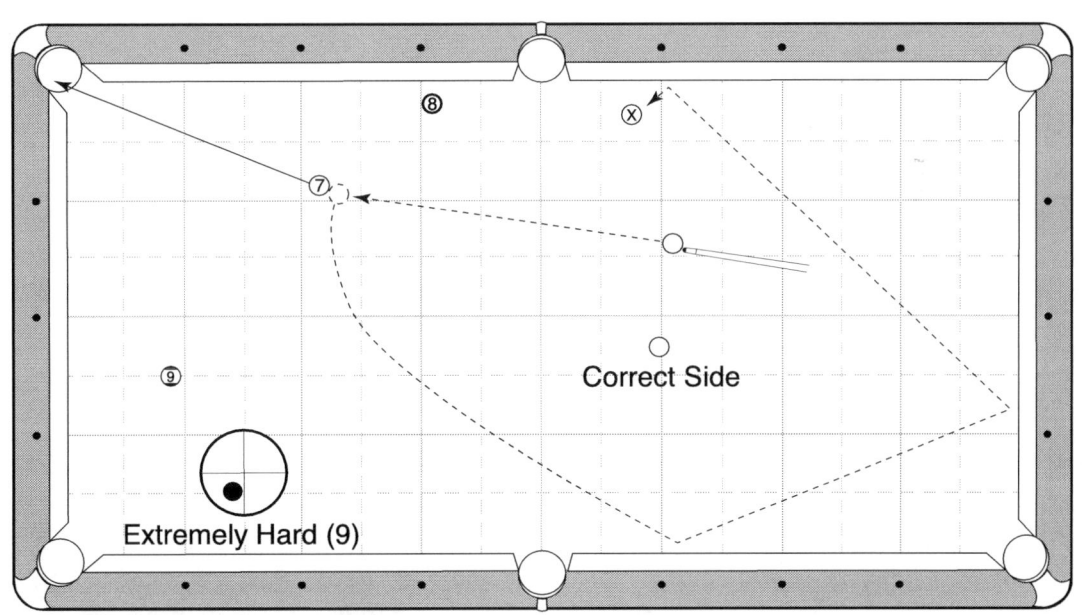

Massive Three Rail Draw (A)

Efren Reyes would have preferred to have position on the other side of the 7-ball as this would have made it much easier to get shape on the 8. But this was no problem for the Magician! Just cue it low and let 'er go with a massive three-rail position play! Notice the huge arc as stun and draw battled it out until the draw spin took over. This action took place at the Sands Regency Open 23, 1996, against Johnny Archer.

Chapter 3 - Position Routes

Four-Rail Position Routes

In my study on the pros, four-rail routes appeared once in every 150 position plays (0.7 percent). This means that **you will face a four-rail route about once in every 35 games** or so (assuming that you shoot about half of the time). So, even though four rail routes are uncommon, it is still necessary for you to know the position plays in this section and others when they come up in competition.

Four rail position plays are typically very exacting because the cue ball will be traveling a long distance across and around the table, so you must be very precise in your planning and execution. While I don't recommend that you don't spend a lot of your valuable practice time on these routes, you should at least play them a few times so you will be familiar to you because any one of them could win a big match for you.

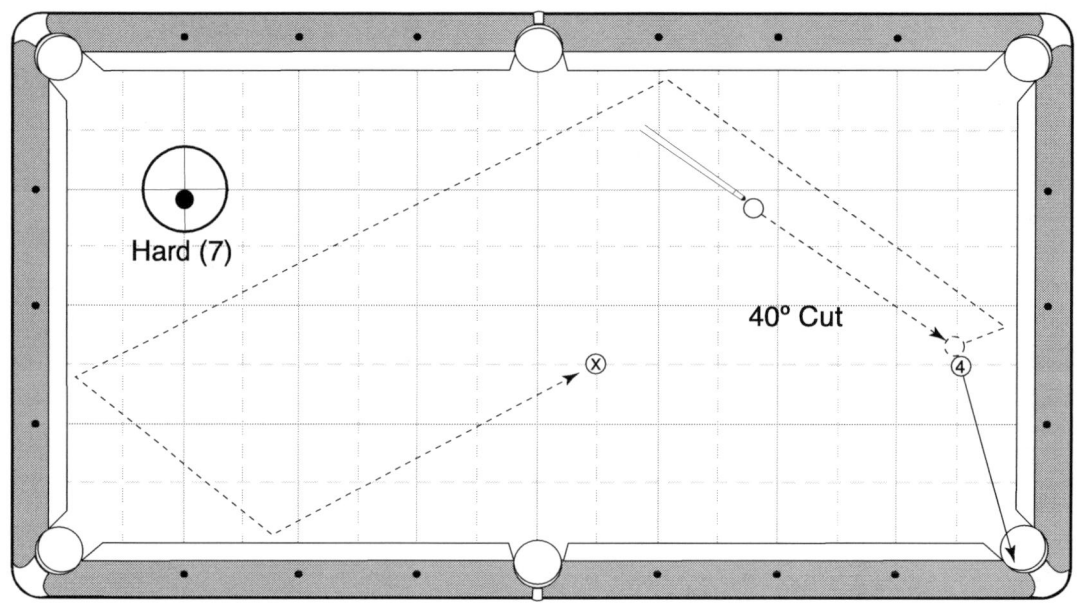

Draw Four-Railer (A)

A hard stroke and a half tip of draw will produce the four-rail route above. The key is to hit the second rail below the side pocket, avoiding a scratch. **When plotting your course for a four-rail route, there is often one pocket that presents the risk of a scratch.** If you can avoid that pocket, the rest of the route will take care of itself.

Four Rails to the Short Side (A)

Mike Sigel was playing Earl Strickland at the Sands Regency Open 17, 1993 when he came up against this challenging position play from the 4-ball to the 6-ball. Multi-rail routes like this are used when you are facing a thin cut in which the cue ball is going to roll a long distance after contact. If the cue ball had been in Position B, Sigel would have played a conventional two-rail route to the 6-ball to Position B-1.

However, with the cue ball in Position A, the 67-degree cut angle prevented Sigel from playing that route. So, he chose to play to the short side of the 6-ball via the imaginative route shown in the diagram. The shot was played with draw and a half tip of outside (running) english. The english opened the cue ball's rebound angle considerably off the second rail and the spin accelerated its roll down table. Even though the cue ball traveled over 13 feet to its final destination at Position X, this shot was mostly about precision, not power.

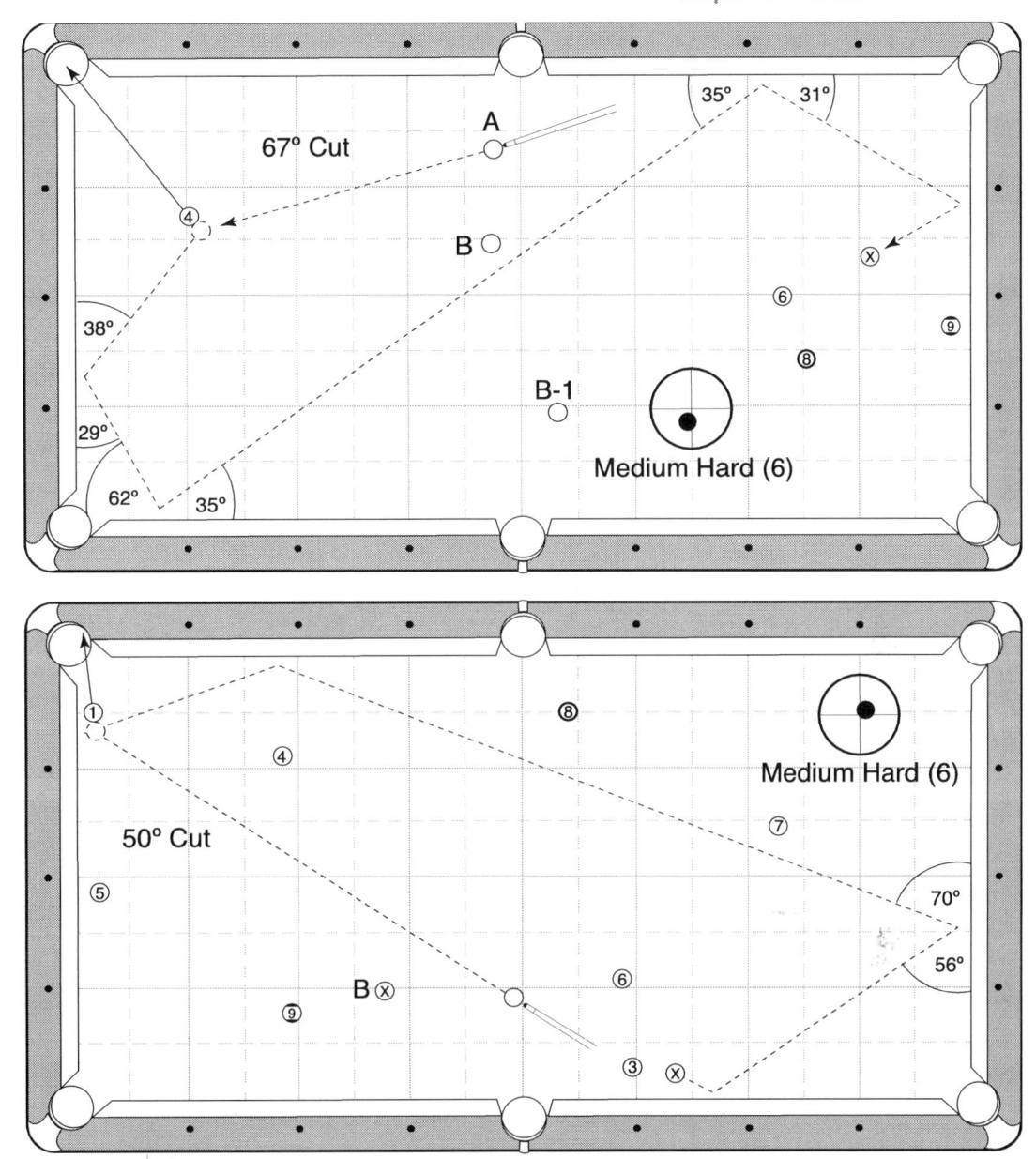

Inside English Four Rails to the Short Side (A)

Earl Strickland used high inside english and a medium hard stroke in playing this creative four-railer against Efren Reyes at the Sand Regency Open 21, 1995. The english really took off the third rail just when the cue ball was losing speed, propelling it to Position X. The distance of the shot and the thin cut on the 1-ball kept him from playing a more conventional route to the long side at Position B.

110   Chapter 3 - Position Routes

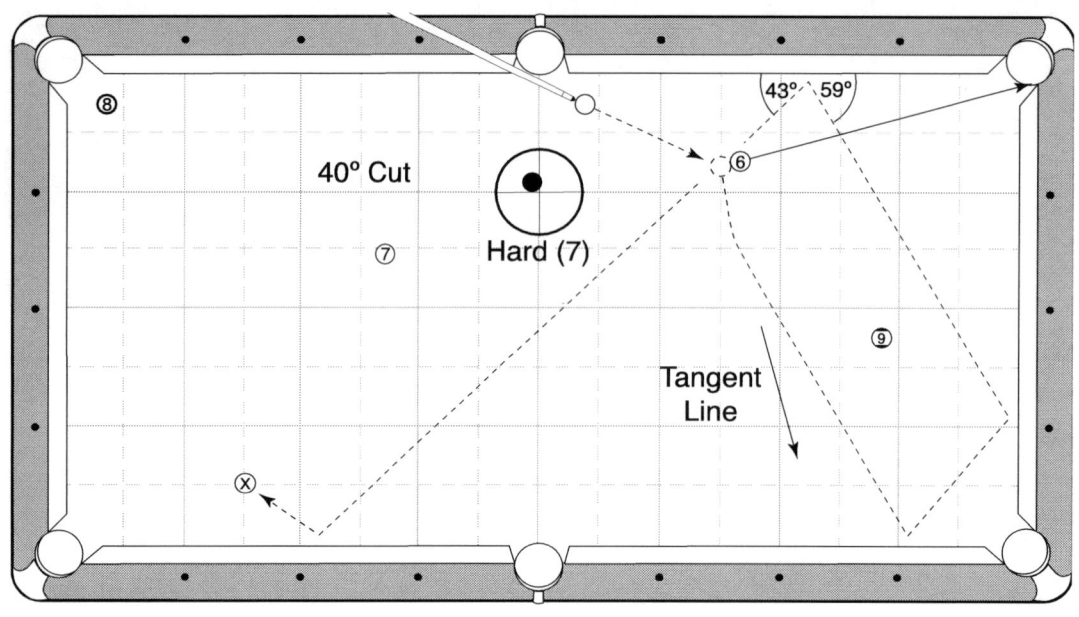

Four Rails with Inside Spin (2) (A)
Allison Fisher orchestrated this beautiful four-railer against Loree Jon Jones at the 1999 Prescott Resort Classic. Ms. Fisher used a hard stroke and high left english. The follow turned the cue ball towards a lower hit on the side rail while the inside running english shot the cue ball down table off of the third rail.

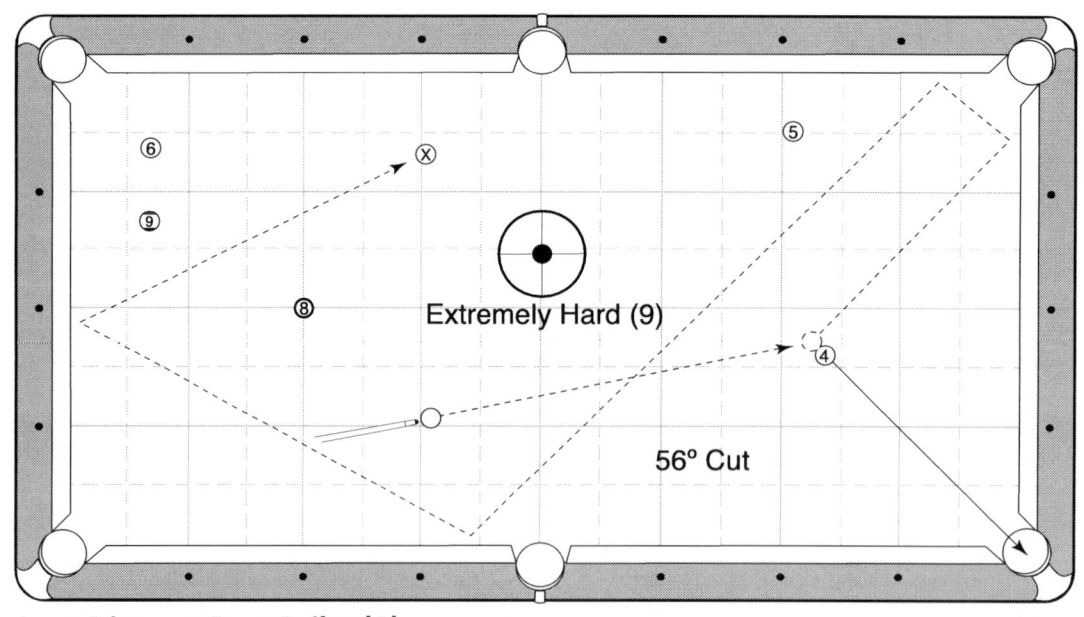

Long Distance Four-Railer (A)
Corey Deuel demonstrated exceptional planning and skill on this powerhouse four-railer against Fong-Pang Chao at the 1999 World 9-Ball Championships. The cue ball traveled over 16' while narrowly avoiding two pockets! The shot was played with an extremely hard stroke, which enabled the cue ball to bounce so far out off of the fourth rail.

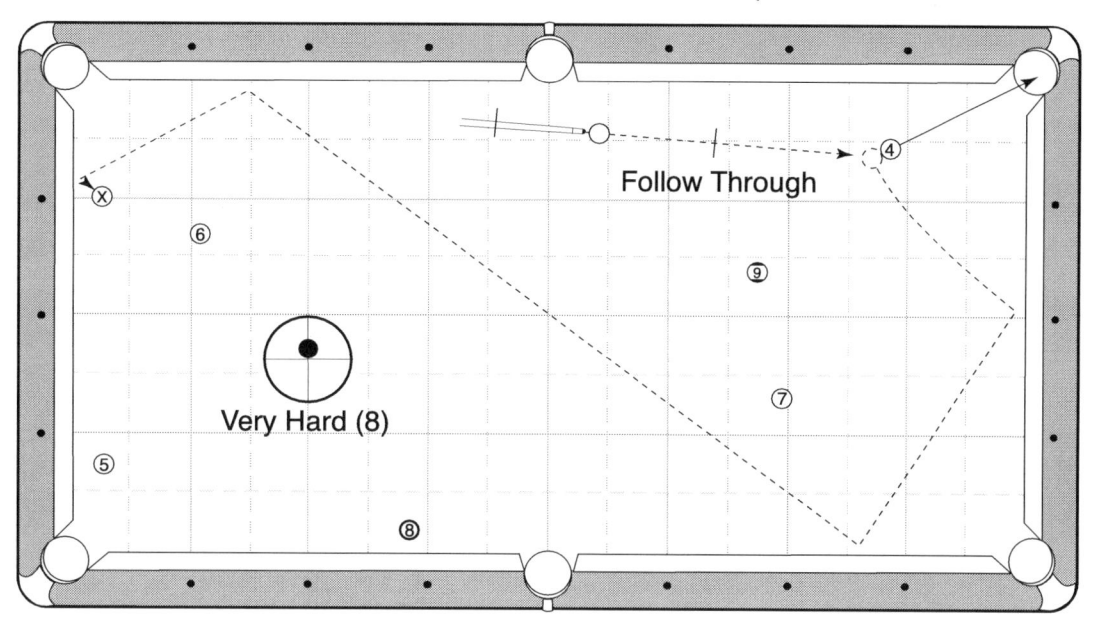

Follow/Pound Around the Table (A)

Rodney Morris employed a 10 inch bridge and a 13 inch follow through to power the cue ball four rails for position on the 5-ball. The cue ball was never in danger of scratching as it struck the third rail 1.5 diamonds up from the corner pocket. This shot took place in the finals of the 1996 U.S. Open as Morris was rolling to the title against Efren Reyes.

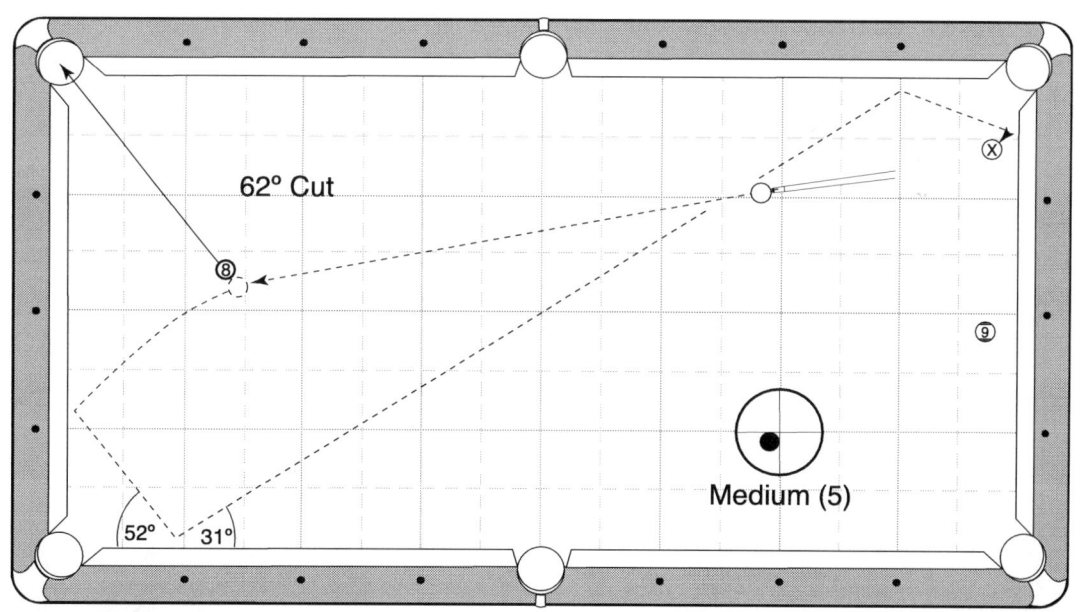

Thin Cut Four Rail Route (A)

The cut angle to the upper left corner is 62 degrees while the cut angle to the lower left pocket is "only" 55 degrees. Still, **sometimes it is better to play a thinner cut** because it offers the opportunity for excellent cue ball control, which explains why Steve Mizerak chose the more difficult shot for this four-rail position play at the 1994 U.S. Open.

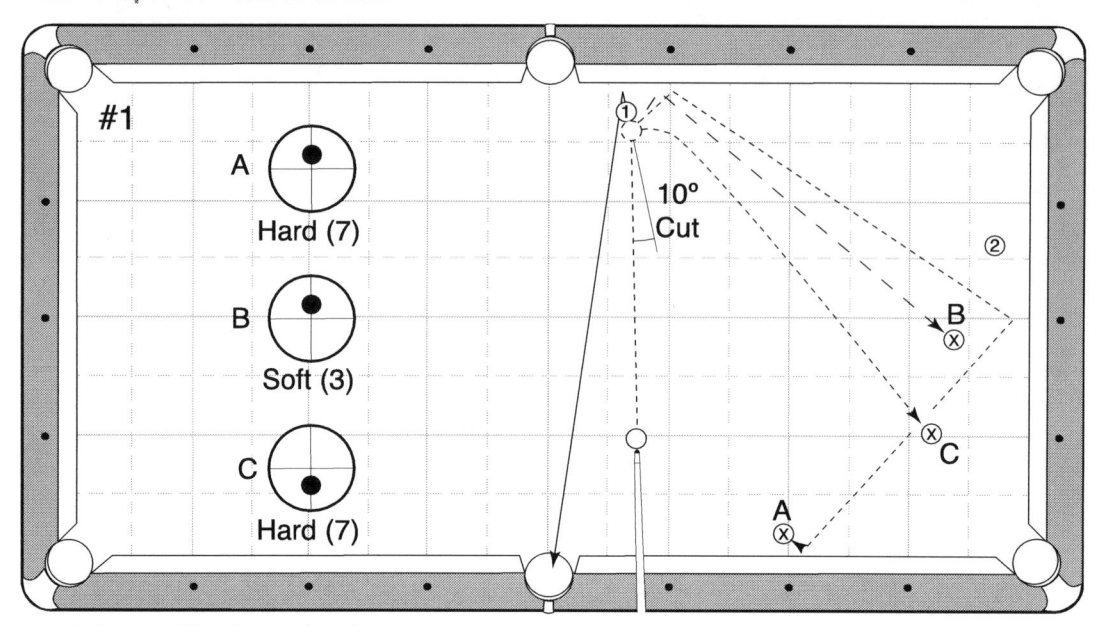

Position off of Bank Shots

Most banks that you choose to play in 9 Ball should be the easier ones that enable you to make the ball a very high percentage of the time and to play good position – or that lead to an excellent safety.

Diagram #1 shows three ways for playing shape on this routine cross-side bank. A hard follow stroke will send the cue ball three rails to Position A. A soft follow stroke will send the cue ball to Position B, giving you shape for a ball on the same end rail. You can also get position for a ball on the end rail by using a hard draw stroke to send the cue ball to Position C.

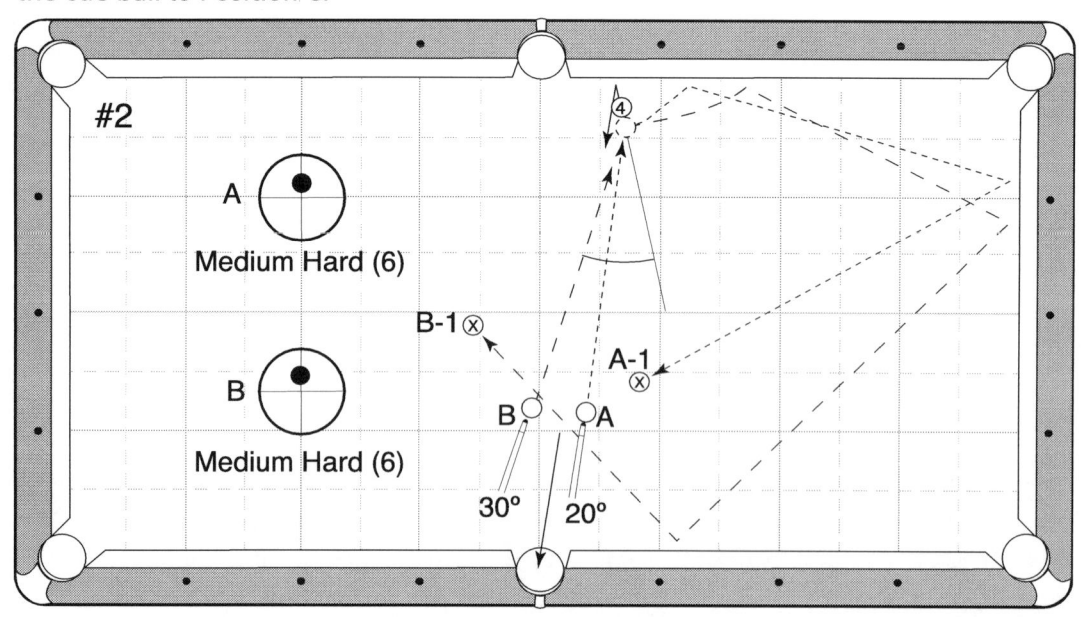

Diagram #2 shows two routes for banks with thinner cut angles. A medium hard follow stroke will send the cue ball from Position A to A-1. When the cue ball is at Position B, which is a 30-degree cut, the cue ball will continue to Position B-1 when it is hit with a medium hard follow stroke.

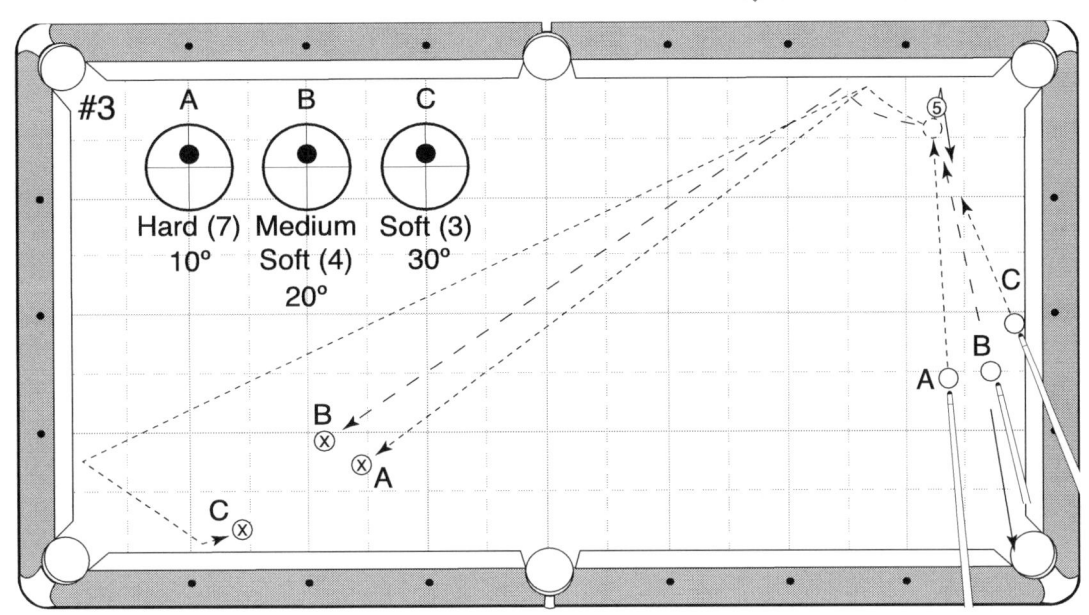

The cue ball will typically travel far up the table when playing backcut bank shots into the corner, as shown in diagram #3. The cue ball ended up in about the same location on all three shots, which were played from three different cut angles at Positions A, B, and C. Each was hit at a different speed.

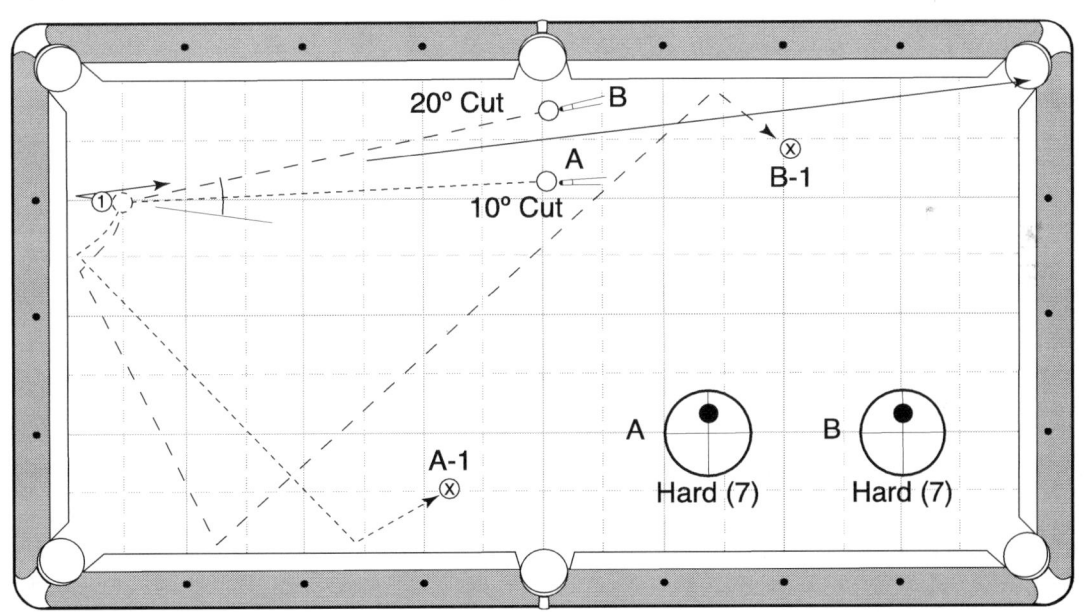

Long Rail Bank Routes

The long rail banks that are played in 9 Ball have very small cut angles, typically no more than 15-20-degrees. The cut angle is only 10 degrees with the cue ball in Position A. It takes a hard stroke just to send the cue ball to Position A-1. The cut angle is 20-degrees in Position B. Now you can send the cue ball to Position B-1 with a hard follow stroke.

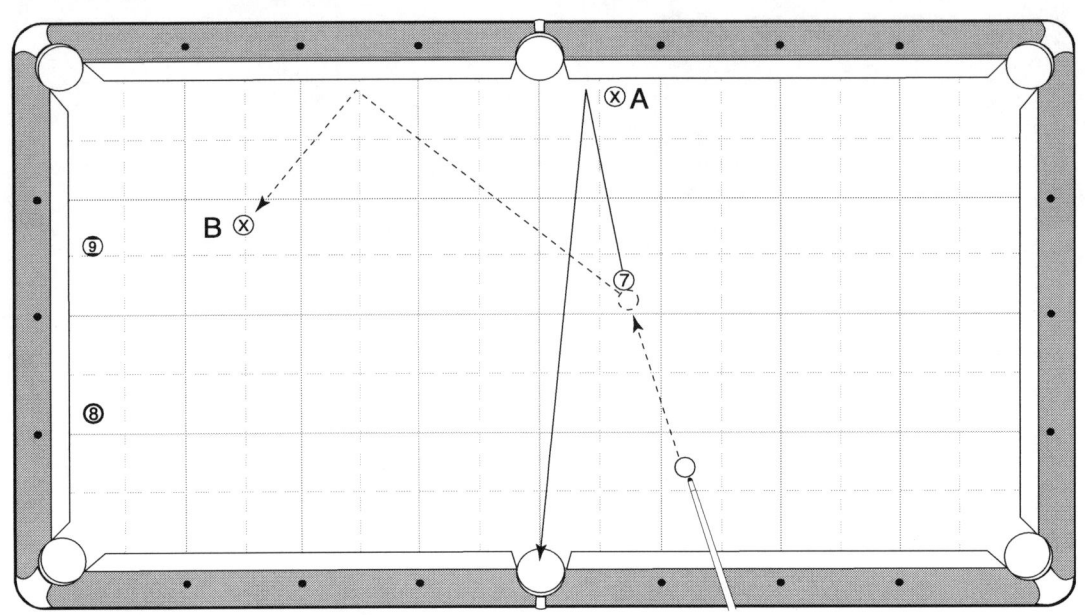

Crossover Side Pocket Bank

You could play a soft follow shot to Position A for shape on the 8-ball. But if you choose this route, you will have to send the cue ball to the opposite end rail and back for position on the 9-ball. A better choice is to play the simple crossover bank in the illustration The cue ball will end up at Position B, which enables you to play shape on the 9-ball with a simple soft follow shot.

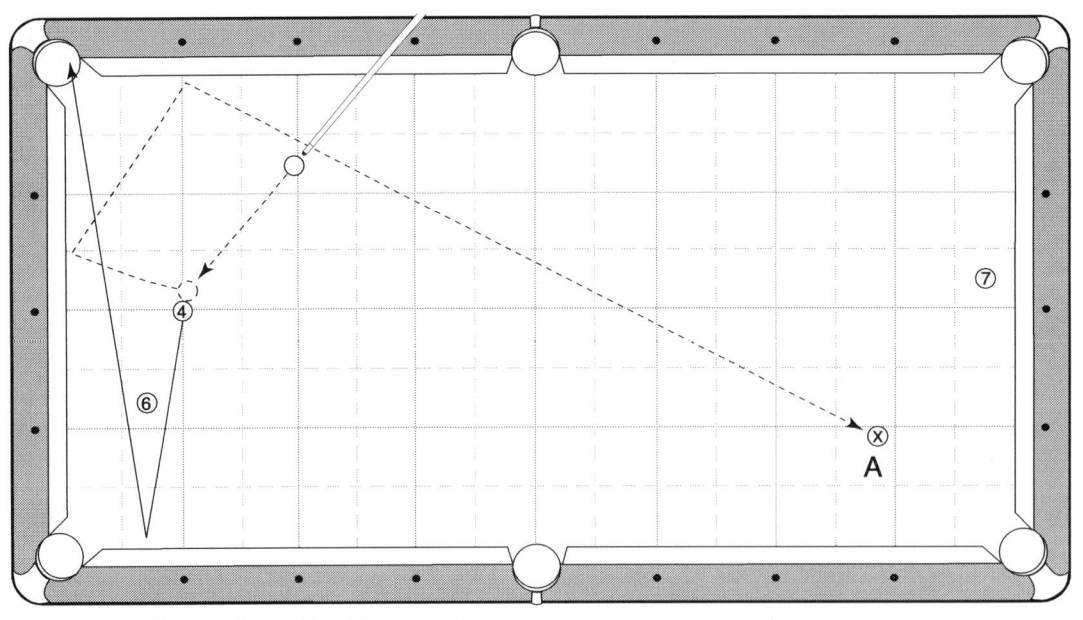

Intentionally Banking for Shape

The 6-ball is blocking the pocket, but you can still make the 4-ball and send the cue ball to the opposite end to Position A for position on the 7-ball by banking the 4-ball cross corner. A bank will increase the cue angle to 30-degrees, adding tremendous speed to the cue ball. Play this shot only when you are feeling confident in your banking and/or you need to build some momentum with a well-calculated risk.

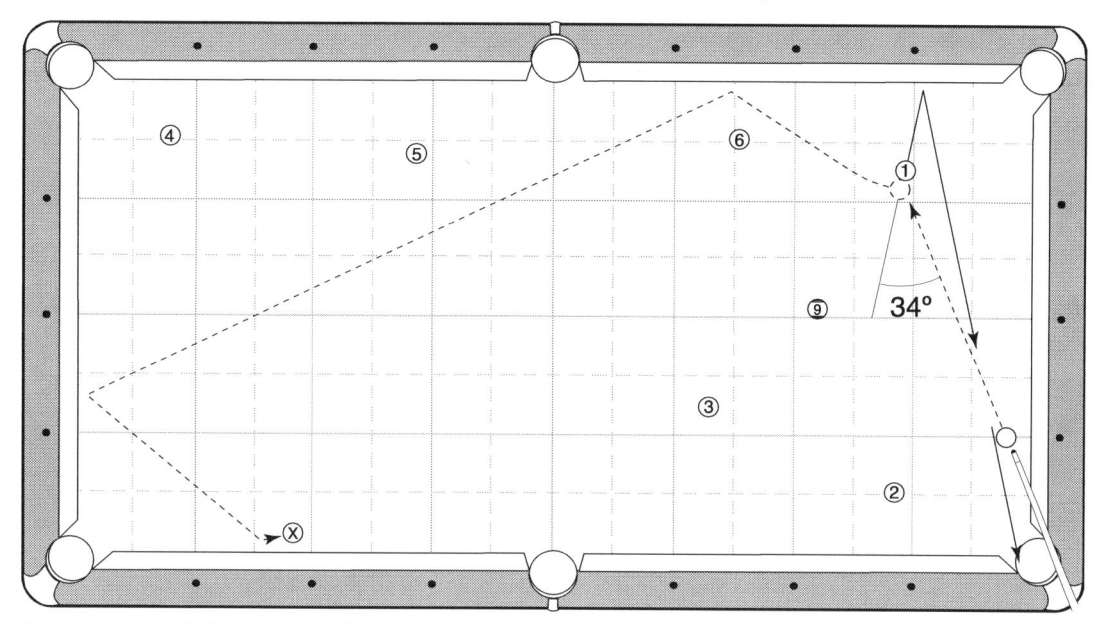

Around the Table Bank Shape

Mike Sigel sent the cue ball three rails for position on the 2-ball after pocketing this difficult cross corner bank shot. The cut angle on the bank was 34 degrees, thin enough that Sigel was able to send the cue ball a long distance with a medium soft stroke. This shot took place at the 1990 U.S. Open against Nick Varner.

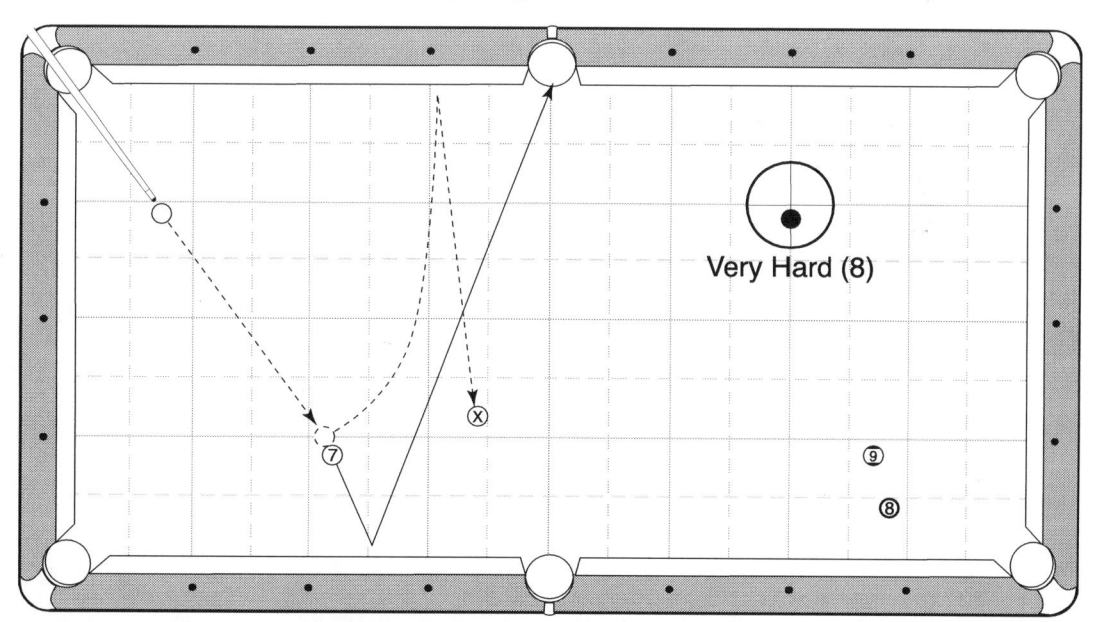

Draw to Rail and Out off of a Cut Bank

Earl Strickland hammered home this cross-side bank on the 7-ball against Takeshi Okumura at the 2000 U.S. Open. He used a very hard draw stroke, which bent the cue ball away from the side pocket and gave it enough steam to bounce back across the table for position on the 8-ball.

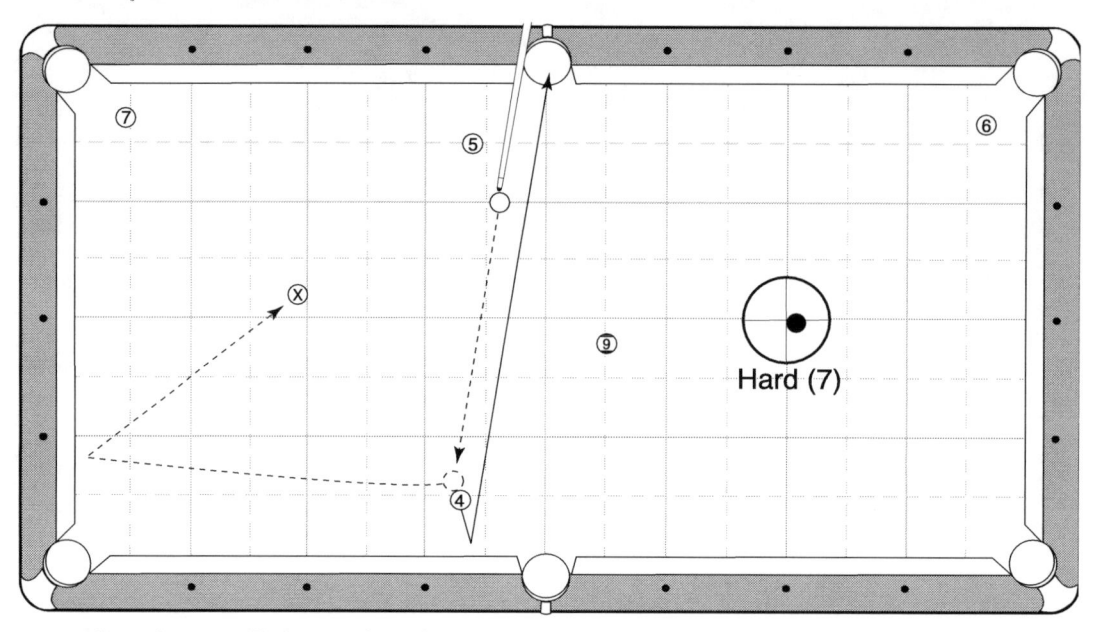

Draw for Shape off the End Rail

Jeremy Jones could have sliced the 4-ball into the near side pocket, but he might have overrun shape on the 5-ball, so he instead chose to bank the 4-ball. This enabled him to end up with an easy shot on the 5-ball. The shot was played with a hard stroke just a hair below center with outside english. The shot is from the finals of the 1999 U.S. Open against Johnny Archer.

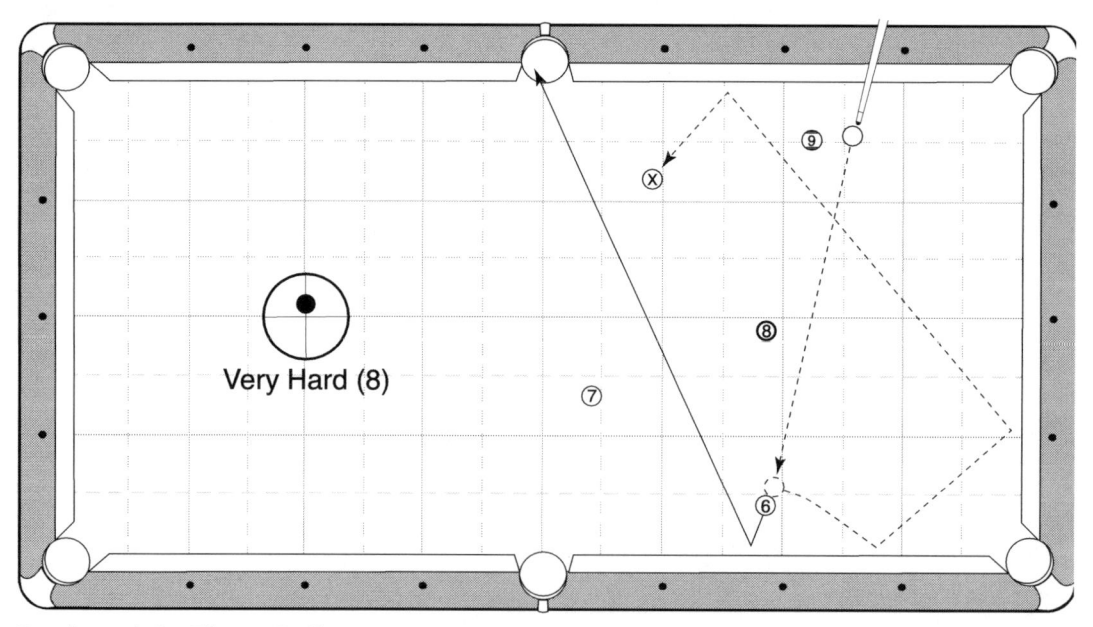

Bank and Go Three Rails

Even though a safety was available, Efren Reyes chose to slam home this cross side bank and to send the cue ball three rails for shape on the 7-ball. Sometimes an aggressive shot like this can loosen you up and build some momentum. This shot was played at the Sands Regency Open 23, 1996, in a match against Johnny Archer.

Position Play Errors
9 Ball is unlike other games which enable you to play position on any of several balls at the same time. **Because you can only play shape on a specific ball, 9 Ball really illuminate your mistakes**. You either get position on the next ball or you don't. Since your mistakes should be obvious to you, it will be no secret which position plays you need to work on.

Why Errors Happen
Poor Execution
You planned the right shot, but executed it poorly. This happens because:
- Your execution skills are deficient.
- You don't know where to hit the cue ball, or the correct speed for that particular shot.

Poor Planning
You select the wrong routes. In this case, your execution could be perfect, but you still end up with a poor result. Worse yet is a failure to take enough time to plan properly for position. Planning errors happen because:
- You do not (yet) know the correct route for the particular shot.
- You know where you want the cue ball, but you don't know the route required to send it there.
- You know where you want the cue ball and the route it must take, but you don't figure out the cueing and speed for the shot.

Poor Planning and Poor Execution
The worst mistake is to combine poor planning with poor execution. Strangely enough, however, you may occasionally plan the wrong shot, execute it poorly, and yet end up with the position you would have gotten with proper planning and execution! But don't count on accidents like this happening too often.

The Corrective Cycle
It is crucial for you to learn from your mistakes in order to play consistent run out 9 Ball. You can correct errors by following these simple steps:
1. **Recognize the mistake**. This is no place for denial or for lack of attention.
2. **Adjust how you play the shot**. Change your cueing and/or routing.
3. **Learn the shot, and commit it to memory**. Practice the shot until you own it.
4. **Play the shot correctly from now on.** Have the confidence to play the shot correctly when it comes up in competition.

Chapter 3 - Position Routes

Specific Error Tendencies
Most players tend to make the same errors on certain shots. These are position plays where it is difficult to compensate sufficiently for an error factor that is built into the shot. One example would be coming up short of the position zone when using inside english to reverse the direction of the cue ball. Players at all levels also have their list of position plays that give them the most trouble. Error tendencies on specific position plays occur because:
- You don't really know the shot or you are unable to execute it consistently, even though you know what you want to do.
- The shot encourages errors by almost players because of the shot's degree of difficulty.
- There is something troublesome about the shot even though it does not appear too difficult.

General Error Tendencies
These are errors that are typically made on a variety of position plays.
Repeatedly overshoot position. This could result from a tendency to stroke excessively hard and/or a tendency to play position on shots with excessively thin cut angles.
Repeatedly come up short of the position zone. This could happen because your angles may be too shallow, or because your stroke lacks authority.

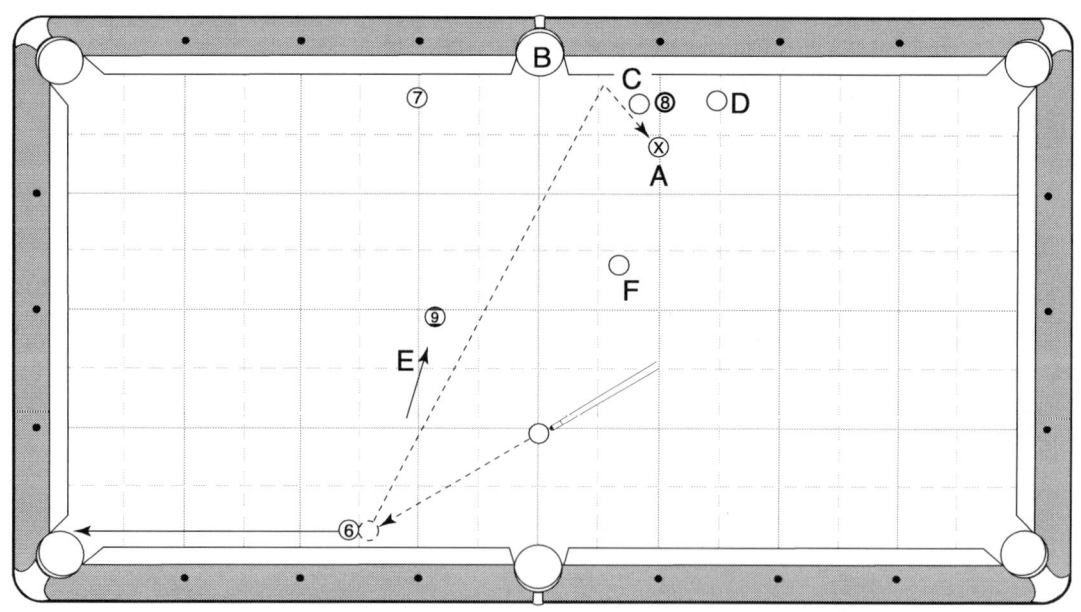

Shots with High Error Potential
Some position plays are simply riskier than others. As a result, you must take into account several things that could go wrong. Consider the one at the top of the next page, which is loaded with danger. Position A shows ideal shape for the 7-ball, but to send the cue ball there you must flirt with a scratch in Side Pocket B. If the cue ball stops near the rail, you could be jacked up over the 8-ball (see Position C).

If you use too much left english, you could get hooked behind the 8-ball at Position D. Another mistake would be to run into the 9-ball at Position E. Finally, the 9-ball could be in your way if you come up short at Position F and have to cross the table and back for the 8-ball.

This example may seem a little extreme, but you will face even more demanding position plays that will require you to take several measures in order to avoid a disaster.

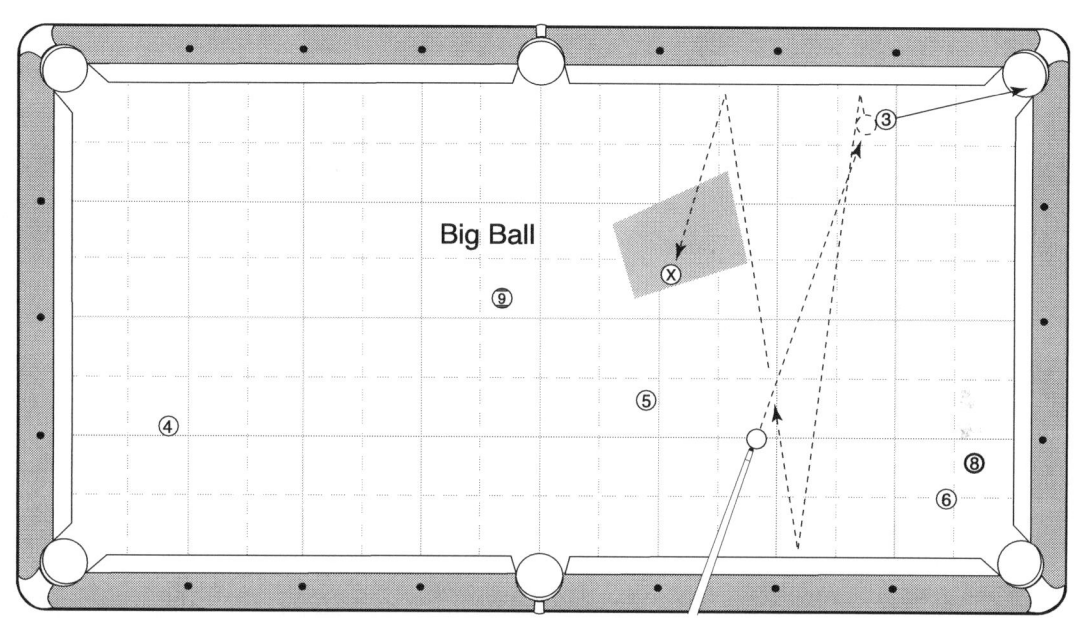

Landing Behind the Big Ball
A solitary ball stationed in the middle of the table can wreak havoc with your position, and speed control is not easy when you are crossing the table over two times. When you combine this with the large 9-ball blocking a 9 inch wide portion of the table, you have the makings of a position play disaster. When you are faced with a situation like this, try to overplay the shot to either side of the potential obstructer.

Other Instances When a Hook Is Likely
- You run into a ball and then get stuck behind it.
- Obstructers near your position zone cause you to play safe on yourself.
- You make a ball in the wrong side of the pocket, which changes the cue ball's path, creating a hook.

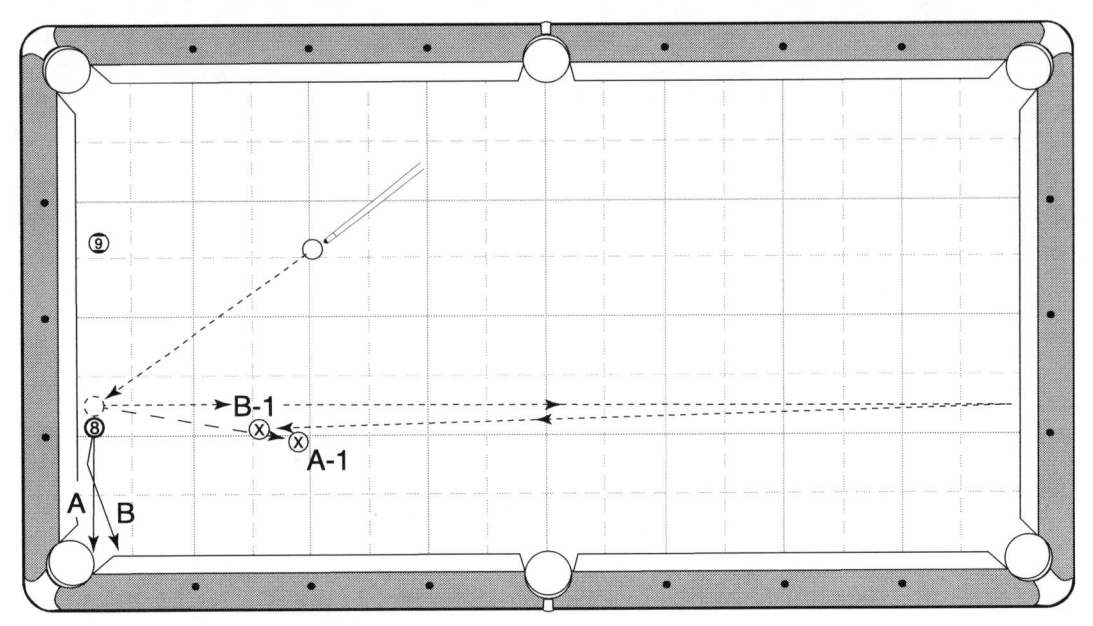

Undercutting for Position

When you have a thin cut and you need to minimize the cue ball's rolling distance after contact with the rail, there is a tendency to undercut the shot. The illustration shows a 50-degree cut angle. If you undercut the shot, the cue ball will stop at Position A-1, giving you great shape for the 9-ball. The trouble is that you will be sitting in your chair!

Often you will hear a player who has missed exclaim, "at least I got my shape." In truth, they may not have gotten anywhere close to the same position if they had made the ball. Pocketing and position are linked together, so don't think that you "at least played shape" when you miss. The correct play is to send the cue ball down Route B to the opposite end rail and back to Position B-1.

Overcutting for Position

The opposite mistake of the one discussed above is to overcut a shot for position. This is done to create additional speed when you have left yourself an overly shallow cut angle.

Hitting Another Ball

The diagram shows two errors, each of which involves running into the next ball. In Part A, the cue ball clipped the 8-ball after bouncing off the side rail, which turned a fairly easy cut shot into a razor thin slice. You can avoid this error by allowing for a sufficiently wide margin for error when passing by the next ball, or by playing the next shot into a different pocket if possible.

The blunder in Part B is far worse because the cue ball is now frozen against the 8-ball. When this happens the balls could be lined up towards a pocket. But 9 times out of 10, you will have to play safe. You can prevent errors like this by having a definite plan for position and playing area shape, which gives you a larger margin for error.

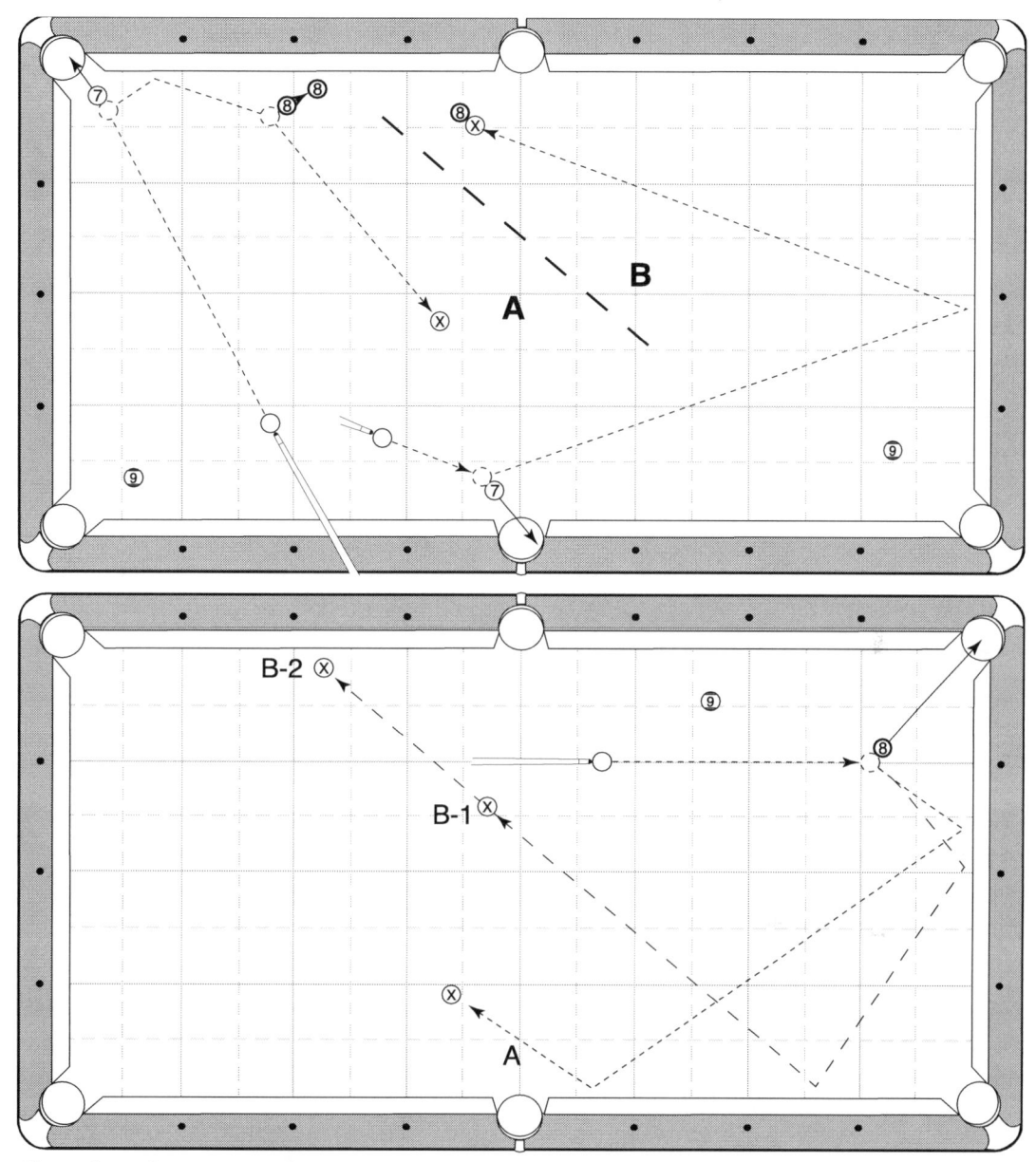

Choosing the Wrong Route
Lack of knowledge or poor execution could be the reason that the cue ball stopped at Position A, which results in a missable cut on the 9-ball. The correct route will take the cue ball to the zone between Positions B-1 and B-2. The player could have intended to send the cue ball down Route B, but failed to apply the necessary draw. A less experienced player might have executed their chosen route correctly, but made the mistake of playing Route A.

Some Other Routing Mistakes
- The cue ball has a tendency to die off the last rail on several multi-rail routes, which can keep it from reaching the position zone.
- When you are playing to the short side you must guard against coming up with an overly steep cut angle.

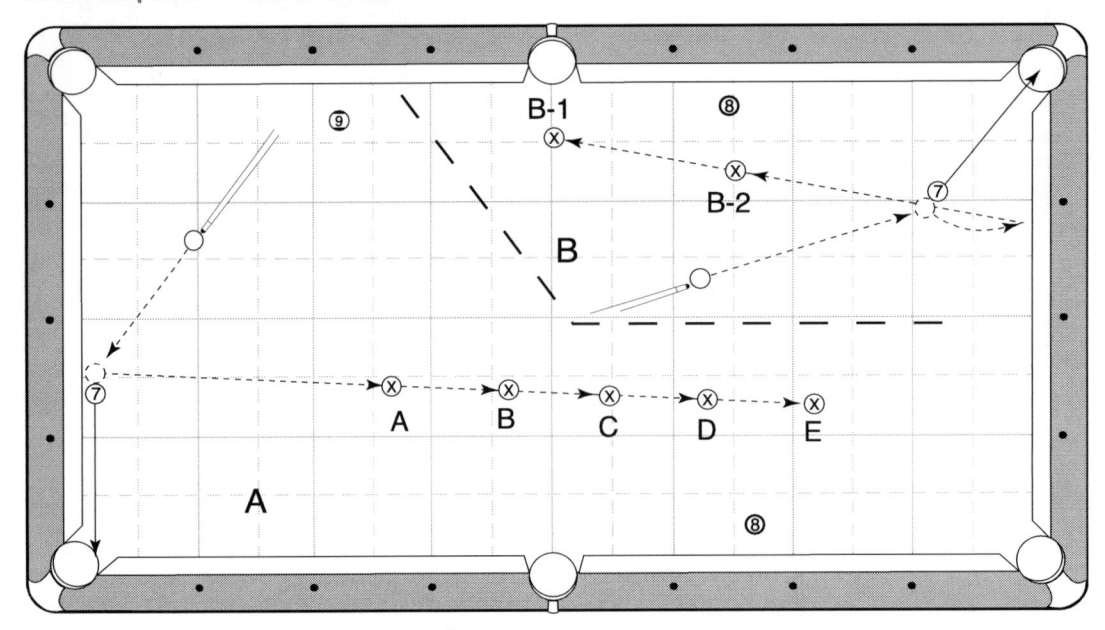

Speed Control

The biggest cause of position play errors is poor speed control. This can be unfortunate when it happens after the player has chosen the correct route and has struck the cue ball in the right location with a straight and authoritative stroke. In Part A good speed control will send the cue ball anywhere between Positions A and C for position on the 8-ball. It is a very common error among amateurs to overrun their shape zone, sending the cue ball to Positions D or E.

In contrast, Part B shows a position play that gives even experienced players trouble on occasion. The cue ball must reverse course with inside english, which creates a tendency to come up short at B-2. The target is Position B-1.

CHAPTER 4

Principles of Position

On two-rail shape: "As soon as you hit the second rail you're in line."
Buddy Hall

My 22 Principles of Position Play, which first appeared in *Play Your Best Pool*, are a must for successful position and pattern play. Position play varies with each game, so I have adapted the principles for this book to the special needs of 9 Ball players.

You may already be using a good number of these principles. When you incorporate the others, you will add a whole new dimension to your play. I advise that you take your time in learning the principles. **Apply one or two principles at a time in practice until they become an automatic part of your planning process**. In time you will learn to quickly evaluate the table, and to use the principles that apply to each shot.

Several principles typically apply to each position play. And the principles are designed to complement one another. However, there are exceptions to the principles – cases where one principle takes precedence over another. In sum, the purpose of the principles is to help you to think like a player when you are planning and executing your patterns and position routes.

#1 Speed Control

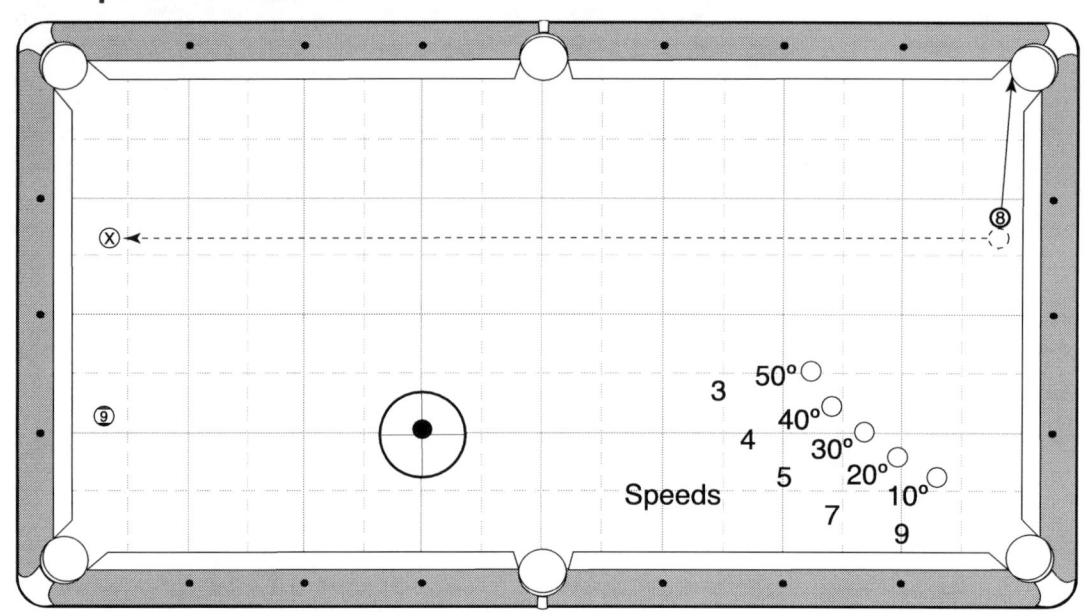

The Importance of Speed Control
The ability to consistently apply the correct speed on your position plays is one of the most critical skills in pool. When you combine proper speed with expert directional control, you have the ingredients for pinpoint position.

9-Ball are played over the entire table, so you will routinely face a wide variety of position plays, from the softest bunt to ultra-hard pound shots. So, you must learn to play shots across the Spectrum of Speeds, a scale that I developed to quantify speed of stroke.

The softest shots are a 1, while the break is a 10. Break shots are hit anywhere from about 14-30+ miles per hour (MPH). Position plays range from a stroke speed of 1.5 MPH for extremely soft shots (1 on the scale) to speeds of 10-12+ MPH for shots played with an extremely hard stroke (9 on the scale). According to my research, **about 4 out of every 5 position plays fall in the 3-6 speed range**. Nevertheless, you must be able to play position at either end of the spectrum in order for your game to be complete.

The Spectrum of Speeds

Speed	MPH	Speed	MPH
1 Extremely Soft	1.0	6 Medium Hard	6.0
2 Very Soft	2.0	7 Hard	7.0
3 Soft	3.0	8 Very Hard	8.0
4 Medium Soft	4.0	9 Extremely Hard	9.0
5 Medium	5.0	10 The Break	10.0

The diagram on the previous page is an example of the Spectrum of Speeds. The play is to send the cue ball straight down the table for position on the 9-ball. Each cut angle corresponds to one of five different speeds of stroke. Start with the 50-degree cut angle and work your way to 10 degrees. Play the shot as close to the vertical axis as possible. Don't worry if you come up short on the shot from 10 degrees as it takes time to develop a stroke powerful enough to cover this distance using an angle this shallow. I advise you to **first learn the basic speeds of stroke including soft (3), medium (5) and medium hard (6)**. Once you've got these mastered, start filling in the gaps.

Importance of Speed Control Varies from Shot to Shot

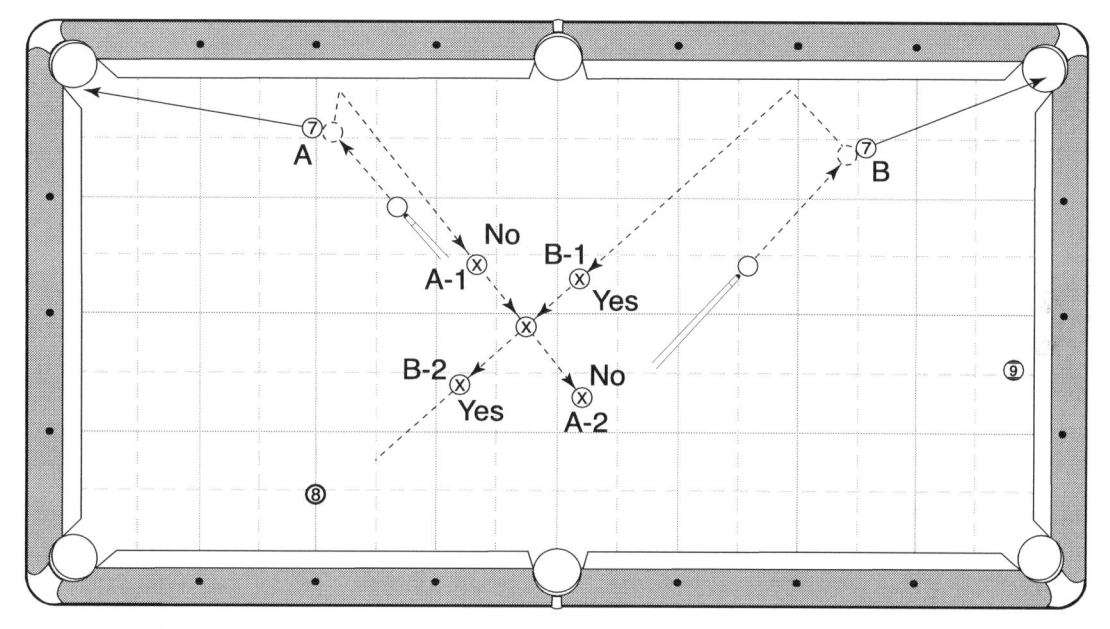

The importance of achieving good speed varies from shot to shot as shown by the two shots on the 7-ball. In each case the goal is to get the correct angle on the 8-ball. In Position A, speed is the critical element to the shot. If the cue ball comes up short at A-1, or long at A-2, it will be much tougher to get from the 8-ball to the 9-ball. When the 7-ball is in Position B, speed control is not nearly as important. Positon anywhere from B-1 to B-2 is ideal for sending the cue ball across and down the table for the 9-ball.

Speed Control versus Pocketing the Shot

Perfect speed is of great value in playing position, but do not obsess on speed control to the point where you sacrifice accuracy for the sake of position. **On soft shots, be careful to use the minimum speed needed to get the object ball to the pocket**. A little extra force can eliminate roll offs and ensure stroking accuracy, especially when the object ball is more than a foot from the pocket. On firmly stroked shots, balance positional requirements with the need to pocket the ball.

#2 The Correct Cut Angle Optimizes Position

Angles are critical to position play in 9 Ball because of the distances you must send the cue ball. The correct angle will give you the high percentage position route, and it will enable you to use the speed that maximizes the accuracy of the shot. In sum, leaving yourself with a workable cut angle is one the most important requirements for consistently running out in 9 Ball. You also want to position the cue ball a comfortable distance from the object ball whenever possible. Remember: **great position is about angles and distance**.

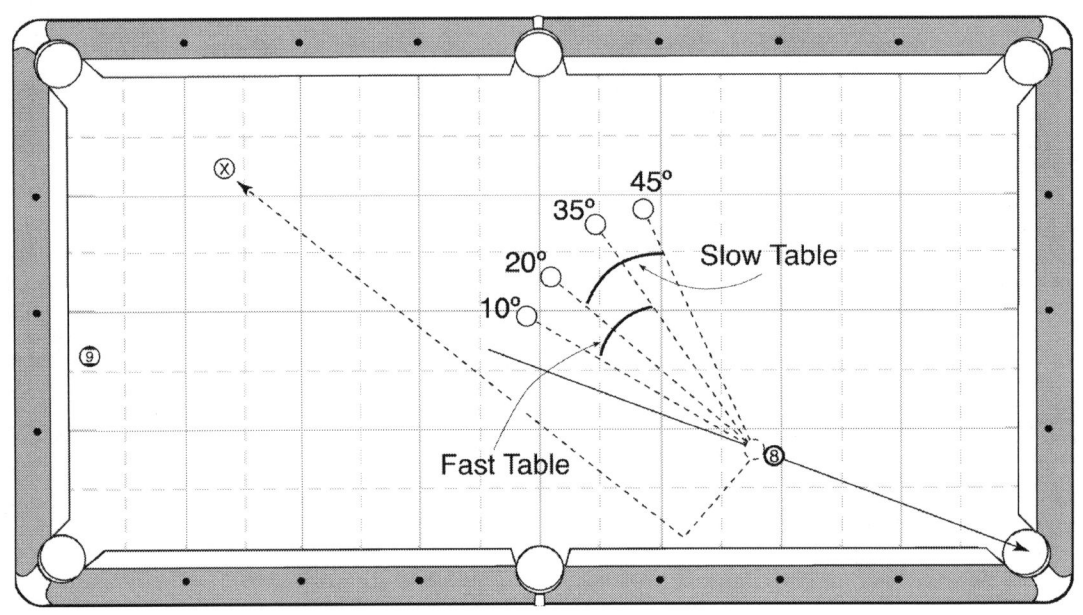

Table Speed and Preferences Affect Cut Angles

You can accomplish the same objective in more than one way on most position plays. The correct choice depends on your style of play, and on the conditions. The diagram shows several possible cut angles for a typical position play. The cue ball is going off the side rail and down table for the 9-ball to Position X.

- If you prefer to use a hard stroke, play for a shallow cut angle (20 degrees in this position).
- If you like to use an easy stroke, play for steeper angles (35 degrees in this position).
- If you like to use running english (right in this example), you'll need less angle on some shots.
- If you prefer to cue on the vertical center axis, you'll need a slightly greater angle.

Your Ideal Angles are also determined by your preference for cueing on the vertical axis, or for using english. Here are some guidelines:

- Small angles go with a hard stroke and running english
- Medium angles go with a softer stroke and running english
- Medium angles go with a harder stroke and no english
- Large angles go with a soft stroke and no english

The conditions will have an influence on the ideal angle.
- On a fast table, play for smaller cut angles.
- On a slow table leave yourself larger cut angles.
- Lively rails require less of a cut angle, while spongy rails require a larger cut angle than normal.

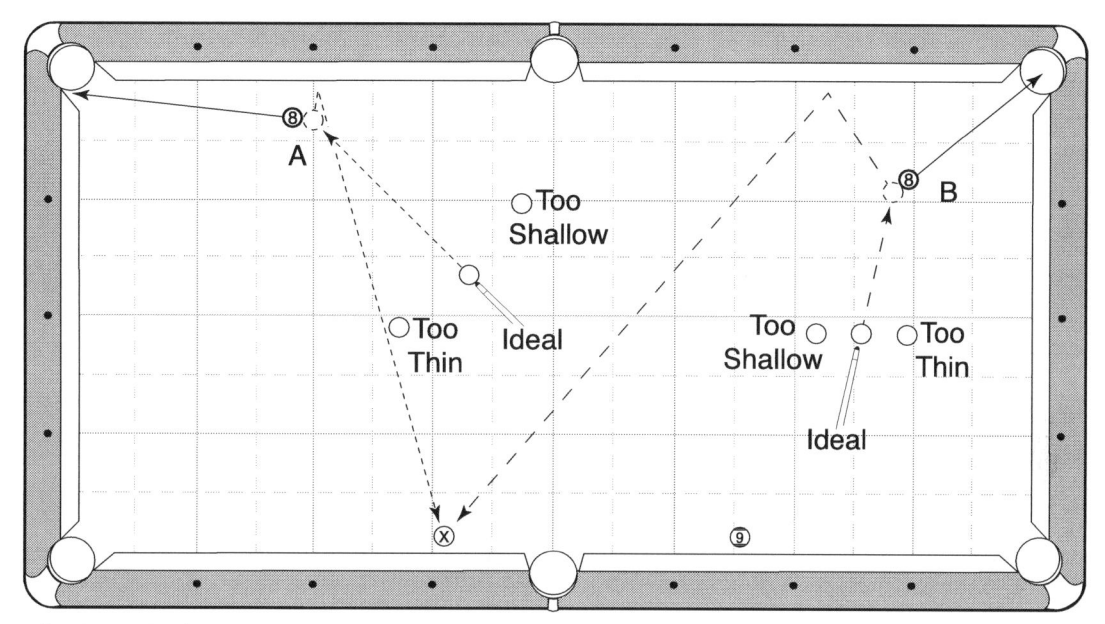

Ideal Angle for Speed Control
The correct cut angle enables you to play the shot at the speed that maximizes your chances of pocketing the ball. The correct angle also makes it easier to send the cue ball within inches of the bull's eye for shape. In Parts A and B the objective is to send the cue ball across table for position on the 9-ball. The ideal angle creates the ideal speed without compromising the accuracy of the shot.

In Part A, pocketing and speed will be much more difficult if the cue ball is not at the ideal angle. In Part B, pocketing the 8-ball is not a problem, but speed control will not be as easy without the cue ball in the ideal position.

Low Risk and High Risk Cut Angles
Low-risk angles fall between the extremes of those that are either too sharp or too shallow. The best angles enable you to use a speed of stroke with which you are comfortable, and allow you to easily send the cue ball to the position zone.

High-risk angles require you to use an extra firm stroke when the cut angle is shallow. You will be forced to use an exceptionally soft stroke when the angle is too sharp, or to send the cue ball across and/or around the table.

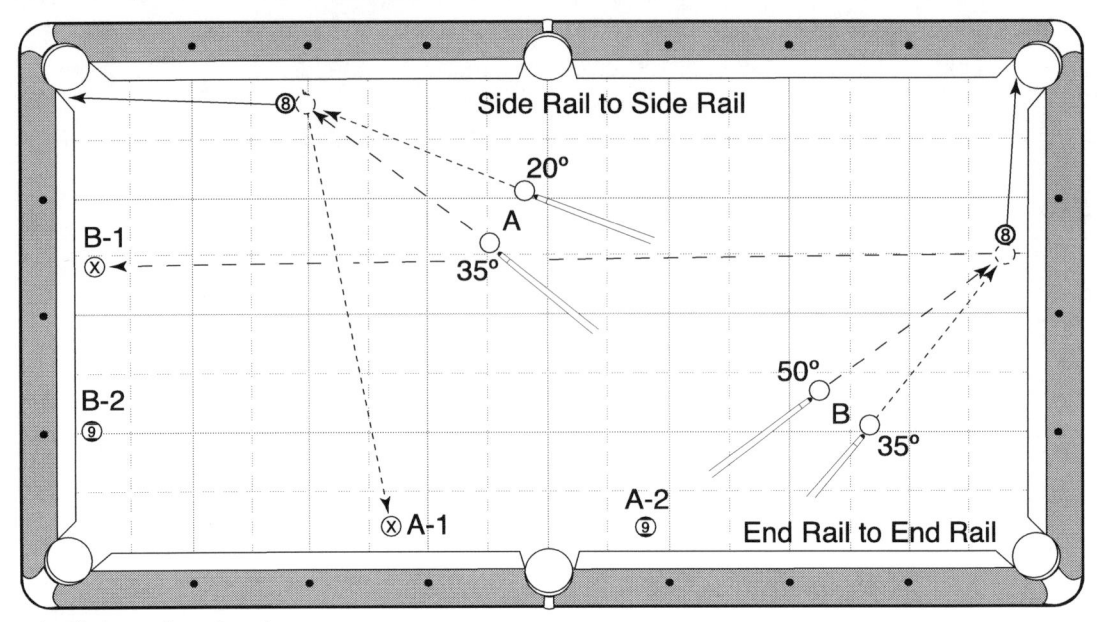

Ideal Crossing Angles
There is an ideal range of cut angles for each position play. The diagram shows two of the most common routes. When the cue ball is in Position A, a 20-35 degree angle is ideal for sending the cue ball across the table to A-1 for the 9-ball, which is at A-2. A 35-50 degree cut angle is optimal for sending the cue ball from Position B to B-1 for shape on the 9-ball at B-2.

#3 Know the Boundaries of a Position Zone
Speed and Direction Create the Zone
Part A in the diagram at the top of the next page shows how the boundaries (and size) of a position zone are created. **Direction establishes the width of the zone while speed is responsible for its length.** Amateurs have wider margins for error than the pros, which explains why their position zones are larger. Part B shows a soft follow shot where speed is the primary ingredient in establishing the zone. The cue ball's path is very predictable on this type of route, so the zone is quite narrow.

Your boundaries for a position zone are based on the requirements for the shot. You also need to factor in your level of skill when setting your boundaries, or target zone.

The maximum size of a position zone is one that enables you to make the second ball and proceed to the third ball. I recommend that you **play for zones that you can hit with an average to above average shot**. In addition, always be striving to upgrade position play no matter what your level of skill. Your goal is to consistently send the cue ball to zones that enable you to continue your run, and it will help you meet that goal if you can hit targets that are more precise.

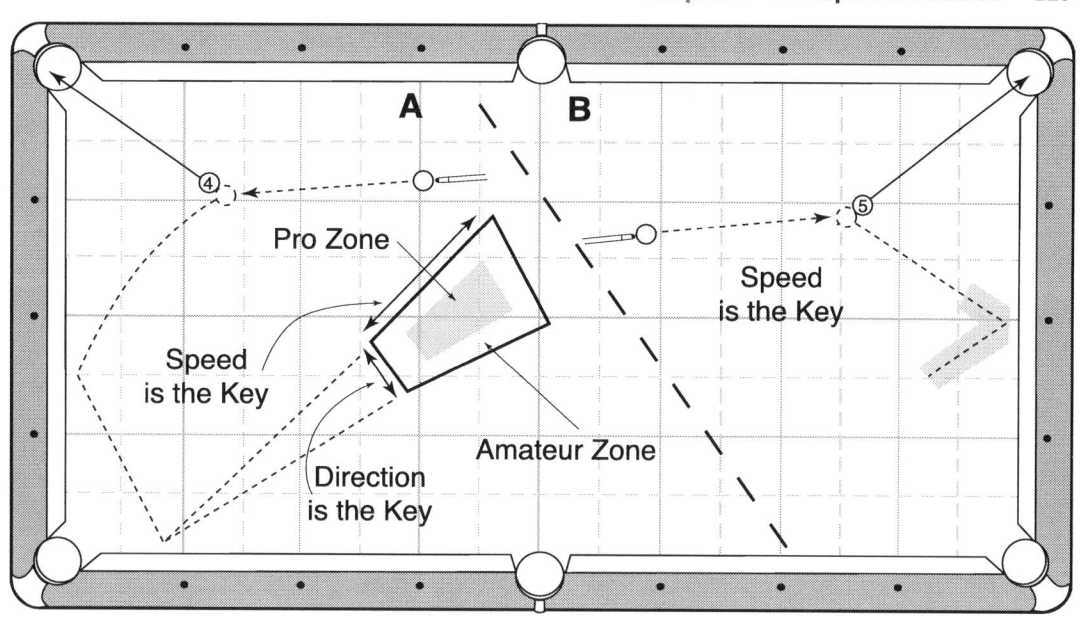

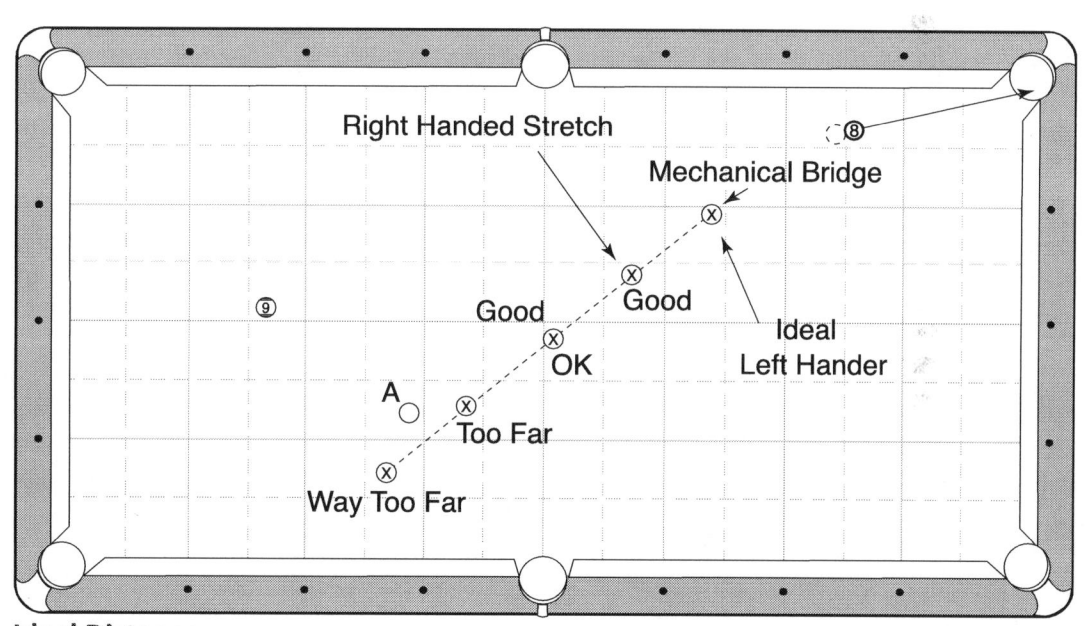

Ideal Distance

You need a well-developed sense of distance when playing position in 9 Ball. The diagram above shows position on the 8-ball for cross table shape on the 9-ball to Position A. A right-handed player has a much more limited zone for playing this shot than a left-hander. When planning shape:

- Take into account the stretch factor. Often you must purposefully play for longer shots.
- Consider the distance you feel comfortable shooting from before your accuracy begins to drop off significantly.
- Calculate the minimum distance you want the cue ball from the object ball.

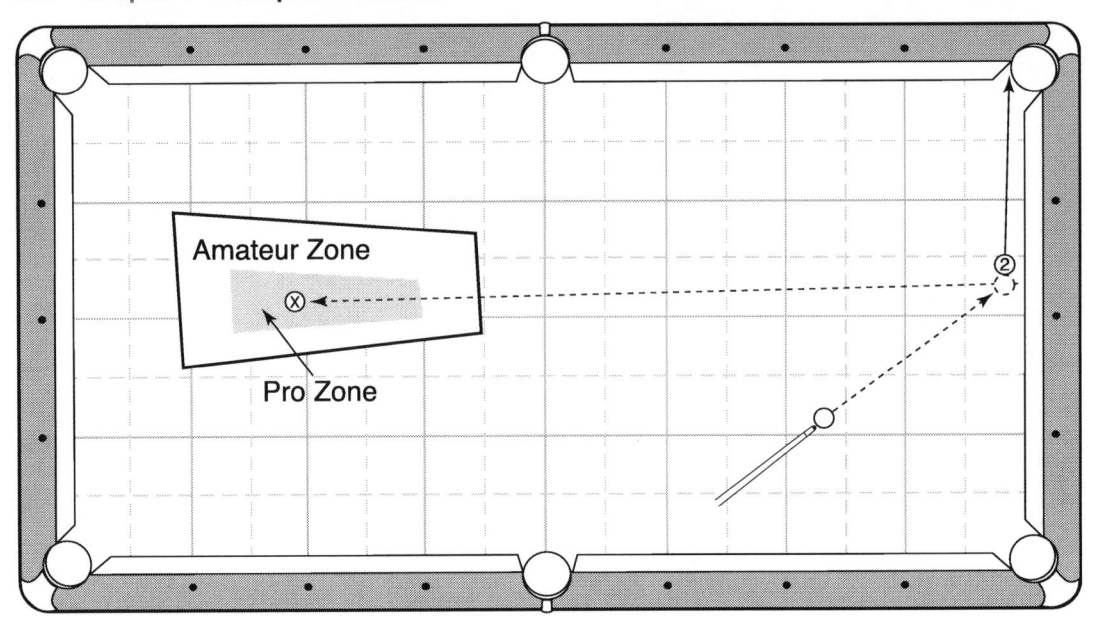

Long and Narrow Zones
The width and length of a position zone depend on the difficulty of controlling speed and direction. When it is easy to control the direction of the cue ball, the zone will be narrow. When speed is easy to control, the length of the zone will be short. When the object ball is close to the rail, then direction is easy, and speed becomes the critical element of the shot. In this case, the position zone is long and narrow.

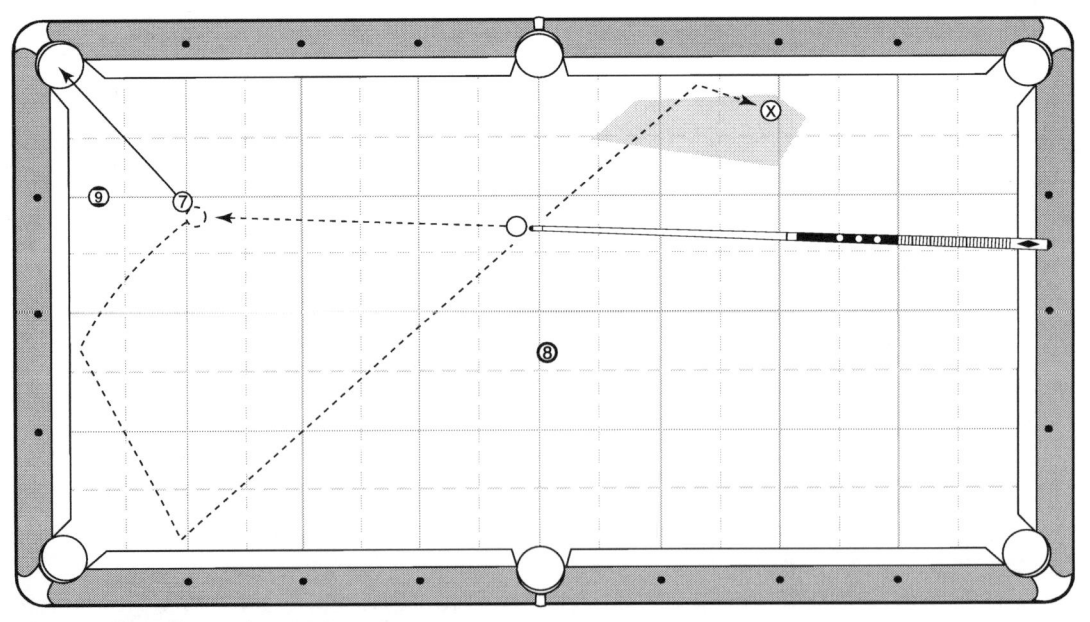

Unusually Shaped Position Zones
Position zones have mistakenly been identified as circles, squares, rectangles, and triangles when, in fact, they come in a variety of shapes. The shape depends on the layout. The diagram shows an unusually shaped zone for playing position on the 8-ball. Notice that the zone does not include the area next to the rail!

#4 Margin for Error

If your cue ball control was perfect, you wouldn't need to plan for a margin for error. But we all make mistakes, so **factoring a margin for error into your routes gives you insurance against disaster**. This policy will protect you from scratching, getting hooked, or otherwise missing shape. The "premium" for this insurance is a slightly more difficult shot than the one you would have with perfect position. The size of your margin for error depends on:

- The dangers surrounding the shot.
- Your skill as a position player.
- Your skill as a shotmaker.

If you are a skillful shotmaker, you can play further away from danger because a slightly tougher shot is no problem. If you have great cue ball control, then you can build a smaller margin for error into your position plays.

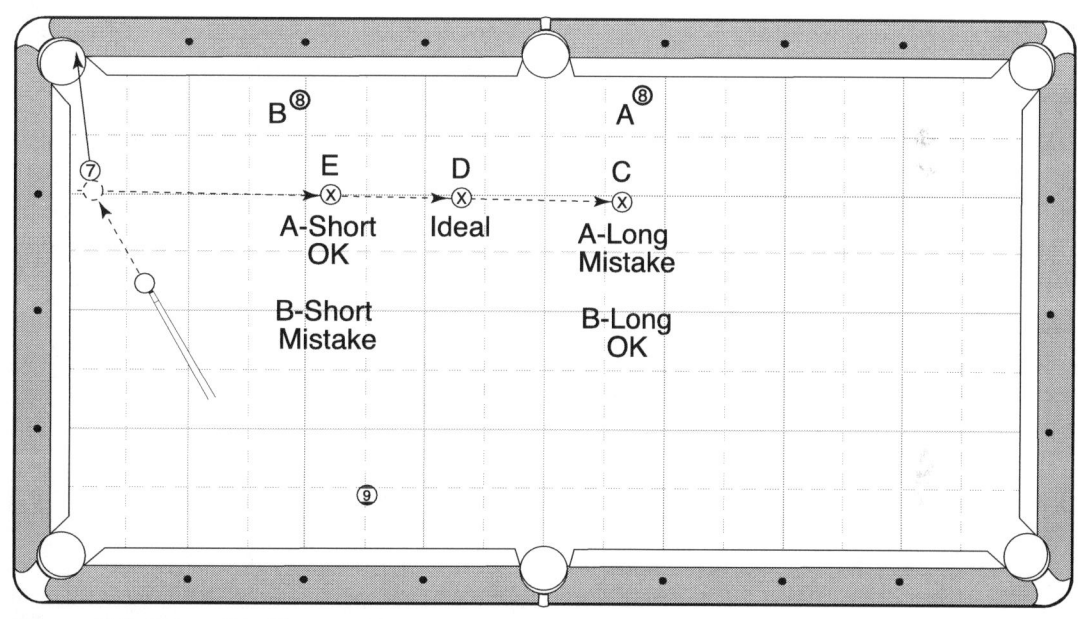

Know When to Go Short or Long

This three ball run out is not difficult as long as you play it with care and build a safety net for your position on the 8-ball. With the 8-ball in Position A, the big mistake is to send the cue ball to Position C, well past ideal shape at Position D. Now you would have to bank the 8-ball. The smart play is to allow for a larger margin for error by targeting Position E. If you hit the shot a little too hard, you could wind up with perfect shape at Position D!

Now let's assume the 8-ball is in Position B. In this case, the smart play is to go long to Position C. If you hit the shot too easy, you could end up with perfect shape at Position D! The pros call this strategy dog-proofing the layout.

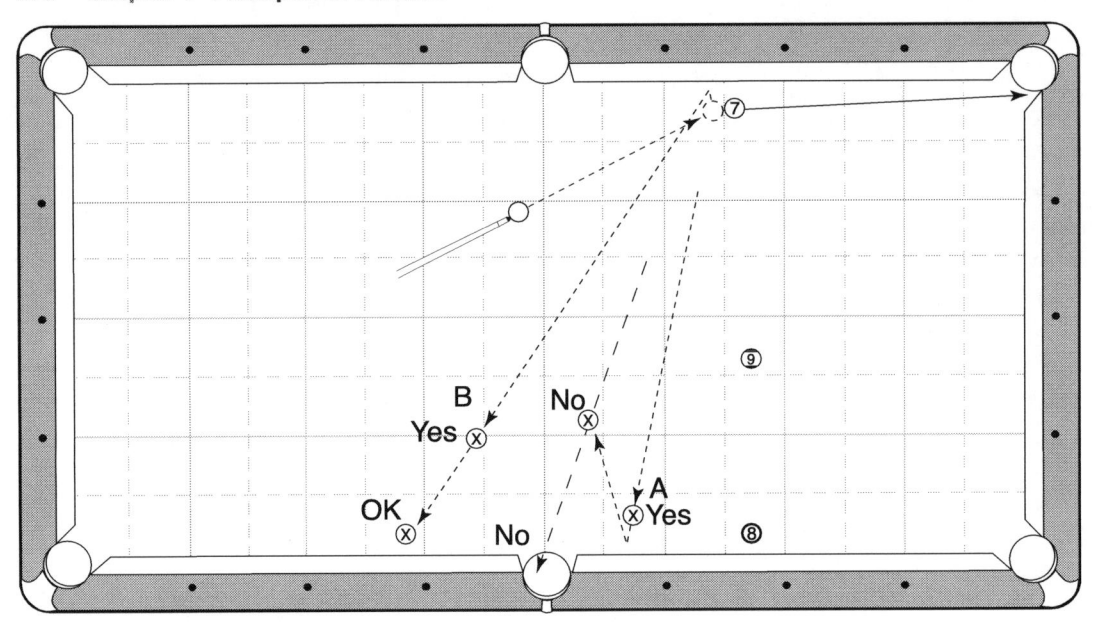

Allowing for a Margin for Error
Using a margin for error eliminated the chance of a scratch in the side pocket on the position play from the 7-ball to the 8. Those with superb cue ball control may play for a closer shot on the 8-ball down Route A, but this requires expert speed and directional control. Route B is better for most players because it gives you a larger margin for error. The price for the safer route to the 8-ball is a shot from Position B that is roughly 18 inches longer than the one from Position A.

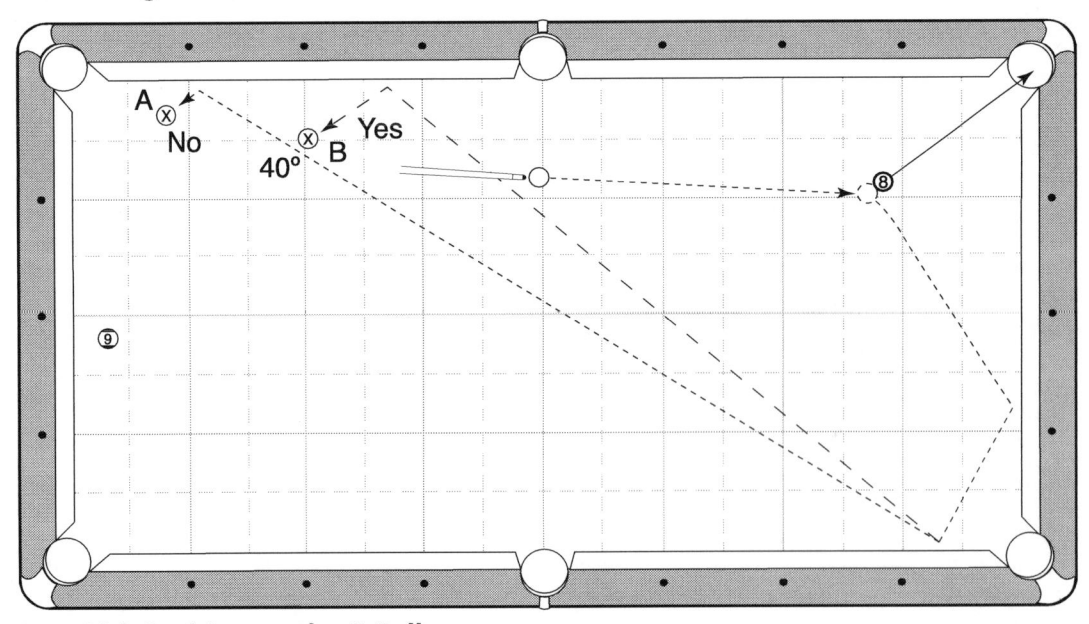

Low Risk Position on the 9-Ball
The big risk on this three-rail position route is a scratch in the upper left corner pocket. You could play for a nearly straight in shot on the 9-ball from Position A, but getting this close to the money ball is not worth the risk. The percentage play is to send the cue ball higher up on the third rail and to accept a modest 40-degree cut shot on the 9-ball at Position B.

#5 When to Play Area Shape
When your position zone is a big one and you only need adequate position for the next ball, aim for the center of the zone. This gives you the largest margin for error and it guarantees that you will complete the next sequence of shots. Area shape eliminates any risk of not having a shot, or of having to play a difficult recovery route.

When Conditions Favor Area Shape
- The next ball is close to a pocket.
- There are very few balls on the table.
- Trying to get close to the next ball could result in disaster.

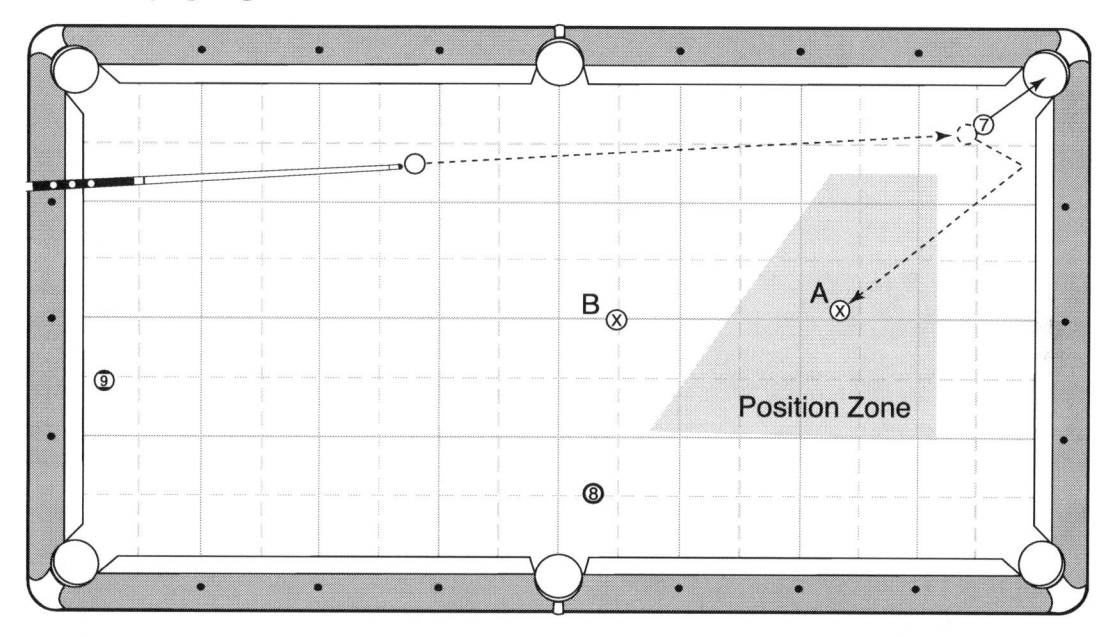

When the object ball is close to the pocket and the cue ball is a long distance from it, then pinpoint position is not easy. In the example, the low risk move is to play for area shape on the 8-ball. Just make sure that the cue ball lands anywhere within that huge position zone. It will be easy to play shape on the 9-ball from Position A. If you get greedy or careless with your position and the cue ball rolls to Position B, you will be faced with a difficult 4-rail route to the short side of the 9-ball.

Going with the Flow
When your game is "on" you can play for larger position zones than normal providing they don't endanger the shot. The idea is to let your shotmaking carry a larger part of the burden. However, you must not get sloppy with your position and let the cue ball venture outside of the limits of a larger zone. When your game is in top gear, you may happily discover that your position play is on target with no special effort on your part.

#6 Survey the Table Before Shooting

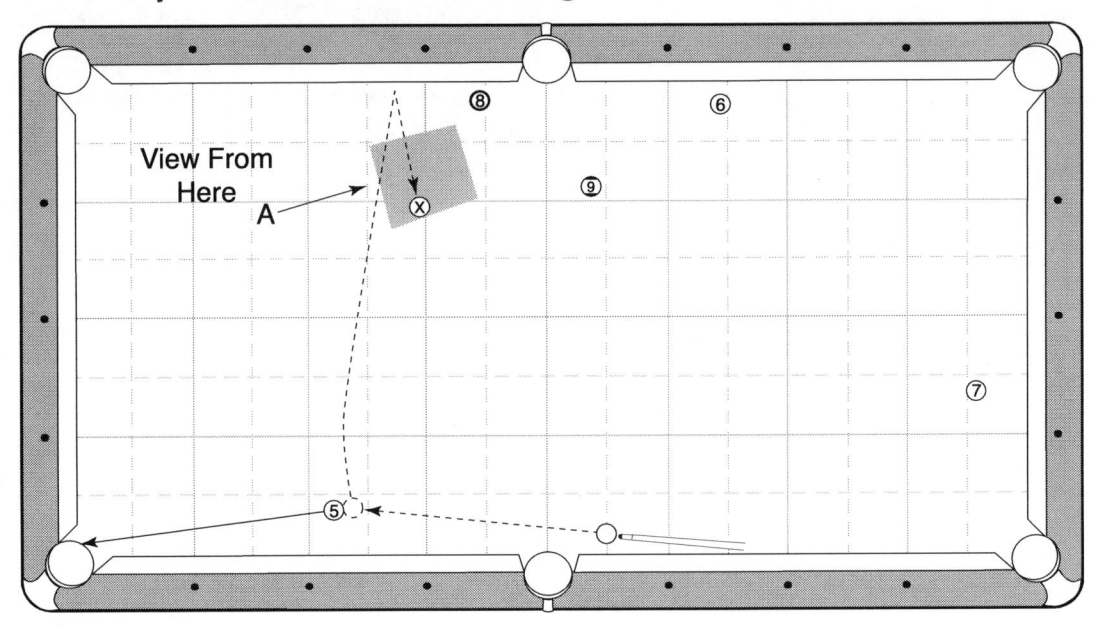

Sometimes you can acquire the information you need to plan a shot by just looking around the table from where you will be taking your stance. If so, you can complete your planning from that position. But **don't commit a blunder just because you were too lazy to walk to another vantage point or two**.

The best view is from straight above the table, but since that area is inaccessible, the next best thing is to view your shots from those positions that will give you all of the information you need to plan the shot as well as you can. Below is a list of things to look for during your survey:

- When the next ball is close to other balls, you discover if it will go into the pocket.
- You find unseen dangers, such as a scratch off of another ball.
- You confirm that the shot you are considering is the best one, or that it only needs a small modification.
- You identify the rail targets more precisely for your position route. (See principle #16).
- You size up the dimensions of your position zone and the plan for the ideal angle for the next shot.
- You reduce the chance of a miss by getting the answers to all other possible questions prior to playing the shot.

Before playing the 5-ball, walk over to Position A and get a good look at the position zone for the 6-ball. This will tell you exactly where you need to send the cue ball. This is much smarter than playing the 5-ball first and then walking over to your shot on the 6-ball, only to discover you are hooked! **Remember this sequence: survey, plan, execute.**

#7 Playing for Three Balls (or more) at a Time

Playing for three balls at a time is the heart and soul of pattern play in 9 Ball. Once you master this concept, your ability to run racks will take a quantum leap forward. The key is to **carefully plan your shape on the second ball because the shape you play on it must enable you to continue to the third ball**. The process rolls forward until you arrive at the last two balls. The process of playing for three balls at a time must become ingrained in your mental computer until you can execute it easily and effortlessly.

Before shooting the first ball determine:
- What options are available for playing position on the second ball?
- What route among those possible choices for the second ball will enable you to then play position on the third ball?
- After you shoot the first ball, the process repeats itself.

A soft follow shot on the 5-ball will send the cue ball to Position A for the 6-ball. This cut angle on the 6-ball makes it easy to escape the end rail and send the cue ball up table for the 7-ball. If the player had only planned for the 6-ball, the cue ball might have stopped at Position B, leaving him with a straight in shot, and likely ending his attempt to run out. Again, when playing the 5-ball, the idea was to plan for getting position on the 7-ball!

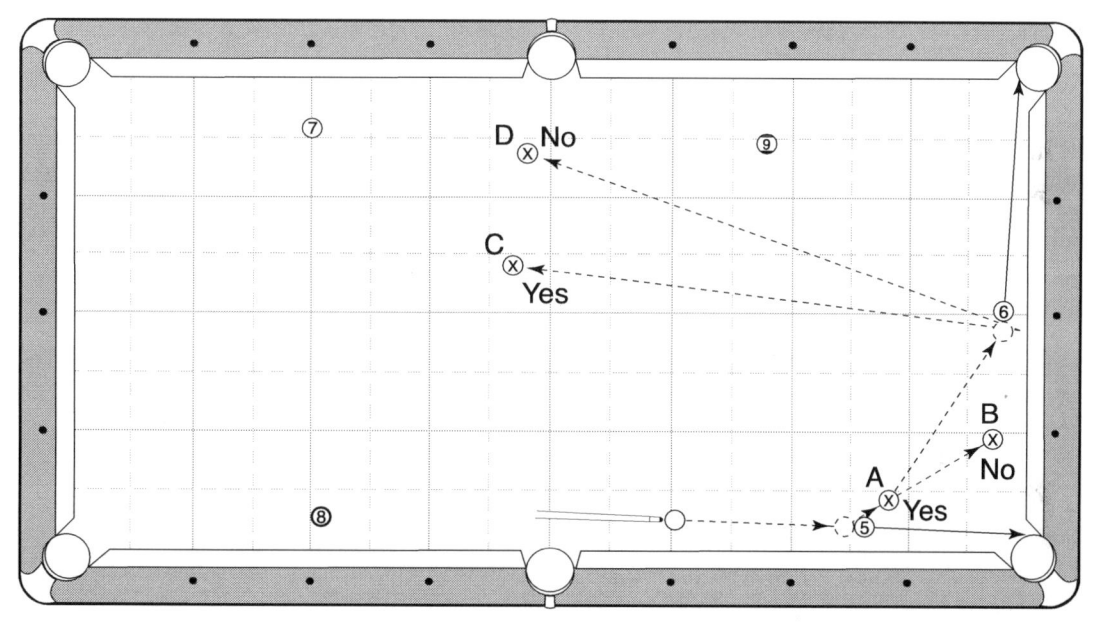

Now the process rolls forward. When playing the 6-ball, you must determine how to get from the 7-ball to the 8-ball. The example shows both the correct and incorrect positions. Question: Why is Position C preferable to Position D?

#8 Play the High Percentage Sequence

Playing the high percentage sequence is about balancing your shots. When you apply this principle correctly, you optimize your chances of completing any given sequence of shots. The following table is for purposes of illustration. It breaks down three broad sequences into cold, hard percentages. Under the ideal sequence you would face two high percentage shots in a row (90 percent and 80 percent). The worst sequence in our example is to play a simple shot (100 percent) followed by a very difficult shot (50 percent) because your overall odds of running out drop from 72 percent to 50 percent.

Sequence Rating	#1 Shot Difficulty(%)	#2 Shot Difficulty(%)	Cumulative Percentage
Ideal	90%	80%	72%
Fair	95%	70%	67%
Poor	100%	50%	50%

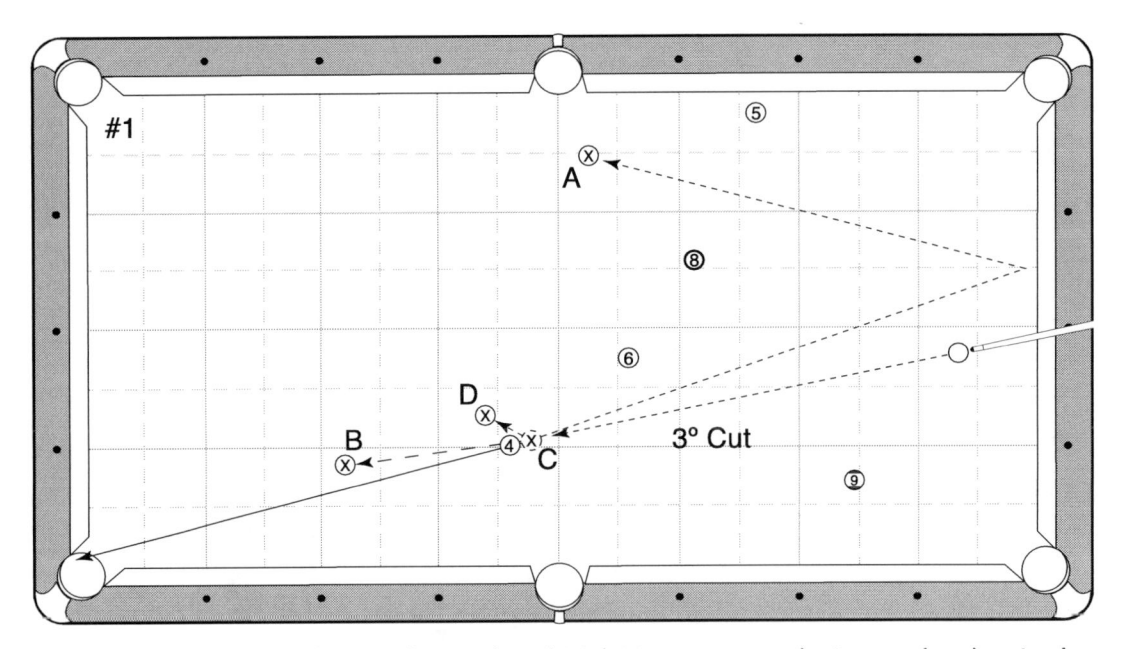

BCA Hall of Fame members Mike Sigel and Nick Varner were playing each other in the 1990 U.S. Open when Sigel left himself with the challenging position play in Diagram #1. Sigel considered drawing to the end rail and back out as shown. Accu-Stats commentator Buddy Hall, however, insisted that Sigel would avoid shooting a power draw shot even though it could have left Sigel with an easy 10-15 degree cut on the 5-ball at Position A. Furthermore, completing the run from Position A would have been a cinch. But Sigel would have had to shoot that long and difficult draw shot to make the next shot extremely simple, a decision that would have violated the principle of playing the high percentage sequence.

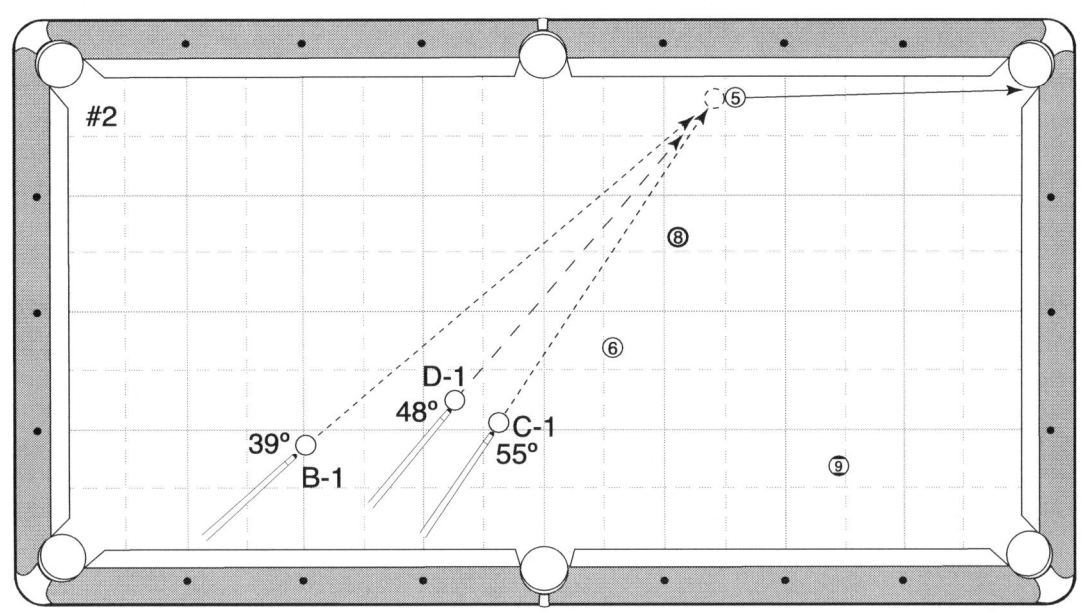

Another possibility was to roll forward 1.5 diamonds to Position B. This would have left a longer 39-degree cut shot on the 5-ball. This option, however, increased the chances of missing the 4-ball because it is difficult to slow roll the cue ball with great accuracy over long distances.

If Sigel played a medium speed stop shot, which would give him the highest probability of pocketing the 4-ball, the cue ball would have come to rest at Position C,. It also would have left him with a 55- degree cut on the 5-ball. Instead, Sigel chose to lower the odds slightly of making the 4-ball by pounding it with an extremely hard stroke. The cue ball crawled a few precious inches forward and to the right to Position D. The pound shot raised his odds of pocketing the 5-ball by reducing the cut angle to 48-degrees.

In sum, Sigel had four viable options for playing this two ball sequence. After much deliberation he chose the one that gave him the best chance of completing his runout.

Diagram #2 shows the shots that correspond to three of Sigel's options. Position C-1 resulted from the stop shot while Position B-1 came after the soft follow shot. Position D-1 shows the location for Sigel's actual shot on the 5-ball.

At the pro level, balancing a sequence of shots is a matter of shifting the odds of success a few percentage points in either direction. I will guess that Sigel lowered his pocketing percentage 2% with the pound shot so that he could raise his odds of making the cut shot by 5%. For a B player, the percentages on this shot may have been a loss of 10% on the pound shot, which would be more than offset by a gain of 15% on the cut shot. A C Player might be better off playing the stop shot and accepting the thinner cut.

Pros are very sophisticated in the way they balance shots. They are experts at adding and subtracting a few percentage points for shots in a given sequence. They know that those percentage points add up over time. So, when choosing the first shot of a sequence, keep in mind that **your goal is to select the shot that gives you the maximum probability of successfully completing the entire sequence**.

Chapter 4 - Principles of Position

#9 Correct Side/Wrong Side

A master key to position play is the principle of correct side/wrong side. On every shot, a line runs from the pocket through the object ball and out the other side. You can, obviously, have a straight in shot, in which case the cue ball is right on the line. On most shots, however, the cue ball is on one side or the other of this straight in line.

Positioning the cue ball on the correct side of the straight in line can make playing shape on the next ball a far more easy and natural process. When the cue ball is on the wrong side, position on the next ball becomes more difficult, if not impossible. You can incorporate this concept into your game by programming yourself to choose the better side of the straight in line for most position plays.

When the object ball is within an inch or so of the rail, there is essentially only one side of the ball on which the cue ball can be positioned. Furthermore, as a rule of thumb, you'll almost always want to be shooting towards the rail when the object ball is within about 6 inches of the rail. There are exceptions, of course, to these rules.

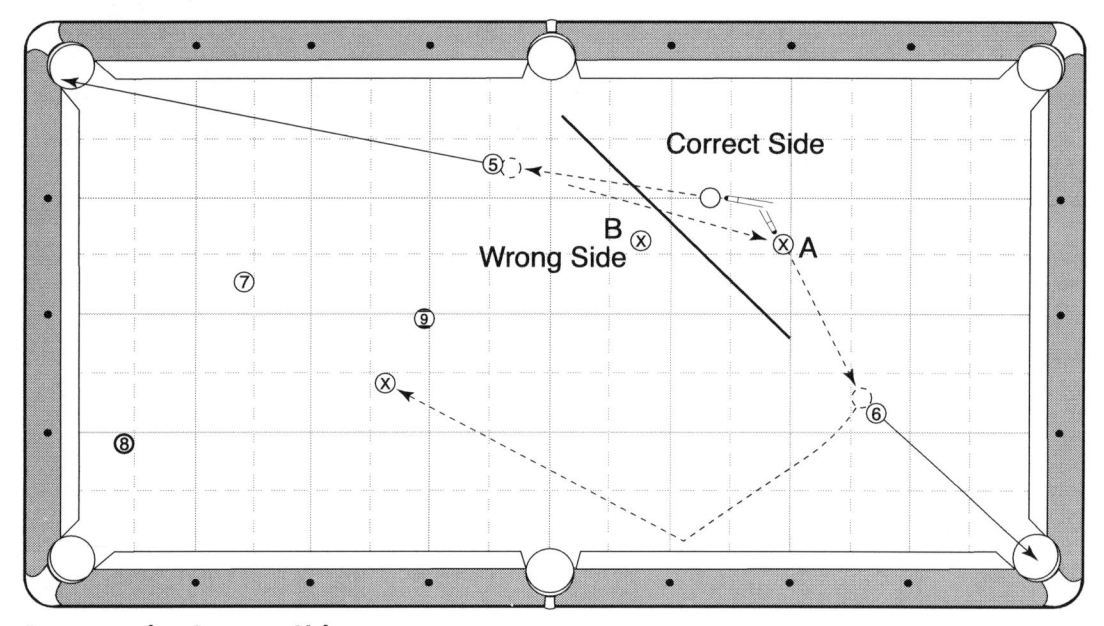

Draw to the Correct Side

Our first example shows a typical draw shot in which the cue ball is going to come nearly straight back down the table after pocketing the 5-ball. The heavy line is an extension of the line that goes directly from the 6-ball to the pocket. It is better, when playing the 5-ball, to draw back to Position A, which is on the correct side of the straight in line. This sets you up for a relatively easy positon play off the side rail and up the table for shape on the 7-ball as shown.

Position B shows the wrong side of the heavy solid line. If the cue ball stops in this position, you would have to use a hard follow stroke with a little inside english, which would greatly increase your chances of missing the 6-ball. In addition, it would have been much tougher to get the correct angle on the 7-ball.

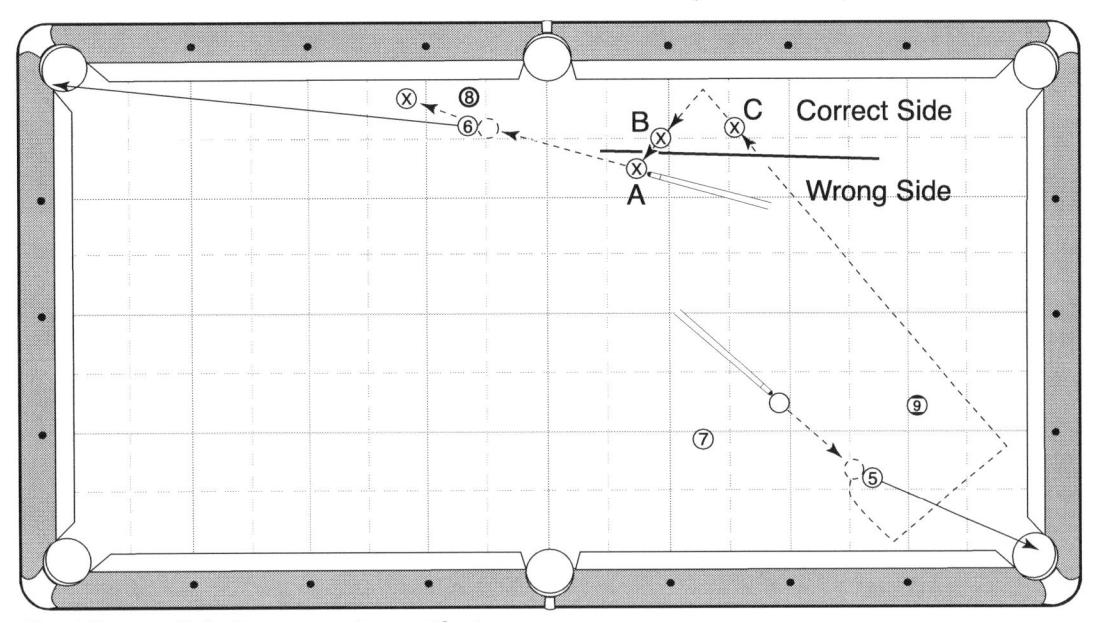

The Wrong Side Leaves a Long Shot

Efren Reyes picked the correct route but struck the cue ball a little firmly, sending it to the wrong side of the 6-ball at Position A. Anywhere on the other side of the line, such as at Positions B or C, would have been ideal. Notice that the cue ball entered the correct side, was briefly in the ideal zone, and then reemerged on the wrong side. Reyes recovered from this error and ran out against Earl Strickland at the Sands Regency Open, June, 1995.

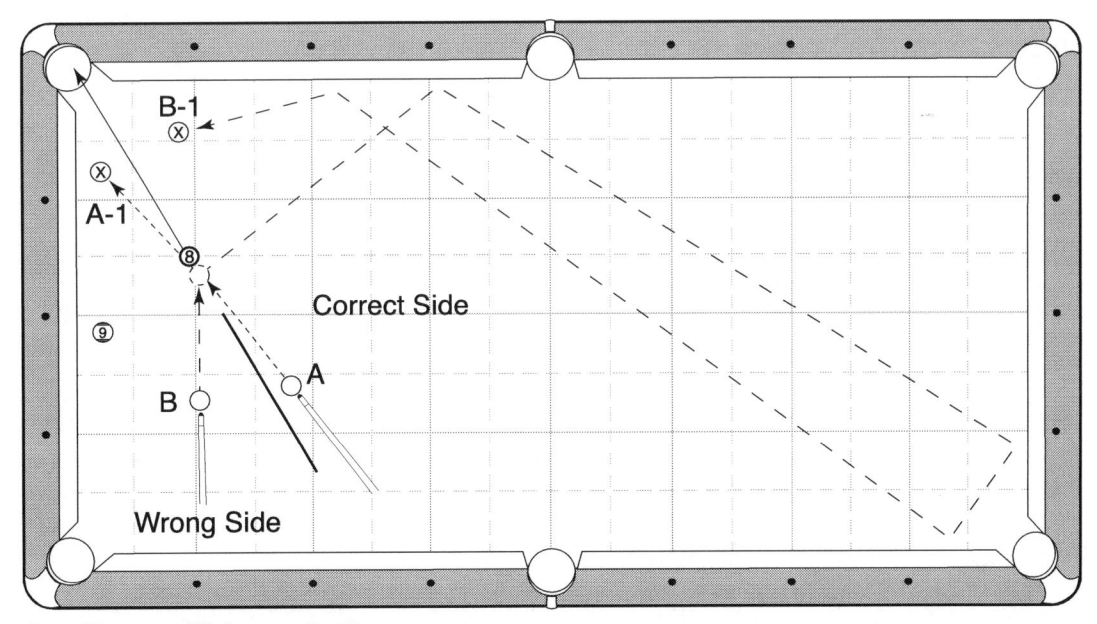

One Foot vs. Eighteen Feet

The position play error in this illustration comes up quite often, usually because of poor planning or execution. With the cue ball on the correct side at Position A, shape on the 9-ball at Position A-1 is a cinch. With the cue ball on the wrong side at Position B, the cue ball must now embark on an 18 foot long journey around the table to arrive at Position B-1 for a shot on the 9-ball.

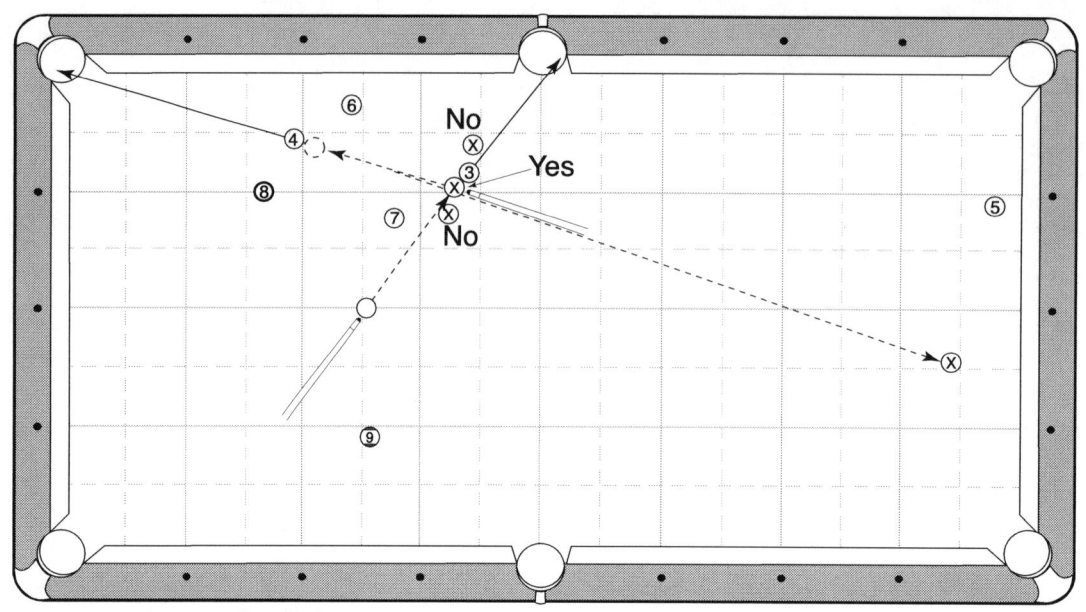

An Exception to the Rule
When balls are stationed on either side of the ball you are about to play, they could easily block your position route to the next ball. The 6, 7 and 8-balls are conspiring to prevent you from sending the cue ball back up table for the 5-ball. A stop shot on the 3-ball into the side pocket will leave you with a straight in shot on the 4-ball. With the cue ball in this position you can draw straight back past the obstructers to the 5-ball. The lesson: sometimes a straight in shot is the correct "side."

#10 Play to the Long Side When Possible and Practical
In 9 Ball you must often send the cue ball on a lengthy journey to the position zone, so **it is usually better to play for the largest shape zones**. This means that you should send the cue ball to the long side of the object ball because this side gives you a bigger position zone. In addition, **the object ball's distance to the pocket is shorter when the cue ball is on the long side**.

    Part A of the diagram at the top of the next page illustrates the concept of long side/short side. The 2-ball is well past the mid-point towards the upper right corner pocket, so the position zone is considerably larger on the long side as shown. It will be much easier to send the cue ball into a long side zone on most occasions because it is generally much larger. You will discover, however, that there are exceptions to this rule.

    Part B shows an exception to the long side principle. Notice that the 6-ball has reduced the size of the long side position zone. In addition, there is now the risk of getting hooked behind the 6 if you play shape on this side. As a result, in this case the short side is preferable.

    In Part C the 1-ball is stationed directly opposite the side pockets, and it is much closer to the top side pocket. The short and long side position zones on a side pocket shot typically don't extend to either side of the ball because one side is almost always the wrong side! This is why the zones in this example stop the line that runs between the two side pockets.

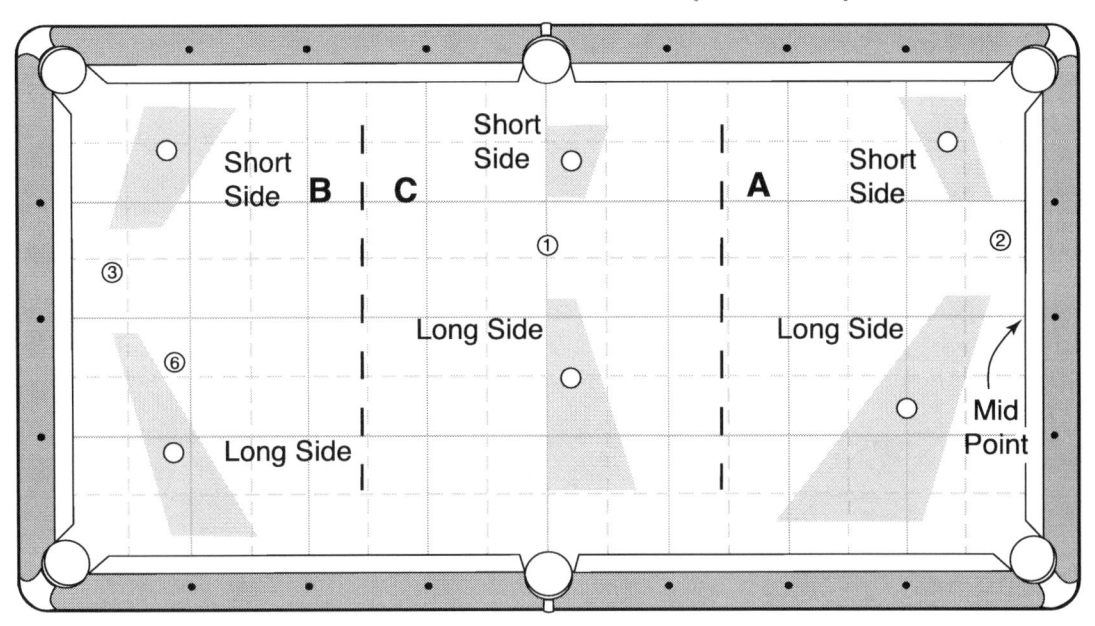

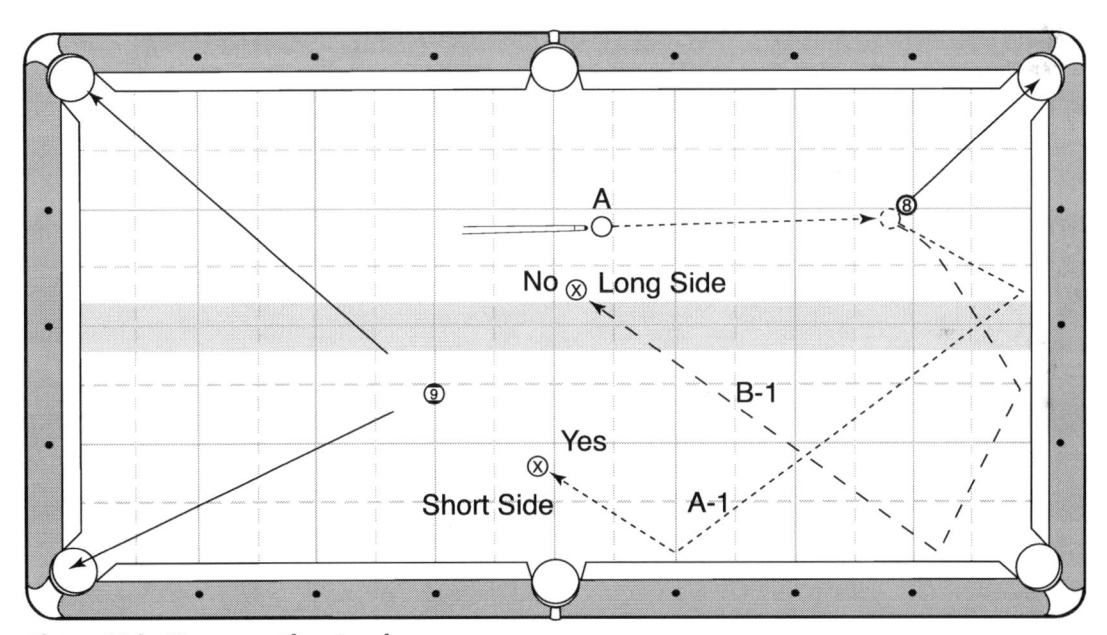

Short Side Ensures the Angle

The channel down the middle of the table is a neutral zone. When the object ball rests in this zone, there is no great advantage to playing on the long side versus the short side. When the next ball rests outside this zone, then the long side is generally preferable. The position in the above diagram is an exception. In this example, you need only pocket the 8 and 9-balls. When the cue ball is in Position A, the short side down Route A-1 is better because the cue ball will be traveling directly at the 9-ball. It is a mistake to play Route B-1 to the long side because the cue ball would be crossing through the position zone (see principle #12).

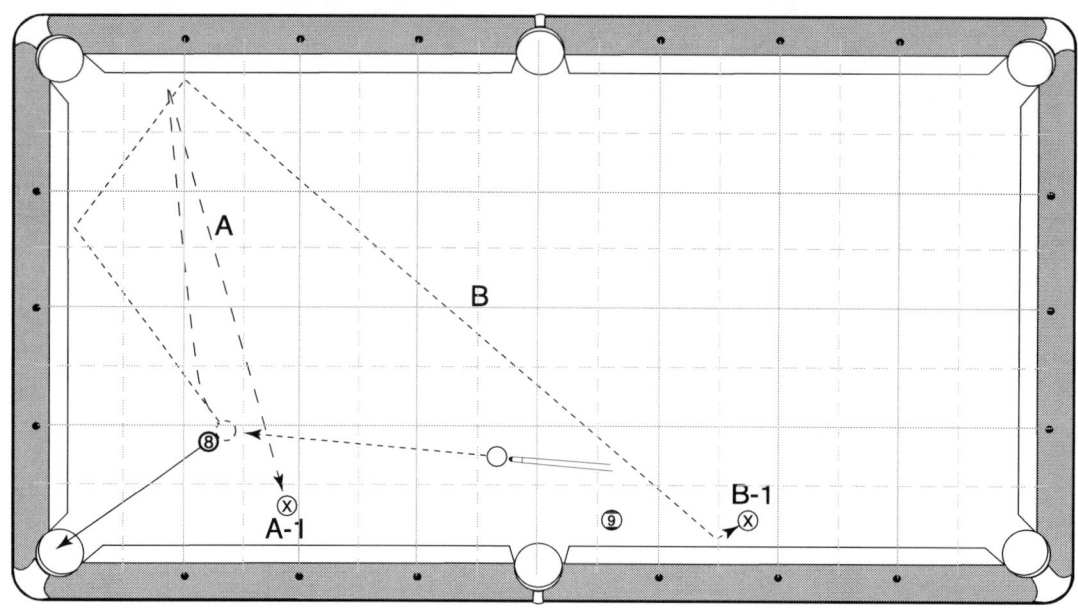

Other Principles Override the Short Side
The principles of position play usually work together to create successful position plays. However, **at certain times one principle takes precedence over another**. It requires a near perfect stroke to play a draw shot across the table and back along Route A to the long side at A-1 for position on the 9-ball. It is much easier to send the cue ball to the short side by using Route B, which is the natural path to B-1. (See principle 14).

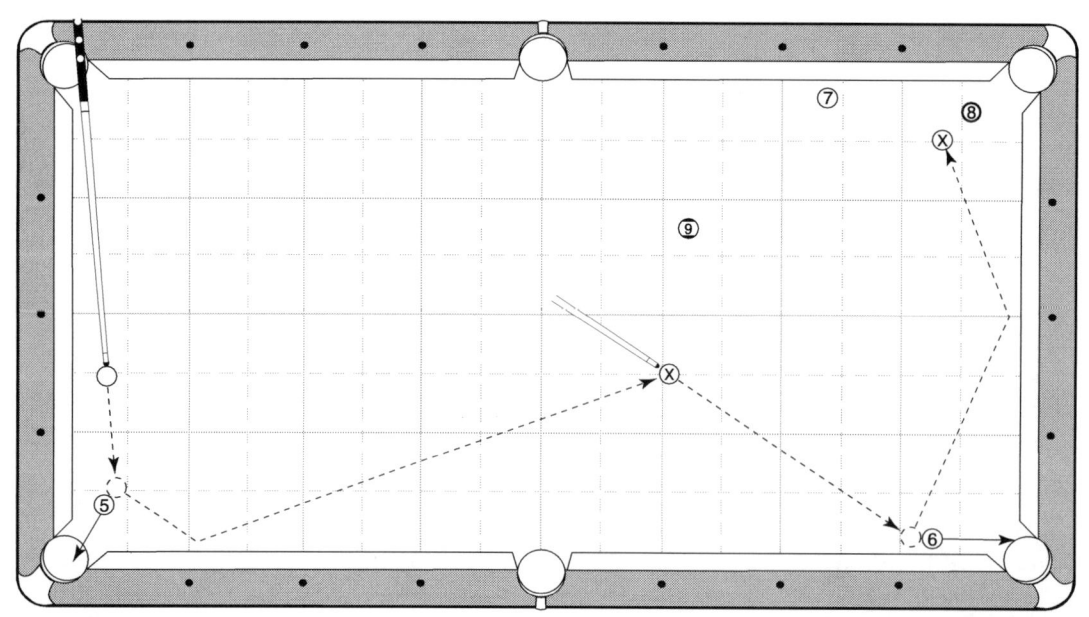

Avoiding a Combo
The 7-ball won't go past the 8-ball, and the 7-8 combo is quite difficult. The alternative is to play the pattern shown in the diagram, which results in short side shape on the 7-ball for the upper left corner pocket. The key is to execute two relatively easy position plays to near perfection.

#11 Ball in Hand Shape

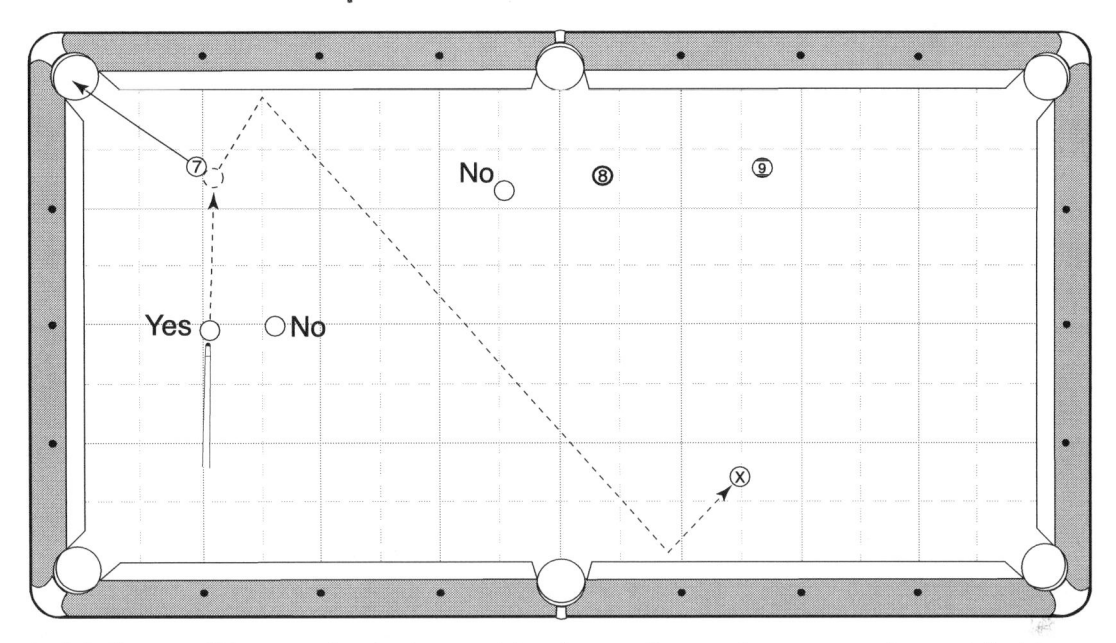

In 9 Ball you will be mostly playing position for medium to long range shots while hopefully getting the correct angle on the next ball. When you have ball in hand, however, you don't have to worry about making the ball or playing for the correct angle. Indeed, **with ball in hand you can put the cue ball as close to the object ball as is possible and practical – a distance that usually ranges from about 6-18 inches.**

You have much more latitude in choosing your cut angle with ball in hand. In the position above, a 50-degree cut angle enables you to play the shot with perfect speed and with great precision. In essence, the position you create with ball in hand almost plays the shot for you before the cue ball has even been struck!

On certain routes **ball in hand enables you to be more exacting in your position**. You can set the angle to precisely match the requirements of the route. This allows you to avoid using excess english or a stroke with which you are not comfortable. You can also play closer to obstacles and hazards when you are certain of the direction the cue ball will be traveling.

You can speed up the position play learning process by watching where excellent players place the cue ball with ball in hand. Did they get good position on the next ball? What route did they take? You will learn many of the best routes, which you will hopefully remember when you encounter them. If you can't consistently get shape on the next ball with ball in hand, you have a strong indicator that your ball placement and/or execution needs work.

TIP: The size of the ideal position zone with ball in hand is not much larger than the cue ball. Be a perfectionist. Perfect shape on the first ball should enable you to get excellent shape on the next ball, which could kick start a run out through the 9 or 10 ball.

144   Chapter 4 - Principles of Position

#12 Playing Down the Line of a Position Zone when Possible

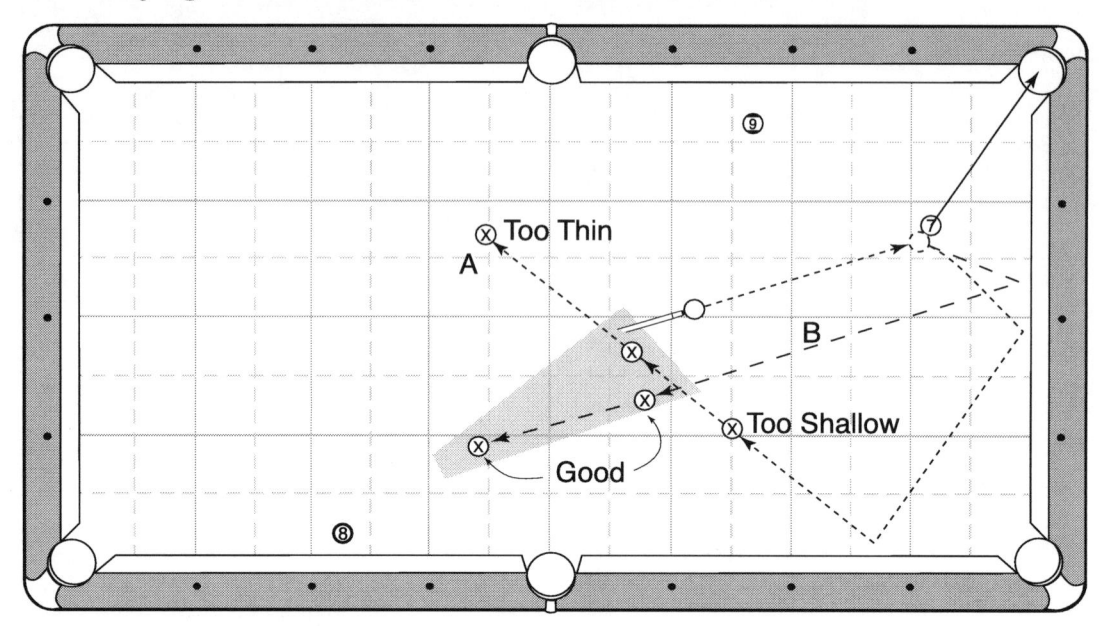

We have talked about the importance of leaving yourself with the ideal angle. Now, **if you follow the Playing Down the Line When Possible principle you will increase your chance of creating the correct angle**.

Three balls remain in the diagram above. If you get the correct angle on the 8-ball, then completing the run will be easy. Players who believe that two-rail position is the big secret to 9 Ball might choose Route A. The problem with this route, however, is that the cue ball will be traveling across the zone, making it play very small. If your speed is off just a little, you could wind up with a cut that is too shallow or too thin. The high percentage route is to send the cue ball down Route B. The cut angle is nearly the same no matter where it stops in the zone. With the correct angle, it will be easy to pocket the 8-ball and send the cue ball across the table for the 9.

Maintaining a Constant Angle

The ideal angle for the 8-ball is 30 degrees in the position at the top of the next page. If you extend the cut line to the bottom side rail, you will discover where the cue ball must hit the rail to maintain a constant 30-degree angle as it travels down the position zone towards the ghost ball next to the 8-ball. The cue ball must also rebound at the appropriate angle so that it will travel at a constant angle to the next ball. Notice that the cue ball entered at 54-degrees and rebounded at 40 degrees. Ideal position lies all the way from Point A to Point C. Point B is the position play bull's-eye!

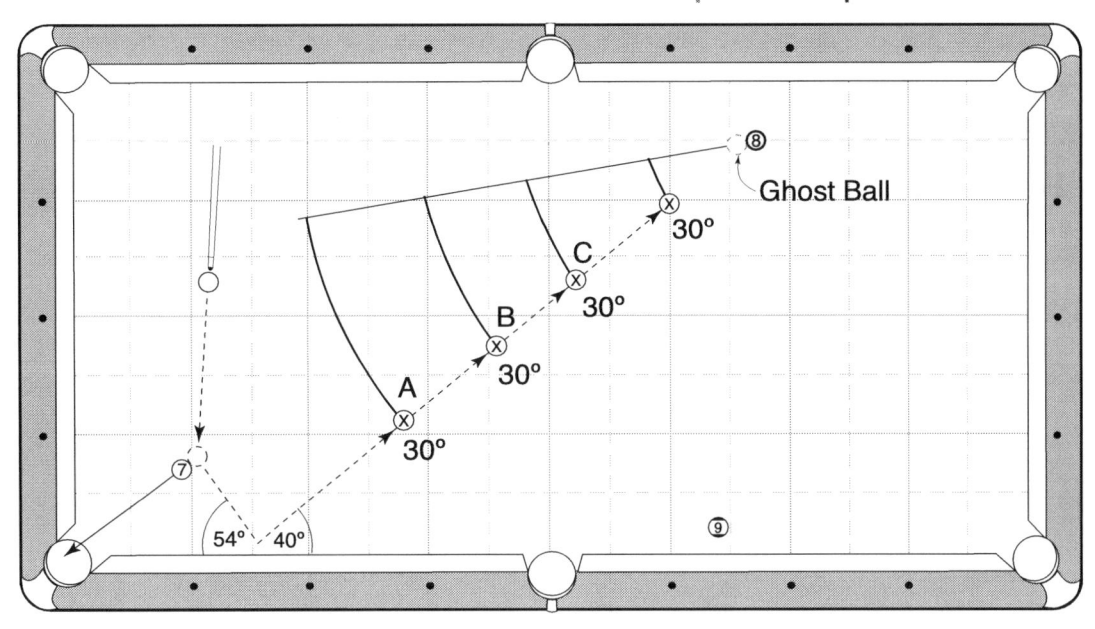

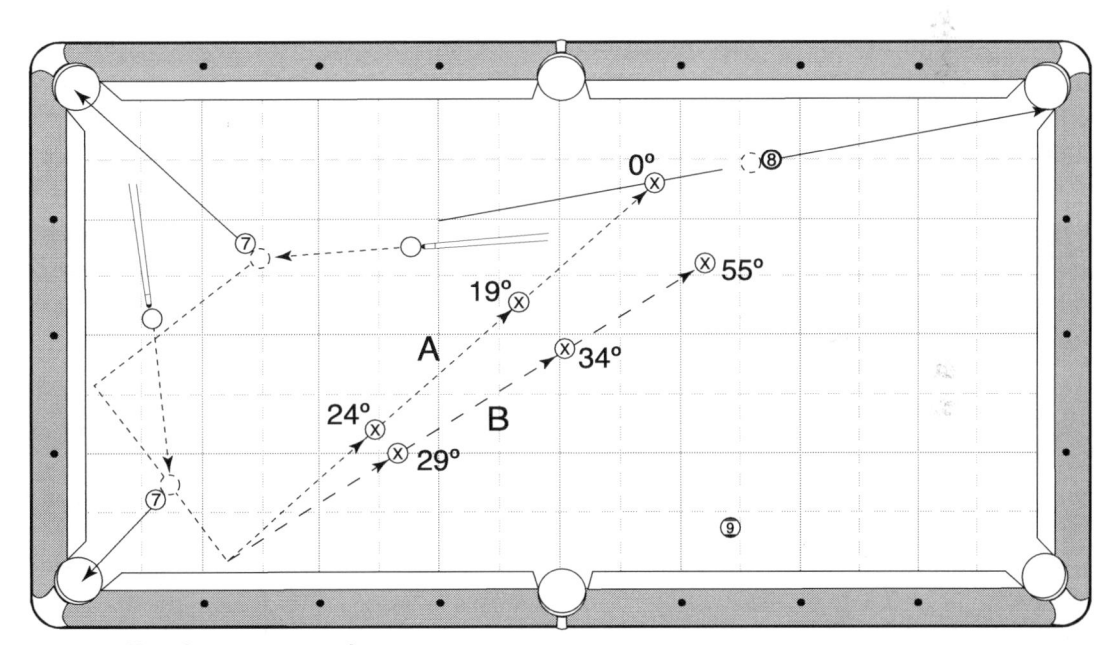

Gradually Changing Angles
On most position plays it is not possible to set up an angle that stays perfectly constant as the cue ball travels down the position zone. A close second is to send the cue ball down a path in which the angle changes little in route. Route A shows a cut angle that is decreasing at a slow rate while the cue ball travels across the table. Route B demonstrates a route where the angle is growing in size as the cue ball rolls toward the 8-ball.

When you have a choice like this, you can use either route. If you don't mind a longer shot, or if you might have trouble stretching for the shot (assuming you are right handed), then Route A would be better. If you are left-handed, or are a tall player with a long reach, or prefer a thinner cut when playing position, then Route B is preferable.

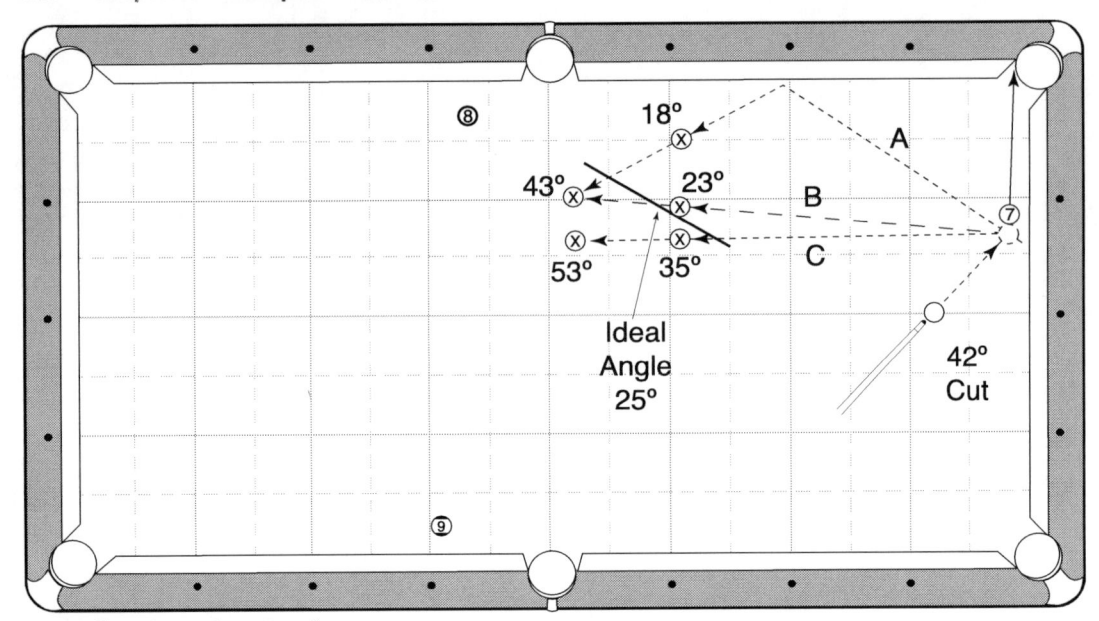

Rapidly Changing Angles

The diagram shows three routes from the 7-ball to the 8. The ideal angle for the 8-ball is about 25-30 degrees. Route A is the riskiest of the three because the cut angle changes from 12 to 43 degrees within a span of only 12 inches! The angle on Route B increases from 23 to 43 degrees within the space of one diamond.

Players who prefer using a soft stroke to cross the table from the 8-ball to the 9 might choose Route C, in which the cut angle grows from 35 to 53 degrees within about a foot. When playing position in a similar situation, **plot your route with care to optimize your chances of having a workable angle – and to give yourself the one that is best suited for your game**.

#13 Enter the Wide Part of a Position Zone

When you must send the cue ball across a position zone, you have less margin for error than if you were able to play down the line, as we discussed in the previous principle. Playing across a zone is a disaster waiting to happen if you don't plan carefully, and if your speed is off even just a little.

You can improve your odds of success by entering the zone at its widest part. The widest part is always further from the object ball. You may give up a little accuracy on the next shot, but this is a good trade because it can ensure that you wind up with a workable cut angle on the next ball. The keys to playing across the line position are:
- Recognize the danger.
- Plan to play to the wide side.
- Execute the shot as precisely as possible. Speed control is crucial.

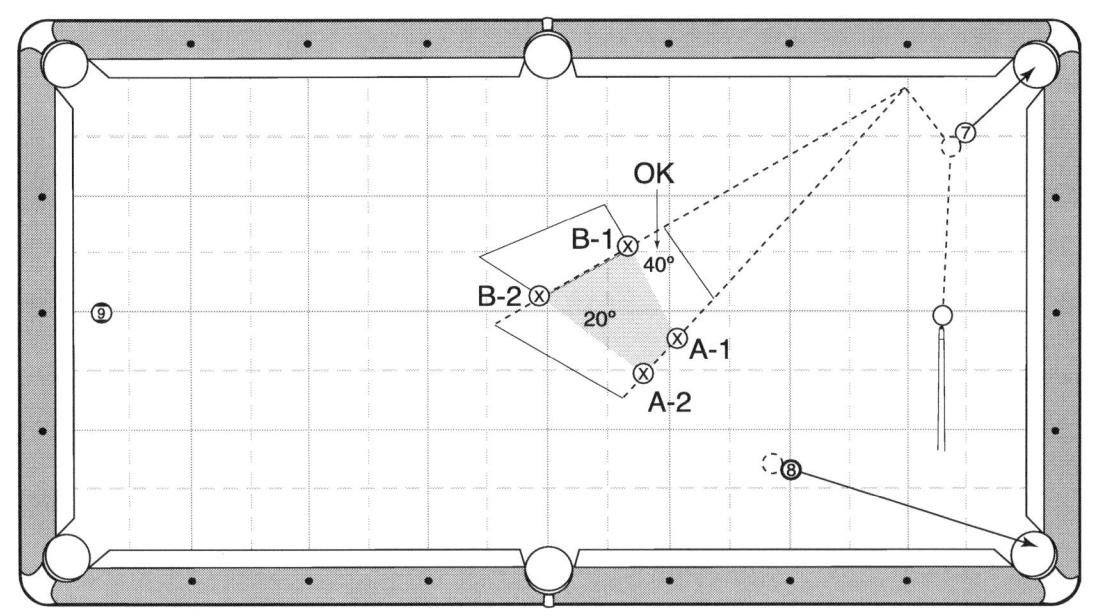

Enter the Wide Side

You must send the cue ball across the width of the zone when playing position from the 7-ball to the 8-ball. The ideal angle on the 8-ball is between 20 and 40 degrees as shown. The zone is only six inches wide from Position A-1 to Position A-2. If you enter at the wide side at B-1, you have an 11 inch long zone that extends from B-1 to B-2. This extra five inches increases your target by 83%!

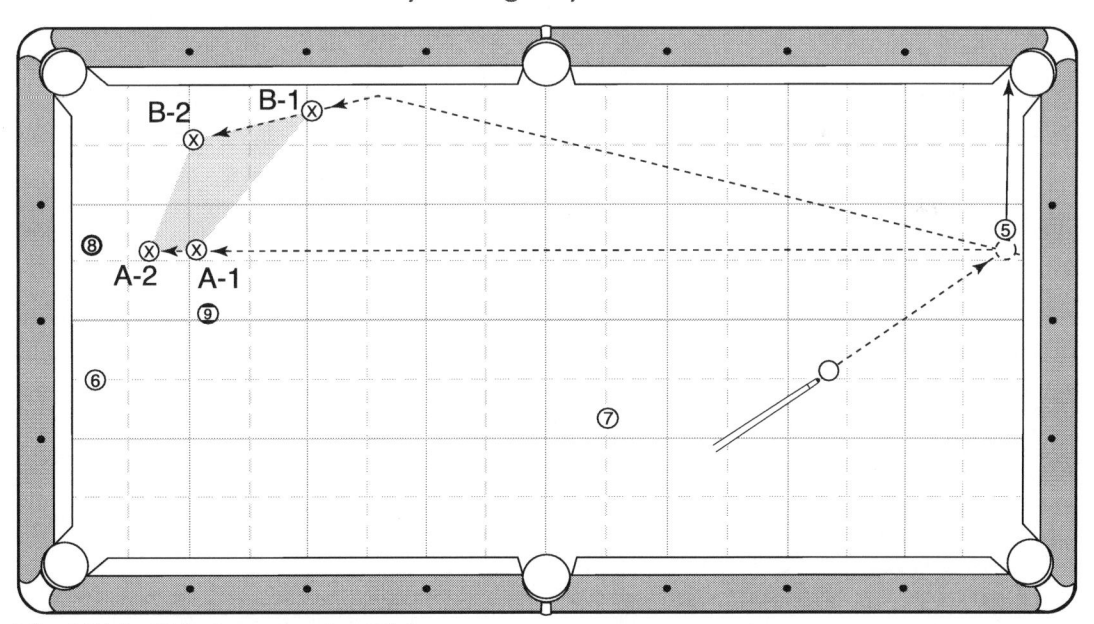

The Wide Side Lowers the Risk

This position play to the 6-ball is fraught with danger because you could easily get hooked behind the 8-ball or the 9. When the object ball is near the rail it is usually easier to control the cue ball by sending it straight down the table. Not this time, though, because the position zone from A-1 to A-2 is only five inches long. Sending the cue ball off the side rail will produce a longer shot on the 6-ball, but this route increases the width of the zone by over eight inches, as shown by the area from Position B-1 to B-2.

#14 Play Natural Shape as Often as Possible

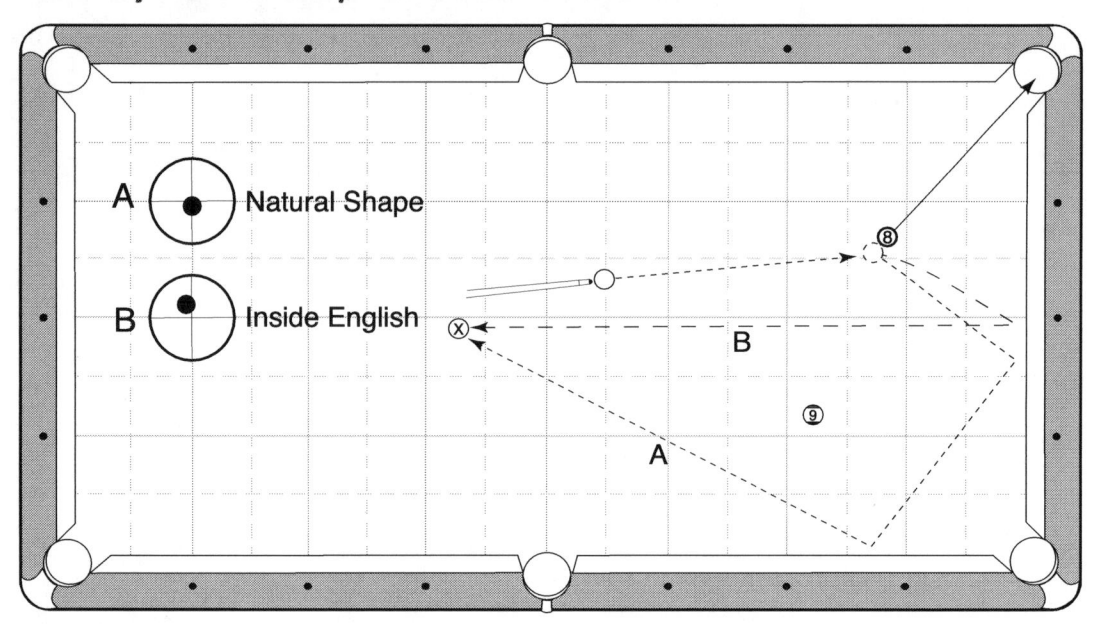

Both 9 Ball require that you shoot with great accuracy while sending the cue ball long distances for position. So, to maximize your accuracy, consider playing natural shape whenever possible. **You can discover the natural way to play a variety of routes by using the speed with which you are most comfortable, and by cueing on the vertical axis** (no sidespin).

Route A shows a natural two-rail path from the 8-ball to the 9. The shot was played with a half tip of draw, a medium soft stroke, and on the vertical axis (no english!). Route B forces you to go against the cue ball's natural roll by using high inside english. This makes it much tougher to pocket the 8-ball.

#15 Plan Your Route and Avoid Obstructions

The balls are typically spread across the entire length of the table after the break in 9 Ball, which often creates an obstacle course that is fraught with danger. **The six pockets can produce scratches, so they should also be treated as obstacles.**

Obstacles appear most often in the early stages of a game when there are more balls – and more opportunities for them to disrupt the cue ball while it's on its travels. The other balls also reduce the size of position zones and can lead to getting snookered. Finally, obstacles can still be a problem even when there are only a few balls left on the table.

If there were no obstacles, you could play simple routes and patterns most of the time. But obstacles do exist, which is part of the reason why I covered a wide variety of position routes in Chapter 3. Your ability to plan your route and to adapt your cueing and speed to the situation will take you a long ways towards helping negotiate the obstacle courses and to arrive at your zones unscathed. Skill at avoiding obstacles will also build your run out power.

Tips for Running the Obstacle Course
The following items help you to plan your way through an obstacle course:
- The obstacle only requires a slight modification from the ideal route.
- There is only one obstacle, but it is a major hurdle.
- There are multiple obstacles to avoid. These could be two balls en route, or a ball and a possible scratch.
- You might have to play a difficult route because an obstacle prevents you from using a simple position play that you would normally use.
- The obstacle is so big that a safety is the better choice.

Rate Your Chances of Avoiding the Obstacle
Before forging ahead with a questionable position play, weigh the alternatives. Your possible choices include:
- Playing a position route that is comfortable, but that has an obstacle that you might hit.
- Playing a less familiar route that allows you to avoid any obstacles. This choice may require that you compromise your shotmaking accuracy.

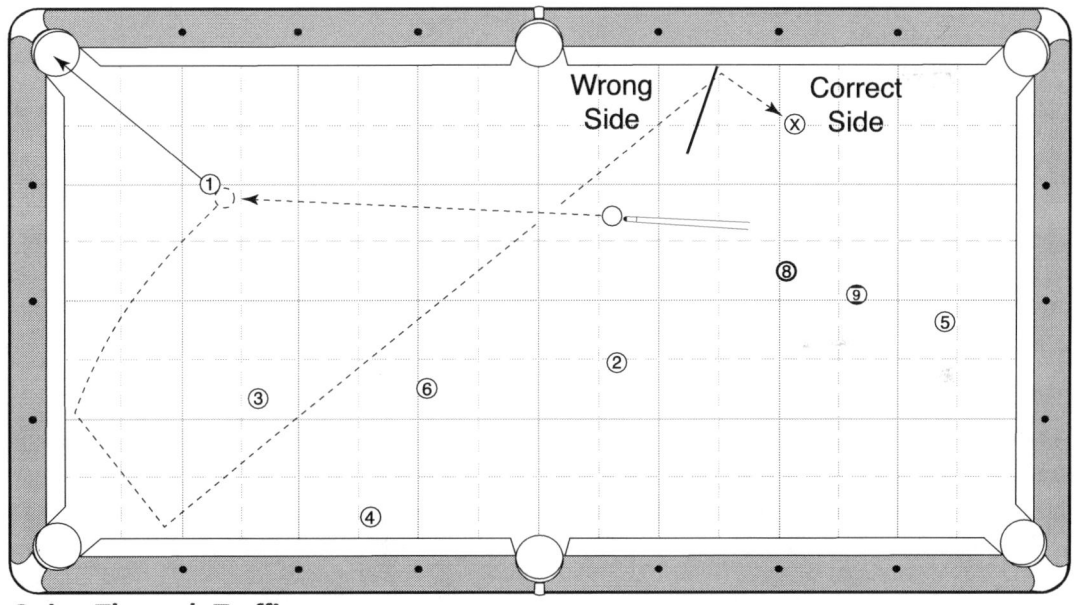

Going Through Traffic
Nick Varner's perfect cueing and speed enabled him to negotiate this obstacle course to the correct side of the 2-ball (remember Principle #9). If he had used a little more draw, the cue ball would have run into the 3-ball. If he had used follow, the cue ball would have run into the 6-ball. When you possess the skills of a Nick Varner, you can cut things close because you just know that the cue ball will arrive safely at its destination. This action took place in a match against Mike Sigel at the 1990 U.S. Open.

#16 Use Rail Targets

Before the cue ball arrives at its resting place, it could contact one or more rails. Each rail that the cue ball contacts en route is a useful target. You can **pinpoint your rail targets by using the diamonds**. When you are planning multi-rail position routes, aim to hit the first rail target precisely where intended because this will establish the direction for the remainder of the cue ball's path.

When playing, and especially in practice, identify where you want to hit the rail. Carefully **observe your results, and then file the information away for future reference**. In time you will become proficient at hitting these intermediate targets, and this will improve your shape while keeping the cue ball out of trouble!

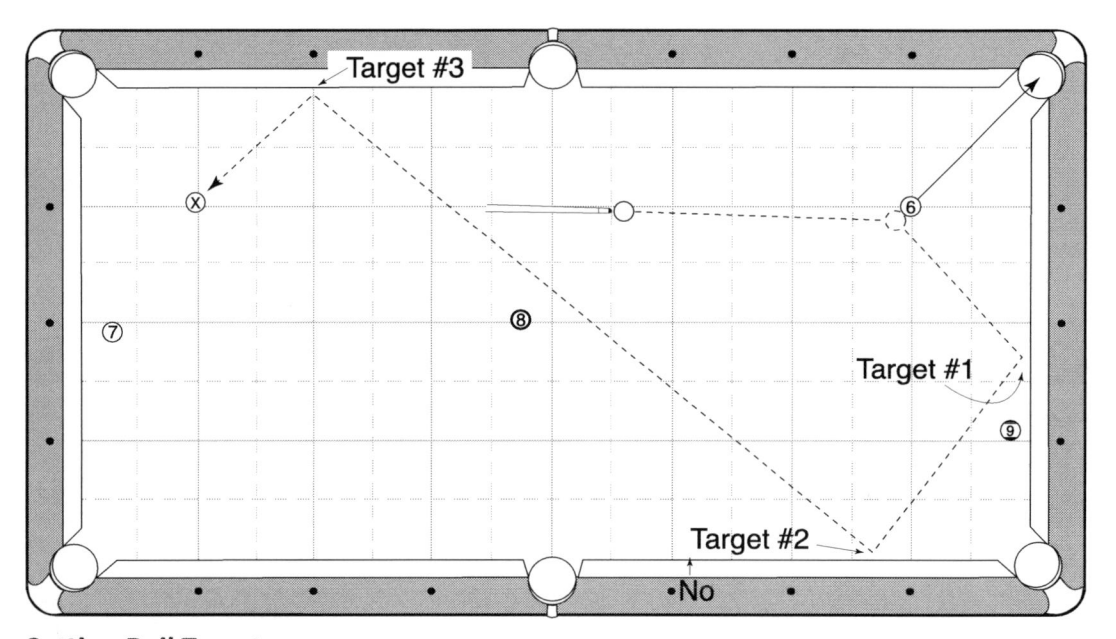

Setting Rail Targets

Rail targets can help you play common three-rail routes with great precision. Target #1 is key because it establishes the direction of the shot. You must make sure that the cue ball avoids the 9-ball on its way to the first rail. If the cue ball hits too far up the second rail, it could hit the 8-ball up table. The third rail target is two diamonds up the rail, and far from the corner pocket. This target was dictated by the need to miss the 9 and 8-balls.

Rail Targets in Small Increments

In the example at the top of the next page, the cue ball must avoid the 9 and 8-balls for position on the 7. **On exacting position plays, it helps to divide the area between the diamonds into small increments because this will give you a more precise rail target**. If you can hit this smaller target, the cue ball will arrive safely at Position X. If the cue ball had hit the rail a quarter diamond above the target, it would have run into the 8-ball. The cue ball would have hit the 9-ball if you had aimed to hit the second rail one quarter diamond below the ideal target.

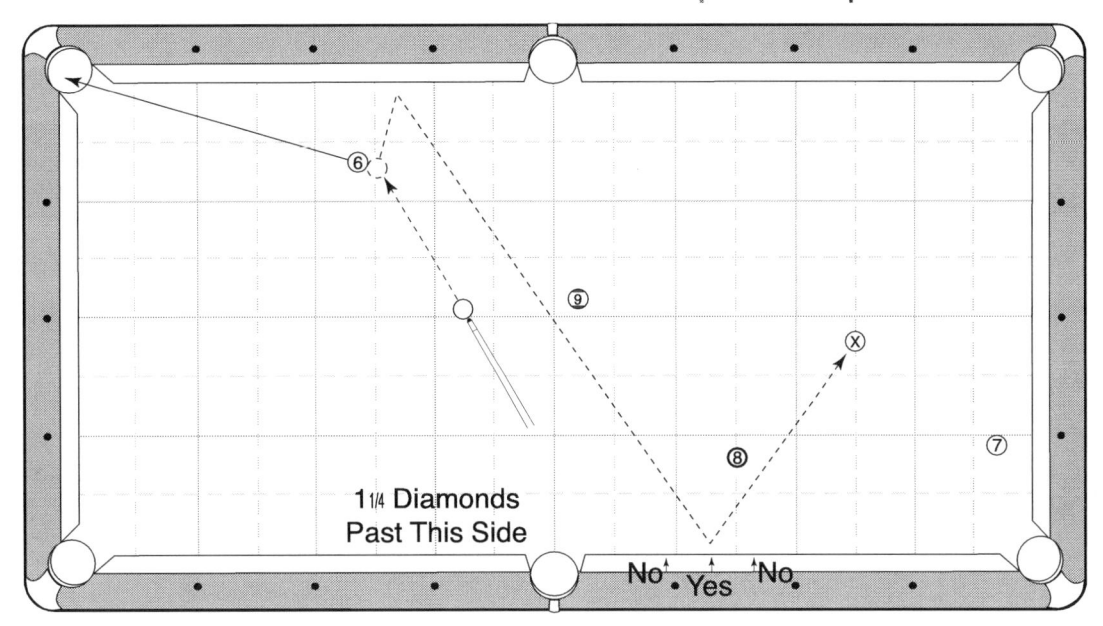

#17 Avoid Scratching

Fouling is the biggest mistake you can make in 9 Ball because it enables your opponent to place the cue ball anywhere on the table. Fouls that follow a tough safety by your opponent are understandable – even pros are guilty of these infractions. In contrast, bad fouls are those that result from scratches on position plays where things are under your control. While some players feel the pool gods are against them when they scratch, the cold hard truth is that bad luck has nothing to do with most of the scratches that come on position plays. The blame falls on the player for their lack of knowledge and/or for their faulty execution. The diagram below shows three common scratches that can be avoided with proper planning and execution.

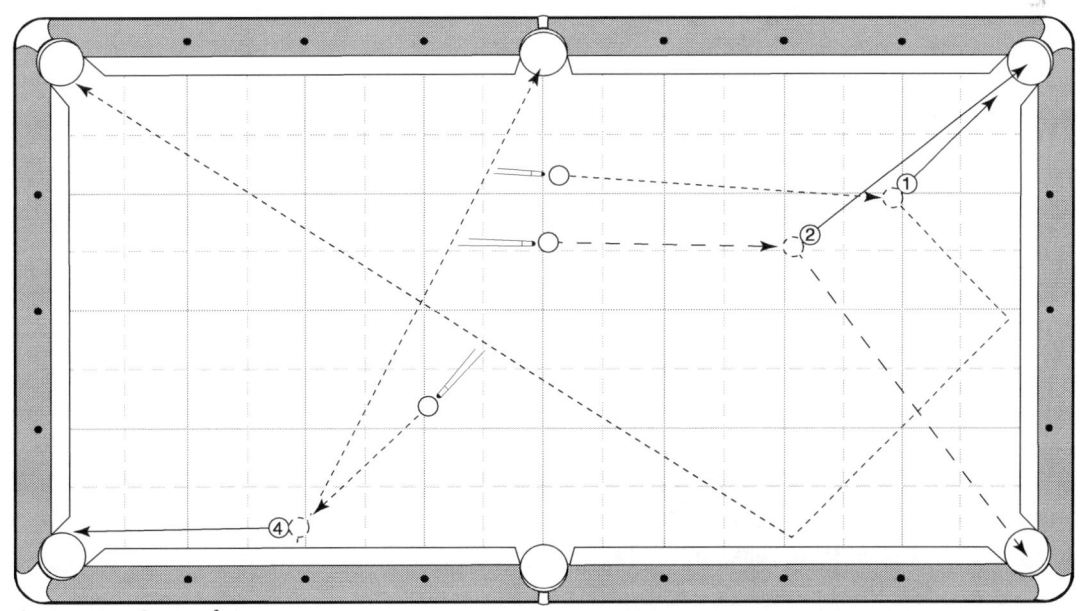

Common Scratches

152   Chapter 4 - Principles of Position

How Scratches Happen
- Natural scratches – the cue ball is going towards the pocket and there is little you can do to eliminate the possibility of scratching.
- Poor execution – you can avoid these with proper execution.
- Poor planning – these result from choosing a high-risk route that places the cue ball in danger.
- The conditions – while you are adjusting to a table you may be vulnerable to scratching because the cue ball follows an unexpected path.
- Bad luck – difficult position plays may involve an element of risk. For example, the cue ball must, by design, narrowly miss scratching. A very slight miscalculation or a rolloff could result in a scratch.

If you scratch too often, begin to start learning from each one so that you don't repeat that scratch again. And pay attention to other players' scratches. How do they unfold? What can be learned from their mistakes so that you can avoid a similar error? Your powers of observation can enable you to familiarize yourself with the shots that carry the highest risk of a scratch, and how to prevent them before they happen – to you!

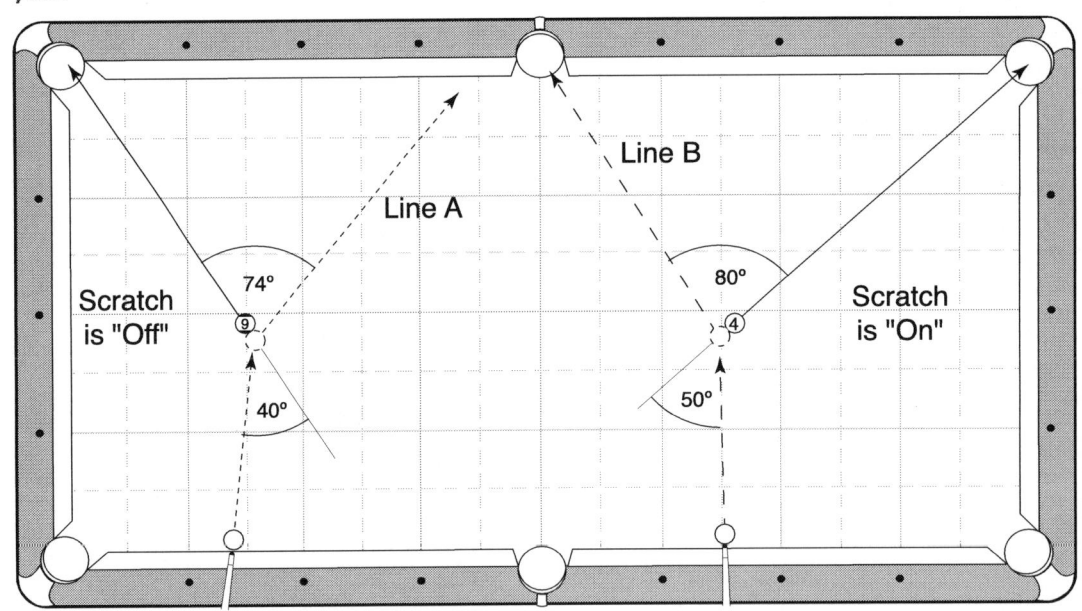

When Scratches are "On" or "Off"
On certain shots a scratch is "on," and there is little you can do to avoid them. Among the most common types are thin cuts where you can do little (or nothing) to alter the cue ball's path after contact. Another common scratch happens on shots off the rail, which limit your choice of cueing. Part A shows a rail shot where the scratch is "off." It pays to know when a scratch is off because then you can shoot the shot with confidence, and not pass on it because you think it will result in a scratch when it won't! Part B shows a thin cut off the rail in which a scratch is "on." Again, knowledge is the key – and in this case that means have a sharp eye, and memory, for this kind of foul.

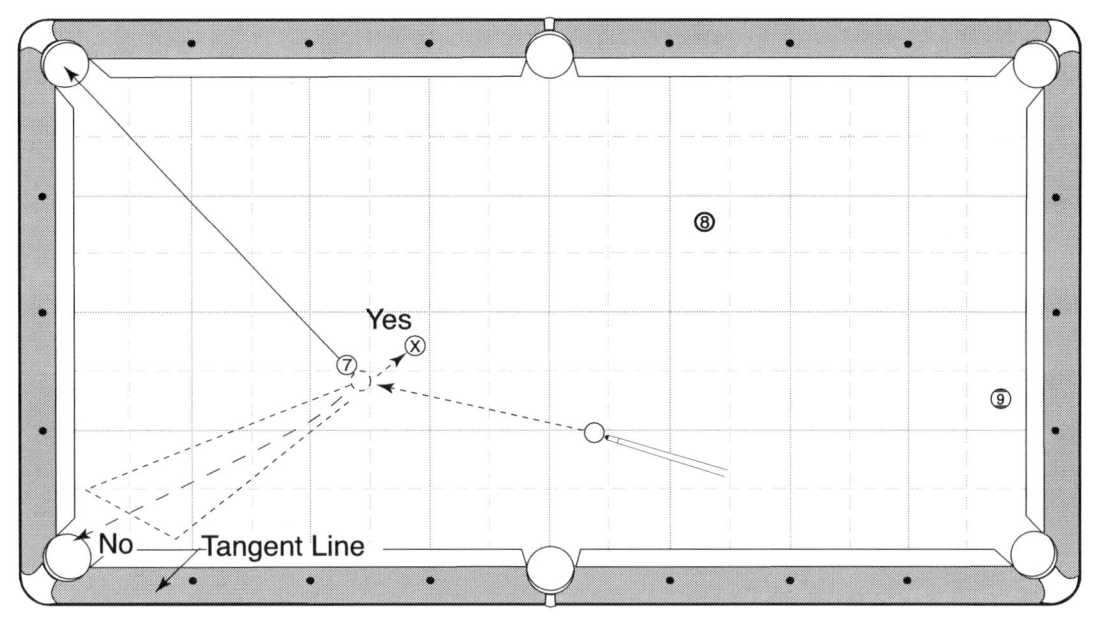

Close But no Scratch with Pro-Like Control
Earl Strickland narrowly avoided a scratch while playing this two-rail beauty against Buddy Hall, at the Sands Regency 12 Open, in December 1990. Turn the book to look at the shot from Strickland's perspective. Does it look like a scratch shot to you? Notice that the tangent line points at the opposite side of the pocket The shot was played with follow, so the cue ball had to bend forward to keep it from scratching.

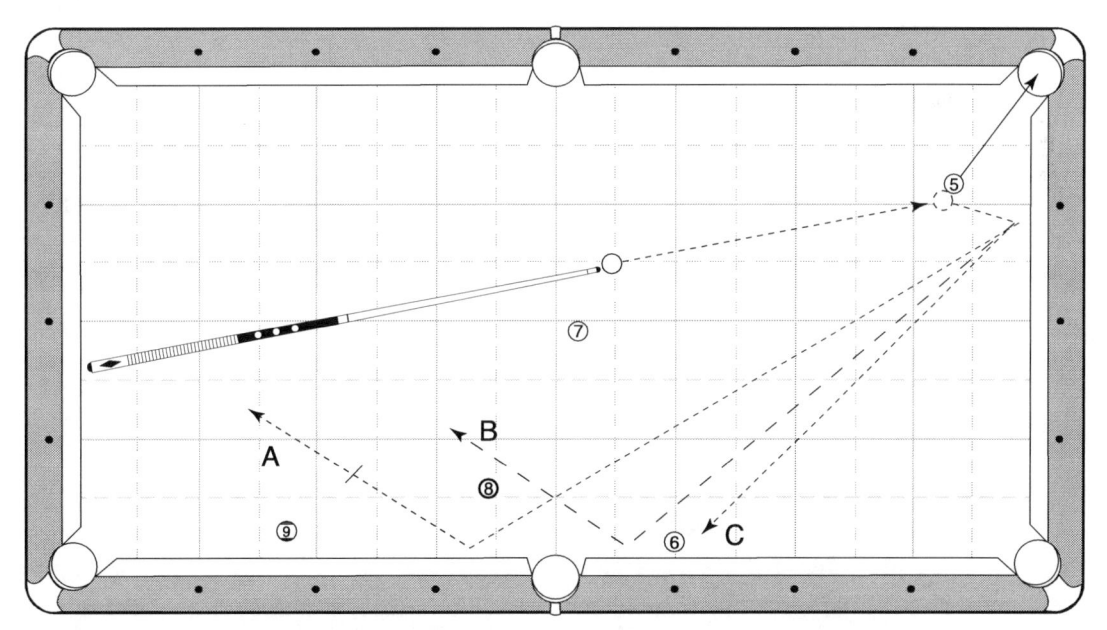

Avoiding an Obvious Scratch
This position play from the 5-ball to the 6 is loaded with danger no matter which route you choose. If you go long down Route A, you could get hooked. Route B could easily result in a side pocket scratch. Route C eliminates these dangers, but you may not have a shot on the 6-ball after running into it. You must pick your poison, and hopefully avoid a disaster with superlative execution – and maybe just a little luck!

#18 Keep the Cue Ball Away from the Rails and Other Balls

About 55 percent of all position plays in 9 Ball require at least a medium speed of stroke. You will, however, severely limit your ability to apply the power that you need on a good number of your shots if you make a habit of leaving the cue ball close to, or against, the rails. The worst mistakes happen when you leave the cue ball on the rail and, on the next shot, you need to:

- Apply english.
- Send the cue ball a long distance.
- Use draw.
- Play a long shot.

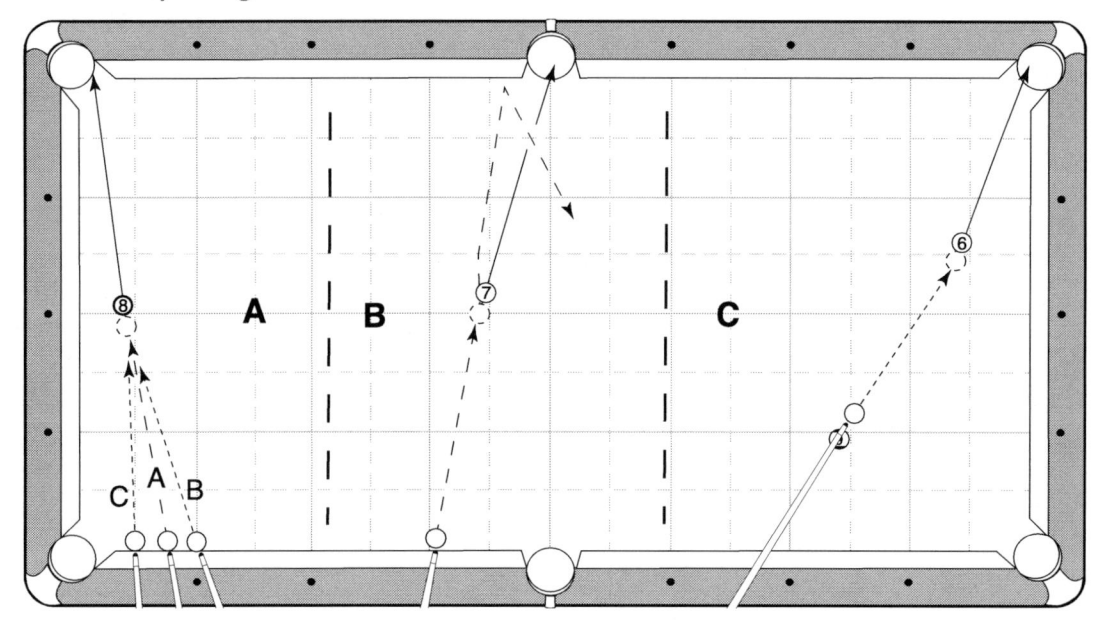

Part A shows one of the worst mistakes: you have a straight shot or one with a small cut angle and the cue ball is frozen to the rail. Many players are, oddly enough, better off with the cue ball in Position A (than with a slight cut angle as in Positions B and C) because they will tend to accept their fate and roll in the shot. This puts them in position to play the next ball with the cue ball a few inches off the end rail.

When the cue ball is in Position B or C, many players will attempt to use those small cut angles for all they are worth by trying to power the cue ball up table. This often results in a miss. When you have a small cut angle, use it to escape the end rail if you can, but don't get greedy and try to muscle the cue ball several feet up table.

It is tempting to use english to send the cue ball further across and down the table when it is frozen to the rail as shown in Part B. However, once again, I advise that you respect the limitations of the shot. Use very little if any sidespin when the cue ball is on the rail because english may cause the cue ball to curve, which could easily lead to a miss. Furthermore, cuing off the rail with english can easily lead to a miscue.

In Part C, the cue ball is next to the 9-ball, so you will have to jack up to play the 6-ball. Once again, accept your fate and use a speed of stroke that does not compromise your accuracy.

#19 Pay Attention to Details

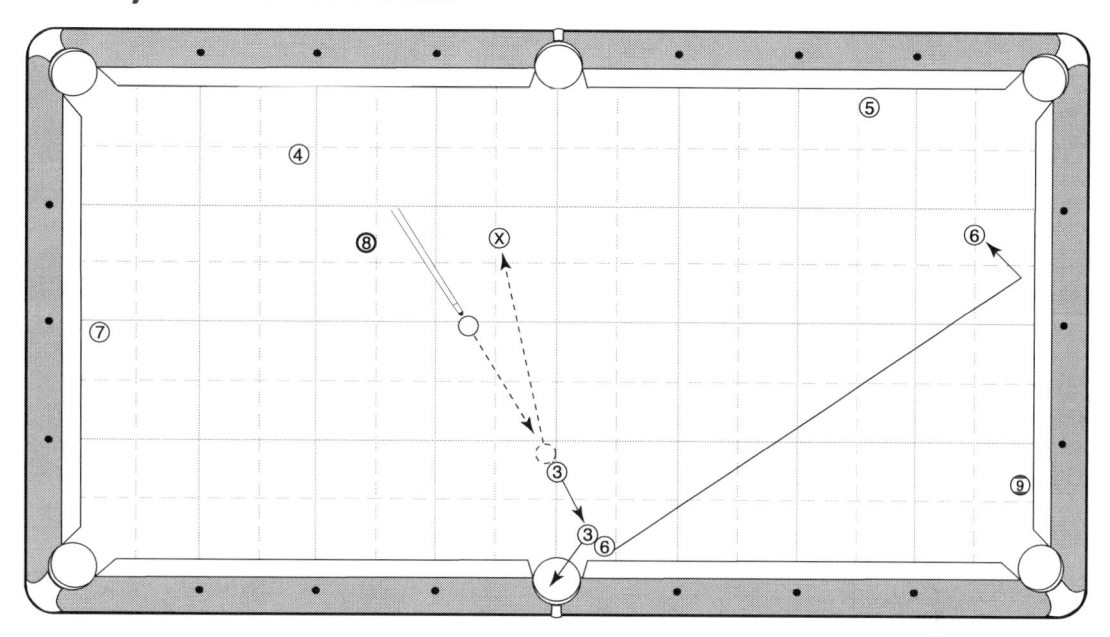

I once saw Joe Salazar, a very fine player, take ball in hand and adjust the position of the cue ball 6-7 times within a 1-2" circle until he got it just where his instincts told him it needed to be. The lesson: **small details often spell the difference between success and failure**. They can also be your insurance policy against disaster.

When you have an easy rack, attention to detail will guarantee that you will finish it off with little or no trouble. **Easy shots give you a chance to hone your execution, and the position play skills that you develop while playing easy layouts will be useful when you play tougher versions of the same position routes**.

The 3-ball is in a perfect position to be played off the 6-ball into the side pocket, which will remove the 6 from the worst spot on the table. Hopefully most players would take this opportunity to solve this problem. And those who pay attention to details will also look for even more ways to improve the layout – like playing the shot with draw and good speed for position on the 4-ball.

A player who pays attention to details will notice that the 9-ball is slightly off the rail and it is near the pocket, making it an ideal candidate for a combo. If the 6-ball is hit with the correct speed, it could lead to a 6-9 combo. Astute observers will also notice that the 5-ball is in ideal position to play shape on the 6-9 combo! Finally, playing the easy 6-9 combo eliminates the need to play shape from the 6-ball to the 7-ball, which is on the middle of the opposite end rail. The lesson: **little things very often make a big difference, so make a habit of looking for them.**

#20 Play Your Game

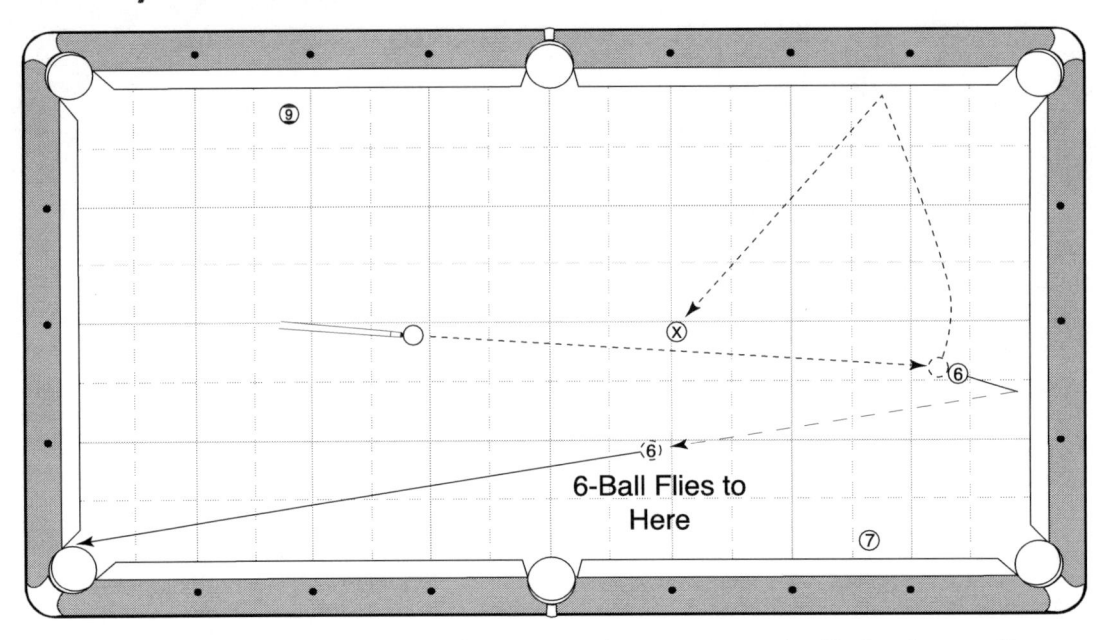

6-Ball Flies to Here

We discussed how certain players like to use a firm stroke and will play for smaller cut angles while others prefer to use a softer stroke and a larger angle. Some players prefer to play on the center axis while others like to spin cut balls whenever possible. Shotmakers play for larger zones while other players strive for pinpoint shape. The point is that after you have gained ample experience playing the games, you will develop your style for playing position.

When it comes to playing your game, you've got to do what works for you, and you must know your limitations. If you don't like limitations, then you must work to expand your skills. And just because you play one style right now doesn't mean "your game" can't change. The more variety in "your game," the greater your ability to handle any situation that arises.

One of the most dramatic examples of a person playing their game came in the 1992 U.S. Open finals between Tommy Kennedy and Johnny Archer. The 62-degree cut on the 6-ball was a thin but makeable shot into the lower right corner pocket. The cue ball could have followed a natural four-rail route to the 7-ball. However, Kennedy chose to play his game, which favored position for the 7-ball off of a long rail bank. The cue ball flew into the 6-ball at over 13 MPH, and the 6-ball was airborne for nearly half of its journey down the table as shown. The shot enabled Kennedy to grab a 2-1 advantage on his way to winning the title.

#21 Use Your Imagination

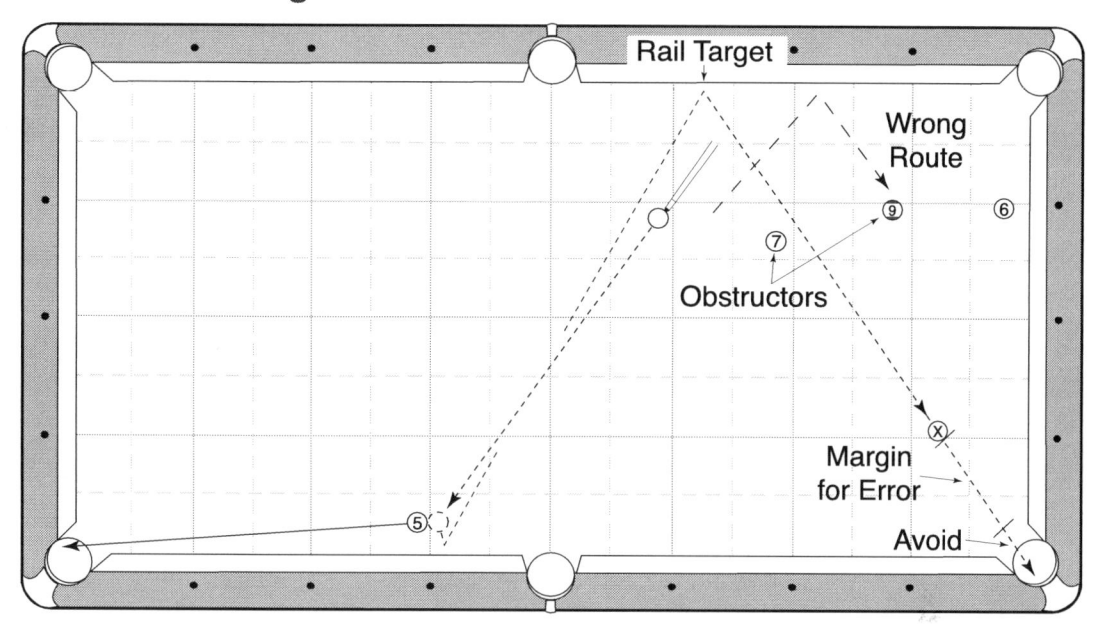

No book can cover every possible position play, so you've got to use your imagination and knowledge of how the balls behave to fill in the gaps, and to construct position plays that are out of the ordinary. Imaginative shots take superior planning and execution, and a super shot may often incorporate a half dozen or more of the principles we've covered in this chapter.

Finland's Mika Immonen was the architect of the brilliant position play in this illustration, which came up in a match against Keith McCready at the Crystal Park Casino near Los Angeles. He was faced with the challenge of sending the cue ball back down table from the 5-ball to the 6. Immonen had to contend with the 7 and 9-balls. Should the cue ball run into either ball, he could have easily failed in his effort to get on the 6-ball. Let's see how he put together the shot.

In this position many amateurs will hit and hope to get past the 7 and 9-balls. Immonen, on the other hand, began to **survey the table** from several vantage points (Note: The Principles of Position are in bold type). At first he considered the route labeled "wrong."

He then checked out the shot from several angles, all the while using his imagination to **plan a route** that would avoid the obstructers. You could see the wheels turning as he calculated the angle of departure off the first rail. He then carefully set a **rail target** that, if hit precisely with just the right amount of spin off the top rail, would enable the cue ball to **avoid the obstructers**.

The route past the obstructers meant that the cue ball would be rolling straight towards the corner pocket. To **avoid scratching** he would have to calculate the **correct speed** for the shot. Nobody's perfect, and the shot required a very powerful stroke, so he allowed for a **margin for error**. After all of this planning was complete, Immonen executed the shot perfectly as shown, and he was rewarded with a warm ovation from the knowledgeable crowd.

#22 Know the Exceptions to the First 21 Principles

The majority of layouts contain familiar position plays in which the first 21 Principles of Position can be applied. However, 9 Ball (like all pool games) are full of exceptions to the rules. Hence, we have Principle #22, which is to Know the Exceptions to the First 21 Principles! Experience and a healthy dose of pool sense will tell you when to ignore one or more of the not-always-sacred principles in this chapter. For example, at times you must:

- Play a risky route when a scratch is possible.
- Run into an obstructer because it can't be avoided.
- Play shape on a shot that allows for virtually no margin for error.
- Turn the cue ball loose and hope for the best because there is no viable safety, and the position route is unfamiliar, or is difficult to control

The principles are designed to work with each other to produce successful position plays. We identified seven of the ones that went into producing Mika Immonen's superlative position play on the previous page. Quite often, however, the principles may be at odds with one another. On page 162 we learned that the Principle of Playing Natural Shape took precedence over the principle of Playing to the Long Side Whenever Possible. Below are some additional instances where one principle may override another.

- You may have to play Area Shape on a difficult shot, which may be at odds with playing for the Correct Side.
- Ball in Hand Shape enables you to violate several of the principles on one shot because of the precision that it gives you in controlling the path of the cue ball.
- The principles of Playing Down the Line and Entering the Wide Side are always in conflict with one another.

CHAPTER 5

Pattern Play

"Anytime you can eliminate anything (that can go wrong) do it."
Buddy Hall

One of the best compliments that a pool player can get is that he plays his patterns well. Good pattern players make sense out the complex jumble that a typical layout of 9 Ball presents. Good pattern players make the game look easy. They move in concert with the layout, and there is a certain flow to their runouts. This is in sharp contrast to those players who always seem to be fighting for position, ball after ball. A good pattern player's ability to run out easily and effortlessly stems from their skills at position play (see Chapter 3), their skills at pattern recognition (this chapter), and their ability to combine patterns to create runouts.

The Run Out Game Plan
Position Play is how you get on the next ball. This includes the route, the target zone, and measures to reduce risk.
Patterns are recognizable sequences of shots that tend to repeat themselves.
Run Outs result from stringing position plays and patterns together.

Pattern Recognition
An infinite number of positions are possible on every rack, and yet **a number of highly recognizable configurations appear repeatedly**. These patterns typically consist of two or three consecutive balls that present a special problem or opportunity. One pattern may require that you handle two consecutive balls on the same rail. On another the key may be choosing whether to play a ball in the corner or side pocket. In this chapter you will be shown how to plan and execute the most commonly recurring patterns. Once you learn to recognize these patterns, you will begin to say things to yourself like: "If I play the 5-ball using a natural two-rail route to the end rail, I will have the correct angle on the 6-ball to send the cue ball back up table for the 7-ball."

Chapter 5 - Pattern Play

The Primary Skill of Pattern Play
To play patterns well you must be able to construct a plan comprised of a series of position routes that enables you to run several balls with the minimum degree of difficulty. These **patterns are linked together with connecting balls to form a complete run out**.

Position Routes as Tools
We covered a variety of position routes in Chapter 3 that enable you to play position from one ball to the next. These are the tools used to execute patterns, which are a series of position plays. When planning the first shot of a sequence, you will often have a choice between two or more potential position routes to the next ball. Your selection must give you position on the next ball, and it must also fit the pattern of the layout. So, you have to plan for two or more successive shots at a time – which we talked about in principle #7 in the previous chapter.

Choosing the correct route will:
- Create a pattern and a run that flows.
- Give you the high percentage route.
- Avoid trouble (scratching, getting hooked, hitting obstructers, etc.).
- Ensure that the cue ball lands on the correct side of the next ball.
- Result in the optimal angle for the next ball.
- Provide a recovery route just in case it is needed.
- Largely enable you to avoid having to play recovery routes.
- Solve problems with difficult balls.

Key Principles of Position for Planning Patterns
The 22 Principles of Position Play covered in Chapter 4 are vital to playing top caliber position. The following eight ones are crucial to planning and executing your patterns successfully:

- #1 Speed Control (see page 124)
- #2 The Correct Cut Angle Optimizes Position (see page 126)
- #3 Know the Boundaries of a Position Zone (see page 128)
- #7 Playing for Three Balls (or more) at a Time (see page 135)
- #8 Play the High Percentage Sequence (see page 136)
- #9 Right Side/Wrong Side (see page 138)
- #12 Playing Down the Line of a Position Zone (see page 144)
- #15 Plan Your Route and Avoid Obstructions (see page 148)

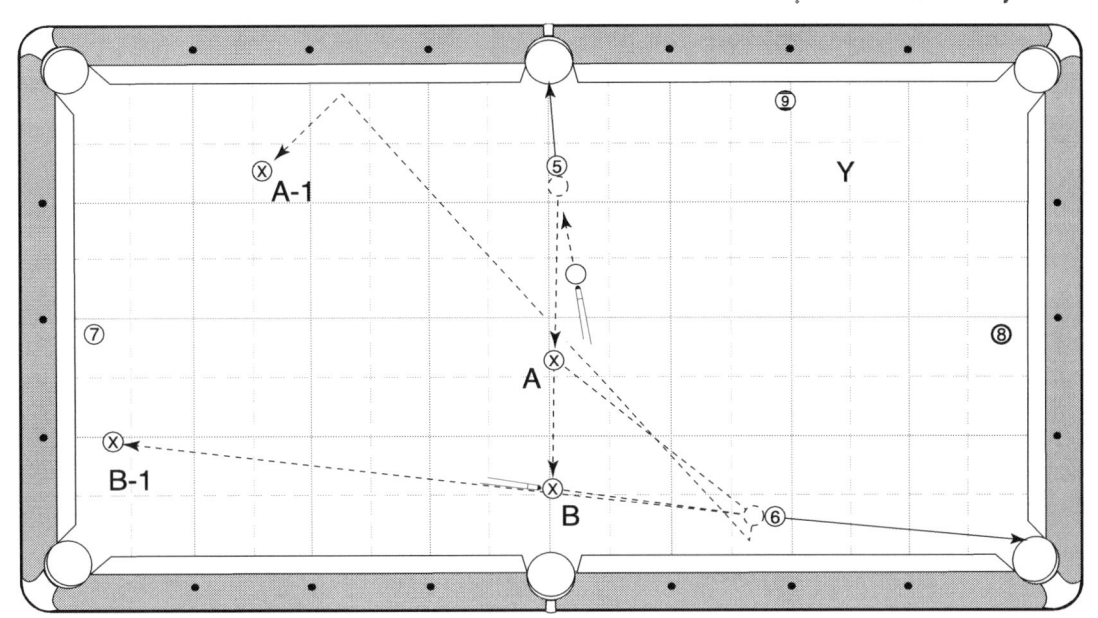

A Tale of Two Players

Good pattern players make the game look easy on layouts where others struggle to run out. This example, which is a contrast in styles, shows the essence of good and poor pattern play. The 5-ball is played with a draw shot. Player A brought the cue ball to Position A, leaving himself with a 30-degree cut on the 6-ball. Player B drew back to Position B for a straight in shot on the 6.

To the novice, Position B looks better because the shot on the 6-ball is easier. But patterns are a series of shots, not shots played in isolation. Player B must now draw back to the short side for position on the 7-ball. His speed was off a little on the 6-ball, which often happens on long straight in draw shots. With only a 10-degree cut angle on the 7-ball, Player B is now facing an extremely difficult recovery route with little chance of arriving at Position Y for the 8-ball, which is at the opposite end of the table.

Now back to Player A. With the cue ball in Position A, he can easily send it across and up the table for excellent position on the 7-ball at Position A-1. The angle on the 7 makes it easy for him to send the cue ball down table to Position Y for excellent shape on the 8-ball.

By the time you are finished with this book, I hope that you have become Player A, and not Player B.

Become a Skillful Navigator

The biggest mistakes in pattern play usually happen in the planning process – before the cue ball has even been struck! You can largely avoid these errors by relishing the challenge of navigating your way around and past the hazards that appear in nearly every rack of 9 Ball. **Every rack can be viewed as a puzzle that needs solving**. If you plough ahead without a plan, your runs are doomed to failure. But if you map out your course with care, and execute well, the cue ball will arrive safely at each of its ports of call until your voyage is complete.

Choosing the Optimal Route

Choosing the correct position routes time after time enables you to execute your patterns in the simplest and most effective manner. Your decisions should be based on: 1) the chances for playing the route successfully, and 2) how the route fits into the pattern or sequence of shots that follows.

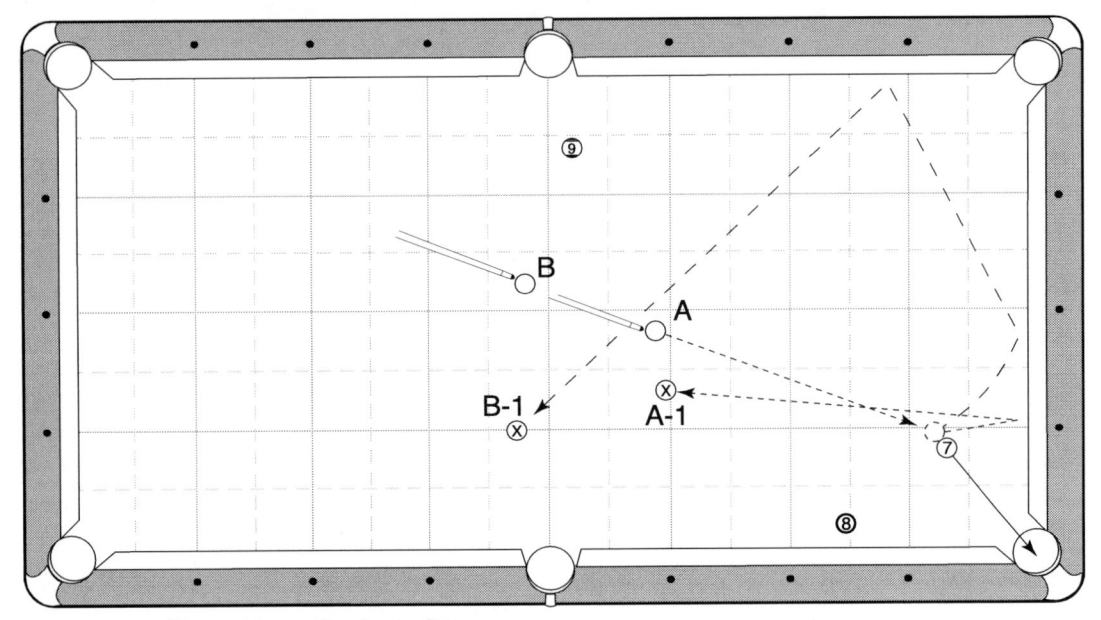

Distance Affects Your Choice of Routes

The cue ball's distance from the object ball is often the deciding factor when choosing which route to play. With the cue ball in Position A, a soft follow stroke with a half tip of inside english (right) will produce a simple route to Position A-1 for the 8-ball. From this distance, using inside english is not difficult because the soft stroke minimizes deflection.

The cue ball is 15 inches further from the 7-ball in Position B – far enough to alter the complexion of the shot. If you used inside english now, the chances of missing the 7-ball would go way up. The better choice from Position B is to draw the cue ball two rails to Position B-1. The remainder of the rack is a cinch from Positions A-1 or B-1, indicating that the pattern was played correctly in both cases.

Obstruction Creates a Gap in Position Zones

Obstructers can have a huge bearing on your choice of possible routes. The 8-ball is blocking an attractive two-rail route from the 6-ball to the 7-ball that could have taken the cue ball to Position A. However, you can still play position on either side of the gap. Route B is the logical choice because it gives you a much larger position zone, and therefore a larger margin for error.

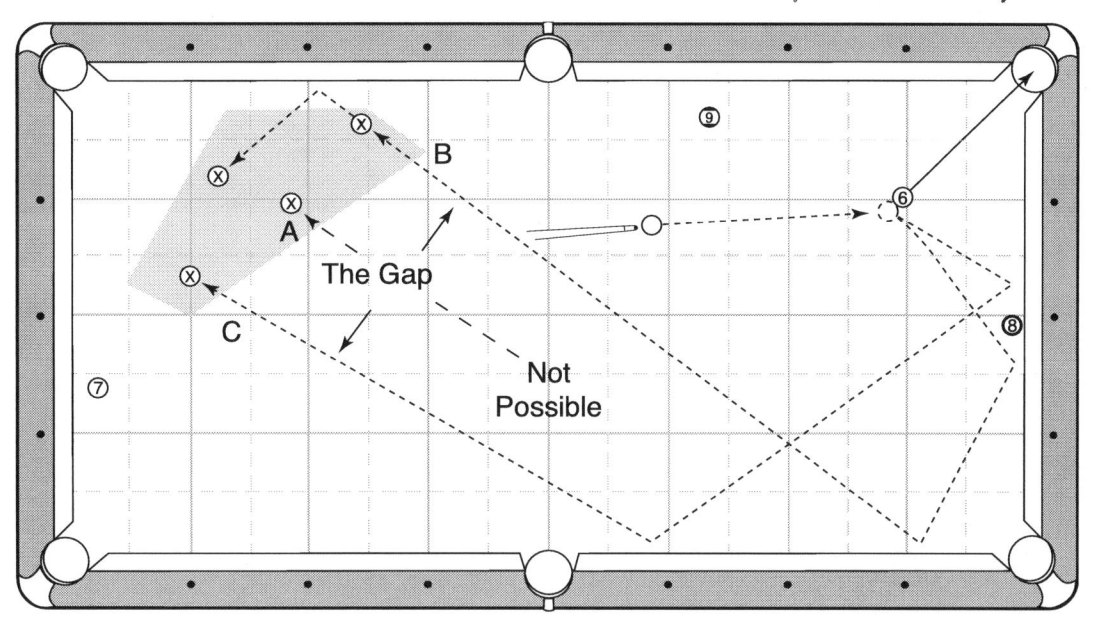

You can get much closer to the 7-ball using Route C. But this advantage is offset by the damage that would be incurred if you came up long or, worse yet, short of the position zone. The lesson: **when a blocker prevents you from playing the ideal route, you must choose the next best one**. This includes considering what is needed to play the pattern.

Connecting Naturally to the Next Ball

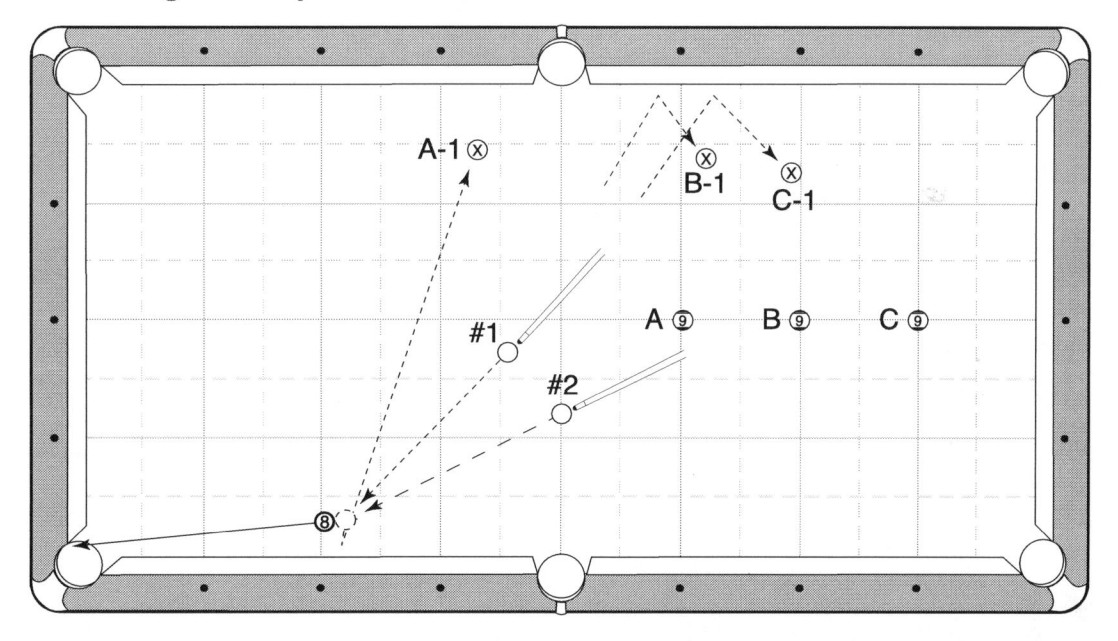

When the cue ball is in Position #1, the logical position for the 9-ball labeled A is at Position A-1. When the 9-ball is at Position B, Position B-1 is best. Finally, when the 9-ball is at C, then Position C-1 is best. Problems arise when you play a route that does not correspond to the object ball's position. Route C-1, for example, doesn't match up with the 9-ball at Position B.

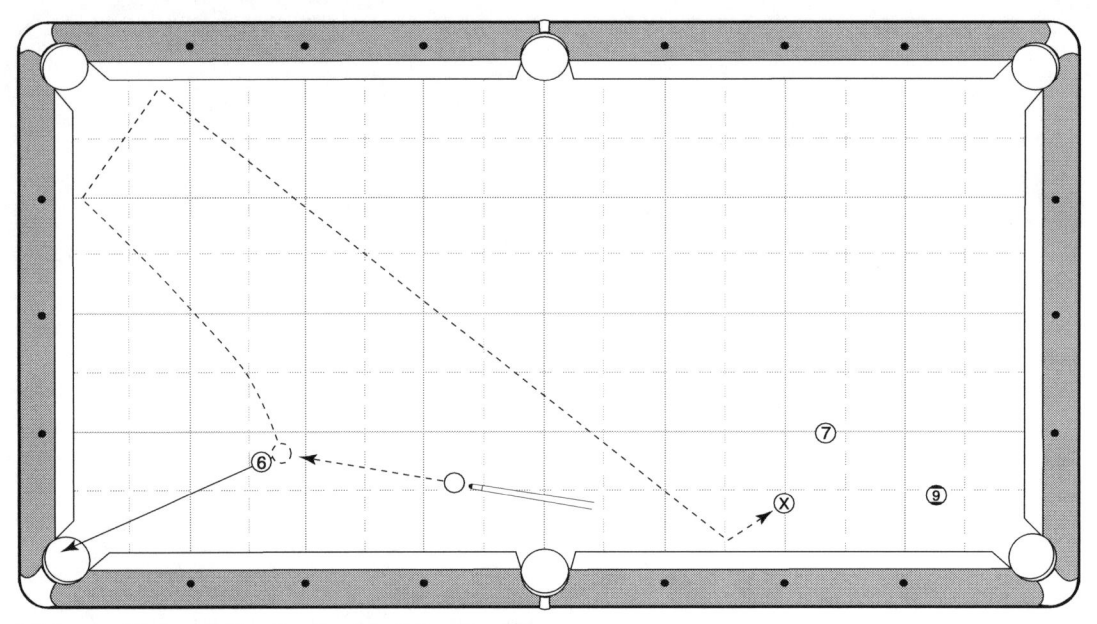

Using a Natural Route to Avoid a Combo

Before playing the 6-ball, Earl Strickland had to decide between the 7-9 combo or shape for a run out in the 1999 U.S. Open against Cliff Joyner. In most cases combo shape would have been the better choice, but not here because a natural three-rail route led to the short side of the 7-ball. The lesson: **long distance shape is not necessarily that difficult when you can play a natural route**, so use this route when it is part of a high percentage sequence.

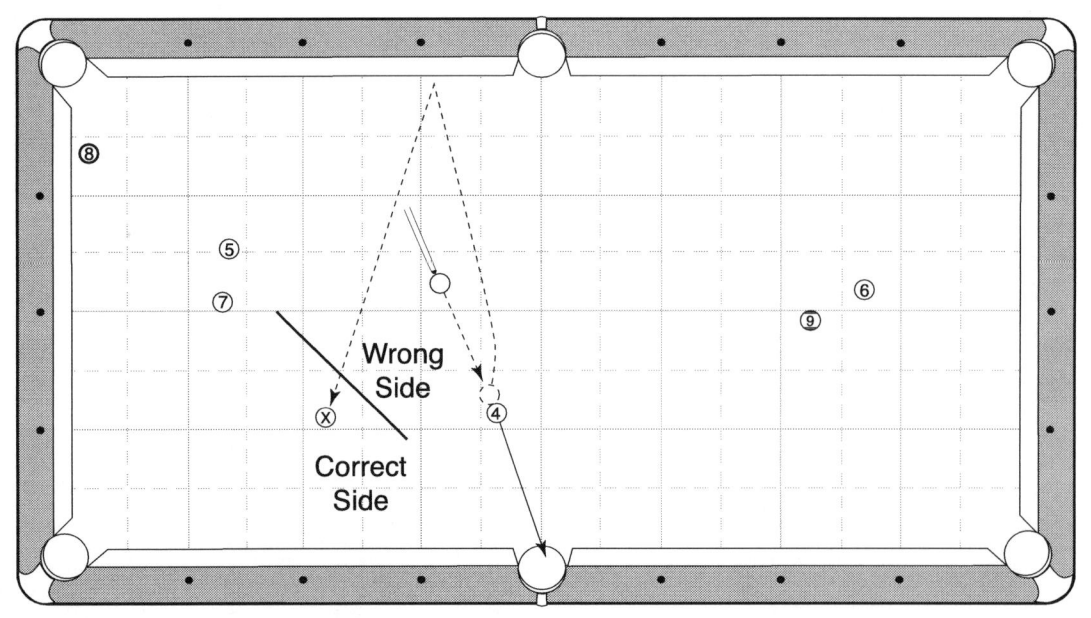

Drawing to the Correct Side

Buddy Hall, a master of pattern play, showed great table sense when he sent the cue ball to the opposite side rail and back to the correct side of the 5-ball. The correct side enabled him to avoid hitting the 7-ball, and to send the cue ball down table for the 6-ball. This shot was played at the Sands Regency Open 15 against Grady Mathews.

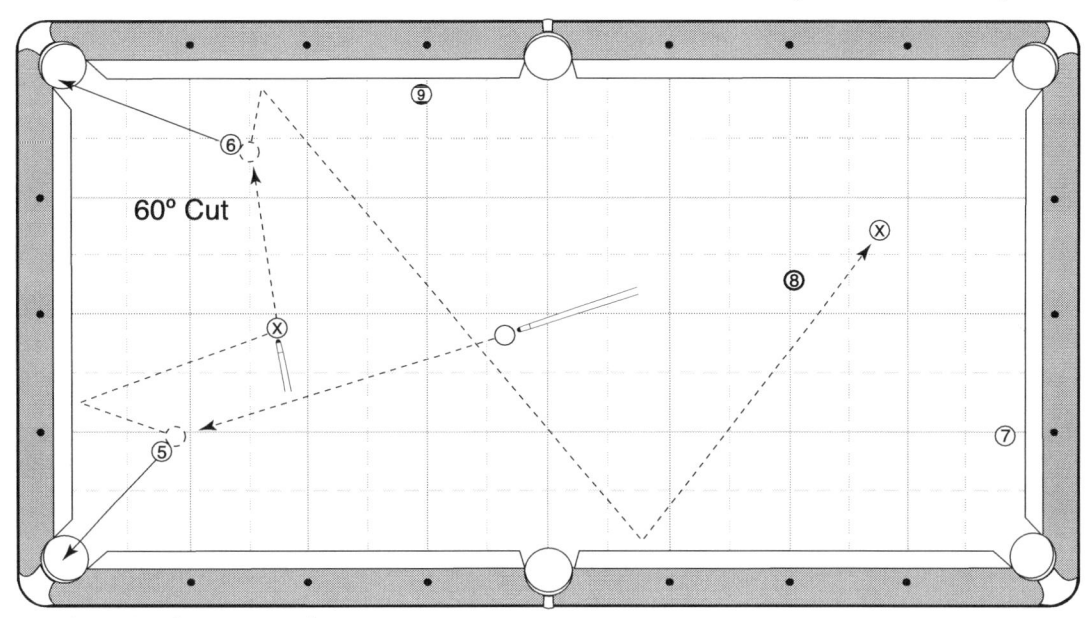

Setting Up the Zorro Shot

Zorro was one of my favorite TV shows as a kid, and the Big Z is also one of the most useful position routes. Kunihiko Takahashi meticulously set up the optimal angle for the Zorro shot with a 60-degree cut on the 6-ball, an angle that enabled him to play shape on the 7-ball with great precision. This pattern and the next one occurred at the 1999 U.S. Open against Chuck Altomare.

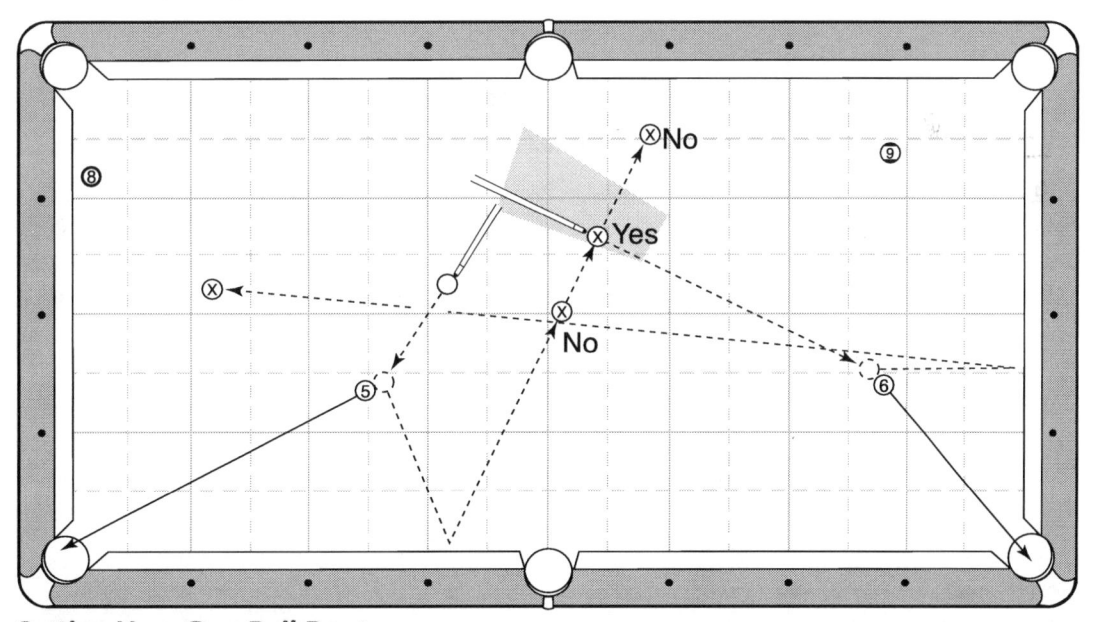

Setting Up a One Rail Route

The 9-ball was blocking a three-rail route from the 6-ball to the 8-ball. Realizing this, Takahashi again showed his knowledge of pattern play by setting up the ideal angle for one-rail shape from the 6 to the 8. His speed on the 5-ball was perfect, and it needed to be because the cue ball approached a narrow position from the side!

Three Ball Patterns

Three-ball patterns, which I introduced in Chapter 4 (see Principles of Position Play #7, page 135), are at the heart of pattern play. When playing for three balls at a time, you must first determine:

- What options are available for position on the second ball?
- What route will enable you to then play position on the third ball?
- After playing the first ball, the process repeats itself.

Three ball patterns are so vital to running racks of 9 Ball that, if you learn nothing else from this book, you must at least master this principle.

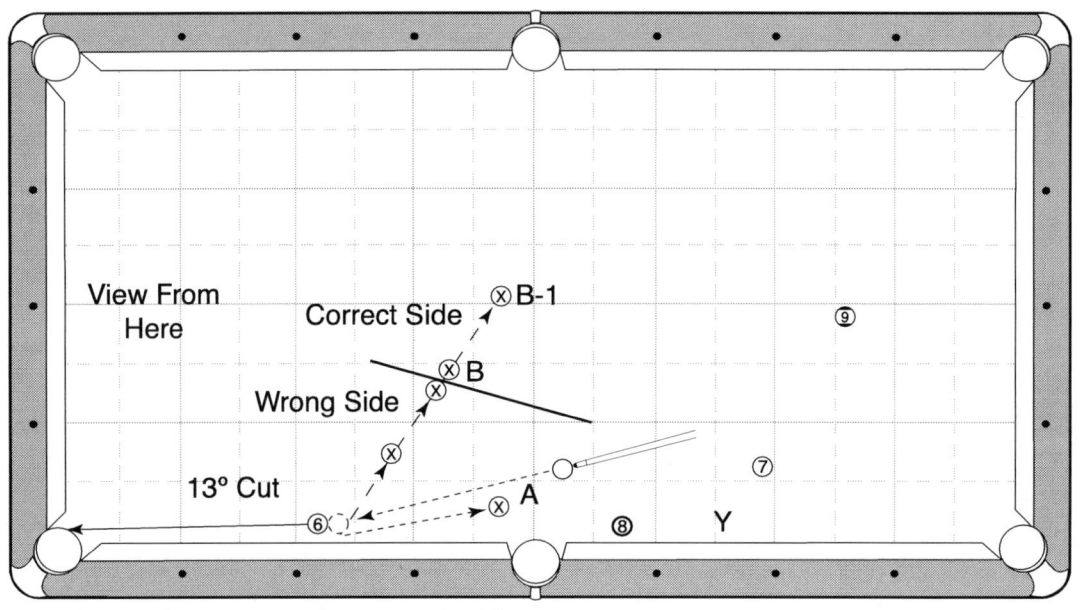

Good Speed to Get on the Correct Side

When two consecutive balls are on the same rail, you may be facing a difficult layout – like the 7 and 8-balls in our example. You could draw to Position A for the 7-ball, but this would force you to send the cue ball across the table and back for shape on the 8.

An easier three-ball pattern is to force the cue ball away from the rail to the zone from that runs from Position B to B-1. The cue ball would now be on the correct side of the 7, enabling you to float the cue ball over to Position Y for shape on the 8-ball. If you came up short of the correct side, you would have to play a recovery route to the 8. The key is to play the 6-ball with enough speed that the cue ball reaches the correct side. So, the smart play is to build a margin for error by favoring the middle of the zone from B to B-1.

Setting up Two Way Position

The big challenge is to get back up table for the 9-ball when playing the 8-ball. The 50-degree cut on the 7-ball makes speed control difficult – and the cue ball will be crossing the position zone – so this is one tough pattern! But you have do have an opportunity to play two-way position, which widens the position zone. If the cue ball stops at Position A, Route A-1 will take you to the 9-ball. If the cue ball continues to Position B, you can use Route B-1. Set the positional bull's-eye in the middle so you have a margin for error to either side.

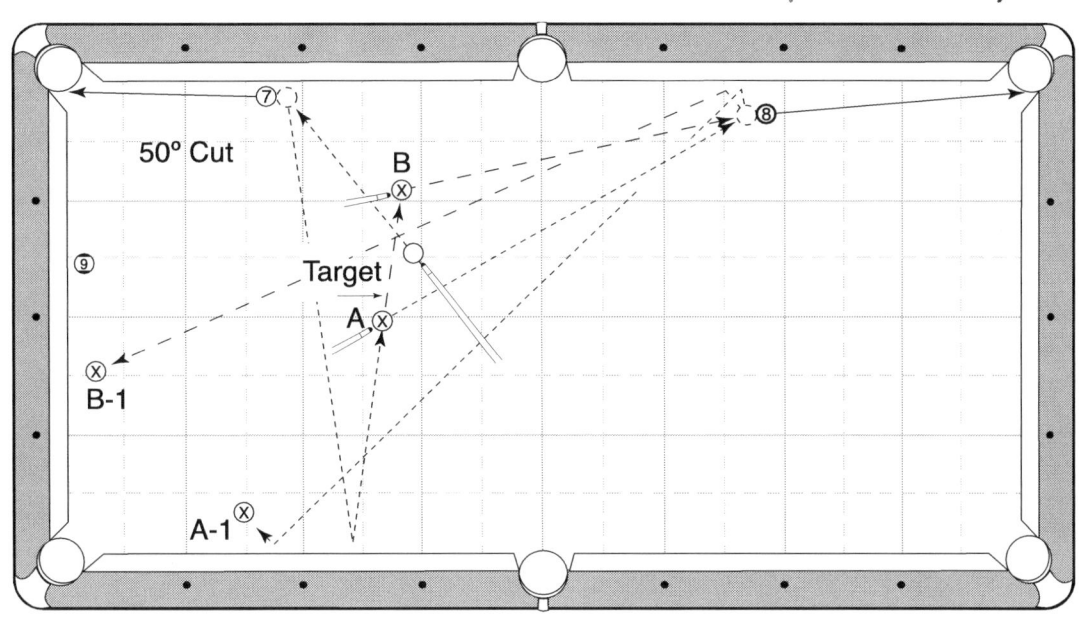

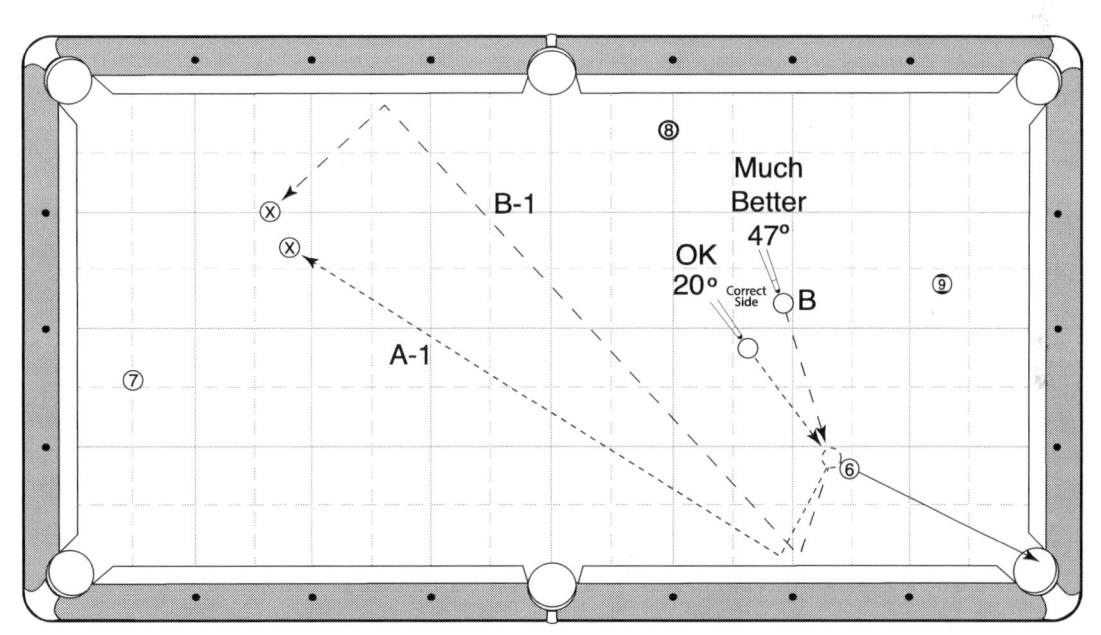

When a Sharper Angle Works Better

Positioning the cue ball on the correct side of the ball with the ideal angle is best, even if that means setting up for a thinner cut shot. The moderate cut angle in Position A leads to a natural path to the 7-ball down Route A-1. However, this route means the cue ball will be crossing through the zone and will be traveling toward the corner pocket. Route B-1 shows the natural path to the 7-ball. Even though the cut is steeper, this route enables you to play down the line shape on the 7-ball – and it eliminates the chance of scratching!

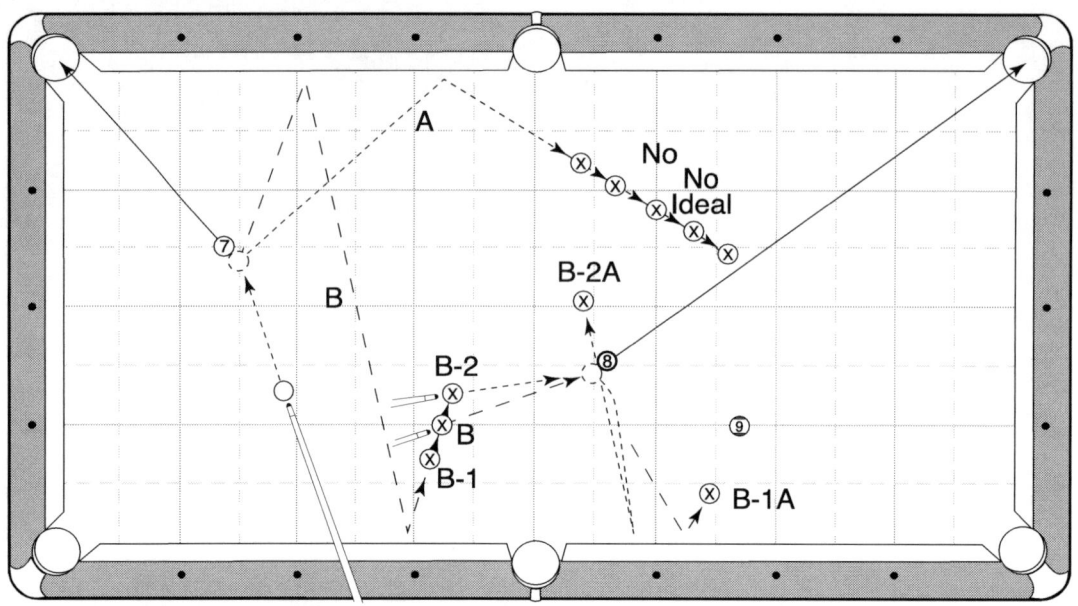

A Multiple Option Pattern - Two Way Position

On both routes to the 8-ball you must play across the line shape. Route A leads to a very awkward position play on the 8-ball if the cue ball stops short of ideal. And, if the cue ball goes past the ideal zone, you will have to play to the end rail and back for the 9-ball.

Route B offers a much better series of routes from the 8-ball to the 9, even if you miss ideal shape at Position B. It is easy to draw from B-1 to the short side at B-1A. From B-2 you can play off the rail to B-2A. These alternative position routes are preferable to those available when you miss ideal position while following Route A.

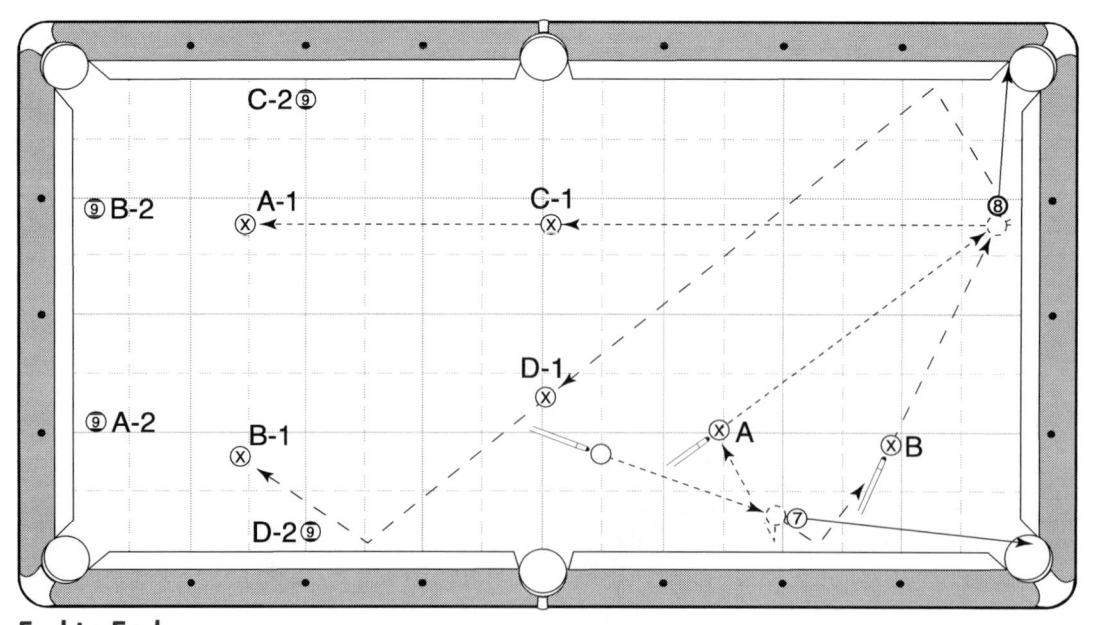

End to End

The 9-ball has been placed in four locations. The key to getting on each 9-ball is to carefully plan your position from the 7-ball to the 8-ball. Drawing off the rail to Position A will set up a sharper angle on the 8-ball. This will make it easier to send the cue ball straight down the table to A-1 for the 9-ball at A-2, or to C-1 for the 9-ball at C-2. A soft follow shot to Position B will set up the two-rail position route to B-1 for the 9-ball at B-2, or to D-1 for the 9-ball at D-2. Notice that the position played on the 8-ball was dictated by the need to get on the 9-ball in the best way possible.

4 Ball Patterns

Planning for three balls is essential to pattern play, but often you must take the planning process one big step further. **At times you must play shape on the second ball with an angle that will enable you to get on the third ball, and that allows you to get on the third ball in a way that ensures you'll be able to continue to the fourth ball!** I know – this may sound a bit complex, but the idea should become clear after you've studied the four diagrams that follow.

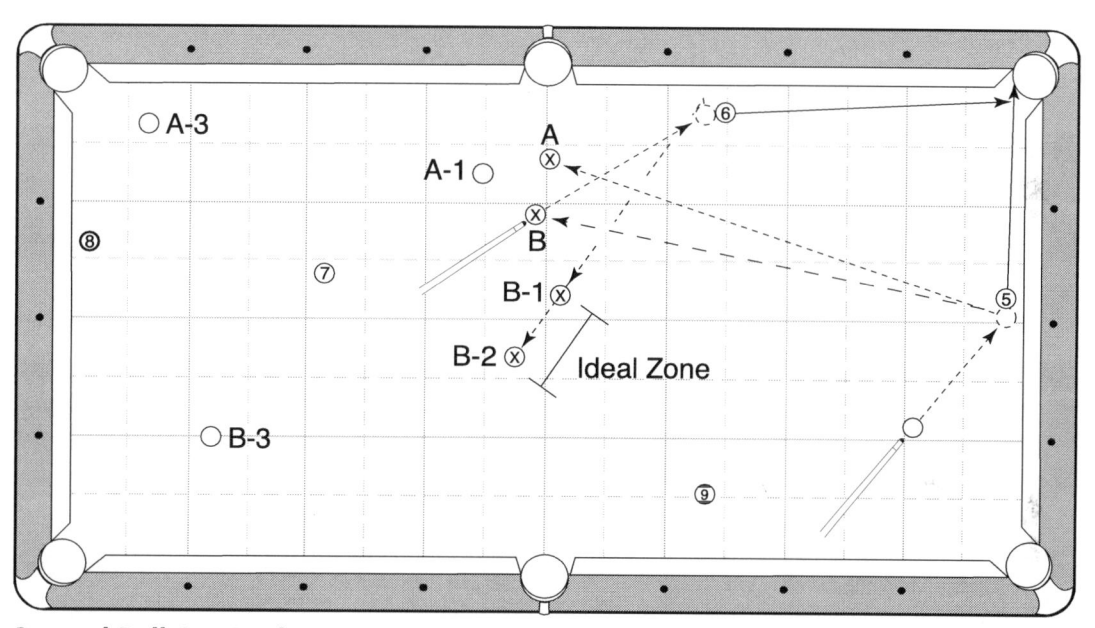

Second Ball Cut Angle

Position from the 5-ball to the 6-ball is no problem. If the cue ball stops at Position A, you will have no trouble making the 7-ball. That takes care of three balls, but what about the 8-ball – the fourth ball? With the shallow angle on the 6-ball, it will be hard to bounce very far from the rail, so you will likely wind up at or near Position A-1 for the 7-ball. Now the cue ball is going to flirt with the upper left corner while playing short side position to A-3.

Now let's assume that you play to Position B for the 6-ball. The larger cut angle makes it easier to float the cue ball across the table to the position zone from B-1 to B-2. Now you can play to the long side of the 8-ball near Position B-3. This also gives you an angle to get to the 9-ball, and the cue ball will be bouncing off the side rail, so there is no chance of scratching!

To recap, the cut angle on the second ball (the 6-ball) ensures that you will easily get position on the third ball (the 7-ball). And that, in turn, enables you to play excellent shape on the fourth ball (the 8-ball).

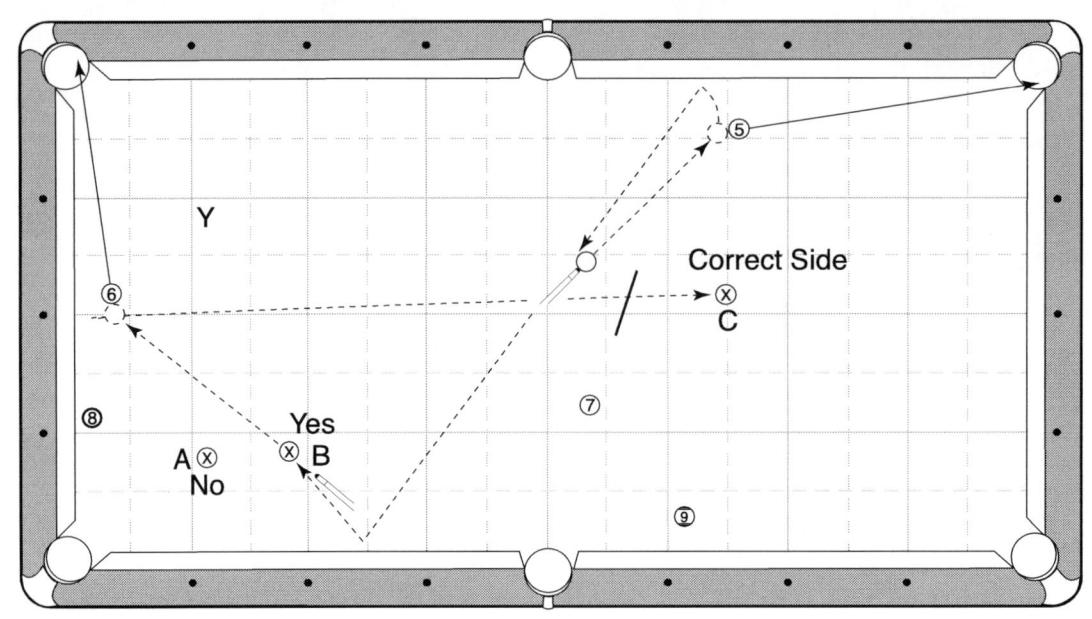

The Second Ball's Cut Angle is Key

Position from the 5-ball to the 6-ball is no problem. As long as you have an angle on the 6, you can escape the end rail and send the cue ball down table for the 7-ball. If you were only planning for three balls, the cut angle on the 6-ball at Position A would be fine. However, the key to this run is getting from the 7-ball to the 8.

The first step in our four ball pattern is to leave a larger angle on the 6-ball as shown by Position B. This angle allows you to use a speed of stroke that can be controlled with precision. When playing the 6-ball, you must get to the correct side of the 7. Position C is ideal. Now it will be easy to play a stun shot off the end rail to Position Y for the 8-ball.

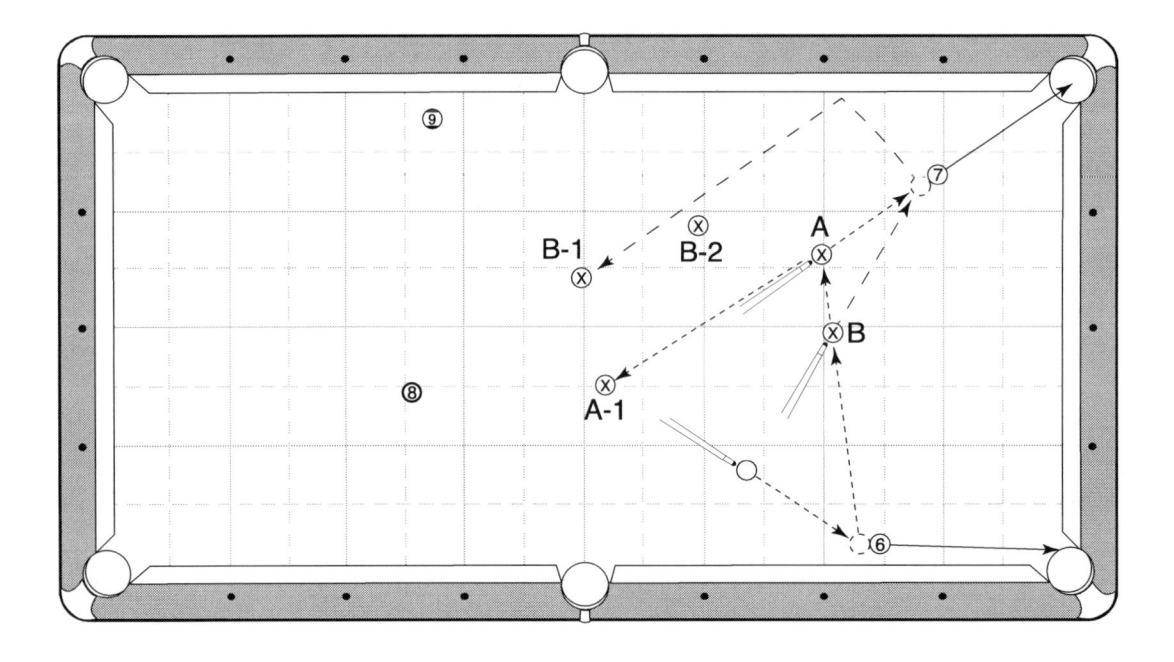

Setting Up Down the Line Shape

The 8-ball is in the middle of the table, which always draws a yellow flag, and the 9-ball is high up on the side rail, so this pattern must be planned with great care. If the cue ball stopped at Position A for the 7-ball, you could draw back to A-1 for the 8-ball. That takes care of the first three balls. However, it will be difficult to get good shape on the 9-ball from Position A-1.

The solution is to plan for four balls. Step one is to leave an angle on the 7-ball at Position B. Now you can draw off the side rail and play down the line for straight in shape on the 8-ball at B-1. From B-1 you can draw straight back to B-2 for excellent

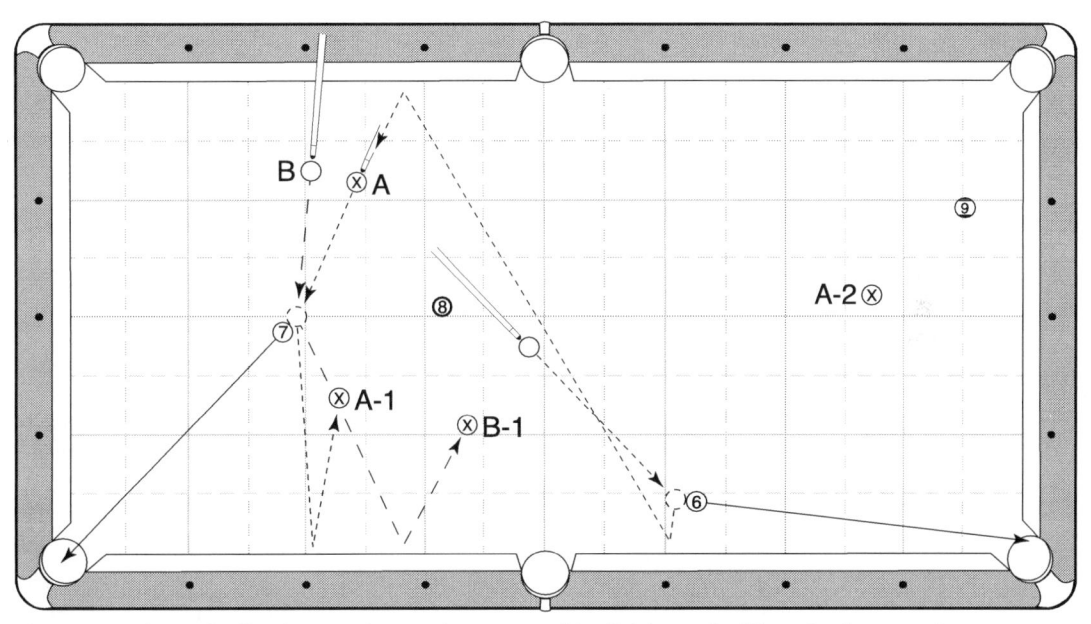

shape on the 9-ball. The angle on the second ball (the 7-ball) is the key to this pattern.

One Good Angle Leads to Another

When you play one good angle after another, running out seems easy. Good angles eliminate the need for recovery shots and heroics that may be entertaining to the fans, but that grate on the senses of a well-schooled observer. This example is a case in point.

The cue ball crossed the table after pocketing the 6-ball and continued out to Position A for a perfect angle on the 7-ball. A soft follow shot on the 7-ball resulted in Position A-1 for excellent shape on the 8-ball. Another soft follow shot will send the cue ball to A-2 for a simple shot on the 9-ball. Notice how the ideal angle turned every shot into a virtual hanger. The key to this pattern was to play the correct position on the second ball (the 7) so you could easily get to the fourth ball (the 9).

Now let's assume on the 6-ball that the cue ball traveled past our ideal angle to Position B. A soft follow shot on the 7-ball would now result in Position B-1, or somewhere even worse! Now it will be a struggle to get on the 9-ball. The lesson: **planning for three balls works most of the time, but if you plan for four balls, your patterns will, at times, be far more precise.**

Chapter 5 - Pattern Play

Don't Fight the Table

When the layout is not completely to your liking, you must still play the hand you've been dealt, as card players would say. That means that you shouldn't force the situation, or try to essentially make something out of nothing. Play the table and make your decisions based on the layout as is, not as how you would have preferred it to be.

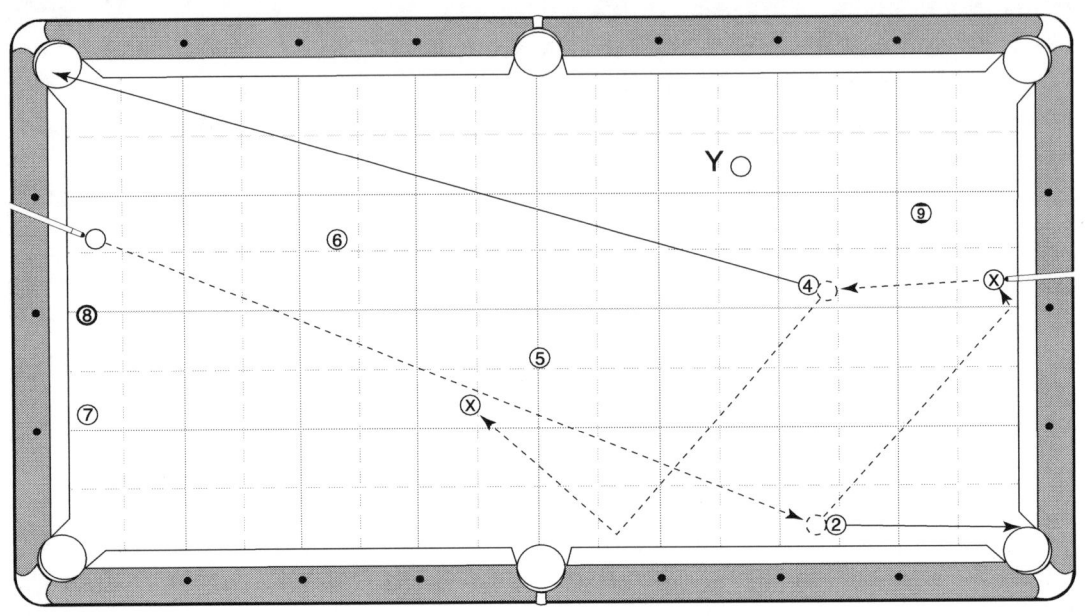

Accept what the Table Gives You

Earl Strickland was faced with a table length shot off the rail on the 2-ball in a match with Johnny Archer at the Sands Regency Open 16, 1992.

He could have powered in the 2-ball and sent the cue ball two rails to Position Y, but he knew that this would be forcing the issue, and that his pocketing percentage would suffer a big drop. So, he wisely used a medium speed of stroke off the rail, insuring the accuracy of the shot. Playing the 2-ball like this also meant that he would next be looking at a table length shot on the 4-ball. So be it. The high percentage sequence (remember this principle?) was to play two moderately difficult shots rather than overplaying the 2-ball in the hopes of having a hanger on the 4-ball.

Cinching Position with a Long Shot

The hard part of this layout is getting from the 4-ball to the 5 because of the 9-ball, which has severely reduced the position zone for the 5-ball. Efren Reyes, our star in this example, could have drawn to Position A when playing the 3-ball, which would have made the 4-ball much easier – to pocket. But this would have forced Reyes to send the cue ball through traffic to get on the 5-ball. Reyes recognized the danger and decided to play a short-range draw shot on the 3-ball, leaving him with a long stop shot on the 4-ball from Position B. Accepting the layout and playing this pattern assured Reyes of a clear shot on the 5-ball from Position C. This took place in the finals with Ralf Souquet at the Sands Regency Open 27, 1998.

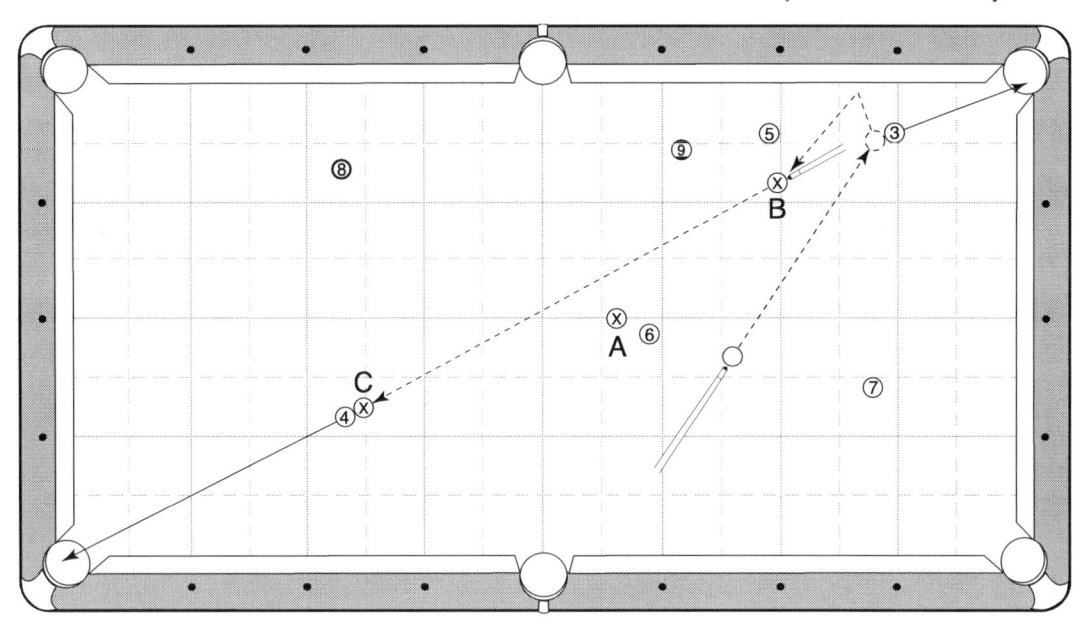

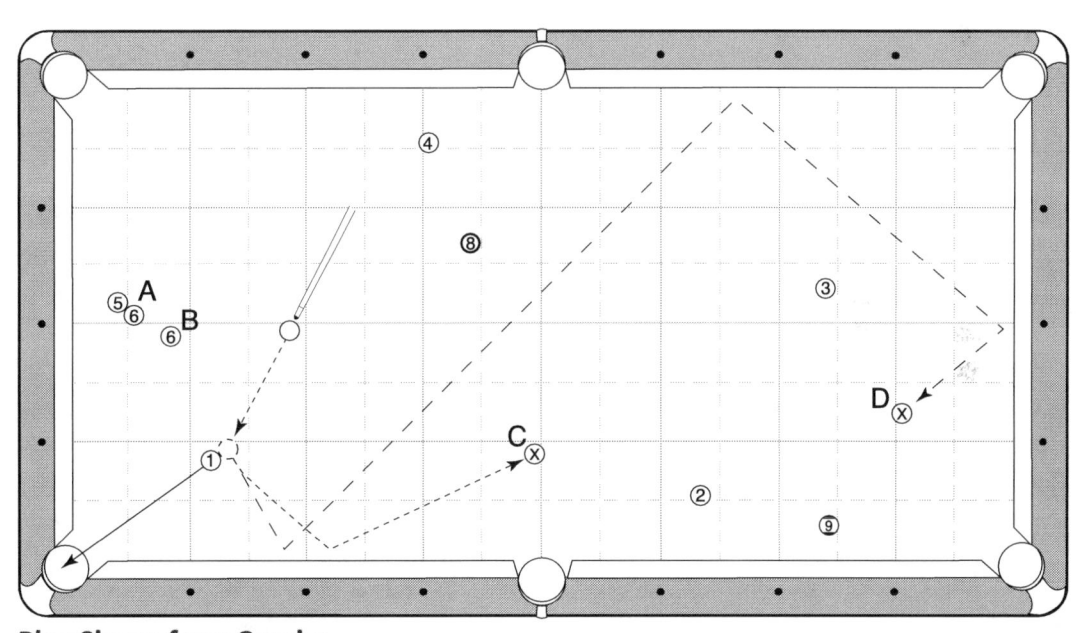

Play Shape for a Combo

The 5 and 6-balls are clustered in Position A, making a runout unlikely. The smart choice for many players in this position is to send the cue ball to Position C for the 2-9 combo. If the 6-ball had been in Position B, then the best strategy would be to play for the run out by sending the cue ball three rails to Position D for shape on the 2-ball. In both positions, the strategy was dictated by the layout. Remember: **don't fight the table. Play what you're given and go with the flow**.

Simple is Often Best

A number of players have a tendency to complicate matters when playing position even though the best approach is often the simplest one. No frills position routes and patterns may not look as impressive to some observers, but they can be very, very, very effective.

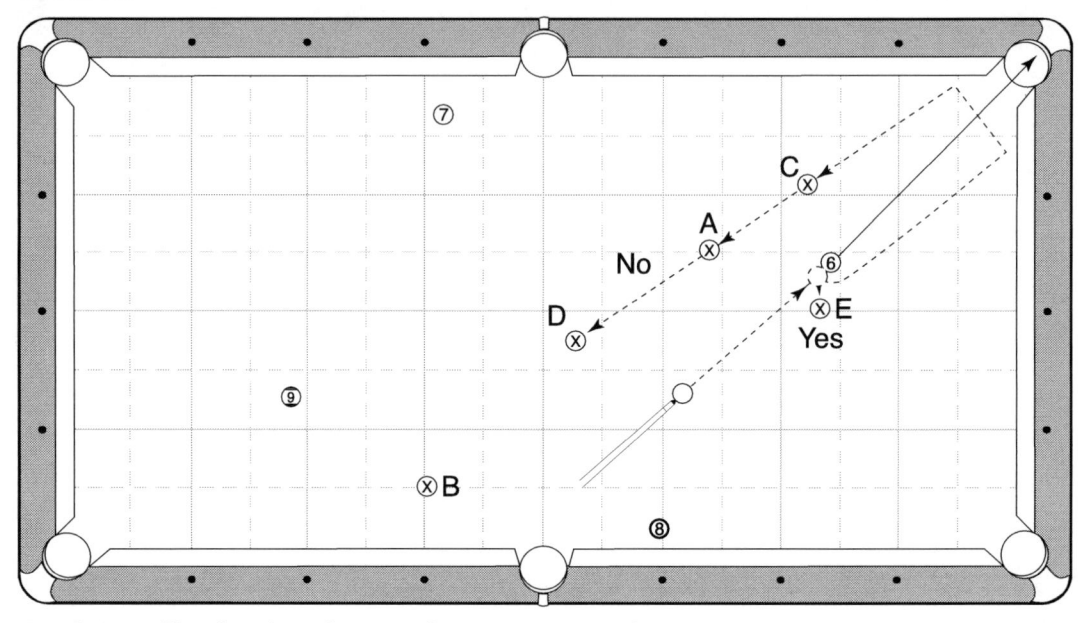

Don't Needlessly Play Shape When You Have Shape

The most important rule of the no frills, keep it simple method of pattern play is **do not play position when you already have position** – a concept that was coined by Buddy Hall, the master of pattern play. His maxim sounds kind of funny when you first hear it, but it will become crystal clear in a few moments.

The key to completing this runout is in getting an angle on the 7-ball that will allow you to send the cue ball across the table for the 8-ball. You could use top left (inside) english to send the cue ball two rails to Position A, which is an ideal angle (25 degrees) for sending the cue ball to Position B for the 8-ball.

If the cue ball stopped short at Position C, you would have to play a difficult two-rail recovery route to the 8-ball, which would require a hard follow stroke with left english. You would be in even worse shape if you hit the cue ball very far past Position A. And, if you misjudged the speed and it continued to Position D, you would have to play safe. As you can see, "playing" shape is a risky proposition in this situation.

Now let's go back to our shot of the 6-ball. A three inch draw shot to Position E would give you the same cut angle as in Position A. Yes, the shot on the 7-ball is about a foot longer (than from Position A), but the extra length is worth it because you have eliminated the risk of missing position on the 7-ball. You didn't have to play position for the 7-ball because it was sitting there right next to the 6-ball!

Keep it Simple to Avoid Trouble

Ismael "Morro" Paez chose the position route chosen in this illustration, which is a single shot clinic in keeping things simple. Paez could have left himself with a shorter shot on the 7-ball by using Route A or B, but each of these choices would have opened him up to getting hooked behind the 8-ball. So Paez chose to keep things simple by following Route C for short side position on the 7-ball. This shot took place in a match with Johnny Archer at the 1997 U.S. Open. Archer, who did a player review of this match for Accu-Stats, totally agreed with Paez' shot selection.

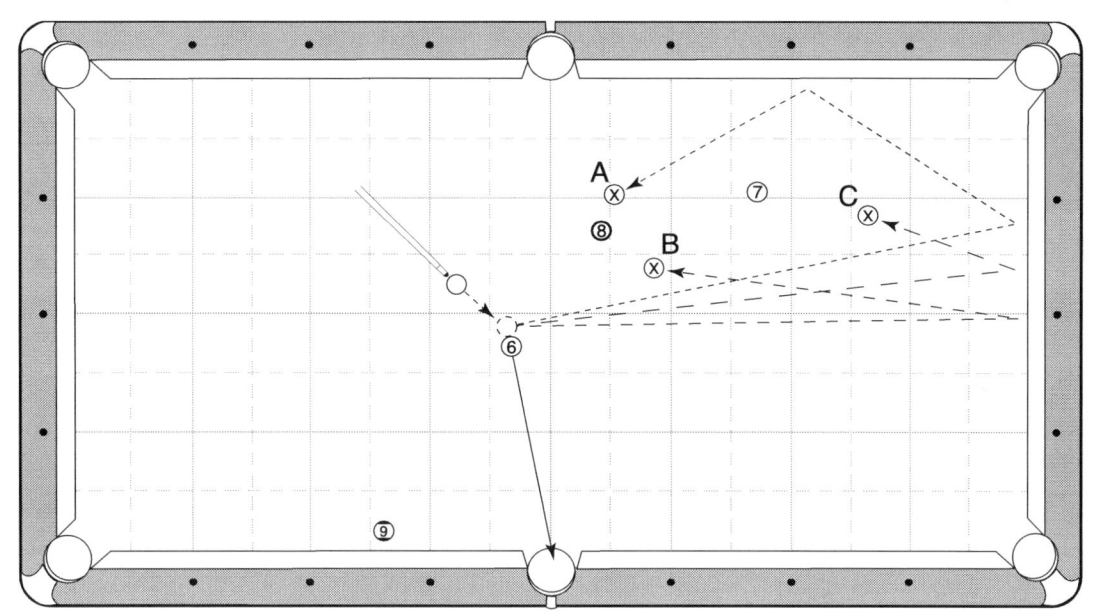

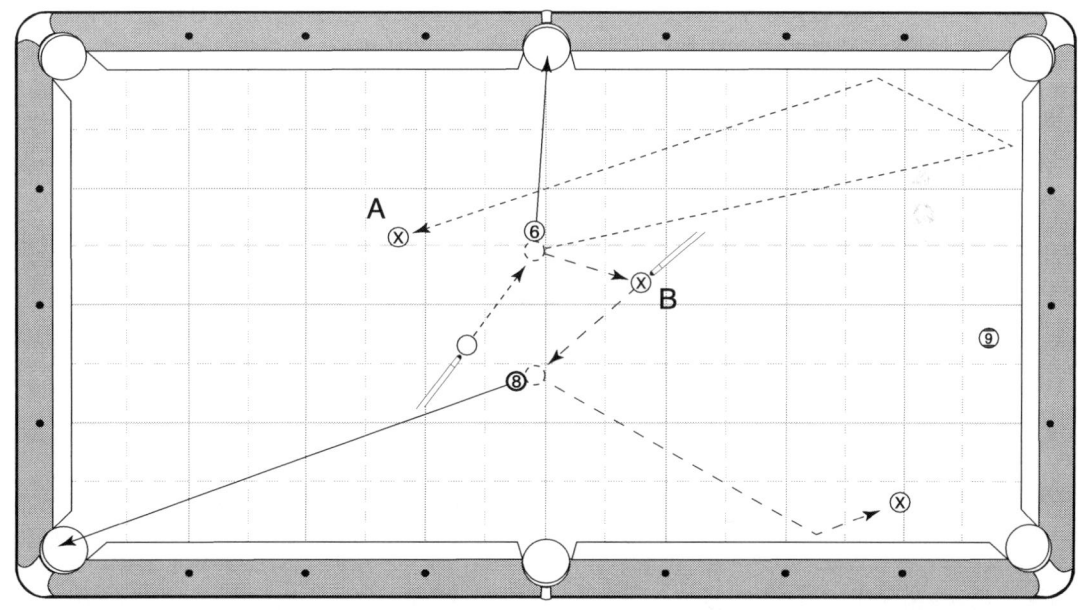

A Sensible but Overlooked Pattern
The pattern above shows another way of keeping things simple. You could send the cue ball two rails for an easy side pocket shot on the 8-ball at Position A, but it would be easy to stop on the wrong side of the 8, or to overrun your position zone. The better play is to drift the cue ball about one foot to Position B for a relatively simple route from the 8-ball to the 9-ball.

Chapter 5 - Pattern Play

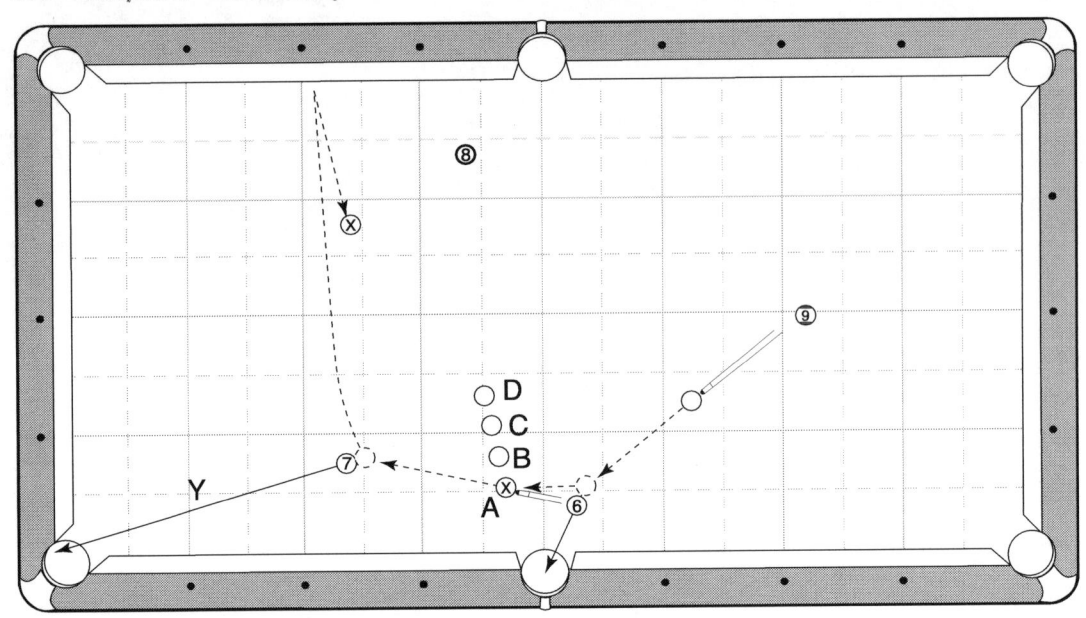

The Easiest and Best Sequence

Johnny Archer was in the finals of the 1999 U.S. Open against Jeremy Jones when he came across this four-ball layout. The pattern is a breeze for a top pro in part because he knows the little details that keep things simple.

When playing the 6-ball, Archer floated the cue ball forward to Position A. This simple maneuver provided him with a large enough angle on the 7-ball so that he could draw across the table and out for the 8-ball. The rest of the run is easy enough.

Now let's consider some alternative routes from the 6-ball to the 7. Position B is ok, but it requires that you use a finesse draw shot to float to Cue Ball X. You could also pound the cue ball to the top side rail and back out. Either of these routes will work, but neither is nearly as playable as the one that Archer played from Position A.

The fun really begins if you were to send the cue ball to Position C after pocketing the 6-ball. One option is to follow down to Position Y for a tricky shot on the 8-ball into the side pocket. Another option is to play a stop shot on the 7-ball, and then send the cue ball three rails for shape on the 9-ball. With the cue ball in Position D (following the shot on the 6-ball) you could follow off the side rail and out to Position Y. Another option is to pound the cue ball off the rail and across for position on the 8-ball. Neither of these choices is very appealing.

The lesson: **simplicity is often the result of paying close attention to the little things that make a big difference in pattern play**.

The Right Choice is a One Railer

Excelling at two-rail position is vital to playing runout 9 Ball, but one rail position is still used on nearly 50% of the pros' position plays because they know that it enables them to maintain maximum control over the cue ball.

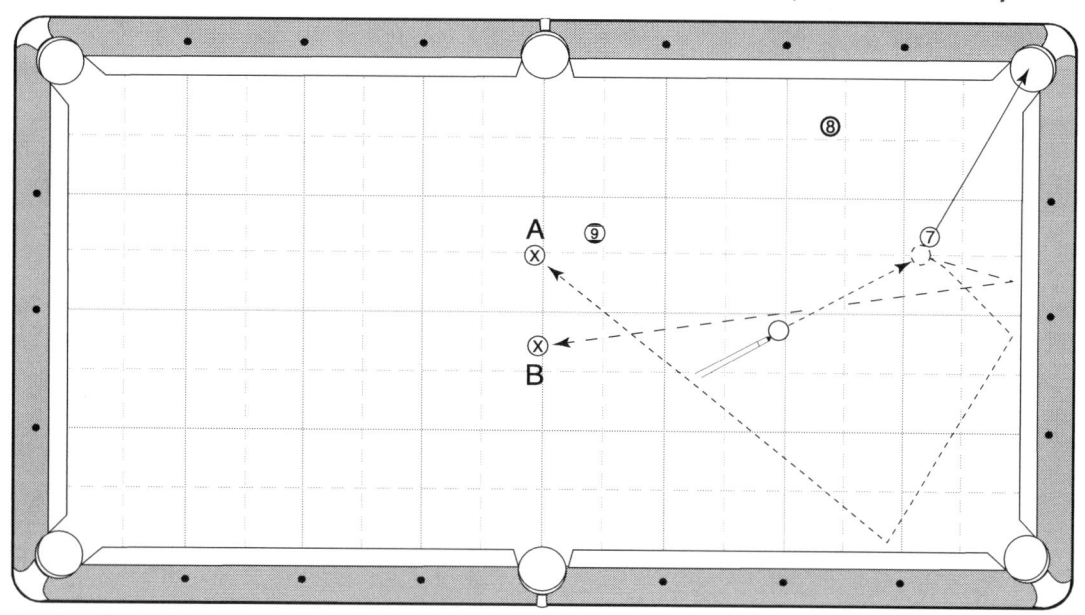

You could play two rails for shape on the 8-ball, but if you overran your position zone, you could get hooked behind the 9-ball as shown by the cue ball at Position A. The one rail route to Position B for the 8-ball is much safer.

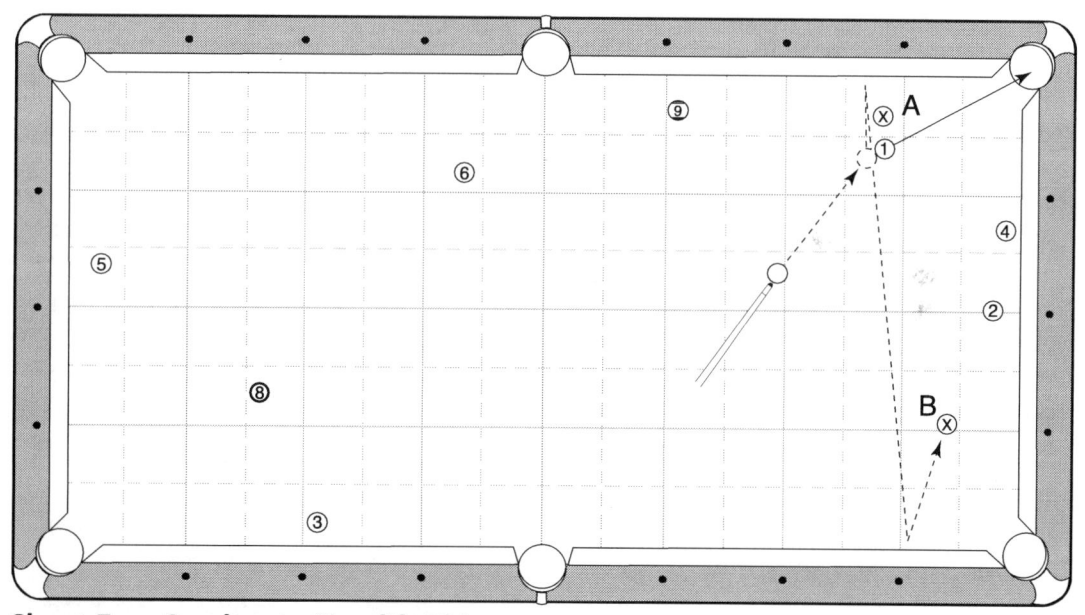

Shoot Easy Combos to Simplify Things

If you rolled the cue ball very softly so that it stopped at Position A after pocketing the 1-ball, you would have to bring the cue ball back down table for the 4-ball when playing the 3, which is not very easy to do from its position on the lower side rail. And, when playing the 4-ball, you would have to send the cue ball to the opposite end of the table for the 5-ball. Both of these positional nightmares can be eliminated if you play the 2-4 combo from Position B after pocketing the 1-ball. The 4-ball is close to the rail, which makes this an easy shot. The lesson: **play easy combos when shooting them can greatly simplify the layout**.

Pocket Choice

Since there are six pockets on a pool table, you might as well make full use of all of them. Don't restrict yourself with theories that say silly things like "avoid the side pockets." And, on certain occasions you will want to violate principle #10 of position play that advises you to play on the long side. The bottom line is this: **use the best pocket for the shot at hand no matter how offbeat that choice may appear at first glance.**

Setting Up the Short Side

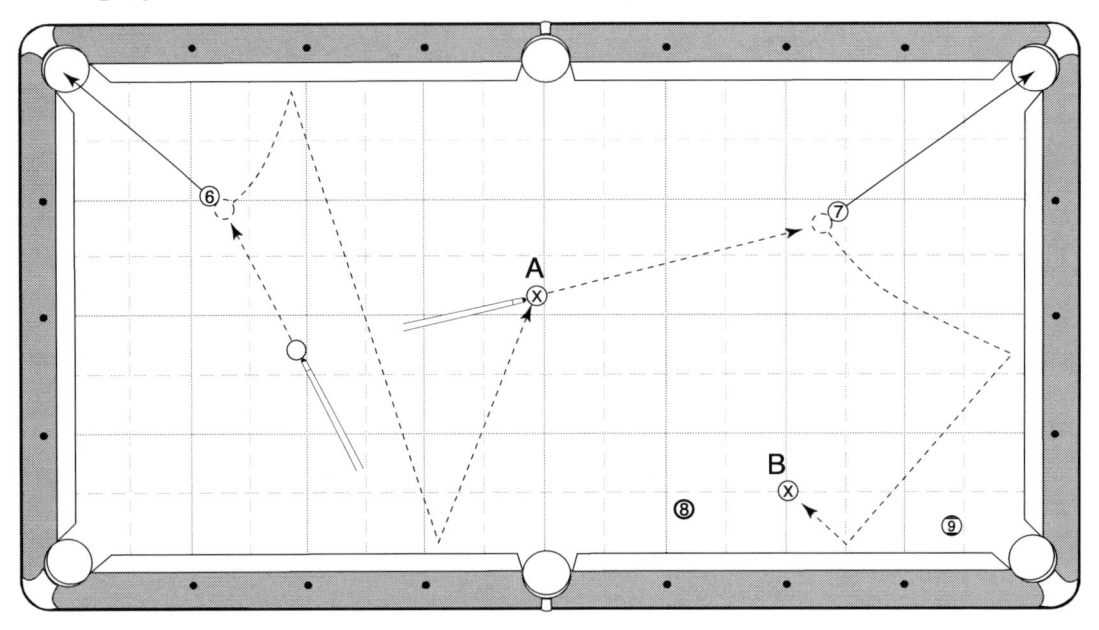

The 8-9 combo is not easy, but many players would go for it because the 9-ball is not far from the corner pocket. Rafael Martinez, however, elected to pass on the combo and run out in the finals against Efren Reyes at the Sands Regency Open 15, 1994. Martinez figured that the percentages favored the run, providing he could get on the short side of the 8-ball. The shot on the 6-ball was key because it set him up with the ideal angle on the 7-ball at Position A. A follow shot off the end rail resulted in perfect shape on the short side of the 8 at Position B.

Use All Six Pockets

Efren Reyes was playing Francisco Bustamante in the semi-finals of the Sands Regency Open 29, 1999 when he came across this fascinating study in pattern play. Reyes could have followed standard operating procedure on the 5-ball by sending the cue ball between the 6 and 9-balls to Position A for the shape on the 6-ball. Reyes instead exercised his creative powers by playing shape for the lower side pocket at Position B. He minimized the cue ball's traveling distance, which usually leads to better position. Finally, he ended up with shape on the correct side of the 6-ball to go down the table for the 7-ball.

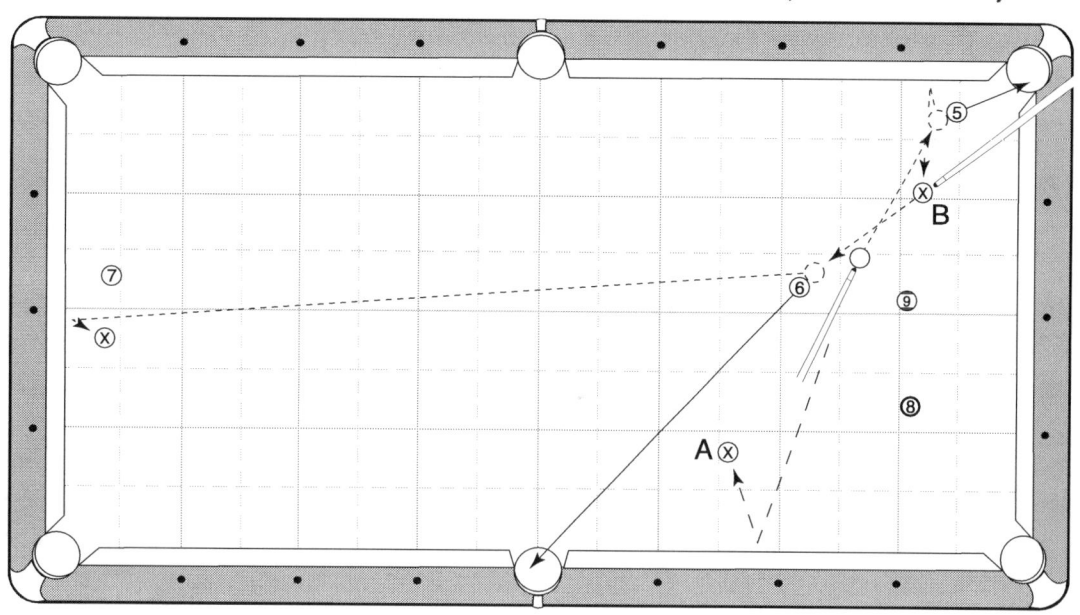

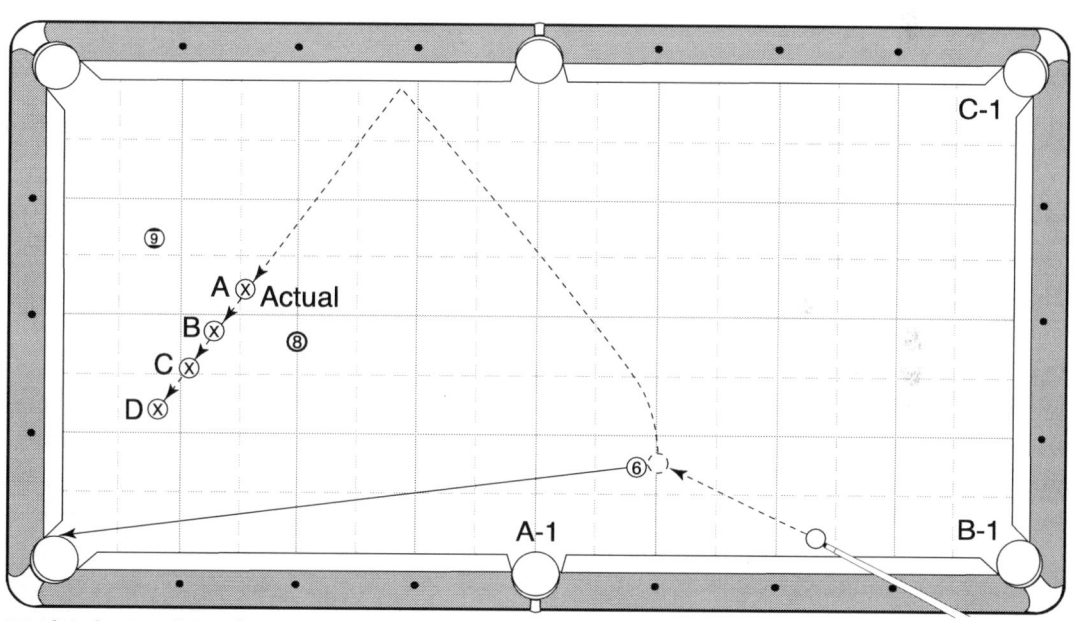

Multiple Pocket Shape

Tommy Kennedy faced the awkward position play above in the finals of the 1992 U.S. Open against Johnny Archer. Kennedy sent the cue ball across the table and down to Position A for straight in shape on the 8-ball into the side pocket A-1. If the cue ball had rolled to Position B, Kennedy could have shot the 8-ball into Pocket B-1. And, if the cue ball had stopped at Position C or D, he could have played the 8-ball into Pocket C-1.

When it is difficult to predict the cue ball's rolling distance and its ending location, it is nice to have the luxury of playing position for several pockets.

Chapter 5 - Pattern Play

Managing Risk and Avoiding Trouble
When planning your patterns, you must carefully weigh the risks and potential rewards of any position route, or series of routes. Should you play it safe, or go for the more aggressive route? Sometimes your choice is between which route to play, while other times the choice could be between a risky position play and a sure safety.

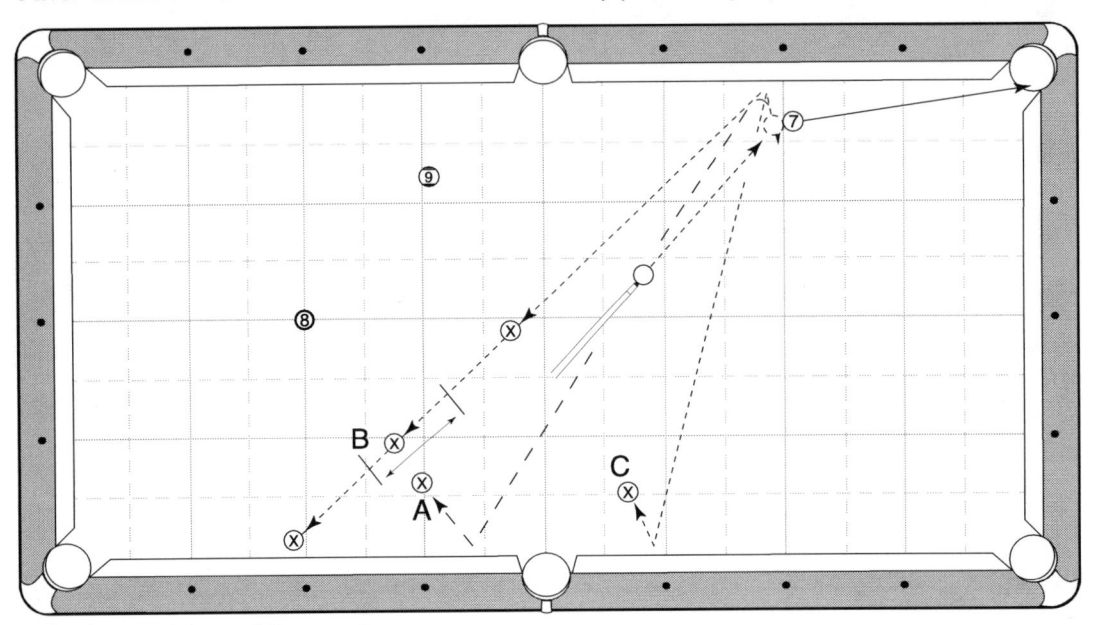

Weighing Risk and Reward
The last three balls are the crucial time in any rack of 9 Ball, and yet this is exactly the point at which many runouts break down because of poor planning or execution. This three ball runout should not pose any special problem as long as you choose the correct sequence. The key is avoiding a side pocket scratch but, at the same time, you want to make the shot on the 8-ball as easy as possible.

Route A offers the best chance of having an easy shot on the 8-ball because the cue ball will be traveling down the line of the position zone after hitting the side rail. The trouble is that this route brings the side pocket into play. Route B enables you to avoid a scratch, but if you come up short or long of the position zone, you will have a very difficult shot on the 8-ball.

Route C eliminates the risks of the previous two shots, but this safer route leaves you with a longer shot on the 8-ball. Now the best route is a medium hard draw shot to the side rail and out for the 9 in the side.

The best choice for you depends on your set of skills. A player with exceptional directional control who is not a great shotmaker might consider Route A. A player with superb speed control might opt for Route B, but this is the toughest position play. A fine shotmaker is better off using Route C.

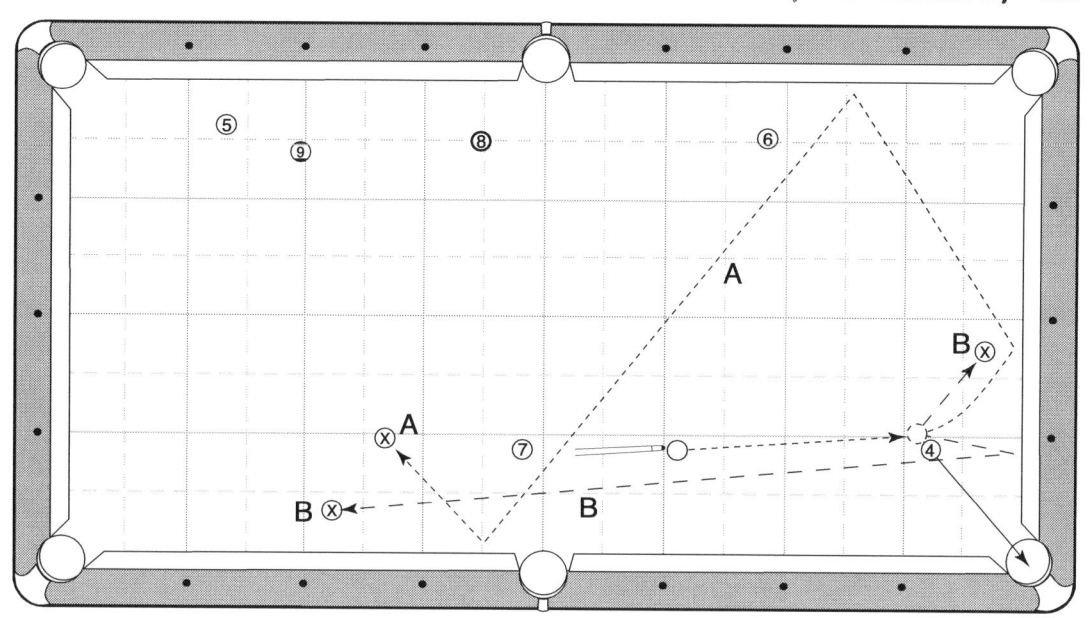

Going Near a Pocket for Shape
Route A is the only way to get on the 5-ball, but it involves a high degree of risk. You'll need to thread the cue ball past an obstacle course and narrowly miss the side pocket. If you feel uncomfortable with this shot, the better choice is to play safe by banking the 4-ball down Route B while using the 7-ball as a blocker.

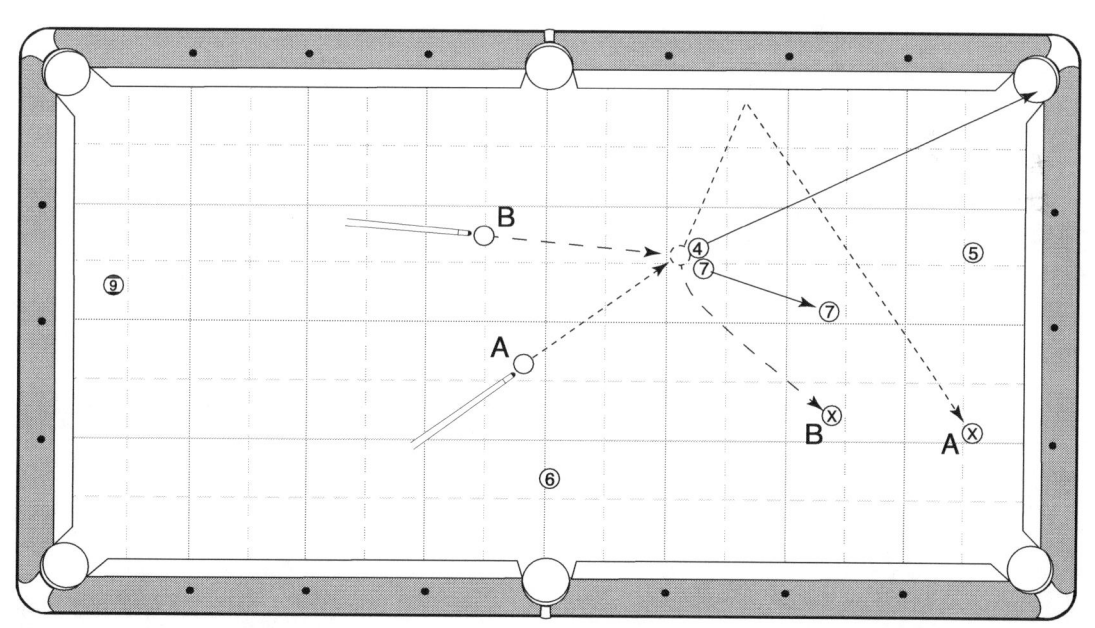

Balls Together Away From the Rail
When two balls are close together in the middle of the table, this can add an element of risk to your runout. It is usually better to avoid contacting the second ball (the 7-ball) by shooting away from it, as shown by Route A. If you must play the 4-ball from the other side as in Position B, and contact is unavoidable, then **you must estimate the ending position of the cue ball and the second ball, especially if there is a chance that it might get in the way of the next shot**, as in the example.

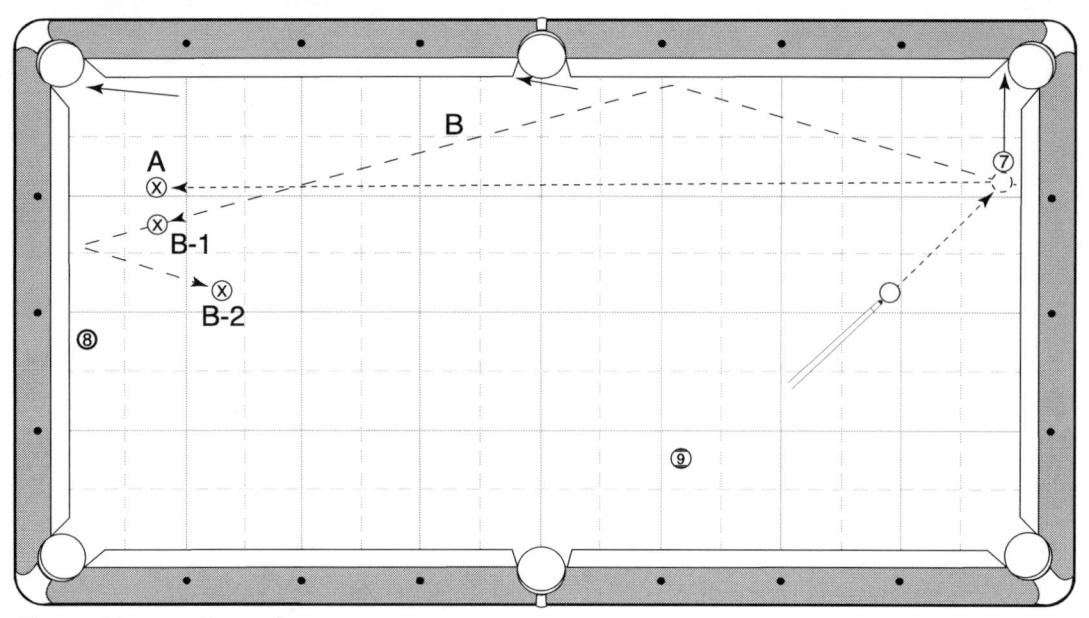

Shape Versus Scratch

Playing position from the 7-ball to the 8 is a risky proposition. You could easily scratch in the corner if you send the cue ball directly down the table using Route A. Route B off the side rail eliminates the scratch, but now the cue ball could hit the point and rebound backwards! You could also end up without a shot if the cue ball rolls past Position B-1 and bounces out to Position B-2. In situations like **this you must weigh each shot and then choose the route you feel you can execute best – knowing that your result is not guaranteed**!

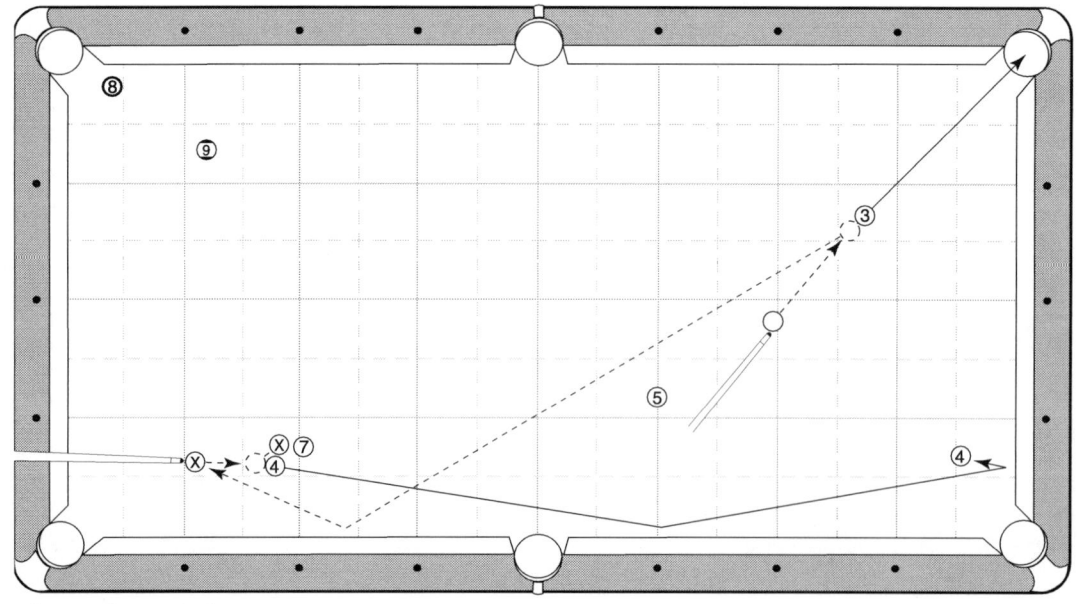

Shape for a Safety

Tommy Kennedy faced a long draw shot into the 4-7 cluster at 1992 U.S Open against Johnny Archer in the finals. He wisely passed on the breakout and played position for a safety, and then went on to win this game. The lesson: **sometimes it is best to runout – to a safety**!

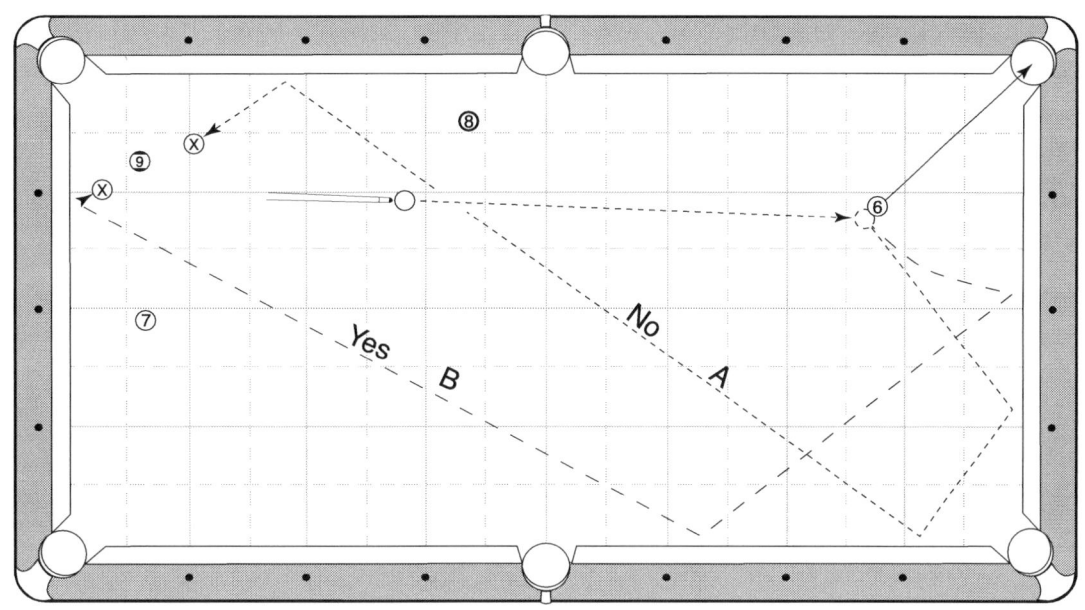

Avoiding Trouble by Using the High Percentage Route
The inclination for many players is to use Route A, which is a natural three rail position play from the 6-ball to the 7. However, if the cue ball hits too far down the side rail, it could end up behind the 9-ball. Francisco Bustamante eliminated this risk by using Route B in this match with Johnny Archer at the 1999 U.S. Open.

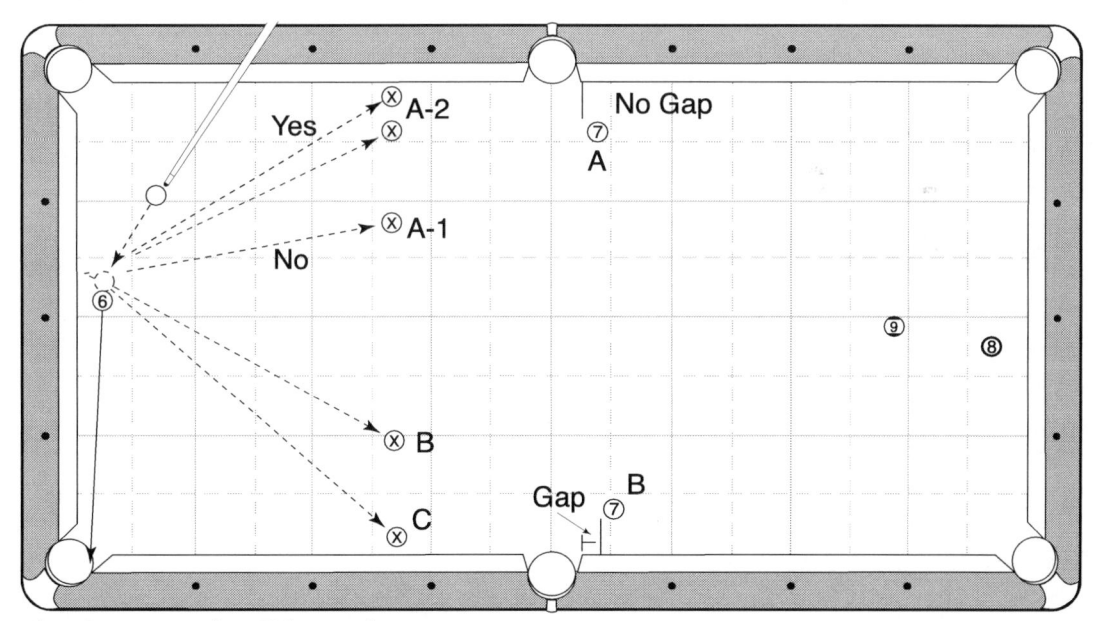

The Gap Past the Side Pocket
Check the position of any ball that is near the side pocket. If there is no gap, as in Position A, the risk of a scratch is a certainty if you get on the wrong side of the ball, such as at Position A-1. The cue balls at Position A-2 are okay. Position B shows a gap between the front edge of the 7-ball and the rail, so you can play to either side of the 7 down Routes B or C and still get to the 8-ball. Route C, incidentally, is the better choice!

Precision Pattern Play

Sometimes the only solution to a pattern is to play precision shape. If you can get on the next ball in a small position zone, your run remains intact. And if you miss your shape by a few inches, or less, it could result in failure. Possible errors include missing the zone, scratching, getting hooked, or missing the correct cut angle.

One big problem with many precision patterns is that a recovery route may not be available. As a result, you either execute the shot exactly as planned, or you suffer from a number of possible consequences. The examples in this section show the degree of precision with which some of the world's leading professionals play this game!

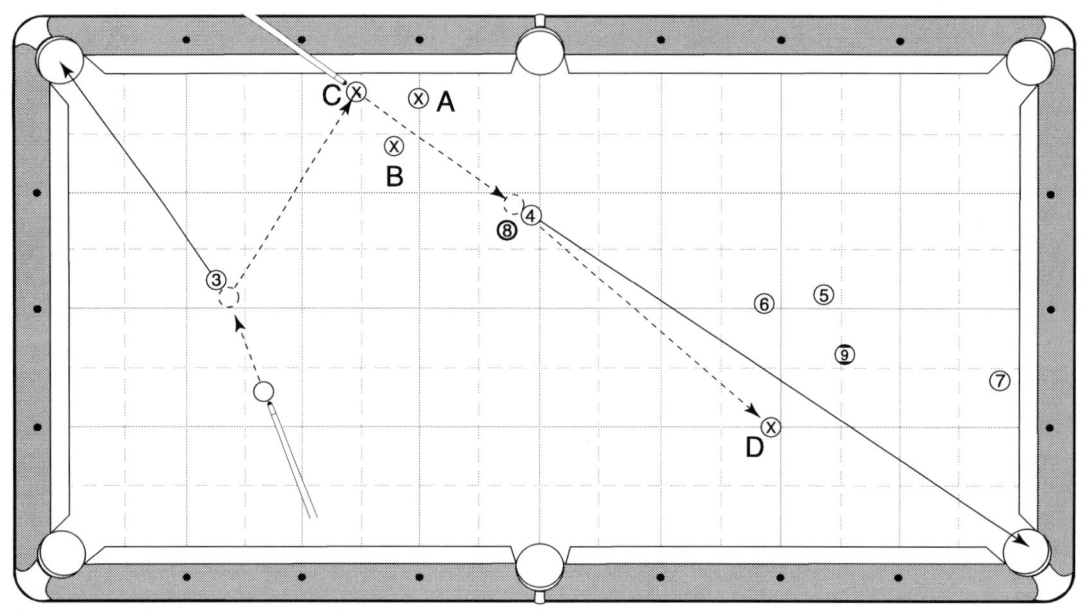

Precision Pattern Play - Varner

Nick Varner was locked in a tense battle with Buddy Hall at the Sands Regency Open 15, 1992 when he pulled off this precision play. Getting to the 5-ball, which was nestled amongst the 6 and 9 balls, was the big hurdle. The lower right corner pocket was the logical choice for the 4-ball, but playing it in this pocket meant that Varner had to leave himself with an almost dead straight in shot to then get shape on the 5-ball. If the cue ball stopped at Position A, it would run into the 8-ball on the next shot. Varner also would not have been able to get to the 5-ball with the cue ball in Position B.

The solution was to play for a dead straight in shot on the 4-ball, which is super hard to do when the cue ball must travel more than a few inches. Varner, however, was up to the task as stun followed the ball over two feet to Position C. He then played a follow shot to Position D and ran out. **The two big keys to this precision runout were: 1) identifying the need for a straight in shot; 2) perfect execution.**

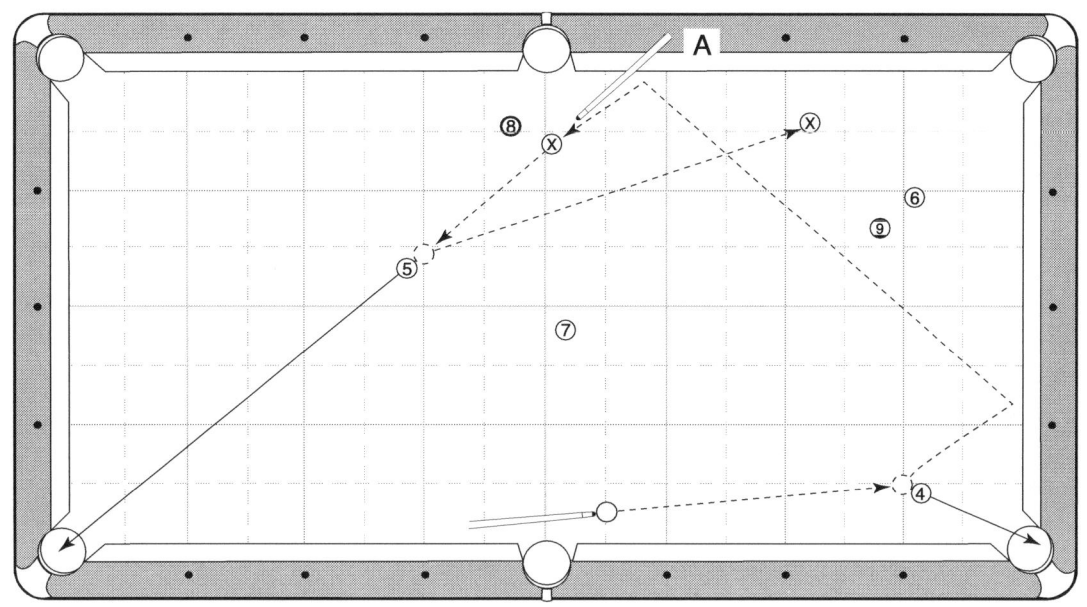

Top Flite Planning and Execution

Buddy Hall showed his mastery of position and pattern play in his duel with Efren Reyes at the 2000 U.S. Open. Before playing the 4-ball, Hall surveyed the table from Position A (on the top side rail) to determine the position he needed on the 5-ball to get to the 6 (three balls at a time). He then played a perfect two-rail route for a slight cut to the right on the 5-ball. This set him up for a precision long-range draw shot to the 6-ball. Bravo!!

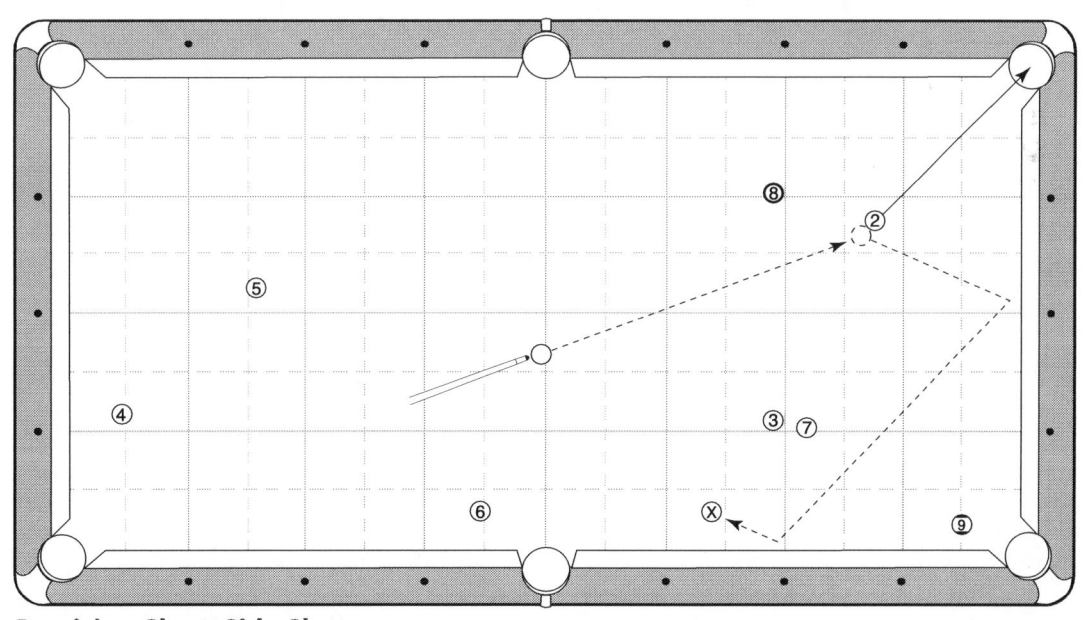

Precision Short Side Shape

Takeshi Okumura from Japan was in the finals of the 2000 U.S. Open with Earl Strickland when he encountered this position. The only place the 3-ball would go was in the upper right corner pocket. Okumura displayed exceptional touch in sending the cue ball two-rails to the short side for pinpoint shape on the 3-ball.

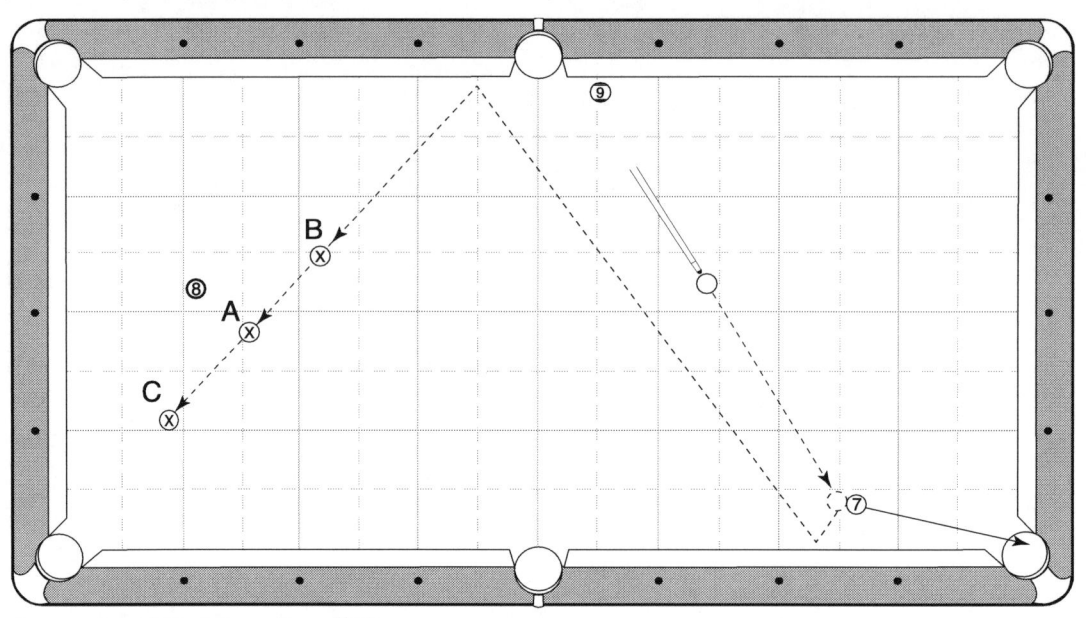

Across and Out to a Small Zone

Francisco Bustamante had no choice but to attempt the superb position route from the 7-ball to the 8-ball in this match with Efren Reyes at the Sands Regency Open 29, 1999. He narrowly avoided a side pocket scratch, and the cue ball proceeded to Position A. Perfect! Notice the difficult time that he would have had getting to the 9-ball if the cue ball had stopped short at Position B, or long at Position C.

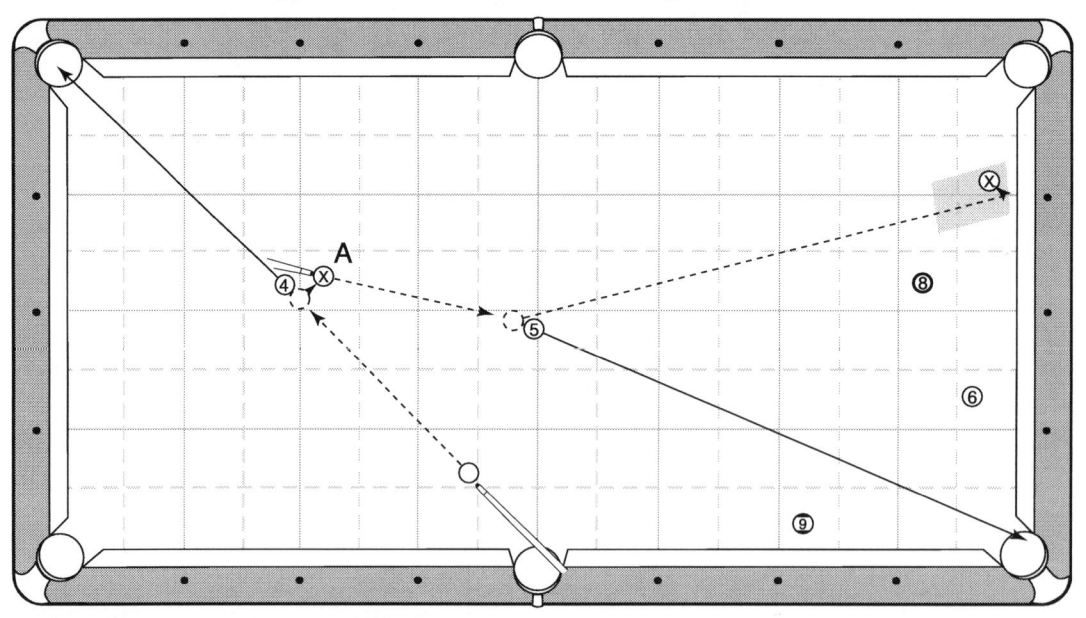

Setting Up a Precision Follow Shot

Ralf Souquet was seeking his first major title in the U.S. in the finals against Efren Reyes at the Sands Regency Open 27, 1998. The key to this pattern was in getting position on the 6-ball on the opposite end rail. Souquet prepared for the 6-ball by setting up the ideal angle on the 5-ball with a stop shot on the 4. From Position A, he demonstrated expert speed control as the cue ball drifted lazily down near the end rail for shape on the 6-ball.

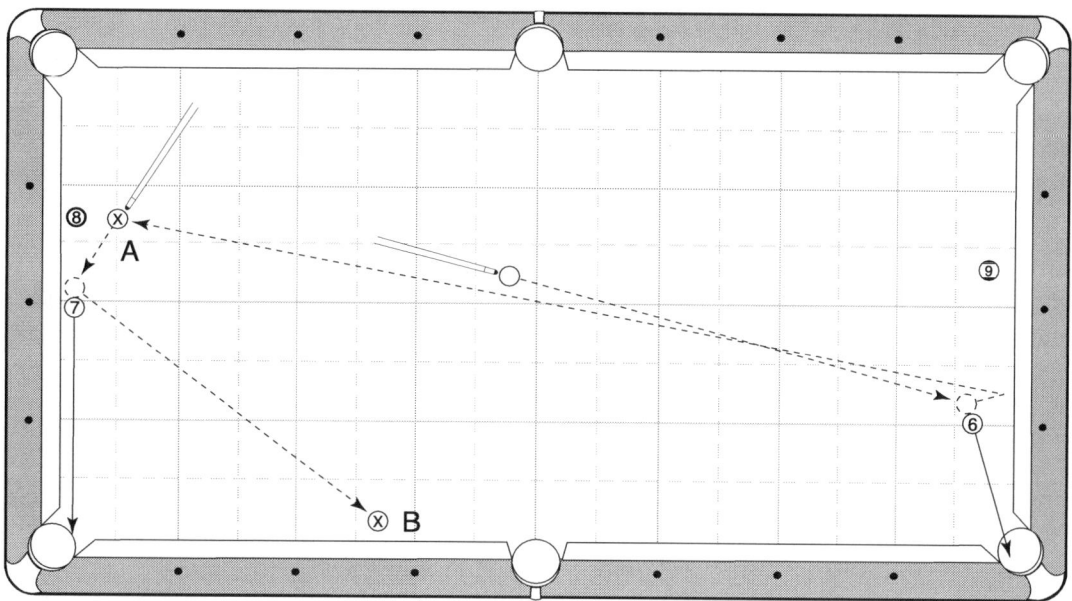

Ultra Precise One-Railer

When two balls are close together on the same end rail, you have the ingredients for big trouble. Mika Immonen answered the challenge with this fine position play from the 6-ball to the 7. The cue ball stopped at Position A, which enabled him to play the 8 in the opposite corner from Position B. If the cue ball had stopped an inch short of Position A, he would have had to go up the table and back for the 8-ball! This wonder shot took place at the 1998 U.S. Open against Jim Rempe.

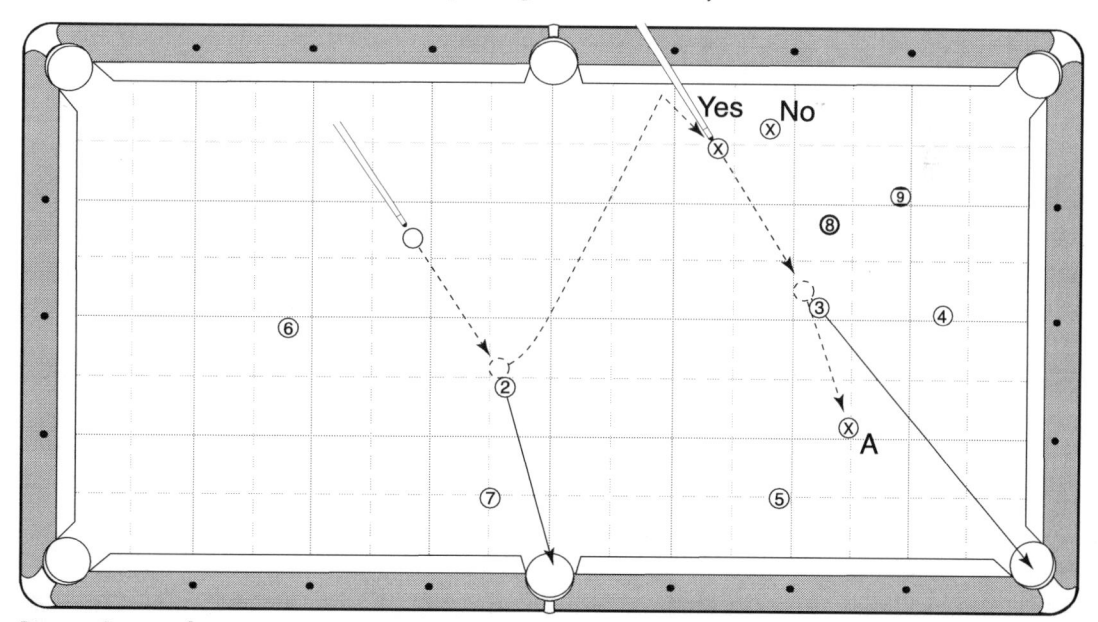

Draw Control

Kim Davenport drew the cue ball to the side rail and out for perfect position on the 3-ball in his match with Shannon Daulton at the 1999 U.S. Open. **Precision position using draw separates the pros from top level amateurs**. His shape on the 3 made it easy for him to send the cue ball to Position X for the 4. If the cue ball had stopped at the position labeled No, getting to the 4 from the wrong side of the 3 would have been a nightmare!

Improving the Layout by Moving a Ball

It is not generally a good idea to run into balls when playing position because the cue ball can be knocked off course, often resulting in a scratch or a hook. **However, at times you can significantly improve a layout by hitting a ball with little or no risk**. And sometimes purposefully contacting another ball is the best move even if it entails a fair amount of danger.

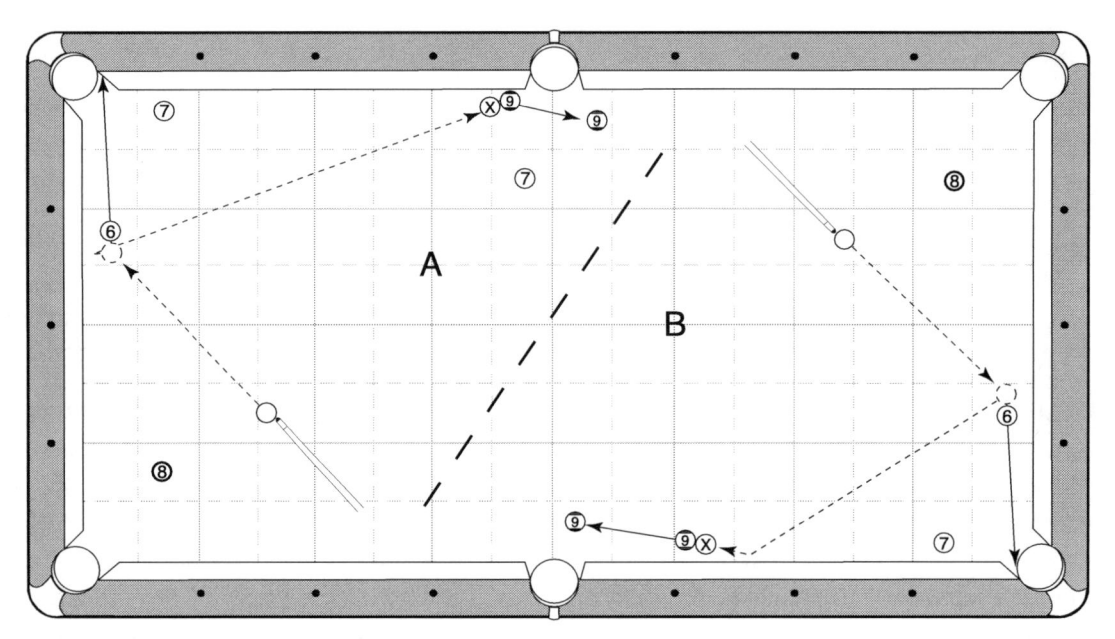

Mandatory and Optional Layout Improvement
A ball frozen to the rail near a side pocket spells big trouble. In Part A you have no choice but to knock the 9-ball off the side rail — that is, unless you want to subject yourself to an extremely difficult shot on the 9-ball. Follow with a quarter tip of right english will send the cue ball into the 9 as shown. There is little risk to this maneuver because shape on the 7-ball is guaranteed, and it is impossible to scratch in the side pocket thanks to the 9-ball.

The 9-ball is in a much easier spot in Part B, so it is not mandatory that you bump it from its position. Nevertheless, you have a golden opportunity to dogproof this runout if you knock the 9-ball in front of the side pocket. This eliminates a possible side pocket scratch when playing shape on the 9-ball. And, if the pockets are tight, you will appreciate not having to send the 9-ball three diamonds down the rail to the pocket. Once again, there is little risk to this shot.

Looking Ahead
Smart 9 Ball players identify the stumbling blocks to their runouts well in advance. The key in this layout is getting from the 7-ball to the 8. While shape on the 8-ball is possible, it will not be easy thanks to the 9-ball, which is next to the 7-ball. You can easily eliminate this possible problem with a three inch draw shot on the 2-ball, which gives you a slight angle on the 4.

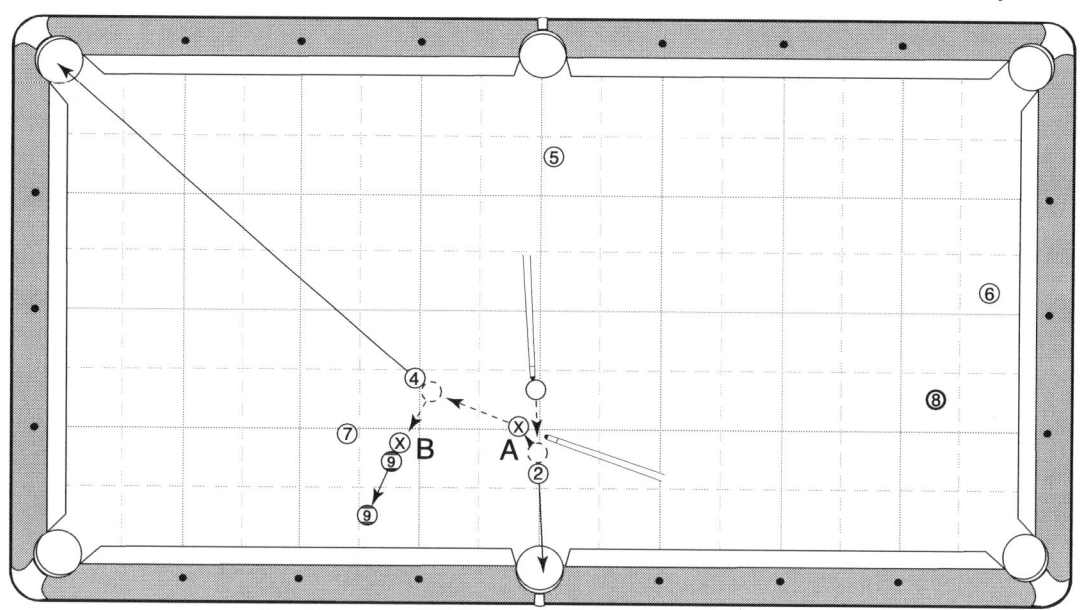

With the cue ball in Position A, a soft draw shot will bump the 9-ball away from the 7. This will clear the way for sending the cue ball off the rail and down for shape on the 8-ball. Getting from the 5-ball to the 6 is no problem with the cue ball in Position B. Once again, moving a ball carries almost no risk, and offers a huge benefit.

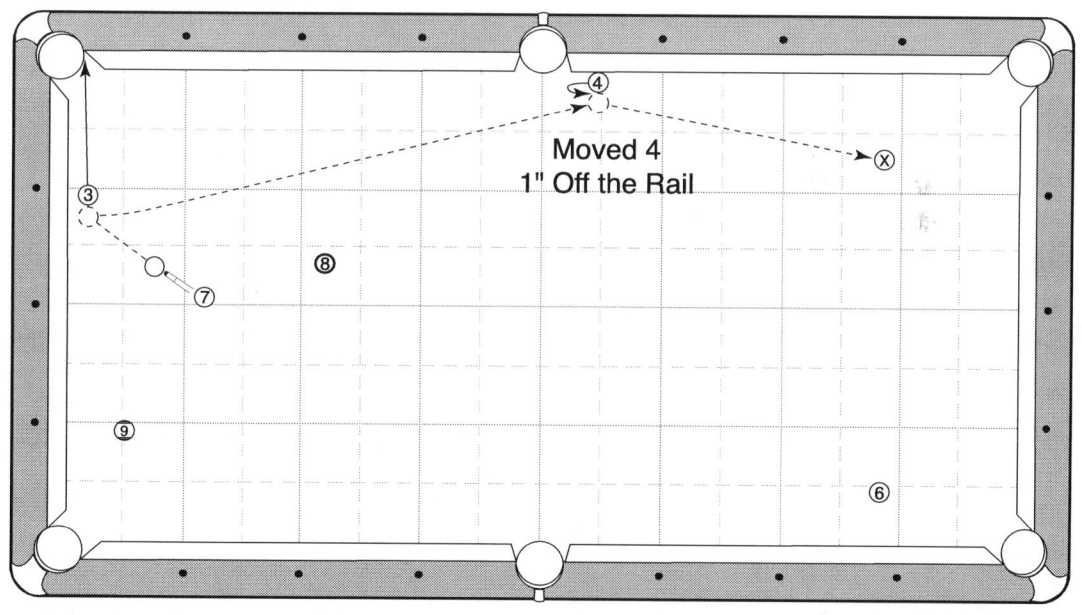

Moved 4
1" Off the Rail

Getting a Ball off the Rail
Alex Pagulayan was in a duel with Ismael Paez at the 2000 World 9-Ball Championships when he came across this incredibly difficult layout. For starters, Pagulayan was jacked up over the 7-ball for this shot on the 3, which was a challenge all by itself. Adding to the difficulty was the 4-ball, which was frozen to the rail near the side pocket. He played the high risk, high reward shot in the illustration, removing the 4 from the cushion, and it paved the way for his runout.

Chapter 5 - Pattern Play

End of Rack Pattern Play

Running a full rack is not easy no matter how well you play. Furthermore, the vast majority of game ending runouts between amateur players commence with only 3-5 balls on the table. Still, no matter what your level of play, end of rack pattern play is crucial to your success.

When you get to those final 3-5 balls, the congestion factor is usually gone, leaving you with a clear path to the game ball. You run out when you are supposed to, or you don't. It is as simple as that. In this section, we'll cover a few of the zillions of possible end of rack patterns so that you will develop a feel for how the game should be played at this crucial stage. And I encourage you to practice these layouts, and others.

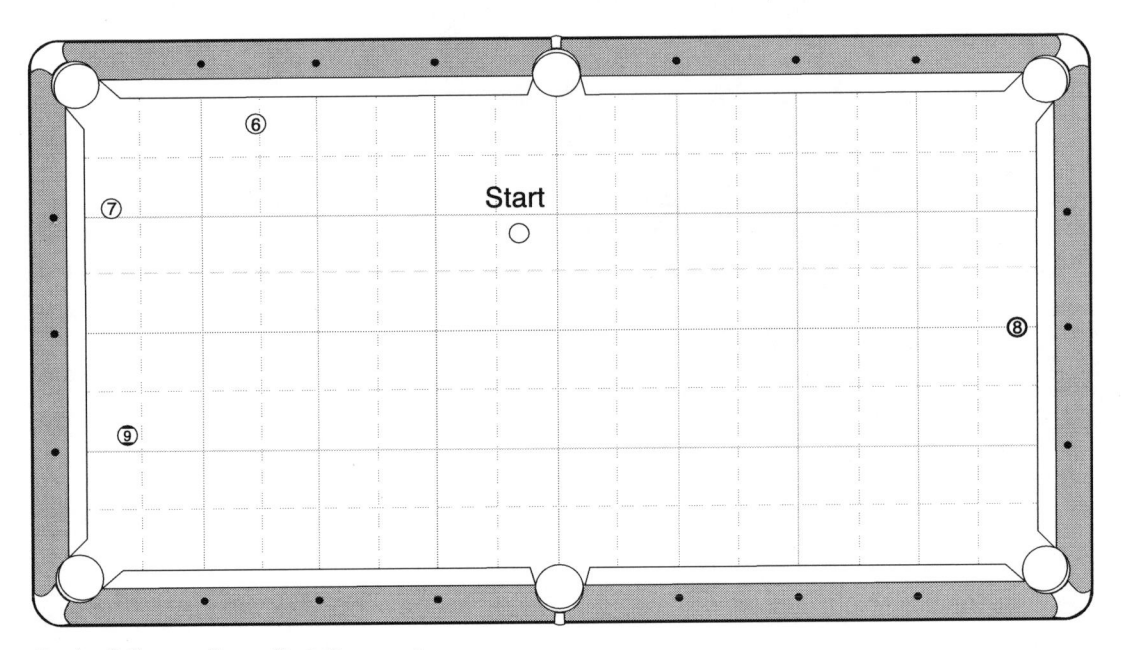

End of Game Run Out Percentages

Here's a pop quiz that is designed to test your level of skill at running out in the end game. Place the balls on the table as shown and run out. Did you run out? While this pattern is not all that difficult, it is typical of the kind of layouts that amateurs fail to convert all too often. I would estimate that a C Player would run out 30-50 percent of the time while a B Player would get out on 70-85 percent of his attempts. An A Player should run this table 95 percent of the time.

The 9-Ball Determines the Correct Route

Three-ball pattern play is crucial in the later stages of a rack when the game is on the line. This is the time to carefully plot the pattern that enables you to arrive at the game ball in the simplest and most efficient manner possible. When playing the 7-ball (page 191), ask what position on the 8 is best for getting to the 9-ball? When the 9-ball is in Position A, send the cue ball across the table to A-1. Now all it takes is a soft follow shot for shape on the 9-ball.

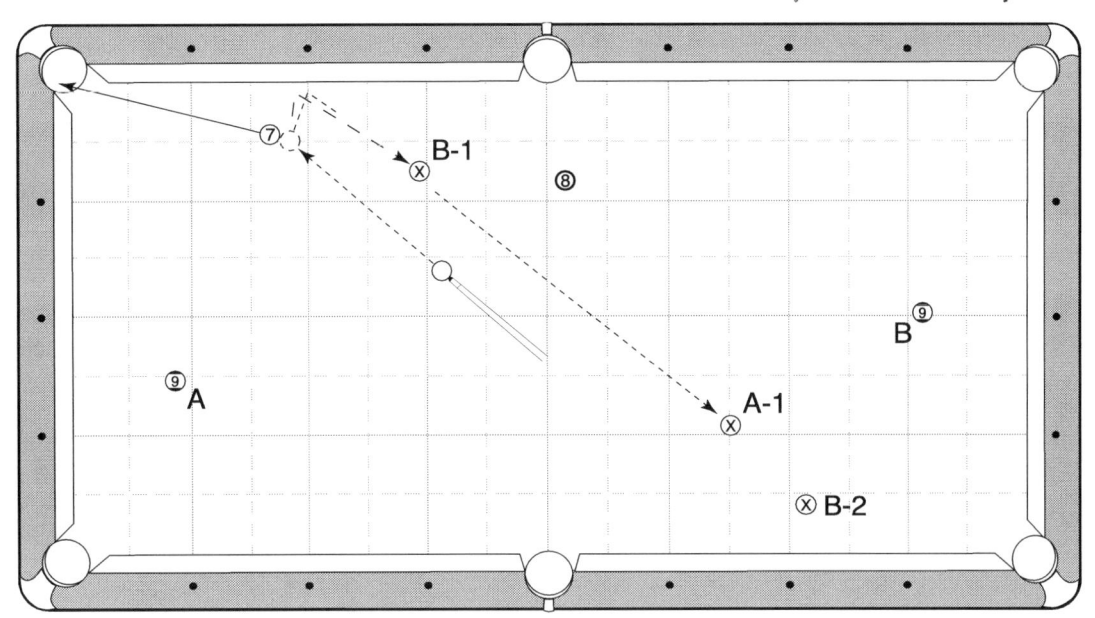

If 9-ball is in Position B, this changes things considerably. Now the percentages favor drawing back to Position B-1 so you can play the 8-ball in the upper right corner pocket. A stun/follow shot on the 8-ball will give you excellent position on the 9-ball at B-2.

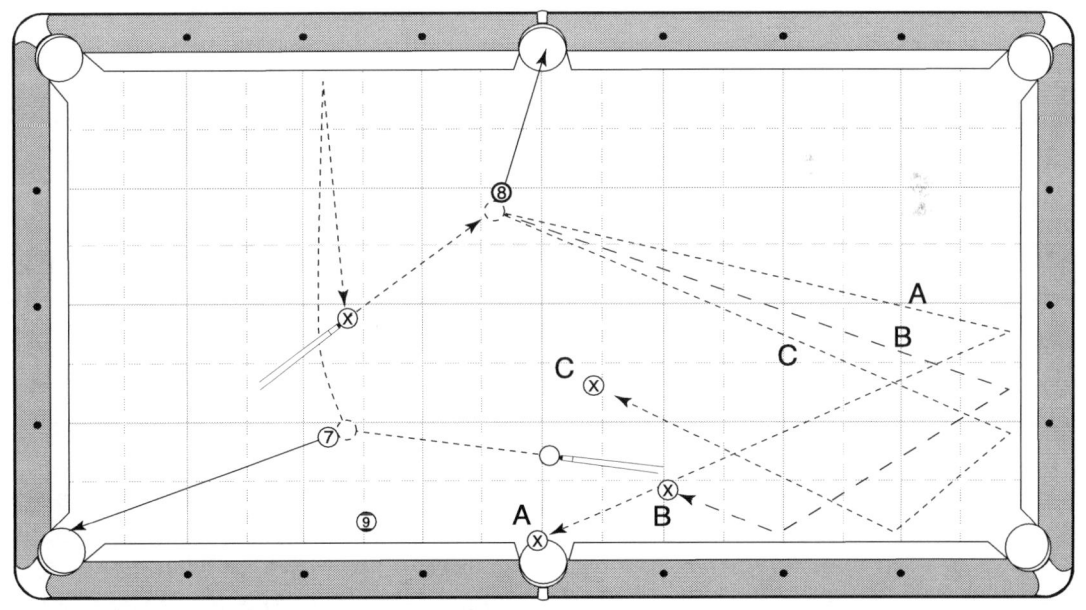

When to Play for a Cut on the Last Ball

Most players favor a near straight in shot on the last ball, but sometimes playing position for a small cut angle puts the game in jeopardy. The 7-ball has been played perfectly, setting up a very workable angle on the 8-ball. If you tried to get straight in on the 9-ball using Route A, you could easily scratch in the side. Route B gives you a large margin for error. If you applied too much draw and the cue ball traveled down Route C, you would still have a relatively easy shot on the 9-ball.

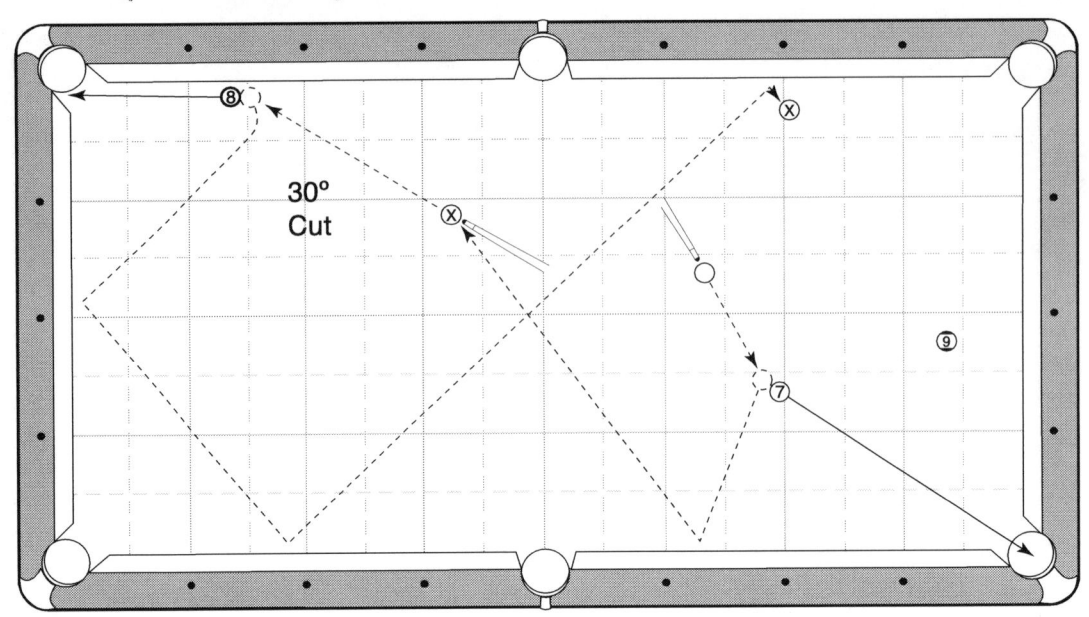

End to End on the Last Three Balls

When the balls are lying tough you have anything but a roadmap runout to the 9 or 10 ball. This happens. Difficult end of rack patterns appear regularly with amateurs because of their opponent's errors. So, **the next time you begin to bemoan your fate when left with a tough shot after your opponent's blown an easy runout, remember to be thankful that you have a shot and a chance at winning.**

Efren Reyes' best pattern was to play the exacting route from the 8-ball to the 9 in this match with Johnny Archer at the 2000 U.S. Open. He used the 7-ball to set up a 30-degree cut on the 8-ball. This angle is perfect for playing three-rail position with inside (left) english – one of his favorite position routes. Remember the principle to Play Your Game!

The Last Two Balls are on the Same Rail

When the last two balls are close together on the same rail, an alarm should go off. When planning your route for the 6-ball, the big question is whether to draw to Position A or Position B for the 7-ball. At Position A you can draw across the table and down to Position A-1 for the 8-ball, ending this game. However, this route is very risky as you could easily scratch or get hooked behind the 9-ball.

A long distance draw shot from Position B to B-1 would give you ideal shape on the 8-ball, but this plan is also loaded with danger. If you drew too far back, you would be hooked behind the 9-ball. And, if the cue ball stopped at B-2, you would have to play a super kill shot or send the cue ball to the opposite end rail and back. The lesson: **sometimes there is no easy solution to an end of rack position. Good planning and great execution are the keys. And it often pays to go with the shot you know best**.

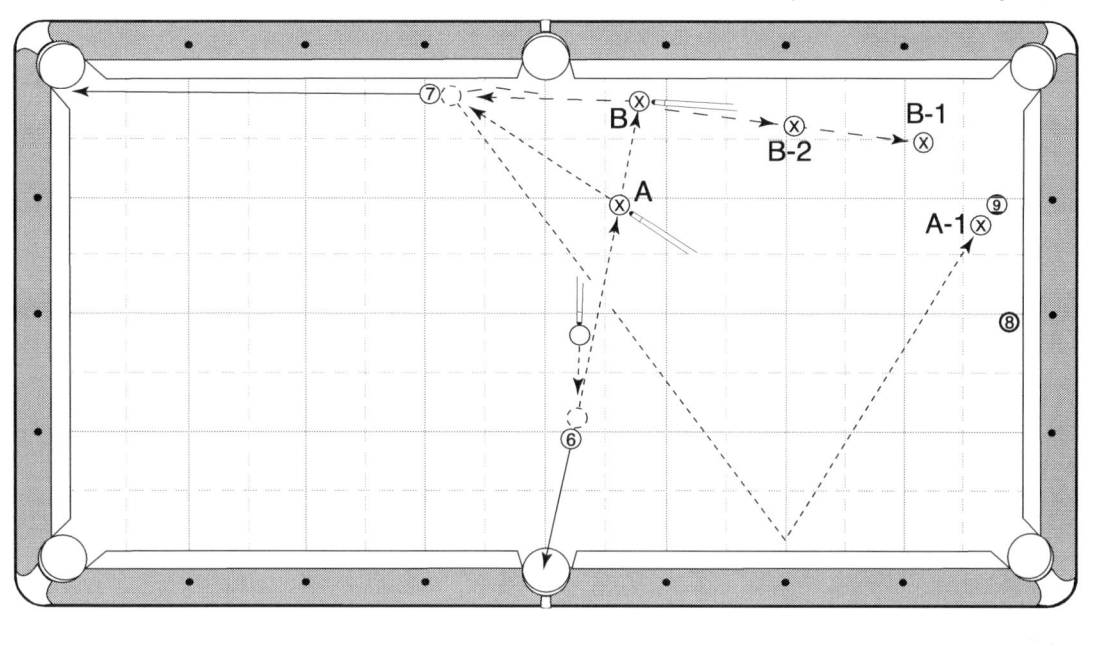

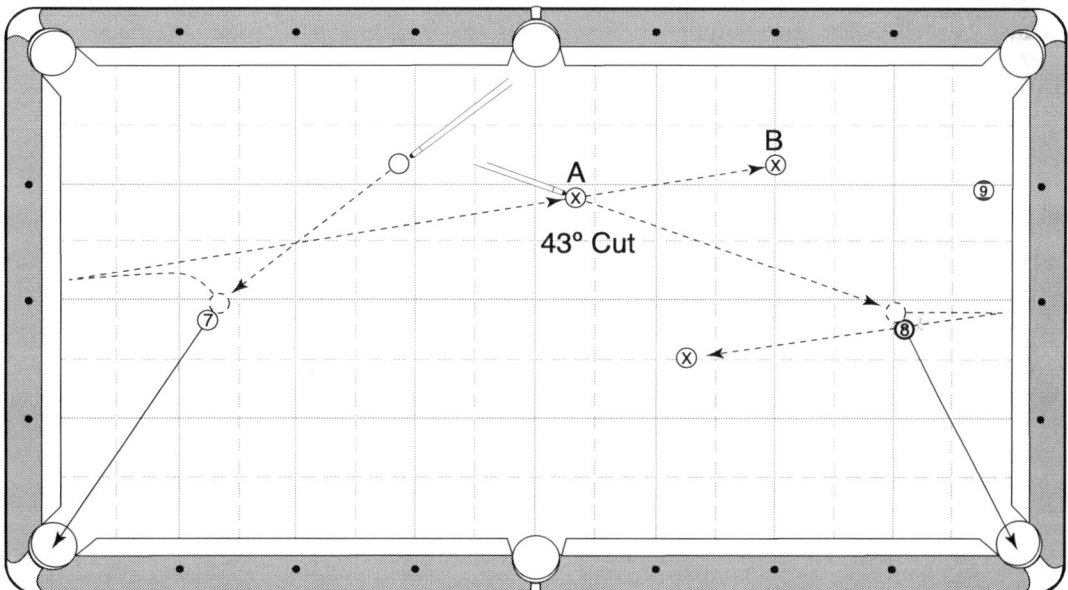

End of Rack Pattern

Keith McCready, widely known for his role in *The Color of Money*, was in a close match with Nick Varner, at the Sands Regency Open 12, 1990, when he came across this end of rack layout. Even great players like McCready make mistakes in their end of rack pattern play and so, in this case, he came up short at Position A when playing the 7-ball. This error was understandable considering the difficulty in controlling the speed on this awkward follow shot.

Though Position B would have been ideal, McCready still got out thanks to his impressive recovery route, which required a soft stroke and the skillful use of inside english. The lesson: **it helps to have an arsenal of recovery routes at your disposal in the end game as they can enable you to save your run** when you miss your ideal position zone.

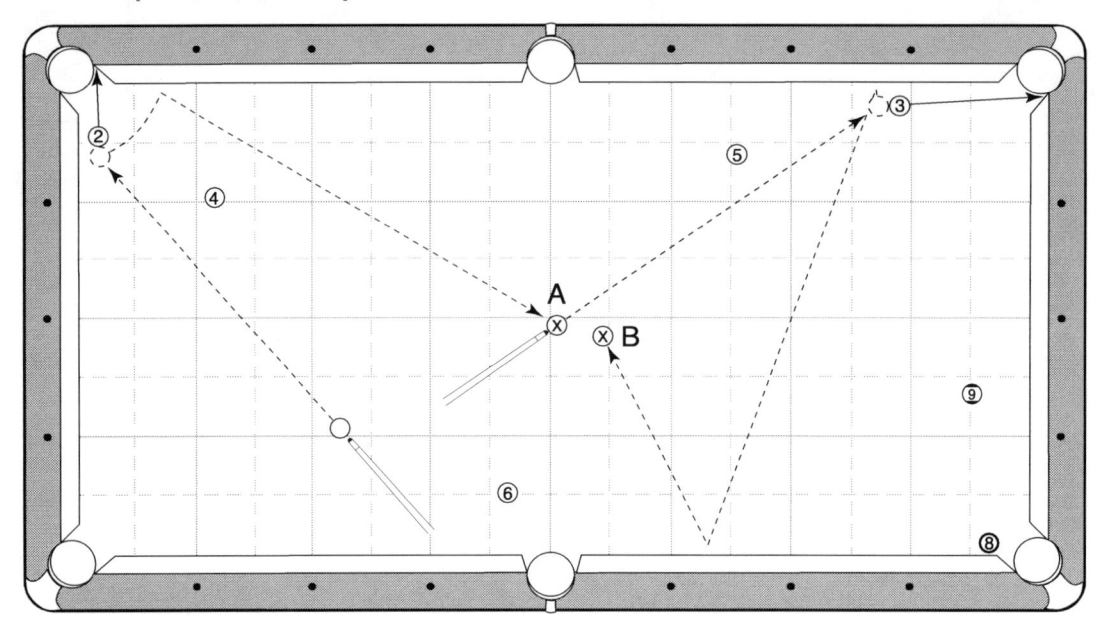

Sending the Cue Ball to Center Table

The center portion of the table is a much used target for the cue ball in 9 Ball, especially when you consider that 1) the majority of the balls are less than a diamond from the rails after the break, and 2) it is generally easier to send the cue ball to a rail and out for position. That said, I couldn't agree less with those who counsel you to return the cue ball to the center whenever possible. Instead, I advise that you **play position in the center portion of the table only when the next ball and the pattern dictate that it is the best place for the cue ball**, period.

Kim Davenport demonstrated how to use the center against Shannon Daulton on his way to a fourth place finish at the 1999 U. S. Open. His two-rail route from the 2-ball to the 3 at Position A set him up perfectly for a crossing route to the 4-ball, which again resulted in ideal shape at Position B – in nearly the same spot in the middle of the table!

Side Pockets Versus Corner Pockets

Some contend that you should play shape for the corner pockets whenever possible, while others favor the side pockets. Average players are suckered into using the sides too often because they make pocketing some shots exceptionally easy. The downside of this strategy is that improper use of the side pockets can, at times, force you into playing long and dangerous position routes.

Let's take a look at the three ball pattern on the top of the next page. If the cue ball traveled down Route A, you would have good shape on the 8-ball to the 9-ball from the positions shown. Route A adheres to Principle # 12, which advises you to play down the line shape when possible.

Despite the advantages of playing corner pocket position, many players would play for the side pocket. Notice that you only have a small position zone. If the cue ball stops short or long of the position zone, you would have a tough time getting from the 8-ball to the 9.

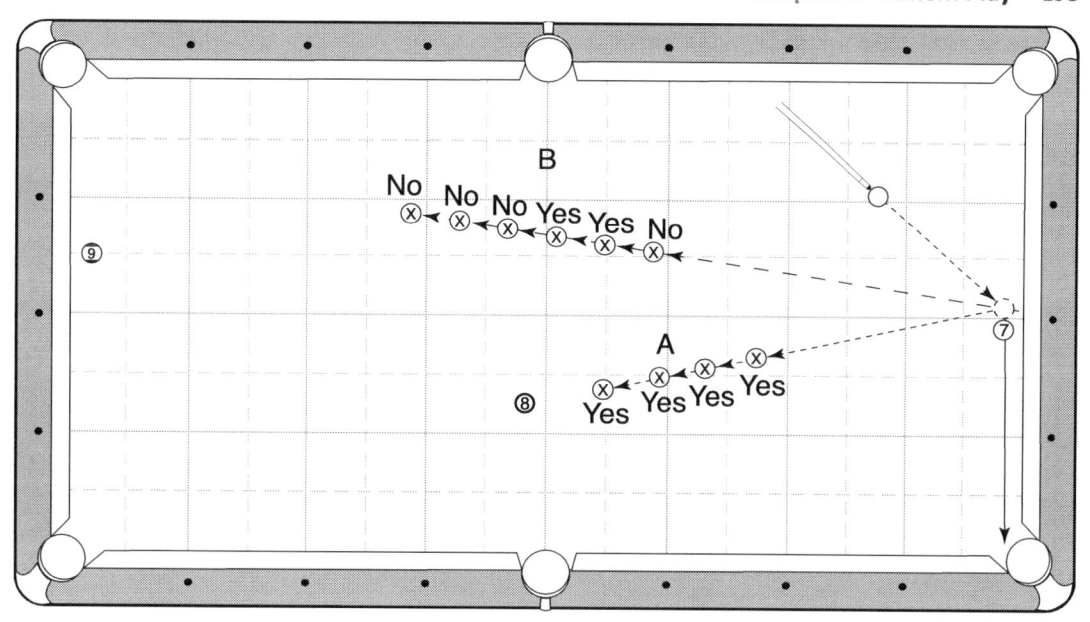

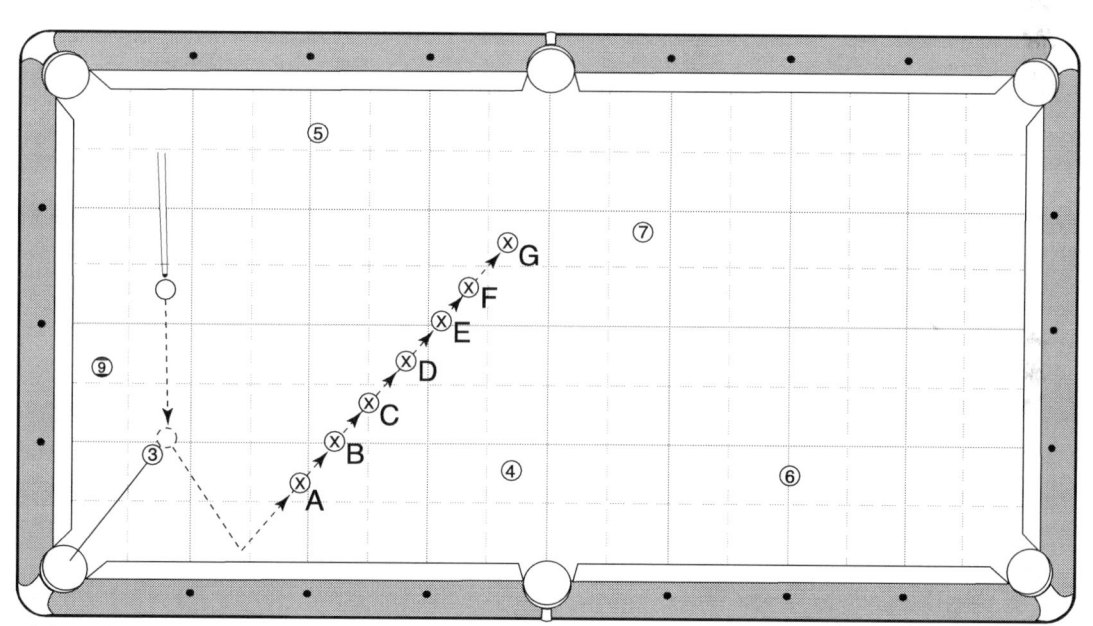

Side Versus Corner

In this example, please consider the many possible position routes from the 4-ball to the 5 after the 3-ball has been played. Ask yourself these questions:
- Do you like Position A for the corner and, if so, why?
- Should you play to the side or corner from Positions B and C? How would you get to the 5-ball?
- Positions D-G are played in the side pocket. How would you get from the 4-ball to the 5-ball from each position?

Now for my recommendation: I feel Position A is best because it allows you to float the cue ball to the middle of the table (about to where Position G is) for a cut shot on the 5-ball. This will make it easy to get on the 6-ball.

Patterning Balls in the Middle

Playing position on balls in the center of the table is one the more difficult maneuvers in 9 Ball. The diagram shows the boundaries for the trouble zone in the middle of the table. **When a ball is in the middle, the long distance that the cue ball must travel to a rail after contact makes it difficult to control the cue ball, and you must keep your cut angles relatively shallow**. As a rule of thumb, you are almost always better off avoiding a backcut when playing position for a ball in this zone.

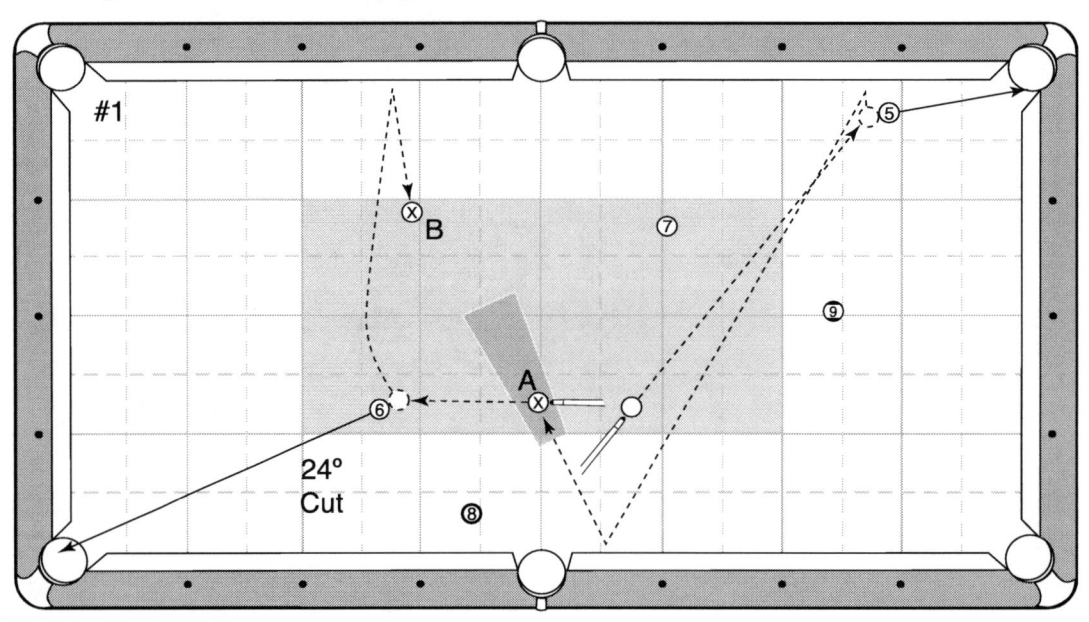

Ball in the Middle

Jim Rempe gave a single game clinic on how to play balls in the dangerous middle with this runout at the 1999 U.S. Open against Francisco Bustamante. In diagram #1, he sent the cue ball across the table and out on the 5-ball, setting up a perfect angle on the 6-ball. Rempe could have worked the cue ball into position for the 7-ball from a big slice within the zone, but the cue ball landed perfectly at Position A. The 24-degree angle gave Rempe maximum control for sending the cue ball to Position B for the 7-ball.

Diagram #2 shows that Rempe ended up with a 26-degree angle on the 7-ball, which was also stationed in the danger zone. He then floated the cue ball to the rail and out for position on the 8.

While this sequence was very acceptable, Rempe would have preferred that the cue ball had stopped at Position A for the 7 because this would have led to a shallower cut angle on the 8, possibly at Position B. Rempe's thin cut on the 8-ball forced him to send the cue ball across the table and back for the 9. He executed this recovery route with an uncanny degree of accuracy!

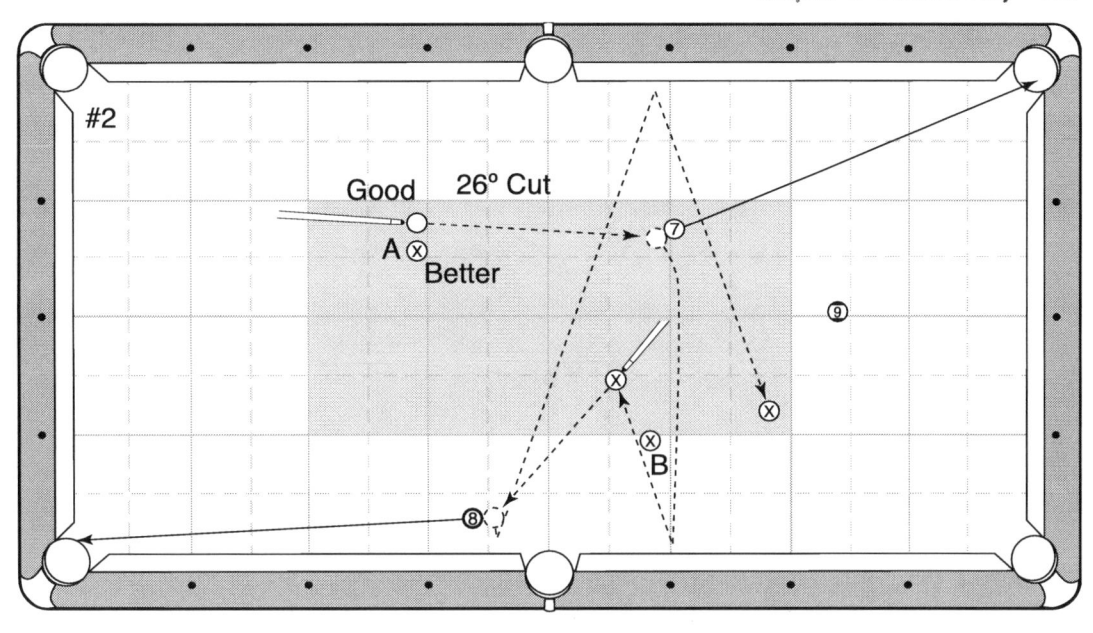

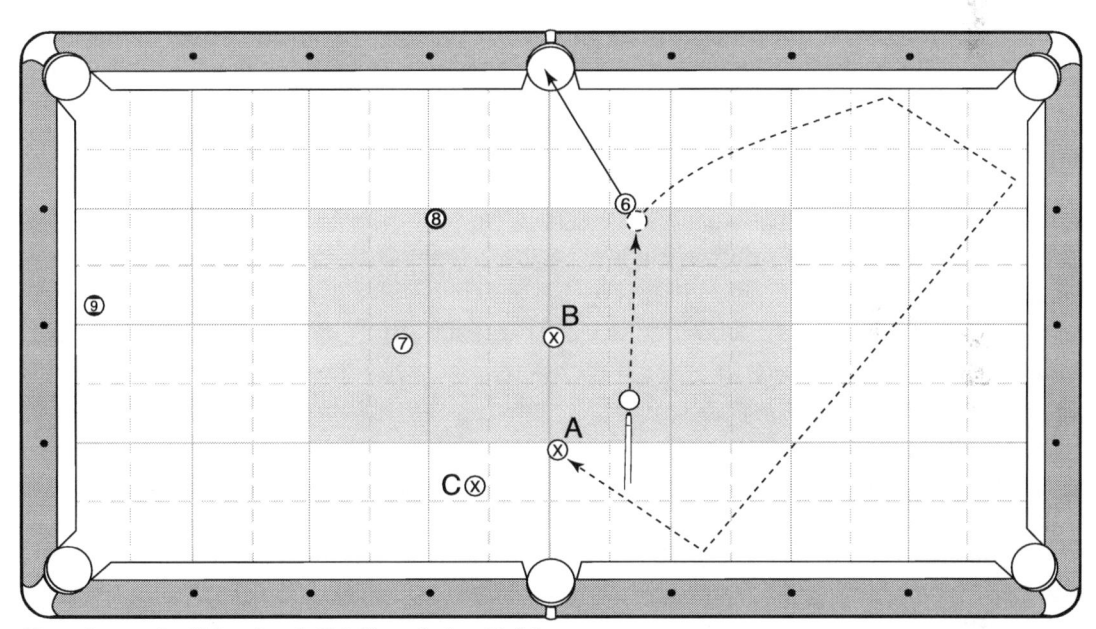

Shaping a Ball in the Middle of the Table

Efren Reyes ran this rack in a match with Johnny Archer in the semifinals of the 1995 U.S. Open thanks to his planning for a ball in the middle of the table. After pocketing the 6-ball, Reyes sent the cue ball on a two-rail route down the position line for shape on the 7-ball. With the cue ball at Position A, Reyes had no trouble getting on the 8-ball.

Now imagine what problems he might have encountered if the cue ball had stopped at Positions B or C. The big lesson: **when playing shape on a ball in the middle, play down the line shape whenever possible** because of the urgent need to control the angle on the next ball.

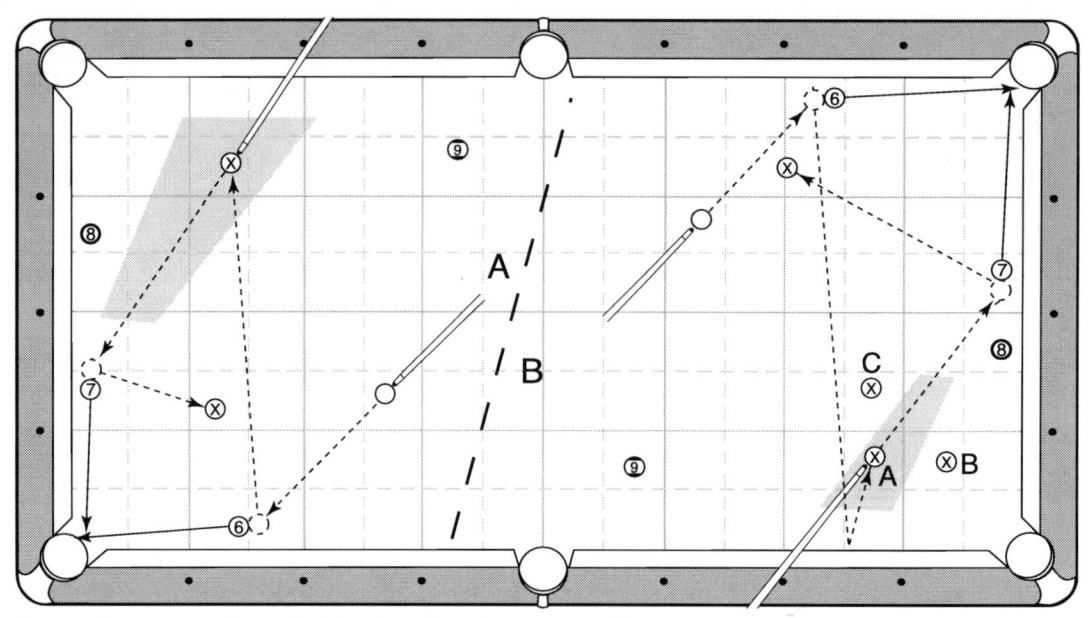

Two Consecutive Balls on the Same Rail

In Part A, the 7 and 8 balls are on the same end rail. The position zone is quite large because of the distance between the two balls. The objective is to leave a shallow cut angle on the first ball on the rail (the 7) without getting hooked behind the second ball in the sequence (the 8).

This position zone was accessed by playing a soft follow shot on the 6-ball with a quarter tip of inside (right) english. A small angle on the first ball keeps you from having a thin cut on the next shot after the cue ball bounces off the rail. A lag shot on the 7-ball with a quarter tip of inside (left) english led to excellent position on the 8.

The 7 and 8 balls are seven inches closer to each other in Part B, creating a much smaller position zone than the one in Part A. The cue ball needs to stop at Position A (after the 6-ball), so you can get on the 8-ball by using a soft stroke with a half tip of inside english as shown. The cue ball in Position B is behind the 8-ball – a mistake that might happen if you played for an overly shallow angle on the 7 and missed the mark.

The sharp cut on the 7-ball in Position C would force you to send the cue ball to the opposite end rail and back. This error happens often on a layout like this, but it is obviously preferable to getting hooked! This pattern is not easy, but it is often the best or only way to handle two balls that are close together on the same rail.

Two Consecutive Balls on the Same Side Rail (1)

When the cue ball is in Position A, a stop shot on the 5-ball will leave it in the middle of the zone at Position A-1. The 6-ball can now be rolled into the upper left corner pocket for position near the rail. The 7-ball goes into the upper right corner pocket.

With the 5-ball in Position B, the play is to draw into the sizeable position zone in the center of the table. Position B-1 gives you a 50-degree cut angle, which enables you to send the cue ball across and back to where the 6-ball now rests! The 7-ball goes into the upper right corner pocket, as in the previous example. The gap between the two position zones is no man's land. If the cue ball stops here, your cut angle will not be sharp enough nor shallow enough for easily getting on the 7-ball.

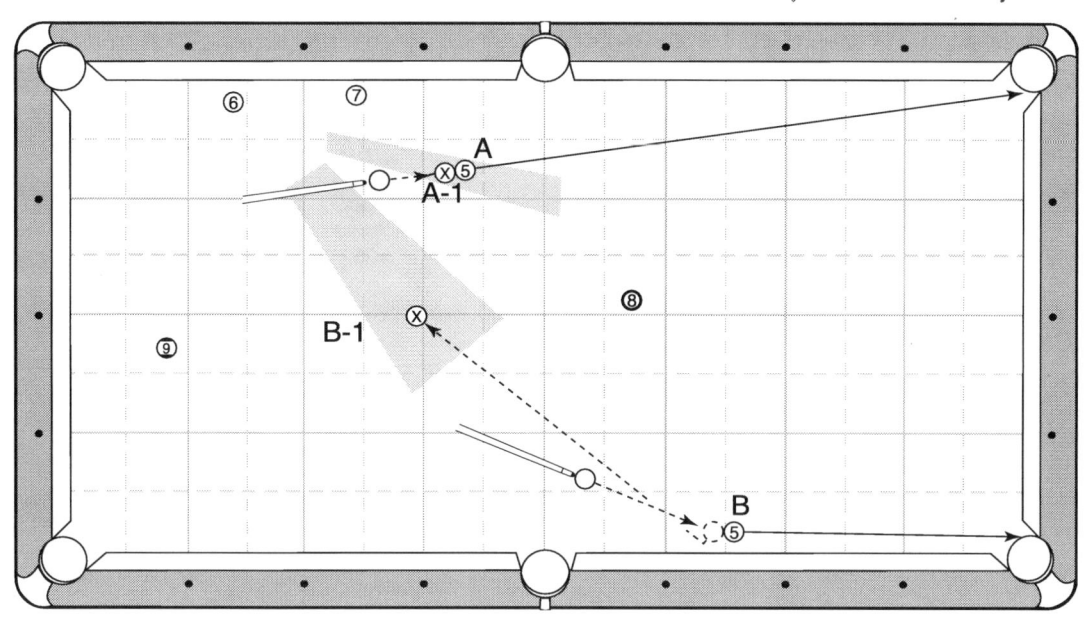

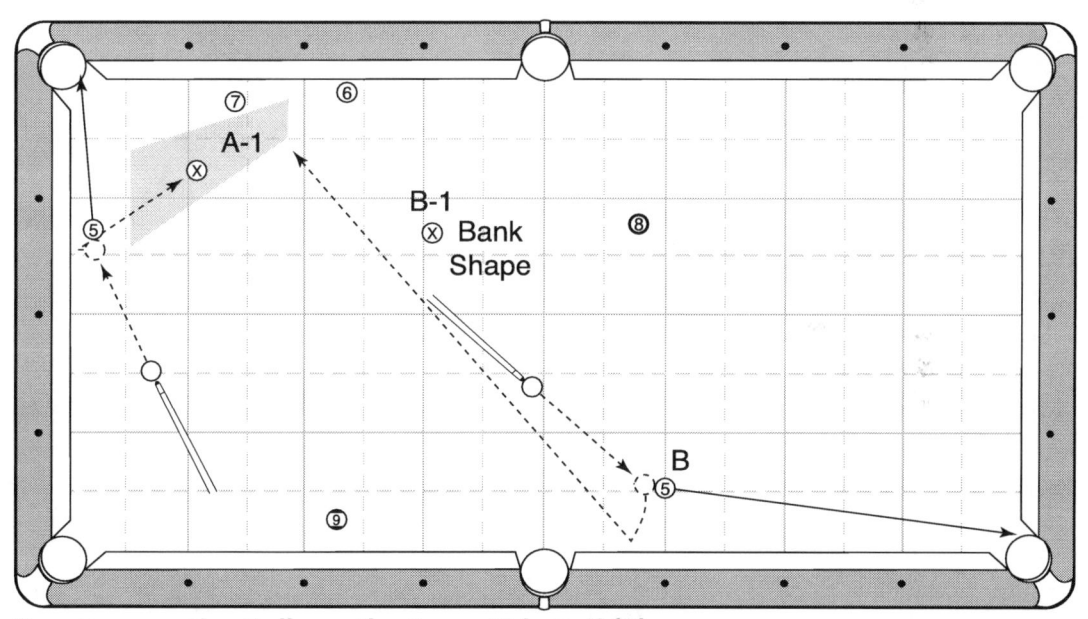

Two Consecutive Balls on the Same Side Rail (2)

This layout spells double trouble because the first ball (the 6-ball) is now on the other side of the second ball (the 7-ball). When the 5-ball is in Position A, you could follow to Position A-1 for a long shot, but it would force you to send the cue ball across and back for the 7-ball. You could also attempt to knock the 6-ball into a better location when playing the 5-ball, but this will not be easy because the shallow cut on the 5 makes it hard to control the cue ball's path.

If the 5-ball was in Position B, you could try hitting the side rail just above the 7-ball (or even bumping it lightly), but this shot takes phenomenal speed and directional control. Another approach is to play for bank shape at Position B-1. **Betting a game on a bank shot can be a good idea if banks are one of your strong suits – and even better when safety play is not.**

Either Side of the Ball Can Work

On most position plays you are much better off with the cue ball on one side of the object ball than on the other. But **it will fine tune your patterns if you can recognize those situations where you can easily play position from either side of the object ball**.

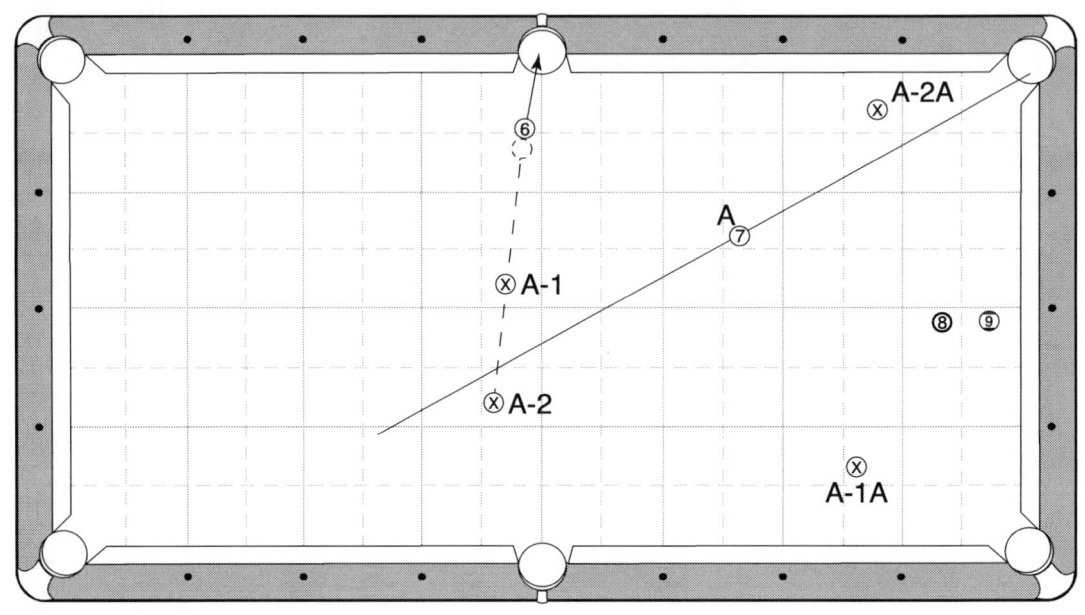

Either Side Works Just Fine

A draw shot leads to position on the 7-ball after pocketing the 6 into the side pocket. If the cue ball stops at Position A-1, you could play shape on the lower side of the 8-ball at Position A-1A. And, if the cue ball comes to rest at A-2, you could play a follow shot to Position A-2A for shape into the opposite corner. There is no great advantage to playing from either side. Your decision should be based solely on personal preference: do you feel more comfortable playing the route to Position A-1A, or the one that leads to Position A-2A? The lesson: **when you can play to either side of a ball, it is heads you win and tails you're the victor**!

One Side Is Better

When you can play to either side, you should still try to stack the odds even more in you favor. **Choose the better side when doing so can increase your chances of running out by 2%, much less 10-20% or more**.

The 8 and 9 balls for our layout on the next page are in the same positions as in the example above, but the 7-ball is now at the opposite end of the table. You can still play shape on the either side of the 8-ball.

When the cue ball is in Position A, play three-rail shape to Position A-1. From Position B, the best route is to send the cue ball to the long side of the 8-ball for shape at Position B-1. (Note: those of you with a sharp eye will have noticed that the position zone for the 8-ball is slightly larger on the top half of the table! Both routes led to down the line shape for the 8 off of the last rail.)

When playing the route to Position B-1, it is easier to lose the cue ball, which could result in a scratch into the upper right corner pocket. So, while both routes will work, the route to Position A-1 appears to be the better choice because, in my opinion, it reduces the chances of scratching. Practice them both and see which one works better for you!

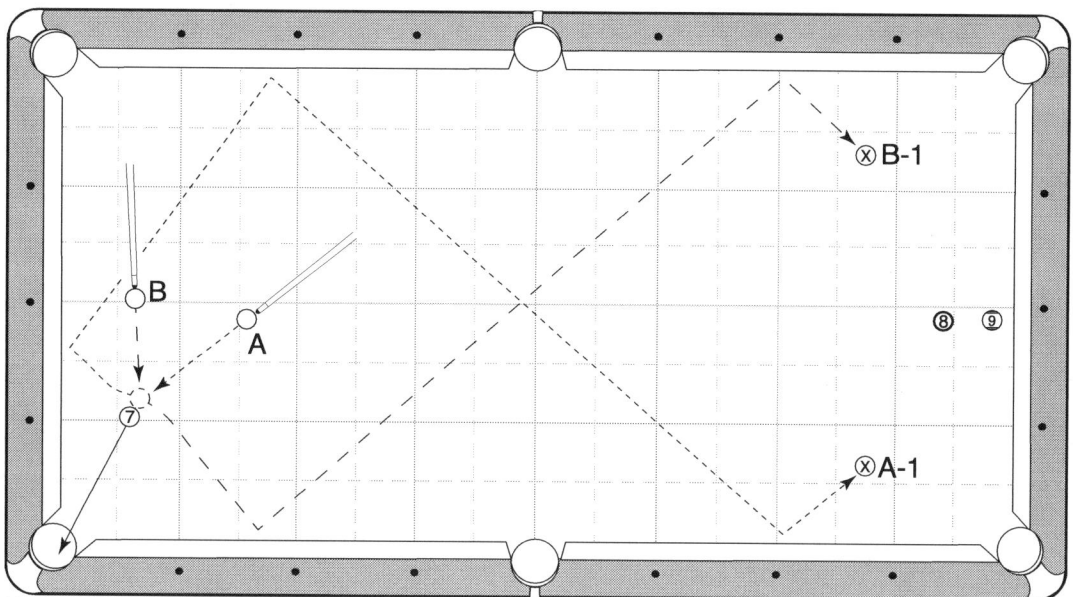

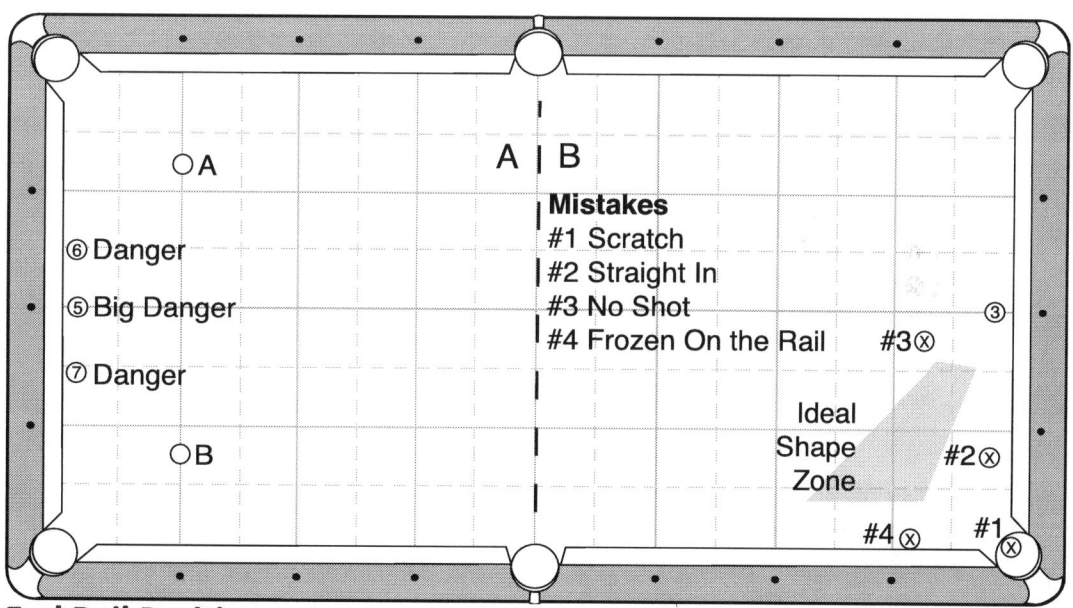

End Rail Position

When a ball is on the end rail, plan and play position on it with great care. In Part A, the shape zone is small on either side of a ball that is at the middle diamond, such as the 5. When the object ball favors one side of the middle diamond by a few inches or more, first consider playing position on the long side if possible. The cue ball in Position A is well placed for a shot on the 7-ball. The cue ball in Position B is ideal for the 6. When you must play to the short side of a ball on the end rail, this often requires precision play. Part B shows the ideal shape zone for the 3-ball. Notice the possible mistakes that could lead to run out failure should you miss this small zone by about eight inches, or less.

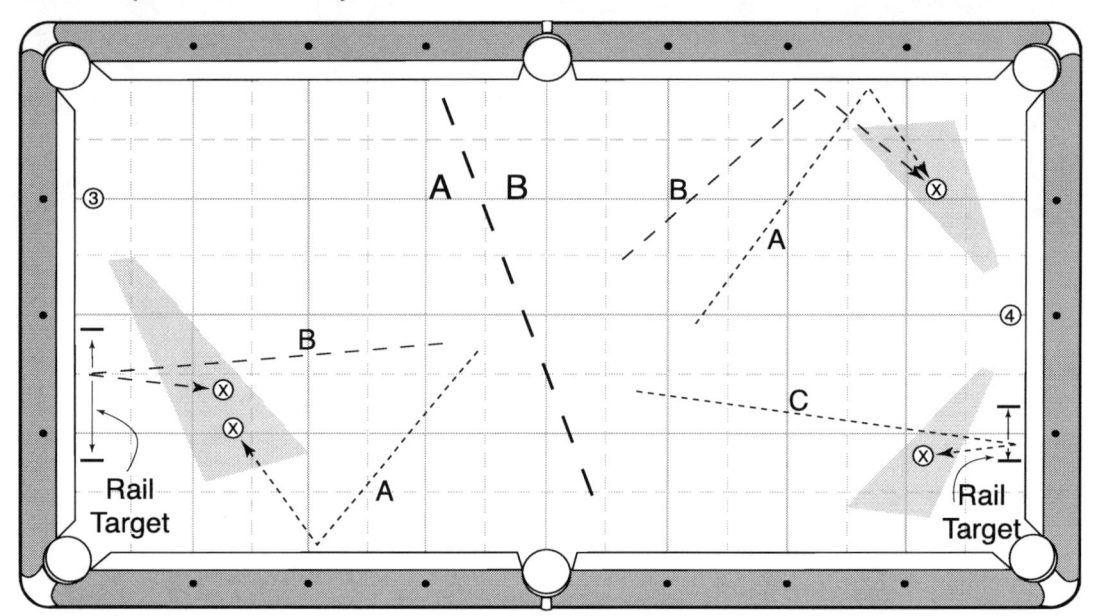

End Rail Position (2)
Here are two methods for playing shape on balls on the end rail. In Part A, the 3-ball is at the diamond closest to the upper left corner pocket, so shape on the long side is better. Route A off the side rail takes the cue ball down the position line and through the heart of the zone. If this route is not possible or practical, then you must play across the zone down Route B. **Most players find it easier to bounce off the rail and back into the zone** as shown. Set your rail target a safe distance from the object ball, and from the corner pocket!

In Part B, the 4-ball is at the middle diamond, so the position zone is the same size on either side. Route A is best because the cue ball will be traveling down the middle of the position zone. If the cue ball approaches the zone at a sharper angle along Route B, your angle for the 4 will change as it travels across the zone. Route C is more exacting as the cue ball will be traveling across the zone. Again, be sure to set your rail target with care, and play for the bounce off the rail into the zone.

Setting Up for a Bank
I've been preaching that **9 Ball are games of percentages, and the percentages usually favor avoiding bank shots**. But pool is loaded with exceptions to the rules. (See Principle #22!) So, there will be times when you should purposefully play for bank shape when no other viable alternative is available. And there will be occasions when a bank can save your run after you've missed position. So, be sure to add bank position to your planning process, either on purpose, or after missing position.

Bank Shape Zones
The 9-ball is frozen to the rail, so this rules out playing shape on the 8-9 combo. And it is nearly impossible to get to the short side of the 8 for position for the upper left corner pocket. So, to finish off this runout, you have no choice except to play position for a cross-side bank on the 8-ball.

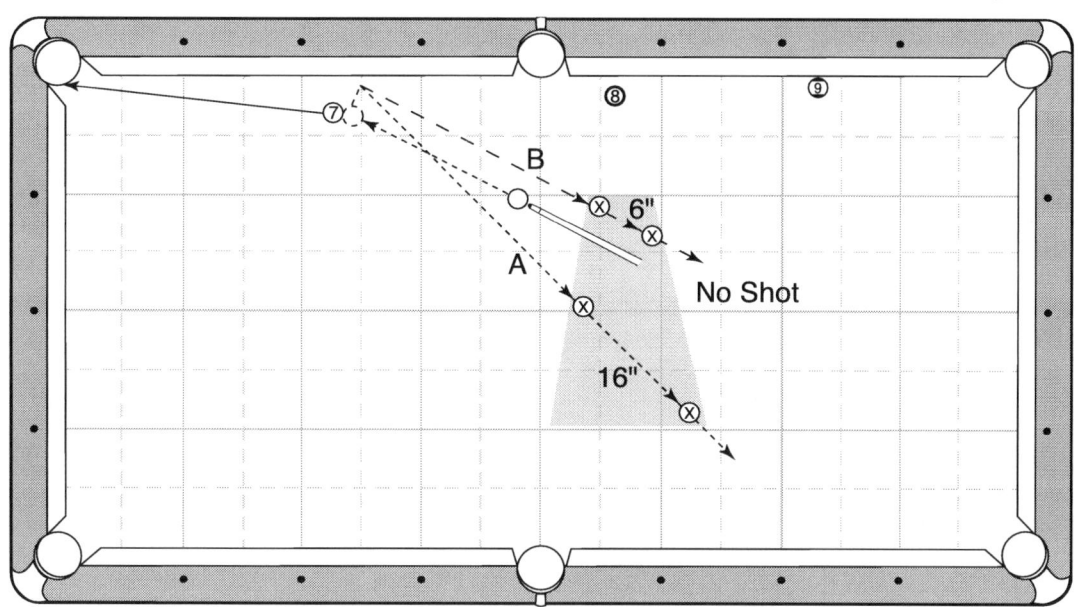

The diagram shows the position zone for a bank shot on the 8-ball. You will have to cross through the position zone on the route from the 7-ball to the 8. Principle #13 of position play advises you to send the cue ball across the wide part of the position zone. Notice that the zone is 10 inches longer on Route A compared to Route B. If you stroke the shot too firmly and roll past the zone, the bank becomes impossible due to a double kiss. Your route from the 8-ball to the 9 depends on where the cue ball stops. There is a good chance that you will have to send the cue ball three rails for position on the 9.

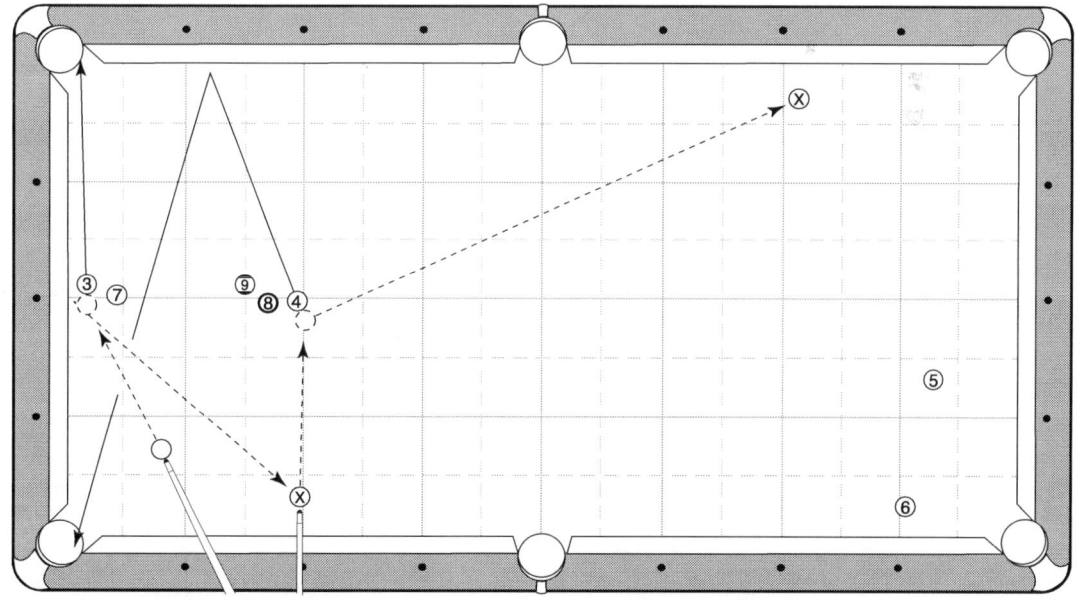

Playing for a Bank - Ortmann

German sharpshooter Oliver Ortmann played shape for a bank on the 4-ball in a match with Fong-Pang Chao at the 2000 World Pool Championships. This looks like a risky shot, but the 4-ball would have probably ended up behind the 8 and 9-balls if he had missed the shot – and Ortmann seldom misses!

Miss Position then Play a Bank

Ismael Paez, who was locked in an emotion packed semi-final duel with Earl Strickland at the 2000 World 9-Ball Championships, missed position on the 6-ball by getting straight in when he needed an angle to cross the table for the 7. After surveying the damage, Paez went to Plan B, which called for bank shape on the 7-ball. His speed on the 6-ball was perfect, setting up a cross side bank. Paez proceeded to run out on his way to staging an upset, and he eventually finished in second place.

CHAPTER 6

Cluster Management

"If you go close to a ball you can get behind, bad things can and often will happen."
Grady Mathews

Cluster management is the art and science of dealing with those annoying groups of balls that could keep you from executing picture perfect run outs. Cluster offer you the opportunity to exercise your offensive or defensive prowess. Sound cluster management enables you to run racks that a less knowledgeable opponent would stall out on. Clusters can also give you the chance to lock up your opponent with a killer safety.

Sound cluster management helps you to avoid costly blunders at critical junctures. The secret lies in accurately appraising the layout, and then precisely executing your plan – a strategy that runs counter to "the blast and hope for a roll" method of dealing with problems. Indeed, the skilled practitioner approaches clusters with the precision of a diamond cutter because they know that one false move can spell disaster

Cluster Management
You need to consider a number of factors that can influence how you deal with the various clusters you'll encounter:
- How the table is playing. If you are comfortable with your cue ball control when sending it off of a cushion, you may go for break outs that you might not otherwise play.
- Aggressive players go for break outs where defensive types would play a safety.
- The risk/reward ratio of the cluster break. Weigh the odds before making your decision to play a break shot or a safety.
- You might play a safe against an opponent who kicks poorly rather than going for the break out.

- When assessing the table, ask 1) do you have a cluster that needs breaking? 2) when can you break the cluster? 3) how can you break it?
- Your goals for a cluster break could be 1) to run out, or 2) to set up a safety, 3) either of the above, depending on the outcome of the breakout.

Reading Clusters
Breaking clusters involves weighing the risks and rewards. The lists below give you the go signs and the pitfalls to breaking high-risk and low-risk clusters. Keep these ideas in mind as you evaluate clusters and **you will soon develop an eye for the clusters you should break, and for those that require a defensive approach**.

High Percentage Breakouts
- The table is open near the cluster, which means there is little or no chance of getting hooked.
- The cluster is not close to a pocket and/or the cue ball will not be traveling toward a pocket after contact, eliminating a scratch.
- The tangent line points to the cluster (no draw or follow is needed). This enables you to control the cue ball's path with great accuracy.
- The cue ball is traveling a short distance into the cluster, so you will 1) not miss it, and 2) possibly hit it exactly where intended.
- Precise contact with the cluster allows you to predict where the balls are going to relocate.
- ou can play shape on a ball that's not in the cluster. This ball is preferably close to a pocket and away from other balls.
- he cluster can be hit softly, reducing or eliminating the chance that the balls roll to undesirable locations.
- The cue ball's path is highly predictable, even if it's going to travel a long distance to the cluster.
- The balls in the cluster need only be bumped lightly to achieve favorable positioning.
- Options are available after the break out: 1) you can continue the run, or 2) you have a safety available.
- The penalty for missing the break out is not substantial.

Risky Breakouts

- The balls are wedged against the rail, which could lead to a double kiss, or to a hook.
- The cue ball will be traveling a long distance to the cluster, which increases the odds that you fail to separate the balls.
- You could easily get hooked by a ball that is stationed close by.
- A precise hit on the cluster is not likely, which increases the chances of not gaining favorable position.
- You could easily scratch after contacting the cluster.
- Good position is not likely despite a successful breakout.
- You must finesse the cue ball very well to break the balls.
- The penalty for missing the cluster is high, which gives this breakout a poor risk/reward ratio.

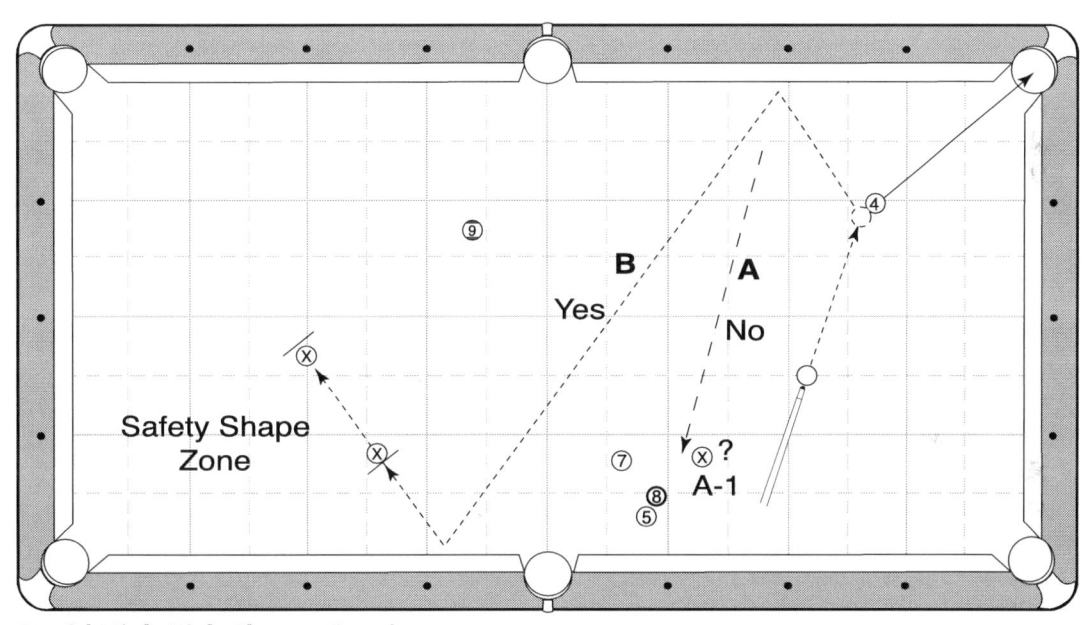

Avoid High Risk Cluster Busting

Route A leads to a cluster break. But even if you succeed at separating the 8 and 5 balls, a good shot on the 5 is not guaranteed. At this distance, you could easily miss the cluster with the cue ball stopping at Position A-1. Now you would have to kick at the 5, which could lead to a sell-out.

A much better choice is to play past the side pocket to the safety shape zone. A softly hit stop shot using draw will leave your opponent hooked behind the (proverbial!) 8-ball. The lesson: **Some clusters should be broken as part of a safety, not as part of a run out**. This is especially true when the distance to the cluster is great, as in our example.

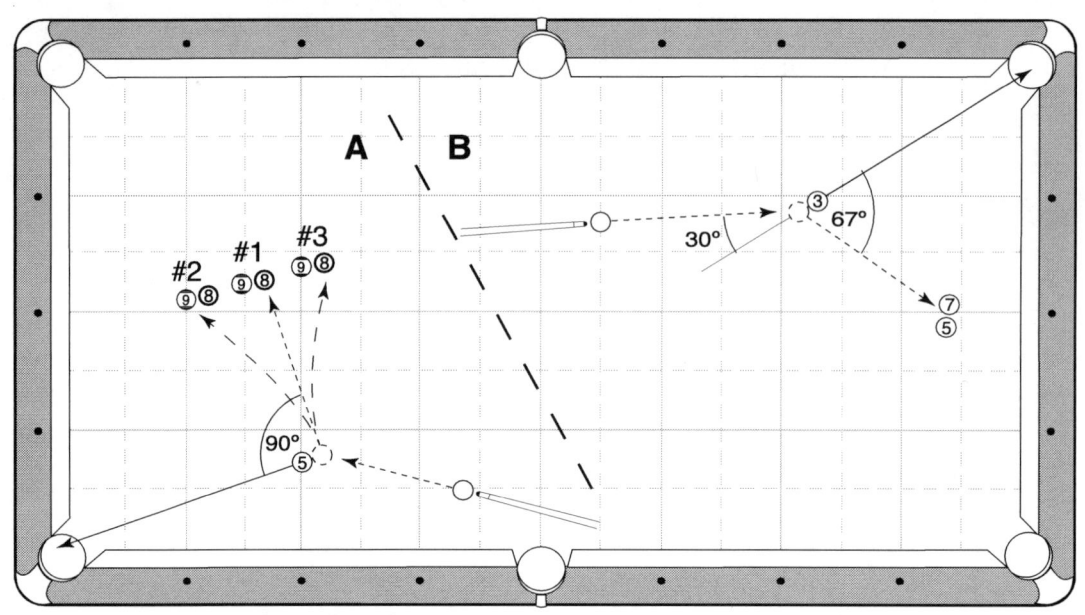

Controlling the Path to the Cluster
The combination of a reasonably short distance from the object ball to the cluster and a stun shot enables you to break clusters with great precision. If the tangent line points directly at the cluster, a stun shot can be used to send the cue ball directly into the cluster as is shown in Part A with the 8 and 9 balls in Position 1.

When the cluster is located a little below the tangent line, as in Position 2, use a medium firm stroke with a tip of follow. If the cluster lies above the tangent line, as shown in Position 3, use draw.

At a soft follow shot can be used to hit the cluster with precision. This occurs when the cue ball's path of departure following contact is lined up directly at the cluster. In Part B, a 30-degree cut angle corresponds with a 67-degree angle of departure when the shot is played with a soft follow stroke. The cue ball will roll directly into the 5-7 cluster. **Soft cluster breaks are usually best because they allow you to exert maximum control over both the cue ball and the object balls**.

Timing a Break Is Critical
The 6-8-9 ball cluster must be broken, so the big question is when? You could pocket the 1-ball and bust the cluster right away, but there is a chance that the cue ball could stop behind one of the balls, leaving you with no direct shot on the 2-ball in Position A. A wiser plan is to clear the 1, 2 and 3 balls. The cue ball should stop near Position B for a cut shot on the 4-ball. The cluster can now be easily broken, and a shot on the next ball (the 5) is virtually guaranteed!

Now let's return to our original shot on the 1-ball. If the 2-ball is in Position C, you should break the 6-8-9 cluster right away when playing the 1-ball because you would almost certainly have an open shot on the 2. The lesson: **When breaking a cluster, ignore those who say to do it as soon as possible and, instead, do it when the timing is right!**

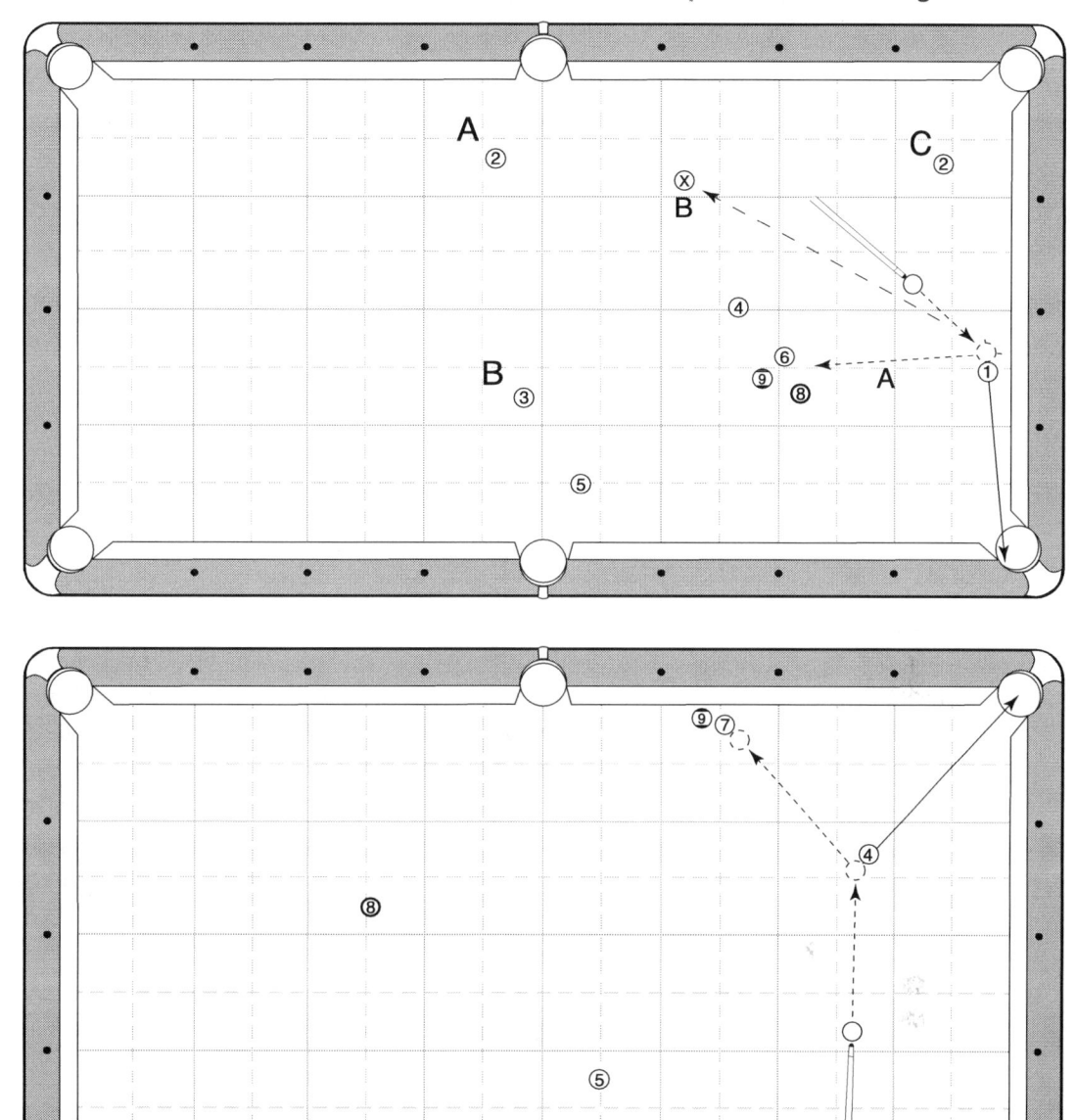

The Ideal Cluster Busting Scenario

This is the ideal scenario for breaking a cluster. The shot on the 4-ball is not difficult. But **do NOT make the mistake of looking up too soon to see if you've broken the cluster**! The short distance from the point of contact to the cluster should help you to hit the 7-ball precisely where intended. The chances of getting hooked are close to zero. Finally, you should have an easy shot on the 5-ball, which is in front of the opposite side pocket.

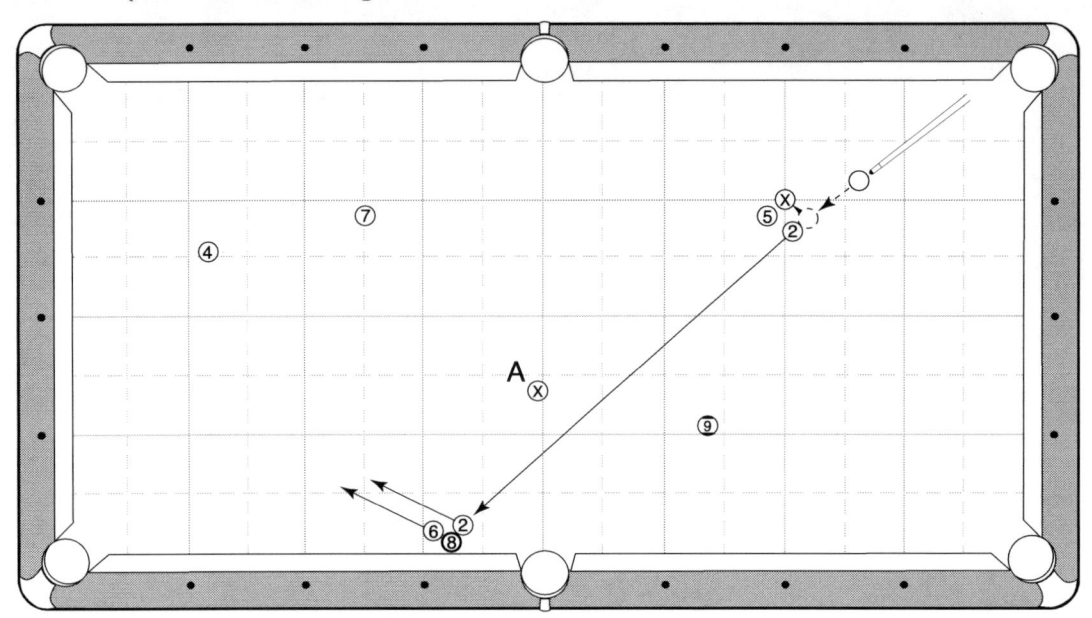

Use Ball in Hand to Break Clusters

You have ball in hand. One option is to play the 2-ball and follow to Position A for a break shot on the 4-ball. After playing the 4, you just might wind up with a shot on the 5-ball, but you could also get hooked behind the 6-ball, or be stuck with an awkward shot off of the rail. The smart move is to shoot the 2-ball into the cluster while pinning the cue ball behind the 5. Now you have an excellent chance of running out after your opponent plays a kick shot, especially if he fouls and you get ball in hand.

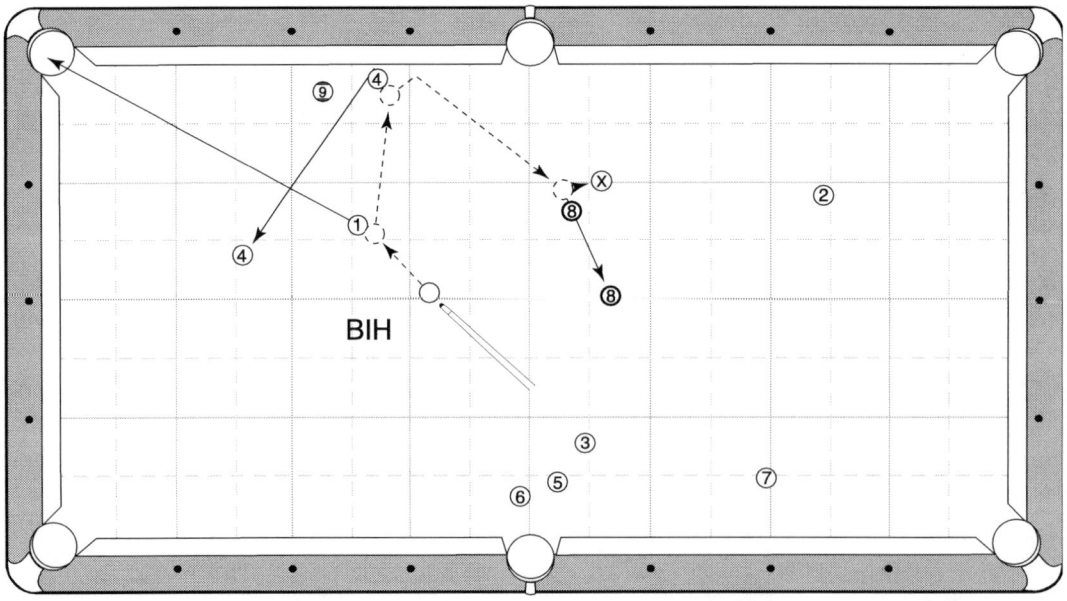

Breaking a Cluster with BIH

Francisco Bustamante showed excellent cue ball control on this break shot against Earl Strickland at the 1992 Bicycle Club Invitational. He placed the cue ball so that he could roll it into the right side of the 4-ball, separating it from the 9-ball. The cue ball bumped the 8 and stopped at Position X for the 2-ball.

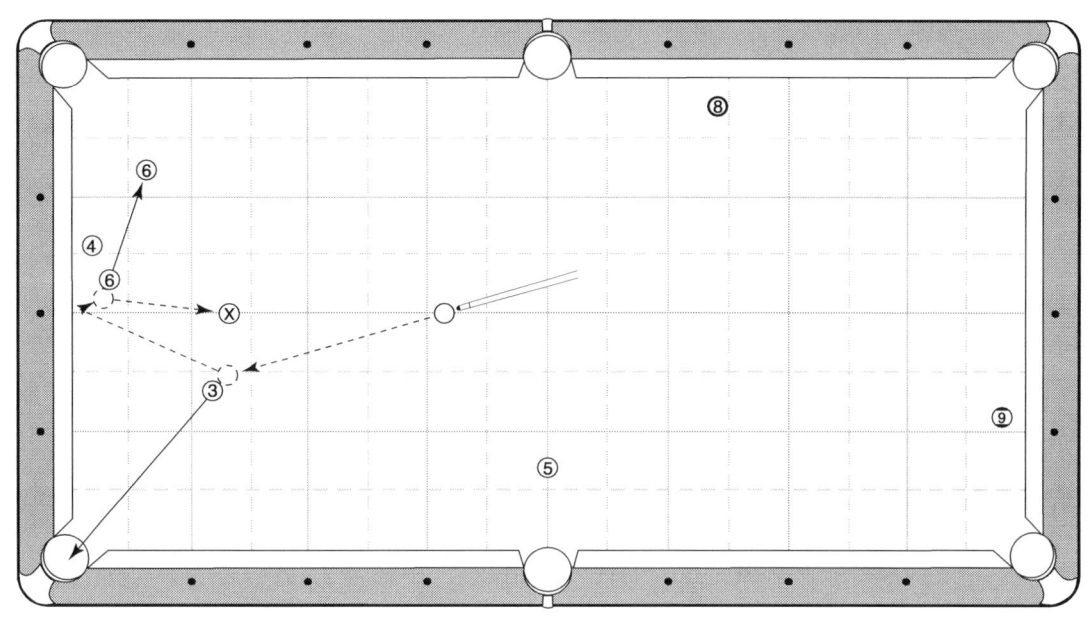

How to Break a Cluster

Mika Immonen played this precise cluster break against Jim Rempe at the 1998 U.S. Open. A soft follow shot sent the cue ball off the end rail and into the right side of the 6-ball, leaving Immonen with a relatively easy shot on the 4-ball. Hitting the correct side and the right portion of the 6-ball at a slow speed were the ingredients for success on this shot.

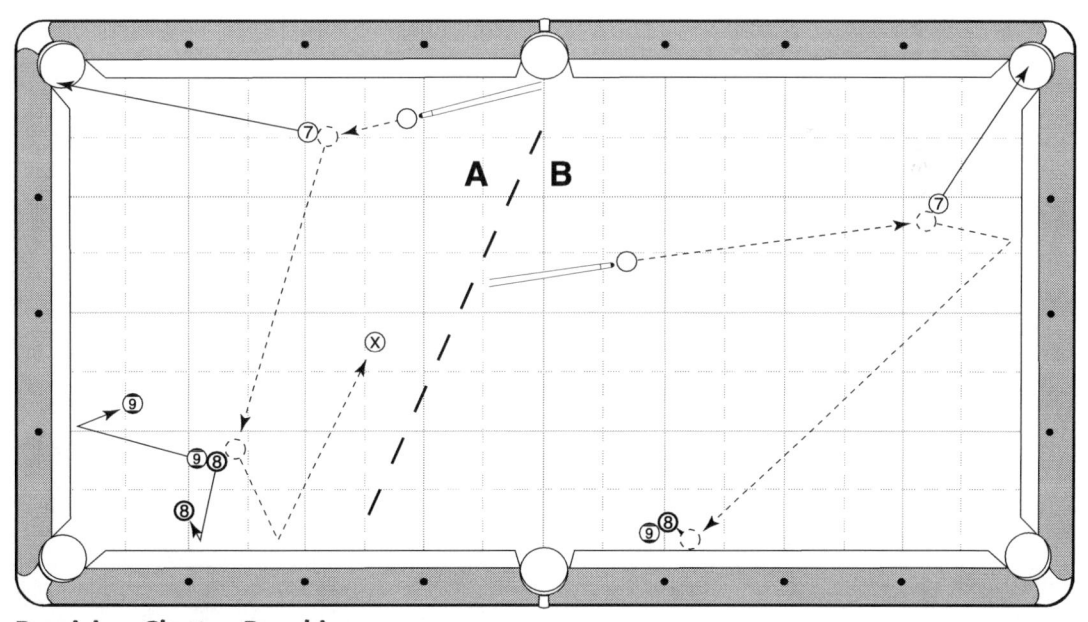

Precision Cluster Breaking

IIn Part A, controlling the path of the cue ball with the correct speed enables you to predict the contact point on the 8-ball and the ending locations of the balls with accuracy. In Part B, this long-range cluster break is worth the risk if your cue ball control is above average. If the 8 and 9-balls were switched, there could be a post break shot hook.

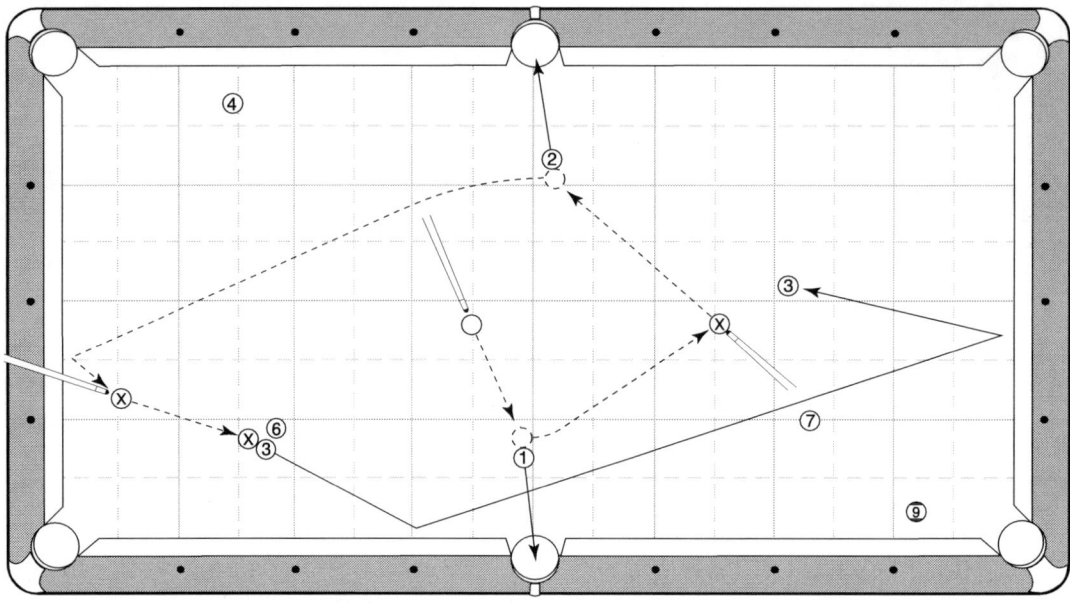

Break a Cluster with a Safety

Earl Strickland played shape for a safety rather than taking a chance on missing the cluster in this match with Cliff Joyner at the 1999 U.S. Open. The route to the cluster break and to a safety were nearly identical, but the safety zone was a couple of feet long, giving Strickland a big margin for error. In addition, the penalty for missing the break was so severe that this shot was not worth the risk.

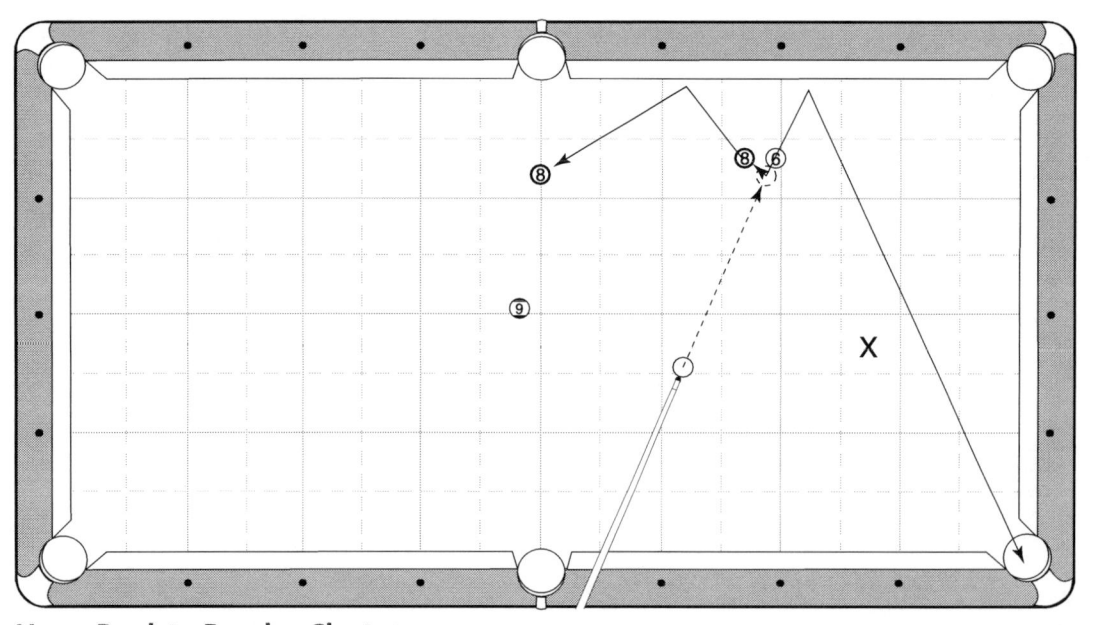

Use a Bank to Break a Cluster

An offensive shot is sometimes the best way to break a cluster. The cue ball was hit with a hard stroke so the 6-ball could be hit slightly to the left of center and still make the bank and drive the 8-ball off the rail and out. This is the right choice if you excel at bank shots. Other players might be better off playing shape on at Position X on the 6 for a safety.

CHAPTER 7

Reading the Table

"You have to be fairly intelligent when you're playing Nine-Ball."
Bill Incardona

Reading the table is how you make sense out of the jumble of balls that makes up a typical layout in 9 Ball. As you improve at evaluating the table, your decision-making skills will become a strategic weapon. When you can consistently pick the course of action based on the position of the balls, your game will have taken a huge step forward. You will start making the most of your offensive opportunities while, at the same time, keeping your opponent's game in check with your defense. Basically, **reading the table boils down to deciding whether the odds favor playing offense or defense**.

The Football Analogy
When a football team takes possession of the ball, they hope their drive will result in a score. If it stalls and they are facing fourth down and long yardage, they will almost always punt, giving their opponent possession. Similarly, when your drive begins with the first shot, you are also hoping to score by eventually sinking the game ball.

Like in football, **you should be willing to give the ball away when your "drive" stalls**, possibly due to poor position. Your "punt" is designed to contain your opponent's offense. In pool, your defensive efforts may keep your opponent from a clear-cut offensive opportunity. And yet, strangely enough, **many players choose to go for it on pool's equivalent of fourth and 40, often when a safety is readily available**!

The Stop Light Analogy

The stop light analogy can help you to accurately assess the potential of a rack as it enables you to quickly assign a rack to one of the three categories below:

- **Green Light** – There are no significant obstacles to running out, so it is all systems go. Now it's all about offense and execution.
- **Yellow Light** – A run out is possible, but one or more minor problems must be solved. Perhaps there is a difficult shot or position play that must be executed with a high degree of accuracy.
- **Red Light** – The rack has one or more problem areas that will keep you from running out. Now is the time to look for a safety that can help you to win the battle for control of the table.

A Simplified Decision Matrix

When you are thinking like a player, the decision making process is automatic most of the time. Until you acquire the experience and knowledge required for making decisions in a *Blink*, as Malcolm Gladwell calls it, you should find it useful to employ the matrix below.

#1 – Do you have a reasonably solid offensive opportunity?

Yes. Continue with Step #1. **No.** Proceed to Step #2.
A - Does your reading of the table suggest that a run out is very possible?
B - Is a combo, billiard, or some other shot at winning available right away?
C - Even if there is an offensive opportunity, is there a safety that gives you a better chance of winning than either of the above?

#2 – Is there a good defensive opportunity?

Yes. Continue below. **No.** Proceed to Step #3
A - Consider your options for playing safe and then chose the best one.
B - If the balls have just been broken, should you push out?

#3 – What options are there for avoiding a foul?

A - Should you play a kick shot? Is there a safety built into the shot?
B - Is a jump shot the best choice?
C - Does an intentional foul give you the best chance of winning?

Know Your Game and Play Your Game

When playing 9 Ball, no one strategic approach is right for all players. Your unique set of skills determines when to play offense or defense. You will go a long way towards increasing your winning percentage by learning to play the highest percentage shot in all situations, always keeping your game in mind.

Don't let your ego cause you to shoot shots that simply aren't in your arsenal (yet!). Be realistic about your chances of running out, playing a specific safety, or making a combination on the game ball. As an example, amateur players should play many more safeties than pros because of positional errors and lack of shotmaking power.

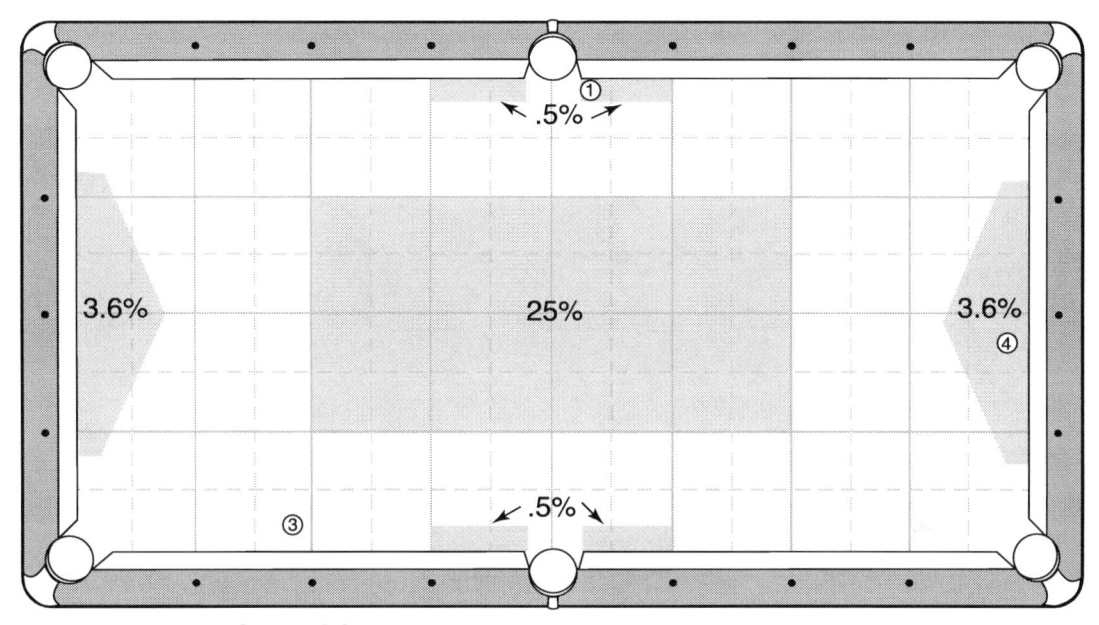

Get to Know the Table

Since 9 Ball is a full table game, the balls will typically be spread across the table after the break. Any ball could be in an advantageous or poor location – an assessment that largely depends on the location of the other balls. As a rule of thumb, however, certain ball positions do tend to cause more trouble than others.

The illustration shows the problem areas. The most troublesome position for a ball is on the side rail near the side pockets. The 1-ball frozen to the rail next to the side pocket is in the spot that causes more headaches than any other location. When you are inspecting the table after the break, look for balls that happen to reside in these problem zones, because they will have to be handled with care. Luckily, this trouble zone only occupies 2 percent of the table.

Balls on or near the end rails also cause their share of problems. A ball in the end rail zone is particularly troublesome when you must get shape on it from the opposite end of the table, such as from the 3-ball to the 4-ball. You must also avoid getting straight in on balls sitting in these zones. Each "end zone" each occupies 3.6 percent of the table.

The center portion takes up 25 percent of the table. Balls in this zone cause problems with position because the cue ball must travel a long distance to the rail on routes that require one or more rails, and because it is difficult to get the correct angle on balls in this area.

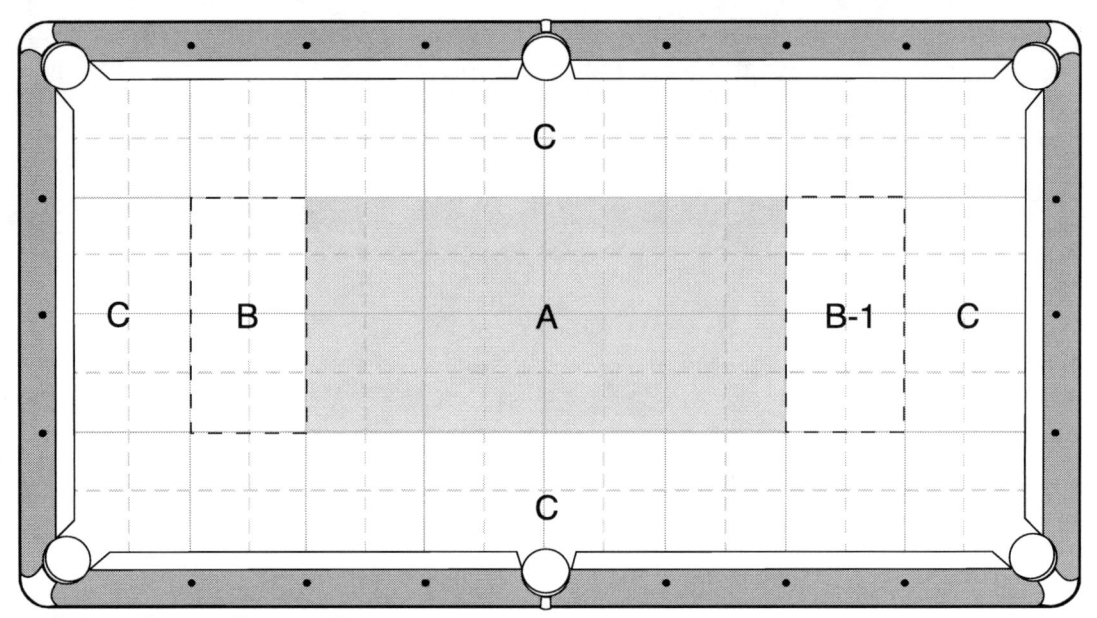

Where the Balls Tend to Locate

Ball location after the break is fundamental to reading the table. With that in mind, I conducted a brief study of 25 pro games of Nine Ball to determine where the balls are most likely to come to rest. The center portion of the table (A) takes up 25 percent of the playing surface, but only 17.5 percent of the balls remaining on the table ended up in this area. Sections B and B-1 at either end of the center make up 12.5 percent of the table, but are home to 13.5 percent of the balls after the break. This is not too surprising as Section B is where the balls are racked. Section C is made up of the playing surface that is within a diamond of the rail. This section covers 62.5 percent of the table, and yet 69.0 percent of the balls ended up there. This may be due to the fact that the balls tend to lose speed quickly as they strike the final cushion.

The value of this research is in alerting you to the fact that most shots are played with the object ball within a diamond of the rail. This may also warn you about the special problems created by balls that end up close together near or on the rails. Knowing that most of the balls are near the rails should also be useful in planning your runouts. Balls near the rail are also good for playing safe. Finally, less than 1.5 balls per rack locate in the center portion of the table, which is the location that creates problems with position play.

Reading the Table

When you are playing position, you are concerned with that one shot. And, when you are playing a pattern, you must plan for a sequence of several balls. Reading the table takes it a step further as its purpose is to give you a realistic assessment of the entire rack, no matter when your turn begins.

Part of your skill at reading the table is correctly assessing the type of rack you are facing. Some are roadmaps that say, "Please run me," while others are ugly configurations that make you want to rack the balls and start over again. Regardless of whatever the breaker (you or your opponent) and the Pool Gods dish out, you must learn to make the most of each and every rack – the good, the bad, and the downright ugly!

How to Read the Table

While you are reading the table, look for things you can do on offense or defense. This involves a realistic assessment of the layout and an awareness of your unique skills. Weigh the risks and rewards, then make a decision on your course of action.

Your results in competition are the best indicator of your current ability to read the table. Are your choices making things difficult for your opponent, and are they giving you your share of offensive opportunities – and then some? Or, are you making life easy for your opponent with low percentage shots and poor safeties that are allowing them to seize the advantage?

In the sections that follow, we'll cover situations that come up repeatedly – real life examples where you must read the table and make a decision. With experience, you will discover that your options fall into three broad categories:

- The layout offers a clear-cut offensive opportunity.
- A defensive maneuver is obviously called for.
- You must weigh the situation before choosing offense or defense.

While common themes run throughout a typical rack, most will also present you with a special challenge or subtle nuance. So, you must learn to decipher the special characteristics of each rack that must be handled in a specific way. Often a minute difference in a single ball's position can change the entire complexion of the rack. For example, a rack could offer the opportunity for a runout or a safety based on whether or not two balls are clustered, or are just an eighth of an inch apart!

The Various Types of Layouts

The balls can take any of a zillion positions after the break. Nevertheless, a number of themes repeat themselves on a regular basis. You will, in due time, learn to quickly size up the kind of layout you are facing. This will enable you to move smoothly on to selecting the offensive or defensive plan that maximizes your chances of winning the game.

TIP: **While you are sitting in the chair waiting your turn or when watching other matches, "practice" reading the table**. Keep asking what you would do if it was your turn, and evaluate the shooter's decisions.

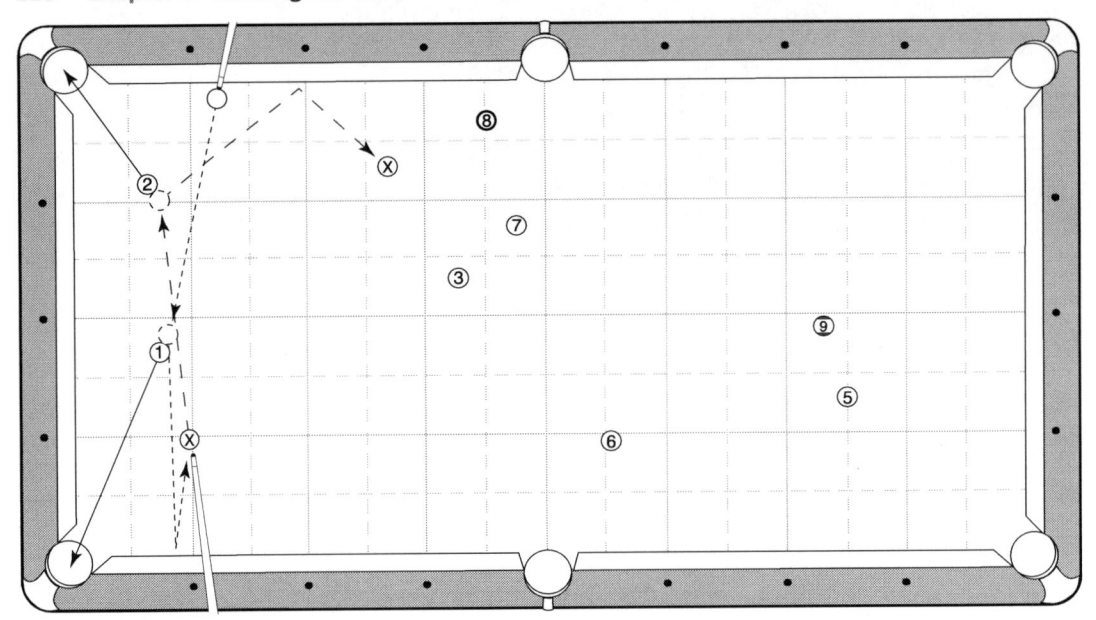

The Roadmap (or Cosmo)
Nick Varner broke and ran this simple layout at the 1990 U.S. Open against Mike Sigel. A quick survey reveals that no clusters stood in his way, and the balls were evenly spread. The big "problem" was getting on the 3-ball, which Varner managed with precise position play. Racks like this are known as "Cosmos." **When you are faced with an easy rack, consider it a chance to polish your position play skills**.

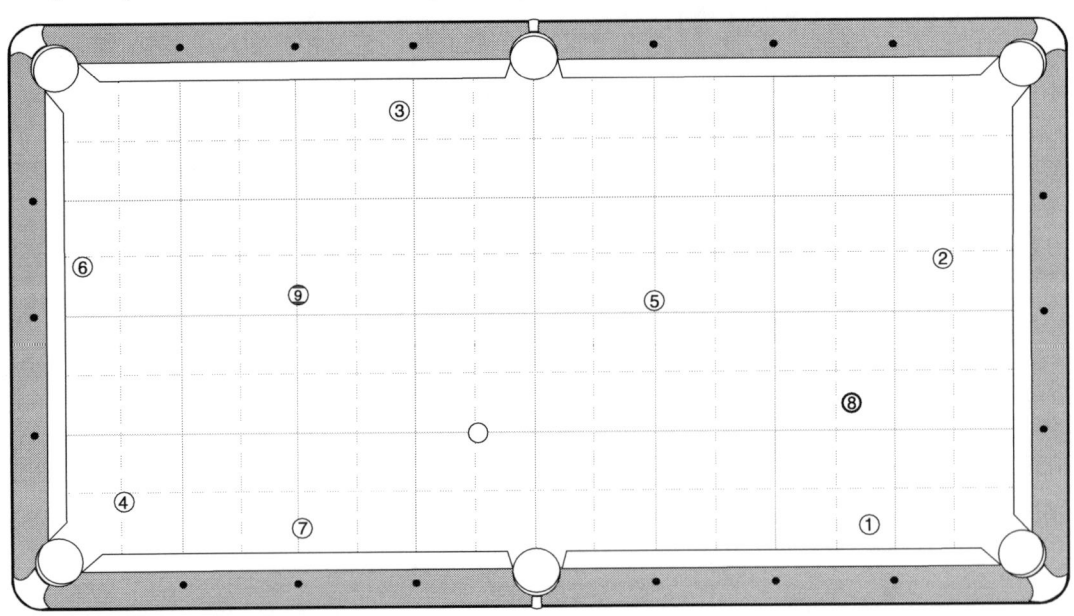

Tough Racks that Appear Easy
When the balls are spread evenly across the table, **don't be lulled into a false sense of security**. Always be on the lookout for trouble: 1) you need an angle on the 2-ball without getting hooked behind the 8, 2) you need to avoid the 9-ball when playing position on the 4-ball, 3) position on the 6-ball will not be easy. The lesson: **proceed with caution because simple looking racks can have their share of problems**.

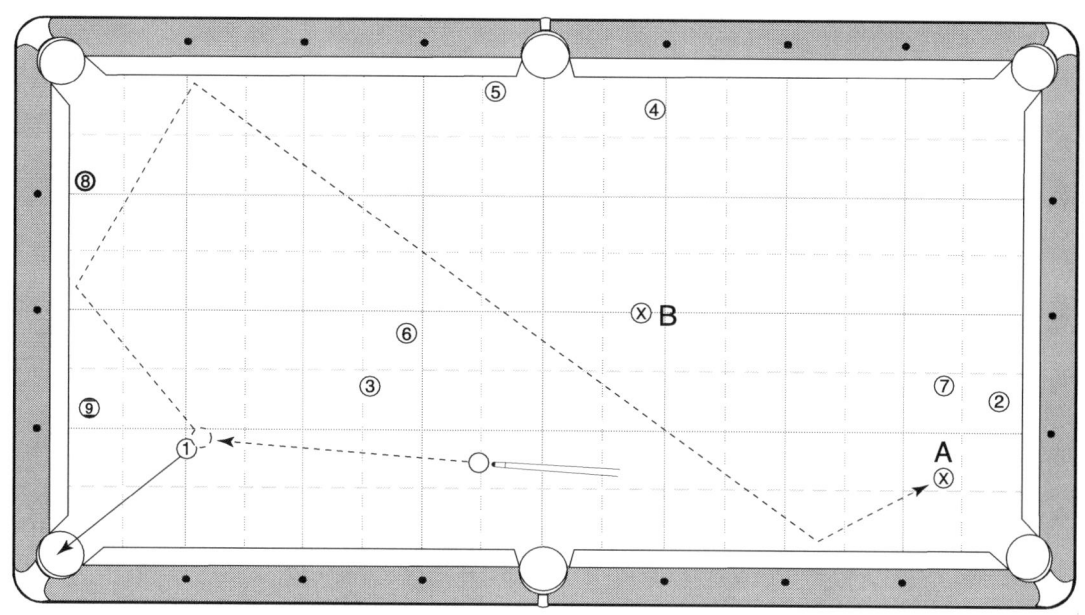

Precision Run Out is Possible

This rack can be run providing you exercise pinpoint cue ball control, shot after shot. On the 1-ball, you must avoid scratching. You also need an angle on the 2-ball at Position A so you can continue to Position B for the troublesome 3-ball. Try planning the rest of the rack with an eye towards the precise execution that it requires.

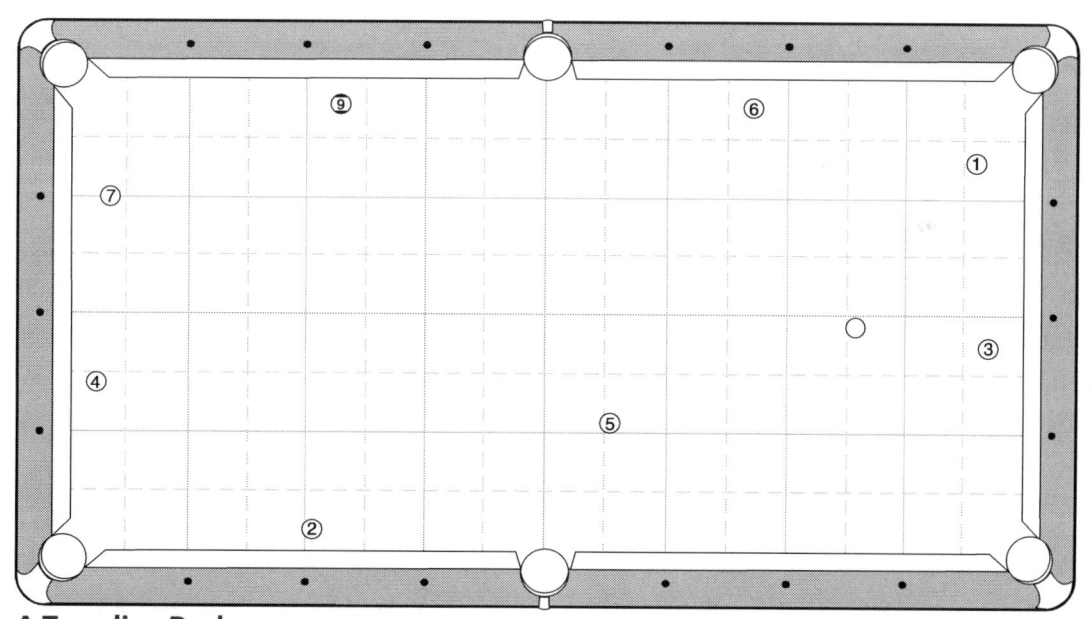

A Traveling Rack

An opponent who knows how to gain separation with his ball placement in the rack and/or the luck of the break can result in a traveling rack. Playing shape on the 2, 3, 4, and 7-balls is going to require some expert long distance cue ball control. If you read this rack correctly, you know the cut angles on the key shots that will be needed to move the cue ball across and down the table.

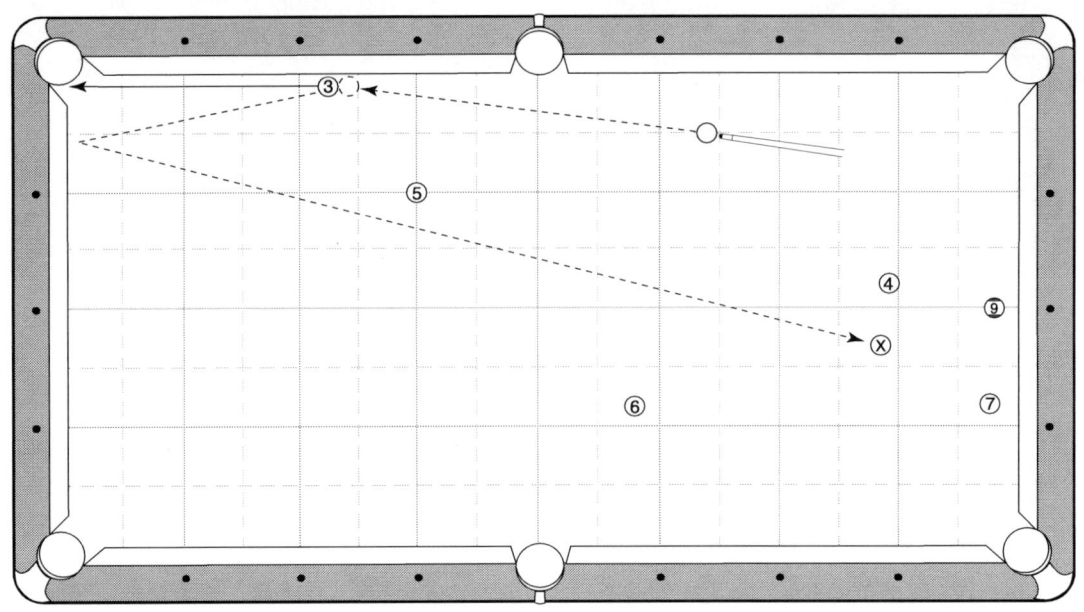

A Tough Position Play

Francisco Bustamante faced a difficult route from the 3-ball to the 4 late in a close match with Efren Reyes at the Sands Regency Open 20, 1994. After surveying the table, he let loose with a very hard follow stroke, sending the cue ball two-rails and down the length of the table for excellent position.

Sometimes the only key to completing a runout is to make a very difficult or unfamiliar position play, such as the one above. If you are feeling confident, give shots like this a go. If you can pull it off, it will further boost your confidence, send a message to your opponent that you came to play, and score a bead for your side!

If you have any doubts, however, about your ability to execute a shot like this, consider playing safe. Remember, **a good safety is better than a less than confident attempt at making a difficult shot**.

The Out Shot

A game can ride on a very difficult shot, which can ignite a run out. The goal is to pocket the ball and end up with a shot that you can work with. Jeanette Lee ably demonstrated this concept against Robin Dodson at the 1994 U.S. Open with this long thin cut shot on the 5-ball.

A couple of safeties were available, but Lee took an aggressive approach and went for the shot, slicing in this off the rail table length 73-degree cut and sending the cue ball nearly 1.75 table lengths for position on the 6-ball. Wow!! Ms. Lee was rewarded with a run out. The lesson: **on tough shots you must be completely honest with yourself**. Your decision to go for it or play safe is often based on the state of your game at that very moment, how you feel about your chances of making the shot, and the score of the match.

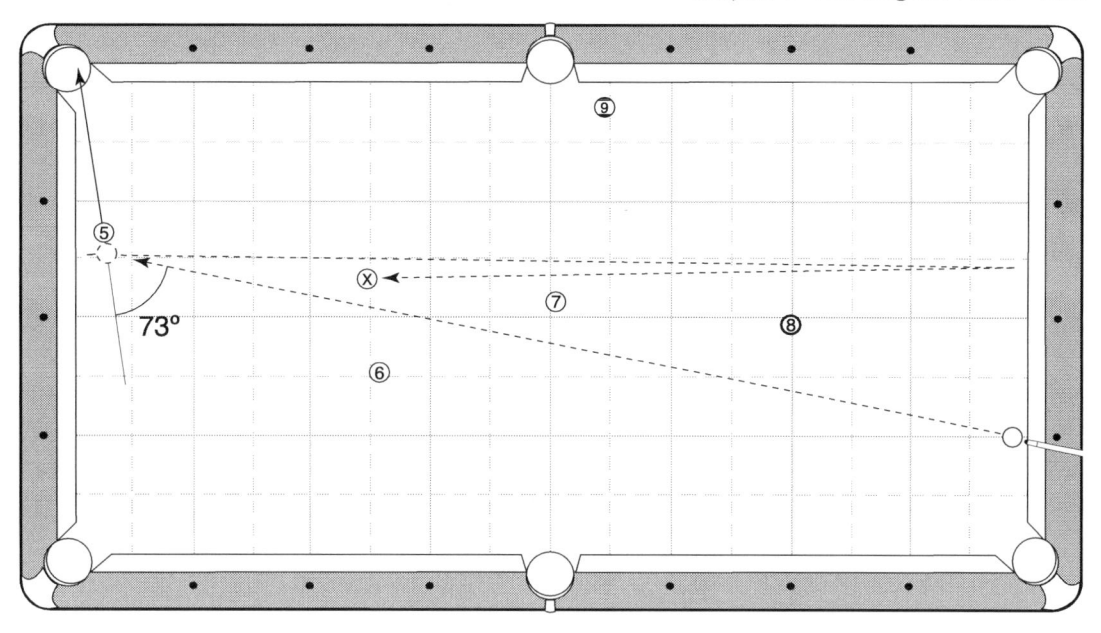

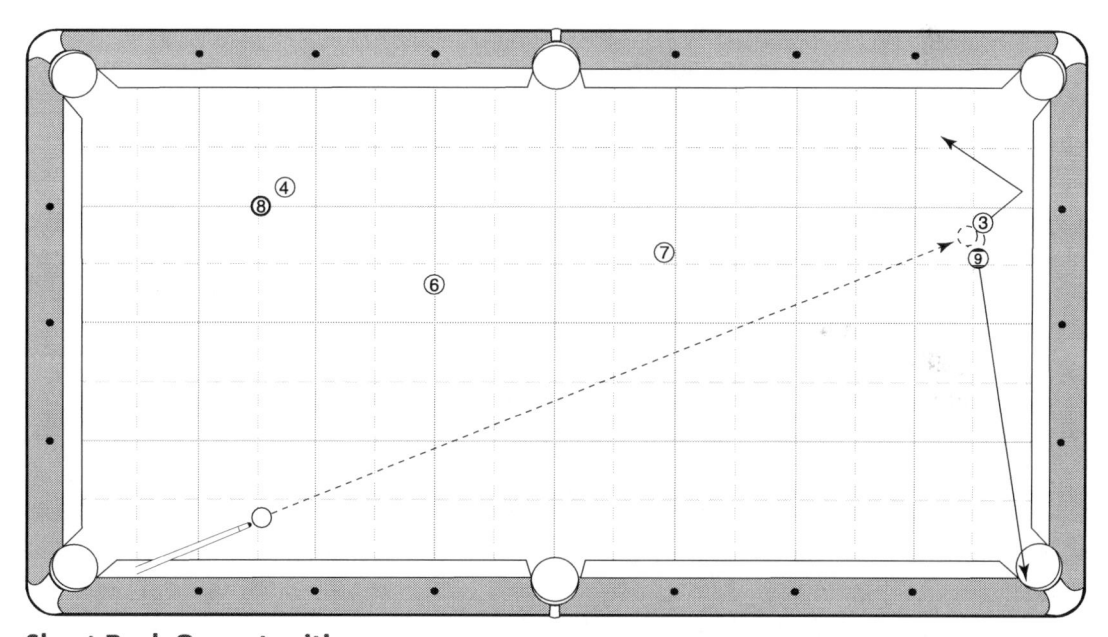

Short Rack Opportunities

Nothing much can lift your spirits and demoralize your opponent more than a quick and easy win. I'm sure you know to keep an eye out for high percentage combos, billiards, and intelligent "cheese rides" that can result in an instant victory. And you will want to develop a sixth sense for the kind of offbeat shots that are lying dead, or near dead, but that are not the kind that you normally come across.

Kunihiko Takahashi spotted this backwards billiard on the 9-ball in a match with Chuck Altomare at the 1999 U.S. Open. The shot required an extremely hard stroke and a very full hit on the 3-ball. PS: **Don't get bullied out of playing legal shots by an opponent who is known for calling "bad hit."** Explain that it is impossible to make the 9-ball straight in with a 100-degree cut angle – because of the billiard, of course! And get a ref if you feel that it is necessary.

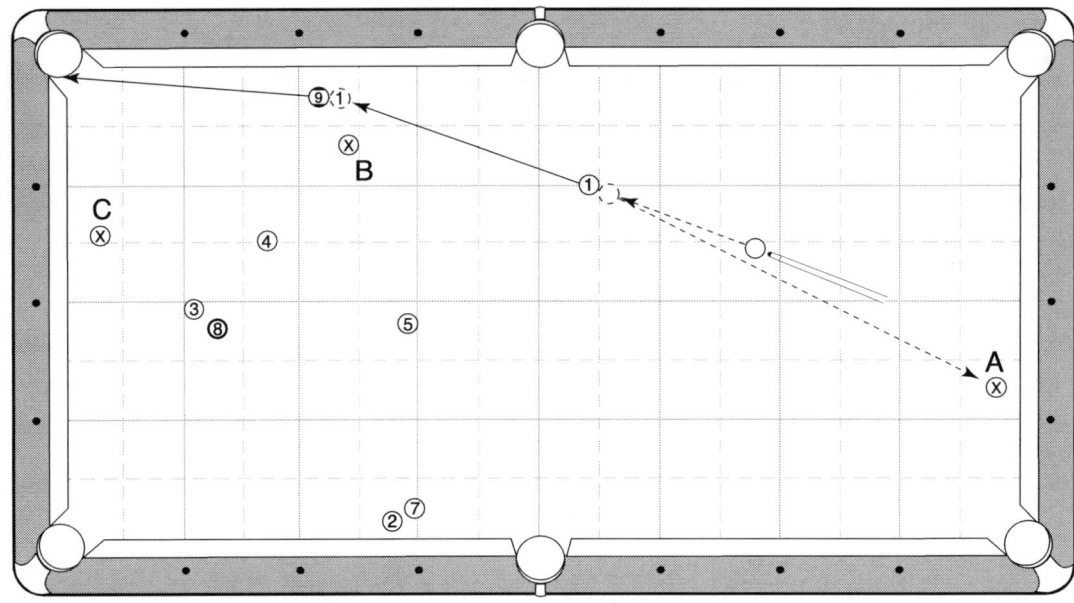

Congestion Rules from the Start
There is a tendency to half-way give up on "ugly" racks just to get them over with. Remember that every game counts the same. So hang in there, play safe, massage the rack, and do whatever it takes to win. Patience is a game winning virtue in some situations, and it may be something that your opponent is lacking!

This kind of layout often results from a weak break, a poor hit on the 1-ball, or an opponent who is using a soft defensive break, which is, of course, a cowardly tactic (or is smart!). The 2-ball is tied up with the 7 on the side rail and there is no way to break it open on this shot. In addition, position on the 3-ball will be difficult (after breaking the 2-7 cluster) because of the 4, 5, and 8 balls nearby. And finally, if you get on the 3-ball, it will be tough to follow this up with good shape on the 4-ball!

When a rack can't be run, look for a shot on the game ball. This time the 1-9 combo is available. When playing a shot like this, build some defense into the shot. Drawing back to Position A will make things super tough for your opponent in the likely event of a miss. Another option is to play position for a safety by pocketing the 1-ball and sending the cue ball to Position B. From here you can break the 2-7 cluster and send the cue ball behind the 3-8 cluster or the 4-ball to the vicinity of Position C.

TIP: A poor break = congestion = opportunities to play safe.

When evaluating a layout where the balls are close together, don't assume that the congestion factor will prevent a run out. In some cases, there will be room to make all the balls as long as you maintain exquisite control of the cue ball.

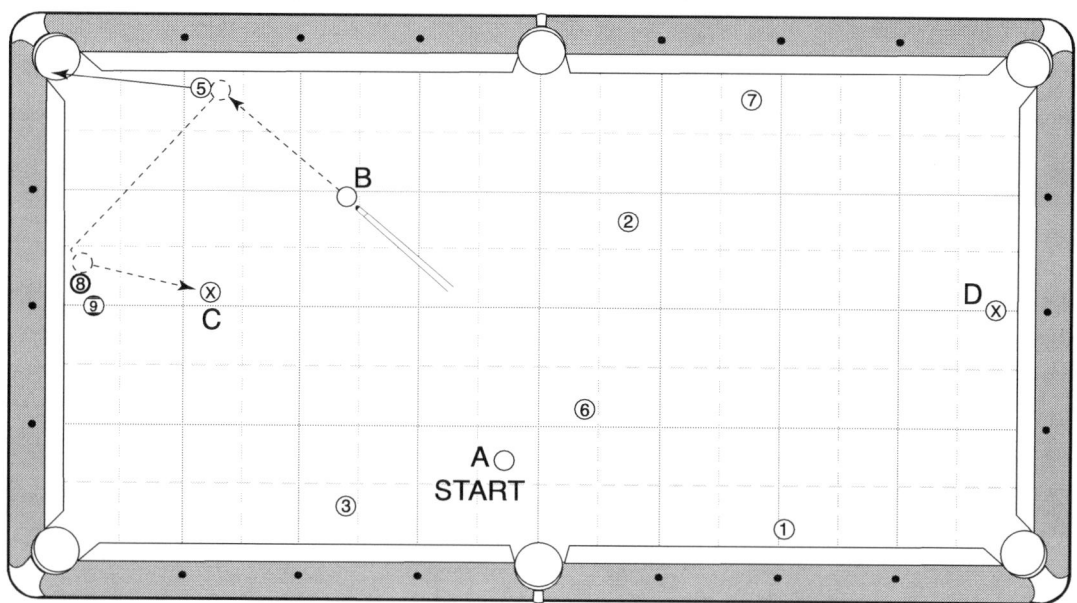

Congestion at the End

We all hate it when the last two balls are tied up and in a position to thwart an attempt to run out. This time the 8 and 9 balls are clustered on the end rail. If you wish to run out, you will have to break this cluster. Timing is crucial because you want to have a makeable shot after separating the balls. That rules out breaking the cluster when playing the 2-ball or the 3. If you run the first three balls and maneuver the cue ball into Position B, you could break the 8-9 cluster and send the cue ball to Position C for shape on a long shot on the 6-ball. This would require near flawless execution.

  Now back to our original layout with the cue ball in Position A. Another choice is to run through to the 7-ball and play shape for a safety. Skim the right side of the 8-ball and break the cluster while sending the cue ball to the opposite end of the table near Position D.

224 Chapter 7 - Reading the Table

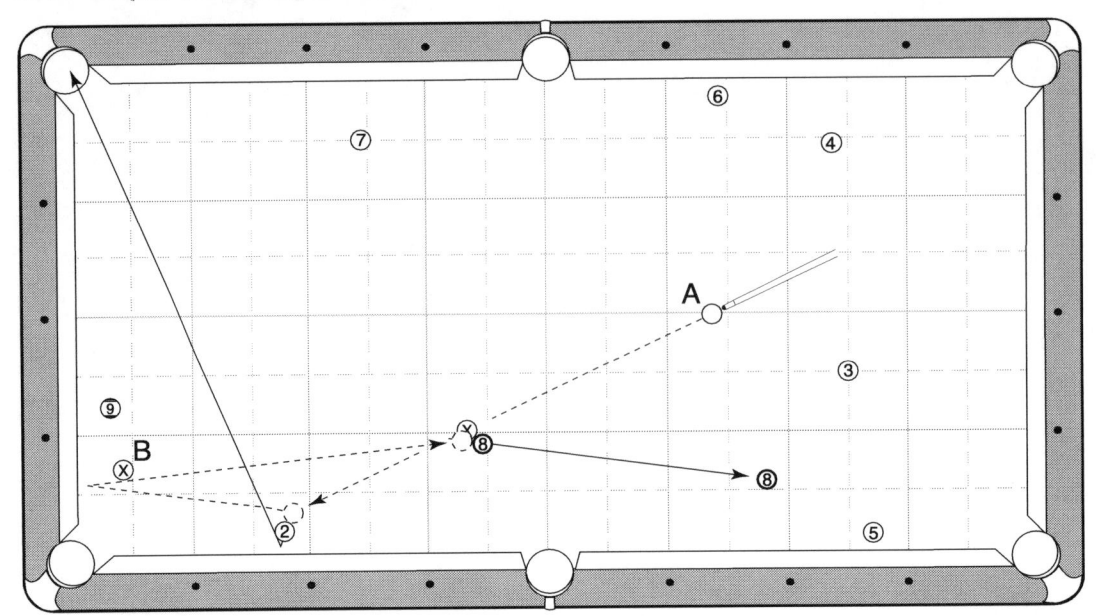

The Improbable Dream

British sharpshooter Steve Davis took a commanding 10-5 lead over Kunihiko Takahashi by running the layout above on his way to an impressive tie for fifth place at the 2000 World 9-Ball Championships. Davis' first shot with the cue ball in Position A was a difficult crossover bank on the 2-ball. Next came a long 58-degree cut on the 3-ball followed by a table length shot on the 4-ball from Position B. Davis never was able to get completely in line during the entire run, so he had to keep making one spectacular shot after another till the very end.

Davis' lack of position was not due to poor position. Instead, he simply had encountered one of those racks where the balls were lying "funny." When this happens, you can still run out providing you keep making difficult shots with just enough position for the next shot. So, when you encounter a rack like this, don't despair (too much). After all, layouts like this give you the opportunity to showcase your shotmaking abilities!

It occurred to me later that the run out Davis played is the way many players proceed through nearly every rack who have not yet learned to control the cue ball! Don't you be one of them (but in the off chance that you think you are, please see Chapter 3).

CHAPTER 8

Push Out Strategy

*"Any time there is indecision (after a push out)
you know you have done your job."*
Bill Incardona

The player with possession of the table after the balls have been broken may be faced with a hook, a very tough shot, or another difficult situation. At this point, they have the option to pass on the shot and play a push out. The shooter must inform their opponent that they are going to push out. A legal push out is any shot on which the cue ball does not scratch or knock any ball off the table. On the most common push, the player rolls the cue ball a few inches, often without it hitting a rail or contacting another ball. However, the cue ball can hit any other balls or pocket any ball on the table. If the 9-ball is pocketed, it is placed on the foot spot.

After a push out, the opponent can take the shot or let the pusher shoot. A push out is not an intentional foul, so the player who pushes out is not on a foul, even if the second player accepts the shot. Once a push out has been played, the "regular" rules of 9 Ball apply for the remainder of the game.

The table below is for newcomers who are unfamiliar with the timing for playing a push out.

Your Push Out Opportunities Come When:
- You've made a ball on the break.
- Your opponent hasn't made a ball on the break.

Your Opponent's Push Out Opportunities Come When:
- You haven't made a ball on the break.
- Your opponent has made a ball on the break.

Professionals' Use of the Push Out

Professionals view push outs as a necessary evil. Their dislike for this tactic is because it often puts them at a disadvantage as their opponent will: 1) accept the push if it offers something good to work with or 2) refuse the push if the pusher has left them with a low percentage shot or safety.

Push outs at the pro level offer a fascinating study into each player's decision-making process since push outs test a player's shotmaking, safety play, and knowledge of their opponent's capabilities.

In a study I conducted of 500 pro games, the pusher won 41.9 percent of the 43 games with a pushout. Their opponent (who made the decision to receive or reject the push out) won 58.1 percent of the time.

When a pro has to push out, he is hoping for a 50/50 chance of winning the game but, as my study showed, they fall short of this goal. The pusher knows their opponent also knows the moves, so they will not likely be able to "pull something over" on them. If a pro gives his opponent even the slightest advantage by making the shot or safety opportunity just a bit too easy, he will shoot. And if he pushes to a position that is a hair too difficult, he is going to have to shoot.

The Push Out is a Valuable Strategic Weapon

The push out is a strategic maneuver that involves sophisticated decision making by both players. The pusher must decide how to push out, and their opponent must then decide whether to accept the push. When you do push out, good things can happen as your opponent may:

- Fail to hook you with their safety.
- Let you play safe when they should have taken the push out.
- Go for a tough shot with no reward when they could have played safe.

Amateur players should use the push out more often than the pros because:

- You or your opponent may exert less control over the cue ball and get a poorer spread on the break, which leads to more potential hooks and tough shots.
- You or your opponent should pass on some of the tough shots, safeties or kicks that a pro would play at the start of a rack.
- Your opponent won't respond to the push out nearly as well as the pros, who have all the shots and knows all the moves.

You can alter the degree of difficulty of the shots you leave your opponent to match your opponent's skills and tendencies. On the next page we'll explore possible weaknesses that you can exploit with a savvy push out strategy. Your opponent is a:

- Poor shotmaker who shoots at everything. Strategy: give them tempting shots that are out of their comfort zone.

- Poor safety player. Strategy: Give them opportunities to play the kind of safeties that they can't execute, but that you can.
- Susceptible to a bluff. Strategy: Push out to a position that makes them think they must shoot, but that offers them little to work with.
- Foolish risk taker. Strategy: Push out to very low percentage shots and combos and other shots on the game ball.

Common Errors

These **strategic blunders must be avoided** when pushing out:
- Pushing to easy shots that your opponent will accept and make.
- Pushing to easy safeties that your opponent will play, leaving you hooked.
- Pushing to your weaknesses. Your opponent may pass the shot back to you when they know that your odds of success are far less than theirs.
- Pushing to your opponent's strengths. You can avoid this mistake by paying attention to your opponent's game.
- Pushing to sure sellouts.
- Thinking that distance alone makes a push out acceptable.

The 40-60 Rule of Push Outs

Your objective against a smart player is to gain a slight advantage when pushing out. In the long run, you cannot expect to win control of the table more than 50-60 percent of the time against a knowledgeable opponent. When your pushout leaves your opponent an easy shot or safe, you lose. The same goes when you pushout to an overly difficult shot or safety. So, **when pushing out, look for the middle ground where you and your opponent have a 40-60 percent chance of winning control of the table**.

The matrix below shows the probable results for push outs that leave your opponent with a shot or safety in any of five levels of difficulty. Avoid pushing out to levels 1 and 5. If your opponent is a poor strategist, you may get away with occasionally playing a pushout in levels 2 or 4. Against a smart opponent, your pushouts should be confined to level 3.

Push Out Decision Making Matrix

Difficulty	Who Shoots	Probable outcome	Strategy
1 - Very tough	You'll have to shoot	A loss is very likely	Very poor
2 - Tough	Hope your opp. takes	Odds favor non-shooter	Bluff/Poor
3 - Average	Favors neither player	Game is up for grabs	Realistic
4 - Easy	Hope you get to shoot	Odds favor shooter	Bluff/Poor
5 - Very easy	Opponent will shoot	A loss is very likely	Very poor

Developing a Winning Push Out Game
Shots
- **Master long distance safeties** that you can push out to, or that you are likely to encounter after a push out.
- **Learn to pocket two or three different types of difficult shots** that you can make after a push out. These could include: jump shots, shots off the rail, jacked up shots, etc. You want to create a situation where it is heads you win (if you must shoot) and tails you win (if your opponent shoots)!
- **Execution is the key.** You must be able to execute what you leave yourself, or what you chose to accept from your opponent.

Your Push Out
- **Tailor your strategy to your opponent's game**. The better they play, the tougher you must make things, and vice versa.
- You should expect your opponent to take your push outs most of the time.
- **Bluffing can be used effectively against lesser players**, but don't overdo it.

Your Opponent's Push Out
- **Accept most of your opponent's push outs**.
- **Avoid falling into a pattern** of accepting or rejecting certain shots, as your opponent will use this against you.

Strategy
- When you are the shooter after a push out, **look to play safe most of the time against above average players**. C Players can fire away against other C Players because their games are usually won on the last 3-4 balls.
- **Distance is a key element in push out strategy.** Most shots and safeties you push to or consider accepting are tougher versions of the shots that appear routinely during the rest of the game.
- **Keep your opponent guessing**.
- Consider strategies for dealing with additional money balls when you are getting or giving up weight.

Strategy Against Lower Level Opponents
- Accept their push outs and play a devastating hook.
- Let them sell out if you sense they don't know what to do or they have left themselves in a jam.

Strategy Against Better Players
- Realize that **they could be bluffing**. Ask yourself if they have really left a reasonable shot or safe? If not, pass.
- They will test you to see what you know, or don't know.
- Think through a reasonable solution and give it your best.
- If you pass, **take note of your opponent's move**s. Learn from your experiences so you'll know what to do next time when a similar situation arises.

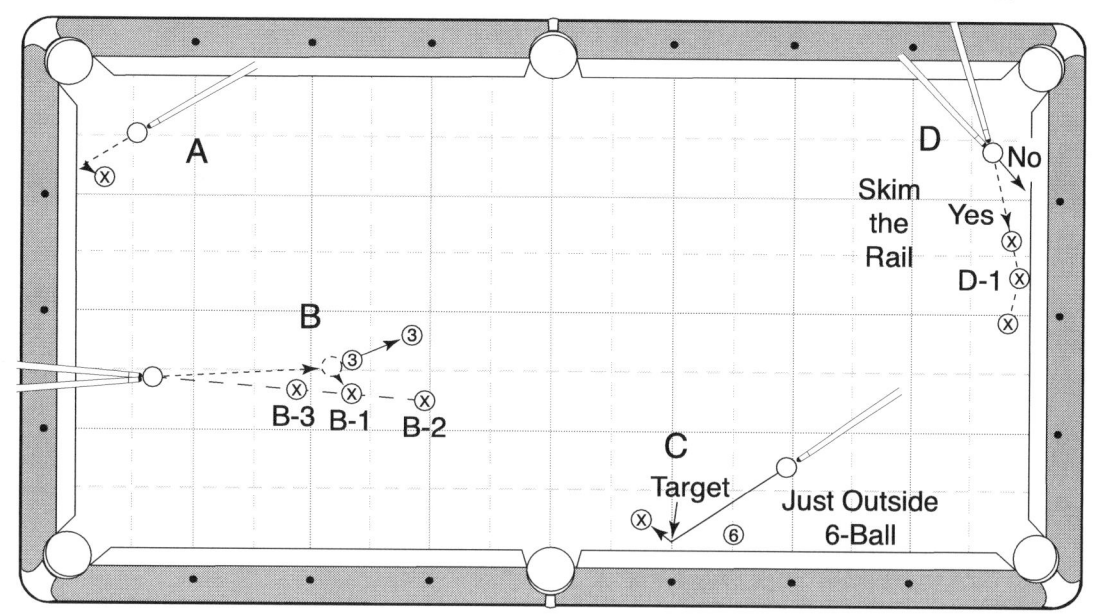

Basics of Cue Ball Control

A valuable skill for the push out is the ability to roll the cue ball a short distance to within an inch or two of perfection. This is easier said than done. Not convinced? Place the cue ball a diamond or two from a rail and try to lag it softly so it dies on the rail. If you can stop the cue ball less than 2.25 inches from the rail (a ball's width), you have a soft touch. If the cue ball stops within an inch, you have a great touch. Now you can pinpoint your pushouts and execute expert maneuvers like:

- Leaving the ball frozen to the rail.
- Leaving the cue ball an inch off the rail (if that is your objective).
- Hooking your opponent by a precise amount for the purposes of regulating the difficulty of a jump shot.
- Precisely regulating the length of a shot.
- Exposing the edge of a ball for a curve shot or safety.

Position A shows a push out where the goal is to leave the cue ball an inch off the rail so you can elevate easier for a jump shot.

In Position B, the objective is send the cue ball to Position B-1 by rolling it straight ahead. If the cue ball rolled to Position B-2, your opponent would have an easier response. And, if the cue ball came up short at Position B-3, the shot may be too tough. The easiest way to control this shot is to hit part of the 3-ball and let the contact kill the cue ball so it stops where intended.

Other balls or the diamonds on the rail can be used as targets when pushing out. In Position C, the cue ball was sent a quarter inch past the outside edge of the 6. The objective in Position D is to leave the cue ball close to the rail. **Skimming the rail gives you a longer target**.

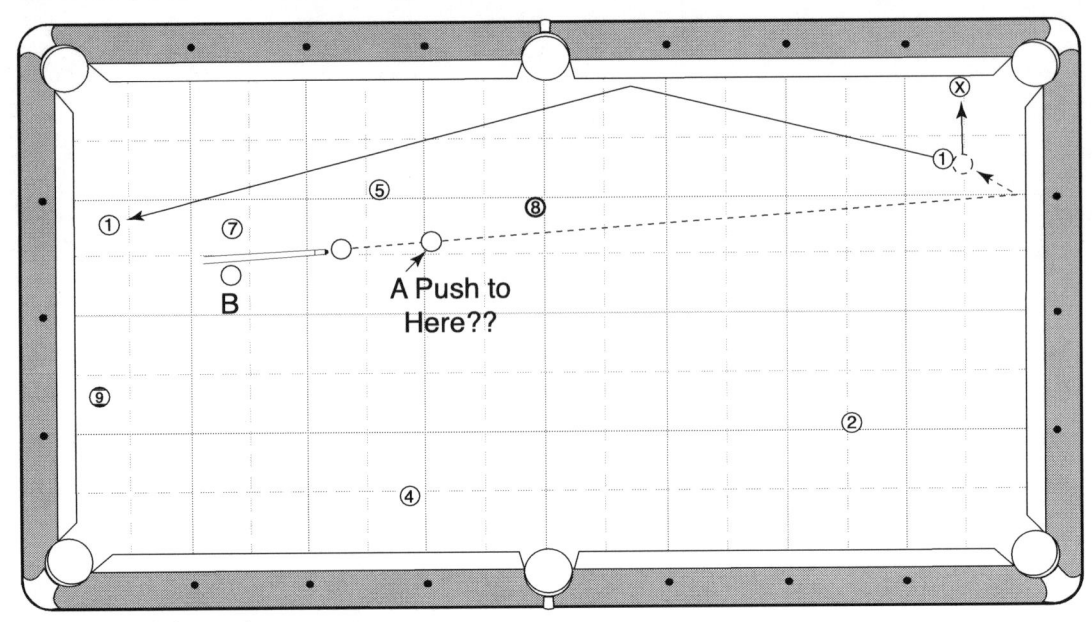

Shoot, Don't Push

The 1-ball is in front of the pocket so you can't push to a shot. If your opponent passes on all hooks, roll up a little further to Position A to make the kick safety a little easier. Against a skilled kicker you could push to Position B to make the kick/safety a little tougher. Ideally they will take the shot and sell out. **In many cases it is best to avoid a push out and play a kick safety** as shown, especially against A Players.

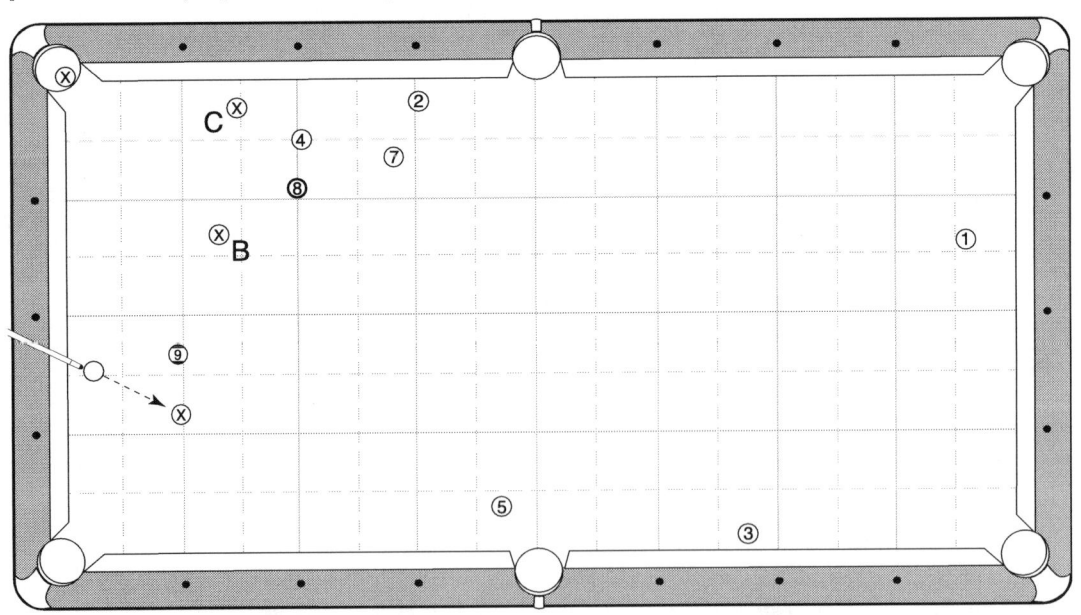

Leave Two Tough Shots

Tempting your opponent with a makeable shot wins games against certain kinds of players. The hard part is making the ball and getting shape. The possible positive outcomes are A) they miss the 1-ball, B) they make the ball and get hooked. If they make the ball and the cue ball stops at Position C, they'll still have trouble getting out, but they could play safe.

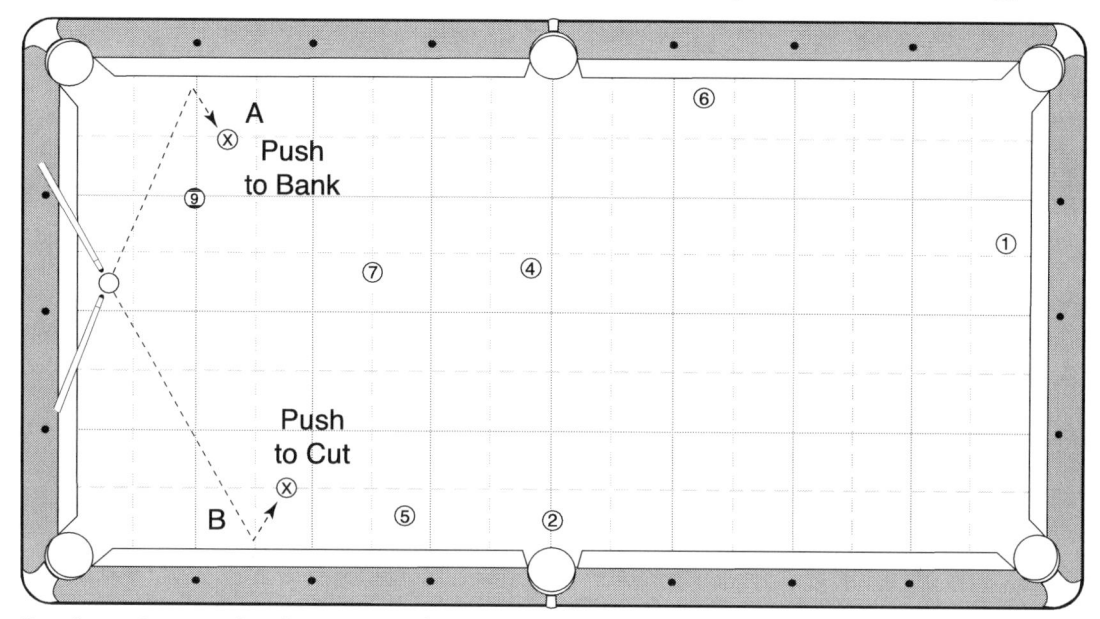

Bank or Cut – What's Your Preference?
When a good safety is not available, push to a tough shot you can make, and that your opponent is likely to miss. If you are good at banking and your opponent isn't, push to Position A, which offers a bank/safety (a two-way shot). Push to Position B, if cut shots are your strong suit and your opponent is weak at them. **Make sure that you will get a reward for making a tough shot** such as: 1) keeping your opponent from winning, 2) good position on the next ball, or 3) position for a safety.

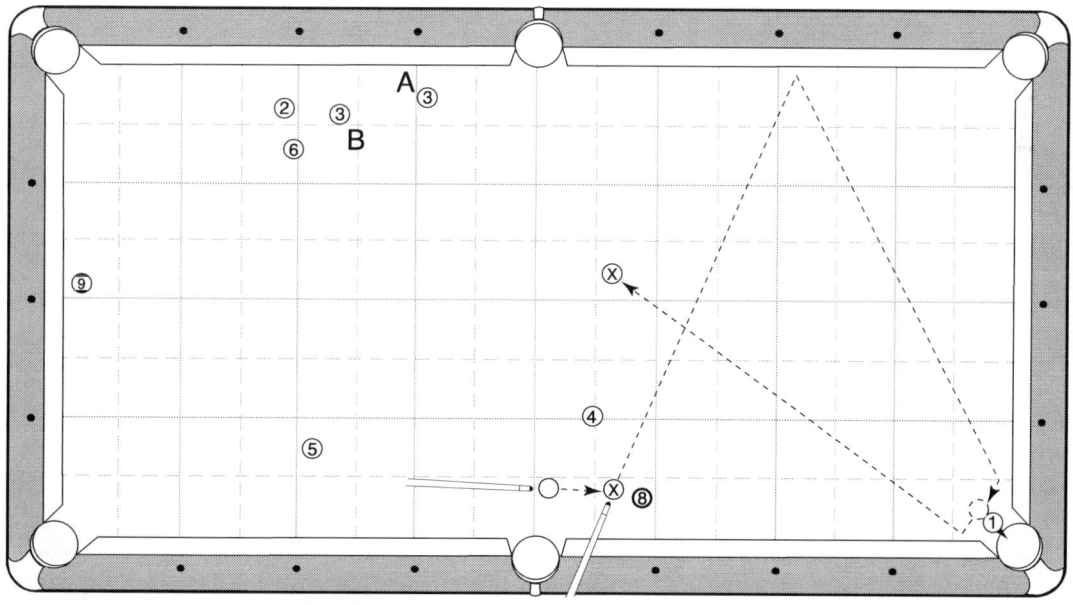

When to Kick at a Pocket Hanger
Your opponent has pushed out, tempting you with a kick shot to a pocket hanger kick. Go for it if the 3-ball is in Position A, but not if the 3-ball is part of a cluster, and in Position B. **Any decision to accept or reject a push out must be made within the context of the entire layout.**

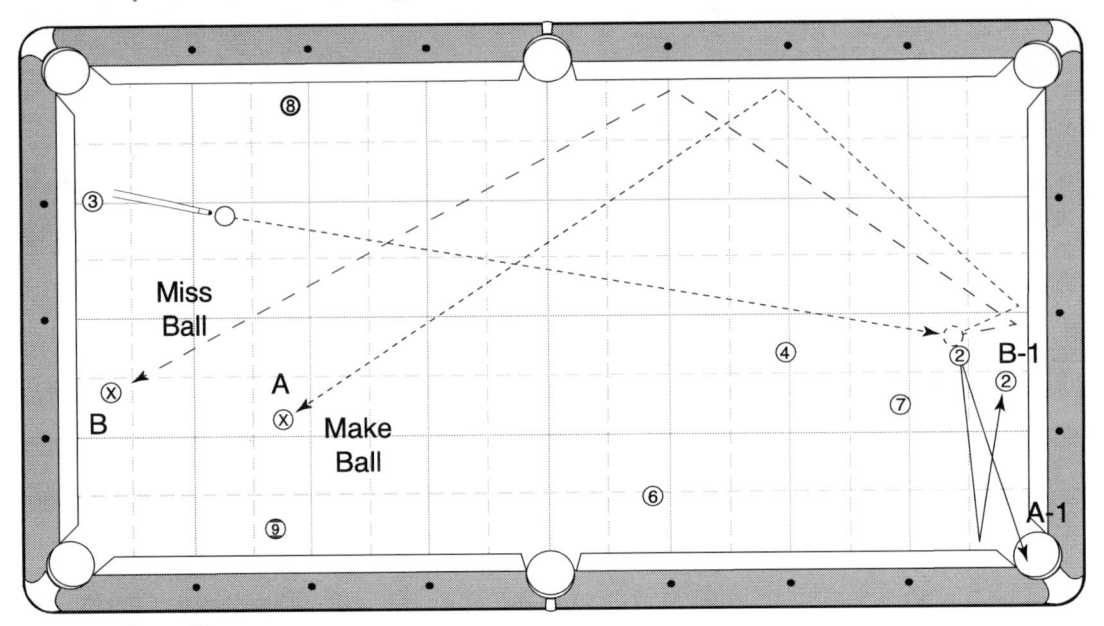

Accept Free Shots

You should take full advantage of your opponent's failure to build a penalty for missing into a push out. You have a free shot on the 2-ball. If you slice in the 2-ball (A-1), the cue ball will stop near Position A, giving you excellent shape on the 3-ball. If you overcut the 2, the cue ball will stop near Position B, while the 2 will be stationed behind the 4 and 7 balls near Position B-1.

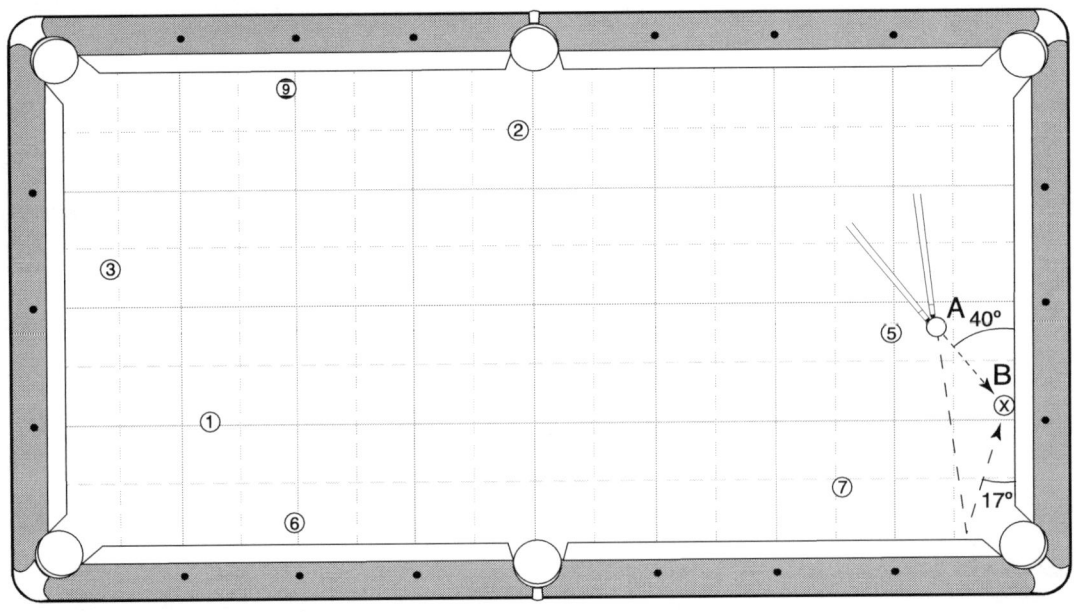

Get It Close to the Rail

If you like jump shots, pushing to Position A could give you an edge in playing a jump to make the ball or play safe. Another choice is to freeze the cue ball on the end rail, leaving a difficult shot off of the rail. You have a better chance of leaving the cue ball on or very close to the rail by sending it to the side rail and out rather than shooting directly at the rail.

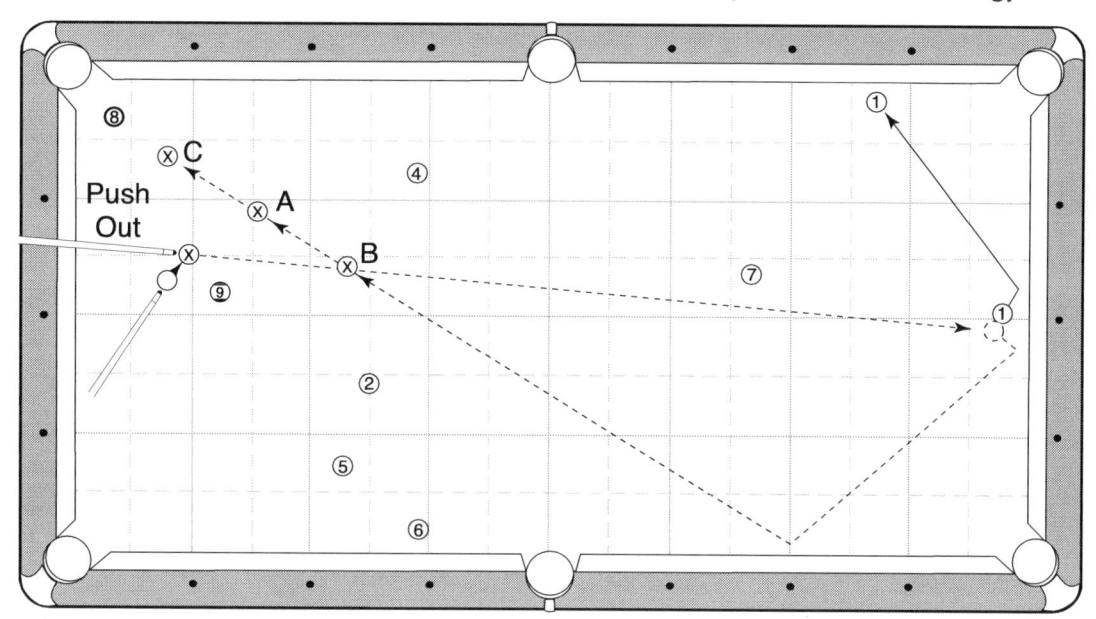

Push to an Uncertain Hook
If your opponent knows the moves, set up situations where execution is the key. Wager your skills against theirs. The 4-ball is a big ball, so it can serve as a blocker. Still, a hook after hitting the 1-ball is uncertain. Position A is a hook while Position B is a sellout. Position C leaves your opponent a tough shot. So, if your chances of creating the safety are good, and his are not, you push may lead to a win.

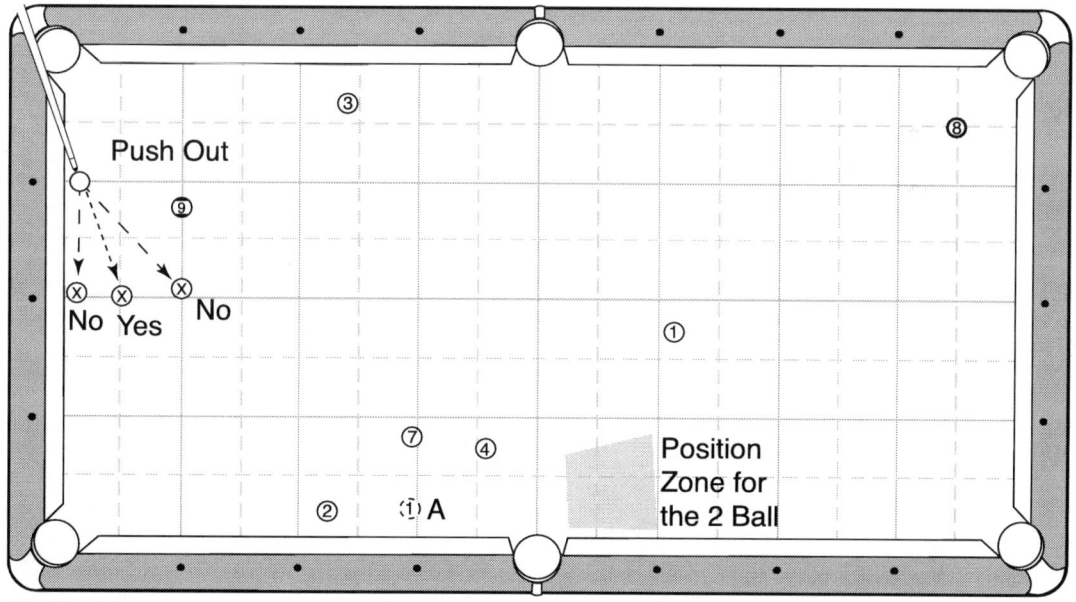

Sucker Shot versus Smart Safety
Let your overly aggressive opponents beat themselves by offering some tempting bait. Leave a shot they think they can make (like the one on the 1-ball), but that is hard to get on the next ball. And, getting from the 2-ball to the 3 will not be easy. If they pass on the shot, play a safety by banking the 1-ball to Position A. If your opponent plays the safety, you may have to reevaluate your strategy because he may play a little smarter than you thought.

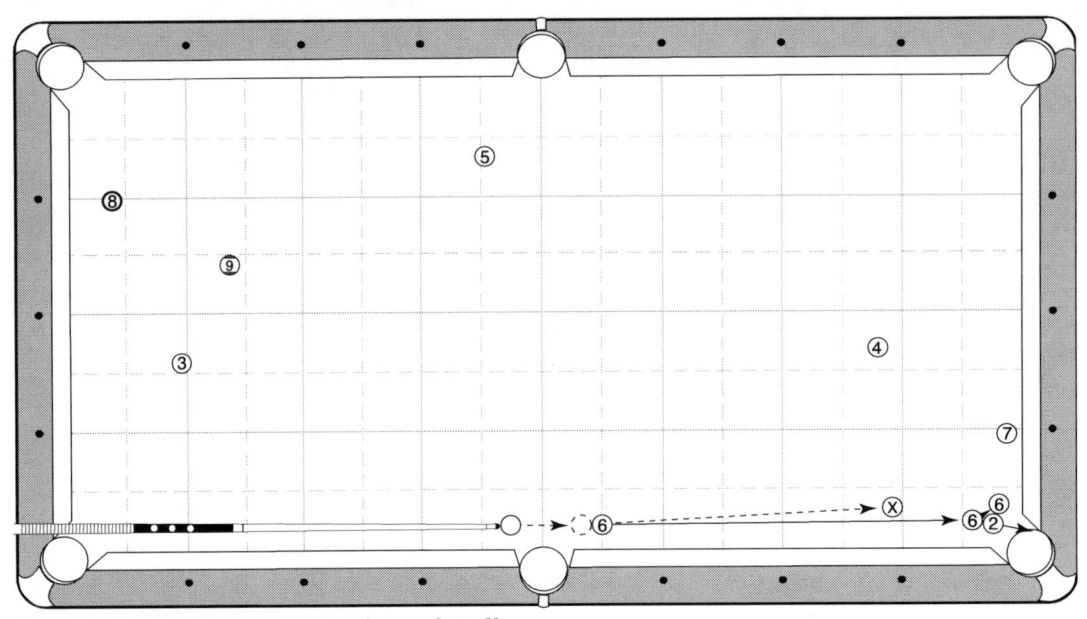

Combo in the Lowest Numbered Ball
The rules allow you to pocket the lowest numbered ball on a push out, and it is not respotted. The 2-ball is near the pocket and is the lowest numbered ball. Even if you kicked it in, you would not be rewarded with much of a shot on the 3-ball. So, the move is to shoot the 6-ball into the 2-ball, and to send the cue ball to Position X. Now either you or your opponent will have a challenging safety or bank shot on the 3-ball.

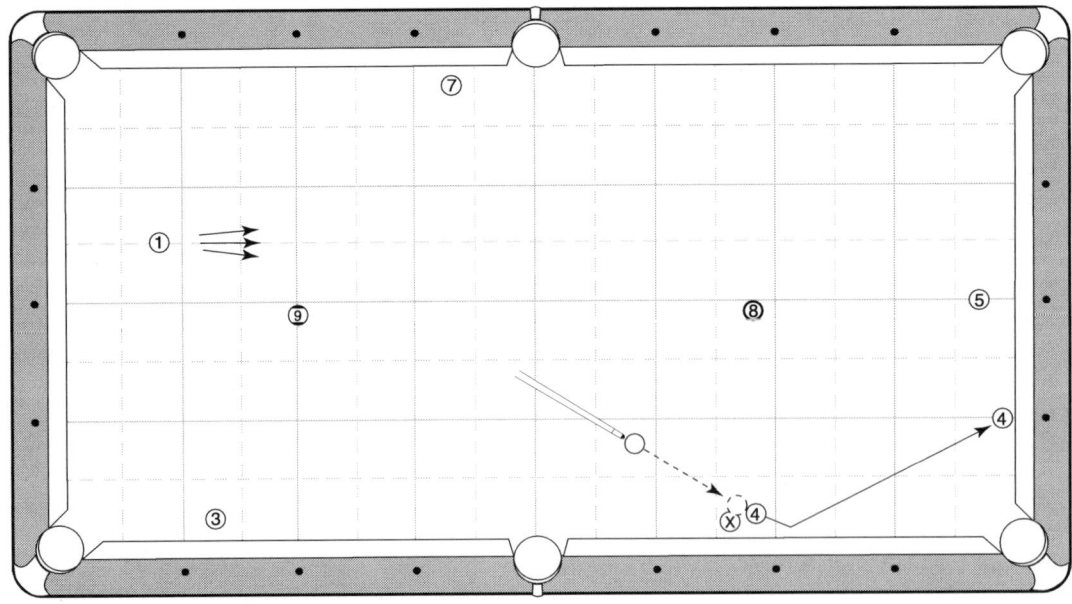

Make the Run Much Tougher
When there is no good place to push to a potential safety, see if you can make the layout more difficult. A soft and accurate bank on the 4-ball will send it to the end rail opposite the 5-ball. Now it will be very difficult for him to run out even in the likely event that you leave a shot after he makes you kick at the 1-ball and you miss kicking it in.

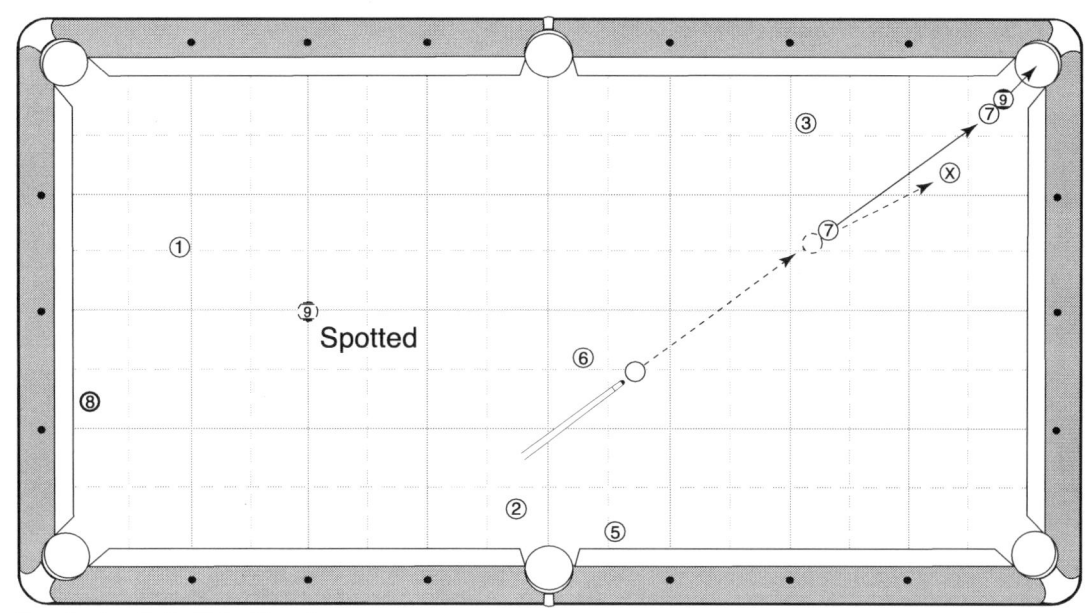

Pocket a 9-Ball in the Jaws

No player ever likes for his opponent to win a game without a struggle, but this can happen when the money ball ends up in the jaws after the break. The solution is to make that ball as part of your push out! Play the 7-9 combo and roll forward to Position X, leaving a tough shot or safety. The 9-ball is then respotted.

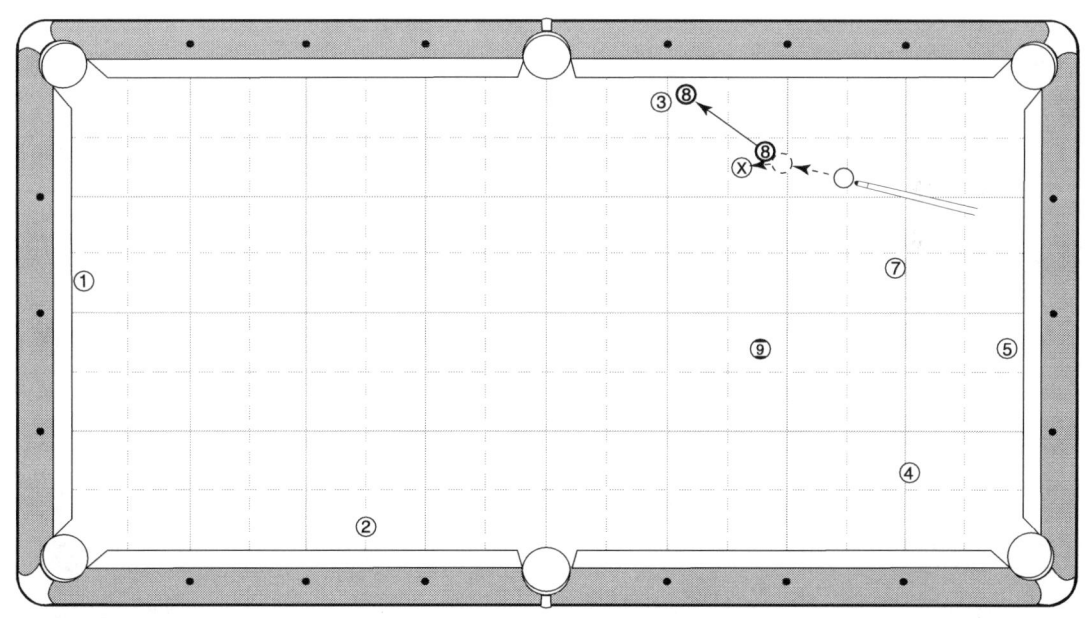

Tying Balls Up

A safety will not be easy with the 1-ball frozen to the opposite end rail. If you push out, you can assume you will be shooting. So, before you play a safety that could easily leave a shot, gently roll the 8-ball next to the 3 as a part of your push out. Now it will be hard for him to run out even if you leave a shot on the 1-ball after your safety.

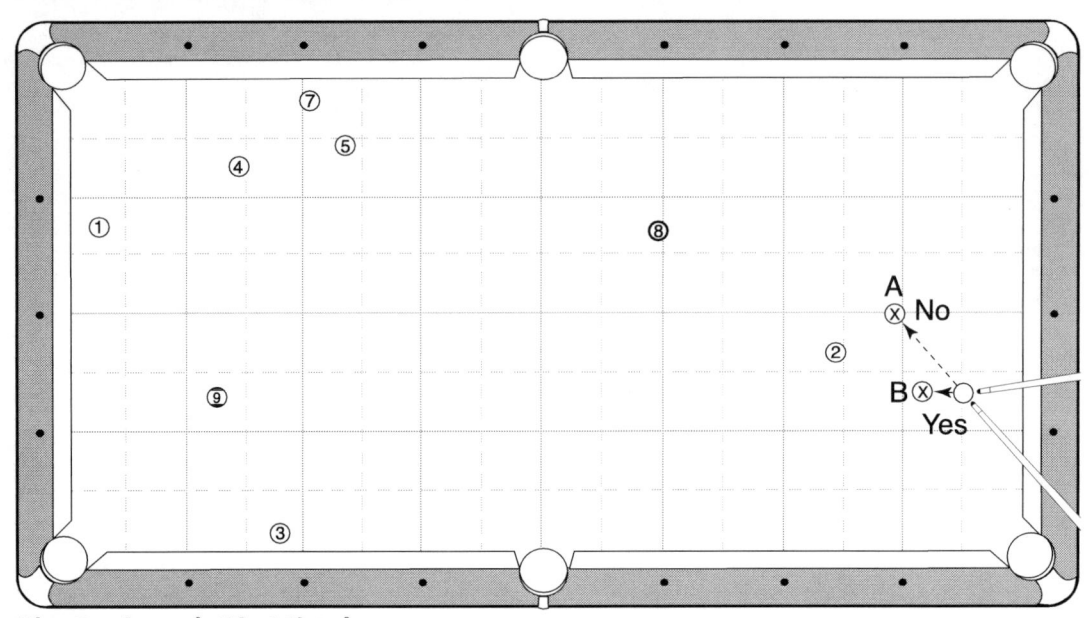

The Beginner's Big Mistake
New players often think that distance alone makes a good push out. But pushing to Position A gives your opponent the chance for an easy hook behind the 4, 5, and 7 balls. A better choice is to push to Position B, which is a moderately difficult kick safety.

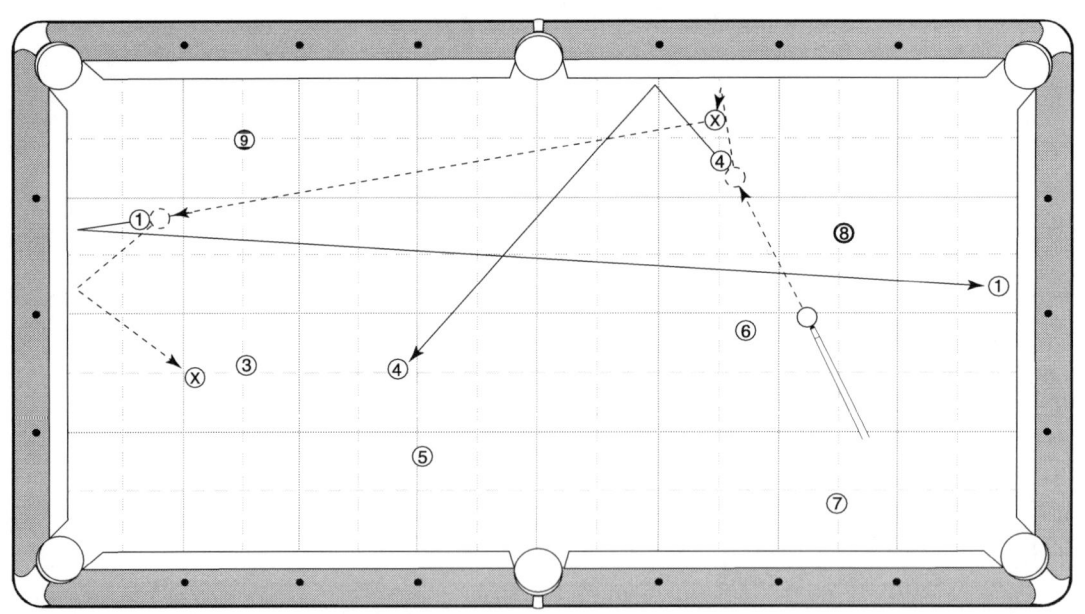

Pushing to a Semi-Easy Hook Opportunity
When pushing out, carefully consider your opponent's skills and chances for hooking you. Cliff Joyner played this push out against Earl Strickland at the 1999 U.S. Open. Strickland promptly took advantage of Joyner's generosity by hooking him behind the 3-ball while sending the 1-ball to the opposite end of the table.

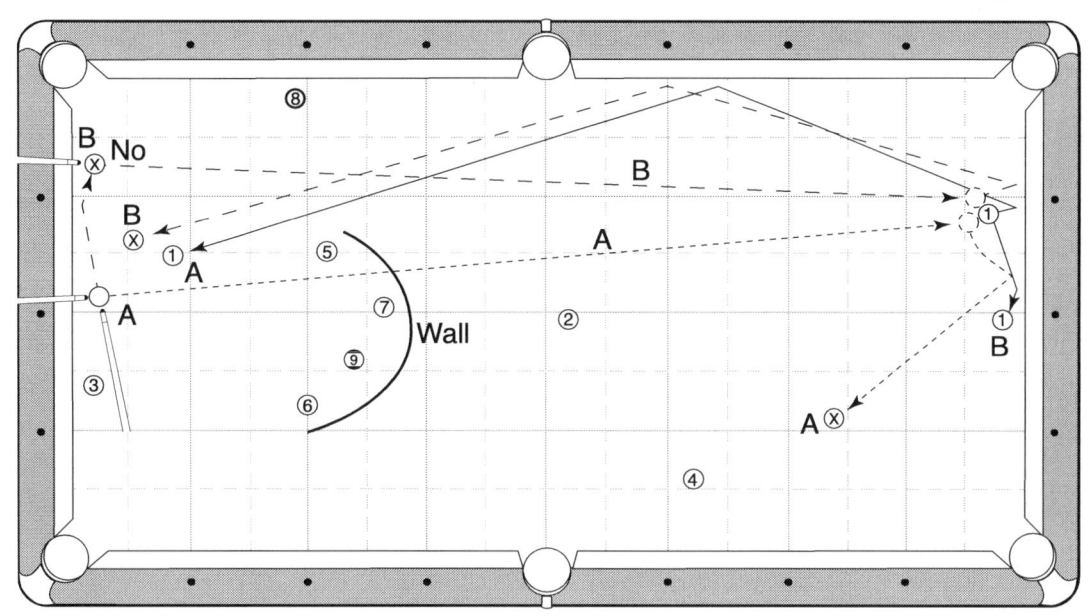

Be Wary of the Congestion Factor
Congested racks can create ample opportunities for safeties, so you must be careful not to push out to a place where your opponent can hook you – even if it's from long range. In this case, use the wall of blockers (the 5, 6, 7, and 9 balls) by playing Safety A. If you push out to Position B, your opponent has the opportunity to play Safety B by thinning the 1-ball and bringing the cue ball back behind the wall.

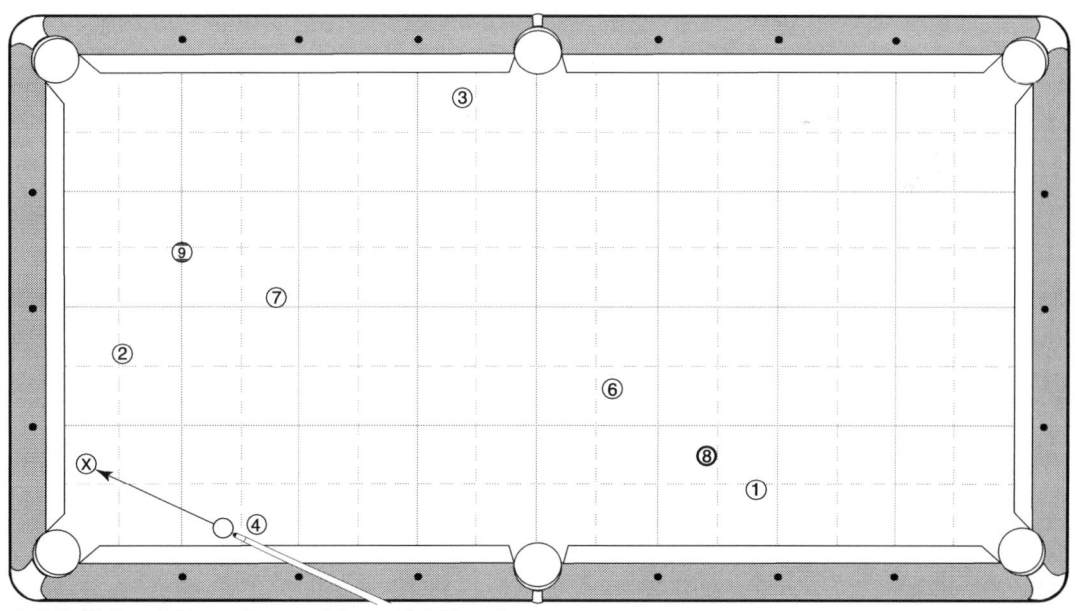

A Bluff Could Lead to a Mental Mistake
A push out to Position X will leave your opponent with a tough shot on the 1-ball (good), and with even tougher shape on the 2-ball (also good). In this position, many players might overestimate their game and try the monster shot on the 1-ball. Or they could fear your game and feel they must shoot. The lesson: let them think their way into an error.

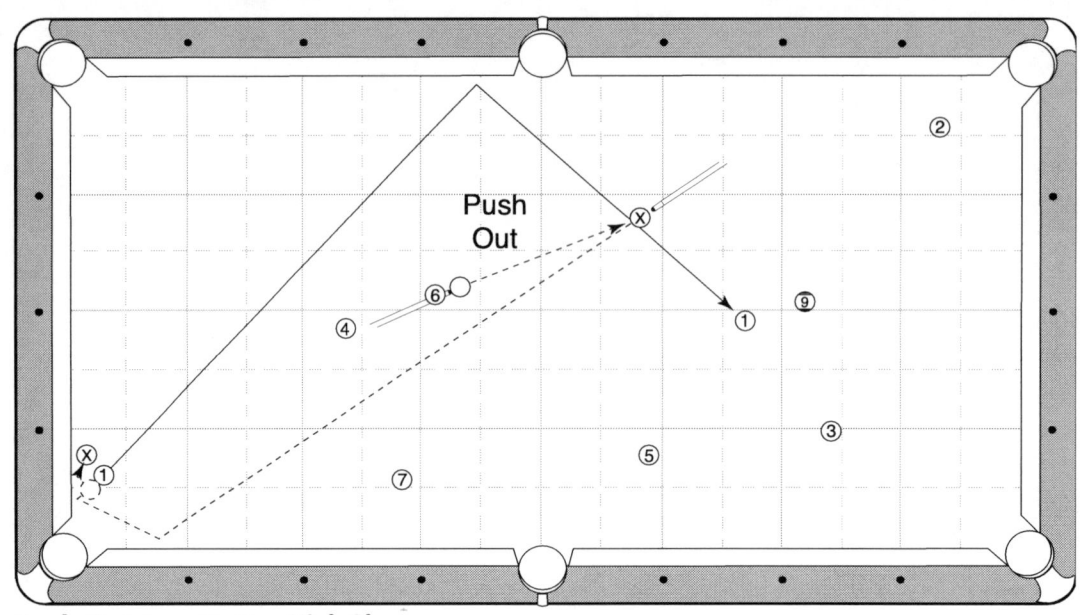

Push Out to a Better Kick Shot

Johnny Archer played this push and kick sequence against Jeremy Jones in the finals of the 1999 U.S. Open. He pushed out to an easier kick, but not so easy that Jones would choose to play it. What made Archer's shot possible was 1) seeing it, 2) rolling the cue ball 18 inches to the perfect spot, 3) executing the kick shot to near perfection. Jones was left with no shot on the 1-ball.

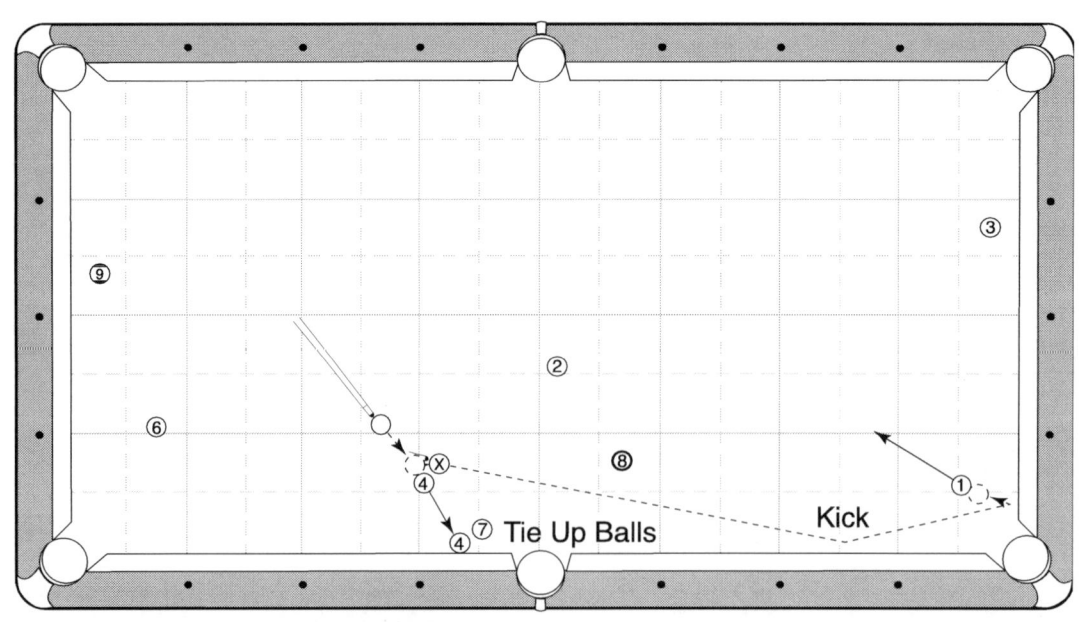

Combining Elements of a Push Out

Look for chances to combine elements to create a winning push out. In this position, the 1-ball is in front of the pocket, so you must push to a kick or jump shot. The kick could leave a shot, so the smart play is to tie up the 4 and 7 balls before kicking at the 1-ball.

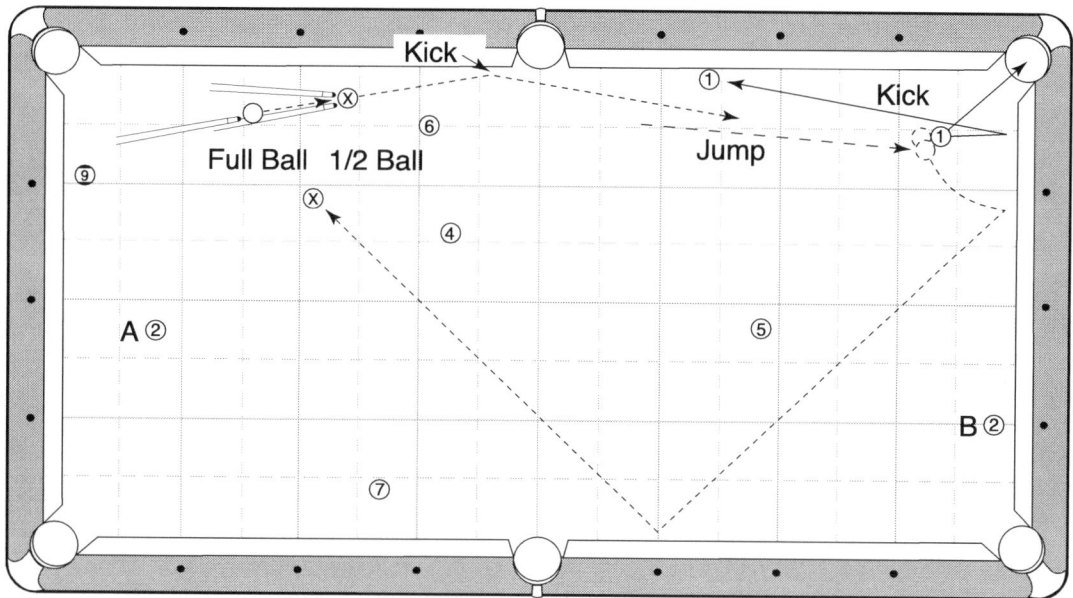

Jump or Kick?

If you are skilled at jump shots and your opponent isn't, pushing out to a jump shot can lead to a win if you shoot, and a loss (for them) if they shoot! However, if jumping isn't your strong suit, tempt them with jump shots that could result in a foul. And try to build a playable kick shot into the push out.

The cue ball is directly behind the 6-ball. In this position, even a skilled jump shooter might pass on this shot. Pushing to Position X would be a:

- Poor strategy if your opponent is a good jump shooter and the 2-ball is in Position A.
- Good strategy if your opponent is a good jump shooter, but the 2-ball is in Position B, because this makes position on the 2-ball difficult.
- Good strategy in any case if your opponent is a poor jump shooter but loves to pull out their fancy jump cue, thinks they are the jump king, and always plays them.
- Good strategy if your opponent is the conservative type who passes on these kinds of push outs, you are a good jump shooter, and the 2-ball is in Position A.
- Good strategy if your opponent dislikes jump shots, but thinks they are the second Efren Reyes and plays kick shots that offer little chance of success.
- Poor strategy if your opponent is a skilled kicker who can hit the proper side of the 1-ball if they miss, sending the 1-ball up the side rail as shown, leaving you with a tough safety.

This exercise shows that there is not always a clear-cut strategy on a push out. To make the best choice, you must carefully weigh both your and your opponent's skills.

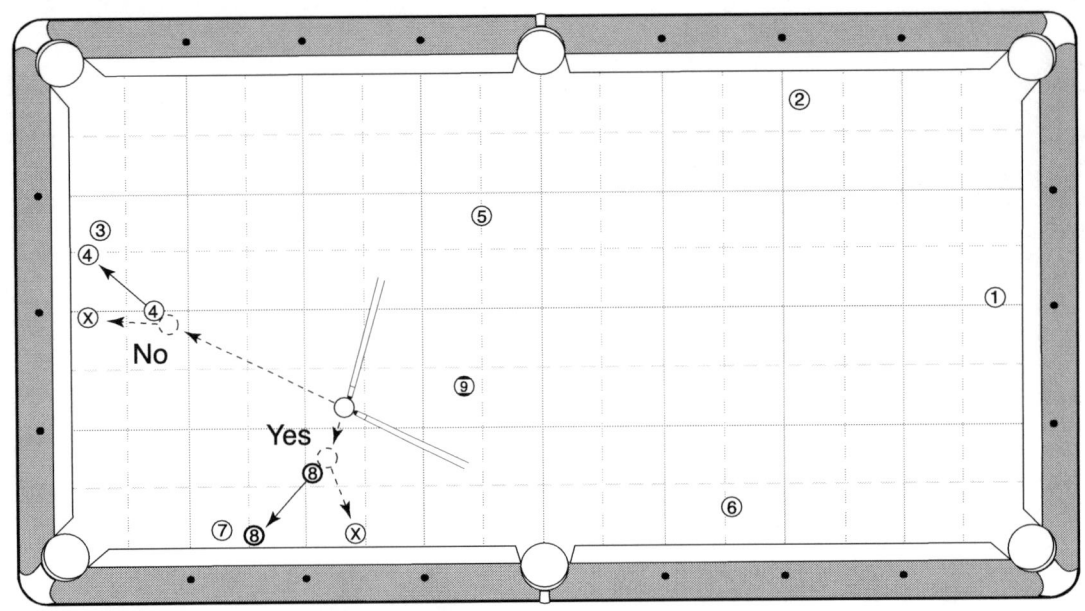

Cluster Balls Past Your Money Ball

You can employ the tie-up-the-balls strategy to great effect when you are being spotted the 7-ball or more in 9 Ball. The move is to tie up the balls past your money ball, making it more difficult for your opponent to run out while leaving the balls you must run in the clear. In the example you are getting spotted the 6-ball. When pushing out, tie up the 7 and 8 balls, not the 3 and 4 balls.

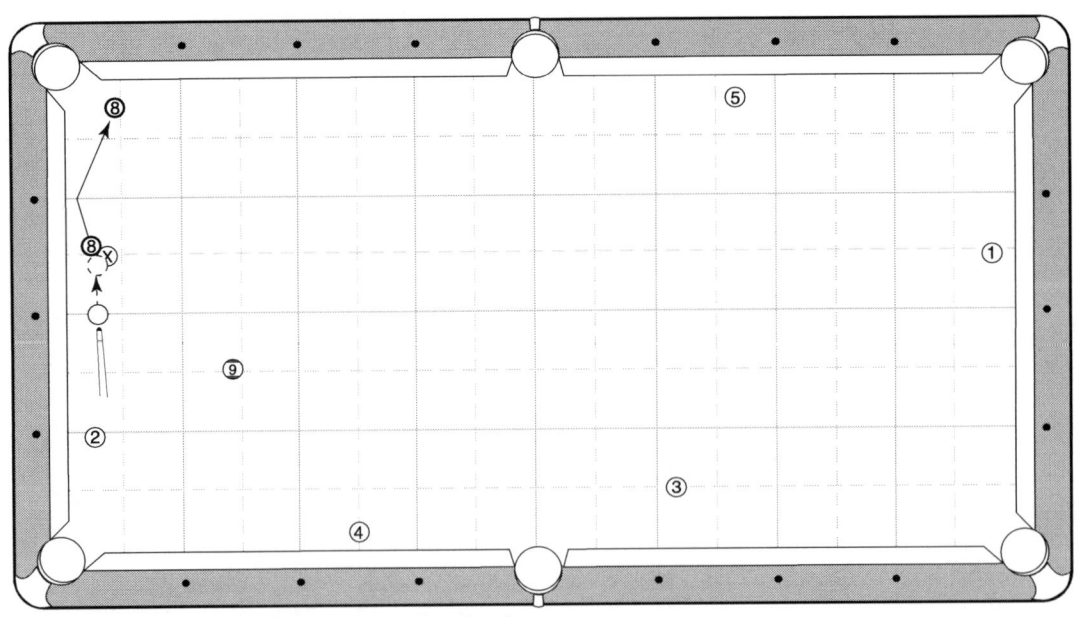

Get Your Money Ball in Front of a Pocket

When you are receiving a spot, you can force your opponent's hand when pushing out by bumping a money ball close enough to a pocket. Now they must think hard about letting you shoot. Let's assume that you are being spotted the 8-ball. Bumping it in front of the pocket sets up a winning bank combo that your opponent will hate to shoot, but that he will dislike having you shoot!

CHAPTER 9

Safety Play

"Sometimes you can kind of stutter step them (your opponent) into submission with a series of aggressive safeties."
Grady Mathews."

"Now if I'm playing good and thinking correctly I like my opponent to really have to work for even the semblance of a good shot."
Grady Mathews

A golfer with a 270 yard carry over water is better off laying up short than trying for the putting surface. The golfer is playing the percentages while trying to avoid a disaster. Pool players facing similarly long odds will, strangely enough, try heroic shots that have close to zero odds of success.

Pool players are a little more foolhardy, perhaps, than other sportsmen because the penalty for failure does not seem as great, nor is it as obvious. After all, when you miss, you get to sit down and sip on your favorite beverage. If, however, your goal is to win, you must avoid taking unrealistic chances, especially when a solid safety is readily available.

You must give up the table and play safe, even though this may go against the grain. Those of you who dislike playing defense must understand that if you develop a strong safety game you will get the table back quickly enough. So, when you are faced with a choice between a safe and a shot, coldly calculate the odds. If the situation clearly suggests that a safety is the better choice, quell your urge to fire away and instead send the cue ball snugly behind a well-positioned blocker.

Mindset for Safety Play

If you are gravitating to 9 Ball from the world of 8 Ball, you may be accustomed to playing with people who look down on safety play. To be successful at 9 Ball, you will need to adopt a new mindset towards defense. If you opponents cry that you are playing dirty pool, take that as a compliment that your safety skills are improving. Besides, in today's world, knowledgeable opponents will say nothing, or even "good shot" when you lock them up tight because they know it's all part of the game. And they'll certainly return the favor when the opportunity presents itself.

In 9 Ball, safeties are used by players of all levels, so you might as well join them in making full use of these defensive maneuvers. And once you've adopted a mindset for safety play, you will begin to see that your defensive skills give you a chance to ignite your offense. **In most situations where there is a choice between a safety and a hard shot, the skill required to play the safety is far less demanding** – and yet a well-played safety can go just as far, if not farther, towards helping you win a game as the most heroic of super shots.

Good safety play will help you win the battle for the table, and an airtight safety game can frustrate and demoralize your opponent. For many of you, the ability to consistently recognize and execute a few basic safeties can improve your game by perhaps 10-20 percent, almost overnight.

Safety battles are like tennis rallies or pitcher/batter duels. They can be decided on one shot, or they may last several turns. You should look forward to safety battles, especially if you are the superior defensive player.

Defensive Goals
When playing offense, the object is to make the ball and play good shape, ball after ball. On defense, however, the many possible objectives are determined by the position of the balls and your level of skill. Possible goals include:
- Hiding the cue ball behind a blocker.
- Leaving a long and difficult shot or safety.
- Separating a cluster while hooking your opponent.
- Setting up a combo on the game ball.

You will see these objectives and others come to life over and over again as we proceed through this chapter. These safeties will appear in your games and, when they do, you will know what objectives you should be looking to accomplish.

Rating the Quality of Your Safeties
The best safeties will give your opponent little or no chance to hit the next ball, which of course means that you will likely be returning to the table with ball in hand! The worst safeties provide your opponent with an easy shot or chance to hook you in a way that you wished you had hooked him in the first place. **The results of your safeties largely speak for themselves.**

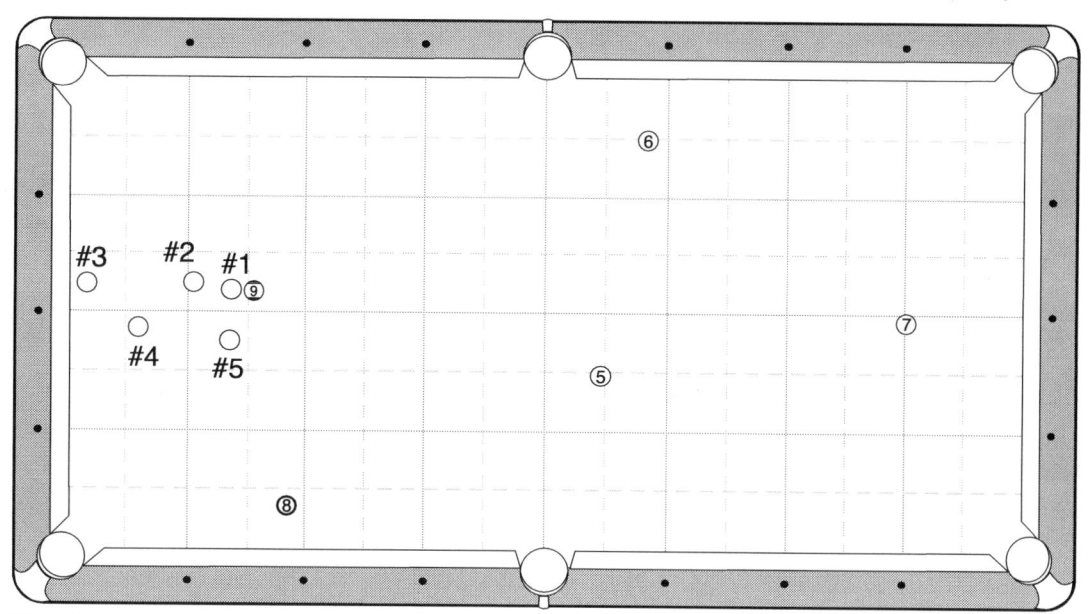

The Spectrum of Safeties

The illustration shows five cue ball locations that resulted from an attempt to play safe on the 1-ball. They are graded on the Spectrum of Safeties below.

1 **Excellent** - You will almost certainly get ball in hand on your next turn.
2 **Good** - Your opponent is hooked, but he has a fair chance of hitting the ball. Still, the odds are good that he will leave you a shot or an easy safety.
3 **Average** - Your opponent may be hooked but he has a reasonably good chance to hit the ball and quite possibly return the favor. He may also have a clear shot at the ball which gives him a fair chance at making a tough shot or hooking you with a well-played safety. The outcome of the game is 50/50 with a so-so safety.
4 **Poor** - Your opponent is the favorite to win the game thanks to a below average safety.
5 **Awful** - The lowest quality safeties turn your opponent into the heavy favorite to win the game. A poor safety has about the same effect as missing a shot that leaves an easy run out.

The Spectrum of Safeties gives you a method for evaluating the quality of your safeties. If most of your safeties rate a level 1 or 2, you are playing solid defense. Accu-Stats considers safeties rated at levels 3-5 as mistakes when computing their performance average. If an appraisal of your safety play shows that most result in a level 3 or worse, you have discovered an area that can provide you with substantial improvement. Here are some steps for improving your safety play:
- Raising your ability to execute the safeties you choose to play.
- Learning to recognize additional opportunities to play safe.
- Exercising your imagination when a defensive maneuver is not obvious at first glance.

Skills for Excelling at Safety Play
Mastering the Basics
Cue ball control is the foundation for good safety play, just as it is when playing position on offense. You must be able to send the cue ball along the correct path at the required speed so that it will arrive in the safety zone. On the following pages we'll discuss the many skills that can enable you to control the cue ball, and that can provide the foundation for a solid safety game.

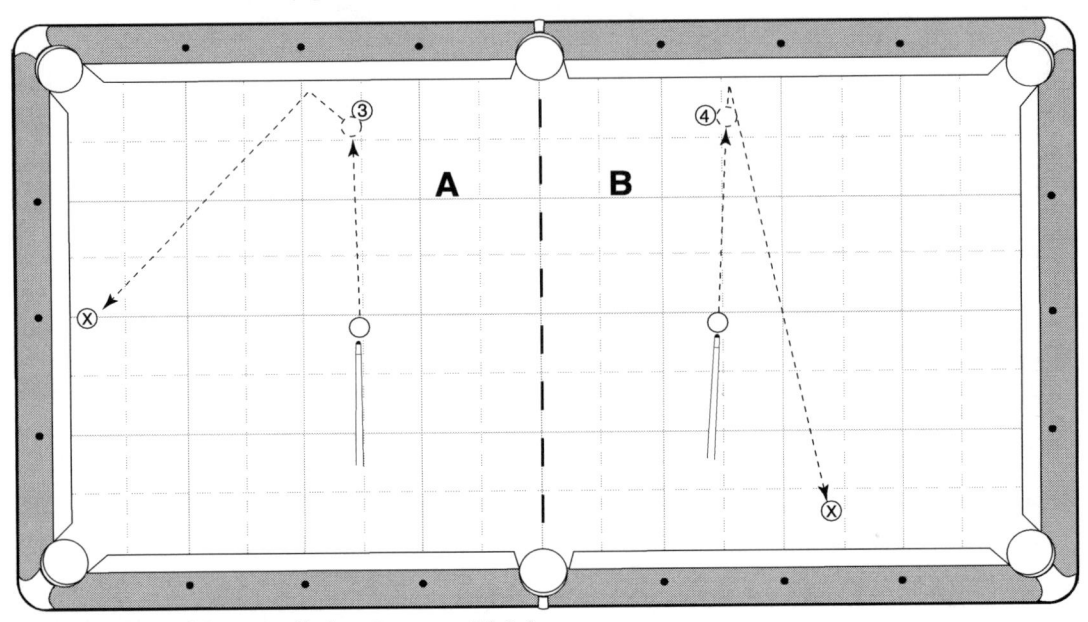

Hitting the Object Ball the Correct Thickness
Hitting the correct amount of the object ball enables you to control the cue ball's direction and rolling distance. Part A shows the cue ball's path after a half ball hit on the 3-ball. In Part B, a thin hit on the 4-ball led to a far more direct path across the table as shown. Sometimes it helps if you look at the object ball as a pie that can be cut into several sized pieces. The recommended sizes come in these increments: full, 3/4, 2/3, 1/2, 1/3, 1/4, 1/8, and 1/16 (for those with great vision). Once you master the cue ball's path after it contacts various amounts of the object ball, you will be able to access a variety of safety zones with the skill of a first rate pool surgeon!

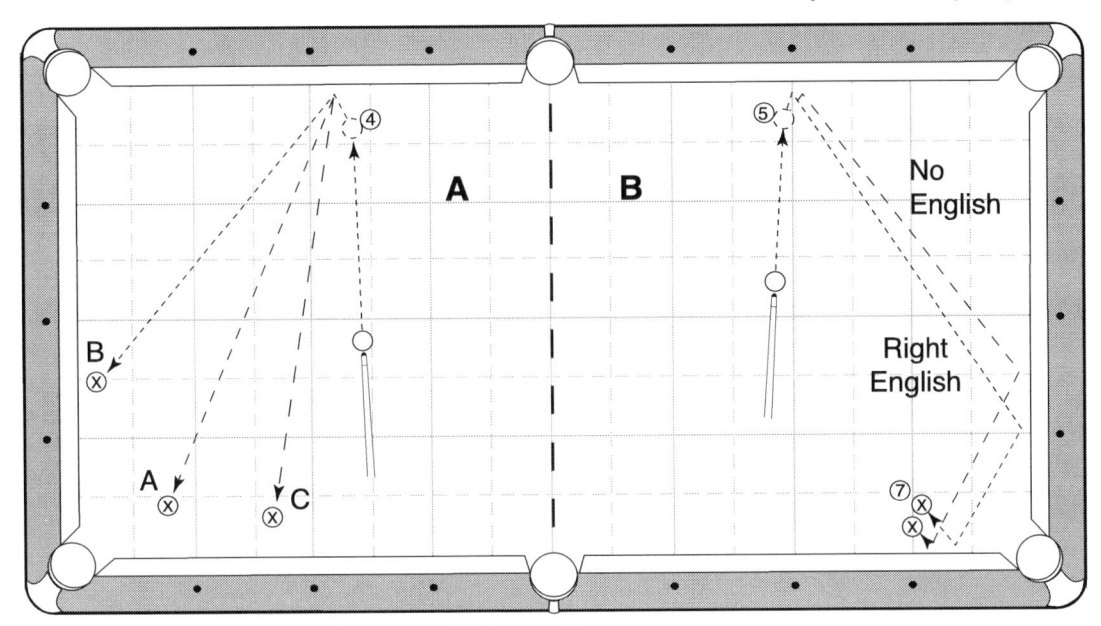

Controlling the Cue Ball's Path off the Rails
English enables you to pinpoint the cue ball's ending location after it has contacted one or more rails. In Part A, Route A shows the cue ball's path after a thin hit on the 4-ball using a tip of follow and no english. When you apply outside english (left) and a tip of follow, the cue ball will rebound at a wider angle as shown by Route B. Outside english is commonly used on off-the-rail safeties to better control the cue ball's direction and rolling distance. This kind of shot requires a fine touch – if you use too much english, the cue ball could overrun the safety zone.

Inside english (right) with a tip of follow is demonstrated by Route C. Notice how the cue ball's path is narrower than when no english was used. Inside english slows down the cue ball on certain safeties like this, so you must guard against hitting this type of shot too softly.

Part B shows a familiar three rail safety. Most players find it easier to control the speed and distance by hitting the object ball (the 5) thinner with a half tip of right english and follow. The alternative is to hit the 5-ball a bit fuller with a slightly firmer stroke and a tip of follow. Now the cue ball will travel down a slightly different path before once again arriving behind the 7-ball.

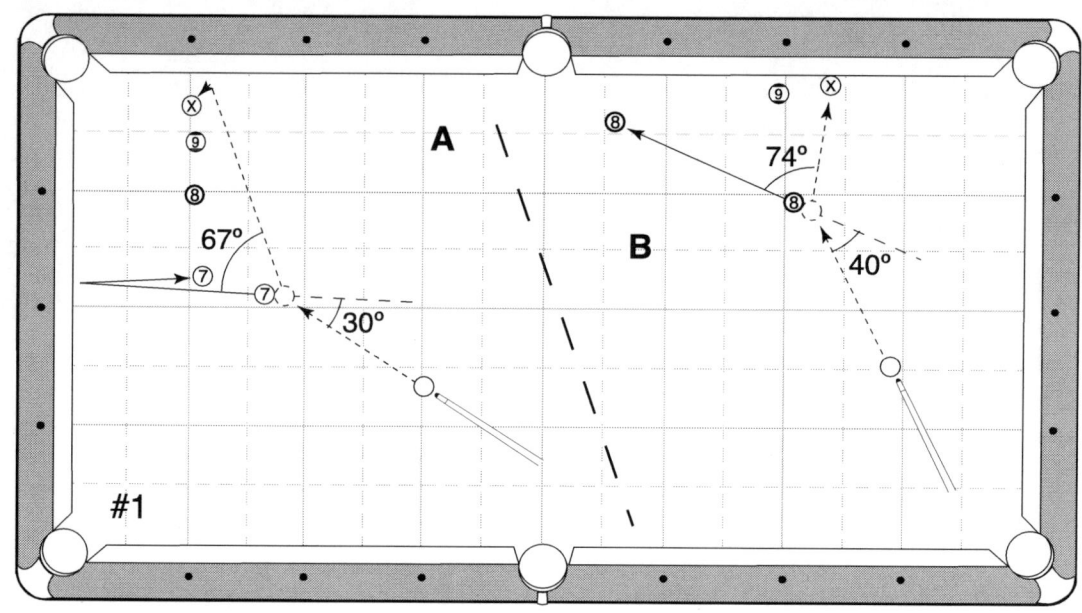

The Angle of Departure

The most accurate method for controlling the cue ball's direction on safeties is by using the angle of departure. **On cut shots hit with a very soft follow stroke, the cue ball leaves the tangent line a fraction of an inch after contact and then follows a path that corresponds to the cut angle.** In Part A of Diagram #1, the 7-ball is a 30-degree cut, which leads to a 67-degree angle of departure. The cue ball will follow the path exactly as shown and snuggle up behind the 9-ball. Part B shows a 40-degree cut on the 8-ball, which corresponds to a 74-degree angle of departure. On this safety, a fine touch is required to keep the cue ball from bouncing too far off the rail.

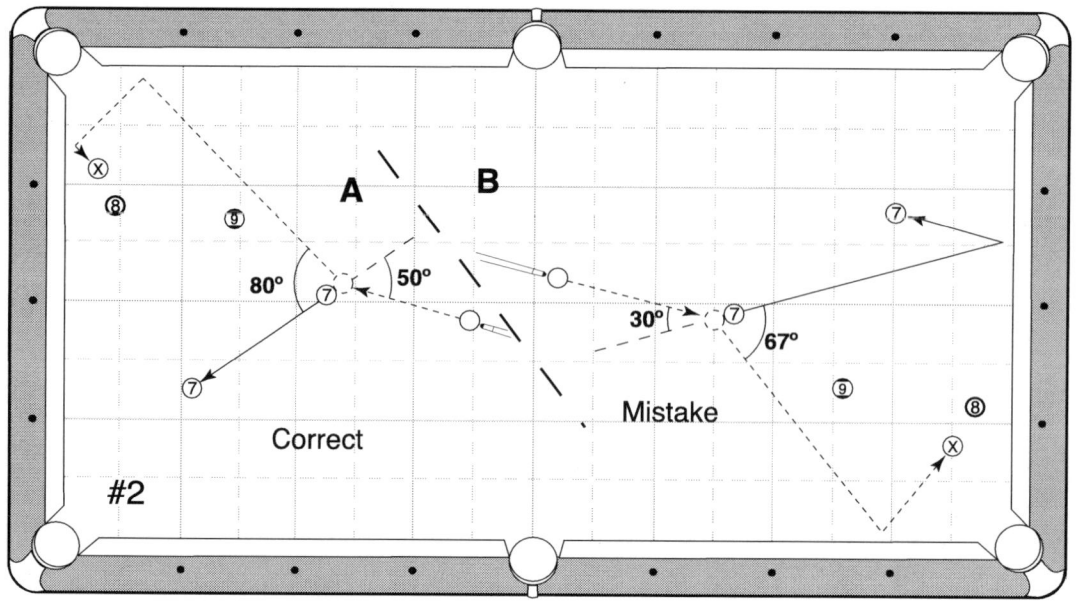

You can adjust the cut angle on the object ball when using the angle of departure to match the desired path for the cue ball.

In Part A of Diagram #2, the 50 degree cut angle led to the cue ball's two-rail path to behind the 8-ball. Part B shows a too full hit on the 7-ball (a 30-degree cut). This resulted in an overly shallow angle of departure, and the safety failed to result in a hook behind the 8-ball.

Angles of Departure (degrees)

Cut angle	Angle of departure	Cut angle	Angle of departure
10	33	30	67
15	25	40	74
20	33	50	80

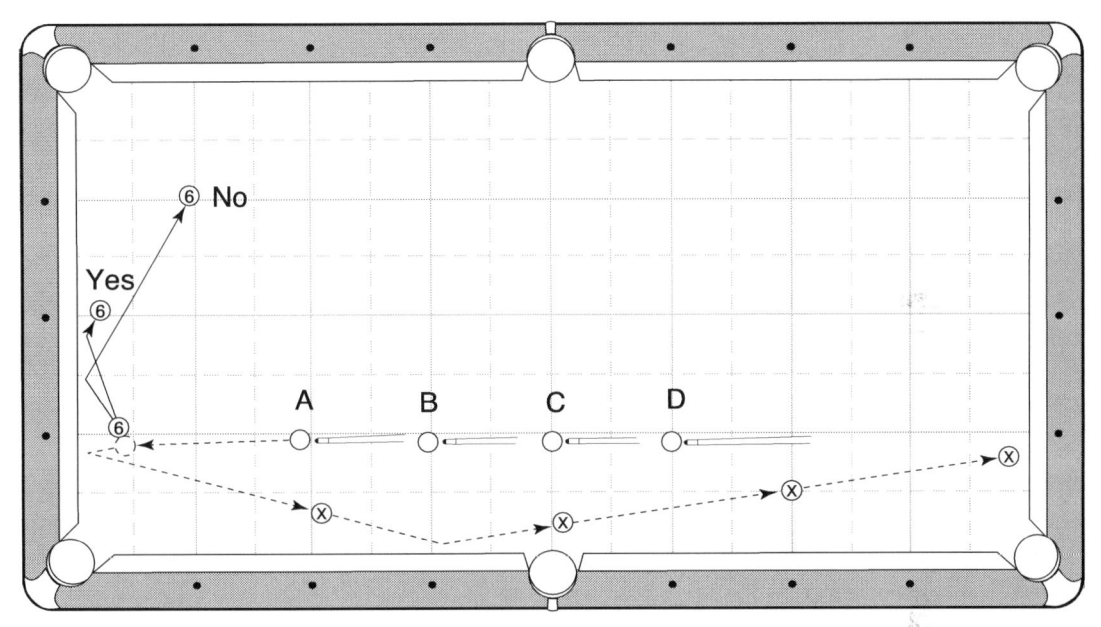

The Thin Hit

The ability to hit the object ball thinly is a valuable skill in 9 Ball. Thin hits can enable you to play tight safeties, and they can bail you out of a jam when there is a long distance between the cue ball and object ball. Two common mistakes when playing these safeties are: 1) hitting the ball too fully because you fear that you might miss it, and 2) trying to hit the ball so thin that you miss it entirely.

You can cure these maladies and master thin hits by practicing the safeties shown below. Start with the cue ball in Position A and work your way back to Position D, or beyond. (Lefthanders should practice this on the other side of the table.)

Shoot at different speeds so that the cue ball lands in the four positions as shown. Observe the object ball's position once it's stopped. Your goal is to hit it as thinly as possible to keep it near the end rail. A too full hit on the object ball will result in the error labeled **No**. The two main purposes of this drill are: 1) to improve your skill at thin hits, and 2) to understand the practical limits of this shot, taking into consideration your level of skill.

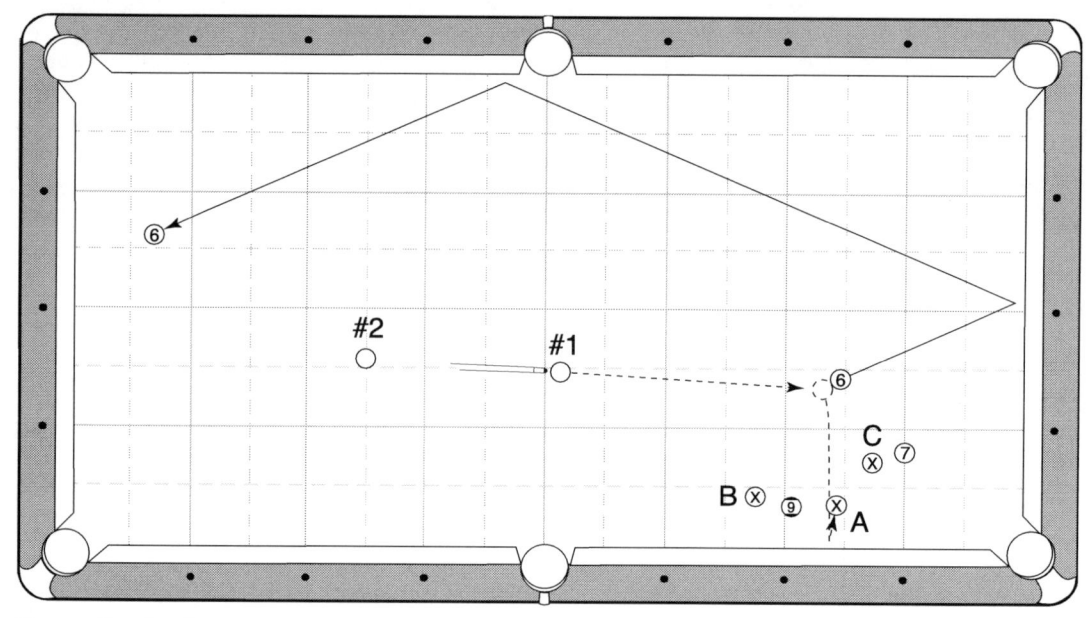

Draw Control

Sending the cue ball a long distance to the object ball with draw when playing safe takes expert technique so, on most draw shot safeties, you will do better by using a relatively soft draw stroke to send the cue ball a short distance to behind a blocker. Most draw safeties require a nearly full hit on the object ball. The cue ball will drift sideways behind a blocker, as shown in Position #1. When this safety is played correctly, the cue ball will nestle in behind the 9-ball in Position A. If the 6-ball is hit too fully, the cue ball will end up in Position B, leaving a direct hit or shot at the 6-ball. If the 6-ball is hit too thinly, the cue ball will end up in Position C, again resulting in a direct shot at the object ball.

The cue ball in Position #2 is considerably further from the object ball. To play this safety, use a drag draw shot. This requires a very low hit on the cue ball with a medium hard stroke. Don't become discouraged if you have trouble at first with the drag draw shot. This is an advanced safety that takes time to master.

Safety Skills Inventory

You will need to acquire a broad range of skills for a complete safety game. So make a copy of the skill list below and then rate yourself from not much skill (a 1) to pro (a 10). The safeties you rated 1-3 require your immediate attention. Those in the 4-6 range need work as time is available, but many could be good enough for you to play in a game. The safeties that you rated 7-10 can win you games right now.

Take your list to the poolroom to practice the areas where you are weak, and to maintain your skills in the ones that you have mastered. **The plan is to systematically build your skills on all types of safeties**.

__Hit the object ball the correct thickness.
__Control the cue ball's path off the rails without english.
__Control the cue ball's path off the rails using english.
__The angle of departure.
__The thin hit.
__Draw control.
__Drag draw shots.
__A soft touch.
__A very soft touch.
__Stop the cue ball dead in its tracks.
__Float the cue ball a short distance with a firm stroke.
__Control the object ball's path when required.
__Send the cue ball through traffic to the chosen destination.
__Kick shot safeties.
__Others that you encounter (the possibilities are endless)!

Knowing When to Play Safe

One of the main skills in safety play is to know when you should even play one! Sometimes a safety is obviously the best play. At other times you must weigh the odds of going for a run versus turning the table over to your opponent.

Consider playing safe when:
- You have no shot.
- You have a very difficult shot.
- You have a makeable shot, but can't get position.
- You can improve a layout by separating a cluster, or by sending a ball to a more advantageous location.
- You can set up an easy combo on the game ball.
- A safety is readily available.

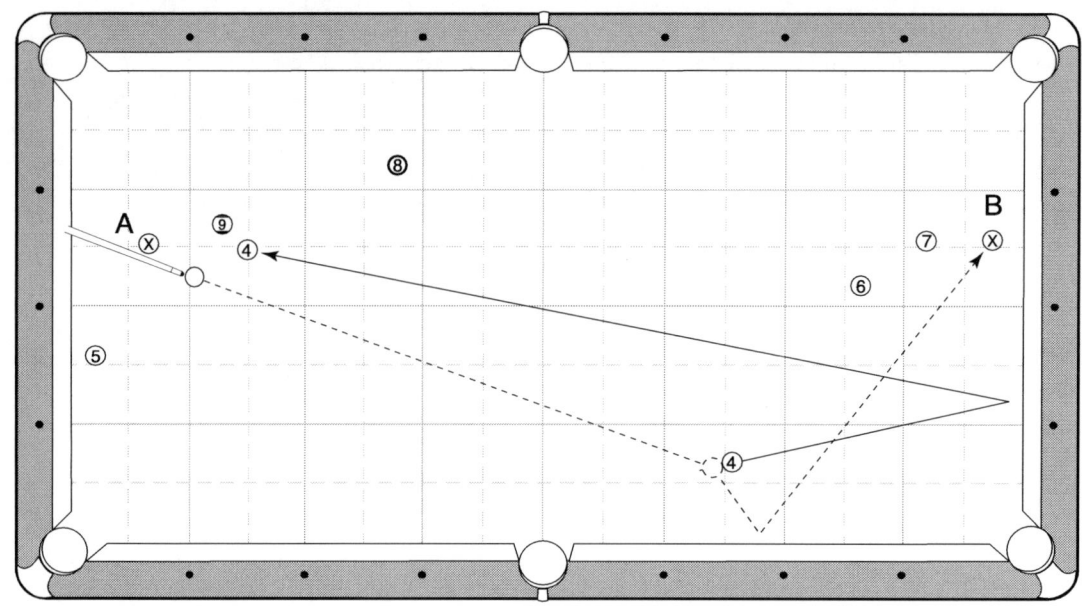

Safety Over a Shot
You could attempt to pocket that difficult shot on the 4-ball and draw back to Position A for the 5-ball. On the 1-10 scale, this shot is at least an 8. If you miss, a loss is very likely. The percentage play is to bank the 4-ball to the opposite end of the table while sending the cue ball to Position B behind the 6 and 7 balls.

You will have many opportunities to play safeties like this that enable you to avoid difficult shots that, even if pocketed, will likely lead nowhere. Many players are so offensive minded that they fail to capitalize on chances to lock up their opponent.

Selecting the Best Safety
The ideal safeties are easy to execute, and they leave your opponent a tough, if not impossible, kick shot. The worst safeties are tough to execute and have a good chance of resulting in a sellout. Most safeties fall in between these extremes, so you will need to weigh the risks and rewards of each option like you do when choosing between several position routes.

The 7-8 combo is a difficult shot, so a safety the logical choice. Part A shows a safety that is easy to execute. A 2/3 full hit on the 7-ball results in a hook, as shown. Your opponent should not have much trouble hitting the 7-ball by kicking off the end rail. And, if they make a good shot or get lucky, the 7-ball could go to the opposite end rail, leaving you with a tough shot or safety. This safety is easy to execute, but the reward is not great, and the outcome could still be in doubt.

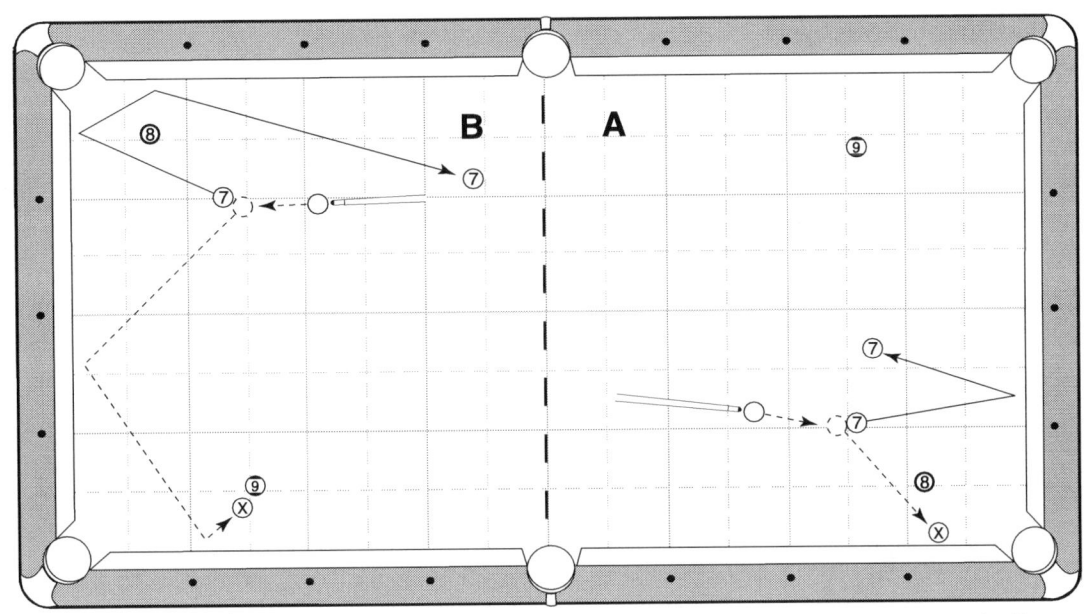

The balls are in the same relative positions in Part B. This time the cue ball was sent two rails over behind the 9-ball. Now your opponent is faced with a much tougher kick on the 7-ball. Even if they do manage to hit the 7-ball by kicking off the end or side rails, a sellout is very likely. The safety in Part B was more difficult than the one in Part A, but it also had a much higher reward.

Which Safety is the Better Choice?
Below are some of the factors that could influence your decision:
- **Your skill at playing safe**. Can you execute the safety in Part B most of the time? If so, go for it.
- **Your opponent's skill at kicking**. If your opponent kicks poorly, then the safe in Part A may be better. But if they are highly skilled at kicking, then you need to make things tough on them by playing the safe in Part B, even if you are not totally sure that it will result in a hook.
- **The score of the match**. If both of you need one game, you may pick the easier safe, for example, rather than risk the match on the high risk/high reward safe in Part B.

When considering a safety in competition, the key questions are:
- Do you really know the safe?
- Can you execute it a high percentage of the time?
- Are you confident that you can execute it under pressure?
- What is your opponent's expected response?
- Is the safety the high percentage choice, all things considered?

TIP: Don't delay the inevitable hook. Know when to take a chance.

Basic Hook Safeties

The fundamental goal of safety play is to leave an obstacle between the cue ball and the lowest numbered ball. Once you are sure that a safety you are considering can meet this basic goal, then it is time to consider additional objectives that can make your opponent's job of avoiding a foul even tougher.

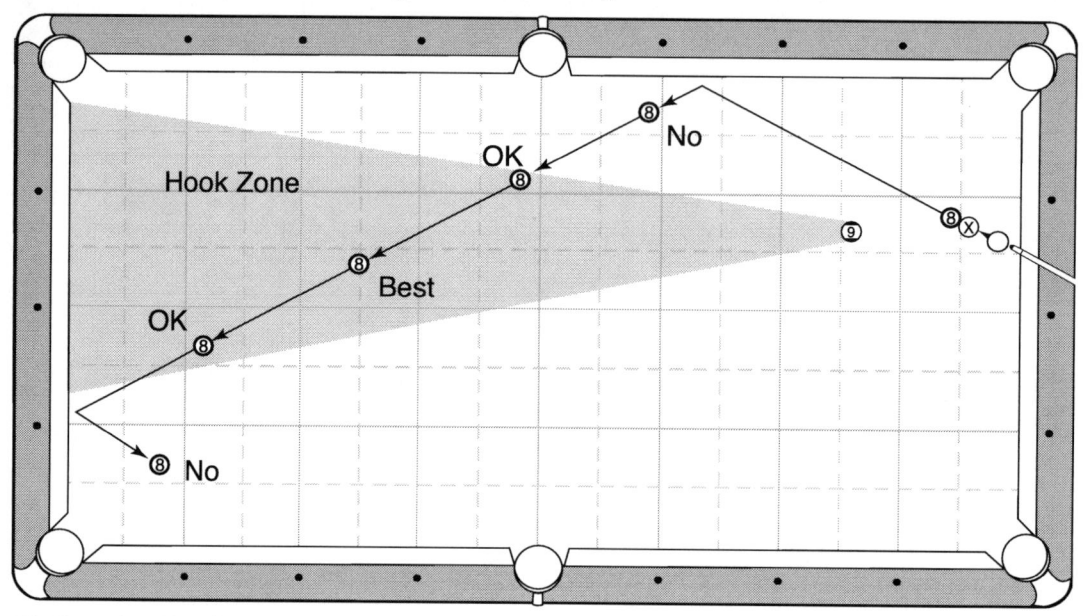

Hitting the Hook Zone

Missing the shape zone for the 8-ball could result in this end game position. There is no reasonable shot at the 8-ball, so it's time to play safe. A stop shot at the correct speed will leave the 8-ball and the cue ball on opposite sides of the 9- ball.

A hook zone is the area where the object ball is shielded from direct contact by the cue ball. The 8-ball is shown in three locations within the hook zone. If the object ball rests in the hook zone, then your opponent will have to play a jump, kick, or curve shot to make contact.

A key feature of stop shot safeties is that you know exactly where the cue ball will soon be residing. When you can predict the cue ball's resting spot with complete accuracy, you can also determine the precise location and size of the hook zone.

Sending the 8-ball into the hook zone should not be too difficult because the portion that it will be crossing is over three feet long. Try to send the 8-ball into the middle of the zone because this will give you about a 20 inch margin for error on either side of the bulls-eye. If the 8-ball is hit with too little force, it will stop short of the zone, and if it is hit too hard, it will leak out of the opposite end of the hook zone.

This safety is the high percentage play. Among amateurs, this safe will win most games, especially if your opponent is not skilled at kick, curve, or jump shots. Advanced players and professionals dislike leaving the outcome in doubt, even when the odds are in their favor. In this position, an A Player may choose to cut the 8-ball slightly left of center with a stun-follow stroke to make the cue ball float up against the 9-ball. If successful, he would eliminate the jump shot. This safety would also force his opponent to kick two rails for the 8-ball, which is way more difficult than a one-rail kick. The floater safety should be mastered in practice before you use it in serious competition. Remember, **a well-executed safety of "average" difficulty is normally much better than a "hero" safety that backfires**.

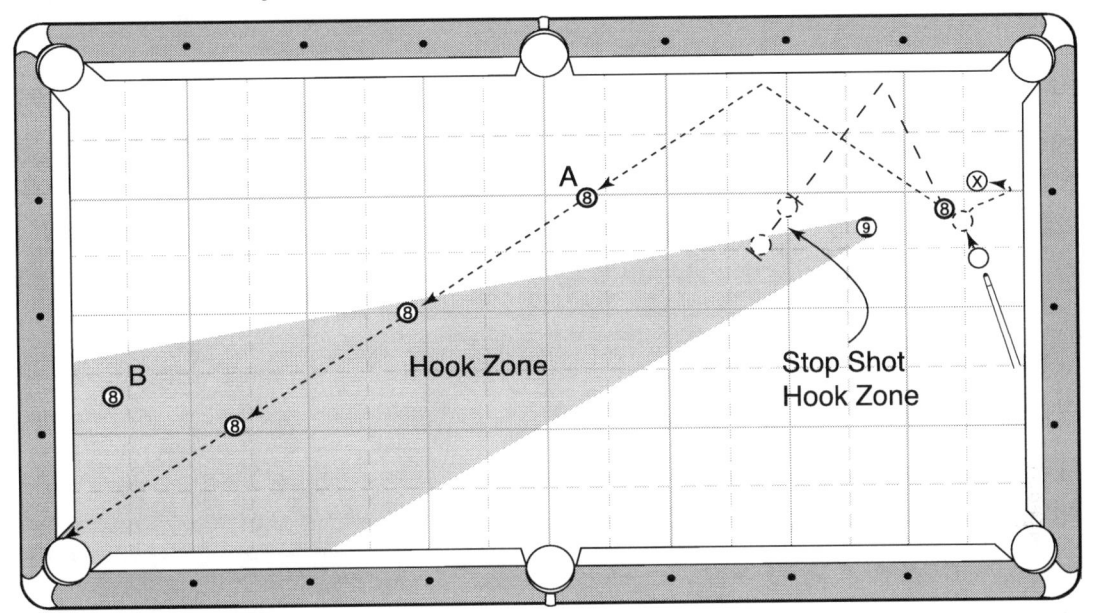

Hitting the Hook Zone (2)

The 8 and 9 balls are in the same locations as in the previous example, but the cue ball is 2 1/4 inches towards the bottom side rail, and is further from the cushion. This small difference in the cue ball's position makes a huge difference in how this safe is played. A stop shot is no longer feasible because the hook zone along the path that the 8-ball will be traveling is only five inches long as shown. A player would need a superhuman touch to consistently hit this tiny target.

The better choice is to cut the 8-ball on the right side with draw. This safety produces a much wider hook zone, similar to the one in the previous illustration. The challenge is in calculating how much of the 8-ball to hit, and choosing the speed of stroke. If the 8-ball is hit too easily, it will stop short of the hook zone near Position A, leaving a shot. When cutting the object ball with draw, the hook zone cannot be so easily forecast like it can with a stop shot. So, do not attempt to send the 8-ball too far down the hook zone (to Position B, for example) because the thinner hit on the 8-ball makes it more difficult to control the cue ball.

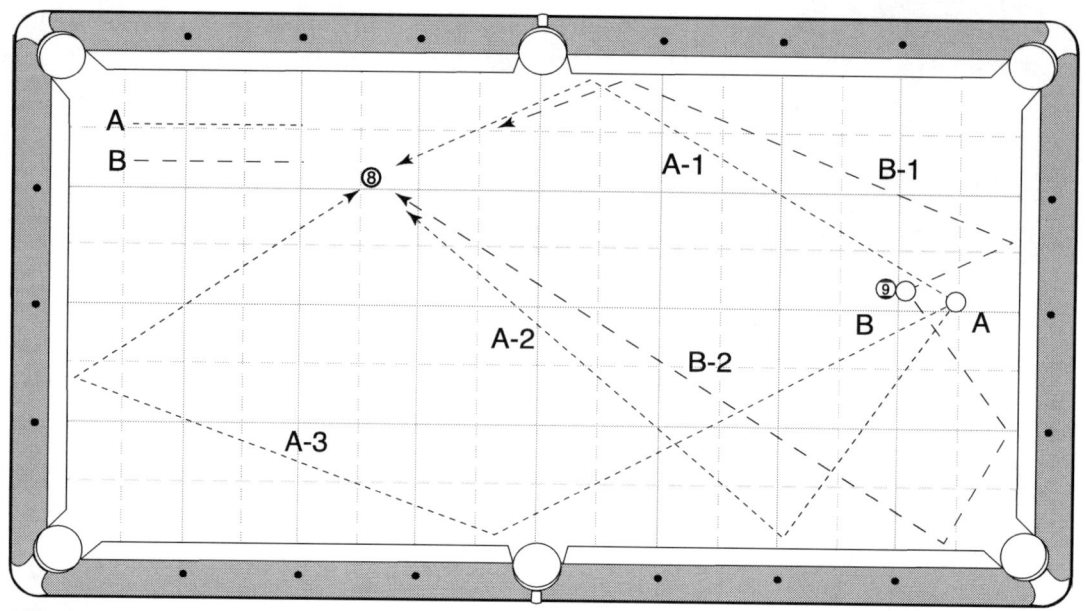

Eliminating Options

Eliminating as many of your opponent's options as possible for replying to a safety is always a solid strategy. This example dramatizes the difference between a so-so safety and a "pro" safety. When the cue ball is in Position A, which is five inches from the blocker (the 9), your opponent can hit the 8-ball more often than not by sending the cue ball down Route A-1. If this safety had appeared earlier in the game and Route A-1 was not available (because of a blocker), your opponent would have to kick down Route A-2, which is much more difficult. Route A-3 is another possibility.

Now let's look at a pro safety. The cue ball is snuggled up against the 9-ball in Position B, so your opponent's chances of hitting the 8-ball have been drastically reduced. Options A-1, A-2, and A-3 have all been eliminated! Now he must choose between a two-rail kick off the short rail down Route B-1, and a two-rail kick along Route B-2. In both cases the player will have to elevate, which sends the degree of difficulty through the roof. I would rate an average player's chances of hitting the 8-ball from Position A at about 70-80 percent. With whitey in Position B the odds are no more than 20 percent. The lesson: **a few inches can make a huge difference in the quality of your safeties. When you leave the cue ball close to the blocker, your odds go way up.**

Block the Natural Kick Route

You can make life difficult for your opponent by cutting off the natural kick route because this forces him to play a much lower percentage route to avoid the obstructer. The 8-ball is on the natural one-rail kick route to the 7-ball. If he chooses Route A, he will have to open the rebound angle by over 20 degrees with a liberal dose of outside (left) english. It is difficult to regulate large amounts of english, which reduces his chances of hitting the 7-ball.

Your opponent's other choice is to send the cue ball on the opposite side of the 8-ball down Route B. Reverse (right) english or a hard stroke is needed to hit the 7-ball. Most players have far more trouble hitting the object ball when they have to reduce

Chapter 9 - Safety Play   255

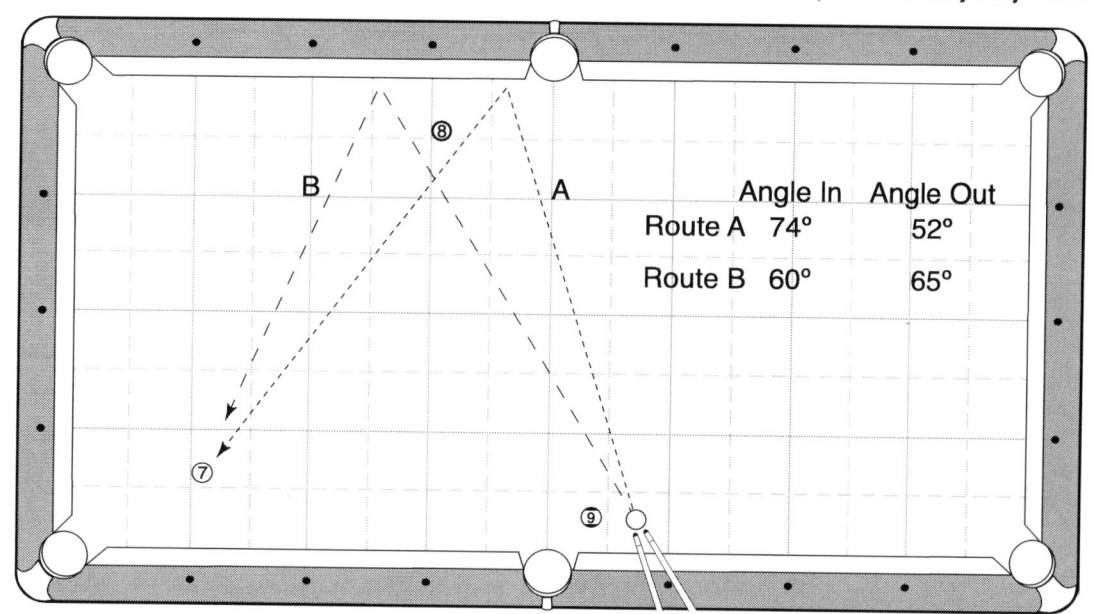

	Angle In	Angle Out
Route A	74°	52°
Route B	60°	65°

the rebound angle. **When playing safe, it is usually better to eliminate the route that enables your opponent to use outside english.**

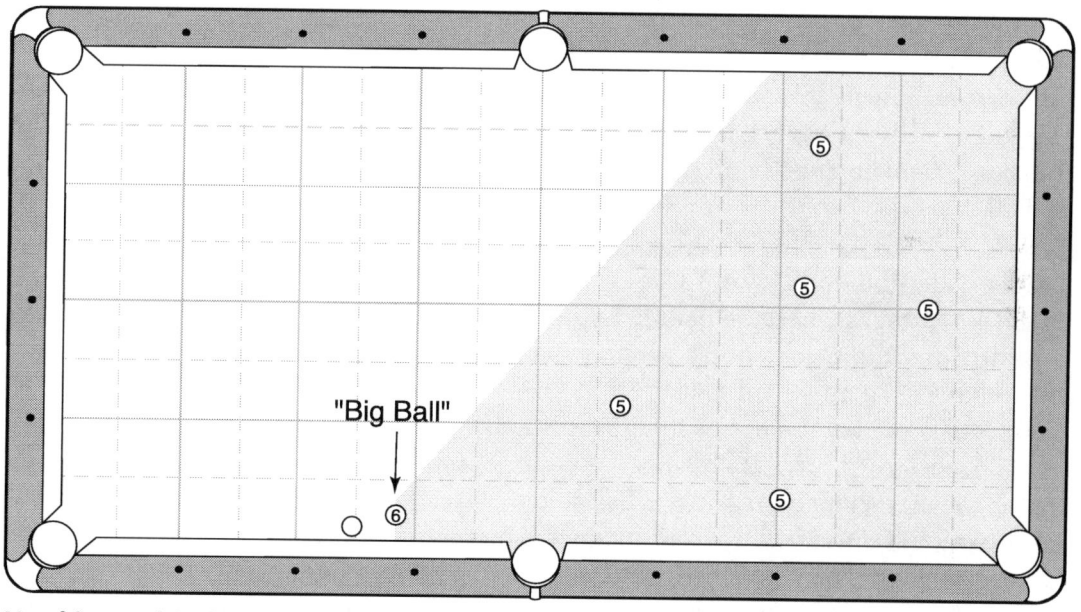

"Big Ball"

Hooking Behind the "Big Ball"

When a blocker is within a ball's width of the rail, it is said to be in the "Big Ball" position. Blockers in this position are very effective at shielding the cue ball from the object ball in a large area of the table. Notice that the 5-ball is blocked no matter where it lies within the gigantic hook zone thanks to the cue ball's position behind the "big" 6-ball.

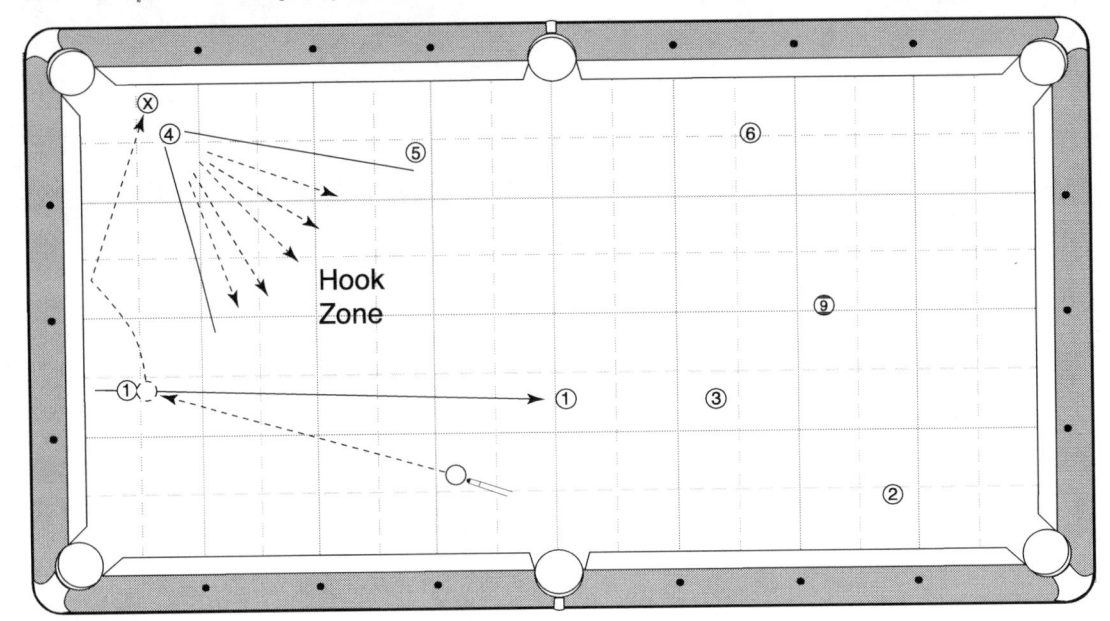

Basic Hook

A basic and yet highly effective safety is to bank a ball down the table while using follow and a soft touch to send the cue ball behind a nearby blocker. Mike Sigel, who is known as Captain Hook for his defensive skills, executed this lethal safety to perfection against Nick Varner at the 1990 U.S. Open. Sigel blocked almost the entire table from Varner's view. When playing this safety, a nearly full hit makes it easier to control the speed of the cue ball. This is especially important for players who dislike using soft stroke. The 1-ball was banked directly up the table, which made it easier to control its ending location.

Off the Side Rail and Down Table

In the early stages when the balls are spread across the table, a grouping of balls may offer an opportunity for a hook. **When you can couple a hook with distance, you have the makings of a powerful safety.** Efren Reyes took advantage of the layout in playing the safety shown at the top of the next page at the 2000 U.S. Open.

The keys to its success are speed and direction. Reyes controlled the direction by hitting the correct amount of the 1-ball, and by his skillful use of running english. **When you must send the cue ball a long distance off one or more rails, running english helps to control the speed.** The correct application of english enables you to use the speed with which you are most comfortable. To fully appreciate the strength of this safety, put yourself in Johnny Archer's position (Reyes's opponent). How would you go about hitting the 1-ball? Note: aren't the 4 and 9 balls a real pain?

TIP: The best route to the object ball after an opponent's safety could be to send the cue ball along the same route it just traveled to the hook zone. In the example, it leads almost exactly to the 1-ball's new location!

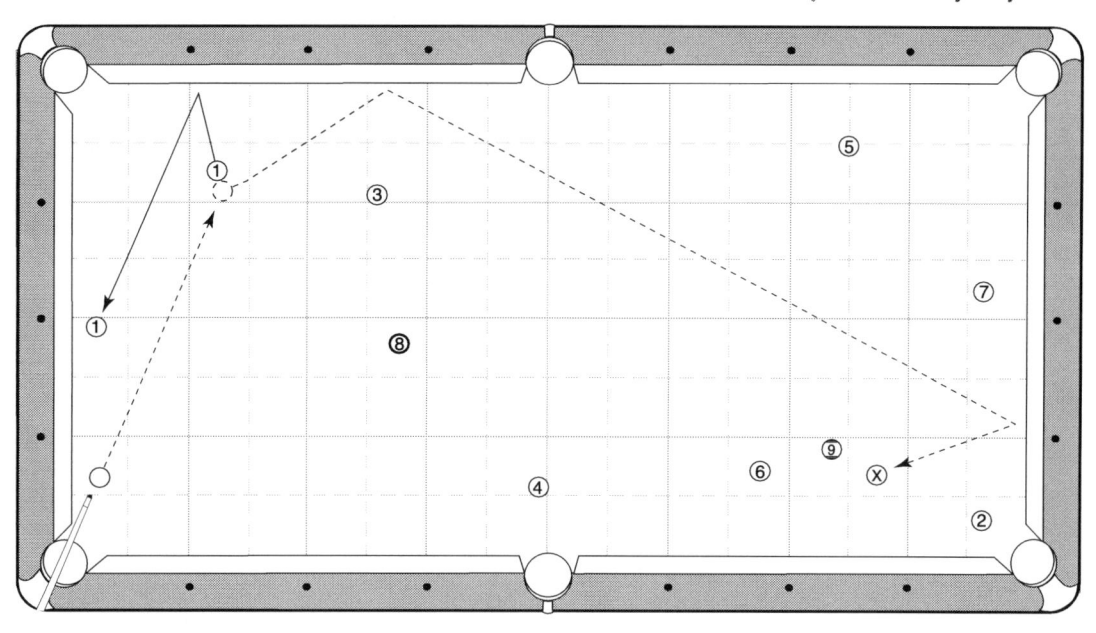

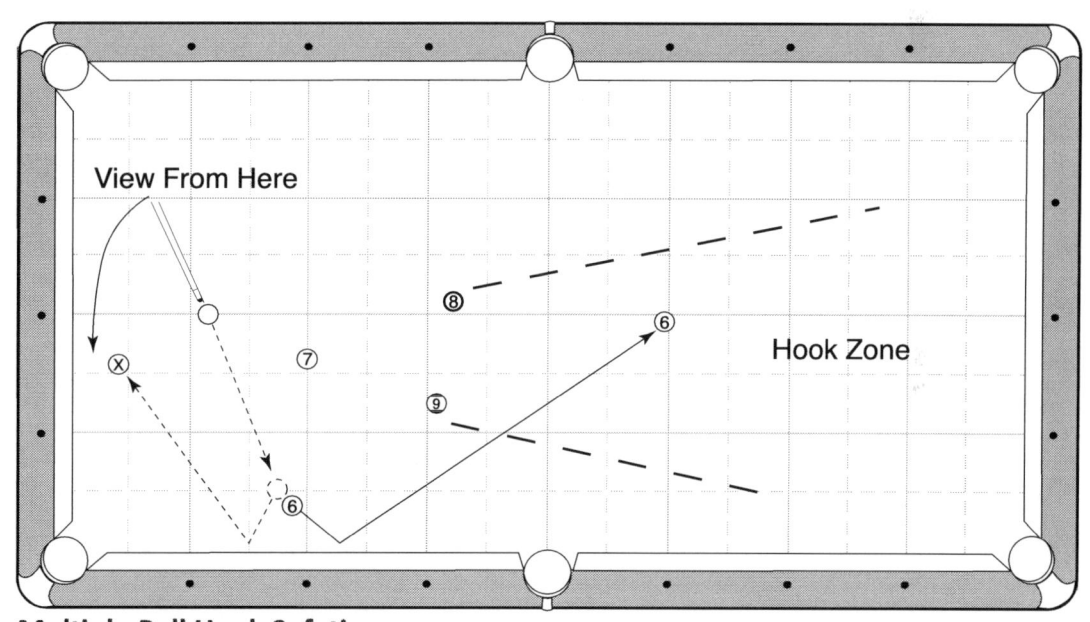

Multiple Ball Hook Safeties

A number of balls may combine to block a large portion of the table even when they are not in close proximity. This safety is not difficult to execute, and yet it is very effective thanks to the location of the potential blockers. The key is to walk over to where you think you would like to send the cue ball. Then look up table to see if there are any gaps between the balls. In this case, the 7, 8, and 9 balls provide a solid wall of protection. Notice the huge hook zone that they have formed!

Chapter 9 - Safety Play

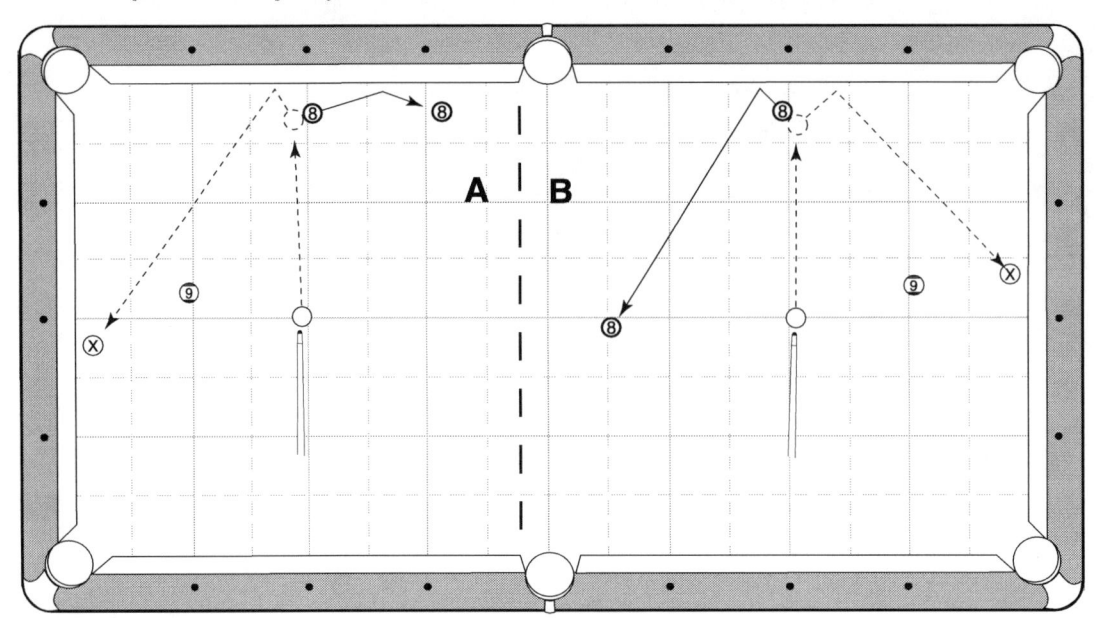

Risk Versus Reward

The risk of a safety is often commensurate with the reward. In Part A, a thin hit on the 8-ball with a little left english will result on a hook behind the 9-ball. The keys to this commonly played safety are speed control and hitting the correct amount of the object ball so that the cue ball follows the path to the end rail. The 8-ball's ending location near the side rail is very predictable, and it is generally easier to control the cue ball when you don't have to worry much about the object ball.

The balls are in the same relative positions in Part B. This time the 8-ball is hit more fully, so it travels to the middle of the table. Now your opponent is faced with a far tougher kick than in Part A. The tradeoff for leaving a tougher kick is that this safety is more difficult. The big key is in matching the speed of stroke with the fullness of the hit on the 8- ball.

In sum, when playing safe, risk often equals reward. If you are playing a poor kicker, the safety in Part A might be good enough to result in a foul. However, the safe in Part B might guarantee that you get ball-in-hand. Against a strong kicker, you might go for the sure hook in Part A because they are going to hit the ball no matter which safe you play!

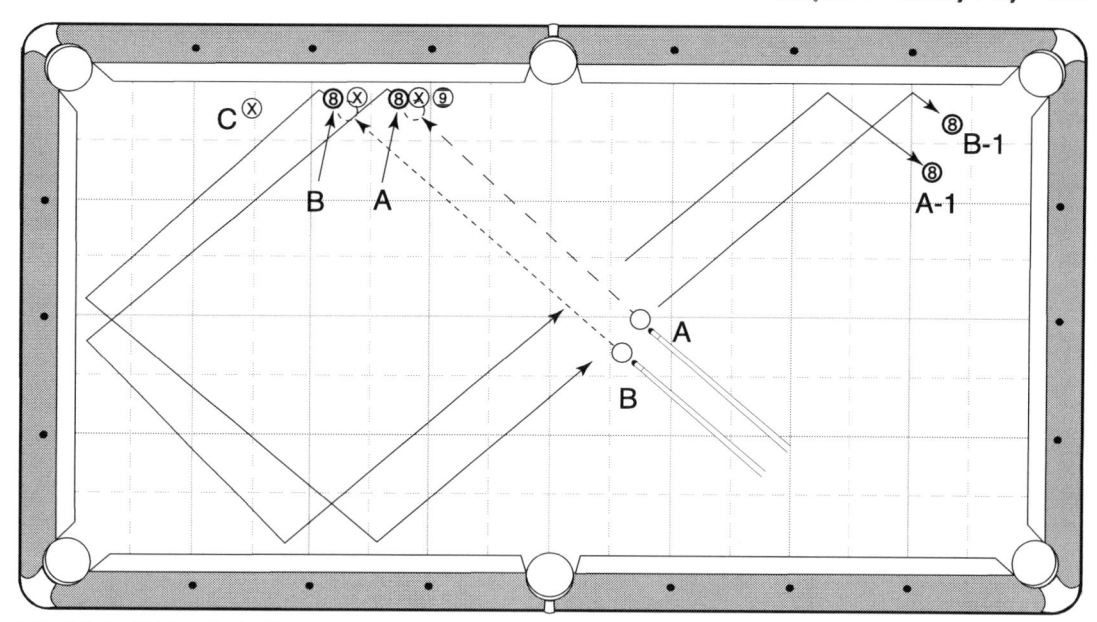

Multi Rail Hook Safeties

This is a classic safety that you will play countless times during your career. The 8-ball in Position A will not go in the upper left corner pocket because it is too close to the 9-ball. You could play a bank into the lower left corner pocket, but this shot would require a very hard stroke and/or inside (left) english. So, the odds favor a three-rail safety down Route A. Use a firm stroke and hit the cue ball a small fraction below center. You should also aim a hair to the right of straight at the 8-ball, which will cause the cue ball to drift up against the 9-ball as shown. The cue ball will travel 3 or 4 rails to somewhere close to Position A-1.

Let's assume the 8-ball is six inches further down the rail in Position B. Now you could attempt to run out by sending the cue ball across the table and back to Position C. However, this difficult position play requires near perfect speed control. A more conservative approach is to play a stop shot while banking the cue ball three-rails to Position B-1. Hit the 8-ball just a shade to the right side so the cue ball will drift closer to the cushion. This subtle move dramatically increases the size of the hook zone, and it also makes the kick much tougher. The Lesson: **Never overlook the chance to add the little extras to a safety that will make it much more effective – especially when you can do them with little or no ris**k.

All levels of players should play the safety with the 8-ball in Position A. When the 8-ball is in Position B, the correct decision depends on the situation, how you are playing, your skill, and your opponent's game. If you are a C Player, the safety is probably the best choice. A B Player may go for the run out if he is playing very well, or he might pass if he is out of stroke. An A Player may feel that his best chance of winning against a strong opponent who excels at the kicking game is to go for the run rather than leaving the game up for grabs, even if the odds are not in his favor.

Controlling the Right Ball is Key

Success depends on controlling the cue ball, the object ball, or (possibly) both. Once you have mastered a variety of cue ball routes across and around the table, you can access blockers and play killer safeties from countless positions. This takes care of the cue ball.

You may be unaware of how far a ball could roll when pocketing a shot because its roll is abruptly halted when it enters the pocket! However, **when playing certain safeties, controlling the rolling distance and direction of the object ball is the big key to the success of the shot**.

The most challenging safeties require you to control both the cue ball and the object ball. These shots confuse many players because of the need to control the ending location of two balls. You can solve this problem by planning exactly what you must do with each ball prior to assuming your stance. The final step is to decide on cuing and on speed. Once you get over the shot, your thoughts should be focused on aiming and executing the shot as well as possible.

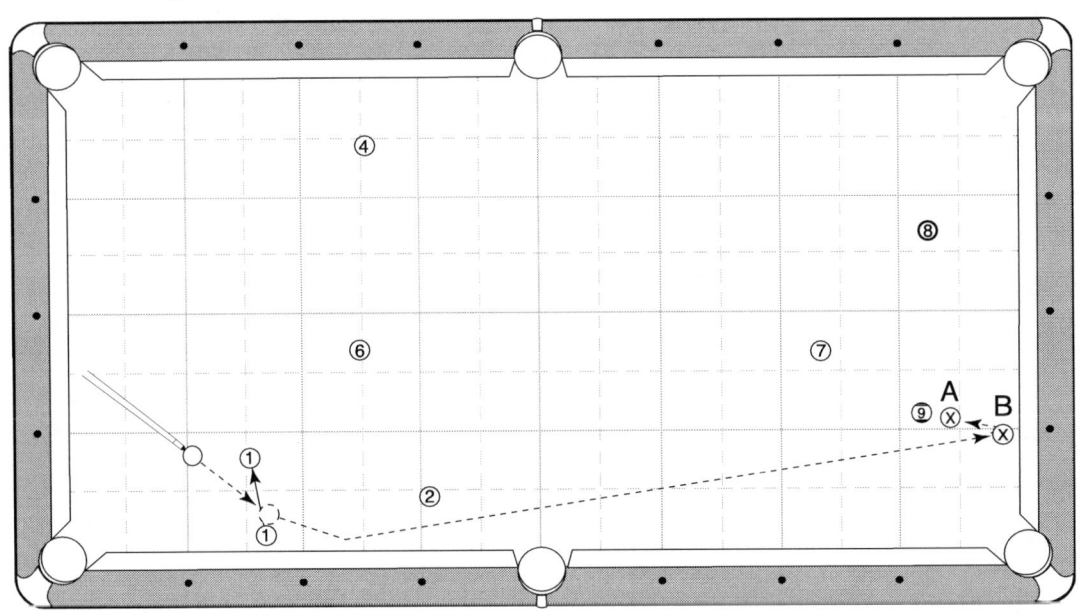

Airtight Safety

Steve Mizerak put on a clinic in safety play on his way to a 13-10 victory over Earl Strickland at the 1994 U.S. Open. Mizerak, the 1978 U.S. Open Champion, finished in a tie for ninth. Among his gems was this precision two-rail safety, in which the cue ball came to rest behind the 9-ball at Position A. The keys to this type of safety are a thin hit and superb speed control. If the cue ball had stopped six inches short of Position A at Position B, Strickland would have had a clear shot at the 1-ball! Mizerak was able to pull off this shot in part because of his skill at Straight Pool, which teaches you how to finesse the cue ball.

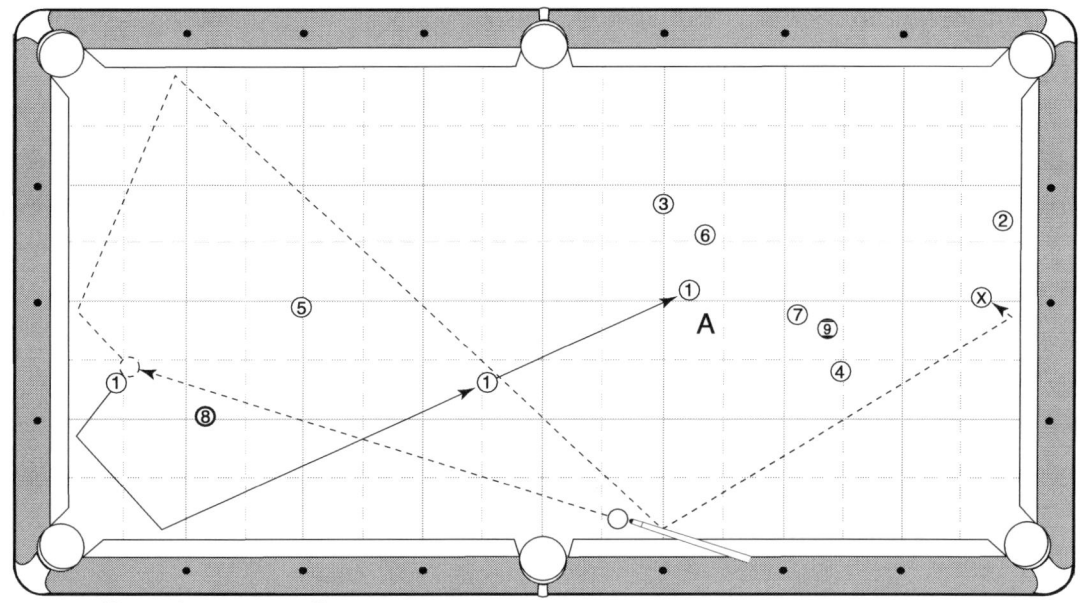

Controlling the Cue Ball at Long Range

Keith McCready executed this creative safety to perfection against Nick Varner at the Sands Regency 12 Open in 1990. A firm stroke with a tip of right english propelled the cue ball four rails to behind the wall of blockers at the opposite end of the table. The 1-ball traveled two rails to the middle of the table, but the shot was still under his complete control thanks to the precise routing of the cue ball. The 1-ball could have continued to just short of Position A before it would have come out from behind the wall. The secret was in properly routing the cue ball. Speed control on the cue ball was not overly critical due to the wide coverage provided by the wall of blockers.

Chapter 9 - Safety Play

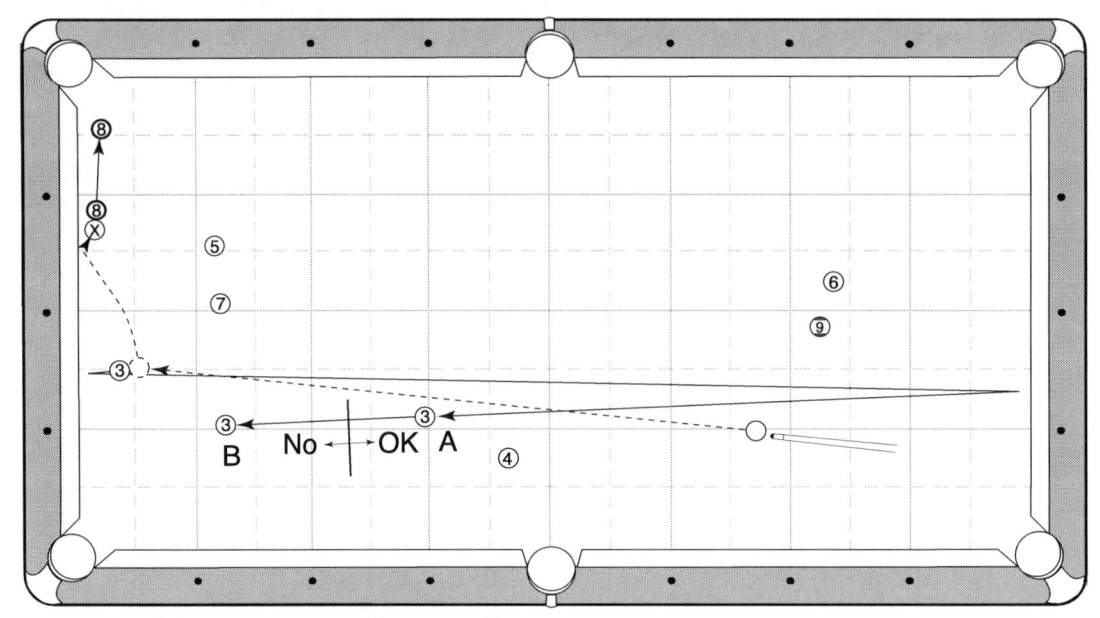

Beware of the Returning Object Ball

The plan is to bank the 3-ball down the table while leaving the cue ball behind the 5 and 7 balls. The 8-ball helps to contain the cue ball, so its ending location on this safety is very predictable. The key is in banking the 3-ball at the correct speed so that it stops on the opposite side of the blockers. Position A is okay. If you fail to control the object ball's rolling distance, it could wind up at Position B, leaving your opponent with an easy return safety. And, if the 3-ball rolls any further, he would have a shot!

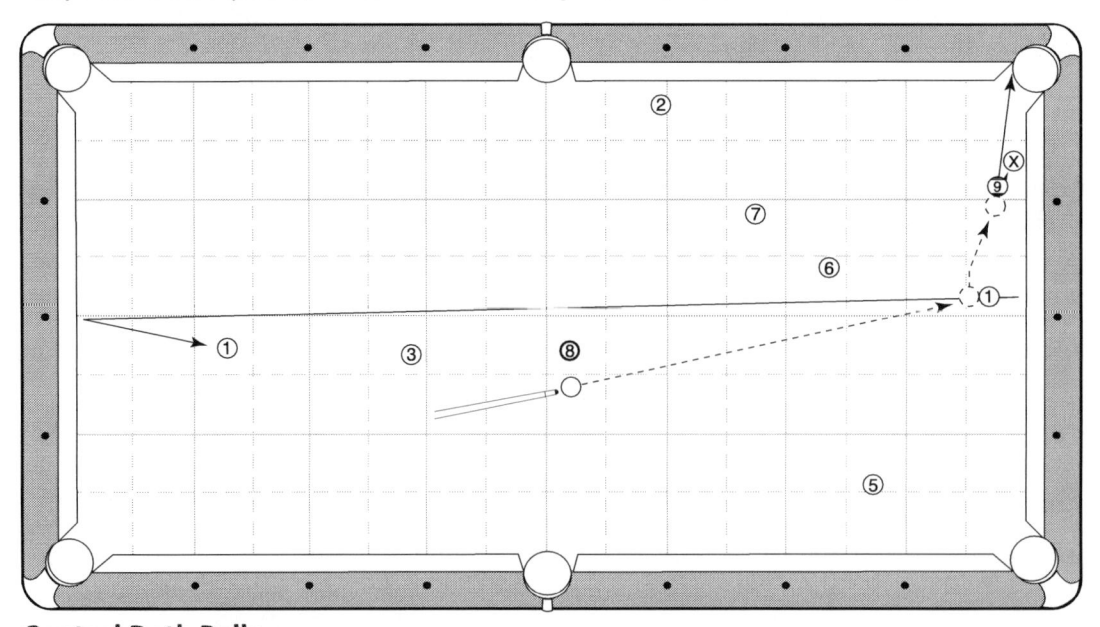

Control Both Balls

Tony Robles opened his match with Jose Garcia at the 1998 U.S. Open with this exacting billiard on the 9-ball. The cue ball was nearly four feet from the 1-ball, so Robles had to exert superb speed control for the 9-ball to be struck fully. In addition, he had to contact just the right amount of the 1-ball, which meant hitting it 2/3 full. That takes care of the cue ball.

Robles also built a safety into the shot by deftly controlling the path of the 1-ball past the 6, 8, and 3 balls. The 7-ball wound up as a blocker, separating the cue ball and the 1-ball. The big key to this shot was controlling the cue ball, but Robles' control of the 1-ball should not be overlooked. If he had missed the billiard, the chances were good that Robles would have hooked Garcia. At worst, Garcia would have been facing a long tough shot or safety on the 1-ball.

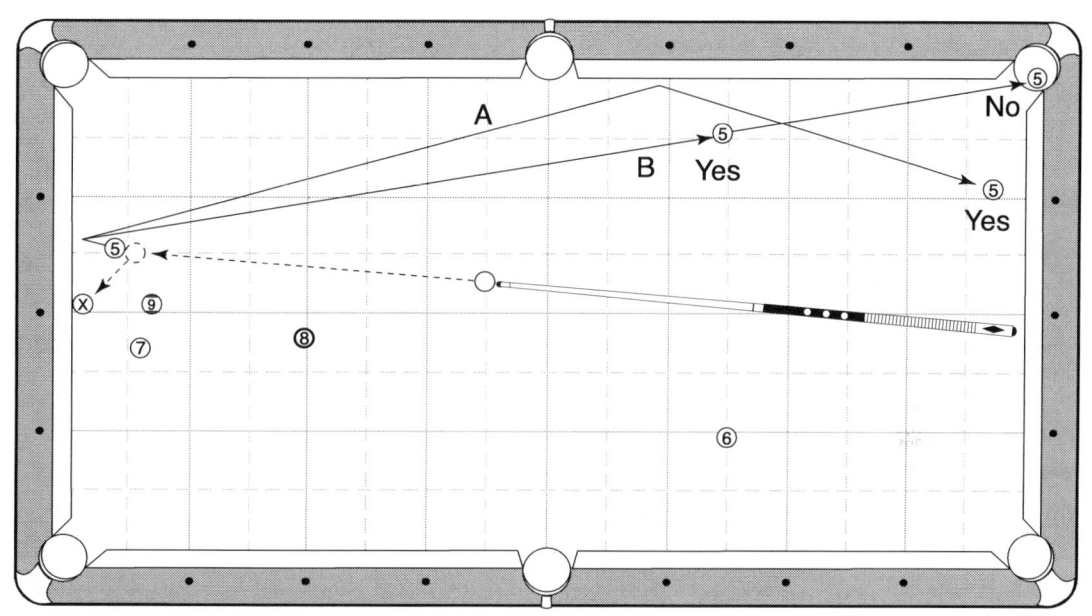

Don't Accidentally Make a Bank
The goal is to bank the 5-ball at least 1.5 diamonds past the side pocket, eliminating the possibility of your opponent having a direct hit or shot at the 5-ball. If you hit the shot a little too hard, you might make the 5-ball. You can avoid this disaster by making sure to bank the 5-ball with good speed down Route B. You could also play it off the side rail down Route A. Notice that the 9, 7, and the 8-ball two diamonds down the table combine to make the wall between the cue ball and the 5-ball. **One of the biggest mistakes is to play a safety on yourself by accidentally pocketing a ball**. But after studying this shot, it is not going to happen to you.

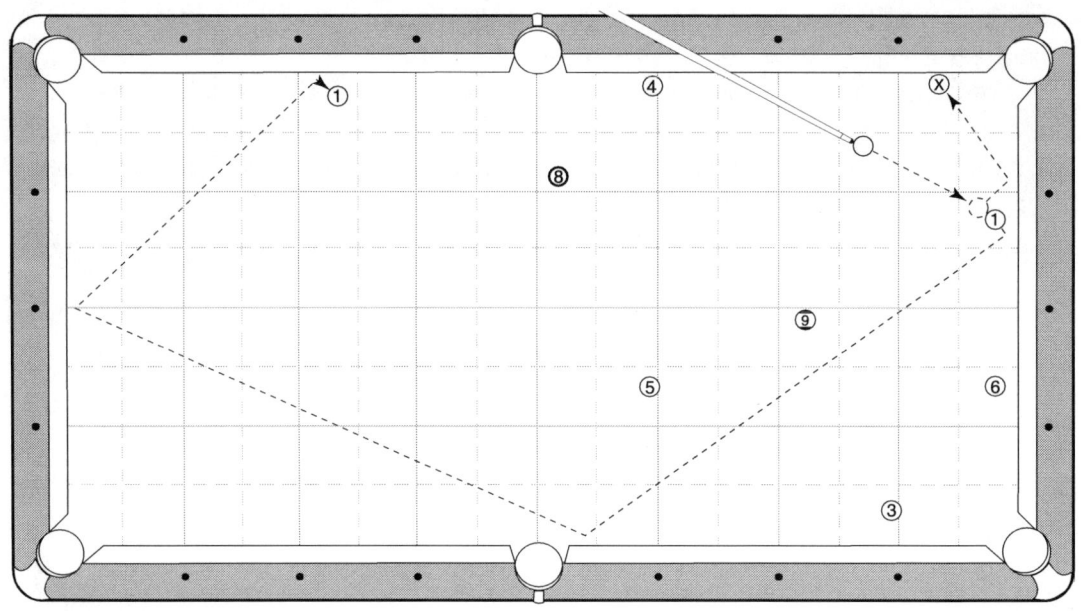

Control Both Balls

George "Ginky" SanSouci chose this aggressive safety against Earl Strickland at the 2000 U.S. Open, and was rewarded with a win. The 1-ball traveled 12.5 feet to the upper side rail with perfect speed. At the same time, SanSouci exercised great cue ball control by sending it a short distance to the top rail with a hard stroke, which is a difficult assignment. Luck played about a two percent role in this safety as SanSouci carefully plotted the course of both balls, and then executed the shot to perfection.

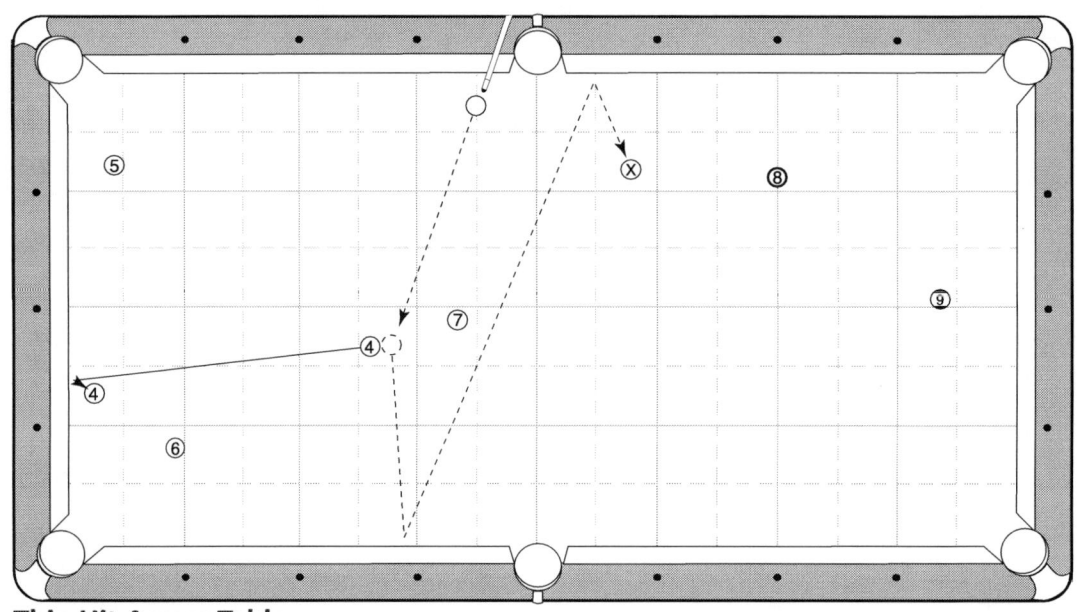

Thin Hit Across Table

This safety does not look overly impressive at first glance because it did not even result in a hook, but Steve Mizerak used it to win this game against Earl Strickland. Mizerak's first concern was to leave the 4-ball near the end rail, which he did thanks to his near perfect speed control on the object ball. It was difficult to gauge the cue ball's rolling distance, but Mizerak was able send it down the table far enough to leave a 64-degree cut shot.

Strickland would be expected to make this shot more often than not when he is at his freewheeling best. But at this particular moment, Mizerak correctly sensed that his conservative style had taken Strickland out of his rhythm, making a miss more likely – and that is just what happened.

Sharp-eyed students may have noticed that getting to the 5-ball would not have been easy even if Strickland had pocketed the 4-ball. The success of this safety rested partly in its execution, and partly on Mizerak's ability to sense a temporary weakness in his supremely talented opponent. The lesson: **be aware of the fluctuations in your opponent's game and use them to your advantage when plotting your defensive maneuvers.**

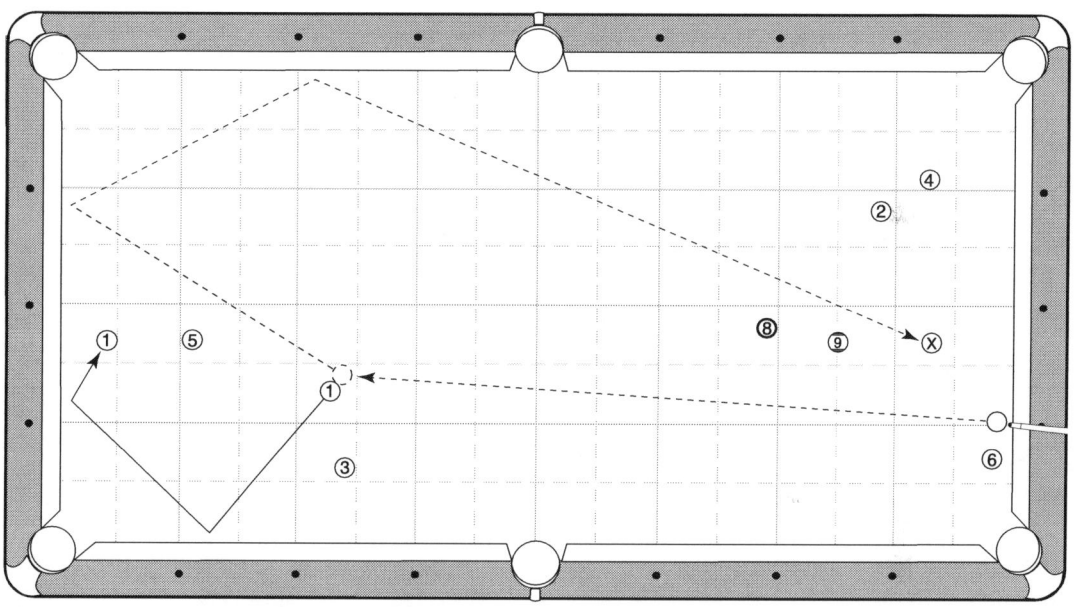

An Effective Long Distance Safety

Two-Time World Nine Ball Champion Robin Dodson played this beautiful long distance safety against Jeanette Lee at the 1994 U.S. Open. The cue ball and the object ball each came to rest behind blockers. If Ms. Dodson had mishit the shot ever so slightly, a sellout could have easily resulted. The degree of difficulty was heightened by the cue ball's initial position just off the end rail! You will have opportunities to play safeties like this, so keep this one in mind.

Using Available Blockers

A ball or group of balls may have the potential to act as a hiding place for the cue ball. It depends on their location and if you can send the cue ball behind them with an acceptably high rate of success. When you are surveying the table, look for a ball or balls you can employ as blockers, and ask yourself how you could leave the cue ball and object ball on opposite sides of the defenders. **Once you have determined that a safety is available, take a moment to see if there is a little step or two that can improve its effectiveness.**

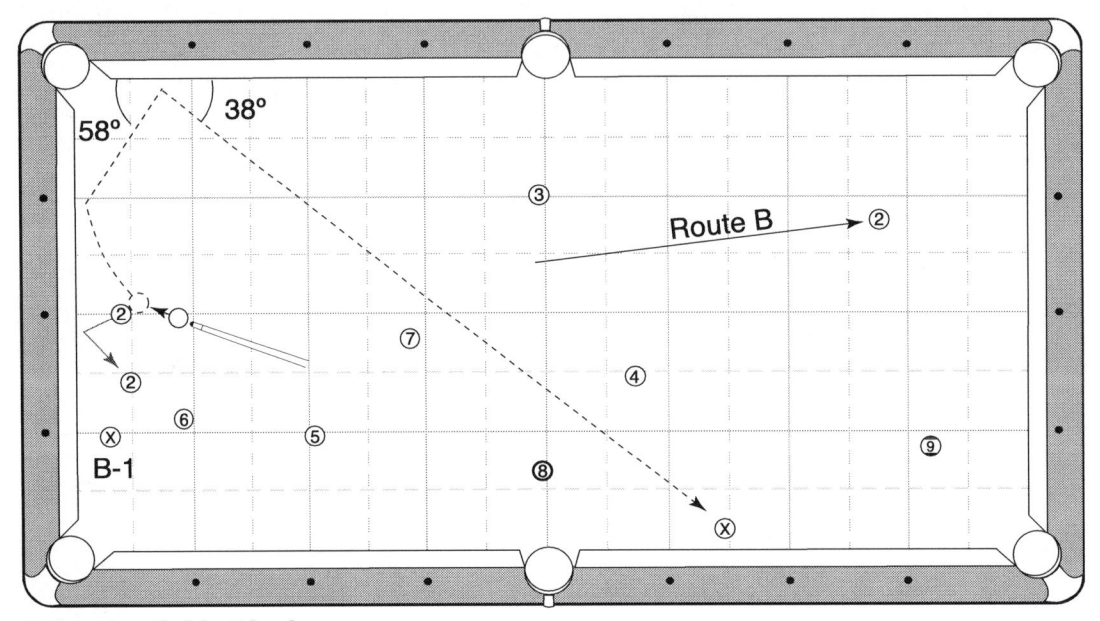

Using Available Blockers

Efren Reyes played this safety while on his way to a victory in the semi-finals over Francisco Bustamante at the Sands Regency Open 29 in 1999. The big clue that this safety was available was that the balls were almost all on the same side of the table. Reyes used outside english to control the cue ball off two rails, enabling him to thread the needle through the blockers and on to the opposite end of the table. The cue ball entered the second rail at 58 degrees and departed at only 38 degrees. The second rebound angle was much shallower than the first thanks to the english. Skill at using english to control the cue ball's path can enable you to send it behind blockers that other players would crash into.

If you were in this position and didn't mind using the mechanical bridge, you could bank the 2-ball down Route B while sending the cue ball to Position B-1.

Window Free

Takeshi Okumura played this fine safety in the finals of the 2000 U. S. Open. The cue ball was a table length from the 1-ball, but this was not a super difficult safety thanks to the line of widely spaced blockers strewn along the topside of the table. When preparing for a safety with widely spaced blockers, walk over to where you wish to send the cue ball. Besides being good exercise, walking will enable you to see if there is a window between the balls that could result in a direct line to the object ball. If Okumura had hit the 1-ball too far on the right side, it could have ended up at Position B, and the cue ball might have stopped at Position B-1, leaving a 1-9 combination.

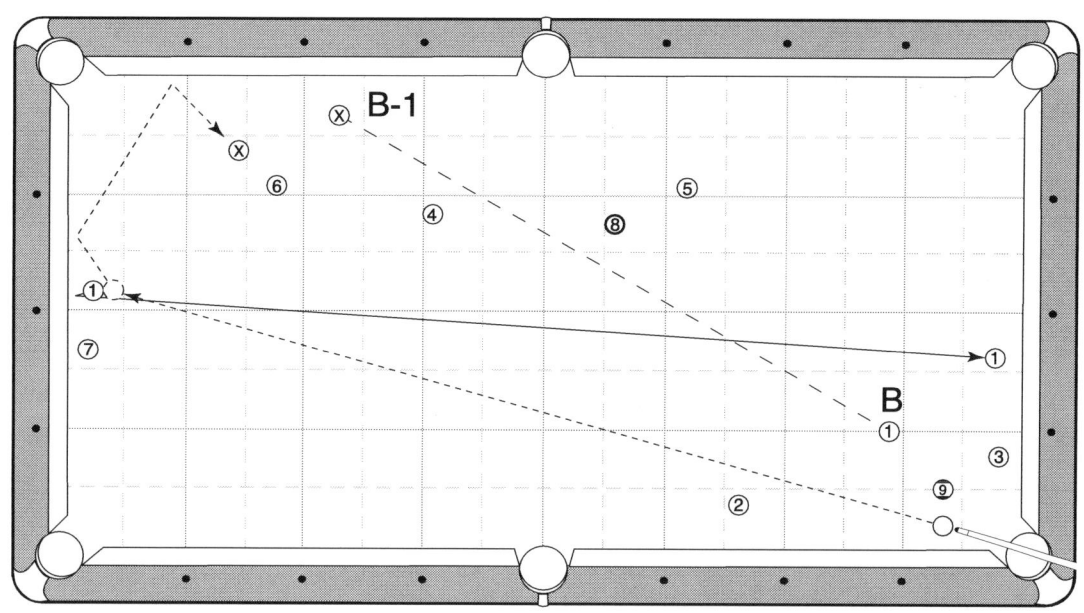

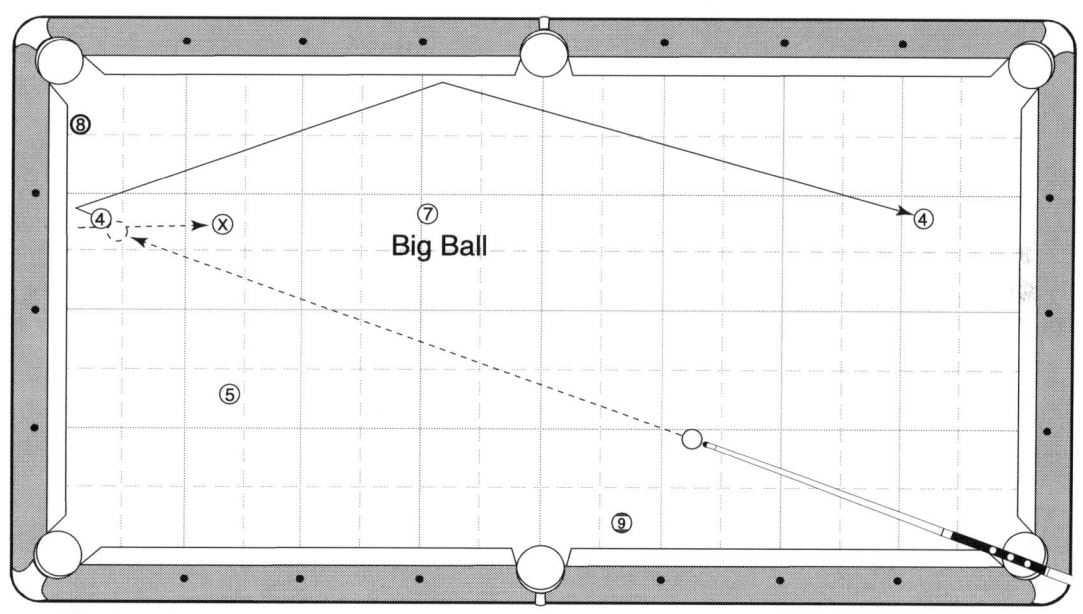

Banking Past a Big Ball
A solitary ball in the middle of the table can block a big part of the table, shielding the object ball from direct contact. The 7-ball is a big ball because it has the potential to obscure a large portion of the right side of the table. The key to this safety is an accurate hit on the 4-ball. It must be struck just a hair left of center with follow so it will not veer off to either side of the 7-ball, which could leave a direct hit on the 4-ball.

Soft Follow Shot Safeties

Playing safeties with a soft follow stroke allows you to control the cue ball with great precision, which enables you to play killer safeties with little effort. The big keys to this kind of safeties are a soft touch and knowing where you must hit the object ball in order to send the cue ball where required.

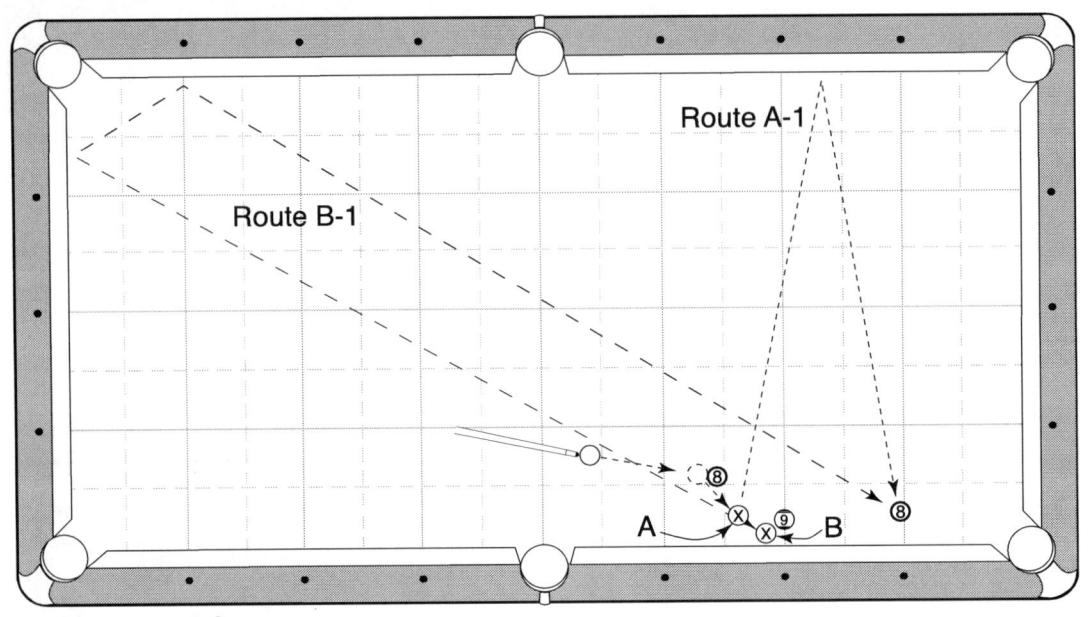

Lock'em Up Tight

The 8-9 combo is a very difficult shot, so a safety is the smart play. The safe is quite easy because the 9-ball is slightly less than a ball's width from the rail, providing you with a big hook zone.

When playing safe in the "short game" there are average safeties, and then there are the you've-got them-in-jail safeties that greatly multiply your chances of winning. An average safety would leave your opponent with an easy one-rail kick from Position A at the 8-ball down Route A-1. He should have little problem hitting the 8-ball – and he might make the 8 or possibly leave you with a tough shot or safety.

A soft follow shot to Position B will increase the difficulty of the kick shot enormously. Your opponent must now kick two rails into the 8-ball down Route B-1. Those extra three inches that you sent the cue ball forward made a huge difference in the effectiveness of this soft touch safety. Chalk one up to the player with a keen eye and a well-developed sense of touch.

Super Soft Hit Safety

The rather mundane looking safety at the top of the next page is actually one of the finest safeties ever played. Nick Varner was clinging to a 10-9 lead in a race to 11 against Johnny Archer in the finals of the Sands Regency Open 23, 1996, when he was confronted with a possible table length combo on the 8-9. After much deliberation, Varner slow rolled the cue ball into a near full hit on the 8-ball. He used an extremely soft stroke – a speed that is often reserved for pool's top surgeons! The 8-ball caressed the rail and stopped less than a quarter inch after contact. The cue ball also did its play, crawling up behind the 9-ball. Archer missed the hit and Varner won the title. The two big secrets were perfect speed control and hitting the correct portion of the 8-ball. This shot was way more difficult than it may have appeared to the untrained eye.

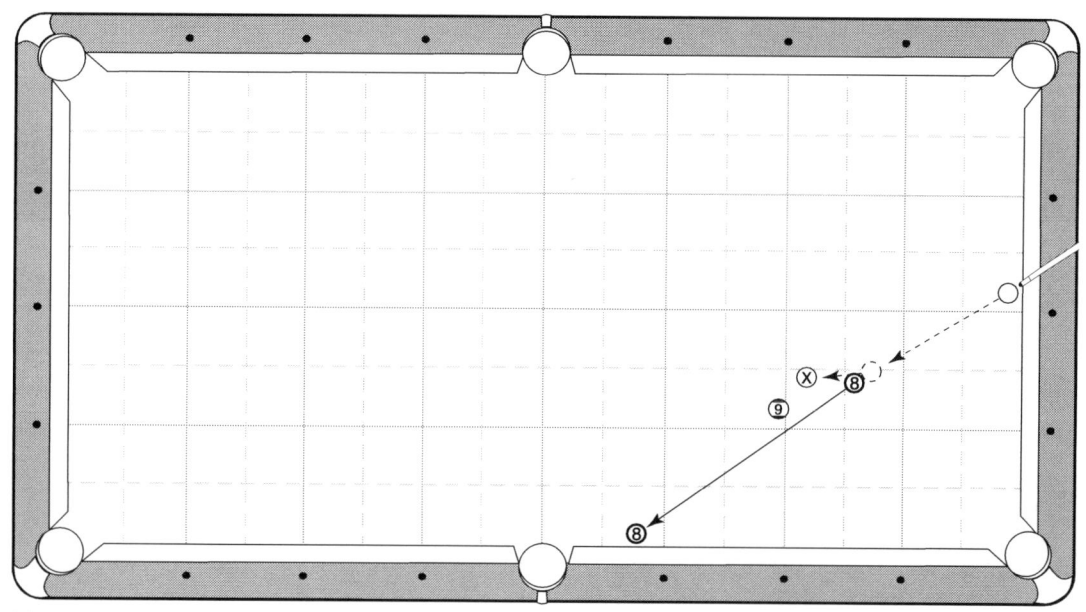

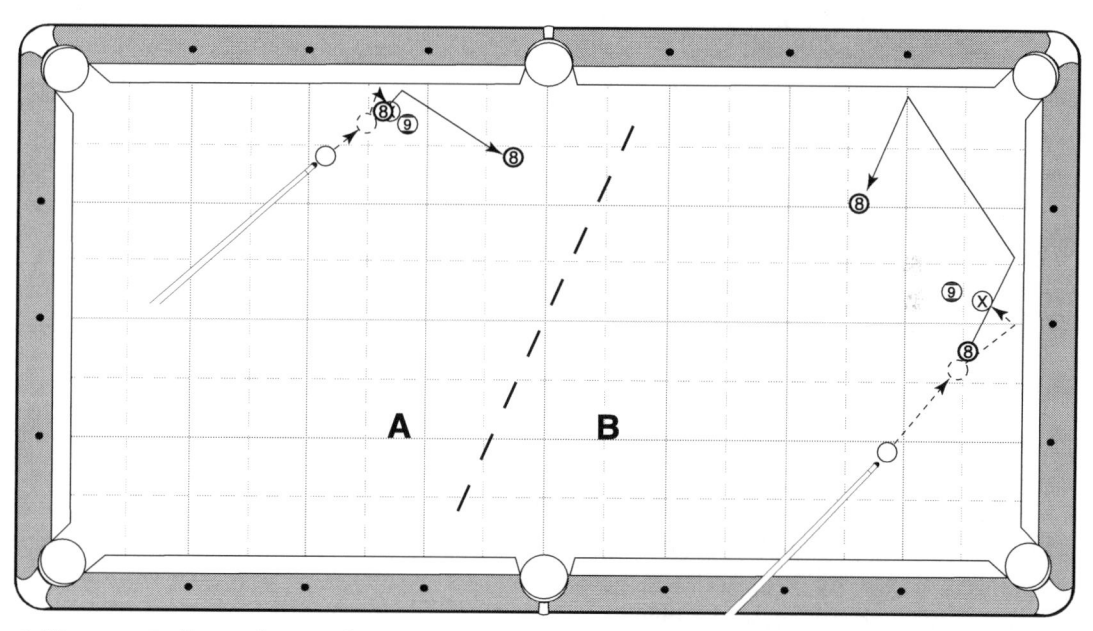

A Finesse Follow Shot Safety

In Part A, the 8-ball must be cut a hair to the left using a very soft follow stroke. The cue ball will come directly off the rail, creating a devastatingly effective hook safety! The concept is the same in Part B, only this time the 8-ball must be hit a little less fully with a soft follow stroke. The lesson: **on nearly fully hit soft follow shots, small differences in the contact point can have a big influence on the cue ball's path**!

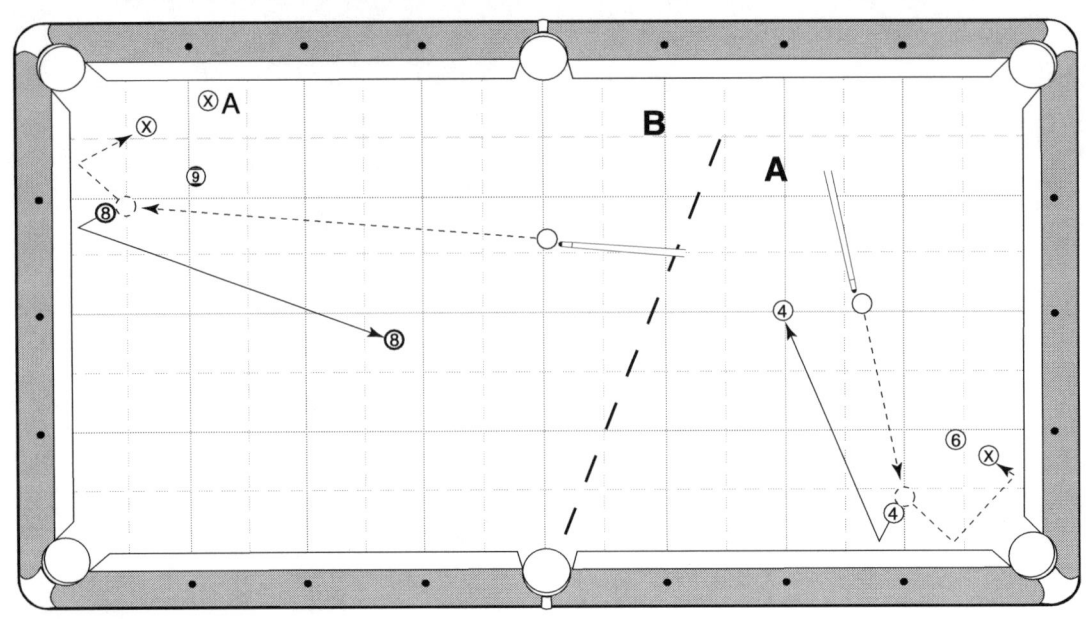

Inside English Kill Shot Safety

Controlling the cue ball's speed is not always so easy to do even when it will be traveling a foot or less to behind a blocker. **When a couple of inches spell the difference between leaving a hook and a direct hit, you need to employ the best possible techniques.** One effective method for putting the brakes on the cue ball is a combination of inside english and a soft follow shot. The move in Part A is to bank the 4-ball to the middle of the table. The right english will kill the cue ball's speed as it strikes the two rails as shown.

In Part B, inside (left) english makes it far easier to contain the cue ball's roll after it strikes the end rail. Still, this safety still requires a soft touch and just the right hit on the 8-ball. If the 8 is hit a little too thinly, the cue ball could leak out to Position A, leaving a shot.

Finesse Draw Safeties

Most players find it more difficult to control speed on position plays when using draw. The same holds true on safeties. But if you master finesse draw safeties, you will gain an edge on your competitors who have not bothered to learn the fine points of playing defense. **Finesse draw safeties are played with a stroke that is both authoritative and soft.** You can't baby a finesse draw shot because the draw won't take properly. And, if you use too much speed, you will lose control of the object ball.

Soft Draw Hook Safety

Robin Dodson played the safety at the top of the next page in a match with Jeanette Lee at the 1994 U.S. Open. The 1-ball traveled six feet while the cue ball slid a couple of inches over behind the 7-ball after contact. The shot was played with a soft stroke with a full tip of draw. The secret was a perfect hit with the perfect speed. The cue ball was hit hard enough so that the draw spin would keep it from rolling forward. At the same time, the speed needed to be soft enough so that the 1-ball would not come back down table to around Position A. **Controlling the cue ball and the object ball** often requires that the speed fall in the happy middle – not too hard, and not too soft.

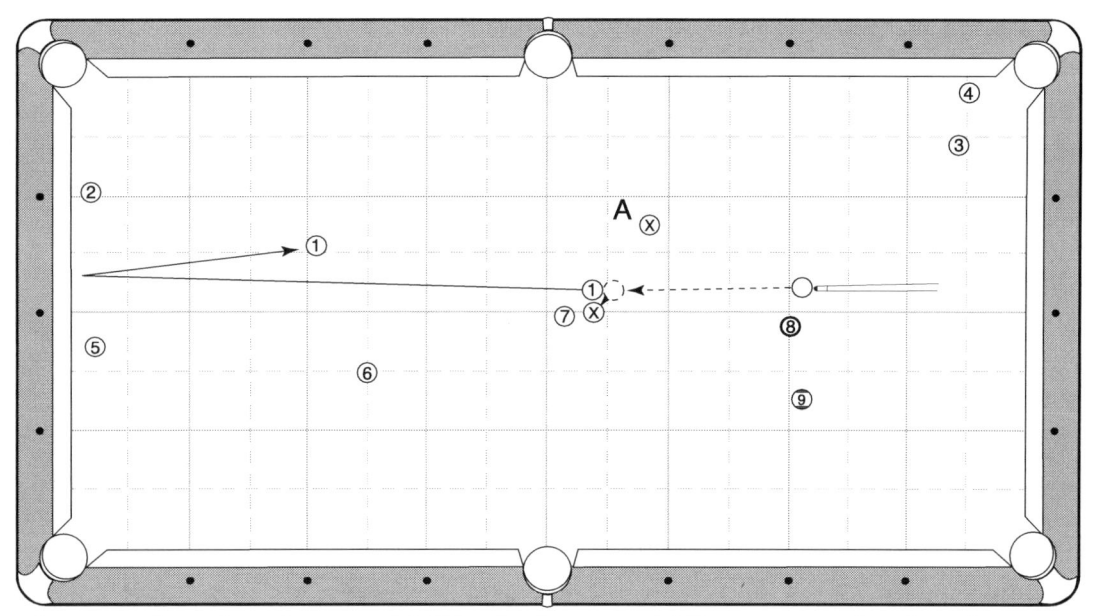

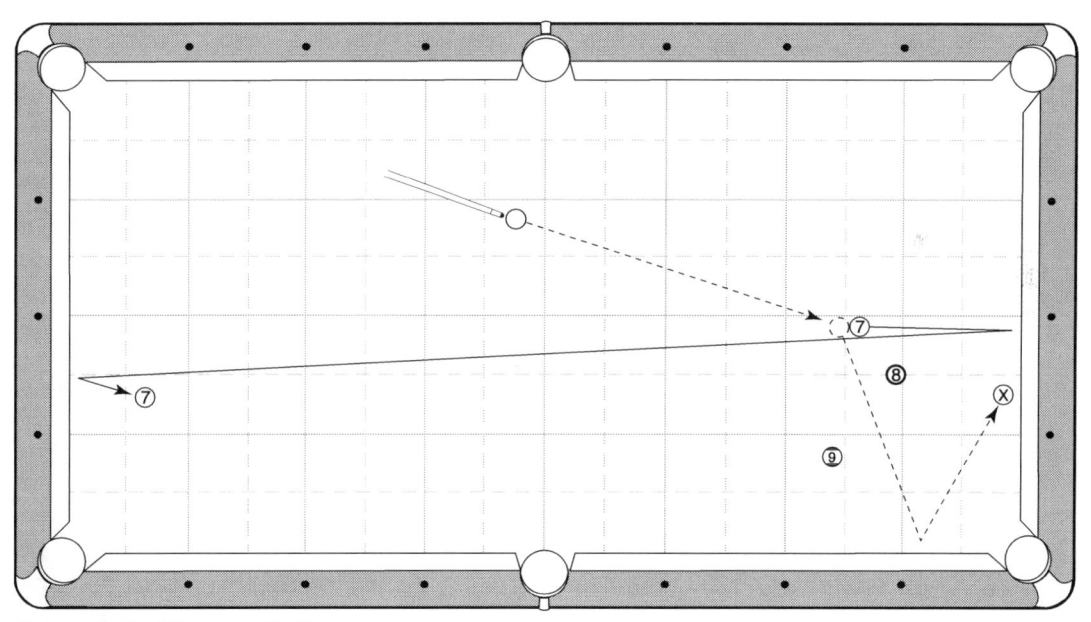

Draw Spin Finesse Safety

The 8-ball is blocking the 7-ball and shooting the 7-8 combo is out of the question because the cue ball is too far down the table. The solution is to play a draw/spin safety using a medium soft stroke and a tip of draw and a half tip of inside (left) english. The side spin will turn the cue ball off the side rail and down behind the 8-ball. The draw holds the cue ball's line to the side rail, and it prevents it from scratching. Once again, **the skillful combining of cueing and speed leads to a killer safety**!

Chapter 9 - Safety Play
Thin Hit Safeties
The big challenge in playing thin hit safeties is to contact a very small slice of the object ball without missing it entirely! Furthermore, to play these safeties well you must be comfortable stroking in the lowest ranges (speeds 1-3) of the Spectrum of Speeds (see page XI) A dose of english can also be useful in sending the cue ball to a precise ending location.

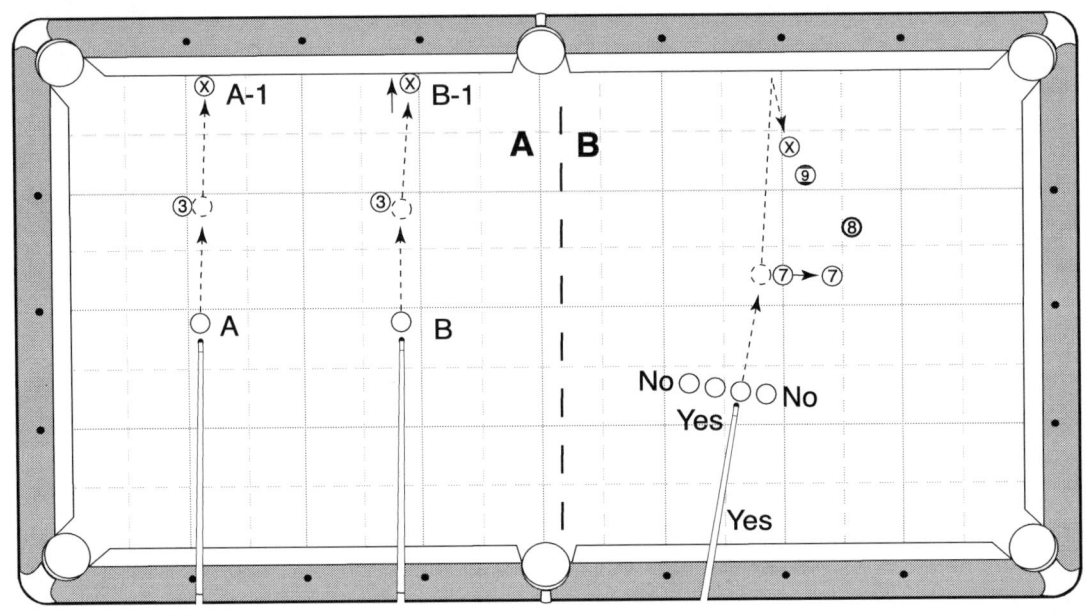

Thin Hit at Short Range
A the big challenge in thin hit safeties is to figure how far the cue ball will be diverted from its original path after contacting the object ball. In Part A, if you brush the 3-ball as thinly as possible with Cue Ball A, the 3-ball would barely move, and the cue ball would continue on its initial line to Position A-1.

The 3-ball and cue ball are in the same relative places in Position B. This time the 3-ball was hit very thinly, but noticeably greater than before. The cue ball was diverted 2 inches to the right of its initial line of travel to Position B-1. This may appear to be a small and insignificant distance, but when you are playing precision safeties to super small targets, an inch or two can make a huge difference.

The safety in Part B shows how hitting the object ball thinly with good speed and english produces a lethal safety. **A small difference in the location of the balls determines whether a safety is "on" or "off."** In the example, the safety is a go from an area about 5 inches wide (about two ball widths, as shown).

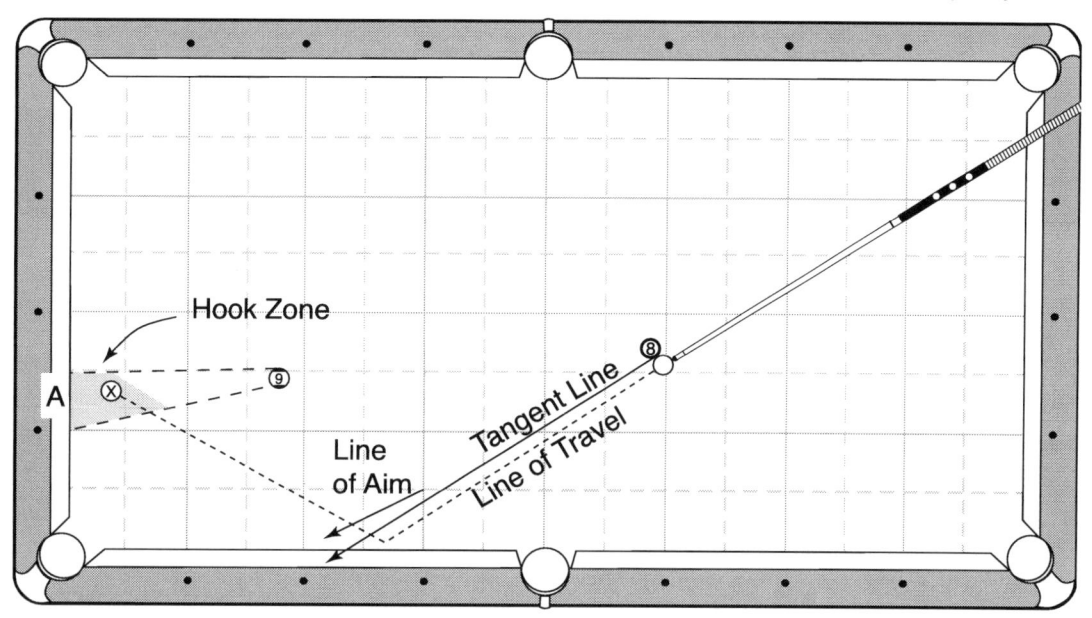

Frozen Ball Safety

The cue ball is frozen to the 8-ball and there is no practical offensive shot. However, a devilish little safety is available thanks to the position of the 9-ball. The plan is to brush the 8-ball while moving it as little as possible. The 8-ball should not move more than about an inch, so you can predict its position with great accuracy, which then enables you to identify the hook zone behind the 9-ball. Before playing the shot, walk over to Position A to calculate exactly where the hook zone lies.

Establish your point of aim by first drawing a tangent line between the cue ball and 8-ball. Locate the point where it intersects the rail. Aim a couple of inches inside this line, which guarantees that you "hit" the 8-ball. What you are really doing is not shooting away from the 8, which would result in a foul.

These maneuvers should be carried out in full view of your opponent, and **you may wish to explain why your shot will be a legal safety before you play it**. The cue ball shown ended up in the hook zone using follow. You could use english if needed to send the cue ball along a shallower path to a position behind the blocker.

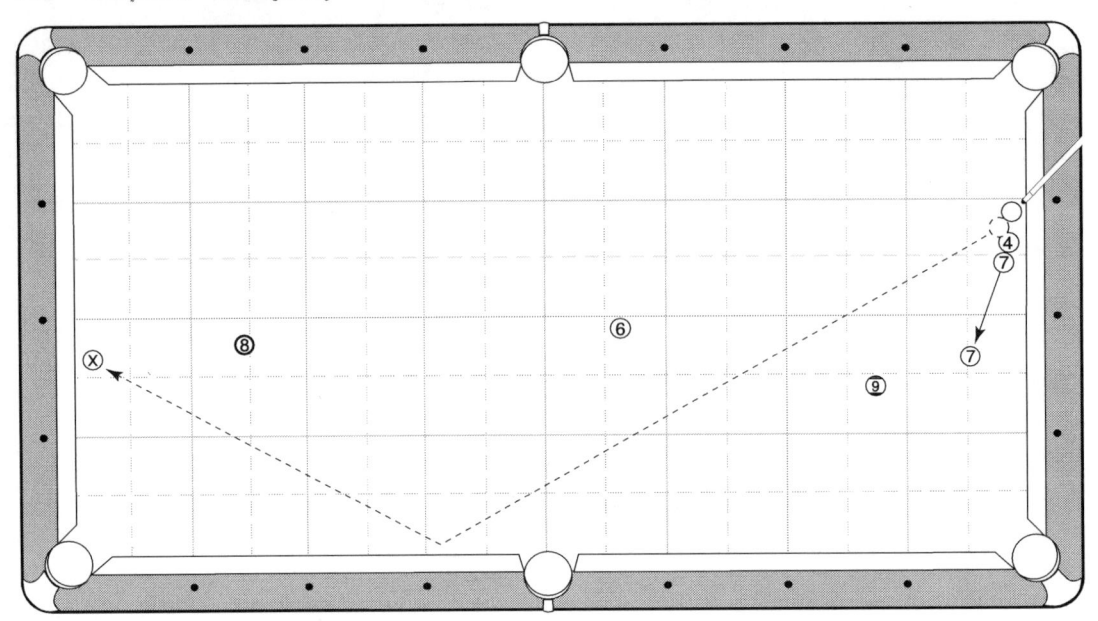

Ball in Hand Thin Hit Safety
You could have ball in hand and still not have an offensive shot if the balls are clustered together. This situation arises after your opponent has used an intentional foul to tie up the balls. When you are in this position, look for a route to a blocker, and try to separate the balls as constructively as possible.

The play is to hit the 4-ball thinly so you can control the cue ball's path to behind the 6 and 8 balls, which are going to serve as blockers. Another big goal is to separate the 4 and 7 balls. If your opponent fouls again, you can use a second ball in hand to position yourself for a runout.

Thin Hit Safety or Bank Shot?
The 9-ball is the only ball left in the two positions shown on the next page — a situation that frequently occurs in games between amateurs. Your choice is usually between a thin hit safety and a table length bank shot. The decision is based on the position of the balls, and on the skills of the players. The long rail bank is not overly difficult when the cue ball is in Position A. **If you are confident in your banking and wish to avoid a safety battle against a crafty opponent, go for the bank.** However, a thin hit safety is an easy shot from this distance and could be the better choice if your opponent is a poor safety player.

When the cue ball is in Position B, the bank may be the better choice because the thin hit safety from this distance could be even tougher to execute successfully. Position C is the mirror image of the one above except that the cue ball is in between Positions A and B. A thin hit safety is probably better because it is not too difficult from this distance, and because the bank is very missable.

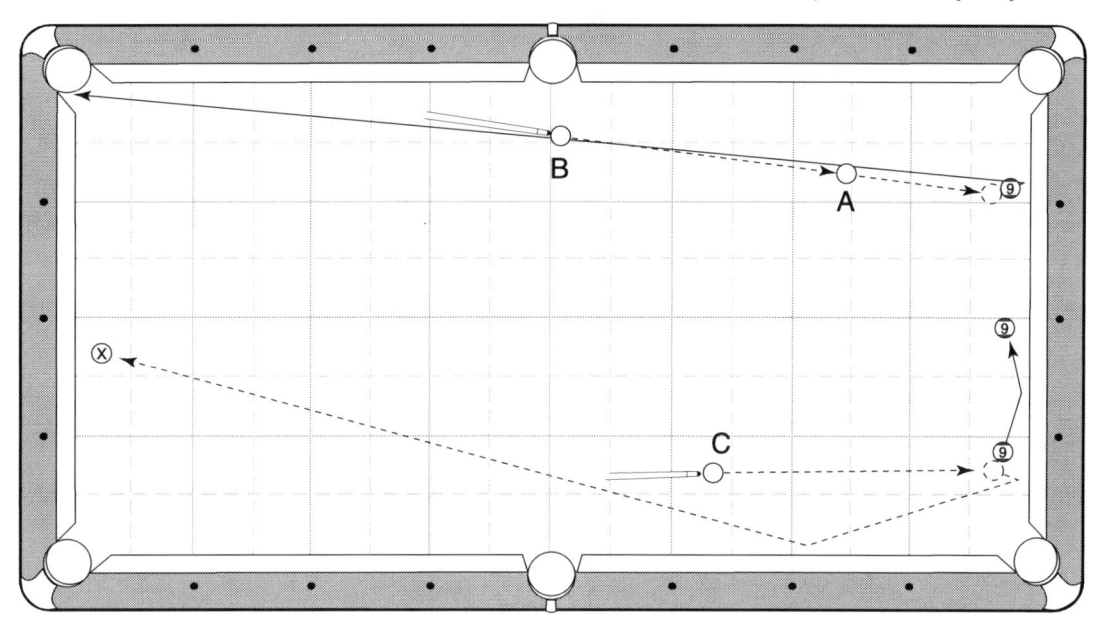

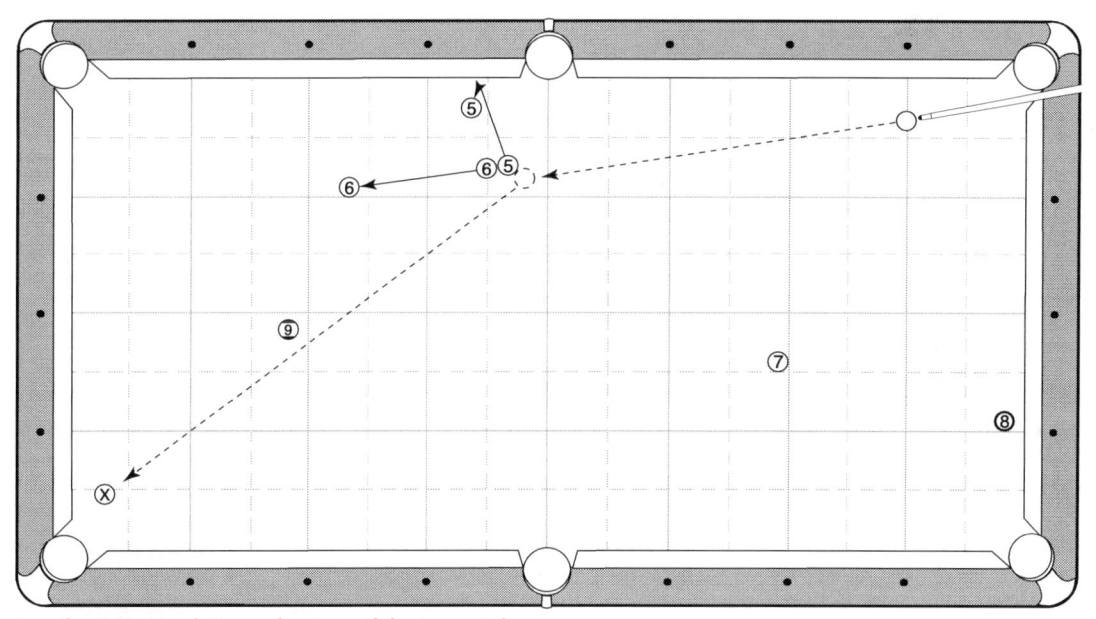

Perfect Speed Avoids Possible Scratch

Distance is a strategic weapon that is designed to leave the toughest shot or safety possible. Ewa Laurence, the 1991 U.S Open champion, was confronted with a long-range safety against Robin Dodson in the finals of the 1992 U.S. Open. The 6-ball was the key to controlling the 5-ball. Ms. Laurence used the perfect speed as the 5-ball made it to the rail with a little room to spare while the cue ball stopped inches short of a near scratch. She probably knew that a scratch was possible, but had enough confidence in her speed control to send the cue ball in the direction of the pocket, knowing that it would fall short. **Knowing precisely how far the balls are going to roll is a skill than enables you to play ultra precise safeties.**

#1

Blockers

90°

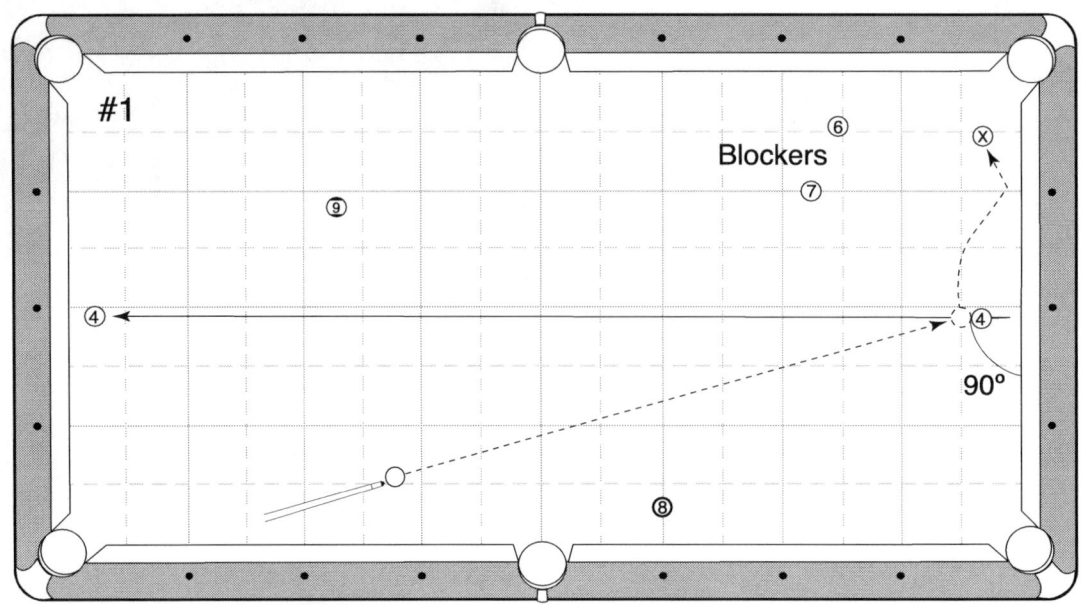

Crossover Bank Safeties

Crossover bank safeties come up very often, and they are usually very effective. The play is to bank a ball down the table while the cue ball crosses over the path of the object ball as it rebounds off the rail. Diagram #1 shows a long distance crossover safety. The 4-ball is banked straight down the table while the cue ball crosses over and behind a wall of blockers. It is much easier to control both balls when you bank the object ball at a 90-degree angle (perpendicular to the end rail). Knowing the exact line on which the object ball will be traveling enables you to focus your attention on speed of stroke. If your speed is right, the 4-ball will arrive near (or on) the end rail. This safety leaves your opponent with a table length two-rail kick shot on the 4-ball.

Crossover bank safeties are very effective in the end game. Let's assume that the 4-ball is the 9-ball, and the other balls are gone. You could play a thin cut or a bank on the 9-ball, but either of these shots could easily be missed. If you are not sure of pocketing either shot (and even pros wouldn't be), then play a crossover bank safety. Your goal is to leave your opponent in a similar predicament. They may go for the shot and sellout, or play a poor safety. If you are playing a knowledgeable player, he could return the favor. If so, at least you gave him the opportunity to commit an error. And, if he also showed you a little more of his knowledge of safety play, then you have a read on his game, which is especially important at the amateur level when skill sets vary so widely.

Diagram #2 at the top of the next page shows an advanced version of the crossover bank safety. If you bank the 9-ball straight back down the table, you might leave a cut shot if your speed and direction are slightly off. The 9-ball is a few inches off the rail, so you can cut it a little to the left and still avoid a double kiss. When the object ball is this close to the rail, and this far from the upper right corner pocket, you need not worry about scratching.

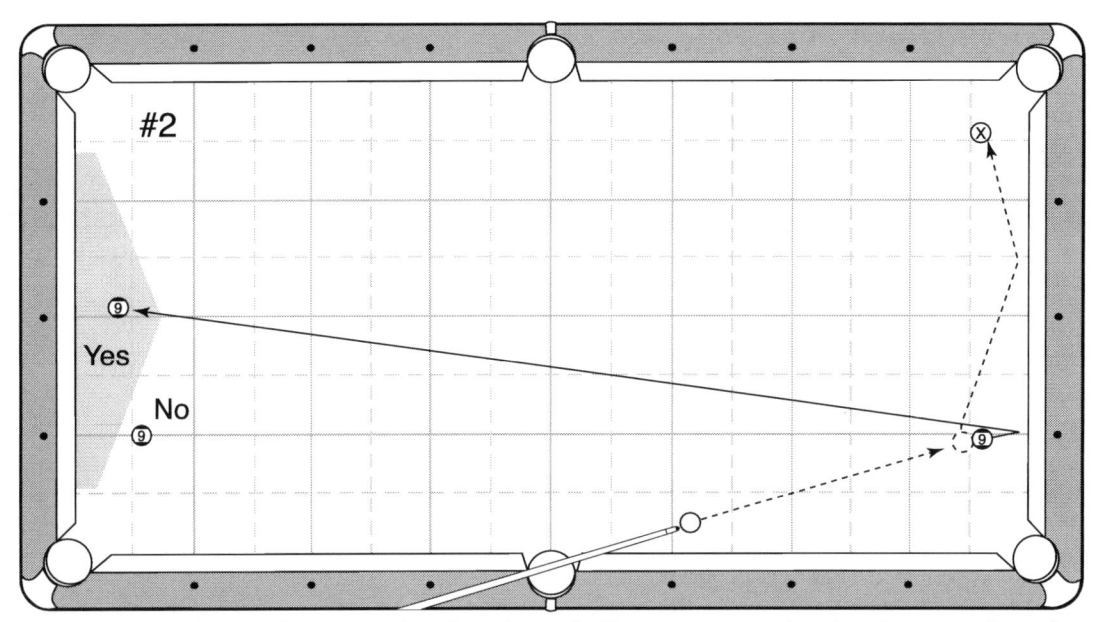

The zone shows the target for the object ball on crossover bank safeties. When the ball you are banking is about a diamond or more from the end rail, you must guard against scratching. Most crossover bank safeties are played with a medium soft follow stroke, so the path of the cue ball after contact is very predictable. The only reason for scratching is a lack of knowledge about the cue ball's path after contact, a problem that can quickly be eliminated with sufficient practice.

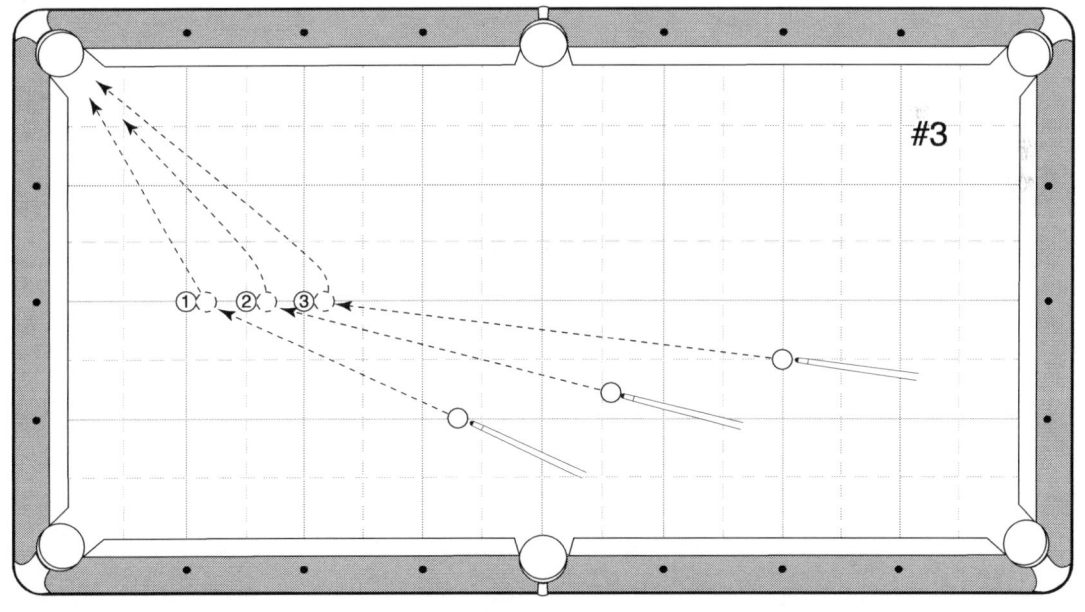

Set up the three balls in Diagram #3, one at a time. Start with the 1-ball. Shoot crossover safeties with the cue ball in the position that corresponds with each object ball. Try to send each ball to the middle diamond of the opposite end rail. Each shot is a dead or near dead scratch. Now, adjust the cue ball's position in small increments to both the left and right. This exercise will teach you what a crossover scratch shot looks like, and how to avoid scratching.

Safes with a Carom

When the balls are lying a little funny and you are wondering how to play safe, it is time to get creative. Put on your thinking cap and draw upon your knowledge of a variety of shots, any one of which may be employed to construct an effective safety. One such concept is the carom safety. **To play a carom safety, shoot the lowest numbered ball off another ball so that it will continue to a safe location.**

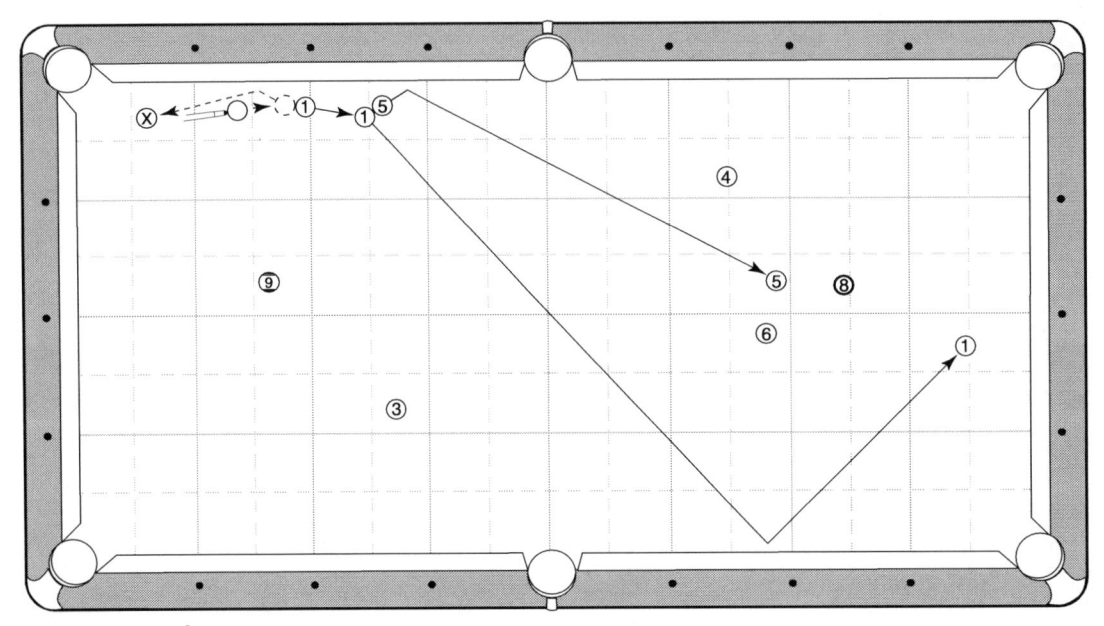

A Carom Safety

You could hit the 1-ball thinly on the right side and send the cue ball to the other end of the table, but you would run the risk of scratching. A better choice is to carom the 1-ball into the 5-ball and draw back to Position X. The 1-ball should bounce off the side rail and behind the blockers up table. The key is to calculate how much of the 5-ball to hit to get the 1-ball started on the correct line. In this case, a 1/3 hit on the 5-ball is required. Warning: **only attempt certain carom safeties when the cue ball, object ball, and the second ball are in a relatively straight line**. Otherwise, aiming is quite difficult.

A "Dead" Carom Bank Safety

The 5-ball is frozen to the 8, which is a familiar position for playing a carom to pocket a shot. In this position, use the 5-ball's predictable path to play a deadly carom safety. Preshot planning indicates that the 5-ball will follow the path as shown to behind the row of blockers. If the 5-ball is struck between 2/3 and 1/2 full, it should have the speed needed to stop behind the blockers. The key is to hit the correct amount of the 5-ball with draw and enough speed so that the cue ball stops near the end rail at Position X.

Chapter 9 - Safety Play 279

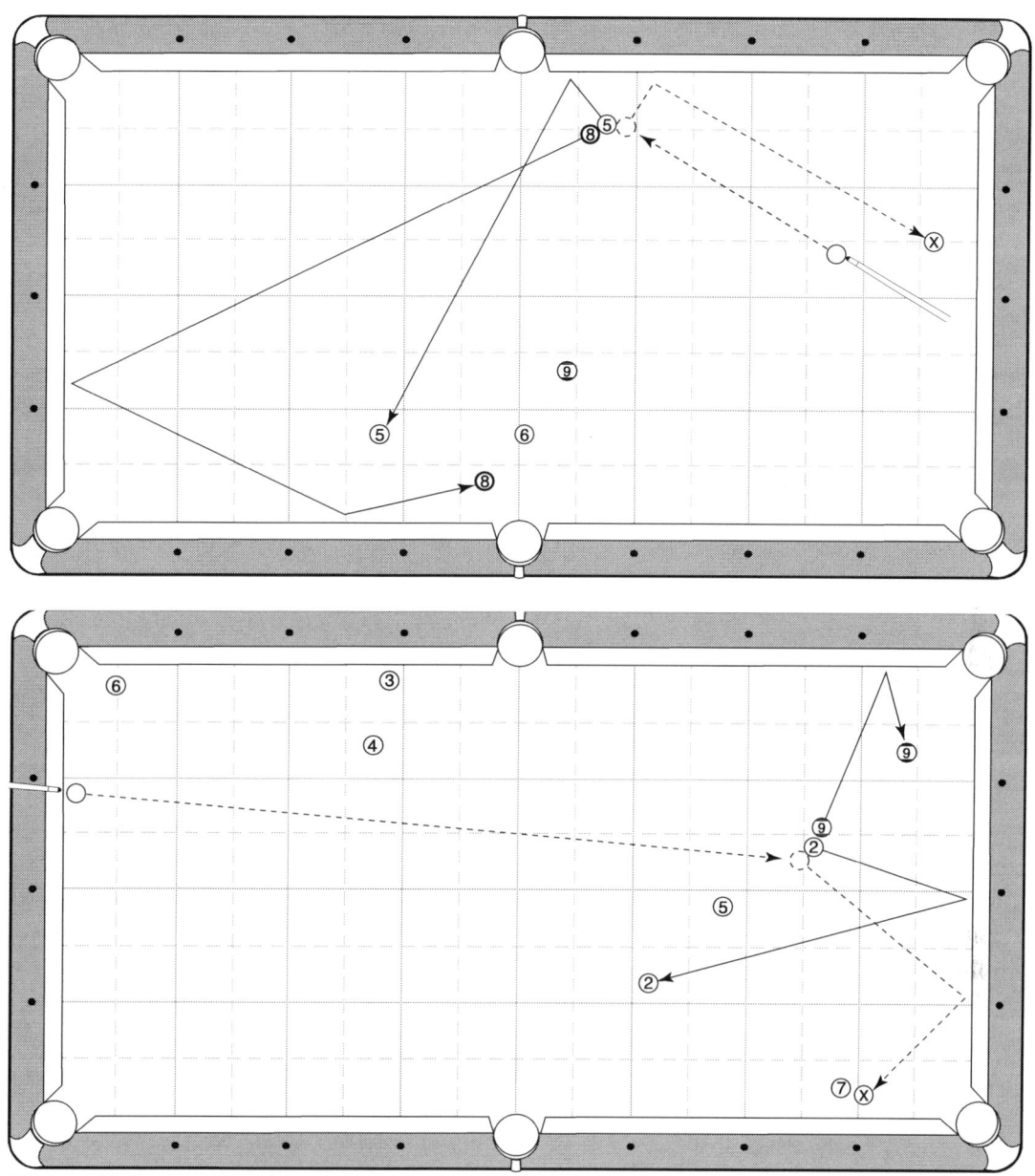

Carom Safety at Long Range

When Kunihiko Takahashi of Japan stepped to the table, he was facing this puzzler at the 1999 U.S. Open. His solution was a very creative and well executed carom safety. The 2-ball hit only a small portion of the 9-ball, so it retained much of the force from its contact with the cue ball, enabling it to roll three diamonds up table after contacting the end rail. The cue ball contacted the 2-ball perfectly and continued to behind the 7-ball. The secret to this safety was Takahashi's extensive knowledge of how the balls interact, which comes with experience, a sharp eye, and a good memory.

Kick Safeties

While the outcome is somewhat uncertain on most kick shots, there are times when a kick shot safety has a very high probability of success. In this section we'll cover some of the most commonly played kick safeties. For a more complete discussion of kick shots, please refer to Chapter 10.

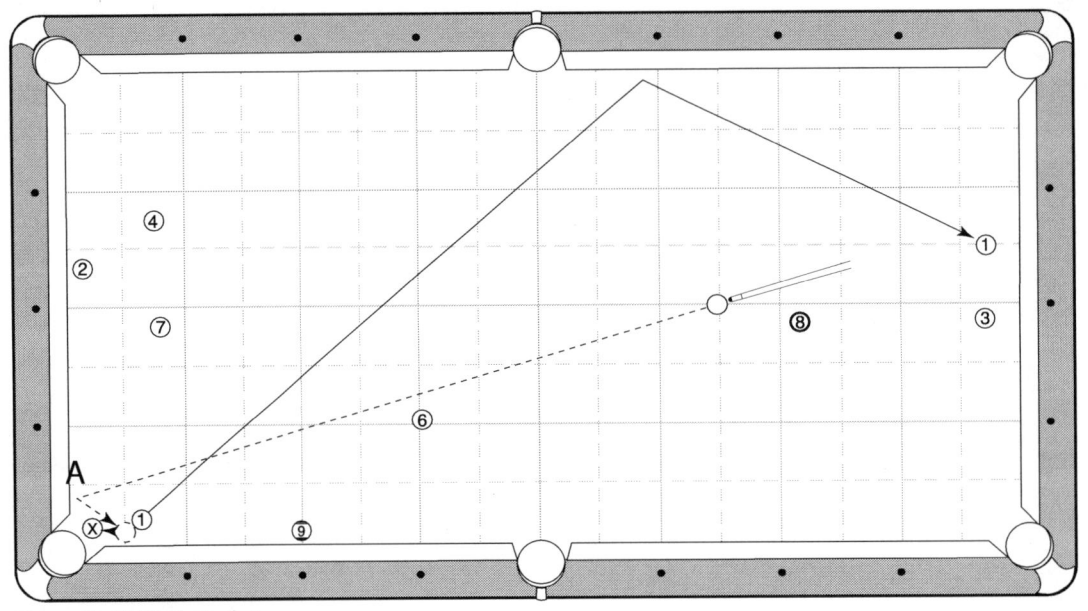

Two Rail Kick Safety

Nick Varner was hooked on the 1-ball after the break in a match with Keith McCready at the Sands Regency Open 12, 1990. There was no place to push out except for a jump shot, so Varner played this two-rail kick safety. He walked over to Position A to inspect the cue ball's position at contact and to determine the 1-ball's initial direction. He used a medium speed follow stroke to execute this kick safety to perfection. The 1-ball is less than a ball's width from the rail, which allowed Varner to predict contact with confidence. The Lesson: **whenever you are kicking at a ball that is close to the rail, you may have an opportunity to play a high percentage kick safety**.

Short Rail Kick and Stick

Open spaces abound on the left side of the table, so it would be a mistake to kick softly at the 4-ball while just trying to make a good hit. Instead, hit the 4-ball firmly and drive it around and down table, hopefully behind any of the blockers. Use a hard draw stroke and a quarter tip of reverse english, which will cause the cue ball to stop dead upon contact with the 4-ball. This shot is not too difficult because the 4-ball is only a few inches from the rail. If the 4-ball was an inch or two further from the cushion, the degree of difficulty would rise substantially. The lesson: **when blockers are absent on one end of the table, kick the object ball to the opposite end**.

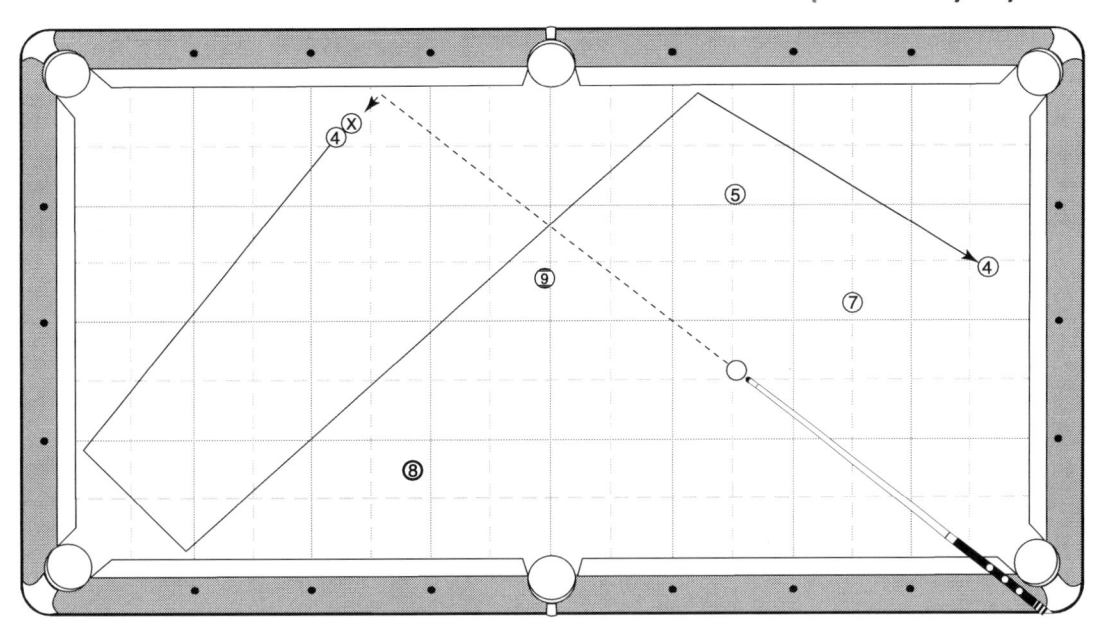

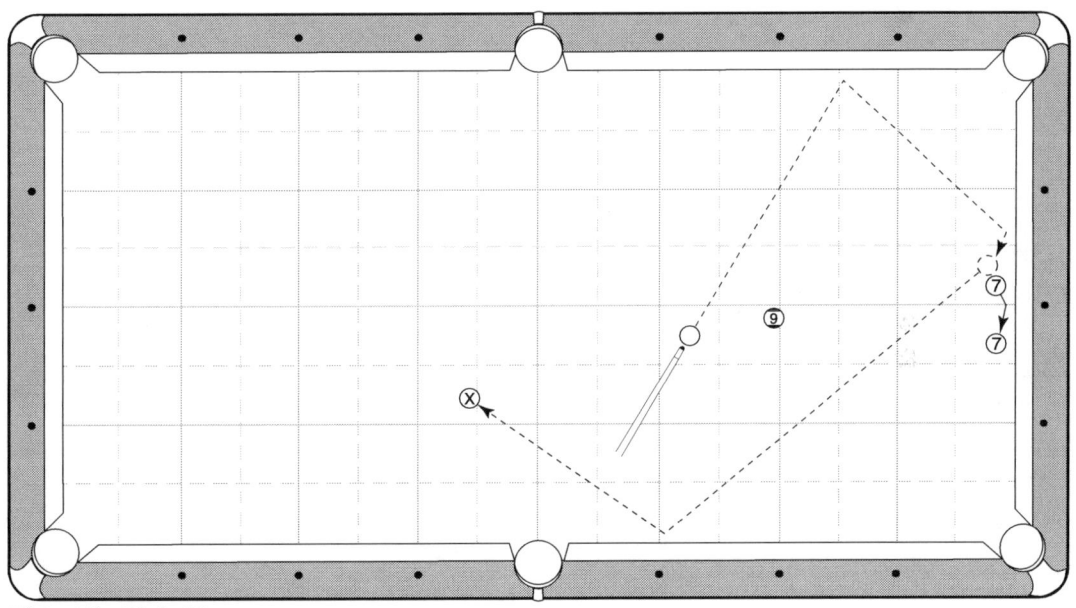

Thin Hit Kick Shot

This kick shot offers three basic choices: 1) you can try to pocket the 7-ball in the lower right corner pocket, 2) you can blast into the 7-ball and try to drive it up table, or 3) you could play the two rail thin hit safety shown in the diagram. The kick to pocket is a high risk shot that could easily result in a sellout. Blast and hope is a good choice if your kicking game is only average. **Soft kick safeties are for advanced players who are skilled at the kicking game**.

The margin for error on this safety is not very big, but it is still much larger than on the kick to pocket shot. Use a soft stroke, and be sure to hit the 7-ball thinly enough that you don't knock it in front of the pocket. And do not bail out in the other direction and miss the ball altogether, which is a common mistake on this safety.

Missing Safe (1/2 Safe, 1/2 Shot)

Missing a shot is not a pleasing thought, but the realities of pool dictate that you must allow for a miss when playing difficult shots. **If, during your planning process, you build in the possibility of a miss, you give yourself two chances to win the game**: with the shot or a safety. The Two Way Shots (1/2 Safe, 1/2 Shot) that we'll be covering are on the 9 and 10 ball even though they can be used at any time. Amateurs will find them particularly valuable during the end game when one to three balls are on the table.

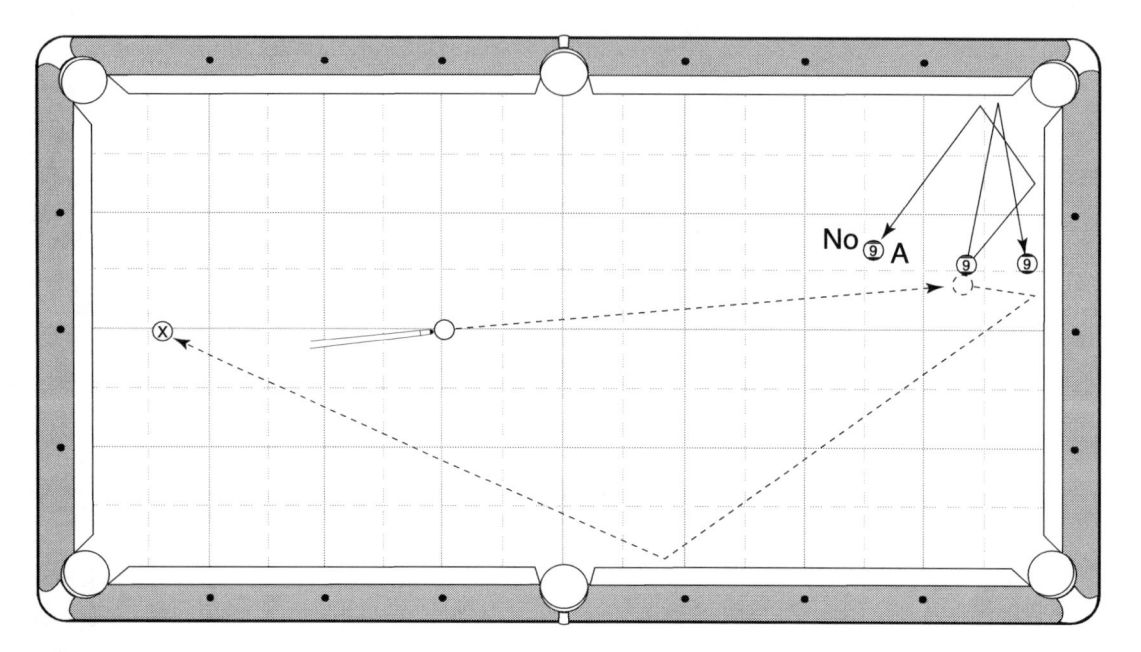

Overcut to Miss Safe

Suppose your opponent left you with a long thin cut shot like this on the 9-ball. You can stack the odds in your favor by aiming to miss the shot just a shade above the pocket as shown. If you hit the shot as planned, you'll leave your opponent in a bind. If you cut the shot more than you planned, you should still leave him safe. And, if you undercut the shot, the 9-ball will disappear into the pocket! In short, it's heads you win, tails you win!

If you play to make the 9-ball and fail to cut the shot enough, which is a common mistake on thin cut shots, the 9-ball will rebound two rails to Position A, leaving your opponent with a shot. The diagram shows the cue ball's path when outside (right) english was used. If you prefer to use a shade of inside (left) english, the cue ball will return to about the same location, only it will travel down the middle of the table.

Miss Short Rail Banks on the Pro Side

This 20-degree backcut short rail bank is not difficult, but it is also no sure thing. So **your best bet is to aim slightly above the pocket**. When you miss this way and the 10-ball stops at Position A, you have missed it on the "pro side," and you have not left a shot. A miss on the amateur side would leave your opponent with a shot on the 10-ball at Position B.

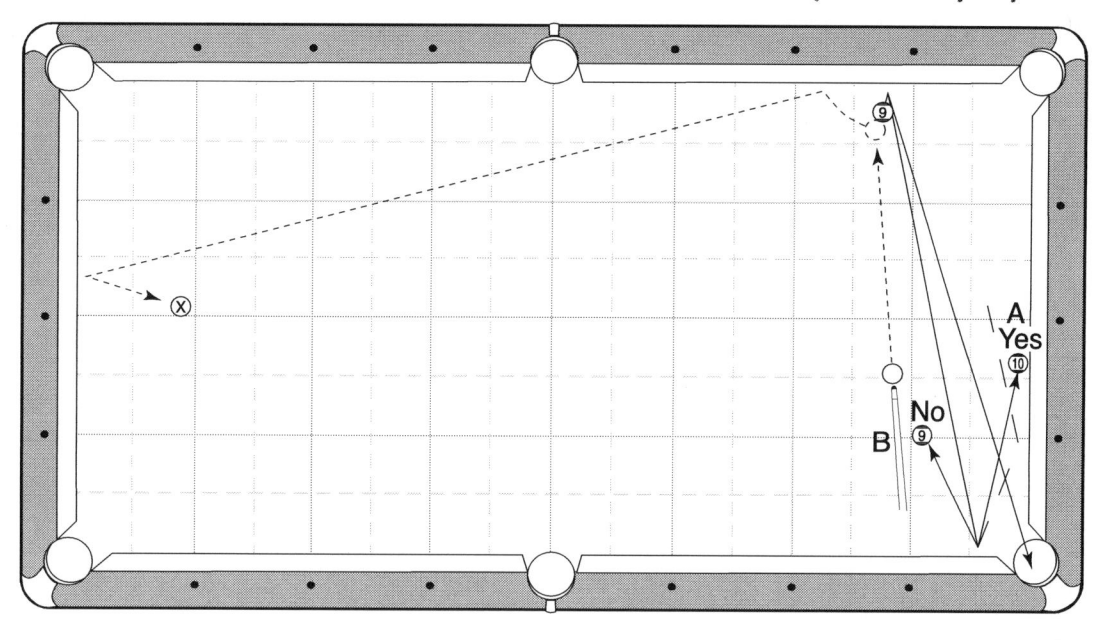

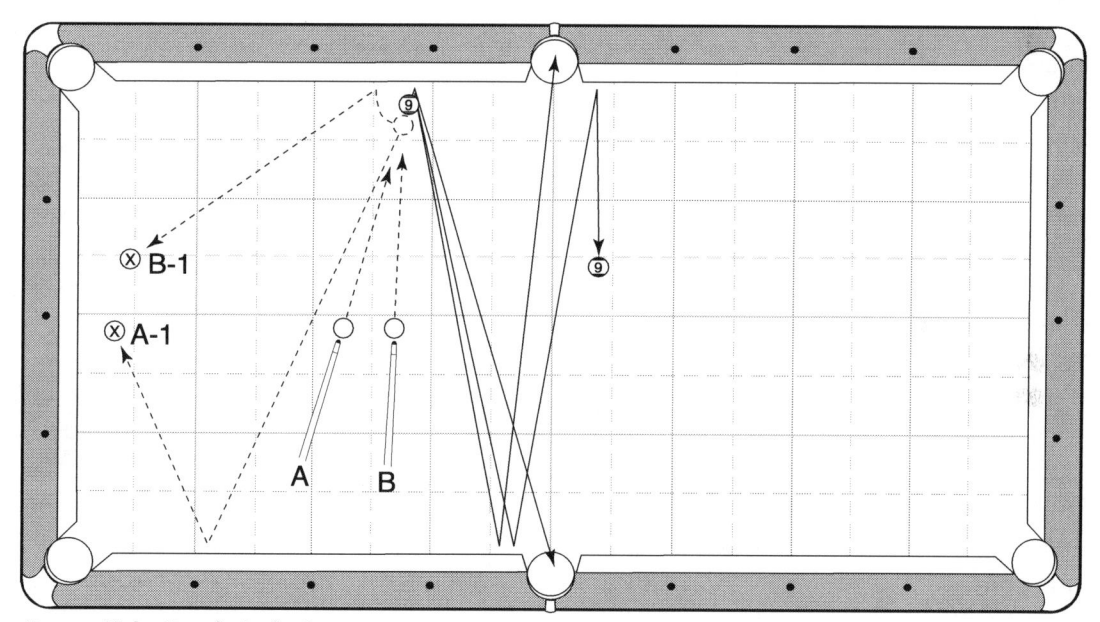

Cross Side Bank Safeties

This is the kind of bank you expect to make most of the time. If you are uncomfortable with the rails or your bank shots are off, you can build a safety into the shot. Use a hard draw stroke when the cue ball is in Position A to pull it back to Position A-1. When the cue ball is in Position B, use a hard stun/follow stroke to send it to Position B-1.

If you play this bank a little short of the side pocket, you give yourself three chances to win: 1) bank it straight in, 2) make it in the opposite side pocket, and 3) leave your opponent with a tough shot.

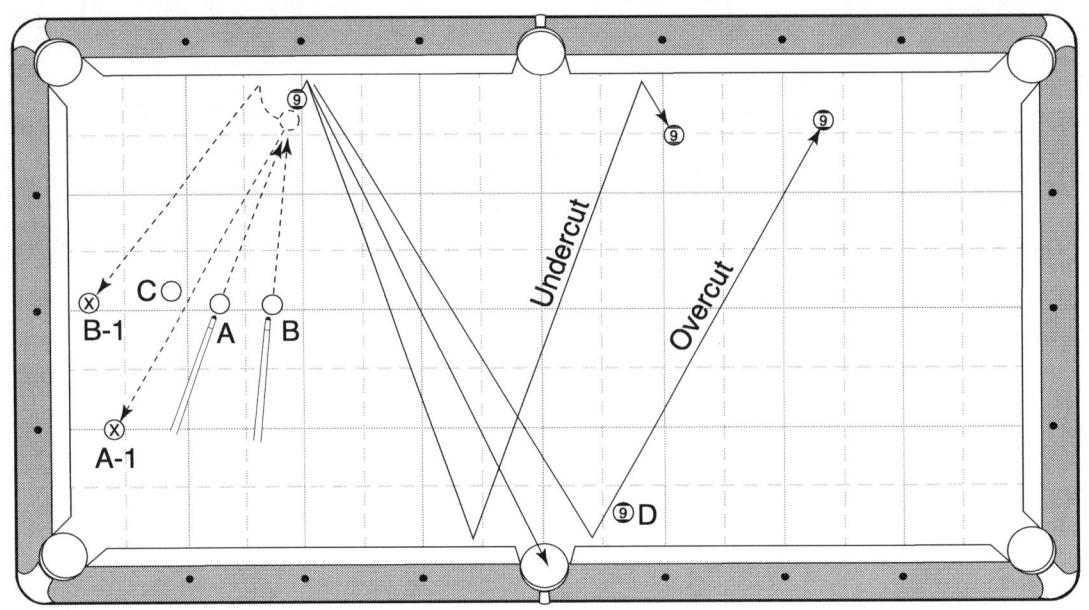

Cross Side Safety Bank
On certain banks you will want to shoot for the pocket even if you could leave your opponent with a shot if you miss. With the cue ball in Position A, most players at the C Player level or better would make this bank upwards of 40-50 percent of the time while pros might make it on 80 percent of their attempts. Your primary goal is to pocket the ball, and a secondary objective is to leave your opponent with a difficult shot should you miss. The 9-ball will land closer to the middle of the table if you undercut the shot, so this miss is preferable to missing long.

You can also make things tough by sending the cue ball to the end rail. When the cue ball is in Position A, draw back to Position A-1. With the cue ball in Position B, a follow shot will send it to B-1.

When the cue ball is too far to the left of a full hit, as in Position C, you can no longer play safe by sending the cue ball to the end rail. Play the bank with a soft draw stroke and a half tip or more of inside (right) english. Your goal is to make the ball or miss to the far side of the side pocket. You want the cue ball on the top rail near the point of contact, and the 9-ball at Position D, leaving your opponent in a very difficult position.

Missing Long Rail Banks on the Pro Side
The diagram at the top of the next page shows a long rail bank. **Many players fear long rail bank shots because they believe these shots will result in a sell out when missed. But such is not the case if you miss on the pro side**, and you maintain control of the cue ball. Notice that the cue ball stopped on the bottom side rail, indicating that the shot was hit with the proper speed.

The biggest factor in playing a long rail bank Shot/Safety is the location of the object ball. The 10-ball in Position A gives your opponent a relatively tough cut shot. Position B is even better because he now has no reasonable chance to win the game. The 10-ball in Position C is a sellout, which occurred because the bank hit the side rail first on its way down the table.

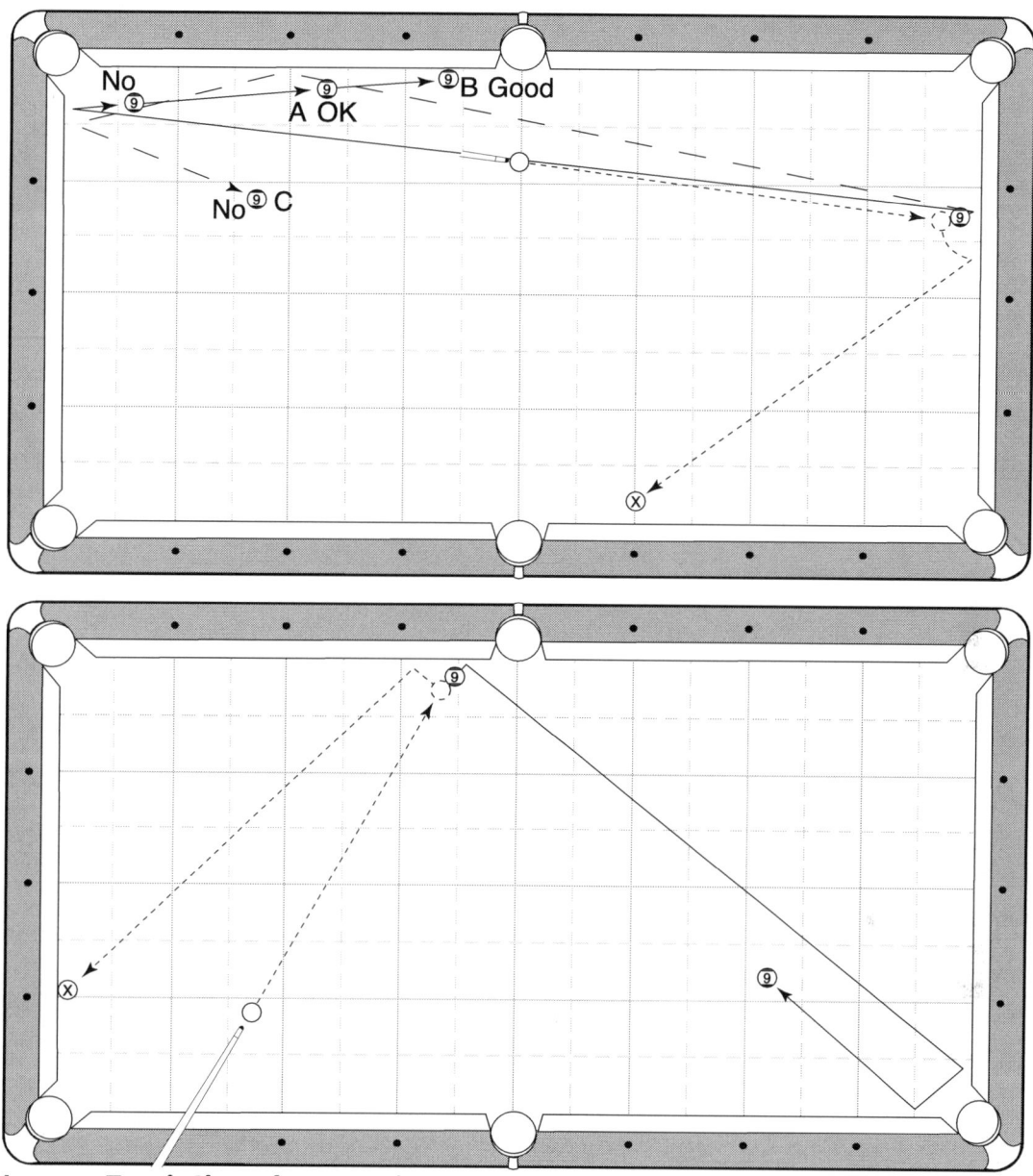

Leave a Tough Shot after a Bank

We've seen that superb cue ball control can swing the odds heavily in your favor, even after a missed shot. Now we'll advance that concept to the ultimate degree with this offensive/defensive super shot, which Johnny Archer executed in a match against Nick Varner at the 1991 World Championships.

Varner had just missed the 9-ball, but he left Archer in a jam. Archer responded by going for a difficult cross table bank. Even though he missed by a couple of inches, he did two things that kept him in the game: 1) he hit the bank with enough speed that it exited the vicinity of the corner pocket, and 2) he demonstrated exceptional control over the cue ball's distance and direction. Varner missed the shot from the end rail, but he eventually won the game and the match.

End Game

The end game typically begins when there are three or fewer balls on the table. A high percentage of games between amateurs are won and lost in the end game because of missed shots and positional errors. Once a game gets down to the last three balls, there is an impulse to go for it among most players. But **the end game is a time when games can be won with smart safeties rather than spectacular shots no matter what your level of play**.

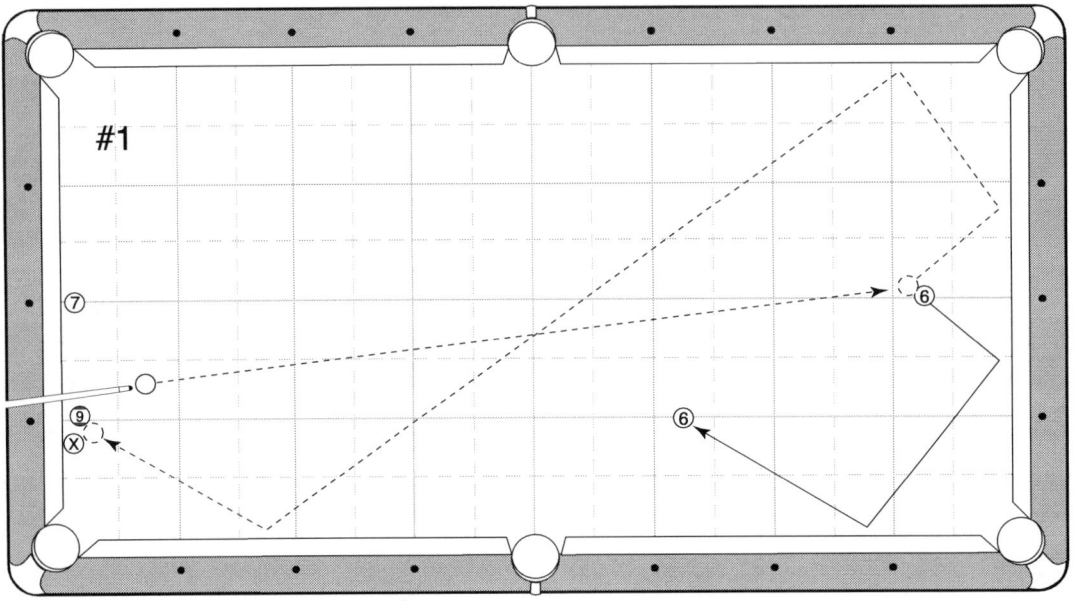

Long Distance End Game Warfare

Pro players relish the opportunity to engage in some end game warfare. Shannon Daulton, who was pitted against Kim Davenport at the 1999 U.S. Open, faced what looked like a do or die shot on the 6-ball in Diagram #1. Rather than take a flyer on the 6-ball, he purposefully left Davenport a difficult shot as shown. Daulton felt confident in his chances of returning to the table because he knew that running the last three balls would be an incredibly difficult chore for any player — even a top pro like Davenport. Daulton came up with a safety that is not obvious to most observers until after it has been played. His execution was perfect as he left the cue ball snuggled up against the end rail.

Davenport's response is displayed in Diagram #2 on the next page. He failed to take the bait and opted for a crafty two-rail bank safety that left the 6-ball near one end rail, and the cue ball close to the other. This game of cat and mouse continued for another four innings before Davenport came out on top. He went on to finish in fourth place in the event.

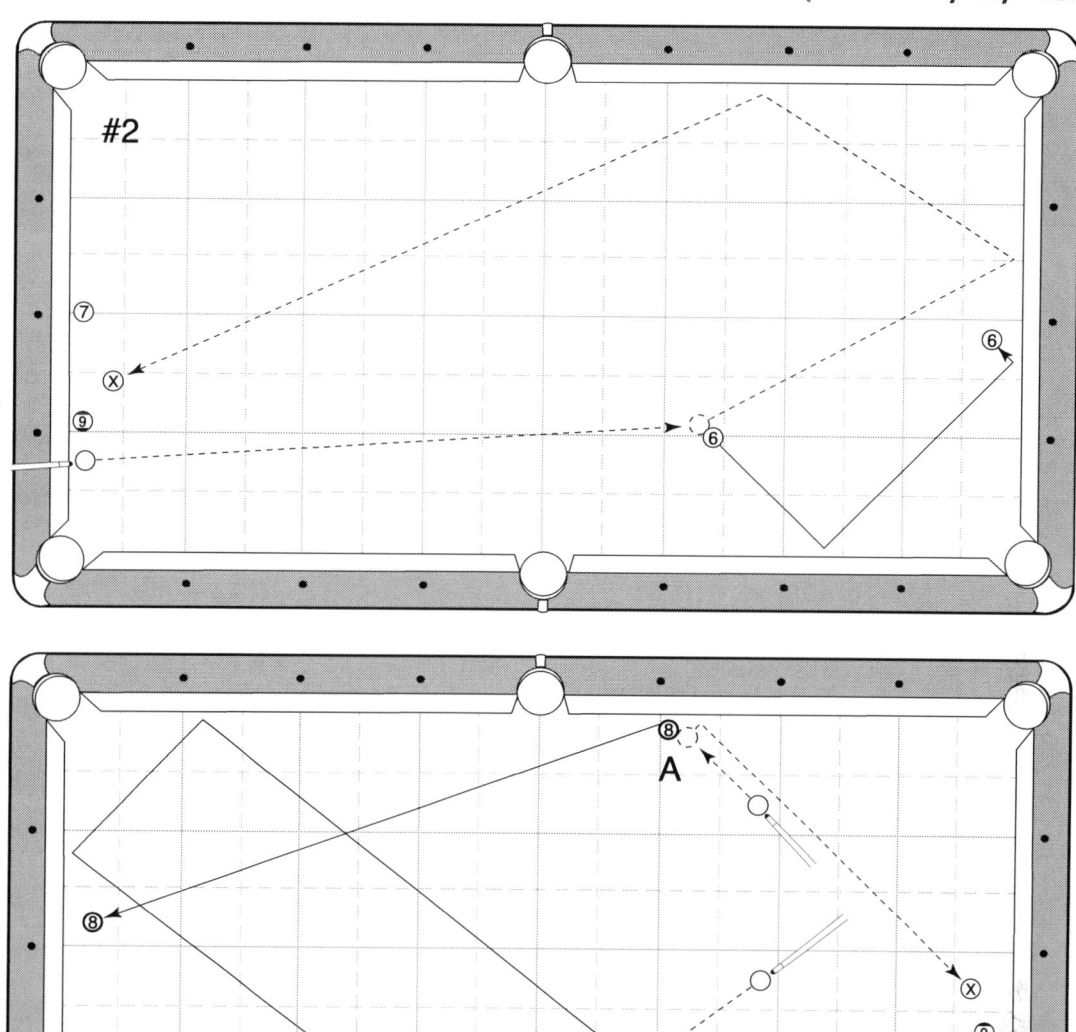

Two End Game Bank Safeties

Here are two end game safeties. You could attempt to end the game in Position A with a 48-degree cut past the point of the side pocket. A more conservative approach is to bank the 8-ball down table. Now your opponent is forced to beat you. This is better than handing over the game, which would have likely happened if you had missed the cut shot.

There is no offensive shot in Position B, but the balls are lying perfectly for a four-rail safety. This 9-ball must be hit squarely with a very hard stroke. It is nearly impossible to hit this shot too hard because the 9-ball will slow down quickly after it hits the fourth rail. **When you are in a tough spot during the end of a game, take a moment and let your creative juices flow**. Perhaps you'll discover a bank safety like these that can turn the odds back in your favor.

Strategic Safeties

On many occasions you will face a very makeable shot and you will hear that little voice that urges you to run out. However, there could be a maneuver that can improve your odds of winning the game. **When you have ball in hand or are facing a shot where it will be tough to get on the next ball, your best bet may be a strategic safety.**

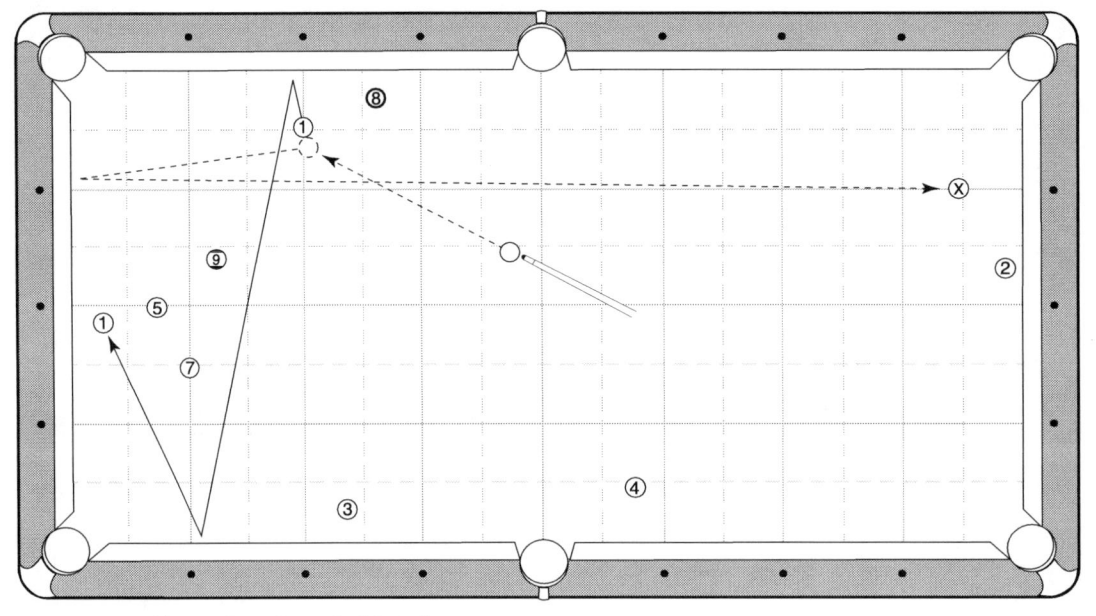

Pass on a Shot that Leads Nowhere

Pocketing the 1-ball is no problem, but getting shape on the 2-ball is very difficult thanks to the 8-ball, which blocks the position route. Even though shape is impossible, many players will still pocket the 1-ball, and only then will they stop to consider the 2-ball. This mistake is especially common among amateur players.

When you have a simple shot that leads nowhere, your must decide whether to play safe right away or to pocket the ball and then play safe. In our example, the move is to play safe right now, as shown, leaving a very difficult response. If you pocketed the 1-ball, it would be hard to then get close enough to the 2-ball to play an effective safety. Besides, if you pass on the first ball and play safe, your opponent will have one more ball to make if you do leave a shot.

Pass on Shot, Hook at Long Range

Earl Strickland, one of the straightest shooters to ever play the game, was faced with a long cross table shot on the 2-ball in a match against Efren Reyes at the Sands Regency Open 21, 1995. In a post-match interview Strickland confided that he was a little off his game, which explains why he chose to play a safety even though Reyes has the best kicking game in pool. The Lesson: **if a world champion can pass on an open shot, even if it would lead to shape on the next ball, so can you.** Amateur players should consider playing a safety like this at all times if: 1) they are not a particularly straight shooter, and 2) their opponent has a poor kicking game.

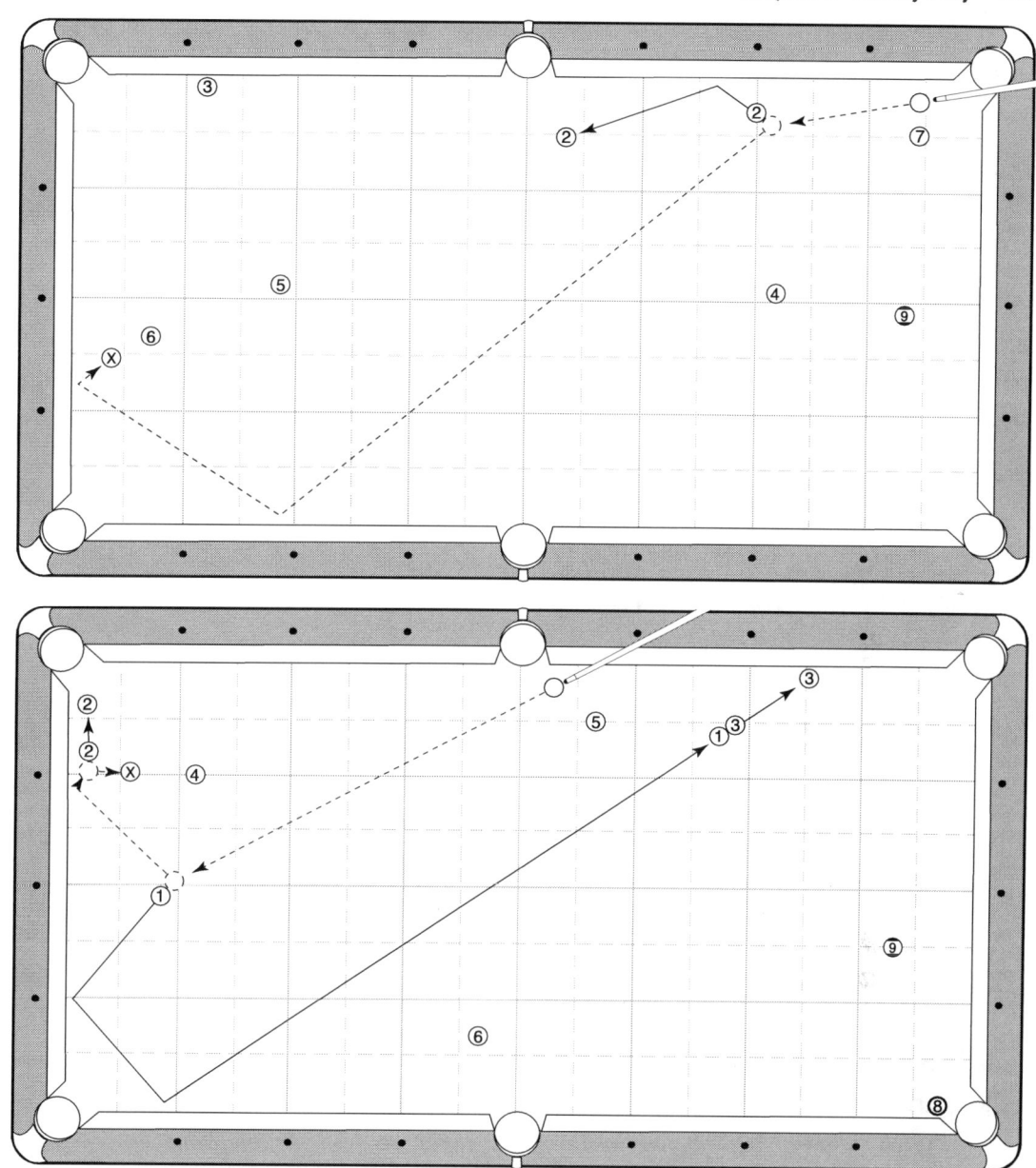

Pass on Shot for Sure Safe

After making a ball on the break, Kim Davenport was confronted with a lengthy shot on the 1-ball that would have to be played with a soft stroke and inside english. He wisely passed on the run out and instead played safe. A nearly full hit on the 1-ball with a medium hard stroke enabled him to slide the cue ball behind the 4-ball. The 2-ball helped to hold the cue ball in place. Davenport subsequently ran out in this match that took place at the 1999 U.S. Open. Once again, **if passing on an open shot is good enough for the pros, it is a strategy all players should consider.**

290   Chapter 9 - Safety Play

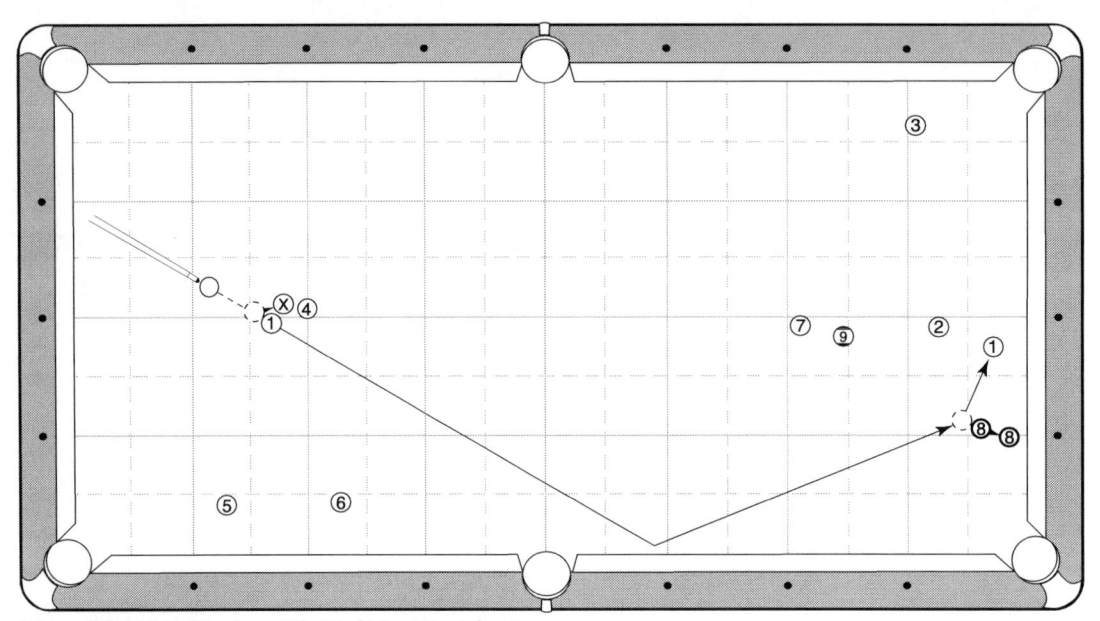

Simplify the Rack with Ball In Hand
When most players are awarded ball in hand, their first impulse is to set up a combo on the game ball, or to try to run out. However, it is often better to delay gratification and instead play a safety. Ball in hand enables you to get close to your work, exercise great control over the cue ball, and to achieve any number of strategic objectives while locking your opponent up tight.

Steve Mizerak employed this tactic by taking ball in hand and hooking his opponent behind the 4-ball, accomplishing his main objective of getting the 1-ball close to the 2-ball and simplifying the runout. He then ran out after Earl Strickland missed the hit on a difficult kick shot. This action took place at the 1994 U.S. Open.

Leave Shots Your Opponent Doesn't Like
Effective safeties do not always require that you hide the cue ball. Thin cuts, banks, shots off the rail, and long shots pose a problem for any player, much less an amateur who is not a consistently straight shooter.

The decision to leave a tough shot is based on your knowledge of the difficulty of the shot, your opponent's game, and his tendencies. The timing for employing this strategy can also be influenced by the situation. A big factor to consider is his ability to respond to the challenge and to pocket difficult shots under the heat, particularly at the end of a close contest.

The illustration shows three shots that can bring out your opponent's worst form. The 1-ball is a table length 76-degree cut shot. If this shot was on the 9-ball, it would be plenty tough, but if he had to make this and play shape on anything but a hanger, then his odds of winning drop even lower.

The cut on the 3-ball is only 30 degrees, but this shot is a monster thanks to the cue ball's position on the end rail. The 5-ball keeps the 2-ball from being played in the upper left corner pocket. This 41-degree cut is a very tough shot because of the distance and the fact that most players rarely play cross table cuts.

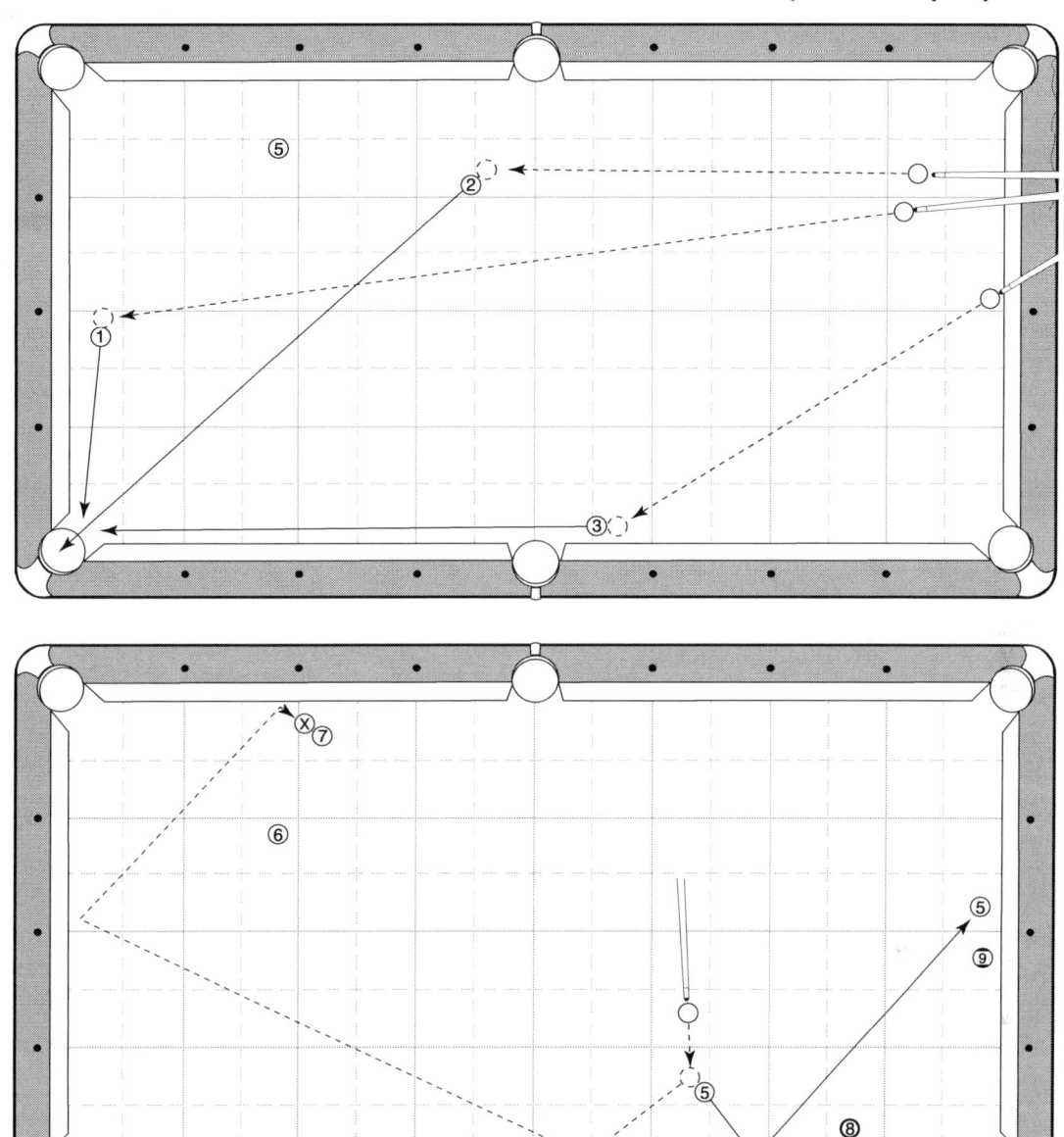

Set Up Combo on the 9-Ball

Steve Mizerak again showed his skill in the safety game at the 1994 U. S. Open when he tied up his opponent while, at the time, setting up an easy 5-9 combo. On his next turn he was well rewarded for his maneuver and his exquisite long range cue ball control with an easy win. The big key to this safety was routing the cue ball with perfect speed up next to the 7-ball. He was also able to send the 5-ball into perfect position for an easy combo. With ball-in-hand on his next shot, Mizerak would have still had a simple five ball runout even if the 5-ball had stopped short of the position in the diagram.

Creative Safety Play

After you have played 9 Ball for some time and have really studied the safety game, your arsenal of weapons should enable you to handle 90 percent of the situations that require a safety. Still, there will be times when your knowledge of safety play and of how the balls interact will be put to the test. So, **when you find yourself in an unfamiliar position take a few extra moments to see if you can conjure up a creative solution** rather than settling for a safety that you just know is less than your best.

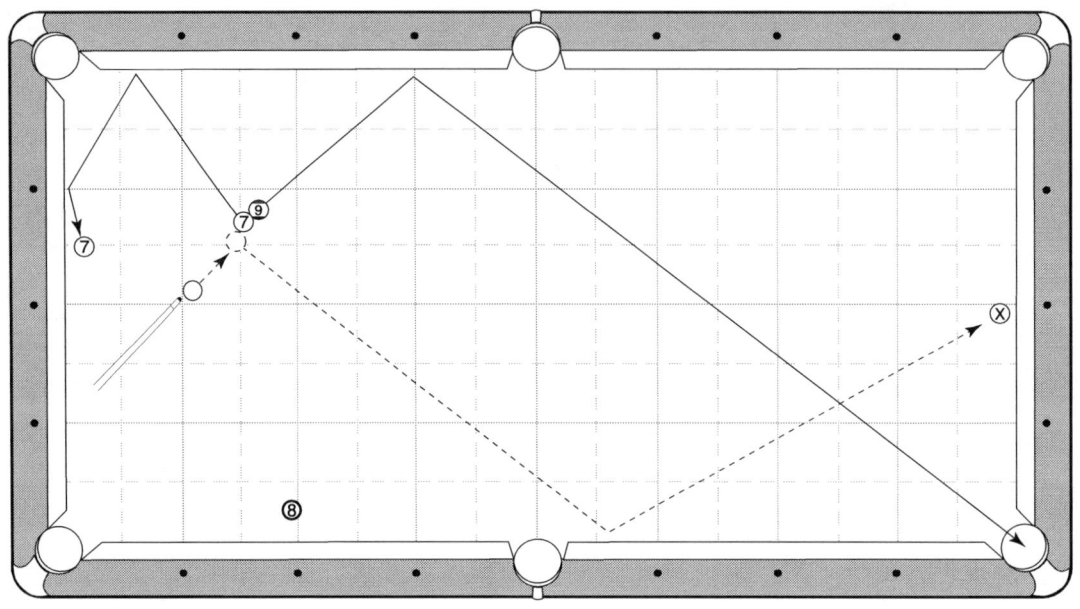

Imagination Creates a Winning Safety

I was faced with this bleak looking position after I missed position by a mile on the 7-ball. After a long inspection, I finally concluded that the 7-ball could be caromed off the 9-ball and sent to the end rail. The shot had to be struck rather firmly, so the problem was to keep the cue ball from returning back down the table. My solution was to go against my instincts and play a draw shot with inside english. The full hit neutralized the cue ball's speed and the spin sent it along a path to the opposite end rail. As a bonus, the 9-ball continued into the lower right hand corner pocket! My opponent cried about my luck, but **you are often rewarded with good fortune when you execute a shot exactly as planned**.

Grady's Near Masterpiece

Grady Matthews was faced with the task of computing a response to a lucky kick shot by Buddy Hall at the Sands Regency Open 15, 1992. Mathews drew on his extensive knowledge and composed this super creative safety. The 3-ball traveled about 18 feet to the middle of the table while the cue ball rolled to a stop a long distance from the 3-ball. As luck would have it, the cue ball stopped 2 inches short of a hook. Hall pocketed the difficult cross table cut on the 3-ball and ran out. Still this was a great safety that would have won the game most of the time from 99.99 percent of all other pool players on the planet.

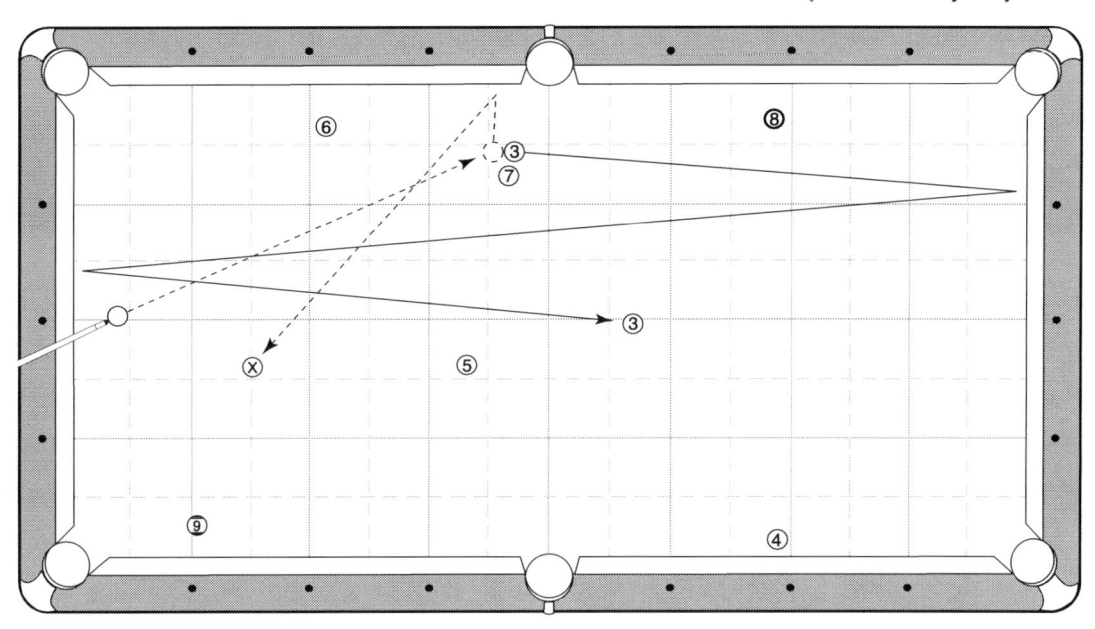

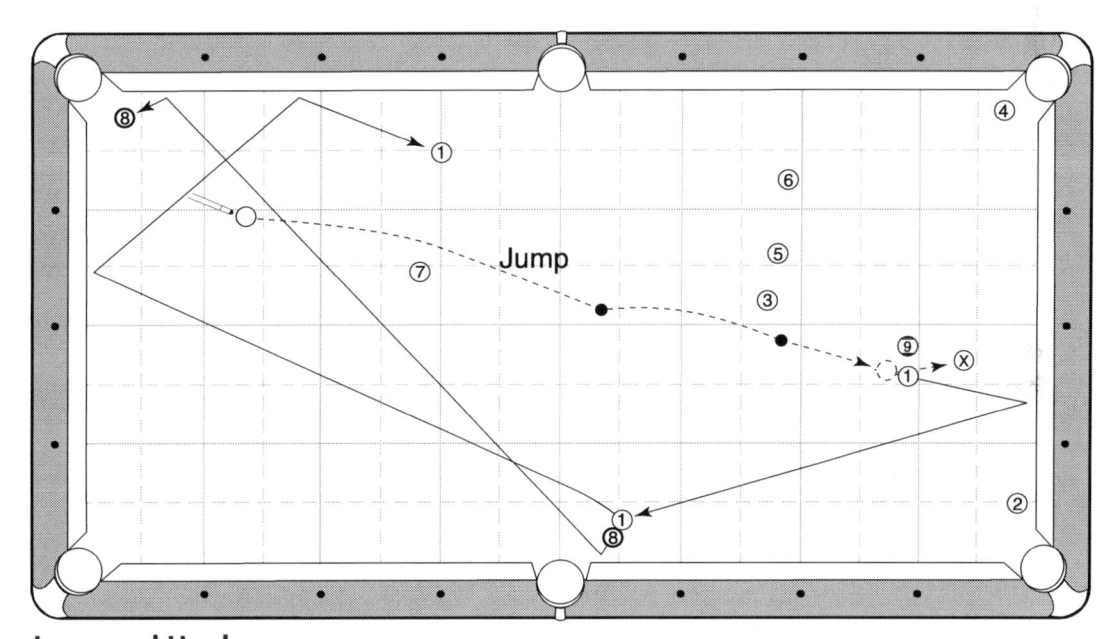

Jump and Hook

Loree Jon Jones left Allison Fisher hooked behind the 7-ball at the 1999 WPBA Prescott Resort Classic. The 8-ball blocked the natural kick route to the 1-ball and the 2-ball took away the two-rail path. Ms. Fisher could have aimed below the 8-ball at the third diamond on the side rail and played a kick shot with a hard stroke and draw, but this is a very difficult way of hitting the 1-ball. Her creative solution was to jack up to 60-degrees and send the cue ball skyward. It hopped twice and struck the 1-ball solidly, driving it up the table. Meanwhile, the cue ball drifted to a stop behind a row of blockers!

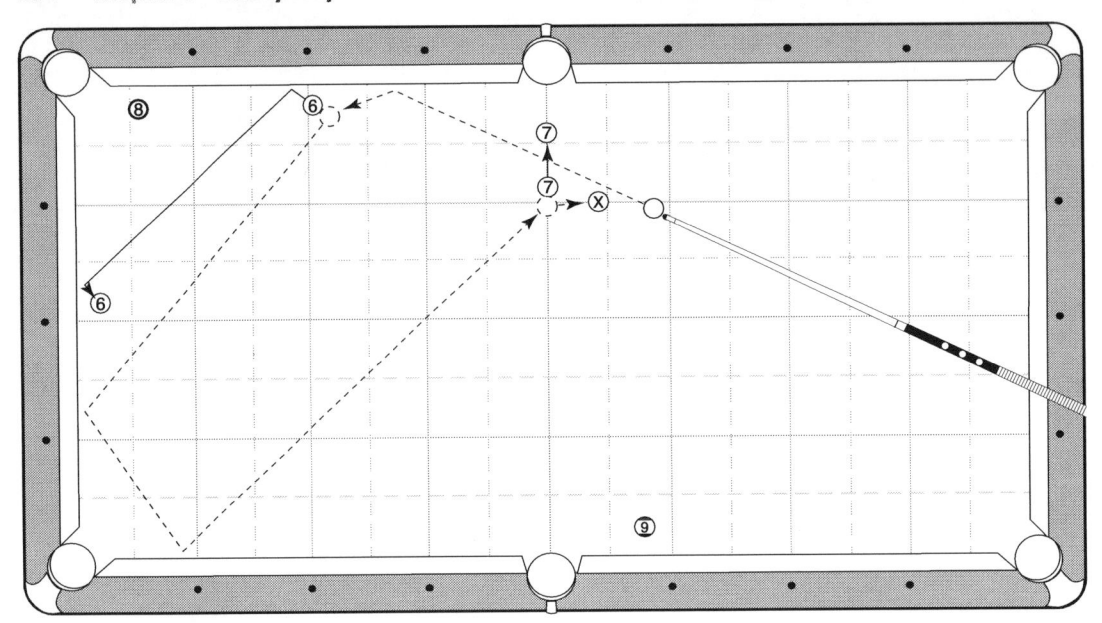

Rail First Safety

Keith McCready played this creative safety against Nick Varner at the Sands Regency Open 12, 1990. Rather than slugging away at the kick shot, McCready played a finesse safety by hitting the 6-ball thinly after contacting the top side rail. Running english (left) accelerated the cue ball off the second and third rails and down to Position X, leaving Varner with a difficult bank or safety.

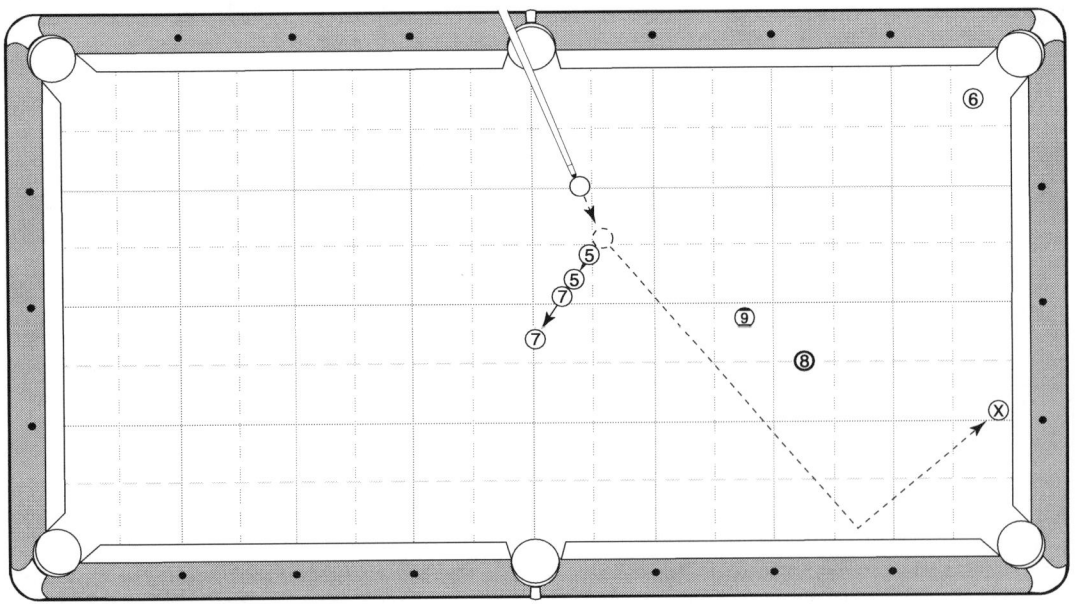

Use a Second Ball as a Stopper

You normally should be a little concerned with the object ball's ending location when you are attempting to hook your opponent on most safeties. Such is not the case when **a stopper ball can be used to hold the object ball in place after contact**. In the example, your energies can go towards sending the cue ball to Position X, which is on the opposite side of the 8 and 9 balls from the 5-ball.

CHAPTER 10

The Kicking Game

"I get more satisfaction out of a great kick shot than I do out of running the table."
Allison Fisher

A kick shot is played by banking the cue ball off of one or more cushions before it contacts the lowest numbered ball. Kick shots can appear when: 1) you are hooked after the break, 2) your opponent got lucky after a miss, 3) your opponent played a safety, and 4) you make a mistake playing position and hook yourself. You are going to be constantly facing kick shots so a strong kicking game is a vital skill in 9-Ball.

A kick shot must hit the lowest numbered ball and then drive either an object ball or the cue ball to a rail. Failure to meet these requirements is a foul, and it results in ball in hand for your opponent. This rule encourages safety play. In fact, excellent safeties are now being played by amateurs at the C Player (average) level and above.

If your kicking skills are not up to par, your opponents will take advantage of this deficiency by hitting you with an endless barrage of safeties. After all, why should they take a chance on a moderately risky shot when they feel certain that a safety will result in ball in hand? Hopefully this discussion is motivating you to hone your kicking skills. If not, you'll discover the incentive after losing enough matches to players who are beating you with hook safeties even though you are superior to them most facets of the game!

The luck factor is an inherent part of all but the easiest of kick shots. This disturbs many players. When faced with a kick shot, those with a negative attitude towards kicking prefer to bemoan their fate, so they play kick shots in a halfhearted manner. When you come up against one of these types, you've got the green light to safety them into submission.

Your Attitude Toward Kicking

I advise that you **adopt an attitude of positive expectancy as you prepare for a kick shot**. If you plan wisely and execute the shot to the best of your ability, good things will happen often enough to justify your efforts. A sense of fascination should accompany every kick shot. I like to think of them as a golfer does when he is preparing for a putt outside of "gimme" (can't miss) range. A golfer knows he may not make the putt, especially if it is longer than 10 feet. But that doesn't stop him from giving the longer putts his best effort. So, try approaching kick shots with the same attitude: plan the shot as well as you can, give it a good go, and be pleasantly surprised when the shot turns out the way you wanted it to.

Convince yourself that kicking is not punishment handed down by the Pool Gods. Enjoy the challenge, and try to make something good happen. Don't just go through the motions while expecting the worst.

When you execute a devastating kick shot in response to your opponent's safety or lucky leave, the effect can be devastating. After all, they were expecting ball in hand. Act as though you expected to lock him up. This tactic could unnerve him and get him to wondering how he can beat someone who kicks like Efren Reyes!

The #1 Basic Requirement

The #1 basic requirement of the kicking game is the ability to consistently make contact with the object ball. If you hit the ball and drive it or the cue ball to a rail without scratching, you have a chance for something good to happen. From this point on, skill at kicking becomes increasingly complex. Among the extras that add depth to your kicking game are: 1) kicking with the proper speed, 2) kicking to hit a certain side of the ball, and 3) kicking to meet a specific strategic objective.

"You can't get lucky if you miss it." **Pat Fleming**

The Possible Outcome – How You View a Kick Shot

Kick shots almost always carry a more uncertain outcome than shots in which you are aiming directly at a ball, including position plays and safeties. Because of this, you should at times incorporate your feelings about the possible outcome into the planning process. This will free you up to give it your best effort, and you won't fret so much about the outcome when it does not go in your favor.

A Game Plan for the Kicking Game

The concepts below will help you in developing a solid approach to the kicking game. This game plan is based on playing the percentages as much as possible, as opposed to just pounding away and hoping for the best.

Build a Solid Foundation
Construct a solid foundation by mastering the basic concepts and kick routes that you will encounter most often.

Your Style
Most kick routes can be played without using english. Still, many players are more comfortable applying a little running english to most of their kick shots.

Your Goals Will Change
A new players' goal is to hit the ball. As your skills progress, you can adopt more sophisticated kicks, goals, and strategies.

The Conditions
Playing conditions can have a large effect on the kicking game. With enough experience and attention to detail, you will learn how to quickly adjust to the table.

Early Versus Late Game Strategy
Kick battles are most common early in the game when blockers abound. You will likely have to adopt a different approach to kicking in the later stages of a rack.

The Main Objective
On most kick shots your objective is to play a safety. However, when the object ball is directly in front of a pocket, or it is very close to the cushion in a big ball position, pocketing the kick could become your primary goal.

Kicking Battles
Kick/safety battles can last several innings, so be mentally prepared to battle long and hard for control of the table. If your opponent is a skillful kicker, it doesn't hurt to appreciate his artistry, and to learn from his shots!

Speed Control is Crucial
Speed control is a critical component on most kick shots. Still, there are those rare occasions when the blast and pray approach is your best choice.

Play the Percentages
There are few certainties when playing most kick shots. The idea is to stack the odds as much as possible in your favor.

Basics of Kicking
The Importance of Speed Control
The two main components to a kick shot are the route and speed of stroke. When playing a kick shot, hitting the ball and avoiding a foul is usually not good enough by itself – the shot must also meet a specific strategic objective. This is accomplished with the hit on the object ball and your speed of stroke. Later in the chapter are kicks that range from a very soft stroke (a 2 on the Spectrum of Speeds) all of the way to those that are hit with an extremely hard stroke (a 9).

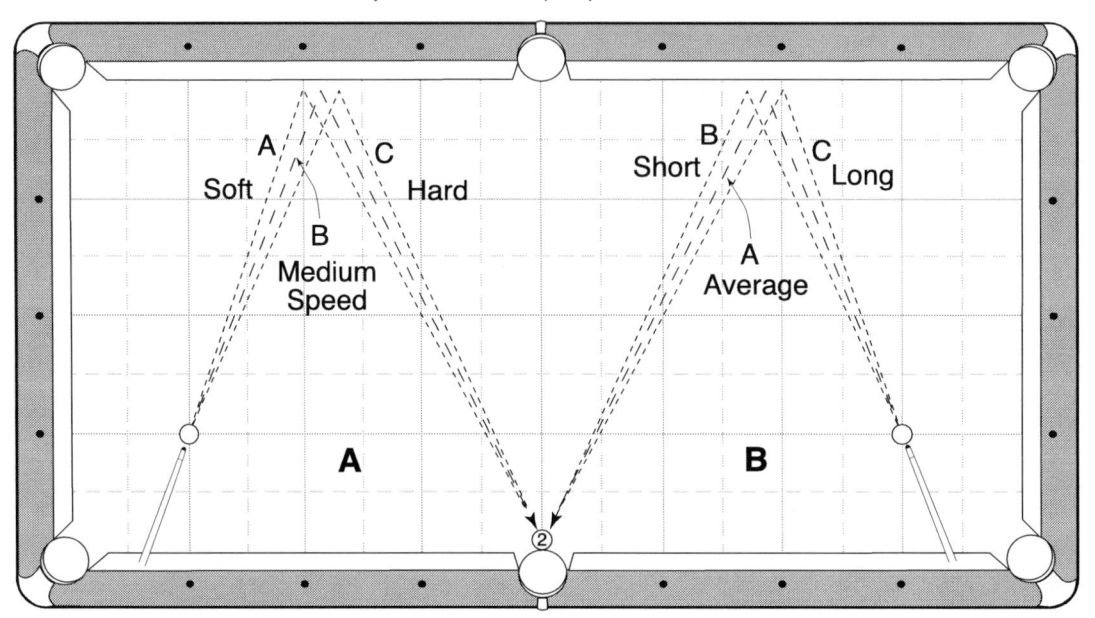

Adjusting for Speed and the Table
Speed has a significant impact on the cue ball's rebound angle on kick shots. Part A shows its rebound path at three very different speeds of stroke. A soft stroke will send the cue ball into the rail and out towards the 2-ball down Path A. The cue ball will rebound at a sharper angle when hit with a medium speed of stroke, as shown by Path B. The sharpest rebound angle is created by a hard stroke, which leads to Path C. The goal is to hit the 2-ball with each kick shot, but the aiming line must accommodate each speed of stroke.

Similar adjustments are made when you are playing on unfamiliar tables. In Part B, every kick was hit at the same speed. Route A shows the cue ball's path on your "average" table. If a table banks "short," your kick shot will travel down a shallower path than you expected, or are used to. You must compensate for this by aiming further down the rail, as shown by Route B. A table plays "long" if the cue ball rebounds at a wider angle than normal. In this case, you need to adjust your aim to hit the first rail closer than usual. Route C demonstrates how to compensate for a table that plays long.

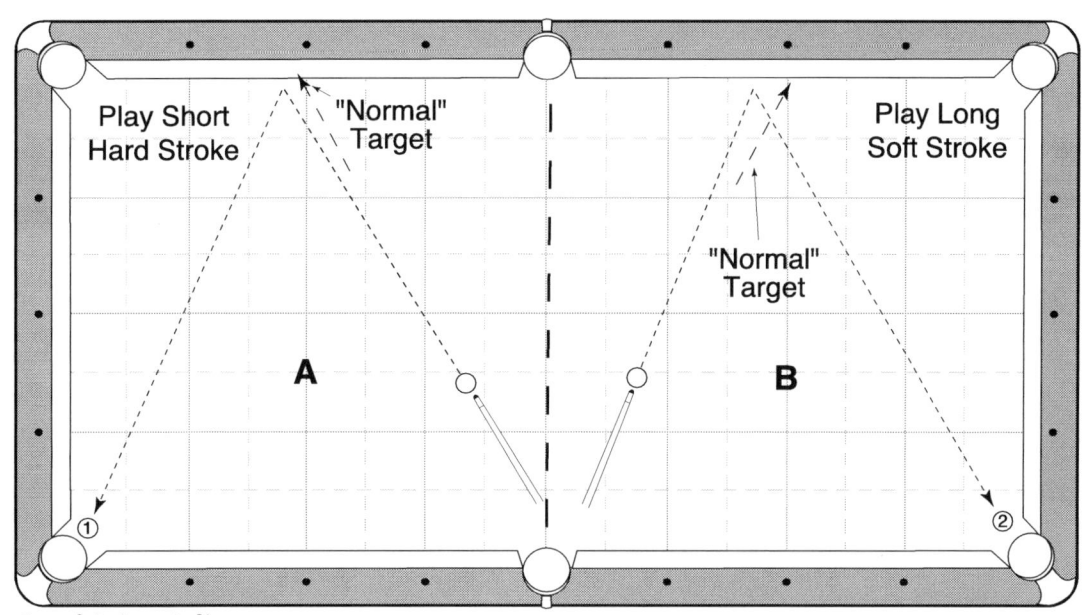

Combining Adjustments

We've talked about how to make a single adjustment for speed of stroke, and one for the table. When **in actual play, you must often make multiple adjustments**. Sometimes these adjustments may cancel each other out. For example, if a table plays long, you can offset this with a hard stroke. And, if a table plays short, you could cancel this by using a softer stroke than normal.

Most of the time, however, you will not have the luxury of matching the speed of stroke to the table. For example, even if a table plays short, it might not be practical to use a soft stroke on a certain kick shot. Remember, **you are usually better off playing a kick shot at the speed that the shot calls for**. If a table plays short and the kick calls for a hard stroke, you must aim well past the normal point of aim to compensate for both the table and the hard stroke. This is shown by Part A of the diagram above. The aiming equation is reversed in Part B. When a table plays long and you are using a soft stroke, you will have to aim much further towards the near side of the rail to allow for both the table and the soft stroke.

How to Adjust to the Table

Shot Requirements	Table Plays	Do This
Hard stroke	Long	Aim normally (cancel out)
Hard stroke	Short	Aim very long
Soft stroke	Long	Aim very short
Soft stroke	Short	Aim normally (cancel out)
Medium stroke	Long	Aim short
Medium stroke	Short	Aim long

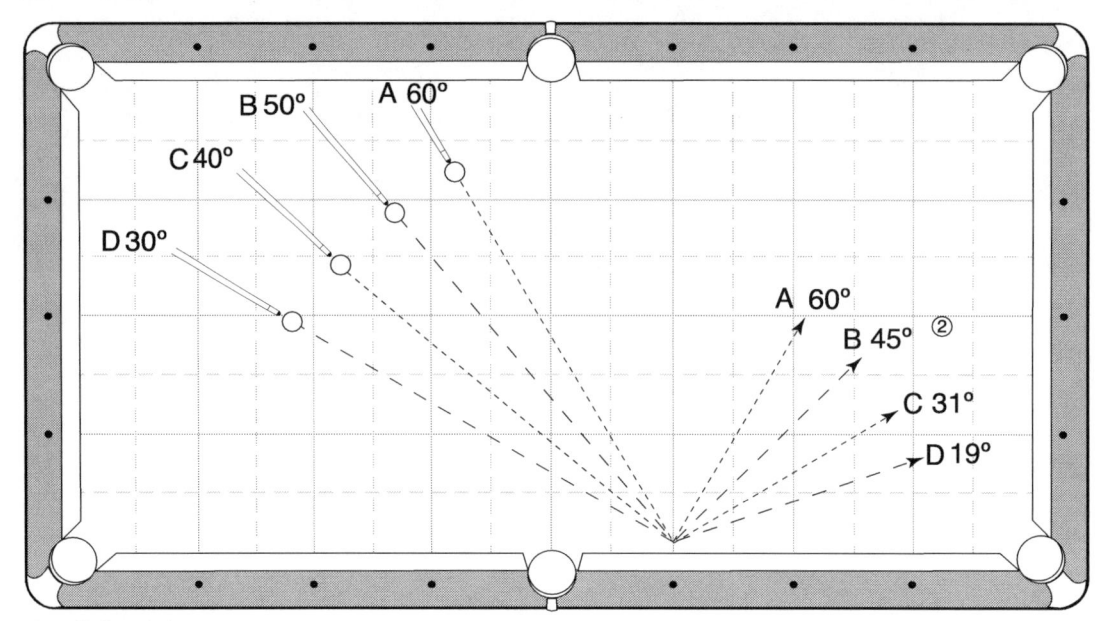

English Pickup

"The angle of incidence equals the angle of reflection" is a fancy way of saying that the cue ball rebounds from the rail at the same angle at which it entered the rail. While this may be true some of the time, on most occasions there is a (sometimes large) difference in the two angles.

When the cue ball enters the rail at a 60-degree angle down Route A, it rebounds at the same angle when shot with a medium speed. **When the entrance angle dips below 60 degrees, the cue ball starts to rebound at a shallower angle**. The cue ball on Route B entered the rail at 50-degrees and exited at only 45-degrees thanks to a slight pickup of english off the side rail. In Route C the cue ball entered at 40 degrees and exited at only 30 degrees. Finally, the cue ball on Route D entered the rail at 30 degrees and departed at only 19 degrees.

English pickup is the main reason why so many players have trouble kicking at balls in the middle of the table. The tendency is to miss on the far side of the ball because of a failure to adjust for the natural opening of the rebound angle. In the example, a player kicking for the 2-ball from Position C would have a tendency to miss the ball on the far side.

Testing a Table

Before you begin a match, take a few moments to run a few tests that can inform you of how a table is playing. You'll want to run these tests on unfamiliar equipment, but also consider conducting them on the table(s) you play on regularly as conditions do change thanks to humidity, temperature, and the aging of the cloth.

Illustration #1 shows a couple of kick routes that can alert you to the current playing conditions. Route A is a common three-rail kick route that was played with a medium speed and a half tip of follow. No english was used. The cue ball will travel directly toward the corner pocket on a so-called "average" table. If the table is playing short, the cue ball will strike the side rail first. And, if the table is playing long, it will hit the end rail first. If the table is playing long or short, adjust your point of aim and try the kick again. Keep adjusting until you make the ball.

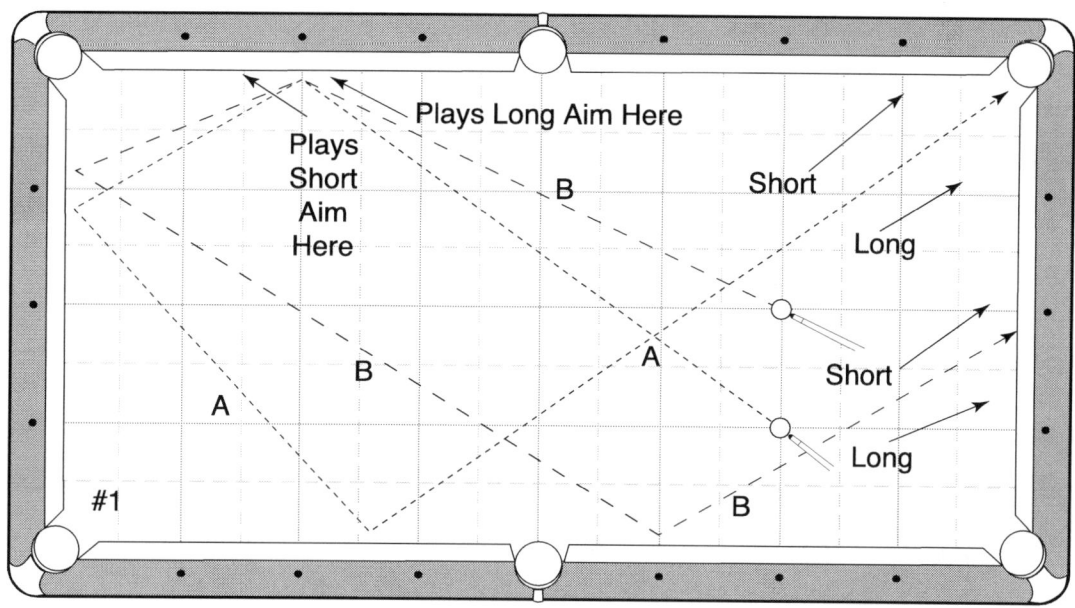

Route B is played with a medium speed and half tip of follow. The cue ball should strike the fourth rail a few inches from the middle diamond. If the cue ball hits to either side, make an adjustment and try again until you are hitting the target.

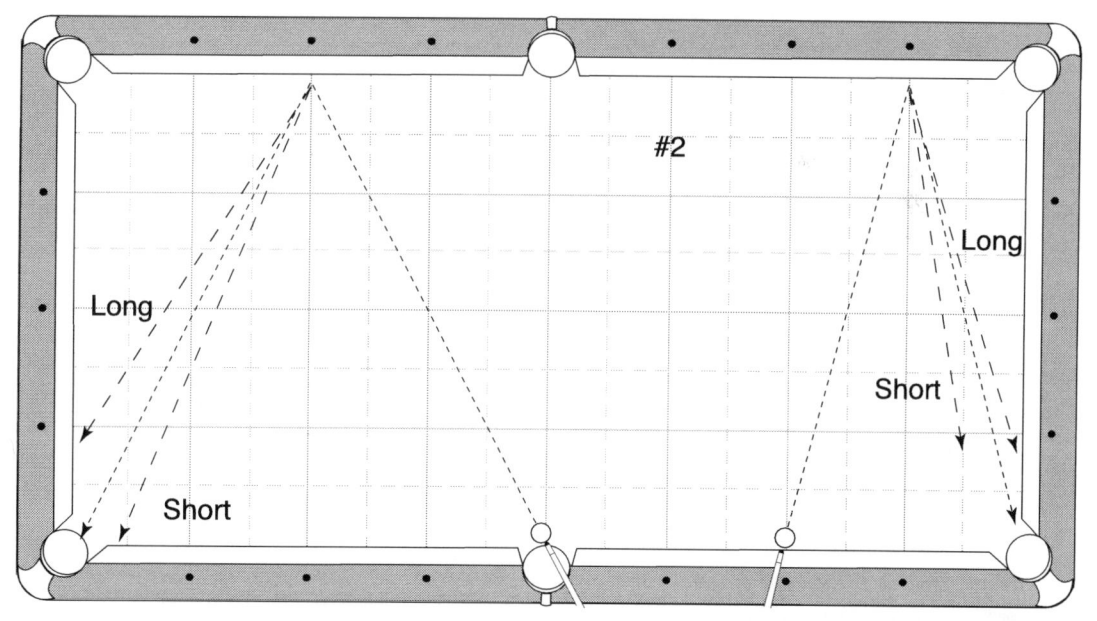

Illustration #2 gives you two additional tests that will only take a few moments to run, but that could make the difference between winning and losing.

The ABCs of Kicking Targets
An accurate assessment of your level of skill can help you make better decisions and be useful in managing your expectations. The first step is to rate your current level of skill at the kicking game using the ABC rating scale below. Remember, an A Player is an expert, a B Player is at the intermediate (advanced) level, and a C Player is an average player. When you are competing, **base your targets on your level of skill, and on the degree of difficulty of the shot you are about to play**.

Targeting Based of Your Skill and the Degree of Difficulty
Easy to Hit (but not a pocket hanger)
- **C** Players go for three quarters hit on the correct side.
- **B** Players go for a half ball hit on the correct side.
- **A** Players go for the pocket or a precise safety. Hit the desired fraction of the object ball.

Medium Difficult to Hit
- **C** Players go for a hit using the easiest route possible.
- **B** Players go for a side of the ball.
- **A** Players go for a half ball hit or less on the correct side.

Hard to Hit
- **C** Players go for the hit.
- **B** Players go for the hit.
- **A** Players can slightly favor one side of the ball.

Very Hard to Hit
- **C** Players consider other options, such as tying up balls or moving money balls away from the pocket.
- **B** Players go for the hit or consider other options.
- **A** Players go for hitting the ball or, in extreme cases, playing an intentional foul while tying up some balls.

Kicking to Hit
The Triangle Method
The triangle method is a reliable measuring tool for determining an aim point on the rail. The method works best when the rebound angle is above 60 degrees because english pickup is not a factor in your calculation.

In Part A, the cue ball entered and exited the rail at 70 degrees along a path straight to the 4-ball. The contact point on the rail was set by using the diamonds to create the triangle as shown.

The first step is to estimate a contact point on the opposite rail. Then draw line C-D, which runs perpendicular to the rail at your estimated point of contact. Now hold your cue over the middle of the cue ball with the tip pointing at the estimated contact point. Measure Distance A between the cue's contact point on the bottom rail and Point D. Now duplicate this distance on the opposite side of Point D. This will give you the point where the right side of the triangle contacts the bottom rail (B-1).

Hold your cue from B-1 to the estimated contact point at C. If the object ball is under your cue, you have correctly estimated the point of aim. You will usually not be far off with your original guesstimate. As a result, a small adjustment to the point of aim is all that is necessary to establish the correct contact point with the rail.

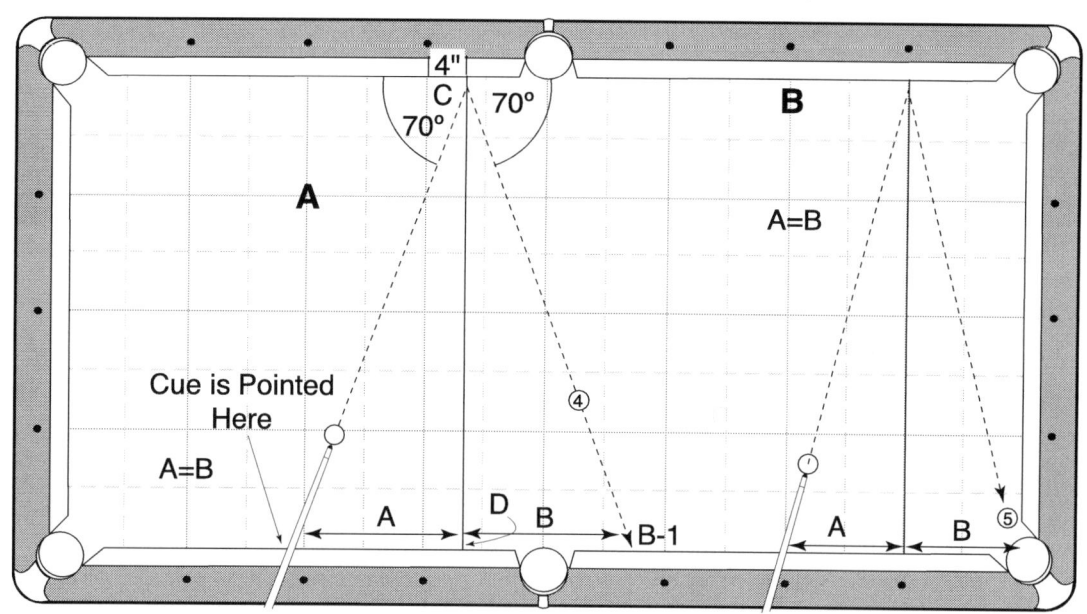

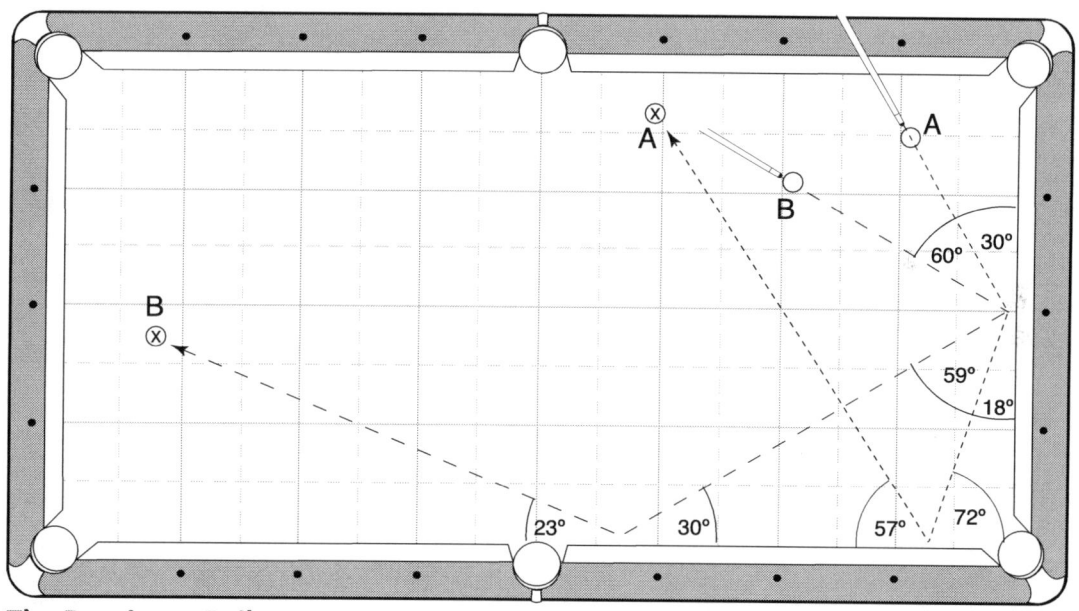

The Dominant Rail

When a kick shot covers two (or more) rails, either the first or second rail will dominate the cue ball's path. When the cue ball was sent into the rail at 30 degrees (Route A) it rebounded off the first rail at 18-degrees. It then entered the second rail at 72 degrees and exited at 57 degrees. The second rail exerted a slightly greater influence on the path of the cue ball.

When the cue ball entered the first rail at 60-degrees, it exited at 59 degrees. The dominant rail was the second rail because the cue ball entered it at 30 degrees and rebounded at only 23 degrees. The lesson: **the rail at which the rebound angle differs most from the entrance angle is the dominant rail because it has the biggest impact on the cue ball's path.**

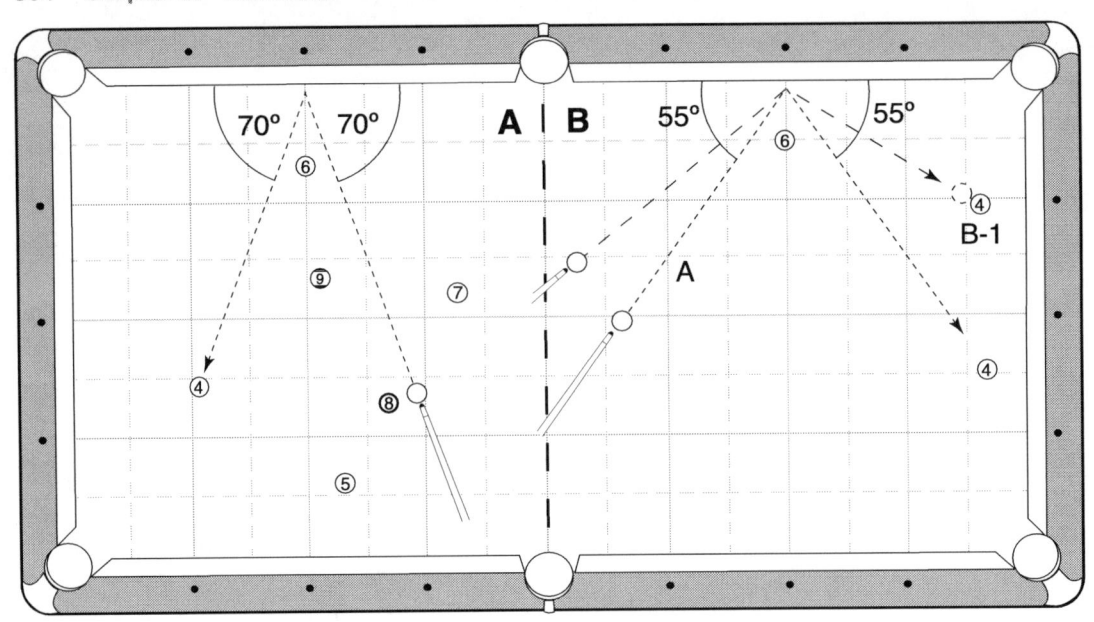

Kicking Past Obstructers

In Part A, the only route to the 4-ball is past the 6. When an obstructer is 7 inches from the rail, you can enter and exit at a 70-degree angle or less without hitting it. In Part B, the 6-ball is only 4 inches from the rail. Now the entrance angle must be 55-degrees or less to clear the 6-ball.

The cue ball was hit with follow down Route A to the 4-ball in Part B. If you have a little room to spare, you can aim wide of the obstructer and spin past it with outside english. This is shown by Route B to the 4-ball in Position B-1. The lesson: **it pays to know when you can kick around an obstructer that is positioned near the rail**.

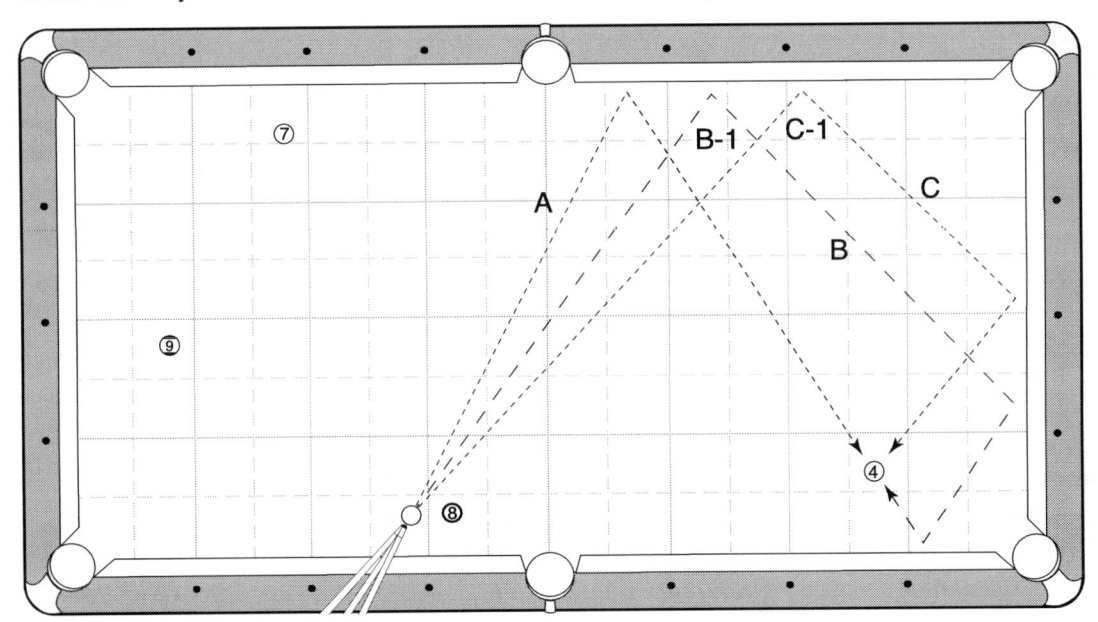

Two or Three Rails is Better than One

The 4-ball (the target) is several inches from the rail. It can easily be missed using Route A and, even if you hit the 4-ball, a sellout is likely. Route B, a three-railer into the 4-ball, is the high percentage play. Route C gives you a good chance of hitting the ball, and should be used if Route B is not available.

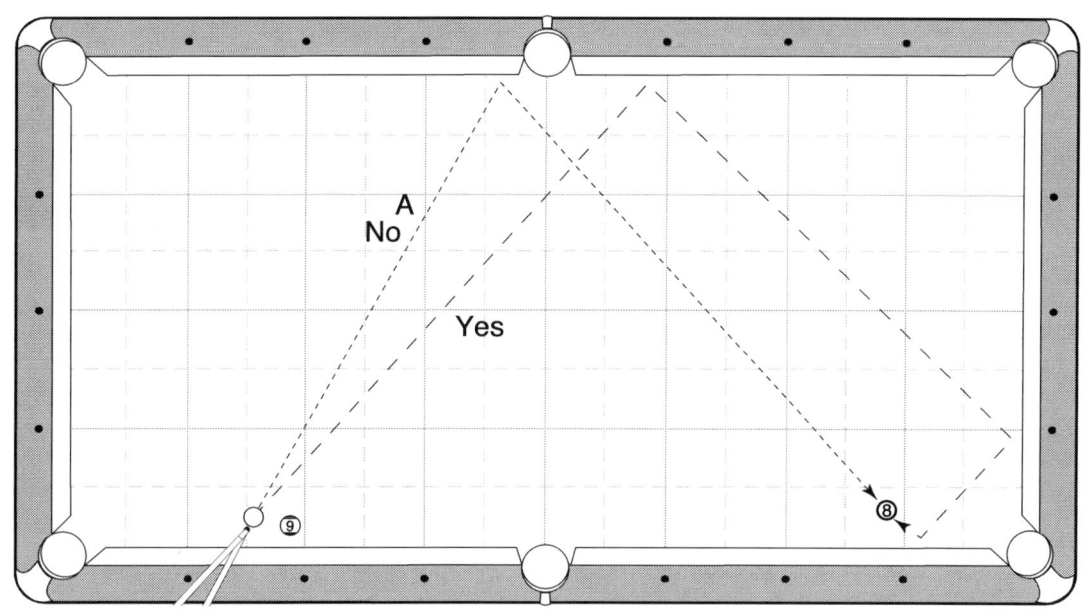

Aim at the Big Ball

The one-rail route to the 8-ball is the most direct path to the 8-ball, but it is loaded with danger. You could scratch by squeezing the cue ball between the 8-ball and the rail, or by hitting the 8-ball on the left side. Both balls could also remain at the right side of the table, leaving your opponent with a strong response.

The percentage play is to kick three rails for the 8-ball. Hitting the 8-ball is all but guaranteed, and you could drive the 8 to the opposite end of the table, making life much tougher for your opponent.

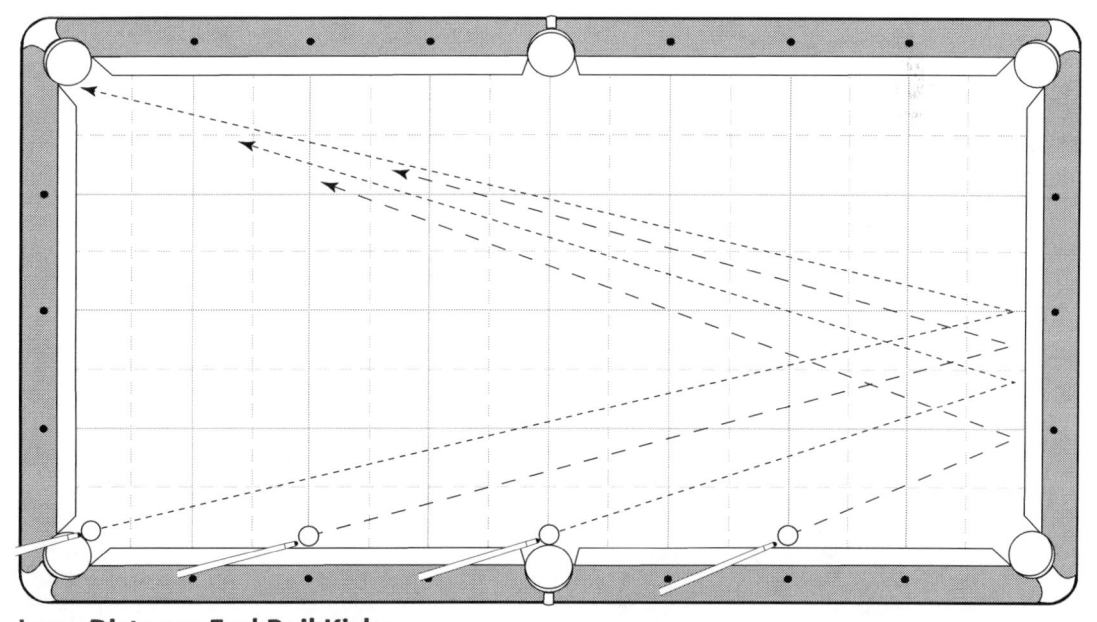

Long Distance End Rail Kicks

The cue ball is entering the rail at a steep angle in each of these four positions, so the exit angle off the end rail is very predictable. These kick routes will be useful for hitting or pocketing a ball that is located near the upper left corner pocket.

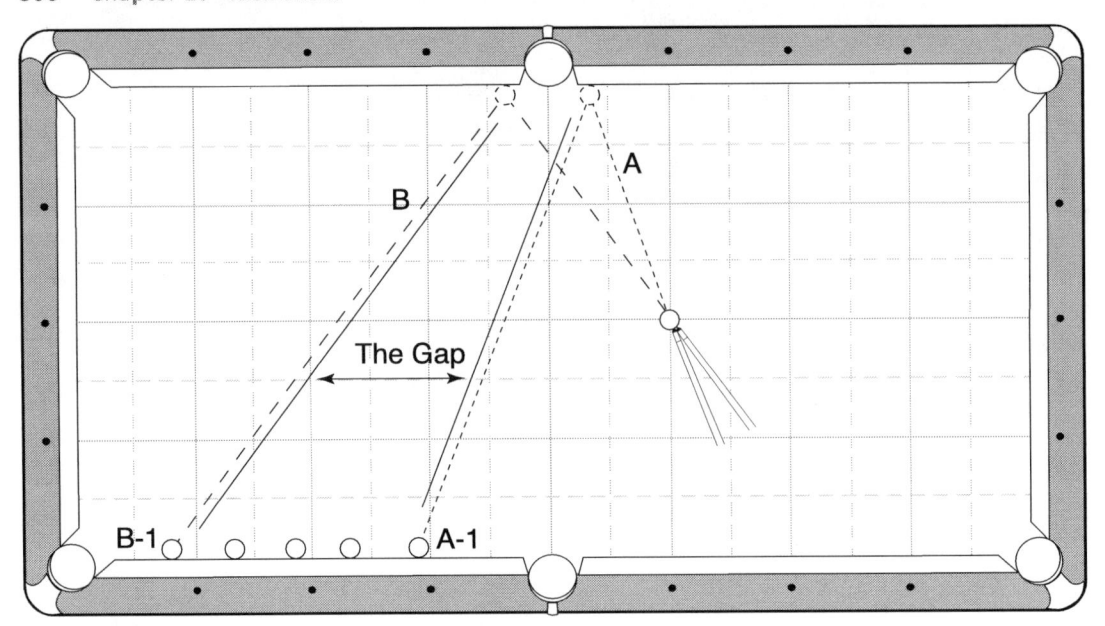

The Side Pocket Gap

Three-cushion players don't have to contend with obstructions like pockets, unlike us poor pool players. So be it. **The side pockets can effectively block a huge portion of your potential aiming points when playing kick shots off the side rails**.

The 5.5 inches wide side pocket effectively removes about an 8.75 inch wide target zone from the side rail. This figure comes from adding up 5.5 inches for the pocket, a half inch on both sides for a margin for error, and 1.125 inches on each side for the cue ball's radius.

The diagram shows the impact that that missing chunk of the rail has on kick shots. A kick to the top rail along Route A leads to the bottom side rail at Position A-1. Kicking down Route B leads to contact with the bottom side rail at Position B-1. Both of these shots were played with a half tip of follow and a medium hard stroke. The two lines drawn down the inner edges of the cue ball's contact points on each side rail give you the boundaries for the gap. You would miss hitting any ball located within the gap if you played a kick shot using the same speed and cuing as above.

If your target resides within the gap, you must adjust the route by: 1) varying the speed of your stroke, 2) applying english, 3) using draw or follow, and 4) by using some combination of these adjustments.

Practice Routes A and B while trying to hit various targets between A-1 and B-1. Mark the positions where the cue ball hits the side rail. Now place several target balls along the bottom side rail as shown. Try to hit them by kicking on both sides of the side pocket. This will teach you the effects of english, speed and how to alter the cue ball's path off the rail.

Corner Pocket Gaps

Obviously you can't kick all the way into the corner because the pocket is in your way, so you have to allow for the gap created by it. **You can only kick so close to the corner pocket before you start flirting with the point of the pocket adjacent to the second rail** as shown in Part A.

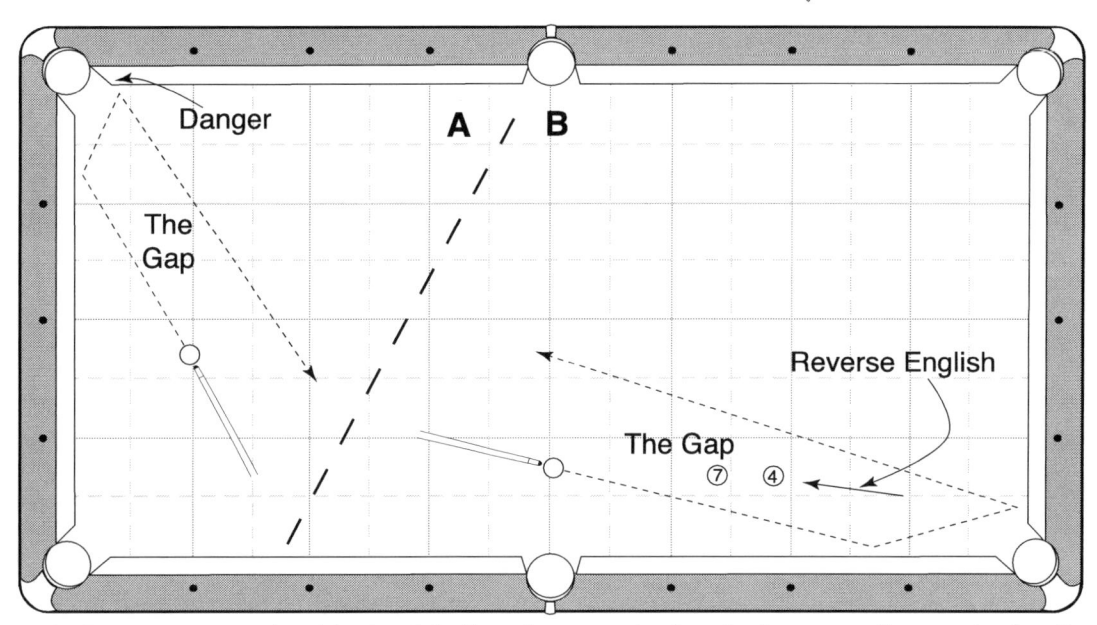

In Part B you need to hit the 4-ball and your only shot is the two rail route in the diagram. You have to use right english (reverse) even though this type of kick shot is extremely difficult to regulate.

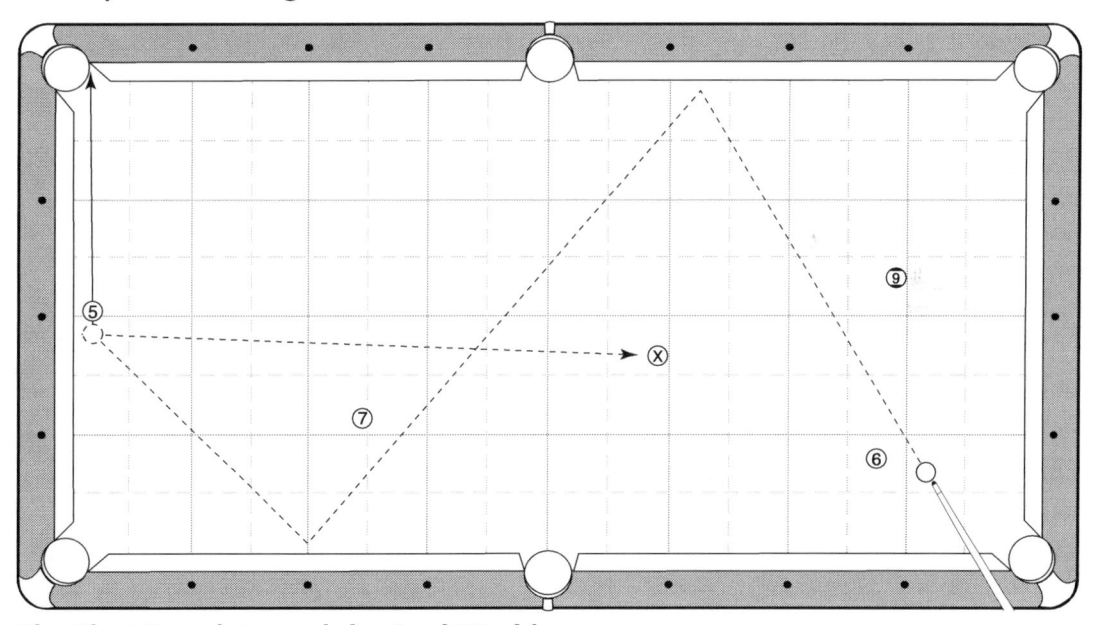

The Shot Heard Around the Pool World
The final match of the Sands Regency Open 21, 1996 was tied at 12 in a race to 13 between Efren Reyes and Earl Strickland when Reyes hooked himself. After a few moments of contemplation, he uncorked a monster "Z" shaped kick shot, making the 5-ball! Reyes then ran out for the title. The moral: **never give up, cause you never know what might happen if you make a good hit**.

"I can't think of a greater shot and I've made millions of them."
Earl Strickland

Kick to Separate the Balls

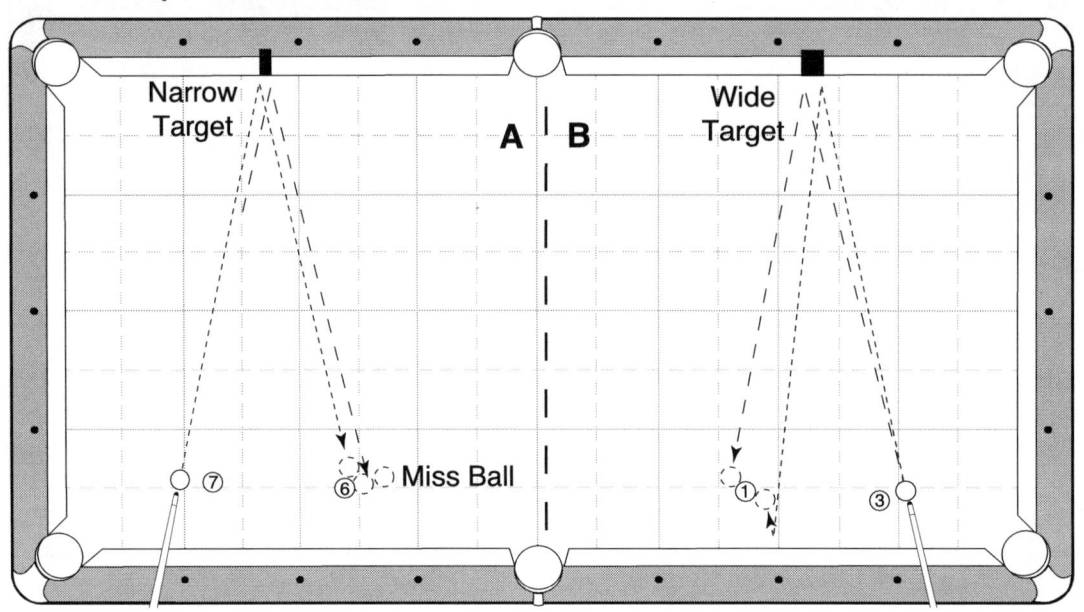

The Big Ball Ensures a Hit
In the early stages of learning kick shots you want to **make sure that you hit the object ball**. Experienced players with a solid kicking game may also choose to go for a sure hit on certain occasions:
- For strategic purposes when they are playing someone of their caliber.
- When they are playing a less skilled opponent who is no threat to run out except with ball in hand.
- When they are trying to avoid having their opponent line up a combo or ride a money ball with ball in hand.

In Part A, a player who kicks well could aim to hit the outside edge of the 6-ball. His narrow target is shown on the top side rail. If he is successful in hitting the 6-ball, it would travel towards the left end rail while the cue ball goes to the opposite end of the table. The penalty for missing is ball in hand.

The balls are in the same relative positions in Part B. Notice that the target on the rail is much wider when you are playing for the cue ball to hit the ball first, or to strike the bottom side rail before making contact. Use a hard stroke on this kick to make sure a ball strikes a rail if the cue ball hits the second rail before contacting the object ball.

Separate the Balls
Often the goal on a kick shot is to put distance between the cue ball and object ball by sending each ball to the opposite ends of the table. This shot is a bit of a gamble, but less so than the kick shot in Part A of the previous section.

Aim for full contact with the object ball. Hopefully your aim will be slightly off in either direction! If you kick down Route A into the lower half of the 1-ball, it will travel to Position A-1 while the cue ball relocates to Position A-2. If you "miss" down Route B on the upper side of the 1-ball, it will rebound to Position B-1 while the cue ball rolls down table to Position B-2.

Chapter 10 - **Kick Shots** 309

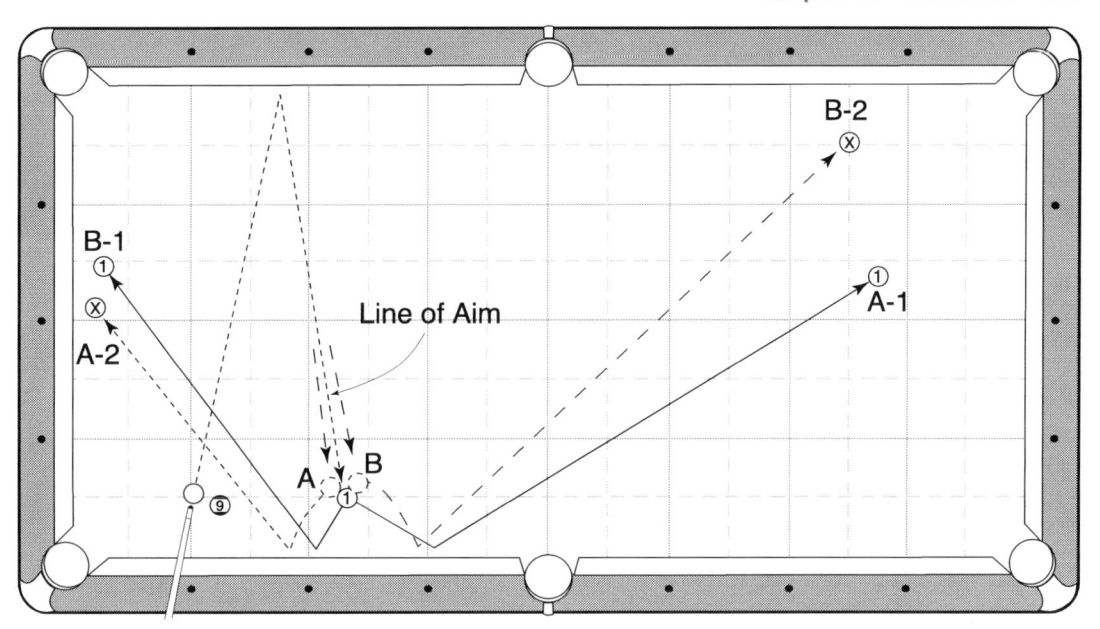

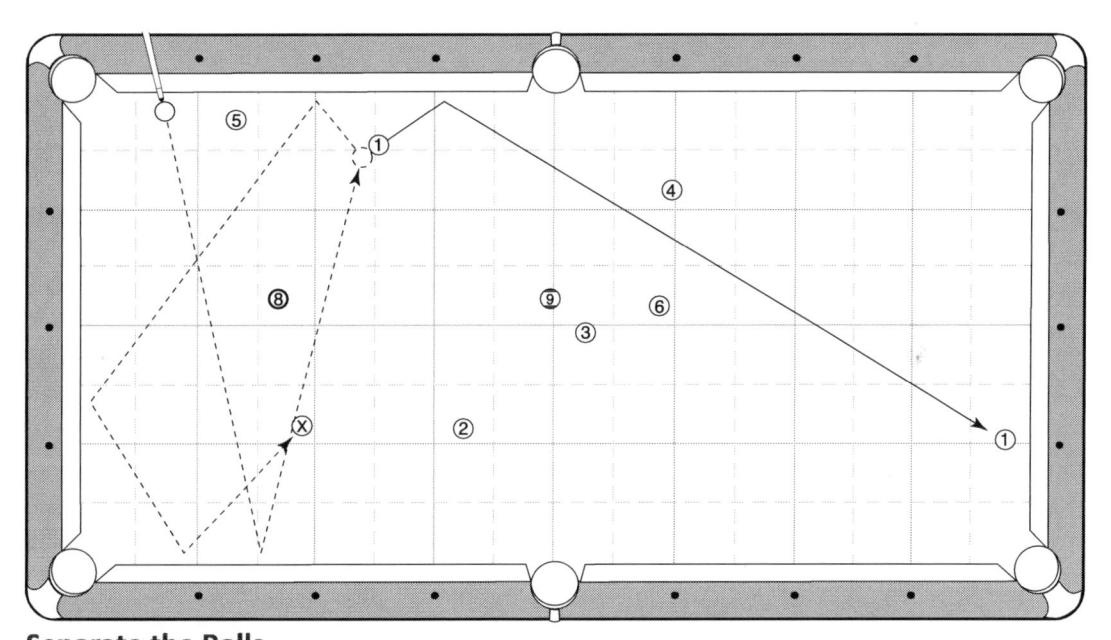

Separate the Balls
Jim Rempe was in big trouble during his match with Francisco Bustamante at the 1999 U.S. Open. He rifled the cue ball across table and back into the left side of the 1-ball, sending it to the opposite end rail. The cue ball traveled three rails to behind the 2-ball. Rempe won this game and the match on his way to a tie for fifth place.

Kick to Hook

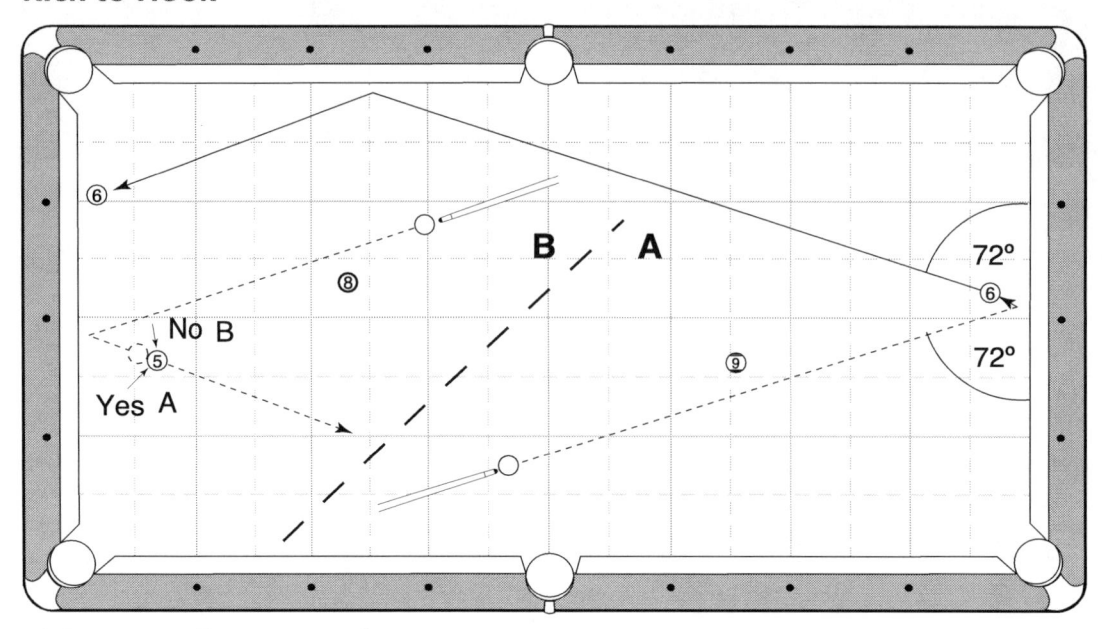

Kicking at Balls Near a Rail
On some kick shots the odds are stacked heavily in your favor! In Part A the 6-ball is close to the rail, there is room to go in behind it, and the angle of attack is steep, which makes it easy to hit the ball fully. Use a medium hard follow stroke. The follow will turn into draw when the cue ball bounces off the rail, causing it to stop dead upon contact. The 6-ball will travel to the other end of the table, leaving your opponent in worse shape than he left you! Be sure not to push out to useless hooks like this unless you are playing a novice who has not yet learned that it is an advantage to be hooked like this!

When the ball you are kicking for is close to the rail, the obstructing ball is always adjacent to your line of aim, so you can use it to help you establish your line of aim.

The 5-ball in Part B is only a couple of inches further from the rail than the 6 was in Part A, but this greatly raises the degree of difficulty on this kick safety. Now you must aim with great care. This kick is no sure thing, so favor Side A of the 5-ball as this usually avoids a complete sellout. If the cue ball hits Side B, an unfavorable result is more likely.

Kick and Stick
Nick Varner was stuck behind the 4-ball in a match with Mike Sigel at the 1990 U.S. Open when he played the outstanding kick and stick shot shown on the next page. Varner hit the 1-ball square on the nose, and he used a hard draw stroke to stop the cue ball dead. Varner unfortunately hit the shot a just a hair too hard and the 1-ball crawled just past the blockers. Sigel cut the 1 into the upper right corner pocket and ran out. The lesson: **sometimes our best is very good, but just not quite good enough.**

Chapter 10 - **Kick Shots**

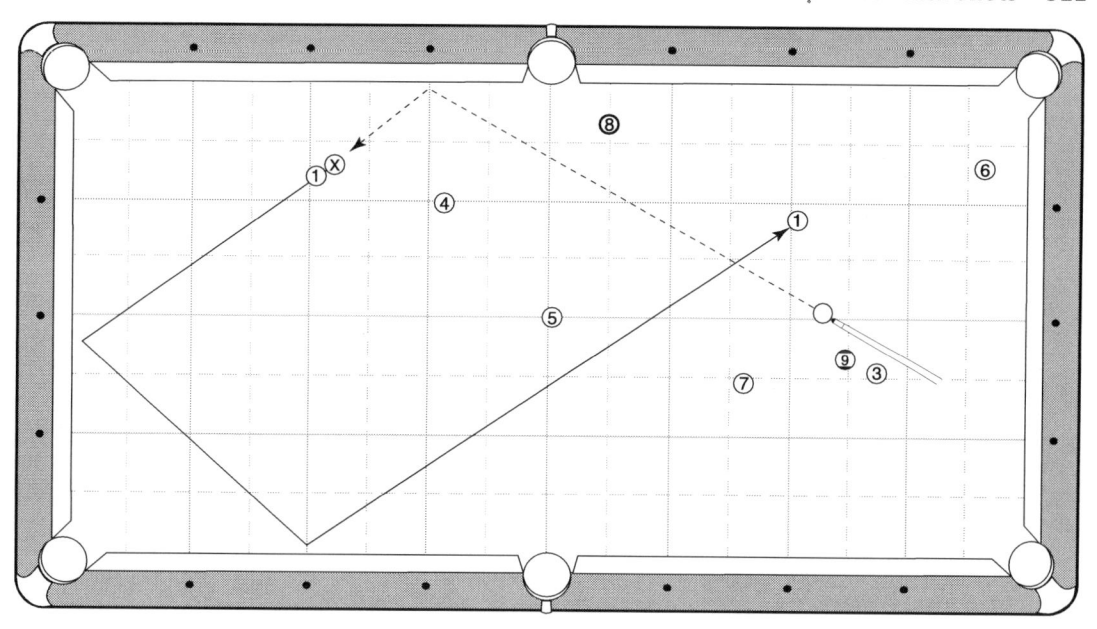

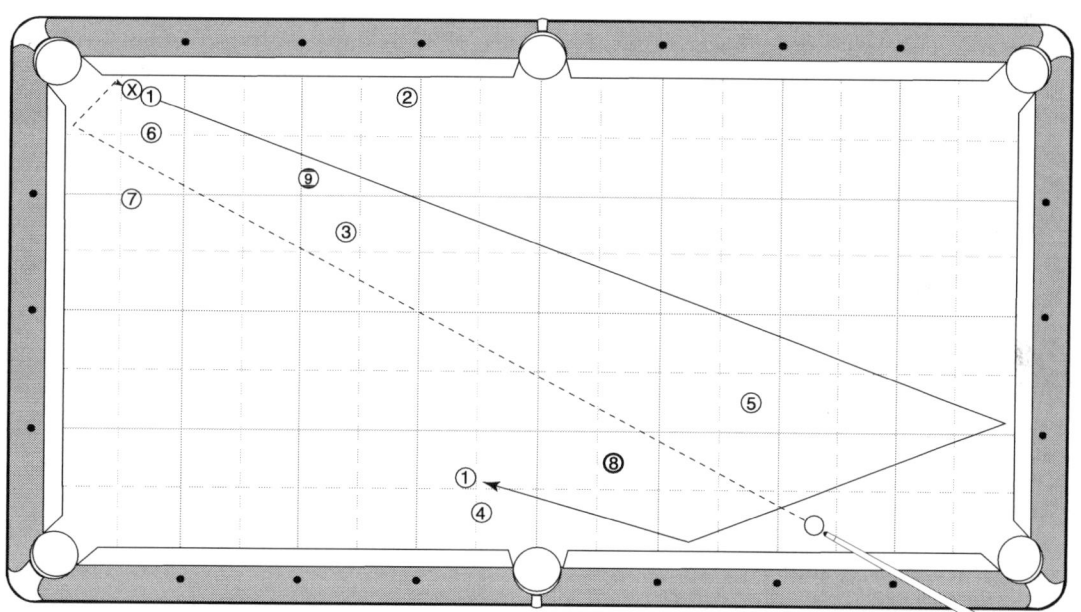

Two Rail Stick and Hook at High Speed

This kick and stick shot enabled Efren Reyes to grab a 3-1 lead over Nick Varner on his way to winning the finals of the 1994 U.S. Open. He loaded up the cue ball with topspin and used a hard stroke before sending the cue ball two-rails in behind the 1-ball. The cue ball stopped dead behind the 6-ball while the 1-ball traveled over 12 feet before stopping on the other side of the 6.

312   Chapter 10 - **Kick Shots**

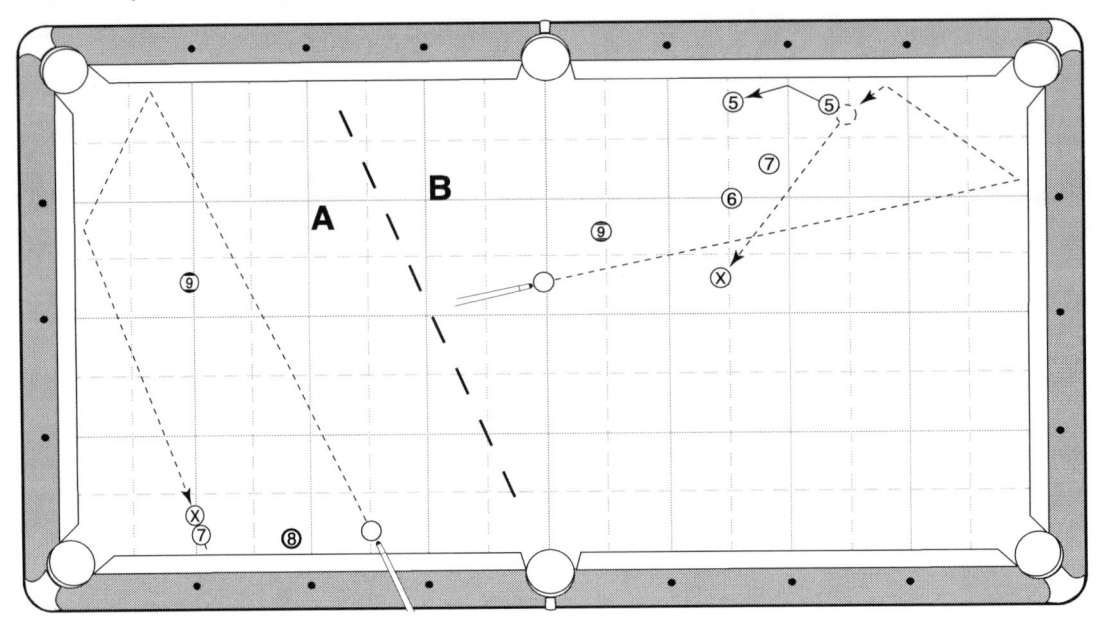

A Soft Hit Kick Safety

The kick shot in Part A calls for a very soft stroke and a near perfect two-rail route to bump the 7-ball to the rail without leaving a shot. This kick is for advanced players who have a fine touch and excellent directional control. The two-rail kick route to the edge of the 5-ball in Part B is played with left english and a soft stroke. The lesson: **be on the lookout for blockers nearby that make a soft kick safety a viable choice**.

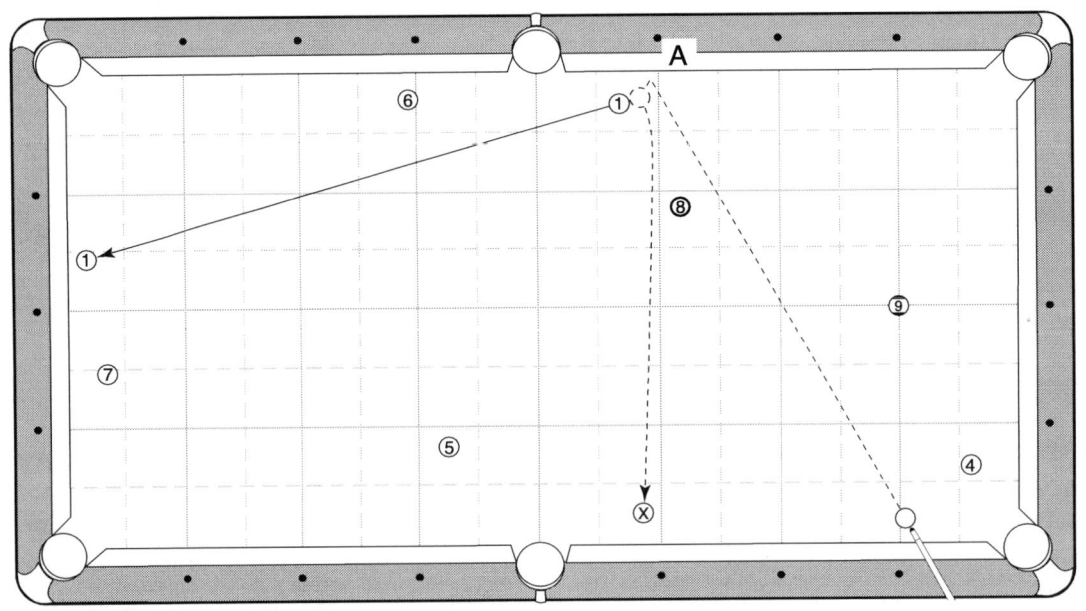

Kick and Hook One-Rail

Efren Reyes and Johnny Archer went double-hill at the Sands Regency Open 23, 1996. The final game was a 13-inning duel that included this precision one-rail kick by Reyes. The key was hitting the correct part of the 1-ball. When you are kicking for a ball that is close to the rail, you can hit it with great accuracy. I suggest that you walk over to the contact point (Point A in this example) to plan kick shots like this.

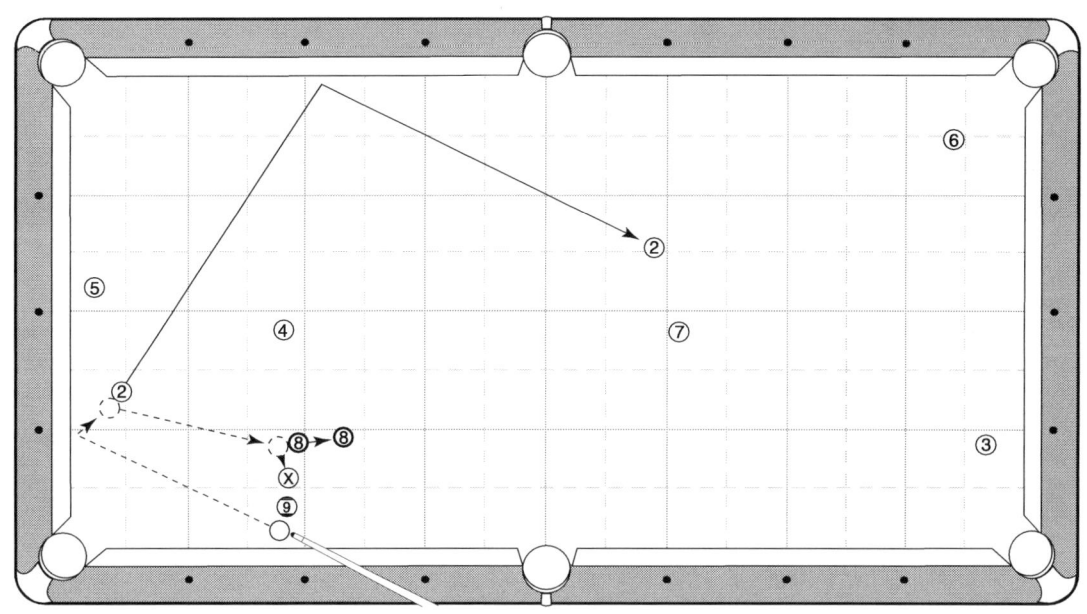

Kick and Hook

Buddy Hall played this masterful kick against Earl Strickland at the Sands Regency Open 12, 1990. Hall jacked up, applied right english, and sent the cue ball off the end rail and into near full contact with the 2-ball. The 2-ball headed down table while the cue ball nestled in behind the 8-ball. The key was in regulating the english so that the cue ball hit about 80 percent of the 2-ball.

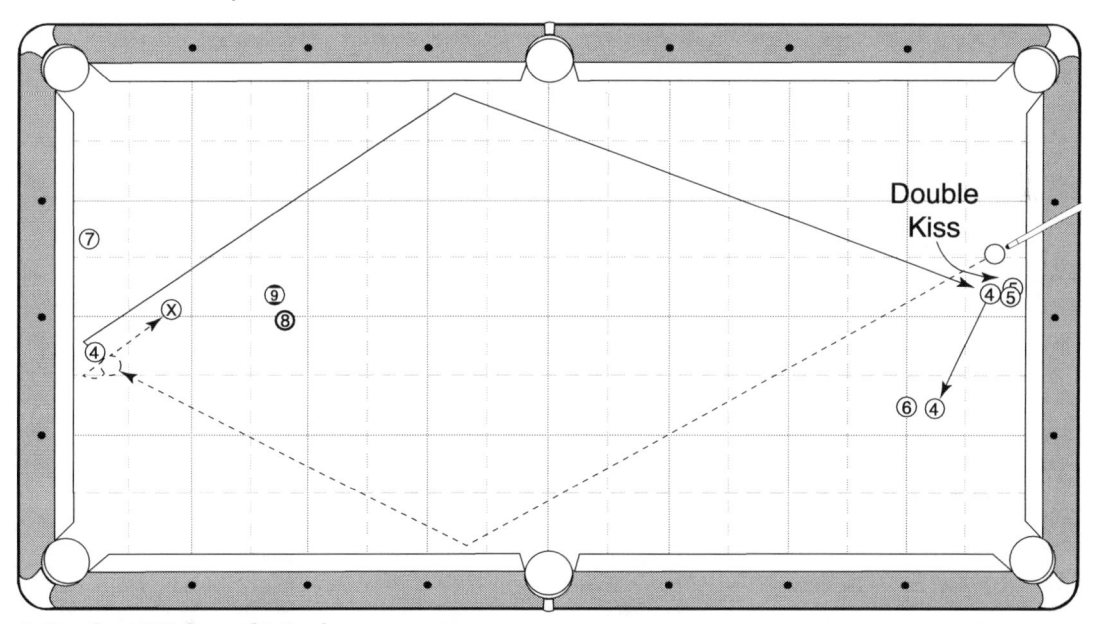

A Perfect Kick and Hook

Corey Deuel was up against Fong-Pang Chao at the 2000 World 9-Ball Championships when he came across this direct path to the 4-ball. Deuel chose instead to play a powerful one-rail kick shot – resulting in this mind-boggling kick/safety. Deuel used a very hard stroke. Notice how the cue ball curved forward to the left behind the blockers after making perfect contact with the 4-ball, leaving Chao with a difficult table length kick shot.

Kick to Pocket

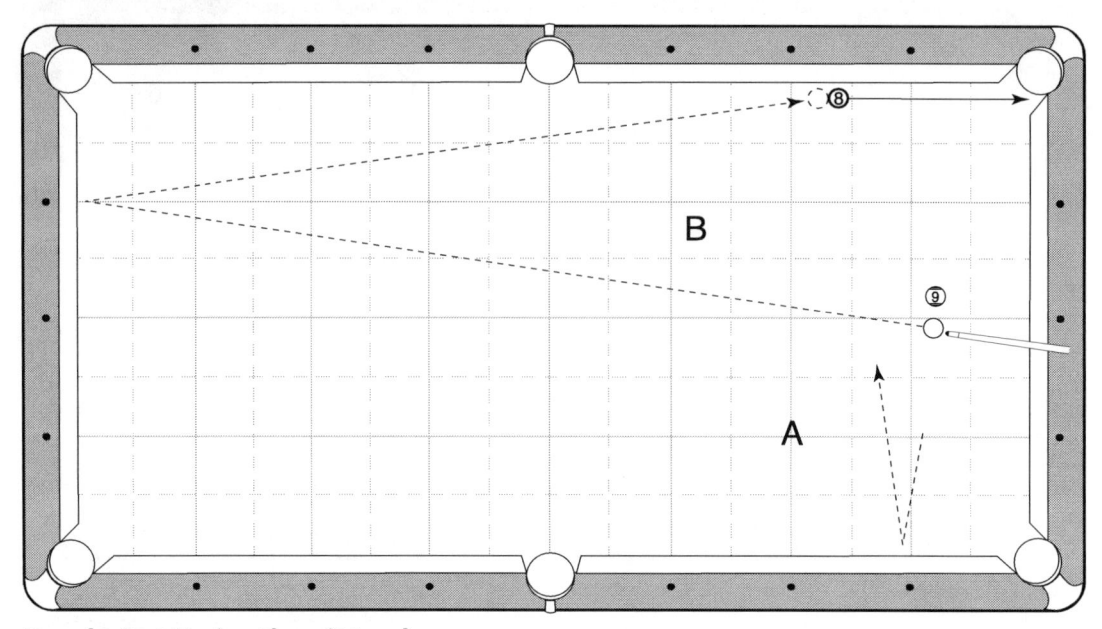

Tough, But Easier than it Looks
Your objectives on most kick shots are to hit the ball and leave your opponent tough. Sometimes, however, the kick to pocket is not difficult, or you have no choice except to go for the pocket! In this end game position, you could kick down Route A, but a sellout is likely. Kicking down Route B gives you a chance to win. This shot is not as difficult as it looks because the 8-ball is slightly off the rail, in the big ball position.

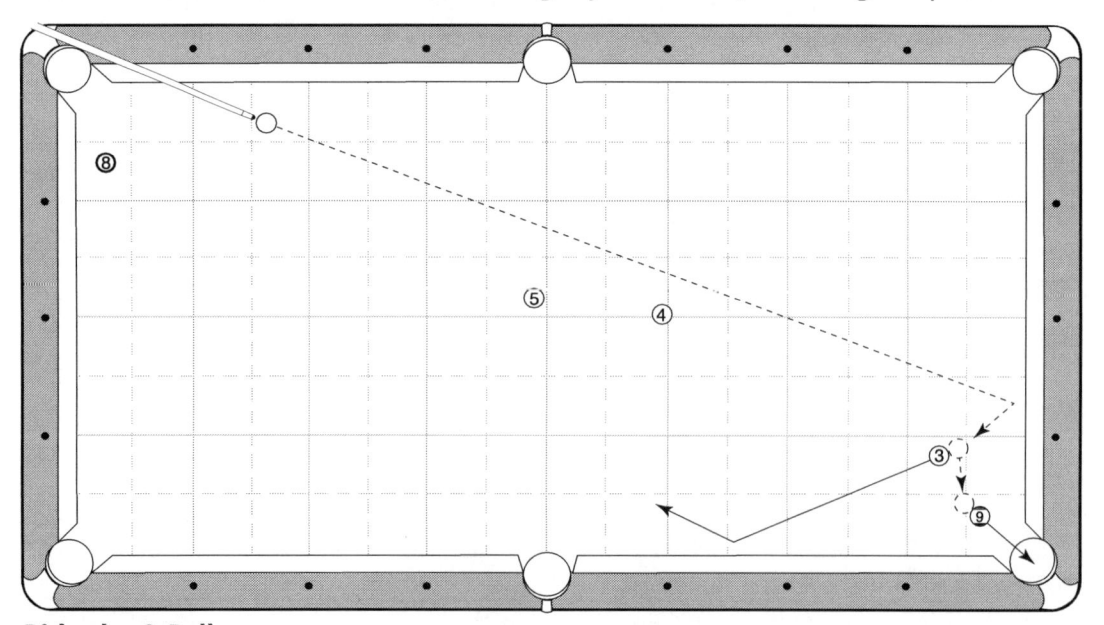

Ride the 9-Ball
When the game ball is close to the ball you must hit, you may have a chance to ride the money. Earl Strickland was in the finals of the 2000 U.S. Open against Takeshi Okumura when he employed this tactic. Strickland used a very hard stroke in producing this spectacular kick/billiard!

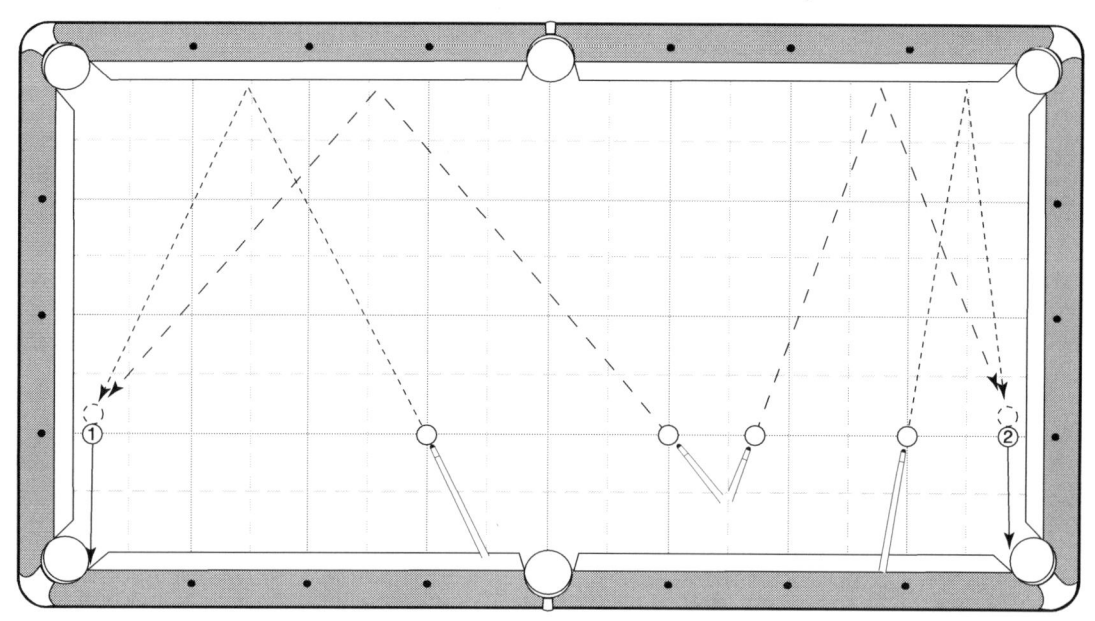

Kick to Pocket off the Side Rail

When the object ball is close to the rail and is within a diamond or so of the pocket, your chances of pocketing a kick shot are reasonably good. You can pocket these shots 1) with a perfect hit, 2) by going rail first, 3) by hitting the gap, and 4) by hitting the ball a little too fully and cheating the pocket. The diagram shows a number of candidates for a kick-to-pocket shot. You may have to adjust your aim slightly to allow for the table. These kicks go in quite often, so you should also consider how you are going to play position on the next ball.

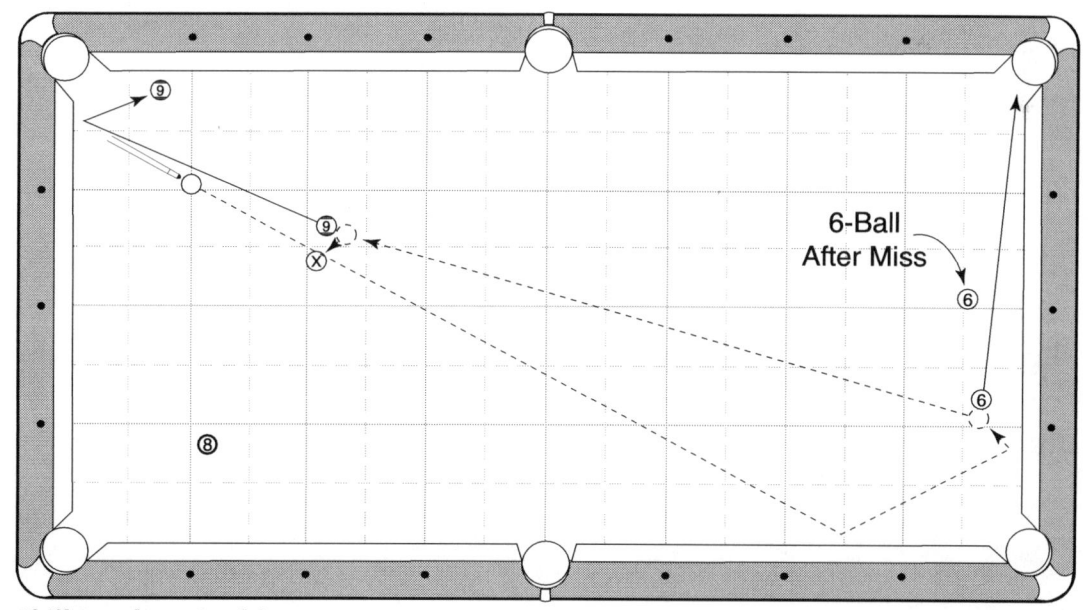

Skill Leads to Luck!

Efren Reyes was in the semifinals of the 1994 U.S. Open against Johnny Archer when he was faced with this challenging kick shot. Reyes' skill enables him to "get lucky" at times, as shown by this kick shot. If Reyes had missed, he might have left Archer a table length bank shot on the 6-ball. The lesson: **skill gives you a chance to get lucky**!

Creative Tactics

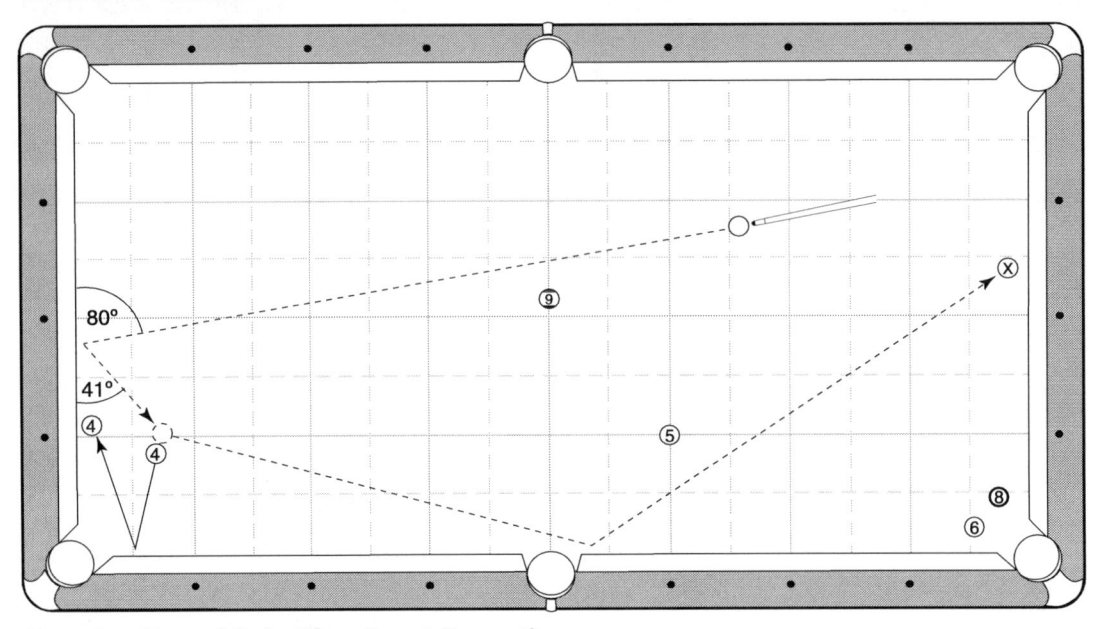

Creative Use of Spin Plus Great Execution

Johnny Archer was confronted with this potential sellout in the finals of the Sands Regency Open 22, 1995 against Rodney Morris. Archer pondered the situation a moment while devising this ultra precise kick safety. He used a medium soft stroke and a tip of left english. The 4-ball was hit very thinly while the cue ball grazed the point of the side pocket and continued to Position X, leaving Morris with a difficult reply.

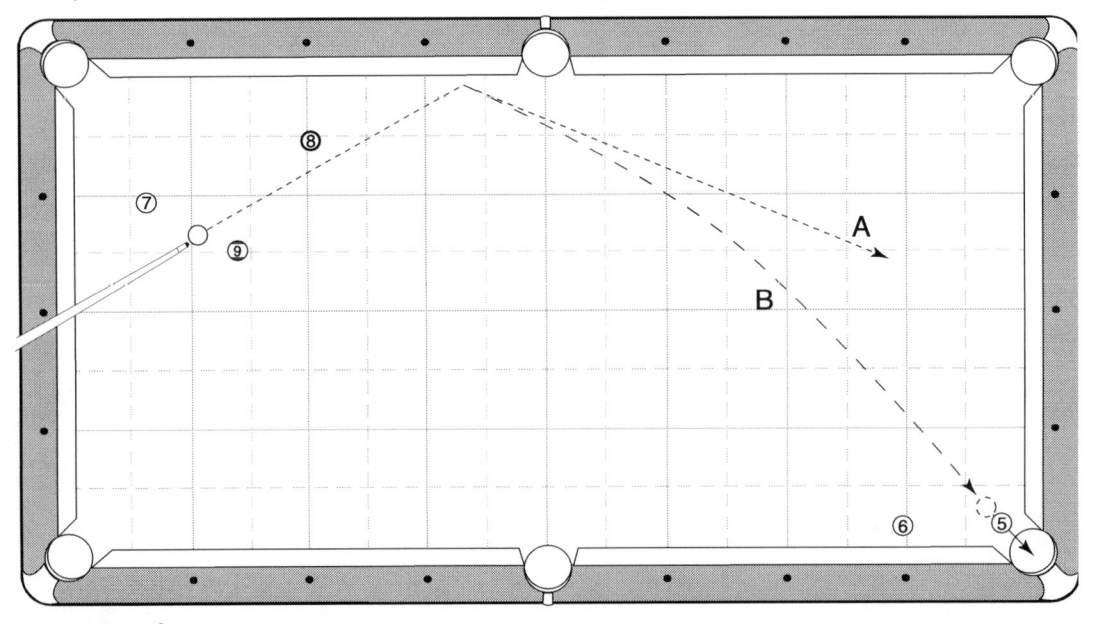

Draw Bender

The blockers have eliminated the standard kick routes. Path A shows the cue ball's line of travel if you use follow, which won't work, and you can't alter the cue ball's path enough to hit the 5-ball with inside english. The solution is a hard draw stroke, which will cause the cue ball to bend radically to the right as it comes off the rail, sending it down Path B into the 5!

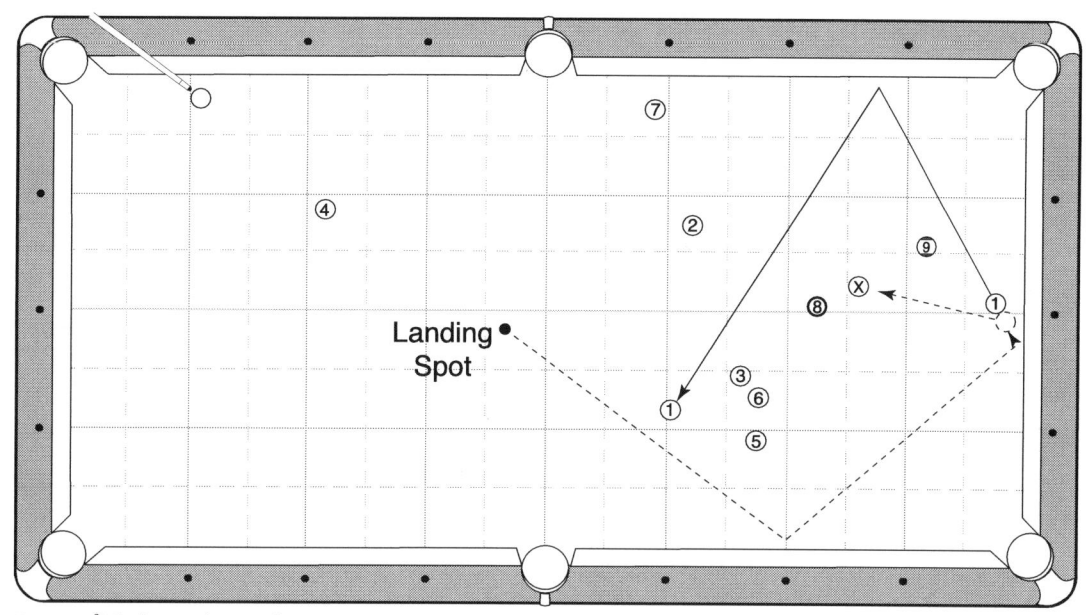

Jump/Kick and Hook

The ideal kick route to the 1-ball was blocked by the 4-ball, but Jim Rempe had the solution: a jump/kick shot over the 4 and two rails into the 1-ball! As a bonus, he snookered his opponent! The keys were Rempe's imagination and the long landing strip, which lowered the chance that the cue ball might jump off the table. This took place against Mika Immonen at the 1998 U.S. Open.

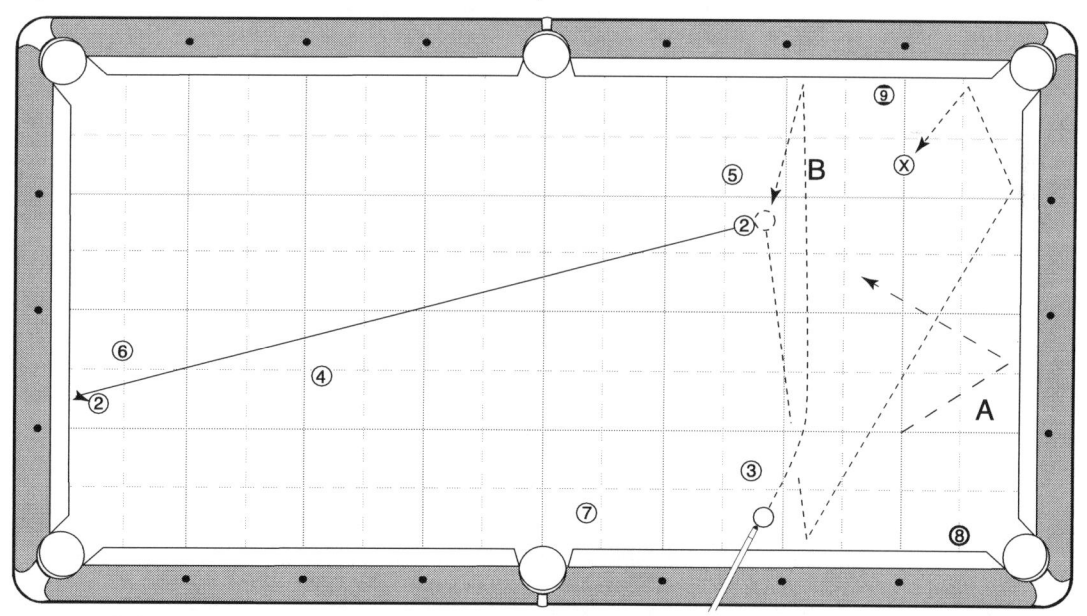

Curve Kick Shot

Sometimes the best (or only) way to hit the object ball is with a curve/kick shot. Efren Reyes was in combat with Kim Davenport at the 1995 Pro Tour Championship when he was left with this testy kick shot on the 2-ball. If Reyes used Route A, he would have been kicking the 2 to the open side of the table. So he played a curve/kick shot down Route B, leaving Davenport with a long tough cut shot on the 2-ball from Position X.

Kicking Errors

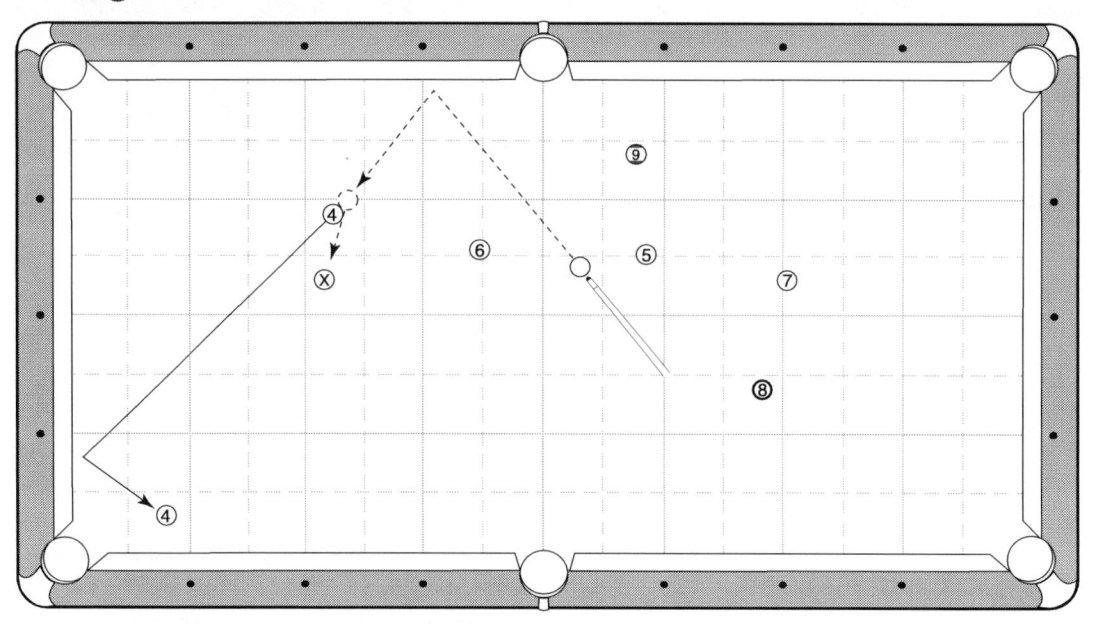

Don't Kick Softly to an Open Area of the Table
It is a mistake to kick softly at a ball that is sitting by itself at one end of the table as shown by this shot on the 4-ball. A player who commits this kind of blunder may have intended to pocket the ball, but the odds say that the shot will be missed and a sellout will result. The lesson: **hit a solitary ball hard and try to drive it to the other end of the table.**

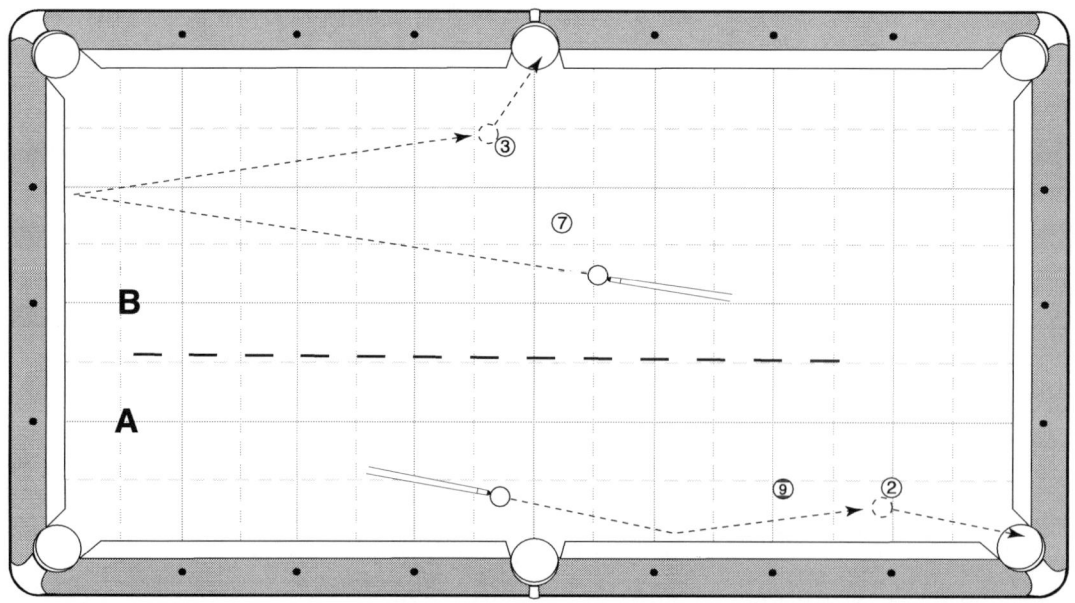

Avoid Scratching
When the object ball is several inches or more from the pocket, the risk of scratching can still be high when the cue ball will be approaching it from certain directions. In Part A, the 2-ball is several inches from the rail, and yet a scratch is very likely if the cue ball hits too far down the rail. A scratch is very possible if you hit the left side of the 3-ball in Part B.

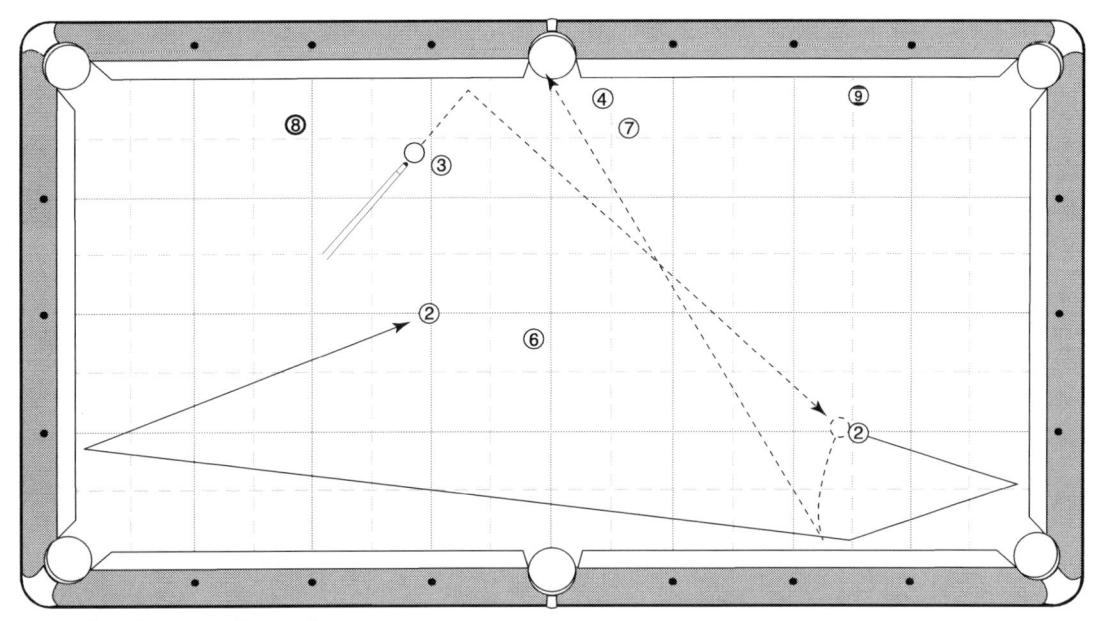

Use the Correct Speed
Kunihiko Takahashi made a full hit on the 2-ball but used excessive speed, as the 2-ball rebounded three diamonds off the end rail and the cue ball which banked into the side pocket. When playing kick shots, you must take care to match your speed to the requirement of the shot. This shot took place in the 1999 U.S. Open in a match with Chuck Altomare. The lesson: **watch where the balls stop to learn speed of stroke for the cue ball and the object ball when playing kick shots**!

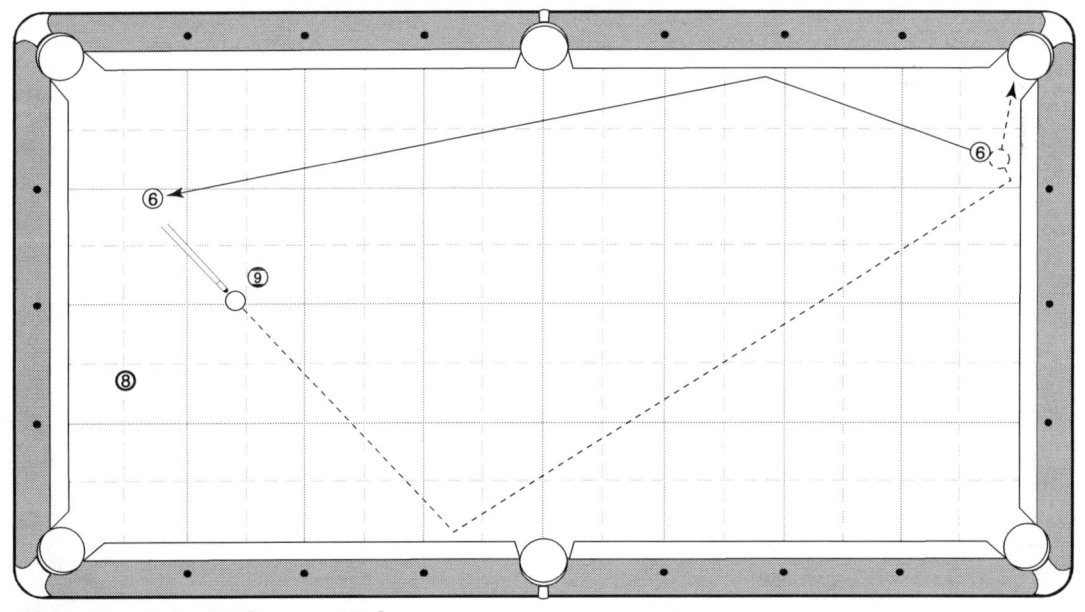

A Common Scratch on a Kick
Some kick shots are long enough and difficult enough that you simply must turn the cue ball loose, increasing the chances of scratching. A world champion committed this error by contacting the far side of the object ball when it was only a little more than a ball's width from the rail.

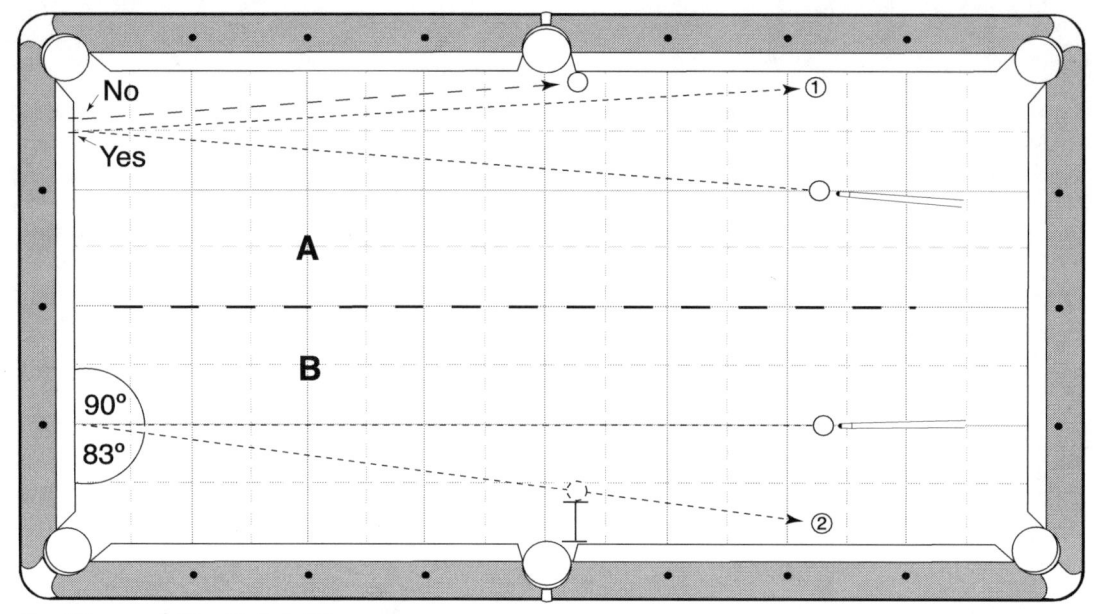

Be Wary of the Point #1

All players hate to see the cue ball bounce off the point of the side pocket when kicking down the side rail because it eliminates the chance of something good happening – and it results in ball in hand. In Part A, the cue ball was sent a scant inch off line, but this was enough to send it into the point. **You can avoid the side pocket point by aiming wide of the corner pocket and using a quarter tip of english**, as shown in Part B.

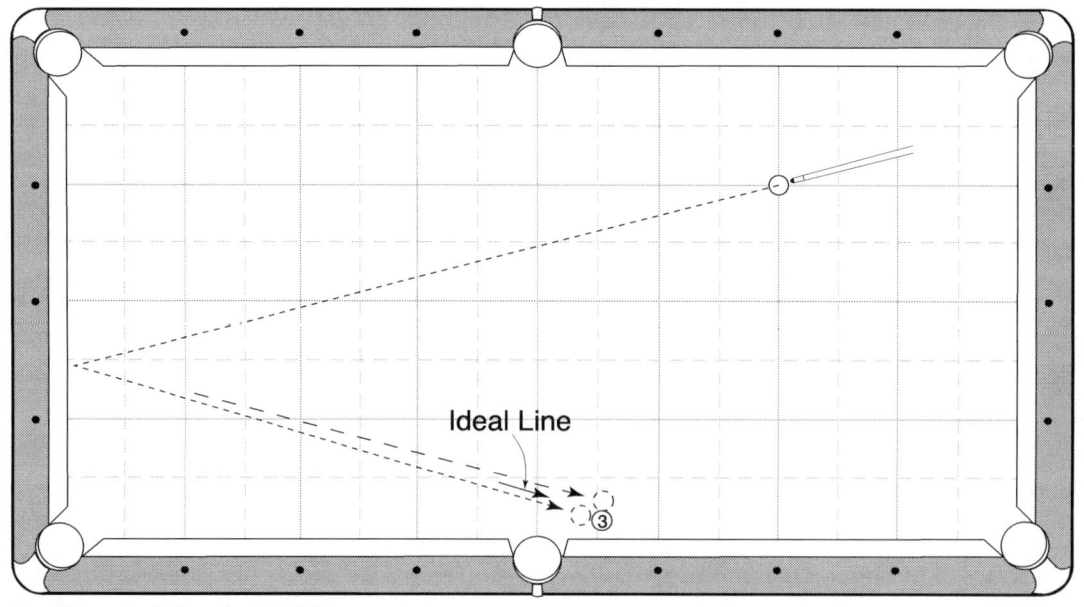

Be Wary of the Point #2

The object ball is next to the side pocket. To avoid hitting the point, aim for a half ball hit on the object ball. This will give you a small margin of error between hitting the point and missing the ball entirely.

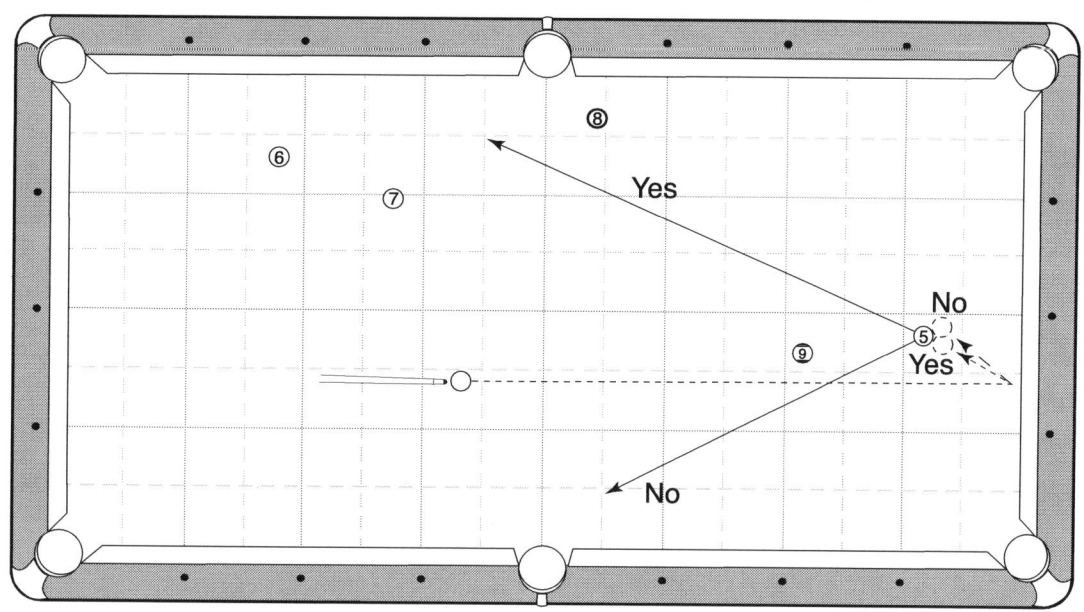

Hitting the Wrong Side
When you must use english to hit the object ball, exercise great care to avoid hitting the wrong side of the ball. Left english is needed to spin the cue ball off the end rail into the 5-ball. If the 5-ball is hit on the correct side, it will head towards the blockers down table. If too much spin is used, the 5-ball will be struck on the wrong side, sending it towards the open end of the table.

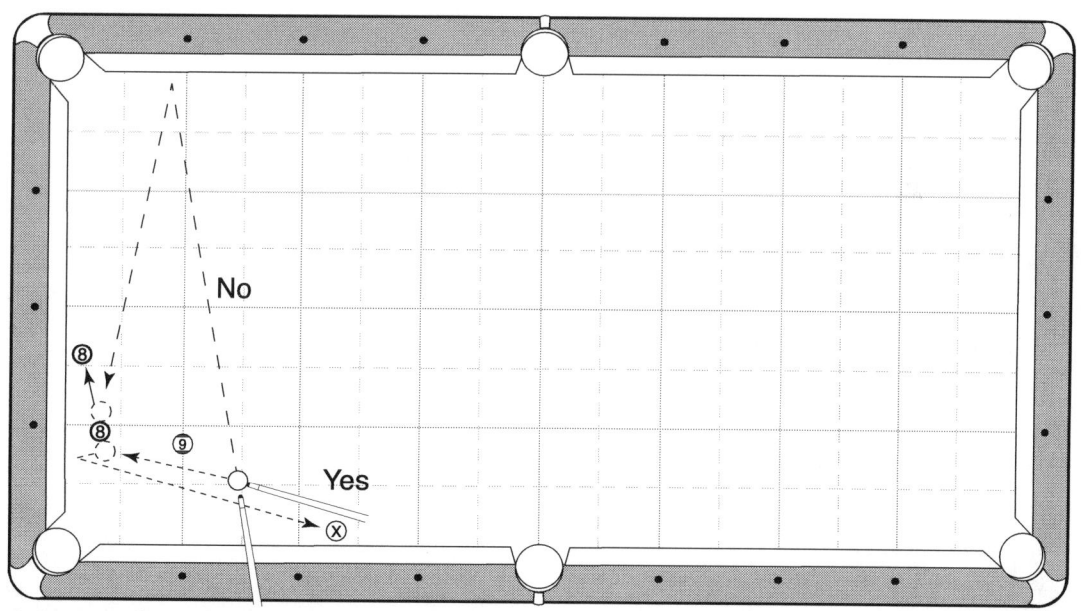

A Sure Safety Beats a Sucker's Kick Shot
It is a huge mistake to kick to make a ball that is near the end rail when the ball is more than a quarter inch from the cushion, and when you can skim it and play a safety! These shots looks like they shouldn't be too difficult, but I would guess that they are missed at least 8 times out of 10. The smart play is to skim the object ball and go for a safety.

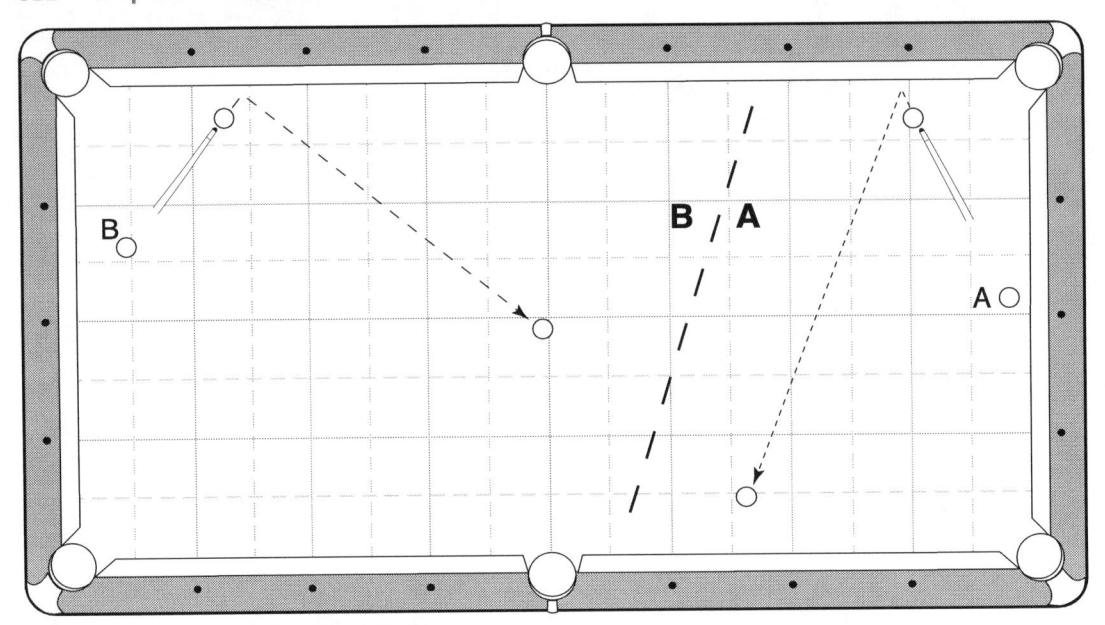

Short Distance to the First Rail
Kick shots in which the cue ball will be traveling only a few inches to the first rail are among the game's toughest. In Part A, the cue ball will only travel about 2 inches before hitting the cushion. The rebound angle is fairly sharp, but this kick is still tough to judge. The problem is magnified in Part B because of the shallower rebound angle. When playing this kind of kick shot, avoid english unless it is necessary. When aiming, try visualizing the route as if the cue ball was further from the rail, such as at Positions A or B.

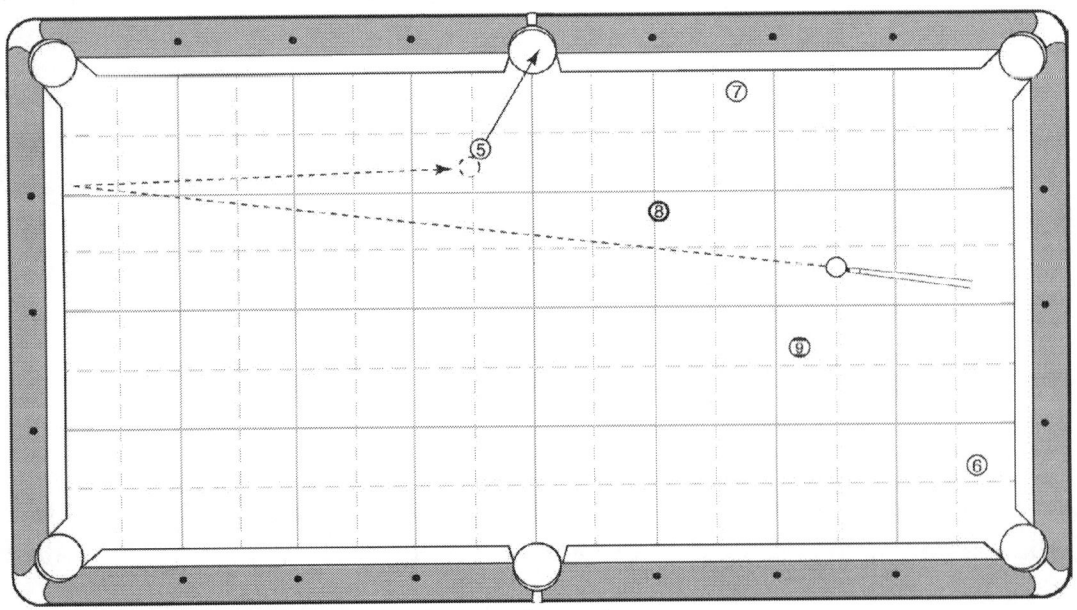

Trying to Hit Balls Thinly and Missing Altogether
You could try to kick/cut the 5-ball into the side pocket, but this requires a very thin hit on the 5-ball. The reward could be substantial, but the risk of missing a thin hit far outweighs it. The correct shot is to go for a solid and hard hit on the 5-ball and hope for a hook.

CHAPTER 11

The ABCs of Strategy

"It's all a game of percentages."
Jim Rempe

Both 9-Ball and 10-Ball are demanding games that require a level of shotmaking and position play that is unlike the other popular games. **Big differences in players' skills lead to a larger variety of ways that certain shots should be played.** In this regard, these games are a lot like sports where significant differences in the skills of even the very best performers set them apart. Legendary golfer Jack Nicklaus played long shots with a high trajectory to distant greens that his peers couldn't match. However, he often lost shots to competitors who had stronger short games.

In pool, Philippine superstar Efren Reyes is known for his strong kicking game and position play. But he loses ground to competitors with more powerful break shots. A very few players have complete mastery of every facet of pool. In today's game, Shane Van Boening is an example of a player who has no weaknesses.

Your game could be strong where your opponent's is weak, and vice versa. So don't let your admiration for their areas of expertise lead you into thinking you can't win. Instead, adopt strategies that enable you to take advantage of your skills, and to exploit your opponent's weaknesses.

You can maximize your strategic decision-making by first making a realistic appraisal of your game. Identify your strengths and weaknesses. When competing, your self-knowledge will help you to make the most of your strong points while minimizing the impact of your weak spots. You may dislike admitting your weaknesses, but you must if winning is your goal. Besides, your weaknesses need not be permanent. In fact, **I recommend that you systematically eliminate them in practice, one by one**.

In today's world of amateur competition, **players of all levels are likely to face each other in tournaments and leagues, or even for a friendly wager.** Blind draw tournaments, handicapped leagues, and negotiated money games often result in an A Player matching up against a C Player one moment, and an A Player in their next match.

All opponents are not created equal, so you should adjust your strategy to match the level of your opponent's game. Changes in strategy can be quite subtle when an A Player is playing an A- Player. In contrast, a major change in tactics is required when a B+ Player faces a C Player rather than a fellow B+ Player.

Rating Your Game and Testing Your Skill

You may have a good idea of your standing compared to other pool players in your region. Furthermore, you may have a ranking and/or handicap from participating in a local or national league, or in a series of tournaments. **A big problem with pool is that the ranking systems are not all created equal**. A C Player in one region could be a B- in another area of the country, or even across town. An 8 rated player might be a 7 somewhere else.

I will not be making any attempt to create a universal rating system below. Instead, I will be suggesting that the number of racks or balls you regularly run in 9-Ball is a reasonably accurate indicator of your current level of play. Later in the chapter I will present strategies based on how you rate yourself (A, B, or C) against the criteria below, regardless of your rating in your league or poolroom.

Measuring Your Ability By the # of Racks Run

The number of balls, or racks, that you can break and run when you are playing reasonably well is a solid indicator of your skill. Because these games are so challenging, it is difficult to exceed your norm by a significant amount, just as it is not likely that a 90 shooter in golf will break 80. Your lifetime best may not be an accurate indicator of a level of skill, but it does give you an idea of your potential.

How to Measure a Run

I'm going to spend a moment discussing how to measure your runs in 9-Ball because I believe this can help you in gauging your level of play. The method for measuring the racks you've run is quite crude compared to how runs are measured in Straight Pool, in which your total is a precise number. **Measuring racks run in 9-Ball is somewhat imprecise** because:
- Your runs can start with part of a rack.
- You can break in the game ball.
- You can make the game ball on a variety of shots during any part of the game.

The high run gauge is meant to be a measure of your skill, so I suggest that you not count 9 or 10 balls on the break as part of your best run. A run of a half of a rack is about 4-5 balls. If your run starts on the 4-ball and continues through that rack and you break and run the entire next rack (minus any balls on the break, of course) that would be run of 1.5 racks. If your run had started on the 2-ball and continued through that rack and two more complete racks, that would be a run of three racks. You do not get credit for balls made on the final rack that do not lead to the completion of the rack. For example, let's say you started a match by breaking and running the first rack and you continued through to the 7-ball of the next rack before missing. That would count as a run of one rack, not 1.5 racks.

Your Typical Good Runs

A typical good run doesn't occur every day, but it will happen on most days, providing you play for at least an hour or two.

C Player – Your best daily runs are usually 5-7 balls, and are comprised mostly of routine shots. You seldom break and run a complete rack. When you do run a complete rack, it is usually an easy layout with no problems. An average run is 3-4 balls.

B Player – You can occasionally break and run out. You will sometimes run two racks if the balls are lying well. An average run is 5-6 balls.

A Player – You run one to two racks quite often. A typical run is 7-8 balls. Runs of three or more racks happen far less often than most otherwise knowledgeable observers think that they do. An A Player's ability to run three racks is a very perceptible dividing line between pretty good players (B-B+) and really good players (A- and above). To run three or more racks with any regularity, you need:

- A great break.
- Excellent cue ball control.
- The ability to consistently make tough shots to continue your run.

Personal Bests

The personal bests do not include making the 9-ball or 10-ball on the break. It is also debatable whether or not a personal best should include quick wins that come by a combo, billiard, or some other shot on the game ball at the beginning of a rack. Remember, the main purpose of this gauge and the one above is to give you an accurate measure of your skill.

	9-Ball	**10-Ball**
C Player	1-2 racks	1 rack
B Player	2-3 racks	1-2 racks
A Player	4-5+ racks	3+ racks

The Three Phases of a Rack

Your strategy for playing a rack depends on the number of balls left on the table, the challenges and opportunities the layout presents, and your and your opponent's levels of skill. As a matter of convenience, I have broken the rack into three phases. The number of balls in the first two phases depends on the number of balls that went in on the break. The last phase almost always consists of three balls, since it is nearly impossible to make seven or more balls on the break. Using **a three ball end game makes planning this critical phase a uniform process**. Besides, in amateur competition, many games are not decided until the last 3-4 balls no matter how many balls are made on the break.

Length of the Phases – 9-Ball

Balls on the break	0	1	2	3	4	5	6
Phase 1: Beginning	3	2	1	0	0	0	0
Phase 2: Middle	3	3	3	3	2	1	0
Phase 3: End	3	3	3	3	3	3	3

Length of the Phases – 10-Ball

Balls on the break	0	1	2	3	4	5	6
Phase 1: Beginning	3	3	2	1	0	0	0
Phase 2: Middle	4	3	3	3	3	2	1
Phase 3: End	3	3	3	3	3	3	3

The composition of the layout may go through many changes as you progress through a rack. Please understand that **there will be plenty of exceptions to these rules thanks to the fact that no two racks are exactly alike**.

When I am discussing the two games, please remember that I am talking about both of them at the same time. For example, when I say 9 or 10 ball, I mean that the strategy holds true for the 9-ball in 9-Ball, and the 10-ball in 10-Ball. It does not mean that it is true for the 9 and 10-balls in 10-Ball.

Phase 1: The Beginning
When in Phase 1, the key to running out is to avoid the many obstacles on your position routes. When 7-9 (or 10) balls are on the table, you have ample opportunities to play safe. The first phase is also a time for taking shots on 9 or 10 balls (or other money balls, if you are getting spotted), providing these shots have little risk of costing you the game if you miss. The game is still young for C Players. B Players may or may not have an opportunity to win in this phase, depending on the difficulty of the layout. A large majority of games between A Players are decided in Phase 1 or 2.

Phase 2: The Middle
The outcome is decided in this phase for the vast majority of games between B Players. Most games between A Players that have not been decided in Phase 1 are settled in Phase 2. In games between C Players, the game may or may not yet be on the line. It all depends on the difficulty of the layout.

Phase 3: The End
When a game between A Players reaches Phase 3, it has usually been decided. Games between B Players should have also been decided at this point, but errors often leave the game up for grabs. A very high percentage of racks are won and lost by C Players in Phase 3. It's like watching a 50 percent free thrower: the ball might go in, but it could just as easily be missed.

The ABCs of Strategy

Games of 9-Ball take on a much different complexion for players of varying levels of skill. The following sections provide strategic guidelines for the three broad categories of players discussed earlier. Each one emphasizes strategies for playing those in your category of skill, and the sections also give you some guidelines for competing with those in the other categories. While you only need to read the section that applies to the group(s) you will be competing against, I do recommend that **serious players study the tactics that the players in other skill groups will employ against them!** For example, a C Player who is about to play a B Player should read the section called C Players vs. B Players. Serious competitors, however, will also want to read the section titled B Players vs. C Players so you will understand the tactics your opponent will be employing against you.

No matter what your level of play, **you need to recognize your limitations if you wish to have a chance of competing successfully**. Remember, winning at 9-Ball largely depends on managing your game. Make the most of what you've got. And do not try world beater shots that you saw Earl or Efren make in professional matches.

Spots – typical ones – games on the wire – Wild balls – call balls – ETC. OR – See the chapter – Competitive 9 Ball Maybe switch chapters 13 and 14

Strategies for All Levels of Players
Quick and Easy Wins 9-Ball are unique in that both games offer the opportunity for quick and easy wins via combos, billiards, and other specialty shots. Most players find it difficult to resist the chance to "ride the cash." Still, you must make intelligent use of this tactic no matter what your level of skill. Keep an eye out for easy wins because they are a tonic to your psyche, and they can demoralize your opponent. But remember that a high penalty is often paid for missing these shots, and that pool is a game of percentages.

The Break I'll repeat a rule that holds for all opponents: Don't scratch on the break!!! After a foul on the break good players will run out or play safe, and lesser players will ride the game ball (or any other balls if they are receiving weight).

Racking Money Balls If you are receiving a spot, rack your money balls in the row behind the 1-ball. The same holds true when you are racking for someone who is receiving an extra money ball or two from you. Racking the money balls in this position lessens the chances that your opponent will make a spot ball on the break.

Strategies for C Players
C Player vs. C Player
The ebb and flow of games between C Players is astounding. At any moment, anything can and does happen. You may receive a gift at any time. Learn to manage your expectations and try to stay on an even keel, which is not easy given the highly volatile nature of these contests. Your ability to manage your emotions, and to make shots while not testing your limitations in Phase 3, will largely determine your success or failure.

Weight It is difficult for a C Player to give another C Player a spot. So think twice before giving weight, but almost always be grateful for a ball spot, even if it is only the last two.

Intimidation Don't overestimate your opponent's play just because they made an impressive shot or two. Recognize that you have a great chance of winning most matches, and that your opponent will give you many chances to win most games.

Expect Mistakes Don't worry about having to play perfect pool.

The Rolls C Players torture one another with the luck factor, which plays a significant role in many games. Realize that many of the good rolls are neutralized by poor play, and by the abundant opportunities to win that are present in most games.

Phase 1 Look for ways to make the game ball, especially if you are playing another C Player. Ride the money with ball in hand, especially if you can play safe at the same time.

Target Practice Unless the entire rack is lying easy, realize that the first three balls are largely target practice for getting you in stroke for the later phases when the game is on the line.

Shotmaking Your primary weapon is shotmaking. It pays to know your shotmaking capabilities, and your opponent's, because good or poor shots (as opposed to position plays) decide most games.

Run Out Range You may be within run out range with 4-6 balls on the table. It depends on the layout and on how well you are playing. In this phase, you may continue to play position with the idea of running out, but you don't want to run 2-3 balls, then miss, and hand the table over to your opponent with three easy balls to run.

End Game Errors Be prepared for tough shots and safeties in the end game that result from your opponent's errors.

Safeties "Average" safeties can lead to ball in hand thanks to your opponent's lack of kicking skills. Emphasize safeties starting with the last five balls, and especially when the game gets down to the last three balls or fewer. Playing smart can give you a huge advantage when playing another C Player. Remember, safeties have a larger margin for error than do shots, which often makes them easier to execute under end of game pressure.

Kick Shots Emphasize hitting the ball. Don't get too fancy trying to skim the edge because you don't want to give your opponent a chance to ride the game ball with ball in hand.

Jump Shots Unless you have actually learned the jump shot, trying them can do more harm than good. So, consider jumping only when a kick is next to impossible, or you only have to clear the edge of the ball.

Running Out If you have decided that the rack is within your run out range, keep things as simple as possible when playing shape.

Don't Be a Hero Don't give away games by attempting difficult runs on the last three balls. Play safe and let your opponent beat themselves.

C Player vs. B Players

Unless the format favors upsets or you are receiving weight, realize that you are a substantial underdog. You may have a chance to score an upset if you have a great day, get a few rolls, and your opponent is off their game. So relax and enjoy the opportunity to play a better player. And try to learn from them while in your seat, which will be more than half of the time.

Ride the Money Look for ways to make any money balls against B Players early in Phase 1, and possibly in Phase 2 if the layout is difficult and a run out is not likely, even for them.

Safety Play safeties early in the game even when the layout is easy. You can't run out yet, but you have to keep them from running out, so play the first safety of the game if possible. Play safe in Phase 3 in situations where you might normally go for a low percentage shot.

Unnerve Them C Players' unique style can unnerve better players who have forgotten their modus operandi, or are not used to it. Your go for the gusto, riding the money, and shotmaking style of play may throw a B Player off guard, and a couple of "lucky" shots could have them mumbling to themselves!

Make it Tough B Players can often run out when 6 balls or fewer remain. So tie up balls, play safe, and do what you can to keep them from running out until the game gets to within your run out range.

Spot Balls B Players seldom give a C Player more than one extra money ball. Remain conscious of its position while looking for ways to make it out of rotation.

Tie Up Balls If you are receiving a spot, tie up balls past the spot. For example, if your opponent is giving you the 7-ball in 9-Ball, tie up the 8 and 9-balls. This kind of insurance can prevent them from running out should you miss the 7-ball later in the game.

Time of Possession You will spend less time at the table than when playing a C Player. You can overcome the tendency to grow cold in the chair by following your shooting routine and playing every shot to the best of your ability.

C Player vs. A Player

When there is a huge gap in skill between two players, then the outcome usually depends on how the better player is playing. Unless you are receiving a huge spot and your opponent is having a bad day, then look at matches with A Players as learning experiences. Enjoy watching good pool, and see if some of their game might rub off on you.

Ride the Money Look for ways to make the money balls early in the game when a run out is less likely, especially if you are getting multiple wild balls. When you can move two or three of them at a time and one is lined up somewhat at a pocket, let'em rip!!

The Break It is often your best chance if you are receiving weight. When you make a ball on the break other than a money ball, scour the table for a way to pocket a money ball on the first shot, or within a couple of shots. And look for a shot on the cash when your opponent fails to make a ball on his break.

Set Up Money Balls When you have nothing better to do, try moving your money balls to places where you can make them with a combo or some other kind of shot while playing safe at the same time.

Tie Up Balls If you are receiving a big spot, tie up balls past the spot. If your opponent is giving you the 6-ball, tie up the 7 and 8-balls, or the 8 and 9-ball, for example. And in 10-ball, tie up the 10. This strategy could prevent them from running out later in the game.

Safety Play Play more safeties at all times during the game in an attempt to thwart your opponent's offense. You will lose most battles, but you can't let this frustrate you – this is better than just handing them a runout, and it will sharpen your defense for future encounters with your fellow C Players.

Pushouts Be cautious when evaluating your opponent's pushout. He will offer bait, or play safeties you don't see. It is usually better to take the shot than let him shoot. When you push out, make it as tough as possible. Do not push out to easy safeties!

The Chair Don't be surprised if you spend upwards of 70-80 percent of your time in your chair. And don't become frustrated if you play less than your best, because you are going to spend plenty of time cooling off in your seat.

Move Balls The 7, 8, or 9-balls (and 10-ball) should be moved to a location that will make running out much tougher. Do this when you are likely to miss a kick shot, or on push outs. Hopefully he will then miss at the end of the rack because you made his job tougher – just when it is within your run out range.

Strategies for B Players

B Player vs. B Player

You and your fellow B Player are capable of shooting some very fine pool, and are thus very dangerous and unpredictable. You could be paired against a B Player who looks like a C Player one minute and an A Player one rack later! You must understand that a B Player's game averages out to the B level over the long haul, but that it can vary widely in the short term. Contests between B Players are often decided by who is on their game, and/or by who can sustain a higher level of play than normal through an entire set.

Know the Gaps B Players have many well-developed skills and several gaps in their arsenal. Play around your opponent's strengths and force them to do the things that they hate doing — for example, shooting long shots or short rail kick shots.

Intimidation Your opponent is capable of playing fine pool. Don't let his great pool lead you into thinking that you don't have a chance, as he most likely will cool off soon enough — then you will have your chance!

The Rolls In a short race, the rolls could definitely favor one player. However, there are usually enough innings in matches between B Players that the outcome is decided by who is playing better. So don't fret about luck, and stick to making the most of the opportunities that come your way.

Pace of Play You must guard against conforming to his pace of play, whether it is faster or slower than your normal tempo. If you are up against a slow player, don't let him take you out of your game, even though you will be spending more time in the chair.

Weight There is enough difference between members in this category that upper level B Players can give other B Players a single ball spot, such as the 8-ball (or the 9-ball in 10-ball). If you are giving or getting weight, you must plan accordingly.

The Score Avoid losing confidence at those critical junctures when your opponent has jumped into a lead of 2-3 games and is playing well — especially if you made a poor shot or two that helped him to get started.

Push Outs You can gain an edge on push outs with your skill in some area, such as hiding the cue ball on long distance safeties.

Safety Play B Players with a strong defensive game can gain a significant advantage, enabling them to pick up a number of the games that are up for grabs. If that describes your game, take full advantage of your skill. If not, get to work on bringing your safeties up to par.

Kick Shots Skill at kicking is another area that can separate you from your fellow B Players — especially when you consider that relatively strong safety play is a common characteristic of many B Players. Adjust your strategy to match the defensive skills of your opponents.

Jump Shots There is a wide range of skill among B Players on jump shots. You should quickly assess your opponent's ability to play jump shots as this may alter your strategy when playing safe or pushing out. If your opponent jumps well, force him to play kick shots by leaving the cue ball up close to blockers.

Phase 1 A low percentage of racks are run in this phase unless the balls are lying well. Play safe often and use ball in hand to improve difficult layouts.

Ride the Money Consider combos or other shots on the game ball when the rack is lying tough, especially when a safety is built into the shot. If you are getting a wild ball, play it when it has a good chance of going and when a miss won't cost you the game.

Phase 2 This is winning time for most B Players as the rack is now well within your runout range. Tighten up your safety play and initiate the safety battle, as this is the critical juncture in the battle for control of the table.

Run Outs You will win a high percentage of matches against fellow B Players by running out the last 3-6+ balls when you know you are fully capable of doing so. In other words, get out when you know you are supposed to!

The End Game Positional errors may force you to abandon a run. You may wind up facing a tough shot or safety in the end game as a result of an opponent's error. So be prepared to come with a big shot or creative safety when the game is in Phase 3.

B Player vs. C Player

You are the prohibitive favorite, providing that there is no handicap and the contest is long enough to neutralize the luck factor. The three main things that could cause you trouble are: 1) failure to close out easy racks, 2) dealing with odd ball leaves at the end of the game, and 3) rides on any extra money ball if a ball spot is being given.

Phase 1 This is a dangerous phase because you may not be able to run out, and your opponent may realize this and take shots at the 9-ball or 10-ball and the spot balls, if any.

Push Outs You can gain an advantage over a C Player by outfoxing him with your push outs. Offer shots and safeties that you can execute but he can't, or that he doesn't recognize.

Safety Play Play safe whenever you have the slightest doubt about making a shot. Your main objective is to hook your opponent, because there is a good chance that a C Player will miss hitting the kick shot.

Money Balls If you are giving up an extra money ball or two, be very conscious of their positions, especially in the first two phases when C Players like to take them for a ride.

B Player vs. A Player

Relish your role as an underdog. An upset is not likely in a long race, but you could pull one off with a handicap or in a short race format. Let you confidence soar and let your best game come out. This is your chance to realize a whole new level by playing well against an A Player. And even if you don't win, you could score a moral victory by keeping things close, and you might discover that you are a better player than you may have realized. At your level of skill you could make life difficult for an A Player if you are playing your best and/or he is off his game. Most of all, enjoy the match and learn from it. Think that way and you will always end up a winner.

The Break Really bear down on the break because it gives you a chance to get off to a good start in your battle for control of the table.

Kick Shots You may have to gamble and go for a tougher objective than normal, such as hitting a side of the ball, because a "normal" kick could leave an easy response for an A Player.

Push Outs A Players are good at bluffing, so be wary of what he offers you on his push outs. However, don't be afraid to go for a shot or safety if you feel your opponent has a good chance of taking control of the table. When you push out, make sure you don't leave him with an easy safety, even from long range.

Phase 1 This is a crucial stage for you now because you can easily lose due to your opponent's skill at running out. Unless the rack is lying easy, emphasize defense and wait for your opportunity to get out. If you are getting the 7-ball or more, go for the win from the start.

Run Outs Keep playing safeties until the rack is within your run out range. Avoid failing on heroic run out attempts because this will often leave an easy run for your opponent. When you have a high percentage run, get out! Remember, against A Players, execution is key.

Safeties Try to limit his responses by sending the cue ball up closer to the blockers than usual. It is generally better to hide the cue ball instead of the object ball.

Strategies for A Players
A Player vs. A Player

Against a fellow A Player, the main factors that determine the winner are: the break, execution, attitude, and adaptability to the conditions. With top players, successful 9 Ball is largely about executing what you know to near perfection. If you can stay in line, your position plays and shotmaking requirements become somewhat repetitious. Then it all comes down to execution. In sum, you must take charge of the table and run out – over and over again.

You should be psyched up for a very good performance, but understand that both of you will make mistakes – even the pros do, as shown by Accu-Stats Video Productions, which rates the performance of top pros at major tournaments. In 44 rated matches at the U.S Open, from 1998-2000, the 88 winners and losers averaged .841. That's about 3 mistakes in every 20 shots by the best players against the best under pressure on tough tables.

The Score You should have a chance to fire back even if your opponent jumps to a lead of several games in the early going, so remain patient and get mentally prepared to make the most of your opportunities. In a short race format, make every effort to jump out ahead, especially if you are a habitual slow starter.

Pace of Play Use your well-rehearsed shooting routine to keep from mimicking your opponent's pace of play. Guard against going cold or hurrying your shots when you return to the table against a slow-playing opponent.

The Rolls Most matches between A Players are decided in far fewer innings than those between less skilled players, so there are fewer opportunities for the breaks to even out. So, the impact of a few rolls in either player's favor is magnified. Don't get upset if the Pool Gods seem to be conspiring against you. Make the most of what you are given to work with.

Intimidation You may derive an edge from your reputation. If your opponent is favored, you still have an excellent chance of winning, so relax and enjoy your role as a spoiler. Your opponent may feel pressure to win against someone he feels he is supposed to beat. Either player may be subjected to the forces of intimidation during the course of the match due to their opponent's fine play.

Safety Play The best safeties lead to ball in hand (for you) or a difficult kick (for your opponent). The rest leave the outcome very much in doubt. So be prepared to gamble a little when playing safe in an attempt to nail down a winner. You must also take into account your opponent's ability to jump out of a hook.

Kick Shots The first rule is to hit the ball. But you must go beyond that against a fellow A Player. Your goals (make a ball, safety, leave a long shot, etc.) should be correlated to the difficulty of the shot and the layout.

Jump Shots The games of A Players are well rounded, but this is one area where you can find some major differences in skill. Try to make an accurate assessment as to their ability to play jump shots on their first couple attempts – and if they pass on a potential jump in favor of a kick shot.

Phases 1 and 2 The majority of racks are decided in Phase 1 and a lesser amount in Phase 2. Be prepared to run out or to play a killer safety.

Target Practice The last three balls (Phase 3) are the easiest part of the rack because the obstructions are gone, and the balls are almost never close together. The last three balls are not much more than target practice. Focus, execute, do what you know how to do, get the job done, and be a closer.

The Break The break is often the single biggest factor in determining the outcome among upper level players. Monitor your break and adapt quickly to the table by changing positions and speeds if necessary. Pay attention to your opponent's break and consider copying it if it is working particularly well. Conduct periodic rack inspections.

Battle for Control You must battle for every chance to ignite your offense against a skilled player. Don't expect anything to be handed to you, but be grateful when it happens.

Push Outs Never underestimate the knowledge of a fellow A Player by pushing out to situations that are either too easy (they'll shoot) or too difficult (you'll have to shoot).

Neutralize Your Opponent's Strengths While an A Player's game is well rounded, he may count on a couple of areas to win a game here and there. Discover these as quickly as possible (unless you already know his game) and deny him the opportunity to beat you with his strengths.

A Player vs. B Player

Your strategy should resemble that which you use against an A Player. B Players can be very dangerous when they catch a couple of rolls and their best game kicks into gear. You are a substantial favorite, even when giving up a spot (within reason, of course), but you cannot afford to play in a haphazard manner, especially if the race is not a long one. Don't play down to your opponent's level because that is a recipe for an upset.

Time of Possession You should play well because you should be doing 60-70 percent of the shooting. Your advantage in table time could weaken your opponent's game.

Avoid Frustration Guard against frustration if you fall behind a player you feel you should beat easily. B Players can run out, especially when things are working in their favor. Put your ego aside and do not worry about the potential consequences (embarrassment) should you suffer an upset.

His Strong Suit A B Player usually has a strong shot or two which he loves playing, such as the jump shot. He thinks these shots give him an edge, and he is willing to shoot them with little hesitation. If he really is strong in a particular area, you must deny him the opportunity to use it. But if he thinks he is Sky King, the cue ball will often descend on the poolroom floor; so, give him all the jump shots he thinks he can handle.

Money Balls You will likely be giving up one or more balls as a handicap. You must therefore manage their positions on the table to minimize or eliminate any easy wins. Make him earn every game.

Phase 1 Play a B Player tough from the start, like you would an A Player, because he is a threat to beat you in any game if given a chance. Try to break up trouble when playing safe.

Phase 2 This is the segment where you must nail down the game if the layout in Phase 1 was not conducive to a run out.

An Off Day Your knowledge of strategy and tactics, and your skill at running basic patterns, should be good enough for you to beat a B Player even when your game is off.

Safety Play A number of games against a B Player feature a turnover in Phase 3. Safeties in Phase 3 are about using distance, freezing the cue ball on the rail, creativity, and controlling both balls. Pros and top amateurs use several cagey maneuvers to avoid selling out in end game positions where less knowledgeable players will go for the most heroic and/or foolish of shots.

A Player vs. C Player

If you are playing a C Player even up in a race to three or longer, you should virtually never lose. However, most match ups between these two disparate levels involves a handicap, often substantial, which can be enough to put the outcome in doubt. Still, one of the laws of pool is that the better player will usually win as long as the weight is reasonable and the match is long enough to neutralize the rolls factor.

The Basic Strategy When an A Player is playing a C Player with no ball spot (although there could be games on the wire), the game plan is to avoid losing the game with a stupid mistake on the last 3-4 balls.

Time of Possession You will get 70-80 percent of the table time, so you should get in great stroke providing you don't get complacent. And, your opponent will play less than their typical because of lack of table time and the intimidation factor.

The Luck Factor A Players, who give up big spots, must get used to the C Player's apparent advantage in the luck. Sure he will win some games by smashing the balls around the table, but he will lose even more games when these shots fail to produce wins.

Manage the "Money Balls" You will probably be giving up a handicap in a tournament or league play, and you certainly will be when playing for money. When this weight is an extra money ball, or two or three, you must eliminate your opponent's chances for short rack victories. Again, this line of thinking may be foreign to A Players who mostly play opponents at their level.

Kick Shots Reduce your goals when kicking on all but the easiest kicks. Avoid giving up ball in hand because the last thing you want is to have him take dead aim on one or more money balls.

Break Clusters When pushing out, see if you can separate clusters in the later phases of the rack that could keep you from running out.

When to Gamble You can take chances on combos or tough run outs in the early stages when the game is out of his run out range.

The Last 3-6 Balls Your strategy in this phase is more about avoiding losing than about beating your opponent. You should win even when giving up a handicap providing you play your game and play smart. You needn't take the aggressive approach that must be used against A Players.

Phase 3 Tighten up your game when it reaches the mid-point. This is the time where you want to take control and eliminate any chance of losing. Let the C Player beat himself in the end game.

Strange Happenings in Phase 3 If you are playing a C Player without a ball spot (which happens in a tournament where games are given on the wire) and he is shooting in the end game, you are in for a unique experience – especially if you are used to playing only A Players. Be prepared for long distance shots, safeties, and a wide assortment of situations that you'll seldom encounter in the world of precision run outs where the game is over much earlier in the rack.

Big Ball Spots When you are giving away a multiple ball spot, you must play tight from the start because your opponent's end game starts a lot sooner than yours.

Safeties Use your skill at safeties to control the game. In many cases, you can play safe to larger zones if your opponent is especially poor at kicking.

Ball In Hand You may use it to play a shot at the game ball when a safety is built into the shot in a situation where you might normally try to run out.

Avoid the Barrage If you are giving away a big spot, you must learn to withstand an occasional barrage when his money balls can't seem to stay out of the pocket. You've got to suck it up, fade his barrage, and be prepared to assume command once again.

CHAPTER 12

Competitive 9 Ball

The highly competitive nature of 9-Ball draws so many to these action packed games. Every few minutes a new game begins, bringing with it a unique layout with fresh new challenges and the possibility of victory. The games have skyrocketed in popularity as players at every level have more opportunities to compete than ever before, as the number of leagues and tournaments has proliferated throughout the land. And, of course, the games are perfectly suited for those who enjoy a friendly wager.

You've got to love matching skills, shots, and strategies against a worthy opponent who may be your superior in many facets of the game. **Your best chance to gain the upper hand in the mental game is to let your cue do the talking**. When you are competing at these games, your ability to get lost in the game is what largely enables you to emerge in the winner's circle. Your talent for playing one shot at a time and a strong will to win are mandatory operating equipment.

Your mental strength will be tested many times during the course of any contest. A bad roll, a poor shot, or your opponent's fine play could cause you to doubt your ability to win. At times like this, **you must show your "heart," the quality that players ascribe to players who don't get rattled when things are not going their way**. You must be able to rekindle your fighting spirit, and signal to your opponent via your play that you are a force to be reckoned with – all of the way until the finish line. And, when you are ahead, you must demonstrate a killer instinct and be able to close out a match, especially one that goes double hill. You want your opponent to begin to feel that they have no chance of getting back into the contest.

"It's not how good you play but how good your opponent plays on you."
Jim Rempe, voicing a quote from **Irving Crane**

Intimidation – The Mental Side of 9-Ball and 10-Ball

When two players compete, one usually has an edge in the mind game. One player feels a degree of intimidation while the other feels like he is the better player, or that this is his time to win. The intimidation factor becomes quite obvious when you see an unknown compete against a great player.

Your emphasis should be on making the most of your opportunities during a match, and on playing each shot to the best of your ability. A big part of the win/loss equation, however, also falls on the quality of your opponent's game. That's why Rempe's quote above rings so true. If you are the type of player who puts others in top gear, then your intimidation factor is rather low, which obviously makes winning that much tougher. On the other hand, if you can turn your opponent's arms to stone, you have a huge advantage going into every match.

Any advantage that you gain in the intimidation department should come from your game, your confident demeanor, and other positives that combine to elevate the fear factor in others. You should not try to intimidate your opponents with tactics that exceed the boundaries of good sportsmanship. In short, **you can be a consummate sportsman and still intimidate the hell out of your opponents**! Excellent examples of intimidating sportsmen are Johnny Archer, Efren Reyes, Shane Van Boening, and Allison Fisher.

Your quest to create an intimidating presence leads to a fascinating paradox: part of you wants to compete with a formidable opponent who motivates you to play your best, while the other part wants your opponent to make mistakes so you can get to the table and run-out! The ideal scenario is to play someone whose game you respect because this will motivate you to play your best. You want them to play well, but to make just enough mistakes so that you can win an exciting and memorable contest! So, while blowouts are nice, **your sweetest victories will result from those close encounters with a skilled opponent where you emerge victorious**.

Qualities that Opponents Find Intimidating

A big part of winning is doing all of the little and not so little things that intimidate your opponent, and that get them to thinking they can no longer win. A number of elements in your game (other than blatant sharking) can signal to your opponent that you are a force to be reckoned with.

Style of Play

Most players have a few opponents whose style grates on them like chalk on a blackboard - intimidating them or throwing them off their game. This explains, in part, why some very fine players have a problem with certain opponents.

Fast and Flashy Players

Fast and flashy players intimidate some opponents, especially if this style is combined with superior shotmaking. This form of intimidation works well on less experienced players who are unaware of the benefits that come from playing a fast player. So, **if fast players intimidate you, take the cure by remembering that they are more prone** to making errors. In addition, you have to spend less time waiting for your turn, which helps to keep you from cooling off. Remember also that **pool is a game of yin and yang – a strength can be a weakness, and vice versa**.

Cold and Methodical
Emotionless and methodical players are among the most intimidating kind of opponents. They take their time, plan each shot carefully, make few mistakes, and keep you waiting in your chair. In addition, they almost never show any signs of mental weakness, even if they are feeling vulnerable inside. The best way to combat this type is to take your time (but not too much time), bear down on every shot, and get fully into the match. And do not make the mistake of fussing in your chair between turns. Instead, study the table and plan for your next turn.

TIP: Whether you play fast or slow, don't change your tempo to match that of your opponent. Play at your ideal speed and your ideal rhythm.

Your Arsenal of Skills
Players, even at the pro level, are at least a little intimidated by an opponent who is super skilled in one department, especially if this is a weak spot in their game. For example, Shane Van Boening intimidates players with his break while Efren Reyes' ability to kick his way out of trouble is a source of frustration to most everyone who plays him.

A Single Shot
A single shot can signal to your opponent that you have come to play, and that you are a force to be reckoned with. In many cases, **a big shot can turn a match around or establish momentum that carries through to the end of the match**. If you are on the receiving end of a potentially intimidating shot, you need to quickly put it into proper perspective: remind yourself that it takes more than a single shot to win or lose the match. Enjoy your opponent's great play and let it inspire you to give your best effort.

A Picture Perfect Run Out
Knowledgeable opponents will be most impressed by your run outs which feature near perfect cue ball control from start to finish. A well-executed run gives your opponent the dubious pleasure of watching you play great pool for several minutes. And **a couple of well-executed runouts can have a lasting impact** because your opponent may start thinking that every time he misses he will have to sit and watch you run out yet another game.

Your Reputation as a Player
Your name often precedes you in competition, as does that of your opponent. Most players in a tournament will read the board to see who they are going to play next, and in future rounds, should they keep on winning. If your opponent sees your name, what do you think he will be thinking? And what are your thoughts when you know you are going to be playing a fine player?

If your upcoming opponent views you as a tough draw, the advantage could be worth a couple of games in a race, especially if you back up your psychological edge with a strong start. If he sees you as an easy match, you need to make a statement early on that you are no soft touch.

Your reputation and respect for your game can take a sudden leap when you knock off a fine player or two. If you have just beaten an excellent player, your next opponent will know who you beat, and possibly by how much. This could instill an element of doubt as to the outcome of his upcoming match with you.

Your Mental Strength

A savvy opponent will look at more than your game for signs that you can be beaten. He will evaluate your composure when you are behind, your ability to deal with bad rolls, and your demeanor following a poor shot. He will also notice how you respond to his good play. Any weakness will signal to him that your mental game is less than rock solid, and that it could continue to erode. This will give him additional confidence that he can win, which is not exactly what you want to have happen.

Experience in pressure situations is the best antidote for intimidation in the long run. In the early stages of your career, expect to take your lumps while learning how to deal with the various scenarios that you will encounter. In time you will learn how to put things into the proper perspective and to view events in a way that makes a positive contribution to your game. With enough seasoning and a positive outlook towards the learning process, a day will come when little, if anything, that your opponent does (within the boundaries of acceptable sportsmanship) will cause your mental game to weaken.

The Battle for Intimidation

One of a number of possible mindsets could be at work as you and your opponent prepare for a match. As the match wears on, confidence levels rise and fall for several reasons, including each player's performance. In most cases, one player will gain an edge in the beginning, or by the time the match is in the later stages. Broadly speaking, there are five possible levels of intimidation.

Levels of Intimidation – the Spectrum

1 – Your Opponent is Very Intimidated.
You are the heavy favorite, and you and your opponent both know it. Focus on playing your best game as insurance against what would be a tough loss to swallow. Avoid playing down to his level because this could give him a much needed boost of confidence, and a shot at an upset.

2 – Your Opponent is Somewhat Intimidated.
At Level 2, you know you are the favorite, which should give you confidence. You must not become overconfident or take your opponent for granted because this could lead to an upset. Your opponent knows he is the underdog, but not by much, so you don't want to give him breathing room or else his best game may come out.

3 – There is Mutual Respect and Little or No Intimidation
Level 3 can lead to your best game because you know you must really play well. As the

match wears on, one player may emerge with the edge while the other feels the pressure of trailing, missed shots, bad rolls, their opponent's fine play, or their less than stellar effort.

4 – You are Somewhat Intimidated.
If mind is in Level 4, you still have a chance, but you are going to have to work hard at impressing your opponent – and yourself! You are the underdog, but you have enough confidence to know you do have a chance. If things go your way, you turn the dynamics around and gain an edge on your opponent.

5 – You are Very Intimidated.
The highest level of intimidation occurs when you know, going into a match, that your opponent is the overwhelming favorite. You could drop down to Level 5 from Levels 2-4 if you totally break down during a match. When your mind is in Level 5, defeat is almost guaranteed. You are ready to roll over and play dead. You have all but conceded the match to your opponent. Respect for a superior player's game has turned into mind numbing fear. When you are in the frame of mind, you have nothing to lose, so you might as well lighten up, enjoy your role as the underdog, and give it your best shot.

9-Ball are Battles of Skill Sets

When competing at 9-Ball or 10-Ball, it is your break, position play, patterns, shotmaking, safeties, jumps, and kick shots versus those of your opponent. When you do something well, your opponent could be thinking he can't match your superior skill in that area. So, if you continually bombard him with a wide array of shots that demonstrate your skill in several parts of the game, **he could break down and mentally concede the match even though several games are remaining**!

Your opponent may be an outstanding shotmaker, play pinpoint position, or possess a powerhouse break shot. Even so, **do not be overly impressed with any one element of your opponent's game**, especially if you are confident in your areas of expertise. Remember, whatever you give up in one area, such as the break, you may more than make up for with your superior skills in another.

Scouting Your Opponent

You can up your chances of winning by learning about your opponent's game in advance of your match. **Your "intel" will help you establish a game plan for winning**, and for developing a healthy respect for his game. Information comes from a variety of sources:
- Your knowledge from previous encounters.
- Watching them compete against other players.
- A scouting report from a knowledgeable source.
- Observing their play during your match.

Below are samples of the kinds of information that can give an edge:

Intelligence Report #1
Intel: He can't kick but he can jump like Earl.
Strategy: Play tight safeties.

Intelligence Report #2
Intel: Misses long pressure shots at the end of the game.
Strategy: You can push out to a long shot at the end of a match, especially when no hook safety is available.

Intelligence Report #3
Intel: Has a weak break that leads to congestion at the foot end of the table.
Strategy: Be prepared to play a defensive game.

The Mini-Max Strategy

A realistic assessment of your skills and your opponent's will enable you to fine-tune your strategy. The goal is to **maximize the impact of your strengths while minimizing the damage of your weaknesses**. And you want to minimize your opponent's ability to use his strengths and force him to play shots he dislikes playing. I call this the Mini-Max Strategy, which is an easy way to remember to play strategic 9-Ball.

The Mini-Max Strategy
- Maximize the impact of your strengths.
- Minimize the damage of your weaknesses.
- Minimize the impact of your opponent's strengths.
- Maximize the damage of his weaknesses.

Your Kicking is:
- **Good:** Try to hit the better side of the ball with the proper speed and go for the pocket when a reasonable opportunity presents itself. Consider kicking instead of pushing out when hooked after the break.
- **Poor:** Aim your kicks for the center of the ball to avoid giving up ball in hand. Consider using higher speeds to try to separate the balls. Try to "make something happen."

Opponent's Kicking is:
- **Good:** Play tight safeties to reduce his possible responses. Take riskier shots rather than leaving him with easy to hit kicks with which he can easily turn the tables.
- **Poor:** Play safeties much more often instead of going for run outs.

Your Safety Play is:
- **Good:** Play more safeties that give you an good chance of getting ball in hand rather than always trying to run out.
- **Poor:** Go for the run out more often. Be aggressive with your offense.

Opponent's Safety Play is:
- **Good:** Try to avoid safety battles. Accept the shot more often when your opponent pushes out.
- **Poor:** Be prepared to execute the tough shots, easy kicks, and return safeties

they leave you with. Initiate safety battles. This kind of player often specializes in non-safe safeties!

Your Shotmaking is:
- **Good:** You can afford to play further from the object ball to give yourself a bigger position zone for the correct angle.
- **Poor:** Play closer position on the object ball. Concentrate on pattern play and on getting the best angle possible on each shot.

Opponent's Shotmaking is:
- **Good:** Be careful what you leave him on a pushout. Play two-way shots (part offense, part safety).
- **Poor:** Tempt your opponent on pushouts with shots that you can make and he can't (depending on their skill at safeties). Play more offensively on tough racks when there is a shot or two that should prevent him from running out if you miss.

Your Position and Pattern Play is:
- **Good:** You can attempt to run-out much more often.
- **Poor:** Play more safeties. Be patient. Try to rearrange the rack if possible. Avoid giving a stronger opponent a chance to exercise his skills.

Opponent's Position and Pattern Play is:
- **Good:** Avoid attempting low risk runouts that leave the table with a relatively easy run out. Learn about the game and the table from watching his game.
- **Poor:** Play more aggressively in the early stages of a typical rack, and in the middle stages of difficult layouts because you have little fear that he will run out if you miss.

Your Break is:
- **Good:** Look forward to breaking the balls. Try to take full advantage of this critical component of the game.
- **Poor:** You can still win by skillfully executing the other parts of your game up to your usual standards. Make certain you get good racks. Play smart pushouts.

Opponent's Break is:
- **Good:** Even the best breakers often run in streaks, so be ready to run out if they hit a cold spell. (Slip them a slug rack – just joking!)
- **Poor:** Seize the initiative at the start of the game. Be prepared to deal with clusters and obstacles at the break end of the table.

The Score – All About Pool's Most Vital Statistic

The score exerts an inordinately large impact on the play of many players. Some players play well with the lead, in part because of the confidence that it engenders. A player in this category can be a quick starter. If you let him jump out to an early lead, he can be hard to catch. A player who gets out in front early may then play too cautiously in an often futile attempt to protect what he feels is his match. A player who adopts this mindset is often in for a rude awakening when the rolls turn and/or his opponent's game kicks into gear.

In the other camp is the slow starter, who likes the thrill of coming from behind. While his ability to play well from arrears is admirable, falling behind makes no practical sense, especially if he is playing against a seasoned competitor. With the short race format used in most leagues and tournaments, you are asking too much of yourself if you have to consistently overcome 2-3+ game deficits.

If you are a member of the frontrunner or comeback-artist club, then you have just discovered a part of your mental game that needs work. A quick starter needs to keep playing with the same aggressiveness he has shown in the beginning clear through to the end. He must also know his limitations to keep from throwing away the match due to recklessness or running out of fuel.

A slow starter must quell the urge to spot his opponent an early lead. He needs to warm up properly, deal more successfully with early match jitters, and start playing his game from the beginning. **Your ultimate goal is to play your best game under any circumstance, no matter what the score**.

"You cannot let the score affect how you play the game."
Johnny Archer

Categories of Games
The five basic categories include the games:
1 – You figure to win, and you do win.
2 – You are supposed to win, but you lose.
3 – Your opponent figures to win, and he does win.
4 – Your opponent is supposed to win, but they lose.
5 – That are up for grabs.

In the ideal scenario, you always win the games you are supposed to (the 1s), and more than your share of the games that are up for grabs (the 5s). And you would seldom give away "sure" wins (2s). At the same time, your cause can be aided by an opponent who gives away games he is supposed to win (the 4s), perhaps because of the pressure you are applying with your fine play!

When analyzing your matches, you will discover games that could be added (the 2s) or subtracted (the 4s) from your total if you and your opponent had performed up to expectations. Your analysis should also include the games that were up for grabs (the 5s). It is important to recognize what shot or series of events leads to your either winning or losing those games. Your analysis can serve as a valuable learning tool, and it will reveal areas that you need to work on.

Accessing Your Top Gear and Closing a Match
The mantra that has become a religion to so many instructors, me included, is to **play one shot at a time. And give every one your best. Your games and matches are a collection of individual shots**. In the real world, however, you will experience fluctuations in your concentration, which have an impact on your ability to execute. The result is that your level of play is occasionally less than your best.

The great champions in all sports recognize these fluctuations, but they also know when and how to shift into top gear when a contest is on the line. Joe Montana was famous for his ability to rally his team to victory late in the fourth quarter. Jack Nicklaus was known for his ability to play his best golf while his peers were folding like lawn chairs. In tennis, Roger Federer has won 68 percent of his trips to the final. And in pool, Mike Sigel was the best at playing under the heat as shown by his astounding record in the finals, where he won about 75 percent of his matches while accumulating over 100 professional victories.

You may be wondering why these athletes didn't give a fourth quarter kind of effort to the whole contest? Well, **it is impossible to sustain an end-of-game kind of effort for the entire contest**. Top athletes know that their intensity varies from time to time, and they also know how to consciously turn up their game on command. They have a top gear and they can access it when the time is right. When the game is on the line, winners can:

- Call on the special powers.
- Put their game into overdrive.
- Beat the percentages.
- Get the job done.
- Run out for the cash.

Skill at closing out a match should not be taken lightly. It is one thing to win the last couple of games against a weaker opponent when you have a big lead. But closing out a match is a whole different matter when you are on the hill and your opponent is running racks and is threatening to pass you at the finish line.

A favorite line of mine from *The Hustler* comes when Bert Gordon (George C. Scott) counsels Fast Eddie (Paul Newman) after Eddie lost a big lead (and his money) that "The game isn't like football. Nobody pays you for yardage." At that time, Fast Eddie lacked Minnesota Fats' ability to close the deal. He learned, however, and won the rematch later in the movie.

The ability to close (win!) comes from putting yourself in the position often enough that you gain experience in dealing with the pressure. Eventually you will be able to maintain the style of play and that got you close to the goal – and to run with it all of the way to the winner's circle. **You will have so much trust in your game, and yourself, that you can execute the way you know you can when the match is on the line.**

"You don't get any consolation for having a big lead and losing."
Johnny Archer

Rolls, Mistakes, and Great Shots

"The rolls" is pool lingo for the luck factor, both good and bad. Both 9-Ball are completely fair games in the long run, but they can also be excruciatingly unfair in the course of a race to 5, 7, or even 11 games. **The Pool Gods simply do not dole out the rolls evenly in the short run**. In the long haul they are eminently just – but it may not seem that way because most players filter out their own good rolls, but can recite every one of their bad rolls, or their opponent's good rolls!

No in-depth study of the rolls has been made to determine how they are dispersed throughout a typical match. Still, it is safe to assume that **the rolls often play a substantial role in deciding the outcome of the short races** (7 games or fewer) that are popular in tournaments throughout the country. In longer races you have a much better chance of overcoming your opponent's edge in the rolls department by simply out playing him.

A few good rolls can assist your opponent in gaining a lead from which you cannot recover if you focus on bemoaning your fate. If, however, you choose to fight back, you may prevail in spite your early misfortune.

Each bad roll can be counteracted by eliminating a mistake, or by making a great shot. Let's assume that your opponent won a match with you, 9-7. And he led in the rolls, 6-3. It is possible that you could have won if he had failed to take advantage of his good fortune. You could also have come out on top by making fewer errors than normal, or by making a great shot or two.

The list below shows five ways in which the rolls may be dispersed over a short session.
1 – The rolls greatly favor you.
2 – The rolls are slightly in your favor.
3 – The rolls are about even.
4 – The rolls slightly favor your opponent.
5 – The rolls greatly favor your opponent.

When the rolls fall into category #1, the Pool Gods have decided to shine on you today. When everything is going your way, winning is easier, providing you don't get complacent. But don't count on this lasting forever. And you will have a tougher time beating your opponent when the rolls are heavily stacked in their favor (category #5). The rolls can remain lopsided in one player's favor throughout a match. In most instances, however, the rolls fall into categories 2-4. **When the rolls are about even, or when one player holds a slight advantage, both players usually have a chance at winning**.

"The balls will not stay loyal to any one person." **Bill Incardona**

Developing the Killer Instinct

If you compete against the same crowd of people, you may play well against some opponents and slack off against others. For example, you might lighten up against people you like. Remember, however, that playing less than your best takes away from their victory. In addition, your opponent may be aware that you are playing beneath your ability, and this will rob him of the satisfaction he would have received from beating you at your best.

You may also slack off because you feel bad that your opponent is not getting to play much. If this is the case, you need a reminder that **pool is the most selfish sport yet devised by man. The idea is to stay at the table for as long as possible, and to deny your opponent the opportunity to shoot**! You can't afford to feel guilty because you are doing most of the shooting. If you play the nice guy once too often, your opponent may take advantage of your generosity and go on to win the match.

You've simply got to develop a killer instinct. **You've got to want the table all for yourself**. You have to take great pleasure in running out and playing the kind of safeties that give you ball in hand so you can run out all over again. You cannot feel bad because your opponent, who came to play some pool, has instead turned into your personal racker, and into a spectator. Rest assured that as you move up the competitive ladder, you will be playing more and more opponents who have trained themselves to think this way.

Men and Women in Today's World of Pool

Men are highly competitive by nature, thanks to the hunter instinct that dates back to our beginnings – and to our upbringing, which emphasizes sports. Men, by nature, have a killer instinct. Men dislike losing even if it is to their best friend. Furthermore, since pool is really an enlightened form of hand-to-hand combat, the game magnifies men's competitive instincts to an extremely high level. It is me versus you, survival of the fittest, and may the better man win.

The majority of women who are new to pool may not have the same competitive drive as men players. Some women may even feel bad for their opponent when they conclude a winning match. As women gain experience and their games improve, they learn to become much more competitive, but this process can take years to unfold.

Women who are new to competition may compete with men who they know at a local poolroom or tavern. Initially this is a non-threatening environment when playing the men. Competing against another woman as a beginner may bring additional pressure, however, especially if the men are watching the contest.

As a woman player starts working on her game and improves, she becomes more competitive, and the desire to win begins to grow in earnest. When a female player starts playing in important ladies events that may last 2-3 days or longer, the expectations rise – along with the pressure to do well. When a woman player enters this phase, her competitive mindset is becoming closer to that of male players.

Men and Women Competing Together

The sizeable gap between the number of men and women who participate in organized competition has been closing for at least a couple of decades now as the number of leagues and tournaments has proliferated. A high percentage of competitive events now encourage participation by both sexes, which means that men and women will be facing each other more often at the table. These mixed gender match-ups have a tendency to bring forth issues that are not present in matches involving competitors of a single sex.

Let's face it, most men don't want to lose to a woman. The male player has their big fat ego on the line when playing a woman, and they hate the thought of being teased by their buddies after losing to "a girl." This thinking may have been understandable 30 years ago when there were few women in the game and fewer still who could be classified as C Players (using the same standards as for the men) or above.

The times have changed as the quality of women's pool has risen dramatically. Want proof? Just tune in to the ladies playing on TV. Allison Fisher, the dominant women's player for about 15 years, scored a near perfect .970, according to the Accu-Stats scoring system, in a match with Loree Jon Jones at the 1999 WPBA Prescott Resort Classic, a score seldom matched by the best male players. BCA Hall of Fame member

Jean Balukas beat several of the best male players at Nine Ball and Straight Pool, which was her best game. Several years ago Jasmine Ouschan finished fifth in the World 14.1 Championship in 2006. Karen Corr has won several times on the highly competitive Joss Tour, while Jennifer Barretta won an event against the men pros on Tony Robles' Predator Tour.

While the number of highly skilled women players is still far below the men, they are gaining ground. Nowadays it is no surprise for a male player to play a female who plays well enough to beat him in tournament or league competition. I would therefore advise my male counterparts to put aside this ego thing. Start viewing women who play pool as pool players. Give them the respect they deserve. And don't be too surprised if they play well enough to send you packing!

Women who have the skill to compete with men in amateur events may still view their male opponents as the favorites. This may take some of the pressure off of these mixed gender matchups if the women approach them with low expectations. This mindset may enable the ladies to play well for part of a match, but pressure always appears at the end, which can sabotage your efforts. So, **I suggest to women players who have built a reasonably solid game that you should go into any contest with the attitude that you are going to play your game, and that you are playing to win**. View yourself as a very capable pool player who has every right to expect to win.

Tournaments
Types of Tournaments
Nine Ball is so popular now that you can compete in a tournament seven days a week if you live anywhere close to a major metropolitan area. And now Ten Ball is also in the midst of a growth cycle as more and more pro events are being played, and as interest in it is spreading amongst amateur players.

Weekly tournaments are one of the greatest bargains in pool – and in amateur sports for that matter! These events enable you to compete against a variety of players, gain valuable experience, and win prize money for entry fees that typically range from $5-$20. And, there is a tournament for every pocketbook and level of skill. There are several types of weekly events:
- Open events where players of all levels of skill are welcome.
- Handicapped events that are open to all levels of play.
- Restricted events that only allow players up to a certain level of skill, such as B Players and below.

A C Player's entry will be accepted almost anywhere he goes. Most events are also open to B Players. A Players will often be required to give substantial handicaps, if they are even allowed to compete with the C and B Players. In recent years there has been a substantial growth in the number of regional tours that cater to advanced players (see the appendix for details). The entry fees for regional events usually range from $30-$100. These are still a great deal because they allow upper level players to compete for substantial prize money in fields that may occasionally feature several top pros!

Prize money usually depends on the number of entrants. Some tournaments subtract a green fee, which is fair considering that table time is usually included in the price of your entry. At some of the most popular events the house and/or outside sponsors will add money to the pot. At most billiard room tournaments you will usually get at least an hour of free practice time, which further sweetens the deal.

You will likely be paired against players of all levels of skill over the course of a few tournaments. In some open events, A, B, and C Players will be competing with one another, with or without handicaps. If you are new to 9-Ball, open tournaments give you a chance to play better players for much less than it would cost you if you played them in a money game. And if the event is handicapped, you could learn from your opposition while winning at the same time. What could be better?

Manage Your Expectations
It is a good idea, when playing in tournaments, to manage your expectations. Do your best to win against better players, but accept losses as learning experiences. When competing with players at your level, you have an opportunity to improve your ability to play under pressure. Again, your ability to close out a match is one of the most important lessons you can learn from playing competitive pool.

How to Win a Tournament
The best player does not always win – otherwise they wouldn't continue to hold tournaments. While skill is important, **a host of variables can enter into the win/loss equation that are not in any player's control**. When top pros win, they usually acknowledge the role that luck played in their victory. There are usually one or two close matches that easily could have gone the other way. For example, Corey Deuel completed the monumental task of capturing 11 matches in a row (including 10 in a row on the loser's side) on his way to winning the 2001 BCA Championship. One match went double hill while two others were decided by scores of 11-9.

I suggest that you try to play your best pool in every event you enter. When you play great pool, however, **don't be surprised if the Pool Gods conspire against you** somewhere along the way. They may rob you of a title that should have been yours. However, there will also be time when you win with less than your best game.

Below are many of the factors that can aid in your march to a title. Your mental approach and your game are in your control. The other factors are in the lap of the Pool Gods.
- You play great pool.
- You beat the players you are supposed to beat.
- You pull off an upset or two.
- You never give up.
- You receive a bye in your first round.
- The best players are on the other side of the chart.
- You start with a series of easy matches that help to put you in stroke.
- Players you would have trouble beating lose to players who you can beat, even if you aren't the favorite.
- You get great rolls match after match.
- Your opponents get terrible rolls.
- The format encourages upsets. Single elimination, short races.
- You win a match or two despite a sub-par effort.

Single Elimination

In single elimination tournaments, you must keep winning or you're out. You must also be prepared to play one match right after another because there is no waiting for the loser's bracket matches.

If you like odds, then the following calculations should be of interest. If you play in a 32 player field and you are a 70 percent favorite to win every match, your odds of winning a single elimination event are 1 in 5.9 tries. In a 64 player field, your chances would drop to a win in every 8.5 tries.

Double Elimination

The winner's side of a double elimination bracket is the high percentage route to victory. You need to win fewer matches on your path to the title as long as you can stay on it, but you must cope with a steady diet of players who are on their game, and who are feeling confident after their recent victories. Your matches will attract more attention as you proceed further in the winner's bracket. And you may have to deal with the intimidation factor because you will be competing against better and better players.

As you continue further into the winner's bracket, it helps to have a plan for spending the often vast amounts of time between your matches. Four obvious choices are: 1) get some rest, 2) eat, 3) practice, and 4) scout future opponents.

If you lose a match and go to the one-loss bracket, don't let this get you down, especially if a defeat happens sooner that you anticipated. A good attitude and some solid play can take you a long way on the "losers" side. You could face players who are off their game, or who are bummed about being on the loser's side. Many will have one foot out the door, so it is your job to open it for them!

Your survival is at stake so the loser's side is no place for complacency. You must play more matches than those on the winner's side, so you will have a chance to get in stroke and to adapt to the conditions. It will help if you are in good shape, physically and mentally.

You will need every edge, because your matches will only get tougher. After a couple of wins you will begin to play tough opponents who have just won a contest (or more) on the loser's side and have some momentum, or who are smarting from their first loss after a string of victories. And then there is the money – once you have made it into the cash, the stakes and the motivation escalates with every match.

Preparing for a Big Tournament

Your pre-tournament preparations should enable you to **bring your game to a peak just before the event**. The proper preparations will enable you to arrive at the tournament with complete confidence in your game. The time to begin your preparations is an individual matter that is related to the importance of the event, your available time, and how much practice is required to get your game into top form.

Solitary Practice

- Practice your fundamentals and evaluate your technique.
- Work with your instructor to correct any flaws.
- Use practice exercises to get in stroke, and to stay in stroke.

- Emphasize trusting as the tournament nears. You should no longer be too concerned with your mechanics.

Competing to Get Ready
- Only compete in the game you will be playing (9-Ball or 10-Ball) to sharpen your shotmaking skills.
- Compete with lesser players so you can practice running out.
- Play races the same length as the tournament for a friendly sum against a player at your level or slightly better.
- Simulate tournament conditions as closely as possible.
- Compete in local events to gain confidence and to build your immunity to pressure.

Mental
- Visualize playing great pool and executing one fine shot after another. Imagine the surroundings as vividly as possible.
- Make a realistic assessment of the field and establish a goal of where you would like to finish. It could be winning, fifth place, or a moral victory against a tough opponent – whatever suits your game and the occasion.
- Set goals that ensure a rewarding experience no matter what happens, such as: learning from your mistakes and successes, watching and talking to good players, meeting new people, and having fun!

Practical Matters
- Make all preparations well in advance, especially if you are traveling from out of town. This includes: hotels, travel, and things to be taken care of before you leave home.
- Make a checklist for your equipment and accessories such as: shapers, tappers, cleaners, towels, bridge heads, chalk holders, gloves, cue holders, extenders, etc.

At the Site
- Arrive early so you will be relaxed and well rested.
- Eat properly – not too heavily – and don't abuse alcohol.
- Practice and get used to the conditions. Test the tables and make any refinements in your strategy.
- Tell yourself you that like the conditions. If the conditions are not ideal, let your opponents be bothered by them, not you.
- Consider the distractions and other challenging elements. Be prepared to deal with them and eliminate all excuses for losing.

Before Each Match
- Know when you will be playing and be ready.
- Schedule enough time to warm up before each match (20-30 minutes) on the practice tables and/or the table on which you will be playing.
- Follow a routine that enables you to concentrate 100 percent on playing great pool.
- Don't let prematch nerves be a source of concern. A little anxiety is a sign that you are up for the contest. All players feel it.

Money Games

Playing pool for money provides enjoyment for countless participants, and it always will for as long as the game is played. Playing for money is an accepted practice at golf clubs across America. In addition, casino gambling, lotteries, and wagering on football, basketball, and other sports are sources of pleasure for tens of millions of upstanding citizens. As a result, it would be sheer hypocrisy to expect pool players to be held to standards that those who participate in America's other mainstream activities are not.

As for the big money games that certain pros play, it is a shame that these incredibly skilled performers must supplement their tournament earnings by gambling. I believe that most of those who gamble would not feel the need to do so if tournament prize money was even 10 percent of the purses in golf or tennis.

Handicapping

9-Ball are played for money far more than any other pool games. These games provide fast action with the average game lasting 4-5 minutes. And **both games are easy to handicap**. When you are making a game, you will likely be giving or getting a handicap. Handicaps are referred to as a spot, or as weight.

The theoretical goal of the pre-match negotiations should be to arrive at a game in which each player has close to a 50 percent chance of winning. In the real world, this seldom happens. One player may want to play and is not concerned with winning. His opponent, in contrast, usually won't play unless he is the favorite, often the heavy favorite. Skilled negotiators are known to win upwards of 80 percent of their "contests." **Some players grossly overestimate their skills and/or underestimate their opponent's games**. They are lucky if they walk away with the cash 20 percent of the time. Those who play for money can be broadly lumped into three categories:

The Winners – Their games and/or negotiating enable them to win 70+ percent of their encounters.
The Sportsmen – They win roughly 40-60 percent of the time. They like winning, but they like playing and the action even more.
The Losers – They would like to win, but they come out on the short end most of the time, due to poor negotiating skills and poor play. They also enjoy the company of better players, and do not mind paying for "lessons."

If you are a philanthropist and don't mind losing, you will find people in a poolroom who are more than happy to relieve you of your funds. **Should you wish to make pool a money making enterprise, or if you want to avoid being labeled a sucker, then you will need to hone your negotiating skills**. Classes are in session daily at many rooms across the land.

Before you wager your dough, eavesdrop on the conversations of the more articulate poolroom attorneys. Listen to the lines and the responses. You will soon learn the answer to every objection. The skills you learn can also prepare you for a career as a salesman!

Some players are famous for having short memories, so I suggest that you **reach an understanding with your opponent on the critical points in your negotiations** so that you avoid any disagreements. There are many components to the negotiating process, the most important of which are discussed below.

Spotting

An adroit game maker derives a large part of his advantage from skillfully manipulating the elements below to arrive at his winning edge. He knows which bargaining chips – such as the break, or a game on the wire – hold special appeal to a certain audience. He also knows better than to give up multiple wild balls to a player who incessantly rides the money.

Wild Ball – The player being spotted has an additional game ball. When a player is getting the wild 8-ball, for example, he wins anytime the 8-ball is pocketed on a legal shot, just as he would with the 9-ball (or 10-ball). Other common wild ball spots are the wild 7-ball and the wild 6-ball (and the wild 9-ball when playing 10-Ball).

Called Balls – The concept is the same as for the wild ball except that the player getting the spot has to call the pocket when playing his spot ball(s). This reduces or eliminates his chances of winning with a slop shot.

Multiple Wild Balls – When one player is significantly better than the other, the lesser player may receive two or more wild balls, or called balls. For example, an A Player might spot a B Player the call 7-ball and wild 8-ball. The possible combinations are endless. If you are giving multiple wild balls, try to keep them from counting on the break. If you are getting this spot, then you want them to count on the break!

The Last Two – The game is over when the player receiving his spot makes the ball before the 9-ball (or before the 10-ball in 10-Ball), when the 9-ball (or before the 10-ball in 10-Ball) is the only other ball on the table. This spot basically eliminates the need to play shape on and pocket the 9-ball (or the 10-ball). This spot can be extended to the last three, etc. This is one of the smallest spots that a B Player or an A Player can give another. However, the last two is a huge spot for a C Player to give to another C Player because their games are largely decided on the last two or three balls.

Games on the Wire – Let's assume two players are racing to 9 games. If Players A gave Player B a two game head start, Player B would be receiving two games on the wire. This spot is commonly used in tournaments (instead of the ball spots discussed above) because it is less confusing, and it reduces misunderstandings.

The Breaks – One player may have the privilege of breaking every rack while his opponent is assigned the duties of rack boy. A stronger player uses the break as a big bargaining chip to entice players of far less ability into a game. He is confident that his opponent cannot often win from the break, and that he will quickly take control of the table after the break. The breaks are often given in combination with a wild or called ball, in an attempt to create an even game.

Combination Spots

Spots can be combined in a thousand different ways. Here are a few samples:
- The wild 8-ball and the breaks.
- The called 7-ball and the last two.
- The last three and the breaks.
- The wild 6-ball and a game on the wire.

Format

A big part of your money game negotiations will be focused on the format. **The most common format used today is a race to X number of games**. The most common lengths are 5, 7, 9, or 11 games — but I see no reason why they can't be to an even number of games! Here are some tips for choosing the number of games that gives you the best chance of winning.

- Slow starters should bargain for long races.
- Fast starters should request short races.
- Better players should extend the race, while lesser players should keep the sets as short as possible.
- Players giving weight should extend the races, while players receiving weight should make them as short as possible.
- The larger the wager, the longer the set.
- The length should also be a function of the time available and how many sets you want to play.

Many players prefer to play sessions that conclude when one player gets X number of games ahead. For example, in a five ahead set, a player could win by taking the first five games. If the players are evenly matched, they could battle back and forth for hours before one player pulls five games ahead.

Another format is to pay after every game, which allows for the greatest flexibility in changing the wager, the spot, and the length of time that you are going to play. This format is not nearly as popular as it was 20-30 years ago, and it is frowned upon in establishments (the vast majority) that do not like to see money constantly changing hands.

Money Management

When you are playing poolroom regulars and your pals for friendly wagers, money management is not as much of an issue as it is for those who wager large sums. Still, **you can increase your enjoyment no matter what your budget by following sound principles of money management**.

Let's assume you have $100 that you have set aside for wagering at pool (after groceries, the rent, etc.). Do not bet it all on one game the moment you enter the poolroom. Instead, divide your stake into a sufficiently large number of units, otherwise known as barrels. If you are going to play someone by the game, you might be wise to play for $10 per game. Your opponent would have to get 10 games ahead before you run out of money, which is not easy unless you are in a bad game, or are suffering from extremely poor play. If you are going to play races to 9 games, for example, you consider playing for $50 per set. This enables you to make a comeback in a second set should lose the first one.

Your wagers are a personal matter. Most players are content playing for nominal sums. For them, the game is of primary importance. Those who feel that they must bet large sums to get a thrill from playing pool are gamblers first, and pool players second. In sum, there is no single answer for establishing your wagers. One hundred dollars is a small fortune to some, while to others it is tip money. Your pocket book and your common sense should enable you to wager sensibly.

When negotiating for a game, the amount of the wager is another bargaining chip. For example, if your opponent wants to play for an amount higher than you've been offering, you may agree to the figure only if he reduces (or increases) the spot, lengthens (or shortens) the set, or agrees to play on a different table. **When selecting a table, be sure it is one you like**. Also, be sure that it isn't the table that your opponent practices on for eight hours daily, and on which he plays like a world-beater!

The Rules
Discuss the rules with your opponent to make sure you are in agreement. Primary topics include the three-foul rule, who will act as a referee on close hits, cue ball and/or object ball fouls, and the use of jump cues, to name a few. For a more complete discussion of the rules, please see the appendix.

Time
You can save yourself from some grief if you **set a firm time limit before play begins**. If you are winning when your quitting time arrives, your opponent may insist that you keep playing, perhaps until the room closes. One of my favorite phrases is, "You've got to give me a chance to get my money back." Well, guess what – when you've won fair and square and it is in your pocket, whose money is it really? Remind him of your agreement and tell him you'll be glad to play again, but on another day.

Backers
You will have truly moved up in the rankings when someone is willing to finance your money games. **The typical split of the winnings is 50/50**, while the backer assumes all losses. **Treat your backer like a king** and only make games where you have an excellent chance of winning. And never, ever commit the dastardly act of losing on purpose (dumping, doing business). If the word gets around that you dumped a match, you will lose your backer, and your reputation will go straight down the toilet.

Hustles and Shark Moves
Books and DVDs have been devoted to the art of relieving your "opponent" of their cash as quickly and efficiently as possible. Their words of wisdom cover the usual gamut of strategies including the stall, every hustler's favorite. You begin the stall by playing well beneath your ability until your unsuspecting opponent believes he has a chance of winning – and may even think that he is the heavy favorite!

Once the bet is to the hustler's liking, balls start finding the pockets, and he emerges with the cash. If trickery and deceit is your thing, you may wish to purchase guides on this subject. Better yet, **why not spend your time and energy perfecting your game** so you can win with your newfound skills – at actually playing the game.

The Collection Department
When you are playing friends and regulars for nominal stakes, you needn't worry much about getting paid. Even if your opponent "forgot their wallet," or their spouse "emptied out the ATM", they will most likely pay you soon enough rather than have you hounding them.

If you gamble with strangers and/or for big stakes, you should take precautionary measures. At a minimum, insist on getting paid after every game or fifth game (if you are playing by the game), or at the end of every set. In the world of high stakes pool, it is standard procedure for the money to be posted prior to the beginning play. If the wager is sufficiently high and/or trust is low, **a neutral third party is often enlisted to hold the money** – and he is compensated for his service.

If you are not averse to extending credit, realize how your game could be affected playing on the "owsies." When you are not going to be paid right away, there is a tendency to let down. This is fueled by the feeling that you don't want to have to worry about collecting a debt in the future.

League Play

League pool has exploded in popularity - probably because this format combines the rugged individualism of pool with the highly social nature of pool players, many of whom grew up playing team sports. While Eight Ball was initially the game of choice for league pool, 9-Ball is catching up fast, and I am expecting big things from 10-Ball as well.

Many players view league night as an enjoyable night away from home – one that gives them a chance to socialize with others who like to enjoy a beverage or two, and to shoot a few games of pool. That is all fine and dandy. This section, however, is for those of you who are out to win and to grow as pool players.

My ideas below have been adapted from *A Mind For Pool,* which can provide you with a far more detailed presentation on how to compete successfully in league pool.

An Introduction

A typical season lasts from 10-30 weeks. It is comprised of a series of home and away matches between teams of 4-5 players plus substitutes. Women are making their presence felt in competitive pool, and this is very much the case in league pool, where many leagues and teams are made up of players from both sexes.

Your experience will benefit you the most if you play in a league that closely mirrors your level of skill. In leagues that use a handicap system, this is not an issue. In fact, I encourage newer players to compete in handicap leagues so that they can learn from better players. And choose your home poolroom or tavern with care. Make sure it is a place in which you feel comfortable playing, and that has an owner who supports league pool.

Your Team

The best teams are put together when the team's captain takes his duties as chief recruitment officer seriously. **The captain should have a clear idea of the kinds of players that he feels would make for good teammates.**

The captain will naturally want to recruit the best players he can, unless it is a handicap league. **Team chemistry is an important ingredient for success**, and for having a good time. Teammates have to get along over the course of a long season. Captains who want to construct a winning squad must put some effort into the selection process rather than simply rounding up a group of friends. A captain should pick those who share their commitment to the team, and who are dedicated to the sport. If you don't want the captain's job, look for a team and a captain who are serious about winning, and who support each other's efforts.

Team captains often derive great pleasure from their role as leaders. In exchange, they must take care of the mundane details, such as collecting money, arranging for substitutes, and record keeping. Their teammates should show their appreciation for his efforts by showing up on time, playing hard, and maintaining a good attitude.

Team Goals

The team should get together before the season starts to establish its goals for the season, and to devise a plan for reaching them. The captain should write down the goals, make copies, and distribute them to his teammates prior to the first match. Email can also be used for this, and in many other ways, to keep teammates in touch with one another.

Some possible goals include:
- Contend for first place.
- Improve on last year's performance.
- Win the league title.
- Beat the top teams, or an arch rival.
- Qualify for the nationals.
- Help each other improve.
- Learn to play as a team.
- Compete successfully in the nationals.
- Have fun.

Individual Goals

Team goals come first, but some individual goals are also worth striving for. You and your teammates must not become at odds with one another should you be competing for the same honors. Individual goals include:
- Improve your game.
- Increase your winning percentage over last season.
- Become skilled at coaching and instructing your teammates.
- Win the league MVP.
- Win or at least play very well in a season ending tournament.

League Night

Try to **arrive at least 30 minutes before the start of play**. You will reduce your captain's stress level, and you will give yourself time to get in stroke and to get used to the tables. Your team can share ideas on how the table(s) is playing. In addition, you may spot a flaw in a teammate's game that can easily be corrected prior to the start of play.

The whole team should meet briefly to discuss the other team, especially if you know their players from previous encounters. This session can help to refine your strategy and to arrange your line up.

Before play starts, the captain or another team member should **devise a motivating statement to set the tone for the evening's play**. Be creative, since the same line may lose its effect if used week after week. Your motivation could come from wanting to beat the #1 team, keep a winning streak alive, or to secure a place in the nationals. Before each game, one or more teammates should make a positive comment to the person who is about to play.

In one-on-one play, you obviously have only one person to worry about. In league play there could be upwards of 10-20 people crowded around the table. Under these conditions **don't expect total peace and quiet**. League pool offers a stern test of your powers of concentration because it is futile to keep quieting the crowd, so it is best to stick to business unless the other team is blatantly sharking you.

Some leagues permit coaching on at least one shot each game. These sessions can help your team win, and to educate the player at the table. Your coach should be knowledgeable, an excellent communicator, and be familiar with the other players' games. **Mid-game advisory sessions should be fast and effective**. If they become drawn out lectures, they could disrupt a player's rhythm.

After each game is over, your teammates should congratulate the winner – this signals to your opponents that your squad is united in a common cause. Losing players should be consoled and encouraged about their game.

It is pointless to criticize a player while his match is in progress. If, however, a player is missing due to an obvious flaw, he can be offered a quick cure (such as "stay down on the shot") prior to his next turn. The time for evaluating mistakes in position, strategy, or shot selection is after a match. Any criticism should be offered in the most constructive manner possible. This objective is most easily met when you and your teammates have made it a priority to help each other to improve.

Ideally your teammates will still be around at the end of your match, especially if it comes last. After the match is over, hold a brief meeting to discuss what went right and wrong, what you can learn, and any plans for next week, including any practice sessions in between matches.

CHAPTER 13

Practicing 9 Ball

*"I've picked every weakness out and worked on them
until they matched the rest of my game."*
Jeanette Lee

The great players you've witnessed in live or recorded action running racks with apparent ease and pocketing unbelievable shots put in long hours of practice developing and refining their skills. Although you may lack the time or inclination to practice as much as the pros, your game will still benefit from a few hours or more of practice every week.

If you are serious about improving, you will make time for practice. And, a routine that is enjoyable and productive will have you to looking forward to your sessions, not seeing them as a form of torture. Don't forget that while you are practicing you are stroking and hitting pool balls – so, how bad can that be?

One way to improve critical areas of skill is to **schedule your practice sessions as closely together as possible**. This enables you to make the corrections needed, remember what is working, and to really learn each shot – something that obviously can't take place in a match.

As you enter your matches, you will have created a skill set that gives you advantages over your opponents in several departments, which combine to give you the winning edge. Any advantages that you possess are largely acquired in practice. If your practice sessions are well thought out and conducted in a workmanlike manner, you will build your storehouse of skills more quickly.

In short, **if your practice sessions are different and better than those of your fellow competitors, it will show in your performances**. So let's get to work on your game, starting with a complete evaluation of your skills.

Rating Your Game in the Key Competencies
Your 9-Ball games are the sum of your skills in a wide range of critical competencies. You can compete successfully at lower levels with only a modest level of skill in a few

key areas. An average player who is a skilled shotmaker, and who has mastered a few basic safeties, can compete successfully against players at his level. **As you move up the ladder, you must fill in the gaps**. Your opponents will take advantage of those skill gaps in your game which, of course, results in unnecessary losses.

A big step towards improving your game is to **conduct a skills inventory**. Use the 1-10 scale. If you wish to add precision to your rankings, you can fill in the gaps between whole numbers with decimal points. For example, you could rate your stroke at 6.5 – in between 6 and 7. Be as objective as possible. If you are not sure how you rate in certain areas, have a knowledgeable friend or instructor evaluate your game.

You can **use a simplified or detailed approach to rating your game**. For example, you could rate yourself in the overall category of shotmaking knowing that there are many different shots that make up this area of skill. You can add precision to your evaluation by breaking the major categories into subcategories – this enables you to pinpoint specific areas for improvement. This more painstaking approach will lead to better results.

The list below will help get you started. You can amend it as needed. The list below could be broken down even further, but there is a practical limit to what you can evaluate and practice regularly, or as needed.

Champions Checklist

Fundamentals
__Grip
__Stance
__Bridge
__Stroke
__Aim
__Preshot routine

Basic Shotmaking
__Cut shots
__Thin cut shots
__Off the rail
__The long green
__Jacked up over a ball

Specialty Shots
__Banks – short rail
__Banks – long rail
__Caroms
__Billiards
__Combinations
__Curve shots

The Break
__Power break
__Control break
__Adaptability to the table

Kick Shots
__Basic routes
__Using english
__Using speed

Position Play
__Stop
__Draw
__Follow
__No rail routes
__1 rail routes
__2 rail routes
__3 rail routes
__4 rail routes
__Use of outside english
__Use of inside english
__Recovery Routes

Pattern Play
__Basic 3 ball patterns
__Advanced patterns

Safety Skills
__Full hit safeties
__Thin hit safeties
__Control of the cue ball
__Control of the object ball
__Knowledge of a variety of safeties
__Imagination

Push out
__Strategy
__Skills

The Lag for Break

After completing your inventory you will have a blueprint for developing your game. You will know your strengths and weaknesses. Then it is time to go to work on any glaring deficiencies in the key competencies. At the same time, work on refining your strengths, and on keeping them honed to a fine edge.

Developing and keeping a variety of skills at an acceptably high level is really like a juggling act. The goal is to keep as many balls (skills) as high up in the air as possible. In short, **learn, perfect, maintain**!

A Sample Comparison of Skills

Skill	Position	Shotmaking	Patterns	Safeties	Break
Pro	9.8	9.2	9.6	9.3	9.4
A	8.6	9.0	8.3	9.2	8.1
B	7.1	8.3	7.0	6.6	8.0
C	4.8	6.0	3.6	2.8	3.4
You	?	?	?	?	?

This table is a sample of what a broad based skills inventory might look like for players of various levels of skill. Our pro rates a 9.2 or better in all areas, as you would expect from a top player. He may win his share of matches and compete very successfully, but shotmaking, which is his biggest weakness, could be the one thing that is keeping him from winning pro events.

The A Player has a solid game. His safety play is his biggest weapon while his comparatively weak break offers room for substantial improvement – especially considering that a player of his skill can run out when given a chance.

Our B Player shows consistent skill for his level of competition in all areas except his safety play. Poor safeties could be costing him games against opponents he would otherwise be beating.

The C Player's skills leave room for much improvement in all areas. He, like many average players, has learned to pocket balls first, which shows by his 6.0 rating in shotmaking. Now he needs to go to work on his safeties (2.8) and pattern play (4.8). The break can wait until his other skills are more fully developed – remember, skills are learned in sequence.

The admittedly simplistic analysis should give you an idea of the process of evaluating your game. **Your goal is to develop a solid, consistent game with no glaring weaknesses. Balance is the key**. Still, no matter how well you play, you will always have areas in which you excel – and these strengths should be exploited to the fullest in competition. **While competing, you must minimize the impact of your weak points until such time as you can eliminate them in practice**. (For more on this, see the Mini-Max Strategy in the previous chapter.)

Practice Environment

Choose your practice environment wisely. **When you want to focus on specific areas and do not wish to be interrupted, practice in quiet surroundings**. This could be on your home table or at the poolroom during the afternoons. If you are using devices, such as the donuts (hole reinforcements), and you wish to practice without feeling self-conscious, choose off hours at the poolroom.

If you want to simulate game conditions, practice in a loud, noisy and crowded environment because this will teach you how to tune out distractions. And you will most certainly face them on a busy league night or during a tournament. This environment may be best when practicing with a friend. I will present some ideas for this later in the chapter.

Good reasons exist for spending most of your practice time on the same table, and for switching tables, rooms and conditions! Such is the yin and yang of pool! When you practice on the same table, it is easier to measure your progress. You can set up identical drills and routines and compare results from one session to the next. Because you feel comfortable with the conditions, playing on the same table can help boost your confidence

In the real world of competitive pool, conditions do change, often radically. So, you need to develop the skill of adapting to strange conditions if you are to compete successfully away from home. And this is something that you can simulate by practicing regularly in a variety of conditions.

Increase Your Awareness

When playing and practicing you want your awareness level to run as high as that of an eagle sighting its prey. **A high level of awareness will help to confirm the things you are doing correctly. Reinforcing the positive builds confidence**. Awareness is also instrumental in turning poor shots into learning experiences. Once you begin to pay attention to the nuances of each shot, a whole new world of sensory experiences will open up to you. So, as you play each shot, tune into things like:

- Visualizing a successful shot before you play it.
- The feel of the tip at contact.
- Your cueing (where you strike the cue ball).
- The feel of your stroke.
- The roll of a well struck shot.
- The cue ball's route to the position zone.
- The speed of the table.
- How english takes off the rails.
- The sound of the ball hitting the pocket.

Solitary Practice

Most of your practice time should be spent alone. There are countless ways that you can structure each session. Many things need work, either to master or maintain, so practice should always be enjoyable and educational. I suggest you follow these tips:

- Practice regularly and for 1-3 hours at a time.
- Prepare an agenda for each session.
- Develop short and long-term goals including improvements in the areas you have identified during the evaluation we discussed earlier.
- Keep a journal with results from your drills, new discoveries, and things to work on in future sessions.
- Practice as long as you remain enthusiastic. If your desire begins to slip, switch to something else or end your session.
- Frequent practice is best, especially for newer players, even if that means shorter sessions than I recommended above. Lengthy but infrequent sessions don't work nearly as well.
- Resist the temptation to "play" during practice. Be disciplined.

- Intermediate and advanced players should practice under a variety of conditions.
- Have a knowledgeable friend or instructor watch your game.
- Use the donuts to mark the position of the cue ball and the object ball so you can repeat the same shots. Keep a record of your results over time as a way of measuring your progress.
- Practice components of your game that your opponents ignore in their sessions, such as safeties, kick shots, and the break.

How to Structure Each Session

You can create a highly effective practice routine that works for you by using the ideas below. Each session should include a few core elements. Beyond these, you can custom tailor your sessions to meet both your short and long term goals. And, you can create sessions that are as enjoyable as they are productive.

The Start

Take 10 minutes to get your stroke in the groove. It makes little sense to jump into the tough assignments until you are loose and confident. There are countless ways to loosen up. One is to **shoot easy shots first** so you can build your confidence and experience success at pocketing ball after ball. Gradually increase the difficulty as you loosen up and your stroke starts to feel relaxed and fluid.

The Heart of Your Session

After your warm ups, it is time to work on your specific agenda for this session. This part could include things that you wish to work on in every practice that you need to keep in tune such as:

- Your shotmaking – keep track of your pocketing percentages.
- Certain fundamentals, perhaps with a practice device.
- Basic position routes that you wish to master.
- Safety skills.
- Your break shot.
- The kicking game.

"Every time I go to the table (in practice) I really focus on my technique." "You have to maintain your strengths too." **Allison Fisher**

Specific Items for a Session

You obviously can't work on everything at each session, so you must build your skills one by one. Pick out a specific skill, shot, position play, or other item from the checklist that you wish to emphasize. In one session you may spend 20-30 minutes on bank shots while at the next you may spend that time working on shots off the rail.

Trusting Practice

In the later stages of your session it is time to practice in a way that most closely resembles how you would play in competition – this is your reward for your hard work. When at your best in competition you should be playing with a sense of freedom and trust in your game. The idea is to break loose and let your best game out while playing largely on instinct.

End Strongly
I like to end each session by shooting a long straight in stop shot diagonally across the table. I want the last shot to leave a positive impression. If you execute this shot perfectly, you will feel your stroke at its best, and you will see the object ball split the pocket while the cue ball stops dead in its tracks. I suggest that you use this shot, or some other technique, that will help you leave the table in a great frame of mind.

Practice Tips for Solitary Sessions
You have room for varying your agenda within the heart of your practice session. Any or all of the ideas below can add variety to your sessions, and to expanding your skills.

Work on Your Weak Spots
While playing in a friendly match or in serious competition, make a note of any errors or shots that are consistently giving you trouble. Then systematically remove these weak spots in upcoming practices.

Expand Your Skills
Devote a major part of the post warm up period in a session to a segment of the game. For example, a session may consist of an hour or two of nothing but safeties. Start with the most basic safeties and work your way up to the most difficult versions. Push the envelope. After all, practice is a time to learn the limits of each shot and the extent of your capabilities – and to stretch them!

Take Extra Shots
While you are practicing running out, you may discover that your stroke is slightly off kilter. If so, take a few moments between racks (or shots) to shoot few shots to get back in tune. Replay a missed shot (or position play) during a run until you are satisfied with the result before finishing the rack.

Give Yourself a Head Start
Spend some of your solitary practice on running racks from the break, which enables you to work on your break and runouts. After the break, separate clusters and give yourself ball in hand – but don't necessarily put it in a position where you have a simple shot on the first ball. Instead, set up an "out shot" (a tough shot that leads to a win) where you have a 50-70 percent chance of making the ball. This kind of shot will simulate game conditions where you quite often must make a challenging shot on the first ball to ignite your run.

Experiment with Your Pace of Play
Experiment with your pace of play during the trusting segment of your session. All players have a natural pace from which they should not deviate greatly. And yet, if you are a very fast player who is prone to making mistakes, try a little slower and more methodical pace. Slow paced players may suffer from paralysis of the stroke due to too much analysis. If this describes your style of play, you could benefit from a faster tempo.

Fundamentals
While you are practicing specific shots, patterns, or other non-fundamental components of your game, you may sense that your technique doesn't feel quite right. If so, take a moment to check your fundamentals. On your next couple of strokes, look for the flaws that have a tendency to creep into your game, such as jumping or twisting your wrist at contact.

Play the Ghost

A popular practice technique for advanced players is to play the ghost. Here's how it's done: break open a rack and give yourself ball in hand. After several attempts over several sessions you will get an accurate measure of your run out percentage. This, in turn, will give you a reliable gauge for measuring your progress. Less skilled players who seldom run out can keep an average of the number of balls made after the break. These players might also consider removing the last three or four balls so that they can discover their runout range.

The ABCs of Practicing with a Partner

Regular sessions with a practice partner can be extremely productive. The ideal practice partner shares your devotion to improving, and does not look at practice as a social event. He should respect your time by showing up promptly for your sessions. Candidates include your pool playing friends, family members, teammates, your coach, and anyone with whom you feel can conduct some serious and productive sessions.

You can, of course, have more than one practice partner. In fact, much can be gained from practicing with players of varying levels of skill. Let's consider a sampling of the ways that players of all abilities can benefit from practicing with one another:

A Player and C Player. The A Player will get lots of chances to runout, and he will get plenty of practice on hard shots because C Players leave open but tough shots. The C Player will gain from observing the excellent play of the A Player, getting tips on all aspects of the game, and by getting answers to his questions.

A Player and B Player. The A Player can act as a mentor for the B Player who is looking to refine his game. The B Player's knowledge of the game and of the A Players technique (after a couple of sessions) should enable him to detect when a recurring flaw starts to creep into the A Players game.

A Player and A Player or B Player and B Player

When these knowledgeable players practice together, there should be a mutual exchange of new ideas and information that can help each other's games. In addition, each is well qualified to monitor the other's technique, which can be of great value in avoiding slumps.

B Player and C Player

A B Player will benefit from getting to shoot most of the time when playing with a C Player, which will help him hone his skills. The C Player can learn from observation, and from asking lots of questions. The B Player can also offer suggestions on fundamentals, and on basic position play, safeties, and pattern play.

C Player and C Player

Players at this level will share the table equally, which gives each player ample time to work on his game. These players can help each other by sharing suggestions on technique or position as long as they are aware of their competencies and of those areas where their lack of knowledge could lead to sharing misinformation. If they are unable to objectively evaluate the areas where they are knowledgeable enough to be of help, then a qualified instructor should be enlisted to provide this information.

How to Practice with Your Partner

The techniques below will help you gain maximum value from your practice sessions with a partner. You and your partner(s) should give each a try before committing to a regular program – then continue with those that are the most enjoyable and produtive for both of you. In short, **it's about chemistry and competence**.

Analyze the Game as You Play

When you are uncertain of a position route in the middle of a game, put the donuts under the cue ball and object ball before playing the shot. Then analyze with your partner how to play it. Make a policy that it's okay to interrupt each other as long as the shooter has not begun his preshot routine. Observe how the first shot turns out. If you like the results, but aren't sure how you got them, replay the shot now, or after the game is over. You can take the same approach to shots that are unsuccessful: shoot them now if doing so doesn't disturb the layout, or try the shot after the game is over.

Watch Your Partner's Game

A big benefit of practicing regularly with another player is that you get to know each other's games. This allows you to monitor each other's fundamentals. It also enables you to watch for other negative tendencies, such as overrunning position (due to shooting too hard), sloppy safety play, and missing with inside english to name a few. You and your partner may wish to record these tendencies in a journal.

Concede Easy Outs

A and B Players can create more opportunities to practice the skills that win the battle for control of the table and the game by conceding the easy 1-3 or even 4 ball run outs. Once the rack has been clearly decided (let's assume a 90 percent probability of a run out), stop play and rack the balls. This will give you more time for extra break shots, safeties, shotmaking, and safety practice.

Better Player vs. a Much Weaker Player

When one player is much better than the other, a imbalance in the number of shots each gets to shoot. This problem can be solved by letting the weaker player finish some of the easy runs. The stronger player will get practice doing the things that win games in the early going while the weaker player gets needed practice running the last 3-4 balls, where most of his games are decided when he is playing opponents of his caliber.

Alternating Shots

You can get an excellent feel for your partner's game by alternating shots because you now have to shoot what they leave you. The more knowledgeable player can now offer even better advice on how the shot should have been played. On alternate shots, the stronger player gets to practice harder shots and demanding position plays left by the lesser player. And the weaker player gets to play more shots that are within their range of ability. In addition, the weaker player gets to experience, firsthand, what good shape looks like! In fact, the light bulbs may go off when he steps to the table with excellent position on a shot that he now knows is so much better than the plan he had in mind!

Customize Your Practice

You can further customize your game playing practice by trading skills. For example, An A Player could play all of the break shots, which makes sense because the break is so important for players at his level. In exchange, the C Player gets ball in hand once the rack reaches the 6-ball or 7-ball no matter who is at the table because position and pattern play at this stage is an area where he needs big improvement.

Use your imagination to create a barter system for exchanging any shot or skill at any time during a game when you and your partner agree that one player really needs work on that area while the other has it pretty well mastered.

Play Sets Like You Are in Tournament Competition

Play races to the number of games that you and your partner normally encounter in tournaments, leagues, or in money games. Put something on the set that will encourage both of you to bear down and give the contest your best effort. Bragging rights may suffice for some. For others, a nominal $2-$5 wager or table time should work. But please don't confuse this with gambling and any negatives that may accompany this activity. Remember, you are friends and practice partners first and foremost.

B vs. B in Practice

If you and your partner are B Players, then a lot of your games are decided by the one who, on that day, has the ability to consistently run the last 5-6 balls. To get as much run out practice as possible, break the balls and remove enough of the lowest numbered balls that 5-6 balls are on the table.

Sharking

When you and your partner are competing in the real world, you will occasionally have to deal with opponents who employ gamesmanship or sharking tactics, whether intentional or not. You can prepare for these tactics by engaging in a little shark warfare. You will know what to expect, and you can become hardened to the point where these tactics have virtually zero effect on your game.

Having a Teacher, Coach, or Mentor

You can eliminate much trial and error and speed your progress by enlisting the services of a knowledgeable pool person. In addition, a qualified teacher, coach, or mentor can help you learn things the right way at the start. This will save you the time and trouble of relearning the game when you must uproot several bad habits. But choose your teacher wisely. Make sure the chemistry is right, that he is well qualified, and he is sincerely interested in you and your game. If you have any doubts as to the value of a qualified teacher, mentor, or coach, listen to the words of 1990's Player of the Decade Johnny Archer on fellow pro and friend Jay Swanson:

"I can't begin to tell you how much he (Jay Swanson) helped my game. There wouldn't be enough time on the tape. He was a very smart player." **Johnny Archer**

Tips for Being a Great Student

- Show enthusiasm, which will motivate your instructor.
- Keep an open mind to new ideas, especially in the weakest areas of your game.
- Your pool game will take time to develop, so remain patient.
- Develop a plan with your instructor and stick to it.
- Keep your mind on the business at hand.
- Ask good questions, and remember that there are no bad questions.
- When something doesn't feel right, let your instructor know.
- Practice between each lesson.
- Show up on time for your lesson.

Practicing Your Fundamentals
Practice Drills for Your Stroke
A fundamentally sound and consistent stroke is at the heart of any player's game. This section presents a number of exercises and tips that will help you to hone your technique and put you in excellent stroke for your next match.

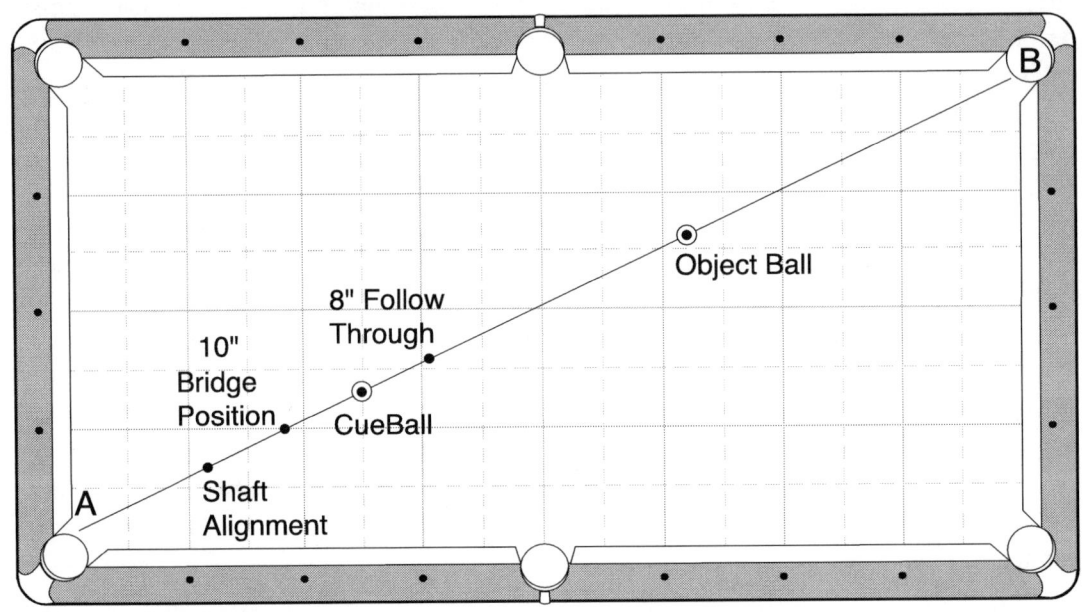

5 Donuts in a Row
Set up for this valuable stroke drill by stretching a piece of string (or dental floss) from Points A to B as shown. Place a donut underneath the string opposite the third diamond up from Point B as shown. The second donut goes underneath the string 2.5 diamonds up from Point A. So far you have prepared the positions for the cue ball and object ball.

Now is the part of the set up where you can exercise some freedom in positioning the donuts in accordance with your unique fundamentals. If your goal, for example, is to follow through 8 inches with a full, medium to medium hard stroke, place the third donut underneath the floss 8 inches past the cue ball's position. Now let's assume you wish to use a 10 inch bridge. Place the next donut 10 inches from the donut for the cue ball as shown.

The final donut goes underneath the string about 10 inches from the donut for your bridge. Now remove the string, place the cue ball and object ball on the appropriate donuts and you're ready to go.

Check Your Bridge
This exercise has a number of valuable components. For starters, assume your stance and check your bridge to see if the distance you've taken is the length you want to use. If not, make the adjustment in the position of the donut for the bridge and then proceed to the next step.

Check Your Alignment
Assume your stance once again and look down at the first donut. Your shaft should obscure the donut from view. If not, your alignment needs to be corrected.

Straighten Your Backstroke
Let's assume that your bridge is the length you desire and your set up is straight. Take several warm-up strokes while looking down at your cue where the first donut is positioned. The donut should remain out of view throughout your warm-up strokes. If not, then your stroke is wavering sideways on the backstroke and/or forward stroke.

Keep warm-up stroking until your cue is tracking above the donut. If you make 15-20 complete warm-up strokes, you will begin to experience what a perfectly straight stroke feels like. One of the beauties of this routine is that it gives you instantaneous feedback on the quality of your stroke.

Play the Shot
The final step is to shoot a stop shot. Stay down and hold your follow through as if you are posing for a picture. The three things to look for are:
- The length of the follow through. Does the tip go to or beyond the final donut?
- The straightness of your stroke. Does the tip rest directly over the last donut?
- Is your cue level?

Cue Over the Diamond Drill
A very valuable part of the drill discussed above enables you to practice without setting up the donuts. Take your stance with the tip of your cue covering the foot spot and the shaft directly over the middle diamond on the end rail. Your cue should cover the middle diamond directly beneath it. Take several practice strokes while looking down at your cue. The diamond should remain out of view. If not, you are twisting your cue off line during your stroke.

You can refine this exercise by drawing a thick line that's the width of your shaft and about three inches long on a "post-it" note. Place the paper directly over the middle diamond in line with your cue. When you take your stance and stroke, even the slightest deviation in your stroke will be readily apparent. The line on the paper should remain mostly covered from set-up to follow-through. A slightly wavering in the back part of your stroke is okay, as we are not robots, but your cue should track perfectly as the tip nears the front half of your stroke.

After practicing this routine for 10-15 minutes, alternate between the exercise and shooting at object balls. Shooting four-to-five shots each time works well.

Shotmaking Practice

Accurate shotmaking is a must for playing 9-Ball. No matter how well you control the cue ball, you will still be required to make your share of thin cuts, long shots, and the other challenging shots that the game demands. It is hard to know exactly how accurate you are on specific shots because you don't have a scorekeeper recording your percentages, like they do in basketball on free throws, three-pointers, and so on.

You can learn the shots you play well and those that need work by practicing the exact same ones from session to session. Record your number of attempts and successes each session, compare your results to previous practices, and note your progress. Let's assume that your shotmaking practice consists of 10 different shots, each played 10 times. This totals 100 shots. You can compare your results in specific categories, as well as your overall rating from session to session.

IMPORTANT: On the exercise below, and others to follow, I recommend that you also do the mirror image version of the shots and position plays. This will ensure that you are equally skilled when cutting shots to the left and the right, and when you are using left and right english.

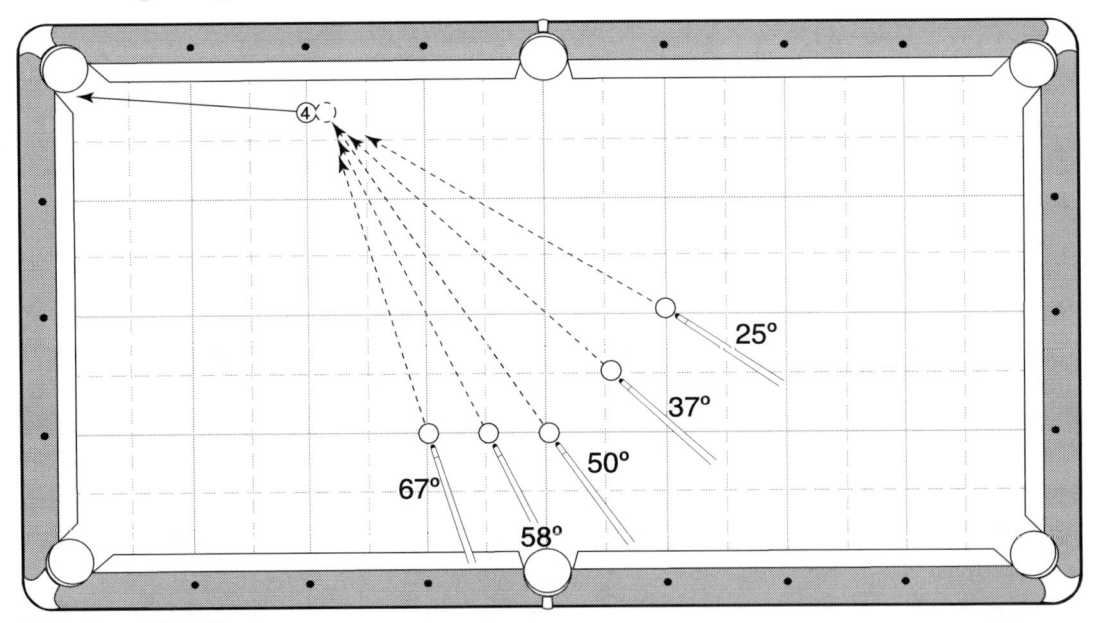

Test Your Cut Shots

Here is an example of a part of the program that we discussed above. This exercise is comprised of shots ranging from 25 to 67 degrees. Shoot each shot 5 or 10 times in each session, recording your results as you go. Start with either the thin cuts or the thicker one. Use your imagination and knowledge of your game in choosing the shots you want to work on until you feel you have them mastered. Then put them in the maintenance mode and pick out a new group of shots, and work on them in the next series of practice sessions.

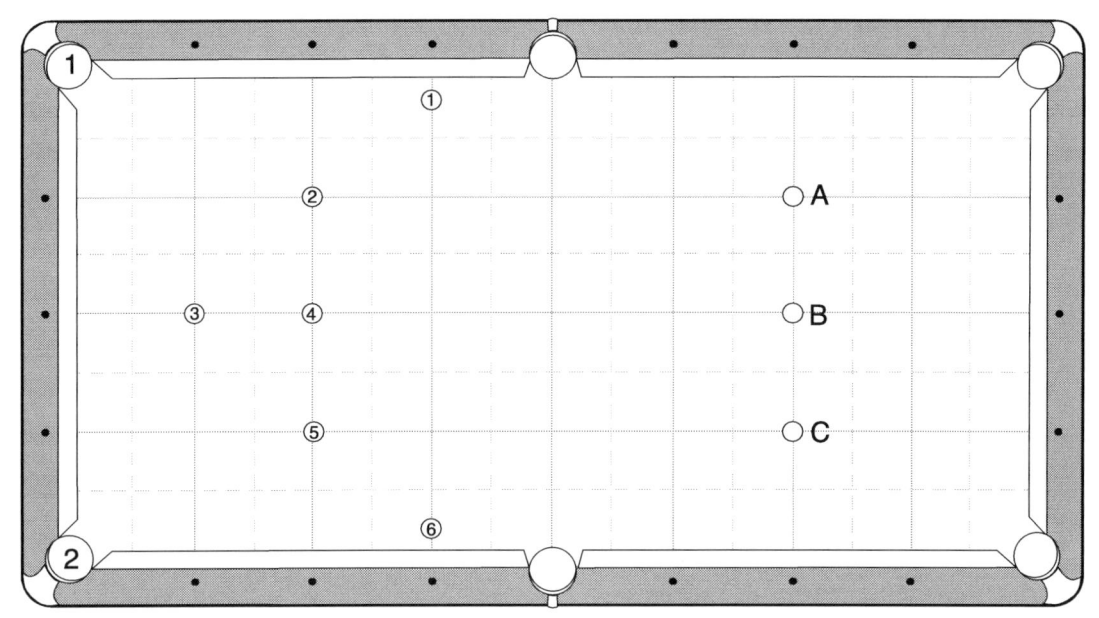

The Long Green Practice Drill

Proficiency at long green shots may be the single most important factor in determining the winner at 9-Ball. To play your best, you must approach these shots with total confidence in your ability to put the ball in the pocket.

These cue ball and object ball positions are easy to set up because the balls are on the intersections of the diamonds – except the 1-ball and 6-ball, which are a half of a ball's width from the rail. When you first practice these shots, use the cueing and speed of stroke in the table below. Then try other speeds and other cueing options.

Each shot has a mirror version so you can gain proficiency in cutting balls to the left and right. Mirror shots are also useful in discovering flaws in your technique. You may consistently pocket a ball in one direction, but not in the other. The same shot (distance and cut angle) is not exactly the same because of the direction, so you may discover that you feel more comfortable cutting in one direction than the other. A slight loss in confidence could cause you to miss – but once you are aware of the visual challenge that your "bad" direction presents, you can take steps to correct this flaw.

The cut angles range from 0 to 62 degrees. The number in parentheses indicates the pocket for each shot.

O.B.	Cue Ball A	O.B.	Cue Ball B	O.B.	Cue Ball C
1 Draw –	Medium hard (1)	1 Draw –	Medium hard (1)	1 Follow –	Medium hard (1)
2 Follow –	Medium (1)	2 Follow –	Medium hard (1)	2 Draw –	Medium (1)
3 Follow –	Medium (2)	3 Follow –	Medium (1 & 2)	3 Follow –	Medium (1)
4 Draw –	Hard (2)	4 Draw –	Hard (1 & 2)	4 Draw –	Hard (1)
5 Draw –	Medium (2)	5 Follow –	Medium hard (1)	5 Follow –	Medium (2)
6 Follow –	Medium hard (2)	6 Draw –	Medium hard (2)	6 Draw –	Medium hard (2)

Position Practice

Excellent shotmaking and good position play feed off each other. If your position play is excellent, it takes some of the pressure off your shotmaking. And if your shotmaking is one of your strengths, you can get away with minor mistakes in position. That said, solid position play will add a degree of consistency to your game. The exercises in this section can help you to significantly improve your cue ball control. I also encourage you to practice the position routes in Chapter 3.

IMPORTANT: On every exercise, I recommend that you also do the mirror version of the shot.

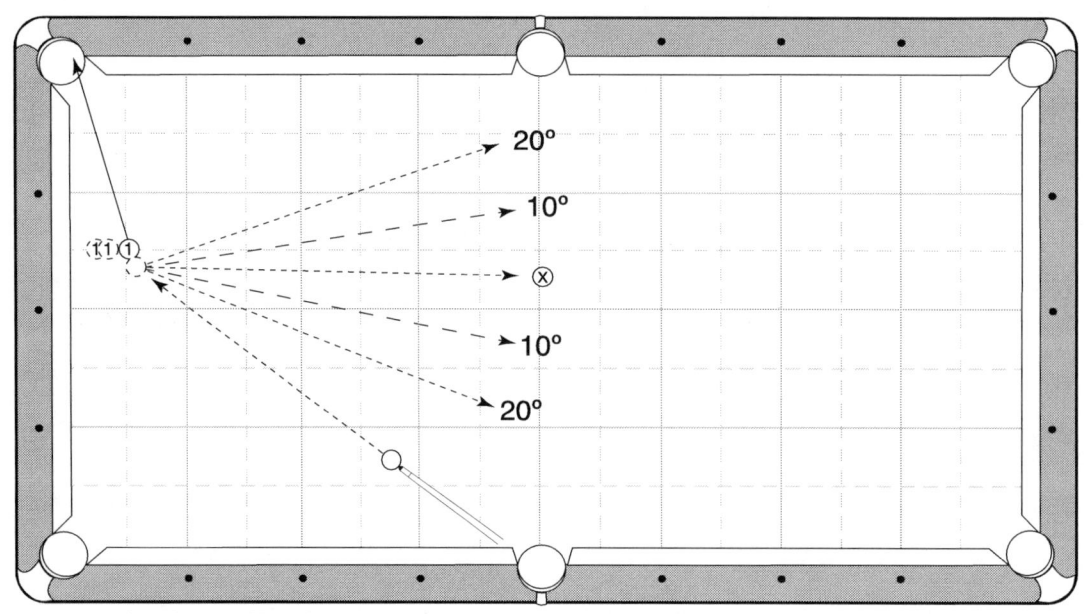

One-Rail Rebound Pathways
One-rail shape is used on 49 percent of all position plays by leading professionals, so these position routes must be mastered. This exercise will increase your awareness of the cue ball's rebound path off one cushion and it will improve your speed control.

The 1-ball is placed two ball-widths off the rail with a 40-degree cut angle. The other positions are one ball's width and a half ball's width from the rail as shown. The goal is to learn to control the cue ball's distance and direction. There are 5 basic directions as shown. Practice each variation until you can send the cue ball within a few inches of each directional line. This will teach you to use the correct cueing for each shot. You can learn speed control by setting up donuts a diamond apart along each route. You can extend the donuts even further down the table. Try to stop the cue ball as close as possible to each donut.

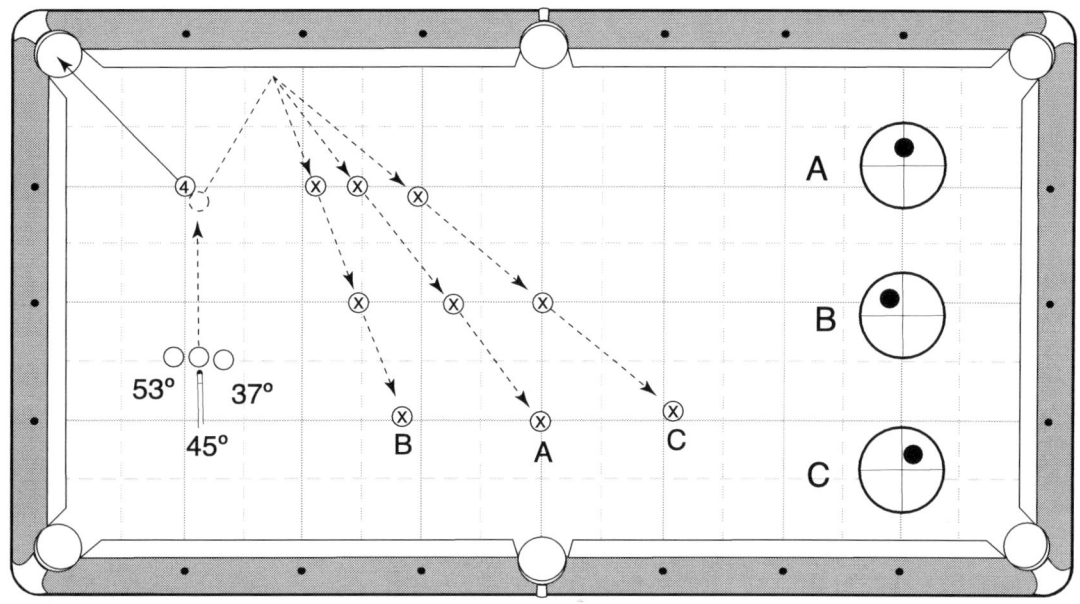

Soft Follow One-Rail

This one-rail position exercise will improve your touch and speed control on soft follow shots. Play the shot at 45 degrees with follow, then follow with outside english, and then follow with inside english. Try to stop the cue ball at the three positions shown on each path. After playing it at a 45-degree cut angle, repeat with cuts of 37 and 53 degrees (one ball width to the left and right). Notice the difference in the cue ball's route and traveling distance, and it will give you **an appreciation of the difference that a cue ball's width makes in playing position**.

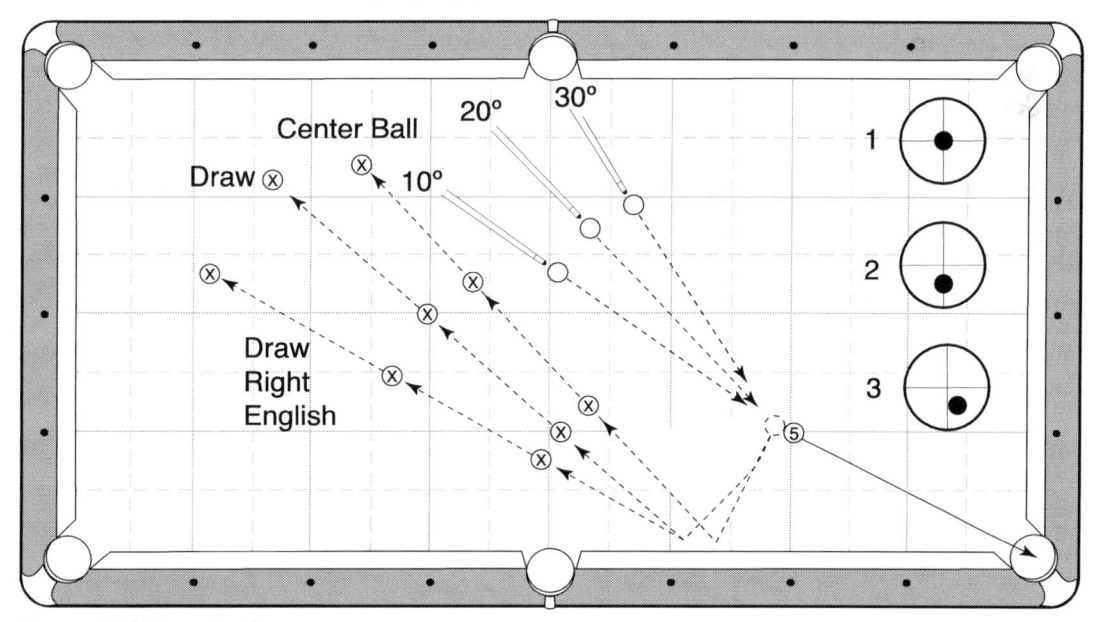

Draw Off One Rail

This exercise will help you master several of the most common one-rail position routes. Repeat the routine three times using: 1) centerball, 2) 1 tip of draw, 3) 1 tip of draw with outside (right) english. Try to send the cue ball to the three locations on each route.

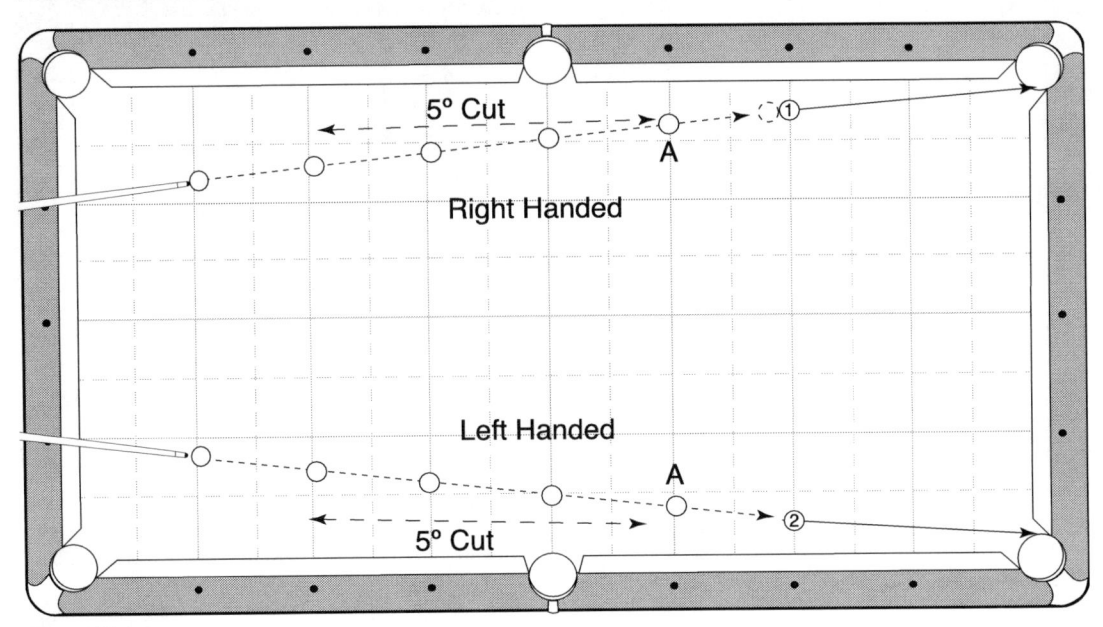

No-Rail Position

Stop Shot
The ability to control the cue ball without contacting a rail is second in importance to playing 1-rail position. According to my research, the pros play no-rail shape on nearly 24% of their position plays. Common no-rail position plays include stop shots, soft follow shots, small angled draw shots, follow/stun, and draw/stun.

The stop shot is the foundation of position play. Begin with the cue ball a diamond from the object ball in Position A. Use a medium-firm stroke while cueing in the dead center. As the distance increases, begin using draw – and at just the right speed – to stop the cue ball in its tracks. Next, practice stop shots at a 5-degree cut angle. Pay attention to just how far the cue ball drifts sideways after contacting the object ball.

Follow Shots
Soft follow shots are very useful for developing speed control. Line up the cue ball and object ball at a 5-degree angle – then practice getting shape at Positions A, B, C, D, E, and F. Keep playing for each ending location until you can consistently stop the cue ball near or on the target.

I chose the 5-degree angle because **most soft follow shots are not lined up directly at the pocket**. It is useful to become familiar with how much the cue ball veers to the opposite side of the line to the pocket after contact. This long shot forces you to shoot with accuracy and touch.

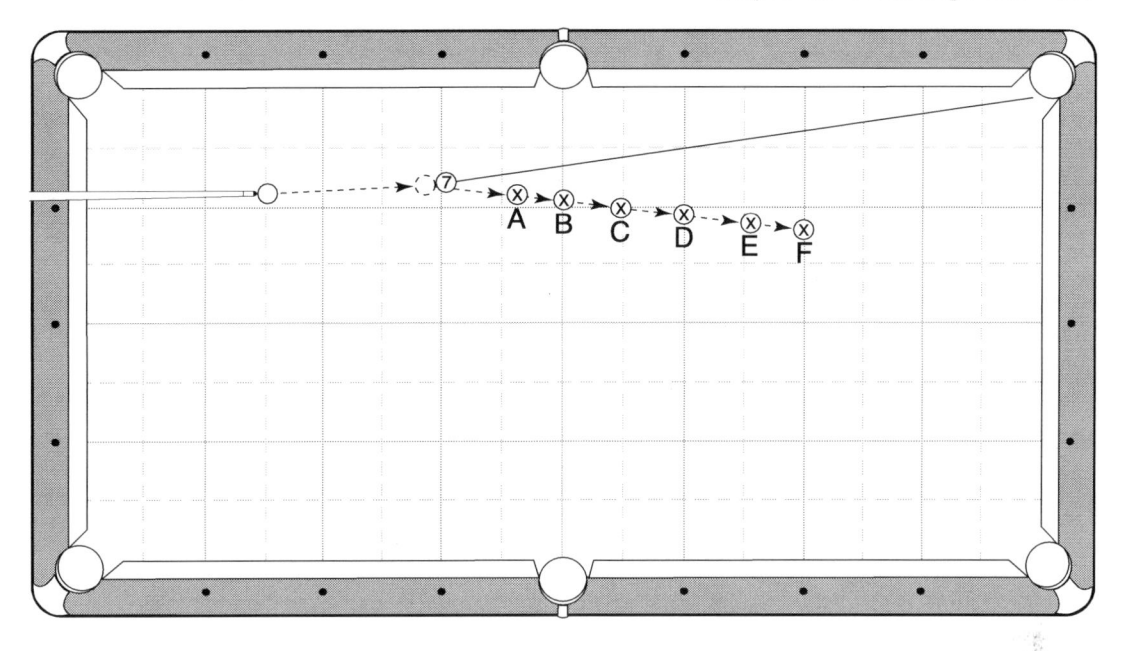

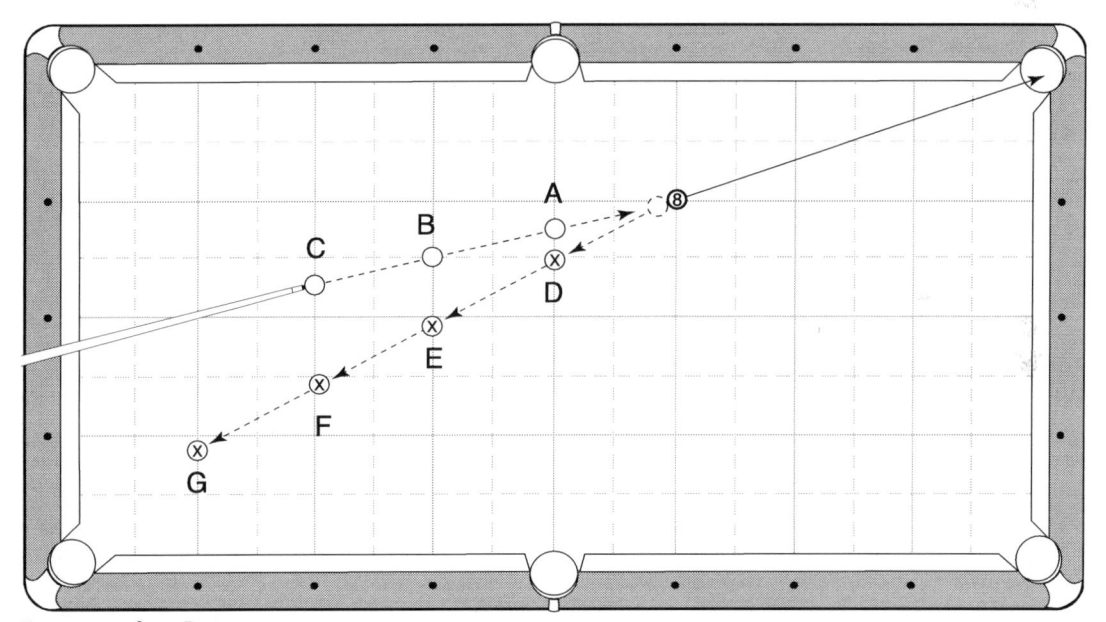

Progressive Draw

Progressive drills are useful for developing your draw stroke. The object ball is placed in the same position for each shot. Start with the cue ball in Position A. After drawing to Position D, the goal is to draw the cue ball a foot further back on each successive shot to Positions E, F, and G. This takes expert technique and speed control.

To generate decisive draw spin, you must strike the cue ball one tip below center (one and a quarter tips is the maximum). Use a smooth stroke, especially during the transition, and follow through completely. Avoid the temptation to overpower the cue ball because this produces excessive cue ball speed and minimal backspin. After completing phase one, repeat the exercise with the cue ball at Position B, and then at Position C. A small cut angle of 5 degrees will teach you how the cue ball's path widens out on draw shots.

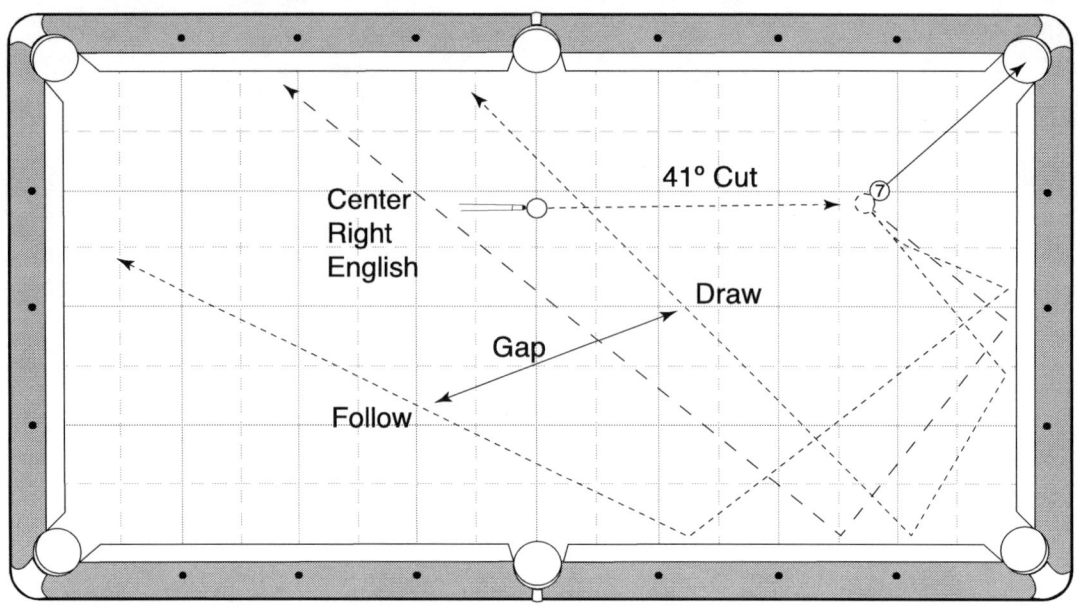

Two-Rail Position

Pros use two-rail shape on 22% of all of their position plays, so skill at these routes is a must. Three two-rail routes are shown. In each case, the route would technically turn into a three-rail route if the cue ball traveled further and hit the third rail. **Most three-rail routes are extensions of two-rail position routes**.

The 41-degree cut shot and slight variations of it are among the most common two-rail position plays in 9-Ball. Notice the path taken by the cue ball when a tip of draw and a tip of follow are used. The wide gap between these two routes can be filled by a variety of speeds and cueing.

A third route was played on the center axis with right english. Notice that it fills part of the gap. Set up the shot as in the example and practice using different speeds and cueing. An hour spent practicing these routes should have a noticeable impact on your position play.

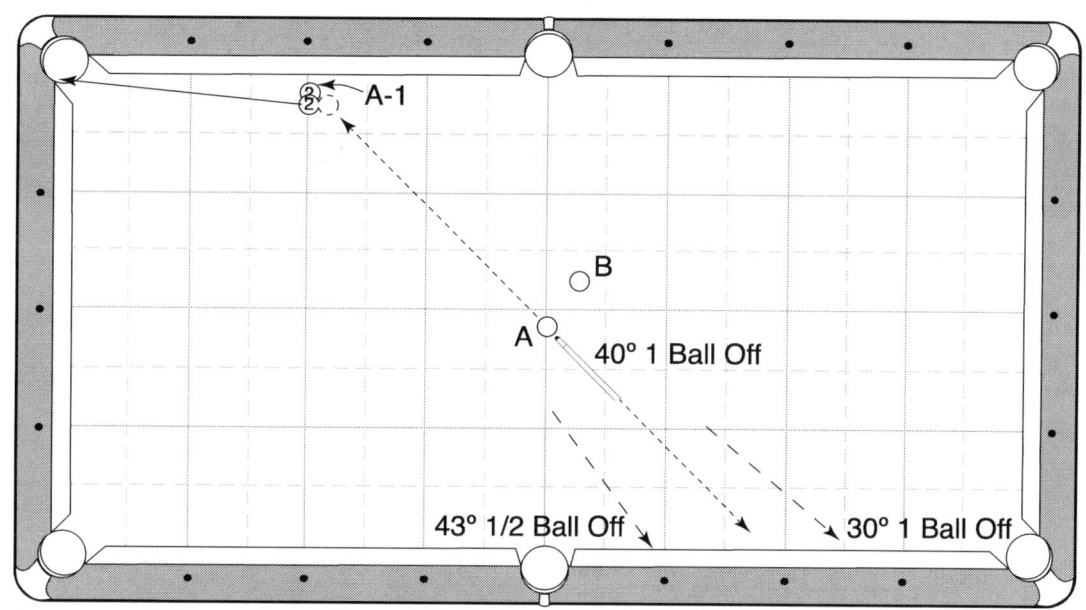

Across and Down the Table

This exercise will help you master a series of the most valuable and troublesome two-rail position routes. The goal is to bring the cue ball safely past the side pocket and to the opposite end of the table on a cut shot with the object ball close to the rail.

A 40-degree cut is shown with the 2-ball a ball's width off the rail and the cue ball in Position A. The arrow pointing two diamonds up the rail from the lower right corner pocket shows the expected return path on a well stroked shot using draw with outside (right) english.

The arrow pointing towards the rail closer to the side pocket shows where the cue ball would hit when playing a 43 degree cut on the 2-ball. On this shot, the 2-ball is a half of a ball's width off the rail at Position A-1.

The cue ball in Position B shows a cut angle of 30 degrees. The 2-ball is one ball width off the rail. The cue ball travel towards the first diamond when hit with low right english. The key to these shots is a high quality spin draw stroke, not brute force. The following tips will help you to match the cue ball's route across and back down the table:

- As the object ball gets close to the rail, its rebound angle will become sharper – that is, you won't be able to send it as far back down the table.
- You estimate the cue ball's path back across the table by drawing a line from the point where the cue ball hits the first rail through its original position and then extend it to the bottom rail. The cue ball will usually return at a little sharper angle than this directional line that you have created.

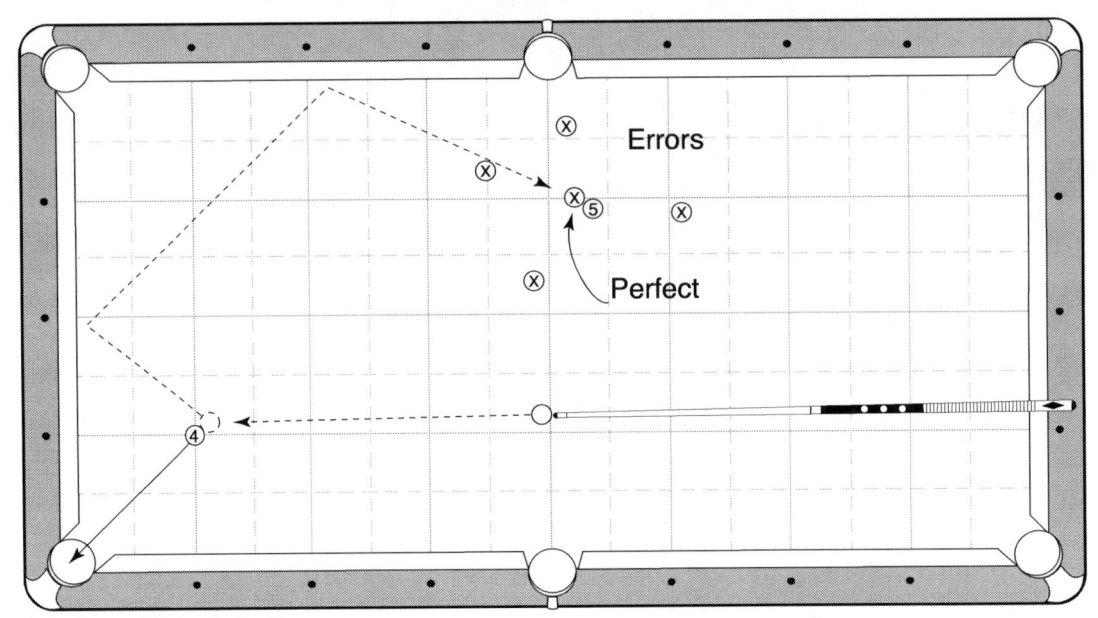

Hitting a Target Ball

This exercise will help you **detect errors with your speed control and/or directional control**. Set up a series of the most commonly used position plays, such as this two-rail route. Place an object ball exactly where you would like to send the cue ball. Your goal is to have the cue ball stop as close to the target ball as possible. A bull's eye is a direct hit on the target ball just as the cue ball is about to stop. The diagram shows several possible kinds of errors: poor direction, hitting the shot too easy, and using excessive force. Try playing each shot at least 8-10 times.

Every player has a tendency to make the same kind of error on each position play. To cure this problem, place a donut where the cue ball stops after each shot. Your dispersion pattern will show your error tendencies. For example, if you are overrunning a shot consistently, you need to remind yourself to use a softer stroke until you develop the right touch for the shot.

TIP: **You may wish to copy the diagram in the appendix and mark the ending positons of each shot**.

Avoid Obstructers

Your skill at position play depends on your ability to avoid obstructing balls on the cue ball's journey from Point A to Point B. When practicing a specific position route, place one or more object balls within two to three inches off the cue ball's pathway. This will teach you to control the cue ball like a pro! The illustration shows two of the many commonly used position routes where you must avoid sending the cue ball into another ball. The obstructers make avoiding contact a challenging proposition.

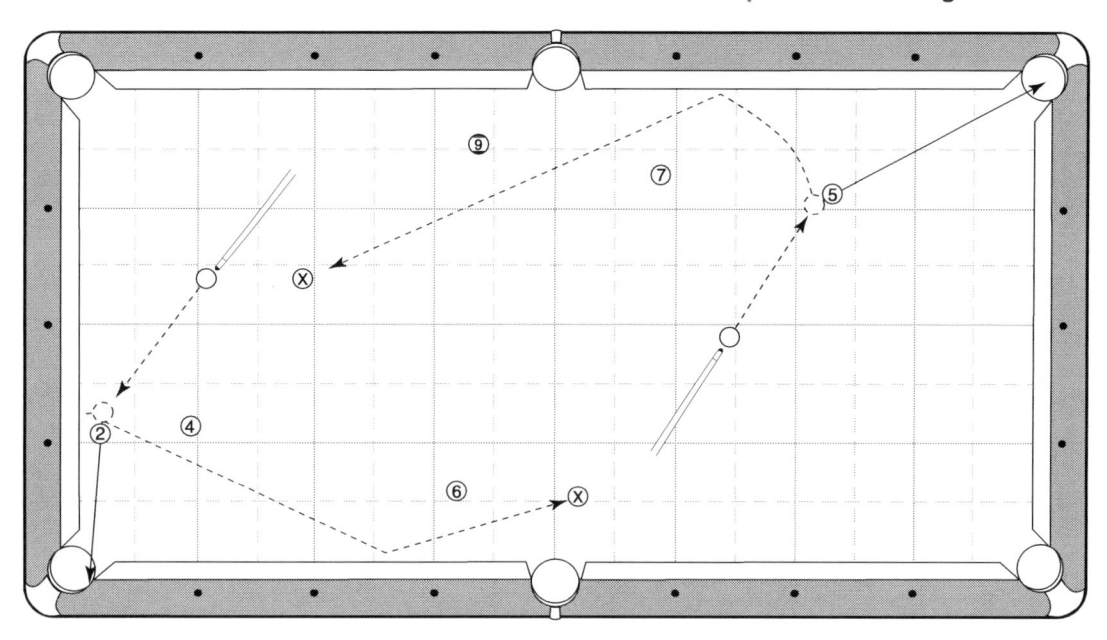

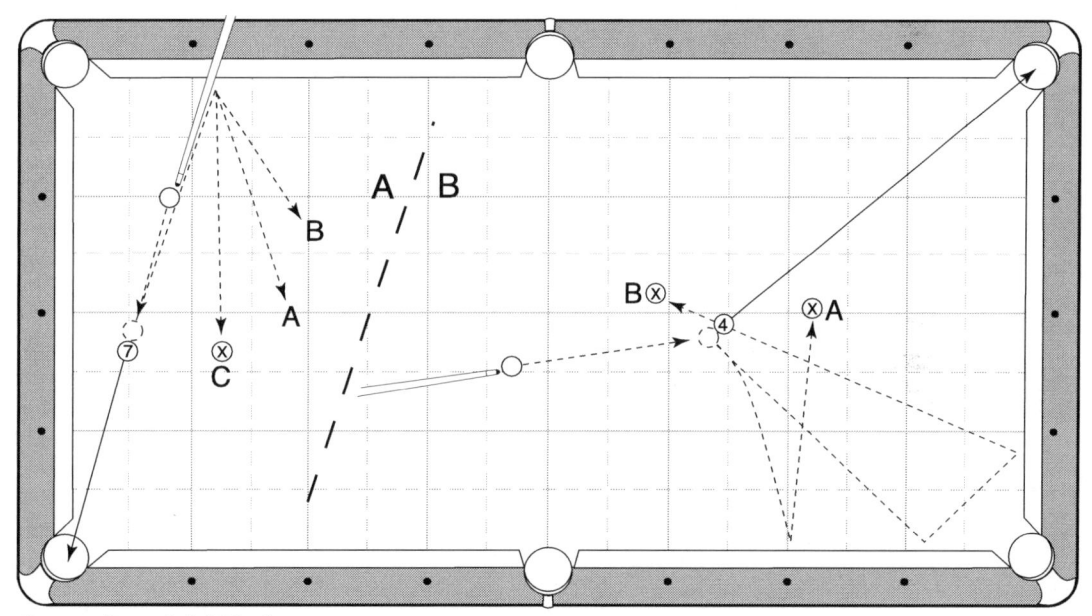

Opposites Add Variety

The nine basic contact points on the cue ball, along with the different speeds of stroke, combine to offer you a wide variety of position play possibilities. You can expand your skills by playing a certain shot with center-ball, follow, draw, and then with both right and left english.

In Part A, the draw to the rail and back out shot is normally played along Line A using straight draw, or with draw and outside english down Line B. You can add another route to your arsenal by leaning to play it with draw and inside (left) english! This cuing will sharpen the rebound angle, sending the cue ball down Line C.

In Part B, the shot is usually played with draw, which will send the cue ball near Position A. Now try this position play with a center right english and a firm stroke. The cue ball will travel down Route B.

Pattern Play

The position play exercises we've just covered and those in Chapter 3 are the building blocks for pattern play. If you can consistently play your routes correctly, you will be able to string together several position plays into patterns, which will enable you to run out regularly.

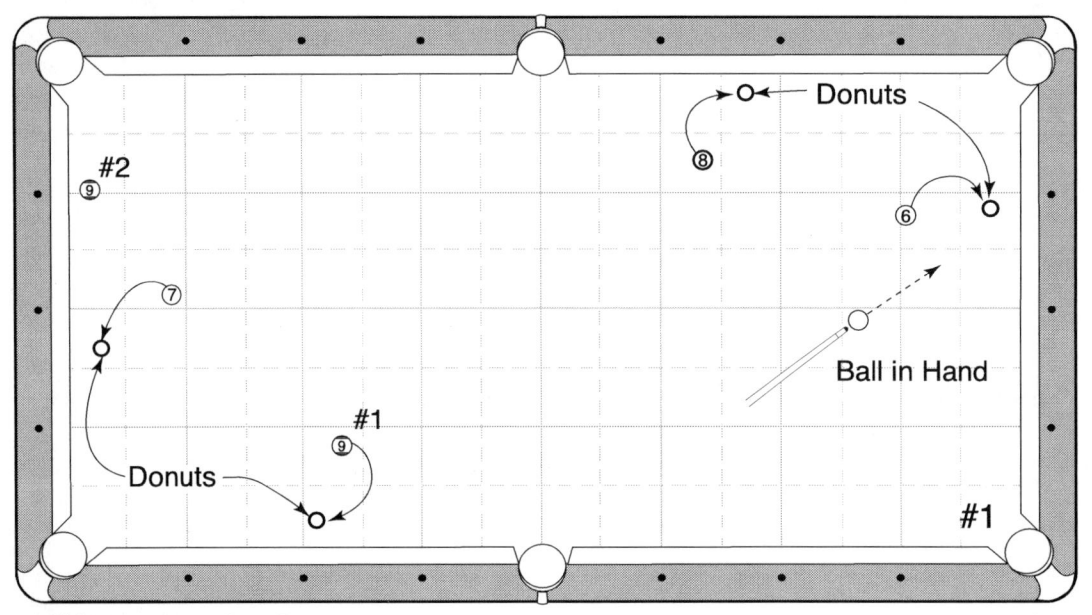

Build Your Run Out Power

Our first pattern play exercise will help you to build your run out power. Set up 3-5+ ball patterns with the donuts, such as the one in Diagram #1. Play the pattern over and over until you get it just right. This one requires that you excel at one-rail shape from end to end, and from side to side. Notice the position plays that give you trouble and adjust your cuing and/or speed until you play them just right. **Observe your successes and internalize the results**.

The next step is to move one of the object balls. Now play the pattern again. In the example the 9-ball, which was originally in Position #1, was moved to Position #2.
On each pattern, move one ball to a different position, give yourself ball in hand, and try to run out. Be sure you cover some of the more troublesome locations. These include:
- A ball frozen to the rail.
- A ball opposite the middle diamond on an end rail.
- A ball in the middle portion of the table.
- A ball near or on the rail near a side pocket.

In Diagram #2, the 8-ball has been moved to the center of the table. Evaluate the pattern, and then devise a plan for running out. After the 8-ball, was moved the 7-ball was still in its original location at Position A. Now let's move the 7-ball to Position B. Again, notice how the complexion of the run has changed.

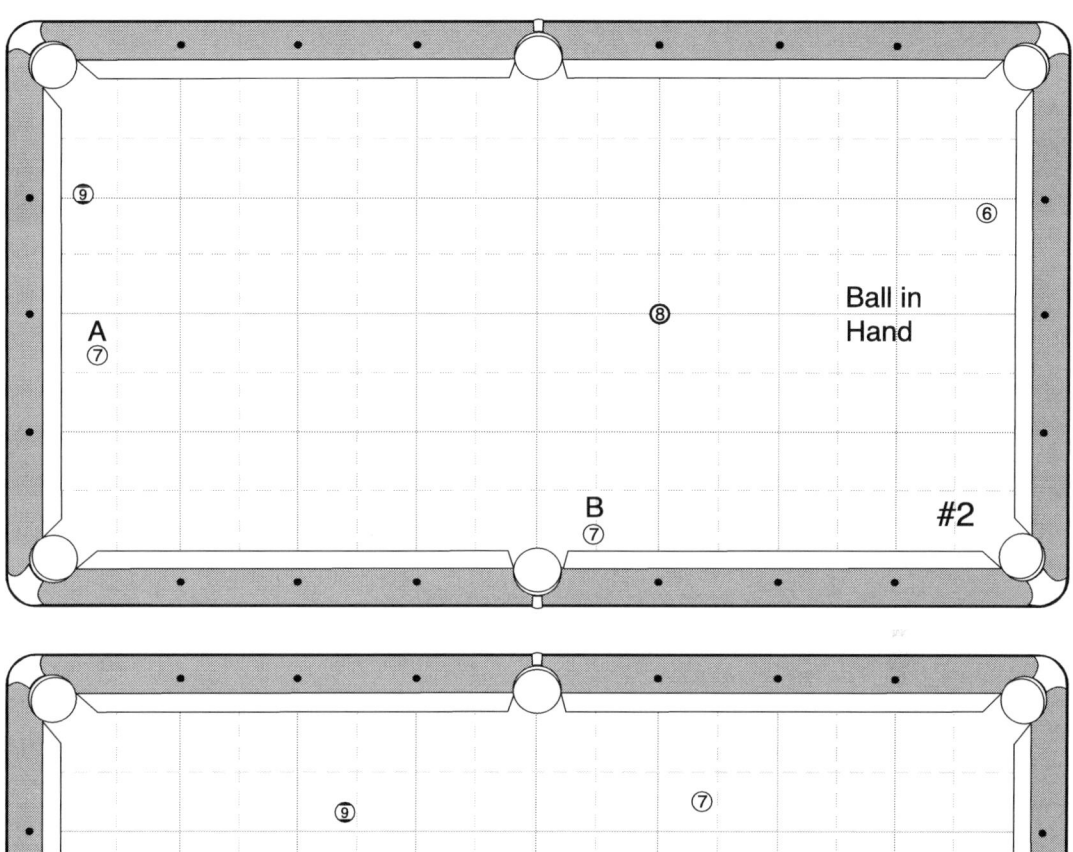

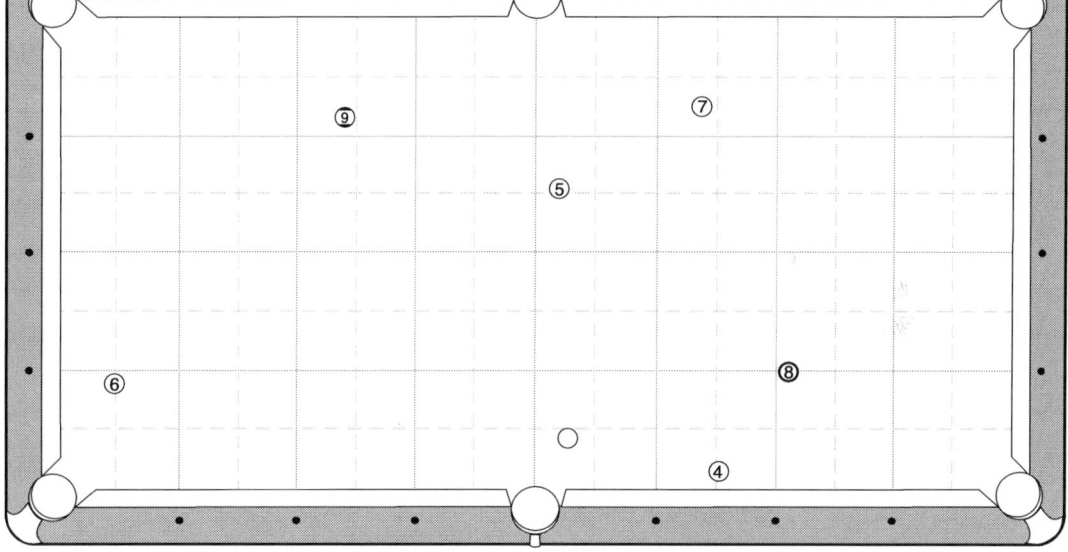

Use Cosmos to Build Concentration

A cosmo is a layout that is so easy that you have to commit a major blunder to not get out. But blunders do happen. To cure blunderitis, practice easy 5-6 ball run outs where none of the balls is in a difficult position. The layout in this illustration is not difficult. The shots are easy, and the routes are simple. Still, this is the kind of layout that amateurs fail to complete because of poor planning and/or execution.

The key is to treat each shot and position play with complete respect. Seek perfection when running a cosmo. This exercise in concentration will keep you from throwing away games that you "should have won." The discipline you develop practicing cosmos will help you with tougher layouts.

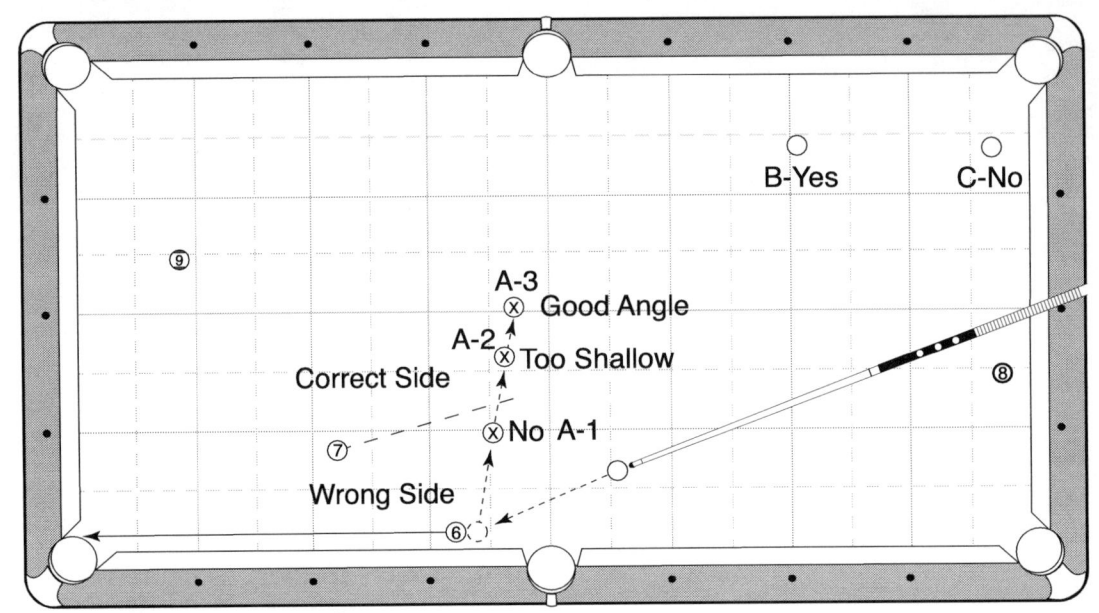

Practice the Key Principles

The Principles of Position Play (see chapter 5) are critical to playing patterns effectively. To run out consistently you have to know them and be able incorporate the key ones into each position play. This does not happen overnight, but the learning has to start somewhere. So, I suggest that you begin by incorporating the following three principles into your planning process on every shot:

- Which side of the ball do I need to be on? (Principle #9. Note: in some instances you may wish to have a straight in shot.)
- What angle do I need? (Principle #2.)
- How can I play 3 balls at a time? (Principle #7.)

Take the time you need while working on this exercise, even if it means playing slower than normal. Complete the planning process before your preshot routine, and then play each shot. Don't worry if your execution is off – this is only natural because you will be focusing more energy than normal on planning, which may disturb your natural rhythm. Eventually the planning process will become so natural to you that it will have no effect on your game.

The example will acquaint you with the thinking process. The cue ball is going to rebound off the rail after playing the 6-ball. But where, and why? If it stops short of the dashed line, you will have trouble getting from the 7 to the 8-ball. This would violate the need to play for three balls at a time, so Position A-1 must be the wrong side. If the cue ball travels to the opposite side of the dashed line to Position A-2, it would be on the right side but with the wrong angle. Position A-3 is the winner because it is on the right side with enough angle to send the cue ball off the rail and down to Position B for the 8-ball.

When playing the 7-ball, you wouldn't want to send the cue ball to Position C because this would violate the principle of playing for 3 balls at a time. It would take a monumental effort to get good position on the 9-ball. However, it would be easy to get to the 9-ball with the cue ball at Position B.

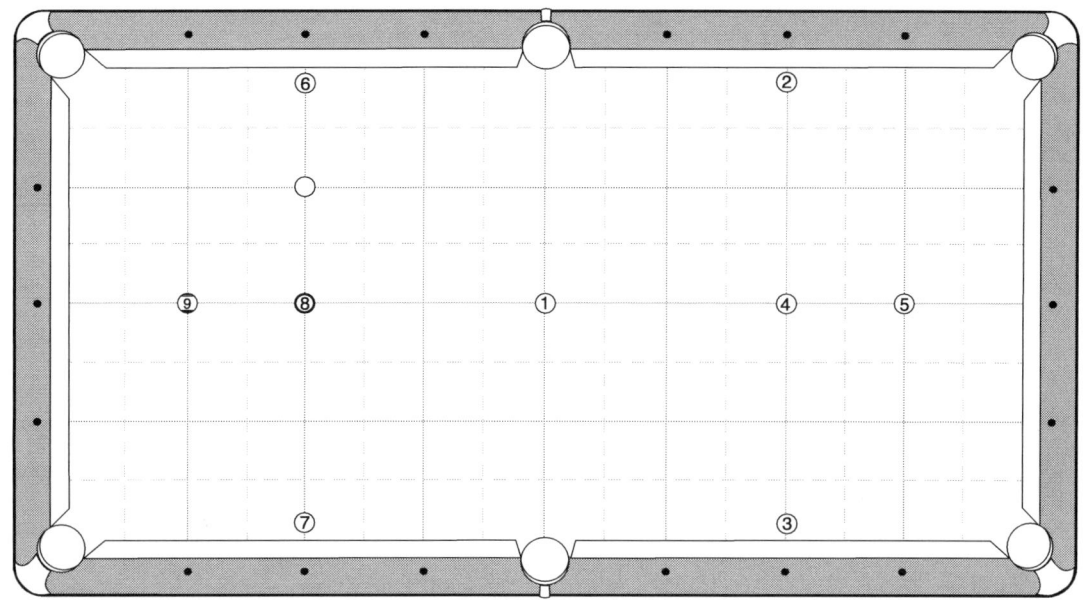

A Useful Run Out Drill

This one is for advanced players courtesy of my fellow instructor, Ed Smith. Start with cue ball in hand. The object balls next to the rails should be a quarter to a half inch off the rail. Run the balls in order. If you hit another ball, that is a miss and you must start over. After successfully completing this version, alternate ball positions. For example, you could exchange the 4 and 8-balls, or the 3 and 7-balls. A considerably more difficult version is to freeze the balls to the rails.

Additional Pattern Play Drills:
Center Axis Only

Practice running out while cueing only on the center axis. This will teach you the natural roll of the cue ball, lessen your dependence on english, and improve your shotmaking. As a variation, limit yourself to using english only once or twice per rack.

No Side Pockets

Many players do not make the correct choices when shooting in the side pocket. You can help solve this problem by not shooting into the side pockets during practice. This will teach you some new patterns and position routes. And, when you play and can obviously use the side pockets, they will seem like such a welcome addition, and they will greatly simplify your patterns.

Practice Drills for Safety Play

Smart safety play can lead to ball-in-hand and makeable shots which can translate into victory. Safeties demoralize your opponent, which further increases your chances of success. So, you should have ample incentive to develop this critical facet of the game – one that many of your peers mistakenly neglect to practice.

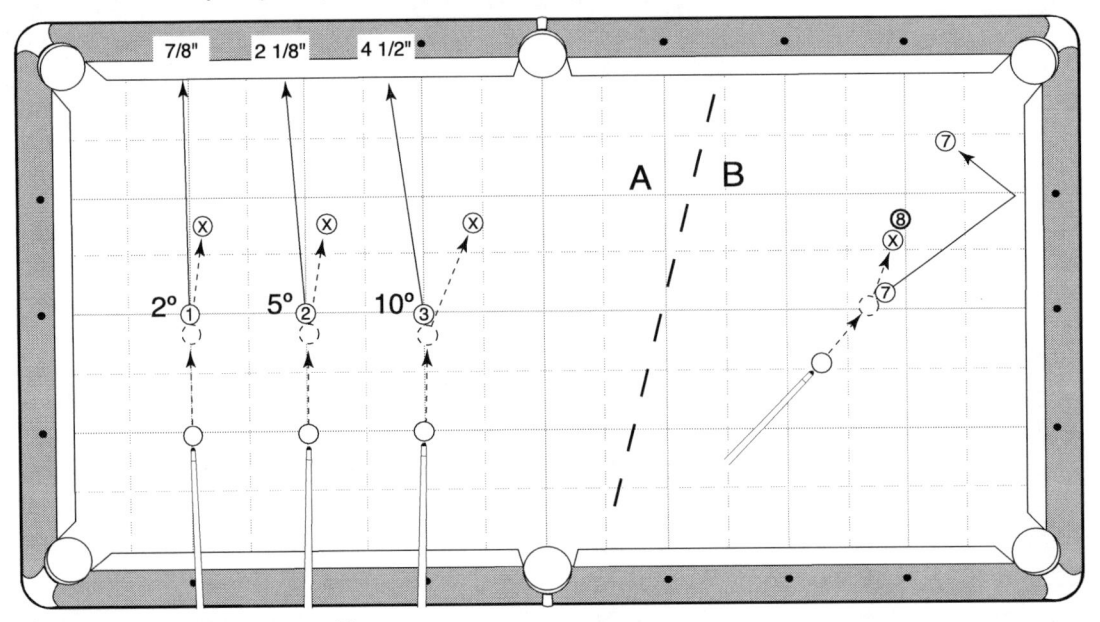

Controlling Sideways Drift

A big key to safety play is a delicate touch that enables you to control the cue ball's rolling distance with great precision. Another vital skill is the ability to hit the right amount of the object ball so the cue ball follows the proper course, possibly to behind a blocker.

The exercise in Part A will help you discover how far the cue ball veers off to the side on soft follow shot safeties when you are hitting a little less than a whole object ball. Set up the cue ball and object ball as shown. Place a piece of chalk on the rail below each diamond at the distances shown. This will give you a precise point of aim for cut angles of 2, 5, and 10-degrees. Play a series of soft follow shots while trying to stop the cue ball various distances past the object ball's original location. Notice how far the cue ball veers off to the side, as well as the cue ball's ending position on each shot.

Part B shows a practical application of this safety. Set up a number of positions similar to this one. Your initial goal is to send the object ball to the opposite side of the blocker, creating a hook. The advanced version of this safety calls for pinning the cue ball up against the blocker as shown.

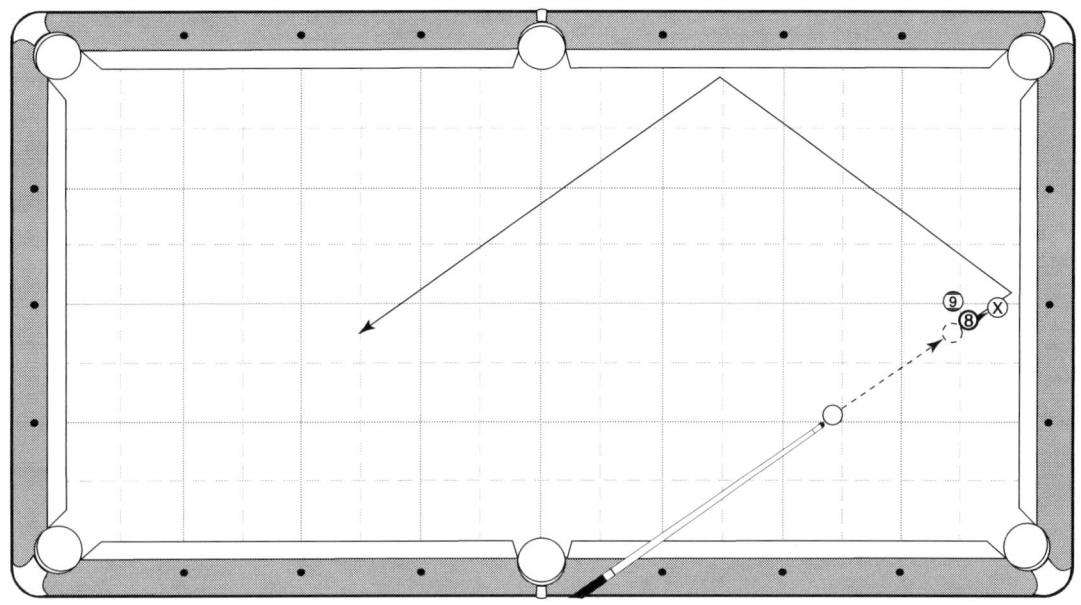

Float and Hook

The ability to stroke the cue ball firmly and yet have it travel a very short distance forward after it contacts the object ball is a valuable skill that will separate you from the pack. In the example, your goal is to send the object ball around the table and have the cue ball float forward behind the 9-ball. The trick is to stroke the cue ball firmly and just a quarter to an eighth of a tip above center. Be sure to hit the 8-ball fully because even the slightest bit of cut will cause the cue ball to veer off course, eliminating the hook safety.

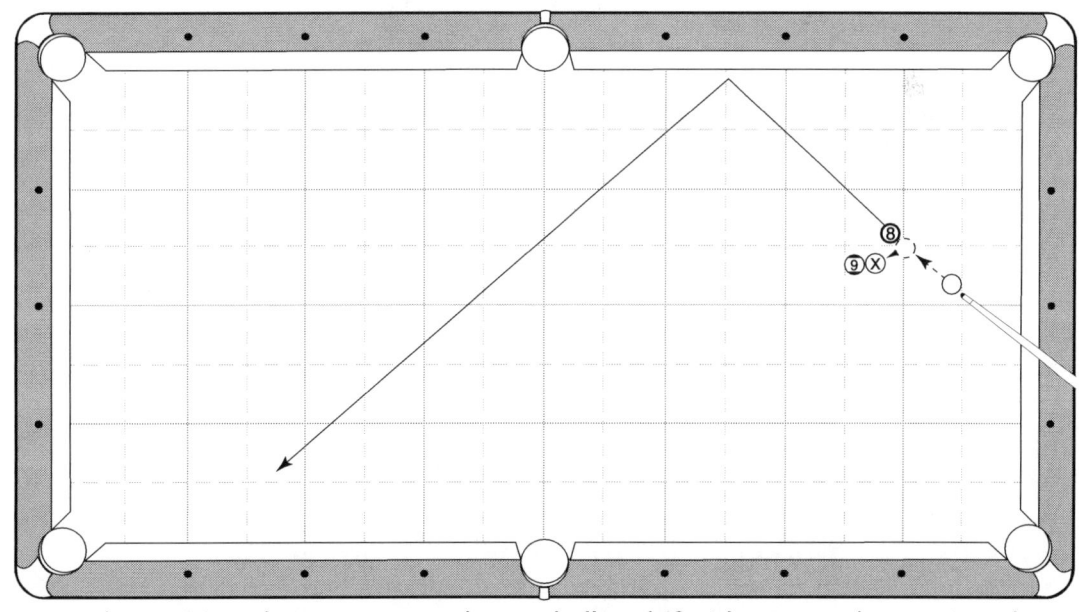

In the position above you want the cue ball to drift sideways and up against the 9-ball after sending the 8-ball up table. Use a medium stroke and strike the cue ball in the dead center. Aim just a shade left of center on the 8-ball. Try both of these exercises from a variety of positions.

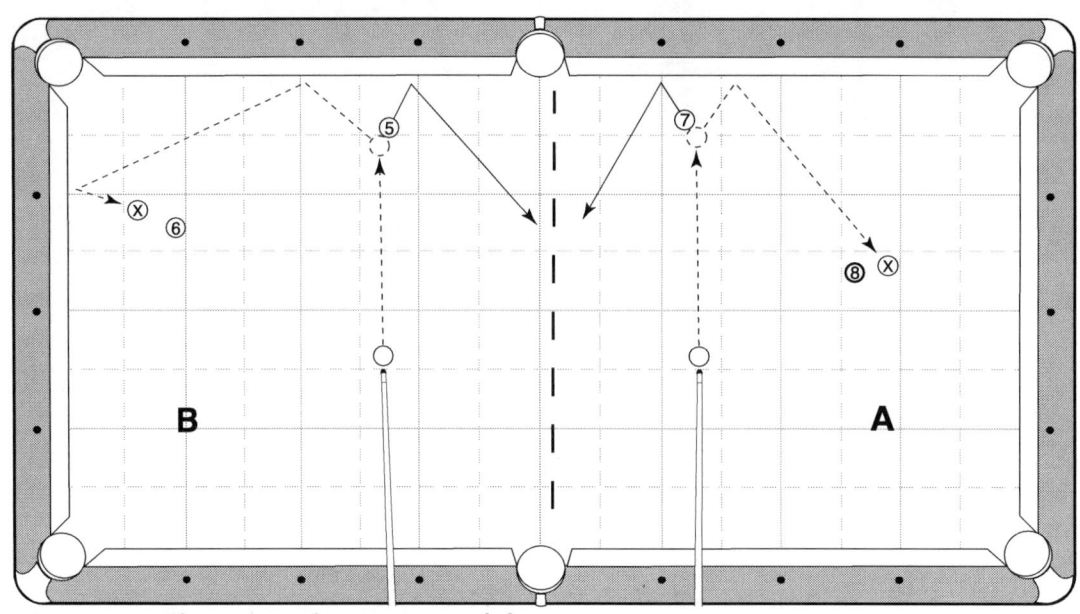

The Cue Ball's Route After Contact (1)

Playing safe is a lot like position play, only your target is a hook zone instead of a shape zone. Although **safety hook zones come in all sizes and shapes, they tend to be smaller than position zones**. So, you will need to perfect your routing skills if you intend to consistently hit the hook zones.

The exercises in this section require expert cue ball control. You needn't worry about the object ball as long as you take care of the cue ball. The cue ball and object ball are in the same relative positions in Parts A and B. In Part A, the goal is to cut the 7-ball just the right amount using follow so the cue ball rolls behind the 8-ball. Set up several variations by changing the hit on the object ball and the location of the hook ball.

In Part B, a soft draw shot with just the right speed and cuing on the 5-ball will send the cue ball two rails in back of the 6-ball. Again, I suggest you set up several variations of this shot so you can master a variety of safety routes.

The Cue Ball's Route After Contact (2)

These exercises can further elevate your routing skills. In Part A, a thin hit on the 5-ball with a soft stroke and follow results in the three pathways as shown. Notice how english changes the cue ball's direction. Set up the cue ball and object ball in the same locations and play several safeties using the three cueing options. Hit the same amount of the object ball each time. Then place a potential blocker in a position behind which you would like to send the cue ball. Practice playing hook safeties. Next, change the amount of contact on the object ball and repeat the shot.

Part B shows a medium range thin hit safety. Set up this shot and others like it and go for a hook behind the blocker. Speed control and directional control are essential ingredients of this safety.

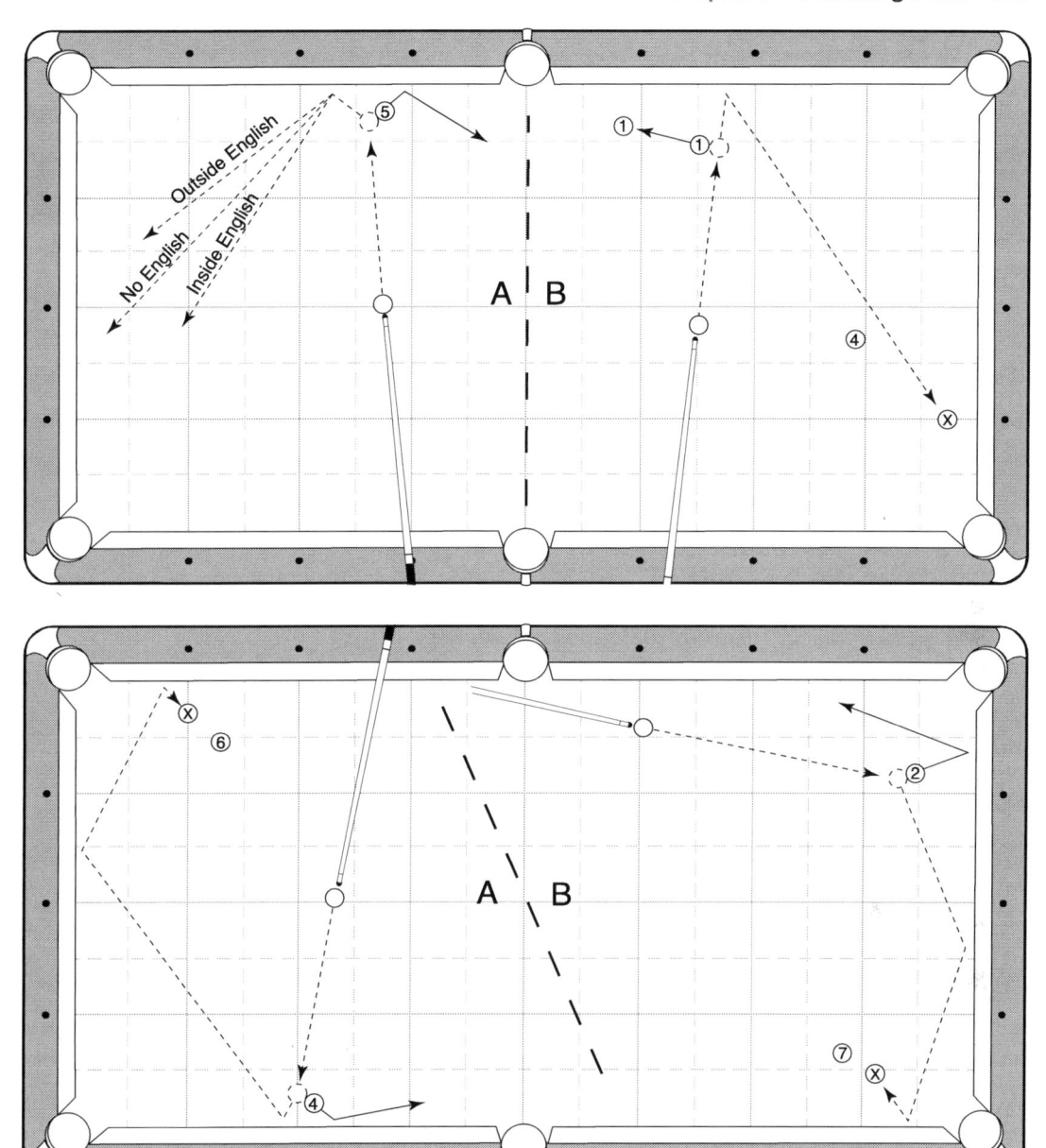

Long Distance Hook Safeties

When the blocker is a long distance from the object ball, you must exercise exquisite control over the cue ball's direction and speed. Part A shows a typical three-rail route to a blocker using follow, outside english, and superb speed control. Part B shows a tricky two-rail safe that requires draw, proper contact on the 2-ball, and great touch. These are the kind of safeties that appear regularly in competition, which makes them of great value to your game. They are also misplayed because few players are willing to take the time to practice them.

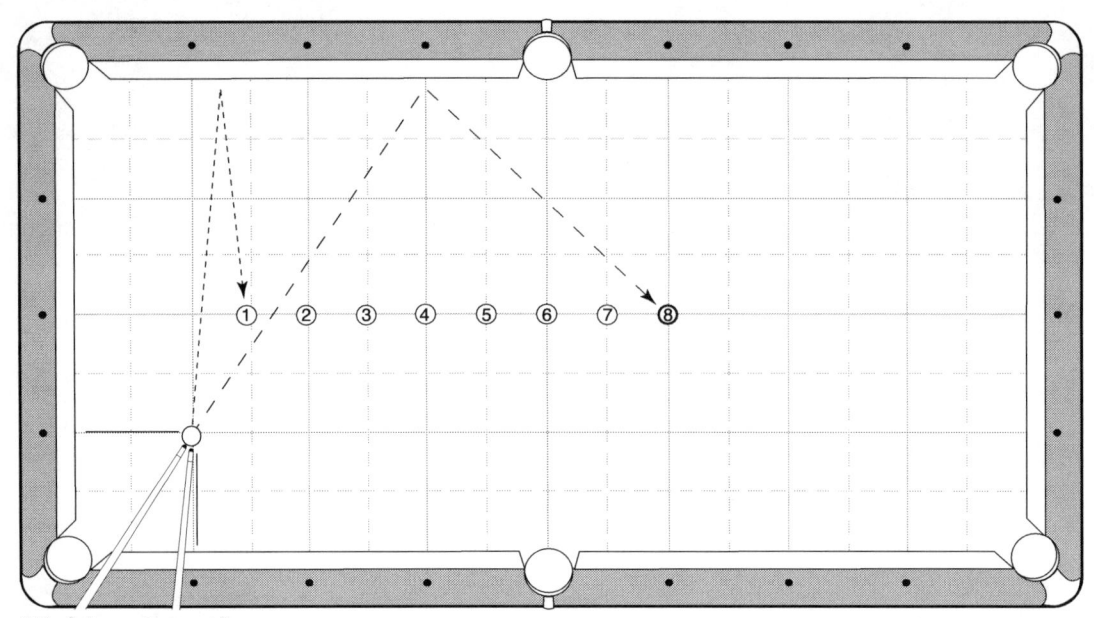

Kicking Practice

You can develop your eye for kick shots, as you have done for aiming regular shots. It just takes practice. You could pick out several of the shots in the chapter on kicking as practice exercises. Another method to develop your skills is with a series of progressive exercises. The one above resembles an exercise that players use for practicing bank shots.

Place the cue ball and 1-ball where shown and kick for the 1-ball off the side rail. When you can hit it three times in a row, place a ball a half diamond further up the table where the 2-ball is located. When you have hit it three times in succession, proceed to the next ball, and then the next. The kick shot to the 8-ball is one of the most troublesome in pool. If you can hit this on three consecutive shots, your kicking practice is really starting to pay off!

If you make this routine a regular part of your practice sessions, keep score so you can measure your progress. One way is to keep shooting each ball until you hit it. A perfect score would be an eight. Advanced players should keep shooting each one until you hit it three straight times. A perfect score would be 24 (3 x 8). You can add variety to the exercise by using difference speeds of stroke and by aiming for different sides of the ball.

Break Shot Practice

You simply must strike the cue ball solidly on the break shot. You can check the quality of your contact by lining up the dot or circle on the cue ball in the exact position where you would like to hit it. Chalk up, play your break shot, and check the cue ball to see if you are hitting it on the bull's eye. If you are hitting it correctly and the cue ball is following past the rack or drawing back too far despite a solid hit on the 1-ball, you need to adjust your contact point in one direction or the other.

BOOK 2

Play Your Best
10 BALL

CHAPTER 14

About 10 Ball

The Game

The game of 10 Ball, which is a very close cousin to 9 Ball, has been growing in popularity over the last 10-15 years, especially among the professionals and upper level amateur players. Pool tournament directors like to adopt certain rules for their events, such as "call shot" and "rack your own rack." But, for the most part, the rules are the same as for 9 Ball – shoot the balls in numerical order, and you win on a legal shot on the 10 Ball, even if it comes via a combination, billiard, or carom.

In 9 Ball, there are five rows of one to three balls – 1, 2, 3, 2, 1, with the 9-ball in the middle. In 10 Ball, there are four rows – 1, 2, 3, 4. The 10 Ball goes in the middle of the third row.

Since 2001 the list of winners of the UPA International Ten-Ball Championships includes a who's who in pool with names like Buddy Hall, Mika Immonen, Johnny Archer (three years in a row), Thomas Engert, Shane Van Boening, Tony Drago, Dennis Orcullo (two times), and Efren Reyes. WPA World Championship winners include Darren Appleton, Mika Immonen, and Huidji See. And at the CSI U.S. Open the winners since 2010 have included Shane Van Boening, Dennis Orcollo, and Rodney Morris. Pin-Yi Ko was the winner of the 2014 CSI Invitational.

The big differences in 10 Ball are, again, that extra ball and the shape of the rack. That ball does not change the relevancy of the concepts that we talked about in the previous chapter on 9 Ball – you can apply the position routes, patterns, safeties, kick shots, and other techniques that you learned for 9 Ball to the game of 10 Ball. But what does change, especially among the pros, is the relative value of certain aspects of the game. For example, the break is less important in 10 Ball, while creative position play and defense are even more valuable.

Who Should Play 10 Ball

I am going to assume that you are an improvement oriented player or else you would not be reading this book. You have probably been playing 9 Ball and you are now thinking of adding 10 Ball to the games that you play regularly (if you haven't already). Before you do, let me present this analogy – in golf, the best players play from the back tees, which increases the challenge of the game. In pool, 10 Ball is like playing our sport from the back tees. In short, you should be a reasonably accomplished player before you add 10 Ball to your repertoire. However, even if you don't play 10 Ball, you can still apply the lessons in the two following chapters to 9 Ball!

The table below shows the nine basic levels of amateur players who are far beyond the beginner level. Within these levels there are three broad groups – those who should stick to 9 Ball (at least for now), those in the transition zone, and players who are definitely ready for 10 Ball.

If you are in the C- to B- category and you still want to play 10 Ball, I think you will have more fun if you follow my suggestion in games with your friends: award a point for the 5-ball, and 2 points for the 10-ball. This will give you more practice at closing and defense, and solves the problem of having to wade through so many balls before getting to the place where the game is now on the line.

Who Should Play 9 & 10 Ball

C-	C	C+	B-	B	B+	A-	A	A+
9	9	9	9	9/10	9/10	10	10	10

C- to B-   Definitely 9 Ball
B to B+   Either game (transition zone)
A- and up   10 Ball

My 424 Game Study: 9 Ball vs. 10 Ball

In 2001 I conducted a 500 game study of professional 9 Ball. It resulted in a battery of statistics for the first edition of this book. For the second edition I studied 424 games of 10 Ball from the Derby City and Make It Happen events and computed statistics that should be of value in comparing the two games. Let's get started!

The two stats that capture most players' interest are break and run out percentage, and how often does the breaker win. In 9 Ball, the breaker wins 13.6% more often than the second player, so the break is obviously a much bigger advantage in that game. In 10 Ball, the odds are about 50/50! Part of the breaker's advantage in 9 Ball results from the pros impressive break and run out average of 28.0% – this is 11% greater than that posted by the 10 Ball players. If you compare the two averages with each other (28% vs. 17%), you will see that 9 Ball players break and run out 64.7% more often than 10 Ball players!

	Breaker Wins	Opponent Wins	Break and Run out
9 Ball	56.8%	43.2%	28.00
10 Ball	50.3%	49.7%	16.98

Balls on the Break	1 or more	B&R %	Conversion %
9 Ball	68.00%	28.00	41.18
10 Ball	60.38%	16.98	28.12
Derby City 10 Ball	63.46	17.95	28.28
Make It Happen 10 Ball	51.79	14.29	27.58

It is great to see several balls drop on the break, especially when you have an easy first shot and a Cosmo awaits you. For the pros, however, the real key is in making at least one ball and having a shot. On the times when the pros made at least one ball on the break in 9 Ball, they ran out over 41% of the time. In contrast, when they made one or more balls on the break in 10 Ball, they only ran out about 28% of the time, or 13% less!

The two big reasons for their significantly lower runout conversion percentage in 10 Ball are: 1) that extra ball really does cause problems, and/or 2) the break leads to a different spread in 10 Ball – for example, on many breaks the balls tend to congregate along one rail, or in the middle of the table.

Innings per game stats show another big difference between the two games. It is expected that 10 Ball games would last more innings, but it may surprise you to know how big, or little, the difference really is. The average 10 Ball game took 12.5% more innings than a game of 9 Ball. The average game in the Make It Happen event lasted 22.4% more innings, showing the impact that tougher conditions and that additional ball can have on the length of the game.

A fast game could be defined as one that lasts three innings or less. In 9 Ball, 68.40 % of all games are finished with three innings compared to 61.32% in 10 Ball.

Drawn out defensive battles that last six or more innings are far more prevalent in 10 Ball – they occur in 16.74% of all games (1 in 5.97) compared to only 10.4% (1 in 9.6) of all games in 9 Ball! If you are going to be a top notch 10 Ball player, you really need to sharpen your safeties and kick shots.

Innings Per Game			Length of Game	9 Ball	10 Ball
9 Ball	3.03		Quick – 1-3 innings	68.40	61.32
10 Ball	3.41		Mid-range – 4-5 in.	21.20	21.93
Derby City	3.31		Long games – 6+ in.	10.40	16.74
Make It Happen	3.71				

Winning Inning!

	9 Ball %	10 Ball %
1	28.20	17.92
2	25.40	26.65
3	14.80	16.75
4	11.80	11.79
5	9.40	10.14
6+	10.40	16.74

The Break in 10 Ball

It has been assumed for many years now that Shane Van Boening (SVB) and Francisco Bustamante (FB) have been the sport's two best breakers. Because stats on key skills in pool are lacking, I decided to create my own for this book, so I conducted the 424 game study on 10 Ball, which I introduced earlier in this chapter. The results of my break shot sample are presented below.

The average number of balls made by Van Boening was 1.63 at Derby City, almost twice the number that the other pros, excluding Bustamante, were able to make. Bustamante beat the average, 1.03 to .83. Conditions can have an astounding impact on the number of balls made on the break as shown by a comparison between the Derby City and Make It Happen events. Even though both were played on Diamond tables and under the lights (for filming), .93 balls per break were made at Derby City compared to only .68 at the Make It Happen event. At the Make It Happen, Van Boening's average dropped in half!

Balls on the Break

	Games	Balls	Ave.	SVB	FB	Ex. SVB,FB
Derby City	312	291	.93	1.63	1.03	.83
MIH	112	76	.68	.78	—	.65

Derby City has been a showcase for both players' incredible skill at making balls on the break, and for then converting these games into run outs. The break and run (B&R) percentage for the 219 racks broken by their peers — and these are world beaters — was only 13.70%. Van Boening's B&R average in 24 games was 25.00% while Bustamante's, in 69 attempts, was an astounding 28.57%! In addition, he put together break and run out streaks of six and four straight racks.

Break and Run Average

	Games	B&R	%	SVB	FB	Ex. SVB,FB
Derby City	312	56	17.95	25.00	28.57	13.70
MIH	112	16	14.29	18.52	—	12.94

Practicing Your Break

If you are like most players, you probably do not practice your break much, if at all, so your break during competition is also your practice! As a result, you need a routine that enables you to perform as well as possible given this limited number of reps. I am not sure how much time each pro spends working on their break, but the stats show that each game lasts an average of six minutes, so each player breaks an average of five times an hour. I will guess that an average amateur would then break about four times an hour because their games take longer to complete.

Shane Van Boening's break is so well grooved from his many hours of practice and play that he only needs about five seconds to complete his in-stance, preshot routine. If you were to copy his break, I would add a few seconds to your routine to give you time to groove your stroke and to loosen up. Francisco Bustamante, who is 19 years older than Van Boening, does not practice his break as much, but he makes up for that, in part, by taking 8-9 seconds and about 9 warm-up strokes to prepare for his final forward stroke. I would suggest that you use a similar length of time.

In Stance Activities
While in their stance, Van Boening and Bustamante zero in on their line of aim while actively loosening themselves up for the final stroke. They always line up for a full ball hit on the 1-ball (give or take a millimeter or two to the side to compensate for breaking away from the head spot). The line of aim is almost always the same (unlike cut shots), so they can focus extra hard on it, and on orienting their arm and body to the cue ball's line of travel.

Van Boening moves his head and body a little during his warm up strokes as he gets ready and relaxed for his final stroke. He does little with his grip hand until the final stroke, when he greatly relaxes his grip hand in the transition (see photo #10). Bustamante, in contrast, cocks and uncocks his wrist during his warm-up strokes as he mimics the action that he will be using on his final stroke.

The Transition
The transition to the final stroke is the key move in any player's break stroke, and these two players make the switch from backwards to forwards as well as any players in the world. Each begins his transition by moving his body forward while keeping his grip hand as far back as is possible.

Each player's front knee moves forward while their head begins to elevate, clearing the way for their body. Van Boening's head elevates more prior to contact than Bustamante's, but Bustamante moves harder forward. Van Boening's transition appears to proceed at a leisurely pace while Bustamante changes directions with a quick and athletic move that features his pronounced wrist cock.

Follow Through
Van Boening follows through with his cue level to the table while Bustamante's cue is also very level through contact – then he begins his famous leap and his grip hand goes almost straight up to avoid contact with the table. He concludes his follow through with his famous leg kick!

Both players' cues are level, and are moving very fast at impact, but how they get to this position, and how they follow through, results from a series of moves that are unique to each player.

Developing Your Break
As for how to develop your break, I suggest that you study the photos of both players on the following pages (or some others), and try different parts of their technique. Piece together a style that works best for you. And take it slow – that is, try breaking at slower speeds and gradually increase your speed as your ability to hit the 1-ball squarely improves. If the cue ball is not stopping in the center portion of the table (excluding when it gets kissed elsewhere), then you need to work on accuracy and your overall motion before you can ramp up the power.

Shane Van Boening: Pool's Most Powerful Second!

Van Boening's break is a well-choreographed series of complex moves that combine to give him a break that appears to proceed at a leisurely, but that packs a ton of power. The captions below correspond to the photos on the next page.

1 – He is at the starting point
2 – He is half way back
3 – His cue it starting to elevate
4 – The end of the backstroke
5 – Starting forward
6 – Head goes much higher
7 – He is very upright at contact
8 – Follow through is complete
9 – Grip hand at address
10 – Grip hand at transition

Pre-Shot Routine

Van Boening uses a glove, to reduce friction and a closed bridge with his fingers pulled in so he can hit slightly down on the cue ball. His feet are about 18 inches apart. His grip hand is about five inches forward of 90 degrees when at address while on non-break shots he holds it much farther back. His knees are flexed and in a position that enables him to spring forward. His head is about 6 inches above his cue, which is pointing in a distinct angle because he places his tip right on the cloth!

You can see a couple of inches of daylight between his cue and the rail.

Warm-Up Strokes

His warm-up strokes feature a lot of motion as he loosens up his shooting arm! His five second long routine includes a couple of slight raises of his head to preview the elevation that is coming. He lowers his head for to establish an even better line of aim and, at the end of his final forward warm-up stroke, his tip is very low to the table, just like he does on his draw shots, and he is intently looking forward. He pauses for about a full second before beginning his final backstroke.

Final Back Stroke

His chin is a barely above his cue as he begins his final backstroke, and he appears to be super focused on aiming. As he swings his cue back, it levels out. He then begins to elevate his cue and the angle becomes even steeper as he is starting to move forward. His knees are still flexed during this long and leisurely transition.

An Extended Transition

He moves forward an up with great timing and pace while clearing the way for his shooting arm to swing forward. His head has elevated well above his cue, which is still at a sharp angle to the table. His hand has not begun to move forward – his tip is still at the end of his bridge loop! At transition his body has cleared and his head goes up another couple of inches further WHILE his arm drops!

The Final Forward Stroke

His leisurely looking transition quickly becomes a blur. He continues to move his up and the finally begins to swing his arm forward! His grip hand is well in back of his elbow and shoulder, and he is now accelerating into contact. At contact his arm is a blur, and his arm is almost straight at contact, and his right leg has straightened out.

Follow Through

Past contact, his arm has dropped so much that his cue is pointing up and his hand is traveling towards the rail. Then he lifts his grip hand at the last split second to avoid contact with the table and his cue is about level with the table.

Chapter 14 - **About 10 Ball** 397

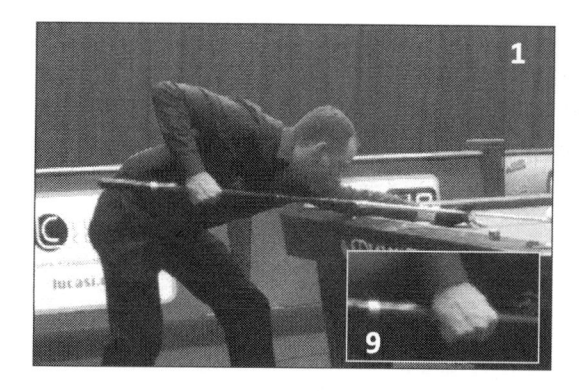

Francisco Bustamante's High Powered Break Stroke

Bustamante's break stroke is arguably the most powerful and athletic in the game. The captions below go with the corresponding photos on the next page.

1 – Starting position for his final stroke
2 – Half way into his back stroke
3 – Full backstroke is complete
4 – He is beginning to elevate
5 – He is beginning to drive forward
6 – Into his forward stroke
7 – Two thirds towards contact
8 – Past contact
9 – Beginning his leap
10 – Jumping follow through is complete

Pre-Shot Routine
He assumes his stance from directly behind the ball. He uses a closed bridge, is resting his bridge arm on the rail (!), and is standing with his legs straight. His head is two inches above his cue. His grip hand is just in front of 90 degrees, as it is for regular shots. It would be a little forward of that if he didn't position it 1-2 inches from the cue ball. His shaft points a tip to the left of center as it does for all shots, but he will reroute if to the vertical axis at contact. He uses a loose cradle as shown by the daylight between his cue and the V formed by the thumb and index finger.

Warm-Up Strokes
He took nine full warm up strokes on the video I studied, and his preshot in-stance routine lasted for nine seconds. His fluid motion and the cocking and uncocking of his wrist during his warm up strokes is to loosen up his shooting arm. After he his warm-up strokes he, unlike Van Boening, goes right into his final backstroke.

Final Back Stroke
His chin is a barely above his cue, and he is super focused on aiming as he prepares to take his cue back. He swings his cue quickly back and, as it goes up, it gets closer to his chin! He elevates his cue sharply, and the angle becomes even steeper as he begins to move forward. His knees are now flexed and his wrist is fully cocked.

An Extended Transition
For the regular stroke, most instructors think of the transition as a momentary changing of directions. With Bustamante, on his break stroke it is a far more complex move in which he begins to drive his body forward while holding his arm back until he has established some momentum and the ideal position for his body to whip it forward into the cue ball. At the end of his backstroke his knees are starting to bend as he moves his upper body first. His cue is right under his chin now and is quite elevated. He **is now driving very hard with his legs and his knees are bent.**

The Final Forward Stroke
When his tip is a couple of inches out of his bridge there is now 8-9 inches of separation between his cue and his chin. His back arm is a blur as it is moving very fast even though he has only completed about 2 inches of his 12 inch stroke! As he moves from the beginning to the end of his final stroke, his head continues to go up, and yet his bridge arm is continuing to rest on the rail!

Follow Through
His cue is very level with the table after contact – so his patented leap is intended to avoid hitting the rail – it has no impact on the action of the cue ball!

Chapter 14 - **About 10 Ball**   399

An Introduction to the Following Sections and Chapters

The remaining sections in this chapter will 1) offer ideas on what it takes to excel at 10 Ball, 2) prepare you to get the most from your study of the following two chapters, prepare you to use the book as a guide to Accu-Stats' DVDs of these events (which I highly recommend), and 4) instruct you on how to practice the run outs in the illustrations.

The Derby City and Make It Happen Tournaments

I would like to thank Pat Fleming and his crew at Accu-Stats for filming the events that provided the basis for the illustrations of the top pros in the chapters that follow. Though this book is a stand-alone product, I do encourage you to buy and watch any and all of the tapes of the 19 matches that I will be analyzing.

Bill Incardona, Danny DiLiberto, and the other announcers for Accu-Stats did a fine job of providing commentary for the matches. If you watch the tapes, you will hear some agreement in our opinions (which can't be helped), and some differences. In addition, I was able to add so many of the details that make up much of the descriptions of the shots because I had the benefit of time: I could look at each shot as many times as I wished, and I used slow motion and freeze frame – luxuries that the commentators did not have.

The 424 games in those 19 matches are comprised of more than 4,500 shots by top pros, so narrowing them down to the 121 diagrams and 180 shots that appear in the next two chapters was not easy. I finally decided that the best plan was to watch the matches in chronological order and present them that way. Whatever caught my eye, I chose for the book. Besides, this is how the game really works – when you are playing you never know what will come next! As proof, in one game Efren Reyes played five straight shots into the side pockets. I was joined by Todd Fleitman during the selection process, an instructor from New Jersey with one of the sharpest eyes and keenest minds in the game.

I wanted to showcase all of the players in the DVDs and I focused mostly on the kind of shots that you may encounter in a game, and from which you can learn something. Another goal was to entertain you with shots with the WOW Factor – that is, highlight reel shots that make you want to jump up out of your seat and clap, and that may inspire you to great deeds of your own. Most of all, I wanted to provide you with a representative sample of the shots (and the thinking behind them) that go into playing a world class game of 10 Ball in the hopes that you will further develop your pool sense and your feel for the game.

Derby City and Make It Happen Shot Titles

The introduction of the book includes an explanation of the diagrams for those of you who are beginning your studies with the chapters on 10 Ball. A few items appear on the subject line in the following two chapters that need to be discussed. Below are some examples:

The Best Shot Ever!   (4/12 – 54:05)   BCB: 7, 8, 9, 10 - A
The first item is, of course, **the name of the shot**.
The **4** before the slash is the match number in the book's series of 19 matches. Derby City matches are numbered 1 to 13. Make It Happen's are numbered 1 to 6.
The **12** refers to the game number on the Accu-Stats DVD of that match. You can use the menu when watching the DVDs to quickly navigate to a particular game.
54:05 refers to the time on the DVD when the shot appears. Once you get to the game, you can fast forward to the shot.
BCB: 7, 8, 9, 10 refers to the Black Cue Ball practice exercises. A complete description of these exercises appears at the end of this chapter. The last letter is the difficulty of the patter. A is difficult, B is moderately difficult, C are less difficult. Almost none are what I would consider to be easy!
(Note that the **BCB** feature appears on 70 of the 121 illustrations.)

Terrific Kick Shot!   (4/19 – V2 – 37:23)   BCB: 7, 8, 9, 10
Matches numbered 1, 4, 7, and 11 in the Derby City chapter are on two DVDs. A **V2** will appear in the subject line when a shot comes on the second DVD. The time starts at 00:00 on each DVD, so **37:23** in our example refers to the time on that DVD.

A Super Draw Shot!   (Diag. A – 6/6 – 26:05)   BCB: 7, 8, 9, 10
Fifteen examples come in two parts. On these series of shots, you will see **Diag. A** (or **Diag. B**) in the subject line before the match number. This will alert you to the fact that there are two parts to this presentation.

Capelle's Analysis

A dissertation could be written on every shot and pattern in the following chapters, but the realities of book publishing (and your patience!) dictate that I only include certain information. For example, I may talk about the cue ball's path off of the tangent line on one shot, or give the speed of stroke, but not on the next. That does not mean that these elements are not important – it just means that other items that are particularly relevant to this shot were chosen for discussion.

In cases where certain information is missing, I leave it up to you to fill in the gaps. One of the big objectives of the 10 Ball section is to get you to think like a pool player who sees all that is necessary when planning and executing each shot.

Besides their obvious skill at pocketing balls, what really makes the pros so great is their attention to the details that make up every shot. Their skill at planning comes from much experience, and tons of thinking at the conscious and non-conscious levels. In a moment I am going to describe the categories of ideas and concepts that will be appearing with the diagrams. This will alert you to what you can expect, and it will serve as a primer on the thinking that goes on in the planning and execution of professionally played pool shots!

Now let's get into the specifics of the presentation and the type of information that you can expect in each shot and series of shots.

Features of the Presentations

Common Features

The Diagrams – A full description of the diagrams appears in the introduction to the book (see page ix). The grid lines add perspective to each ball's position, and they are helpful in setting up the shots in your practice sessions.

The First Sentence – It is often used to set the stage and provide context for the shot. Did it result from an opponent's foul? Is the player in the midst of a runout? Must he respond to a safety? I want you to feel like you are getting out of your chair, or are continuing to execute a run of your own.

Elements of a shot – The situation, planning, execution, speed, cueing, angles, distance, principles at work, alternatives, Plan B, etc.

Mistakes – On some positions the incoming player is poised to take advantage of an opponent's mistake.

Partial Mistakes – The pros are experts at recovering from small mistakes by playing recovery routes, getting back in line, and continuing their run out.

Technique – I comment periodically on techniques such as short and long bridges and strokes, and on shots with various degrees of elevation. I also talk about the time that the pros spend playing a shot (see below).

Planning

The Feeling of a Top Player – Immerse yourself in the process of being, or becoming, a top 10 Ball player.

Every Game is Unique – You never see the exact same layout or play the exact same shot twice, so look for the differences in various positions, no matter how small. Remember, pool is largely about nuances and creativity, and about applying what you know to every situation and shot.

The Situation – Look for the special challenge in each position. Think about it, your game, and how you can adapt to it and make the most of each shot.

Ball In Hand – You can learn so much from studying where the pros place the cue ball after an opponent has fouled. Why did they put it there? Would you have put it in the same place? What route did they play? Indeed, the questions are endless!

Obstacles – The typical 10 Ball layout is an obstacle course, which is proven by the significantly lower runout average when a ball is made on the break compared to 9 Ball. Study the obstacles, and how they influence position routes and shape zones.

Alternatives – The pros often face several choices and possibilities due to their vast skills and knowledge. Amateurs, ironically, often have even more choices because their level of skill varies so greatly from player to player. As a result, a shot may be right for a pro, but not for you or another amateur. So keep an open mind to the possibilities and try to make decisions that are based on your level of play. Part of the commentator's job is to make their choices known in real time, and they must stick their necks out, so they occasionally make errant calls. I get to act as a Monday morning quarterback – and so I do play that position in the book!

Position and Pattern Play

Position Routes – Appreciate the masters as they execute the simplest to the most complex routes with consummate skill. What path did they choose? What speed, cueing, and stroke did they use? What impact did the cut angle have on the shot?

Patterns – Learn to recognize and work your way through the three phases of a rack: 1) the beginning, with all of its complexities, 2) the middle, which may also have its complications, and 3) the close! Chapter 5 presents a complete discussion on pattern play.

Principles of Position – I regularly mention the principles of position which appeared in chapter 4, so plan on referring to this chapter as needed. These include margin for error, speed control, position zones, natural position, and many more.

Runouts – I often will show you the tough part, routine shots that were played extremely well, critical position plays, and recovery routes.

The Out Shot – A tough shot that kick starts a run out, or is the last major hurdle.

The Out Pattern – A sequence of difficult shots that lead to a typical closing pattern.

Statistics Help the Learning Process

I believe that statistics are valid for teaching and for putting certain activities in perspective. When you are playing a shot, however, you never want to thinking about numbers.

Time for Planning – When a pro stops to study a shot, and when he walks around the table, there is a good reason why!! In pro pool 40-60 seconds is a long time, so when I mention a certain instance when they took a long time before playing a shot, they must have been facing a tough decision over what shot to play and/or how to play. The pros will also take extra time to plan a series of shots – then they may move quickly from shot to shot on the next few balls.

Time for Execution – The time that a player stands over the ball is such a useful statistic that I feel that this piece of advice alone is worth more than the price of the book! Time is needed to prepare, while in your stance, for every shot. And the time required depends on the difficulty of a shot and a player's relative skill. I've seen the pros take anywhere from two seconds to 15 seconds to play a shot.

Speed of Stroke – The pros' speed of stroke is based on their experience with the type of shot they are about to play. It is never, to my knowledge, based on a number that describes that speed. However, I believe that my Spectrum of Speeds is a good teaching tool, and it is far more precise in describing the power needed than simply saying that "he used a medium stroke." For more on the Spectrum of Speeds see the introduction and Principle #1 in chapter 4.

Angles – We humans do not come equipped with onboard protractors, and I do not expect you to look at a shot and say "That is a 37 degree cut so I must ..." But angles do have value in learning about cut shots for shotmaking and position play, so I use them quite often in the book. In addition, a few angles are very useful as guides to playing certain types of shots. For example, 40 degrees – give or take a few degrees – is a great angle for moving the cue ball a long distance while not being so thin as to make shotmaking too difficult.

Distance the Cue Ball Travels – This stat gives you a sense of perspective and appreciation for the speed and directional control that is needed to send the cue ball a long distance.

LESSON

A lesson appears at the end of every example. Some of them are self-contained while others require that you read the text above it. The lessons include instruction on planning, position play, recovery routes, patterns, safeties, technique, angles, decision making, difficult shots, problem balls, specialty shots, and much more.

Pool's Unique Challenge

Earlier I talked about the elements that go into the shots and patterns that appear in the following chapters. While you will encounter similar positions during your career, you will never face exactly the same ones as those in the illustrations. As a result, the great challenge of pool is to plan and then execute a particular shot and sequence of shots that you have never seen before, and will never see again!

Great pool players have the ability to figure out new problems, game after game, and to devise solutions to complex positions. They are problem solvers who can think on their feet in tension filled competitions – and then execute their plans with great precision. In my opinion, 10 Ball, a relative newcomer to the cue sports, has taken its place as one of the most interesting and demanding of all pool games.

Thinking Pool: The Possibilities are Endless

Pros know so much that, in many positions, their choices are limited! They may know five ways to play a push out, but only one is correct because their opponent knows as much as they do, and can execute equally well. In contrast, an amateur may have more choices in the same positon because he can leave shots for his opponent that a pro would not think of giving to his foe! In short, part of what makes pool so difficult is that you must learn to think for yourself because, in so many situations, the only rule that really applies is to play YOUR game!

On Becoming a Top Thinker

In sports much credit goes to the player with limited physical talent who uses his greater mental strength and strategy to beat his opponent. To compete at the highest levels in pool, you need great technique which many think of as a gift that you are born with. This may be true for world beaters, but amateurs can improve your physical game by thinking better about your technique Once your technique is reasonably sound, then you are in position to benefit from your deep knowledge of the game.

So, to those of you who aspire to be excellent 10 Ball players, I would advise that you develop a reasonably dependable method for pocketing balls. Then concentrate your efforts on becoming a top thinker – a player who sees the options available, can chose the best one for his game, and then execute it at your usual standard of play in the events that matter most to you.

Black Cue Ball Practice Exercises

The key to winning at 10 Ball for the pros often involves winning the battle for control of the table before they run out. If the layout is relatively trouble-free, a pro can be expected to run out regularly with 8, 9, or even 10 balls on the table. Again, their key to victory is to win the battle for the table so they can then put their high octane offense to work.

A high percentage of the examples in the following two chapters feature the battle for the table, or they key position plays and patterns that set the stage for a routine closing runout – at least, it is routine for them.

The key to winning for the pros is the battle for the table. For amateurs below the A- Player level, the key to winning and improving is to more consistently run out those games when the opportunity presents itself – to become a better closer.

Black Cue Ball

In 46 of the examples in the Derby City chapter and 24 more in the Make It Happen chapter are my Black Cue Ball (**BCB**) practice exercises. The examples with a **BCB** on the right side of the subject line are followed with a series of numbers that correspond to the balls that remain on the table when the close begins.

The Black Cue Ball is in the identical position that it was when the pro started his closing run. I naturally chose positions in which they were successful, so you know that these closing positions are very runnable. Some are not difficult, but that is no excuse for letting up, or for passing over them – remember, part of closing well is executing the routine extremely well and staying out of trouble.

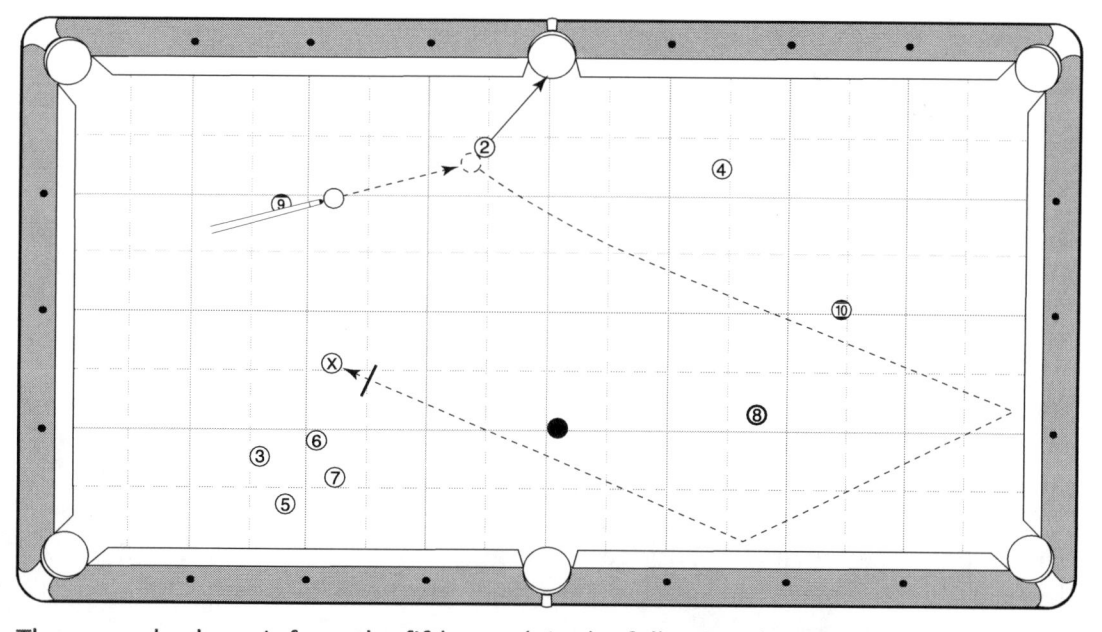

The example above is from the fifth match in the following chapter. You are instructed to begin your closing run on the 7-ball, and then finish with the 8, 9, and 10 balls. The cue ball is placed where the BCB is located. It looks like the 5-ball is in the way, but remember that all of the balls with a lower number than your starting ball (the 7-ball in this example) have already been pocketed!

Chapter 14 - About 10 Ball

Ideas for Your BCB Practice Sessions

You are encouraged to practice these closing positions on your own, and to keep records of your progress. You may also wish to practice these **BCB** patterns with a friend. You can analyze the patterns, teach each other about position play, and engage in some friendly competition!

The BCB exercises can be modified as you wish. For example, players at the A- level and above can begin one or two balls sooner, while a B Player might choose to start his close with ball-in-hand, or one ball later in the run.

Here is another idea for starting with ball-in-hand. Let's say that a closing pattern has five balls, but you are working on running the last three of four. Take ball-in-hand, only this time place it where you think ideal position would be if you had to play for position, not if you are given ball in hand. This will lead to longer shots at different angles, possibly larger ones — and you might even play the shot from a different side of the ball, or at another pocket! This method of practicing: 1) enables you to practice more difficult and more realistic shots, and 2) it trains you to exercise your creative powers.

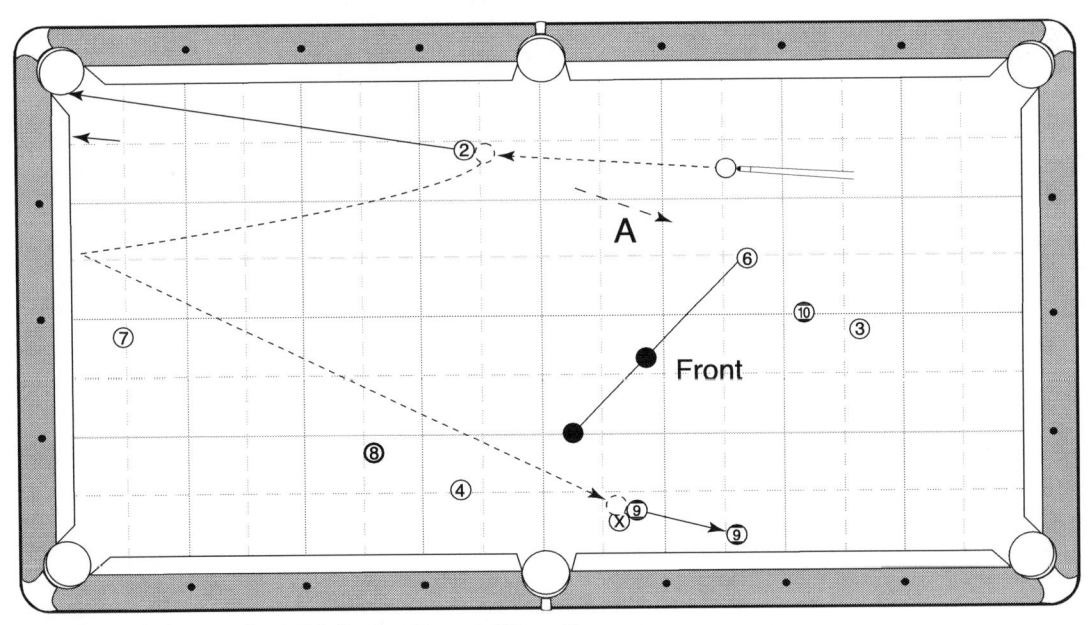

Play From the Back, Middle, or Front "Tees"

Even though we pick up the action after the pro has done the hardest work, a good percentage of these closes are not sure things, such as the pattern above. Pocketing the 6-ball and drawing across and down the table for the 7-ball is no simple matter. So here is an idea: keep the same angle on the 6-ball, but move it 6-10 inches or so closer to the 6-ball. Now you have a shorter and more makeable shot, but you are still essentially playing the same closing pattern — but just from the front tees!

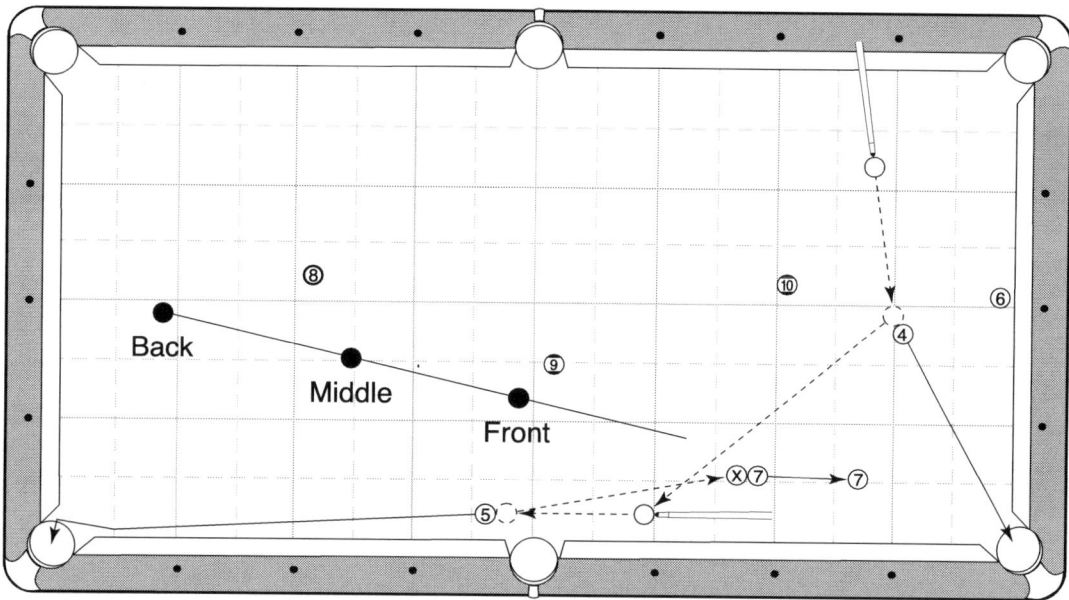

This position is a prime example in the concept of the Front, Middle, and Back Tees! Souquet ended up with the cue ball in the BCB position A, which resulted in a long shot on the 7-ball (from the "Back Tees.") He pocketed the 7, avoided getting hooked behind the 9-ball, and completed his runout. You might wish to shoot this from the Back Tees, Middle Tees, or Front Tees. Again, a major concept is to modify the exercises as needed to match your current level of skill. You can always do the harder versions once you passed your exams on the less difficulty ones.

A Rated Black Cue Ball Exercises

Those of you who want to test your closing skills to the maximum will have fun with the following 19 closing patterns. They include those that I rated A - which are the most difficult.

DERBY CITY
#2 – Efren Reyes (15) vs. Johnny Archer (11)
4 Balls at a Time! (2/20 – :08:05)	A-BCB: 5, 7, 8, 10
Precision Draw Position (1:15:10)	A-BCB: 7, 8, 9, 10
A 4-Rail Escape (1:24:50)	A-BCB: 6, 7, 8, 10
Like a Diamond Cutter! (1:56:35)	A-BCB: 8, 10

#3 – Efren Reyes (15) vs. Brandon Shuff (8)
Efren's Two-Rail Reverse (08:45)	A-BCB: 7, 8, 9, 10

#4 – Shane Van Boening (15) vs. Ralf Souquet (14)
Send in Souquet! (1:00:00)	A-BCB: 7, 8, 9, 10
Set that Angle! – 4/25 (59:25)	A-BCB: 6, 7, 8, 9, 10

#5 – Francisco Bustamante (15) vs. Rafael Martinez (1)
A Certified Jaw Dropper!! – 5/12 – (55:55)   A-BCB: 4, 5, 9, 10

#6 – Lee Vann Corteza (15) vs. Stevie Moore (8)
Corteza's Reward – Diagram B – 6/18 – (2:06:50)   A+-BCB: 4, 5, 6, 7, 8, 10

#7 – Darren Appleton (15) vs. Francisco Bustamante (13)
Straight Back Power Draw!! – 7/22 – (40:00)   A-BCB: 7, 8, 9, 10

#8 – Rodney Morris (15) vs. Darren Appleton (11)
Three Rails in the Side – 8/10 – (45:45)   A-BCB: 4, 5, 6, 7, 10

#11 – Stevie Moore (15) vs. Alex Pagulayan (12)
Closing the Deal in Style   (Diagram B – 11/24 –1:27:25)   A- BCB: 6, 8, 9, 10

#12 – Francisco Bustamante (15) vs. John Morra (5)
Identify the Big Hurdle   (Diag. B – 12/14 – 1:23:00)   A- BCB: 7, 8, 9, 10

MAKE IT HAPPEN

#1 – Shane Van Boening (11) vs. Thorsten Hohmann (9)
Hohmann's Extravaganza!   (1/3 – 19:10)   A-BCB: 6, 7, 8, 10
Incidence Equals Reflection!   (1/11 – 1:01:45)   A-BCB: 4, 6, 7, 8, 9, 10

#2 – Dennis Orcollo (11) vs. Thorsten Hohmann (9)
Power Follow Shot   (2/14 – 1:29:40)   A-BCB: 6, 7, 8, 9, 10

#5 – Shane Van Boening (11) vs. Darren Appleton (5)
Classic Side Rail Stun Shot   (5/1 – 05:45)   A-BCB: 6, 7, 8, 9, 10

#6 – Darren Appleton (11) vs. Thorsten Hohmann (8)
Draw Outside Special   (Diag. B – 6/7 – 53:20)   A-BCB: 5, 6, 8, 9, 10
On the Wrong Side   (6/16 – 1:53:40)   A-BCB: 5, 6, 7, 8, 9, 10

CHAPTER 15

Derby City 10 Ball Challenge

Greg Sullivan of Diamond Billiard products is the founder of the Derby City Classic, which is held every January at the Horseshoe Southern Indiana in Elizabeth , Indiana, right across the river from Louisville, Kentucky. The Classic is comprise of three main events – 9 Ball, 1 Pocket, and Bank Pool – that attract huge fields of top pros and leading amateurs alike.

In 2009 they add an event initially called the Derby City Classic 10-Ball Fat Boy Challenge. Fat Boy's name is Eric Peterson, who added a substantial amount of money to the purse. The field is made up of 16 elite players, including several world champions and members of the Hall of Fame. The list of winners from the inception through 2014 includes a Who's Who lineup of super players that is made up of Lee Van Corteza, Efren Reyes, Rodney Morris. Francisco Bustamante, Dennis Orcollo, Shane Van Boening!

The 10 Ball event was played on a 4.5' x 9' table for the first four years, then they switched to a 5' x 10' table. I like watching the pros play on the bigger table because it puts a premium on shotmaking and execution, and it showcases who is really on their game. Nevertheless, I have confined the examples in this chapter to the events that were played on the 4.5' x 9' because the vast majority of 10 Ball is played on this sized table, so this makes the analysis more relevant to most players. Furthermore, this enabled me to create a more uniform set of statistics that include the first four contests at the Derby City and the Make It Happen All Stars, which are featured in the following chapter.

#1 – Lee Vann Corteza (15) vs. Ralf Souquet (11)

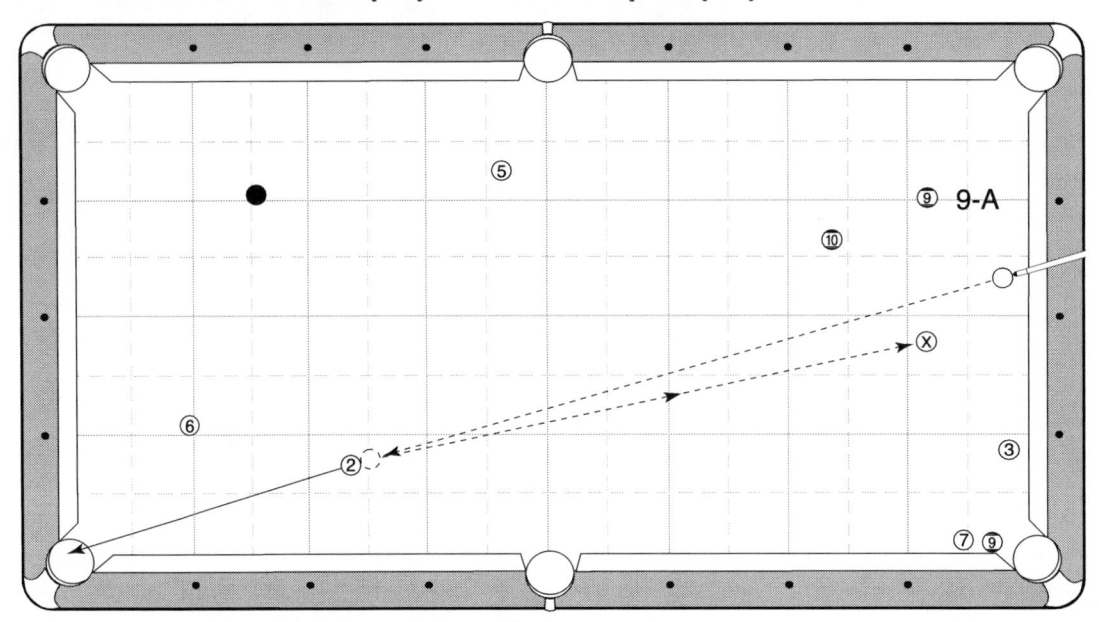

Corteza Makes a Statement! (1/1 – 6:00) C-BCB: 6, 7 (where it is), 9-A, 10

Lee Vann Corteza, in the first game of the match, stepped up to the table for the 2-ball and uncorked this long draw shot, sending the cue ball back to near its original position for excellent shape on the 3-ball!

Corteza used an elevated closed bridge and took three attempts to get positioned for the shot. After failing to capture "the feeling," he got back up and stretched out his shooting arm, perhaps trying to relax his muscles for the massive effort ahead. He again assumed his positon and, six seconds later, unleased a six inch long power jab-like stroke into the cue ball that featured an incredible burst of acceleration.

An alternative shot is to play a safety, perhaps by banking the 2-ball to the left end rail, and sending the cue ball to the opposite end of the table.

LESSONS: 1) Take more than one attempt to get set if needed, 2) loosen up that shooting arm, and 3) a short power jab stroke can result in a surprising amount of draw off the rail, and may be your best bet when a longer bridge is not feasible.

Balls in the Middle (Diag. A – 1/5 – 32:50) C-BCB: 7, 8, 9, 10

Ralf Souquet is one of the great surveyors as he is always stalking the table with his eyes glued to the balls, calculating his next shot and series of moves like a true German engineer.

The 8-ball was in an awkward position out in the middle of the table, so he needed to get a good angle on it to proceed to the 9-ball. The one big error he avoided was leaving a big cut to the left on the 8-ball because then it would have been all but impossible to get on the 9-ball. Souquet played a precise draw shot on the 7-ball, floating over a few inches for the 8. His small angle on the 8-ball made it easy for him to roll forward to Position X.

LESSON: When a ball (like the 9) is at, or near, the middle of the end rail, consider playing position on either side of it – and, in this case, on either side of the 8 as well! This adds great flexibility to your pattern, and it can increase your margin for error.

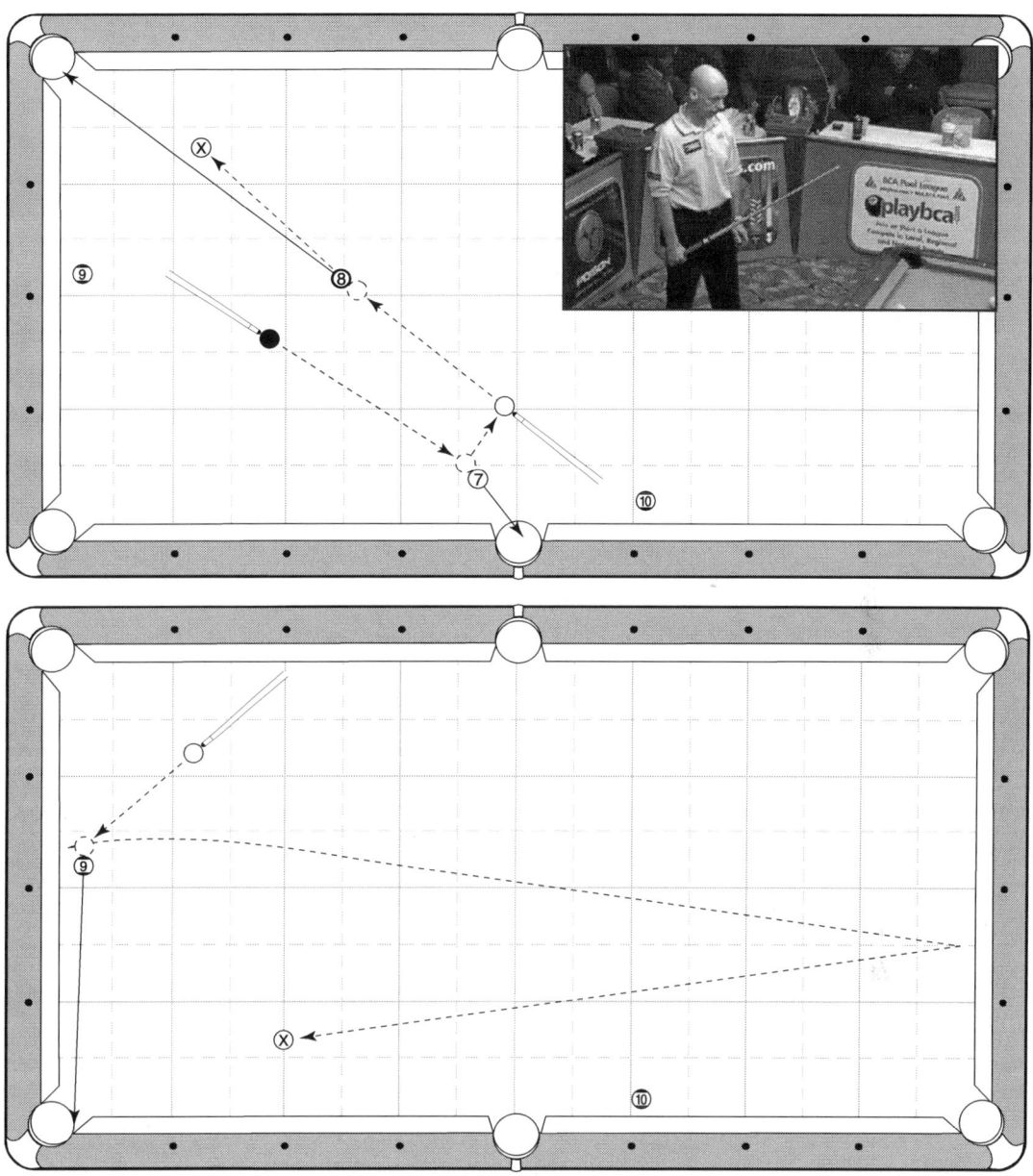

Balls in the Middle (Diag. B – 1/5 – 33:45)

Souquet wisely chose to play the 9-ball in the lower left pocket because this view, gave him a better look at his route to the 10-ball. If he positioned the cue ball on the other side of the 9, the 10-ball would have been out of his peripheral vision!

Souquet checked out the angle for the 9-ball, but came up six inches short of ideal position, leaving him with a 48 degree cut shot. This forced him to play a recovery route to the opposite end and back to Position X. If Souquet had left himself with a shallower angle on the 9-ball, he could have followed directly towards Position X. About a diamond past it would have been just right.

LESSON: If you have a choice of sides for position, try to get on the one that enables you to see the position route in your peripheral vision.

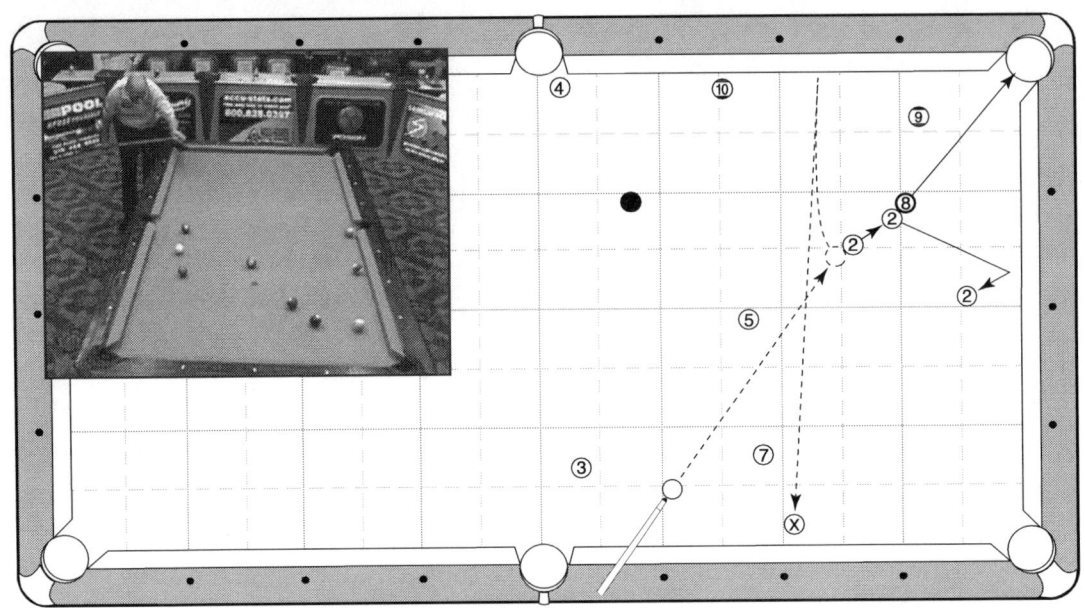

Shape After the Combo (1/10 – 1:06:20)   B-BCB: 5, 7, 9, 10

Making a combo like the 2-8 in this illustration is a big challenge, but Souquet, being the professional that he is, took it a big step further and planned for shape on the lead ball. I watched him and counted his vantage points - there were seven, and the process took him 45 seconds. Then he spent another seven seconds over the shot, zeroing in on the target.

The 2 ball relocated a half diamond off the end rail, and Souquet had a relatively easy shot and route to the Black Ball. You can pick up the action from here and close out the rack. Warning: the last two balls near the same rail make this a challenging end-of-rack runout.

LESSON: When you have a complex shot, take the time YOU need to consider all of the relevant variables. Only then are you ready to pull the trigger.

Souquet's Combo Clinic (1/13 – 1:23:25)

I had no plan for showing certain types of shots in a specific order, opting instead for a more natural selection process. This partly explains why I am showing you two straight combos by Ralf Souquet. The other, of course, is that both of these shots are very instructive.

A pro will usually choose a runout over a combo, especially when the balls are as far from each other and the pocket as the 2 and 10 balls are. However, playing great shape on the 2 for the upper right pocket was not easy, nor was getting from the 4 ball to the 5. So, Souquet opted to play shape on the 2-10 combo. He got on it well enough to make the shot, but if he hadn't, he could have played a safety.

He cut the 2 and the 10 balls slightly to the right – which is so much easier than trying to see a right-left or left-right combo. In addition, he used a medium hard (6) stroke for accuracy.

LESSON: Amateurs should go for more combos like this early in the game when they, and their opponent, are not yet in runout range.

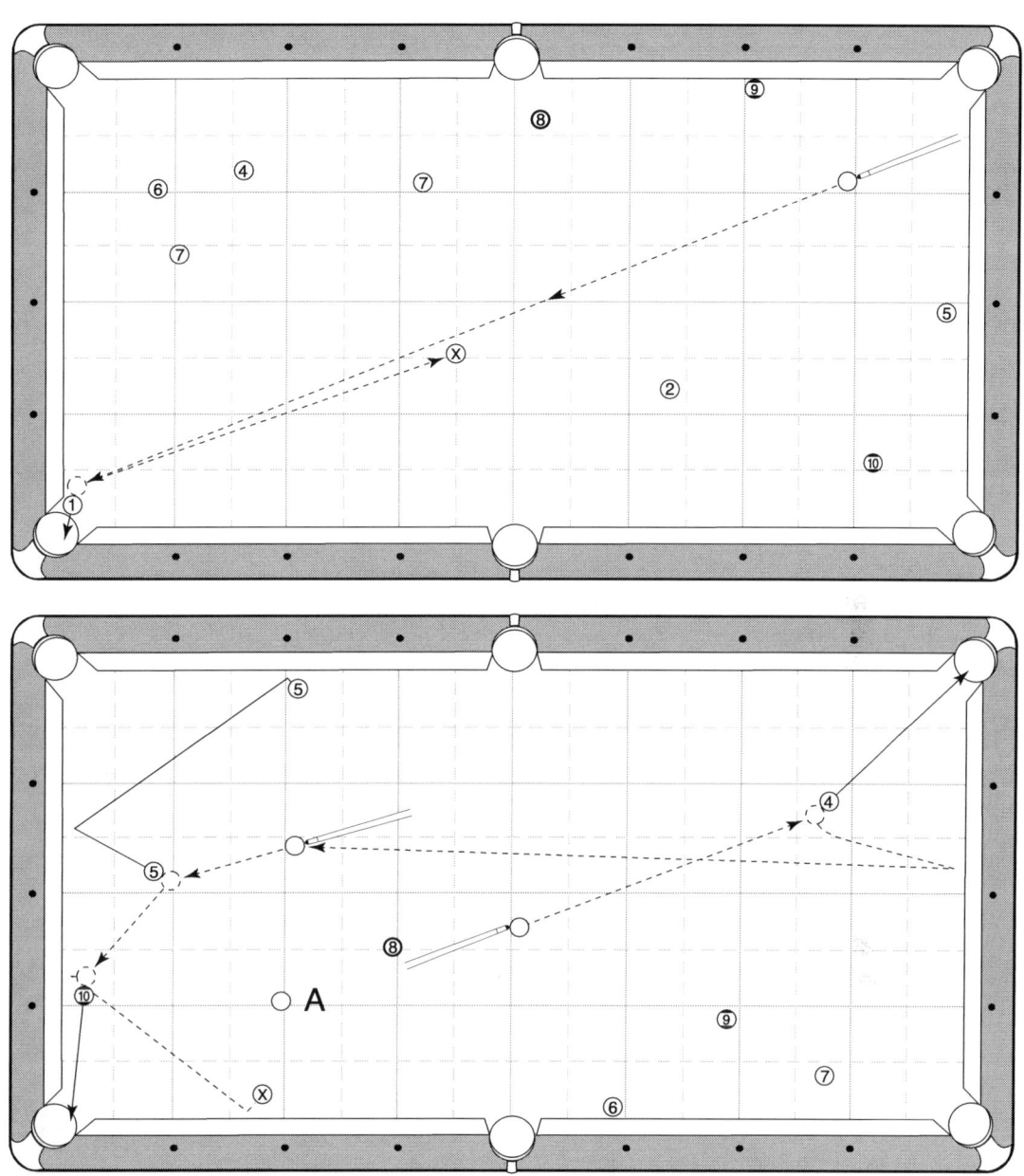

Two-Way Billiard is a Winner   (1/17 – V2 – 21:35)
Corteza is facing a cut to the left on the 4-ball, so the natural route is between the 8-ball and side rail to Position A for the 5-ball into the upper left pocket. If he had succeeded – and he had a huge position zone – a player of his caliber could be expected to run out the rest of this rack at least 9 times out of 10.

The cue ball, however, passed on the opposite side of the 8-ball, leaving Corteza with the 5-10 billiard. He wrapped his cue around his back, stretched across the table – both moves characteristic of Filipino players – and made the billiard, scoring a bead for his side. Note that the cue ball and the 5 positioned themselves on the opposite rails, so Souquet would have been facing a safety should Corteza have missed!
LESSON: Ironically, the billiard is the right choice to play for lower level players!

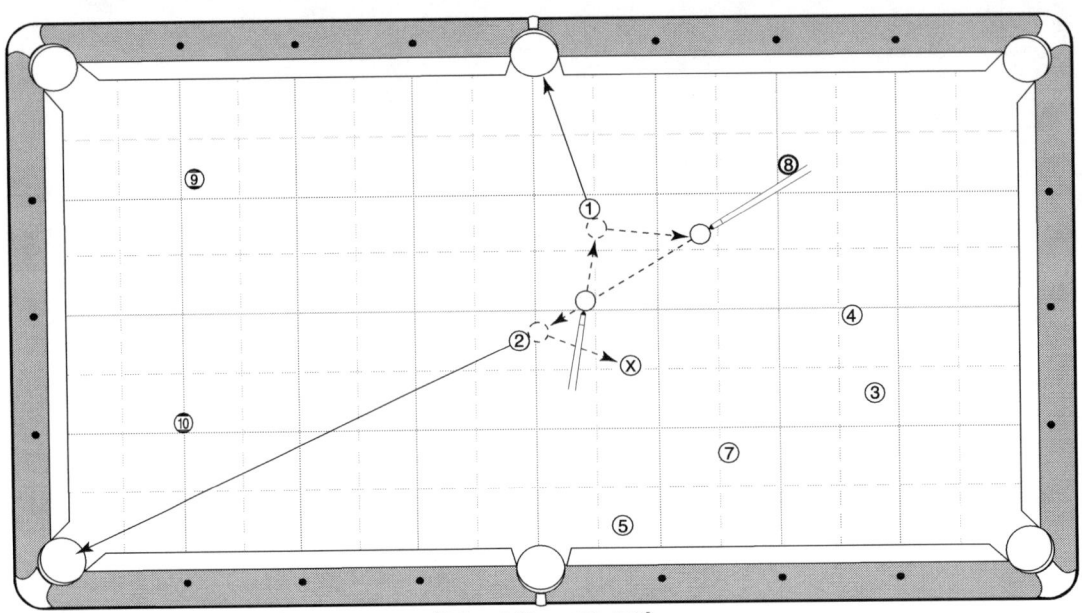

Souquet: Phase 1 - (Diag. A – 1/20 – V2 – 40:30)
We pick up the action with the first shot of a break and run after Souquet has just pocketed a ball on the break. The 1-ball requires a soft finesse draw stroke to contain the cue ball's movement for the 2-ball, and to get nearly straight in on it – which he did. This shot is hit as low as you dare with the softest stroke that will still hold the line. Again, Souquet restricted the cue ball's sideways movement by using low outside english when playing the 2-ball to get on the 3.

LESSON: Balls in the middle are tough to get position on when you aren't going to a rail because you must use very small angles, or be straight in.

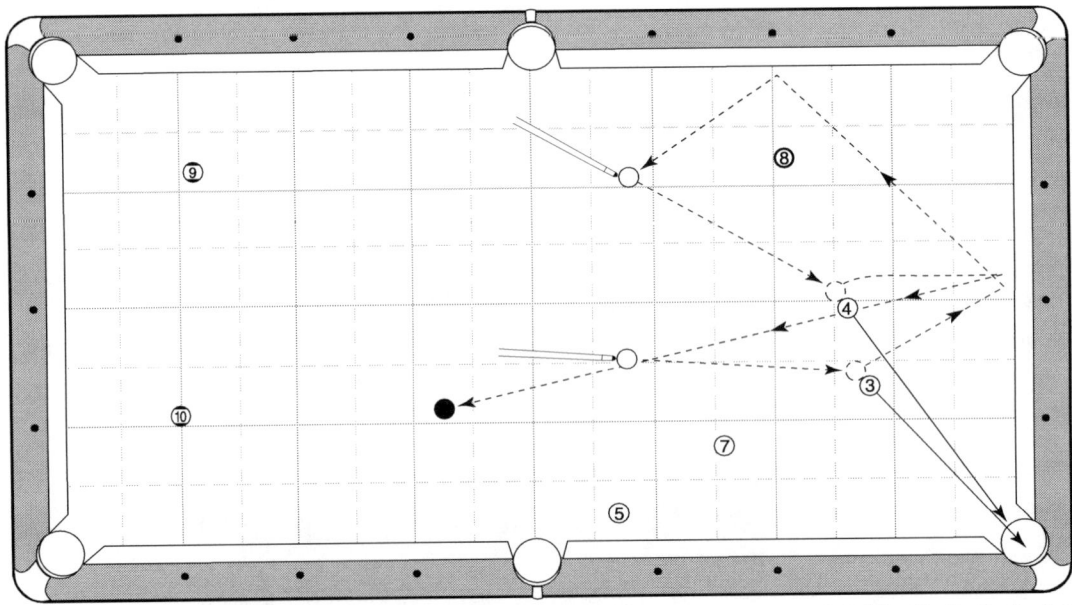

One Pocket in 10-Ball (Diag. B – 1/20 – :41:40)   C-BCB: 5, 7, 8, 9, 10
Souquet is now going to play the next four balls into the same pocket, starting with the 3-ball. Because of the somewhat thin cut (42 degrees) he was able to hit this shot with a medium soft stroke, which helped him to dial in the speed. He might have pre-

ferred to have a little fuller angle on the 4 for this one rail route to the 5-ball, but he was still able to reverse the cue ball off the end rail with inside english.
LESSON: Most players tend to overcut certain shots using inside english.

#2 – Efren Reyes (15) vs. Johnny Archer (11)

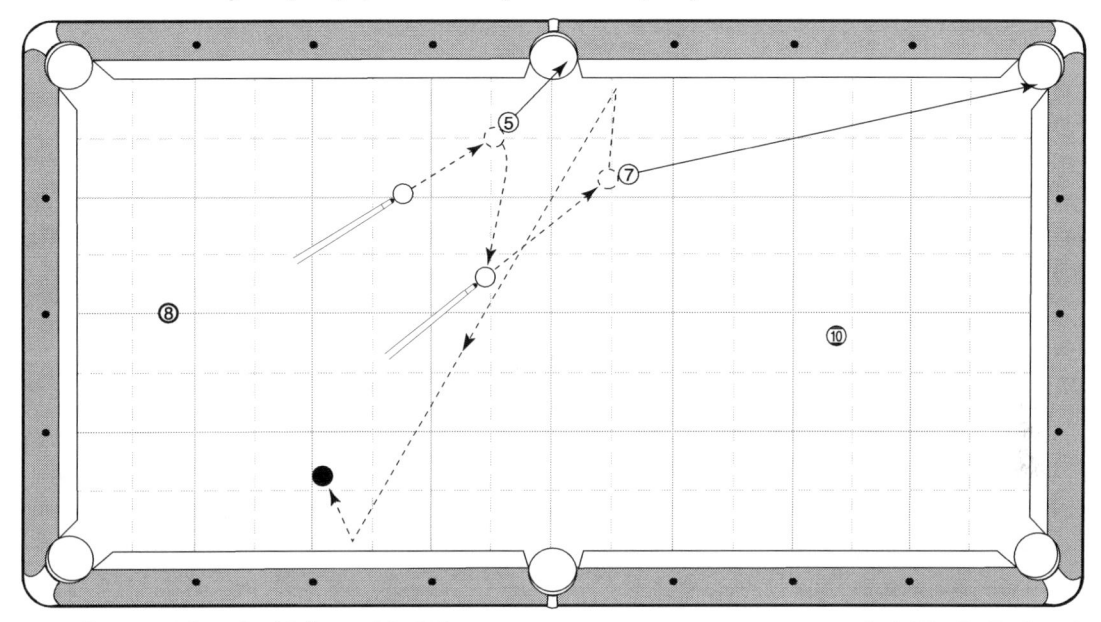

4 Balls at a Time! (2/1 – :08:05)   **A-BCB: 5, 7, 8, 10**

Johnny Archer is meticulous, but with good reason. While he is looking at the table his mind is whirling away, considering his options and making sure that he makes the best choice – which he invariably does. Take this closing pattern. He is down to the final four, and his big remaining hurdle is to get on the 8-ball with a good angle to travel back down table for the 10-ball.

If he was playing for three balls at a time, as conventional wisdom (including mine) advises you to do, he would make the 5-ball and get an angle to take him from the 7-ball to the 8.

But that is not good enough as there are good and bad ways to go from the 7 to the 8-ball. He wanted an angle to get back down for the 10-ball without having to resort to a recovery route – which is why he meticulously planned for the angle on the 7-ball that would enable him to cross the table for very playable angle on the 8. And, he was kind enough to put his tip down on the table and show us his target!

LESSONS: 1) At times you will need an angle for an angle – and for yet another angle that will take you from the third to the fourth ball! 2) Put that tip on the zone!
PRACTICE BCB: Try Archer's close. See if you can see what he did when he plotted his closing pattern – how well did you execute it?

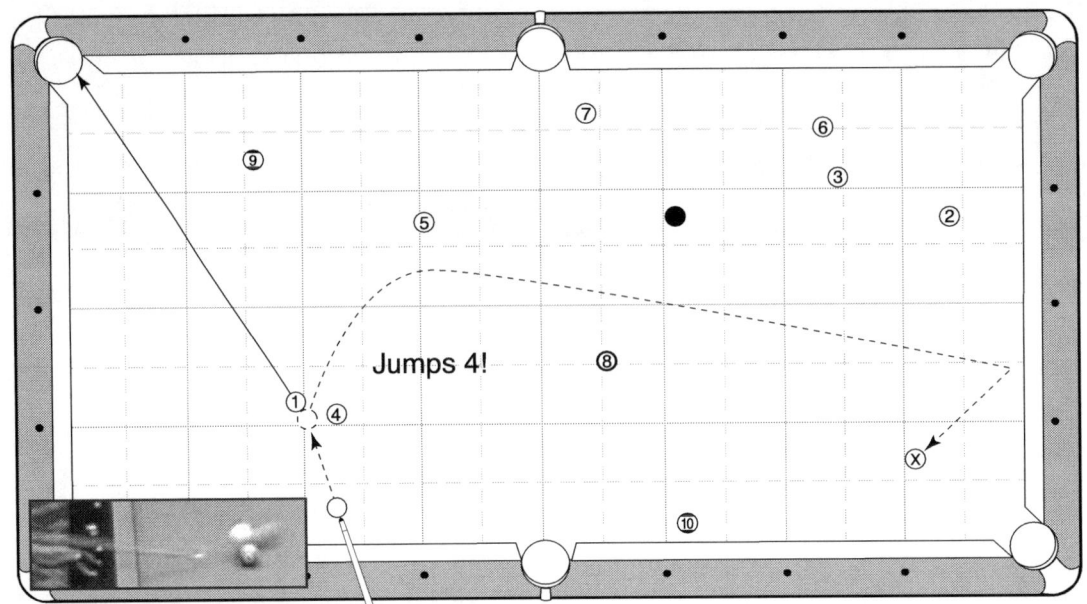

The Magician Plies his Trade (2/2 – 10:15)   C-BCB: 6, 7, 8, 9, 10

If pool was featured on ESPN or the major networks, miracles like Reyes' jump/draw/curve shot (with position) would be replayed to death so that everyone in the sporting universe saw it – and it would go viral on YouTube and the like! But, in case you missed it, here is the recap!

The two big keys to this shot are 1) seeing it in the first place, and 2) being able to execute it – not in 20 tries on the practice table, but right then and there in the heat of big time competition! Indeed, shots like this are a reminder of why Efren Reyes has long been hailed as The Magician – the coolest nickname in our sport!

Most everyone who plays pool has never made this shot, but Reyes proved that it can be done. There was no exact blueprint for this, not even for Reyes. Indeed, while he was over the ball he tested several angles for his cue before settling in on the one that must have felt right. He used a hard stroke with outside english – but how hard? Did Vladimir Horowitz know how hard he hit the keys? No, he just played!

LESSON: There is magic in each of us – maybe not like Reyes', but enough so that we can, on occasion, pull off a shot that even we did not know we knew!!

Efren Threads the Needle (2/6 – 30:10)   C-BCB: 7, 8, 9, 10

Reyes missed position on the 6-ball, but he got back in line (sort of) with this superb recovery route to the 7-ball. If he had a larger cut angle to the right on the 6-ball, he could have played a soft draw shot off the side rail with outside spin while maintaining complete control of the cue ball.

In fact, his shallow angle forced him to create one by 1) cheating the pocket, and 2) playing a pound/draw shot. The big challenge was to thread the needle through the gap (as shown) without hitting either obstacle!

The cue ball traveled further down the table than was ideal (to the Black Ball position) thanks to the high speed shot he was forced to play. This, in turn, forced him to use a soft stroke with outside spin on the 7-ball so that the cue ball would stay close to the rail for the 8-ball! The 7-ball is a good place to start your runout.

LESSONS: The size of the gap between two balls depends on the angle of approach, not how far they are apart. It is always less than the distance between the balls!

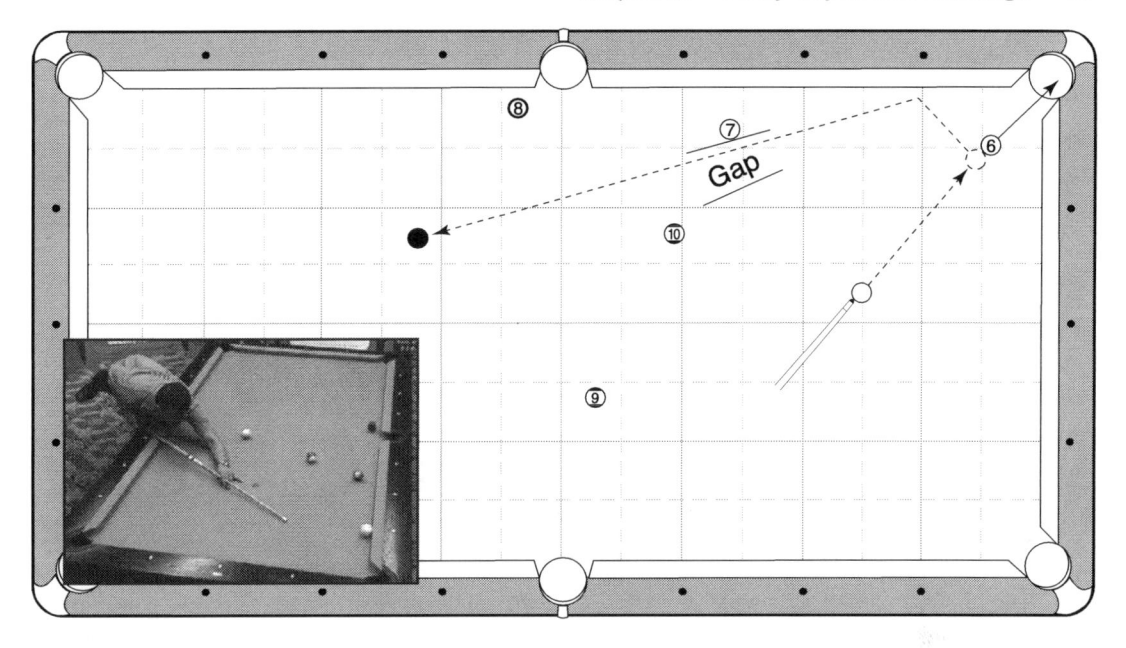

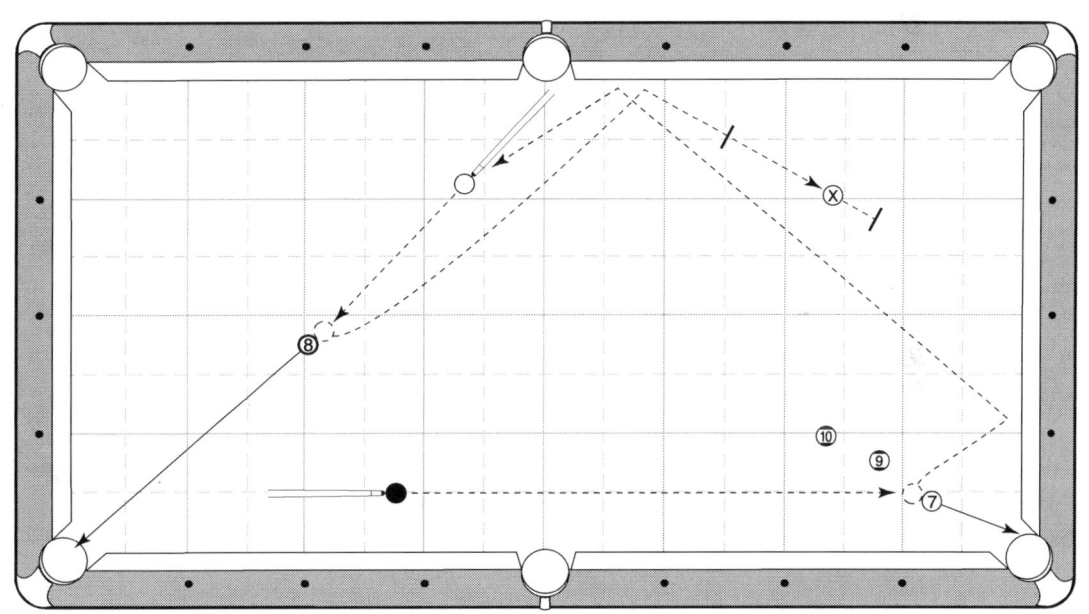

Precision Draw Position   (2/13 – 1:15:10)   **A-BCB: 7, 8, 9, 10**

Archer once again makes a tricky closing sequence look far easier than it really is. Imagine what the shot from the 8-ball to the 9 would have been like if the cue ball had stopped a couple of inches to either side of where it actually did.

Give this one a try, starting with the 7-ball. The key is that two-rail route to the 8 as shown, sending the cue ball Down the Line (P#12) rather than across the zone. He also followed the Natural Route (P#14). Notice the size of the shape zone for the 9-ball. Archer hit the bull's eye at Position X.

LESSON: Keep it as simple as possible, and execute extremely well, just like Archer!

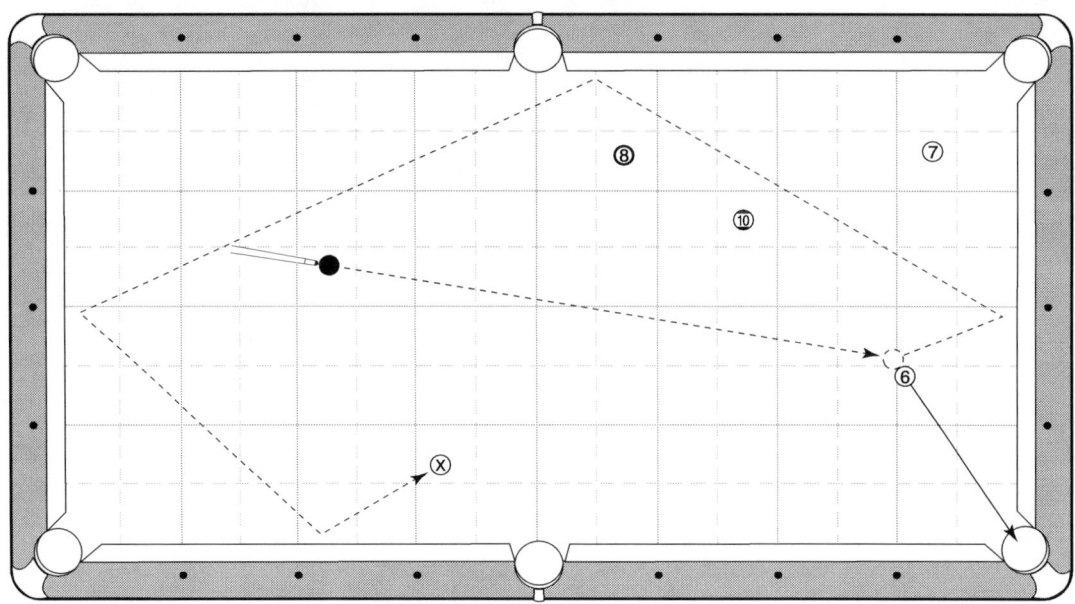

A 4-Rail Escape (2/15 – 1:24:50)   A-BCB: 6, 7, 8, 10

The Magician is the Magician in part because he has to be. I know – it is heresy to suggest that Reyes ever misses position, but he does – and a little more than most people might imagine given his typical brilliance. But when he does, he is able to recover from a mistake as well as, if not better, than anyone who has ever played the game. Take this shot, for example.

Reyes got a little thin on the ball before the 6, hit the point of the side while trying to send the cue ball down table, and ended up with this lengthy 46 degree cut shot (a shade more than a quarter ball hit) on the 6-ball. No problem – he speared it in and sent the cue ball on a 14.5 foot journey for an open shot at the 7, avoiding a hook behind the 10-ball.

LESSON: You may wish to copy Reyes' disciplined shooting routine. He takes about five seconds for a shot of average difficulty, and about two to three more on tougher ones. This gives you a little extra time to dial in your aim, stroke, and speed. Note: On this shot Reyes took seven seconds, and eight warm-up strokes!

Like a Diamond Cutter! (2/21 – 1:56:35)   A-BCB: 8, 10

Reyes hid Archer, forcing him to play an awkward kick, which he missed giving Reyes ball in hand. If an amateur player had ball-in-hand, he should try to hit the 2-ball lightly in an effort to manufacture a shot. If unsuccessful, he can play safe.

As for Reyes, he saw that microscopic position zone for the upper left pocket, went for it using a soft follow shot with inside spin (!), and stopped the cue ball on a dime for near perfect shape! Precision shape like this shows what a world class player is capable of when they are literally given a license to steal! I wonder, even among the pros, how many would have seen this route, and played for it?

LESSON: There should be more opportunities for ball-in-hand in 10 Ball than in 9 Ball simply because there is that extra ball. It is also possible that the way that the balls break in 10 Ball could lead to more chances for tough hook safeties.

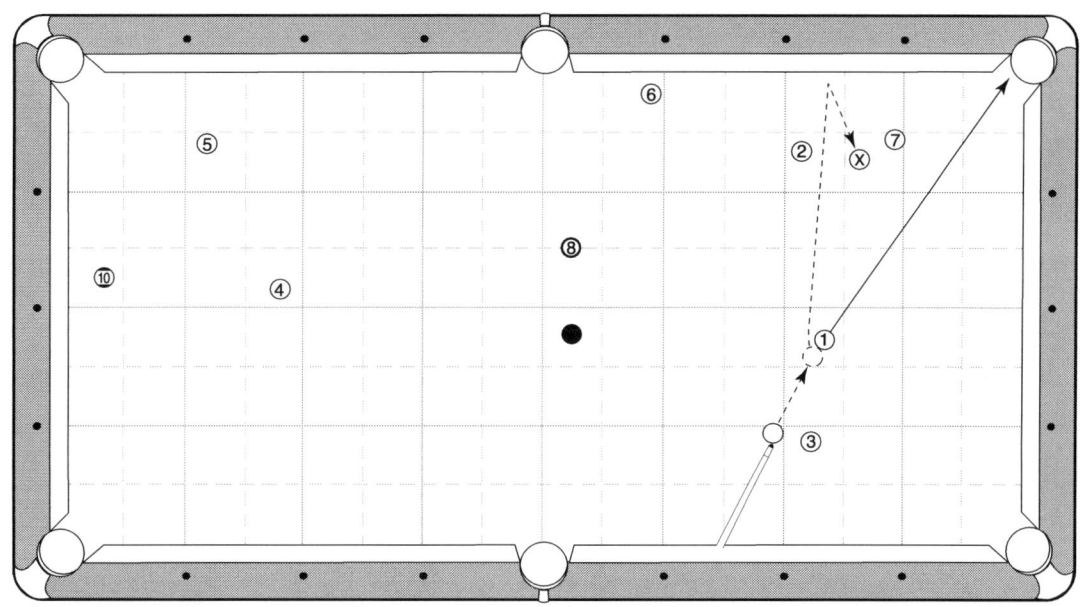

PRACTICE: Reyes got on the wrong side of the 8-ball with a small angle – one of the worst mistakes in pool – but ramped up his power/follow/spin stroke and managed to send the cue ball four rails to the 9-ball. See if you can match the Magician's shot!

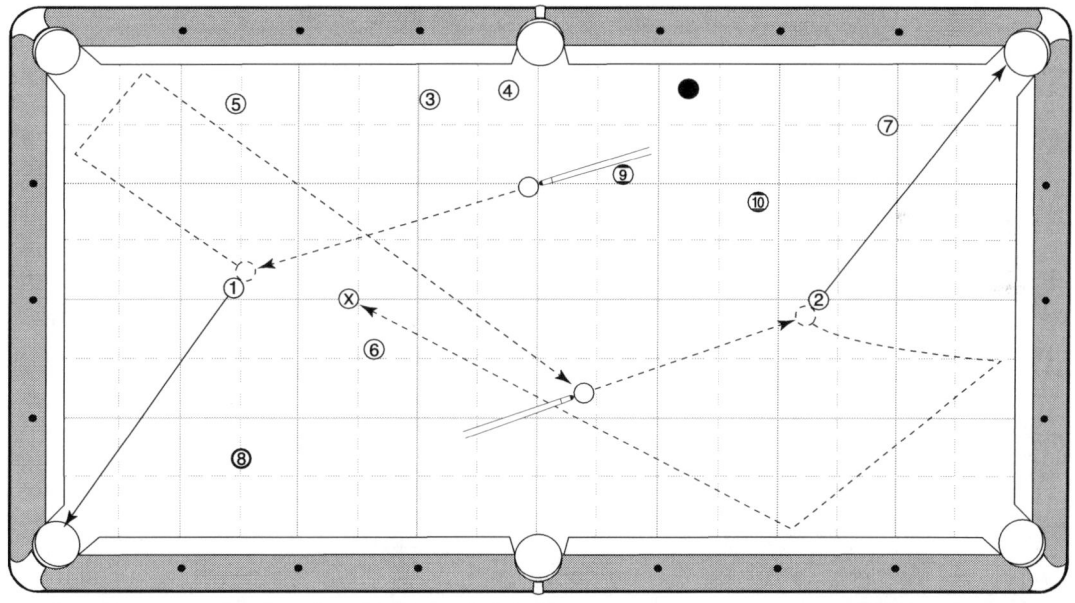

Archer Runs to the Bank (2/24 – 2:14:40) **B-BCB: 7, 8, 9, 10**

This beginning pattern is vintage 10 Ball at its best. Two excellent position routes led to perfect bank shape on the 3-ball. When Archer played the 1-ball, the cue ball barely avoided the 5, leading to an ideal angle on the 2-ball. And that angle on the 2-ball was a half ball hit – 30 degrees – which was what Archer needed to get his speed just right for the 3. He speared it in and ran out!

LESSON: If your speed control is generally superb, or you are playing a route in which you feel very confident, then you can play across the line shape as Archer did on for that bank. Otherwise, play shape for something like the 3-4 billiard.

#3 – Efren Reyes (15) vs. Brandon Shuff (8)

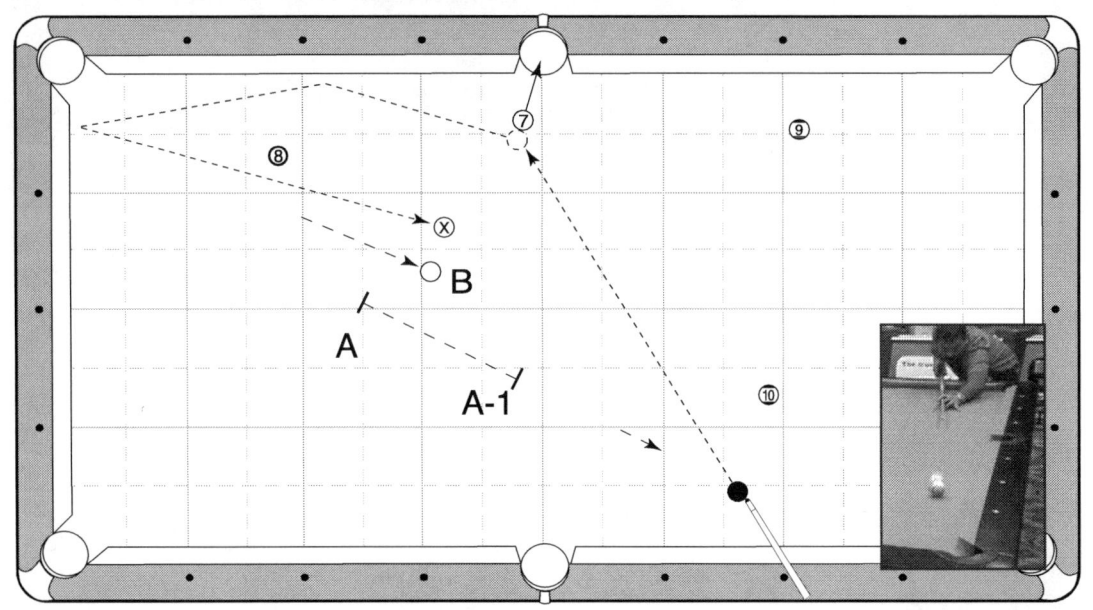

Efren's Two-Rail Reverse (3/1 – 08:45)   **A-BCB: 7, 8, 9, 10**

A bomb went off in Reyes' hand when playing the 6-ball, and he overran the A to A-1 position zone by a mile, stopping at the Black Cue Ball! Now a routine runout had become an adventure, necessitating a recovery route.

So Reyes elevated slightly off the rail, used a medium (5) draw stroke with inside (right) english, and played the two rail route to the 8-ball. Notice that he barely missed the 8 in passing. He probably intended to send the cue ball to Position B, but he used up his entire margin for error. Reyes eventually missed the 10-ball, but it banked two-rails into the upper left corner pocket – so I guess he didn't miss it!

LESSON: There is usually more than one way to get on a ball. So, try Reyes's route to the 7-ball, and try cheating the right side of the pocket and going three rails. This is not as difficult to execute, but it will leave you with a longer shot on the 8-ball.

Use those Blockers (3/9 – 48:55)

In this early rack layout blockers abound, and there is no reasonable shot on the 2-ball, so the table is screaming out SAFETY! The question is which one to play, and how to play it – questions that caused Brandon Shuff to ponder his strategy for 60 seconds from several angles before he settled on the one in the illustration.

Shuff loaded up the cue ball with right english and propelled it four rails on a precise path to behind that wall of blockers. Meanwhile, the 2-ball nestled in behind the 9. As an alternative, Shuff could have possibly banked the 2-ball three rails behind the 3-6-8-10 wall, and sent the cue ball behind the 5 and 9.

LESSON: When planning a safety with separation like this, consider sending either ball to each end of the table. One will usually emerge as the clear favorite.

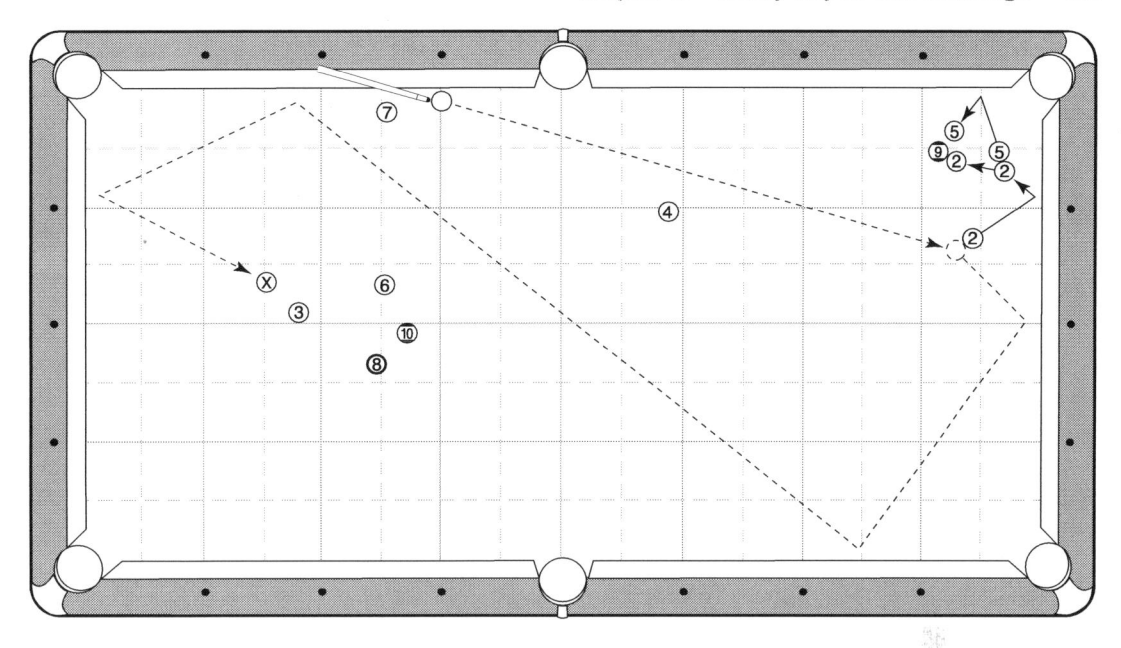

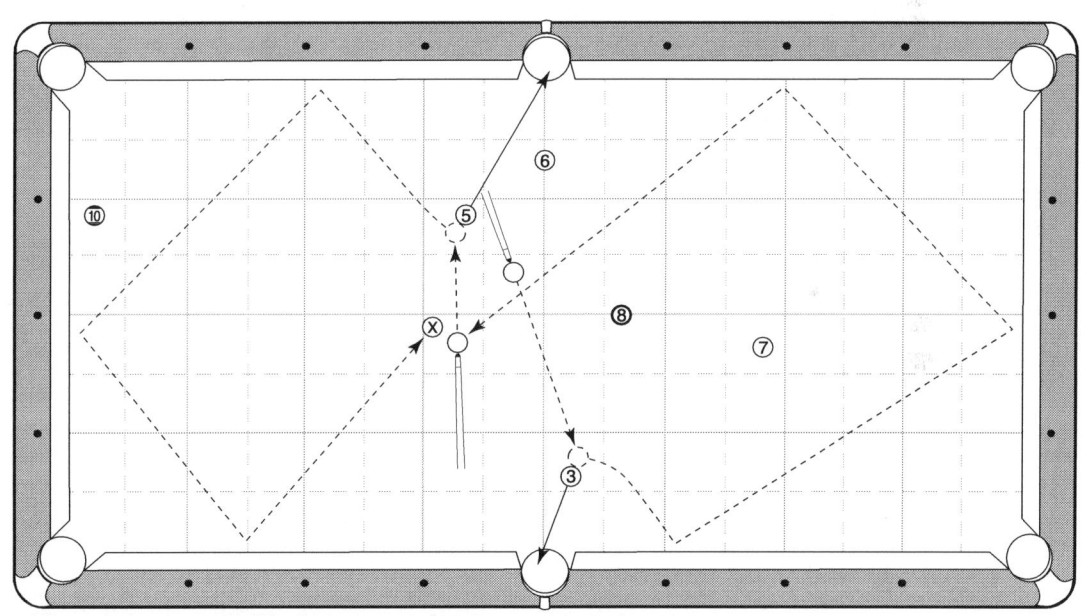

Side Pocket 10 Ball!   (Diag. – 3/12A – 1:12:55)
We will pick up the action on the second shot of Reyes' break and run. He played the 3-ball into the side and went three cushions to the 5-ball, but came up about a diamond short of ideal position. He covered this half mistake with another side pocket three rail position play to the 6-ball. There is a certain symmetry to these twin three railers that I find particularly appealing – perhaps you will as well!

LESSON: Imagine the position play Reyes would have had on the 6-ball if the cue ball had rolled another diamond when playing the 5. You can learn to play better position next time by studying non-lethal mistakes like this.

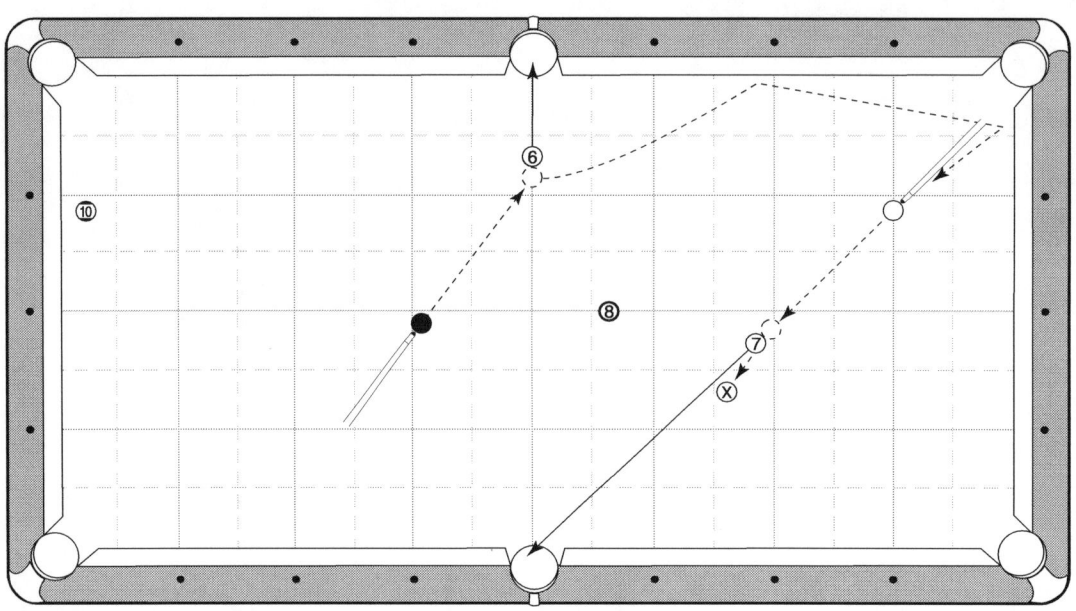

Side Pocket 10 Ball!   (Diag. B – 3/12B – 1:13:20)   B-BCB: 6, 7, 8, 10

Your practice pattern starts with the shot on the 6-ball into the side pocket. Reyes played a two rail route for nearly straight in shape on the 7-ball into the lower side pocket. Perfect! He then shot the 8 into the upper side pocket and floated down for the 10-ball on the end rail.

   Add them up – that is five consecutive position plays into the side pockets. Reyes, the king of 1-Pocket, might also be the master of Side Pocket 10 Ball!

LESSON: There are some instructors who will tell you to avoid the side pockets. Reyes just showed you why that is nonsense! Play each ball to whichever pocket is best for making it, and for creating your pattern.

#4 – Shane Van Boening (15) vs. Ralf Souquet (14)
Half Ball Bank Safety   (Diag. A – 4/3 – 12:30)

Shane Van Boening just made a ball on the break and has no reasonable shot at the 1-ball, but he does have the widely spread wall of blockers to work with. After only 20 seconds of study, which is not a long when planning a safety, he settled into his stance and took aim at the 1-ball.

   This is not a common safety, so aiming is a bit of a challenge. I did a freeze frame analysis, which showed that he hit about half of the 1-ball (he aimed the center of the cue ball at the left edge of the ball).

   The 1-ball was destined to roll a long distance, but there was no chance that it would return to the same end of the table. Meanwhile, the cue ball came to rest in the jaws after nearly scratching! This fact alone points to the difficulty of aiming and playing unusual safeties like this. Van Boening was no doubt targeting the end rail, probably at Position A. Souquet missed this difficult kick on the 1-ball on the near side, which is the opposite of how this shot is typically missed.

LESSON: Aiming can be a challenge on some safeties because there is no pocket to shoot at, so be comfortable using a bit of guesswork and your intuition, which will improve over time with experience.

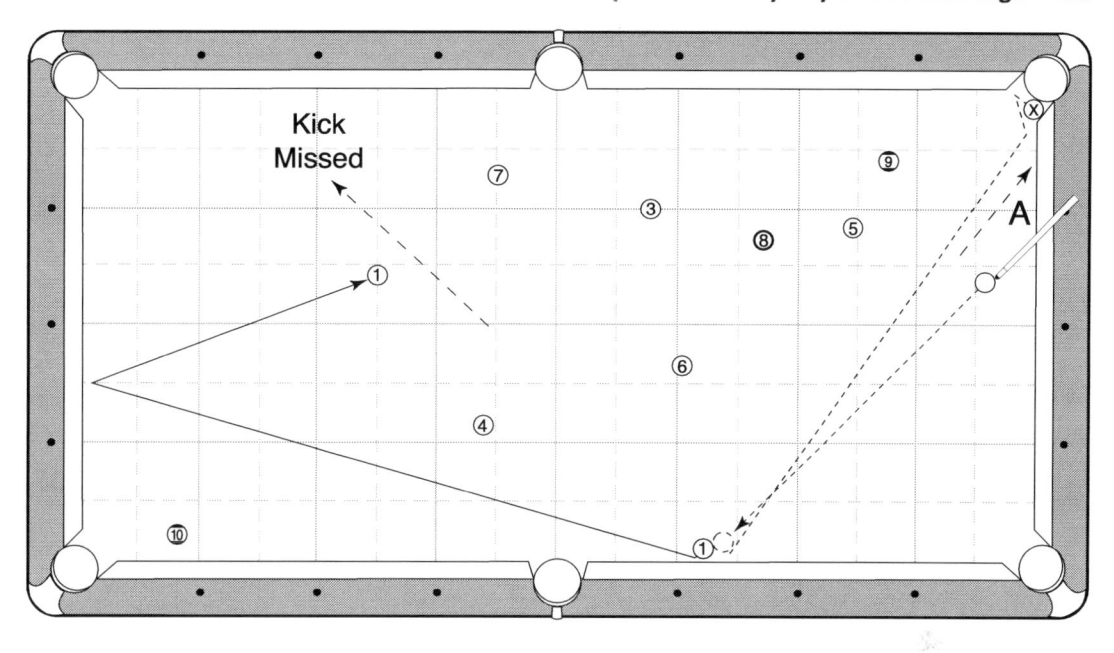

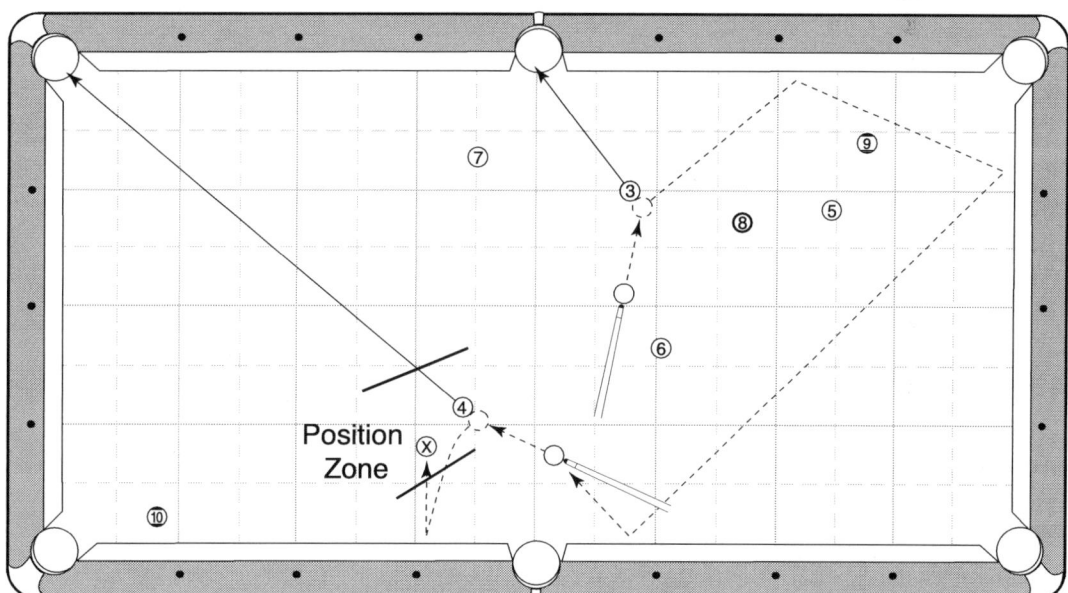

Shane Opens the Window (Diag. B – 4/3 – 14:30)

Van Boening won control of the table thanks to his skill (and a little luck) on the shot in the previous diagram. Ball in hand enabled him to set up a short range position play to the 3-ball, so he could have ended up with close to any shot that he wanted on the 3-ball – and he selected this cut for playing shape on the 4.

There was much to like about his position play to the 4-ball: 1) the 50 degree cut angle – which makes pocketing easy enough from this range – enabled him to dial in his speed, 2) the route to the 4-ball was a natural one, 3) the cue ball was traveling down the line to the 4-ball, and 4) he was able to access the position zone (in the window), as shown, for shape on the 5-ball!

LESSON: On exacting position plays, you may need to stir several ingredients into the stew – so make sure, like Van Boening, that you leave nothing out.

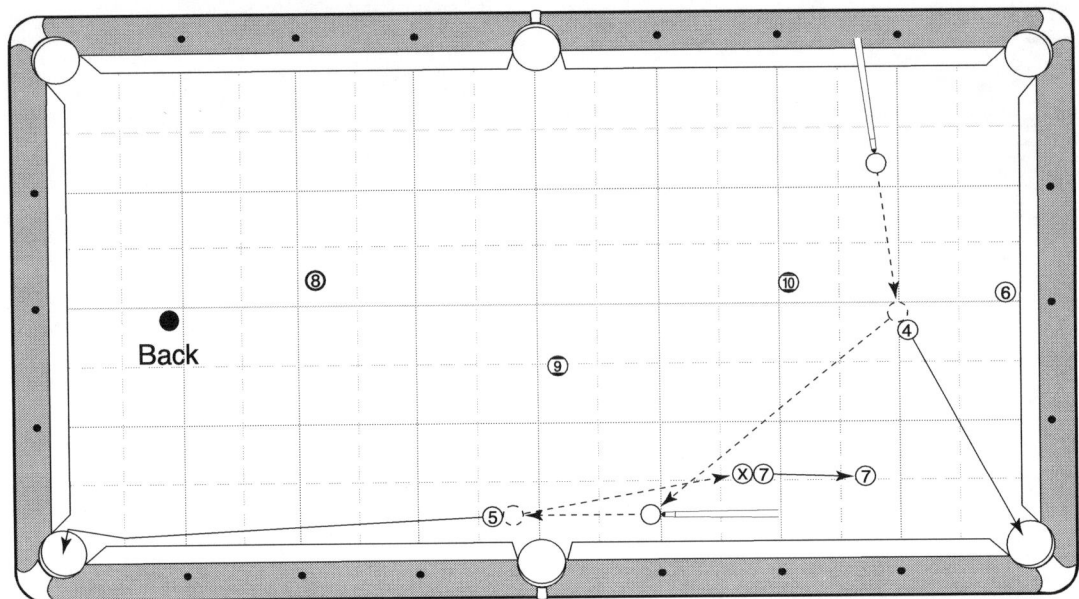

Send in Souquet! (4/12 – 1:00:00)   A-BCB: 7, 8, 9, 10

If pool was like football and you could send in a player for a specific task, like a long field goal – and you had a tough pattern that required planning, position, and shot-making – you'd want Ralf Souquet on your team.

He faced a difficult sequence in using the 4-ball to get on the 5 just right so he could draw back for the 6-ball on the end rail. The potential paths to the 6 are blocked by the 7, 9, and 10, so when planning the shot on the 5, he had to take these balls into consideration.

He opened the sequence with a stun/follow shot on the 4-ball. He wanted to get straight in on the 5-ball so he could draw back between the 7 and the rail – but he got a little angle to the right. He hit the 7-ball squarely, but came away with a playable shot on the 6 at Position X (the 7 was hit out of the way), and went on to complete this challenging layout. Notice that the 5-ball brushed the rail – perhaps he was trying to keep from hitting the point. If he had made it in the right side of the pocket, he would have missed the 7-ball and had a far easier shot on the 6.

LESSON: Difficult patterns showcase how the pros manage to get out. Their position is not always perfect, but it is usually good enough to allow them to continue from ball to ball to get to the gamewinner.

Ultra-Thin Safety! (4/20 – 16:30)

Van Boening had three options: he could 1) push out, 2) try to fan the 1-ball in the side, which would force him to send the cue ball on a wild and perilous journey with no guarantee that he would emerge with position on the 2-ball, and 3) employ one of his specialties – the thin hit – to play a safety. He chose #3.

His goals were to graze the 1-ball and to send the cue ball behind the wall made up of the 2, 4, and 10 balls. He used a soft (2) and short stroke to gently roll the cue ball to the end rail and out for a hook. If he had hit the 1-ball a little fuller, it could have rolled past the 2-ball to Position A, possibly leaving Souquet with a safety. This was the second inning of an 11 inning game that Souquet eventually won.

Chapter 15 - Derby City 10 Ball Challenge   425

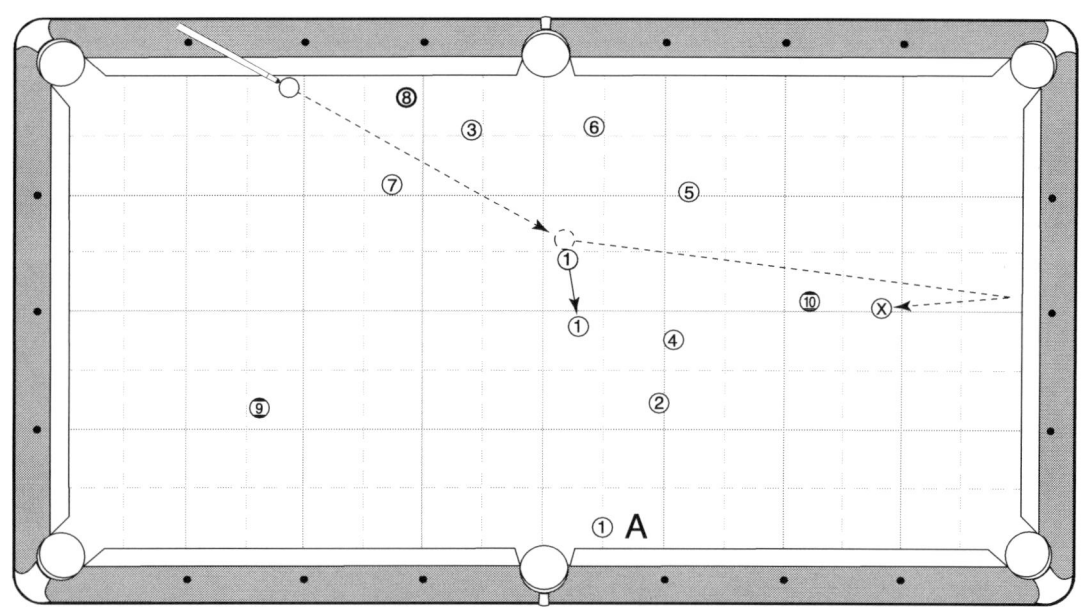

LESSON: All of these little skills, like the ability to hit balls thinly, add up, and they are what turn you into, as Billy Incardona would say, "an upper echelon player."

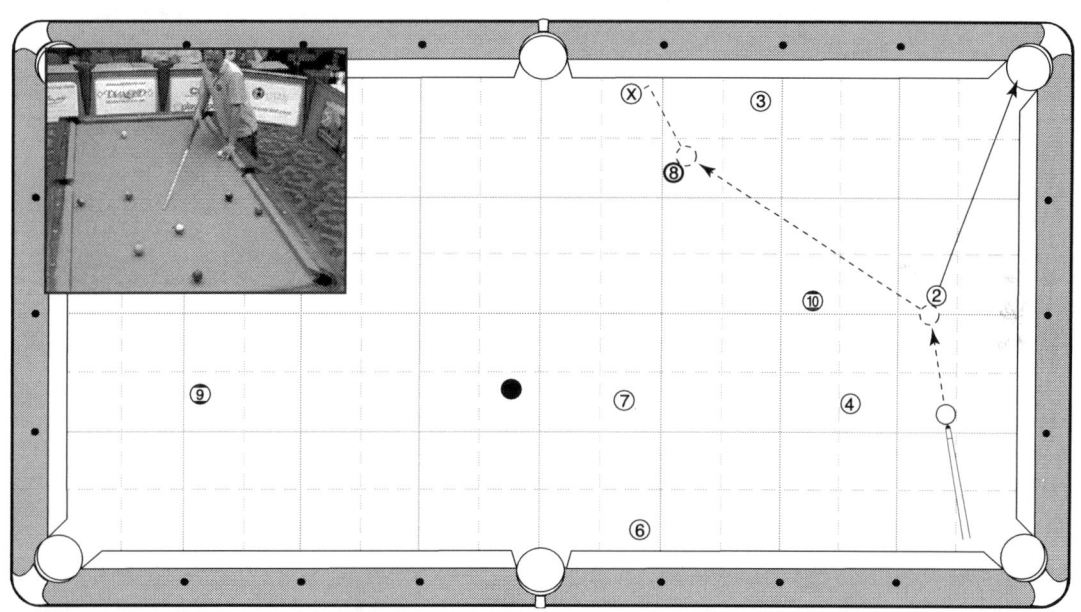

Set that Angle! (4/25 – 59:25)   **A-BCB: 6, 7, 8, 9, 10**

Van Boening placed the cue ball with ball-in-hand so that he had to do no more than softy roll it to the rail for shape on the 3-ball. He subsequently drew back for the 4-ball, then played a precise two –rail route to where the Black Ball is stationed.

   Now it is your turn to finish off the rack. I have marked the 6-ball as the key shot. It is a 50 degree cut that is best played by sending the cue ball across to the left side of the upper side pocket and back for the 7-ball. If you are a C Player, you can move the cue ball a little closer to the rail!

LESSON: Set up angles with ball-in-hand that enable you to roll the ball in for maximum control.

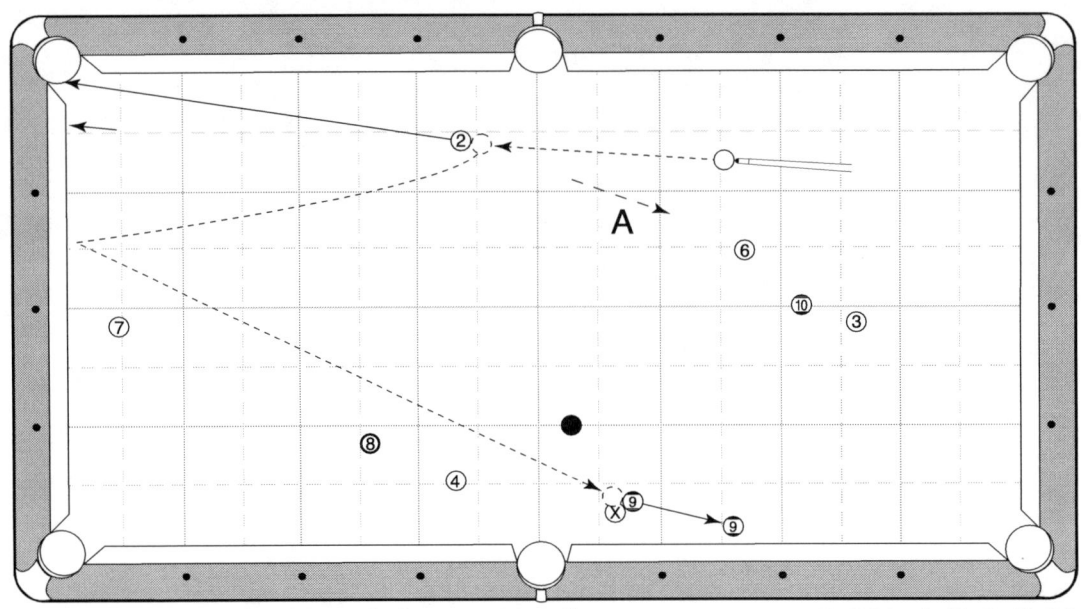

Power Follow and Across   (4/27 – 1:13:05)   B-BCB: 6, 7, 8, 9, 10

Souquet eyeballed his angle for the 2-ball before shooting the 1-ball down the same rail. However, the cue ball crawled out a couple of critical inches further than he intended, leaving him with an overly shallow cut on the 2-ball. So, after playing the 1-ball, Route A is about the best he could do on the 2, so that plan was aborted.

The other choice was to follow to the distant end rail and back and across the table. The arrow to the left of the pocket shows the line of the cue ball and 2-ball. Souquet used top left english and a hard stroke, and was still able to pocket the 2 from long range – a shot that is not for amateurs. The side spin caused the cue ball to rebound at a wide angle, and it went all of the way across and down the table into the 9-ball for position on the 3! He was rewarded with a runout!

LESSON: Souquet crouched low like a baseball catcher to get a better view of his angle on the 2-ball, which confirmed that he had about a 3-4 degree cut. The table level view gives you another perspective that can be very helpful in planning shots like this, and when looking to see if one ball will pass another.

#5 – Francisco Bustamante (15) vs. Rafael Martinez (1)
Off to the Races!   (5/4 – 21:40)   B-BCB: 5, 6, 7, 8, 9, 10

The fun begins with a 41 degree cut on the 1-ball. This angle is good for generating enough speed to easily cross the table and go nearly three quarters of the way back without compromising accuracy. Bustamante played it superbly and ended up with great shape on the 3-ball.

Sharp angles when the object ball is close to a rail make it easy to control the cue ball's direction when your objective is to send the cue ball straight down the table. Bustamante did just that, setting up an inside english two rail follow shot on the 4-ball. In this position, players who feel uncomfortable using inside english could use Route A as shown. This route makes it easier to pocket the ball, but the position zone narrows as you get closer to the 5-ball.

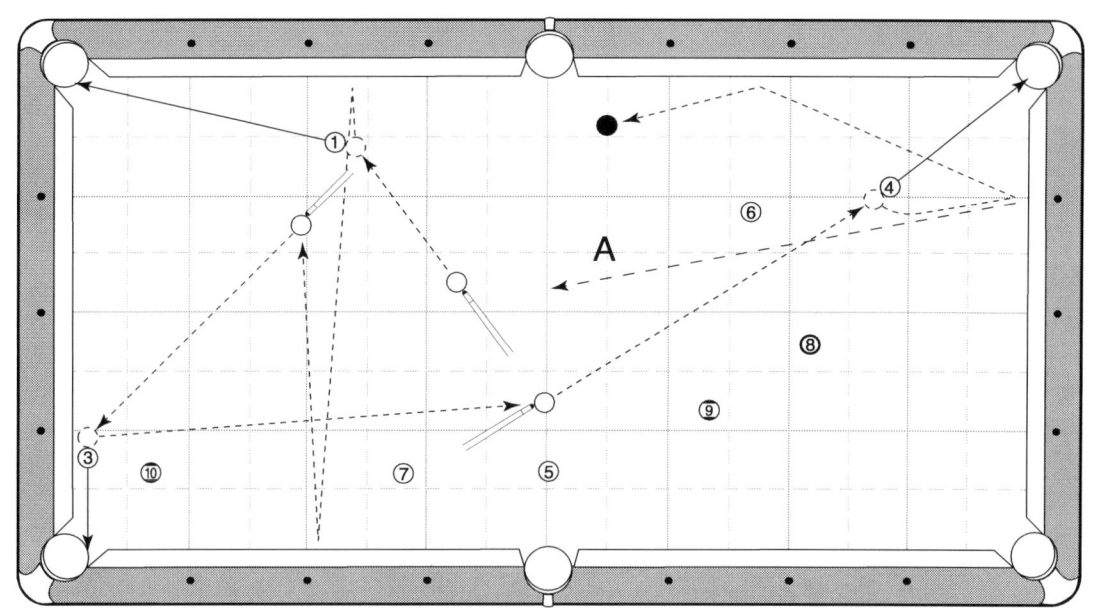

LESSON: Each time you remove a ball, you simplify the layout by eliminating potential obstructers! This means that the game gets easier as you approach the game ball – but tougher for some who have issues with end-of-game pressure.

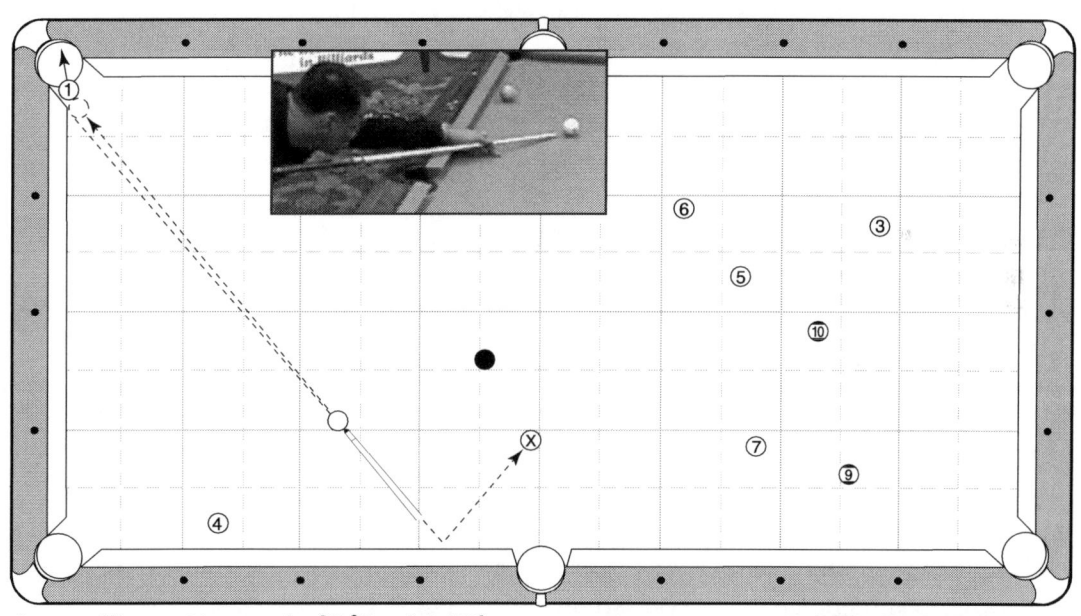

Controlling a Hanger! (5/7 – 34:35)   **B-BCB: 5, 6, 7, 8, 9, 10**

Bustamante's first shot on this break and runout was a super deep pocket hanger on the 1-ball. He used the rail-after-contact method as opposed to trying to hit the 1 full in the face. The cue ball approached the 3-ball down-the-line. He did not want to get greedy with his position because the 5 and 10 balls act like pincers – the closer the cue ball got to the 3, the narrower the position zone became.

LESSON: It is usually best to go to the rail after making a deep hanger for control.

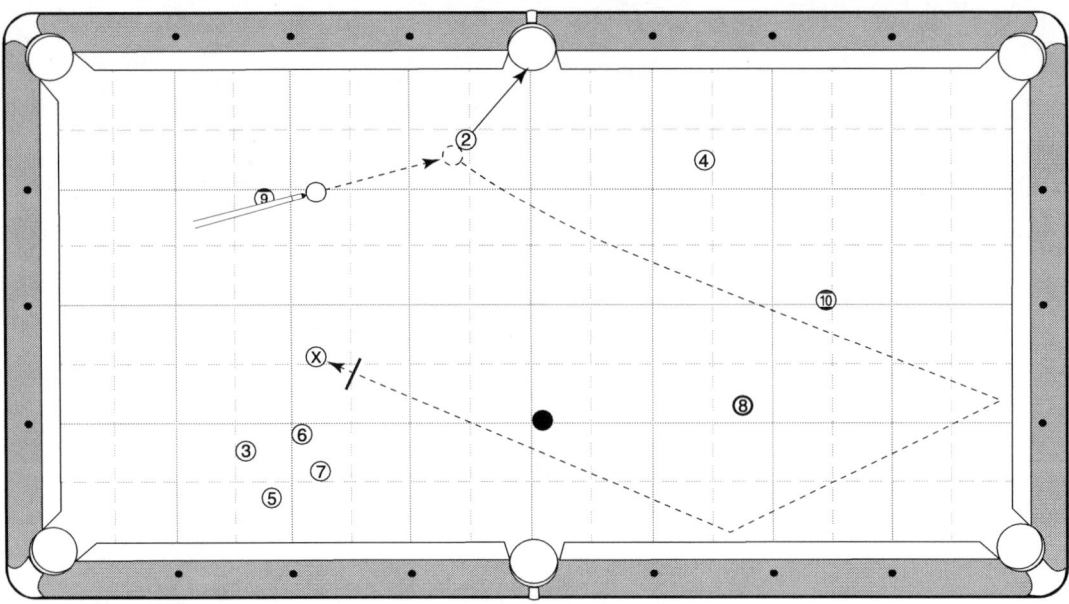

This Judge Gives it a 10!! (5/11 – 52.10)   C-BCB: 7, 8, 9, 10

Crowds in stadiums across America have cheered madly for deeds far less impressive (IMO) than this position play from the 2-ball to the 3 by Bustamante.

Consider the factors that combine to make this a 10 on the degree of difficulty scale: 1) he's shooting in the side pocket at an angle, 2) he's jacked up over the 9-ball, 3) he must avoid hitting the 10-ball, 4) he must apply enough power to send the cue ball 12.5 feet after contact, AND 5) the position zone is microscopic! If the cue ball comes up short he will be hooked. If it goes long he will have to play a thin cut, a bank, or a safety!

EPILOGUE: He pocketed the 3, sending the cue ball off the 5-ball for excellent shape on the 4, and ran out! This was his third straight break and run!

LESSON: Every now and then we should go for a tough shot just to satisfy that little voice that says "I can do it" even when we know better. The same is true for super tough position plays like this – give it a try!

A Certified Jaw Dropper!! (5/12 – 55:55)   A-BCB: 4, 5, 9, 10

Here is another "10" by Bustamante! This time he slammed home the 1-ball using a very hard stroke (8) from long range. The cue ball hit the side rail and went across the table for shape on the 2, which was heavily guarded by the 10 and 5 balls. The cue ball was traveling directly at the pocket, so his speed had to be near perfect!

This route was so tough that one commentator said he would do well to get on the 2-5 combo, and he was right. I wonder if Bustamante was actually trying to hit a little lower on the side rail and send the cue ball to the 2-ball on the other side of the 10! He ran out to extend his B&R streak to four racks. He went on to run 6, the most in the 19 matches I watched while conducting research for this book. Next best was Bustamante, with a run of four!

LESSON: Bustamante spent more time than usual over the ball (eight seconds) to gear up for this shot, which is a good practice for all players.

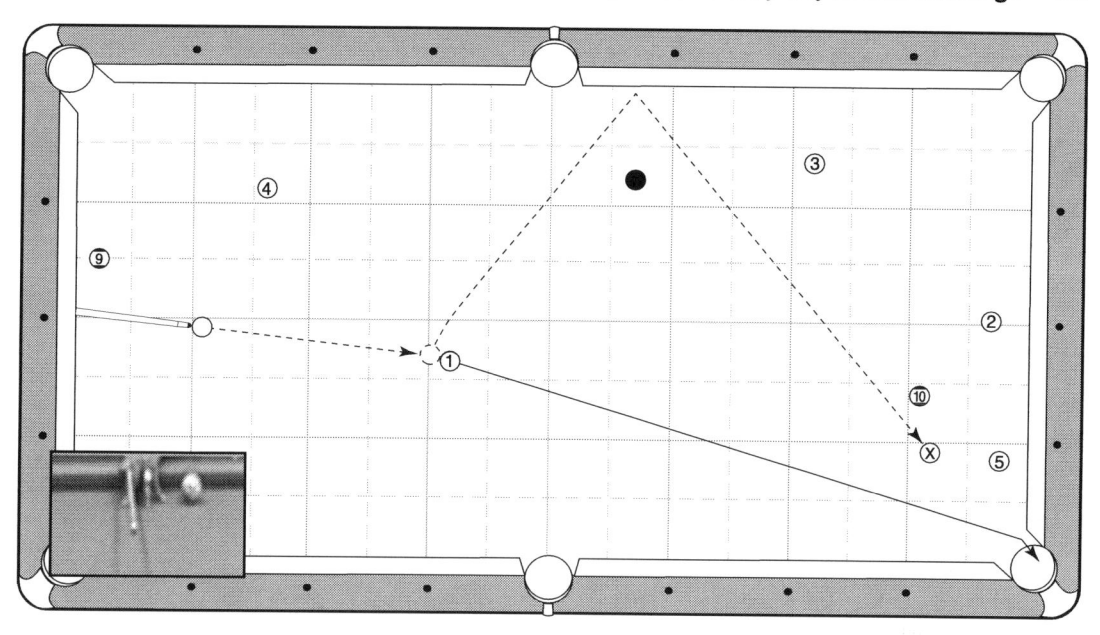

#6 – Lee Vann Corteza (15) vs. Stevie Moore (8)

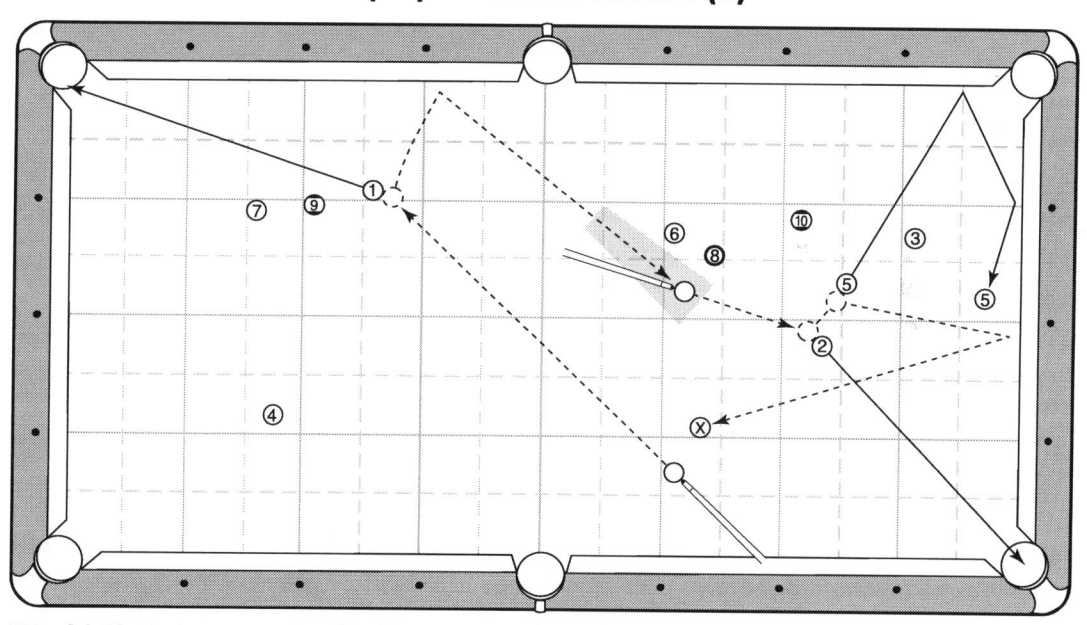

World Class Pattern Play!!   (Diag. A – 6/4 – 30:50)

Moore spent 30 seconds studying the table before embarking on this unrunnable looking mess! Moore's first hurdle was to pocket the 1 past the 9, which was a distractor, and draw back for a shot on the 2 while avoiding a hook behind the 6-8 duo. He spent 15 full seconds over the ball – but the diagram shows that it was time well spent! Next up was the 2-ball. He knew he was going to hit the 5 after contact, so he carefully planned his route off of it to the 3, and made sure that the 5 would not interfere with his next shot. Results speak for themselves. To be continued …

LESSON: An unrunnable looking rack may only need your creative solution, so exercise your thinking cap when deciding whether to run out or play safe.

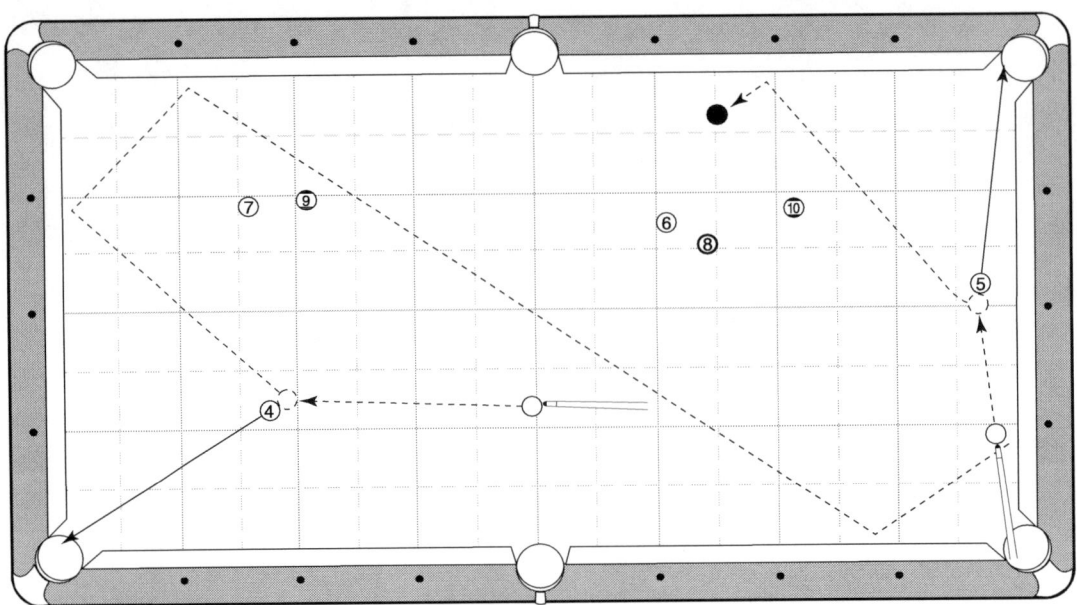

World Class, Part II   (Diag. B – 6/4 – 33:20)   B-BCB: 6, 7, 8, 9, 10

We pick up Moore's run on the 4-ball. He played a picture perfect four rail route to the 5-ball. The cue ball died off the last rail, leaving Moore with an ideal angle to travel to the side rail and out for short side shape on the 6. Now the picture is clear on the role for that ball, which would have been big trouble for most players, but nor for Moore thanks to his precision planning and execution.

You are now authorized to finish Moore's spectacular run from the Black Ball, but feel free to try it starting wherever you please!

LESSON: When a ball is perhaps 12 to 20 inches from the rail and it looks like it is part of a cluster, see if there is a route that can take you to the short side, like Moore did on the 6-ball in this example.

That 40 Degree Angle!   (6/5 – 42:05)   B-BCB: 4, 5, 6, 8, 9, 10

Stevie Moore made an uncharacteristic blunder, leaving Corteza with a huge hurdle to jump. He needed to spear in the 2-ball from long range and set himself up for the key position play in the rack – from the 3 to the 4-ball on the opposite end of the table.

He could have used a variety of speeds to send the cue ball sideways for an angle on the 3-ball, but he chose a speed between 6 (medium hard) and hard (7) so he would have the correct angle for 4-ball. The 42 degree cut was just right for generating speed, and the correct direction – and his four rail position play turned out perfectly! He hit it with center left english and a hard stroke.

The overhead view showed that Corteza, who normally uses a short stroke, took his cue back 10 inches so he could smoothly generate sufficient power, and he followed through a full 12 inches. He also aimed well to the left the "normal" aiming line for this cut to allow for a huge amount of deflection!

LESSON: On big position plays where you need to send the cue ball a long distance, a 40 degree cut (plus or minus a few degrees) could very well be your best choice because it allows you to generate speed without sacrificing the shot.

Chapter 15 - **Derby City 10 Ball Challenge** 431

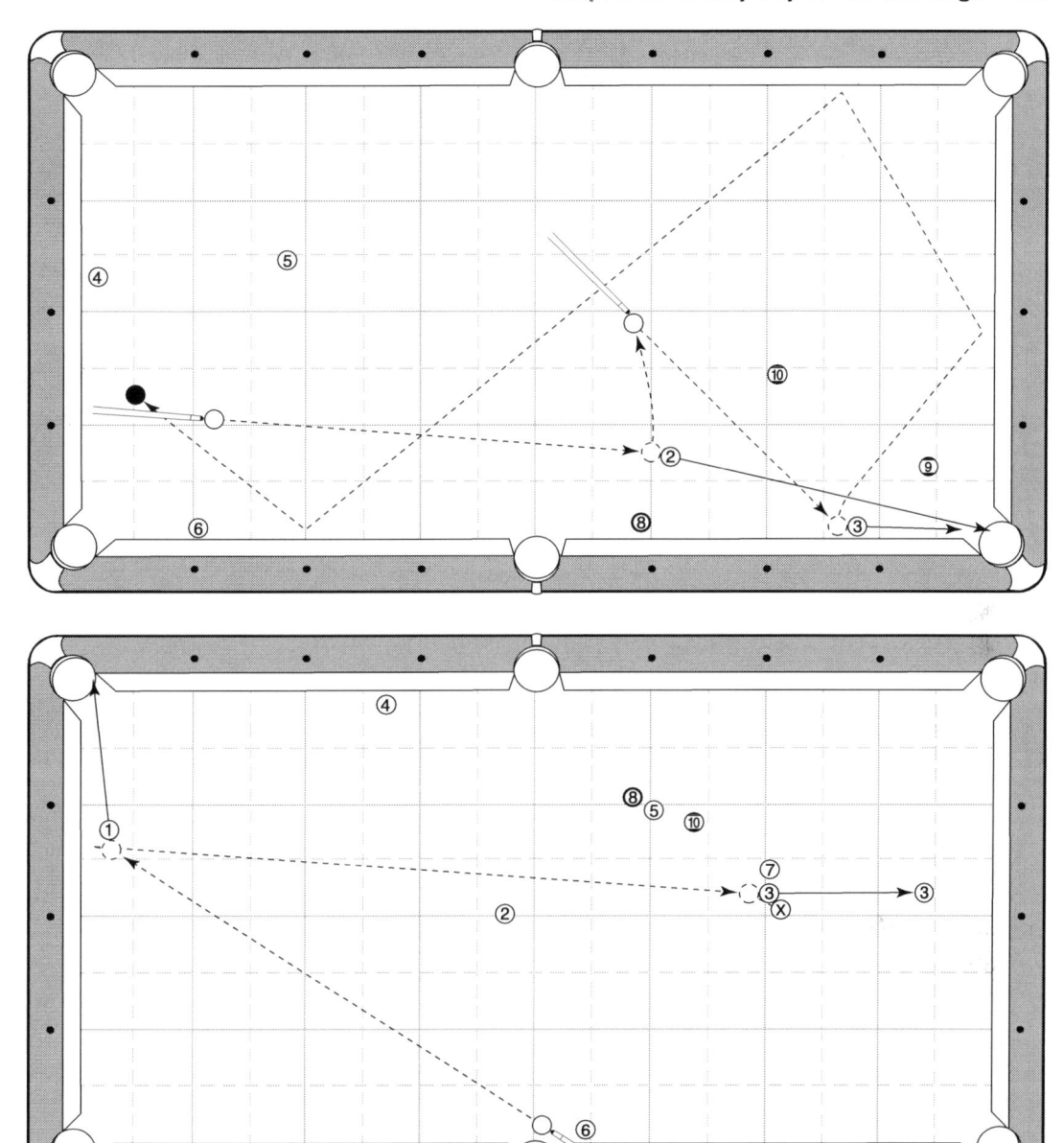

An Impossible Runout!   (Diag. A – 6/18 – 2:06:20)
Corteza has just broken the balls and is facing this seemingly unrunnable nightmare – but appearances can be deceiving as he soon shows us while on his way to a World Class B&R! Step 1 is to slice in the one ball while bridging on the rail and to send the cue ball six diamonds into the 3-7 cluster. Corteza knew that if he was successful he would be facing a tough shot on the 2-ball, but that didn't faze him one bit.

LESSON: When the object ball is this close to the rail and you need to send the cue ball on a direct (or nearly direct) line down the table, cuts from 40-50 degrees enable you to exert great control over the cue ball's path while not sacrificing shot making accuracy. One big reason is that the rail acts as an aiming device on these shots, so you can zero in on a cut angle without worrying about where the pocket lies. To be continued ...

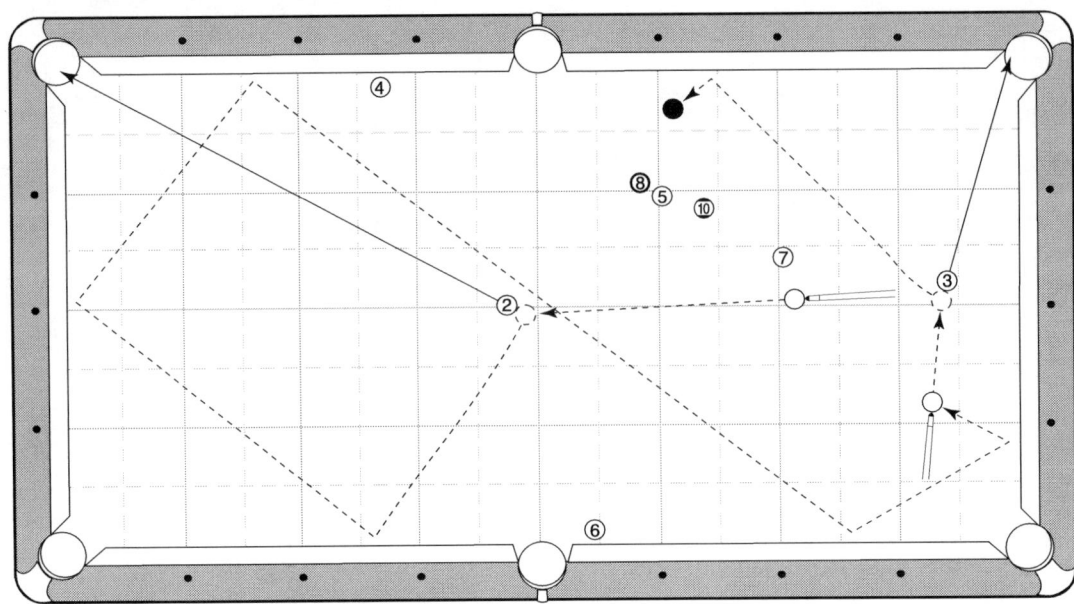

Corteza's Reward (Diag. B – 6/18 – 2:06:50) A+-BCB: 4, 5, 6, 7, 8, 10

Corteza's precise break out on the last shot earned him the right to play this monster five-rail route from the 2-ball to the 3 on the opposite end of the table. But he executed it brilliantly, using a very hard follow stroke (an 8) to send the cue ball on its long journey to the 3-ball. Shots like this showcase his upbringing in the Philippines, where the players must combine power with precision when competing at rotation on slow cloth.

Corteza played the 2-ball about as well as could be expected, but he ended up with a little shallower angle on the 3-ball than he hoped for. So he again reached into his bag of tricks for this high powered stun/follow shot (an 8) for workable position on the 4-ball. He has done most of the heavy lifting – now it is your turn!

LESSON: Power stun/follow shots (like the one on the 3-ball) require a rapid and almost violent acceleration into the cue ball – which is a radical departure from the typical stroke used on almost every other kind of shot.

Two Way Position off a Combo (6/21 – 2:21:25) C-BCB: 6, 8, 9, 10

After making a ball on the break, Moore had no choice but to play shape on the 2-3 combination. The 1-ball was fortunately well positioned for him to play almost directly at the combo while sidestepping the 8-ball. His two rail route to the combo was very well played as it left him with a slight cut to the left.

The 2 and 3 balls are lined up straight at the pocket, the 3 is not far from the pocket, and the 2-ball will have a fair amount of topspin when, and after, it hits the 3-ball. All of these conditions point to the possibility of Moore making both balls on his next shot – and that's what happened as the 2 crawled in on top of the 3! After making the combo, the cue ball stopped at Position A for good shape on the 4-ball.

LESSON: On straight in combos, when the first ball to drop (the 3 in our example) is close to the pocket AND they are lined up straight in – plan for what you will do if both balls go in!

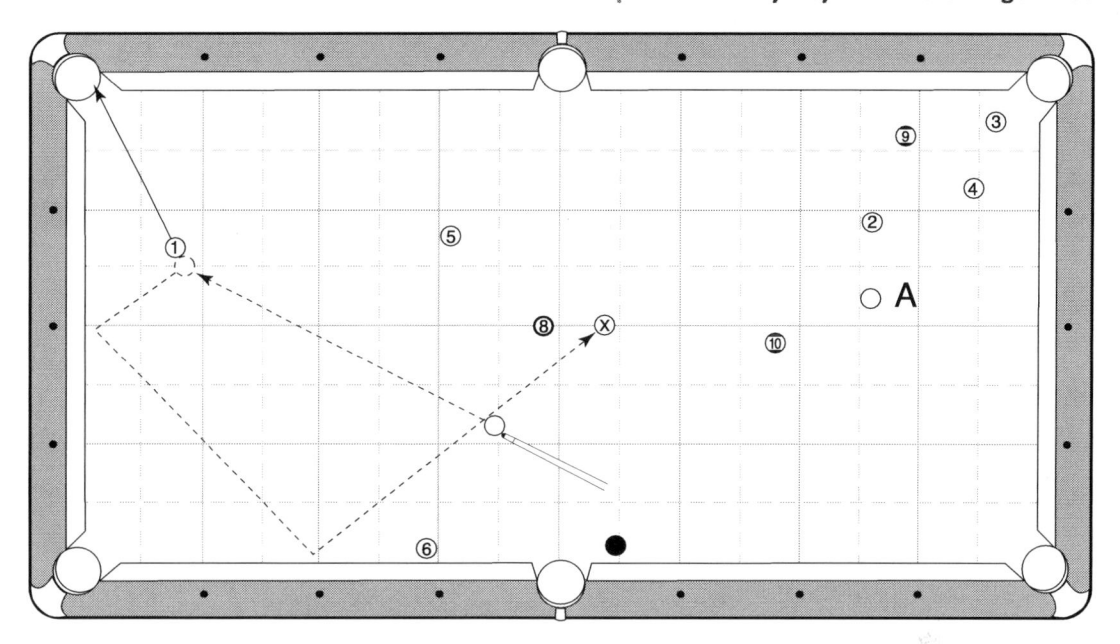

#7 – Darren Appleton (15) vs. Francisco Bustamante (13)

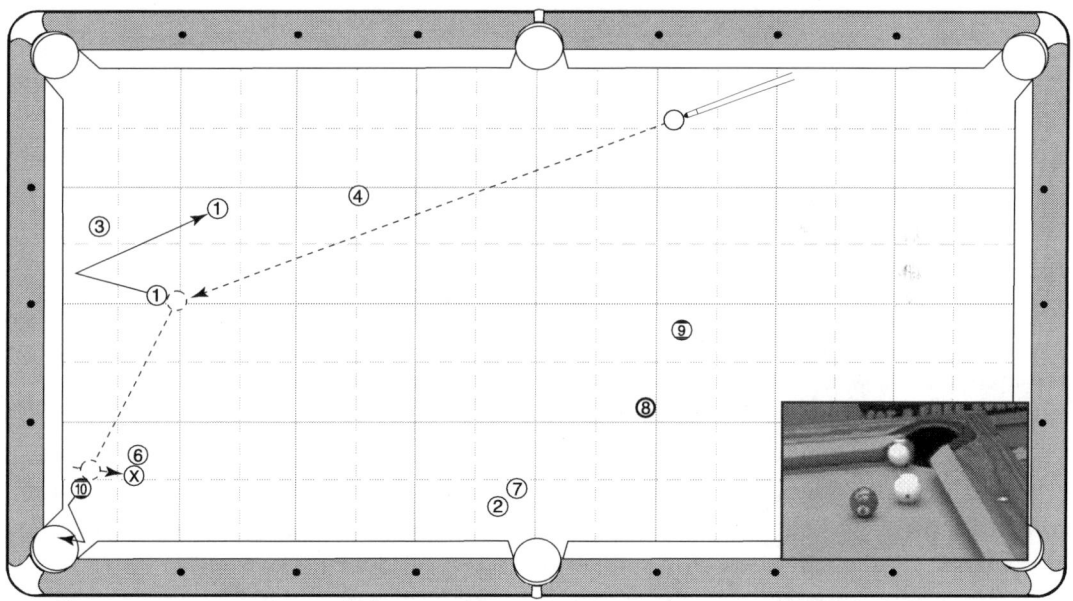

"Banking" in a Billiard   (7/6 – 26:50)

A softly hit billiard from this distance is tough to play with complete accuracy, as Bustamante showed by wobbling the 10-ball into the pocket – even after lining it up carefully with his cue. The cue ball snuggled in behind the 6-ball, so it is easy to assume that this was a successful two-way shot – heads the 10 goes in, and tails it's a hook. While Appleton might have hooked Bustamante if he missed, it is also possible that the cue ball might have snuck out, leaving him with a shot.

LESSON: Quick and seemingly easy wins are momentum builders, and they work on the minds of your opponent – especially if he has had to work his way through a difficult run out on the preceding rack – as Bustamante had just managed to do!

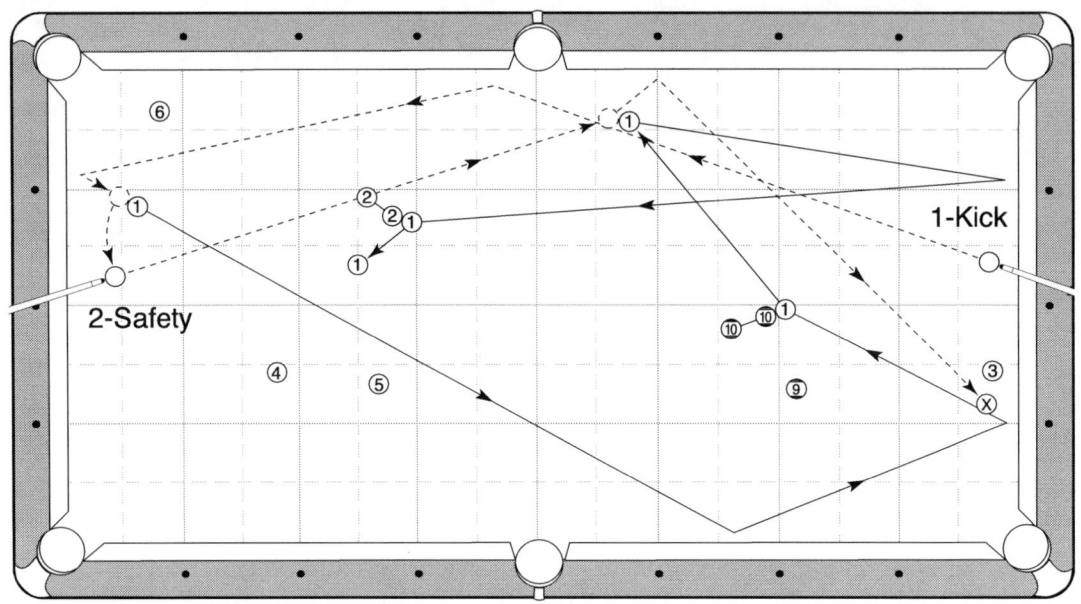

Matching Wits on Defense (7/15 – 1:13:05)

Bustamante opened with a precise two-rail kick with a top of high left english into the back of the 1-ball. The top spin acted like a stun shot, and the cue ball drifted about eight inches to the right, leaving Appleton a lengthy safety on the 2-ball.

Appleton went into a crouch to get a better view of the cue ball's path to the one past the 2-ball. He could not pocket the 1-ball, so he chose to play a crossover bank safety. The 1-ball banked to the left side of the table while the cue ball stopped at Position X. At the point where the cue ball and 1-ball's paths cross, Appleton's timing was perfect as the cue ball barely got out of the 1-ball's way! Bustamante was left with a long distance jump shot over the 10-ball.

LESSON: Appleton took 60 seconds to prepare for his safety. While watching great players stalk the table, try to figure out what they are thinking about.

Pushing Out to a Shot (Diag. A - 7/18 – V.2 – 9:35)

Appleton made a ball on the break and then studied this unappealing situation for 70 seconds before coming up with a mistake. He pushed out to a long shot on the 1-ball, and Bustamante accepted it. He then cut in the 1-ball and sent the cue ball off four rails around the table before it ran into the 8-ball, leaving him with a bank or safety on the 2-ball. Bustamante chose the safe, and hooked Appleton, sending the cue ball behind the 3-ball. Now, imagine the shot that Bustamante would have had if the 8-ball had been over to the side a couple of inches!

At the pro level, Appleton's push was a poor choice, but it is a good one for amateurs. But what could he do? One choice would be to roll the cue ball past where he did and make the shot on the 1-ball even tougher. Another is to roll the cue ball to between the 2-ball and the rail, setting up a kick into the 1-ball. I like this because, after the kick shot, the 1-ball should be on one end of the table, and the cue ball and the 2-ball would be on the other!

LESSON: Remember, at the upper levels of the game, you must get in the habit of looking for a push to a kick shot, especially when the other options that leave a direct path into the object ball are so unattractive.

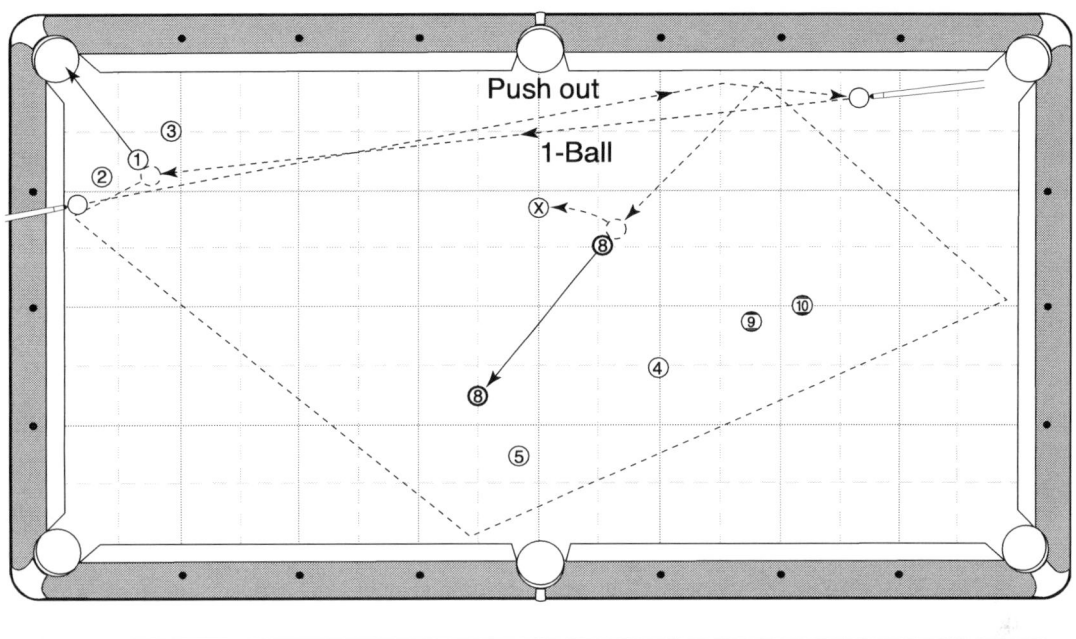

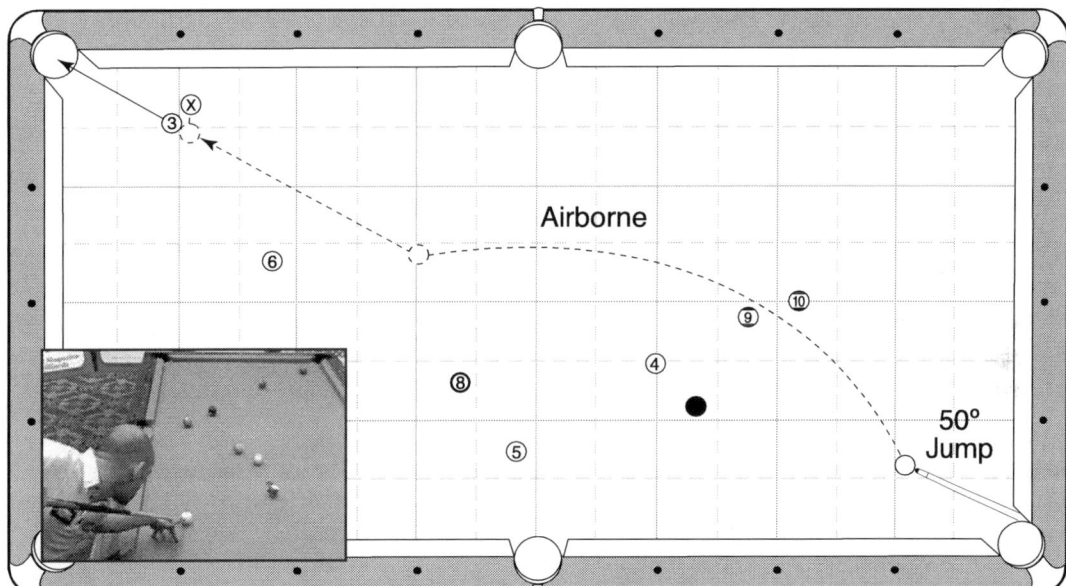

Going Airborne! (Diag. B - 7/18 – V.2 – 15:05)　　　　　　　　　C-BCB: 6, 8, 9, 10

The sequel to the position in Diagram A was a hook by Bustamante followed by an incredibly good (and lucky) kick/safety by Appleton. Bustamante kicked and hit, Appleton then made a thin cut, but ended up with the shot above.

   He chose to jump over the entire 4-ball because: 1) he is great at jumping balls, 2) the 3-ball is close to the pocket, 3) the shot is straight in, giving him control of the cue ball after contact, 4) a long landing strip reduces the chance that the cue ball will fly off the table, and 5) he should have a shot on the 4-ball if he makes the 3. Appleton's unique 12 second routine for setting up for this jump shot included a lesser elevation for aiming, and a steeper one for the shot. The cue ball flew over the 4-ball with four inches to spare, hopped once, and then flew into the 3-ball!

LESSON: Before you pull out your jump cue, carefully weigh the pros and cons.

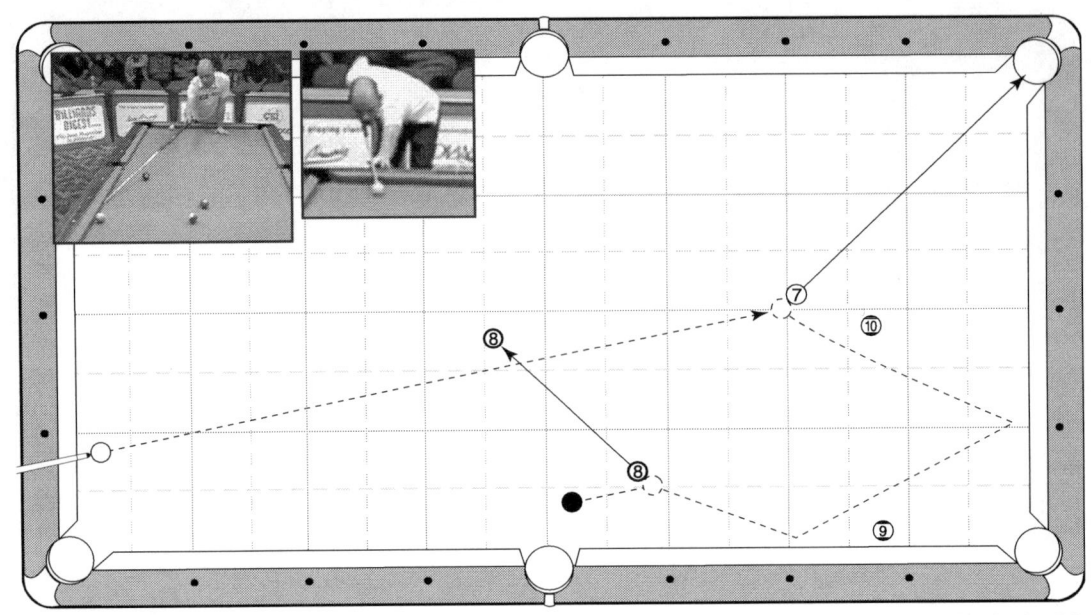

Coming with a Big Shot (7/19 – 24:20)   C-BCB: 8, 9, 10

Darren Appleton has a much deserved reputation as a big time shotmaker, and it is shots like this one have earned him that distinction.

So, how did he make it? He started by swinging his cue back and forth a few times before settling into his stance. He got very low over the ball, his chin is directly over his cue, and his upper arm in near perfect alignment. He spent a full 11 seconds over the shot, far more than usual, to lock in his aim. In comparison, he only took five to six seconds to play each of the final three shots, which were far more routine. He used a medium speed (5), which is ideal for accuracy.

Amateurs might consider playing a safe in this position, but the safe is so tough that you are probably better off going for the shot, and hoping for a roll if you miss!

LESSON: Ignore the advice that says to use the same number of warm up stroke or the same amount of time on every shot! Each shot requires a process that must meet the special needs of that shot, and that changes from shot to shot. Always take enough time or even a second more – but never rush a shot!

LESSON: On extremely hard shots you can eliminate some of the pressure by just giving it your best effort. Nobody will think any less of you if you miss – they know that anyone can miss a shot like this. So have fun with it, give it your best, not your worst, and see what happens – you might be pleasantly surprised!

Straight Back Power Draw!! (7/22 – 40:00)   A-BCB: 7, 8, 9, 10

When drawing the diagram for this shot on the 7-ball, I put a clear triangle over the table and watched the cue ball in regular speed and slow motion. Its path was so straight to and from the object ball that I was forced to use one line for each direction! Appleton drew off the end rail and out for excellent position on the 8-ball.

LESSON: Appleton showed that an open bridge can be very effective in playing a power draw shot – which is in opposition to the old school, which favors a closed bridge on these shots. He stayed down on the shot in perfect position with his cue on his bridge loop until after the 7-ball disappeared into the pocket!

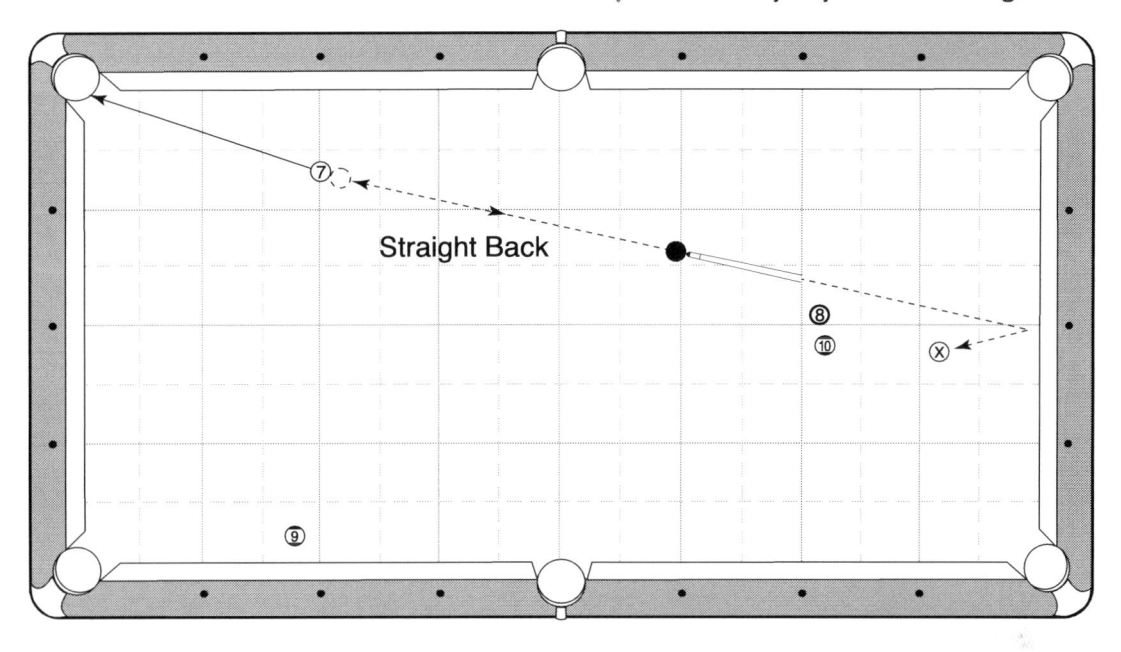

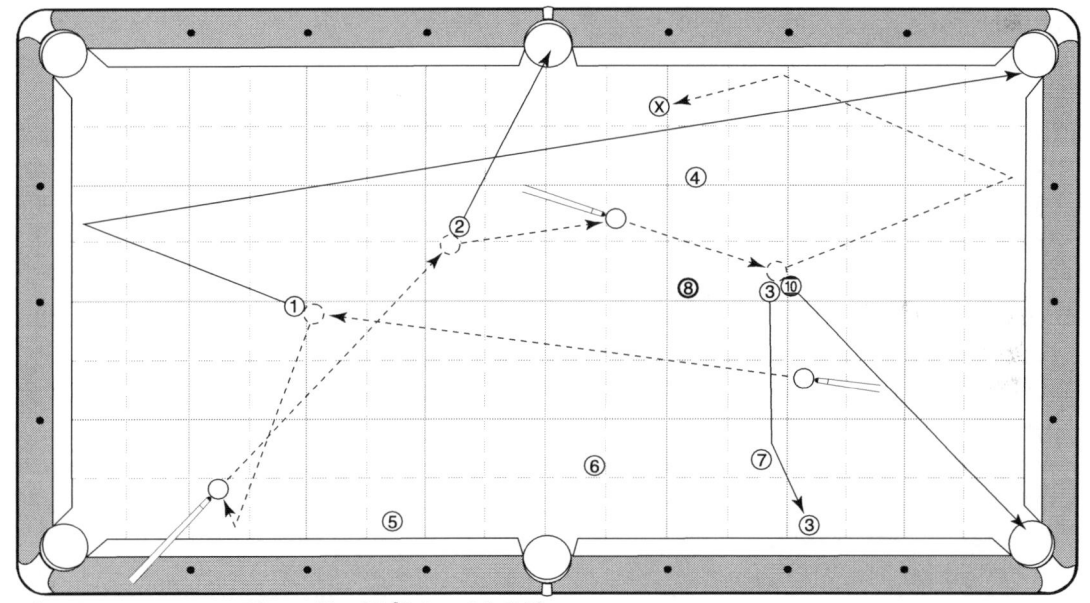

The Bustamante Show!! (7/24 – 46:30)

Bustamante broke, made a ball, and then leaned against the table and pondered his fate. The future 2013 Derby City bank pool champion then rifled home a table length bank on the 1-ball, setting him up for a soft follow shot to the 3-10 billiard, which he made. If he had missed it, the positions of the cue ball and 3-ball show that Appleton would have been facing a kick shot!

LESSON: Players of all levels should look for, and play, these kinds of specialty shots because you will see even more of them in 10 Ball than in 9 Ball. And always call a referee for close hits like this even when there is zero chance that the ball you are calling could be made on a bad hit, as in this position.

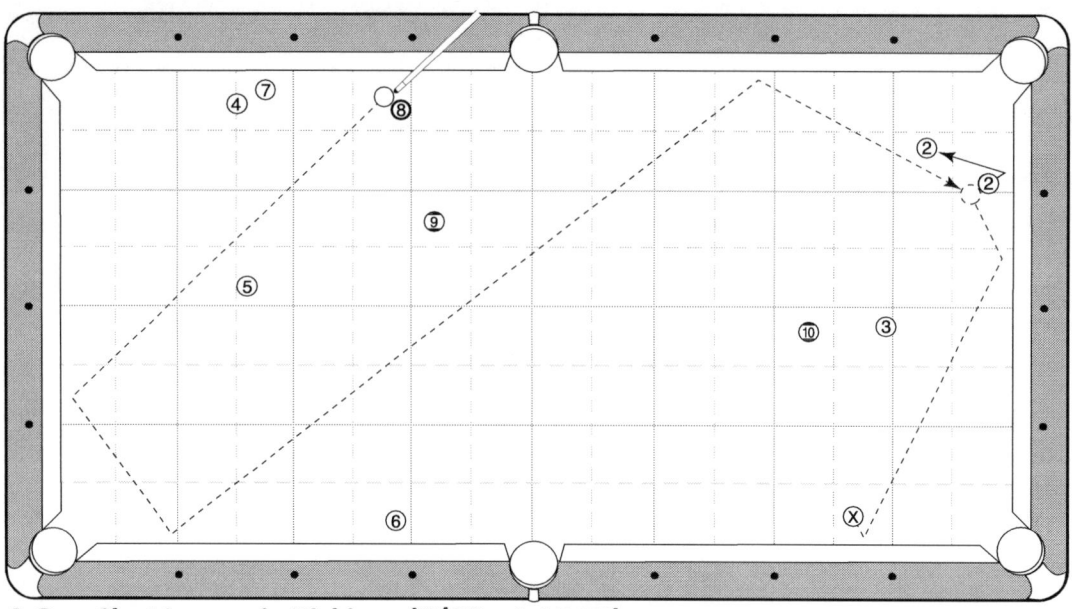

A One Shot Lesson in Kicking   (7/27 – 1:12:25)

This kick/safety occurred in the ninth inning of a 16 inning, 21 minute battle which saw Appleton take a 14-13 lead in a race to 15. He then broke and ran for the win! Note: this was also the longest game of the 424 that I studied for this book. As a consolation prize, I'm going to analyze Bustamante's fabulous kick shot.

Appleton has just made the most of ball-in-hand, softly rolling the cue ball forward and pinning his opponent against the 8-ball, cutting off all escape routes except for the one you see – but it was enough!

Bustamante loaded up the cue ball with running english, pulled his cue 12 inches back, and then fired away, sending the cue ball three rails and into the right side of the 2-ball, which was in the big ball position near the end rail. His perfect contact and speed led to separation between the cue ball and the 2-ball, with each one stopping on opposite sides of the 3-ball!

LESSON: Kicks are part skill, part luck. As a result, you (and yes, your opponent) deserve to be a little lucky when you show this much skill. So, while there is almost no way that Bustamante could repeat this shot as shown given another attempt, he did do it when he needed to!

#8 – Rodney Morris (15) vs. Darren Appleton (11)
Pattern Play Genius   (Diag. A – 8/6 – 24:05)

Rodney Morris is an offensive machine who shoots with the casual air of someone who is practicing while carrying on a conversation with a friend. Meanwhile he chews through racks with the precision of a Swiss watchmaker.

Appleton scratched on the break, so Morris had ball-in-hand. He set up the 1-ball to create that all-important 40 degree angle (actually, it's 42 degrees) on the 2-ball. This angle enabled him to play a super exacting route across the table between the 6 and 10 balls and out for a superb angle on the 3-ball. He used the 3-ball to get on that pesky 4 on the top side rail, which was the major hurdle in this rack.

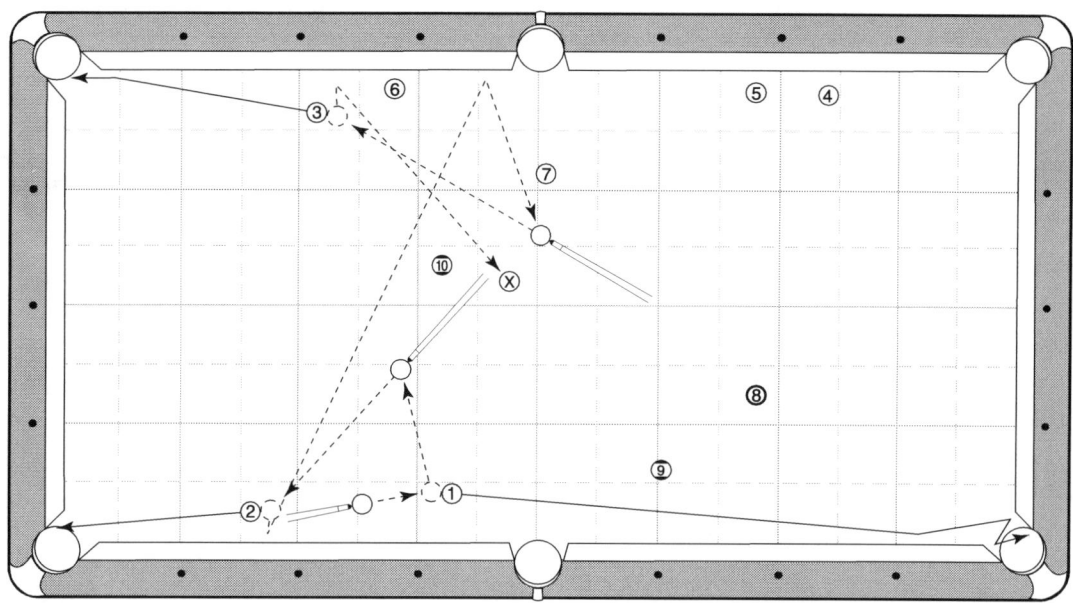

LESSON: I am awarding an A+ to those who saw the four-balls-at-a-time principle at work here (see game 2/1). The angle on the 1 was key to getting on the 2, which enabled him to get the angle on the 3 that allowed him to come out for the 4-ball!

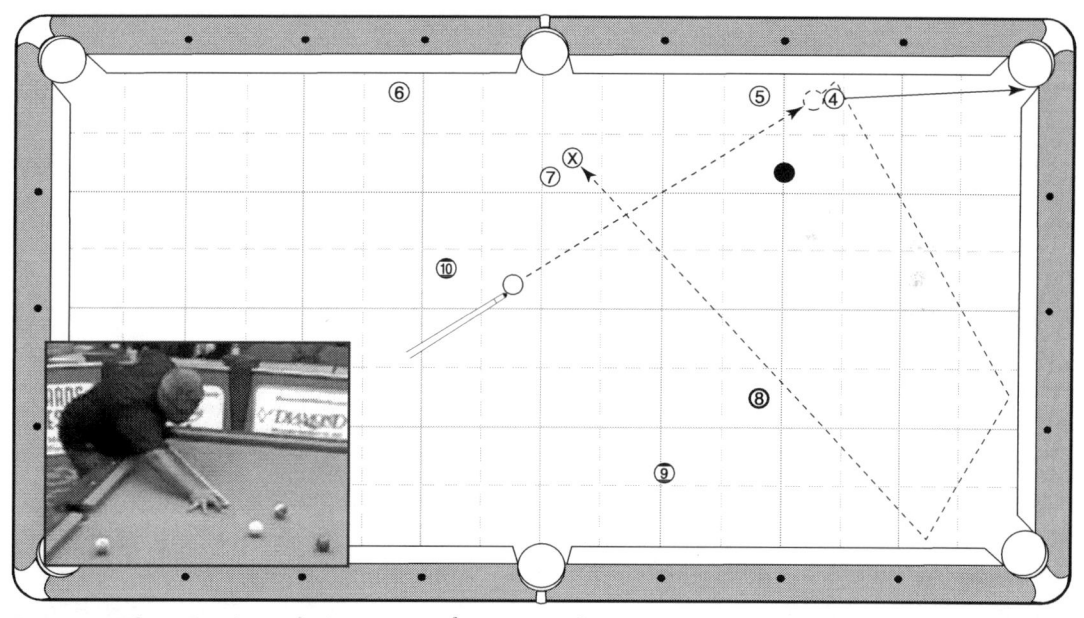

Pattern Play Genius   (Diag. B – 8/6 – 25:00)   **B-BCB: 6, 7, 8, 9, 10**

Morris had already exhibited an otherworldly knack for position and pattern play in this runout, but it was all just a prelude to this three rail route from the 4-ball to the 5! It required the ability to pocket a ball with a ton of inside spin from long range – but The Rocket was up to the challenge. Lesser players might play a stop shot and bank the 4-ball four rails while stationing the cue ball behind the 5-ball.

LESSON – Pocketing has big impact on position. Morris cut the 4 into the far side of the pocket, increasing the speed enough so that the cue ball reached the zone.

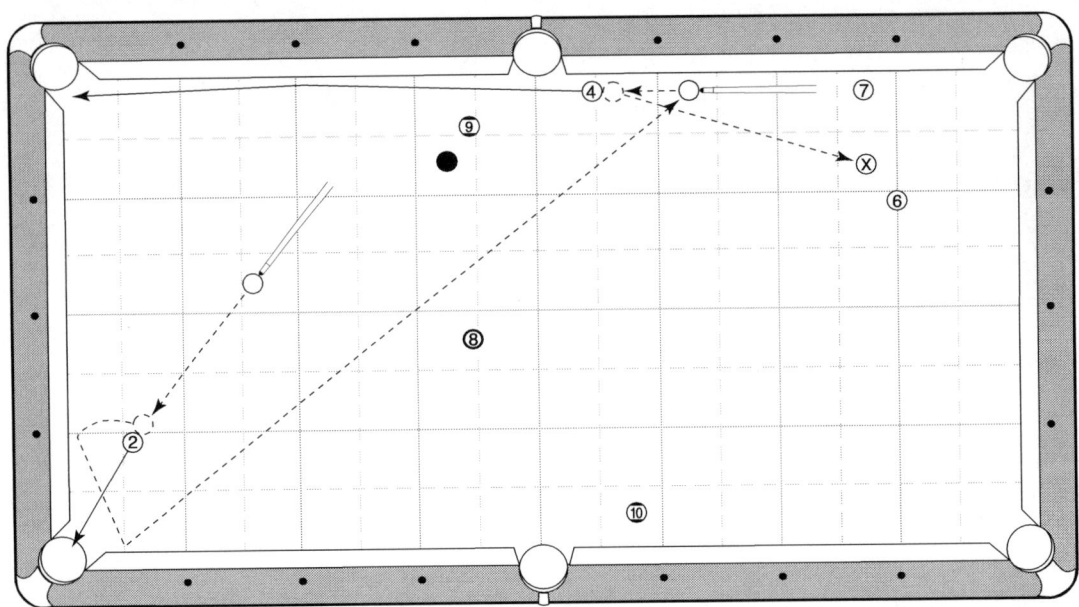

Unusual, But Very Effective! (8/7 – 29:25)   B-BCB: 7, 8, 9, 10

Appleton scratched on a kick shot, so Morris began figuring out what to do with ball-in-hand. And, when the super-fast and efficient shooting Morris take 45 seconds to plan his position route from three different positions, you know there are issues that must be dealt with – and that we should prepare to see something special.

Once the planning was done, Morris wasted no time in the execution phase of the shot cycle, landing on the 2-ball and firing away after spending only two seconds in his stance. This is evidence of a pool shooting savant at work, and should not be copied by most anyone else on the planet! Now for the best part – he applied high inside english and sent the cue ball two-rails and across the table to the third rail and out for superb short side shape on the 4-ball.

Now, if the 8-ball hadn't been in its current location, Morris might have chosen to cut the 2-ball to the right and go off the side rail and across to the 4.

LESSON: Even super-fast players must, at times, stop to consider their options.

Three Rails in the Side (8/10 – 45:45)   A-BCB: 4, 5, 6, 7, 10

Morris attempted to play a safety, but three-rail banked in the 2-ball. After taking 30 seconds to assess the situation, he fired in this three-rail route into the side pocket. He used a medium hard (6) stroke and a full tip of right english – which is never easy when the cue ball is near the rail. And though the cut was only 35 degrees, it was made more difficult by the location of the 3-ball which, as the diagram shows, was a full diamond down from the center line between the two side pockets.

The cue ball traveled three rails with great speed to the gap between the 6 and 10 balls, setting Morris up for yet another side pocket three railer. Notice that this is a longer version of the 35-degree cut that he just played!

LESSON: Morris jumped up a split second after contact, did a knee dip, and his cue left his bridge before contact was made with the 3-ball. Do not follow his example – stay down even when you are not 100% sure of a shot and give it your best effort.

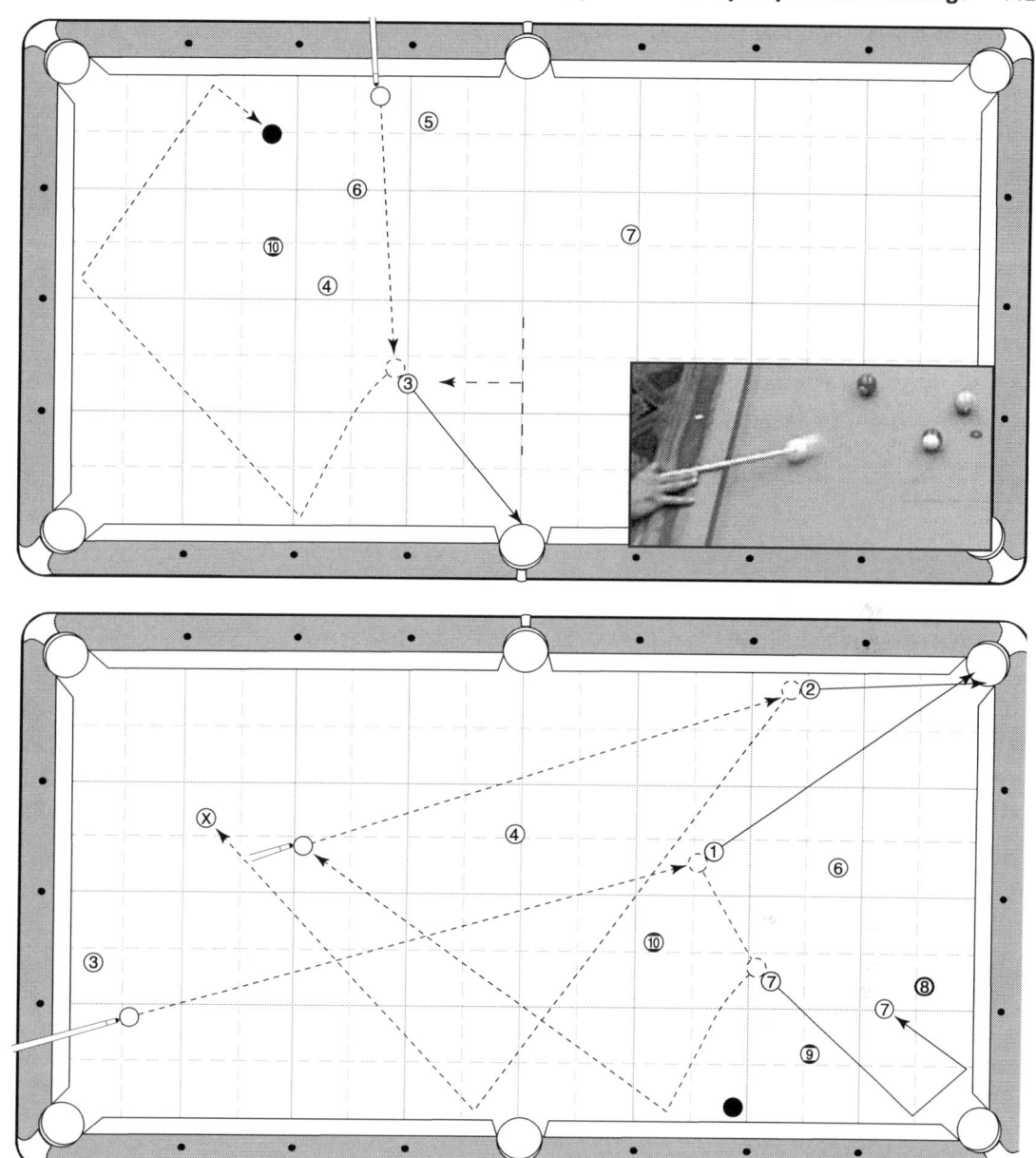

High Speed Firepower! (8/13 – 59:15) C-BCB: 6, 7, 8, 9, 10

Morris played a subpar safety after the break, leaving Appleton with this monster shot on the 1 ball. After taking 33 seconds to assess the situation, he fired in the 1-ball using a very hard (8) draw stroke and sent the cue ball off the 7-ball, which acted like an end rail, and out for another long shot on the 2-ball! He loaded up with low left on the 2, drew past the side and out for superb shape on the 3-ball, and proceeded to run out. The 2-ball showed how difficult it is to bring the cue ball across and back down the table when it is well below the side at a modest cut angle.

LESSON: Appleton narrowly avoided disaster on the 2-ball because he can operate with a small margin for error when needed. As your position play becomes more and more precise, your margin for error will also start shrinking – at which point you can begin to contemplate playing difficult and imaginative routes like this one.

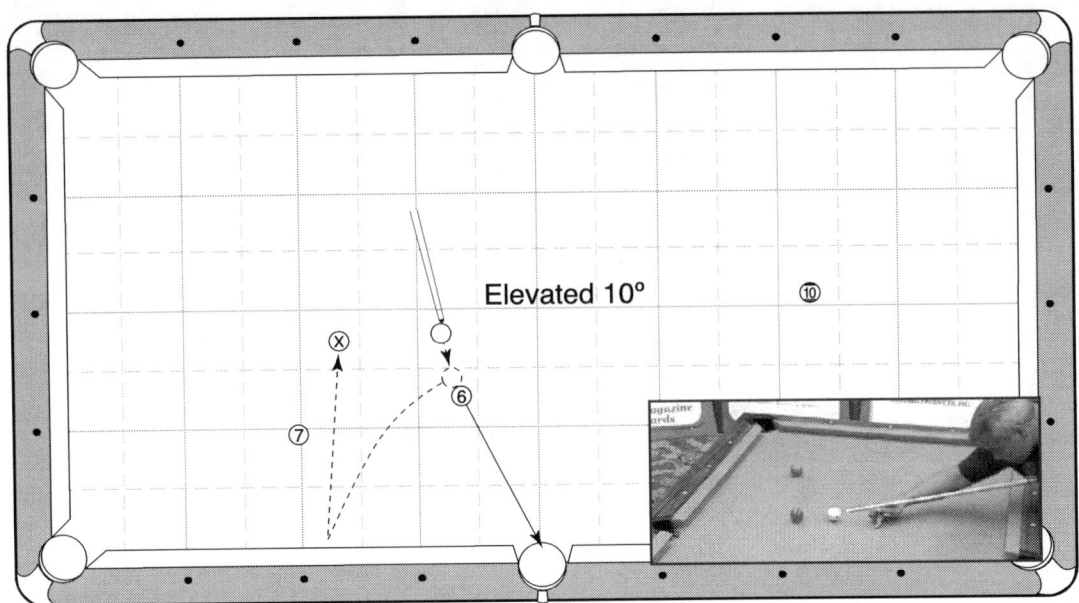

Super Spinner! (8/20 – 1:35:05)   C-BCB: 6, 7, 10

Morris overran his position zone for the 6-ball by a few inches, leaving him with a slightly larger cut than he wanted. He had three choices: 1) slow roll the 6 and play shape for the 7-ball into the upper left pocket, 2) use a hard follow stroke with outside english and go three rails to the center portion of the table, or 3) play a jacked up super spinner for shape in the lower left pocket!

Morris opted for the third route. He elevated his cue to about 10 degrees, drew his cue back only three inches and jabbed down on the cue ball with top left english! The cue ball bent forward off the tangent line, hit the rail not far above the 7, reversed its course off the side rail, and rolled out for ideal position on the 7-ball.

LESSON: It takes a certain knack to see and play a shot like the 6, but creative shots like this can up your odds for a run. I included this shot in the Black Ball run out. So give it and the other choices a try and see what works best for you.

#9 – Francisco Bustamante (15) vs. Shane Van Boening (9)
Punch and Counterpunch! (9/1 – 3:50)

Van Boening had no offensive shot on the 1-ball so he played a safety. He might have been able to bank the 1-ball along the side rail behind the 2-ball while sending the cue ball behind the 8 and 9 balls, but he quickly chose to play off the right side of the 1-ball. He then executed this beautiful four-rail route to the opposite end rail while hiding the 1-ball behind the 8 and 9 balls. Now, imagine the kick Bustamante would have faced if the cue ball had bounced two-three more inches off the rail!

Bustamante responded with a precise two-rail kick which resulted in another hook as the cue ball and 1-ball swapped positions on each end of the table.

LESSON: A positive result is usually proof that you made the right choice on a safety, and that you have just played one that belongs in your memory bank.

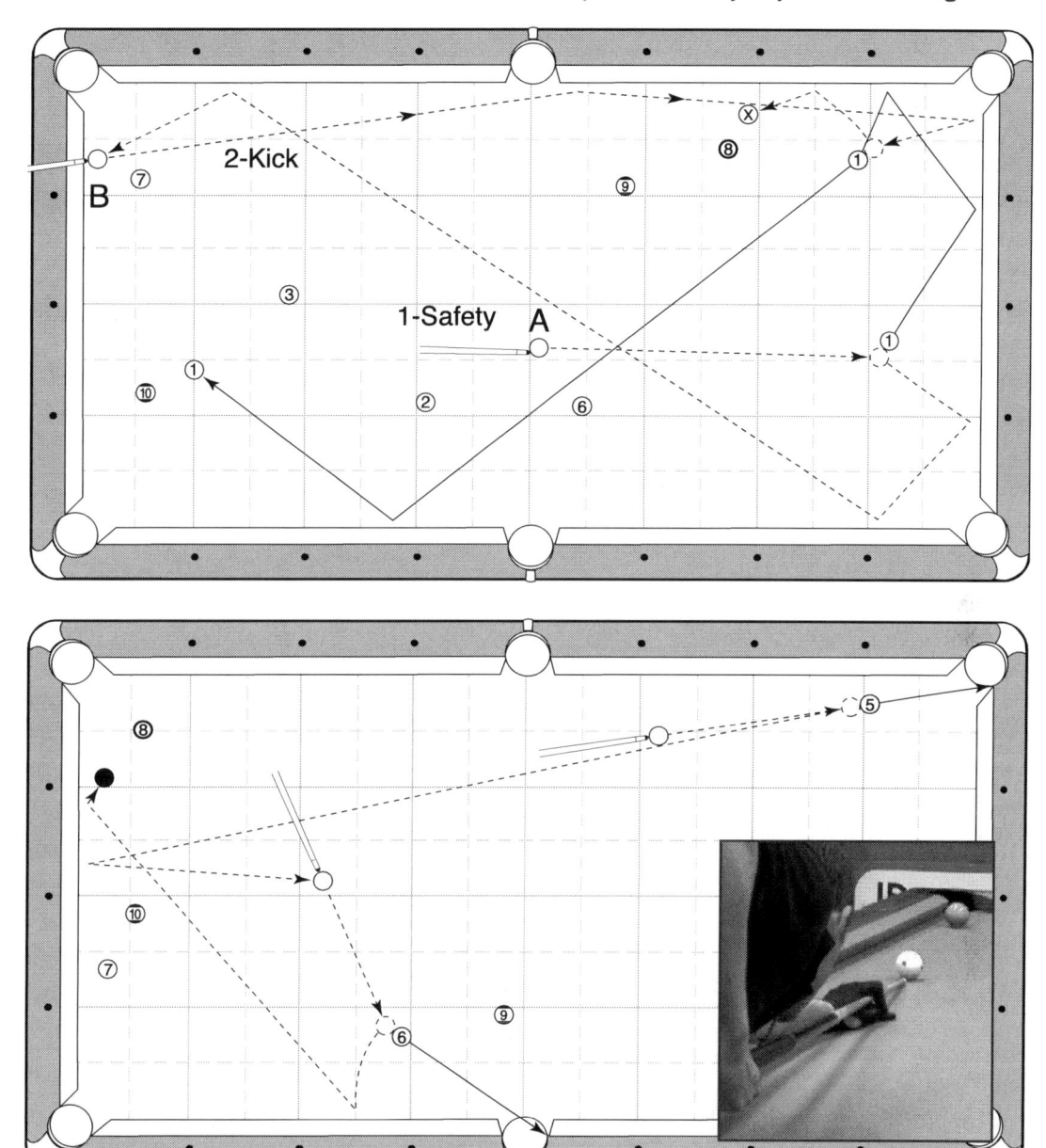

Squeaking in the Widow   (9/6 – 29:55)   **C-BCB: 7, 8, 9, 10**

Van Boening set up for this draw shot on the 5-ball with his tip almost on the cloth, but he rerouted his cue to about a tip below center at contact. The cue ball shot back and off the end rail for position on the 6. The extra rail helped with his speed control and he was able to stop the cue ball about eight inches closer to the 6-ball. The 30 degree (half ball) hit was the ideal compromise between pocketing and position. Yes, the angle made the shot harder to see, but is also made it easier to dial in the speed and direction to that small zone on the end rail for the 7-ball.

LESSON: On some position plays like the 6-ball you must focus sharply on three elements during your routine – shotmaking, direction, and speed. If even one of these had been off, Van Boening's position play to the 7-ball would have failed.

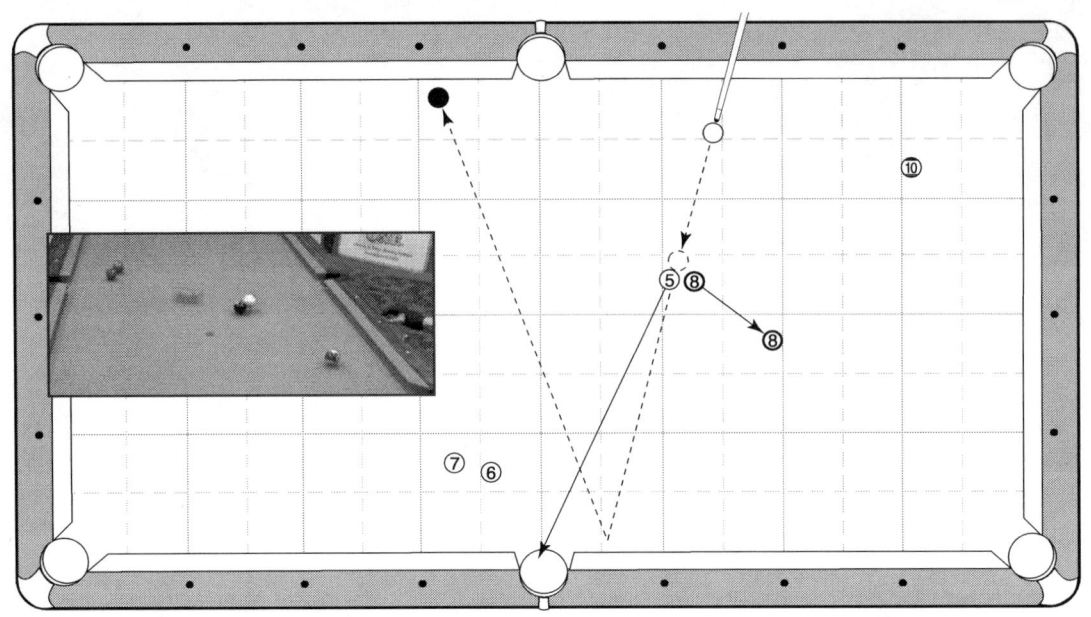

Power Hop and Run! (9/9 – 51:15)   C-BCB: 6, 7, 8, 10

I suppose that Van Boening could have gotten on the other side of the 5-ball – then getting from the 5 to the 6 would have been easy. But what fun is that?

With the 8-ball in his path, he powered up and powered up and shot the cue ball into the 5-ball and then up onto the 8-ball (visible in freeze frame) and past it – and it continued to the side rail and across the table for position on the 6. So even though the cue ball was on the rail this shot is still a masterpiece! As for your practice, you get to close out the rest of the run following his super shot.

Van Boening used a 14 inch long stroke and elevated a few degrees to produce a slight jumping action, and a hard (7) to very hard (8) stroke.

LESSON: Reyes and Van Boening have shown us that sometimes the best way to get past an obstructer is through it, or over it!

Targeting the Cue Ball (9/13 – :13:15)

Pool tables do, of course, have pockets that are the obvious targets for the object ball, but they do not have a hole in the ground like they do in golf. As a result, you must conjure up images for the cue ball's ending position using your imagination, and any available landmarks.

One of the best images is when you would like the cue ball to stop exactly where it is right now for your next shot. This gives you a very definitive target – something that Billy Incardona mentioned in the telecast when he said "He would like to end up where he is now for the 9."

Though the 8-ball was close to the pocket, at this distance and angle, returning the cue ball to its current location would not be easy, but Bustamante came very close. The diagram shows that he was on the same cut angle for the 9-ball, and was a little closer! GREAT speed and direction!!

LESSON: Other possibilities for targeting the cue ball include straight back draw shots, draw shots across the table and back, and small angled one-rail position plays, to name just a few.

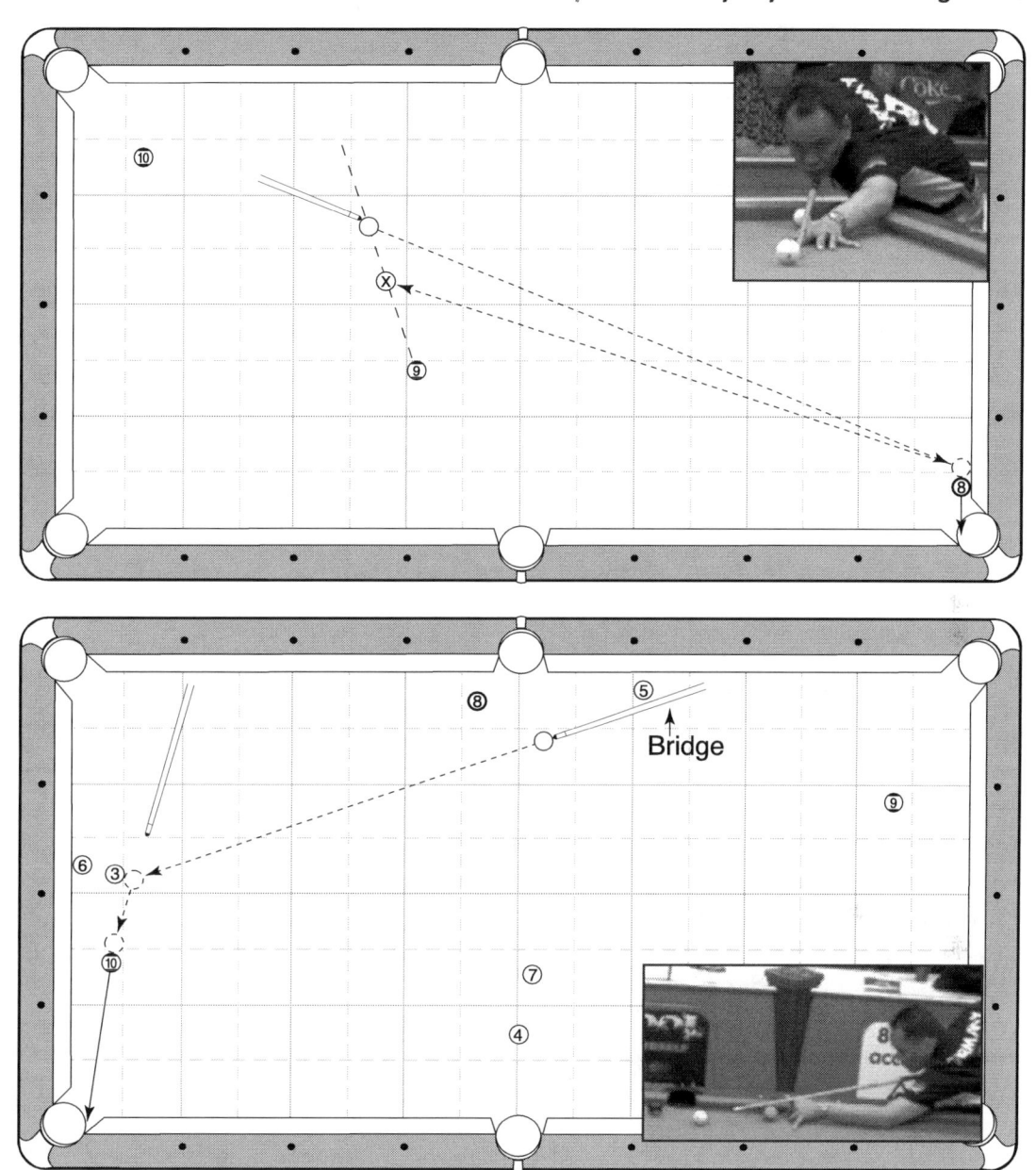

Game Winning Billiard! (9/14 – 1:15:30)
Bustamante, as part of his 40 second long planning process, walked over to line up the billiard with his cue as shown. He was checking for a high speed contact with the 3-ball so the cue ball will follow the tangent line as closely as possible into the 10-Ball. This is the most predictable way of shooting this shot when there is a long distance between the balls. Bustamante appeared to have room to bridge in front of the 5-ball, but he chose to use a slightly elevated 12" super long bridge. He overcut the shot and barely made the 10 where indicated.

LESSON: The announcers questioned the wisdom of this shot, but it is definitely the right one for amateurs when there are eight balls on the table – and it is evidently the correct one for Filipino billiard experts as well!

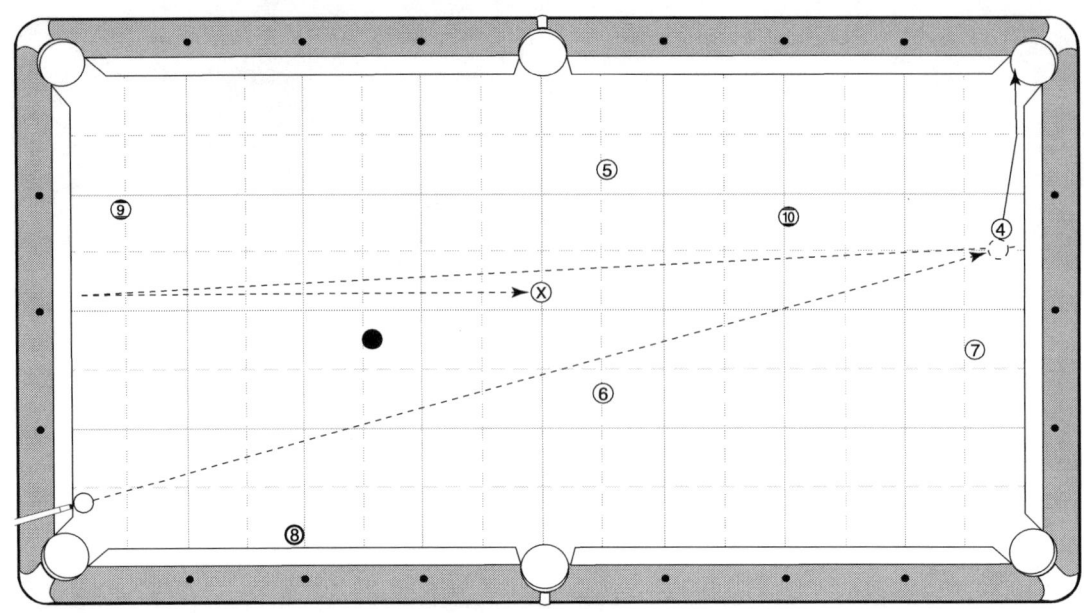

70-Degree Table Length Cut (9/16 – 1:27:20) C-BCB: 6, 7, 8, 9, 10

The shot in the illustration looks all but impossible, but it is a fact – Bustamante did pocket it, though the 4-ball did graze the rail first. Let's see now – the cue ball is on the rail, it's the maximum distance from the object ball, the 4 is not exactly a hanger, and the cut angle is 70 degrees – which means that he needs to slice off about 1/16 of the pie!

On one of my many viewings of this shot I focused on Bustamante's actions. He took seven seconds over the ball lining it up, then watched intently as the cue ball took its sweet time (about three seconds) to arrive at the edge of the 4-ball. Bustamante employed some extensive body english AFTER the cue ball had rolled two diamonds – indicating that he had a little apprehension about the outcome! He then swung his cue to the left like an expert swordsman!

LESSON: It's okay, on occasion, to let your body engage is some post contact histrionics – but only well after contact lest these gyrations work their way back into the moment before contact.

Inside Spin Power 4-Railer! (9/21 – 1:58:25) C-BCB: 6, 8, 9, 10

Bustamante did not play for this small angled cut shot off the rail on the 5-ball (nor the 6-10 combo), so he got back in line for the runout with this spectacular four rail route to the short side of the 6-ball. The stroke that it took to play this shot is in pool what a tape measure home run is in baseball, or a 60 yard field goal in football.

Bustamante has the most powerful break among the top pros, so it stands to reason that his ability to whip his cue through the cue ball would lead to high powered position plays like this! The cue ball spun like a top off the second rail and shot down the table. As an aside, the rest of us are better off shooting the 6-10 combo in this position. Now, set up the last four balls and finish his run.

LESSON: He used an extremely hard stroke (9) and a ton of inside english. A key to a power shot like this it to fight the urge to begin your big move too soon – wait until after you've completed your backstroke to start your rapid acceleration.

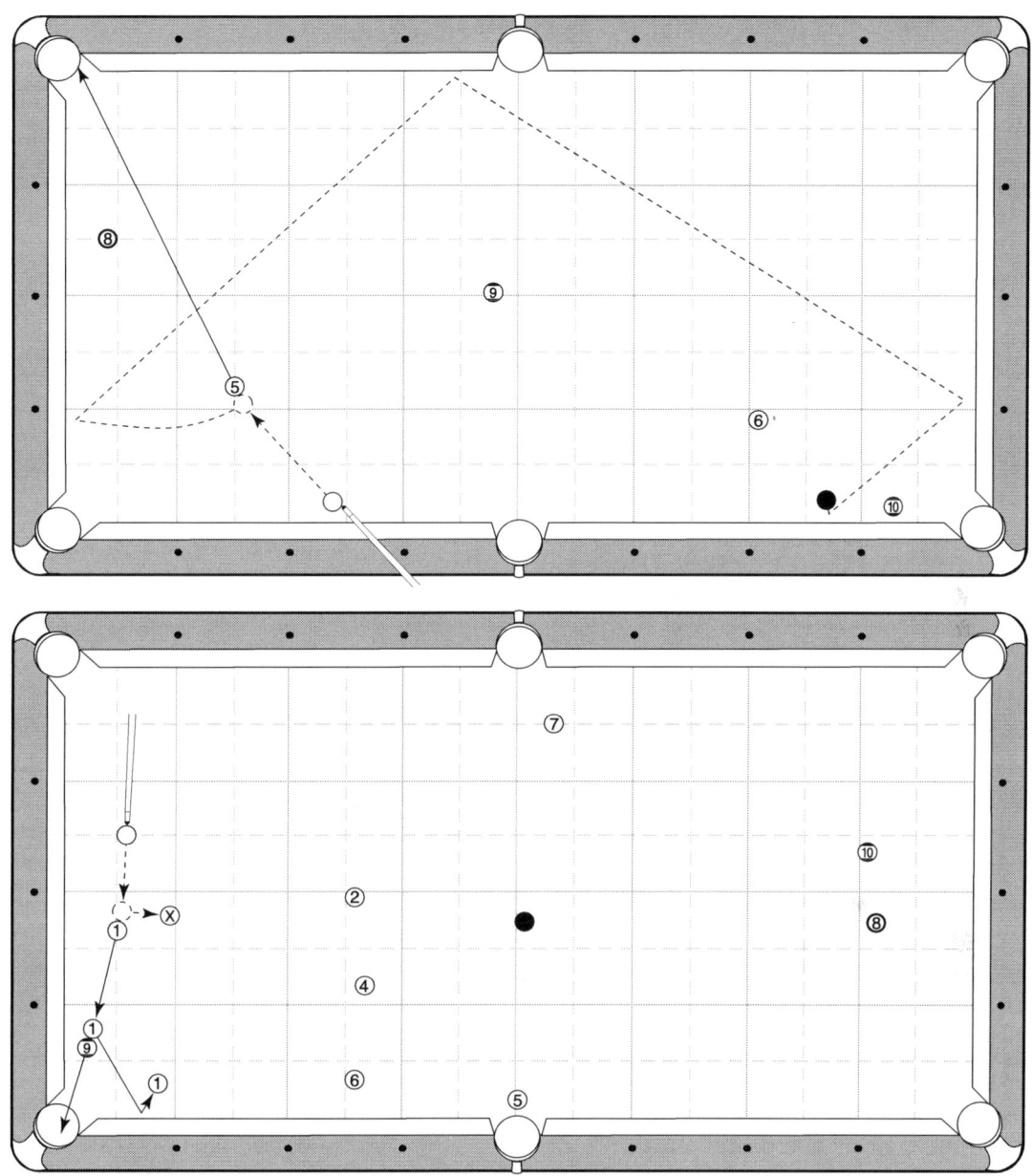

Combo Simplifies the Pattern (9/22 – 2:01:20)　　　　　　　　C-BCB: 6, 7, 8, 10

With ball-in-hand, Van Boening chose to play the 1-9 combo. Why? Because he was thinking like a pool/chess player, planning several moves ahead.

If he shot the 1-ball into the top left pocket, he would have to use the 8 to come back down for the 9-ball, then to the other end for the 10-ball. With his plan, he can finish the run at one end of the table with three short and simple position plays. He did place the cue ball an inch too far from the rail. If he had a little more angle on the 1-ball, he could have avoided playing that easy bank – which he made.

LESSON: When faced with a difficult layout, look for a chance to simplify the position. Take a little harder – but very makeable – shot so that, later in the rack, you will not have to send the cue ball all over the table.

#10 – Alex Pagulayan (15) vs. Rodney Morris (9)

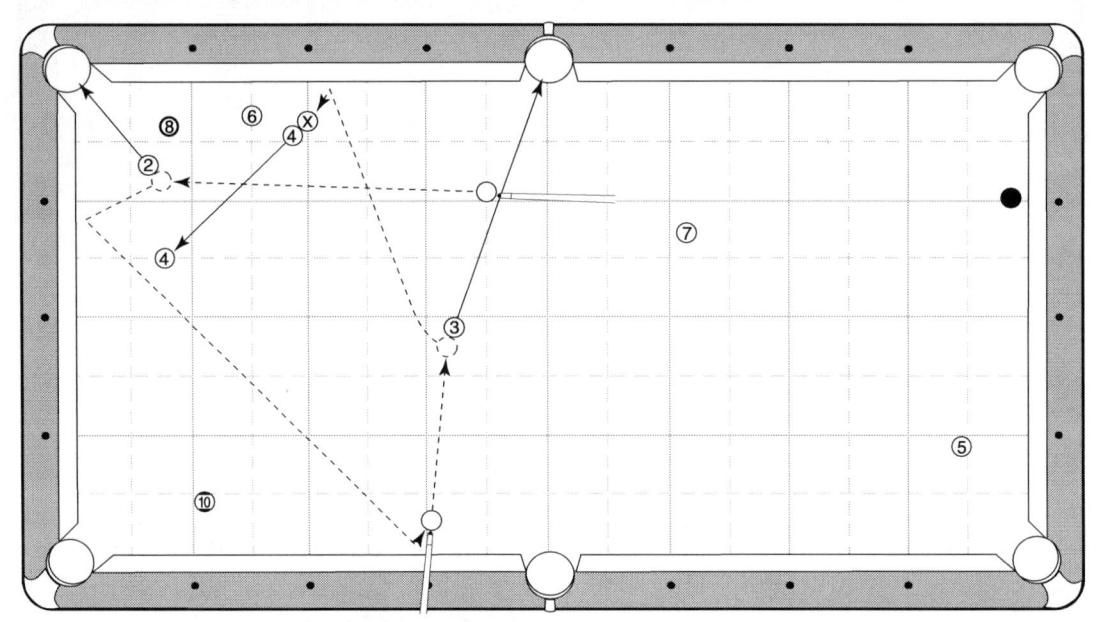

Position for a Breakout (10/1 – 3:45) B-BCB: 5, 6, 7, 8, 10

The 4-6-ball cluster is a big problem, but Morris has the solution. The 3-ball can be used to separate the two balls providing he can obtain the correct angle on it when playing the 2-ball. While direction is important, his speed control from the 2-ball to the 3 will determine the success of this pattern.

He used a very short and soft stroke (2) with outside english on the 2-ball, and his two rail route to the 3-ball left him with a shot off the rail. However, the good news was that he had a workable angle for breaking the cluster.

He used a medium hard (6) follow stroke so he could force the cue ball a little further to the left after contacting the 3-ball. His results indicate that this was a perfect pool shot because: 1) he broke the 4-ball out, 2) he stopped the cue ball dead for an angle to go up table for the 5-ball, and 3) he left the 6-ball alone.

LESSON: When playing a cluster break like this and your next shot is the ball you are breaking loose, it is good to have a Plan B in case you don't end up with a shot. In this example, a hook behind the 8-ball might have been the play if the 4 had been knocked to the end rail.

Runout Over Combo (10/9 – 46:15) BCB#1: 1-10 B-BCB#2: 4, 5, 6, 7, 8, 9, 10

It would be fascinating to see a well-researched table of the odds for a pro and a reasonably skilled amateur in this position. Pagulayan is the pro, and he has ball-in-hand. The 10-ball is only eight inches from the pocket, and he can line up the cue ball perfectly with the 1-ball. We'll guess that he can make it 50% of the time, but that's not good enough because he probably feels he has a 90+% chance of running out! And that is just what he did! Our amateur may have a 30% shot at the combo, but only a 20% chance of running out, so he is better off playing the combo!

LESSON: Know your game and your odds of success. And when the odds say go for the gamewinner, put pride aside and play the higher percentage shot. I have two Black Ball set-ups here – the combo, and a runout starting at the 4-ball.

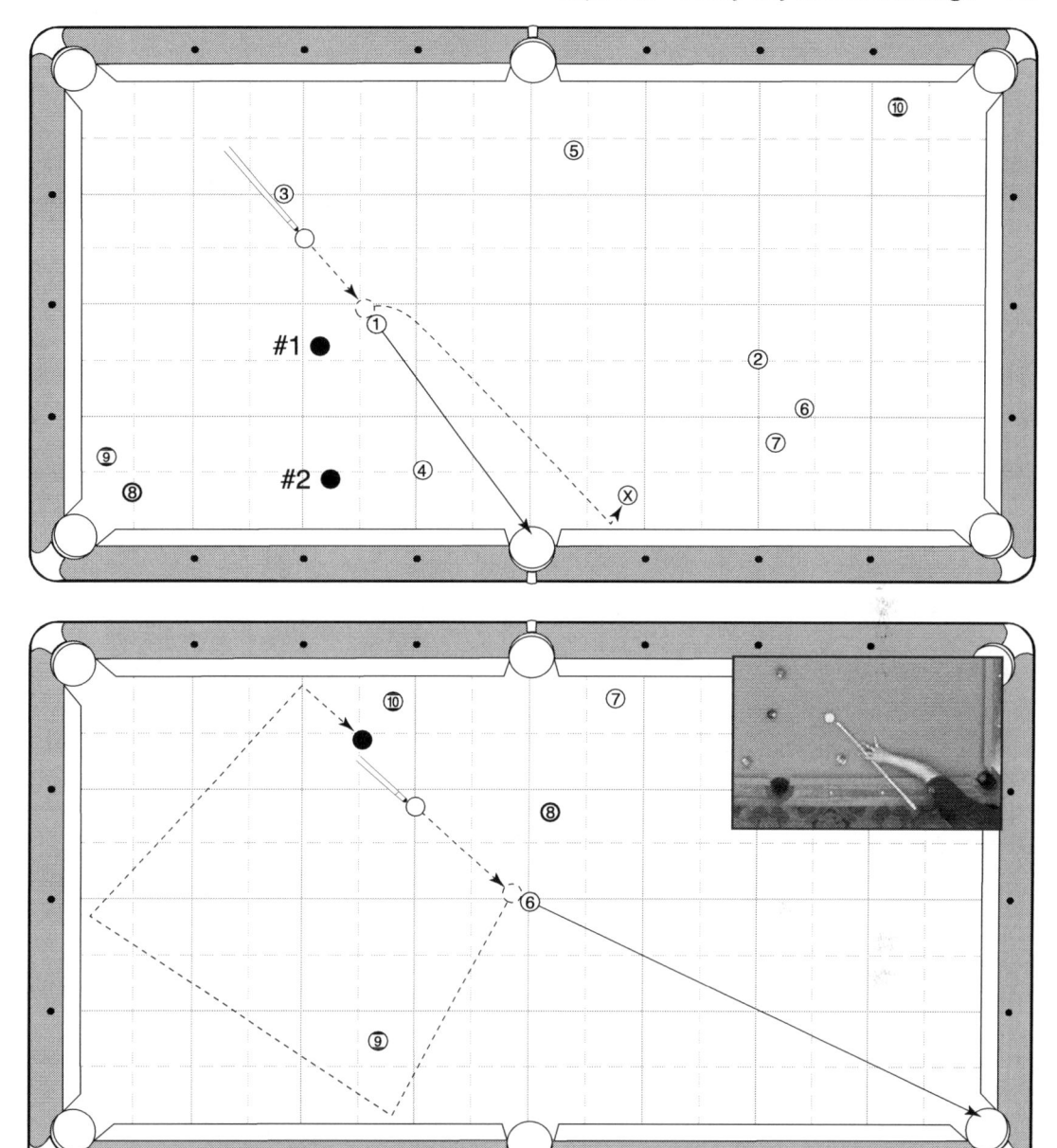

High Octane Recovery Route (10/10 – 53:35)   B-BCB: 7, 8, 9, 10

Morris needed less angle on the 6-ball for the side, or to have position on the other side of the 6-ball for the upper right pocket. Now he has two choices: 1) a thin cut on the 6-ball into the side while sending the cue ball to the right end rail and back – with the side pocket and the 7-ball as potential hazards, and 2) a three rail power stun shot. He chose the latter, and got excellent shape on the 7-ball while barely avoiding a hook behind the 10-ball.

LESSON: This position really underscores the principle of playing your game. If you have a big power stroke and love using it, Morris' shot may be for you. If thinner cuts and softer strokes with precision speed and direction are your strong suit, go with the cut into the side. I suggest that you set these up and give both routes a try!

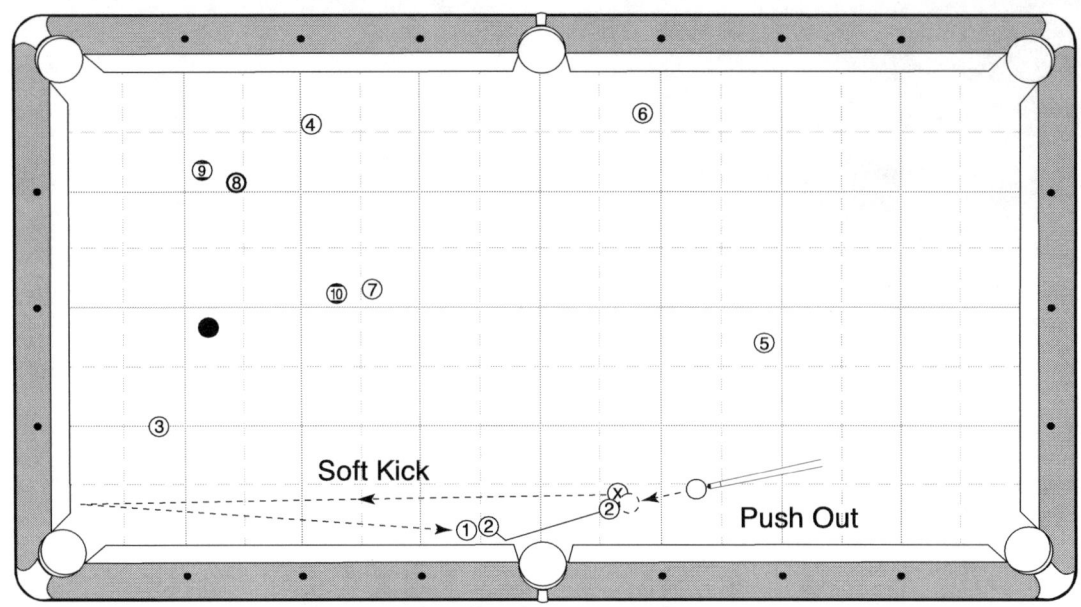

The Cluster and Hook Bunt Shot! (10/11 – 57:00)

After Morris came up empty on the break, Pagulayan spent 55 seconds studying this position before deciding to tie up the 2-ball with the 1-ball while purposefully leaving himself hooked. He used an extremely soft stroke (1) to roll the 2 into the 1.

He had to know that Morris would pass on this soft kick shot – so when he did, Pagulayan used a very soft stroke (2) to kick to the end rail and back into the 1-ball, leaving the two balls in a cluster. His patience was rewarded as he went on to win this game in the sixth inning.

LESSON: Don't be in such a big hurry to win. When you don't like the layout and are unsure how you can win the battle for control of the table, use strategies like tying up the balls that make it hard for both players to win right away, and that prolong the game. If you are a crafty strategist, you will enjoy these little battles, win many games this way, and frustrate your opponents!

Super 4 Rail Route (10/12 – 1:07:15)

Morris had to play for an angle on the 4-ball because the 8-ball blocked a two-rail crossing pattern to the 5-ball. Besides, as he's shown us before, inside english four-rail position plays like this one are definitely in his arsenal. On this shot he has a 40 degree angle, which we've learned is ideal for building speed while retaining your accuracy on long distance position plays.

While planning the shot, Morris walked over to his target zone for the 5-ball and pointed down his anticipated shot on it. That is building positive expectations! He then applied center left and used a medium hard (6) stroke to send the cue ball to Position X. While Position A would have enabled him to play a two rail route down the line to the 6-ball, it is hard to find much fault with his shot – especially since he went on to run out this rack.

LESSON: On inside english multi-rail position plays with the object ball near the rail, you generally want the ball no more than about one and a half diamonds up the side rail, and you want a reasonably thin cut of about 30 to 50 degrees.

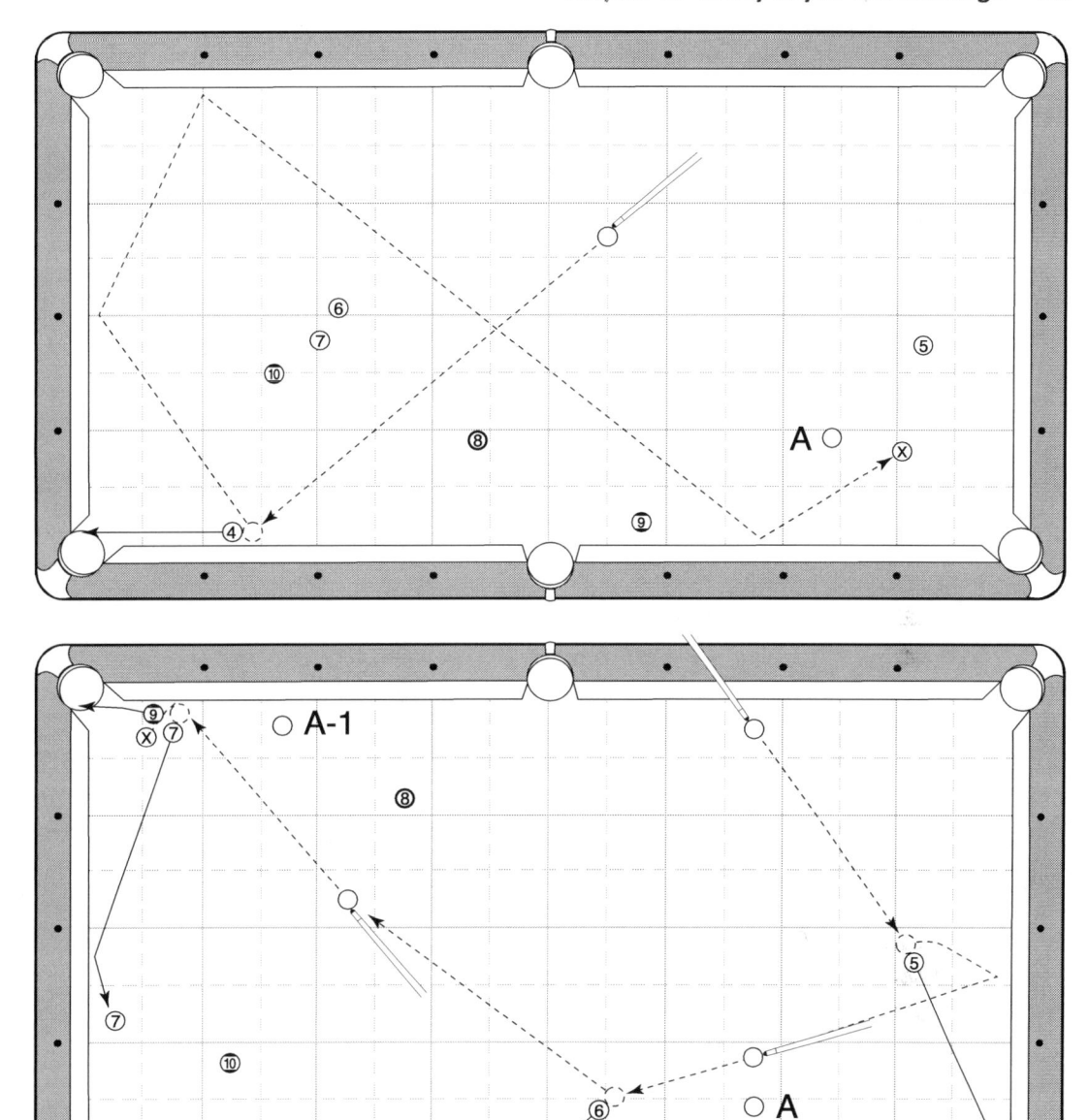

A Rail First (Kick) Billiard (10/13 – 1:13:20)
On the 5-ball, Pagulayan could have chosen to send the cue ball to Position A, setting up a cross table route to Position A-1 for the 7-9 billiard. But he chose to set up the shot in the illustration with the cue ball two diamonds in from the side rail. He used a tip of left english and hit the rail first, then 7-ball (barely) before billiarding the 9 into the corner. The 7-ball rolled across the end rail to a position where he was able to get on the 8-ball in the far corner and finish his runout.

LESSON: Watching the shot in freeze frame and slow motion showed that Pagulayan definitely made a good hit on this shot. Still, it did not appear as if he summoned a referee to make the call, which is something you should always do, especially when playing less knowledgeable players who are not very skilled at judging hits.

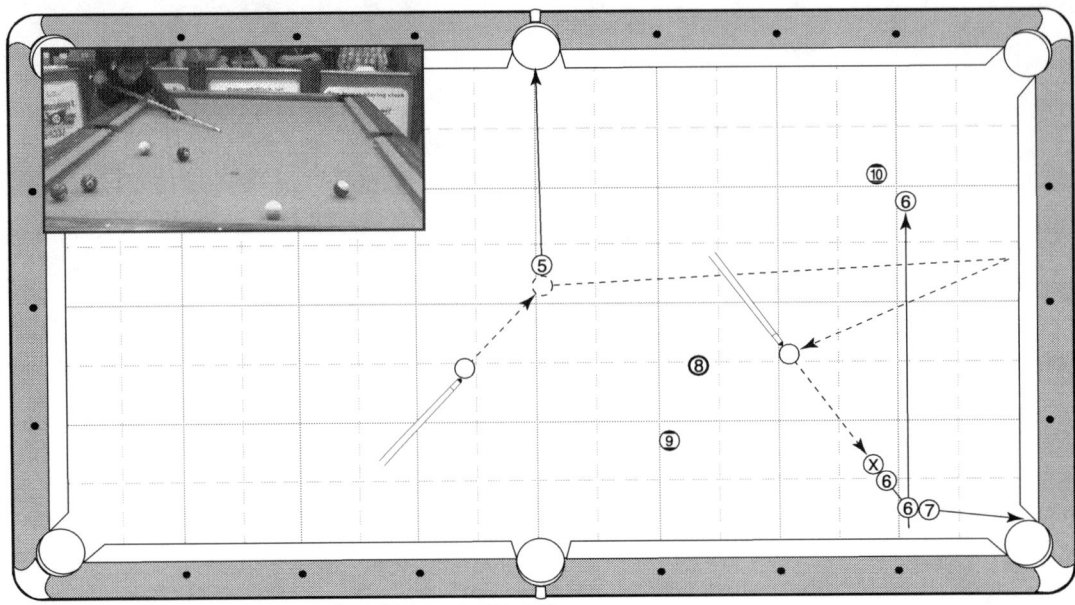

Draw + Spin = Position (10/20 – 1:55:10)

Pagulayan set up this angle on the 5-ball, which he used to float to the end rail and out for ideal positon on the 6-7 combo. While this route may look simple, it is actually an exquisite blend of draw, speed, and english. Let's look a little closer.

On thin cuts, draw is often used so the cue ball will stick to the tangent line after contact, not to bring the cue ball back like on straight shots. And that was the purpose of the draw spin on this shot. The right english was used to swing the cue ball back towards the combo and to get him closer to his work. Speed was the most important element because he was crossing his position zone, which is never easy. If he had used more draw and no english, he could have gotten a similar result, but it would have been much harder to control the speed. Notice that he was perfectly in line for the 6-7 combo, and that the 6 was now well positioned for the next shot.

LESSON: You can add much richness and precision to your position play by learning to play "small ball" by carefully mixing vertical axis cuing (center, draw, follow), english, and speed in the exact proportions needed for that particular shot.

#11 – Stevie Moore (15) vs. Alex Pagulayan (12)
Precision Push Out (11/9 – 1:10:50)

Pagulayan failed to make a ball on the break, leaving Moore to figure out what to do with this mess. He was hooked and had no reasonable kick shot on the 1-ball. And, with the 1-ball out in the open like this, pushing to a kick or jump shot was out of the question. As a result, he was forced into pushing out to a direct line to the 1-ball, which is seldom a desirable situation when facing upper level competition.

Even though Moore eventually lost the game, he did demonstrate superior knowledge and control of both balls with this soft cross table bank on the 5-ball, which tied it up with the 3, and sent the cue ball to the end rail.

LESSON: Players at all levels can expect good things to happen most of the time when they can 1) tie up balls, and 2) leave the cue ball on the end rail.

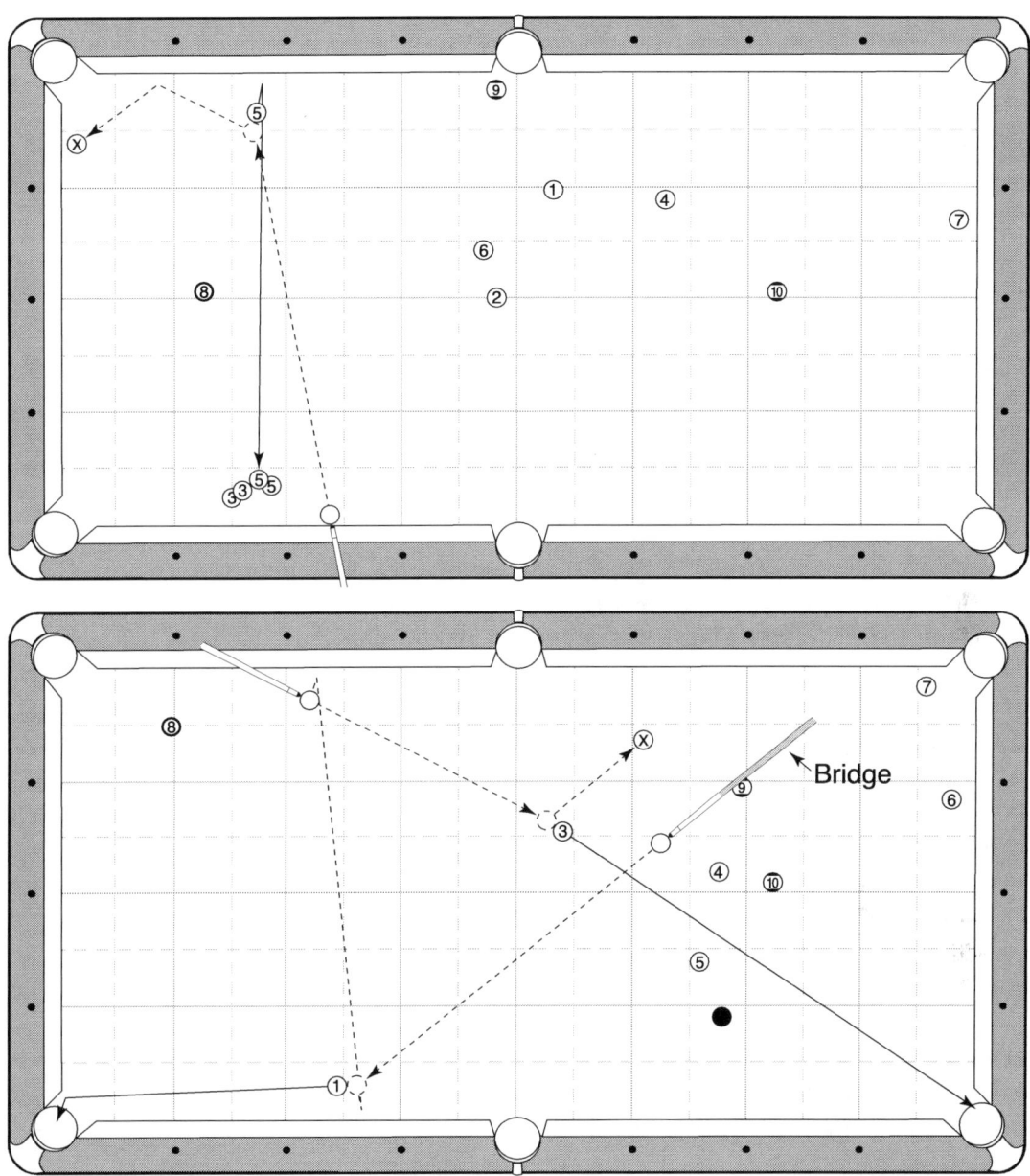

Duel "Out Shots" (11/14 – 1:40:45) B-BCB: 6, 7, 8, 9, 10

Moore made a ball on the break and then opened this run out with two difficult long shots. In pool, an "out shot" is one that, when made, is supposed to get you "in line" to run out a game. In this case, Moore had to open with twin "out shots" before he could establish close and playable shape on the 4-ball.

Moore's 12 inch open bridge over the 9-ball enabled him to get a great look at the 1-ball, but he used only a four inch stroke for accuracy. So, instead of using low left to try to get closer to the 3-ball, he accepted a long shot by rolling in the 1 with a medium soft (4) stroke. He used another short stroke in pocketing the 3-ball.

LESSON: This is another example of the principle of playing the high percentage sequence – don't try to do too much on one shot to make the next one so easy.

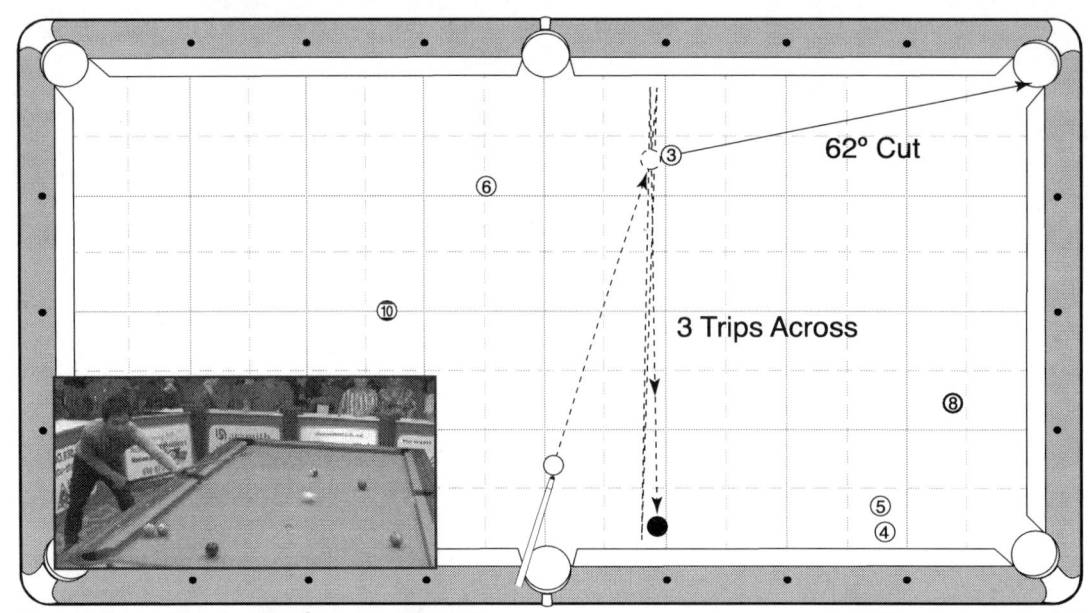

Fan it in to Win! (11/15 – 1:54:55)   **B-BCB: 4, 5, 6, 8, 10**

Moore probably felt that his kick shot would earn him another turn after Pagulayan played a safety – but that was before he opted for offense, fanned in the 3-ball, and sent the cue ball on three trips across the table for perfect position on the 4-ball.

   Pagulayan typically takes about 6-8 seconds over a shot, but on this one he spent 14 seconds – which is indicative of a long and complex aiming process. He then sliced in this 62 degree cut, which is about the practical maximum with the balls this far apart and the object ball this distance from the pocket.

   He used an open bridge for sighting accuracy, and took only a six inch backstroke, but he accelerated fully. His cue remained on his bridge and his eyes were glued to the balls until the 3 was in the pocket. His elbow drop was massive on his follow through as his grip hand went far below the rail and his tip finished about 10 inches above the cloth – all signs that he made a free and full stroke.

LESSON: Only when he could see that the 3-ball was in did Pagulayan then shift his attention to the object ball. Staying with the shot like this will confirm your successes, and reveal your errors should you miss.

More Gems by Moore! (Diag. A – 11/24 – 1:25:50)

Here is another A+ rated runout by Stevie Moore. He avoided the side pocket and the 9-ball with this precision position route to the 3-ball. While he did leave himself with a 60 degree cut on the 3-ball, he could not have hit the shot any harder or else he would have scratched – he needed the slower speed for the right english to work, and to keep the cue ball from rebounding more directly off the side rail.

   His position play from the 3-ball to the 4-ball was a demonstration in distance and directional control. The cue ball should have been a diamond closer to the top side rail for the 5, but he played a strong recovery route, as we'll see in the next diagram.

LESSON: When you must send the cue ball across the table and past the side, and it is going a long ways, you must still hit it slowly enough that the spin can do its work.

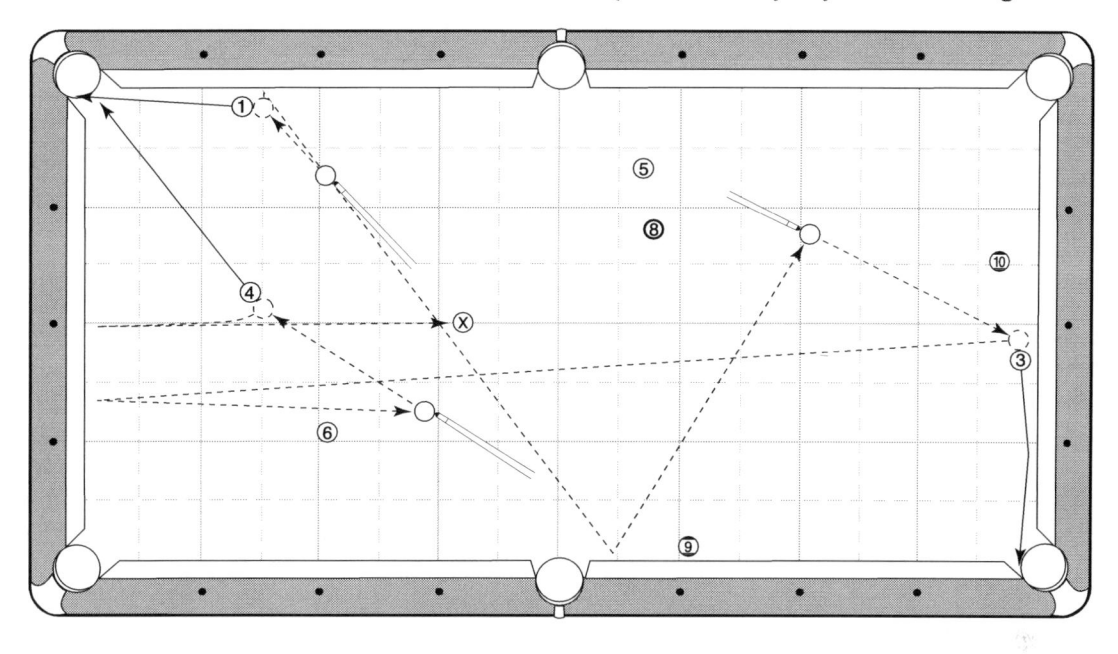

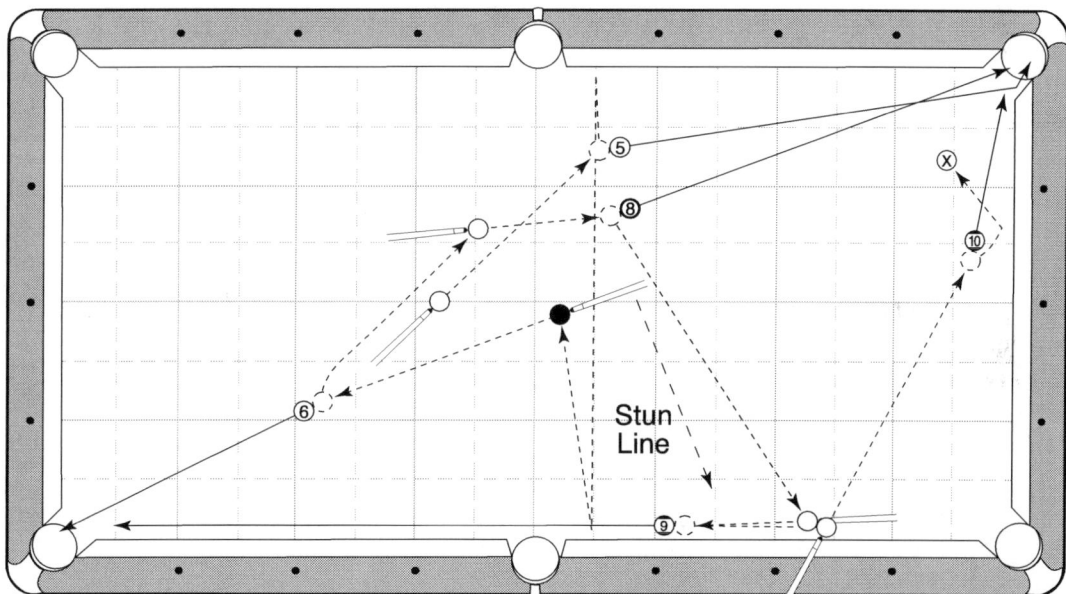

Closing the Deal in Style (Diag. B – 11/24 –1:27:25)   A-BCB: 6, 8, 9, 10

After those two tremendous position plays to open the rack, Moore failed to apply sufficient inside spin on the 4-ball and, as a result, got a little thin on the 5-ball.

Top pros specialize in playing strong recovery routes after partial mistakes, so it was no surprise that he was able to get across the table and out for position on the 6-ball – making excellent use of inside english on this shot!

Moore indicated during his planning process that he intended to send the cue ball off the top side rail and across for the 9-ball, but he drew too far over and back on the 6-ball, leaving him on the wrong side of the 8. But wrong can be right as he showed with this well played stun/follow shot to the short side of the 9-ball.

LESSON: There is usually a correct side and a wrong side for a certain position play, but on occasion either side does offer a way to the next ball – just a different one!

#12 – Francisco Bustamante (15) vs. John Morra (5)

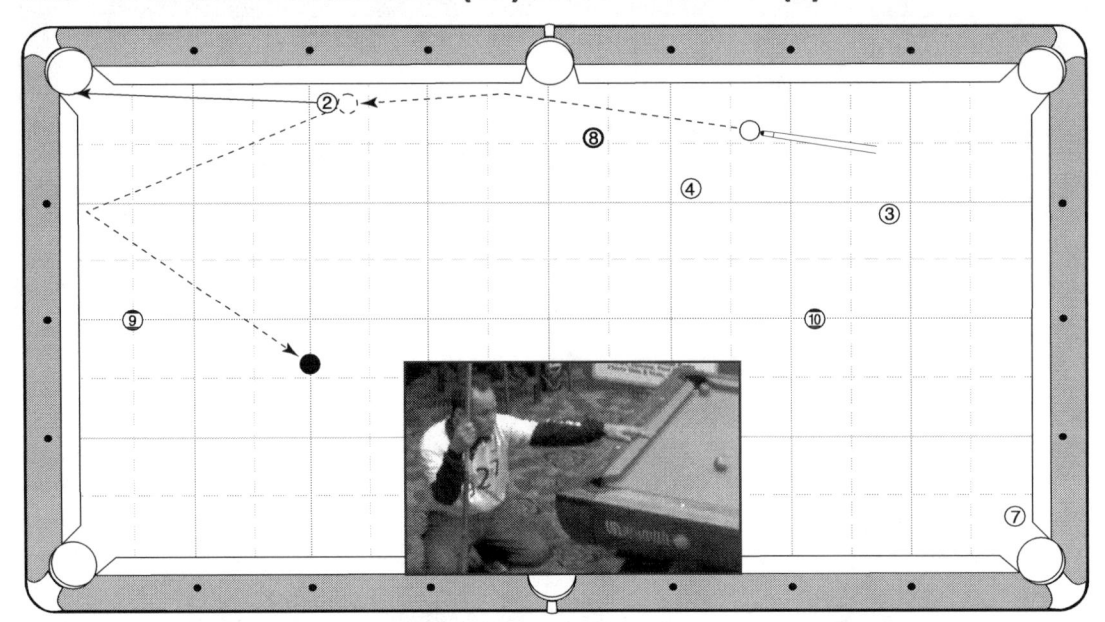

Rail First at Long Range (12/2 – 13:45)   B-BCB: 1, 4, 7, 8, 9, 10

John Morra played what would have been a fine safety IF the cue had bounced another couple of inches off the rail. But he left the door slightly ajar, and Bustamante waltzed right in with this superb rail first shot on the 2-ball.

Most players prefer to play rail first shots with follow, and in this case it was the only way he could get the cue ball far enough across the table for an open shot on the 3-ball. He did not need to use english because the cue ball would pick up some from its contact with the side rail, the object ball, and the end rail. This added spin helped open the angle of the end rail, which was a must for position.

Bustamante could have gotten close to the 3-ball, but he chose to use a play long distance shape because: 1) it gave him an angle to go two rails for the 4-ball, 2) it kept him from possibly scratching in the side or being hooked behind the 10-ball and, most importantly, 3) it improved his pocketing percentage.

LESSON: It is important to know the reasons (see above) why you use certain speeds and routes because these factors are integral to the success of the shot.

Through Traffic to a Combo (12/3 – 17:40)

I could not tell if the 2-ball was partially blocked by the 8-ball, but I suppose that it was, or else Morra didn't like this layout, because he chose to go for the 2-10 combo. I recommend that amateurs go for the combo as well because their chances of running this rack are slim. Morra went for it because he could play great shape on the combo and, being a young sharpshooter, he felt that he could make it.

I mentioned before that combos are best played when you must cut both balls in the same direction (here it is slightly to the right) or when your path from the cue ball to the first ball, or from the first ball to the one being pocketed, is straight.

LESSON: Sometimes it is better to just put all of your energy into making the shot as Morra did rather than factoring in a safety – and then, like Morra, don't miss!

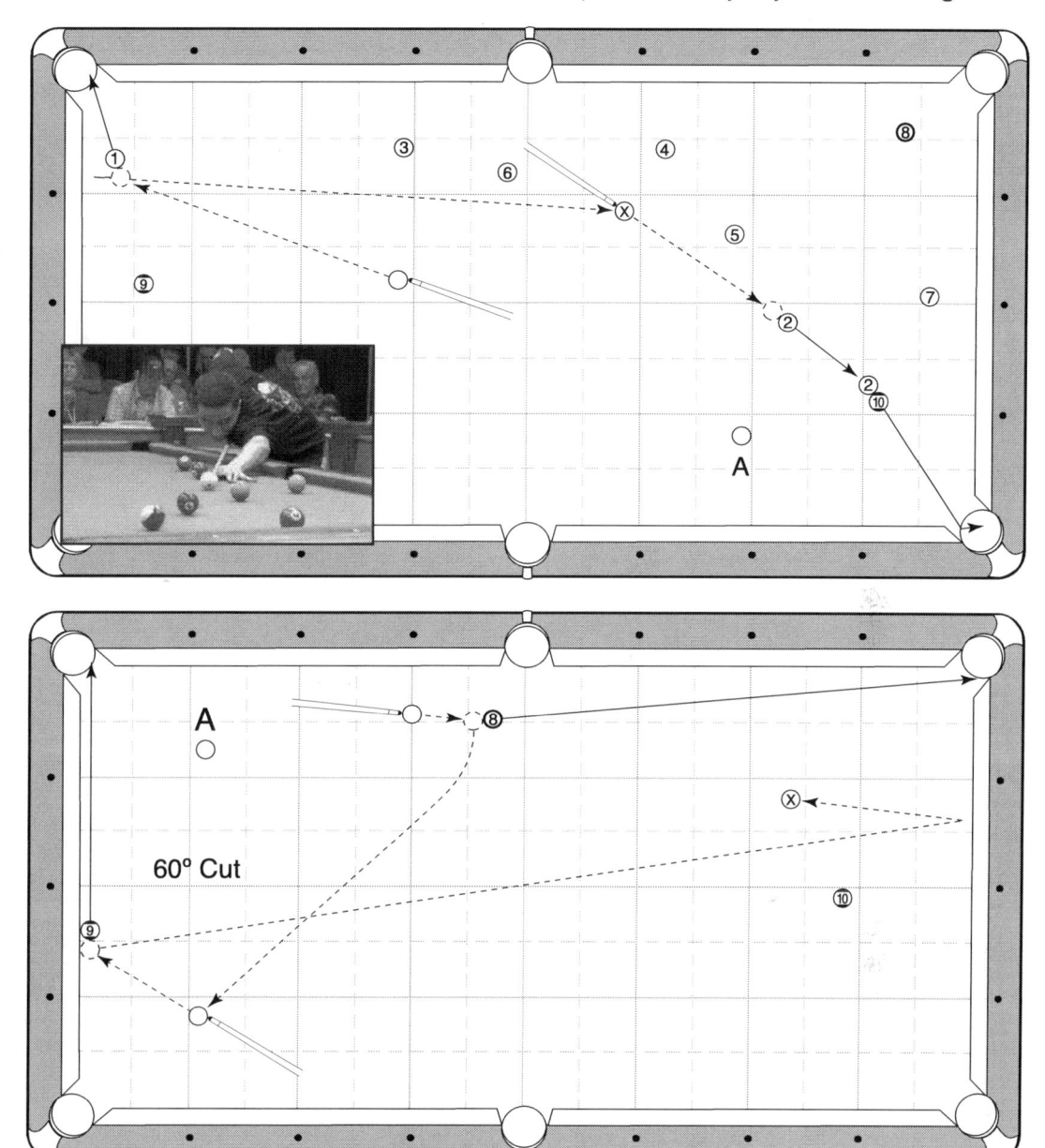

Draw/Stun to a Frozen Cut   (12/13 – 1:19:35)
Bustamante wanted straight in shape on the 8-ball because then he could have drawn straight back to Cue Ball A for the 9-ball. But he got that small angle to the left which forced him to play to the short side of the 9-ball. He used a draw/stun shot with a medium hard (6) stroke and came up a little short. He was unperturbed by his error as he sliced in that thin frozen cut on the 9-ball by hitting the rail a hair before the 9 and came off the end rail and out for Grade AAA shape on the 10-ball.

LESSON: There is a tendency to come up short when playing draw/stun shots. So, try to determine what would be the more damaging mistake – to come up short, or to go long. In this example, the cue ball was headed right at the corner pocket!

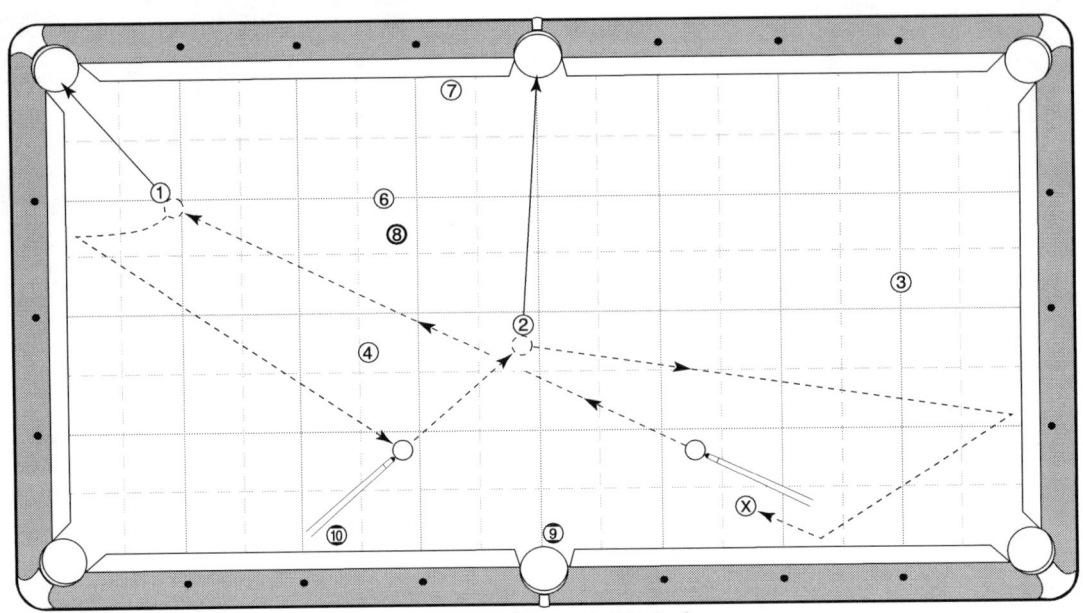

Identify the Big Hurdle (Diag. A – 12/14 – 1:22:00)
After the break you want to immediately identify the Big Hurdle which, in this case, is the 7-ball, which is frozen to the rail near a side pocket. Now, can he get on it? The 6-ball is close by, but getting on it will take super planning and execution.

On his opening shot on the 1-ball Bustamante came up a little short on the 2-ball, but short is okay with that side pocket looming so large! Besides, he had a huge and uncluttered position zone, so he was able to recover quickly with a two-rail route to the 3-ball, setting up an inside english two railer to the 4-ball.

LESSON: You can afford minor mistakes in position when your next position zone is large and your route offers flexibility and the chance to quickly get back in line.

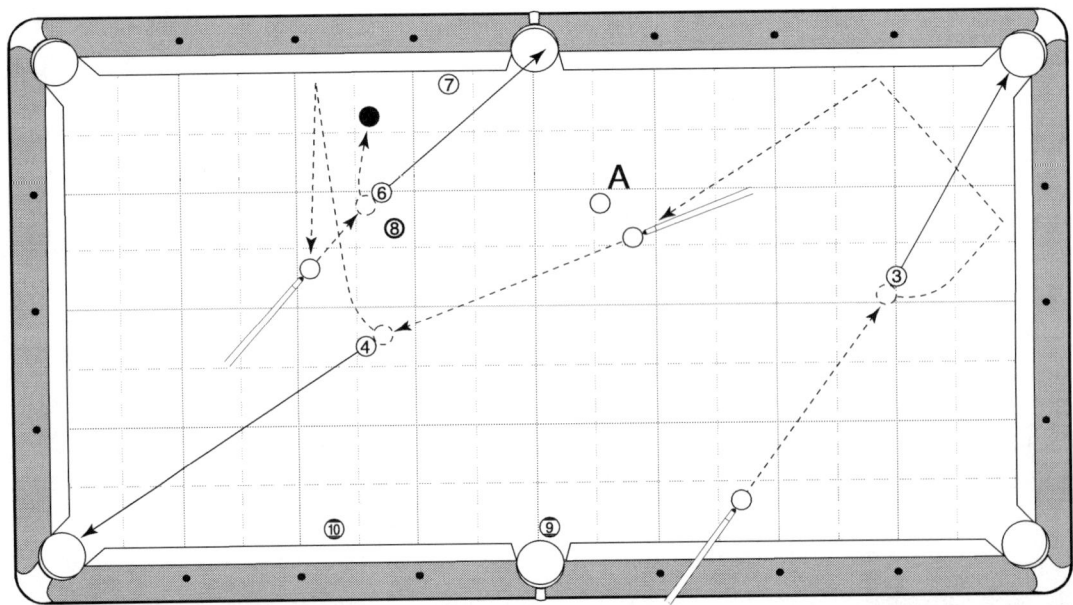

Identify the Big Hurdle (Diag. B – 12/14 – 1:23:00)   A-BCB: 7, 8, 9, 10
Cue Ball A shows the ideal place for position on the 4-ball because it fits the pattern better. However, the natural two-rail route with inside english resulted in the position

as shown! Now completing the 4-6-7 sequence would be an even bigger challenge.

Bustamante's angle on the 4-ball forced him to go to the side rail and out for the 6. A slight cut to the left on the 6-ball would have been better because then he could have sent the cue ball above the 7-ball for shape in the upper left pocket.

The cue ball came out a little too far off the rail, forcing him to improvise. He played a stun/follow shot for the short side of the 7-ball – and came up short. If he had used more speed on the 6-ball to get a smaller angle on the 7 closer to the rail, he would have risked missing because of the sharp angle into the side pocket.

LESSON: It appeared as if his shot on the 6-ball went in the middle of the pocket. Most misses to the side pocket at severe angles like this are wide of the far side!

#13 – Francisco Bustamante (15) vs. Stevie Moore (5)

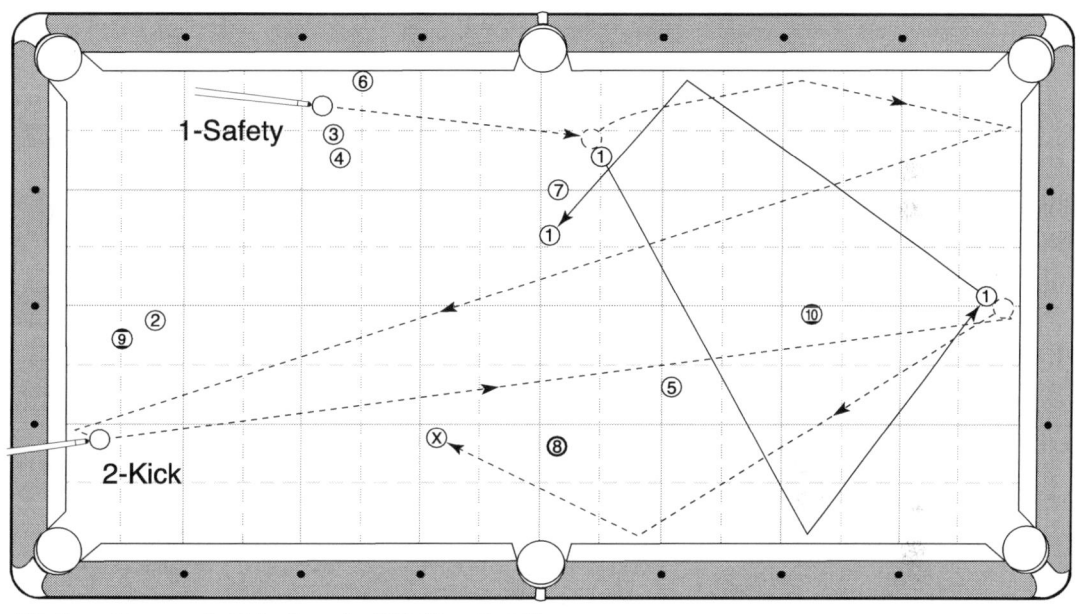

All Out Strategic Warfare! (13/2 – 5:40)
Moore peeked past the 3-ball to make sure he could hit the 1-ball and concluded that he could skim the left side of it. He then conjured up this all-pro safety – sending the 1-ball off the side rail and down to the end rail while propelling the cue ball off two cushions and then down off the opposite end rail. This was a complex job that was well done!

If Bustamante had hit the 1-ball more fully, the cue ball would have stopped near the end rail. However, he also did not want to hit the 10-ball in passing, so he allowed for about a half inch margin. It also appeared that he did not use any english. If he had used a little left english and/or come closer to the 10-ball, then he might have stuck the cue ball near the contact point with the 1-ball.

LESSON: When sending the cue ball past obstructers to pocket a ball or play safe, how close can you come to the ball before you feel the need to alter your line of aim?

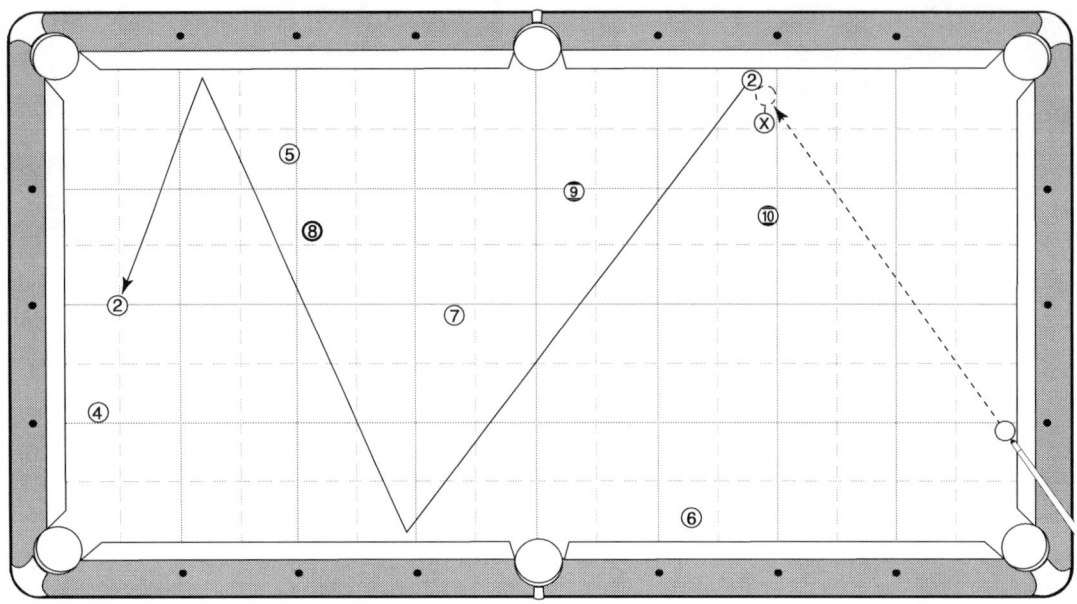

A Big Z Safety! (13/9 – 52:50)

Bustamante faced this early rack position in the third inning of what would be the second nine inning slugfest of three that occurred in this match (and one other game lasted eight innings).

After 50 seconds of study time, he was finally prepared to shoot. He set up with an open rail bridge, jacked up to about 10 degrees, cued a little below center, and fired almost directly at the 2-ball with a hard stroke (7). In freeze frame you can see that the cue ball flew almost half way to the 2, slammed into it, and bounced slightly off the rail to Position X. Meanwhile, the 2-ball traced out a Big Z shaped path before stopping near the opposite end rail with the 8-ball in between it and the cue ball.

LESSON: I advise that you tilt the book clockwise and that Big Z will really jump out at you. Then commit this one to memory so that you, too, can one day pull off one of the game's coolest moves – and maybe win a game in the process.

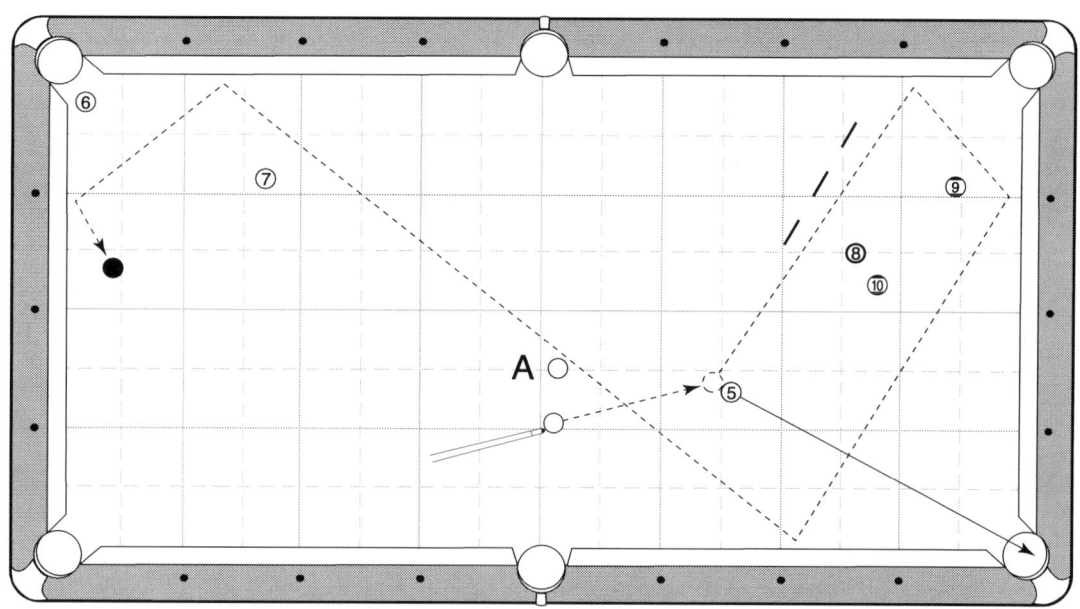

Five Rail Position Play   (13/19 – 1:45:45)   B-BCB: 6, 7, 8, 9, 10

Moore sent the cue ball to the side rail and out for the 5-ball when playing the 4-ball, but was undoubtedly planning for it to stop near the center of the table, perhaps near or at Position A. But if he had gotten his wish, we would have been deprived of the chance to see this spectacular five rail position play!

   Moore was now looking at a 38 degree backcut, the kind that many players have trouble with because the pocket is so far to the side of their line of aim, and is a test of their peripheral vision. He also needed to avoid hitting the 8 or 9 ball, but that should not be a problem considering that the cue ball should be following just below the tangent line to the first rail, and it is pointing well above the 8-ball.

LESSON: Freeze frame shows that the 5-ball entered the pocket just about when the cue ball hit the side rail, Moore's cue was still on his open bridge, and his head had shifted to the right to watch that 5 go into the pocket. This was a world class demonstration in how to watch a shot after contact! And, as the diagram shows, he did get great shape on the 6-ball!

LESSON #2: The cut was 38 degrees, so the cue ball was going to retain a little more speed than it transferred to the object ball. (At 30 degrees the energy is evenly divided.) So, it figures that the cue ball had traveled about 38" to the side rail during the time when the 5-ball had gone only 34" to the jaws of the pocket!

CHAPTER 16

Make It Happen All-Stars

The Accu-Stats All-Star Invitational, held during Easter week in 2014, was the fourth in an ongoing series of Make It Happen events that are produced by Pat Fleming, the owner of Accu-Stats. The field was comprised of three of the winners of previous Make It Happen events, and one player who finished second. The participants included Shane Van Boening, Thorsten Hohmann, Dennis Orcollo, and Darren Appleton – arguably the four best players in the world at the time that the event was held.

The event was held at Sandcastle Billiards in Edison, New Jersey, and was hosted by the room's owner, Ed Liddawi. The overall event was a round robin **comprised of matches in 10 Ball, 8 Ball, Straight Pool, and 1 Pocket. Darren Appleton won the overall competition. In 10 Ball** Van Boening, Dennis Orcollo, and Darren Appleton tied with records of 2-1 while Thorsten Hohmann lost three very close matches.

The average score was 11 to 7.67. The table was very stingy on the break, so this lead to fewer break and runs, and to more defensive battles and 10 ball second player runouts. The greatest opening sequence was Thorsten Hohmann's sequence of shots in Match 2, Game 9. The best shot goes to Dennis Orcollo's amazing effort in Match 2, Game 14 (no spoilers).

#1 – Shane Van Boening (11) vs. Thorsten Hohmann (9)

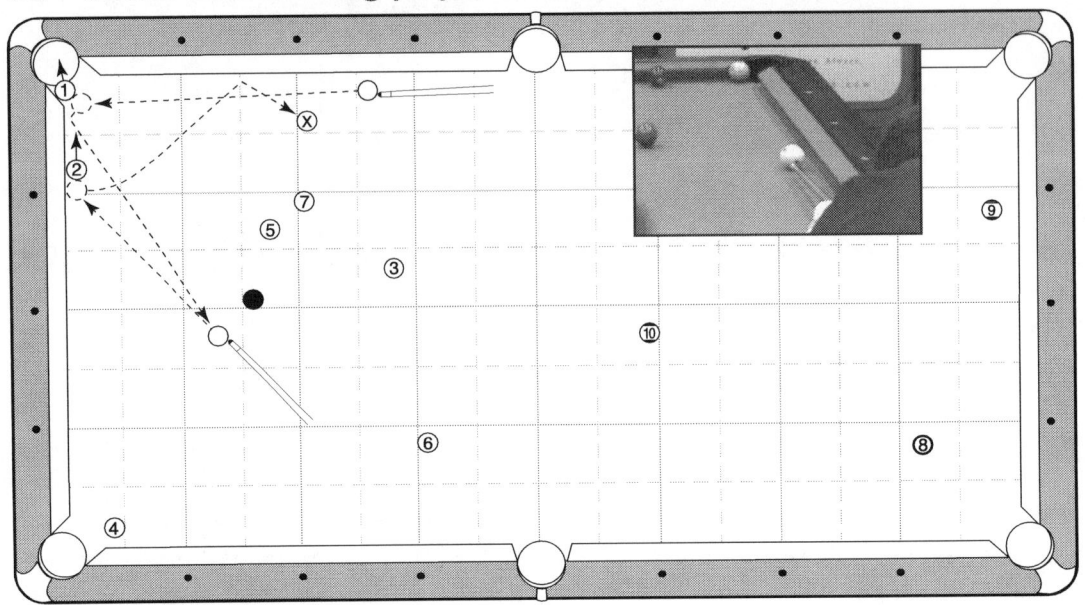

Super Soft Position Play (1/1 – 7:30) C-BB: 6, 7, 8, 9, 10

After Hohmann failed to make a ball on the break, Van Boening pulled his cue back only two inches and played an extremely soft follow shot (a 1 speed) on the 1-ball using a full tip of left english. When a ball is in the jaws aiming is not easy, and yet it is the key to the shot! And accurate aiming results from understanding the cue ball's rebound characteristics on various hits – this one being a half ball hit. Van Boening spun the cue ball past the 2 and out for the ideal angle on it.

Van Boening again showed off his soft touch with a very soft stroke (2) with inside english to go two rails and out for the 3-ball. He used a six inch stroke, about half the length that he uses for power shots. He could have played shape by coming straight off the end rail, but his path increased his margin for error.

LESSON: English was especially made for shots like these two where deflection and the evils of english are at a minimum, and its benefits are most strongly felt!!

Shane's Draw & Jump Show! (1/2 – 14:30) C-BCB: 7, 8, 9, 10

Hohmann again left Van Boening with a ball in the jaws, but this time he chose to hit the ball fully and play a massive draw shot on the 5-ball. From a distance of 6.5' he was able to bring the cue ball back nearly 9' – and was rewarded with a hook!

No problem! He elevated his jump cue to at least 40 degrees, struck the cue ball sharply below center, and sent it flying over 10-ball with an inch to spare. It then bounced and flew into the top half of the 6-ball (pocketing it, of course), and then over the 9-ball before it spun around the table for a shot on the 7-ball. Whew!

LESSON: He wanted to use a closed bridge on the cloth for his big draw shot, so he restricted his bridge to about 10 inches. After only five seconds over the ball, he began his final stroke. His head elevated about 3.5" before contact like he does on his break to create clearance so that his arm could swing powerfully through the shot! His follow through was surprisingly short - about 5 inches! Note: some players would go to the rail after hitting the 5-ball.

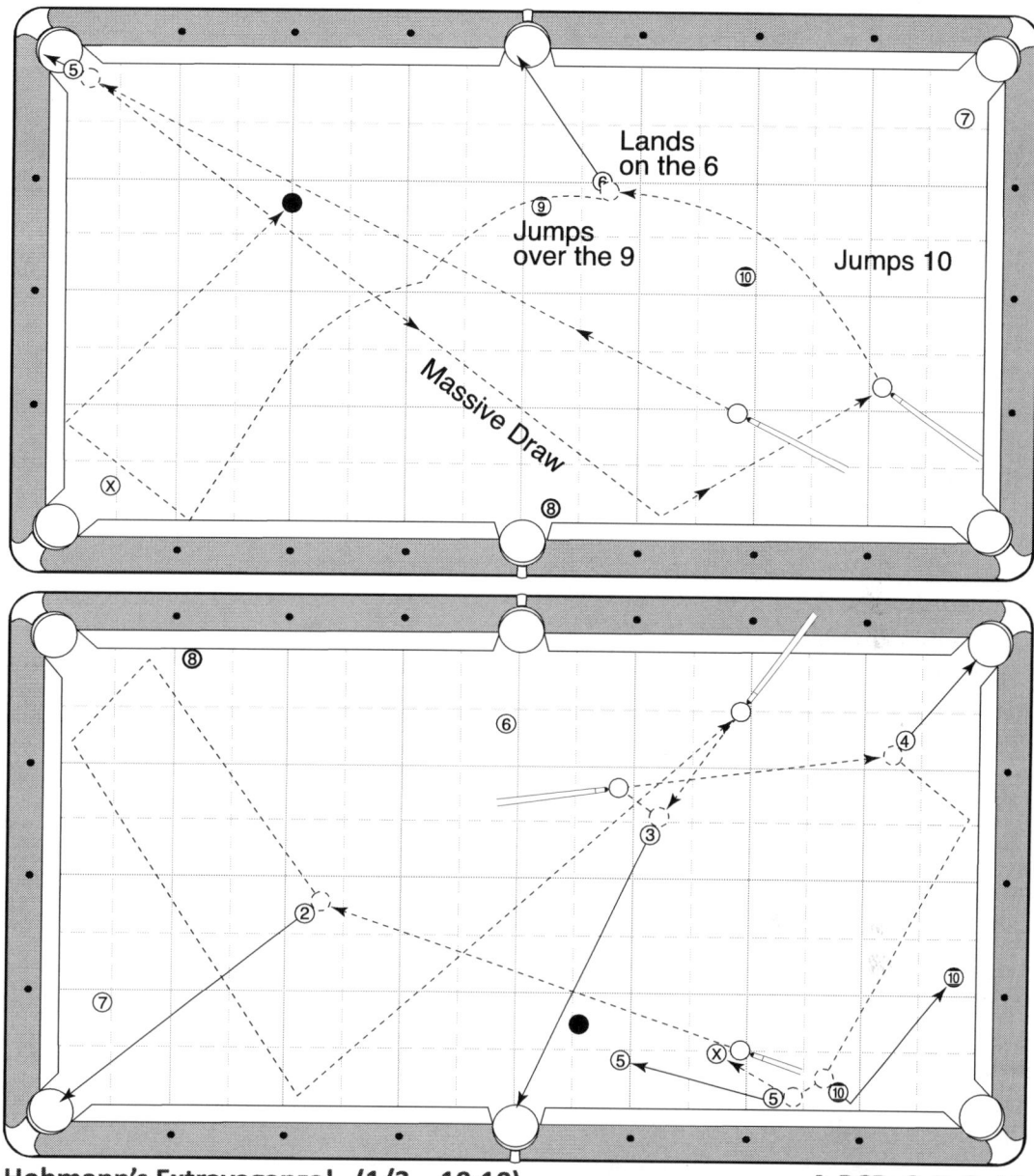

Hohmann's Extravaganza! (1/3 – 19:10)   **A-BCB: 6, 7, 8, 10**

Hohmann's inning began with this long distance 58 degree back cut on the 2-ball. He needed to send the cue ball to the middle of the table for the 3-ball, and he was also jacked up over the 10-ball, so this one definitely rates at least a 9. The good news was that he only needed to use a medium hard stroke (6) because the cue ball was going to retain so much of its energy after contact. This shot was therefore more of a test of his shotmaking accuracy. The cue ball followed the stun line (90 degrees) to the first rail perfectly, and he got great shape on the 3-ball. He then played a soft draw shot for just the right angle on the 4-ball to break up the 5-10-ball cluster, which he did to perfection!

LESSON: Hohmann prefers to use a short stroke on most shots, but with a much longer bridge for aiming accuracy. This is the stroke that he uses to run 100s in 14.1 like a well-oiled machine. There are pros and cons to this method, but it may work for you if you are having trouble using a longer backstroke.

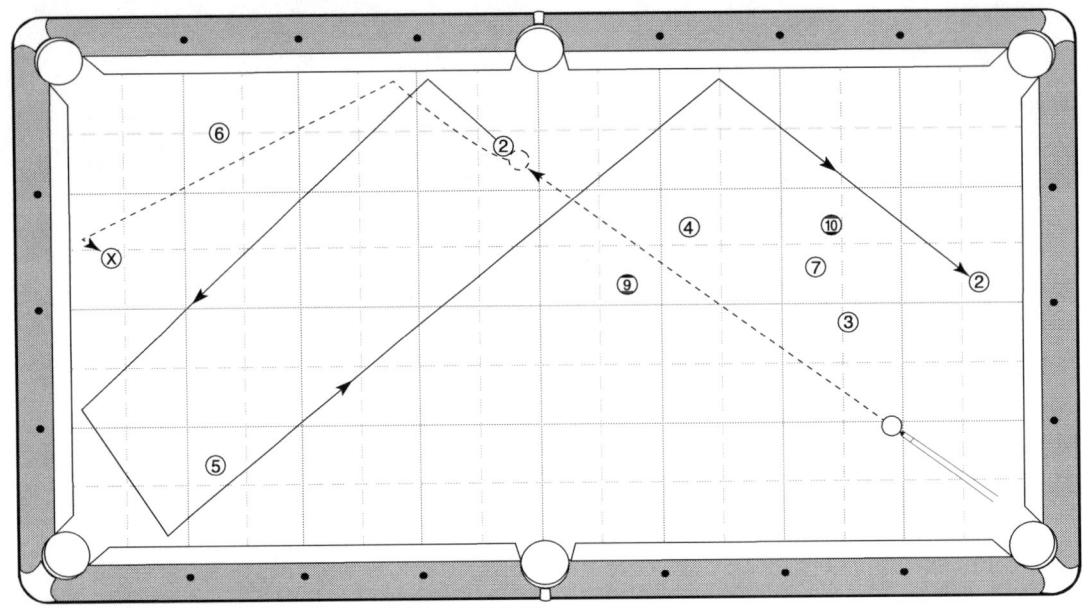

4-Rail Super Bank Safety! (1/6 – 37:30)

Van Boening made a rail first shot on the 1-ball, but hit a ball, which is a distinct possibility on a crowded table in the early going, and had to turn it over to Hohmann – but after first playing this super four-rail bank safety!

After 40 seconds of planning from several angles – including a view from the 2-ball's path past the 5-ball, he formed a 16 inch long bridge, took a 15 inch long stroke, and uncorked a high speed (7) force follow shot.

The 2-ball narrowly missed the 5 in passing, but it did because – well – because he's Shane Van Boening – and the cue ball and 2 took their places at opposite ends of the table with a wall of blockers between them.

LESSON: Super safeties are the product of a top player's experience, imagination, creativity, and ability to execute what he envisions. Van Boening knew how to play this shot because of his knowledge of similar situations and his ability to adapt to the position on the table. Imagination + Execution = A Pool Shot!!

Incidence Equals Reflection! (1/11 – 1:01:45)   A-BCB: 6, 7, 8, 9, 10

Hohmann has left Van Boening with the third pocket hanger in the match – each with its own set of challenges. This time Van Boening is hooked, so he must kick to pocket the 3-ball and send the cue ball away from the potential obstructers for a shot on the 4-ball. The kick to the side rail is out because the 10-ball is in the way, so he would have to create an angle using tons of draw and/or english.

A law of geometry states that the angle of incidence equals the angle of reflection – so the cue ball should rebound from a rail at the same angle that it enters it. But this is true in pool only when the approach angle is steep, the shot is hit softly, and no english is used. Van Boening used a three inch soft follow stroke (3) and sent the cue ball rail first into a thin hit on the 3-ball – in short, a perfect pool shot!

LESSON: I noticed that Van Boening stared holes through that distant end rail, so he obviously had picked out a target even though there was no ball and no specific target to aim at. Possibly he was aiming just to the left of the first diamond.

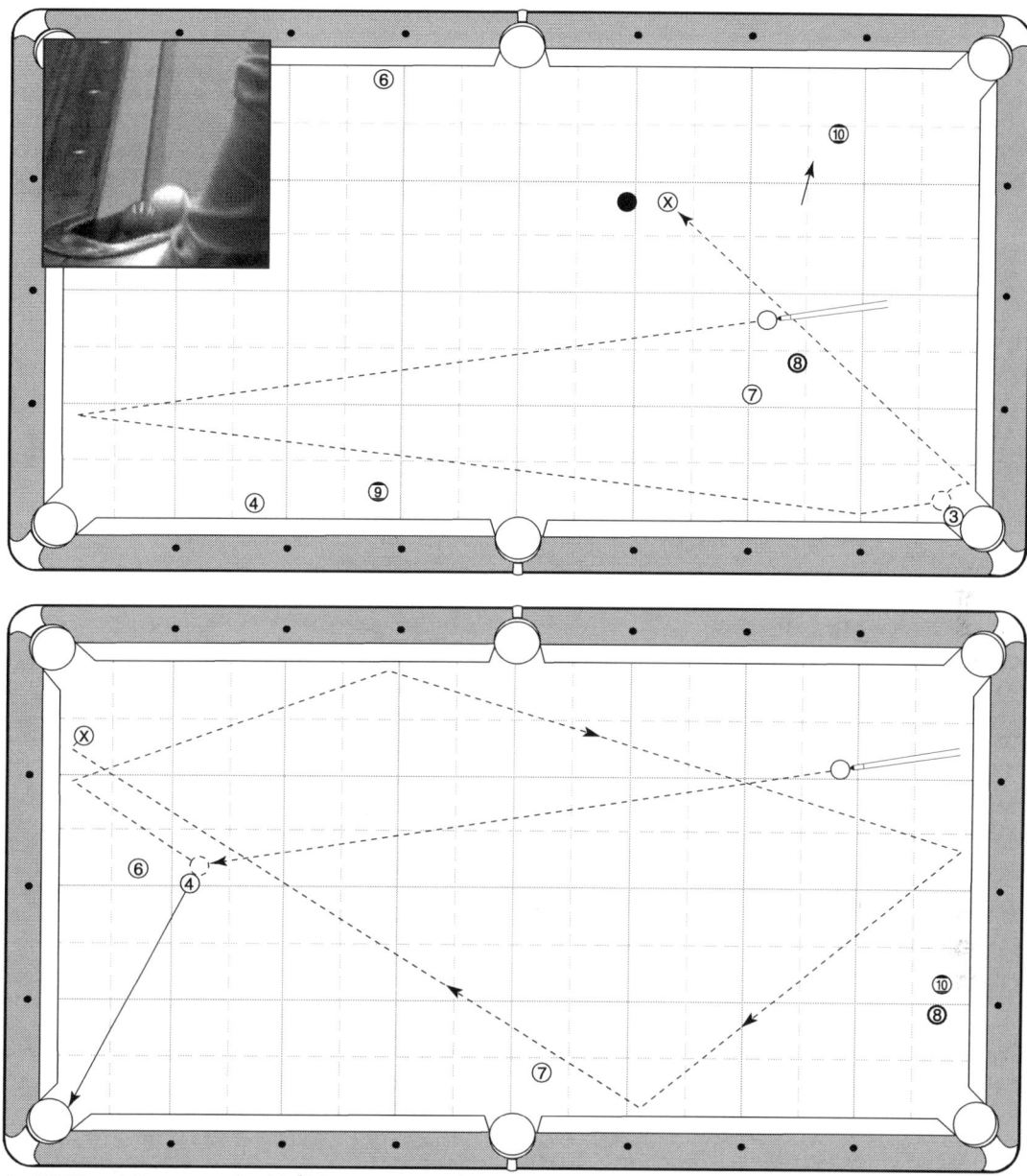

A 26 Foot Journey! (1/13 – 1:15:45)

Hohmann's mid-rack safety would have worked against most pros, but he was playing Van Boening, who began the eighth and final inning of this marathon game with this shot on the 4-ball. Van Boening is a master at long range thin hit safeties and there appeared to be an opportunity here to play one – but something in his pool playing mind told him it was a better idea to play a long distance 52 degree cut in which the cue ball would travel 6 feet before contact, 20 more feet after hitting the 4-ball, and hit five rails before stopping for a shot on the 6! Such are the thoughts of a pool playing genius! The cue ball barely missed the 7-ball and he got a little thin on the 6-ball, but his shot was good enough to win the game!

LESSON: At certain times you should think about taking on shots that are out of your comfort zone because you are on top of your game, you want that boost of confidence, it could have an impact on your opponent – and lastly, for the thrill of it.

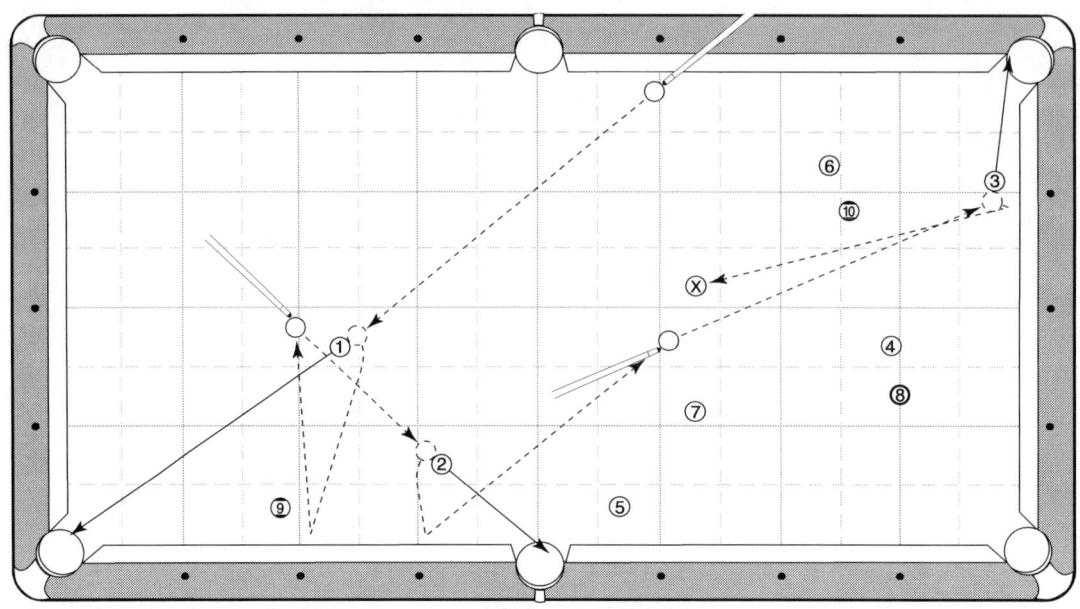

Shane's Variety Act! (Diagram A – 1/18 – 1:41:15)

Van Boening dug deep into his bag of tricks and pulled out several treats on his way to running this challenging layout. First off was this long shot off the rail on the 1-ball on which he used a very hard stroke (8) and played a small angled pound/follow shot. He would rather have been on the other side of the 2-ball, but it was still a great shot, all things considered.

On this follow shot into the side he applied a heavy dose of inside english to the cue ball, and it rebounded at a severe angle, enabling him to get closer to the 3-ball. He then played a super soft cut shot with outside english on the 63 degree cut on the 3-ball to keep the cue ball close to a billiard on the 4-8. His cue appeared to glide into the cue ball in slow motion on this very softly hit shot (2).

LESSON: Pros dislike rolling balls in at a distance, which explains why Van Boening played that power shot on the 1-ball. Amateurs might, in that same situation, be better off rolling the 1-ball into the pocket. If this shot is hit softly enough, it could result in a cut on the 2-ball from the correct side of the ball!

Rail First Cheat Shot! (Diagram B – 1/18 – 1:42:25)   B-BCB: 5, 6, 7, 9, 10

Van Boening clearly signaled his intention to play the 4-8 billiard shown when he surveyed the shot from two locations before playing the 3-ball. After rolling in the 3-ball (see previous illustration) he then scoped out the billiard from a couple of locations to reconfirm his plans before rolling in the 8-ball AND setting himself up for the 4-ball.

He got a little unlucky to end up with a straight in shot on the 4-ball, but he sent the cue ball far from the rail for the 5-ball by creating an angle by going rail first, by cheating the pocket on the 4-ball, and by using draw!

LESSON: Sometimes you need a small roll, like Van Boening did on the 4-8 billiard. But if you don't get one – and he didn't with that straight in shot – you must resist the urge to get angry and instead deal with the next shot as well as you can.

Chapter 16 - Make It Happen All-Stars   469

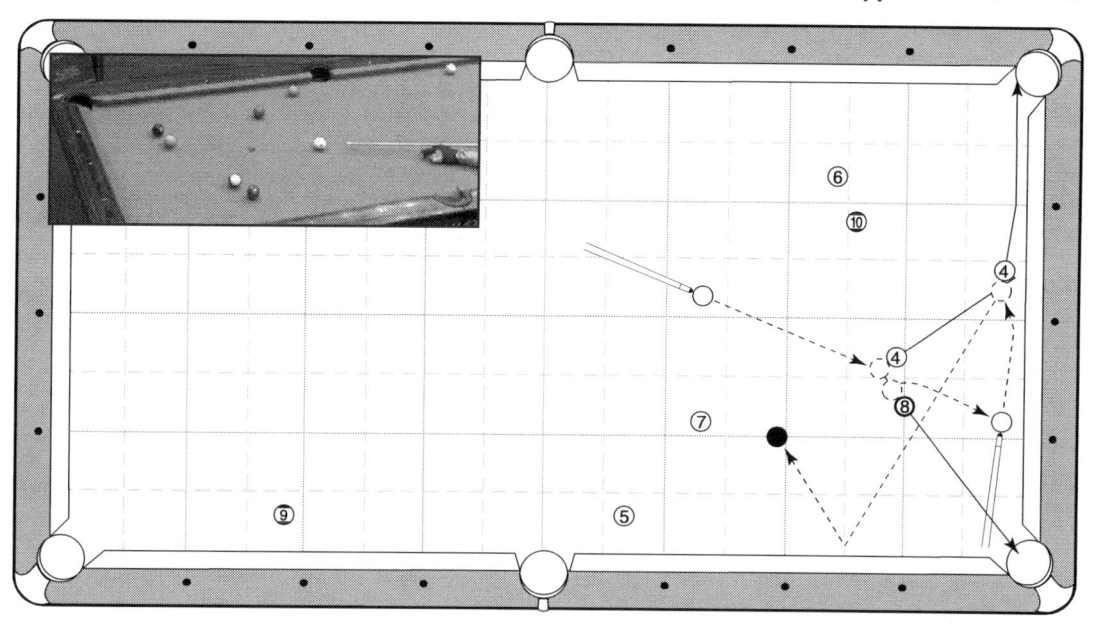

#2 – Dennis Orcollo (11) vs. Thorsten Hohmann (9)

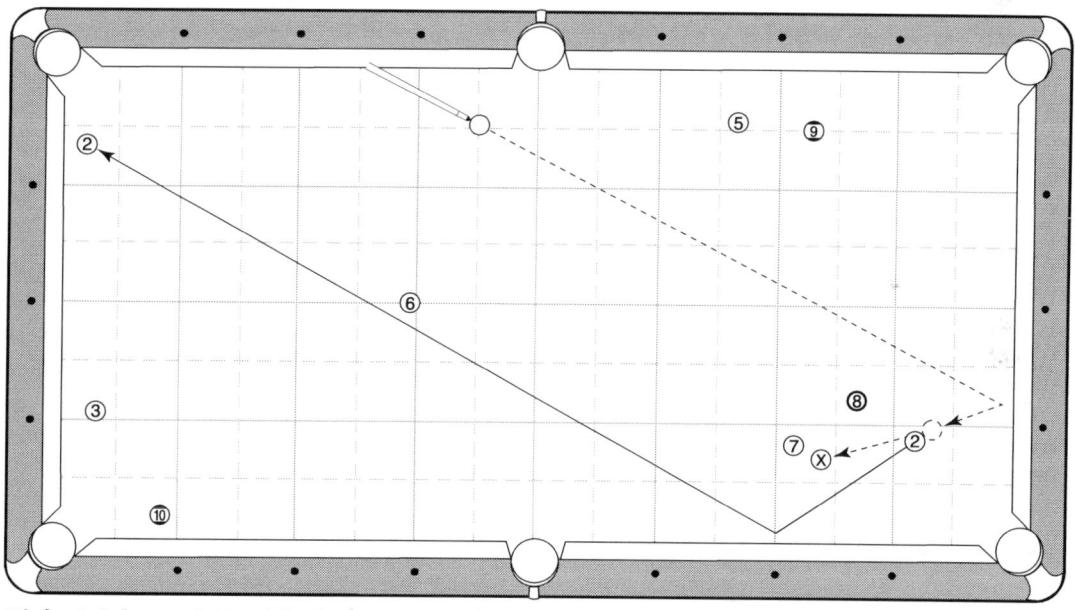

Kick, Stick, and Hook! (2/2 – 17:20)
Orcullo demonstrated the perils of the typical opening position play in a rack of 10 Ball when he tried to sidestep an obstructer while sending the cue ball around the table, hit the 5-ball in the face, and hooked himself. A kick from this distance is no sure thing, but the pros look at positions like this as an opportunity to play safe.

The 7 and 8 balls were not well spaced to act as a wall, but the odds were good that the cue ball would stop behind one of them if he made solid contact with the 2-ball, which he did. The cue ball crawled forward behind the 7-ball while the 2-ball relocated at the other end of the table.

LESSON: The odds of sticking the cue ball behind a blocker drop dramatically with every inch that the object ball's distance from the rail increases. In our example, the 2-ball is nine inches off the cushion, so Orcullo did well to get the result that he did.

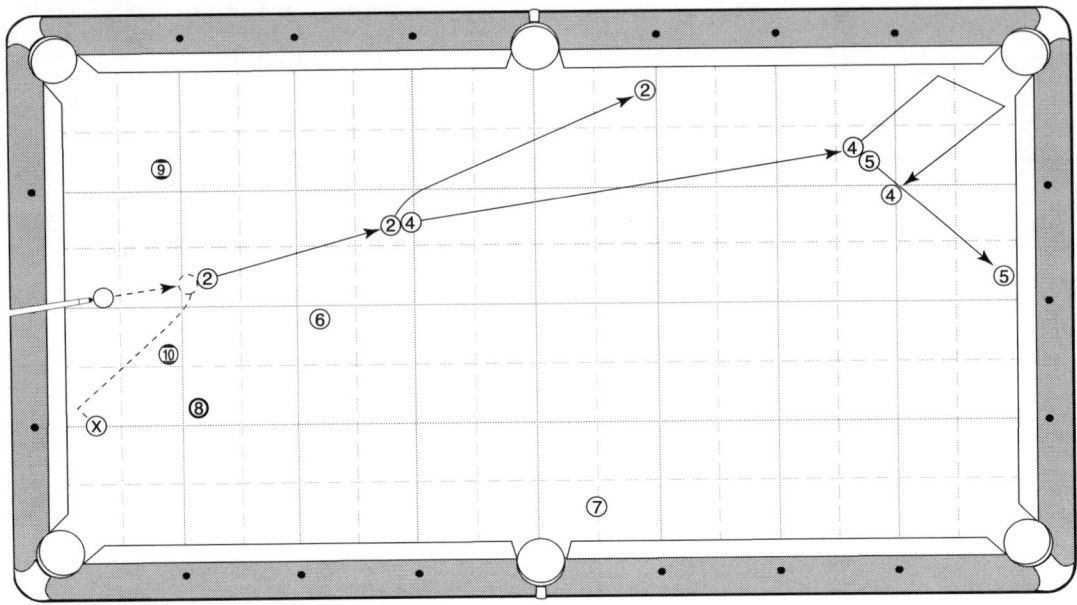

A Pinball Safety (2/5 – 39:00)

Hohmann attempted to get shape on the 2-ball into the upper left pocket, but he overran his position zone. After 65 seconds of study, he finally settled into his stance, then got back up for another quick look, and then returned to the execution phase of the shot cycle for this unusual but effective safety.

He comboed the 2-ball into the 4-ball, which then went down table into the 5-ball. The 2-ball stopped near the side rail while the other two balls came to rest on the opposite end. He drew back to the end rail, hooking Orcullo behind the 10-ball. If the 2-ball had traveled further down table, the 6-ball was ready for guard duty.

LESSON: The cue ball's route was important, but the big key was in controlling the other three balls, especially the 2-ball. It is impossible to predict the path of every ball – with a little bad luck he might have made the 4 or 7, and then there was a chance that the 2-ball would have followed into the side after hitting the 4! If he accidently made a ball, he would have still played a safety – on himself! In sum, there was a little luck to this shot – still, all in all this was a very creative and well played safety!

Great Opening Sequence!! (2/9 – 1:03:40)

Orcullo missed a long rail bank and left Hohmann with this long shot on the 1-ball. This shot dictates that he play the 2-ball into the lower left pocket. Position A would have been better, but he would have had to hit that 1-ball harder with outside english, or play a long distance two rail follow shot, upping the chances of a miss, so he accepted a long small angled cut shot on the 2-ball.

His shot on the 2-ball forced him to play a soft draw/stop shot for a long thin cut on the 3-ball. Notice that the cue ball drifted sideways about a foot. If it had gone much further he would have been hooked behind the 8-ball! Hohmann could play for this sequence because he is a super skilled and confident shotmaker. He naturally followed this up with a superb four rail position play to the 4-ball.

LESSON: Sometimes the balls dictate the pattern. It is then your job to follow the instructions the table has issued, and then to execute hard shots extremely well.

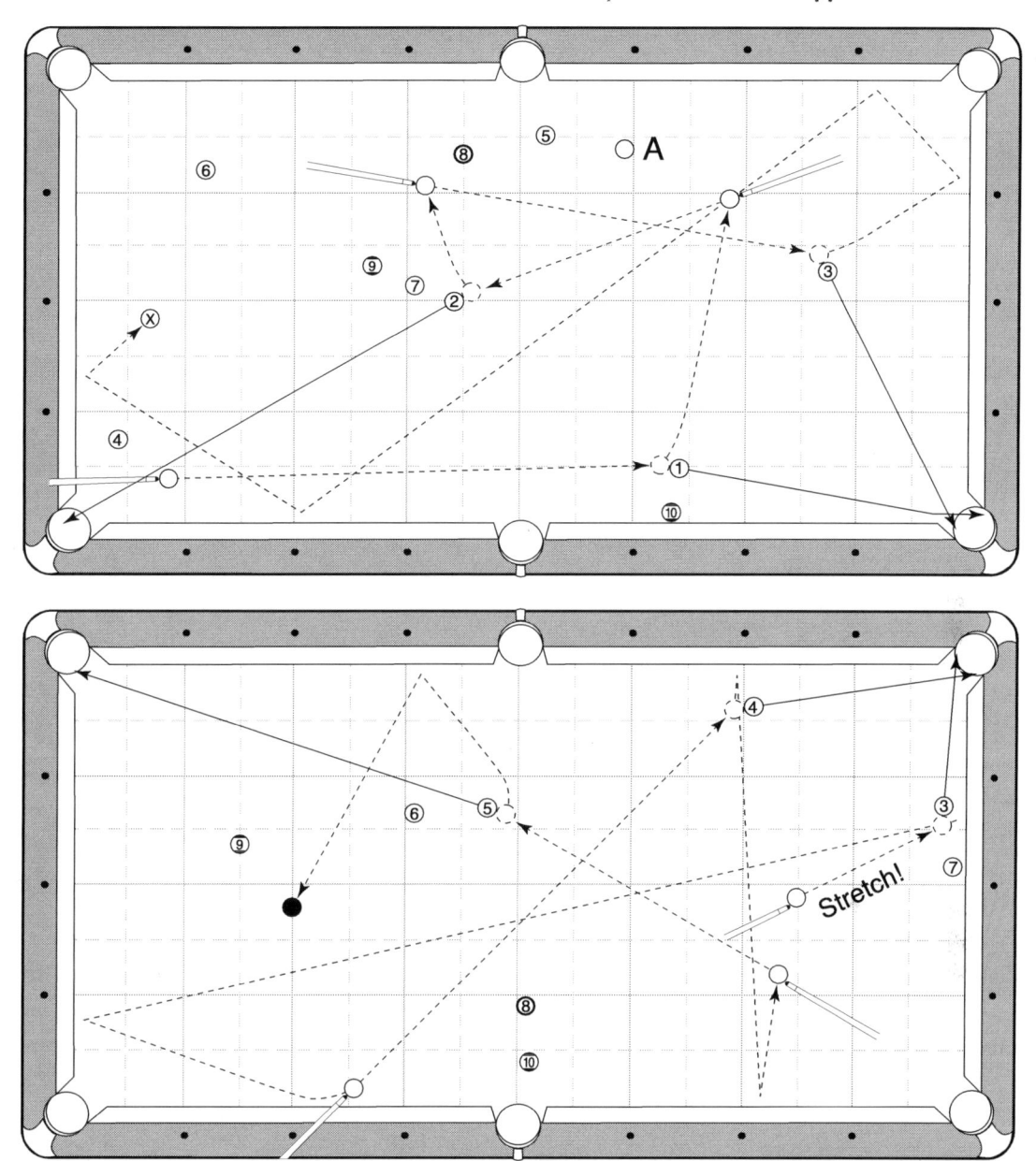

Middle of a Super Tough Run   (2/10 – 1:10:00)   **B-BCB: 6, 7, 8, 9, 10**

Hohmann had to stretch across the table for this 60 degree cut shot on the 3-ball. If the angle had been less severe, he would have used inside english for an easy shot on the 4-ball. However, he had to again accept less than ideal position so that he would be sure of pocketing the shot. The 5 and 6 balls also dictated that he send the cue ball down the opposite side of the table. The result was a long cross table cut on the 4-ball off of the rail. Hohmann used a four inch stroke with a super level cue to roll in the 4-ball for a long shot on the 5-ball. This time he had to play a long follow shot with inside english to get on the correct side of the 6-ball to go down table for the 7-ball on the end rail! The hard part is over, so it is your turn to close the deal!

LESSON: Some people deride 9 Ball and 10 Ball as pool by the numbers. In truth, planning and executing position plays and patterns is often anything but routine!

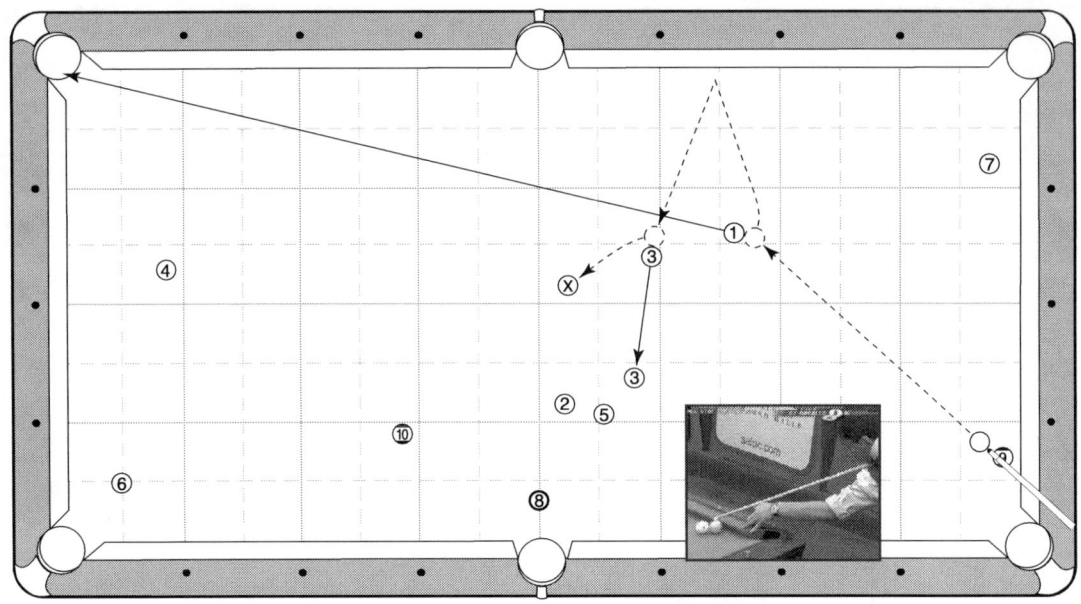

The Hardest Shot of All!!! (Diagram A – 2/12 – 1:20:00)

I watched over 4,500 shots of all types in doing my research for Book 2 on 10 Ball and this is, without a doubt, rates a 10 and is the toughest one of all. Let's see why.

The diagram tells part of the story – now I'll try to fill in the rest. For starters, the 1-ball is six feet from the pocket, and the cue ball is another three feet from the 1. In addition, this is a 30 degree cut, and the cue ball is only two inches off the rail.

Now it gets really interesting. The cue ball is right next to the 9-ball, so Orcollo has to jack up to about 30 degrees, use an awkward and short bridge, and develop sufficient power with a super short stroke. Accu-Stats zeroed in on the balls so I could measure his backstroke – it was only a three and a half inches long! The transition was unusually quick, and his cue went up and out of his bridge a split second after contact, and, after the cue ball had rolled about 15 inches, his cue was parallel with the table and a foot above it! In sum, he used a short, quick, precise, jabbing upstroke to make this shot! Finally, he had to control the cue ball for a shot on the 2-ball, which he managed to do despite bumping into the 3-ball.

LESSON: You never shoot certain shots like this in practice because you would be wasting your time trying to learn them. And yet, when they do appear in a game, you must find a way to make them – or hope that a good safety is available.

The Hardest Shot of All!!! (Diagram B – 2/12 – 1:21:40)   B-BCB: 4, 5, 7, 9, 10

We now pick up the action later in the rack with this 53 degree cut shot on the 4-ball. Orcullo had to stretch and roll the 4-ball in softly enough that the cue ball did not travel past his position zone for the 5-ball.

He used an open bridge, cued low, and deftly rolled the 4 in at pocket speed plus. His handling of the 4-ball increased his margin for error when playing to the 5-ball as the cue ball could have rolled another eight inches and he'd still have been fine.

LESSON: Using draw on thin cuts help many players in aiming the shot, and the draw spin transfers a little follow to the object ball, helping it to roll a couple of inches farther. This enables you use a softer stroke to contain the cue ball's roll.

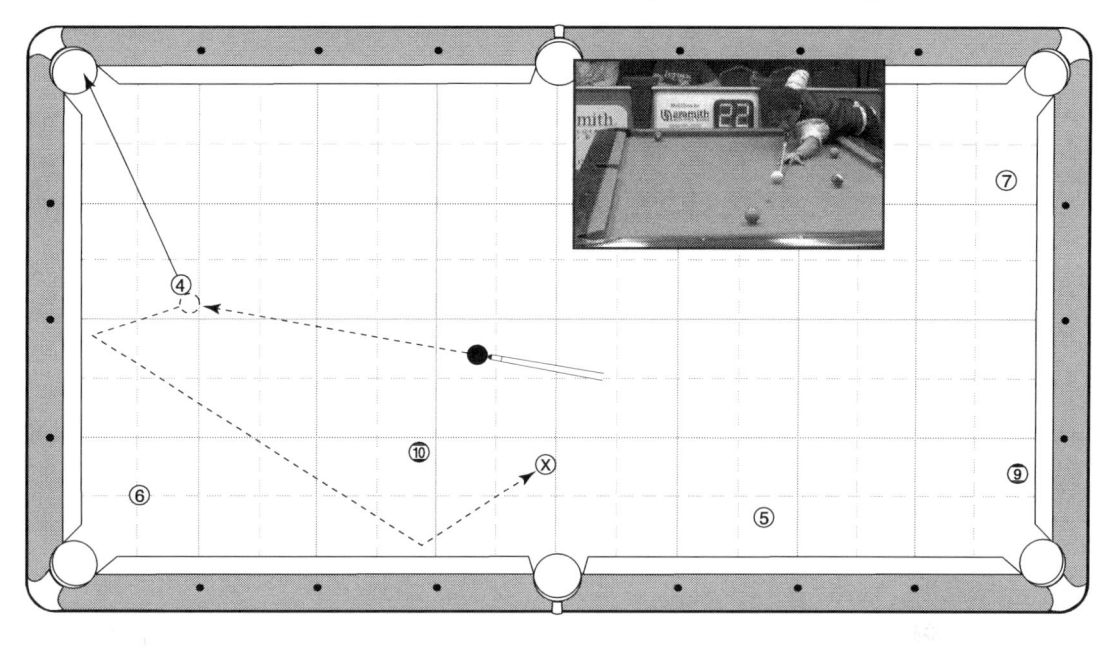

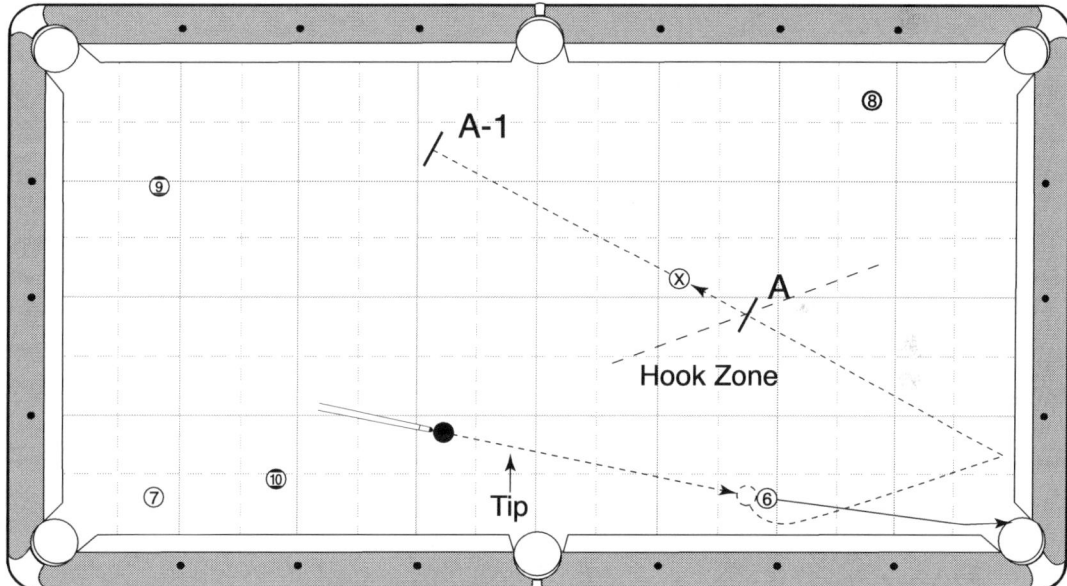

Power Follow Shot (2/14 – 1:29:40)   A-BCB: 6, 7, 8, 9, 10

Hohmann got too straight on the 5-ball and could not escape the rail, so he was forced to play a recovery route from the 6-ball to the 7. The 10-ball acted as a shadow ball, cutting out a big part of the potential zone for the 7-ball.

    Hohmann could play a pound/draw shot with a very hard stroke to escape the rail for shape on the 7, but that six degree cut elevated his chances of a miss. However, he chose to play a two rail follow shot to that huge zone from A to A-1 as it required only a medium hard (6) stroke, and was a more reliable path to the 7-ball. He used an open bridge, and his tip stopped opposite the side pocket!

LESSON: To use follow or draw, that is the question. The answers depends on which gives you the best chance to make the ball and get position – an advanced art of odd-smaking that is not always so easy to calculate just right.

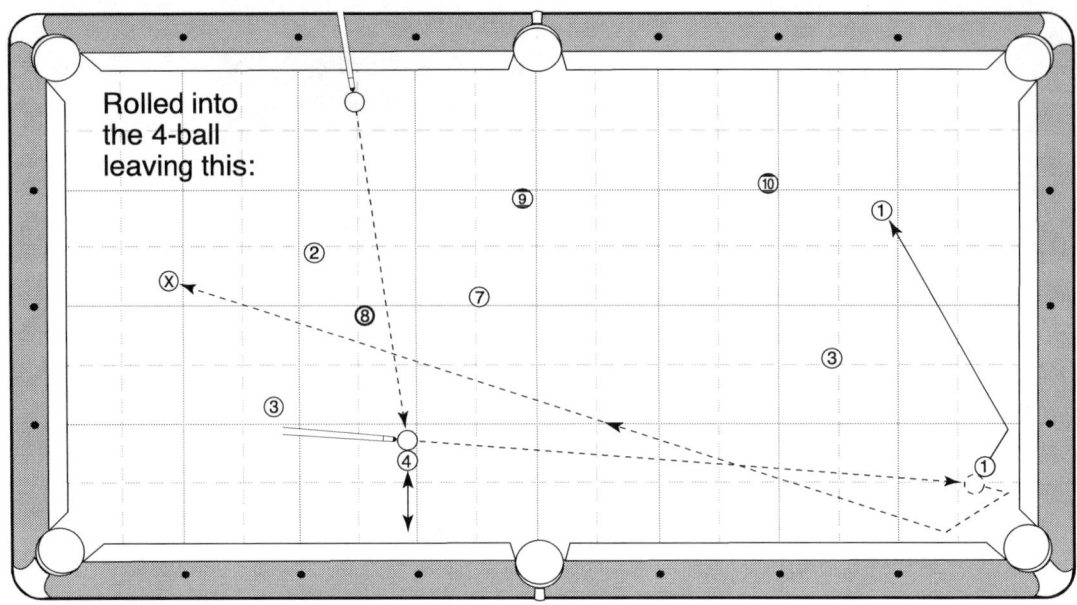

Bad Push to Textbook Safety   (2/15 – 1:32:20)
Hohmann was hooked after the break, so he chose to push out, leaving Orcollo with a direct path to the 1-ball. This safety might work against certain amateurs who do not know the response, or cannot play the safety that follows. But Orcollo is obviously a top pro, so he knew just what to do – accept the push and play the thin hit two rail safety shown above. Notice that he made good use of the 2-7-8 wall of blockers, which were ideally suited for such a maneuver.

So, what could Hohmann have done? First off, he should have known what was coming next, and so he should never have pushed next to the 4-ball. Then he should have devised another push, perhaps by rolling the cue ball gently into the 2-ball, setting up a two-rail kick shot that did not offer such a predictable result! Epilogue: Though Orcollo won this skirmish, Hohmann went on to win in seven innings.

LESSON: When pushing out, remember the 40-60 Rule. Never make it so easy that your opponent will jump at the shot, and do not make it so tough that they would not consider accepting the push out.

#3 – Dennis Orcollo (11) vs. Shane Van Boening (7)
Playing Perfect Pool   (3/3 – 16:30)
Dennis Orcollo made the hardest shot in this book. Now he's shown us the best cluster break. To get to the break he pocketed the 3, came off the rail and hit the 8-ball, which contained the cue ball's travels, resulting in perfect shape on the 4-ball.

His shape had to be perfect so he was able to draw and spin down the table for perfect position on the 5-ball to break that 6-10 cluster. Incardona said "I wouldn't be surprised to see him go into the balls right here," and I agree because that would have given him a much bigger target. Note: he did go on to run out!

LESSON: When you attempt to play super precise position to an extremely small zone – especially one that is this far away – you are gambling on your speed and directional control. But maybe it is not that big of a gamble when you have the skills to make it work. Besides, if he got on the other side of the 5-ball, he could have played safe!

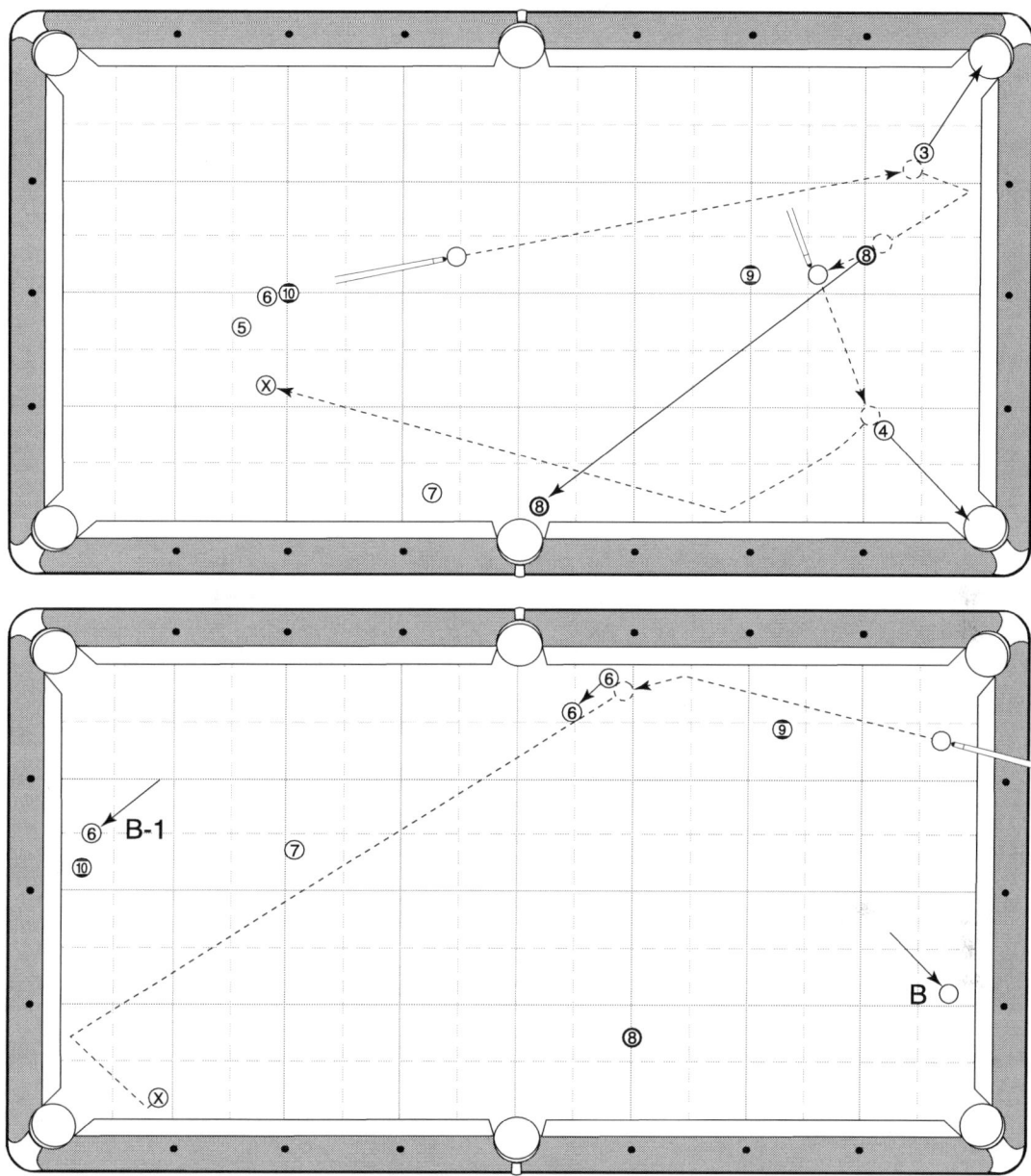

A Great Exchange: Kick and Safety (3/5 – 28:15)

Orcollo missed shape on the 6-ball, played safe, and left Van Boening behind the 6. He had three choices: 1) kick to the far end rail and back with the hope that he makes the 6 in the upper right pocket or gets lucky with the leave, 2) kick across the width of the table, and 3) a rail first safety. Options #1 and #2 have sellout plastered all over them, so he went with #3 even though he knew that this shot gave him no chance of hooking Orcollo. Van Boening elevated slightly, barely missed the 9-ball – which he needed to do to hit the 6 – and then followed the shot intently until well after contact. His speed was excellent as he left the cue ball near the side rail.

LESSON: Orcollo responded with a four rail bank on the 6-ball, sending it to Position B-1, while the cue ball stopped at Position B. Sometimes you must leave your opponent a shot, knowing that they have a chance for a strong reply. In amateur competition, Van Boening's shot is probably a sure winner!

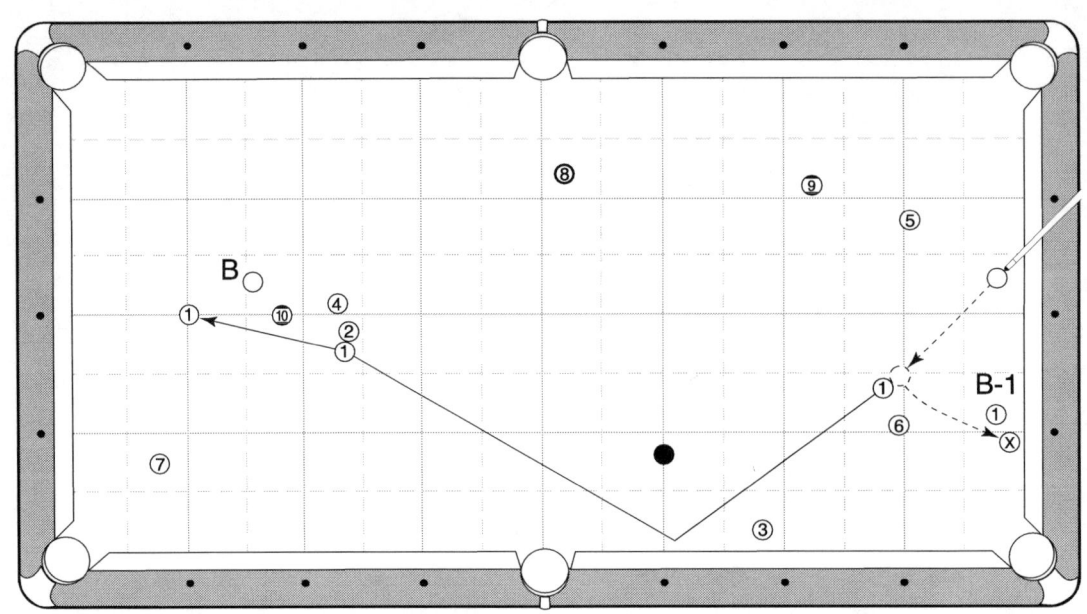

Multiple Objectives!   (3/8 – 38:20)   **B-BCB: 5, 6, 8, 9, 10**

After making a ball on the break, Van Boening played this beautiful safety on the 1-ball that resulted in a hook and a cluster break. (Note: The position of the 4-ball is after the break). He jacked up to about 20 degrees and used a precise jab-like draw stroke to pull the cue ball to the end rail behind the 6-ball. Meanwhile, the 1-ball banked off the side rail and softly nudged the 2-ball, separating it from the 4-ball. **LESSON:** Van Boening's tip recoiled slightly after contact. While this is not a good idea on most shots, this follow through apparently goes well with his jab like stroke.

Orcullo answered with a masse kick shot that curved around the 6-ball, hit the rail a diamond and a half from the lower left pocket, ran into the face of the 1-ball and left Van Boening with the cue ball in Position B, and the 1-ball in Position B-1!

LESSON: When you are playing a top pro, it is hard to ever feel secure, even after you've played a world class safety!

OBVIOUS CONCLUSION DEPARTMENT: It sure looks like fun playing these guys, doesn't it? Yeah, about as much fun as getting in the ring with Manny Pacquiao!

Fortune Favors the Bold!   (3/14 – 1:11:45)   **B-BCB: 6, 7, 8, 9, 10**

Orcullo played an excellent kick shot to leave Van Boening with this shot on the 4-ball – whatever it might be! At first glance it looks like an excellent opportunity to sell-out, but Van Boening turned this lemon into lemonade with this difficult cross table bank. The cue ball crossed the table for excellent position on the 5-ball AND the cue ball stopped behind the 8 and 9-balls. He used a medium speed (5), so there was no chance that the 4-ball would have bounced out of the hook zone if he had missed the shot. To recap, he made the shot, played position, and got a hook just in case he needed it.

As an alternative, he could have softly banked the 4-ball to his right and sent the cue ball to the side rail and off with the 7-ball as an obstructer between the balls.

LESSON: When the three objectives to a shot are making the ball, playing position, and playing safe, you better meet the first two, or the third one.

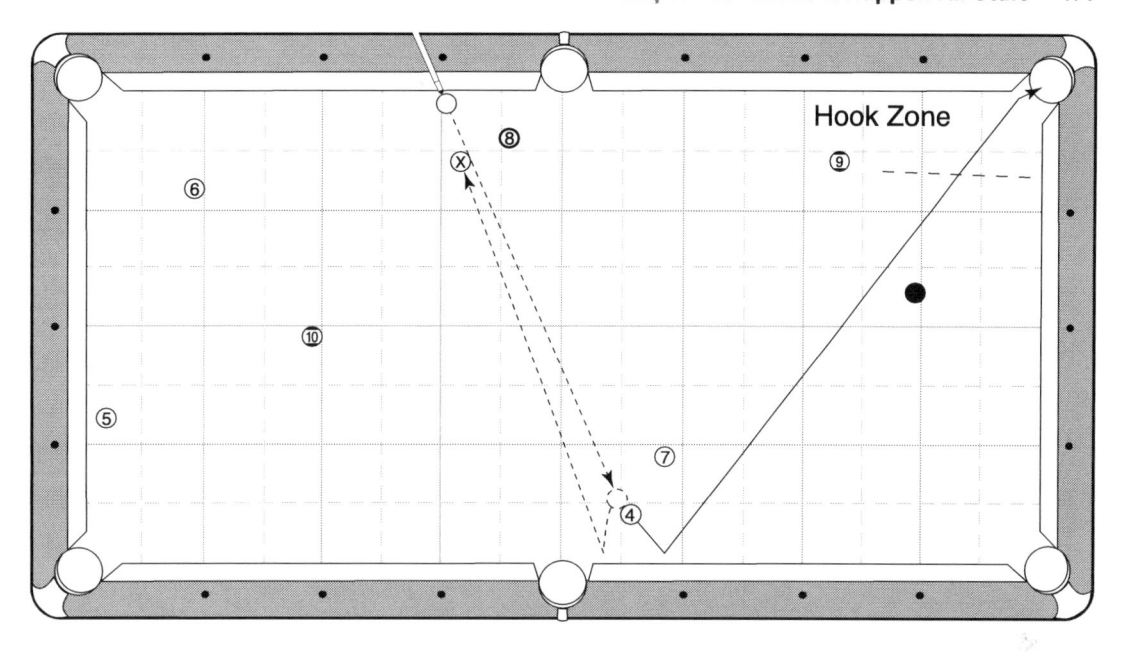

#4 – Darren Appleton (11) vs. Dennis Orcollo (8)

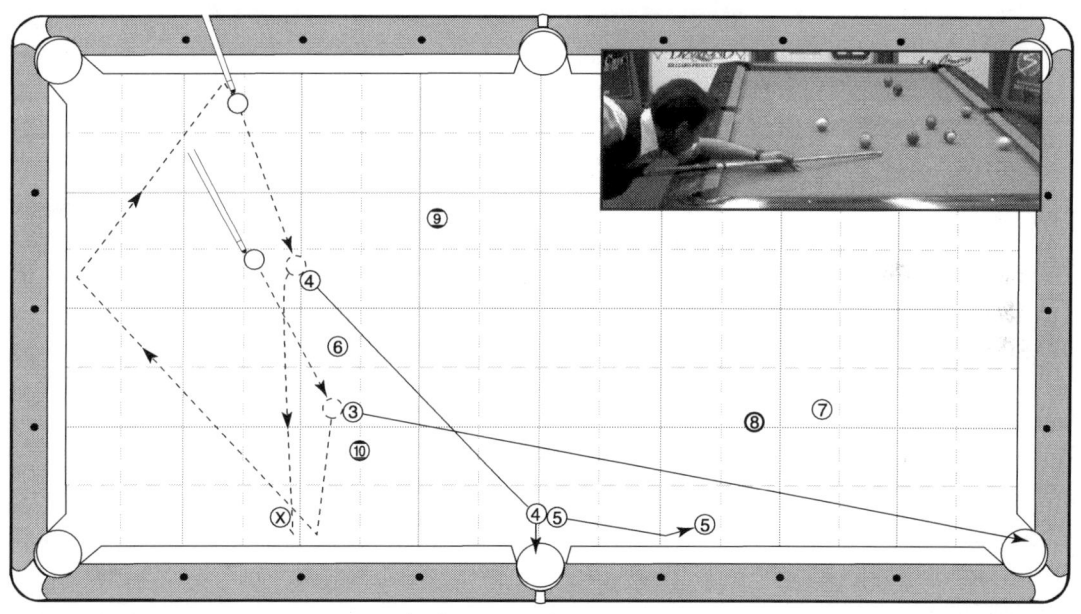

Spectacular Recovery Route (4/1 – 5:25)
Orcullo surveyed the table before playing the 2-ball to see where he wanted the cue ball for his shot on the 3-ball (in the lower right pocket), but the cue ball stopped a diamond short of his target. He was facing a lengthy 52 degree cut, but he split the pocket and got on the 4-ball. Orcollo took his stance before shooting the 3 for a quick look at the shot, got up, and then settled in for good. He then took 10 full seconds to complete his nine warmup stroke routine. On his next shot he softly caromed the 4 off the 5-ball setting up his next shot, and ran out.
LESSON: Orcollo went for the 3-ball because he is confident in his shotmaking, and pros hate to give up the table because most safeties, at this level, do not guarantee a win – they only avoid handing over the table on a miss, which could be instantly fatal.

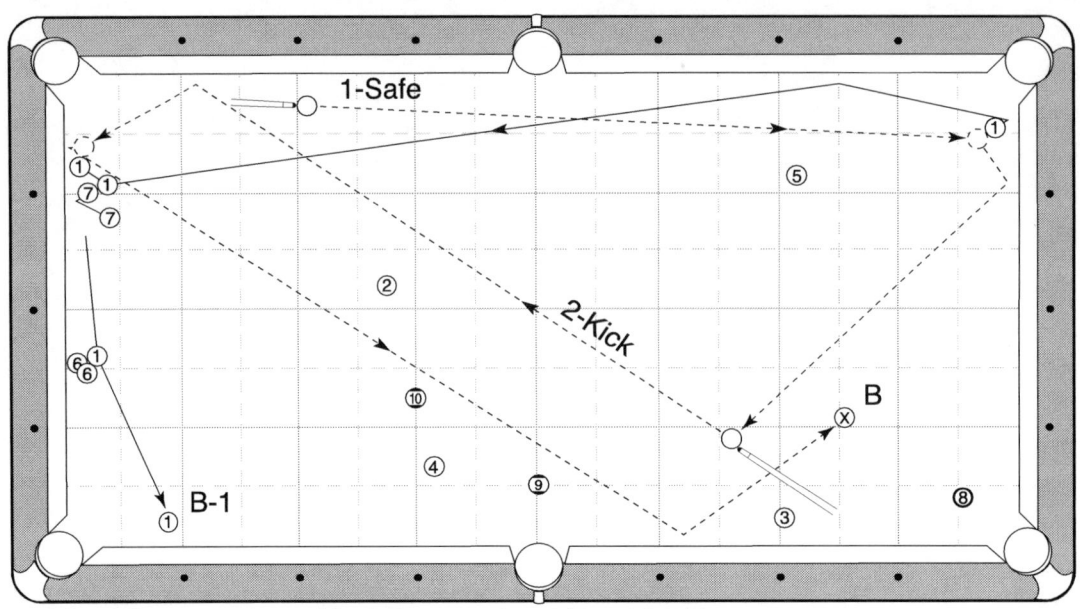

Hook and Counter-Hook! (Diagram A – 4/2 – 10:50)

Appleton overcut the 1-ball and left Orcollo with a long safety. He again got over the shot before his final routine (see the previous shot), and then skillfully banked the 1-ball to the opposite end rail while sending the cue ball behind a single ball, the 2. The 1-ball softly ran into the 7-ball, which now acted as added protection.

The balls told Appleton what to do: play a kick/safety off the side rail first and go for separation. The cue ball bounced off the side rail and hit the 1-ball first, knocking it across the table to Position B-1. The cue ball fortunately snuck between the 2 and 10 balls and ended up behind the 9 and 4 balls at Position B. If he had hit the second rail before the 1-ball, the 1 would have barely moved, and the cue ball might have rolled far down the table with the 2-ball and/or the 8-ball as blockers.

LESSON: When you are playing a long distance safety, it is better to have a wall of two or more balls to ensure a hook. When you only have one ball, as Orcollo did, your execution needs to be especially good.

Precision Long Range Draw! (Diagram B – 4/2 – 13:30)   C-BCB: 6, 7, 8, 9, 10

Appleton needed to use the 4-ball to set up the 5-ball so he could send the cue ball six diamonds down the table to between the 6 and 7 balls! He chose to cut the 4-ball to the left because that made it easier to control his route to the 5-ball. He used a soft draw shot and sent the cue ball a few inches inside of the stun line to the 5!

Proof that he got the perfect angle on the 5-ball was provided by his position play to the 6-ball. He made that 18 degree cut using a low/outside draw and run shot. The angle opened up off the side rail, and the draw/spin combo propelled the cue ball to Perfect Position. A++! Now, study his angle on the 5-ball and try to imagine how the shot would have played if the cue ball was 2-3 inches to the left or right!

LESSON: Appleton was kind enough to share one of his planning techniques with us when he positioned his cue in line with several angles on the 5-ball while deciding which one was best to get to the 6-ball. Pool is a very visual game, and the pros like to use their cues as a visual aide – and so should you!

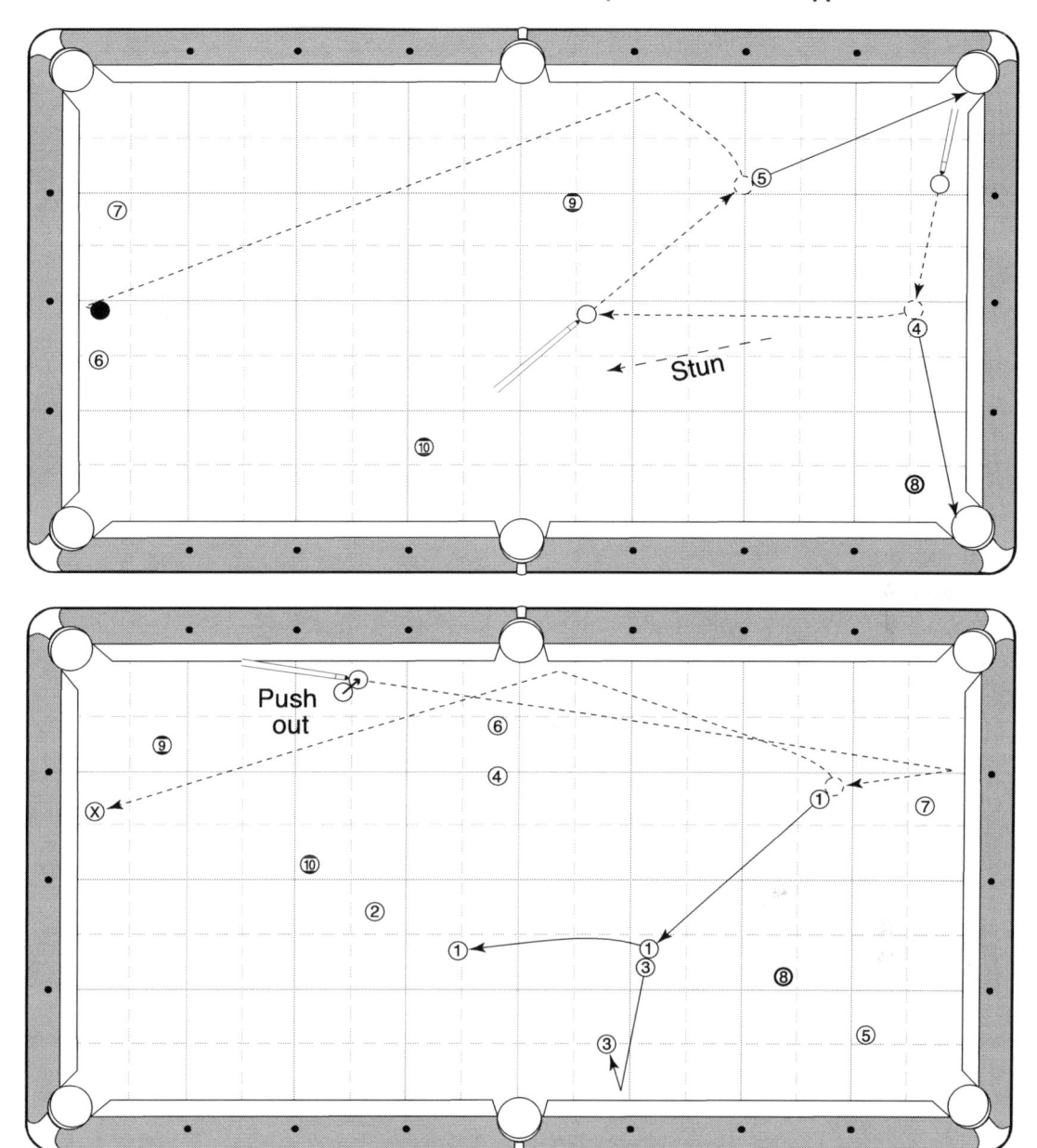

The One Inch Push Out (Diagram A – 4/3 – 16:50)

Appleton failed to make a ball on the break, but left Orcollo hooked behind the 6-ball. He studied the layout for about 35 seconds before tapping the cue ball an inch. He was still hooked, but at least he could now kick for the 1-ball, which was out in the open, without having to use left english – which, at this distance, is not easy. Appleton refused the shot, as expected. Orcollo used a medium follow stroke (5) and no english, hit the 1-ball, and left his opponent with a kick to the end rail. After Appleton missed the 1-ball, Orcollo took ball-in-hand and ran out.

LESSON: On my Spectrum of Speeds, 1.0 is extremely soft. A ball rolled at this speed will go about 10 inches. Tapping a ball an inch must be about .1! The point is that on certain pushouts you must be able to roll the cue ball a very short and precise distance – just as Orcollo did.

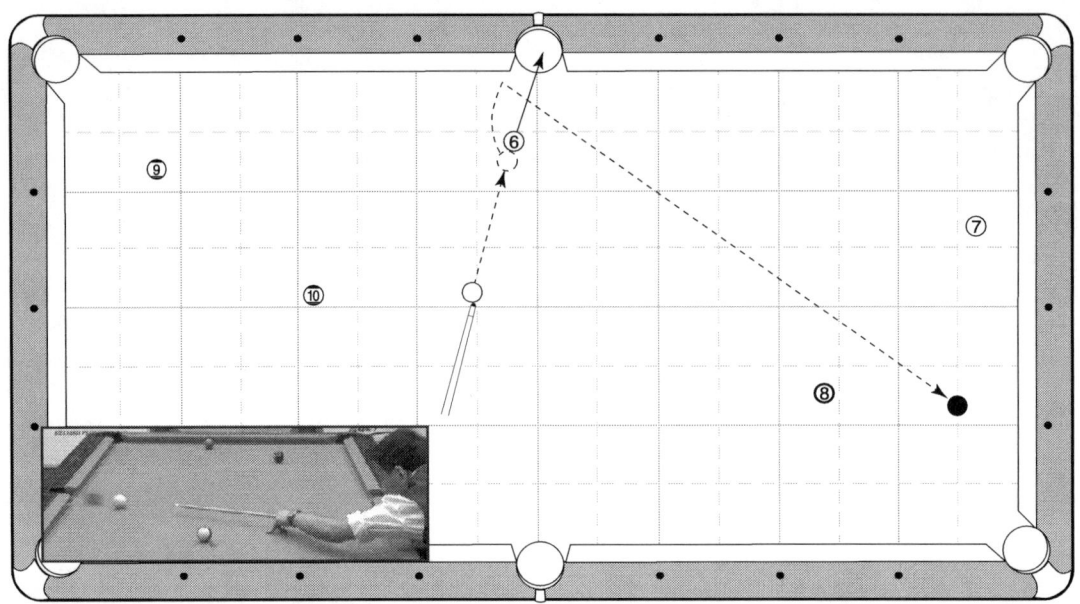

Wrong Side Position Play (Diagram B – 4/3 – 21:05)   C-BCB: 7, 8, 9, 10

This layout is a continuation of the one above in which Orcollo earned ball-in-hand with his maneuvers. When playing shape on the 6-ball, the cue ball stopped a few inches short of the correct side – he wanted to cut the 6 to the left, not the right!

Orcollo uses a short stroke on most shots, but on this one he took his cue back 10 inches, elevated his cue slightly, applied a ton of follow AND right english to the cue ball with a medium hard stroke (6), and forced the cue ball off its natural path – across and down for the 7-ball.

LESSON: The inside english super spin recovery route; is not a shot that you would purposefully play for, any more than Tiger Woods would want to play a shot from a sand trap. But when you have played yourself into an awkward position, it is nice to be able to have a shot like this waiting in your bag of tricks.

Play that Combo! (4/6 – 35:40)   C-BCB: 6, 7, 9, 10

Appleton had ball-in-hand and a problem in need of an answer. He had to get on the 4-ball next, but the 7-ball was covering up a big part of the position zone and the 5-ball prevented him from playing the 1-ball in the bottom side pocket – or did it?

It the 5-ball could have magically been turned into the 1-ball, he could have played it and gained access to the 4. After a minute of study, Appleton was satisfied with his solution – play a combination and replace the 5-ball with the 1-ball! He carefully lined up the cue ball with the 1-ball and the 5-ball and softly rolled the 1 into the 5. The 1-ball then took its place in front of the side pocket, and Appleton moments later sank the 10-ball.

The key to this shot was to send the 1-ball directly into the 5 so that it would die in front of the pocket. He placed the cue ball close enough to the 1-ball for extreme accuracy, and yet far enough away so that he could see the line for all three balls! He used a very soft (2) to extremely soft (1) stroke and a two inch tap stroke!

LESSON: Pool players must think outside the box so here's another solution: Shoot the 1-ball in the lower right corner and billiard the 5-ball in the middle to left side of the pocket. If you hit the 5 or barely miss long, you will have position on the 4-ball!

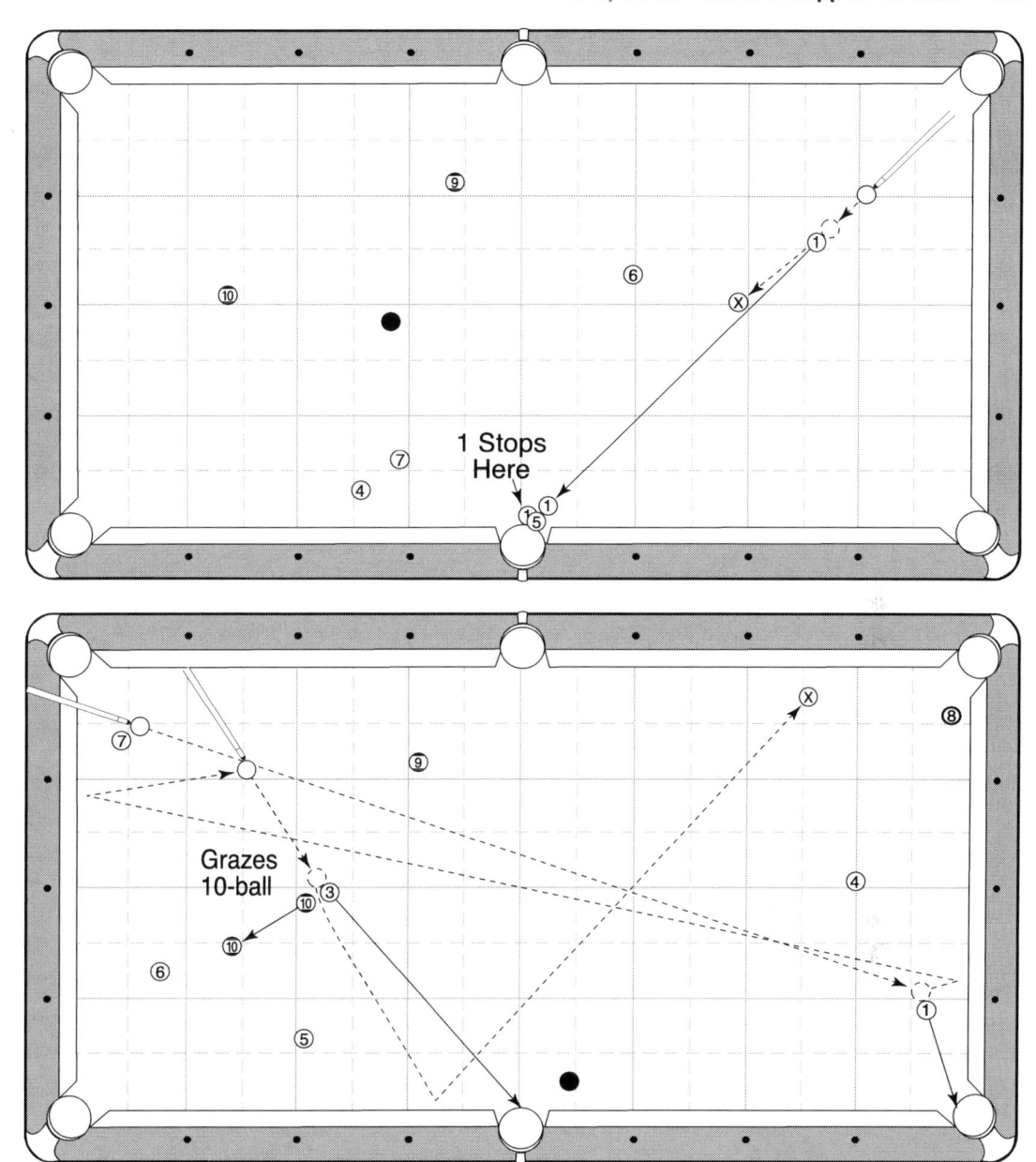

Super Strong Opening (4/9 – 51:20) B-BCB: 5, 6, 7, 8, 9, 10

Appleton opened this break and run with a table length cut on the 1-ball that was a shining example of natural position (Principle #14) – that is, basically make the ball with good speed and you will have shape on the next shot. Before preparing to get down into his stance, he stroked his cue seven times in midair, perhaps in an effort to loosen up his shooting arm for the upcoming shot!

The cue ball traveled 124 inches after contact, about 6 inches too far – putting him on the wrong side of the 3-ball. But his follow shot on the 3-ball grazed off the left side of the 10-ball, and redirected the cue ball into contact further up the side rail. This new path enabled it to continue across and down the table to the 4-ball.

LESSON: The wrong side of a ball can turn out all right if you can change the cue ball's path by sending it off the side of an intervening object ball.

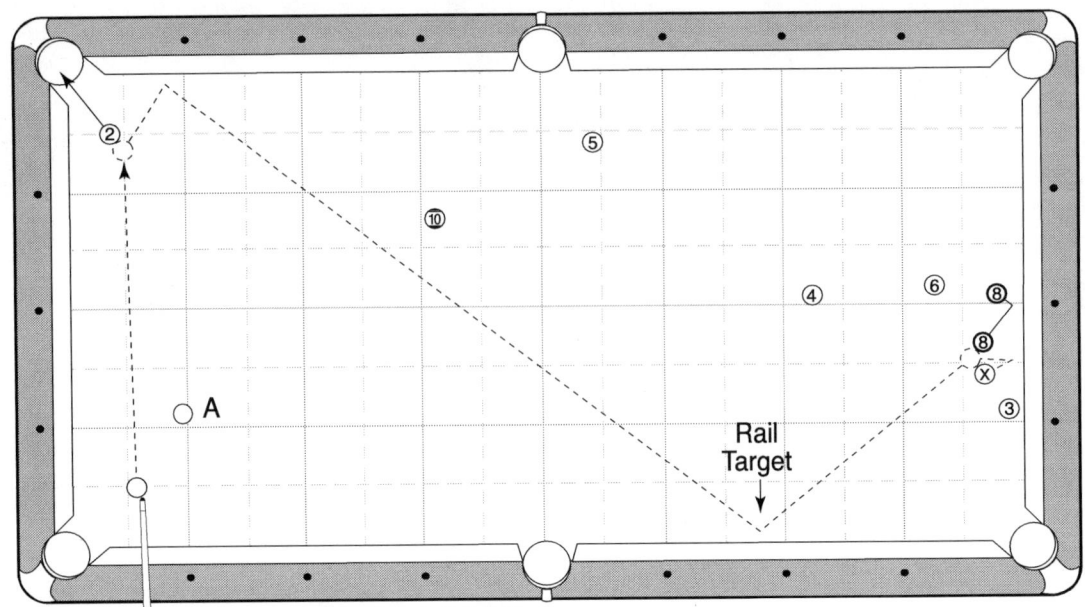

Setting a Rail Target! (4/11 – 1:07:00)

Orcollo played an intentional foul, sending the 8-ball up close to the 3-ball from a long distance. Appleton then took over with ball-in-hand, made the 1-ball and a 2-9 combo, leaving himself with this shot on the 2-ball.

While plotting his journey to the 3-ball he pointed to his rail target (Principle #16) as shown. If he could send the cue ball off this rail, he stood a good chance of getting on the 3-ball. He again used his cue as a pointer while planning his route from one side rail to the middle of the next, and down for the 3-ball.

Appleton applied a liberal dose of right english to the cue ball and sent it across and down the table, hitting the rail within an inch of his target. He got a little thin on the 3-ball, which hurt his efforts to get on the 4-ball, which he missed from Position A.

LESSON: Most of the shots in these chapters on 10 Ball are part of a winning effort, but the planning that went into his shot on the 2-ball was too good to pass up. Besides, there is something to be learned from our near success. On this shot, imagine the outcome if the cue ball had hit the 8-ball a hair fuller? It would have died near the 3-ball with a much smaller angle, and he would have likely run out.

Winning Won Games! (4/12 – 1:12:10)   C-BCB: 7, 8, 9, 10

Appleton was cruising to the finish line when he got poor position on the 6-ball and ended up a little thin on the 7-ball, but he recovered well and finished off this game.

Indeed, when a rack gets to a position like this, it is a Won Game – one that you have marked on your side (mentally) because you believe that it is yours. And it should be considering that the hardest work has almost certainly been completed.

His speed was excellent in crossing the table and out for the 8-ball, and he used that angle on the 8 to go two rails and out for yet another very playable angle on the 9-ball. He then sent the cue ball across the table for great shape on the 10-ball.

LESSON: Yogi Berra, the great Yankee catcher and sports philosopher, once said that "It ain't over till it's over." And so that is part of the purpose of these Black Cue Ball exercises – to give you practice in closing and in the Art of Winning Won Games.

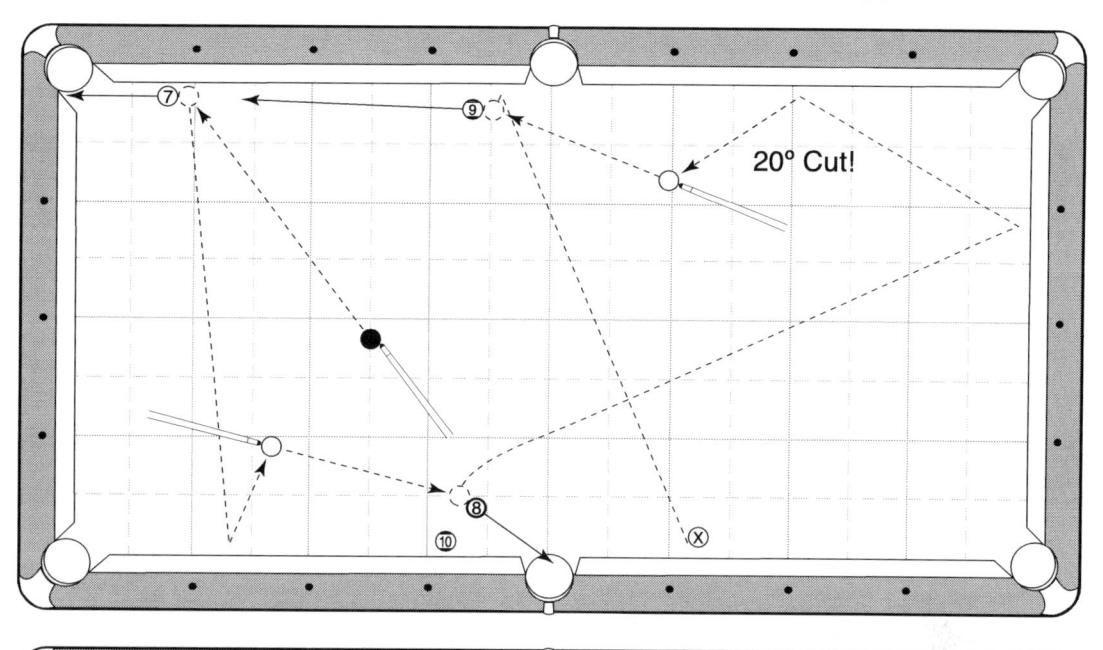

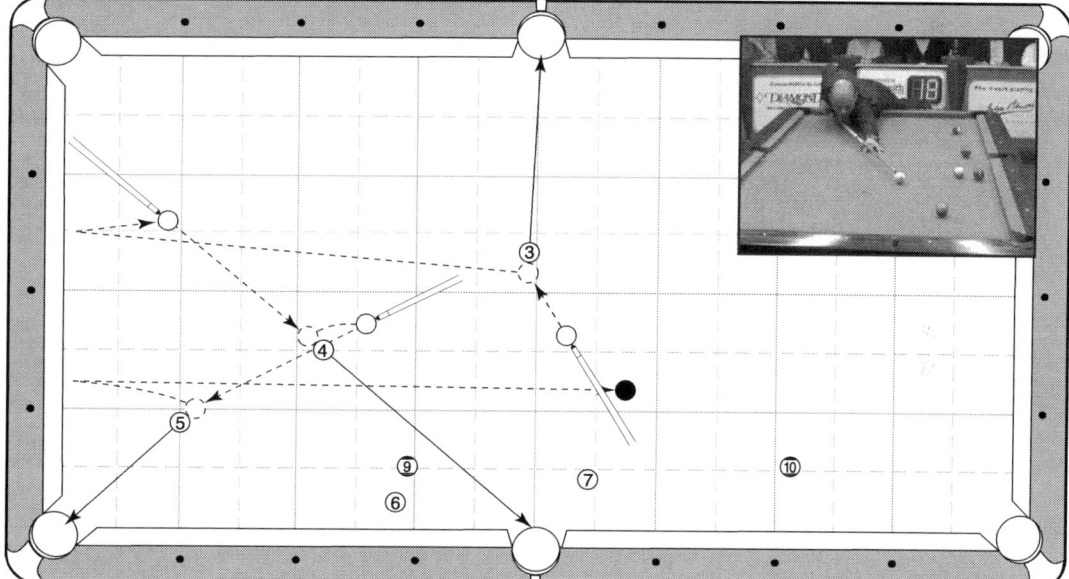

Setting Up the Key Shot! (4/17 – 1:51:40)   C-BCB: 6, 7, 9, 10

The keys to this mid-rack pattern are precision planning and execution. Appleton played for this cut angle on the 3-ball so that he could get to the 4-ball in the side. When you see a route to a shot in the side at and it works out so well, there is a tendency to dismiss it as no big deal. But it was huge – because most players would never think of playing shape for a side pocket with the ball in this position, and if they did, they would not have the speed control to pull it off.

Appleton got nearly straight in on the 4-ball, which enabled him to play a stop shot for the 5-ball. He screwed on his extender, stretched out, rolled in the 5-ball, and came out for the 6-ball. The 6 was the trouble ball in this pattern, and all of his work on the 2, 3, and 4 balls was a big set up for his route from the 5-ball to the 6!

LESSON: The ability to plan and execute complex mid rack patterns is a skill that can be learned, and that can enable you to distance yourself from your peers.

#5 – Shane Van Boening (11) vs. Darren Appleton (5)

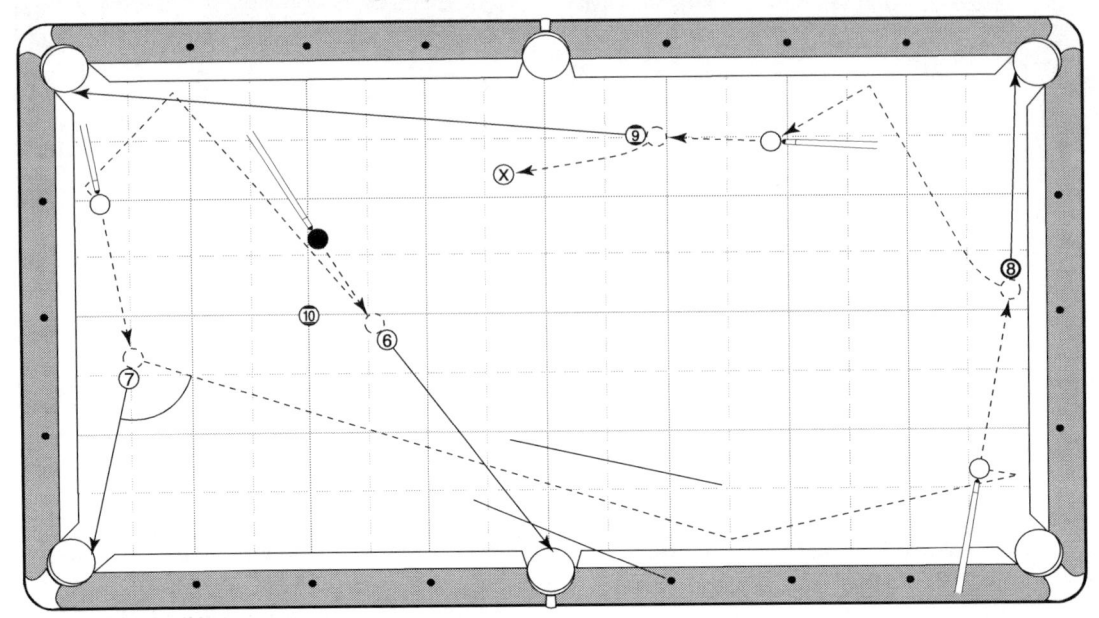

Classic Side Rail Stun Shot   (5/1 – 05:45)   A-BCB: 6, 7, 8, 9, 10

Van Boening opened up this impressive five ball closing sequence by fearlessly spearing the 6-ball into the side and drawing two rails for the 7-ball. He is a man of many strokes, and on this shot his cue recoiled about three inches after contact. Furthermore, his cue was still on the table when the cue ball rolled past it, so the recoil was obviously not to get his stick out of the way of the returning cue ball. I have never used this technique, but he does, so it might be worth a try.

He has a 27 degree cut on the 7-ball, which is within the ideal range (not too thin or thick) for playing a long distance stun shot with great precision. He needs to send the cue ball down the length of the table and avoid the side and corner pockets. The lines show the gap between the pockets, and how the cue ball went down the middle of it! Now it's your turn, starting with the 6-ball.

LESSON: You may know that the cue ball takes off down the tangent line after contact, but can you accurately line up that path at a 90-degree angle to the object ball's path to the pocket? If you can, then you can plan, and execute, precise stun shots like this one!

Long Range Recovery Route   (5/7 – 35:15)

Appleton slopped in a ball on a kick shot and was left with a shot on the 2-ball that called for the use of a mechanical bridge. When you are using a bridge over a ball from long range, there is a tendency that the shot will not come out exactly as planned – and it didn't as the cue ball stopped about 15 inches short of ideal shape. Position A would have enabled him to play a simple follow shot for the 4-ball, but now he had to play a tough recovery shot/route to the 4-ball, which he did!

LESSON: Appleton had to come up with a long range shot on the 3-ball with an unfamiliar Shot Picture, and he was jacked up over the 10-ball! The ability to draw upon your memory bank and to see the less common shots well enough to make them is a sure sign that you are becoming a confident and capable shotmaker.

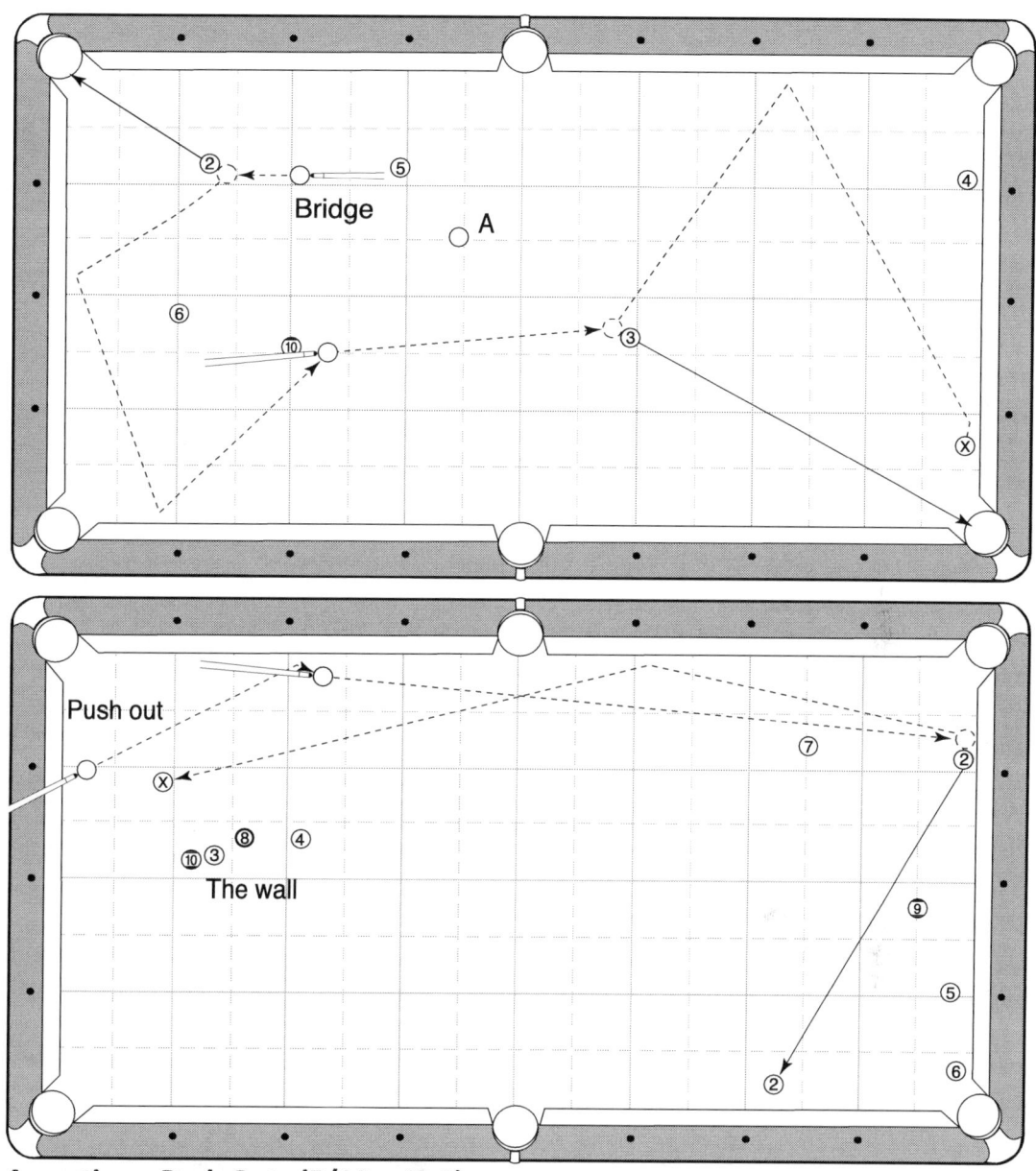

Accepting a Push Out (5/10 – 48:0)

Appleton made a ball on the break but the 7-ball stood between him and the 2-ball, so he pushed out as shown. Most amateurs should let the pusher shoot in this position, but Van Boening knows the moves and has the skill to execute them. In this case, he predictably hit the 2-ball thinly and sent the cue ball to the opposite end of the table behind that fortress of blockers. Appleton missed the kick and Van Boening got ball-in-hand and proceeded to runout, making that push look even worse.

Appleton could have pushed directly towards the 7-ball and set up a kick on the 2-ball. This may also not turn out well, but it could have been better than pushing to a hook safety.

LESSON: As I've said, Van Boening is a master at hitting balls thinly from long range. It is Appleton's duty (and yours) to know, and remember your opponent's strengths. So, if he'd thought about Van Boening's skill set, and had considered what he might do from where he pushed to, he would have surely chosen another place to push to!

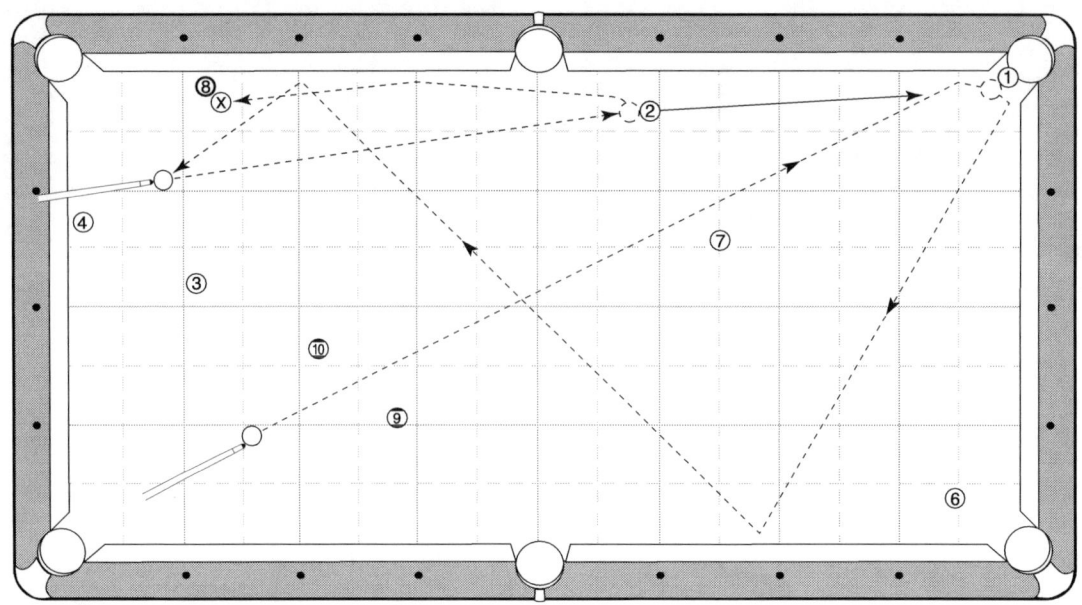

Big Draw Leads to a B&R   (5/12 – 56:20)
Van Boening had just broken the balls and was faced with the daunting task of getting on the 2-ball so that he could then can come back down table for the 3. The 7-ball blocked a direct hit on the 1-ball, preventing him from cutting it thinly on the right side and playing one rail shape.

He was forced to play rail first on the 1-ball, which did offer the chance for position in that zone surrounding the arrow. Then he could have drawn across the table and past the 9-ball, on either side of it, for shape on the 3-ball. However, the cue ball traveled far down the table. But this was no problem as he unleashed his power draw stroke and brought the cue ball back to Position X. As an aside, in freeze frame you can see that his tip struck the cue ball one tip below center – enough for decisive draw spin, but not so low as to risk a miscue!

LESSON: The cue ball tends to run long, often very long (as in this example) on position plays off of a pocket hanger. The trouble is that the cure – trying to get ideal shape – could result in your coming up very short, and ending up with no shot!

Power Follow Past an Obstructer   (5/13 – 1:01:45)   C-BCB: 5, 6, 7, 8, 10
Appleton has just had his turn playing shape off a hanger (see above) and he also ended up with less than perfect position. Now he faced a recovery route that had several difficulty factors: 1) The cut was only 7 degrees, which made it hard to get the cue ball across the table, 2) he was shooting down the rail with a very hard (7) follow stroke, so the pocket played smaller, and 3) the 8-ball was in the way of his cue.

After staring down the aiming line for 30 seconds while pondering this shot, he then landed on the table and uncorked this gem of a position play!

LESSON: When the cue ball is going past another ball after contact while on its way to the first rail, you must determine if it can pass that potential obstructer – or not! In this position the cue ball took off to the left down the tangent line after contact before the top spin caused it to swing back to the right, barely missing the 7-ball.

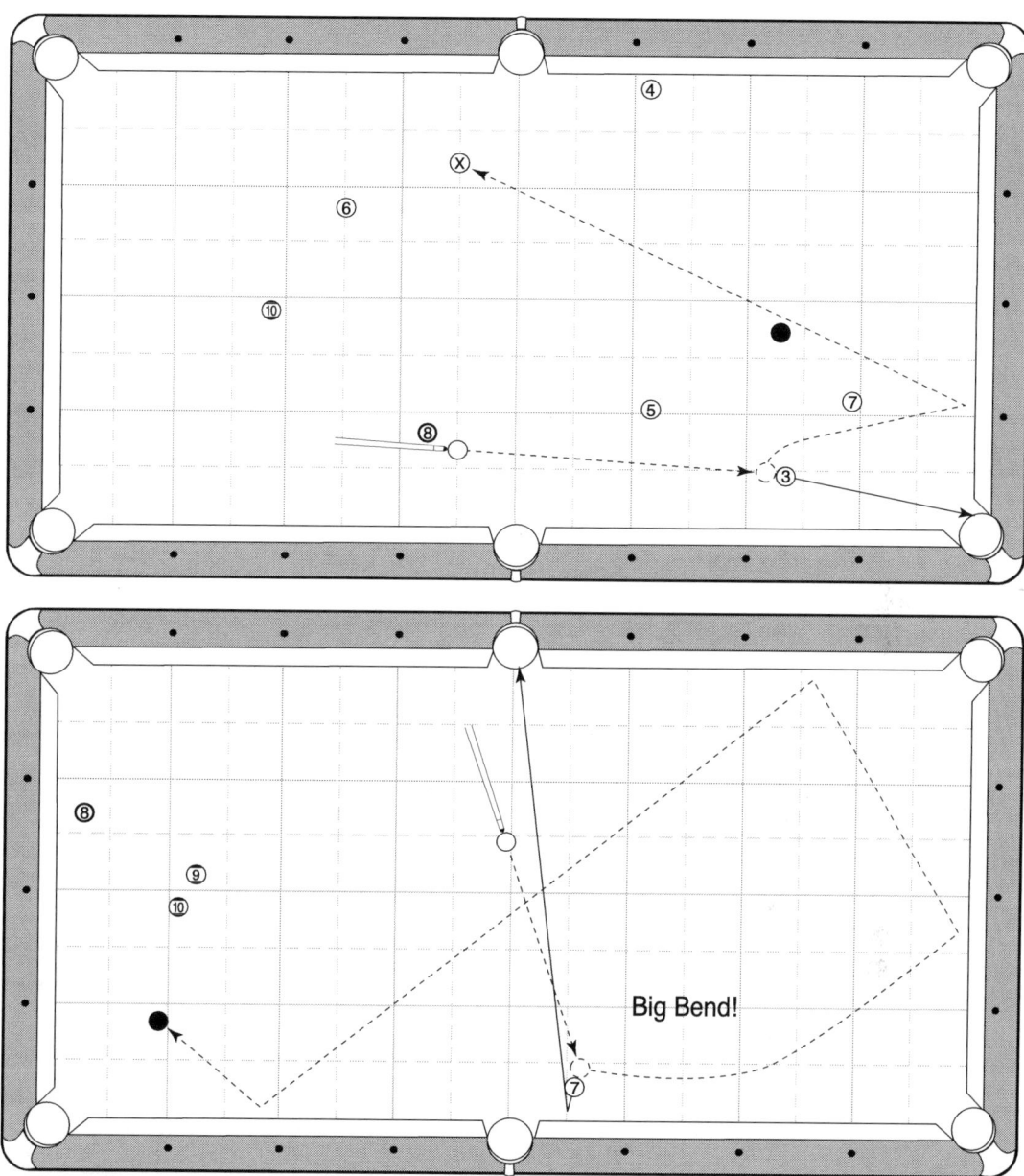

Super Draw/Bender Shot (5/15 – 1:12:25) C-BCB: 8, 9, 10

I studied the path of Van Boening's position play from the 6-ball to the 7 (which followed the line in the illustration) I have no idea what he was trying to do. But he covered his position play error with this spectacular draw/bender shot in which the cue ball started off to the right of the lower right pocket after contact, then swung radically to the left and hit near the middle diamond on the end rail before traveling to the opposite end of the table for ideal shape on the 8-ball!

What else could he have done? Draw off the other side of the 7-ball and try to get behind the 9 and 10 balls? I wouldn't want to have to play that shot. Any ideas?
LESSON: The natural inclination of most players in this situation would be to use follow and hit the side rail first after contact, but this would bring a scratch in the lower left corner into play. Van Boeing's route had a large margin for error as shown by the cue ball's path, which took it into the second diamond on the side rail.

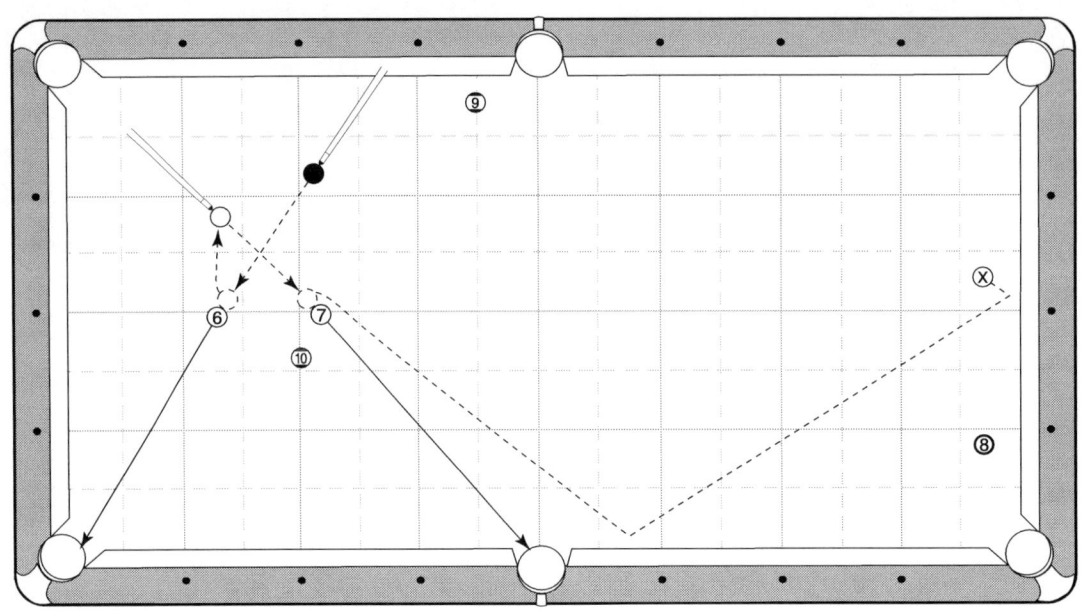

Setting Up the Angle (5/16 – 1:16:35)   B-BCB: 6, 7, 8, 9, 10

I have been emphasizing repeatedly that there is often one shot on which it is crucial that you get the correct angle, and that the preceding shot, or series of shots, is designed to set up that key position play. Well, here is another one.

Van Boening has just played a long cross table route to the 6-ball, so it is time to plan how he can use that ball to set up the angle that he needs to go down the table for the 8-ball. He has three choices: 1) follow six inches and play the 7-ball in the upper right pocket, 2) draw three inches and play in the 7 lower right pocket, and 3) draw about eight inches and play the 7-ball in the side. The side pocket is closer than the corners but, at this angle, it plays smaller.

Van Boening walked over to where his line was for the next shot and tapped his cue where he planned for the cue ball to stop. He smoothly followed through on this precision draw shot (no recoil this time), got good shape on the 7-ball, and ran out.

LESSON: On patterns with several choices, you have the luxury of choosing the sequence that plays to your strengths, and/or avoids a weakness. You may also be able to build a Plan B into your selection. For example, if you intended to play for the side like Van Boening, but came up short, you would still have a shot in the far corner! When practicing this close, I suggest that you try all three pockets.

#6 – Darren Appleton (11) vs. Thorsten Hohmann (8)
Pattern to a Safety (6/2 – 14:05)

Hohmann failed to make a ball on the break, so Appleton went to work on a run out – to a safety. After making the 1-ball, he had this shot on the 2, which was used to set up the 3-ball for a superb two rail route to the 4-ball for excellent shape for a safety. He could have ended up with a few different options for a safety, but the one he ended up with looks like the best one. It certainly passed the Results Test, which is administered on the next shot. Notice that he was in position to play a simple but highly effective soft (2) follow shot that tied Hohmann up in knots. After he failed to hit the 4-ball, Appleton took ball-in-hand and completed his win in two acts!

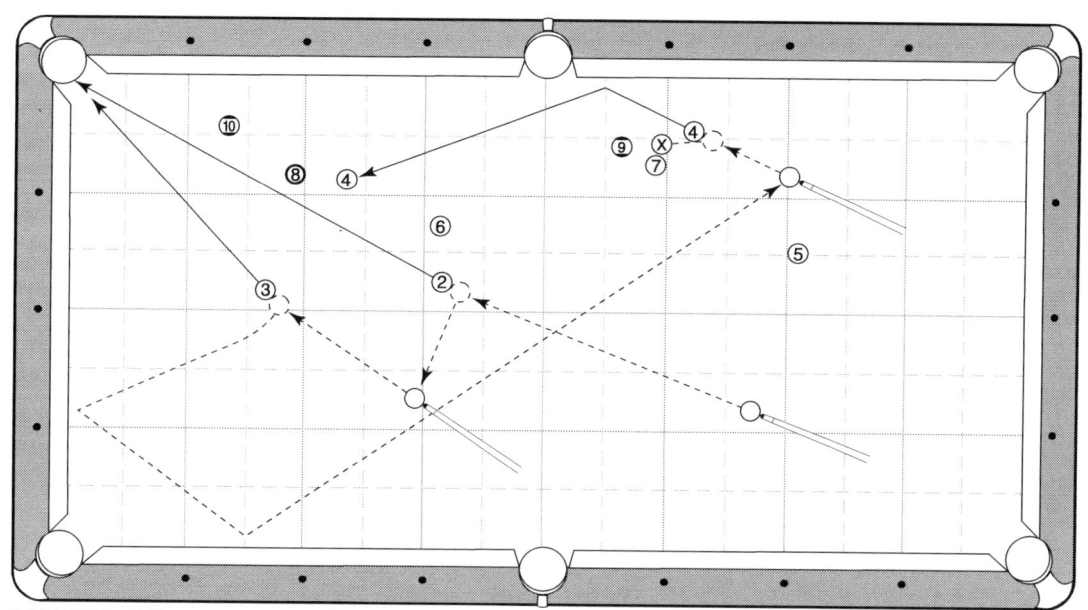

LESSON: When a runout looks impossible, and the best safety comes by using a ball that is several shots away, plan your pattern to that ball as you would when running out. Only your objective is shape for a tight safety, not a shot (yet) on the 10-ball.

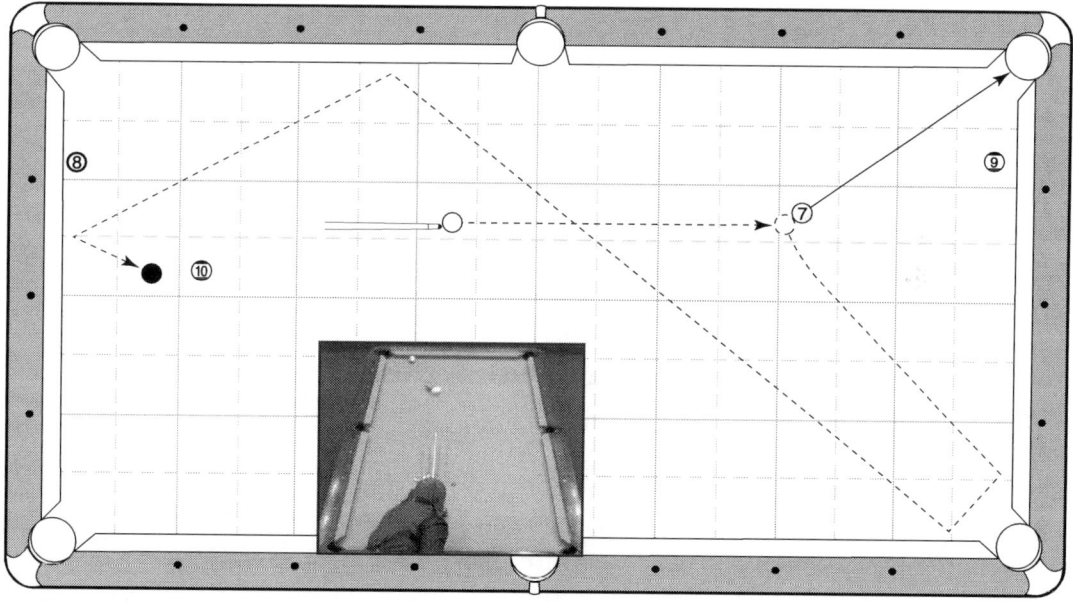

Going Deep into the Corner   (6/5 – 40:40)   C-BCB: 8, 9, 10

Hohmann's position play from the 7-ball to the 8 is a big challenge because: 1) it is a long shot, 2) he is using a full tip of right english, which makes aiming difficult, 3) the tangent line points towards the lower right corner pocket, so a scratch looms large and must be avoided, and 4) he must hit the shot hard enough so that the cue ball reaches the fourth rail and bounces out for an angle on the 8-ball. He used a hard (7) stroke, and his speed control and direction were perfect. And so was his technique as his cue tracked right at the point of contact until contact was made!

LESSON: In real estate it is all about location, location, location. In pool a shot like this makes the case that our sport is largely about execution, execution, execution!

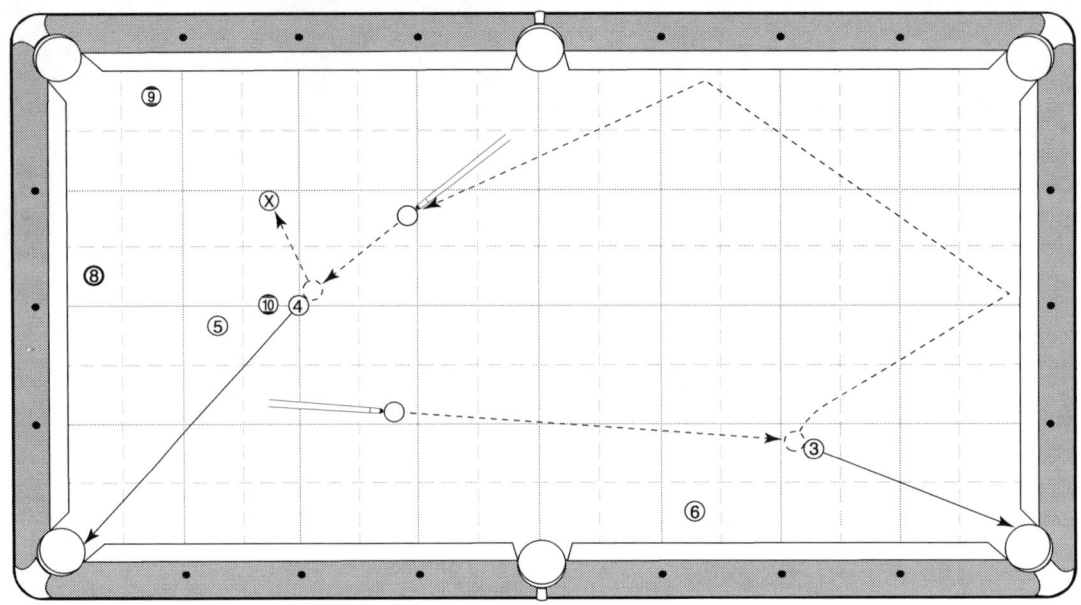

Big Position Play   (Diag. A – 6/7 – 52:35)

Hohmann has just opened this break and run out with shots on the 1 and 2 ball, setting up the lengthy route from the 3-ball to the 4. Now imagine for a second if you could remove the 10-ball and instantly convert this into a game of 9 Ball. In that case, Hohmann would not have that much of a problem

The 10-ball is such a cause for concern that Hohmann looked to see if the 4-ball would go by it three times before he played the 3-ball. Then, after playing that superb shape on the 4, he bent down and eyeballed the shot from table level to reconfirm that it would, in fact, pass the 10-ball – got up, and dropped down again to check it once more, even in the absence of an earthquake. As a final safeguard against the 10, he shot the 4-ball in the far left side of the pocket. It is of interest that cheating the pocket also improved his angle on the 5-ball!

LESSON: When the ball on which you are about to play shape is partially blocked by another, or if that non-blocker is a distraction, get the shortest and straightest shot that you can on your next shot. And double check it to see if it goes.

Draw Outside Special   (Diag. B – 6/7 – 53:20)   A-BCB: 5, 6, 8, 9, 10

We continue Hohmann's superb mid-rack pattern play with his shot on the 5-ball, which he used to set up a shot that took him from the 6-ball to the 8. He had two good choices: 1) play for a moderate cut shot on the 6-ball (25 degrees) and draw back and across the table for the 8 in the lower left pocket, and 2) play for a small angle, or no angle, on the 6-ball and come back down that side rail. He chose #2, which enabled him to play position on to the long side of the 8-ball.

LESSON: The key to Hohmann's route to the 8-ball was to hit the ball with plenty of draw and outside spin. He hit the 6-ball a little fully which, when combined with low outside english, maximized the draw creeper effect, and minimized the sideways bounce off the rail. If he had slightly over cut the ball into the left side of the pocket and used a little too much speed, the cue ball might have stopped near Position A. He would then have had to abandon his run and play safe.

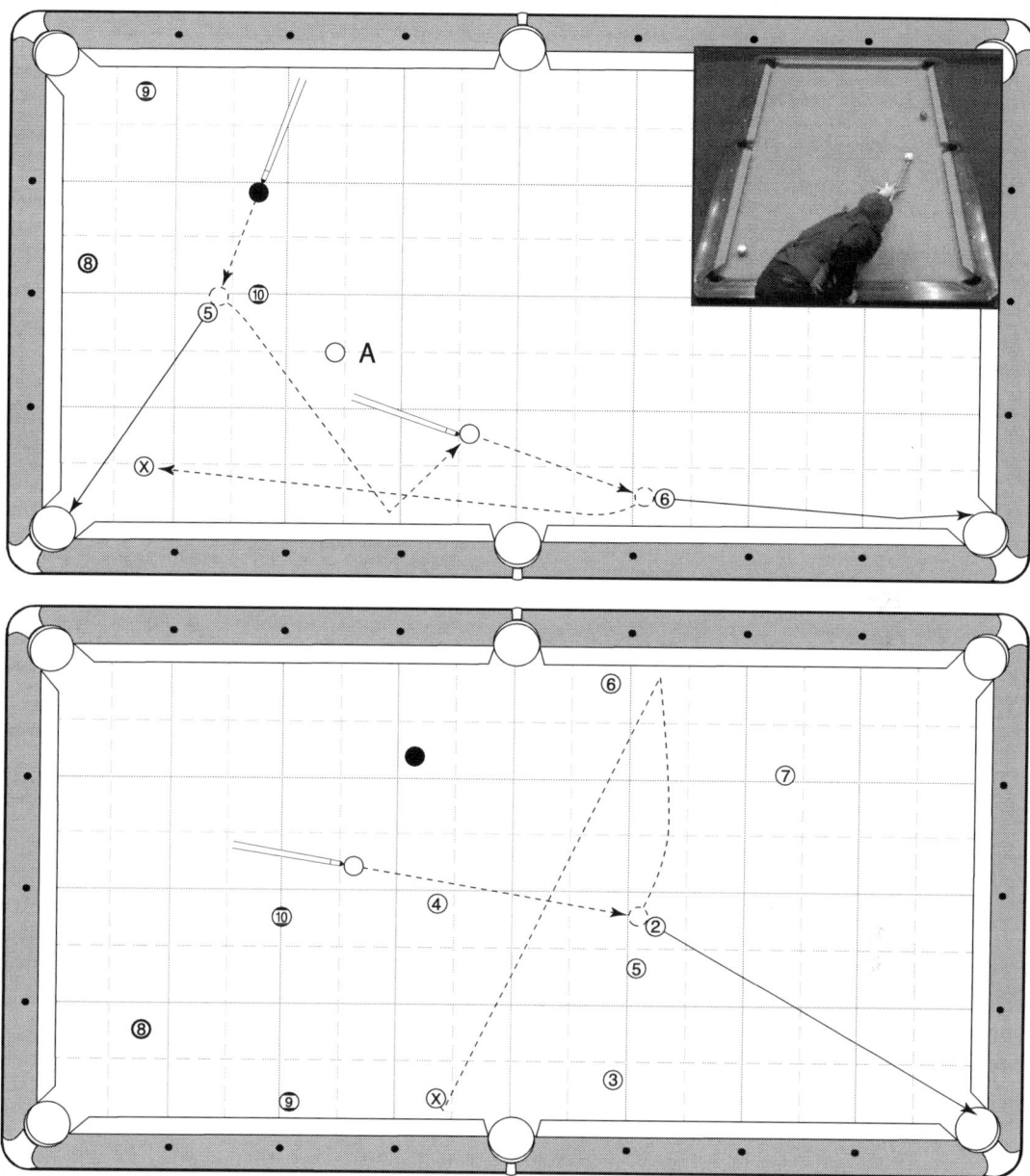

An Aiming/Power-Draw Shot! (6/11 – 1:17:15)   **B-BCB: 6, 7, 8, 9, 10**

Hohmann's powers of concentration were again put to the test – this time by the 4-ball, which was almost directly in his line of sight to the 2-ball. Complicating factors include the distance of the shot and his need to use a hard (7) stroke to cross the table and back for the 3-ball. With the 4-ball in his peripheral vision, it was a hard-to-ignore part of the Shot Picture that is made up of the cue ball, 2-ball, and the pocket (including the rails). Hohmann once again, as in shot #6/7, got down low to the table to see if the ball would go, and by how much. He then unleashed his precise and powerful stroke and I did a freeze frame, which showed that the cue ball passed the 4-ball with no more than about a quarter inch to spare!

LESSON: One way to test your powers of concentration and to increase your ability to see the Shot Picture is to practice a variety of shots and place a few balls just wide to the cue ball's path to the object ball, and the object ball's path of the pocket.

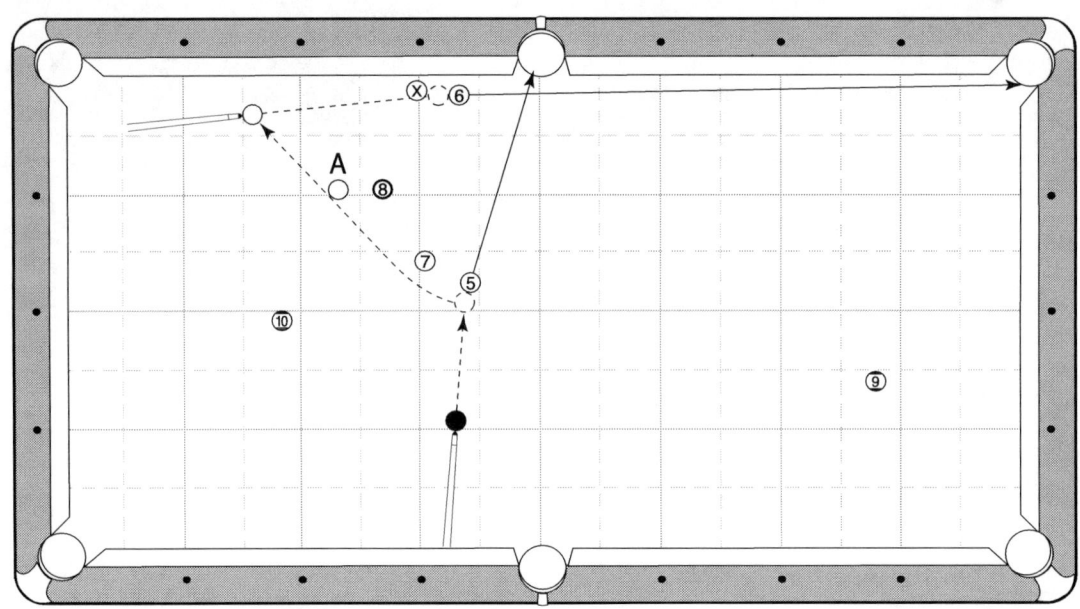

On the Wrong Side (6/16 – 1:53:40) A-BCB: 5, 6, 7, 8, 9, 10

If the cue ball had rolled a few inches further on his position play from the 4-ball to the 5, then Hohmann could have cut the 5 slightly to the left and followed over to the side rail for the 6-ball. If the cue ball had stopped even further to the left of the 5-ball, then he would have had no trouble going to the end rail and back for the 6-ball.

However, pool is literally a game of inches – and fractions of an inch. So he had to play short side shape on the 6-ball into the upper right corner pocket. His stun/follow shot narrowly missed running into the 7-ball. If he'd had a slightly larger angle on the 6, then he would have played the 7-ball in the lower left corner.

With that small angle on the 6-ball, Hohmann was content to draw a couple of inches for the 7-ball into the side. He sent the cue ball three rails to Position A and completed his runout.

LESSON: Small differences in position often lead to a big difference in the route we must play. Straight pool players know this only too well, but we can see from these shots on the 5 and 6 balls how inches influence our decisions in 10 Ball as well.

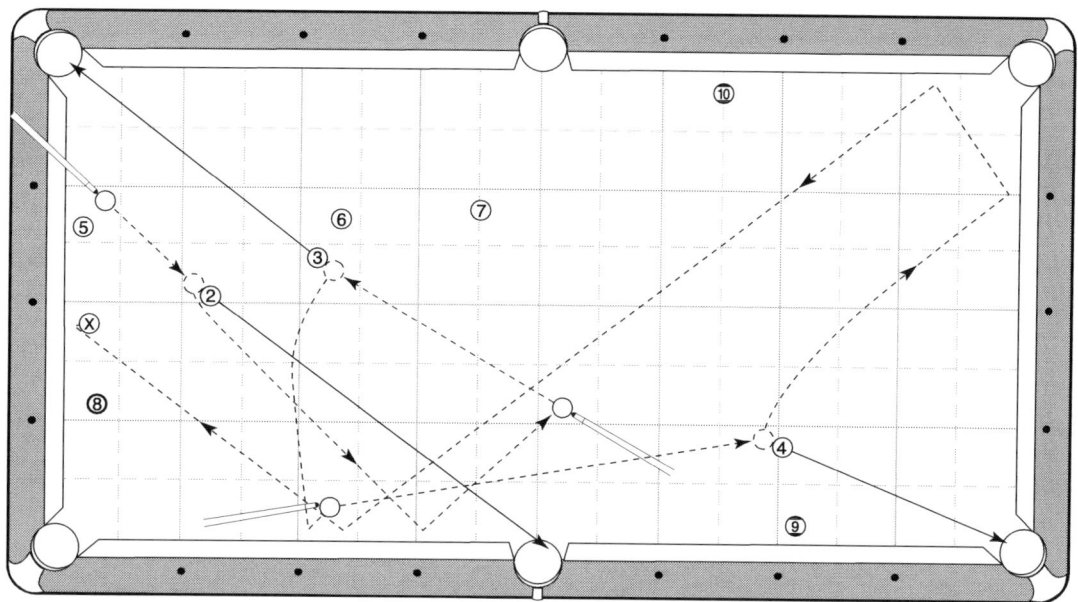

A Strong Opening Act (6/17 – 2:00:05)

An excellent safety earned Appleton the chance to run out this game, which he did thanks to super strong shots on the 2 and 4 balls. The side pockets are obviously in the middle of the table, so his shot is about the longest shot that you can have into one of them. It is also one of the toughest because, at that angle, the opening is about two thirds as big as it is when a ball is directly in front of the pocket.

Appleton, however, is one of the game's best and most fearless shotmakers, so he had no trouble firing the 2-ball into the side with a medium (5) speed follow stroke and coming off the rail for the 3-ball. His rather mediocre stun/draw shot on the 3-ball left him with a long backcut on the 4-ball. While he could have tried to get closer to the 4, the good news is that that larger angle helped him to get to the 5-ball.

He used a medium hard stroke (6) to play from the 4 to the 5, and he was able to generate the speed that he needed thanks to that bigger cut on the 4. However, he got straight in on the 5-ball when he wanted an angle. So perhaps he would have come up a few inches short of Position X if he'd had a shallower angle on the 4-ball!

LESSON: The Yin and Yang of position play is constantly at work. So before you bemoan your fate when you fail to get the shape you wanted, or thought you did, look for the positive in your alternative route, or variation. Even if it is not as much to your liking, you could learn something new, or understand how to avoid making the mistake that led to less than ideal position when a similar situation arises.

Appendix

The Rules of 9 Ball and 10 Ball

When the first edition of this book was published in 2001 there was a more uniform agreement as to the rules of play. Today many associations, leagues, and tours employ rules that may be unique to their organization. And the rules are in a state of flux even amongst many prominent providers and sponsors of high level competitions.

I had a lengthy discussion about today's rules for 9 Ball and 10 Ball with John Leyman, one of the nation's leading tournament directors and rules officials when writing the rules section of this book. The biggest piece of advice that he gave me was to learn the rules that are in force every time you play in events where you are unfamiliar with their rules. Attend player's meetings, read handouts, study league rulebooks, and take a proactive approach to knowing the rules. This will enable you to maximize your strategy, and avoid to losing games due to technicalities or ignorance.

I am now going to present the primary rules that are generally in force, and some of the most common local rules.

9 Ball

Nine Ball is played with nine balls, numbered 1 through 9. The balls are shot in numerical order. The player who sinks the 9-ball on a legal shot is the winner. The 9-ball can be made on the break, or on a combination, billiard, carom, and by other means, including lucky shots.

The balls are racked in a diamond shaped pattern. The 1-ball is positioned up front, and is racked on the foot spot. The 9-ball goes in the middle. The rest of the balls are racked randomly.

10 Ball

Ten Ball is played with 10 balls, numbered 1 through 10. The game is typically played as a call shot game. The balls are shot in numerical order. The player who sinks the 10-ball on a legal shot is the winner. The 10-ball can be made on a combination, billiard, carom shots and other shots as long as it is called. The 10-ball is spotted if it is made on the break.

The balls for 10 Ball are racked in a triangle shaped pattern. The 1-ball goes up front, the 10-ball in the middle. The rest of the balls are racked randomly.

Local Rules: Racking the Balls

Sometimes the 2 and 3-balls are racked on the corners of the rack. Spot balls are usually racked behind the 1-ball.

Local Rules: The 10-ball Goes on the Break

In some events, the 10-ball counts when it is made on the break.

Local Rules: Additional Gamewinning Balls in 9 & 10 Ball

Some matches are handicapped by giving one of the players an extra ball (known as weight, or a spot) or more with which they can win the game. The player receiving a spot, such as the 7-ball, would win whenever the 7-ball is pocketed on a legal shot, just as they would after sinking the 9-ball (in 9 Ball) or the 10-ball (in 10 Ball).

Local Rules: The Break Box
In some events, players can only place the cue ball for the break is a designated area near the head spot. This eliminates breaking off the side rails.

Local Rules: Racking Rules
Some tournament directors are choosing to rack the balls in 9 ball with the 9 ball on the spot as opposed to the one. Some tournament directors are choosing to rack the 2 behind the 1 or behind the 9.

The First Break
In most serious competitions, the players will lag for the opening break. An object ball is shot from behind the head string to the opposite end rail and back to the head rail. The player whose ball stops closest to the head rail wins the lag. The players stand side by side and play the lag at the same time. In some competitions the players may flip a coin for the first break.

The Break
The breaker must hit the 1-ball first. The cue ball is placed behind the head string. Four balls must be driven to the rail and/or pocketed for a legal break.

Local Rules: Winner Breaks or Alternate Breaks
In some events, the winner breaks, while in others they will alternate breaks.

Local Rules: The Breaks as a Handicap
In some tournaments and money games, one player gets to break every game as their weight, or part of their weight.

Legal Shot
For a shot to be a legal shot, either the cue ball or an object ball must hit the rail after the cue ball has made contact with the lowest numbered ball. The failure to meet the requirements of a legal shot includes scratching and jumping the cue ball or an object ball off of the table. When a foul has been committed, the incoming player can place the cue ball anywhere he wishes on the table.

A Player's Turn
A player's turn (inning) goes on as long as he continues to legally pocket balls through the game ball, and he may stay at the table if he has the next break (because the format is winner breaks, or it is his turn to break using the alternate breaks).

Push Out
Push outs can only take place on the very first shot after the break. The breaker has the option to push out when he makes a ball on the break. If a ball has not been pocketed on the break, his opponent can push out. On a push out, the player must designate that he is going to play one. He can then shoot the cue ball any place he wishes. His opponent then has the option of accepting the shot or not. If his opponent refuses, the player who pushed out must now shoot. For the remainder of the game, all shots must meet the requirements of a legal shot, or a foul has been committed. (For more on legal push out strategies, see chapter 8).

Local Rules: On Spotting Handicap Balls
If the player giving weight pockets the ball he is spotting his opponent on a pushout, that

ball is respotted. If the player getting weight pockets his spot ball on a pushout, it is not spotted.

Fouls
- Scratching the cue ball.
- Failure to meet the legal requirements of a shot.
- Shooting without at least one foot on the floor.
- Driving a ball off of the table.
- Making a double hit, or a push shot.
- Touching a ball.

Rules sometimes allow for a touching an object ball, and the opponent can insist that the ball be returned to its original position. Many major competitions make it a foul to touch either an object ball, or the cue ball.

Local Rules: Touching Balls
A tournament director or players in a money game may elect to not play object ball fouls (known as playing cue ball fouls only). If a ball is disturbed, the opponent has the option of replacing it as close to its original location as possible or having it remain in its new location.

Local Rules: Touching Balls, Part II
You may only touch 1 object ball at any time. If you touch 2 or more it is an instant foul. This is true for all touching rules. A new rule for touching balls : You may touch an object ball prior to a shot as long as you can get up off the shot and ask your opponent if they wish it to be replaced. Once you stroke the cue ball, anything touched after that the point of tip to cue ball contact becomes a foul. This is done to alleviate the 7 inch circle and trying to determine whether the touched ball had impact on the shot.

Three Consecutive Fouls
If a player commits three consecutive fouls, that is loss of game. A warning must be given between the second and third fouls.

Local Rules: Waving the Three Foul Rule
A tournament director or the participants in a money game may elect to waive this rule.

Spotting a Ball
Generally the 9-ball (in 9 Ball) and the 10-ball (in 10 Ball) are the only balls spotted in these respective games. They are spotted when they are made on a non-legal shot. They are spotted on the foot spot, or on the foot string as close to the foot spot as possible.

Major Associations – For Further Study
Further information on the rules can be found at the following web sites and associations. The various tours also have their rules (see the listing in the appendix).

World Pool-Billiard Association	wpa-pool.com/web/the_rules_of_play
American Poolplayers Association	media.poolplayers.com/TMRB/2014-Rulebooklet.pdf
CSI	playcsipool.com/AboutUs.aspx
VNEA	vnea.com/111111new-page.aspx
ACS	americancuesports.org/uploads/ACS_Rulebook.pdf
TAP – 9-Ball	tapleague.com/files/pdfs/8_9_ball_rulebook.pdf
TAP – 10-Ball	tapleague.com/files/pdfs/10_ball_rulebook.pdf

Glossary for Nine Ball

To be a complete player, you've got to know the lingo. The glossary contains the standard items you would expect to find, such as head string, draw shot and english. It also includes the many colorful terms that serious competitors and those who wager at pool use on a regular basis. I'm not encouraging you to become a pool hustler, but I believe that a working knowledge of the pool player's lingo can add to your enjoyment of the game.

A

Across the Line A position play in which the cue ball is traveling across the position zone. It is very difficult to accomplish.

Action When a money game is in progress.

Ahead Session A money game in which you win by getting a certain number of games ahead of your opponent.

Air Barrel When the losing player in a money game plays a final game or set even though he doesn't have the money to pay if he loses.

Area Shape An extra large position zone that is used to keep the cue ball out of trouble.

Around-the-World A position play in which the cue ball travels up and down the table off all four rails.

B

Back Cut When the cue ball is closer to the rail than the object ball which is being played.

Backer One who finances a money game in exchange for a share of the winnings, if any.

Bad Hit Failure to hit the designated object ball first. It is a foul.

Balance Point The point where the cue is in balance, which is the point where 50% of the weight is in front and behind.

Ball in Hand A rule that allows a player to place the cue ball anywhere on the table (in Nine Ball) after his opponent has scratched or committed a foul.

Bank Pool A pool game where you only score when you pocket a bank shot.

Bank Shot A shot in which the object ball contacts one or more cushions before going into a pocket.

Bar Box Tavern sized tables. 3 ½' x 7'. Coin operated.

Barking Using loud and/or abusive language in order to rouse a potential opponent's manly instincts so they will play you for money.

Barrel A gambling unit ($20 equals 4 barrels at $5 per game).

Bear Down Give a shot your 100% undivided attention. Playing with great determination.

Bed The playing surface of the table.

Behind the Line Any ball that's between the head string and the head rail.

Big Ball 1) An oversized cue ball that's used on some bar tables. 2) A ball that is easy to hit on kick shots because it is near a rail. 3) A ball that blocks a direct hit on a large portion of the table

Big Table A 4 ½' x 9' table.

Billiard A shot in which the cue ball glances off one ball before driving another ball into the pocket.

Body English Twisting and turning the arms and/or body in an attempt to influence the shot.

Brazilians When a player is in a game they have little or no chance of losing.

Break (The) The first shot of the game.

Break Out Separating a cluster.

Bridge Using the front hand to support the shaft of the cue.

Bridge Hand For a righthanded player it's their left hand. Vice versa for lefties.

Broken Down A player who is mentally defeated before the contest is over.

Bumping A delicate shot that sends a ball a short distance to a more advantageous location.

Bust A wide-open break shot.

Busted A gambler who has lost all of their money.

Bye When a player, through the luck of the draw, advances to the next round without having to play an opponent.

C

Calcutta Selling players at a tournament through an auction to create a separate prize fund for the spectators.

Call The act of designating a specific pocket for a shot.

Called Ball The designated shot.

Call the Hit A referee or neutral party judges whether a hit is good or a foul (bad hit).

Called Pocket The designated pocket for a shot. On rare occasions, local rules may call for the shooter to designate the pocket for the Nine-Ball

Carom A shot in which the object ball glances off another ball on its way to the pocket.

Chalk A small cube with a tacky substance that

is applied regularly to the cue tip to help prevent miscues.

Cheating the Pocket. Shooting the object ball into either side of the pocket.

Chirping When a player converses with the crowd in an animated manner.

Choke Up Shot A shooting technique for playing hard to reach shots.

Cheese (The) A money ball in Nine Ball.

Choke To miss a shot or play poorly because of the pressure.

Cinch To place all or nearly all of your attention on making the ball with little consideration to the positional requirements of the shot.

Cling The momentary contact of the cue ball and the object ball. It can vary slightly depending on the condition of the balls.

Close the Angle When the cue ball rebounds off the cushion at a greater angle than the angle of approach.

Closed Bridge A bridge with a loop for the cue, formed by connecting the tips of the thumb and index finger to the middle finger.

Cluster A group of object balls that are touching or are very close together.

Combination A shot that involves two or more object balls. Two ball combinations in which the first ball drives the second into the pocket are the most common.

Combo (See combination).

Come Up Dry When you fail to make a ball on the break.

Complementary Angles A cut shot with an angle that makes it ideal for playing position on the next shot.

Connecting Ball A straight-in shot which, when played with a stop shot, leaves you with a straight-in shot on the next ball.

Contact Induced Throw Friction between the cue ball and object ball on cut shots that alters the path of the object ball.

Contact Point The spot on the object ball that the cue ball must hit to make the shot.

Corner Hooked When the cue ball is deep in the jaws and the edge of the pocket blocks the cue ball's path to the object ball.

Cosmo A very simple run out.

Cross-Corner A bank shot into the opposite corner pocket.

Cross-Side A bank shot into the opposite side pocket.

Crutch (See mechanical bridge).

Cue The stick with which you shoot.

Cue Ball The all white ball which you shoot with the cue.

Curve What happens when you hit down on the cue ball with english.

Cushion The raised surface that surrounds the edge of the playing surface.

Cut Break A control break in which the cue ball glances off the side of the 1-ball and then goes to the side rail and out.

Cut Shot Any shot that has an angle to it.

Dead Combination A combination shot that's lined up to the pocket which virtually can't be missed.

D

Dead Punch (See dead stroke.)

Dead Shot A shot that's lined up to the pocket. A shot that can't be missed.

Dead Stroke When a pool player is playing at peak levels and his stroke is on automatic pilot. When a player is in the zone.

Deflection Hitting the cue ball with english, which causes it to take off to the opposite side of the english.

Diamonds Markings along the top of the rails that are useful in calculating bank shots and kick shots and as targets for position routes.

Dime A thousand dollars.

Dirty Pool The practice of using underhanded tactics.

Dogged It When a player misses because of choking.

Dog Proofing Playing a layout in such a manner that your success is virtually guaranteed.

Domino Effect (The) When one seemingly little mistake can cause your whole pattern to begin to unravel.

Double Elimination A tournament in which a player must lose twice to be eliminated.

Double Hit Hitting the cue ball two or more times in succession. It's a foul.

Double Kiss When the cue ball strikes an object ball two times in one shot.

Down the Line Shape A principle for playing position that ensures that you will have position.

Draw (the) Used to determine the pairings at a tournament.

Draw Shot Hitting the cue ball below center and applying backspin. On a straight-in shot the cue ball will come directly back towards you.

Draw/Stun Shot A shot that is part draw and part stun.

Duck 1) A very easy shot. 2) Play a safety.

Dump The crime of losing a money game on purpose which is being financed by a backer. The two players then split the winnings. Also known as doing business.

Dutch Doubles A format in which teams are comprised of a male and female player that alternate shots.

E

Eight Ball A game in which each player shoots either the solids or stripes. When their group is pocketed the 8-ball is the gamewinning shot.

Elevated Bridge Raising the palm of the bridge hand off the table so you can shoot over an obstructing ball.

End Rail Either the head rail or the foot rail.

English Side spin that results from stroking the cue ball on either side of its vertical axis.

Even-up 1) Paying an outstanding debt. 2) Playing a money game with no spot or weight.

F

Fade It The ability to handle adversity and continue to play well.

Fan It In To make a very thin cut.

Feather Shot A very thin cut shot.

Ferrule The hard white piece of plastic or ivory at the end of the shaft to which the tip is attached.

Fish Somebody who loses money a very high percentage of the time they gamble.

Float the Cue Ball A shot that sends the cue ball a short distance after either a firm or soft stroke.

Floating Follow A shot in which the cue ball rolls slowly forward after being hit with a firm stroke.

Flow Chart It is used to keep track of the progress of a tournament.

Flush A gambler or player who has a big bankroll.

Follow Top spin that causes the cue ball to roll forward after contacting the object ball. It's applied by striking the cue ball above the horizontal axis (above center).

Follow/Stun Shot A shot that is part follow and part stun.

Follow Through The final phase of the stroke. Extending the cue tip past the cue ball's original location.

Foot of the Table The end of the table on which the balls are racked.

Foot Rail The rail at the end of the table where the balls are racked.

Foot Spot The spot on the table that's on the middle of the foot string. It's where the head ball of a rack is located and where balls are spotted.

Foot String An imaginary line that crosses the table two diamonds up from the foot rail. It goes directly over the foot spot.

Force Follow Hitting the cue ball extra hard above center creating lots of top spin.

Force Shot Making the cue ball travel a good distance sideways when the cut angle is shallow.

Foul Scratching or not meeting the legal requirements of a legal shot or legal safety.

Frame A player's turn at the table.

Free Shot A shot that does not hurt a players chances of winning a game if he misses. If the shot is missed the opponent is left safe.

Free Wheeling Very close to dead stroke. When a player is loose and confident, partly due to their opponent's poor play.

Freeze out When two players agree to play for a specific sum of money. This establishes a minimum amount that either player can win or lose.

Freeze up the money Putting up the money for a freeze out in a neutral location (such as above the light) or giving it to a neutral party.

Front runner A player who plays well with a lead.

Frozen Ball A ball that is in contact with another ball or a cushion.

Full Ball Sending the cue ball into 100% contact with the object ball.

G

Gear A player may have several levels of play to their game. Their "top gear" is their best game.

Getting Down When two players agree to a serious money match.

Getting In Line A demanding shot that puts the cue ball into good position for the next shot.

Good Hit When the cue ball makes contact first with the intended object ball.

Go Off Losing a lot of money, possibly all of a player's bankroll.

H

Hanger A ball that's sitting in the lip of the pocket.

Head of the Table The end of the table from which you play the opening break shot.

Head Rail The rail between the two corner pockets on the end of the table at which you break.

Head String An imaginary line that runs across

the table two diamonds up from the head rail.
Heart The quality of mental toughness. The ability to come through in the clutch. All great players have it.
Heat (the) Playing competitive pool under pressure. Feeling the pressure.
Hit (the) The sensation a player feels from using a particular cue.
Hold-up English Spin that sharpens the cue ball's rebound off the cushion. It also slows the cue ball down.
Hold-up A technique that retards the roll of the cue ball.
Hooked When another object ball is blocking the cue ball's direct access to the designated object ball.
Hook Zone An area of the table where the object ball is blocked from a direct hit by the cue ball.
Hot Seat The winner of the winner's bracket in a double elimination tournament. They are guaranteed no worse than second place.
House Cue A cue provided by the establishment.
House Pro The resident pro whose duties usually include giving lessons and running tournaments.
House Rack (See slug.)
House Rules A set of local rules which you are expected to follow.
Hug the Rail When a ball frozen to the cushion remains frozen as it rolls towards the pocket.
Hustle Conning an opponent into playing a money game when he has little or no chance of winning.

I

In Jail When the cue ball is in a position where your opponent has neither a shot nor a safety. Pool's equivalent of checkmate.
Inning A player's turn at the table.
Inside English Applying sidespin on the same side of the cue ball as the direction of the cut shot.
Intentional Foul A strategic maneuver in which you deliberately give your opponent ball in hand.

J

Jack-it-up The act of raising the bet in a money game.
Jacked Up When you must raise your bridge to shoot over an obstructing ball. Raising the backhand and shooting a draw shot when the cue ball is near a rail.
Jam Up When a player is shooting very well. A very good player's game.
Jawed When the object ball barely misses and comes to rest in the pocket opening.
Jaws The area of the playing surface that is inside the edges of the pocket.
Jelly Roll A sum of money that is paid to someone who has helped another to win money. This could include setting up a game or letting the player use your cue.
Joint The midsection of the cue that holds the shaft and butt together.
Jump Shot A downward stroke that causes the cue ball to leave the bed of the table and sail over obstructing balls.
Jumped Ball An obstructing ball that's been cleared.

K

Key Ball A shot in Nine-Ball that largely determines whether a run will be successful.
Kick Shot Shooting the cue ball into one or more cushions before contacting the object ball.
Kill Shot A type of draw shot that checks the cue ball's roll after it rebounds off the cushion. Sometimes english is also used with the draw.
Kiss When the object ball glances off another ball.
Kitchen The area of the playing surface between the head string and the head rail. It's the area from which you break.
Knock The act of dispensing information that ruins a players chances of getting a game.

L

Lady's Aide (See mechanical bridge).
Lag A very soft stroke. Easing the ball into the pocket.
Lag for the Break At the start of a match each player simultaneously rolls the cue ball down the table and back. The player whose ball stops closest to the head rail wins and gets to break the first rack.
Lamb Killer A player who specializes in beating less skillful players for money.
Leave The position of the balls that one player receives as a result of another's shot.
Lemonading The art of stalling or playing less than your best in the hopes of raising the wager.
Let Your Stroke Out Shooting one or more shots

with a full, loose and free stroke.
Liking it   When you are in a money game that you believe you can win.
Line   The word on how well a stranger plays.
Lock   A game that is so one-sided that the better player has little if any chance of winning.
Locksmith   A player who specializes in making games where he is the heavy favorite.
Long   When a bank shot misses to the far side of the pocket. Also when a player runs the cue ball past the ideal position zone.
Long Green (the)   Long shots on a big table that are considered difficult.
Long Rail Bank   A table length bank shot.
Long Side Shape   When the cue ball is positioned so you can shoot to the closer pocket.
Long String   An imaginary line that runs down the middle of the table. Balls are spotted along the long string, starting at the foot spot.

M
Mark (a)   Somebody who loses money a very high percentage of the time they gamble.
Masse   A shot in which the cue ball curves radically as a result of a nearly vertical stoke on the side of the cue ball.
Match   A contest between two players.
Matching Up   The negotiations that precede a money game.
Mechanical Bridge   A long handled implement with an attachment that has several ridges in which the cue is placed. It is used for shots that can't otherwise be reached.
Miscue   What occurs when the tip fails to stick properly on the cue ball at impact.
Miss   A shot that fails to go into the pocket.
Money Ball   A ball that, when pocketed, results in victory.
Move   A strategic maneuver.
Mushroom   When a tip spreads out and become wider than its original shape.

N
Nap   The degree to which parts of the cloth rise above the rest of the playing surface.
Natural Position   Shape that results from allowing the cue ball to roll without using English.
Nine Ball   A pool game played in rotation with balls 1-9. The first player to sink the 9-ball wins.
Nip Draw   A special draw stroke in which you use a short punch-like stroke.
Nit   A player who always wants a lock and bets low even though he is a good player.
Nut Artist   Someone who plays only when they have a game they can't lose.
Nuts (the)   A money game in which you have little or no chance of losing.

O
Object Ball   The ball at which you are shooting.
Off Angle   When you have played position on the wrong side of the object ball.
On the Hill   When you are one game away from winning the match.
On the Break   Making the money ball on the first shot (the break shot) of the game.
On the Snap   (See on the break.)
Open Bridge   A bridge formed by laying the hand flat on the table and placing the cue in a vee formed by the thumb and index finger.
Open the Angle   English that causes the cue ball to rebound from the cushion at less of an angle than the angle of approach.
Opening Break (The)   The very first shot of a match.
Open Your Nose   In a money game the losing player continues to play and lose more money. A loss, however, is not a certainty.
Out of Line   1) When you fail to play ideal position. 2) When a player's behavior is unacceptable. 3) When you have made a money game that is going to be very tough to win.
Out of Stroke   When a player is off their game and their stroke does not feel right.
Out Shot   A difficult shot that, if made, should result in victory even though there are several balls that still must be pocketed.
Outside English   Applying sidespin on the opposite side of the cue ball from the pocket to which it is being played.
Overdrive Follow   A technique for applying extra follow to the cue ball. It is used for breaking clusters.
Over Cut   Missing a shot because the object ball was hit too thinly.

P
Parking   When the cue ball comes straight back to the center of the table on a break shot. It happens on well struck break shots.
Pattern Play   Playing the balls in a specific order and/or a certain style of playing position.
Pinch   1) Using inside english to make a bank shot that could not otherwise be pocketed. 2)

Using a kill draw stroke to minimize the sideways movement of the cue ball on a small angled cut shot.

Plan B Resorting to a different shot or pattern as a result of a shot not being executed exactly as intended.

Player A person who plays very well, especially under competitive conditions.

Pocket Billiards The formal name for pool.

Pocket Speed Hitting a shot with just enough force so that the object ball drops with a few inches to spare.

Pocket Speed Plus Hitting a shot with a little more force than is necessary to send it to the pocket to avoid a roll off.

Point (the) The sharp edge where the pocket ends and the rail begins.

Pool Games that are played on a rectangular table with six pockets, a cue ball and several colored balls.

Pool Detective A person who makes a point to know various players' games and who passes that information on to others. He is regularly guilty of killing off action.

Pool Gods Mythical characters who control the rolls and the luck factor in each contest. It is not wise to upset them.

Position Where the cue ball is located in relation to the next shot.

Position Zone An area of the table in which the cue ball is well placed for the next shot.

Post up (See freeze up.)

Pound Shot A shot that uses a very hard stroke to send the cue ball off a cushion when the cut angle is very shallow.

Pounding the Ball The act of using a pound shot.

Process of Elimination Planning A technique for planning patterns which involves sifting through your options and eliminating the least likely choices until you arrive at the best choice for playing the shot..

Proposition Offering a wager on an unusual and/or very difficult shot that the person offering the wager knows very well. It can also be an offer to play a variation of a regular pool game.

Pro Side (the) The act of missing a shot to the side of the pocket that minimizes your opponent's chances for winning or at least avoids a complete sell out.

Push Out The option to send the cue ball anywhere on the table on the first shot after the break without incurring a foul.

R

Race A match that's decided by the first player to win a specific number of games (i.e., a race to seven games).

Rack 1) A triangular shaped object that is used to put the balls in place at the start of the game and for each new rack. 2) The position of the balls once they've been placed in position and the rack had been removed. 3) The position of the balls after the break.

Rake (See mechanical bridge).

Rail The raised surface that surrounds the playing surface. It includes the cushions.

Rail Bird A spectator at a competitive game.

Rail Bridge A bridge that's formed by placing the bridge hand on the rail.

Rail Shot When the cue ball is frozen to the cushion or is very close to it.

Rail Target A spot on the rail that is chosen as a place where you want the cue ball to hit.

Rain Table Playing under extremely humid conditions, which affects the rails and speed of the table.

Recovery Position A challenging position play that is used to get back in line after playing poor position.

Regulation Sized Table A 4½' x9' sized table.

Reverse English Sidespin that causes the cue ball to rebound off the cushion at a sharper angle than the approach angle.

Riding the Cash Hitting the lowest numbered ball first with a powerful stroke and sending the ball into a money ball. The object is to make the money ball with a lucky shot.

Riding the Cheese A forceful shot at a money ball that is largely dependent on luck to be successful.

Ring Game A money game of Nine Ball with three or more players, all competing against one another.

Road Map (See cosmo.)

Road Player A hustler or skillful player who travels around the country playing pool for money.

Rock The cue ball.

Roll Off When an irregularity in the table or a not perfectly level playing surface causes a slow moving object ball to roll off line.

Roll Out See push out.

Rolls The breaks of the game. There are good rolls and bad rolls.

Rotation A pool game that uses all fifteen balls.

They are played in order, 1 through 15.
Run The number of balls made on any particular turn.
Run Out Making several ball in succession to win the game.
Run Out Player A player who runs out with great regularity.
Running English English that opens up the rebound angle and adds speed to the cue ball
Run the Rack Breaking and running the entire rack.

S
Safety A defensive maneuver that's designed to leave your opponent with a tough shot or safety, or perhaps no shot at all.
Safety Zone A place on the table where your opponent cannot pocket a ball.
Saver A deal between two players at a tournament in which they share each other's winnings. The percentage is negotiated.
Sawbuck Ten dollars.
Score 1) How a match stands at any time. 2) An amount that is won in a money game.
Scotch Doubles A format in which two players alternate shots.
Scratch When the cue ball disappears into any of the six pockets.
Scratch Shot A shot in which a scratch is very likely or is unavoidable.
Sell Out A poor shot that results in the loss of a game.
Session A lengthy money game.
Set A single race. One race that is a part of a series of races, such as 2 out of 3 sets for the match. It could also refer to playing under the ahead format.
Shape (See position).
Shark A tactic that's designed to distract or throw an opponent off their game. A player who hustles pool.
Sharking The act of using shark tactics.
Shim Thin slices of wood that are placed in the pocket openings to tighten the pockets.
Shooting the Lights Out When you are shooting very straight and playing perfect pool.
Short A bank shot that misses on the near side of the pocket. When the cue ball fails to reach the intended location for good position.
Short Side Shape Playing position for the more distant pocket.
Short Stop A very capable and experienced player who is just a couple of notches below the very best.
Shot Clock A timer that is used to restrict the length of time players can take on a shot. It is used mostly at major pro tournaments.
Short Rack A game that is won with a combo, billiard, 9-ball on the break or other shot so that there are several balls on the table when the game is over.
Short Rail Bank A bank across the width of the table.
Shotmaker A very straight shooter who emphasizes making balls over playing position.
Sideboards When a ball that is near a pocket makes a shot play much easier.
Side Rail One of the rails that run along the length of the table.
Side Rail Break Shot A break shot where the object ball is close to or on the rail.
Skid When the cue ball and object ball maintain contact for a fraction of a second longer than normal. This almost always results in the shot being under cut. Skids can also happen on straight or nearly straight in follow shots that are hit with a soft stroke.
Skimming Balls Rolling the cue ball very softly off the edge of an object ball. It is a defensive measure.
Single Elimination A format for tournament play in which you are eliminated after one loss.
Slate The hard playing surface that rests under the cloth.
Slop Shot A lucky shot that involves little or no skill.
Slug A rack in which there are gaps between the balls. It is given by unscrupulous players to neutralize their opponent's break.
Snatch See draw shot.
Sneaky Pete A two piece cue that looks like a house cue. Hustlers often use it.
Snookered When the cue ball rests behind a ball which blocks a direct hit on the designated ball.
Snow Slang for the cue ball.
Specialty Shots Combinations, billiards, caroms and some banks are the four most commonly played specialty shots.
Spectrum of Speed A 1-10 scale used for measuring the various speeds of stroke.
Speed The level of a persons game.
Speed Control The ability to control the cue ball's rolling distance. Good speed control is essential for playing good position.

Speed of Stroke The force that you apply to the cue ball.

Spin Your Rock Applying English to the cue ball.

Spot A location on the table. The foot spot and the head spot.

Spot Up Placing a ball on the foot spot. Usually it occurs after a money ball has been pocketed and a foul had been committed.

Squatted (See parking).

Squirt (See deflection).

Staking Financing a money game.

Stakehorse A person who finances money games.

Stall Play less than your best in the hopes that you can raise the bet.

Stance The position that you take for a shot.

Stealing When a player is in a money game which they have little or no chance of losing.

Steering When a knowledgeable pool person advises another on who to play for money and on who to avoid playing.

Stick It Stopping the cue ball dead in its tracks upon contact with the object ball.

Stiffed When the winning player in a money game fails to collect the wager.

Stone Slang for the cue ball.

Stop Shot (See stick it)

Straight In Refers to a shot where the cue ball and object ball are lined up directly at the pocket.

Straight Pool Also known as 14.1. A game played to a designated number of points. A point is scored for each ball pocketed.

Stroke The swing of the arm, wrist and hand that propels the cue through the cue ball.

Stun Shot A firmly hit shot in which the cue ball slides across the cloth.

Sweat Watching a pool game. For example, sweating the action.

Sweater A person who is watching a pool game.

Sweet Spot (The) The position for the cue ball that yields the most balls on the break.

T

Table Leaks (The) A table on which it is easy to make balls on the break.

Table Roll (See roll off).

Thin Cut A shot in which very little of the cue ball contacts the object ball.

Throw Friction between the object ball and cue ball that changes the path of the object ball.. English can cause throw, as can contact.

Ticky When an object ball hits one rail, then hits an object ball, and then goes on to accomplish some worthy objective.

Time Shot A lucky shot in which the balls roll around the table in a series of collisions before the object ball is pocketed.

Tip The small round leather item that is attached to the ferrule. Also refers to how much English is used on a particular shot.

Trap When a player is engaged in a losing game.

Triangle Another term for the device used to rack the balls. The area in which the balls are racked.

Through Traffic Skillfully maneuvering the cue ball past a number of potentially obstructing balls.

Two Piece Cue A cue that has a joint in the middle.

Two Way Shots A position play that gives you the luxury of playing position on either of two possible targets.

2 ¼" Rule (The) It states that everything about a shot can and very often does change within the space of 2¼".

U-W

Under Cut Missing a shot because the object ball was hit too fully.

Warm Up Strokes A series of movements of the arm, hand and wrist that prepares the shooter for the final stroke.

Weight A handicap that one player gives another in a money game.

Whitey Slang for the cue ball.

Wild Ball A ball that a player is receiving as a spot that does not have to be called.

Window A gap between two closely spaced balls which exposes the object ball to a direct hit

Wing Ball The two balls that are on either side of the rack in Nine Ball.

Wire (on the) 1) A string above the table with beads or balls for keeping score. 2) A spot that consists of games, as in 1 on the wire in a race to 9.

Woofing See barking.

World (The) A huge spot or handicap.

A Pool Player's Cue Case

Players today are using several cues, which has led to the growth in sales of large cue cases, which can accommodate 2-3 cues and several shafts. The larger cases have big pockets, which can hold the wide range of accessories that have become necessary operating equipment. Perhaps you already own a cue case that can accommodate the items from the list below that are vital to your game. If not, before you purchase a new case, I suggest that you assemble the items from the list below that you want to have available when you play, and then see if they fit in the case you are considering for purchase. Keep in mind that three cues is the maximum number permitted in competition according to BCA rules.

Regular Cue – One or two shafts.

Jump Cue – Make sure it meets the legal minimum of 40".

Break Cue – This cue typically features a slightly larger tip, which is flat, but rounded at the edges. Break cues typically weigh about 19 ounces.

Jump/Break Cue – This is a break cue that allows you to unscrew about 1/3 off the end to quickly turn it into a jump cue.

Joint Protectors – These screw on to the end of the butt and shaft to protect your cue.

Cue Holder – Today's Nine Ball player typically uses 2-3 cues, and may also carry their own mechanical bridge. These items can be held securely in place with devices that are affixed to the edge of a table (not the pool table) next to where you are playing

Chalk – Carry a couple of pieces in your case just in case you wind up playing in a place where there is nothing but a few worn pieces available.

Chalk Holders – You can avoid having to hunt down chalk or the games that some opponents like to play with the chalk. In addition, you can use pieces that are broken in just the way you like them.

Gloves – If you use a glove, consider carrying two in case something happens to the one you are wearing.

Powder – If you use powder, you probably have a difficult time playing without it, so you should make sure to carry your own container.

Sandpaper – Some players like to use a fine grade of this to clean their cue.

Cleaners and Conditioners – They are extremely useful in removing chalk and dirt from your shaft, which of course enables the cue to slide smoothly through your bridge.

Towel Wipe down the cue regularly to prevent buildup of chalk, which gets into the pores and creates unwanted friction. You may also consider carrying a towel to clean the balls.

Shaper – There are numerous devices on the market for restoring your tip to the proper curvature.

Tapper – They open the pores on your tip so they will hold chalk better.

Tip Repair – Extra tips, holders, and adhesives.

Rulebook – A copy can help settle any disputes regarding the rules.

Glasses for Pool – These are glasses with high rims that are made for shooting pool.

Bridge Head – The quality of mechanical bridges varies from place to place, so you may wish to carry a bridge head that can be attached to the end of a cue in just a few seconds.

Cue Ball – Since the cue ball gets the most use, you can ensure that the most important ball is in great condition by carrying your own cue ball.

Training Devices – There are a variety of balls with markings on them that are valuable practice devices. Aiming trainers are also available.

The Donuts – Be sure to include a package of donuts (hole reinforcements), which enable you to easily mark the position of the balls.

Pool Notebook – A small notebook in which you can record shots, strategies, and things to work on.

Bar Table 9 Ball

Nine Ball has long been a popular game on bar tables, but it is now being played more than ever before on the smaller tables thanks to the tremendous growth in the number of leagues and tournaments. The lessons in this book, which were all shown on a regulation sized table, also apply to 9 Ball on a bar table with but a few modifications. Any differences in strategy are due primarily to the size of the table. Other factors which can also influence your strategy and shot selection include: pocket openings, type of cue ball, and the overall playing conditions.

There are three main categories of 9 Ball players: 1) those that play only on big tables; 2) those that play only on bar tables: 3) those that switch back and forth. This section is for categories 2 and 3. Those of you who switch back and forth have a special challenge, as you must be constantly adapting your strategy. When playing on a big table, the 5,000 square inch playing surface dictates that you emphasize execution. On a bar table, which measures 3,200 square inches, you must deal with the congestion factor.

Many big table players make the mistake of thinking there is nothing to playing on a bar table. They are often in for a rude awakening, once they discover that their big table style does not universally apply to the smaller table.

Fundamentals

Basic Strategy Even though you can be rather successful with a "bar stroke", that does not mean you should slack off on your fundamentals. You must make shots that have a reasonable degree of difficulty. In addition, everything is relative: if you only play on a bar table, what looks like a hanger to a big table player could be a long green shot to a bar table player.

The Congestion Factor The size of the table dictates that your bridge will be closer to the rails. This means that your cue will tend to be slightly more elevated on a larger number of draw shots compared to a big table.

A Common Mistake: Many amateur bar table players make the big mistake of placing their regular closed bridge on top of the rail. This leads to a mini jump shot, which creates the tendency to overcut the shot. Remember, you always want to keep your bridge as level as possible.

The Conditions

Basic Strategy: You will encounter a wider variety of playing conditions on bar tables due to: 1) Management's attention to the conditions varies much more in taverns than in pool rooms; 2) Smaller tables tend to be harder to keep level than big tables; 3) differences in cue balls. As a bar player, you must be able to quickly adapt to the conditions. In addition, you cannot let less than perfect equipment affect your attitude. If your opponent starts complaining about the conditions, you can gain an edge in the mental game.

Lopsided Cue Balls At times you will encounter a weighted cue ball that has a disturbing tendency to do a semi-circle as it slows to a halt. You will need to allow for this when plotting your position and safety zones.

Obstructions You at times will need to be able to shoot with a short cue. Use a short stroke when obstructions force you to shoot with a short cue.

The Big Ball
The big cue ball is still used on many bar tables, although it is far less common than it was twenty years ago. If you have played on tables using a big ball, then you are already aware of the special challenge of shooting with the big ball. If not, the suggestions below will help you adapt more quickly to the big ball.
- Aim for a thinner hit on cut shots to compensate for the larger cue ball.
- Use a considerably more powerful draw stroke than normal when the cue ball is more than a couple of feet from the object ball.
- Avoid long draw shots when possible.
- You don't need to overpower the break as the big ball will do plenty of damage by itself. Play more of a controlled break.
- You can shoot with confidence because the cue ball holds its line of travel to the object ball better than a lighter and smaller regulation sized ball.
- Use very little english unless you shoot regularly with the big ball.
- The cue ball will have a tendency to run much further on follow shots.
- The cue ball's path off the tangent line will bend forward quicker on follow shots.

Position Play
Basic Strategy You can more easily play to zones on a bar table at times because the shots are shorter and the pockets tend to be more forgiving. You must also be able to play pinpoint shape because of the congestion factor.

English Use english to refine the cue ball's route through traffic. You generally don't have to allow for as much deflection as on a big table because 1) the shots are shorter; 2) bar table cue balls tend to weigh more.

Area Shape Be sure to leave yourself a shot on a bar table by playing area shape as much as possible, providing it doesn't impact the quality of your position. This is an especially valuable tactic when you do not trust the roll of the table.

Cheat the Pockets There are many routes you can play on a bar table that are not as readily available on a big table thanks to the fact that the corner pockets are quite generous.

Play More Corner Pocket Shape You should play more of your shots into the corner pockets than on a big table because 1) bar table side pockets are smaller; 2) corner pocket position often improves the pattern.

Roll Offs Factor in any roll offs in planning your position routes and zones. You may need to hit the shot more firmly and go an extra rail to avoid the possibility of a roll off. You should also consider playing for smaller cut angles and using a firmer stroke if a table rolls off badly.

Scratching You must be acutely aware of the possibility of scratching in the corners when playing shape on balls on the end rail. This is especially true when you are playing short side shape to a ball on the end rail. You also need to factor the conditions into your routes to avoid scratching.

Pattern Play It tends to be very intricate on a bar table.

Cut Angles When the cue ball is rolling towards the position zone, the angle on the next ball can change very rapidly. You can offset this tendency by playing for a little longer shot.

Safety Play
Basic Strategy You can play tight defense on a bar table because of the closeness of the balls and the congestion factor.
Clusters Be sure to consider clusters as hiding places, especially when the balls are largely in the area of the rack.
Set Up Combos This is a very productive strategy when playing safe on a bar table, especially if you are getting weight.

Strategy
Basic Strategy Bar sized tables dictate that you play more offense on certain shots that you would pass on if playing on a big table. However, the congestion factor leads to more opportunities to play safe. **Offense** You should go for shots on which you'd play safe on a big table
Lucky Shots You should occasionally play to luck in a money ball early in the game when the odds are in your favor and your opponent likely won't run out if you miss. You should also take advantage of opportunities to ride several money balls when getting spotted.

Shotmaking
Basic Strategy You must be better at certain shots like combos and banks than you are on a big table because you are expected to make them on a bar table. In short, you must go for more shots. And you must be sure to make all of the shots you are supposed to make, so don't let up on the easy shots just because you are playing on a small table.
Banks You will have to play more long rail banks since there is less margin for error on skim the ball safeties.
Combos Proficiency at combos is a major weapon on bar tables, especially if you are a player who regularly receives weight.
Billiards The congestion factor will give you ample opportunity to play billiards.
Over a Ball You will have to use an elevated bridge quite often, so shooting over a ball is a necessary skill.
Jump Shots These shots carry a higher degree of risk than do jump shots on a big table because of: 1) the smaller landing areas; 2) cue balls that tend to be heavier; 3) thinner slate that makes it tougher to get the cue ball airborne.
Learn to shoot well over balls
Side Pockets The side pockets are smaller, so you should avoid sharp angled cuts to the side pocket.
Rail Shots The cue ball is going to wind up on or very close to the rail much more often, so you must get used to using a rail bridge.

Push Outs
Use of Distance You must be very careful when using distance to make a push out difficult because your opponents will have more opportunities to either play an offensive shot, or to use congestion in the area of the rack.
Kick Shots When planning a push out, be sure to consider pushing to kick shoot.

Kicking

Strategy Can be precise with your kick shots since the distance to the object ball is not too great. Try to play strategic kick shots rather than just going for the hit.

Kick Routes You may have to play imaginative routes as it is easy for normal big table kicking lanes to be cut off by congestion

Tie Up the Rack Pass on kick shots and tie up the rack if you are not playing the 3 foul rule and the kick shot is extremely difficult.

The Break

Racking The thicker cloth on some bar tables can make racking difficult, especially when there are several sets of pit marks. So be sure to conduct periodic inspection. You and your opponent should reach an agreement on what is an acceptable rack.

Solid Contact The short distance to the 1-ball should enable you to hit it squarely.

Soft Break Since you have a greater chance of making a ball on the break than on a big table, you should consider backing off on the speed and using a softer break for complete control.

Ring Games

A ring game is a 9 Ball game between three of more players. Ring games often spring up when there are a group of players who are seeking some relatively low stakes action or when the players have had no success at making a game between two players. Before play begins, the players must establish the amount of the wager and the order of play, which is by the luck of the draw. In some ring games, the 9-ball is the only money ball, while in others players are also paid for pocketing the 5-ball. A typical wager could be $1 on the 5-ball and $2 on the 9-ball. The 9-ball is typically respotted if it is made out of rotation.

Ring games seem to bring out the best in some players whose games otherwise seem to lie dormant. In addition, many players will jump into a ring game with players who they would otherwise never play without a spot. If you are the best player, you should win in a ring game, but your success is far from guaranteed.

Ring Game Tips and Strategies

- Ring games with three players give you a chance to shoot almost as much as in a regular game, which enables you to stay sharp.
- While opinions vary, I believe a four handed game is best.
- Games with more than four players are a true test of your patience and ability to play when cold.
- You must be able to play your normal speed after waiting long periods for a chance to shoot.
- Safety play is not permitted in a ring game, You must make an honest attempt to hit the lowest numbered ball. If you fail to hit it, the next player usually has the option to shoot or make you shoot again. Rules vary, however, so this is not always the case.
- Combos, billiards and other specialty shots on the money ball are particularly valuable in a ring game. An offensive mindset is mandatory.
- A big break is a huge asset in a ring game.
- Ride your hot streaks for all they are worth, because dry spells are a way of life in ring games.

- When there is a player who is much worse than the others, be thankful if you are following him. And if you are not, insist that the order be changed periodically.
- If you are following the best player, or the one who is following the weakest player, you may face lots of full racks.
- Ring games can break up at any moment, so you must be prepared for the game to end even if you are behind.
- It is easier to quit when ahead in a ring game because the losers can continue playing. In addition, no one person is directly responsible for your winnings. Still, quitting when you are far ahead in a game is not a popular maneuver.
- Avoid a game in which you are pitted against two partners or friends. In other words, don't get stuck in the middle.
- Players with very limited resources have been known to "take a shot" at a ring game.
- Don't be too upset if there is some good natured gamesmanship, as ring games are normally much more vocal than games between two players.

Index of Players - Illustrations

Appleton, Darren - 433, 434, 435 (2), 436, 437, 441, 478, 479, 481 (2), 482, 483 (2), 485 (2), 487, 489, 493
Archer, Johnny
16, 53, 176, 238, 285, 316, 415, 417, 419,
Altomare, Chuck - 104
Bustamante, Francisco
83, 183, 186, 210, 220, 405, 427 (2), 428, 429, 434, 435, 437, 438, 443, 445 (2), 446, 447, 456, 457, 458 (2), 460
Chao, Fong-Pang - 33
Cortez, Lee Vann
410, 413, 431 (2), 432
Daulton, Shannon - 286
Davenport, Kim
187, 194, 286, 287, 289
Davis, Steve - 224
Deuel, Cory - 110, 313
Dodson, Robin - 265, 271
Fisher, Allison - 110, 293
Hall, Buddy - 164, 185, 313
Hohmann, Thorsten - 465, 467, 470, 471 (2), 473, 474, 489, 490, 491 (2), 492
Immonen, Mika
19, 157, 187, 211

Jones, Loree Jon - 107
Joyner, Cliff - 236
Kennedy, Tommy
156, 179, 182
Laurence, Ewa - 275
Lee, Jeanette - 21, 221
Martinez, Rafael - 178
Mathews, Grady - 293
McCready, Keith
193, 261, 294,
Mizerak, Steve
111, 260, 264, 290, 291
Moore, Stevie
429, 430, 433, 442, 453 (2), 455 (2), 459, 461
Morra, John - 457
Morris, Rodney
111, 439 (2), 440, 441, 442, 448, 449, 451
Okumura, Takeshi
26, 185, 267
Orcollo, Dennis
469, 472, 473, 474, 475 (2), 477, 478, 479, 480
Paez, Ismael - 175, 204
Pagulayan, Alex - 189, 449, 450, 451, 452, 454
Rempe, Jim - 196, 309, 317
Reyes, Efren - 101, 107, 116,

139, 173, 179, 192, 197, 257, 266, 307, 311, 312, 315, 317, 416, 417, 418, 419, 420, 421, 422
Robles, Tony - 262
San Souci, George - 264
Shuff, Brandon - 421
Souquet, Ralf - 106, - 186, 406, 407, 411 (2), 412, 413, 414 (2), 424, 426
Sigel, Mike - 104, 109, 115, 136, 137, 256
Strickland, Earl
96 (2), 109, 115, 164, 172, 178, 212, 289, 314
Takahashi, Kunihiko
165 (2), 221, 279, 319
Van Boening, Shane - 397 (P), 423 (2), 425 (2), 443, 444, 447, 464, 465, 466, 467, 468, 469, 475, 476, 477, 484, 485, 486, 487, 488
Varner, Nick - 95, 106, 149, 184, 218, 269, 280, 311

Where to Play 9 Ball and 10 Ball

Below is a partial listing of leagues, tours, and tournaments for those wishing to compete in leagues and tournaments. For more detailed listings, go to azbilliards.com, goplaypool.com, poolmag.com/calendar.cfm, and other listings on the internet.

REGIONAL TOURS

Arizona Desert Classic Tour	desertclassictour.com
J. Pechauer N.E. Women's Tour	jpnewt.com
Joss Northeast 9-Ball Tour	joss9balltour.com
Great Southern Billiard Tour	greatsouthernbilliardtour.com
Gulf Coast Tour	facebook.com/gulfcoast.tour
Lone Star Billiards Tour	lonestarbilliardstour.com
Mezz Pro-Am Tour	mezztour.com
Mezz Tour – West Coast	mezzweststatetour.com
Midwest 9-Ball Tour	9balltour.com
OB Cues Ladies 9-Ball Tour	obcuestour.com
Omega Billiards Tour	facebook.com/omegaBilliardsTour
Poison By Predator Tour	facebook.com/pxptour
Predator Tour	predatorproamtour.com
Simonis Cloth Classic Tour	simonistour.com
Southeast Open 9-Ball Tour	southeastopen.com
The Action Pool Tour	actionpooltour.com
The Tri State Tour	thetristatetour.com
Western NY Pool Tour	westernnewyorkpooltour.com

LEAGUES

American Poolplayers Association	poolplayers.com
American Cue Sports Alliance	americancuesports.org
BCA Pool League	playbca.com
VNEA	vnea.com
TAP	tapleague.com
National Pool League	playnapl.com

PROFESSIONAL and AMATEUR EVENTS

Allen Hopkins Super Billiard Expo	superbillardsexpo.com
CueSports International	Playcsipool.com
Derby City Classic	dcctickets.com
U.S. Open	usopen9ballchampionships.com
WPBA	wbpa.com
Women's Reg. Tours	SEE: wpba.com/regional-tours/list-of-regional-tours.html

Pool Media

Pool & Billiard Mag.	poolmag.com	**Go Play Pool**	goplaypool.com
Billiards Digest	billiardsdigest.com	**Sneaky Pete Mafia**	sneakypetemafia.com
AZ Billiards	azbilliards.com	**On the Break**	onthebreaknews.com
NYC Grind	nycgrind.com	**Professor Q-Ball**	professorqball.com

Accu-Stats DVDs – 9 Ball & 10 Ball

DVDs from Derby City, Make It Happen, and the U.S. Open are listed below. The ones with a star (*) have been chosen by Accu-Stats as being particularly noteworthy. The commentators' names are on the second line of each description below.

DERBY CITY 10 Ball - (researched for this book)
2009
#1 – Lee Van Corteza (15) vs. Ralf Souquet (11) - FINALS
D11-10d - 182 minutes – David Maddux & Mark Wilson
2010
#2 – Efren Reyes (15) vs. Johnny Archer (11) SEMI-FINALS (*)
D12-10a - 154 minutes – Jay Helfert & Mark Wilson
#3 – Efren Reyes (15) vs. Brandon Shuff (8) - FINALS
D12-10b - 148 minutes – Danny DiLiberto & Mark Wilson
2011
#4 – Shane Van Boening (15) vs. Ralf Souquet (14) (*)
D13-10B1d - 171 minutes – Jay Helfert & Danny DiLiberto
#5 – Francisco Bustamante (15) vs. Rafael Martinez (1) (*)
D13-10B2d - 78 minutes – Mark Wilson & Bill Gibbs
#6 – Lee Vann Corteza (15) vs. Stevie Moore (8)
D13-10B3d - 154 minutes – David Maddux & Mark Wilson
#7 – Darren Appleton (15) vs. Francisco Bustamante (13) (*) – SEMI-FINALS
D13-10B4d - 180 minutes – David Maddux & Mark Wilson
#8 – Rodney Morris (15) vs. Darren Appleton (11) – FINALS
D13-10B5d - 123 minutes – David Maddux & Mark Wilson
2012
#9 – Francisco Bustamante (15) vs. Shane Van Boening (9) (*)
D14-10B1d - 148 minutes – Bill Incardona & Mark Wilson
#10 – Alex Pagulayan (15) vs. Rodney Morris (9) (*)
D14-10B2d - 124 minutes – Danny DiLiberto & Mark Wilson
#11 – Stevie Moore (15) vs. Alex Pagulayan (12) – SEMI-FINALS (*)
D14-10B3d - 229 minutes – Danny DiLiberto & Mark Wilson
#12 – Francisco Bustamante (15) vs. John Morra (5) – SEMI-FINALS
D14-10B4d - 110 minutes – Danny DiLiberto & Mark Wilson
#13 – Francisco Bustamante (15) vs. Stevie Moore (5) - FINALS
D14-10B5d - 109 minutes – Jay Helfert & Mark Wilson

MAKE IT HAPPEN ALL STARS 10 Ball (researched for this book)
SET of 2 DVDs includes matches 1 and 2
#1 – Shane Van Boening (11) vs. Thorsten Hohmann (9)   AND
AS14-10B1d - 120 minutes – Bill Incardona & Danny DiLiberto
#2 – Dennis Orcollo (11) vs. Thorsten Hohmann (9)
AS14-10B2d - 130 minutes – Danny DiLiberto & Ken Shuman

SET of 2 DVDs includes matches 3 and 4
#3 – Dennis Orcollo (11) vs. Shane Van Boening (7)
AS14-10B3d - 90 minutes – Bill Incardona & Danny DiLiberto
#4 – Darren Appleton (11) vs. Dennis Orcollo (8)
AS14-10B4d - 130 minutes – Danny DiLiberto & Ken Shuman

SET of 2 DVDs includes matches 5 and 6
#5 – Shane Van Boening (11) vs. Darren Appleton (5)
AS14-10B5d - 80 minutes – Bill Incardona & Danny DiLiberto
#6 – Darren Appleton (11) vs. Thorsten Hohmann (8)
AS14-10B6d - 145 minutes – Bill Incardona & Danny DiLiberto

9 Ball DVDs from the U.S. Open

The U.S. Open celebrated its 40th Anniversary in 2014. Below is listing of the semi-final and final matches of some recent contests, each featuring the best players in the world. The number at the end is the length of the DVD (in minutes). For a complete listing of all Accu-Stats DVDs, please visit their web site.

2013 U.S. Open 9 Ball Championship
389B-18   Lee Vann Corteza (12) vs. Jayson Shaw (10) (*) – SF – 90
389B-19   Shane Van Boening (13) vs. Lee Vann Corteza (10) – F - 115

2012 U.S. Open 9 Ball Championship
379b-19   Dennis Orcollo (11) vs. Alex Pagulayan (7) – SF – 118
379b-20   Shane Van Boening (13) vs. Dennis Orcollo (7) (*) – F - 106

2011 U.S. Open 9 Ball Championship
369b-17   Shawn Putnam (11) vs. Alex Pagulayan (8) (*) – SF – 135
369b-18   Darren Appleton (13) vs. Shawn Putnam (11) (*) –F - 146

2010 U.S. Open 9 Ball Championship
359b-16   Corey Deuel (11) vs. Mika Immonen (3) – SF – 100
359b-17   Darren Appleton (15) vs. Corey Deuel (13) (*) – F – 180

2009 U.S. Open 9 Ball Championship
349b-18D Mika Immonen (11) vs. Donny Mills (10) (*) – SF - 113
349b-19D   Mika Immonen (13) vs. Ralf Souquet (10) (*) – F – 160

How to Order DVDs of the Pros
Accu-Stats Video Productions
P.O. Box 299
Bloomingdale, NJ 07403
PH: 1-800-828-0397
Web: accu-stats.com

- Catalog – Lists 100s of tapes
- Best and most popular tapes are highlighted
- Discounts for multiple purchases

How To Learn from Watching DVDs

Preshot Routines Each player follows a certain procedure prior to playing a shot. This includes evaluating the table and getting set over the shot. Look for players whose style most closely matches yours, and then see if there is something you can add to your favorite's routine.

Take Notes Keep a note pad handy for things you want to work on.

Shotmaking Observe the pros method for playing such key shots as the break, kick shots, banks, billiards, and the jump shot.

Strategy Pay special attention to their pushouts and choice of safeties. Amateurs can gain much from improving their safety play.

Watch them Play Look for their pace of play, changes in momentum, and how the players react to mistakes and great shots by both themselves and their opponent. Observe how each player conducts himself at the table.

Position Play I strongly advise you to play any position route that you wish to master in slow motion to learn the precise path of the cue ball.

Pattern Play Look for the flow, as each shot seems to naturally connect to the next one.

Commentators The commentators are all top players, so it pays to listen to their comments, criticisms, and words of advice

Evaluate their Decisions Before each shot, ask yourself how you would play the shot. Then consider the commentator's choices and observe what the player chose to do. This will train you to think about each shot, and you will learn how closely your thinking matches that of a top player.

Slow Motion If you are a super serious student of the game who loves watching videos, I suggest you purchase a VCR with enhanced special effects. Slow motion and frame advance help you to see the cue ball do things you could never see with the naked eye. This is especially important for learning the cue ball's true path after contact, and for how the cue ball reacts coming off the rails. Slow motion also enables you to hone in on your favorite's mechanics. Slow motion can also teach you how a rack of Nine Ball comes apart on the break.

Rewind Make liberal use of the rewind button. Play over any parts that you didn't fully understand on the first viewing.

Time Log When you come to a part of the DVD that you will want to review at a future date, check your machine's counter and write down the time it appears on the video.

Black Cue Ball Closing Run Out Patterns

In chapters 15 (Derby City) and 16 (Make It Happen) you were presented with the opportunity to close out the racks for some of the world's leading professionals. I did not present the routes and travel lines for the cue ball and object ball as this was your chance to think for yourself. While the pocket is often obvious, on many occasions there were two or more possible targets. Sometimes the pro would choose their pocket because it best fit the pattern while at other times they were forced to change pockets after missing position.

A letter has been assigned to each pocket as shown below. The pocket in which each ball was played comes after each ball. For example, 7(B) means that the 7-ball was played into side pocket B.

Each closing pattern has been assigned a difficulty rating. A is the toughest, Cs are the easiest, but few are what are referred to as a cosmo. The rating comes before the listing of balls and pockets.

I added up the number of balls played into the corners and the side pockets, and separated them into two categories: all shots in these closing runs that came before the 10-ball, and all shots on the 10-ball. At Derby City, only 8.70% of the shots on the 10-ball were played into the side. At the Make It Happen All Stars, 8.33% of all shots on the 10-ball were played into a side pocket. These results are not surprising considering that the 10-ball has a strong tendency to stay near where it is racked after the break. The most commonly played shot is with the 10-ball in or near the rack, and it is played along the diagonal into one of the two corner pockets adjacent to the foot rail.

In sum, 19.22% of all shots on the closing balls before the 10-ball was played into the side pocket. This underscores the importance of actively using the side pockets, and not listening to those who say to avoid them in favor of the corners.

Derby City

	Corner	Side	Side (%)
Non-10-Ball	136	31	18.56
10-Ball	42	4	8.70
	178	35	16.43

Make It Happen

	Corner	Side	Side%
Non-10-Ball	70	18	20.45
10-Ball	22	2	8.33
	92	20	17.86

TOTAL – Both events

	Corner	Side
Non-10 Ball	80.78%	19.22%
10-Ball	91.43%	8.57%

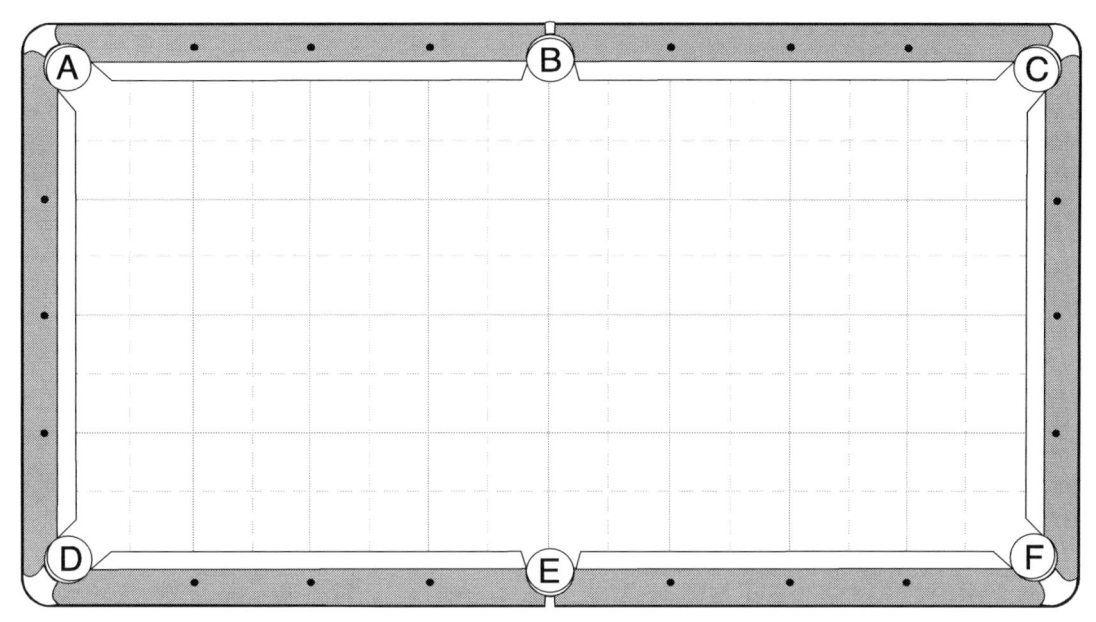

[Pool table diagram with pockets labeled A, B, C (top left, top middle, top right) and D, E, F (bottom left, bottom middle, bottom right)]

DERBY CITY (46)

#1 – Lee Vann Corteza (15) vs. Ralf Souquet (11)
Corteza Makes a Statement (1/1 – 6:00)	**C:** 6(D), 7(F), 9(C), 10(C)
Balls in the Middle (Diag. A - 1/5 – 32:50)	**C:** 7(E), 8(A), 9(D), 10(F)
Shape After the Combo (1/10 – 1:06:19)	**B:** 5(F), 7(F), <u>9(C)</u>, 10(A)
One Pocket in 10-Ball (Diag. B – 1/20 – :41:40)	**C:** 5(F), 7(F), 8(C), 9(A), 10(D)

#2 – Efren Reyes (15) vs. Johnny Archer (11)
4 Balls at a Time! (2/20 – :08:05)	**A:** 5(B), 7(C), 8(A), 10(C)
The Magician Ply's his Trade (2/2 – 10:15)	**C:** 6(C), 7(B), 8(E), 9(A), 10(F)
Efren Threads the Needle (2/6 – 30:10)	**C:** 7(C), 8(A), 9(E), 10(B)
Precision Draw Position (2/13 – 1:15:10)	**A:** 7(F), 8(D), 9(F), 10(F)
A 4-Rail Escape (2/15 – 1:24:50)	**A:** 6(F), 7(C), 8(E), 10(E)
Like a Diamond Cutter! (2/21 – 1:56:35)	**A:** 8(B), 10(D)
Archer Runs to the Bank (2/24 – 2:14:40)	**B:** 7(C), 8(D), 9(B), 10(C)

#3 – Efren Reyes (15) vs. Brandon Shuff (8)
Efren's Two-Rail Reverse (3/1 – 08:45)	**A:** 7(A), 8(A), 9(C), 10(A-2-rails!)
Side Pocket 10 Ball! (Diag. B -3/12B – 1:13:20)	**B:** 6(B), 7(E), 8(B), 10(A)

#4 – Shane Van Boening (15) vs. Ralf Souquet (14)
Send in Souquet! (4/12 - 1:00:00)	**A:** 7(F), 8(A), 9)E), 10(C)
Set that Angle! (4/25 59:25)	**A:** 6(F), 7(F), 8(C), 9(D), 10(F)
Power Follow and Across (4/27 – 1:13:05)	**B:** 6(C), 7(D), 8(F), 9(F), 10(C)

#5 – Francisco Bustamante (15) vs. Rafael Martinez (1)
Off to the Races! (5/4 – 21:40)	**B:** 5(E), 6(C), 7(D), 8(F), 9(F), 10(D)
Controlling a Hanger! (5/7 – 34:35)	**B:** 5(C), 6(A), 7(C), 9(F), 10(C)
This Judge Gives it a 10!! (5/11 – 52.10)	**C:** 7(D), 8(F), 9(A), 10(F)
A Certified Jaw Dropper!! (5/12 – 55:55)	**A:** 4(A), 5(F), 9(A), 10(F)

#6 – Lee Vann Corteza (15) vs. Stevie Moore (8)

World Class, Part II – (6/4 – 33:20)	**B:** 6(E), 7(A), 8(C), 9(A), 10(A)
That 40 Degree Angle! (6/5 – 42:05)	**B:** 4(A), 5(A), 6(D), 8(F), 9(F), 10(F)
Corteza's Reward (Di. B – 6/18 – 2:06:50)	**A+:** 4(A), 5(E), 6(D), 7(C), 8(A), 10(C)
Two Way Position off Combo (6/21 – 2:21:25)	**C:** 6(D), 8(B), 9(C), 10(C)

#7 – Darren Appleton (15) vs. Francisco Bustamante (13)

Going Airborne! (Diag. B - 7/18 – V.2 – 15:05)	**C:** 6(A), 8(E), 9(C), 10(F)
Coming with a Big Shot – 7/19 – (24:20)	**C:** 8(B), 9(F), 10(F)
Straight Back Power Draw!! (7/22 – 40:00)	**A:** 7(A), 8(A), 9(D), 10(F)

#8 – Rodney Morris (15) vs. Darren Appleton (11)

Pattern Play Genius – Diag. B – 8/6 – 25:00	**B:** 6(A), 7(F), 8(F), 9(D), 10(A)
Unusual, But Very Effective! (8/7 – 29:25)	**B:** 7(C), 8(E), 9(B), 10(F)
Three Rails in the Side (8/10 – 45:45)	**A:** 4(E), 5(C), 6(F), 7(E), 10(F)
High Speed Firepower! (8/13 – 59:15)	**C:** 6(C), 7(F), 8(F), 9(F), 10(E)
Super Spinner! (8/20 – 1:35:05)	**C:** 6(E), 7(D), 10(F)

#9 – Francisco Bustamante (15) vs. Shane Van Boening (9)

Squeaking in the Widow (9/6 – 29:55)	**C:** 7(D), 8(A), 9(E), 10(A)
Power Hop and Run! (9/9 – 51:15)	**C:** 6(E), 7(D), 8(F), 10(C)
70-Degree Table Length Cut (9/16 – 1:27:20)	**C:** 6(F), 7(F), 8(D), 9(A), 10(C)
Inside Spin Power 4-Railer! (9/21 – 1:58:25)	**C:** 6(B), 8(A), 9(B), 10(F)
Combo Simplifies the Pattern (9/22 – 2:01:20)	**C:** 6(D), 7(C), 8(F), 10(**F**)

#10 – Alex Pagulayan (15) vs. Rodney Morris (9)

Position for a Breakout – 10.1 – (3:45)	**B:** 5(F), 6(A), 7(C), 8(A), 10(D)
Runout Over Combo – 10/9 – (46:15)	**B:** 4(F), 5(B), 6(F), 7(F), 8(D), 9(D), 10(C)
High Octane Recovery Route (10/10 – 53:35)	**B:** 7(C), 8(E), 9(D), 10(A)

#11 – Stevie Moore (15) vs. Alex Pagulayan (12)

Duel "Out Shots" – 11/14 – (1:40:45)	**B:** 6(C), 7(C), 8(A), 9(C), 10(C)
Fan it in to Win! (11/15 – 1:54:55)	**B:** 4(F), 5(F), 6(B), 8(F), 10(E)
Closing the Deal in Style (D. B – 11/24 –1:27:25)	**A:** 6(D), 8(C), 9(D), 10(C)

#12 – Francisco Bustamante (15) vs. John Morra (5)

Rail First at Long Range (12/2 – 13:45)	**B:** 3(C), 4(C), 7(F), 8(B), 9(A), 10(F)
Identify the Big Hurdle (D. B – 12/14 – 1:23:00)	**A:** 7(C), 8(A), 9(E), 10(D)

#13 – Francisco Bustamante (15) vs. Stevie Moore (5)

Five Rail Position Play (13/19 – 1:45:45)	**B:** 6(A), 7(A), 8(C), 9(C), 10(C)

MAKE IT HAPPEN ALL STARS (24)

#1 – Shane Van Boening (11) vs. Thorsten Hohmann (9)
Super Soft Position Play   (1/1 – 7:30)   C: 6(E), 7(A), 8(F), 9(C), 10(E)
Shane's Draw & Jump Show!   (1/2 – 14:30)   C: 7(C), 8(E), 9(B), 10(F)
Hohmann's Extravaganza!   (1/3 – 19:10)   A: 6(B), 7(D), 8(A), 10(F)
Incidence Equals Reflection!   (1/11 – 1:01:45) A: 6(A), 7(F), 8(F), 9(D), 10(C)
Rail First Cheat Shot!   (D. B – 1/18 – 1:42:25) B: 5(E), 6(C), 7(E), 9(D), 10(C)

#2 – Dennis Orcollo (11) vs. Thorsten Hohmann (9)
Middle of a Super Tough Run   (2/10 – 1:10:00)   B: 6(B), 7(C), 8(D), 9(A), 10(E)
The Hardest Shot of All!! (D. B – 2/12 –1:21:40) B: 4(A), 5(F), 7(C), 9(F), 10(D)
Power Follow Shot   (2/14 – 1:29:40)   A: 6(F), 7(D), 8(C), 9(A), 10(D)

#3 – Dennis Orcollo (11)   vs. Shane Van Boening (7)
Multiple Objectives!   (3/8 – 38:20)   B: 5(C), 6(F), 8(B), 9(C), 10(D)
Fortune Favors the Bold!   (3/14 – 1:11:45)   B: 6(A), 7(C), 8(B), 9(C), 10(A)

#4 – Darren Appleton (11) vs. Dennis Orcollo (8)
Precision Long Range Draw (D. B – 4/2–13:30)   C: 6(D), 7(A), 8(F), 9(B), 10(D)
Wrong Side Position Play   (D. B – 4/3 – 21:05) C: 7(C), 8(F), 9(A), 10(A)
Play that Combo!   (4/6 – 35:40)   C: 6(C), 7(D), 9(B), 10(D)
Super Strong Opening   (4/9 – 51:20)   B: 5(D), 6,(D) 7(A), 8(C), 9(A), 10(D)
Winning Won Games!   (4/12 – 1:12:10)   C: 7(A), 8(E), 9(A), 10(D)
Setting Up the Key Shot!   (4/17 – 1:51:40)   C: 6(D), 7(E), 9(D), 10(F)

#5 – Shane Van Boening (11) vs. Darren Appleton (5)
Classic Side Rail Stun Shot   (5/1 – 05:45)   A: 6(E), 7(D), 8(C), 9(A), 10(D)
Power Follow Past an Obs.(5/13 – 1:01:45)   C: 5(E), 6(A), 7(F), 8(D), 10(A)
Super Draw/Bender Shot   (5/15 – 1:12:25)   C: 8(A), 9(A), 10(D)
Setting Up the Angle   (5/16 – 1:16:35)   B: 6(D), 7(E), 8(F), 9(C), 10(D)

#6 – Darren Appleton (11) vs. Thorsten Hohmann (8)
Going Deep into the Corner   (6/5 – 40:40)   C: 8(A), 9(C), 10(A)
Draw Outside Special   (Diag. B – 6/7 – 53:20)   A: 5(D), 6(F), 8(A), 9(A), 10(A)
An Aiming/Power-Draw Shot! (6/11 –1:17:15)   B: 6(C), 7(C), 8(D) 9(D), 10(A)
On the Wrong Side   (6/16 – 1:53:40)   A: 5(B), 6(C), 7(E), 8(C), 9(F), 10(D)

Phil Capelle

Author of 9 Instructional Books on Pool **Columnist for** *Pool & Billiard Magazine*

I've been continuously involved in pool in several capacities since I took up the game in early 1969. In 1995 I founded Billiards Press with the goal of providing serious students of the game with the finest instructional books on pool. *Play Your Best Pool* was published in late 1995. Since then I have written eight more books and second editions of two of my most popular books. I have also been writing a column for *Pool & Billiard Magazine* since May, 1996.

I began an intensive research project on aiming and the fundamentals in early 2012 and I am planning to produce numerous cutting edge products based on my findings in the years ahead.

I continue to learn new things every day about this fascinating and challenging sport of pool. In the years ahead, I look forward to sharing my findings with you, and I hope they help you to enjoy pool even more. I currently reside in New York City where I conduct research and give lessons.

Billiardspress.com

Billiardspress.com is the companion web site to Billiards Press. The site is packed with features of interest to the pool enthusiast. Below are the contents of the site. You can also visit me at facebook.

Home Page – Late breaking stories and information on our latest titles.
Books – Compete information on instructional books by Phil Capelle.
Reviews – Comments from industry experts, champion players, amateur players, popular retailers, and members of AZ Billiards' forums.
Contact – Write Phil Capelle with your comments.
Laws For Pool – Tips for improving the mental side of your game.
About Us – Profile of Phil Capelle, Billiards Press, and his many discoveries.

Play Your Best 9 & 10 Ball
Your Complete Guide
ISBN-13: 978-0989891745
$34.96 U.S.   544 pages – Spiral Bound
Contents:
- Fundamentals
- Position Routes
- Reading the Table
- The ABCs of Strategy
- The Break
- Cluster Management
- 10 Ball
- Make it Happen
- Shotmaking
- Pattern Play
- Safety Play
- Practicing 9 Ball
- Principles of Position
- Push Out Strategy
- Derby City 10 Ball

Over 550 Illustrations

Play Your Best Pool
Your Complete Textbook on Pool
978-0-9649204-8-4
$29.95 U.S. - 464 pages
For Players of All Levels
Contents:
- Fundamentals
- Position Play
- Nine Ball
- Competitive Play
- How to Use English
- How to Buy Equipment
- Shotmaking
- Eight Ball
- The Mental Game
- How to Improve
- Practicing Pool
- Appendix

Over 400 Illustrations

Play Your Best Eight Ball
Your Complete Guide to Eight Ball
978-0-9649204-7-7
$29.95 U.S. 456 Pages
Contents:
- Precision Cluster Busting
- Maximize Ball-In-Hand
- The Rules
- Learn to Read the Table
- Play Smart Safeties
- Practice Like a Pro
- Outsmart Your Opponent
- Learn to Win
- Master the Cue Ball
- Manage Risk & Avoid Trouble
- Appendix

535 Illustrations

Break Shot Patterns
How to Close 14.1 Racks Like a Pro
978-0-9649204-4-6
$49.95 U.S. - 260 pages
The Book
- Spiral bound – perfect for practicing
- A big chapter on the secrets of closing
- 110 closing patterns
- A description of the pattern
- Ball-by-ball analysis
- Lessons from Capelle's analysis of the pros
- Alternative patterns
- DVD fine points – what to look for

The DVD
- 110 closing patterns – the last four balls
- 2 hours long
- Filmed by Accu-Stats
- 34 world class players including Mike Sigel, Jim Rempe, Thorsten Hohmann, Mika Immonen, Oliver Ortmann

350+ Illustrations

A Mind For Pool
How To Master the Mental Game
978-0-9649204-1-5
$19.95 U.S. - 320 pages
Contents:
Part One: Your Game
Part Two: Competition
Part Three: The Journey
- 120 lessons on the mental game
- 80 lists for evaluating your game
- 295 Laws for Pool
- Over 500 great quotes
- Appendix

Play Your Best Straight Pool
A Complete Course on 14.1
Features a New Player's Guide
978-0-9649204-2-2
$24.95 U.S. - 416 pages
Contents:
- Learning to Play Straight Pool
- Position Play
- Secondary
- Cluster Management
- How to Run a Rack
- Strategy
- All About High Runs
- Pattern Play
- Break Shots
- Break Shots
- Safety Play
- Shotmaking
- Appendix

355 Illustrations

Capelle's Practicing Pool
Take Your Game to the Next Level & Beyond
978-0-9649204-9-1
$29.95 U.S. - 320 pages
Contents:
- Learning to Learn
- Fundamentals First
- Position Play
- Safety Play
- Break Shot Practice
- Practicing with a Partner
- Mental Game Practice
- Fast Start
- Shotmaking - Aiming
- Pattern Play
- Kicking Practice
- Scoring Drills and Games
- League Team Practice
- Practice Programs

200 Illustrations

Mike Massey's World of Trick Shots
Learn Pool's Best Trick Shots
978-0-9649204-6-0
$19.95 U.S. - 300 pages
Contents:
- Hustler's Specials
- Prop Shots
- Crowd Pleasers
- Mystery Shots
- Finger Pool
- Massé Shots
- Stroke Shots
- Bank Shots
- Jump Shots
- Appendix

180 Illustrations

Andy Segal's Cue Magic
Inside the World of Modern Trick Shots
978-0-9898917-0-7
$19.95 U.S.   254 pages
Contents:
Part 1 – Getting Started
- Introduction
- Trick Shot Concepts
- Props
- Terminology and Conventions
- Equipment

Part II – Cue Magic
- Bank / Kick Shots
- Juggling Shots
- Masse Shots
- Multi-Cue Jump Shots
- Miscellaneous Shots
- Speed Shots
- Stroke Shots
- Jump Shots
- Wing Shots
- Partner Shots

Part III – The Lighter Side
- Funny Stories
- About the Author
- Photo Gallery

Capelle on 9-Ball
Archer vs. Reyes
A companion guide to the video of a pro match.
A landmark study on pro pool.
0-9649204-4-1   200 Pages
2 Hours 15 Minutes
Book/DVD $49.95 U.S.

The Book
Part I – The Match
- Capelle takes you shot-by-shot through the match.
- Key shot are diagrammed all perfectly to scale.
- 100+ lessons for your game

Part II – The Pro Method
- Discover how the professionals use their time.
- Archer and Reyes: a contrast in styles.

The DVD
Part I – The Match
- Archer and Reyes fight for survival at the Sands 23.
- Over a dozen superb runouts.
- Learn from Bill Incardona's commentary.

Part II – Lessons from the Pros
- 25 shots analyzed in detail by Phil Capelle.
- Extensive use of special effects.
- Alternative shot selection for amateurs.

To order direct visit us on the web at billiardspress.com
Dealer Inquires Welcomed

Made in the USA
Middletown, DE
26 October 2024